D0075913

Insurance Law and Policy

EDITORIAL ADVISORS

Rachel E. Barkow
Segal Family Professor of Regulatory Law and Policy
Faculty Director, Center on the Administration of Criminal Law
New York University School of Law

Erwin Chemerinsky
Dean and Distinguished Professor of Law
Raymond Pryke Professor of First Amendment Law
University of California, Irvine School of Law

Richard A. Epstein
Laurence A. Tisch Professor of Law
New York University School of Law
Peter and Kirsten Bedford Senior Fellow
The Hoover Institution
Senior Lecturer in Law
The University of Chicago

Ronald J. Gilson
Charles J. Meyers Professor of Law and Business
Stanford University
Marc and Eva Stern Professor of Law and Business
Columbia Law School

James E. Krier
Earl Warren DeLano Professor of Law
The University of Michigan Law School

Tracey L. Meares
Walton Hale Hamilton Professor of Law
Yale Law School

Richard K. Neumann, Jr.
Professor of Law
Maurice A. Deane School of Law at Hofstra University

Robert H. Sitkoff
John L. Gray Professor of Law
Harvard Law School

David Alan Sklansky
Stanley Morrison Professor of Law
Faculty Co-Director, Stanford Criminal Justice Center
Stanford Law School

ASPEN CASEBOOK SERIES

INSURANCE LAW AND POLICY
Cases and Materials

Fourth Edition

TOM BAKER
William Maul Measey Professor of Law and
Health Sciences
University of Pennsylvania Law School

KYLE D. LOGUE
Douglas A. Kahn Collegiate Professor of Law
University of Michigan Law School

 Wolters Kluwer

Copyright © 2017 CCH Incorporated. All Rights Reserved.

Published by Wolters Kluwer in New York.

Wolters Kluwer Legal & Regulatory U.S. serves customers worldwide with CCH, Aspen Publishers, and Kluwer Law International products. (www.WKLegaledu.com)

No part of this publication may be reproduced or transmitted in any form or by any means, electronic or mechanical, including photocopy, recording, or utilized by any information storage or retrieval system, without written permission from the publisher. For information about permissions or to request permissions online, visit us at www. WKLegaledu.com, or a written request may be faxed to our permissions department at 212-771-0803.

To contact Customer Service, e-mail customer.service@wolterskluwer.com, call 1-800-234-1660, fax 1-800-901-9075, or mail correspondence to:

Wolters Kluwer
Attn: Order Department
PO Box 990
Frederick, MD 21705

Printed in the United States of America.

1 2 3 4 5 6 7 8 9 0

ISBN 978-1-4548-7491-1

Library of Congress Cataloging-in-Publication Data

Names: Baker, Tom, 1959- author. | Logue, Kyle D., author.
Title: Insurance law and policy : cases and materials / Tom Baker, William
  Maul Measey Professor of Law and Health Sciences, University of
  Pennsylvania Law School; Kyle D. Logue, Douglas A. Kahn
  Collegiate Professor of Law, University of Michigan Law School.
Description: Fourth edition. | New York : Wolters Kluwer, [2017] | Series:
  Aspen casebook series
Identifiers: LCCN 2016056663 | ISBN 9781454874911
Subjects: LCSH: Insurance law—United States. | LCGFT: Casebooks
Classification: LCC KF1164 .B35 2017 | DDC 346.73/086—dc23
LC record available at https://lccn.loc.gov/2016056663

About Wolters Kluwer Legal & Regulatory U.S.

Wolters Kluwer Legal & Regulatory U.S. delivers expert content and solutions in the areas of law, corporate compliance, health compliance, reimbursement, and legal education. Its practical solutions help customers successfully navigate the demands of a changing environment to drive their daily activities, enhance decision quality and inspire confident outcomes.

Serving customers worldwide, its legal and regulatory portfolio includes products under the Aspen Publishers, CCH Incorporated, Kluwer Law International, ftwilliam.com and MediRegs names. They are regarded as exceptional and trusted resources for general legal and practice-specific knowledge, compliance and risk management, dynamic workflow solutions, and expert commentary.

For Sharon, Matthew, Rachel, and Noa
and
For Ruth Ann, Hannah, Molly, Thomas, Caroline,
Mary Claire, and Feleke

Insurance ideas and practices define central privileges and responsibilities within a society. In that sense, our insurance arrangements form a material constitution, one that operates through routine, mundane transactions that nevertheless define the contours of individual and social responsibility. For that reason, studying who is eligible to receive what insurance benefits, and who pays for them, is as good a guide to the social compact as any combination of Supreme Court opinions.

Tom Baker, *On the Genealogy of Moral Hazard,*
75 Tex. L. Rev. 236, 291 (1996)

Summary of Contents

Contents

CHAPTER 1

Insurance, Law, and Society

CHAPTER 2

Contract Law Foundations

CHAPTER 3

First-Party Insurance: Illustrative
Lines and Issues

CHAPTER 4

Liability Insurance

CHAPTER 5

Liability Insurance Relationship Issues

CHAPTER 6

Insurance Regulation

Preface

This casebook invites students and teachers to reimagine the field of insurance law, reflecting the centrality of insurance to American law, business, and society.

Insurance is already in the mainstream of U.S. law and policy, as well it should be. Entire sectors of the U.S. economy depend on insurance: health care, the housing market, and the civil justice system, to mention just three with particular significance for new lawyers. A large share of federal tax payments goes toward funding government insurance of one form or another. The average American family pays almost as much to purchase the various forms of insurance that make up the private safety net. And for most organizations, insurance is a substantial budget item. As a result, tens of thousands of lawyers make decisions every working day that require a detailed understanding of one form of insurance or another.

Yet insurance remains very much on the margin of the curriculum in most law schools. This marginal status hurts law students by sending them out into practice without a broad, conceptual understanding of insurance law and institutions to help guide them in their work. Further, it deprives the legal profession of the depth of understanding that law teachers have brought to the fields of law at the core of the law school curriculum.

Courses like contracts, torts, civil procedure, property, and criminal and constitutional law are rich intellectual experiences largely because they have been taught by generations of law professors who labored in those fields. The U.S. legal system is among the few in the world that compensates law teachers well enough to free them from the demands of the active practice of law. What the system gets in return is not only well-educated new lawyers, but also legal scholarship and other forms of academic knowledge.

Insurance Law and Policy: Cases, Materials, and Problems aims to make insurance law enjoyable and interesting to teach and learn, so that professors who usually teach torts, contracts, business organizations, health law, civil procedure, and other law school courses will embark into an insurance course—and so that the students who go on that journey will have a worthwhile experience, too.

The goal is to encourage more people to think and write about insurance, risk, and responsibility, so that the field develops the depth of law school subjects traditionally understood to form the core of the curriculum.

So what does this casebook do differently? There are four main things.

First, the book pares down, and in some cases eliminates, some of the arcane aspects of insurance law in favor of presenting a broad and conceptual overview of the field. Lawyers can teach themselves the details when they need to know them. This book focuses on the essential institutional arrangements and enduring tensions that animate the field.

Second, the organization of the book locates insurance law in the law school curriculum. As the book makes clear, insurance is both an upper-level contracts course (see Chapter 2) and an upper-level torts course (see Chapters 4 and 5). Insurance is also an essential aspect of health law (see Chapter 3) and the regulation of financial services (see Chapter 6), as well as a challenging variation on the usual pattern of federalism (see Chapter 6). In addition, insurance provides a window on the distribution of benefits and responsibilities in the United States (see, especially, Chapter 1, but also Chapters 3 and 4). In that sense, an insurance law course has much in common with a tax law course. It is the rare social issue that cannot be seen through a tax or an insurance lens. The difference is, however, that insurance law is more accessible to teachers whose core expertise lies in an allied field.

Third, the book introduces into insurance law many successful innovations from other law school casebooks. There are carefully constructed problems throughout. There are fewer and longer cases, providing students better grounding in the art of extracting useful knowledge from judicial opinions. There are more extensive and pervasive statutory materials, presenting students with a more realistic understanding of the importance of statutes and more practice working with them. There are fresh, contemporary cases, reflecting the major insurance law controversies of the past thirty years, from asbestos litigation to the World Trade Center to the ever-evolving relationship between liability and insurance (as represented in this edition by the extensive use of materials from the ALI's new Principles of the Law of Liability Insurance, for which we are the Reporters).

Finally, although the book continues the trend in insurance law casebooks of organizing teaching units around lines of insurance (e.g., health, liability), it integrates topics to a greater extent. All first party insurance topics are addressed in a single Chapter, with separate sections for different lines of insurance and a single comprehensive subrogation unit at the end. Similarly, after introducing the main types of liability insurance in separate sections in Chapter 4, the book presents liability insurance relationship issues in an integrated fashion in Chapter 5.

Tom Baker and Kyle Logue

January 2017

Acknowledgments

As with any casebook in a developing field, this one stands on the shoulders of others. Two deserve special mention: *Cases and Materials on Insurance Law*, by Spencer Kimball, and *Insurance Law and Regulation*, by Kenneth Abraham. We have taught with both books and both undoubtedly have shaped our understanding and organization of the insurance field more pervasively than we are aware.

Thank you to all of the adopters of the earlier editions for their confidence and their feedback. Thank you, especially, to Rhonda Andrews, Jennifer Bard, Peter Carstensen, Seth Chandler, Stephen Gilles, Stephen Halpert, Robert Jerry, Peter Kochenburger, Jay Naftzger, Chaim Saiman, Adam Scales, Peter Siegelman, Kathryn Sampson, Anthony Sebok, Shauhin Talesh, Jeffrey Thomas, and Jennifer Wriggins for their suggestions and materials. Thank you to the many lawyers who have entrusted us with their insurance problems, keeping us anchored to insurance practice and providing the raw material for many of the topics and problems that (suitably disguised) appear in this book.

Thank you also to the following authors and copyright holders for permission to use their materials:

Adam Scales, Can This Pig Fly? How a Dentist Assaulted a Patient and Made a Million Dollars, http://writ.news.findlaw.com/commentary/20070815_scales. html, FindLaw August 15, 2007. Reprinted by permission. Originally appeared on FindLaw.com

American Law Institute, Principles of the Law of Liability Insurance © 2013 by the American Law Institute. All rights reserved. Reprinted with permission.

Chubb Specialty Insurance, Directors and Officers Liability Policy, Forms 1402-0941 (Ed. 1/92) and 14-02-0943 (Ed. 1/92). Reprinted by permission.

Daniel C. Eidsmore & Pamela K. Edwards, Home Liability Coverage: Does the Criminal Acts Exclusion Work Where the "Expected or Intended" Exclusion Failed?, 5 Conn. Ins. L.J. 707 (1998-1999). Reprinted by permission.

Insurance Services Office, Inc., CGL Declarations Form, CGL Occurrence Form (CG 00 01) and CGL Claims Made Form (CG 00 02). Includes copyrighted and proprietary materials of Insurance Services Office, Inc. or its affiliates with its permission.

Robert H. Jerry II, "Insurance," from Oxford Companion to American Law, edited by Kermit Hall, copyright by Oxford University Press, Inc. (2002). Used by permission of Oxford University Press, Inc.

Kevin LaCroix, excerpt from The D&O Diary, http://www.dandodiary.com. Reprinted by permission of Kevin LaCroix.

John H. Langbein, Trust Law as Regulatory Law: The Unum/Provident Scandal and Judicial Review of Benefit Denials Under ERISA, 101 Nw. U. L. Rev. 1315 (2007). Reprinted by permission.

L. Charles Landgraf, John S. Pruitt & Tom Baker, Modernizing Insurance Regulation in the United States. (2011). Prepared for the Anthony T. Cluff Research Fund of the Financial Services Roundtable. © 2011 Dewey & LeBoeuf LLP.

Oxford Companion to American Law, edited by Kermit L. Hall (2002) c. 1,847 words from pp. 420-423. © by Oxford University Press, Inc. By permission of Oxford University Press USA.

Residual Markets. (2015, March). Insurance Information Institute. Retrieved from http://www.iii.org/issue-update/residual-markets.

Restatement of the Law Liability Insurance, Tentative Draft No. 1 (April 11, 2016) copyright © 2016 by The American Law Institute. Reproduced with permission. All rights reserved. As of the date of publication, this Draft had not been considered by the members of The American Law Institute and therefore did not represent the position of the Institute on any of the issues with which it deals. The action taken by the members with respect to this Draft may be ascertained by consulting the Annual Proceedings of the Institute, which are published following each Annual Meeting.

Susan Randall, Insurance Regulation in the United States: Regulatory Federalism and the National Association of Insurance Commissioners, 26 Fla. St. U. L. Rev. 625 (1999). Reprinted by permission of the Florida State University Law Review.

Tom Baker & Jonathan Simon. (2002). Embracing Risk: The Changing Culture of Insurance and Responsibility. © 2002 by The University of Chicago. All rights reserved. Published 2002. Printed in the United States of America.

Notes on the Text

All omissions from judicial opinions and other materials, except omissions of footnotes and other citations, are indicated by ellipses. Some internal citations and footnotes within cases and other materials have also been removed. All footnotes, including those in the cases and other excerpted materials, are numbered consecutively from the beginning of each chapter.

Insurance Law and Policy

CHAPTER
1

Insurance, Law, and Society

I. INTRODUCTION

For most people, most of the time, insurance operates in the background of everyday life, a dimly understood part of the social infrastructure that is often taken for granted. We have limited attention spans and cannot focus on the inner workings of more than a small fraction of the institutions that we come across. We are content to ignore these inner workings until we need them or are forced to engage with them. Insurance is one such institution.

In fact, the effect of insurance on our lives is profound and pervasive. The vast majority of us are covered by one type of insurance or another, and usually several types. When we buy or rent a home, we purchase insurance against the possibility that the house will be destroyed by fire, wind, or meteorite. We also purchase coverage for the potential lawsuit that might arise if our neighbor slips on the ice on our front porch. When we buy or rent a car, we buy auto insurance to protect us against the possibility of a crash. If there are people depending on our incomes, we get life insurance to replace our earnings. Most of us have some type of health insurance, which—in part because of a subsidy built into the federal income tax laws long ago—is usually provided through our employers. Long-term disability insurance is also sometimes offered as an employee benefit, although surprisingly few employees actually take advantage of it. An annuity is a type of insurance against living beyond one's earning capacity (it might be called longevity insurance), and is also sold by private insurance companies either directly to individuals or through employer-provided benefits.

All of the aforementioned types of insurance are private, in the limited sense that they are the result of contracts between insurance companies and individuals or firms. There is also government-provided insurance. Health, disability, life, and retirement insurance are provided through government programs such as Medicaid, Medicare, and Social Security. And in the unlikely (though perhaps increasingly likely) possibility of a catastrophe—such as earthquake, hurricane, tornado, or terrorist attack—there is government-provided relief of one form or another. For example, the National Flood Insurance Program, provided through the U.S. government, offers policies that cover homes in flood-prone areas against the risk of flood damage; and there are state-run insurance institutions that provide coverage for severe wind or earthquake risks.

For lawyers, insurance has special significance. Insurance is obviously deeply tied up with *risk,* and risk lies at the heart of what lawyers do. Transactional lawyers help their clients plan for the risks of the future. Every contract allocates risks between the parties. Thus, lawyers who draft contracts can be understood as risk managers for their clients. Litigators in turn help their clients address those risks that have matured into harm. In addition, because many lawsuits trigger some form of liability insurance, insurance companies often end up controlling the conduct of civil litigation. For that reason, insurance shapes how the law is administered on the ground: which cases go to trial, which cases settle and on what terms.

For these practical reasons, spending a semester focusing on risk in general and on insurance law and policy in particular is a sound use of time for almost any law student. Most likely, you will run across at least some insurance matters in your professional life. If you are a commercial litigator, you will need to know how the standard commercial general liability insurance policy works. If you advise corporate directors or officers, you would do well to understand the basics of directors' and officers' (D&O) coverage. All lawyers will be purchasing professional malpractice insurance; maybe you should know what the language in those policies means. In your personal life, you will be a significant consumer of insurance and related financial services. Moreover, because the law that governs private and public insurance programs contributes significantly to the type of society we have, every informed citizen should understand the basics of how insurance works. Indeed, with the prominence of public policy issues relating to tort liability, health care, aging, and retirement, we all benefit when more people have a deeper understanding of the insurance systems that finance and, as you will soon come to appreciate, *regulate* these and other important areas of life.

Before diving into insurance law and policy, however, there are some risk, insurance, and responsibility basics that are helpful to understand. This chapter will race you through them. This material is presented up front to help you develop an appreciation for the economic and social functions of insurance as background for the intensely *legal* materials that fill up most of the rest of this book. The goal here is a common vocabulary and a brief preview of what will be found in the materials that follow. If this chapter does that for you, great! If not, don't worry. Just use the chapter to develop a rough sense of the basic points about risk and insurance, as well as the role of insurance in society, and move on from there. There's plenty of law in Chapter 2 and in every chapter that follows it. One piece of advice, though: After you have finished the casebook (but maybe before the exam), reread this introductory chapter. We suspect that you may have a renewed appreciation for the material that is presented here.

II. RISK AND INSURANCE 101

Risk. A risk is something that *can* happen but is not *certain* to happen. A home may be struck by lightning, or it may not. A person may fall from a ladder and injure his back, leaving him unable to work and in need of expensive medical care, or he may step down from the ladder without incident, as he has a thousand times before. A new consumer product may perform exactly as designed and thus make modern life easier, more comfortable, or more interesting; or it can malfunction and explode when plugged into the wrong type of wall socket or fed the wrong fuel, injuring its user and subjecting its maker to a products liability claim. All of these are risks. All are potentially insurable, in part because they are uncertain or probabilistic. Even death, though certain to come eventually to us all, comes at an uncertain time, which makes death itself an insurable risk.[1]

In the insurance field, the word "risk" is sometimes used in more than one way. As just explained, it can be used to signify the possibility of harm to person, property, or enterprise. But risk is also sometimes used to mean the person, property, or enterprise that is subject to the harm. Thus, insurance protects *risks* (in the second sense, the persons or things being insured) against *risks* (in the first sense, the possibilities of harm). In general, these materials will use "risk" in only the first sense — the possibility of harm. We will be concerned with what kinds of risks — what kinds of harm — insurance covers, and for whom; and we will be concerned with how insurance law itself, the rules and doctrines we will be studying, allocates and creates risk.

Risk aversion and risk transfer. Risk aversion helps explain the appeal of insurance. "Risk aversion" is the name given to the preference that most individuals have for certainty over uncertainty with regard to future losses. More technically, a risk-averse individual is one who prefers a certain cost to an uncertain possibility of equal expected value. It is risk aversion that makes people willing to pay a relatively small insurance premium today in exchange for protection against having to bear the financial costs of a much larger loss in the future. The concept of risk aversion is very important to an economic understanding of insurance because it helps explain why insurance is socially beneficial. Without understanding risk aversion, the institution of insurance may seem like a waste of resources. To pay salaries and other administrative expenses, as well as to pay the stockholders a fair rate of return, insurance companies have to charge more in premiums than they pay out in claims.[2] Because of these additional expenses, there are more social resources devoted to losses covered by insurance than to losses not covered by insurance, putting aside for now the possibility that insurers might actually help policyholders reduce losses. The concept of risk aversion helps us understand why these additional resources are not wasted. They are a necessary component of commercial arrangements that provide people with something of great value: security.

To see this basic point about risk aversion, consider the following stylized example. Imagine that you own a home that has a replacement cost of $100,000. And say that the likelihood of the house being destroyed during a particular

---

1. Although risk can have an upside as well as a downside, insurance typically addresses only downside risk. One exception is when insurance products are bundled with investment products. For example, some annuities, which are a type of insurance against living longer than one's assets can sustain, promise returns that vary with the market. Such annuities present some upside risk.

2. This explanation ignores investment gains (i.e., the money the insurance company makes by investing the premiums in the period before paying claims), but it also ignores the benefit that people would have derived from keeping their premium dollars rather than giving them to insurance companies. At the level of generality we're engaged in here, we can think of those two as canceling each other out.

year from any cause is 1/1,000. (This assumed probability is unrealistically high, but it will do for the purpose of our illustration.) Thus, for the relevant policy period, you face a 1/1,000 chance that you will suffer a $100,000 loss due to the loss of your home, and a 999/1,000 chance that no such loss will occur. This means that the expected cost of the risk (the probability-weighted sum of the two possible outcomes) is $100. If you are risk averse, you would by definition rather pay $100 up front and out of pocket than face this uncertain contingency, whose expected cost is also precisely equal to, again, $100. Indeed, depending on how averse you are to risk, you would be willing to pay something greater than $100 to *transfer the risk* to an insurer. This additional value to you of certainty or security is part of what makes insurance worthwhile. This simple example can be generalized to all forms of insurance.

The next obvious question is why people are risk averse in the first place.[3] One possible explanation draws on the idea from economics of the declining marginal utility of money. This idea says that in most circumstances, each additional dollar that you receive, through earnings or gifts or whatever, is worth slightly less to you than the previous dollar received. This is because with your first dollars, you buy the things you really need, necessities such as food, clothing, and shelter. Then, as more money comes in, you buy the things you need somewhat less. When all your so-called needs are met, you buy things you don't really *need* but just want. Next come things you just barely want, and so on. But if something bad happens and you suffer a major financial loss, you suddenly *need* more money: to rebuild your house after a hurricane, to pay for your hospital bills after a heart attack, or to replace the income that you lost when you couldn't work. Because the loss is substantial, you have lost not only the dollars used for trivial things, but also the dollars used for necessities. Thus, the act of buying insurance when times are good, when one is relatively flush with cash, shifts dollars of relatively little value (that is, dollars that might be spent on smartphones or caramel vanilla lattes) to a future state of the world in which the dollars can be spent on absolute necessities, such as food, shelter, and medical care.[4]

Risk spreading. If risk aversion helps to explain why individual insureds are willing to pay something greater than the expected value of their potential losses to transfer risks from themselves to insurance companies, what explains why insurance companies are willing to accept those risks? Put differently, why are insurance companies not also risk averse? The answer is found in the concept of risk spreading. Risk spreading occurs whenever a group of people or firms pool their individual risks in a way that reduces the risk to everyone in the pool. The practice of risk spreading has been around forever. The institution of the family

3. Of course, not everyone is risk averse with respect to all types of risk. Some people are risk preferrers, in the sense that they would rather go uninsured than pay the premium to shift the risk of a large loss to an insurer. But that does not seem to describe most people. It does seem to be the case, however, that many individuals are risk preferrers when it comes to small bets with large upsides. That helps to explain why lotteries, even actuarially unfair lotteries (where the ticket prices exceed the expected value of the potential winnings), are so popular.

4. You can also think of this as a form of intrapersonal redistribution: shifting dollars from the rich me to the poor me through insurance. Indeed, this same sort of argument is the primary justification offered for interpersonal redistribution, such as the progressive income tax-and-transfer system: taxing the richer taxpayers to help the poorer taxpayers because the latter need the money more.

has long provided a way for individuals to share risks with each other. If one family member gets sick and can't work, the others take up the slack, providing a form of informal disability insurance. If a family member dies, the surviving children are taken care of in what amounts to an ancient form of life insurance. Insurance contracts between policyholders and insurance companies provide a way for this sort of risk spreading to be provided on a broader scale, for larger losses to a wider swath of the population.

Although risk spreading can be understood intuitively, it wasn't until the concept of risk spreading was mathematized that modern insurance markets were able to emerge. The basic statistical principle that underlies risk spreading is sometimes referred to as *the law of large numbers*. Put somewhat technically and in terms of insurance, this law means that, up to a point, the larger the pool of insured risks is, the smaller the risk will be to everyone in the pool, on average.

Consider the hypothetical homeowner from above who faced two possible outcomes: loss of house or no loss of house. The expected value of that risk was $100, but the disparity or variance in possible outcomes for the individual insured was huge: she could either suffer a loss of $100,000 or suffer no loss at all. If the homeowner wanted to have "security" for the $100,000 loss without purchasing insurance, she has to put $100,000 in the bank. The same would be true of every individual homeowner. Pooling their risks together through insurance, however, a group of homeowners can substantially reduce their overall risk. This is because if we pool together through an insurance company (say, 50,000 individuals facing precisely the same risk) and we collect $100 in premiums from each of them, the amount of money collected would closely approximate the amount needed to make payouts for actual losses experienced by all members of the pool during the period. (The actual payout for losses would come close to the $5 million of premiums collected from the 50,000 members of the pool.) This is why insurers are willing to accept risk transfers from large numbers of insureds. By providing this risk-pooling function, they are actually reducing the risk to the pool and thus to themselves.[5]

This basic point can be seen in numerous other contexts. Which of the following is more certain: (1) whether a particular 65-year-old male with heart disease will die this year or (b) whether the percentage of 65-year-old males with heart disease in the United States who will die this year will be approximately the same as last year? Or try this one. Which is more certain: (a) whether you will have an auto accident in the next year or (2) whether the number of auto accidents in your region will be approximately the same as last year? In both cases, the answer of course is (2). As these examples suggest, the basic idea of the law of large numbers is that we can be more certain about the future experience of large groups in the aggregate than we can be about the future experience of any particular individuals in that group. Up to a point, the larger the group, the more certain we can be about the future aggregate experience of that group. Thus, the law of large numbers explains that insurance increases social welfare because it provides cheap security.

The law of large numbers does not always work perfectly, though. For example, if all 50,000 of the houses in our homeowners' insurance hypothetical were

---

5. *See generally* Peter L. Bernstein, Against the Gods: The Remarkable Story of Risk (1998); *and* David A. Moss, When All Else Fails: Government as the Ultimate Risk Manager (2002).

built on the same highly volatile fault line (and the insurer were including earthquake coverage in the policy), the law of large numbers in this case would *not* predict that grouping these individual risks together would reduce the overall risk to the pool. Rather, the reverse would be true. Because a single earthquake could destroy all (or at least many of) the 50,000 homes in a single day, grouping the risks together actually concentrates rather than spreads the risk. That is an extreme example, but the point applies generally. And we will see that insurers attempt to deal with these sorts of "correlated risks" contractually, typically using exclusions in their policies. In addition to the problem of correlated risks, some risks are so unusual or infrequent that no reliable data have been gathered with which to make predictions. For these reasons, insurers have techniques other than the law of large numbers for spreading risk. For example, some insurance companies are owned by stockholders who *diversify* their stock portfolios. By owning shares in lots of different companies, whose risks are not correlated with each other, the investors avoid the problem of "putting all their eggs in one basket." Insurance companies themselves also engage in a form of diversification when they insure risks in several different parts of the country or sell several different types of insurance. Also, some insurers actually transfer some of the risk that they assume from their insureds to other insurers, who then slice and dice the risks into small pieces and spread them further over the reinsurance market.

In combination, the existence of risk aversion and the law of large numbers powerfully demonstrates the benefits of insurance. Risk aversion says that people really want protection. The law of large numbers says that insurance can provide that protection at a small fraction of the cost that it would take for people to protect themselves.

III.   BEYOND RISK SHIFTING AND RISK SPREADING

The image of insurance painted so far is that of conduit for the transfer and spreading of risk. But insurance serves other functions as well. This section discusses how insurance performs a regulatory function and actually helps to reduce risk. It also covers some of the market failures and other problems that inhibit insurance from playing both its risk-spreading function and its regulatory function.

A.   *Insurance as Regulation*

To understand how insurance operates as form of risk regulation, we first need to understand the concept of moral hazard.[6] In the insurance context, the term "moral hazard" typically is used to refer to the theoretical tendency for insurance to reduce incentives (1) to protect against loss or (2) to minimize the cost of a loss. An example of the former (which economists call *ex ante* moral haz-

---

6. *See generally* Tom Baker, *On the Genealogy of Moral Hazard*, 75 Tex. L. Rev. 237 (1996).

ard) is leaving a car door unlocked, comfortable in the knowledge that if the car is stolen, the insurance company will pay. An example of the latter (which economists call *ex post* moral hazard) is not caring very much about what it costs to repair a car as long as the insurance company pays for it. *Ex ante* moral hazard can take two general forms. First, an individual or firm can fail to take cost-justified steps to minimize the likelihood or potential magnitude of a loss. In that case, the party's *level of care* would be too low. Second, irrespective of the level of care, the individual might engage in too much of the risky activity. That is, the individual's *level of activity* might be too high. Both of these types of risk-increasing behavior can be caused, or at least made worse, by the presence of insurance.

Moral hazard can also be understood more broadly, as the general problem of individuals and firms failing to take all appropriate measures, in terms of increased care levels or reduced activity levels, to minimize risks. Viewed this way, insurance can actually help to reduce moral hazard.[7] When this happens, insurers perform many of the same functions that are performed by government agencies that are tasked with regulating risks. Indeed, an argument can be made that, at least in some situations, insurance (often together with tort law) provides a more effective form of regulation than does agency-based regulation.

How can this be true? Why would insurers even have an incentive to reduce risks? Don't insurers' profits increase when there is *more* risk, not when there is less? When risks increase, can't they just raise their premiums? While it is true that insurers would be put out of business in the unlikely event that all risks were completely eliminated, there are several reasons why insurers actually have an incentive to help insureds reduce their risks. First, if an insurer can minimize loss payouts, it can hold down the overall cost of insurance for its policyholders, which in turn increases consumer demand for insurance from that insurer. Indeed, if insurance premiums rise too high, individuals and businesses simply will find insurance unaffordable and will, if possible, opt to self-insure instead. Second, keeping premiums within reasonable limits also helps insurers stave off potentially aggressive regulatory intervention. If insurance premiums get too high, ambitious state regulators or angry voters may take steps to force dramatic rate reductions, a possibility that insurers prefer to avoid. Finally, competition among insurers for relatively low-risk insureds forces insurers to try to find ways to distinguish low-risk insureds from high-risk insureds and to charge lower premiums to the former and higher premiums to the latter—a process that can create financial incentives for insureds to increase their care levels and reduce their activity levels.

When insurers take such steps to reduce moral hazard, they are in effect acting as private risk regulators. In some situations, insurance companies may

---

7. This section draws heavily from Omri Ben-Shahar & Kyle D. Logue, *Outsourcing Regulation: How Insurance Reduces Moral Hazard*, 111 Mich. L. Rev. 1 (2012). For an insightful analysis of insurance and loss prevention, *see* George M. Cohen, *Legal Malpractice Insurance and Loss Prevention: A Comparative Analysis of Economic Institutions*, 4 Conn. Ins. L.J. 305 (1997-1998). *See also* Tom Baker & Thomas O. Farrish, *Liability Insurance and the Regulation of Firearms*, in Suing the Firearms Industry (T. Lytton, Ed., 2005) (identifying ways in which liability insurers can operate as regulators in the firearms context); and Tom Baker & Sean Griffith, *The Missing Monitor in Corporate Governance: The Directors' and Officers' Liability Insurance*, 95 Geo. L.J. 1765 (2007) (exploring why D&O liability insurers do not engage in loss prevention efforts and what that fact suggests about why corporations buy D&O coverage).

actually be better at regulating risky behavior than a government agency would be. Given the nature of the insurance business, insurance companies often have an informational advantage over government regulators. Insurers gather a great deal of information in the normal course of their business in order to evaluate claims. As a result of that claims process, they have access to precisely the sort of information that is needed to regulate policyholders' care levels and activity levels, information that a government regulator often will not have. In addition, insurers are motivated by competition to find ever better ways of gathering risk-related information and better ways of using that information to reduce risks. And they are able to get away with some forms of information gathering that a government agency might find politically difficult to do. For one example, auto insurers have begun offering their policyholders the option of having special global positioning system (GPS) devices installed in their cars to gather information about the insureds' driving habits, monitoring both activity levels and care levels. This information can then be used to combat moral hazard and increase incentives to improve safety, as discussed further below.

In their role as private risk regulators, insurers have several strategies or techniques for reducing moral hazard.

1. *Premium differentials.* Insurers give premium discounts to insureds who take steps to reduce risks. Examples of such "premium differentiation" can be found in virtually every area of insurance. Homeowners' insurers give discounts to insureds who install wind-resistant roofing tiles or smoke detectors. Auto insurers charge different rates based on driving experience or on information gathered in other ways. Workers' compensation insurers base premium differentials on the experience of their insured employers. Life insurers charge higher rates to smokers than to nonsmokers. In addition, insurers will sometimes charge differential insurance rates based on an insured's level of care and activity—with auto insurance and the introduction of telematics-based premiums being the best example. That is, with telematically enhanced insurance pricing, insurers are able not only to charge prices that reflect accurate and detailed information about the insureds' driving habits, including how much and how carefully they drive, but also to adjust their premiums automatically in response to risk-reducing or risk-increasing behavior on the part of drivers. According to some reports, this "pay-as-you drive" or "usage-based" auto insurance has produced significant reductions in premiums and in insured accidents, with the biggest gains coming with respect to young drivers.[8] Of course, premium differentiation of this sort is not only about inducing insureds to reduce risks (and controlling moral hazard). Insurers also use premium differentials to attract relatively low-risk and thus low-cost insureds into their risk pools.

Query: To the extent that premium differentials are used primarily for this sort of "skimming" of relatively good risks, are they providing a beneficial regulatory role? Also, some have expressed privacy or "Big Brother" concerns about allowing insurers to have detailed information about precisely where an individual has driven. All existing telematics-enhanced auto insurance programs

8. Lee Boyce, *Blackbox Insurance May Be Cutting Young Drivers' Costs, but I Still Worry About the Spy in the Car,* ThisIsMoney.co.uk, June 25, 2012, *http://www.thisismoney.co.uk/money/cars/article-2161658/ Blackbox-insurance-helps-young-drivers-I-worry-spy-car.html.*

are voluntary, in the sense that each policyholder can decide whether to opt in or opt out. Does the voluntary nature of these programs fully answer the privacy/Big Brother concerns? What exactly are those concerns? How much of a premium reduction would you need to be willing to sacrifice your privacy with respect to where and how you drive?

2. *Deductibles and co-payments.* Another way that insurers reduce moral hazard is to include deductibles and co-payments in their insurance policies. Deductibles require insureds to pay a fixed amount "out of pocket" to cover insured losses before the insurance coverage kicks in to cover insured losses thereafter. Co-payments typically require insureds to bear some fraction of each covered loss claim filed by an insured. The effect of both deductibles and co-payments is to help align the insured's incentives with those of the insurer and thus to reduce moral hazard. There are limits, however, to the extent to which deductibles and co-payments can reduce moral hazard on the part of insureds. Can you see why? And can you see why they nevertheless often make good sense from the insured's perspective?

3. *Exclusions, cancellations, and decisions not to renew.* An "exclusion" is a term in an insurance contract that says that certain types of losses are not covered under the policy. Thus, whereas a deduction imposes on the insured some fixed amount of all insured losses, an exclusion results in the insured bearing *all* losses of a particular type—the excluded type. For example, most insurance policies contain a term that explicitly excludes payment for losses that are intentionally caused by the insured. How could such an exclusion be understood as a regulatory tool for reducing risky behavior by insureds? Think about the *ex ante* incentives created by the existence of the intentional-harm exclusion in the policy. Because the exclusion is present, the insured is discouraged from causing losses intentionally. Other types of exclusions can also have this beneficial incentivizing effect for insureds. Just as fear of the application of an exclusion can create beneficial incentives for insureds to reduce risks, so can the fear of having one's policy canceled for filing loss claims that are excessive in size or number. What are the potential downsides to insureds—and third parties—of the presence of exclusions in insurance policies? What does this suggest about the limits to the regulatory function of insurance exclusions and the threat of cancellation?

4. *Information production and the teaching of safer conduct.* It is often assumed that policyholders have better information about the risks they pose than insurers have, and this is sometimes true. (See the discussion of adverse selection below.) But that is not always the case. Often insurers have better information about the risks confronting particular insureds than the insureds do. This is in part because insurers in some cases have superior information-gathering abilities and in part because insurers have more expertise in assessing the information. For example, the insurance industry established Underwriters Laboratories to test materials for resistance to fire and other hazards. Similarly, the auto insurance industry has long conducted its own crash testing of new automobiles. In addition, insurers, as previously mentioned, gather a great deal of information through the claims process. Some of this information (such as the safety ratings of automobiles) the insurers share with the general public. And some of the information is used by insurers with their own insureds, either through premium differentials (described above) or through programs designed to educate

policyholders about how they can reduce their own risks. Most insurance companies have such "loss control" programs, which provide policyholders with various analytical tools for assessing their own liability risks and identifying ways of reducing them.[9] Despite the (sometimes deserved) bashing of managed health care companies, those same institutions have been behind efforts to develop and disseminate "best practices" in health care.

5. *Insurers as gatekeepers.* Obtaining insurance is often a prerequisite to other activities. You can't register a car without auto insurance, take out a mortgage without homeowners' insurance, obtain a commercial loan without business owners' insurance, bid on a government contract without a surety bond, advertise on network television without media liability insurance, finance a movie without cast insurance, sign a commercial lease without commercial property and liability insurance, get venture capital without "key-man" life insurance, obtain practice privileges at most hospitals without medical malpractice insurance, and so forth.

All these legal or institutional requirements make insurance companies important *gatekeepers* in large sectors of the U.S. economy (and undoubtedly in other parts of the developed world as well). Going through the gate requires meeting the insurance companies' standards, including not running afoul of exclusions within policy (discussed above), as well as paying the necessary premiums. This gatekeeping role gives insurance companies the potential to serve as very significant regulators, while at the same time making access to "private" insurance an intensely "public" issue.[10] One small but revealing example of this "regulation by insurance" came in the form of a report in *The New York Times* following the conviction of a San Francisco woman for murder when her dog killed a neighbor. (The conviction was later overturned.) The *Times* reported that some homeowners' insurance companies refused to issue insurance to people who owned certain breeds of dogs and described a family that gave up their Rottweiler to get insurance for their house.[11]

Because insurers sometimes have informational advantages over government regulators, there have been suggestions to expand the use of insurers as gatekeepers, where government regulation is especially difficult. For example, some have proposed using a combination of tort liability and compulsory liability insurance to regulate the risks posed by imported food products[12] or even to regulate the risks associated with misrepresentations made in corporate financial statements.[13] Do you see how making the purchase of liability insurance mandatory for a given activity puts liability insurance companies in the position of being quasi-private risk regulators? What other advantages do you see in having insurers, as compared with government agencies, as risk regulators?

9. Every major insurer offers such services, as advertised on their websites.

10. *See, e.g.,* Carol Heimer, *Insuring More, Ensuring Less: The Costs and Benefits of Private Regulation Through Insurance, in* Embracing Risk: The Changing Culture of Insurance and Responsibility (Tom Baker & Jonathan Simon eds., 2002); Elizabeth O. Hubbart, *When Worlds Collide: The Intersection of Insurance and Motion Pictures,* 3 Conn. Ins. L.J. 267 (1996-1997).

11. *See* Joseph B. Treaster, *Home Insurers Frown on Many Dogs,* N.Y. Times, Mar. 30, 2002, at A11.

12. *See, e.g.,* Tom Baker, *Bonded Import Safety Warranties, in* Import Safety: Regulatory Governance in the Global Economy 215 (Cary Coglianese et al. eds., 2009).

13. Joshua Ronen, *Post-Enron Reform: Financial Statement Insurance, and GAAP Re-Visited,* 8 Stan. J.L. Bus. & Fin. 39, 48-60 (2002).

What are the disadvantages? Contrast, for example, State Farm and Allstate with the National Highway Traffic Safety Administration as regulators of automobile safety.

While insurance companies have regulated the behavior of private actors for many years, a more recent development has been the role of liability insurers in regulating public police departments. A recent study, involving numerous interviews with insurance-industry representatives and city attorneys, found that municipal liability insurers—through premium differentials based on insurers' superior information from past claim experience—have been able to create incentives for improvements in police conduct. For example, liability insurers have been able to "get police agencies to adopt or amend written departmental policies on subjects like the use of force and strip searches, to change the way they train their officers, and even to fire problem officers."[14] The author of the study considered a number of innovations designed to enhance the regulatory role of police insurance, such as laws mandating the purchase police liability coverage or bans on "first dollar" liability policies (that is, policies with no deductibles). Why might these innovations be a good idea? What difficulties would they present? What about the idea, proposed recently in one state, of requiring police officers to purchase their own professional liability coverage the premiums for which would come out of their own pocket?[15] What are the pros and cons of this approach, compared with liability insurance purchased at the department level or the city level?

B.   Insurance Market Failures

Insurance can be very valuable, both as a system for spreading risk and as a system for regulating risk. This does not mean, of course, that insurance markets are problem free. Insurance too experiences market failures, which is why the insurance industry is regulated. Chapter 6 will address the regulation of insurance companies. Moreover, because many insurance transactions involve contracts between highly sophisticated insurance companies and unsophisticated consumer insureds, there is a potential for insureds to be taken advantage of by insurers. Thus, these contractual relationships themselves require some form of regulatory oversight. Such regulatory oversight of insurance contracts, by insurance regulators, by courts, or both, will be a primary theme that is developed throughout the book. Among the market failures that inhibit market for insurance are the following:

1. *Insurer-side moral hazard.* Insurance can be understood as a form of principal-agent relationship, in which the insured is the principal who appoints the insurance company as the agent responsible for taking care of insured losses. This framework reveals that insurance institutions and intermediaries are also susceptible to moral hazard. For example, in deciding which insurance

---

14. *See, generally,* John Rappaport, *How Private Insurers Regulate Public Police,* 130 Harv. L. Rev. (forthcoming 2017); draft available online at *http://papers.ssrn.com/sol3/papers.cfm?abstract_id=2733783.*

15. *See http://www.npr.org/2016/06/27/483420607/to-stop-police-lawsuits-reformers-want-officers-to-get-insurance.*

company to recommend to a client, an insurance broker might prefer the company that pays the higher commission. (In this example, the "principal" is the person seeking insurance and the "agent" is the broker.) Similarly, in deciding whether to pay a claim, or how much to pay, the insurance company cannot help but be affected by the fact that it gets to keep whatever money it does not pay. (Here, the "principal" is the person who bought the insurance protection and the "agent" is the company that provides it.) These are examples of moral hazard in the broader, principal-agent understanding of the term. As we will see, much of insurance law and regulation is directed at moral hazard by insurance companies and intermediaries.

2. *Insurer opportunism.* Insurance involves the exchange of money for a promise. You pay premiums today. The insurer promises to give you money (or services) in the event that certain bad things happen. The money-for-promise structure of insurance gives the insurer a structural advantage: When the bad thing happens, it is too late for the insured to switch insurers. And there is little that you can do on your own to make the insurer pay. The insurer could simply refuse to pay. As we will see, much of insurance law is directed at preventing insurers from engaging in this kind of opportunism. But the possibility for opportunism never can be completely eliminated, and consumers never will completely trust insurance companies. The potential for opportunism and the resulting lack of trust reduce the demand for insurance. Of course, there can also be opportunism on the part of insureds, such as when insureds misrepresent their risks to insurers, and this sort of opportunism can lead to increased premiums for all who are insured. As we will see, however, there are insurance law doctrines that protect insurers and innocent insureds from such behavior.

3. *Adverse selection.*[16] Another problem with some insurance markets is "adverse selection." In the insurance context, adverse selection typically refers to the (theoretical) tendency for high-risk people to be more interested in insurance than low-risk people are. For example, all else equal, someone with a history of medical problems is more likely to be concerned about losing health insurance than someone who has always been in good health. Similarly, a manufacturer facing a wave of product liability claims will be more likely to look for very high insurance policy limits than will another, similar business (again, all else being equal). The theoretical result of adverse selection is that the average risk level of people who choose to purchase insurance will be higher than the average level of risk of the population as a whole.

Economists also regard adverse selection as an information problem, because insurance companies can address adverse selection if they are able to identify and act on the risk status of potential insureds. The classic illustration of this problem appears in an article on the "lemons problem" that helped George Akerlof win the Nobel Prize in economics: *The Market for "Lemons": Quality Uncertainty and the Market Mechanism*, 84 Q.J. Econ. 488 (1970). Akerlof analyzed a hypothetical market in which used car buyers may buy "peaches" (i.e., good cars) and "lemons" (i.e., bad cars) without being able to determine whether any

---

16. *See generally* Tom Baker, *Containing the Promise of Insurance: Adverse Selection and Risk Classification, in* Risk and Morality (Richard Ericson & Aaron Doyle eds., 2003); *see also* Peter Siegelman, *Adverse Selection in Insurance Markets: An Exaggerated Threat*, 113 Yale L.J. 1223 (2004).

individual car is a peach or lemon. In that situation, the most that a rational buyer will pay is the average price, which is less than a peach is worth. So, owners of peaches will tend to keep them, with the result that the car market becomes disproportionately composed of lemons, so that people will pay even less for cars, driving even more peaches out of the market, and so forth. This "lemons problem" is an information problem because it would be solved if buyers could know whether a particular car was a "lemon" or a "peach." Substituting "low risks" for "peaches" and "high risks" for "lemons" provides the standard account of adverse selection in insurance.

Outside of some health insurance contexts, the evidence for adverse selection by insurance applicants is much thinner than many people think. One reason is that some forms of insurance are (legally or otherwise) mandatory, so that the low risks cannot drop out of the insurance pool. Another reason may be that people who voluntarily buy insurance are, in at least some circumstances, "better" risks from the insurance companies' perspective than people who do not. This latter phenomenon is referred to as "propitious selection." One theory behind propitious selection is that people who buy insurance may be on average more risk averse than people who do not and that higher levels of risk aversion are correlated with more safety-oriented behavior.[17] In other words, there may be a tendency for risk-averse (and therefore safety conscious) people to buy more insurance so that, in contrast to adverse selection theory, the people most likely to buy insurance are low risks, not high risks. For a game theoretic explanation and summary of relevant empirical research on propitious selection, *see* David de Meza & David C. Webb, *Advantageous Selection in Insurance Markets*, 32 Rand J. Econ. 249 (2001).

As with moral hazard, adverse selection can also affect the insurance institution side of the insurance bargain. Policyholders are not the only ones susceptible to adverse selection. The classic example of insurer-side adverse selection is the "race to the bottom" that took place in fire insurance policies before the adoption of standard fire insurance policies in the late nineteenth century. Consumers were ill equipped to tell a "peach" fire insurance policy from a "lemon," and so were unlikely to pay a "peach" price, with the result that the "lemon" policies started to drive the "peach" policies out of the market. The better insurance companies organized and persuaded state legislators to enact state statutes requiring that insurers sell only "peachy" fire insurance policies. It is just this dynamic that many people cite to justify the regulation of mass market insurance contracts today and that, more broadly, explains why insurance regulation can—at least in theory—benefit both insurance consumers and insurance companies.

4. *Externalities.* An "*externality*" is a cost or a benefit that accrues to people who are not in a contractual relationship with the parties that produce the cost or benefit. Pollution is the classic *negative externality*. Pollution is a cost that polluters impose on others who are not in a contractual relationship with them and who, absent government regulation, are not able to make the polluters pay.

17. *See* David Hemenway, *Propitious Selection*, 105 Q.J. Econ. 1063 (1990).

Insurance arrangements also can result in negative externalities. Perhaps the most significant potential negative externalities are costs imposed by behavior that undercuts public trust in insurance arrangements. Because of the money-for-promise nature of insurance just explained, insurance contracts are particularly vulnerable to a decline in public trust. For that reason, substantial aspects of insurance law and regulation are devoted to making sure that insurance companies live up to their promises. For example, much of insurance regulation is devoted to ensuring that insurance companies are financially capable of fulfilling their promises, and much of insurance contract law is devoted to ensuring that insurance companies in fact fulfill those promises.

Another type of externality involves information. As mentioned above, because of the nature of the insurance business, insurance companies have to be repositories of enormous amounts of information about their insureds. The insurers use this information for making important pricing and coverage decisions. This topic is discussed in more detail in "Knowledge Production" below.

C.   *Other Functions of Insurance*

1.   Redistribution and Social Stratification

There are several senses in which insurance is a form of redistribution. How so? First, insurance is at its core *intra*personal redistribution. Recall the discussion above about how insurance can be understood as a means of transferring money across states of the world—from the individual who has not suffered a major financial loss and thus for whom the value of the next dollar earned or spent is relatively small, to the same individual who has suffered a major financial loss and thus for whom the dollars are relatively more valuable. Thus, insurance permits individuals to make transfers from their unharmed selves to their harmed selves with an insurance company serving as the financial intermediary. Second, and relatedly, we can think of insurance as redistribution from the group of insureds who contribute premiums to whichever unfortunate members of the insurance pool happen to sustain a loss-triggering payment. Both of these types of redistribution occur within the insurance transaction even if insureds are charged perfectly "accurate" or "actuarially fair" insurance premiums—that is, premiums that perfectly reflect the risk those insureds bring to the insurance pool.

A third type of redistribution through insurance occurs, however, when premiums are not set perfectly to reflect insureds' objective risk profiles. Imagine, for example, if health insurance companies were forbidden by law to inquire (or in any way consider) whether an individual applicant for insurance has a genetic predisposition to a particular illness that is highly correlated with very high lifetime medical expenses. (This is in fact the law, as we discuss in later chapters.) Absent such a law, health insurers operating in a competitive market would likely be very interested in learning about such genetic predispositions, if doing so could be done relatively cheaply and reliably. The use of genetic markers for disease propensity would allow insurers to charge premiums that more closely approximate the actual risks insureds present to the insurance pool. This would thereby help insurers to prevent adverse selection by individuals who have the disease trait. From one perspective, charging such statistically accurate premiums is fair, because it means each insured pays the full costs associated with her participation in the insurance pool.

From another perspective, however, such a result is unfair — or distributively unjust. Why should an individual who, through no fault of her own, poses a higher risk to the insurance pool — and to society generally — be forced to bear the full brunt of that unfortunate roll of the dice? By forbidding insurers from using the genetic information and thereby forcing insurers to charge the same premiums to both those who have the unfortunate genes and those who don't, private insurance results in a redistributive transfer *from* the mass of insureds lucky enough not to have the trait *to* the relatively few insureds unlucky enough to have it.[18] *Query*: Under such a law, how should insurers, and how should society, deal with the obvious problem of adverse selection, where insureds are permitted to know their own genetic risk profile but insurers are not? Have you ever heard of the "individual health insurance mandate"? The general topic of how the regulation of insurers' risk-classification practices can have distributional and efficiency consequences will be discussed at length in Chapter 6. The individual mandate is discussed briefly in the health insurance unit in Chapter 3.

There is a flip side to the redistributive function of insurance. People who cannot get insurance occupy a different social position than those who can get insurance, and people who have to pay more for insurance have fewer resources to spend on other things. Insurance institutions are hardly the sole "cause" of this inequality, but they can play an important role. Insurance institutions both reflect and create the broader social conditions that lead to social stratification.[19]

2. Capital Accumulation and Allocation

In thinking about insurance as a way to spread risk, it is easy to miss the role of insurance in capital markets. Insurance institutions hold enormous sums of money in reserve to pay claims as they become due. That money does not sit in piles in the basement of the insurance company home office. It is invested — in government bonds, real estate, commercial loans, the stock market, venture capital funds, and almost every place that capital can go in search of a return. This gives insurance companies the potential to exercise significant influence over capital allocation. For historical reasons, and because of government regulation limiting insurance company investment activity, insurance companies have largely been passive investors and lenders.[20] But even behaving in a passive role has significant consequences, for example magnifying the more active involvement of other investors.

18. In fact, an argument can be made that this type of redistribution is more efficient than trying to achieve the same distributive goals through the tax system. Kyle Logue & Ronen Avraham, *Redistributing Optimally: Of Tax Rules, Legal Rules, and Insurance,* 56 Tax L. Rev. 147 (2002).

19. *See* Tom Baker, *Risk, Insurance, and the Social Construction of Responsibility, in* Embracing Risk: The Changing Culture of Insurance and Responsibility (Tom Baker & Jonathan Simon eds., 2002); Regina Austin, *The Insurance Classification Controversy,* 131 U. Pa. L. Rev. 517 (1983).

20. *See* Mark J. Roe, *Foundations of Corporate Finance: The 1906 Pacification of the Insurance Industry,* 93 Colum. L. Rev. 639 (1993); *cf.* Gerald Rosenberg, Allianz and the German Insurance Business, 1933-1945, at 155-157 (2001) (explaining the importance of German insurance companies' purchase of government bonds to the buildup of the Nazi war machine).

Investment regulations can be used to steer capital into preferred fields.[21] For example, French insurance companies are required to invest some of their funds in French real estate, with the interesting result that French insurance companies have become a major force in the French wine industry. On a larger scale, prohibitions on foreign investment in insurance in countries such as India, China, Brazil, and Argentina were long justified as a way to steer capital to indigenous insurance institutions (typically government-owned or authorized monopolies), which would invest the capital locally. Recently, the International Monetary Fund and the World Bank, along with the globalization of the economy, have been significant forces in opening up capital markets—including insurance—to foreign investment.

Understanding insurance as an institution for accumulating capital, it is no surprise to learn that insurance firms compete with banking and securities firms. Yet, banking, insurance, and securities traditionally have been subject to different regulatory regimes. The contemporary "convergence" of the insurance, banking, and securities industries in the financial services marketplace places great strain on the existing regulatory institutions, as they struggle with each other and the firms they regulate, both to achieve regulatory ends and maintain regulatory authority.[22] Convergence and the related trend toward globalization are likely to be among the primary economic forces driving the evolution of insurance regulation in the foreseeable future. This evolution will address such fundamental issues as whether, and to what extent, there will be democratic control over capital and the proper level of governmental control (local, federal, or international) over regulatory decisions.

It is not clear, however, that convergence has been all to the good. Perhaps the most significant event to affect capital accumulation of any kind over the last 80 years has been the "Great Recession," which began with the near collapse of the housing market and the banking industry in the fall of 2008, triggered in part by the systemic failure of an innovative, widely held, and, as it turned out, disastrously risky financial instrument known as the "credit default swap" (which we discuss further in Chapter 6). Interestingly, the insurance industry on the whole, which has large amounts of money to invest, was not threatened by the crisis in the same way that banks were. This is largely because insurance companies, in part owing to state regulations, limit their financial holdings to relatively conservative investments. While it is true that insurance giant AIG required an enormous federal bailout to avoid bankruptcy, an event that would likely have had severe repercussions for the world economy, it was not because of AIG's core insurance operations. Rather, it was AIG's investment branch, which was deeply involved in the market for credit default swaps, and the investment side of AIG's insurance business, which engaged in the risky business of lending its securities as well as purchasing some of the most toxic investment products.

---

21. Much of this section is adapted from Tom Baker, *Insurance and the Law, in* International Encyclopedia of Social and Behavioral Sciences 7587 (N. J. Smelser & Paul B. Baltes eds., 2001).

22. *See* Howell E. Jackson, *Regulation in a Multisectored Financial Services Industry: An Exploratory Essay,* 77 Wash. U.L.Q. 319 (1999).

3.   Knowledge Production

Insurance was among the earliest information businesses. Indeed, from a certain perspective, an insurance company is simply a tool for the collection, analysis, and use of information. The core analytical task of an insurance enterprise is identifying future losses, choosing which of those losses it is willing to insure, estimating the frequency and magnitude of those events, preparing insurance contracts that reflect those choices, and then deciding how much to charge which classes of people in return for this protection. In addition, insurance companies need to learn how to motivate people to buy their insurance, and they ought to learn as much as possible about how to prevent loss. All of this produces knowledge, much of which can have consequences beyond the insurance enterprise:

- A simple life insurance application has the potential to reveal the HIV status of an applicant. Should the insurer have an obligation to inform the applicant? If so, with what safeguards and counseling? How about the public health department?
- Large life and workers' compensation insurers allegedly learned a great deal about the dangers of occupational and other exposure to asbestos years before that knowledge was widespread. Did these organizations have an obligation to inform the public about the risks? Should they be required to contribute to the compensation of people who were subsequently exposed to, and injured by, asbestos?
- Health insurance companies are enormous repositories of health care data. Historically, they used the data largely to predict future costs. Increasingly, they are using the data in pursuit of "cost-effective" medicine and, in the process, altering the traditional relationship between doctor and patient, with significant social and legal consequences.
- Liability insurance companies are similar repositories of data about the tort system. Like health insurance companies, they have historically used the data largely to predict future costs. On the whole, they have been reluctant to provide that information to tort law researchers. When insurance companies join forces with the "tort reform" movement in support of legal reforms such as caps on damages, higher standards for pain and suffering damages, and the like, should they be required to open their data files to disinterested researchers, who can evaluate whether their experience supports the claims they are making in the political arena?

IV.   (WAY) BEYOND RISK SPREADING—INSURANCE AND SOCIAL RESPONSIBILITY[23]

Insurance, we all now know, transfers and spreads risk. Yet what we usually think of as a transfer of risk is also a transfer of responsibility. Without health

---

23. Much of this section is adapted from Tom Baker, *Risk, Insurance, and the Social Construction of Responsibility, in* Embracing Risk: The Changing Culture of Insurance and Responsibility (Tom Baker & Jonathan Simon eds., 2002).

insurance, we are responsible for our medical bills, our choice of doctors, and, in consultation with our doctors, our course of treatment. With health insurance, the insurer assumes some of that responsibility. Insurance, then, not only spreads risk, it also spreads responsibility.

A comparison of two families in quite different circumstances begins to illustrate the relationship between insurance and responsibility. Imagine, first, a professional couple living in Avon, Connecticut, and working in nearby Hartford. If they are typical of others in their social situation, we can easily identify more than 16 forms of insurance that address various risks in their lives. Through payroll taxes, they have rights to a basic level of unemployment and disability insurance, as well as a modest retirement annuity, some life insurance, and generous health insurance for their old age or upon disability (all of which are provided under the Social Security and Medicare Acts). From the private insurance market, they have homeowners' insurance, automobile insurance, term life insurance, and an annuity. Through employment, they have health insurance, sick leave, life insurance, workers' compensation, additional disability insurance, pension plans with significant annuity features, and, possibly, employment severance arrangements that we can understand as a form of supplemental unemployment insurance.

All of this insurance transfers risk from the couple to an insurance fund and, therefore, changes the financial consequences of the events to which the insurance applies. A house fire remains a tragedy to the couple, even with insurance (because of the risk to life and the loss of irreplaceable items), but as long as the company comes through on its promise, the tragedy is not financial. Similarly, an extended illness remains an unhappy event for obvious reasons, but once again the financial effect is muted: Sick leave provides short-term income, disability insurance provides longer-term income, and health insurance covers the medical expenses. Whether living beyond working age is a blessing or a bane depends on many circumstances, but financial need is unlikely to be one of them; the couple will have an income and health insurance for life.

Now imagine a second couple living in the nearby Hartford neighborhood of Frog Hollow. One of them cleans houses in the first couple's neighborhood; the other works for a painting contractor. What insurance pads the sharp corners in their lives? Like the Avon couple, the painter has rights to basic social insurance financed by payroll taxes (unemployment insurance, disability insurance, health insurance in old age or disability, an annuity, and a limited form of life insurance). The house cleaner, however, is paid "under the table," so her only forms of social insurance are means-tested, noncontributory programs that provide a very low level of disability insurance and, in old age or disability, health insurance.[24] As long as both work, she is unlikely to qualify for these income-based benefits. Neither receives any private insurance through employment. They have purchased automobile and life insurance, but their life insurance pays only enough to cover the cost of a funeral and a few months' rent, and their auto insurance provides the mandatory minimum coverage, which does not cover losses to their own car. They don't own their home, and renters' insurance is a difficult-to-find extravagance in their neighborhood.

---

24. If the couple is unmarried, she won't be eligible for social insurance benefits that are derivative of her partner's employment, either.

It takes little imagination to contrast the meaning that sickness has for the two couples. Unwelcome in both places, it is a financial disaster only in Frog Hollow. Because the Frog Hollow couple has less insurance, they bear more responsibility for the consequences of sickness and other unfortunate events. They have no health insurance, no sick leave, and no private disability insurance, and, as a result, all medical costs are their responsibility, as are the rent, the groceries, and the other routine expenses that must be paid in sickness and in health. In the Avon household, in contrast, health insurance, sick leave, and (depending on how long the illness persists) private disability insurance relieve the couple of much of that responsibility. Sickness, along with house fires, disabling injuries, old age, and perhaps even death have different meanings in the two households, according to the presence or absence of a collective, "insurance," that assumes responsibility for the financial consequences of those events.

All these forms of insurance depend on the participation of many to share the burden of those with a qualifying need. Thus, extending insurance asserts a degree of *social responsibility* over the insured against events. In a very important sense, insurance makes the Avon couple *less responsible* for the bad things that can happen in life than the Frog Hollow couple.

Thinking about insurance as a form of social responsibility often founders on the idea of the *social* part of that term. One impediment—an amorphous and confused notion of what "social" means—is readily dealt with by understanding "society" not as an abstract entity, but rather as the group of participants in any particular insurance arrangement. A second, more serious impediment is a vision of insurance as a series of independent, bilateral contracts that leaves out the collective dimension of insurance.

So hidden is this collective dimension in the American perspective on insurance that many people in the United States never realize that most of their premiums for most forms of insurance will go to pay other people's claims. Indeed, one of the most common images of insurance is quite similar to that of a savings account. People recognize that many forms of insurance differ from savings accounts in the degree of flexibility allowed in the timing of insurance withdrawals. Nevertheless, they often expect that over the course of a lifetime, the deposits made by each person should roughly equal the withdrawals on that person's insurance account.

Unless the insurance truly is a form of savings, however (as in the case of annuities and accumulating life insurance), or a very close substitute (as in the case of Social Security retirement benefits), it rarely is desirable for the "withdrawals" to equal the "deposits." Indeed, when it comes to health, disability, property, liability, and term life insurance, if your withdrawals equal your deposits, you have had, in at least some respects, a very unfortunate life. If you are fortunate, your insurance dollars go to pay other people's claims.

Another important stumbling block to understanding how insurance institutions distribute responsibility is the complexity of the set of ideas bound up in the concept of responsibility itself. We can begin with the commonsense notion that insurance is something that responsible people arrange to have. The link between insurance and this sense of responsibility was forged in the nineteenth century in response to strong moral and religious objections to insurance. Yet, if this history means that obtaining insurance is the responsible thing to do, then people with insurance should be *more* responsible than people without insurance, not (as in the comparison of the Avon and Frog Hollow couples) less.

Part of what is going on here is wordplay: "responsible," in the sense of "trust-worthy, loyal, helpful" and the rest of the Boy Scout Law, being played off against "responsible," in the sense of obligated to pay or accountable. It is responsible—in the Scout Law sense—to get insurance precisely because not having insurance makes one responsible—in the financial accountability sense—for any number of bad things that can happen. The linking of these two meanings in the context of insurance, however, extends beyond wordplay. Historically, insurance institutions have tried to become responsible (accountable) primarily for people who are responsible (trustworthy) and to keep the irresponsible out. In the private insurance arena, that effort is manifested in admonitions to agents and underwriters and in opposition to efforts to curtail character underwriting (the latest being directed at the use of credit scores in insurance underwriting). In the social insurance arena, that concern is manifested in the concept of the deserving poor—the notion that children, the disabled, and the elderly poor deserve public support because their present need is not the result of irresponsibility on their part.

As this social insurance example suggests, there is a third, causal meaning to the word "responsible." The able-bodied poor are excluded from noncontributory social insurance programs in part because of a social judgment that they are responsible in this third, causal sense for their poverty, whether because of lack of effort or poor choices earlier in life.

"Responsible" also has a fourth meaning: "free, self-determining, or autonomous." "I'm responsible for X" means that X is my turf, an area in which I am free to act or not. Admittedly, this meaning is difficult to tease out from the first three. Self-determination can be an important element of what it takes to be a trustworthy person, and it can be hard to hold someone accountable for an act that was not self-determined. Yet we do find self-determining people who are not trustworthy, and we do at times hold people accountable for acts that involved no autonomy or free choice. So, freedom is a distinct, if related, sense of the term.

Finally, there is a *relational* sense to the word "responsible" that is captured in the social insurance concept of solidarity. Although this relational meaning may be implicit in some of the other meanings of "responsible," it is also distinct. We can be responsible in this relational sense ("in solidarity with"), whether we are trustworthy or not, for things that we did not cause, and this solidarity is not necessarily coextensive with our moral or legal accountability or our degree of self-determination. Indeed, a mismatch between popular understandings of accountability and solidarity can be a strong social force pushing accountability in a broader or narrower direction.

From these five meanings of the adjective "responsible," we get five corresponding meanings of the noun "responsibility": trustworthiness, accountability, causality, freedom, and solidarity. Can insurance be said to *distribute* all five types of responsibility? To what extent can one or more of these conceptions of insurance as distributing responsibility be seen as overlapping, or perhaps conflicting with, the conception of insurance as regulating risky conduct discussed above?

A. *Insurance and Accountability*

The idea that insurance institutions distribute financial accountability may be the easiest of these aspects of responsibility to understand. Financial accountability for experimental medical procedures provides a ready example. A decision to include experimental medical procedures in health insurance coverage assigns the financial responsibility for these procedures to insurance institutions and, through the institutions, to the "members" of these institutions. A decision to exclude experimental medical procedures from covered health insurance benefits assigns the responsibility for funding experimental treatments elsewhere, either with individual patients or with some alternative medical research funding mechanism.

The health insurance context also helps us to see that insurance institutions distribute accountability in a broader sense than who pays for health care. To the extent that leading U.S. "health insurance companies" transform themselves into "managed care organizations," they assert more control over medical care and become more accountable—certainly in a moral sense and possibly also in a legal sense—for adverse medical outcomes. Similarly, the new phenomenon of "accountable care organizations"—large medical systems that that receive payments based in part on the health of the population and not simply on the amount of care provided—represents a combination of health care provider and insurer.

B.   Insurance and Trustworthiness

Insurance institutions also mark people or organizations as responsible in the trustworthy sense. For example, it is nearly impossible in the United States to obtain financing for a home, a car, or other property without first obtaining insurance covering that property. Having insurance marks a potential borrower as responsible in a sense that is very important to lenders: The borrower can be trusted to repay the loan even if disaster strikes. This is the reason insurance "redlining" (the practice of identifying geographic regions in which an insurance company prefers not to issue policies) is of such concern. A neighborhood redlined by insurance companies is a more risky place for banks to lend. Without good financing opportunities, fewer people invest in the neighborhood, and without investment, the neighborhood becomes an even more risky place for banks, causing further decline.

Insurance institutions also mark people as trustworthy (or not) at the claims end of the insurance relationship. In nearly any claim decision, deciding whether to pay involves a moral evaluation of the claimant. For example, in the workers' compensation insurance context, the question "Does this worker have a repetitive stress injury?" invariably involves the question "Can this worker's story be trusted?" If the answer to the second question is yes, the claim will be paid with less investigation than if the answer is no.

Finally, and perhaps most importantly, insurance institutions distribute trustworthiness by structuring situations so that people act in a more or less responsible—in the Scout Law sense—manner. Workers' compensation insurance provides a number of useful examples of how insurance institutions structure situations in this manner. One common approach is to design and maintain workplaces so that it is difficult for workers to behave in an unsafe manner (and, conversely, easy to be safe). Workers' compensation insurance does this in a direct, command-and-control manner through teams of inspectors employed by insurance companies and consulting firms. It also does this in an indirect manner through experience-based premiums that give employers an incentive to prevent injuries. A second common approach to fostering responsible behavior focuses on injured workers and their return to work. Here, the responsible behavior being fostered is following through with the doctor's or therapist's orders and returning to work as soon as it is physically safe to do so.

A third, less easily documented approach to fostering "responsible" behavior is suppressing claims. Once again, workers' compensation insurance provides a ready example. From the perspective of the workers' compensation regime, an accident is a problem only if it produces a claim, and the size of the problem turns on the amount of benefits paid on the claim. Accordingly, suppressing claims may be the "responsible" thing to do. As this suggests—and this is a very important point—the responsibility fostered by an insurance institution is defined with respect to the internal logic of that institution and not according to an external perspective. In other words, insurance institutions not only structure situations so that people behave in a responsible manner, they also define what behavior is (and is not) responsible.

C.   *Insurance and Causation*

Insurance institutions can also mark people or organizations as "responsible" in the third, causal sense of the word. In deciding when and whether to defend and pay claims, insurance claims personnel regularly decide who or what caused what. Workers' compensation insurance also illustrates this dynamic. Each compensation payment reflects a judgment that an illness or injury was caused by the worker's employment. These judgments are affected by the nature of workers' compensation benefits and the availability of other forms of compensation.

One demonstration of this comes from a study of doctors' judgments about whether an injury or illness resulted from employment.[25] The study compared doctors in health maintenance organizations (HMOs) with those in private practice. The compensation incentives of the two groups differed in a crucial respect: Private health insurance paid more for a given illness or injury than workers' compensation insurance, but workers' compensation insurance paid more than the HMOs. This meant that if the illness or injury was work related, doctors in HMOs were paid more for treating the patient, while doctors in private practice were paid less than they would have been if the condition was not work related. Not surprisingly, the study showed that the HMO doctors were more likely than the doctors in private practice to diagnose an injury or illness as work related.

Of course, the study tells us nothing about which doctors were right. What it shows is simply that payment systems affect judgments about causation. When the payment system favored the work-related diagnosis, more injuries were work related. When the payment system favored a contrary diagnosis, fewer injuries were work related. Absent workers' compensation, even fewer injuries would be "caused" by employment because there would be even less occasion to link

---

25. Richard J. Butler et al., *HMOs, Moral Hazard and Cost Shifting in Workers Compensation*, 16 J. Health Econ. 191 (1997).

employment to work. Thus, workers' compensation produces injuries at work not (only) because of moral hazard, but rather because it gives us a reason to link an event (injury) with a cause (work), where otherwise that event might never have been linked to that cause.

A second example comes from an excellent book by Barry Werth, *Damages* (1998).[26] *Damages* reports the personal and legal saga leading up to the settlement of *Sabia v. Norwalk Hospital,* a medical malpractice case brought on behalf of Tony Sabia, who nearly died shortly before he was born. Tony's twin brother, Michael, did die, and whatever caused Michael's death starved Tony's brain of oxygen long enough to cause profound damage. The defendants in the case were Mary Ellen Humes, the doctor who delivered Tony and Michael, and Norwalk Hospital, the hospital where Tony was born and that ran the maternity clinic that treated Tony's mother.

It becomes clear to Tony's lawyers that (1) if the harm is shown to have been caused during delivery, the jury will put Dr. Hume on the hook and her insurance policy limits ($2 million) will be available to compensate the plaintiff; but (2) if the harm is shown to have been caused earlier, the hospital, with its $17 million of liability coverage, will be on the hook. So how does it turn out? Tony's lawyers skillfully manage this uncertainty about causation to get a settlement that included (1) a major contribution by Dr Hume's insurer, as well as (2) a major contribution from the hospital's insurer. How do you think the plaintiffs were able to get both insurers to contribute to the settlement, given that the accident was caused either during the delivery or earlier?

In addition to such case-by-case approaches to causation, insurance institutions are also involved in shaping public opinion regarding causation. Beliefs about who or what tends to cause what can have a significant impact on political decisions allocating financial accountability. For example, much of the rhetoric of moral hazard in policy debates identifies people as "responsible" in a causal sense for their condition (and thus not deserving of insurance support). We can see this at work in such diverse fields as social insurance, workers' compensation, and products liability. The larger point is that causation and responsibility are *created,* not revealed. Even if we can imagine that there is some "real" or "essential" cause for an injury (or anything else for that matter), we can never even hope to see it except through the perspectives that our history and institutions offer us. Insurance powerfully shapes those perspectives.

D.   *Insurance and Freedom*

Insurance can also affect responsibility in the freedom or self-determination sense. As discussed above, insurance is intimately tied up with social control. The more an insured loss lies within the control of the individual insured, the more strings an insurance company attaches to the promise to insure. What we described previously as "structuring situations so that people act in a more or less responsible — in the Scout Law sense — manner" is a form of social control.

---

26. This discussion is adapted from Tom Baker, *Teaching Real Torts: Using Barry Werth's* Damages *in the Law School Classroom,* 2 Nev. L.J. 386 (2002).

Insurance-based limits on freedom, autonomy, and self-determination (but none of these terms is exactly right) affect not only insurance beneficiaries, but also people and institutions that provide insured services, such as doctors and lawyers. Indeed, both the medical and legal professions are currently engaged in a struggle to maintain their professional autonomy in the face of cost control efforts by insurers. Doctors and managed health care receive the most public attention, but the same dynamic affects tort defense lawyers and liability insurance. Liability insurance companies instruct defense lawyers whether and when to take depositions, whether and when to settle, whether and when to hire experts, and so forth. Moreover, the legal expense accounting systems used by some U.S. liability insurance companies apparently allow them to tell their law firms which lawyers within the firm are the most effective (from a cost efficiency perspective), thereby affecting compensation and promotion within the firms.

E. *Insurance and Solidarity*

Depending on the degree to which premiums or benefits are linked to individual characteristics or choices, the fortunes of members of an insurance group can be linked together to a greater or lesser extent. This sort of solidarity can also be seen as a form of redistribution from the better off (less risky) to the worse (more risky). As the differences between individual life insurance and U.S. Social Security benefits show, there are great variations in the degree of solidarity or redistribution that insurance institutions embody. Individual life insurance, with its underwriting guidelines, risk classifications, and investment choices, epitomizes the individualistic end of the insurance spectrum, and Social Security, with its mandatory participation and income-based premiums and benefits, epitomizes the solidaristic end. A health care plan with "community rating" (everyone pays the same premium) and "open enrollment" (no one is turned away) is more solidaristic than a plan that charges the sick more than the healthy and turns the riskiest applicants away. Thus, as we will see in the health insurance unit in Chapter 3, the individual mandate and other aspects of the Affordable Care Act represent a significant effort to move health insurance in the United States toward greater solidarity.

To the extent that the government forbids insurers from engaging in risk classification, it is in effect compelling a greater degree of solidarity or redistribution than would otherwise exist in insurance markets. As it turns out, individual state governments in the United States differ significantly in their approaches to these risk-classification issues. Does this suggest that there is variation across states in terms of the citizens' desire for insurance solidarity/redistribution? Or does this suggest variation in the strength of insurers' ability to resist such rules? This topic is addressed at greater length in Chapter 6.

V. INSURANCE LAW

As this chapter suggests, the potential scope of an insurance law course is vast. There is the law relating to "social insurance" (a terrible name—all insurance is social) such as Social Security and Temporary Assistance to Needy Families. There is the law relating to workers' compensation. There is the law relating to "private" insurance companies and their products. And, if we treat all forms of risk spreading as forms of insurance, there are tort law, employment law, tax law, and a host of other legal fields.

Of course, no single course could ever cover that kind of ground. So the scope of "insurance law" encompassed here is fairly traditional: the law regulating the insurance functions of private insurance companies. The scope of these materials differs from others, principally in the breadth of attention devoted to insurance regulation and in the more explicit attention given to the relationship between insurance contract law and tort law. To fit those topics into today's slimmed-down casebook, this book leaves out some specialized insurance contract issues. So don't be surprised if your instructor supplements these materials to cover some of those issues.

In yet another way of analyzing what insurance is, the following excerpt from a recent article by Professor Kenneth Abraham describes "four conceptions of insurance." As you read it, think about how the taxonomy that Professor Abraham uses is consistent or inconsistent with the ideas of insurance as regulation, insurance as redistribution, insurance as social stratification, and insurance as responsibility.

> It is worthwhile at the outset to briefly summarize the four conceptions. The *contract conception* understands insurance as a voluntary agreement between an individual policyholder and an insurer, subject to the constraints and rules of construction that are ordinarily placed on such agreements by the law of contracts. This conception supplies the "literal" view of insurance to which the other conceptions, understood as metaphors or analogies, contrast themselves. Under the *public utility-regulated industry conception*, contracts are a mere tool for bringing the regulated relationship into existence. On this view, insurance is a cartelized industry selling a good sufficiently essential that it requires government regulation in the public interest. The *product conception* sees insurance as resembling a tangible good more than a promise to perform financial services, and therefore appropriately subject to rules analogous to those that govern defectively designed products. Tort rather than contract is the therefore core paradigm in this conception. Finally, the *governance conception* views insurance as a surrogate for government in controlling behavior and protecting against misfortune, as well as an organizational arrangement among policyholders. These governance relationships create the risk of abuse by the insurer for its own ends, and for the ends of the majority of policyholders at the expense of the minority. Insurance law rules analogous to those that protect the populace against government, and that protect the minority of the populace against overreaching by the majority, are therefore desirable.[27]

We have thus far said a great deal about what insurance is. But what about insurance law? Of course, this book is all about what insurance law is. However, to give you a brief preview, the short article that follows represents an attempt by one of our leading contemporary insurance law scholars to summarize some of the major aspects of insurance law in a very few words. It's a useful introduction that, like the rest of this chapter, bears revisiting at the end of the semester to be sure that you haven't lost sight of the forest for the trees.

---

27. Kenneth S. Abraham, Four Conceptions of Insurance, 161 U. Pa. L. Rev. 653, 657 (2013).

INSURANCE

Robert H. Jerry II
from Oxford Companion to American Law 420-423 (Kermit Hall ed., 2002)

Insurance law has two major divisions. One focuses on regulating entities that engage in the insurance business. This realm of insurance law is primarily a body of statutes enacted by state legislatures and administrative regulations promulgated by agencies (typically a department of insurance, headed by the insurance commissioner) that exist in every state. The other major division is a set of judicially articulated doctrines that regulate the relationship between an insurer and its policyholder. This aspect of insurance law is predominantly a specialized application of contract law, although tort law (e.g., the law of bad faith) and agency law principles, as well as some statutes and administrative regulations, are sometimes relevant.

CATEGORIZING INSURANCE

Because of its size and complexity, the insurance business can be categorized in several ways: (1) by line, which divides insurance into personal insurance (life, accidental death or dismemberment, disability, and health insurance) and property and casualty insurance (fire, ocean and inland marine, title, errors and omissions, various forms of liability insurance, and various discrete forms of property coverage); (2) by interests protected, which distinguishes first-party insurance (the policyholder insures her own interest in a person's life or in property) and third-party insurance (liability insurance, which pays proceeds to a third party to whom an insured becomes liable); (3) by method of marketing, which distinguishes (*a*) between group policies, purchased by a group representative (e.g., an employer or professional association) for the benefit of members of the group, and individual policies and (*b*) among insurance entities based on the methods used to sell policies (e.g., through agents authorized to act for only one entity; through independent agents, commonly called "brokers," who represent several companies but typically with more limited authority; or through direct marketing techniques, such as Internet marketing); and (4) by insurer organization, which recognizes the myriad structures through which insurance entities operate (e.g., stock companies, mutual companies, reciprocal exchanges, Lloyd's associations, various hospital and medical organizations).

Some insurance law principles apply consistently to different lines of insurance. For example, because insurance policies are often standardized forms drafted by the insurer and offered to the policyholder on a "take-it-or-leave-it" basis, ambiguities in the text are strictly construed against the insurer, and exclusions are construed narrowly while coverage grants are construed broadly. Similarly, a prerequisite to an insurance contract's validity is that the insured loss must be "fortuitous" in some sense, although the precise meaning of "fortuity" varies with the context.

Sometimes, however, insurance law principles have different ramifications in different lines. For example, in both life and property insurance, the owner of a policy must possess an "insurable interest" in the life or property insured as a prerequisite to the contract's validity, but what constitutes such an interest differs in the two lines because of the basic differences between property and lives. The principle of "indemnity," which holds that the benefit from an insurance contract cannot exceed the amount of the loss, is strong in property insurance but weak in life insurance, owing to the difficulties inherent in placing an economic value on an insured's life. A similar distinction is also evident with respect to "subrogation," an equitable principle (and sometimes a right afforded to the insurer by the contract) that enables one party (here, the insurer) who has paid, under some kind of legal compulsion (the contractual obligation imposed by the insurance policy), another's debt (the insured's loss for which a third party is legally obligated) to succeed to the creditor's (the insured's) claim against the third party. Subrogation, which in its application promotes indemnity, is commonly available in property and casualty insurance, where the principle of indemnity is strong, but not available in life, disability, and accidental death insurance, where the principle of indemnity is weak.

REGULATION OF INSURANCE ENTITIES

The first insurance regulations were the restrictions placed by state legislatures in the charters granted to insurance corporations. When the first general incorporation statutes appeared in the early nineteenth century, many states also enacted statutes governing the establishment of insurance companies. These statutes imposed requirements similar to those contained in a typical insurer's corporate charter, such as making periodic reports to state officials, avoiding certain kinds of investments, and maintaining minimum levels of capitalization and reserves. More onerous burdens were typically imposed on out-of-state insurers. By the 1860s, insurers tended to view the patchwork system of state regulation as burdensome, and the industry urged Congress to adopt national standards in which insurers would become federal institutions analogous to banks. This strategy, however, was foreclosed when the Supreme Court ruled in *Paul v. Virginia*, 75 U.S. (8 Wall.) 168, 183 (1869), that "issuing a policy of insurance is not a transaction of commerce," which effectively put the business of insurance outside Congress's regulatory authority and preserved the dominant role of the states.

By 1900 most states had adopted some kind of licensing procedure for insurers and agents, but state regulation was generally quite lax. Public concern over insurer abuses led to an investigation of the life insurance industry by a New York legislative committee. Its highly critical 1906 report prompted the enactment of remedial legislation in New York, which became a model for statutes in other states. By 1919, thirty-six states had created separate insurance departments vested with the authority to administer regulatory statutes. By 1930, insurance departments in most states were authorized to collect information from insurers, to protect insurer solvency, and to regulate reserve levels, valuation of assets, investments, policy forms, and unfair trade practices, such as rebating, misrepresentation, and discrimination. State regulation had become fairly comprehensive by 1944 in all areas except rate-making.

The Supreme Court, in *United States v. South-Eastern Underwriters Association*, 322 U.S. 533 (1944), overruled *Paul v. Virginia* and held that insurance transactions could be subject to federal regulation under the Commerce Clause. Ironically, by 1944 the insurance industry generally preferred state regulation to an unknown federal regulatory scheme and the possibility that federal antitrust laws might be applied in ways detrimental to the industry. Industry lobbying and the efforts of the National Association of Insurance Commissioners led to Congress's enactment in 1945 of the McCarran-Ferguson Act., 15 U.S.C. §§1011 *et seq.* In this act, Congress declared that state regulation superseded federal law to the extent that states chose to exercise their regulatory authority over the business of insurance.

Shortly after passage of the McCarran-Ferguson Act, state insurance departments collaborated in an effort to propose state legislation to regulate the areas Congress indicated it would not enter if the states acted. By 1950, some form of rate regulation had been adopted in every state. A federal inquiry into advertising practices in the accident and health insurance industry in the mid-1950s led to the adoption of unfair trade practices legislation in all states. Public concern over automobile insurance rates in the 1960s and early 1970s prompted federal inquiries, and a majority of states adopted some form of automobile insurance reform (often "no-fault" legislation). By 2000, insurance was the largest U.S. industry (in 1999 employing 2.4 million persons and collecting $677 billion in premiums, exclusive of health insurance, accounting for 7.4 percent of gross domestic product) to have escaped significant federal regulation.

State regulatory frameworks have multiple objectives, pursued through a variety of regulatory devices. Although each state has a unique insurance code, the National Association of Insurance Commissioners, which prepares and recommends model legislation and administrative rules, provides a unifying force for state regulation, and some general observations on regulation are possible.

To promote insurer solvency, state statutes limit the organizational structures in which the insurance business can be conducted; regulate relationships among insurers and their affiliates or holding companies; impose minimum capitalization, surplus, and reserve requirements; require disclosure of various kinds of financial information; regulate rates; control the kinds and proportions of investments insurers can make; and create guaranty associations to cover the financial obligations of insolvent insurers through assessments on all insurers. The solvency objective is also related to preventing excessive competition and monopoly pricing, both of which are sometimes cited as goals of insurance regulation.

To compensate for inadequate information in insurance markets, state statutes regulate the text and substantive content of insurance policies, require disclosures to consumers at the time of sale, and impose standards for accuracy in advertising. Much regulatory activity by state insurance departments might be explained as a government agency using its expertise to act as the consumer's proxy in the face of information neither accessible to nor understandable by the public. To correct unequal bargaining power, state statutes prohibit unfair trade and claims settlement practices. To promote market access, state statutes limit the ability of insurers to refuse to underwrite, cancel, or deny renewals of some kinds of insurance; prohibit insurers from withdrawing from the market; and create residual markets (e.g., access to coverage for high-risk persons).

Some insurance regulation is best understood as paternalism, manifested in the override of undesirable consumer choices. And some regulation is best seen as promotion of social goals not uniquely related to insurance, such as prohibiting underwriting practices that reinforce socially unacceptable or discriminatory classifications; increasing compensation for automobile accident victims by requiring vehicle owners to purchase minimum amounts of liability insurance; and promoting or endorsing (or discouraging or condemning) particular statuses or behavior by requiring (or proscribing) insurance coverage for particular losses (e.g., the costs of abortions or costs of infertility treatments for childless couples).

THE INSURER-POLICYHOLDER RELATIONSHIP

The relationship between insurer and policyholder is established in the insurance contract (or policy), a kind of "private law" stating the parties' reciprocal rights and duties. A typical policy contains coverage-granting provisions, exclusions, definitions, conditions and sometimes warranties (facts or circumstances the insured "warrants" to be true), and claims-processing provisions. In liability insurance, the insurer, in addition to promising to indemnify the insured against judgments or settlements of covered claims, promises to defend the insured against claims within the coverage—which means the insurer appoints an attorney to represent the insured and defend the claim made against the insured. The ability of insured parties to shift their responsibility for tort liabilities to insurance mechanisms has significant implications for the deterrence, corrective justice, and compensatory purposes of tort law. Some state statutes require those who engage in particular activities (e.g., owners of automobiles in almost all states; those engaging in hazardous businesses, such as mining) to purchase liability insurance. The predominant rationale for such requirements is to provide a source of compensation for victims of accidents. By interpreting insurance contracts and making decisions about the relative rights and duties of insurers and policyholders, courts exert significant regulatory influence on the insurance business.

Some insurance law doctrines relevant to the relationship between insurer and policyholder exist outside the text of the contract. Examples include: the requirement that the loss be accidental in some sense (the "fortuity principle"); rules that allocate proceeds among multiple parties having partial interests in insured property; rules that disqualify life insurance beneficiaries who intentionally kill the insured; and rules that provide the insurer with a defense if the policyholder fails to provide accurate information during the underwriting process or during claims processing.

INSURANCE DRAFTING PROBLEM

As you may already have noticed, there are problems in almost every section in this book. The problems are designed to give you the opportunity to apply the principles and precedents discussed in these materials. Take your cue from your instructor regarding how much attention to give the problems in preparing for class. Whether or not you spend much time on them during the semester, they are likely to be quite helpful in preparing for your exam.

Imagine that you have been asked to write the first draft of an insurance policy—a contract between a policyholder and an insurance company—to cover the risks listed below. In actuality, the vast majority of insurance contracts are standard form agreements. For this exercise, however, pretend that you must write the contract from scratch. Try to write the first sentence or two of the agreement. Then make a list of the various problems that would arise, from the insurer's and the policyholder's perspective, if the agreement were limited to those two sentences.

A.   The greatest professional soccer player in the world wants to insure his legs against injury.
B.   A country club that offers a prize of $10,000 to anyone who makes a hole-in-one on the eighteenth hole of its golf course wants to insure the risk.
C.   The owner of a commercial building in New York wants a policy that covers him in case his building is destroyed in a terrorist attack.
D.   A young doctor, just beginning her practice, would like a policy that covers her for the risk of a medical malpractice lawsuit.

CHAPTER
2

Contract Law Foundations

I. INTRODUCTION

Historically, insurance law *was* contract law. Whether conceived as a mutual benefit protecting a fraternal group or as a commercial enterprise promoting trade and investment, insurance was a voluntary undertaking whose obligations were determined almost exclusively according to the rules governing the field of law that came to be known as the *law of contracts.*

Insurance regulation did not begin in earnest in the United States until the latter half of the nineteenth century, when states began forming insurance departments that were chiefly concerned with maintaining the solvency of insurance companies. Insurance regulation created a new statutory and administrative source of insurance law that governed the relationship between insurers and their state regulators and policyholders.

Insurance regulation has developed considerably since then but, with one notable exception, the relationship between insurers and policyholders remains largely the province of contract law. The exception is social insurance. In Social Security, Medicare, Medicaid, unemployment insurance, and, to an important extent, workers' compensation insurance,[1] administrative law has replaced contract law.

In all other forms of insurance, contract law continues to define most aspects of the relationship between insurers and policyholders. There are consumer protection statutes that provide insurance consumers with additional rights and remedies, but the volume of benefits obtained by policyholders under those statutes pales in comparison to the benefits that policyholders obtain through straightforward insurance contract actions. Similarly, there are statutes and administrative processes that mandate that certain benefits be included in certain insurance policies, but, once again, the value of the benefits provided pursuant to those mandates cannot begin to compare to the value of benefits voluntarily provided by insurance companies.

The one field of private insurance in the United States in which the contract law paradigm may be on the wane is employment-based insurance. Because most

---

1. Workers' compensation is like other forms of social insurance in that the benefits to which workers are entitled are set by statute and enforced through an administrative process. Workers' compensation differs from other forms of social insurance, however, in that the benefits are provided in most states by private insurance companies pursuant to contracts between the employer and the insurance company. Contract law plays an important role in governing the relationship between employers and insurance companies.

private health and disability insurance in the United States is provided as an employment benefit, the federal statute regulating employee benefits, ERISA, is very important to health and disability insurance. ERISA (the Employee Retirement Income Security Act of 1974) draws on trust law to create rights and obligations that differ from those of contract law and allows employers to design their plans so that courts do not apply the usual *de novo* standard of review regarding the meaning of the contract at issue. We address ERISA in the employment benefit unit in Section V of Chapter 3.

II.   INSURANCE CONTRACT INTERPRETATION

The first case in this chapter illustrates an extreme example of one traditional approach to insurance contract interpretation. The majority uses (some might say misuses) the doctrine of *contra proferentem* ("against the drafter"), which instructs courts to interpret ambiguous insurance policies in favor of policyholders. Judge Clark's concurrence articulates a common criticism of this approach.

Although the facts may be a bit difficult to tease out at first, please stick with the case, since understanding the competing approaches of the dissent and majority is important. The key is to begin by making a timeline of the events surrounding the application and the ultimate rejection of Mr. Gaunt. Be sure to note the dates of Gaunt's medical examinations, the date he was murdered, and the status of his application in the company at the time of the murder. Then carefully parse the language from the application quoted in the first footnote and apply that language to the facts.

It is probably easiest at first to read the application in the way that the insurance company urged. The hardest part may be understanding how Judge Learned Hand uses the concept of ambiguity to reach the result he does. Having accomplished that, you are well situated to understand how and why Judge Clark takes him to task for that approach.

This is a somewhat difficult first case, but the effort will pay off in the end. The important thing to keep in mind is that the point of starting off with this case has almost nothing to do with the particular interpretive question at hand and everything to do with the approaches of the two judges to that question. Of course, you do need to understand the particular interpretive question at hand to appreciate the moves that the judges are making, so on to that task!

GAUNT v. JOHN HANCOCK MUTUAL LIFE INSURANCE CO.

United States Court of Appeals, Second Circuit
160 F.2d 599 (1947)

LEARNED HAND, Circuit Judge. The plaintiff appeals from a judgment, dismissing her complaint after a trial to the judge, in an action, brought as beneficiary, to recover upon a contract of life insurance upon her son's life. . . . The judge made detailed findings, the substance of which, so far as they are material to this appeal, is as follows.

One Kelman, a solicitor for the defendant authorized to take applications from prospective customers and to give receipts for first premiums, after two preliminary interviews with Gaunt, the insured, on August 3d, procured from him the signed "application," which is the subject of the action. This was a printed document of considerable length and much detail, the only passage in which here relevant we quote in full in the margin.[2] The important words were: "if the Company is satisfied that on the date of the completion of Part B of this application I was insurable . . . and if this application . . . is, prior to my death, approved by the Company at its Home Office, the insurance applied for shall be in force as of the date of completion of said Part B." Number 12 of the answers which the insured was to make in the application was in the alternative: it read: "Insurance effective: (Check date desired) Date of Part B . . . Date of issue of Policy. . . ."

When Gaunt signed the application he had not checked either of these answers; but after he had delivered it to Kelman, Kelman checked the second, so that, as the 'application' read, Gaunt was to be insured only from the issuance of the policy. The judge found that "Both Gaunt and Kelman intended that Gaunt should be covered from the date of the completion of the medical examination"; and that Kelman's checking of the wrong answer "was due to a mutual mistake on the part of Gaunt and Kelman."

At the time of signing the "application," Gaunt paid the full first premium and Kelman gave him a receipt containing the words we have just quoted without substantial change: both the "application" and the receipt were upon forms prepared by the defendant for use by solicitors such as Kelman. On the same day Kelman took Gaunt to the defendant's local examining physician who found him insurable under the rules and who recommended him for acceptance. Kelman delivered the "application" and the premium, and the physician delivered the favorable report, to one, Wholey, the defendant's local agent for Waterbury, Connecticut, who prepared a report recommending acceptance, signed by himself and Kelman, which he sent with the "application" and the physician's report to the "home office," where the documents were received on the 9th.

Since it appeared from the papers that Gaunt had been classified as "4F" in the draft because of defective eyesight, the "medical department" at the "home office" required another physical examination in Waterbury. This took place on the 17th: on the same day the local physician wrote to the "home office" again passing Gaunt; and on the 19th "a lay medical examiner" for the "medical department" at the "home office" approved the "application." Nevertheless the "home office" on the 20th wrote to Wholey asking further information as to Gaunt's classification in the draft; Wholey answered satisfactorily on the 24th by a letter received on the 25th; and on the 26th one of the "doctors of the medical department . . . approved" the application "from a medical standpoint."

The "home office" received news on that day of Gaunt's death, and never finally approved the "application," although the judge found that, if Gaunt had lived, it would have done so. Gaunt left Waterbury on August 19th. He was going

---

2. "If the first premium or installment thereof above stated was paid when this application was signed, and if the Company is satisfied that on the date of the completion of Part B of this application I was insurable in accordance with the Company's rules for the amount and on the plan applied for without modification, and if this application, including said Part B, is, prior to my death, approved by the Company at its Home Office, the insurance applied for shall be in force as of the date of completion of said Part B, but, if this application so provides, such insurance shall be in force as of the date of issue of the policy."

to the Pacific Coast or to Alaska in search of work; he arrived at Chicago on the 21st; and on the 24th he had reached Montevideo, Minnesota, where he was seen traveling in an "army bus" that had been loaded upon a flat car of a west-bound freight train. The only other occupant of this bus was one, Rasch, about whom nothing was learned except that he was later traced to the wheat fields of Wyoming as a casual worker. On the 25th Gaunt's body was found beside the west-bound track of the railroad at Milbank, South Dakota, with a hole in his head made by a 38 or 45 caliber bullet, which had entered his right jaw near the ear and had come out at the top of his skull; and although the record contains no evidence on the subject, we may take judicial notice that this must have caused substantially instant death. There was blood inside and outside the bus, and the bullet was found inside which had killed him. On the testimony the judge found that Gaunt had been intentionally killed. . . .

The first question is whether Gaunt was covered at all at the time of his death. Curiously, neither party has incorporated in the record "Part B," and we do not know what was the date of its "completion." If it was the approval "from a medical standpoint" as "advised by one of the doctors of the medical department," it was not "completed" before Gaunt's death. On the other hand the judge found that "Gaunt was, at the time of the completion of Part B, insurable in accordance with the rules of the defendant company for the plan and the amount applied for," and that is consistent only with the understanding that "completion" was earlier than the 25th. The defendant has not argued to the contrary and we shall so assume.

Thus the question becomes whether the words: "if the application, including Part B, is prior to my death, approved by the Company, at its Home Office," must inescapably be read as a condition precedent upon the immediately following promise: "the insurance . . . shall be in force as of the date of the completion of Part B."

It is true that if the clause as a whole be read literally, the insured was not covered if he died after "completion of Part B," but before "approval"; and indeed he could not have been because there must always be an insurable interest when the insurance takes effect. Yet what meaning can be given to the words "as of the date of the completion of Part B" if that be true?

The defendant suggests six possible "advantages" to the insured which will satisfy the phrase, "the insurance . . . will be in force," (1) The policy would sooner become incontestable. (2) It would earlier reach maturity, with a corresponding acceleration of dividends and cash surrender. (3) It would cover the period after "approval" and before "issue." (4) If the insured became uninsurable between "completion" and "approval" it would still cover the risk. (5) If the insured's birthday was between "completion" and "approval," the premium would be computed at a lower rate. (6) When the policy covers disability, the coverage dates from "completion."

An underwriter might so understand the phrase, when read in its context, but the application was not to be submitted to underwriters; it was to go to persons utterly unacquainted with the niceties of life insurance, who would read it colloquially. It is the understanding of such persons that counts; and not one in a hundred would suppose that he would be covered, not "as of the date of completion of Part B," as the defendant promised, but only as of the date of approval.

Had that been what the defendant meant, certainly it was easy to say so; and had it in addition meant to make the policy retroactive for some purposes, certainly it was easy to say that too. To demand that persons wholly unfamiliar with insurance shall spell all this out in the very teeth of the language used, is unpardonable.

It does indeed some violence to the words not to make actual "approval" always a condition, and to substitute a prospective approval, however inevitable, when the insured has died before approval. But it does greater violence to make the insurance "in force" only from the date of "approval"; for the ordinary applicant who has paid his first premium and has successfully passed his physical examination, would not by the remotest chance understand the clause as leaving him uncovered until the insurer at its leisure approved the risk; he would assume that he was getting immediate coverage for his money.

This is confirmed by the alternatives presented in the twelfth question; the insurance was to be "effective," either when the policy issued, or at the "date of Part B"; there was not an inkling of any other date for the inception of the risk. It is true that in Connecticut as elsewhere the business of writing life insurance is not colored with a public interest; yet in that state, again as elsewhere, the canon *contra proferentem* is more rigorously applied in insurance than in other contracts, in recognition of the difference between the parties in their acquaintance with the subject matter. A man must indeed read what he signs, and he is charged, if he does not; but insurers who seek to impose upon words of common speech an esoteric significance intelligible only to their craft, must bear the burden of any resulting confusion. We can think of few situations where that canon is more appropriate than in such a case as this . . .

Judgment reversed; judgment to be entered for plaintiff for $15,000.

CLARK, Circuit Judge (concurring). I agree that the course of negotiations required and controlled by the insurance company was "unpardonable," and am willing to concur in the decision for that reason. But I do not think we can properly or should rest upon the ambiguity of the company's forms of application and receipt. Had this bargaining occurred between parties with equal knowledge of the business and on equal terms, there could be little difficulty in supporting the condition precedent that the "insurance," i.e., the insurance contract or policy, could not "be in force," i.e., take effect, until approved at the home office, and that then it dated back to an earlier time. Moreover, conditions of this general form are unfortunately still too customary for a court to evince too much surprise at them.

There have been acute discussions of the legal problems involved; thus, most helpful is the article, Comments, *Operation of Binding Receipts in Life Insurance*, 44 Yale L.J. 1223 (1935).[3] There receipts given for the payment of the first premium were held best divisible in two categories, one requiring approval as a condition precedent to the contract, in substance as here, and the other requiring that the company be satisfied that on the date of the medical examination the applicant was an insurable risk, and that the application was otherwise "acceptable" under the company's regulations for the amount and plan of the policy applied for.

---

3. Other references might include Kessler, *Contracts of Adhesion—Some Thoughts about Freedom of Contract*, 43 Colum. L. Rev. 629, 631–635 (1943); Patterson, *The Delivery of a Life-Insurance Policy*, 33 Harv. L. Rev. 198 (1919); Havighurst, *Life Insurance Binding Receipts*, 33 Ill. L. Rev. 180 (1938).

The first form, it was said, was generally held to prevent the existence of a contract before acceptance, except with a few courts which found the provision too inequitable to support. The second, however, gave no difficulty where its reasonable requirements were afterwards found to have been met. A questionnaire to insurance officials showed an increasing trend towards the second or fairer form — a development warmly supported by the author. There was further the acute observation that use of the former form resulted in continuous litigation in a field of law where certainty was essentially indispensable, since it stimulated judicial interpretation to resolve the "ambiguity" against the company, followed by the latter's renewed attempts to revise and refine the technical words.

Hence a result placed not squarely upon inequity, but upon interpretation, seems sure to produce continuing uncertainty in the law of insurance contracts. Even though for my part I should feel constrained to concede the weight of judicial authority against our view. I think the considerations stated are persuasive to uphold recovery substantially as would occur under the second form of contract stated above.

NOTES AND QUESTIONS

1. In his casebook, Professor Spencer Kimball (one of the giants of twentieth-century insurance scholarship) described this case as one in which careful attention to the language of the insurance policy reveals that the insurer was almost certainly correct in denying coverage. *See* Spencer L. Kimball, Cases and Materials on Insurance Law 26 (1992). Do you agree with Kimball's conclusion? Does Judge Clark?

2. A perennial question in applying the doctrine of *contra proferentem* is "What is an ambiguity?" Notwithstanding the strong preferences of many contract law teachers and scholars, most courts persist in employing a "plain meaning" approach to the interpretation of insurance contracts. In this approach, the judge sits down in his or her chambers and reads the policy. If the judge can decide what it means, it is not ambiguous. Yet, as legal scholars from Oliver Wendell Holmes on down have demonstrated, one problem with "plain meaning" analysis is that words mean different things in different contexts. *See, e.g.,* Oliver Wendell Holmes, *The Theory of Legal Interpretation,* 12 Harv. L. Rev. 417 (1899). Something that might appear clearly to have one meaning to a judge sitting in chambers might have an entirely different meaning in the context in which the parties negotiated and lived out the contract. Might *Gaunt* have been such a case? In other words, might the circumstances have led Gaunt and his agent to believe one thing about the meaning of the binder, even though careful reading of the life insurance binder at issue might have led to a different understanding? If so, can we say that the clause was ambiguous in context?

3. What about Judge Clark's challenge? As a purely descriptive matter, he is certainly correct. The insurance field is replete with examples of insurance companies redrafting insurance policies to more clearly exclude a risk that courts have used *contra proferentem* and other interpretive tools to sweep into previous versions of insurance policies. One result is longer and perhaps more carefully written insurance policies. It is quite doubtful, however, that

this process produces better-informed consumers. Do you agree? Why or why not?

4.   In a provocative and insightful article, Professor Boardman raises an additional challenge. *See* Michelle E. Boardman, *Contra Proferentem: The Allure of Ambiguous Boilerplate*, 104 Mich. L. Rev. 1105 (2006). She argues that insurance companies in fact have little incentive to rewrite ambiguous insurance policies, as long as they can live with the pro-policyholder results in the few cases in which policyholders take the insurers to court:

> For the first nondrafter or consumer before the court, the application of *contra proferentem* is a boon, assuming that the drafter's interpretation was rejected by the court in part to protect the consumer. But if the court's construction of the language is *acceptable to the drafter*, it will be used in the future, to the disadvantage of consumers two through two million, who will not understand the language or who will be misled by it into not seeking relief a court would grant.

Id. at 1111. Even a pro-policyholder ruling provides useful guidance for the insurer to use in predicting future losses under the policy, and the fact that it is possible to read the policy in a way that favors the insurance company gives the insurance company room to maneuver in negotiations with the insured in future cases. If Professor Boardman is right, why might insurance industry groups so often redraft insurance policies?

The following case needs no introduction. Although the legal issue is not particularly complex, the amount of money at stake is substantial. Consider to what degree the legal rules governing the interpretation of insurance contracts involving such sums of money and such sophisticated purchasers ought to be the same for contracts sold to individuals and small businesses.

WORLD TRADE CENTER PROPERTIES v. TRAVELERS INDEMNITY CO.

United States District Court for the Southern District of New York
2002 U.S. Dist. LEXIS 9863

JOHN S. MARTIN, JR., District Judge: The terrorist attack on the World Trade Center did damage to human lives for which no amount of money can provide adequate compensation. It also did massive property damage for which monetary compensation is possible. At issue in this litigation is the extent of the liability of various insurance companies to provide that compensation to those who had an ownership interest in the World Trade Center Complex.

In this opinion, the term "Silverstein Parties" refers to entities that, after an extensive bidding process with the Port Authority of New York and New Jersey, entered into 99-year leases for the World Trade Center Complex in July 2001. These entities are controlled by Larry Silverstein, a successful New York-based real estate developer and businessman. In connection with the contemplated leases, the Silverstein Parties were obliged to procure first party property insurance coverage on the World Trade Center Properties, and the Silverstein Parties enlisted an insurance broker, Willis of New York, Inc. ("Willis"), to assemble an insurance program.

The insurance program set up by Willis was designed to be a layered program whereby claims of loss would be initially covered by a primary layer of insurance. When claims of loss exceeded the primary layer, coverage up to specified amounts would be provided by excess layers. The Silverstein Parties' insurance program consisted of a primary layer and eleven excess layers in which over twenty insurers and Lloyd's syndicates participated. Ultimately, the Silverstein Parties purchased property and business interruption insurance for the World Trade Center Properties in the amount of $3.5468 billion. . . .

DISCUSSION

The extent of the liability of the insurance carriers may ultimately depend upon resolution of the question:

Which of the two following statements best describes what caused the destruction of the World Trade Center on September 11, 2001?

1) In a single coordinated attack, terrorists flew hijacked planes into the twin towers of the World Trade Center.
2) At 8:46 A.M. on the morning of September 11th, a hijacked airliner crashed into the North Tower of the World Trade Center, and 16 minutes later a second hijacked plane struck the South Tower.

Since most property damage insurance is written on a "per occurrence" basis—the maximum insured amount will be paid for each covered occurrence—the Court would normally expect to find the answer to the question whether the events of September 11th constituted one or two "occurrences" by looking at how the parties to the insurance contract defined that term in the policy they negotiated. In the case of the World Trade Center, however, with minor exceptions,[3] there were no insurance policies in place on September 11th, although each of the insurers had signed binders setting forth in summary form their agreement to provide property damage coverage. Some of these binders expressly stated that the precise language was "to be agreed upon."

Although Travelers had not issued a policy as of September 11th, three days later, it issued a policy providing $210,620,990 in property damage insurance for the World Trade Center "per occurrence." Despite the fact that the media had already reported the controversy over whether the attack on the World Trade Center constituted one or two "occurrences" for insurance purposes, the policy Travelers issued did not define the term "occurrence."

Plaintiffs now seek summary judgment contending that, since Travelers did not define the term "occurrence" in the policy, it agreed to be bound by the meaning given to that term in the decisions of the courts of the State of New York, where the coverage was negotiated. Plaintiffs argue that, with respect to insurer liability, "occurrence" has a clear and unambiguous meaning under New York law and refers to the "immediate, efficient, physical, proximate cause of the loss, not some indirect or more remote cause of causes."

For its part, Travelers contends that since there was no policy in place as of September 11th, the Court must look to the extrinsic evidence concerning the parties' negotiations, including the fact that Willis, the insurance broker for the Silverstein parties, had circulated to the insurers a policy form that included the following definition:

> "Occurrence" shall mean all losses or damages that are attributable directly or indirectly to one cause or to one series of similar causes. All such losses will be added together and the total amount of such losses will be treated as one occurrence irrespective of the period of time or area over which such losses occur.

While Travelers and the other insurers raise a number of additional legal and factual arguments against the Silverstein Parties' contention that the Court can decide, as a matter of law, whether there were one or two "occurrences" on September 11th, the Court's view is that the dispositive issue on this motion is whether the term "occurrence" has such a clear and unambiguous meaning that the trier of fact should be barred from considering the available extrinsic evidence concerning the meaning that the parties gave to that term when they were negotiating the insurance coverage for the World Trade Center.

Before turning to the specific cases discussing the construction of insurance contracts under New York law, it is useful to look at the larger context in which our system of justice operates.

Several hundred years ago, Lord Chief Justice Coke observed that truth is "the mother of justice." Sir Edward Coke, Second Institute 524. Our system of justice is founded on the principle that litigation is to be a search for the truth; it is not some type of intellectual game that is circumscribed by the inflexible rules that define it. *See* Arthur T. Vanderbilt, Cases and Materials on Modern Procedure 10 (1952) ("The fundamental premise of the federal rules is that a trial is an orderly search for the truth in the interest of justice rather than a contest between two gladiators with surprise and technicalities as their chief weapons. . . .").

In conducting our search for the truth, we sometimes apply rules that may appear to obstruct the search for truth in an individual case because those rules will enhance the likelihood of finding the truth in a majority of cases. For example, by providing that certain types of contracts will be enforced only when evidenced by a writing, the Statute of Frauds seeks to protect against unfounded claims based on alleged oral contracts. Similarly, many states have Dead Man statutes that preclude interested parties from testifying to conversations with a deceased party in order to advance an interest adverse to the deceased.

For similar reasons, some states have adopted a strict rule that courts will not look behind the plain meaning of the words of a contract, no matter how strong the extrinsic evidence that the parties intended something other than that which is indicated by their words. New York is one of the states that rigidly adheres to this rule. As Judge Kaye explained in *W.W.W. Assocs., Inc. v. Giancomteri*, 566 N.E.2d 639 (N.Y. 1990):

> "That rule imparts 'stability to commercial transactions by safeguarding against fraudulent claims, perjury, death of witnesses . . . infirmity of memory . . . [and] the fear that the jury will improperly evaluate the extrinsic evidence.'"

However, the rule that the court will not consider extrinsic evidence that would vary the plain meaning of contract language only advances the search for the truth if the parties' intent can clearly be determined from the words they used. If contract language is ambiguous, then the courts should look to extrinsic evidence to determine the true intent of the parties. As Judge Jones observed in *Hartford Accident & Indem. Co. v. Wesolowski*, 305 N.E.2d 907 (N.Y. 1973):

> The objective in any question of the interpretation of a written contract, of course, is to determine "what is the intention of the parties as derived from the language employed" (4 Williston, Contracts 3d ed. §600, p. 280). At the same time the test on a motion for summary judgment is whether there are issues of fact properly to be resolved by a jury (CPLR 3212, subd. [b]). In general the courts have declared on countless occasions that it is the responsibility of the court to interpret written instruments (Williston, op. cit., §601, p. 303). This is obviously so where there is no ambiguity. *Bethlehem Steel Co. v. Turner Constr. Co.*, 141 N.E.2d 590 (N.Y. 1957). If there is ambiguity in the terminology used, however, and determination of the intent of the parties depends on the credibility of extrinsic evidence or on a choice among reasonable inferences to be drawn from extrinsic evidence, then such determination is to be made by the jury.

Restatement 2d, Contracts, T.D. No. 5, §238.

Is the term "occurrence" ambiguous? As Justice Holmes noted over eighty years ago, "A word is not a crystal, transparent and unchanged, it is the skin of a living thought and may vary greatly in color and content according to the circumstances and the time in which it is used." *Towne v. Eisner*, 245 U.S. 418, 425 (1918). The standard for determining whether a word is ambiguous is found in *Curry Road Ltd. v. K Mart Corp.*, 893 F.2d 509, 511 (2d Cir. 1990):

> A term is ambiguous when it is " 'capable of more than one meaning when viewed objectively by a reasonably intelligent person who has examined the context of the entire integrated agreement and who is cognizant of the customs, practices, usages and terminology as generally understood in the particular trade or business.' "

Walk-In Medical, 818 F.2d 260, 263 (*quoting Eskimo Pie Corp. v. Whitelawn Dairies, Inc.*, 284 F. Supp. 987, 994 (S.D.N.Y. 1968) (Mansfield, J.)).

The history of litigation over the meaning of the term "occurrence" amply demonstrates that its meaning is far from unambiguous and must be divined from the particular context in which it is used. As Judge Stanton of this Court found in *Witco Corp. v. American Guarantee and Liability Ins., Co.*, 1999 U.S. Dist. LEXIS 17279 (S.D.N.Y. November 4, 1999):

> There is no all-inclusive definition of the term "occurrence" or any "formulation of a test [that is] applicable in every case, for the word has been employed in a number of senses and given varying meanings depending on the relative context."

This Court has presided over a sufficient number of insurance coverage cases to be aware that anyone "who is cognizant of the customs, practices, usages and terminology as generally understood in the insurance business" would agree with Judge Stanton that the term "occurrence," standing alone, is ambiguous and, for that reason, is often specifically defined in insurance policies. Indeed, it apparently was because they viewed the term "occurrence" as ambiguous that Plaintiff's insurance brokers circulated a specific definition of occurrence to the insurers they were soliciting.

While cases cited by the Silverstein Parties do construe the term "occurrence" without resort to extrinsic evidence, each of those cases must be read in light of the particular factual record before the court. For example, in *Hartford Accident & Indem. Co. v. Wesolowski*, on which Plaintiffs rely, the court did decide the issue as a matter of law, but only after noting, "As the parties agree, there is no relevant evidence extrinsic to the insurance policy bearing on the intention of the parties at the time of its execution. Thus, there is no question of credibility and there are no inferences to be drawn from extrinsic evidence." *Hartford Accident & Indem. Co.*, 305 N.E.2d 907, 908 (N.Y. 1973).

In sum, none of the relevant cases compels a finding that the term "occurrence" has such an unambiguous meaning that, in its search for the truth, justice should blind itself to the wealth of extrinsic evidence concerning the parties' intentions that is available in this case. This includes the specific definition of the term occurrence circulated by the insurance agent for the Silverstein Parties, testimony and documents relating to the negotiations prior to September 11th and the overall structure of the insurance program from the World Trade Center, and testimony and documentary evidence concerning statements made after September 11th by those who had been involved in negotiating the insurance contracts, in which they expressed their views on the question of whether there had been one or two occurrences.

While the Court is not unmindful of the Silverstein Parties' interest in obtaining a prompt decision concerning the amount of money the insurers will have to contribute to the rebuilding of the World Trade Center, that interest can not outweigh the interest of justice in insuring that the true extent of that liability is fairly and accurately determined.

For the foregoing reasons, the motion for summary judgment as to the liability of The Travelers Indemnity Company is denied.

NOTES AND QUESTIONS

1. In a subsequent summary judgment decision, Judge Martin ruled that there was only one "occurrence" within the meaning of the Willis form quoted in the decision above. 2002 U.S. Dist. LEXIS 17900 (Sept. 25, 2002). Granting summary judgment in favor of three insurance companies that had explicitly bound coverage in a manner that adopted the terms of the Willis form, Judge Martin wrote:

   > The insurers argue that where one of the Twin Towers was struck by a hijacked airplane at 8:46 a.m. on September 11th, and 16 minutes later, the second tower was hit by a second hijacked plane, there can be no reasonable dispute that the Silverstein Parties' losses were the result of "one series of similar causes." The Silverstein Parties limit their response to this argument to a footnote in which they quote a professor's argument that this language could be construed so that two planes hitting the two towers in a sixteen minute period would not constitute one series of similar causes.
   >
   > This half-hearted attempt to dispute the plain meaning of the WilProp definition of "occurrence" cannot defeat the insurers' right to summary judgment on this issue. . . .While an academic may be able to come up with a strained meaning for the definition of "occurrence" in the WilProp Form, "common speech" and the "reasonable expectation and purpose of the ordinary

businessman" can not. The ordinary businessman would have no doubt that when two hijacked planes hit the Twin Towers in a sixteen minute period, the total destruction of the World Trade Center resulted from "one series of similar causes."

Id. The Second Circuit affirmed these decisions and a related decision (involving a question whether certain insurers had bound on the Willis form) in *World Trade Center Properties, LLC v. Hartford Fire Ins. Co.*, 345 F.3d 154 (2d Cir. 2003). The Silverstein Parties' case against Travelers (and the other insurers that bound on the Travelers form or similar forms) went to trial on the question of whether there had been one or two occurrences in this case. The jury decided that there were two occurrences. Although the jury did not give official reasons for its decision, the lore among insurance coverage lawyers is that the jury was heavily influenced by the fact that Travelers had taken a conflicting position on the number of occurrences issue in another case in California. The Second Circuit affirmed this decision as well. *SR Int'l Business Ins. Co., Ltd. v. World Trade Center Properties, LLC*, 467 F.3d 107 (2d Cir. 2006). The "number of occurrences" issue will be discussed again in Chapter 4 in the context of liability insurance.

2. Litigation over the valuation of the World Trade Center loss continued until May 2007, when New York governor Elliot Spitzer announced the final settlement of the World Trade Center claims. *See* Charles Bagli, *Insurers Agree to Pay Billions at Ground Zero*, N.Y. Times, May 24, 2007, at A1 (reporting that the total insurance recovery for rebuilding the World Trade Center would be $4.55 billion, which represents "about half of the $9 billion cost of building five towers, retail space and possibly a hotel"). The *New York Times* reported:

> As part of the deal, the Port Authority and Mr. Silverstein had to relinquish their claim that the companies owed more than $500 million in interest resulting from delays in making the payments. The insurers, in turn, abandoned their claim that they did not owe the money until the project was completed, in 2012. . . . Mr. Spitzer said the agreement, which ends all the litigation, was a collaborative effort on the part of many officials who had lost "patience with the ongoing fighting that didn't serve the public interest or the effort to rebuild."

Id.

The American Law Institute (ALI) has recently embarked on its first insurance law project. The ALI is a law reform organization that publishes the influential Restatements that you may be familiar with from your first-year torts and contracts classes. According to the ALI, a Restatement of a particular area of the law seeks to provide "clear formulation of common law and its statutory elements or variations and reflect the law as it presently stands or might appropriately be stated by a court." A Restatement is drafted by "reporters" and approved by the ALI Council and the ALI membership. The editors of this casebook are the Reporters for the Restatement of the Law of Liability Insurance (RLLI), the first "Tentative Draft" of which (TD1) was approved by the ALI in May 2016.

This casebook contains numerous excerpts from the language of that draft of the RLLI. All of the sections of the RLLI, including those approved by the ALI Council and membership, are subject to further revision until the Restatement is finally completed and approved.

Chapter One of the RLLI addresses much of the contract law doctrine addressed in this chapter of the casebook: interpretation, waiver and estoppel, and misrepresentation. The interpretation sections of TD1 of the RLLI, along with selected comments, are reproduced below. As with other Restatements, the comments are also drafted by the reporters, subject to the approval of the ALI Council and ultimately the ALI membership.

RESTATEMENT OF THE LAW OF LIABILITY INSURANCE

American Law Institute (Tent. Draft No. 1, Approved May 2016)

§2.   Insurance Policy Interpretation

(1) Insurance policy interpretation is the process of determining the meaning of the terms of an insurance policy. Whether those terms as so interpreted are enforceable is determined by reference to other legal rules.

(2) Insurance policy interpretation is a question of law.

(3) Except as this Restatement or applicable law otherwise provides, the ordinary rules of contract interpretation apply to the interpretation of liability insurance policies.

. . .

§3.   The Presumption in Favor of the Plain Meaning of Standard Form Insurance Policy Terms

(1) The plain meaning of an insurance policy term is the single meaning, if any, to which the language of the term is reasonably susceptible when applied to the claim at issue, in the context of the insurance policy as a whole, without reference to extrinsic evidence regarding the meaning of the term.

(2) An insurance policy term is interpreted according to its plain meaning, if any, unless extrinsic evidence shows that a reasonable person in the policyholder's position would give the term a different meaning. That different meaning must be more reasonable than the plain meaning in light of the extrinsic evidence, and it must be a meaning to which the language of the term is reasonably susceptible.

Comment:

a. The plain-meaning presumption. There are two opposing approaches to the interpretation of insurance policy language, both of which find support in the common law of insurance. Under the "plain-meaning rule," if a term is unambiguous "on its face" when applied to the claim in question, then evidence extrinsic to the policy itself is not admissible to show the meaning of the term. The plain-meaning rule can be unduly rigid and is sometimes applied in mechanical fashion. For example, considering the purpose of a term might be considered improper under the plain-meaning rule, even if that purpose were well known and undisputed. A few courts applying the plain-meaning rule have even gone so far as to conclude that it is improper to take the circumstances of the claim into account in determining whether a term is ambiguous. In contrast, under the "contextual approach," any kind of extrinsic evidence may be used to show that a term is ambiguous, with all of the consequences under insurance law associated with the ambiguity determination. The contextual approach, if applied without constraint, accords no special significance to the policy language.

The presumption in favor of plain meaning set forth in this Section does not follow the strict plain-meaning rule's absolute preclusion of extrinsic evidence regarding the meaning of policy terms that on their face have a single meaning when applied to the claim in question. A meaning that appears plain to a judge examining an insurance policy may differ from the meaning that is plain in the circumstances in which such policies are sold. The presumption nevertheless accords the language of those terms a significance that the contextual approach may deny them. Extrinsic evidence is admissible to show the meaning of a policy term that is unambiguous on its face, but the language of the term must be susceptible to the alternative interpretation, and that evidence must be sufficiently persuasive to the court to overcome the presumption in favor of the plain meaning of the term. To overcome this presumption, the meaning that derives from the extrinsic evidence must be more reasonable than the plain meaning.

This approach to extrinsic evidence departs significantly from that of the most commonly articulated contextual approach. That contextual approach requires the court to use available extrinsic evidence to determine whether the term is ambiguous. If the court determines that the term is ambiguous, the court then construes the term in favor of coverage, unless the insurer persuades the court that the coverage-defeating interpretation is significantly more reasonable than the alternative. In that process the court gives the latent meaning revealed by the extrinsic evidence at least the same weight as the plain meaning that the court first discerned, and in some cases more weight. The plain-meaning presumption stated in this Section also permits the use of extrinsic evidence, but the objective is not to determine whether the term has another reasonable interpretation and, hence is ambiguous, but rather to determine whether there is another, more reasonable meaning. In that process the court gives the plain meaning greater weight than the latent meaning revealed through consideration of the extrinsic evidence.

Because of variations in how courts apply the plain-meaning and contextual approaches, there is no majority rule, although there are more jurisdictions with some version of a plain-meaning rule than there are jurisdictions that openly embrace a contextual approach. As a practical matter, courts that apply the plain-meaning approach are willing to consider some materials beyond the insurance policy, such as dictionaries, the decisions of other courts, and, significantly, treatises and other secondary authority written by authors with a deep understanding of the real-world institutional contexts in which insurance policies are sold and administered. Also, some courts that apply the contextual approach give the plain meaning of policy language more weight than extrinsic evidence that merely shows that another meaning is possible. . . .

c. Rebuttable presumption. The presumption in favor of plain meaning has a number of benefits. It reflects the public value of having insurance policies communicate a consistent meaning to a wide variety of audiences, including the judges who ultimately are charged with determining the meaning of insurance policy terms. This is especially important because of the standard-form, mass-market nature of insurance policies. The presumption also provides insurers an incentive to draft those policies to accurately communicate the intended meaning to judges and other nonspecialist readers.

This Section treats the plain meaning determined by the court as the presumptive meaning in the following sense: The plain meaning prevails unless the court concludes, after considering extrinsic evidence in favor of another meaning, that a reasonable person in the policyholder's position would give the term this other meaning, and the language of the term is reasonably susceptible to this other meaning under the circumstances. In other words, for the plain meaning to be displaced, the court must conclude that the plain meaning is a less reasonable meaning. If, after considering extrinsic evidence, the court cannot determine which interpretation is more reasonable in the circumstances, the plain meaning of the term prevails. This presumption in favor of the plain meaning is not a factual presumption, because interpretation of the term is a question of law. The presumption therefore does not refer to a burden of proof, which pertains only to factual issues. Rather, the presumption in favor of the plain meaning is a rule of decision that defines the deference that courts should give to the plain meaning of insurance policy terms. Whether and how to use extrinsic evidence to determine whether to displace the plain meaning is a legal question, except in the unusual situation in which, for example, there is some question about the authenticity or truth of the extrinsic evidence.

While it is possible that this approach may in some cases lead to higher costs of resolving disputes than would an inflexible plain-meaning rule, the notion that the presumption can be displaced after considering extrinsic evidence more closely tracks the actual practices of many courts in insurance cases, avoids strained application of ambiguity rules, and better protects the objectively reasonable expectations of insurance purchasers. A strict plain-meaning rule exposes parties to the risk that the meaning a court gives to a term will not coincide with the meaning that a reasonable person would have been most likely to ascribe to the term in the context in which the policy is sold (unless that objectively reasonable meaning is defined, tautologically, as the plain meaning). Put another way, language that seems reasonably susceptible to only one meaning on its face may, after consideration of extrinsic evidence, turn out also to be reasonably susceptible to a different meaning. In a perfectly operating insurance market, there would be no such differences, but they do exist in the real-world insurance market. The rules followed in this Section are directed at minimizing those differences by providing insurers an incentive to reduce them. . . .

d. Relation of the presumption to ambiguity determinations. Under this Section, if a policy term has a plain meaning—is unambiguous on its face when applied to the claim in question—extrinsic evidence may be used to show that the term has a different meaning in context. However, the plain meaning prevails unless it is displaced under subsection (2) of this Section. By contrast, if on its face a term has more than one meaning to which the language of the term is reasonably susceptible when applied to the claim at issue, then it does not have a plain meaning, and it is interpreted under the ambiguity rules stated in §4, pursuant to which the term may be interpreted against the party that supplied it. The difference lies in the weight given to the different meanings in the two contexts. If the court relies upon extrinsic evidence to determine that there is a second reasonable meaning that favors coverage, in addition to the plain meaning that disfavors coverage, the plain meaning prevails unless the insured can persuade the court that the latent meaning revealed by the extrinsic evidence is more reasonable. By contrast, if there is not a plain meaning, the meaning that favors the non-supplying party (typically the insured) prevails, unless the party that supplied the term (typically the insurer) persuades the court that meaning is unreasonable in light of the extrinsic evidence. . . .

    e. The reasonable person and the reasonable person in this policyholder's position. The plain meaning of an insurance policy term is the understanding of the term that an ordinary, reasonable person would have, if that person took the time to read all of the relevant parts of the policy in the context of the claim at issue, without taking any other circumstances into account. The plain meaning of an insurance policy term does not vary depending on the level of sophistication or insurance-purchasing experience of the party buying the policy, because such characteristics of the policyholder lie outside the insurance policy being interpreted. Thus, for example, a standard definition of the term "occurrence" should have the same plain meaning in a homeowners' insurance policy and a general liability policy sold to a large organization, unless there is another term in one policy, not present in the other, that interacts with that definition to give it a different plain meaning. The plain meaning of any insurance policy term is determined from the perspective of the same reasonable person, an imaginary being that is properly understood as a legal construct.

    When considering whether extrinsic evidence reveals a latent meaning that is sufficiently persuasive to overcome the presumption in favor of the plain meaning, the court necessarily expands its view to consider the circumstances. The legally relevant circumstances include the observable, objective characteristics of the policyholder that identify the policyholder as a member of a relevant class of insurance purchasers, with greater or lesser experience and expertise in the insurance market (or greater or lesser capacity to obtain expert advice in that regard). Taking these circumstances into account assists the court in arriving at the traditional objective of contract interpretation, giving a term the meaning that a reasonable person would ascribe to it under the circumstances. Accordingly, in considering what, if anything, extrinsic evidence reveals about the meaning of the insurance policy term in question, the court should employ a tailored objective standard — that of a reasonable person in this policyholder's position. This standard takes into account the level of sophistication and insurance-purchasing experience expected of the party buying the policy, but not that party's subjective understanding. Thus, for example, if there is a special, insurance trade understanding of a term, and if the policyholder is an organization that would reasonably be expected to be aware of that trade understanding, then the term will be interpreted to have that meaning through the rebuttal of the plain-meaning presumption. . . .

§4. Ambiguous Terms

    (1) An insurance policy term is ambiguous if there is more than one meaning to which the language of the term is reasonably susceptible when applied to the claim in question, without reference to extrinsic evidence regarding the meaning of the term.

    (2) When an insurance policy term is ambiguous, the term is interpreted in favor of the party that did not supply the term, unless the other party persuades the court that this interpretation is unreasonable in light of extrinsic evidence.

(3) A standard-form insurance policy term is interpreted as if it were supplied by the insurer, without regard to which party actually supplied the term, unless the policyholder has agreed in writing to a contrary interpretive rule, in which case any term actually supplied by the policyholder will be interpreted using that contrary interpretive rule.

Comment

a. Definition of ambiguity. An ambiguous policy term is a term that has at least two interpretations to which the language of the term is reasonably susceptible when applied to the claim in question, without regard to extrinsic evidence. An ambiguous policy term, therefore, is a term that does not have a plain meaning in relation to the claim in question. This definition follows the traditional insurance law approach pursuant to which the competing interpretations need not be equally reasonable. All that is required is that the language of the policy be reasonably susceptible on its face to the coverage-promoting interpretation urged by the insured. The concept of ambiguity in insurance law can include what is sometimes called vagueness: a lack of clarity in application that does not easily reduce to multiple competing interpretations. A term that has a plain meaning when applied to one claim may not have a plain meaning when applied to another claim. . . .

b. Relationship to reasonable expectations. This Section is broadly consistent with the principle that insurance policy terms are to be interpreted according to the reasonable expectations of the insured. The term "reasonable expectations" is not used in the black letter of this or other Sections, however, because of the wide variation in the way that courts have employed that term. By requiring that the meaning be one to which the words are reasonably susceptible, this Restatement does not follow the strong formulation of the reasonable-expectations doctrine, pursuant to which an insurance policy is to be interpreted according to the reasonable expectations of the insured even if the insurance policy language is to the contrary. So stated, the reasonable-expectations doctrine is not actually a rule of interpretation. Rather, it is a rule regarding the enforceability of terms that are inconsistent with the reasonable expectations of the insured. As stated in §2, the enforceability of insurance policy terms is governed by legal rules other than those regarding interpretation. . . .

h. Interpretation against the supplier of the term. The rule that an ambiguous contract term should be interpreted against the party that supplied the term is commonly referred to in insurance law sources by its Latin name, *contra proferentem*, which means "against the offeror." In the context of standard-form insurance policy terms the insurer is so regularly the party supplying the form that courts often describe the *contra proferentem* rule as meaning that an ambiguous policy is interpreted in favor of coverage. The standard justification for the *contra proferentem* rule builds on the idea that the supplier of a term in a contract is generally in the best position to avoid ambiguity in the wording of the term, since the supplier drafted or, at the very least, chose to offer a contract containing that term. This rationale applies especially to situations involving standard-form terms, when one party supplies the terms and the other party either accepts or rejects them but is not given the option of suggesting alternative wording. The *contra proferentem* rule gives the supplier of the terms the incentive to take all reasonable steps to eliminate ambiguity in the drafting of terms.

It should be noted, however, that the aim of the rule is not the elimination of all ambiguity. Here the analogy to tort law is helpful. Just as it is not possible for the incentive provided by a tort-liability rule to eliminate all possibility of accidents, it is not possible for the incentive provided by a *contra proferentem* rule to eliminate all possibility of ambiguity. Even insurance policy terms that are relatively simple and clear on their face can become ambiguous when applied to a particular claim. The cost, to insurers and policyholders, of attempting to draft policies that specifically and unambiguously address every conceivable contingency would be prohibitive. Over time, insurance policies would become unacceptably long and, by their very length and complexity, inhibit rather than promote clear meaning. Thus, the *contra proferentem* rule, even when creating positive drafting incentives, should not be expected to eliminate all ambiguity.

i. Residual risk of unavoidable ambiguity. In addition to creating positive drafting incentives, the *contra proferentem* rule allocates to the party supplying the term the residual risk of unavoidable ambiguity. This allocation of risk is especially appropriate in the insurance context, where the parties supplying terms generally are insurance companies whose primary function is the spreading of risks. Thus, the risk of unavoidable ambiguity in insurance policy terms is, through the application of the *contra proferentem* rule, ultimately spread over all policyholders rather than borne by any individual insured. There is also a fairness argument that supports imposing the costs of ambiguity upon the party that benefited from having its preferred term in the insurance policy. This fairness argument applies even when the doctrine works against the insured and, thus, against risk spreading. . . .

NOTES AND QUESTIONS

1. As the title of the ALI Project suggests, the Restatement of the Law of Liability Insurance addresses only liability insurance. However, everything in the material reproduced here and later in this chapter could equally apply to other kinds of insurance. Accordingly, it would be useful to consider the ALI approach to insurance contract interpretation for all lines of insurance, including the life insurance at issue in *Gaunt* and the property insurance at issue in the *World Trade Center* case. How would the facts in *Gaunt* and *World Trade Center* be analyzed under these provisions? What are the advantages and disadvantages of the ALI approach to *contra proferentem*?

2. These provisions reflect a mainstream approach to insurance contract interpretation, one that is more receptive to the use of extrinsic evidence than the courts in states such as Texas and Oregon, while being more committed to the "plain meaning" than courts in states such as California. *See, e.g., Pacific Gas & Electric Co. v. G.W. Thomas Drayage Co.*, 69 Cal. 2d 33, 37 (Cal. 1968) ("The test of admissibility of extrinsic evidence to explain the meaning of a written instrument is not whether it appears to the court to be plain and unambiguous on its face, but whether the offered evidence is relevant to prove a meaning to which the language of the instrument is reasonably susceptible"); *London Mkt. Insurers v. Superior Court*, 53 Cal. Rptr. 3d 154 (Ct. App. 2007) (applying Pacific Gas to a liability insurance coverage action and considering, inter alia, some of the drafting history of the term in question and noting the relevance

of that drafting history to the decision of the trial court on remand). Oregon is a jurisdiction that has taken a strong "plain-meaning" approach. *See, e.g., Holloway v. Republic Indem. Co. of America*, 147 P.3d 329 (Or. 2006) (permitting extrinsic evidence only when there is an ambiguity and not allowing extrinsic evidence to determine whether there is an ambiguity).

3.   New York is generally considered to be a "plain-meaning" state. *See W.W.W. Associates, Inc. v. Giancontieri*, 77 N.Y.2d 157, 162, 566 N.E.2d 639, 642 (1990) ("Evidence outside the four corners of the document as to what was really intended but unstated or misstated is generally inadmissible to add to or vary the writing"). However, consistent with the national trend in contract interpretation, older New York cases apply a more contextual approach. *See, e.g., Hunt Foods & Indus., Inc. v. Doliner*, 26 A.D.2d 41, 43, 270 N.Y.S.2d 937, 940 (1966) (Holding "[t]o be inconsistent the term must contradict or negate a term of the writing, [so] [a] term or condition which has a lesser effect is provable"). Other courts have rejected the "plain-meaning" rule in contract interpretation. *See In re Soper's Estate*, 598 S.W.2d 528 (Mo. Ct. App. 1980) (concluding that the word "wife" referred to a person other than the woman to whom the decedent was legally married); *Hessler v. Crystal Lake Chrysler-Plymouth, Inc.*, 338 Ill. App. 3d 1010, 1021, 788 N.E.2d 405, 413 (2003) ("Illinois law does not require a finding of ambiguity as a condition for the admission of extrinsic evidence"). Many legal commentators have also advocated for a more contextual approach. *See, e.g.*, Oliver Wendell Holmes, *The Theory of Legal Interpretation*, 12 Harv. L. Rev. 417, 417 (1899) ("A word generally has several meanings, even in the dictionary. You have to consider the sentence in which it stands to decide which of those meanings it bears in the particular case, and very likely will see that it there has a shade of significance more refined than any given in the word-book"). Modern contract law also supports a more contextual approach. *See* Restatement (2d) of Contracts §212 Comment b (1981) ("It is sometimes said that extrinsic evidence cannot change the plain meaning of a writing, but meaning can almost never be plain except in a context"); UCC §2-202 Comment 2 ("[W]ritings are to be read on the assumption that the course of prior dealings between the parties and the usages of trade were taken for granted when the document was phrased. Unless carefully negated they have become an element of the meaning of the words used").

4.   In attempting to reduce the role of *contra proferentem* in deciding cases, the RLLI may be fighting an uphill battle. As Professor Kenneth Abraham has observed, in the context of insurance:

> [T]he most frequently employed principle of interpretation, however, is contra proferentem, which roughly translated means 'against the drafter' or 'against the offeror.' This is the rule than an ambiguous provision in an insurance policy—one that is subject to two reasonable interpretations—is interpreted against the drafter. Since the drafter of an insurance policy is almost always the insurer, for practical purposes this translates into a rule that ambiguous policy language is interpreted in favor of coverage. Literally thousands of reported decisions have applied this rule.

Kenneth S. Abraham, Insurance Law and Regulation 37 (5th ed. 2010). *See also* Jeffrey E. Thomas, New Appleman on Insurance Law Library Ed.

§5.02 (Lexis 2012) ("The rule of contra proferentem has been described as 'the first principle of insurance law.' In short, it provides that ambiguous provisions are to be construed against the insurer. Contra proferentem has been cited and used in thousands of insurance cases."). For a discussion of how many courts purport to apply a mechanical "strict liability" version of *contra proferentem* but in fact often apply a version of the doctrine that takes into account other factors, such as the relative reasonableness of competing interpretations, the ease with which the language could be corrected, and whether a majority of insureds would be willing to pay the premium for the coverage provided under the insured's preferred interpretation, *see generally* Kenneth S. Abraham, *A Theory of Insurance Policy Interpretation*, 95 Mich. L. Rev. 531 (1996). For a critique of the *contra proferentem* doctrine's overuse by modern courts, *see* Michelle E. Boardman, Contra Proferentem: *The Allure of Ambiguous Boilerplate*, 104 Mich. L. Rev. 1105, 1127 (2006) ("Compulsive application of contra proferentem to clauses that are not ambiguous, but rather simply disputed, can . . . belittle the role of language").

The following case is regarded by many insurance law teachers as one of the high-water marks of explicit judicial efforts to engage in the kind of lawmaking that Judge Clark called for in *Gaunt*. Consider all three grounds on which the majority finds for the policyholder. Although we have not yet studied waiver or estoppel, you might remember the basic elements of promissory estoppel from the famous §90 of the Restatement (Second) of Contracts: (1) a promise that (2) the promisor should have expected that the other party would have relied on and (3) the other party in fact does rely on to his or her detriment. Consider whether this case could have been decided on the much less controversial grounds of promissory estoppel or the "ambiguity" approach of the majority in *Gaunt*. What might have motivated the court to take the approach it did when there were more traditional approaches available? How would this case be decided under the approach to interpretation adopted in the Restatement of the Law of Liability Insurance?

C&J FERTILIZER, INC. v. ALLIED MUTUAL INSURANCE

Supreme Court of Iowa 227 N.W.2d 169 (1975)

REYNOLDSON, J. This action to recover for burglary loss under two separate insurance policies was tried to the court, resulting in a finding [that] plaintiff had failed to establish a burglary within the policy definitions. Plaintiff appeals from judgment entered for defendant. We reverse and remand.

Trial court made certain findings of fact in support of its conclusion reached. Plaintiff operated a fertilizer plant in Olds, Iowa. At time of loss, plaintiff was insured under policies issued by defendant and titled "BROAD FORM STOREKEEPERS POLICY" and "MERCANTILE BURGLARY AND ROBBERY POLICY." Each policy defined "burglary" as meaning,

> . . . the felonious abstraction of insured property (1) from within the premises by a person making felonious entry therein by actual force and violence, of which force and violence there are visible marks made by tools, explosives, electricity or

chemicals upon, or physical damage to, the exterior of the premises at the place of such entry. . . .

On Saturday, April 18, 1970, all exterior doors to the building were locked when plaintiff's employees left the premises at the end of the business day. The following day, Sunday, April 19, 1970, one of plaintiff's employees was at the plant and found all doors locked and secure. On Monday, April 20, 1970, when the employees reported for work, the exterior doors were locked, but the front office door was unlocked.

There were truck tire tread marks visible in the mud in the driveway leading to and from the Plexiglas door entrance to the warehouse. It was demonstrated this door could be forced open without leaving visible marks or physical damage. There were no visible marks on the exterior of the building made by tools, explosives, electricity or chemicals, and there was no physical damage to the exterior of the building to evidence felonious entry into the building by force and violence. Chemicals had been stored in an interior room of the warehouse. The door to this room, which had been locked, was physically damaged and carried visible marks made by tools. Chemicals had been taken at a net loss to plaintiff in the sum of $9,582. Office and shop equipment valued at $400.30 was also taken from the building.

Trial court held the policy definition of "burglary" was unambiguous, there was nothing in the record "upon which to base a finding that the door to plaintiff's place of business was entered feloniously, by actual force and violence," and, applying the policy language, found for defendant. . . .

The "BROAD FORM STOREKEEPERS POLICY" was issued April 14, 1969; the "MERCANTILE BURGLARY AND ROBBERY POLICY" on April 14, 1970. Those policies are in evidence. Prior policies apparently were first purchased in 1968. The agent, who had power to bind insurance coverage for defendant, was told plaintiff would be handling farm chemicals. After inspecting the building then used by plaintiff for storage he made certain suggestions regarding security. There ensued a conversation in which he pointed out there had to be visible evidence of burglary. There was no testimony by anyone that plaintiff was then or thereafter informed the policy to be delivered would define burglary to require "visible marks made by tools, explosives, electricity or chemicals upon, or physical damage to, the exterior of the premises at the place of . . . entry."

The import of this conversation with defendant's agent when the coverage was sold is best confirmed by the agent's complete and vocally-expressed surprise when defendant denied coverage. From what the agent saw (tire tracks and marks on the interior of the building) and his contacts with the investigating officers " . . . the thought didn't enter my mind that it wasn't covered. . . ." From the trial testimony it was obvious the only understanding was that there should be some hard evidence of a third-party burglary vis-à-vis an "inside job." The latter was in this instance effectively ruled out when the thief was required to break an interior door lock to gain access to the chemicals.

The agent testified the insurance was purchased and "the policy was sent out afterwards." The president of plaintiff corporation, a 37-year-old farmer with a high school education, looked at that portion of the policy setting out coverages, including coverage for burglary loss, the amounts of insurance, and the "location and description." He could not recall reading the fine print defining "burglary" on page three of the policy.

Trial court's "findings" must be examined in light of our applicable rules. Ordinarily in a law action tried to the court its findings of fact having adequate evidentiary support shall not be set aside unless induced by an erroneous view of the law. It follows, the rule does not preclude inquiry into the question whether, conceding the truth of a finding of fact, the trial court applied erroneous rules of law which materially affected the decision.

Extrinsic evidence that throws light on the situation of the parties, the antecedent negotiations, the attendant circumstances and the objects they were thereby striving to attain is necessarily to be regarded as relevant to ascertain the actual significance and proper legal meaning of the agreement. . . .

I.   Revolution in Formation of Contractual Relationships

Many of our principles for resolving conflicts relating to written contracts were formulated at an early time when parties of equal strength negotiated in the historical sequence of offer, acceptance, and reduction to writing. The concept that both parties assented to the resulting document had solid footing in fact.

Only recently has the sweeping change in the inception of the document received widespread recognition:

> Standard form contracts probably account for more than ninety-nine percent of all contracts now made. Most persons have difficulty remembering the last time they contracted other than by standard form; except for casual oral agreements, they probably never have. But if they are active, they contract by standard form several times a day. Parking lot and theater tickets, package receipts, department store charge slips, and gas station credit card purchase slips are all standard form contracts.

W. David Slawson, *Standard Form Contracts and Democratic Control of Lawmaking Power*, 84 Harv. L. Rev. 529 (1971).

With respect to those interested in buying insurance, it has been observed that:

> . . . Few persons solicited to take policies understand the subject of insurance or the rules of law governing the negotiations, and they have no voice in dictating the terms of what is called the contract. They are clear upon two or three points which the agent promises to protect, and for everything else they must sign ready-made applications and accept ready-made policies carefully concocted to conserve the interests of the company. . . . The subject, therefore, is sui generis, and the rules of a legal system devised to govern the formation of ordinary contracts between man and man cannot be mechanically applied to it.

7 Williston on Contracts §900, pp. 29-30 (3d Ed. 1963). R. Keeton, *Insurance Law Rights At Variance With Policy Provisions*, 83 Harv. L. Rev. 961, 966-67 (1970). . . .

It is generally recognized the insured will not read the detailed, cross-referenced, standardized, mass-produced insurance form, nor understand it if he does. . . . The concept that persons must obey public laws enacted by their own representatives does not offend a fundamental sense of justice: an inherent element of assent pervades the process. But the inevitable result of enforcing all provisions of the adhesion contract, frequently, as here, delivered subsequent to the transaction and containing provisions never assented to, would be an abdication of judicial responsibility in face of basic unfairness and a recognition that persons' rights shall be controlled by private lawmakers without the consent, express or implied, of those affected. . . .

The statutory requirement that the form of policies be approved by the commissioner of insurance, neither resolves the issue whether the fine-print provisions nullify the insurance bargained for in a given case nor ousts the court from necessary jurisdiction. In this connection it has been pertinently stated:

> Insurance contracts continue to be contracts of adhesion, under which the insured is left little choice beyond electing among standardized provisions offered to him, even when the standard forms are prescribed by public officials rather than insurers. Moreover, although statutory and administrative regulations have made increasing inroads on the insurer's autonomy by prescribing some kinds of provisions and proscribing others, most insurance policy provisions are still drafted by insurers. Regulation is relatively weak in most instances, and even the provisions prescribed or approved by legislative or administrative action ordinarily are in essence adoptions, outright or slightly modified, of proposals made by insurers' draftsmen.
>
>   Under such circumstances as these, judicial regulation of contracts of adhesion, whether concerning insurance or some other kind of transaction, remains appropriate.

R. Keeton, *supra* at 966-67.

The mass-produced boiler-plate "contracts," necessitated and spawned by the explosive growth of complex business transactions in a burgeoning population left courts frequently frustrated in attempting to arrive at just results by applying many of the traditional contract-construing stratagems. As long as fifteen years ago Professor Llewellyn, reflecting on this situation in his book The Common Law Tradition—Deciding Appeals 362-71 (1960), wrote,

> . . . The answer, I suggest, is this: Instead of thinking about "assent" to boilerplate clauses, we can recognize that so far as concerns the specific, there is no assent at all. What has in fact been assented to, specifically, are the few dickered terms, and the broad type of transaction, and but one thing more. That one thing more is a blanket assent (not a specific assent) to any not unreasonable or indecent terms the seller may have on his form, which do not alter or eviscerate the reasonable meaning of the dickered terms. The fine print which has not been read has no business to cut under the reasonable meaning of those dickered terms which constitute the dominant and only real expression of agreement, but much of it commonly belongs in.

Id. at 370.

In fairness to the often-discerned ability of the common law to develop solutions for changing demands, it should be noted appellate courts take cases as they come, constrained by issues the litigants formulated in trial court—a point not infrequently overlooked by academicians. Nor can a lawyer in the ordinary case be faulted for not risking a client's cause on an uncharted course when there is a reasonable prospect of reaching a fair result through familiar channels of long-accepted legal principles, for example, those grounded on ambiguity in language, the duty to define limitations or exclusions in clear and explicit terms, and interpretation of language from the viewpoint of an ordinary person, not a specialist or expert. . . .

II.   REASONABLE EXPECTATIONS

This court adopted the doctrine of reasonable expectations in *Rodman v. State Farm Mutual Automobile Ins. Co.*, 208 N.W.2d 903, 905-908 (Iowa 1973). The Rodman court approved the following articulation of that concept:

> The objectively reasonable expectations of applicants and intended beneficiaries regarding the terms of insurance contracts will be honored even though painstaking study of the policy provisions would have negated those expectations.

Supra at 906.

At comment *f* to §237 of Restatement (Second) of Contracts, *supra* pp. 540-41, we find the following analysis of the reasonable expectations doctrine:

> Although customers typically adhere to standardized agreements and are bound by them without even appearing to know the standard terms in detail, they are not bound to unknown terms which are beyond the range of reasonable expectation. A debtor who delivers a check to his creditor with the amount blank does not authorize the insertion of an infinite figure. Similarly, a party who adheres to the other party's standard terms does not assent to a term if the other party has reason to believe that the adhering party would not have accepted the agreement if he had known that the agreement contained the particular term. Such a belief or assumption may be shown by the prior negotiations or inferred from the circumstances. Reason to believe may be inferred from the fact that the term is bizarre or oppressive, from the fact that it eviscerates the non-standard terms explicitly agreed to, or from the fact that it eliminates the dominant purpose of the transaction. The inference is reinforced if the adhering party never had an opportunity to read the term, or if it is illegible or otherwise hidden from view. This rule is closely related to the policy against unconscionable terms and the rule of interpretation against the draftsman.

. . . The evidence does show, as above noted, a "dicker" for burglary insurance coverage on chemicals and equipment. The negotiation was for what was actually expressed in the policies' "Insuring Agreements" the insurer's promise. "To pay for loss by burglary or by robbery of a watchman, while the premises are not open for business, of merchandise, furniture, fixtures and equipment within the premises. . . ."

In addition, the conversation included statements from which the plaintiff should have understood defendant's obligation to pay would not arise where the burglary was an "inside job." Thus the following exclusion should have been reasonably anticipated:

> EXCLUSIONS
> This policy does not apply:
>
> (b) to loss due to any fraudulent, dishonest or criminal act by any Insured, a partner therein, or an officer, employee, director, trustee or authorized representative thereof. . . .

But there was nothing relating to the negotiations with defendant's agent which would have led plaintiff to reasonably anticipate [that] defendant would bury within the definition of "burglary" another exclusion denying coverage when, no matter how extensive the proof of a third-party burglary, no marks were left on the exterior of the premises. This escape clause, here triggered by the burglar's talent (an investigating law officer, apparently acquainted with the current modus operandi, gained access to the steel building without leaving any marks by leaning on the overhead Plexiglas door while simultaneously turning the locked handle), was never read to or by plaintiff's personnel, nor was the substance explained by defendant's agent.

Moreover, the burglary "definition" which crept into this policy comports neither with the concept a layman might have of that crime, nor with a legal interpretation. *See State v. Ferguson*, 128 N.W. 840, 841-842 (Iowa 1910) ("It need not appear that this office was an independent building, for it is well known that it is burglary for one to break and enter an inner door or window, although the culprit entered through an open outer door . . .").

The most plaintiff might have reasonably anticipated was a policy requirement of visual evidence (abundant here) indicating the burglary was an "outside" not an "inside" job. The exclusion in issue, masking as a definition, makes insurer's obligation to pay turn on the skill of the burglar, not on the event the parties bargained for: a bona-fide third party burglary resulting in loss of plaintiff's chemicals and equipment. . . .

III.   IMPLIED WARRANTY

Plaintiff should also prevail because defendant breached an implied warranty that the policy later delivered would be reasonably fit for its intended purpose: to set out in writing the obligations of the parties (1) without altering or impairing the fair meaning of the protection bargained for when read alone, and (2) in terms that are neither in the particular nor in the net manifestly unreasonable and unfair.

More than 75 years ago this court, without statutory support, recognized in contracts for sale of tangible property there was a warranty implied by law that the goods sold "were reasonably fit for the purpose for which they were intended." *Alpha-Check-Rower Co. v. Bradley*, 75 N.W. 369, 372 (Iowa 1898). This seminal concept of basic fairness grew by progressive court decisions and statutory enactments into that network of protection which today guards the chattel purchaser from exploitation. . . .

We would be derelict in our duty to administer justice if we were not to judicially know that modern insurance companies have turned to mass advertising to sell "protection." A person who has been incessantly assured a given company's policies will afford him complete protection is unlikely to be wary enough to search his policy to find a provision nullifying his burglary protection if the burglar breaks open an inside, but not an outside, door.

There is little justification in depriving purchasers of merchandized "protection" of those remedies long available to purchasers of goods:

> Although implied warranties of fitness for intended purpose have traditionally been attached only to sales of tangible products, there is no reason why they

should not be attached to "sales of promises" as well. Whether a product is tangible or intangible, its creator ordinarily has reason to know of the purposes for which the buyer intends to use it, and buyers ordinarily rely on the creator's skill or judgment in furnishing it. The reasonable consumer for example depends on an insurance agent and insurance company to sell him a policy that "works" for its intended purpose in much the same way that he depends on a television salesman and television manufacturer. In neither case is he likely to be competent to judge the fitness of the product himself; in both, he must rely on common knowledge and the creator's advertising and promotion.

W. Slawson, *supra* at 546-47.

Effective imposition of an implied warranty would encourage insurers to make known to insurance buyers those provisions which would limit the implied warranty inherent in the situation. These exclusions would then become part of the initial bargaining. Such provisions, mandated by the Uniform Commercial Code to be "conspicuous" in the sale of goods (§554.2316, The Code), should be conspicuously presented by the insurer in the sale of protection. This would be no more difficult than the manner in which they advertise their product's desirable features. *See Henningsen v. Bloomfield Motors, Inc.,* 161 A.2d 69, 93 (N.J. 1960). From a public policy viewpoint, such a requirement (in order to enforce what is essentially an exclusion) might promote meaningful competition among insurers in eliminating technical policy provisions which drain away bargained-for protection. The ultimate benefit would be a chance for knowledgeable selection by insurance purchasers among various coverages. . . .

Ten years ago this court banished the ancient doctrine of *caveat emptor* as the pole star for business. *Syester v. Banta,* 133 N.W.2d 666, 668 (Iowa 1965). In *Mease v. Fox,* 200 N.W.2d 791 (Iowa 1972) we joined a scant handful of courts pioneering the concept that implied warranty relief was not the captive of chattel sales law, but was available to resolve long-standing inequities in the law of dwelling leases. It is now time to provide buyers of protection the same safeguards provided for buyers of personality and lessees of dwellings. . . .

IV.   UNCONSCIONABILITY

Plaintiff is also entitled to a reversal because the liability avoiding provision in the definition of the burglary is, in the circumstances of this case, unconscionable.

We have already noted the policies were not even before the negotiating persons when the protection was purchased. The fair inference to be drawn from the testimony is that the understanding contemplated only visual evidence of bona-fide burglary to eliminate the risk of an "inside job."

The policies in question contain a classic example of that proverbial fine print (six point type as compared with the twenty-four point type appearing on the face of the policies: "BROAD FORM STOREKEEPERS POLICY" and "MERCANTILE BURGLARY AND ROBBERY POLICY") which "becomes visible only after the event." Such print is additionally suspect when, instead of appearing logically in the "exclusions" of the policies, it poses as a part of an esoteric definition of burglary. . . .

The rule of selective elimination of unconscionable provisions is articulated in the tentative draft of the Restatement (Second) of Contracts, *supra* §234, p. 528:

§234.   Unconscionable Contract or Term

If a contract or term thereof is unconscionable at the time the contract is made a court may refuse to enforce the contract, or may enforce the remainder of the contract without the unconscionable term, or may so limit the application of any unconscionable term as to avoid any unconscionable result.

The following statement appears in comment "a. Scope":

Particularly in the case of standardized agreements, the rule of this Section permits the court to pass directly on the unconscionability of the contract or clause rather than to avoid unconscionable results by interpretation.

Comment "d. Weakness in the bargaining process" incorporates the following observation,

Gross inequality of bargaining power, together with terms unreasonably favorable to the stronger party, may confirm indications that the transaction involved elements of deception or compulsion, or may show that the weaker party had no meaningful choice, no real alternative, or did not in fact assent or appear to assent to the unfair terms.

The resources of a court to avoid unconscionable provisions are not exhausted after a determination of inapplicability of the *contra proferentem* rule: "Even in such a case, the court may refuse to enforce an unconscionable provision and may give such remedy as justice requires. . . . A contractor may defeat his own ends by the use of complex printed forms devised with intent to get the most and to give the least." 3 Corbin on Contracts §559, pp. 270-71. . . .

A policy of relying solely on traditional techniques of construction in an effort to avoid the effect of unconscionable provisions ultimately compounds the problem:

First, since they [such techniques] all rest on the admission that the clauses in question are permissible in purpose and content, they invite the draftsman to recur to the attack. Give him time, and he will make the grade. Second, since they do not face the issue, they fail to accumulate either experience or authority in the needed direction: that of making out for any given type of transaction what the minimum decencies are which a court will insist upon as essential to an enforceable bargain of a given type, or as being inherent in a bargain of that type. Third, since they purport to construe, and do not really construe, nor are intended to . . . they seriously embarrass later efforts . . . to get at the true meaning of those wholly legitimate contracts and clauses which call for their meaning to be got at instead of avoided.

Llewellyn, *Book Review*, 52 Harv. L. Rev. 700, 703 (1939). . . .

Reversed and remanded . . .

LE GRAND, J. I dissent from the result reached by the majority because it ignores virtually every rule by which we have heretofore adjudicated such cases and affords plaintiff ex post facto insurance coverage which it not only did not buy but which it knew it did not buy. . . .

While it may be very well to talk in grand terms about "mass advertising" by insurance companies and "incessant" assurances as to coverage which mislead the "unwary," particularly about "fine-print" provisions, such discussion should somehow be related to the case under review. Our primary duty, after all, is to resolve this dispute for these litigants under this record.

There is total silence in this case concerning any of the practices the majority finds offensive; nor is there any claim plaintiff was beguiled by such conduct into believing it had more protection than it actually did.

The record is even stronger against the majority's fine-print argument, the stereotype accusation which serves as a coup de grace in all insurance cases. Except for larger type on the face sheet and black (but not larger) print to designate divisions and sub-headings, the entire policies are of one size and style of print. To compare the face sheet with the body of the policy is like comparing a book's jacket cover with the narrative content; and the use of black type or other means of emphasis to separate one part of an instrument from another is an approved editorial expedient which serves to assist, not hinder, readability. In fact many of our opinions, including that of the majority in the instant case, resort to that device.

Tested by any objective standard, the size and style of type used cannot be fairly described as "fine print." The majority's description, right or wrong, of the plight of consumers generally should not be the basis for resolving the case now before us. . . .

Crucial to a correct determination of this appeal is the disputed provision of each policy defining burglary as "the felonious abstraction of insured property . . . by a person making felonious entry . . . by actual force and violence, of which force and violence there are visible marks made by tools, explosives, electricity or chemicals upon, or physical damage to, the exterior of the premises at the place of such entry. . . ." The starting point of any consideration of that definition is a determination whether it is ambiguous. Yet the majority does not even mention ambiguity.

The purpose of such a provision, of course, is to omit from coverage "inside jobs" or those resulting from fraud or complicity by the assured. The overwhelming weight of authority upholds such provisions as legitimate in purpose and unambiguous in application. Annot. 99 A.L.R.2d 129, 134 (1965); (additional citation omitted).

Once this indisputable fact is recognized, plaintiff's arguments virtually collapse. We may not—at least we should not—by any accepted standard of construction meddle with contracts which clearly and plainly state their meaning simply because we dislike that meaning, even in the case of insurance policies.

. . . Here we have affirmative and unequivocal testimony from an officer and director of the plaintiff corporation that he knew the disputed provision was in the policies because "it was just like the insurance policy I have on my farm." I cannot agree plaintiff may now assert it reasonably expected from these policies something it knew was not there.

These same observations should dispose of plaintiff's claim of implied warranty, a theory incidentally for which there is no case authority at all. The majority apparently seeks to bring insurance contracts within the ambit of the Uniform Commercial Code governing sales of goods. I believe the definitional section of the Code itself precludes that notion. *See* U.C.C. §554.2105. This should put an end to the majority's argument that buying insurance protection is the same as buying groceries. The complete absence of support from other jurisdictions would also suggest it is indefensible. At least it has done so to some courts. *See Drabbels v. Skelly Oil Company,* 50 N.W.2d 229, 231 (Neb. 1951).

The remaining ground upon which the majority invalidates the policies—unconscionability—has also been disavowed by the great majority of courts which have decided the question, usually in connection with public policy considerations. *See Scanlon v. Western Fire Insurance Company,* 144 N.W.2d 677, 679 (Mich. Ct. App. 1966); (additional citation omitted). . . .

NOTES AND QUESTIONS

1. Of the three doctrines that the majority employs, "reasonable expectations" takes most seriously the promise of autonomy often thought to be at the core of private ordering through contract law. *See, e.g.,* Patrick Atiyah, *Contracts, Promises and the Law of Obligations,* 94 L.Q. Rev. 193 (1978). With reasonable expectations, the ideal type remains the individually negotiated contract between two parties of equal knowledge and economic power, and the governing ideal remains consent. Contract law simply adapts to reflect the mass market nature of the contract and the informational advantage held by the insurer. Reasonable expectations is an "information forcing" doctrine that holds out the possibility of an insurer accurately marketing and describing the insurance policy so that the coverage the insurer intends to sell perfectly matches the coverage the buyer understands he or she is buying. Thus, reasonable expectations do not in fact go as far toward judicial lawmaking as Judge Clark would have gone in *Gaunt.*

    Given how close the doctrine of reasonable expectations hews to the contract law ideal of consent, it may be surprising that it has been such a controversial doctrine. Professor (later Judge) Robert Keeton is generally credited with promoting the concept of reasonable expectations through the article cited in *C&J Fertilizer,* although the scholarly roots of the doctrine date back at least as far as the article by Professor Patterson that Judge Clark cited in the footnote to his concurrence in *Gaunt* and the book review by Professor Karl Llewellyn cited in *C&J Fertilizer.* Yet, according to Professor Roger Henderson, only ten states adopted the doctrine in insurance cases. *See* Roger C. Henderson, *The Doctrine of Reasonable Expectations in Insurance Law After Two Decades,* 51 Ohio St. L.J. 823, 828 (1990).

2. The unconscionability doctrine comes the closest to putting the court in the position Judge Clark advocated in *Gaunt.* With unconscionability, the governing ideal is not consent or the accurate dissemination of knowledge but rather fairness. Perhaps because of the elusive nature of substantive fairness, American courts have shied away from unconscionability; it is very unusual to see it employed in an insurance case. As a result, we do not have a very good picture of what it would look like in application. Courts are somewhat more likely to invoke "public policy" than unconscionability: holding that a provision is void because it conflicts with some important public policy. *See Bartlett v. Amica Mutual Ins. Co.,* 593 A.2d 45, 49 (R.I. 1991) (finding that the public policy for which the legislature enacted the uninsured motorists' statute should guide how the court interprets contract provisions); *Unigard Sec.*

Ins. Co. v. Schaefer, 572 S.W.2d 303, 308 (Tex. 1978) ("Because the provision of such mandated coverage is a matter of public policy, a claim of rejection thereof should not be determined simply by reference to the rules which courts otherwise apply to determine the intent and acts of contracting parties").

3. The implied warranty doctrine may be the most intriguing of the three doctrines employed by the court in *C&J Fertilizer* because it reflects an understanding of the insurance policy as a "product," a thing bought and sold in a market, rather than a negotiated relationship. Professor Ian Macneil coined the term "bureaucratic good" to describe complicated mass market goods and services. *See* Ian R. Macneil, *Bureaucracy and Contracts of Adhesion,* 22 Osgoode Hall L.J. 5 (1984). The more that insurance is thought of as a "thing" or "good" rather than a contract, the more obvious the mismatch between what Professor Friedrich Kessler called the "ideology of freedom of contract" (see his article cited in Clark's dissent in *Gaunt*) and mass market insurance. *Cf.* Arthur Allen Leff, *Contract as Thing,* 19 Am. U. L. Rev. 131, 155 (1970) (cautioning that the law should not require contracts or products to be so excellent that people cannot afford to buy them). Interestingly, people in the insurance business regularly refer to what they sell as insurance "products" and sometimes even describe parts of their business as the "manufacture" and "distribution" of those products. What might the doctrine of implied warranty accomplish that reasonable expectations or unconscionability could not? Why might courts resist the application of the implied warranty doctrine to insurance policies? Professor Daniel Schwarcz has argued that product liability theory (which is similar in many respects to the theory behind the implied warranty) provides a useful framework for judicial regulation of insurance policies. *See* Daniel Schwarcz, *A Products Liability Theory for the Judicial Regulation of Insurance Policies,* 48 William & Mary L. Rev. 1387 (2007). He suggests that courts might adopt a defective warning analogy that would better serve the information forcing function currently served by reasonable expectations doctrine and that a defective design analogy could achieve the relationship-shaping role that Judge Clark advocated for judges in his concurrence in *Gaunt.* Of course, it is very difficult to state with any precision what makes an insurance policy defective. The question is whether thinking about an insurance policy as a product that is designed will allow courts to develop a more consistent and practical approach than any of the other policyholder protecting doctrines developed to date. Professor Abraham thinks not. *See* Kenneth S. Abraham, *Four Conceptions of Insurance,* 161 U. Penn. L. Rev. 653, 683 (2013).

4. How might a less adventurous court have used the doctrine of *contra proferentem* to accomplish the same result? Is the "plain meaning" of the burglary provision ambiguous? If not, is there a way to argue that the provision is ambiguous in context? How? Think about the following factors in the court's analysis: (1) the small point size of the type; (2) the fact that the exclusion was in a definition rather than in the exclusions section of the policy; (3) the purpose of the exclusion and how an exclusion that was more narrowly tailored to meet that purpose would have been written; (4) the understanding of people in the trade (evidenced by the insurance agent); and (5) external standards of what "burglary" means.

5. Section 211 of the Restatement (Second) of Contracts adopts a narrow version of the reasonable expectations doctrine that applies to standardized agreements. That section states:

§211.   Standardized Agreements

(1) Except as stated in Subsection (3), where a party to an agreement signs or otherwise manifests assent to a writing and has reason to believe that like writings are regularly used to embody terms of agreements of the same type, he adopts the writing as an integrated agreement with respect to the terms included in the writing.

(2) Such a writing is interpreted wherever reasonable as treating alike all those similarly situated, without regard to their knowledge or understanding of the standard terms of the writing.

(3) Where the other party has reason to believe that the party manifesting such assent would not do so if he knew that the writing contained a particular term, the term is not part of the agreement.

Could the exception in subsection (3) have been used to reach the same result in *C&J Fertilizer*? Note that under the approach of the RLLI, the rule in §211 would be treated as a rule affecting the enforceability of insurance policy provisions, not a rule of interpretation. Thus, the sections of the RLLI addressing interpretation do not address the applicability of the §211 rule to insurance contracts. The courts in only a very few states have ever applied §211 as a basis for refusing to enforce an insurance policy provision.

6. As *C&J Fertilizer* reflects, the vast majority of insurance policies are "standard form" documents, drafted by or on behalf of the insurance company and presented to the purchaser on a "take it or leave it" basis. Even when large commercial policyholders individually negotiate policies (sometimes called "manuscript" policies), most or all of the contract language is taken from standard forms. Often the most that even a large corporate insured can do is pick and choose among the various parts of the insurer's standard form policies. Should the same rules of contract interpretation apply when the policyholders are large corporations rather than individuals or small business owners? Why or why not?

7. In the property/casualty insurance field, many insurance policies are drafted by industry committees, under the auspices of the Insurance Services Office (ISO). ISO is what is left of the insurance rating bureaus that, in effect, organized legal cartels during substantial periods of the twentieth century. For claims that ISO continued to engage in anticompetitive behavior well into the latter half of the twentieth century, *see Hartford Fire Ins. Co. v. California*, 509 U.S. 764 (1993).

There are many advantages to insurers in using ISO standard forms, including that

- the insurer receives the benefit of the "considered wisdom" of the drafters regarding what coverage can profitably be offered on a mass market basis;
- in the event of litigation, the insurer can rely on earlier precedent regarding the meaning and application of disputed provisions;

- ISO members can receive the loss data of other members using the same form, thereby allowing the insurer to predict future losses on the basis of much larger experience; and
- ISO takes care of obtaining approval from state regulators for the use of the forms.

At least theoretically, these benefits accrue to the general public as well, because they lower the costs of entry, thereby making insurance a more competitive business. In addition, standard forms facilitate price shopping among insurers. If one homeowners' insurance policy is pretty much like another, then consumers can be more confident that they are not making a mistake by choosing the less expensive insurer. With the rise of truly massive personal lines insurance companies with national markets, the uniformity of auto and homeowners' coverage has broken down somewhat. Very large insurance groups (such as State Farm and Allstate) do not need to aggregate their personal lines loss experience with other insurers and, accordingly, they have felt more free to vary the language in their policies from that in the corresponding ISO policies.

8. The *C&J Fertilizer* majority regards as utterly irrelevant the fact that the contract language in question had been approved by the Iowa Department of Insurance. Why? There has been no systematic, scholarly study of the effectiveness of state regulation of insurance forms. Nevertheless, the attitude of the Iowa Supreme Court is typical. *See, e.g., Leonard v. Nationwide Mut. Ins. Co.*, 438 F. Supp. 2d 684 (S.D. Miss. 2006) (Hurricane Katrina case rejecting insurer's argument that the insurance policy was unambiguous and enforceable as written because it was approved by the Mississippi Department of Insurance). One wonders whether a court would have the same attitude with respect to federal securities or banking regulators. Isn't the real problem here the fact that even the best regulator could never anticipate in advance all the problems involved in applying a form contract? Given the hundreds of thousands of insurance claims handled in any given year, there inevitably will be circumstances that result in an "unfair" application of insurance policy language that may quite reasonably have seemed fair to the regulator who approved the form. Courts, legislators, and administrative agencies around the world have struggled with the problems inherent in regulating standard form contracts, and no one has arrived at the one best solution. What alternatives can you see? Any mix of prior approval, postclaim policing, and "free market" control you can dream up is almost certain to have been tried somewhere.

9. Think about the policy language at issue in *Gaunt* and *C&J Fertilizer*. What legitimate reasons might there be for the allegedly offensive provisions? Is there any way in which these provisions promote the goal of quality insurance at a reasonable cost? What are the risks that these provisions leave on the consumer? Are those risks more expensive for the insurance company than other risks? Are those risks that most insurance policyholders would want covered? How do you know?

10. Professor Peter Swisher has drawn a useful distinction between "formalist" and "functionalist" approaches to insurance contract interpretation that echoes the distinction between form and substance drawn by Professor Duncan Kennedy in *Form and Substance in Private Law Adjudication*, 89 Harv. L. Rev. 1685 (1976). *See* Peter N. Swisher, *Judicial Rationales in Insurance*

Law: Dusting Off the Formal for the Function, 52 Ohio St. L.J. 1037 (1991). Plain meaning and *contra proferentem* are "formal," in that they focus on the insurance form, while reasonable expectations, implied warranty, and unconscionability are functional (or substantive), in that they focus on the function or purpose of the insurance in question. Can you see how there might be more and less "formal" or "substantive" approaches to each of these doctrines? For example, a "formal" approach to reasonable expectations might state that the only reasonable expectation a consumer would have would be one that exactly matched what the insurance contract said; after all, people should read their contracts (or so the argument would go). Similarly, a "substantive" approach to *contra proferentem* might look at the entire context of the transaction to determine whether the words are ambiguous.

11. In practice, it is safest to begin with a formal approach. For reasons of bureaucratic control, insurance companies almost always insist that claims personnel apply the insurance contract strictly as written. Although an insurance adjuster may in some cases be receptive to the argument that the company should not insist on a "technicality," adjusters are taught that the insurance policy is their bible and that they do not have the authority to "create" coverage that is not explicitly granted in the insurance policy. *See* Tom Baker, *Constructing the Insurance Relationship: Sales Stories, Claims Stories and Insurance Contract Damages,* 72 Tex. L. Rev. 1395 (1994). By far, the vast majority of insurance claims are resolved according to the insurance law of the insurance adjuster, without resort to the courts. Thus, notwithstanding the prevalence of cases with a substantive approach in this and other insurance casebooks, insurance law in action is highly formal and closely tied to the "plain meaning" of the insurance contract, as that plain meaning is determined by the claims departments of insurance companies. For that reason, one might quite reasonably ask whether we should draw any significance at all from cases like *C&J Fertilizer.* Indeed, it might be argued that such cases serve only to legitimate the status quo, by making it appear (falsely) that courts can in fact control insurance companies. Is this too cynical a view? Professor Boardman goes a step further, arguing that cases like *C&J Fertilizer* discourage insurance companies from redrafting insurance policies to make their intent more clear—and thereby informing at least those insurance consumers who are willing to compare insurance forms. *See* Michelle E. Boardman, *Contra Proferentem: The Allure of Ambiguous Boilerplate,* 104 Mich. L. Rev. 1105, 1127 (2006).

12. Even in court, the formal, "plain meaning" approach is the baseline for most lawyers and judges, notwithstanding the more realistic approach of *C&J Fertilizer* and the *Darner* case in the next section. It is important not to let your perspective on insurance contract law be skewed by the selection of cases in this and other insurance law casebooks. In preparing a casebook, there is a bias in favor of "interesting" cases. Cases that carefully apply detailed policy language in a specific factual context are not as interesting as cases that examine the nature of the insurance relationship in more expansive terms. For every *C&J Fertilizer* or *Darner,* there are more than a dozen cases like *St. Paul Fire & Marine Ins. Co. v. Albany County Sch. Dist. No. 1,* 763 P.2d 1255 (Wyo. 1988), in which the Supreme Court of Wyoming wrote:

> If the policy language is clear and unambiguous, the rule of strict construction against the insurer does not apply, and the policy must be interpreted in accordance with the ordinary and usual meaning of its terms. The parties to an insurance contract are free to incorporate within the policy whatever lawful terms they desire, and the courts are not at liberty, under the guise of judicial construction, to rewrite the policy.

Id. at 1258. Do not let the fact that the main cases in this chapter find for the policyholder mislead you into thinking that policyholders always win. The reasons they do not are set forth in the dissenting opinions in *C&J Fertilizer* and *Darner.* Do you find them persuasive? Why or why not? If not, why do you think that courts are so reluctant to find coverage in the teeth of an unambiguous exclusion?

13. Professor Kenneth Abraham has observed that the principle of reasonable expectations may be most significant, not as a controversial and hard-to-apply doctrine of insurance contract interpretation, but rather as a governing ideal for insurance law more broadly:

> Honoring policyholders' reasonable expectations is not something we can always achieve; in fact, it is not something we will always even attempt to achieve. But honoring reasonable expectations as to coverage is a good of sufficient importance that we should continually measure our progress toward achieving that good in a world of insurance that is limited by imperfect information, strategic behavior, the partial incompatibility of that good with other goods, and the practical compromises that markets are always in the process of making.

Kenneth S. Abraham, *The Expectations Principle as a Regulative Ideal,* 5 Conn. Ins. L.J. 59, 63 (1998) (this article appeared in a symposium, *The Insurance Law Doctrine of Reasonable Expectations After Three Decades,* which is worth consulting for those who wish to learn more). Abraham's approach to reasonable expectations is consistent with the approach taken by the ALI in the RLLI. (See RLLI, §4, Comment B, as quoted above.)

THE HURRICANE ANDREW CODE UPGRADE PROBLEM

Hurricane Andrew devastated a large swath of Dade County, Florida, in 1992. Existing Dade County ordinances required homes that were more than 50 percent destroyed to be rebuilt in full compliance with all current building codes. One of the most significant building code changes over the years had been the requirement that the first floor of a home be constructed a specific number of feet above sea level. (South Florida is exceedingly flat, and much of Dade County is less than 15 feet above sea level.) Following the hurricane, a number of insurance companies took the position that the costs of reconstruction attributable to raising the elevation of a house were not covered by homeowners' insurance policies because of the following exclusion:

> We do not insure under any coverage for any loss which would not have occurred in the absence of one or more of the following excluded events . . .

a.   Ordinance or law, meaning enforcement of any ordinance or law regulating the construction, repair or demolition of a building or other structure, unless specifically provided under this policy.

Dade County brought a *parens patriae* lawsuit in Florida state court in Dade County against one of the insurance companies on behalf of affected citizens, arguing that "replacement cost" homeowners' insurance policies require insurers to pay the full costs of replacing a legal home with a legal home. *Metropolitan Dade County v. State Farm Fire & Cas. Co.*, 94-0081 (Dade County Circuit Court). The trial court granted summary judgment for the county and the district court of appeal reversed, each in unpublished opinions.

State Farm and insurance company amici argued that the plain meaning of the exclusion meant that insurers did not have to pay the costs of elevating the homes. They characterized these costs as payments for "upgrades" that provided the homeowner with a better house than the one that was destroyed. Dade County and the consumer group amici argued that the exclusion only applied where the building code violation caused the loss (which, they argued, was not the case here because the damage to the homes would have occurred whether they were elevated or not). They characterized the costs at issue as "replacement costs" and argued that excluding these costs defeated the reasonable expectations of consumers who had purchased a "replacement cost" insurance policy.

Think about this dispute from the perspectives of Judge Hand, Judge Clark, Justice Reynoldson, and Justice LeGrande. Develop arguments on each side of the case that you believe would be persuasive to each of these four judges. How are those arguments different from one another? The same? What kinds of additional information would be relevant to each judge in deciding this dispute? How would this dispute be analyzed under the interpretation sections of the RLLI? How does that analysis differ, if at all, from the approach that would be persuasive to these four judges?[4]

III.   WAIVER AND ESTOPPEL

Insurance contract interpretation lies at the center of most insurance coverage litigation. Nevertheless, deciding what the insurance contract means is not necessarily the end of the litigation. Either the policyholder may have a reason for coverage in spite of the contract limitations or the carrier may have a reason for avoiding coverage in spite of the contract seeming to provide coverage.

For insurers, the most common reasons for not paying a claim that would otherwise be covered by the policy are misrepresentation and breach of an important condition in the insurance policy, such as the requirements that insureds give prompt notice of a claim and cooperate with the insurer. We address misrepresentation in Section V of this chapter and get a taste of insurance policy

---

4. In part as a result of Hurricane Andrew litigation and subsequent legislative activity, many standard homeowners' policies now provide a limited amount of ordinance or law coverage. There is a copy of a standard homeowners' insurance policy at the beginning of the "Property Insurance" unit in Chapter 3.

conditions in Section VI, which addresses disproportionate forfeiture. For policyholders, the most common reasons for demanding payment for a claim that would otherwise not be covered by the policy are the doctrines of waiver and estoppel, the main topic of this section. If these fail, policyholders sometimes have the further recourse of bringing a negligence action against the agent or broker. We address actions against agents and brokers at the conclusion of this section.

Waiver occurs where a party voluntarily and unilaterally relinquishes a known legal right. A party can only waive a contract right that would benefit him or her; a party may not waive a right intended to benefit the other party. Waiver may be either express or implied, and the party waiving the right must (1) be aware of the right being waived and (2) intend (in the "objective" understanding of that term discussed in first-year contract law class) to forgo the right. For example, an insurer that accepts a premium payment, knowing that it is late, waives the right to later deny a claim based on the late payment of that premium, even if the insurer chants continuously as it deposits the check, "I do not intend to waive my right to later deny the claim for late payment." The RLLI states the black letter waiver rule as follows:

§5. Waiver

A party to an insurance policy waives a right under the policy if
   (1) that party, with actual or constructive knowledge of the facts giving rise to that right, expressly relinquishes the right, or engages in conduct that would reasonably be regarded by the counterparty as an intentional relinquishment of that right, and
   (2) the relinquishment or conduct is communicated to the counterparty.

Estoppel occurs when one party's acts or representations reasonably induce detrimental reliance on the part of another. Waiver depends solely on the insurer's conduct. By contrast, estoppel depends on the conduct of both the insurer and the policyholder. The insurer must make a representation or take an action, and the policyholder must reasonably and detrimentally rely on that representation. For example, if an insurance agent assures a policyholder that his or her insurance will not lapse if the payment is a month late, and the policyholder relies on this statement, the insurer will be estopped from claiming that the policy did not cover a loss that occurred during the month period. Estoppel is potentially a very expansive doctrine and, as we will see, not all jurisdictions have embraced its full potential. The RLLI states the black letter estoppel rule as follows:

§6. Estoppel

A party to a liability insurance policy who makes a promise or representation that can reasonably be expected to induce detrimental reliance by another party to the policy is estopped from denying the promise or representation if the other party does in fact reasonably and detrimentally rely on that promise or representation.

In the mid-twentieth century Professor Clarence Morris described the development of waiver and estoppel as part of insurance law's answer to the problem of insurer-side adverse selection:

Indexes to the great nineteenth century insurance texts do not list waiver and estoppel. But times have changed. The 1951 third edition of Vance on Insurance enfolds an excellent and important seventy-six page "Waiver & Estoppel" chapter—about a fourteenth of the book's bulk. What has fostered this growth in the last hundred years? My thesis is that waiver and estoppel are two of several guises that cloak the courts' part in changing insurance from a service safely bought only by sophisticated businessmen to a commodity bought with confidence by untrained consumers. Judges, at the urging of policyholders' advocates, have used waiver and estoppel to convert insurance from a custom-made document designed in part by knowing buyers to a brand-name staple sold over the counter by mine-run salesmen to the trusting public.

Seventeenth and eighteenth century marine insurance contracts were handwritten; hull and cargo owners and their brokers knew insurance as thoroughly as the underwriters. When a marine policy buyer entertained a proposal of a warranty, he bargained for important premium concessions and knew the courts would construe the warranty strictly against him. American draftsmen-lawyers, sometimes in the hire of fly-by-night companies, proliferated fine print in the nineteenth century fire and life insurance policies. Companies, spurred by competition, debased their product (as the Germans did their linen). Restrictions on coverage, not noticed or not understood by policyholders at the time of issue, became painfully clear after uncovered losses which policyholders would have paid to cover. The insurance market might have soured had not the law stepped in and afforded consumer protection greater than companies intended to sell.

Of course this process of favoring consumers can be carried too far. Insurance companies need and are entitled to reasonable limits on their responsibilities; the public is prejudiced when company liabilities are by generous caprice stretched over risks that cannot be profitably underwritten at a just premium. By and large, however, the courts have not been overgenerous to the public. Judges have limited their use of the doctrines of waiver and estoppel because of their awareness of important underwriting realities.

Waiver and Estoppel in Insurance Policy Litigation, 105 U. Pa. L. Rev. 925, 925-926 (1957). As you read the following notes and cases, consider whether you think the courts have gone too far, or not far enough, in this direction.

DARNER MOTOR SALES, INC. v. UNIVERSAL UNDERWRITERS INSURANCE CO.

Supreme Court of Arizona
682 P.2d 388 (1984)

FELDMAN, J. . . . Darner Motors is in the automobile sales, service and leasing business. . . . Darner Motors' various operations were insured under several policies issued by The Travelers Company (Travelers). In October of 1973, Doxsee, an insurance agent who was a full-time employee of Universal, contacted Joel Darner to solicit insurance business. The following month, Darner purchased a Universal "U-Drive policy" through Doxsee. This policy insured Darner Motors and the lessees of its cars for automobile liability risk. Darner Motors was covered in limits of $100,000 for any one injury and $300,000 (100/300) for all injuries arising out of any one accident. The lessees were covered in limits of 15/30. The rest of Darner Motors' business risks continued to be insured under a "dealership package policy" issued by Travelers.

It is unclear from the record, but this situation presumably continued until April of 1975, a renewal date of the Travelers policy. In April of 1975, Universal "picked up" the entire insurance "package" for Darner Motors' various business activities. This "package" consisted of a Universal "Unicover" policy which included coverage for garagekeeper's liability, premises liability, property coverage, crime coverage, customer car coverage, and plate glass insurance. The parties describe this as an "umbrella policy," so it is possible that, in addition to covering multiple risks, it also contained excess coverage over other policies which provided primary coverage. In addition to the umbrella policy, Universal also renewed the U-Drive policy, which provided coverage to the lessees of Darners Motors.

. . . [A]ccording to Darner, he informed Doxsee that renewal of lessee coverage was to be in the same limits as applied to Darner Motors in the original U-Drive policy. When the new U-Drive policy arrived after renewal in April of 1975, Darner examined it and noticed that the limits of coverage for lessees were 15/30. After reading this, Darner claims that he called Doxsee. He was concerned because his rental contract contained a representation of greater coverage (100/300) and because he felt that it would be better for his business operation if his lessees had the higher coverage. Darner told Doxsee that the liability limits of the U-Drive policy did not conform to their prior agreement, and asked Doxsee to come to Darner Motors and discuss the matter. Doxsee did call upon Mr. Darner at the latter's office. Although Doxsee could not recall the subsequent conversation, both Darner and his former sales manager, Jack Hadley, testified about the discussion. Their deposition testimony would support a finding that Doxsee told Darner not to worry about the limits because, although the U-Drive policy provided only 15/30 coverage, the all-risk clause of the umbrella policy would provide additional coverage to limits of 100/300.

At some time after he received the U-Drive policy and, presumably, also after his discussions with Doxsee, Darner did receive a copy of the umbrella policy. That policy was evidently quite lengthy and forbidding. Darner admits never reading it; he explained this omission by pointing out that "it's like reading a book" and stating that, following his conversations with Doxsee, "I didn't think I needed to." Darner's office manager testified that she never really read the policy either and saw little need to do so in view of the fact that Doxsee would occasionally appear, remove pages from the loose-leaf binder and insert new pages. So far as the record shows, the printed, boiler-plate provisions contained in the loose-leaf type, "book length," all-risk policy were neither negotiated before nor discussed after the policy was delivered. The parties seem to have confined themselves to a discussion of the objectives that would be realized from the purchase of the policy rather than an attempt to negotiate the wording of the policy.

Approximately twenty months after the conversation between Darner and Doxsee concerning coverage under the Universal policies, Darner Motors rented a car to Dwayne Crawford. . . . [T]he form used for the rental agreement . . . contained a representation of coverage in the amount of 100/300. While driving the vehicle under this rental contract, Crawford negligently injured a pedestrian and caused severe injuries. The pedestrian sued Crawford, who looked to Universal for coverage. Universal claimed that lessee's coverage on the "U-Drive" policy was limited to 15/30. Crawford then sued Darner Motors under the rental agreement warranty that coverage was provided in limits of

100/300. Darner Motors called upon Universal to provide additional coverage under the umbrella policy. The umbrella policy did contain the higher limits, but Universal claimed that lessees were not parties "insured" as that term was defined in the all-risk policy. Universal was therefore unwilling to provide coverage in excess of the $15,000 limit of the U-Drive policy. Darner Motors then filed a third-party complaint, naming Universal and Doxsee as third party defendants.

Eventually, the pedestrian recovered $60,000 from Crawford. Universal paid $15,000 of this amount, and Darner Motors has either paid or is liable to Crawford for the remainder. Darner Motors claims that Universal and Doxsee are obligated to indemnify it against that loss. To support that contention, Darner Motors advances the following theories:

(1) Universal is estopped to deny coverage for lessees under the umbrella policy in amounts less than 100/300;
(2) The umbrella policy should be reformed so that it does contain such coverage;
(3) If no coverage is found through estoppel or reformation, then the loss incurred by Darner Motors was caused by the negligence of Universal and its agent; Doxsee, and should be borne by them. . . .

After considerable discovery, Universal and Doxsee moved for summary judgment, contending that there was no genuine issue of fact and that they were entitled to judgment as a matter of law. The motion was granted and judgment entered against Darner Motors. The court of appeals affirmed; pointing out that Darner Motors had not claimed that the umbrella policy was ambiguous, the court held that the insured's failure to read the policy prevented recovery on any theory, even though the contents of the policy did not comport with the representations of the insurance agent and those same representations were a part of the reason that the insured failed to read the policy. . . .

CONTRACT LAW AND INSURANCE POLICIES

. . . Implicit in the reasoning of the court of appeals is the concept that the insurance policies purchased by Darner constitute *the* contract between Darner and Universal. Darner is considered to be bound by the terms contained within the documents. The court of appeals held:

> Because Mr. Darner received a copy of the umbrella policy and made no contention that it was ambiguous or confusing, he cannot expand the insurer's liability beyond the terms of the umbrella policy issued by Universal. Basic to this holding is the principle that the oral agreement between Doxsee and Darner cannot be shown to vary the terms of the insurance policy.

This, indeed, was at one time the majority view. Some cases, including those from our own state, hold that since insurance policies are like other contracts, where the meaning and intent of the parties is "clear" from the words used in the instrument, the courts cannot "rewrite" the policy by considering the actual "words" used in striking the bargain. Thus, the rule of interpretation is stated to be that the intention of the parties as derived from the language used within the four corners of the instrument must prevail. *See, e.g., Rodemich v. State Farm*

Mutual Auto. Insurance Co., 637 P.2d 748, 749 (Ariz. Ct. App. 1981) (a vehicle which turned over and was damaged when the driver swerved to avoid an animal was not covered under the "upset" clause of a comprehensive risk policy because "upsets" resulting from attempts to avoid collision with animals were not covered unless there was actual contact).

Rodemich is a good example of the mischief made by applying ordinary contract law to insurance policies. No doubt it would have come as a great surprise to Mr. and Mrs. Rodemich (and, also, to the State Farm agent who sold the policy) to learn that they had formed any intent to delete collision coverage—which covers physical damage even when there is no collision—and to include comprehensive coverage, which generally excludes "collision" damage but covers other physical damage, such as that caused by upset, except upset damage resulting from attempts to avoid birds or animals. In the latter situation there is coverage under the comprehensive clause only if one collides with the bird or animal. It would have surprised the Rodemichs even more to learn of the method by which the court was able to determine, from the four corners of the instrument, their specific intent not to be covered for physical damage resulting from the overturning of their vehicle in a successful attempt to avoid striking an animal on the road. The court reasoned as follows:

> However, [coverage D of the policy includes the clause] a "loss caused by . . . *colliding* with birds or animals shall not be deemed to be loss caused by collision." (Emphasis added). Hence, Coverage D provides that a loss caused by *colliding* with an animal would be within the comprehensive coverage. We believe that the policy's use of the term "colliding," rather than the term "collision" which was specifically defined in the policy, indicates that[] "collision" and "colliding" are not the same thing under policy. "Collision" is defined to include "upsets" of the covered vehicle, regardless of the cause, and therefore does not require any contact between the vehicle and any other object. Because the policy used the different term "colliding" in excluding from the definition of "collision" any "loss caused by . . . colliding with birds or animals," we believe that the terms of the policy indicate that the *parties intended* "colliding with . . . animals" to be read in its ordinary dictionary sense and thus to require an actual striking, clashing, or coming together of the motor home and an animal. Therefore, unless the motor home actually struck the animal, there was no "loss caused by . . . colliding with . . . animals." Instead, the motor home suffered an upset, within the definition of "collision" excluded from the comprehensive coverage.

Rodemich, 637 P.2d at 750 (footnote omitted, last emphasis supplied). At best, such reasoning, based on patently unfounded assumptions of intent, is result oriented; at worst, it makes no sense. If there was some reason why the Rodemichs should not have prevailed, there must be some better way to find and articulate what it might be. Artificial results derived from application of ordinary rules of contract construction to insurance policies have made courts struggle to find some method of reaching a sensible resolution within the conceptual bounds of treating standardized, formal contracts as if they were traditional "agreements," reached by bargaining between the parties. This difficult task is often accomplished by the use of various constructs which enable courts to reach a desired result by giving lip service to traditional contract rules. . . .

Such systems of logic—or illogic—have been criticized by Keeton, *supra*, and others for failing to recognize the realities of the insurance business and the methods used in modern insurance practice. . . .

EQUITABLE ESTOPPEL

The elements of estoppel are "conduct by which one . . . induces another to believe . . . in certain material facts, which inducement results in acts in reliance thereon, justifiably taken, which cause injury. . . ." *Sahlin v. American Casualty Company of Reading, Pennsylvania,* 436 P.2d 606, 608 (Ariz. 1968).

The majority rule is considered to be "that the doctrines of waiver and estoppel are not available to bring within the coverage of an insurance policy risks not covered by its terms, or expressly excluded therefrom." Annot. 1 A.L.R.3d 1149, 1147 (1965). Indeed, the annotation lists only two jurisdictions (Idaho and South Dakota) that clearly take the contrary view. *Id.* at 1150-51. However, since the annotation was published several other states have adopted the view that estoppel may be available under certain circumstances. *Harr v. Allstate Insurance Co.,* 255 A.2d 208, (N.J. 1969); *King v. Travelers Ins. Co.,* 505 P.2d 1226 (N.M. 1973); *Hunter v. Farmers Insurance Group,* 554 P.2d 1239, 1243 (Wyo. 1976).

In adopting the "minority rule" the New Jersey Supreme Court examined the "decisions holding estoppel not available to broaden coverage" and found "many of the cases so stating are confusing. . . ." *Harr,* 255 A.2d at 218. The reason for this is that "in many cases where estoppel is held unavailable the necessary elements have not been made out anyway." *Id.* This conclusion is particularly applicable to the Arizona cases cited by appellee in support of the proposition that Arizona follows the majority rule. Given our view of contract theory . . . there are strong reasons to recognize a rule which allows an insured to raise the issue of estoppel to establish coverage contrary to the limitations in the boiler-plate policy when the insurer's agent had represented the coverage as greater than the language found in the printed policy.

The facts of the case at bench are within the exception to interpretation contained in subsection (3) to Restatement (Second) of Contracts §211. The coverage limits for lessees were separately negotiated. The standard boiler-plate definition of the word "insured," excluding lessees, was not bargained for, not written by and not read by the parties. It need not be allowed to "undercut the dickered deal." We therefore adopt the rationale of the New Jersey Supreme Court in *Harr* and recognize equitable estoppel as a device to prevent enforcement of those boiler-plate terms of the insurance contract which are more limited than the coverage expressly agreed upon by the parties. As applied to this case, the rule adopted means simply that if the fact finder determines that Darner and Doxsee did agree upon lessee's coverage in limits of 100/300, and if, by justifiably relying on Doxsee's assurances or for some other justifiable reason, Darner was unaware of the limitation in the umbrella policy, Universal would be estopped to assert the definitional exclusion which eliminates Darner's lessee from the class of persons insured. Thus, we do not limit the assertion of estoppel by the insured to cases in which an insurance policy has not been delivered prior to the loss. Since the parol evidence rule does not necessarily prevent establishing the true agreement, estoppel may apply where, from the nature of the transaction, the fact finder is able to determine that the insured acted reasonably in not reading the particular provision of the policy.

REFORMATION

"Where reformation is sought because of the mistake of one party only, it is essential that fraud or inequitable conduct be found in the other." *Korrick v. Tuller,* 27 P.2d 529, 531 (Ariz. 1933). "Inequitable conduct which would justify reformation when there is unilateral mistake takes the form of knowledge on the part of one party of the other's mistake." *Isaak v. Massachusetts Indemnity Life Ins. Co.,* 623 P.2d at 14. "Ordinarily, the terms of the policy should control, although the statement of an agent well may ground an action for reformation." 16C Appleman, Insurance Law and Practice, §9167 at 165 (1981). Moreover, one whose inequitable conduct has caused the instrument to be "accepted with provisions at variance with the true agreement may not set up the other party's negligence in failing to read the instrument. . . ." *Lane v. Mathews,* 251 P.2d 303, 305 (Ariz. 1952) (*quoting* 76 C.J.S., Reformation of Instruments §46 at 400).

According to Universal, Darner was simply mistaken about the extent of coverage under his umbrella policy. Darner avers that, if so, this resulted from Doxsee's failure to properly explain the terms of the policy. There is no dispute that Darner told Doxsee he was concerned about having only 15/30 coverage for lessees. There is clearly a factual dispute regarding Doxsee's appreciation of Darner's concern. Arguably, Doxsee had knowledge of Darner's "mistaken" understanding of the agreement. Thus it may be that "the true contract of insurance in this case . . . arose out of the oral agreement between the parties and not that as evidenced by the written policy." *Ranger Insurance Co. v. Phillips,* 544 P.2d 250, 254 (Ariz. Ct. App. 1976); *see also A.I.D. Ins. Services v. Riley,* 541 P.2d 595, 598 (Ariz. Ct. App. 1975).

The same disputed material facts which demand trial on the merits regarding the estoppel remedy can also be marshaled under the reformation theory. Under the provisions of Restatement (Second) of Contracts §211 the form provisions at variance with the bargained deal or contrary to the dominant purpose of the transaction are "not part of the agreement." They should be eliminated, so that the bargains made will be realized. The written agreement may be reformed to state the true agreement. Accordingly, summary judgment on reformation was error. . . .

CAMERON, Justice, specially concurring. I concur in the majority decision and opinion and write only because I believe the dissent incorrectly characterizes the opinion and could lead to a misinterpretation of the holding of the majority.

First, I do not believe that the opinion adopts "virtually every minority position." The majority opinion adopts the rule of the Restatement (Second) of Contracts §211 (1981), and applies to form provisions the same general rules of contract law which we have recently applied to all contracts. *Smith v. Melson, Inc.* 659 P.2d 1264 (Ariz. 1983).

Second, today's decision does not make the contents of insurance policies or other contracts irrelevant. The majority opinion specifically indicates that the terms contained in standardized forms will continue to be enforced as written.

Today's opinion merely articulates the limits of what will be enforced. Most, if not all, of those limits have long been recognized.

Third, the majority opinion does not reward "ignorance of the contents of the document." It applies only to the type of contract which, because of the nature of the transaction, the particular customer was not or should not have been expected to read. Customers are still charged with knowledge and understanding of the forms, even when they do not read them. The majority opinion, then, does not confer on "sophisticated businessmen" any absolute right not to read the policy. Whether this is a transaction in which the consumer (Darner) was not expected to read the policy (and thus one to which the rule applied by §211 is applicable) is a question to be decided at trial. Admittedly, the majority opinion recognizes that in most insurance transactions and many others involving standardized forms, the "boiler-plate" will probably neither be read nor understood. Those terms, however, are still enforceable unless the seller should know that they would not be acceptable. *See* Restatement (Second) of Contracts §211(3) (1981).

The impact of the day's decision is merely to formulate the rules of construction for standardized contracts. These rules do not allow interpretation on the basis of "impression or imagination" of the consumer. Only those reasonable expectations which are induced by the words or conduct of the parties should be considered. 1 Corbin, Contracts, §1 at 2 (1983).

Construction and interpretation of form contracts is no innovation. For years we have interpreted such contracts by reference to the "intent of the parties," even though the parties may not have demonstrated any intent with respect to the terms contained in the printed form provisions. Through today's decision we adopt a more rational set of rules as a basis for interpretation and, in addition, subject form contracts to the same rules of construction as all others. Where there is an expressed intent, it will be given effect. Where the "boiler-plate" conflicts with the intent it will not be enforced. The agent must inform the customer if there is something in the "boiler-plate" that is contrary to the expressed intent of the parties or the purpose of the transaction. I believe this is good law. . . .

For the foregoing reasons we vacate the decision of the court of appeals and reverse the trial court's summary judgment as to the counts of equitable estoppel, reformation of the contract, negligent misrepresentation and fraud. . . .

HOLOHAN, C.J., dissenting. With the stated purpose of reviewing the clarity and consistency of a large body of Arizona law dealing with insurance coverage, the court by this decision proceeds to overrule the major part of past precedent on the subject. Having overruled the past precedent, the court then proceeds to adopt virtually every minority position taken by any court or text writer in the United States. The decision makes the contents of a written insurance policy irrelevant in the determination of the nature and extent of coverage. In place of the insurance policy the nature and extent of coverage will now be decided by a swearing contest between the insured and the insurance company's agents. I cannot agree with the position taken by the court and, therefore, dissent. I believe that the decision of the Court of Appeals in this case should have been approved.

The court's decision is based on the fact, at least as found by the majority, that people do not read their insurance policies, and, if they do, they don't understand them anyway. Apparently the group encompassed within the court's protection includes not only the ordinary citizen but also the successful sophisticated businessman such as the plaintiff in this case. There is no limitation on those who qualify for the benign protection of this court from what is perceived as the obfuscation created by insurance companies. Under today's decision, any person who reads his insurance policy would be a fool since it is far better to plead ignorance of the contents of the policy and claim coverage to the broadest possible extent. The matter will then be resolved by trial based on the most convincing story. The written agreement or policy is to be ignored.

Although the insurance industry is the subject of this court's current efforts to clarify and reform previous precedent, many other business organizations should feel uncomfortable about their future. I have no doubt that experience will show that few people have read their mortgages, deeds of trust, or even the escrow instructions used in various real estate transactions. Under the same rationale advanced by the court in its decision today, the various financing documents used in real estate transactions may be subject to oral modification because they have not been read, or, if read, not understood by ordinary citizens.

The mischief created by today's decision will be far-reaching. Currently the only industry affected is the insurance industry. It can be said without any exaggeration that no insurance company now operating in Arizona can be assured that the written policies currently in effect have the limitations contained in the policy. The extent of the risk which these companies thought they had undertaken is now incapable of calculation. The extent of the risk is limited only by the impressions or imagination of policyholders about the extent of their coverage.

Every insurance company in this state must review its current method of operation because today's decision will significantly affect current policies and future policies written in this state. Of course, a company may elect to cease doing business in this state because of our "enlightened" insurance law, but, hopefully, a more cautious approach may be deemed prudent until such time as appropriate legislation can be sought to establish the insurance policy as a document with some binding effect. In the interim it appears that every insurance agent will be required to do a complete review of the policy with the insured and establish some form of record to support the conclusion that the insured was advised and understood the nature, extent and limitations of the policy which was purchased. The sale of insurance in Arizona may take on much the same formality as the taking of a plea of guilty in a criminal case. The agent, like the judge in a criminal case, will have to advise the insured of his rights and the consequences of taking the policy presented. Hopefully, it will not be necessary for a verbatim record to be made of the negotiations.

Under today's decision it appears that we have come full circle in the development of the law on contracts. Oral contracts were largely the method used in early times. To avoid the disputes which arose out of misunderstandings in oral agreements, the written contract became preferred. In modern commercial practice the written contract is not only preferred, it is essential. It is designed to eliminate disputes, and it is intended to establish some certitude in setting out the agreement of the parties. These concepts may be basic, but they are largely ignored in today's decision because an insured is not allowed to help write the contract. A debtor doesn't write the mortgage or deed of trust or most any other type of financing document, but until now the signing of the document bound the borrower to the terms of the agreement.

Whatever evil the majority is attempting to eliminate, the remedy advanced is like decapitation to cure dandruff—a cure that is far worse than the disease. . . .

NOTES AND QUESTIONS

1. This case provides one example of how reasonable expectations can serve as a regulative principle. The court uses the ideal of reasonable expectations to justify the application of estoppel doctrine in the insurance context. Stepping back and taking a very wide focus, *Darner* looks and sounds very much like *C&J Fertilizer,* even though the courts use different contract law doctrines in the two cases.

2. As surprising as this may seem to students who still remember §90 of the Restatement (Second) of Contracts from their first-year contracts class, the use of promissory estoppel in insurance cases remains controversial in some jurisdictions. In *DeJonge v. Mutual of Enumclaw*, 843 P.2d 914, 916 n.3 (Or. 1992), the Oregon Supreme Court stated:

   > Most jurisdictions have ruled that estoppel is not available to expand the coverage of a written policy so as to protect the insured against risks expressly excluded. *See* Annot., 1 A.L.R.3d 1139, 1143 (1965 & Supp. 1991) (collecting cases from over 30 states, including Oregon, that follow that rule). Courts have stated various reasons for that rule. The most prevalent is that courts cannot create a new contract for the parties. A related rationale is that an insurer should not be required by estoppel to pay a loss for which it charged no premium.

   Are these justifications persuasive? Think back to your contracts class and the use of promissory estoppel to make promises binding in the absence of consideration.

3. Like so many other aspects of contract law, the estoppel cases concern the allocation of risk, in this case the risk of mistaken understanding of the terms of the insurance coverage resulting from statements or actions by insurance companies. Who should bear that risk? Which party is in the best position to prevent such mistakes? What incentive does the rule that estoppel is not available to expand coverage provide insurance companies to train their agents and adjusters? What is the response to the claim that the widespread adoption of estoppel would increase the costs of insurance coverage?

4. Most courts that reject the use of estoppel to avoid "restrictions on coverage" (such as the exclusion at issue in the main case) will nevertheless allow the doctrine to be used to avoid application of a "condition" (such as the requirement that premiums be paid on time or that notice of a claim be filed promptly). This line of cases may reflect the same underlying policy concerns as the disproportionate forfeiture doctrine, which we discuss later in this chapter. Drawing a line between a "coverage restriction" and a "condition" is not always easy. Adopting a firmer rule for one type of insurance policy provision than another encourages insurers to draft their policies so that "conditions" become "restrictions on coverage." The RLLI rejects the

narrow use of estoppel doctrine. See §7, reproduced in the introductory note at the beginning of this section.

5. At one time, the parol evidence rule provided a major obstacle to promissory estoppel. *See, e.g., Union Mut. Life Ins. Co. v. Mowry*, 96 U.S. 544 (1877) (holding that evidence of promise by life insurance agent was inadmissible). Stated a bit simplistically, the core idea of the parol evidence rule is to force parties to put their full agreement into writing to prevent "he said, she said" arguments in the future about the nature of their agreement. Given the adhesive nature of insurance contracts, the difficulty of understanding them, and the widespread role of intermediaries, it is hardly surprising that the parol evidence rule has not provided insurance companies with the protective shield that a first-year contracts class might suggest. Even courts that adhere to the older, more formalistic approach to parol evidence will admit that oral and other evidence is admissible to explain the meaning of ambiguous terms. As a result of this and other exceptions to the parol evidence rule, Professor Robert Jerry concluded, "[I]n only a few instances will the parol evidence rule be used successfully to confine the coverage of insurance contracts to the literal terms of the insurance policy." Robert H. Jerry, II, Understanding Insurance Law 390 (5th ed. 2012).

6. Sometimes the most difficult-to-prove aspect of an estoppel case is detrimental reliance. Think back to *C&J Fertilizer* for a moment. What would be the detrimental reliance in that case? Would the policyholder have to prove that he could have purchased another burglary insurance policy with a different burglary definition? Why? Suppose the policies all had the same definition?

7. One case in which the detrimental reliance requirement proved fatal to an estoppel claim was *Crown Life Ins. Co. v. McBride*, 517 So. 2d 660 (Fla. 1987). In that case the Florida Supreme Court announced that it would permit the use of estoppel in an insurance case but nevertheless found for the insurance company on the grounds that the policyholder had introduced no evidence proving detrimental reliance. *Crown Life* concerned a dispute over whether McBride was a dependent under his father's employment-based insurance policy. When the father started a new job, he asked whether the policy would cover his 20-year-old son, who suffered from a genetic premature aging disease, was financially dependent on his father, and was enrolled in a special high school for slow learners.

    The jury in the trial court concluded that the father was told by an agent of the insurance company that the plaintiff was covered, even though the insurance policy defined "dependents" as "[a]ny unmarried child of an insured employee, who is less than 19 years of age" or "[a]ny unmarried child of an insured employee, who is at least 19 years of age but less than 23 years of age who is enrolled in and in full-time attendance in a recognized college or university." The Florida Supreme Court reversed on the grounds that there was no evidence of detrimental reliance:

    > The sole evidence submitted in proof of this essential element was [the father's] testimony that respondent had been previously covered under [the father's] group coverage offered through his prior employment and that he had the option of converting that coverage to an individual policy. Respondent offered no written policy, memoranda, witnesses, or other evidence to

support this testimony. Further, respondent admitted that he did not know what benefits were offered under the conversion coverage. The record reveals no evidence as to the duration or extent of this alleged prior coverage. In short, respondent did not prove that the lapsing of the prior coverage was to his detriment or that refusal to enforce the alleged promise would sanction the perpetration of a fraud. . . .

Id. at 662. If you had represented McBride, what would you have done differently at the trial court level? Suppose that the father's previous policy had a similar definition of "dependent"? Why do you think group insurance policies define "dependent" in this way? Among other things, this case illustrates one of the perils of relying on employment-based health insurance as the heart of the financing mechanism for the U.S. health care system.

BIBLE v. JOHN HANCOCK MUTUAL LIFE INSURANCE CO.

Court of Appeals of New York
176 N.E. 838 (1931)

CARDOZO, C.J. The defendant issued two policies of insurance, each in the sum of $400, upon the life of Anna Bible, payable at her death to her husband, the plaintiff.

Anna Bible was a patient in Hudson River State Hospital, a sufferer from a "manic depressive psychosis." An agent for the defendant visited her in the hospital and procured her signature to applications for insurance. Later he handed her the policies in the presence of her husband, received payment of the first premium, and at weekly intervals thereafter collected additional premiums at the hospital for a period of three months; the premiums thereafter being collected by another.

Upon the death of the insured, about a year and eight months after the delivery of the policies, there was filed with the insurer a proof of claim in due form exhibiting the condition of her health at the time of the delivery of the policies and earlier. The insurer disclaimed liability upon the ground that the policies had been avoided by the breach of two conditions. The two conditions are the following:

This policy shall not take effect unless upon its date the insured shall be alive and in sound health and the premium duly paid.

This policy shall be void . . . if the insured . . . has attended any hospital, or institution of any kind engaged in the care or cure of human health or disease, or has been attended by any physician, within two years before the date hereof, for any serious disease, complaint or operation . . . unless each such . . . medical and hospital attendance and previous disease is specifically waived by an endorsement in the space for endorsements on page 4 hereof signed by the secretary.

The policies contain also the following general provision as to alterations, erasures, and waivers:

No modification, change or alteration hereof or endorsement hereon will be valid unless signed by the President, a Vice President, the Secretary or an Assistant Secretary, and no other person is authorized on behalf of the company to make, alter or discharge this contract or to waive forfeiture. Agents are not authorized to waive any of the terms or conditions of this policy or to extend the time for payment of premiums or other moneys due to the company, or to bind the company by making any promise not contained in this policy.

Upon the defendant's disclaimer of liability, this action was begun. The jury were instructed that the breach of the conditions might be found to have been waived if the defendant had knowledge through its agent of the state of health of the insured and of her confinement in the hospital when the policies were issued and the premiums accepted. The jury gave a verdict for the plaintiff, and the Appellate Division affirmed by a divided court.

. . . In the absence of warranty or warning, the delivery of the policies by the insurer, and the keeping of the premiums with knowledge of a then existing breach of the conditions as to the health of the insured and her treatment in a hospital, gave rise to a waiver or, more properly an estoppel. *Whipple v. Prudential Ins. Co., of America,* 118 N.E. 211 (N.Y. 1917); *McClelland v. Mutual Life Ins. Co., of New York,* 111 N.E. 1062 (N.Y. 1916); Vance on Insurance 461, 496 (2d Ed.). If the insurer desired to overcome the effect of the estoppel, it should have annexed applications with appropriate recitals of notice and assent.

The question remains whether the agent to whom knowledge was imparted was so related to the defendant as to charge it with his knowledge. As to this our decision in *McClelland v. Mutual Life Ins. Co. of New York, supra,* must be held to be conclusive. Here, as there, the agent was more than a soliciting agent. He was that, but much besides. He was authorized not only to solicit applications, but to make delivery of the policies, and upon delivery and afterwards to collect the weekly premiums. So, at least, it may fairly be inferred from the evidence of his conduct and from the failure of the defendant to prove anything to the contrary. If at the time of delivery and the collection of the premium, he was informed that the insured was in a hospital and ill, he was under a duty to communicate to his employer the information thus acquired. *McClelland v. Mutual Life Ins. Co. of New York, supra;* Vance, Insurance, pp. 413, 419, 518, 520. The employer with that knowledge retained the premiums as its own. . . .

The judgment should be affirmed with costs.

NOTES AND QUESTIONS

1. Is this an estoppel case or a waiver case? At one point in the opinion, Judge Cardozo writes, "In the absence of warranty or warning, the delivery of the policies by the insurer, and the keeping of the premiums with knowledge of a then existing breach of the conditions as to the health of the insured and her treatment in a hospital, gave rise to a waiver or, more properly, an estoppel." Yet at other points in the opinion, he states that the jury was "instructed that the breach of the conditions might be found to have been waived if the defendant had knowledge through its agent of the state of health of the insured." Why is it important to distinguish these points? Why might the court not do so?

2. It might help to compare the elements of waiver and estoppel. Waiver requires the intentional relinquishment of a known right, while estoppel requires a promise or an action that the actor would expect to lead to, and

does lead to, detrimental reliance. Are those elements met here? What would the plaintiff need to show to prove detrimental reliance? Has he made that showing?

3. *Bible,* as well as *Darner* and the next case, *Jenkins,* present questions of agency and whether an insurance company can and should be held accountable for an agent's actions. Agency will be discussed in greater depth in Section IV.

As you read the next case, keep in mind its pedagogical point: the application of the doctrine of waiver. The choice of law and interspousal issues are not the main points of the case. Focus on those issues only as necessary to analyze whether the insurance company's behavior satisfied the requirements of waiver.

JENKINS v. INDEMNITY INSURANCE CO. OF NORTH AMERICA

Supreme Court of Connecticut
205 A.2d 780 (1964)

KING, J. On August 14, 1958, the plaintiff, while operating his automobile in Manchester, Connecticut, collided with several concrete abutments. The collision caused injuries to his wife, Patricia, a passenger in the car. The defendant insurance company, a Pennsylvania corporation, had issued the plaintiff a policy which was in full force and effect at the time of the accident and which insured him against liability for bodily injuries "sustained by any person . . . arising out of the ownership, maintenance or use" of the plaintiff's automobile. The policy was issued in New York.

The defendant denied liability under the policy, and refused to defend any action brought by the wife, on the ground that the wife's claim was an interspousal claim against her husband and, as such, was excluded from coverage by §167(3) of the New York Insurance Law. That section provides that a spouse's injuries are not within the coverage of an automobile liability insurance policy "unless express provision relating specifically thereto is included in the policy."

The defendant does not, and in reason could not, question that the wording of the insurance policy, considered apart from the New York statute, clearly covered any liability of the plaintiff to his wife arising from the accident. On the other hand, if the accident had occurred in New York, the policy, because of the statute, clearly would not have covered that liability. Thus, the real question is whether, under the facts of this case, the New York statute is to be given operative effect.

The plaintiff's wife sued her husband in Connecticut, he personally appeared, and a judgment was recovered against him for $25,000 damages together with costs. The plaintiff brought this declaratory judgment action against the defendant seeking (a) a declaration that the policy covered his wife's claim, (b) injunctive relief to compel the payment to his wife of the judgment recovered by her, with costs, and (c) money damages for himself in the amount of the attorneys' fees and witness fees he had been compelled to expend in defending his wife's action. . . . Judgment was rendered for the defendant on the basis that, since the policy was issued in New York, the New York statute was "mandated into and made a part of" the plaintiff's insurance policy and therefore the policy did not cover the wife's claim. This appeal is from that judgment.

The general rule is that the validity and construction of a contract are determined by the law of the place where the contract was made. But if the contract is to have its operative effect or place of performance in a jurisdiction other than the place where it was entered into, our rule is that the law of the place of operative effect or performance governs its validity and construction.

In the instant case, therefore, the law of New York will apply unless the contract was to have its operative effect elsewhere. The plaintiff's claim is that since the policy was to apply "within the United States of America, its territories or possessions, or Canada," its place of operative effect is wherever, within those territorial limits, an accident occurs. This claim hardly seems consistent with the purpose of the parties in entering into the contract. Presumably, that purpose was to fix in advance their rights and liabilities in the event of an accident, at least so far as the construction and interpretation of the contract are concerned, rather than to leave them dependent upon the fortuitous circumstance of the place of the accident. Indeed, the assumption underlying our applicable conflicts rule is that when parties enter into a contract they do so with the law of a specific jurisdiction in mind. *Chillingworth v. Eastern Tinware Co.*, 33 A. 1009 (1895). There is nothing in the instant case to suggest that this assumption is unfounded with respect to this insurance contract. On the contrary, in the declaration portion of the policy, the plaintiff stated that his residence was in Bronxville, New York, and that his automobile would be principally garaged there. This declaration gives no hint that the parties thought of this contract as other than a New York transaction. In the absence of a showing that the place of the operative effect of this contract was not New York, under our rule the validity and construction of the contract were governed by the law of New York, where the contract was made.

In 1955, in the absence of any relevant New York authority, this court held that §167(3) was not intended to apply to an accident occurring outside the state of New York. *Williamson v. Massachusetts Bonding & Ins. Co.*, 116 A.2d 169, 172 (Conn. 1955). Since that time the New York Court of Appeals has held that (1) §167(3) "is mandated into and made a part of every policy of automobile liability insurance issued in this State [New York]," and (2) the legislature intended that the statute apply "no matter where the accident occurs." *New Amsterdam Casualty Co. v. Stecker*, 143 N.E.2d 357, 359, 360 (N.Y. 1957). As New York law is to govern, the decision of New York's highest court authoritatively determines the construction of the contract of insurance in the light of the statute.

The claim that the words "any person" in the policy satisfy the statute's requirement of specificity in including coverage in interspousal actions is without merit. Coverage for Patricia's injuries is excluded by virtue of §167(3). Nor has the plaintiff shown that it would be contrary to the public policy of Connecticut to apply the law of New York to this particular action, in which a New York resident is the insured, a New York resident is the injured party, and a Pennsylvania insurance corporation is the insurer.

This would be dispositive of the appeal, adversely to the plaintiff's contentions, but for the plaintiff's claims that the defendant has waived, or is estopped to avail itself of, any rights which it might have under §167(3). . . .

On August 15, 1958, the day following the accident, the defendant, through its agents, was informed of the accident and that the plaintiff's wife had sustained injuries and was a claimant under the policy. On September 10, 1958, the defendant was informed by the wife's attorney that there were legal questions as to coverage in interspousal actions where a policy was written in New

York and an accident occurred in Connecticut, and that no additional information would be furnished the defendant's investigators unless it was understood that the defendant would accept coverage of the wife's claim. Accordingly, on September 18, 1958, the defendant wrote the wife's attorney that it agreed to pay, "within the limits of . . . [the] policy and subject to its provisions," any final judgment which was rendered against the insured (the plaintiff herein) arising out of the accident. From September 10, 1958, to October 27, 1958, the defendant was actively engaged in attempting to adjust Patricia's claim against her husband. On October 27, 1958, the defendant first learned of the seriousness of Patricia's injuries and the extent of her medical bills. On November 12, 1958, in a letter to her attorney, the defendant disclaimed coverage and stated that the defendant was not waiving the New York statute.

The plaintiff claims that the court's conclusion that waiver had not been proven is not supported by the subordinate facts found, including those as to the defendant's efforts to adjust the claim, and especially its letter of September 18, 1958, acknowledging coverage. The plaintiff further claims that from the subordinate facts waiver should be found as a matter of law.

Waiver is the intentional relinquishment of a known right. *National Transportation Co. v. Toquet,* 196 A. 344, 347 (Conn. 1937). The [trial] court held that there was no waiver because "it did not appear that the defendant had any certain knowledge of its rights" under the New York Insurance Law. The court specifically found that the defendant was told by Patricia's attorney that there was a question as to the policy coverage in interspousal actions where, as here, a policy was written in New York and an accident occurred in Connecticut. Thus, the defendant knew of its right to claim that the New York Insurance Law denied coverage and of the possible, if not probable efficacy of such a claim. The *Stecker* case had been decided by the New York Court of Appeals long after the decision of this court in the *Williamson* case and some fifteen months before the date of the Jenkins accident. In order to waive a claim of law it is not necessary, contrary to the court's obvious conclusions, that a party be certain of the correctness of the claim and its legal efficacy. It is enough if he knows of the existence of the claim and of its reasonably possible efficacy. Under the [trial] court's theory, waiver of a claim of law could rarely, if ever, be established, since the defendant could always claim, as in effect it did here, that it knew nothing about, or at least did not fully understand, the law of New York, which, according to its own claims, governed the construction of its own contract of insurance. The conclusion that there was no waiver . . . cannot be sustained.

There remains for consideration the claim of the plaintiff that the subordinate facts as matter of law require a conclusion of waiver, and that the case should be remanded to the trial court with a direction to render judgment for the plaintiff in accordance with his claims. The conclusion that a party has waived a right is one of fact for the trier and not one which can be drawn by this court, unless, on the subordinate facts found, such a conclusion is required as a matter of law. *See Kurzatkowski v. Kurzatkowski,* 116 A.2d 906, 908 (Conn. 1955).

In the light of the request of Patricia's attorney for a commitment as to coverage, as well as the defendant's attempts thereafter to adjust the claim, the letter of September 18, 1958, can be construed only as an intentional relinquishment of a known right. Furthermore, once a right is waived, the waiver cannot be withdrawn even if subsequent events prove the right waived to have been more valuable than had been anticipated. *DiFrancesco v. Zurich General Accident &*

Liability Ins. Co., 134 A. 789 (Conn. 1926). The defendant's letter of November 12, 1958, denying coverage because of the New York statute was ineffective to withdraw its waiver, and the court was in error in not drawing the conclusion of waiver from the subordinate facts which it had found. . . .

NOTES AND QUESTIONS

1. The complaint in the case alleged estoppel, not waiver, as grounds for coverage. What arguments can you see for and against the application of estoppel? Where is the detrimental reliance?

2. Some commentators advocate the use of the term "election" to refer to situations in which an objective observer would understand that an insurance company had given up a right even though no one in the insurance company actually intended to do so. One example might be an insurance company that deposited a late payment—thereby suggesting to the objective observer that it had "waived" the defense of late payment—without anyone in the company realizing that it was late or intending to waive the defense. *See, e.g.,* Robert Keeton & Alan Widiss, Insurance Law §6.8(c)(3) (1988). In the editors' view, understanding waiver as subject to an "objective" standard, in the same sense that "acceptance" and "consent" are subject to an "objective" standard, eliminates the need for the doctrine of election (which has never really caught on among courts, anyway).

3. The *Jenkins* court's resolution of the choice of law question is the traditional one, although there is substantial authority under the approach of the Restatement (Second) of Contracts that a liability insurance contract should be interpreted according to the law of the jurisdiction in which the underlying tort claim will be governed. *See generally* Banks McDowell, *Choice of Law in Insurance: Using Conflicts Methodology to Minimize Discrimination among Policyholders,* 23 Conn. L. Rev. 117 (1990).

4. The doctrines of waiver and estoppel perform similar functions; however, there are important differences in the way that those functions are performed. Comment c to §6 of the RLLI addresses these functions and differences as follows:

> Both waiver and estoppel raise two important practical concerns. First, both doctrines reduce insurers' ability to maintain control over the risks that they assume, by allowing their agents to obligate insurers to assume risks that the insurers do not wish to assume. This loss of insurer control in the long run increases the price of insurance for all policyholders. Second, both doctrines create the risk that some policyholders will misrepresent what an agent said to them in order to obtain coverage. In the worst case, insurers may have to go to trial to enforce even the most basic terms in the insurance policy, as the credibility of witnesses is a fact question that requires resolution by a jury. Balanced against these two concerns is the concern that insureds will be harmed by false or incorrect assurances of coverage made by insurers' agents.
>
> Estoppel requires insureds to prove that such harm in fact occurred, in the form of a showing of detrimental reliance. See §6. Such proof is not required by the waiver doctrine. The detrimental-reliance requirement of estoppel doctrine serves two purposes. First, it limits insurers' involuntary assumption of risk to cases in which the insured can prove that the countervailing concern—harm to

the insured—in fact occurred. Second, it serves an evidentiary role. The fact of detrimental reliance makes more credible the insured's assertion that the agent made the promise that the insured seeks to enforce. For that reason, estoppel has broader application than waiver.

5.   Courts often state that waiver by an insurer "cannot expand coverage." However, the law clearly contemplates situations in which a claim that would not have been covered but for a waiver is, because of the waiver, covered. How can these two seemingly contradictory principles coexist? Comment j to §6, RLLI, answers this questions as follows:

> Courts often state that waiver by the insurer cannot expand coverage. What this statement appears to mean is that representatives of the insurer cannot create coverage where none would have existed under the policy, assuming all conditions had been met. Under this understanding, the waiver-cannot-expand-coverage rule is not violated if an insurer expressly or impliedly waives a condition, such as a payment deadline for a premium. In such cases, as shown in Illustration 1, waiver can result in the triggering of an insurer's obligations with respect to a claim, despite the failure to satisfy a condition. The waiver-cannot-expand-coverage rule, however, would apply to a situation in which an insured contends that its general liability insurer, owing to the actions or inactions of a representative of the insurer, has waived the policy's pollution exclusion—or to a situation in which an insured contends that its auto liability insurer has agreed to provide liability coverage for an automobile not listed in the policy. Permitting waiver to require the insurer to provide coverage in such situations would conflict with this rule of insurance law. To recover in such situations, the insured would have to meet the more demanding requirements of estoppel. See §6, Comment *e.* . . .

THE ROSETH PROBLEM

Some courts that allow promissory estoppel to avoid restrictions on coverage nevertheless limit the application of the doctrine to promises that induced the policyholder to purchase coverage. *Roseth v. St. Paul Property & Liability Insurance Co.*, 374 N.W.2d 105 (S.D. 1985), is a classic case. *Roseth* involved a shipment of cattle injured in a traffic accident. The adjuster assigned to the claim—a man named Wattleworth—did not contradict Roseth's (mistaken) belief that he had coverage for calves that were injured but not killed. The adjuster told Roseth that he did not have a copy of the policy, but that St. Paul would meet its obligations under the policy. The court described the facts as follows:

> The trial court found that Roseth had told Wattleworth that he believed he had an all-risk policy and that the decrease in value of the livestock would be covered under his policy; that Wattleworth thought at the time that St. Paul did not have an all-risk cargo policy; that Wattleworth nevertheless allowed Roseth to go on thinking that the coverage existed because Wattleworth did not want to antagonize Roseth; and that Wattleworth told Roseth that he thought it was a good idea to sell the cattle the next day to minimize the loss.

Id. at 107. When it turned out that the policy provided coverage only for livestock that were killed in an accident, Roseth brought a claim under promissory estoppel. The promise was the statement by the adjuster and the detrimental reliance was Roseth's decision to immediately sell the calves at auction (at a loss) rather than nursing them back to health.

As with nearly all the cases rejecting the use of promissory estoppel, the court relied exclusively on precedent, without squarely addressing the injustice that results from the rule:

> The requirement that the estopping conduct occur "before or at the inception of the policy" is consistent with the underlying rationale of the minority rule. The minority rule was born out of the inequities which result where an insured relies to his detriment on an insurer's superior knowledge in purchasing a policy of insurance and consequently is deprived of the opportunity to purchase the desired coverage elsewhere. Under the facts of the case before us, Wattleworth at most indirectly perpetuated a misconception held by Roseth concerning the nature of his coverage. We hold that under these facts the remedy of estoppel is not available to expand the terms of the policy.

Id. Develop arguments in favor of adopting promissory estoppel in this case. Analyze whether Roseth could have used the doctrine of waiver. Consider, as well, whether Roseth might have had a cause of action against Wattleworth. To address this final issue, you'll need to read the following materials and consider whether insurance adjusters should have any duties to the policyholders whose claims they handle.

IV.   THE ROLE OF INSURANCE INTERMEDIARIES

An omitted part of the *Darner* opinion addressed the liability of the insurance agent for failing to adequately represent Darner Motors. As this part of *Darner* illustrated, there is often a close factual connection between claims or defenses based on waiver, estoppel, or misrepresentation and the potential liability of an insurance intermediary. In many waiver or estoppel cases, it is an insurance intermediary who made the statement that serves as the basis for the estoppel claim. Similarly, in many misrepresentation cases, it is the insurance intermediary who put false information in the insurance application. If the policyholder loses coverage because of the misrepresentation or is unsuccessful in obtaining coverage through waiver or estoppel, the insurance intermediary is the logical target.

Cases involving insurance intermediaries raise a predictable set of issues. Are the acts or omissions of the intermediary binding on the relevant insurance company? If they are, do those acts or omissions form the basis for a waiver or estoppel? Is there any basis for holding the intermediary legally responsible for the harm that results?

One complication in these "insurance intermediary" cases is the use of the labels "agent" and "broker." Some purists maintain that the term "insurance agent" should be reserved for entities that have *actual authority* to act on behalf of an insurance company and the term "insurance broker" should be reserved for entities that have *actual authority* to act on behalf of the person seeking insurance. "Actual authority" is the term in agency law for the type of authority that a "principal" intentionally gives to an "agent" to act on the principal's behalf. Thus, even under this purist definition, both "insurance brokers" and "insurance agents" are "agents" in agency law terms. The difference between them is the identity of the principal. The broker's principal is the policyholder; the agent's principal is the insurance company.

There are practical problems with dividing the world cleanly between "agents" and "brokers" in this way. On the one hand, it can be difficult to determine the scope of the actual authority that an insurance company gives to a given intermediary. On the other hand, insurance intermediaries can come to have *apparent authority* to act for a company with regard to something from which the company has made every effort to withhold *actual* authority. "Apparent authority" is the term in agency law for a situation in which a person reasonably believes that someone has authority to act for a principal. Apparent authority is a fact-sensitive concept, and there are many ways that insurance intermediaries can gain apparent authority to act for an insurance company. *See generally* Eric M. Holmes, Holmes' Appleman on Insurance §45.7 (2d ed. and supp. 2002).

The excerpt of the following case briefly addresses the agency question and discusses in greater detail the liability of an insurance agent or broker.

ECONOMY FIRE & CASUALTY CO. v. BASSETT

Appellate Court of Illinois, Fifth District
525 N.E.2d 539 (1988)

LEWIS, J. Sherry Bassett operated a licensed day-care facility at her home at Rural Route 1, Sunnybrook Meadows, Carmi, Illinois. At the time of the incident giving rise to this litigation, Bassett had provided babysitting services in her home for approximately nine years. She received compensation for these services. On any given day, she would have up to eight children in her care.

Among the children for whom Bassett was being paid to baby-sit was three-year-old Dylan Jones. On October 16, 1981, Dylan was at Bassett's home, along with Mandy Sparrow, Carla and Dusty Pritchard, Devon and Deon Erkman, and Jamie and Kathy Mills. At approximately 4:30 P.M., Patricia Mills drove into Bassett's driveway to pick up Jamie and Kathy, her children. As Mills backed out to leave, her automobile struck and injured Dylan.

Dylan's parents brought a personal injury action on his behalf against both Mills and Bassett. Bassett held a homeowner's insurance policy from Economy Fire & Casualty Company, which she had purchased through Connie and Robylee Gott at the Burnett Insurance Agency. Bassett notified Economy of the lawsuit, and it provided her with legal representation under a reservation of rights. At the same time, it filed the action *sub judice* against Bassett, Mills, and Dylan seeking a declaratory judgment that its policy with Bassett did not cover Dylan's accident. The basis for Economy's claim was an exclusion in the policy which provided:

1. Coverage E—Personal Liability and Coverage F—Medical Payments to Others
do not apply to bodily injury or property damage: . . .
   b. arising out of business pursuits of any Insured. . . .
   This exclusion does not apply to:
   (1) activities which are ordinarily incident to non-business pursuits. . . .

Dylan, through his guardian *ad litem,* Doug Dorris, and Sherry Bassett each then brought a third-party action against Connie Gott, Robylee Gott, and Bruce Burnett, d/b/a Burnett Insurance Agency, alleging that the Gotts and Burnett had failed to exercise reasonable skill, care, and diligence in procuring insurance for Bassett which would cover her residence and the babysitting business she conducted there and, in the alternative, that they had breached an oral contract to obtain such insurance for her.

Following a bench trial, judgment was entered in favor of Economy on its complaint against Bassett, Mills, and Dylan, and in favor of the Gotts and Burnett on the third-party claims of Bassett and Dylan. In entering this judgment, the circuit court expressly found, *inter alia:*

1. that the policy issued by Economy to Bassett did not cover the accident on October 16, 1981, in which Dylan was injured because that accident, and the resulting damages, "arose from the business pursuits of Sherry Bassett, and not activities which are ordinarily incident to non-business pursuits";

2. that Robylee Gott, Connie Gott, and Bruce Burnett, d/b/a Burnett Insurance Agency, did not serve as agents of Economy in procuring that policy, and Economy was therefore not bound by any acts or omissions which these parties are claimed to have committed; and

3. that Robylee Gott, Connie Gott, and Bruce Burnett, d/b/a Burnett Insurance Agency, neither breached any contract, nor acted negligently in procuring insurance for Bassett.

Post-trial motions filed by Bassett and Dylan were denied, and Dylan alone now appeals. . . .

Dylan argued that the Gotts and Burnett committed certain acts and omissions and that those acts and omissions should be binding on Economy because the Gotts and Burnett were Economy's agents. As we have noted, the circuit court held that the Gotts and Burnett did not serve as agents so as to bind Economy by their acts and omissions, and Dylan now claims that this finding is contrary to the manifest weight of the evidence. This contention must also fail. The record before us adequately established that the Gotts and Burnett were insurance brokers who represented the insured, Sherry Bassett, and not agents of the insurer, Economy.

Under Illinois law an insurance broker is one who procures insurance and acts as middleman between the insured and the insurer, and solicits insurance business from the public under no employment from any special company, but, having secured an order, places the insurance with a company selected by the insured, or, in the absence of any selection by him, with the company selected by such broker. Insurance agents, on the other hand, are those who have a "fixed and permanent relation to the companies they represent and have certain duties and allegiances to such companies." Although the Gotts and Burnett had the authority to solicit the sale of Economy policies and could "bind" Economy to coverage until such time as a policy application was received by and accepted or rejected by Economy, the evidence also showed that the Burnett Insurance Agency was independent and solicited the sale of policies from a variety of different insurance companies. It had no fixed and permanent relationship to Economy, or any other company.

When Bassett needed insurance she went to the Gotts and explained what her situation was. Robylee Gott then suggested the particular policy that was purchased. Bassett did not direct the Gotts to obtain insurance from a specified insurer, but rather relied on the Gotts' judgment. Connie Gott agreed that "[the Bassetts] more or less placed their insurance needs in [our] hands and [we] took care of them." These factors adequately supported the trial court's conclusion that the Gotts and Burnett were "insurance brokers" not "insurance agents," and their agency relationship was with the Bassetts, not Economy. Because the Gotts and Burnett were not agents for Economy, nothing that they knew or should have known and no negligent act on their part can be imputed to Economy.

A third, and more substantial, claim made by Dylan is that the circuit court erred in finding that the Gotts and Bruce Burnett did not act negligently in procuring insurance for Bassett. As we have just discussed, the Gotts and Burnett acted as insurance brokers for Bassett. Illinois law places a particular burden on an insurance broker to exercise competence and skill when he renders the service of procuring insurance coverage. As a general rule:

> [A]n insurance broker is bound to exercise reasonable skill and diligence in the transaction of the business entrusted to him and will be responsible to his principal for any loss resulting from his failure to do so. *See Kane Ford Sales, Inc. v. Cruz*, 255 N.E.2d 90 (Ill. App. Ct. 1970). In this regard we observe that the primary function of an insurance broker as it relates to an insured is to faithfully negotiate and procure an insurance policy according to the wishes and requirements of his client. *See City of Chicago v. Barnett*, 88 N.E.2d 477, 481 (Ill. 1949); *Galiher v. Spates*, 262 N.E.2d 626, 628-629 (Ill. App. Ct. 1970).

See Pittway Corp. v. American Motorist Ins. Co., 370 N.E.2d 1271 (Ill. App. Ct. 1977).

The relationship between an insured and his broker, acting as the insured's agent, is a fiduciary one even though the broker may be compensated by some third party. A broker is not liable if he acts in good faith and with reasonable care, skill, and diligence to place the insurance in compliance with his principal's instructions. On the other hand:

> If an agent neglects to procure insurance or does not follow instructions when obligated so to do, or if the policy obtained is void or materially defective through the agent's fault, or if the principal suffers damage by reason of any mistake or act of omission or commission of the agent which constitutes a breach of duty to his principal, he is liable to his principal for any loss he may have sustained thereby.

Dylan contends that the Gotts and Burnett should be held liable under these standards because they failed to take reasonable steps to insure that the policy which they sold to Bassett was adequate for her needs. We agree. According to Bassett, she told Robylee Gott that she baby-sat in her home. Although she did not recall any specific conversation with the Gotts regarding coverage for her business, she also explained that she never knew to ask about this in particular. In her words, "I just thought the homeowner's had always covered for me."

That the Gotts did, in fact, know that Bassett baby-sat in her home for compensation at the time they sold her the policy from Economy is clearly established by the record. Connie Gott, who filled out the actual application form for the Bassetts, testified that she lived on the same street with them and had known

Sherry Bassett was baby-sitting for pay before 1979, when the Economy policy was first issued. The testimony of Robylee Gott was to the same effect. There was also evidence that the Gotts had even referred to Sherry Bassett a family member in need of babysitting services. Despite this knowledge, the Gotts admitted that they never warned Sherry Bassett that she might need additional coverage for her babysitting service. . . .

In view of this evidence we fail to see how the circuit court's judgment in favor of the Gotts and Burnett can be sustained. The Gotts knew or should have known that Bassett might need additional coverage for her babysitting service. They could easily have ascertained from Economy whether that babysitting service was covered under the policy which they chose for her. They did not. Sherry Bassett and her husband placed their insurance needs in the hands of the Gotts and the Burnett Insurance Agency. The Gotts and the agency for which they worked agreed to accept this responsibility, but they clearly did not understand or try to understand the product they were selling, and their efforts to ascertain the Bassetts' actual insurance needs were virtually nonexistent. In short, the actions of the Gotts and the Burnett Insurance Agency in selling this policy to the Bassetts were devoid of the reasonable care, skill, and diligence required by the law.

The Gotts and Bruce Burnett, d/b/a Burnett Insurance Agency, claim that they nevertheless cannot be held liable because the Bassetts had a copy of the policy, they had ample opportunity to read it, and they should therefore have brought any discrepancies in the policy to the attention of the Gotts before the accident occurred. . . . In such cases, as this court has previously held, an insured's failure to read his own policy is not an absolute bar to the insured's right to recover against his broker for breach of the broker's fiduciary duty.

NOTES AND QUESTIONS

1. Do you think the Bassetts knew the difference between brokers and agents? Should they? What are the public policy reasons behind the distinction between brokers and agents made in the opinion? Are there ways of satisfying those public policies without leaving insureds empty-handed in the event their "brokers" cannot satisfy a judgment?

2. What is the risk allocated in this decision? Who are the potential bearers of that risk? Who is best able to prevent that risk? Should insurance law take these considerations into account in assigning responsibility for mistakes by insurance intermediaries? Did it in this case? Assume that the law assigns the risk to the policyholders. What can they do to avoid it? How about the agent or broker? The insurance company? How might the existence or nonexistence of liability affect behavior? Consider whether the concept of moral hazard (in the broader principal-agent understanding of that term) is a useful one here.

3. Insurance companies use many different kinds of intermediaries to sell their insurance policies. Some companies use employees. Other companies use "captive" agents who are independent contractors as a matter of employment law but who work exclusively for and largely under the direction of a particular insurance company. Both these types of agents are typically understood as having actual authority to bind the company and, even where

they do not, as having apparent authority. Other companies use "independent agents" who have the ability to place business with more than one insurance company. The insurance agency in *Economy Fire & Casualty* appears to have been an independent agent in this sense. The status of "independent" insurance agents under agency law is more variable. Decisions tend to be fact specific. Consider what would be the consequences of adopting a rule that all insurance intermediaries who deal with ordinary consumers be regarded as having "apparent authority" to act on behalf of the insurance companies with whom they place insurance policies. How might that change the business practices of independent agents?

4. Would your analysis of the case change if you knew that the Gotts carried a $5 million errors and omissions policy that protected them against claims like this? If you knew that the Gotts had no insurance? Should the existence or availability of liability insurance affect liability rules?

5. Some jurisdictions have eliminated the statutory distinction between "agents" and "brokers" and, instead, issue a single license and set of regulations for "insurance producers" on the grounds that the terms "agent" and "broker" harm consumers more than they help them. Should this approach to licensing affect the courts' decisions about whether an intermediary is the agent of the insurance company?

V.   MISREPRESENTATION

Insurance misrepresentation doctrine is the legal tool that requires people to provide accurate answers to the questions that insurance companies use to underwrite and classify insurance applicants. Misrepresentation law is concerned only with false statements that matter: *material* false statements. Typically what makes a false statement matter to an insurance company is that a high-risk entity or person is charged a low-risk price. This implicates public policy concerns because of the problem of adverse selection and the principle of equal treatment among equally situated individuals. As you will recall from the discussion in Chapter 1, there is a risk of adverse selection whenever insurance is voluntary and people have private information about the level of risk that they bring to the pool. Insurance companies try to prevent adverse selection by establishing contracting procedures that require potential insureds to reveal that information. In simple terms, insurers ask questions. Misrepresentation law is what requires insureds to provide accurate answers. Sometimes statements made in the insurance application process turn out to be both false and material, even though the insured had no intention of misleading the insurer. Consider how the following statutes compare in terms of addressing the problem of adverse selection and the problem of unintentional misrepresentations. Consider also the alternative approach to misrepresentation used in the ALI's Principles of the Law of Liability Insurance, approved May 2013, which differs importantly from the other approaches.[5]

5. The Restatement of the Law of Liability Insurance began as a "Principles Project." Whereas ALI Restatements are addressed primarily to common law courts, ALI Principles Projects are addressed primarily to state legislatures or other policymakers.

IOWA CODE §515.101 (2001)

Any condition or stipulation in an application, policy, or contract of insurance, making the policy void before the loss occurs, shall not prevent recovery thereon by the insured, if it shall be shown by the plaintiff that the failure to observe such provision or the violation thereof did not contribute to the loss.

MASS. GEN. LAWS CH. 175 §186 (2007)

No oral or written misrepresentation or warranty made in the negotiation of a policy of insurance by the insured or in his behalf shall be deemed material or defeat or avoid the policy or prevent its attaching unless such misrepresentation or warranty is made with actual intent to deceive, or unless the matter misrepresented or made a warranty increased the risk of loss.

N.Y. INS. LAW §3105 (McKINNEY 2001)

§3105.   Representations by the Insured

(a) A representation is a statement as to past or present fact, made to the insurer by, or by the authority of, the applicant for insurance or the prospective insured, at or before the making of the insurance contract as an inducement to the making thereof. A misrepresentation is a false representation, and the facts misrepresented are those facts which make the representation false.

(b) No misrepresentation shall avoid any contract of insurance or defeat recovery thereunder unless such misrepresentation was material. No misrepresentation shall be deemed material unless knowledge by the insurer of the facts misrepresented would have led to a refusal by the insurer to make such contract.

(c) In determining the question of materiality, evidence of the practice of the insurer which made such contract with respect to the acceptance or rejection of similar risks shall be admissible.

PRINCIPLES OF THE LAW OF LIABILITY INSURANCE

American Law Institute (Tent. Draft No. 1, Approved May 2013)

§7.   Misrepresentation

(1) Any statement of a past or present fact made by a policyholder in applying for or renewing a liability insurance policy is a representation by the policyholder.

(2) An insurer may decline to pay a claim on the basis of a false or misleading representation by a policyholder during the application or renewal process for the insurance policy and may, after returning all premiums paid by the policyholder, rescind the policy only if all of the following conditions are met:

(a) The misrepresentation was either intentional or reckless as defined in §8;

(b) The insurer reasonably relied on the misrepresentation in issuing or renewing the policy as specified in §9; and

(c) The misrepresentation was material as defined in §10.

(3) It is not a basis for rescission or denial of an insured's claim that the policyholder concealed or failed to disclose information that the insurer did not expressly ask about in the application or renewal process. . . .

(5) The conditions stated in Subsection (2)(a) to (c) of this Section and the rules stated in Subsections (3) and (4) of this Section are non-mandatory rules for policies sold to large commercial policyholders.

§8. Intentional or Reckless Misrepresentation by Policyholder

(1) A misrepresentation by a policyholder is intentional only if at the time it is made the policyholder knows or believes that the statement is false.

(2) A misrepresentation by a policyholder is reckless only if at the time it is made the policyholder is willfully indifferent to whether the statement is true or false.

§9. Reasonable Detrimental Reliance Requirement

The reliance requirement of §7(2)(b) is met only if,

(1) Absent the misrepresentation, the insurer would not have issued the policy or would have issued the policy only with substantially different terms; and

(2) Such actions would have been reasonable under the circumstances.

§10. Materiality Requirement

A misrepresentation by an insured during the application or renewal of an insurance policy is material if, in the absence of the misrepresentation, a reasonable insurer in this insurer's position would not have issued the policy or would have issued the policy only under substantially different terms.

§11. Remedy for Misrepresentations That Are Neither Reckless Nor Intentional

If the requirements of §7(2)(b) and §7(2)(c) are met, but the misrepresentation was neither reckless nor intentional, as those terms are defined in §8:

(1) If the insurer would have issued the same policy but at a higher premium if the correct information had been supplied at the time of the application or renewal, the insurer must pay the claim at issue but may collect from the policyholder or deduct from the claim payment the additional premium that would have been charged.

(2) If the insurer would not have issued the policy for any premium if the correct information had been supplied at the time of the application or renewal, the insurer must pay the claim at issue but may collect from the policyholder or deduct from the claim payment a reasonable additional premium for the increased risk.

(3) The insurer may cancel the policy prospectively within a reasonable time after discovering the misrepresentation.

THE AUTO INSURANCE MISREPRESENTATION PROBLEM

Consider what your answer would be to the following questions under each of the three misrepresentation statutes and the Principles Project sections above:

1. Frank Smith, a second-year law student, applies for car insurance. He lives in Detroit, Michigan, but he lists as his residence the town of Ann Arbor, where his parents live, to get a cheaper rate on his car insurance. When he gets in an accident, can his insurance company deny the claim?
2. Frank gets a new policy. When he applies, the agent asks whether he will use the car to drive to work or school. Frank says to drive to school. The agent then asks how far Frank drives to school each day. Frank says three miles, believing that to be correct, but it turns out that his apartment is six miles from school. When he gets in another accident, can his insurance company deny the claim?
3. Frank gets another policy and answers the same questions about driving to school. This time, Frank answers correctly. A year later, he graduates and gets a job in Kalamazoo (a city about two hours away from Detroit). He does not call up the insurance company and tell them about his new, longer commute to work. When he gets in an accident, can the insurance company deny the claim based on the incorrect commuting distance?

NOTES AND QUESTIONS

1. What risks are created by the misrepresentation defense? Who is in the best position to prevent those risks? To spread those risks? Should we spread those risks? How do the statutes differ in how they assign the risks associated with misrepresentations?
2. What are the differences between the statutes' approach to materiality? Which approach is more carefully tailored to the problem of adverse selection?
3. Notice that the Massachusetts statute treats both misrepresentation and fraud ("actual intent to deceive" in the Massachusetts statute). Fraud is a defense at common law, so that defense is available in Iowa and New York, even though the statutes do not include it. Nevertheless, it is important to be aware that fraud is a relatively unimportant coverage defense. As Professor Jerry notes, "although one can find judicial pronouncements that an immaterial but fraudulent misrepresentation will void a policy, these pronouncements are rare." Understanding Insurance Law 810 (3d ed. 2002).
4. Notice as well that the New York statute defines applicants' statements as "representations." This is a liberalization of the common law, which allowed insurance companies to designate certain statements as "warranties" rather than simple representations. In contrast to representations, there was no materiality requirement for warranties. All that was required was that the warranty was not complied with. One famous example of this is *DeHahn v. Hartley*, 99 Eng. Rep. 1130, 1131 (K.B. 1786), *aff'd,* 100 Eng. Rep. 101 (Ex. 1787). In that case the insured "warranted" that a ship would sail "from Liverpool . . . with 50 hands or upwards." The ship in fact sailed out of

Liverpool with only 46 hands and then picked up 6 more hands only six hours out of Liverpool, bringing the total number of seamen on board to 52. When the ship later went down at sea, the insurer refused to pay, and the famous English judge Lord Mansfield concluded that the insurer was perfectly justified in so doing because warranties "must be strictly complied with." Some courts softened this by going to great lengths to find that a warranty was satisfied. *See, e.g., Vlastos v. Sumitomo Marine & Fire Ins. Co.*, 707 F.2d 775 (3d Cir. 1983). The common law warranty rule remains in effect for marine insurance in many jurisdictions. *See* Jerry, *supra*, at 780.

5. Is there a knowledge or intent requirement under the statutes? Does a misrepresentation have to be intentional or negligent to be actionable? Should it? Why or why not? Courts in some states have required that misrepresentations must be intentional in the case of automobile insurance. *See, e.g., Middlesex Mut. Assurance Co. v. Walsh*, 590 A.2d 957, 961 (Conn. 1991). What might be different about automobile insurance? Courts in Texas have required intent for other kinds of insurance as well. *See, e.g., Parsaie v. United Olympic Life Ins. Co.*, 29 F.3d 219 (5th Cir. 1994).

6. If adverse selection is the "problem" to which misrepresentation law is part of the "answer," what knowledge requirements should there be on the part of applicants? Notice that, apart from fraud, the statutes do not make distinctions on the basis of *mens rea*. Does that suggest that more than adverse selection is at issue? If so, what might that be?

7. The quasi-reformation remedy stated in §11 of the Principles of the Law of Liability Insurance is an innovation. For a similar concept, *see* Brian Barnes, *Against Insurance Rescission*, Note, 120 Yale L.J. 328, 347 (2010); *see also* Thomas R. Foley, *Insurers' Misrepresentation Defense: The Need for a Knowledge Element*, Note, 67 S. Cal. L. Rev. 659, 662–663 (1994) ("[I]f a court grants rescission, the insurance buyer may be in a much worse position than existed prior to contract formation. . . . First, the insurance buyer will be worse off if she could have obtained insurance with another insurer or for a higher price had she not inadvertently misrepresented. . . . Second, even if an insurance buyer was absolutely uninsurable at any price on account of the misrepresented fact, had she been uninsured she could have taken greater precautions to prevent the loss or forgone the risky activity entirely").

8. A few states have, by statute or court decision, explicitly adopted a requirement that an insurer seeking to rescind a policy must prove that the falsehood was made either knowingly or recklessly (that is, without any effort to verify that statement's truthfulness). *See, e.g., Middlesex Mut. Assurance Co. v. Walsh*, 590 A.2d 957, 963–64 (Conn. 1991) ("[I]n order to constitute a misrepresentation sufficient to defeat recovery on an automobile insurance policy, a material representation on an application for such a policy must be known by the insured to be false when made."); *Strickland v. Prudential Ins. Co. of Am.*, 292 S.E.2d 301, 304 (S.C. 1982) (requiring the insurer to show "not only the falsity of the statement challenged, but also that the falsity was known to the applicant" and was "made with the intent to defraud the insurer"); and *Shafer v. John Hancock Mut. Life Ins. Co.*, 189 A.2d 234, 236 (Pa. 1963) (reaching similar conclusion). Even in jurisdictions that do not require that misrepresentations be intentional in order for the insurer to be able to rescind a policy, courts may still be reluctant to void the policy of a policyholder who acted in good faith. That is, courts may search for

other pathways to enforce the insurance contract. For example, a court may apply the contribute-to-the-loss approach to materiality or place a low threshold on the circumstances that should alert a reasonable insurer to investigate further before issuing an insurance policy. In addition, if an insurance application contains an ambiguous or unclear question, courts will construe the interpretation of that question against the insurer and in favor of the policyholder, applying the standard interpretive rule to the insurance application. Limiting rescission to cases of intentional or reckless misrepresentations provides a more transparent and predictable rule that better protects policyholders and better informs insurance companies than the ad hoc application of these and other devices to protect policyholders acting in good faith.

Think about these claims after you read the next case.

9. As a technical matter, an actionable misrepresentation makes a policy voidable, not void, and the remedy typically specified in a misrepresentation defense is rescission. Some states have modified by statute the traditional common law right of an insurance company to rescind a policy. Often these statutes address the insurance company's ability to "cancel" a policy. The Connecticut Supreme Court addressed one such statute in *Munroe v. Great Am. Ins. Co.*, 661 A.2d 581 (Conn. 1995). *Munroe* concerned a tort victim's rights under a liability insurance policy issued to a man who engaged in a series of deliberate falsehoods and evasions to obtain automobile insurance. Within a month of issuing the insurance policy, the insurance company's home office discovered the misrepresentations and attempted to rescind the policy. Unfortunately, the insured had caused a serious automobile accident in the interim. The court held that the state's cancellation statute had modified the insurance company's right of rescission and, accordingly, found for the victim. What public policy reasons might have motivated the court in this case? Is automobile insurance different from other forms of insurance in this regard?

10. A material misrepresentation *after* a loss can also be grounds for rescinding a policy. For example, in *Longobardi v. Chubb Ins. Co. of N.J.*, 582 A.2d 1257 (N.J. 1990), the New Jersey Supreme Court upheld a trial court decision rescinding a policy because the insured had lied to an insurance adjuster about circumstances surrounding a burglary claim. Significantly, the court held that the insurance company did not have to prove that the insured intended to defraud the company, only that the misrepresentation was knowing and material. Why might courts require that a post-loss misrepresentation be "knowing"? ("A mere oversight or honest mistake will not cost an insured his or her coverage; the lie must be wi[l]lful." *Id.*) The main issue in the case was the standard of materiality. The intermediate appellate court held that a post-loss misrepresentation was material only if it actually prejudiced the insurer. The New Jersey Supreme Court disagreed, holding that a post-loss "misstatement is material . . . when . . . a reasonable insurer would have considered the misrepresented fact relevant to its concerns and important in determining its course of action." The court stated that the intermediate appellate court's approach would "allow an insured to gamble that a lie will turn out to be unimportant."

11. Health insurance contracts have traditionally provided a source of many interesting misrepresentation cases. *See, e.g., Pum v. Wisconsin Physicians Service Ins. Corp.*, 727 N.W.2d 346 (2006). However, misrepresentation in the

health insurance context is decreasing in importance because of the limitations that the Affordable Care Act has placed on the underwriting practices of health insurance companies. Specifically, because health insurers can no longer deny coverage for preexisting conditions and are severely limited in their ability to charge different premiums to policyholders based on differences in their risk characteristics (as revealed through their answers to questions on insurance applications), insurers ask fewer such questions and insurance applicants' incentives to misrepresentative has diminished. Other types of insurance, however, are not affected by the Affordable Care Act in this way. For example, consider the following case, which involves an application for life insurance.

HARPER v. FIDELITY AND GUARANTY LIFE INSURANCE COMPANY

Supreme Court of Wyoming

234 P.3d 1211 (2010)

HILL, Justice.

Joseph Harper, the husband of Appellant Gail Harper, bought a life insurance policy and died within two months of doing so. Fidelity and Guaranty Life Insurance Company refused to pay the claim because they insisted that Mr. Harper "misrepresented/omitted" the state of his health in the claim application. Mrs. Harper filed suit, the district court granted summary judgment in favor of Fidelity, and this appeal followed.

FACTS

Joseph Harper (Mr. Harper) applied for a $63,000.00 life insurance policy with Fidelity & Guaranty Life Insurance Company (Fidelity) on February 10, 2006, and named his wife Gail (Mrs. Harper) as the beneficiary.

Fidelity's application for insurance required that Mr. Harper answer questions about his health and health history. He indicated that he was born on January 19, 1955, that he was 5'11" tall, and that he weighed 275 pounds. He represented on his application that he had never sought or received treatment, advice, or counseling for the use of alcohol. He listed that he was diagnosed with both high blood pressure and high cholesterol in 1997, and the application noted that he was currently taking medication for both conditions. He responded "no" to whether he had been treated for or diagnosed with "[a]ny circulatory disease, stroke, TIA, aneurysm, or any other disorder of the veins or arteries," "[h]epatitis, gastritis, colitis, or any disease or disorder of the liver, stomach, pancreas, or intestines." Mr. Harper reported that he had surgery on his knee in "1995 or 1996," and that he had "[b]lood tests and an electrocardiogram for complaint of migraine & headaches—complete recovery from symptoms in 1996."

After Mr. Harper signed and submitted the application to Fidelity for approval or denial, Lisa Jones, a senior underwriter . . . for Mid–America Agency Services (MAAS), reviewed the application. The type of life insurance applied for by

Mr. Harper was a "simplified underwritten product," where the underwriter reviews and relies upon only the information and medical history provided by the application plus a single report from the Medical Information Bureau (MIB).

Overall, the information contained in the MIB was consistent with Mr. Harper's application information, but two pieces of information from the MIB were of note to Ms. Jones. First, based upon the MIB information existing for Mr. Harper, Fidelity knew that he had applied for another insurance product, the type and results of which were unknown. Second, Ms. Jones noted a weight discrepancy—the MIB recorded Mr. Harper's weight to be 305 pounds within sixty days prior to January 9, 2006; Mr. Harper's February application represented his weight to be 275 pounds. Under Fidelity's underwriting guidelines, an individual the height of Mr. Harper (5'11") must be less than 301 pounds for an application to be accepted. Ms. Jones concluded that given the time between the date of the application and the date of her review, she assumed Mr. Harper had lost enough weight (four pounds) to fit within the guidelines, so she gave him the benefit of the doubt and "let it go."

Ms. Jones made several other observations about Mr. Harper's application that she ultimately let go as well. She noted that Mr. Harper had been treated for depression in 1996 but had a "complete recovery;" thus she was not concerned about his depression being severe, which would have resulted in denial of the application. Also, she observed his diagnosis for high blood pressure and high cholesterol, but considered both to be under control based on the fact that he was taking medication for both conditions. Based on all of Mr. Harper's answers, Ms. Jones recommended his application for life insurance be approved.

On March 1, 2006, Fidelity issued a life insurance policy to Mr. Harper. On April 20, 2006, Mr. Harper died from sudden cardiac arrest, hypertensive cardiovascular disease, and hypertriglyceridemia, just 50 days after the policy was issued.

In light of Mr. Harper's death, Fidelity conducted an investigation within the insurance company's "two-year contestability period," during which Mr. Harper's medical records were reviewed. Fidelity identified various medical conditions of Mr. Harper's that had not been disclosed on his application for life insurance but that, in Fidelity's estimation, were material to the issuance of the policy. First, Mr. Harper had been treated for a "probable transient ischemic attack (TIA)" in May of 2000. On his application, however, he denied ever being treated for a TIA. Also, Mr. Harper's medical records reflected a history of alcohol abuse, including advice from his physician to quit drinking because his liver tests were abnormal—he denied any such condition on his insurance application. In March of 2000, Mr. Harper was also hospitalized for heart fluttering and chest pains, which he did not disclose. Mr. Harper's weight discrepancies also came up. Although he listed himself at 275 pounds on his application, and although his MIB report listed him to be 306 pounds, Mr. Harper's certificate of death recorded Mr. Harper as morbidly obese at 350 pounds.

Mrs. Harper submitted a claim for benefits, but her claim was denied by Fidelity based on Wyo. Stat. Ann. §26–15–124. Along with its denial, Fidelity refunded the premiums paid on the policy to Mrs. Harper, who nevertheless filed suit in district court, asserting four claims for relief: breach of contract, reasonable expectations, equitable and/or promissory estoppel, and breach of the implied covenant of good faith and fair dealing. She also sought an award of punitive damages, attorney's fees, and costs. The district court granted Fidelity's motion for summary judgment, and this appeal followed. . .

[The Court reviews the summary judgment standard of review.]

Issue I — Materiality

Mrs. Harper contests the district court's finding that there was no issue of material fact as to whether Fidelity properly rescinded Mr. Harper's insurance policy pursuant to Wyo. Stat. Ann. §26–15–109. Mrs. Harper argues that a representation or omission in an insurance application is "'material' if knowledge or ignorance of it would naturally influence the judgment of the insurer in making the contract, or in estimating the character of the risk or setting the premium." Thus, argues Mrs. Harper, this is a question of fact for the jury to decide.

Wyo. Stat. Ann. §26–15–109 (LexisNexis 2009) sets forth when a "misrepresentation, omission, concealment of facts or incorrect statement" will prevent recovery under a life insurance policy and states in relevant part:

(a) Any statements and descriptions in any application for an insurance policy . . . by or in behalf of the insured . . . are representations. . . . Misrepresentations, omissions, concealment of facts and incorrect statements do not prevent a recovery under the policy or contract unless either:
    (i)   Fraudulent; or
    (ii) Material either to the acceptance of the risk, or to the hazard the insurer assumes; or
    (iii) The insurer in good faith, if it knew the true facts as required by the application for the policy . . . would not have:
          (A) Issued the policy or contract;
          (B) Issued it at the same premium rate[,]

One year before §26–15–109 was adopted, this Court considered a case similar to the instant one. In *All American Life & Casualty Co. v. Krenzelok*, 409 P.2d 766 (Wyo.1966), Mary Krenzelok, a foreign woman who could neither read nor write, applied for life insurance. Her son actually completed the application and Krenzelok signed it. The policy was issued, and Krenzelok died from a cerebral brain hemorrhage approximately one year after its issuance. It was then discovered that Krenzelok had failed to disclose a hospitalization for arteriosclerotic heart disease and congestive heart failure. This Court stated on appeal:

> There are numerous cases which hold a concealment or failure to disclose periods of past hospitalization and medical treatment will invalidate a policy, regardless of whether applicant had a fraudulent intent to deceive. . . . A fraudulent intent on the part of the insured is not a requisite of concealment. Consequently, concealment of facts material to the risk will avoid the policy even though the concealment was the result of inadvertence or mistake and was entirely without fraudulent intent.

Id., 409 P.2d at 768.

More recently, the Wyoming Federal District Court interpreted §26–15–109, and discussed *Krenzelok*.

Krenzelok, a case decided one year before the Wyoming legislature adopted §26-15-109, and which influenced the drafting of that statute, therefore stands for the proposition that if the insurer can show that the concealment was "material" to the insurance risk at issue, then any concealment by the insured, even if made in good faith, will justify rescission of the coverage by the insurer. Other courts have reached the same conclusion in interpreting similar state statutes. *Bageanis,* 783 F. Supp. at 1145 ("A good faith mistake does not excuse a material misrepresentation"); *Massachusetts Mut. Life Ins. Co. v. Nicholson,* 775 F. Supp. 954, 959 (N.D. Miss. 1991) ("If the misstatement is material, it can make no difference as to whether or not it was made in good faith") (citations omitted). Stated another way, proof of intent is not necessary to rescind under *Krenzelok* as long as the insurer can prove that the concealment was "material" to the insurance risk involved. While the rule enunciated in *Krenzelok* may be a considered a harsh one, it is nonetheless the prevailing law of Wyoming which this Court must follow and apply in this case.

White v. Continental Gen. Ins. Co., 831 F. Supp. 1545, 1553 (D. Wyo. 1993). "Materiality" is determined by asking whether reasonably careful and intelligent persons would have regarded the omitted facts as substantially increasing the chances of the events insured against so as to cause a rejection of the application or different conditions, such as higher premiums. *White,* 831 F. Supp. at 1554. The materiality of a misrepresentation may be established by the underwriter's testimony or testimony of the insurer's employees. *Bageanis v. American Bankers Life Assurance Co.,* 783 F. Supp. 1141, 1145 (N.D. Ill. 1992). Furthermore, a good faith mistake does not excuse a material misrepresentation. *Id.* The fact that a potential insured does not die from the withheld ailment does not affect the materiality of the misrepresentation. *Hatch v. Woodmen Accident & Life Co.,* 88 Ill. App. 3d 36, 42 Ill. Dec. 925, 409 N.E.2d 540, 543 (1980). Finally, although materiality is usually a question of fact, summary judgment is appropriate where the misrepresentation "is of such a nature that there can be no dispute as to its materiality." *Commercial Life Ins. Co. v. Lone Star Life Ins. Co.,* 727 F. Supp. 467, 470 (N.D. Ill. 1989).

Mr. Harper's application contained omissions and misrepresentations. He did not accurately respond to several of the questions, including the question about his weight; the question regarding whether he had treatment for/was diagnosed with "hepatitis, gastritis, colitis, or any disease or disorder of the liver . . ." (he underwent a biopsy and ultrasound of his liver and was treated for a liver disease/disorder); and the question regarding diagnosis or treatment of "stroke, TIA, aneurysm . . ." (he had been treated for a TIA and he had been diagnosed as suffering from a stroke). Under Fidelity's guidelines, and according to the underwriter, Mr. Harper's application would have been denied had this information been known. Dennis Gunderson, the chief underwriter in Mr. Harper's case, testified that the policy would not have been issued if the true facts had been presented. Mrs. Harper's own witness, John Terry, testified that Mr. Harper's failure to disclose his history was material.

The omissions/misrepresentations on Mr. Harper's application were material. Mr. Harper did not disclose several health conditions on his application. Whether or not he meant to omit them is not at issue. Had he included them, it is clear that Fidelity would not have issued the certificate of insurance. The underwriter testified that if Mr. Harper had correctly stated that he had a liver function test with an abnormal result, or that he had a liver biopsy, or had he disclosed his hospitalizations for heart problems in March 2000, and/or the May

2000 treatment for a probable TIA, his application would have been rejected. This is a case of even though there are material misrepresentations, which usually raises a question of fact, summary judgment was appropriate here because the misrepresentations are of such a nature that there is no dispute as to this materiality. Thus, there being no genuine issues of material fact, Fidelity was entitled to summary judgment, and the district court is affirmed.

Issue II — Duty to Investigate

Mrs. Harper argues that Fidelity had a duty to further investigate Mr. Harper's answers on his insurance application, and that Fidelity should have obtained his medical records rather than rely on the application itself. Fidelity, however, disputes the assertion that it was under a duty to investigate the answers Mr. Harper gave in his application when the application was submitted, especially because Fidelity had no reason to assume that the answers were not truthful or accurate.

An insurer is under no duty to investigate the truthfulness of an applicant's responses unless it has notice that those responses might not be truthful or accurate. *White*, 831 F. Supp. at 1545. A majority of cases interpreting statutes similar to Wyoming's statute have held that an insurer does not have a duty to investigate, and is entitled to rely on the representations made by the applicant on his application. See, for example, *Twin City Bank v. Verex Assur. Inc.*, 733 F. Supp. 67, 71 (E.D. Ark. 1990) (interpreting Ark. Code Ann. §23–79–107(a) (LexisNexis) which is verbatim to Wyoming's statute).

In *White*, 831 F. Supp. at 1553, the Tenth Circuit weighed in on this very issue:

> Although the Tenth Circuit has not spoken to this issue as of the date of this order, this Court is inclined to follow the rulings of the other appellate and trial courts that have considered this issue and have rejected this position, concluding that the insurer is entitled to rely on an insured's representations. . . . [Citations omitted.] As the court in Bageanis said, the insured was the one who had the burden "to supply complete and accurate information to the insurer." . . . [Citations omitted.] Therefore, the Court concludes that the insurer did not have a duty to investigate and thus was entitled to rely on White's representations.

Also, in a case similar to the instant one (and mentioned in *White*), the insured omitted several hospitalizations for psychological problems and a history of suicide attempts from her insurance application (but did disclose three other hospitalizations for mental issues). *Mutual Ben. Life Ins. Co. v. Morley*, 722 F. Supp. 1048 (S.D.N.Y. 1989). She argued that the insurance company engaged in "lax and sloppy underwriting" and had the underwriter been more thorough and ordered medical records, her prior hospitalizations and suicide attempts would have been discovered, precluding her from insurance coverage. The court granted summary judgment to the insurance company, noting that the company was entitled to rely on the representations made by the applicant.

Mrs. Harper insists that there were red flags that were ignored by Fidelity and, rather than investigate, the underwriter simply ignored the signs that warranted more study. Specifically, Mrs. Harper points to the conflicting MIB information versus the application regarding Mr. Harper's weight. The MIB listed his weight at 305 pounds, while his application stated his weight to be 275 pounds.

Contrary to Mrs. Harper's assertions, however, the "red flags" in this case were adequately explained away by the underwriter: Indeed, Mr. Harper indicated his weight was 275 pounds, whereas the MIB reported his weight to have been 305. The underwriter testified that she looked at the different weight on the MIB report and assumed that Mr. Harper would have lost enough weight to fit into the guidelines which, for Mr. Harper, would have been 301 pounds. In the simplified underwriting process that was used in Mr. Harper's case, the underwriter is to rely on the health questionnaire and the MIB, which is what happened in this instance. Furthermore, Mr. Harper represented in his application that "[t]he statements made in this application are complete, true, and correctly recorded." Mr. Harper's knowledge in this instance was not limited to his "knowledge and belief," as in some cases. There, where the insurance application contains "knowledge and belief" language, the insurer must show that the insured intentionally made the misstatement or omission to rescind the contract. See *Joseph v. Zurich Life Ins. Co. of America*, 159 Fed. Appx. 114, 116, fn. 3 (11th Cir.2005).

Based upon the law, and Mr. Harper's own assertions, Fidelity was under no duty to investigate and was entitled to rely upon Mr. Harper's application.

. . .

[The court also addressed the plaintiff's estoppel, bad faith, and reasonable expectations arguments, agreeing with the lower court's decision to grant summary judgment in favor of the insurer.]

CONCLUSION

There is no issue of material fact as to whether Fidelity properly rescinded Mr. Harper's insurance policy pursuant to §26-15-109. Mr. Harper's application contained omissions and misrepresentations, and summary judgment is appropriate where the misrepresentation "is of such a nature that there can be no dispute as to its materiality." Such was the case in this instance. Furthermore, an insurer is under no duty to investigate the truthfulness of an applicant's responses unless it has notice that those responses might not be truthful or accurate. There is no basis to conclude that the equities in this instance require the insurance contract be enforced under the doctrine of promissory estoppel. Finally, the covenant of good faith and fair dealing was not breached, and no claim exists under the doctrine of reasonable expectations. Affirmed.

NOTES AND QUESTIONS

1. Compare the Wyoming misrepresentation statute to the Iowa, Massachusetts, and New York statutes reprinted above. Would the case come out the same way under all three? What result under the approach adopted in the Principles of the Law of Liability Insurance?

2. Hindsight is 20/20. Should courts be skeptical of insurance underwriters' and employees' testimony that an applicant's misrepresentation is material? In *Harper*, the underwriter, Ms. Jones, noted at least two discrepancies in Mr. Harper's application for insurance. Under the company's underwriting guidelines, the weight discrepancy required the underwriter to reject

the application. Nevertheless, Ms. Jones exercised discretion, "gave him the benefit of the doubt and 'let it go.'" *Harper*, 234 P.3d at 1215.

3. Despite the insurer's awareness of potential problems in Mr. Harper's insurance application, the *Harper* court held that it could rely on the applicant's statements and that there was no duty to investigate the claims. The legal standard for this question cited by the court was whether the insurer "has notice that those responses might not be truthful or accurate." Did the insurer have notice that Mr. Harper's responses might not be truthful or accurate? Part of the court's reasoning seems to rely on the "simplified" nature of this insurance product. Which view of insurance does the court ascribe to? Does that view affect the court's decision and reasoning? Can you think of reasons why the court would be hesitant to require an insurer to investigate every application for life insurance containing discrepancies or potential inaccuracies? Does the RLLI's treatment of misrepresentation include a duty to investigate in the context of liability insurance?

4. Perhaps Mr. Harper was simply an unsympathetic policyholder. Not only did he fail to disclose that he was treated for a liver disease and had a stroke, but when he died, only 50 days after receiving the policy, he weighed 350 pounds and was morbidly obese. In most cases, the determination of whether a misrepresentation is material is a question of fact reserved for the jury. Could a jury have fairly concluded that Mr. Harper's misrepresentations were not material?

5. *Cox v. American Pioneer Life Insurance Co.*, 626 So. 2d 243 (Fla. Dist. Ct. App. 1993), reaches a similar result under Florida law, despite the fact that Florida did not have an administrative regulation like Wis. Admin. Code §INS 3.28(5)(c) (2007). The court used materiality to accomplish the same end. In *Cox*, the insured had submitted medical records that, had the company read them, would have revealed that statements in the application were incorrect. The court concluded that the fact that the insurance company did not obtain the applicant's medical records after the company learned that she had a significant medical condition provided "evidence . . . from which the jury could determine that the misrepresentations on appellant's insurance application were not material." 626 So. 2d at 246. Cases like *Pum* and *Cox* establish something that comes close to a "duty to underwrite" before issuing an insurance policy. How, if at all, do the PLLI rules in misrepresentation address the duty to underwrite?

6. In *Chawla v. Transamerica Occidental Life Insurance Co.*, 440 F.3d 639 (4th Cir. 2006), the plaintiffs persuasively argued that the insurance company knew the application contained material misrepresentations. The court nevertheless upheld summary judgment in favor of the insurance company on the ground that the "duty to investigate" was not an independent insurance law doctrine but rather an application of estoppel doctrine. The court wrote:

> As a general matter, Maryland law does not impose on insurers a duty to investigate insurance applicants. *See N. Am. Specialty Ins. Co. v. Savage*, 977 F. Supp. 725, 731 (D. Md. 1997) ("Generally, insurers do not have a duty to investigate insurance applicants and are entitled to believe what an applicant claims to be true."). In "extraordinary situations," however, when an insurer is presented with "a considerable amount of suspicious information," it is under a duty to investigate before issuing an insurance policy. *Id.* (quoting *Clemons v. Am. Cas. Co.*, 841 F. Supp. 160, 167 (D. Md. 1993)). The circum-

stances surrounding the life insurance applications in this case certainly provided Transamerica with a basis for being suspicious. In addition to its files on the three earlier policies—indicating that Giesinger, a seventy-two-year-old man, had a slow-growing tumor on his brain, and drank a bottle of wine every day—Transamerica's examining physician, Dr. Parmelee, noticed a fresh, four-to-five-inch surgical scar on Giesinger's abdomen that Giesinger could not explain. We are unable, in view of these facts, to say that such circumstances should not have raised the eyebrows of a prudent insurer.

We need not actually decide, however, in resolving this appeal, whether the pertinent circumstances of this matter constituted an "extraordinary situation" triggering a duty to investigate on the part of Transamerica. In order to claim the benefit of estoppel, a party must demonstrate that it changed its position for the worse in reliance on the other party's representation. *See Allstate Ins. Co. v. Reliance Ins. Co.*, 786 A.2d 27, 32 (Md. Ct. Spec. App. 2001) ("In order for estoppel to apply, one must have been misled and sustained injury."). We have recognized that, where an insured seeks to estop an insurer from rescinding an insurance policy, he is obliged to show that he could have obtained insurance elsewhere, in order to satisfy the essential element of detrimental reliance. *See Souter v. State Mut. Life Assurance Co.*, 273 F.2d 921, 926 (4th Cir. 1960) (applying Maryland law to conclude that insured failed to demonstrate detriment because he could not show that he could have obtained coverage from another insurer). Chawla has offered no proof that any other insurer, properly apprised of Giesinger's true physical condition, would have issued a policy on his life. She has therefore failed to carry her burden of establishing the elements of estoppel.

Id. at 647–648.

7. The practice of conducting an intensive investigation into insurability after a large claim is presented is often referred to, pejoratively, as "post-claim underwriting." *See* Thomas C. Cady & Georgia Lee Gates, *Post Claim Underwriting*, 102 W. Va. L. Rev. 809 (2000) ("This Article confronts the bane of many an insured: post claim underwriting. It is an underwriting abomination. It is an artificial vehicle for contract avoidance. It is quintessentially opportunistic."). From a cost-minimization perspective, there would seem to be benefits to putting off investigations until after large claims are made. That way, the insurance company only spends money on insureds who turn out to be high risk. *See* Omri Ben-Shahar and Kyle D. Logue, *Outsourcing Regulation: How Insurance Reduces Moral Hazard*, 111 Mich. L. Rev. 197, 215 (2012). In a portion of the *Harper* opinion not included in this excerpt, the Court rejected the plaintiff's claim that the insurer was acting in bad faith because it was engaging in "post claim underwriting." What, if anything, is troubling about post-claim underwriting? After all, the only insureds who will lose their benefits will be those who made material misrepresentations.

8. Although courts in many jurisdictions have adopted some version of a duty to investigate (*see, e.g., Stephens v. Guardian Life Ins. Co.*, 742 F.2d 1329 (11th Cir. 1984)), most states have enacted statutes that place an even heavier burden on life and disability insurance companies, requiring that these policies be "incontestable" after the passage of a specified period of time. Both the duty to investigate and incontestability requirements reduce policyholders' incentives to provide accurate information to insurance companies, and may in fact provide an incentive to lie or conceal damaging information. Given the importance of information to the insurance enterprise, there

must be competing values or concerns motivating the rule in *Pum* and the incontestability statutes. What might those be?

9. *Barrera v. State Farm*, 456 P.2d 674 (Cal. 1969), approaches post-claim under-writing in the context of automobile liability insurance. Based on Califor-nia's Financial Responsibility Law, the court concluded that the state man-dates insurance for the protection of accident victims rather than drivers. The court created a duty to investigate in order to protect third parties, but it held that insurers would nevertheless be able to use misrepresentation as a basis for recovering from the policyholder:

> The insurer may still prosecute a cause of action against the insured for dam-ages for wrongful misrepresentation, after satisfying the injured person's claim, or, in an action brought by the insured after he has satisfied a judgment against him by the injured person, defend on the ground of misrepresenta-tions in the application.

Id. at 681. Courts' and legislatures' understanding of who is the beneficiary of li-ability insurance policies—the insured defendant or the person injured by that defendant—informs the resolution of many liability insurance issues, as we will study in detail in Chapters 4 and 5.

VI.   DISPROPORTIONATE FORFEITURE

Disproportionate forfeiture is a potentially wide-ranging contract doctrine that has received relatively little attention among students and practitioners of insur-ance law. *But, see* Bob Works, *Excusing Nonoccurrence of Insurance Policy Conditions in Order to Avoid Disproportionate Forfeiture: Claims-Made Formats as a Test Case,* 5 Conn. Ins. L.J. 505 (1998-1999). Disproportionate forfeiture attempts to put into practice the idea that contracting parties should not use "technicalities" to avoid having to perform their contractual obligations.

Professor Works has argued that disproportionate forfeiture is especially important in insurance law because of the structure of the insurance rela-tionship. In a contract involving simultaneous performance, there is a simple answer to a party who unreasonably refuses to perform his or her part: "Fine, then I won't pay you the money or give you the goods." Moreover, in many other situations involving sequential performance, the "wronged" party can go out in the market and make a contract with someone else, albeit at a higher price. The insurance situation is very different. By the time the policyholder makes a claim, not only has the insurance company already received the benefit of the bargain, but also the policyholder has nowhere else to go.

AETNA CASUALTY & SURETY CO. v. MURPHY

Supreme Court of Connecticut
538 A.2d 219 (1988)

PETERS, Chief Justice. The sole issue in this appeal is whether an insured who belatedly gives notice of an insurable claim can nonetheless recover on the insurance contract by rebutting the presumption that his delay has been prejudicial to the insurance carrier. The plaintiff, Aetna Casualty and Surety Company, brought an action against the defendant, George A. Murphy III, to recover for damage he allegedly caused to a building it had insured. The defendant then filed a third party complaint impleading his comprehensive liability insurer, Federal Insurance Company, Chubb Group of Insurance Companies (hereinafter Chubb), as third party defendant. Chubb successfully moved for summary judgment on the ground that Murphy, the defendant and third party plaintiff, had inexcusably and unreasonably delayed in complying with the notice provisions of the insurance contract. The defendant appeals from this judgment. We find no error.

The underlying facts are undisputed. The defendant, George A. Murphy III, a dentist, terminated a lease with Hopmeadow Professional Center Associates on or about November 30, 1982. The manner in which he had dismantled his office gave rise to a claim for damages to which the plaintiff, Aetna Casualty and Surety Company, became subrogated. Although served with the plaintiff's complaint on November 21, 1983, the defendant gave no notice of the existence of this claim to Chubb until January 10, 1986. The motion to implead Chubb as third party defendant was filed on May 14, 1986, and granted on June 2, 1986.

Chubb moved for summary judgment on its three special defenses, alleging Murphy's noncompliance with the terms of his insurance policy. Its first claim was that it was entitled to judgment because Murphy had ignored two provisions in the Chubb policy imposing notice requirements on its policyholders. The first of these provisions states: "In the event of an occurrence, written notice . . . shall be given by or for the insured to the company . . . as soon as practicable." The other states: "If claim is made or suit is brought against the insured, the insured shall immediately forward to the company every demand, notice, summons, or other process received by him or his representative." In his answer to Chubb's special defenses, Murphy admitted his failure to comply with these provisions. Accordingly, his affidavit opposing summary judgment raised no question of fact but relied on his argument that, as a matter of law, an insurer may not deny coverage because of late notice without a showing, on its part, that it has been prejudiced by its insured's delay.

The trial court granted Chubb's motion for summary judgment on its first special defense. It found that Murphy's two year delay in giving notice to Chubb was inexcusable and unreasonable, and concluded that such a delay "voids coverage and insurer's duties under the contract [of insurance]. . . ."

On appeal, Murphy challenges only the trial court's conclusion of law. Despite his inexcusable and unreasonable delay in giving notice, he maintains that he is entitled to insurance coverage because Chubb has failed to allege or to show prejudice because of his late notice.

As Murphy concedes, the trial court's decision accurately reflects numerous holdings of this court that, absent waiver, an unexcused, unreasonable delay in notification constitutes a failure of condition that entirely discharges an insurance carrier from any further liability on its insurance contract (citations omitted).

In our appraisal of the continued vitality of this line of cases, it is noteworthy that they do not reflect a searching analysis of what role prejudice, or its absence, should play in the enforcement of such standard clauses in insurance policies. That issue was put on the table, but not resolved, by a vigorous dissent in *Plasticrete Corporation v. American Policyholders Ins. Co.*, 439 A.2d 968, 973-974 (Conn. 1981) (Bogdanski, J., dissenting). The time has come for us to address it squarely.

We are confronted, in this case, by a conflict between two competing principles in the law of contracts. On the one hand, the law of contracts supports the principle that contracts should be enforced as written, and that contracting parties are bound by the contractual provisions to which they have given their assent. Among the provisions for which the parties may bargain are clauses that impose conditions upon contractual liability. "If the occurrence of a condition is required by the agreement of the parties, rather than as a matter of law, a rule of strict compliance traditionally applies." E. Farnsworth, Contracts §8:3, p. 544 (1982). On the other hand, the rigor of this traditional principle of strict compliance has increasingly been tempered by the recognition that the occurrence of a condition may, in appropriate circumstances, be excused in order to avoid a "disproportionate forfeiture." *See, e.g.*, 2 Restatement (Second), Contracts §229 (1981).[6]

In numerous cases, this court has held that, especially in the absence of conduct that is "wil[l]ful," a contracting party may, despite his own departure from the specifications of his contract, enforce the obligations of the other party with whom he has dealt in good faith. In construction contracts, a builder's deviation from contract specifications, even if such a departure is conscious and intentional, will not totally defeat the right to recover in an action against the owner on the contract. *Grenier v. Compratt Construction Co.*, 454 A.2d 1289, 1292-93 (Conn. 1983); *Vincenzi v. Cerro*, 442 A.2d 1352, 1353-54 (Conn. 1982). In contracts for the sale of real property, the fact that a contract states a date for performance does not necessarily make time of the essence. *Kakalik v. Bernardo*, 439 A.2d 1016, 1019 (Conn. 1981). A purchaser of real property does not, despite his knowing default, forfeit the right to seek restitution of sums of money earlier paid under the contract of sale, even when such payments are therein characterized as liquidated damages. *Vines v. Orchard Hills, Inc.*, 435 A.2d 1022, 1027 (Conn. 1980). Finally, despite a failure to deliver contract goods, a seller need not pay an amount contractually designated as liquidated damages to a buyer

---

6. The Restatement (Second) of Contracts §229 (1981), entitled *Excuse of a Condition to Avoid Forfeiture*, provides:

> To the extent that the non-occurrence of a condition would cause disproportionate forfeiture, a court may excuse the non-occurrence of that condition unless its occurrence was a material part of the agreed exchange.

The Comment elaborates on the concept of "disproportionate forfeiture" as follows:

> The rule stated in the present Section is, of necessity, a flexible one, and its application is within the sound discretion of the court. Here, as in §227(1), "forfeiture" is used to refer to the denial of compensation that results when the obligee loses his right to the agreed exchange after he has relied substantially, as by preparation or performance on the expectation of that exchange. *See* Comment b to §227. The extent of the forfeiture in any particular case will depend on the extent of that denial of compensation. In determining whether the forfeiture is "disproportionate," a court must weigh the extent of the forfeiture by the obligee against the importance to the obligor of the risk from which he sought to be protected and the degree to which that protection will be lost if the nonoccurrence of the condition is excused to the extent required to prevent forfeiture. The character of the agreement may, as in the case of insurance agreements, affect the rigor with which the requirement is applied.

who has suffered no damages attributable to the seller's breach. *Norwalk Door Closer Co. v. Eagle Lock & Screw Co.*, 220 A.2d 263, 268 (Conn. 1966).

This case law demonstrates that, in appropriate circumstances, a contracting party, despite his own default, may be entitled to relief from the rigorous enforcement of contract provisions that would otherwise amount to a forfeiture. On the question of what circumstances warrant such relief, no better guidelines have ever been proffered than those articulated by Judge Benjamin Cardozo in the celebrated case of *Jacob & Youngs, Inc. v. Kent*, 129 N.E. 889 (N.Y. 1921). Discussing the interpretation of contracts to ascertain how the parties intended to govern their contractual relationship, Cardozo first notes that "[t]here will be no assumption of a [contractual] purpose to visit venial faults with oppressive retribution." *Id.* at 891. The opinion then continues: "Those who think more of symmetry and logic in the development of legal rules than of practical adaptation to the attainment of a just result will be troubled by a classification where the lines of division are so wavering and blurred. Something, doubtless, may be said on the score of consistency and certainty in favor of a stricter standard. The courts have balanced such considerations against those of equity and fairness, and found the latter to be the weightier. . . . Where the line is to be drawn between the important and the trivial cannot be settled by a formula. 'In the nature of the case precise boundaries are impossible' (2 Williston on Contracts §841). The same omission may take on one aspect or another according to its setting. . . . The question is one of degree, to be answered, if there is doubt, by the triers of the facts . . . and, if the inferences are certain, by the judges of the law. . . . We must weigh the purpose to be served, the desire to be gratified, the excuse for deviation from the letter, the cruelty of enforced adherence. Then only can we tell whether literal fulfil[l]ment is to be implied by law as a condition." *Id.* at 891.

In the setting of this case, three considerations are central. First, the contractual provisions presently at issue are contained in an insurance policy that is a "contract of adhesion," the parties to this form contract having had no occasion to bargain about the consequences of delayed notice. Second, enforcement of these notice provisions will operate as a forfeiture because the insured will lose his insurance coverage without regard to his dutiful payment of insurance premiums. Third, the insurer's legitimate purpose of guaranteeing itself a fair opportunity to investigate accidents and claims can be protected without the forfeiture that results from presuming, irrebuttably, that late notice invariably prejudices the insurer.

There can be no question that the insurance policy in this case is a "contract of adhesion." That term was first introduced into American legal vocabulary by Professor Edwin Patterson, who noted that life insurance contracts are contracts of adhesion because "[t]he contract is drawn up by the insurer and the insured, who merely 'adheres' to it, has little choice as to its terms." E. Patterson, *The Delivery of a Life-Insurance Policy*, 33 Harv. L. Rev. 198, 222 (1919). Standardized contracts of insurance continue to be prime examples of contracts of adhesion, whose most salient feature is that they are not subject to the normal bargaining processes of ordinary contracts. The fact that the notice provisions in the Chubb insurance policy were an inconspicuous part of a printed form supports the characterization of these clauses as a "contract of adhesion." Nothing in the record suggests that they were brought to Murphy's attention or that, if they had been, their terms would have been subject to negotiation.

It is equally clear that literal enforcement of the notice provisions in this case will discharge Chubb from any further liability to Murphy with regard to the present claims for insurance coverage. That indeed is the necessary purport of Chubb's special defense and the consequence of the trial court's ruling on its motion for summary judgment. The operative effect of noncompliance with the notice provisions is a forfeiture of the interests of the insured that is, in all likelihood, disproportionate. *Johnson Controls, Inc. v. Bowes*, 409 N.E.2d 185 (Mass. 1980).

In determining whether an insured is entitled to relief from such a disproportionate forfeiture, loss of coverage must be weighed against an insurer's legitimate interest in protection from stale claims. "The purpose of a policy provision requiring the insured to give the company prompt notice of an accident or claim is to give the insurer an opportunity to make a timely and adequate investigation of all the circumstances. . . . And further, if the insurer is thus given the opportunity for a timely investigation, reasonable compromises and settlements may be made, thereby avoiding prolonged and unnecessary litigation." 8 J. Appleman, Insurance Law and Practice §4731, pp. 2-5 (Rev. Ed. 1981). If this legitimate purpose can be protected by something short of automatic enforcement of the notice provisions, then their strict enforcement is unwarranted.

In our judgment, a proper balance between the interests of the insurer and the insured requires a factual inquiry into whether, in the circumstances of a particular case, an insurer has been prejudiced by its insured's delay in giving notice of an event triggering insurance coverage. If it can be shown that the insurer suffered no material prejudice from the delay, the nonoccurrence of the condition of timely notice may be excused because it is not, in Restatement terms, "a material part of the agreed exchange." Literal enforcement of notice provisions when there is no prejudice is no more appropriate than literal enforcement of liquidated damages clauses when there are no damages. *Norwalk Door Closer Co. v. Eagle Lock & Screw Co., supra*, 220 A.2d at 268.

A significant number of cases in other jurisdictions lend support to our conclusion that, absent a showing of material prejudice, an insured's failure to give timely notice does not discharge the insurer's continuing duty to provide insurance coverage. Most of these decisions place the burden of proof on the issue of prejudice on the insurer (citations omitted). In a few jurisdictions, although prejudice from delay is presumed, that presumption is rebuttable if the insured can demonstrate an actual lack of material prejudice (citations omitted). By contrast to these cases which afford some latitude for factual inquiry into prejudice, some jurisdictions continue to enforce delayed notice provisions literally (citations omitted).

In light of existing related precedents in this jurisdiction, although we are persuaded that the existence or nonexistence of prejudice from delayed notice should be determined on a factual basis, the burden of establishing lack of prejudice must be borne by the insured. It is the insured who is seeking to be excused from the consequences of a contract provision with which he has concededly failed to comply. His position is akin to that of the defaulting purchaser of real property in *Vines v. Orchard Hills, Inc., supra*, 435 A.2d at 1027-28, where we held that, "[t]o prove unjust enrichment, in the ordinary case, the purchaser, because he is the party in breach, must prove that the damages suffered by his seller are less than moneys received from the purchaser. . . . It may not be easy for the purchaser to prove the extent of the seller's damages, it may even be strategically advantageous for the seller to come forward with relevant evidence of the losses he has incurred and may expect to incur on account of the buyer's breach. Nonetheless, only if the breaching party satisfies his burden of proof that the innocent party has sustained a net gain may a claim for unjust enrichment be sustained." Principles of unjust enrichment and restitution bear a family resemblance to those involved in considerations of forfeiture. Under both sets of principles, the law has come to permit a complainant to seek a fair allocation of profit and loss despite the complainant's own failure to comply fully with his contract obligations. The determination of what is fair, as a factual matter, must however depend upon a proper showing by the complainant who seeks this extraordinary relief.

Applying these principles to the present case, we conclude that the trial court was correct in granting summary judgment, although not for the reason upon which it relied. Chubb, the third party defendant, was not automatically discharged because of the delay of Murphy, the third party plaintiff, in giving notice of an insured occurrence. Chubb was, however, entitled to summary judgment because Murphy's affidavit opposing summary judgment contained no factual basis for a claim that Chubb had not been materially prejudiced by Murphy's delay.

NOTES AND QUESTIONS

1. What are the purposes of the notice provision? Are there benefits to the bright-line rule that Chief Justice Peters ignores? The New York courts have rejected the notice-prejudice rule. *See Argo Corp. v. Greater N.Y. Mut. Ins. Co.,* 827 N.E.2d 762 (N.Y. 2005) (declining to reconsider the notice-prejudice rule); *Security Mut. Ins. Co. of N.Y. v. Acker-Fitzsimmons Corp,* 293 N.E.2d 76 (N.Y. 1972) (refusing to adopt a notice-prejudice rule, but noting that insured must have a reasonable time in which to make notice). In 2009 the New York legislature adopted the notice prejudice rule by statute. *See* Eric Tausend, *"No-Prejudice" No More: New York and the Death of the No Prejudice Rule,* 61 Hastings L.J. 497 (2009).

2. The Connecticut Supreme Court recently changed its mind about the burden of proof of proving prejudice, adopting the majority rule that requires the insurer to prove prejudice and overruling *Aetna v. Murphy* in that limited respect. *See Arrowood Indem. Co. v. Pendleton,* 304 Conn. 179, 39 A.3d 712 (Conn. 2012).

3. Like incontestability provisions and the duty to investigate reflected in *Cox,* disproportionate forfeiture is one of a number of ways that insurance law discourages opportunistic behavior by insurance companies at the point of claim. Others include the duty of good faith and fair dealing (which we will explore in Section VII of this chapter), the conversion of warranties into representations (discussed in the notes to the misrepresentation statutes), and some (highly fact-dependent) applications of waiver and estoppel. While much work remains to be done, these contract law doctrines can usefully be analyzed through the lens of institutional economics and relational contracting. See the article by Professor Works, cited at the outset of this unit, 5 Conn. Ins. L.J. at 554 (*citing* George M. Cohen, *The Negligence-*

Opportunism Tradeoff in Contract Law, 20 Hofstra L. Rev. 941 (1992)). The underlying insight is that the structure of the insurance relationship creates the incentive and opportunity for insurance companies to delay, deny, or "adjust" claims in a way that devalues the promise that the insurance company made at the point of sale. *Cf.* Tom Baker, *Constructing the Insurance Relationship: Sales Stories, Claims Stories and Insurance Contract Damages,* 72 Tex. L. Rev. 1395 (1994). In the absence of some legal intervention, this incentive and opportunity would create a classic collective action problem (or, in the language of game theory, a prisoners' dilemma) in which the combination of individually rational actions produces a collectively irrational result. Here, the result would be a public that so mistrusts insurance companies that they avoid purchasing insurance whenever possible. These doctrines can be understood as the legal intervention that prevents this collectively irrational result. Despite the fact that insurance companies resist the application of these doctrines in individual cases, the doctrines are in the interests of insurers as a whole, because they help foster the trust upon which nearly the entire edifice of insurance is constructed, or at least so the argument goes.

4.   As Professor Works explains, *C&J Fertilizer* can also be understood as a disproportionate forfeiture case. Can you see how? *Hint:* Think about the "external marks" language in the burglary policy as creating an evidentiary condition. When the failure of the insured to "meet" that condition does not cause the insurance company any harm (because, for example, the situation makes clear that the loss was not an "inside job"—the purpose of the condition), the resulting forfeiture of the promised benefits is disproportionate. Can you understand *Gaunt* as a disproportionate forfeiture case as well? The Iowa approach to materiality and the rule in *Cox v. American Pioneer* might also be understood as embodying the disproportionate forfeiture concept as well. Both *Cox* and the Iowa materiality rule limit the forfeitures from misrepresentations to cases in which the misrepresentation really made a significant difference.

5.   Recall Professor Abraham's observation that reasonable expectations have been more influential as a regulative ideal than as a doctrine of insurance contract interpretation. Might the same be possible with disproportionate forfeiture as well? Just like honoring reasonable expectations, the ideal of avoiding disproportionate forfeitures might in some circumstances create more problems than it avoids. Can you think why? Try to come up with very specific examples. Nevertheless, this ideal is very important because it focuses on structural dynamics at the claims end of the relationship that are every bit as important to understanding the underlying tensions of insurance law as the more familiar and more carefully studied dynamics at the sales end of the relationship.

6.   Comment *c* to §34 of the RLLI states the following regarding disproportionate forfeiture:

> The prejudice requirement for cooperation and notice-of-claim conditions is an application of the more general contract-law principle of disproportionate forfeiture, pursuant to which a nonmaterial breach of a condition by an insured does not excuse the insurer from performance because the harm to

the insurer from the breach is so much less than the value of the coverage to the insured. See Restatement Second, Contracts §228. Under that principle, the failure of the insured to satisfy these conditions relieves the insurer of its obligations under the policy only if the insured's failure caused substantial harm to the insurer. There are both efficiency and fairness considerations for this principle that have special force in the liability insurance context. The principle is efficient in the sense that it applies these insurance-policy terms in a manner that most insureds would be willing to pay for, if they had the information and bargaining power, because the principle protects insureds from the same kinds of risks for which they buy liability insurance: their own negligence. The principle is fair because it is consistent with widely accepted proportionality norms as well as the public policy in favor of compensation of underlying claimants.

7. One of the main problems with disproportionate forfeiture doctrine is deciding the boundaries of its application. Formal distinctions, such as that between "coverage provisions" and "conditions," are unlikely to be helpful because they can be easily manipulated during the insurance contract drafting process. (We will examine in Chapter 4 one example of this in connection with "claims made" liability insurance policies, in which the notice requirement appears in a coverage provision rather than as a loss settlement condition.) What guidance does the Restatement section cited by Chief Justice Peters in *Aetna v. Murphy* provide? Section 229 states:

> To the extent that the non-occurrence of a condition would cause disproportionate forfeiture, a court may excuse the non-occurrence of that condition unless its occurrence was a material part of the agreed exchange.

When is a forfeiture "disproportionate"? What makes the "occurrence" of a condition "a material part of the agreed exchange"? Should the standard form insurance policy be the exclusive source of information regarding the latter question? If so, how long will it take insurance companies to learn to write their policies so that *every* condition is drafted using whatever language courts decide is adequate to convey materiality? How does Justice Peters answer these questions in *Aetna v. Murphy*?

Professor Works argues that only the payment of premiums should be "material" and, therefore, courts should focus exclusively on whether a forfeiture is "disproportionate." 5 Conn. Ins. L.J. at 599-601. He disagrees with Professors Burton and Andersen, who read Section 229 to require courts to evaluate "the importance of the term to the parties at the time the contract was made," which is a potentially much more open-ended approach. *See* Steven J. Burton & Eric G. Andersen, Contractual Good Faith: Formation, Performance, Breach, Enforcement 194-195 (1995). Professor Melvin Eisenberg takes a middle-ground approach that in practice would likely produce the result that Professor Works advocates. *See* Melvin Aron Eisenberg, *The Limits of Cognition and the Limits of Contract*, 47 Stan. L. Rev. 211, 240 (1995) ("Courts should not require perfect fulfillment unless it is established that the parties had a specific and well-thought-through intention that perfect fulfillment be required in a scenario like the one that actually occurred").

Regarding what constitutes a forfeiture, comment b to Section 229 offers the following:

> "Forfeiture" is used to refer to the denial of compensation that results when the obligee loses his right to the agreed exchange after he has relied substantially, as by preparation or performance on the expectation of that exchange. The extent of the forfeiture in any particular case will depend on the extent of the denial of that compensation.

Professor Works argues that, in the insurance context, this means that any time the insurance company refuses to pay a claim, there is a forfeiture. In the insurance context, "the proper question is whether the extent of that forfeiture is disproportionate to the harms to the insurer that could have been avoided by compliance with the condition." *Supra* at 603. Does this help? How would this approach help answer the issue in *Aetna v. Murphy*? How would this approach address the exclusion at issue in *C&J Fertilizer,* the condition in *Gaunt,* or the exclusion at issue in *Economy Fire & Casualty*? What alternative readings of Section 229 can you see? What are the differences among these readings? The following problem may help you work through some of the problems and challenges in applying the doctrine of disproportionate forfeiture.

WECARE'S PROBLEM

Mr. Green had a health insurance policy with WeCare that stated that WeCare would pay costs relating to an admission to and stay in a hospital only if WeCare had "approved and precertified the admission and stay *before* the admission" or if the hospital care related to an "emergency." Mr. Green was admitted to St. Joseph's Hospital on day 1 because of a sinus condition. He asked to be released from the hospital on day 7 so that he could attend to some personal business. He returned to the hospital on day 10 and stayed there for another week. When Mr. Green filed a claim for benefits relating to the hospital care, WeCare denied the claims on the grounds that the admissions were not precertified and that there was no medical emergency. In litigation, WeCare's medical director admitted that the services were medically necessary and that WeCare would have precertified the admission if it had been asked. WeCare argues that it is not obligated to pay for the benefits because the precertification requirement was a material part of the agreed exchange. Precertification requirements are an essential element of WeCare's cost containment efforts, which are necessary to make health insurance affordable. Mr. Green argues that WeCare is trying to get out of its contractual obligations on a "technicality" that produces a disproportionate forfeiture.

How would you analyze this dispute under Section 229 of the Restatement? What kinds of additional information would you want to obtain if you were representing Mr. Green or WeCare? How do you think you would get that information?

Suppose that WeCare later concluded that the first admission to the hospital was a medical emergency? What additional legal arguments are thereby opened up with regard to the second admission?

VII.   DAMAGES

Contract damages traditionally are determined according to the "expectation" measure—that is, the amount of money that would be required to put the plaintiff into the same position that he or she would have been in if the defendant had not breached the contract. Where the promise that is broken is a promise to pay money—as is usually the case in an insurance contract—expectation damages generally mean paying the money that was owed, perhaps plus the interest that has accrued since the time of breach.

In ordinary contract cases, expectation damages never really make the plaintiff whole because contract damages do not usually include the cost of bringing the breach of contract action. Plus, expectation damages are limited by the requirement that the "consequential" losses to the plaintiff—the collateral damage that results from not performing on time—must be foreseeable and by the refusal of courts to compensate parties for even foreseeable aggravation and inconvenience that does not result in a measurable financial loss. This refusal to make the nonbreaching party whole is justified in contract law by the belief that it discourages needless litigation and encourages parties to get on with their lives. A party that can be made whole through litigation might prefer that route when in fact he or she would suffer very little harm if he or she quickly took care of the problem by finding another source for the contracted-for goods in the market.

Damages may be the doctrinal area in which the law treats insurance most differently from other kinds of contracts. The rules of insurance contract interpretation may seem quite different than other kinds of contracts, but that is because first-year law school contracts classes rarely focus on contracts of adhesion. In truth, there is very little to distinguish insurance contracts from other contracts of adhesion, at least for purposes of contract interpretation. *See* Todd Rakoff, *Contracts of Adhesion: An Essay in Reconstruction*, 96 Harv. L. Rev. 1174, 1268 (1983) (discussing the adhesive nature of many contracts, including insurance).

When it comes to damages, however, the law does seem to draw a distinction between insurance and other contracts of adhesion. For example, many states allow courts to award attorneys' fees to policyholders who prevail in an ordinary insurance coverage action. Typically, there is a state statute specifically authorizing this fee shifting, but the courts in other states have adopted this rule through the common law. *See Olympic Steamship Co., Inc. v. Centennial Ins. Co.*, 811 P.2d 673 (Wash. 1991) (ruling that insureds are entitled to attorneys' fees in any successful coverage action). In addition, many states are far more generous in what is regarded as compensable consequential damages for breach of an insurance contract, especially if the breach is in "bad faith." Finally, breach of an insurance contract can, in particularly egregious circumstances, result in an award of punitive damages.

Some courts accomplish this expansion of damages for breach of insurance contracts by creating a new tort of insurance bad faith. But, as we will see, labels like "tort" and "contract" do not help answer the fundamental question: What is it about insurance that might make ordinary contract damages insufficient to encourage companies to keep their promises?

KEWIN v. MASSACHUSETTS MUTUAL LIFE INSURANCE CO.

Supreme Court of Michigan
295 N.W.2d 50 (1980)

KAVANAUGH, J. [*Editor's Note:* This is an appeal of an appellate decision affirming a trial court verdict against a disability insurance company for bad-faith breach of contract. The opinion summarized the facts of the case in a way that did not reveal what might have led the jury to conclude that the insurer had engaged in bad-faith behavior.]

A jury trial was held, and a verdict in favor of the plaintiff was returned. The jury awarded $16,500 in benefits under the disability insurance contract; $798.40 as agreed cash value of the related life insurance policy; $75,000 for mental or emotional distress; and $50,000 for exemplary damages. The defendant's motions for a new trial, remittitur, and judgment notwithstanding the verdict were denied, and a claim of appeal was filed in the Court of Appeals.

On November 21, 1977, the Court of Appeals held that a disability insurance contract is a contract involving matters of mental concern and solicitude and that, upon proper pleading and proof, mental distress damages are recoverable for breach of the contract. The Court also held that the mental distress damages and exemplary damages awarded by the jury in this case were for the same mental anguish, and accordingly reversed the award of $75,000 for mental or emotional distress. Finally, the Court held that the plaintiff's complaint was insufficiently specific to support either a claim in tort for intentional infliction of emotional distress or a claim in contract for mental anguish damages, but that it did support a recovery of exemplary damages.

The parties do not dispute that a cause of action in contract arises upon a bad-faith breach of a disability insurance contract. Their positions differ sharply, however, on the question of whether and under what circumstances mental distress and exemplary damages are recoverable as a consequence of such a breach.

Under the rule of *Hadley v. Baxendale,* 9 Exch. 341; 156 Eng. Rep. 145 (1854), the damages recoverable for breach of contract are those that arise naturally from the breach or those that were in the contemplation of the parties at the time the contract was made. 5 Corbin, Contracts, §1007. Application of this principle in the commercial contract situation generally results in a limitation of damages to the monetary value of the contract had the breaching party fully performed under it. Thus, it is generally held that damages for mental distress cannot be recovered in an action for breach of a contract.

There are exceptions to the general rule limiting the recovery for breach of contract. We are asked to apply an exception recognized in *Stewart v. Rudner,* 84 N.W.2d 816 (Mich. 1957), to this case involving disability insurance. The plaintiff in Stewart brought suit on a breach of contract theory against the defendant doctor. The defendant had promised to deliver plaintiff's child by Caesarean section, but did not do so. It was asserted that as a result of the breach of the agreement, the plaintiff's child was stillborn.

In writing for four members of this Court, Justice Talbot Smith wrote to allow recovery for mental distress:

When we have a contract concerned not with trade and commerce but with life and death, not with profit but with elements of personality, not with pecuniary aggrandizement but with matters of mental concern and solicitude, then a breach of duty with respect to such contracts will inevitably and necessarily result in mental anguish, pain and suffering. In such cases the parties may reasonably be said to have contracted with reference to the payment of damages therefor[e] in event of breach. Far from being outside the contemplation of the parties they are an integral and inseparable part of it.

The nature and object of the agreement justified the treatment accorded it in *Stewart*. A contract to perform a Caesarean section is not a commercial contract in which pecuniary interests are most important. Rather, such a contract involves "rights we cherish, dignities we respect, emotions recognized by all as both sacred and personal." *Stewart* at 823. Where such interests are invaded by breach of a contract meant to secure their protection, mental distress is a particularly likely result. Flowing naturally from the breach, these injuries to the emotions are foreseeable and must be compensated despite the difficulty of monetary estimation.

Insurance contracts for disability income protection do not come within the reach of Stewart. Such contracts are commercial in nature; they are agreements to pay a sum of money upon the occurrence of a specified event. The damage suffered upon the breach of the agreement is capable of adequate compensation by reference to the terms of the contract. We recognize that breach of the insurance contract, as with almost any agreement, results in some annoyance and vexation. But recovery for those consequences is generally not allowed, absent evidence that they were within the contemplation of the parties at the time the contract was made. . . .

Plaintiff implies and *amicus curiae* policyholders argue that he has pleaded and this Court should recognize an independent tort based on bad-faith breach of an insurance contract. . . . *Amicus curiae* policyholders direct our attention to *Gruenberg v. Aetna Insurance Co.*, 510 P.2d 1032 (Cal. 1973), where the California court recognized a cause of action in tort for the insurer's breach of an implied duty of good faith fair dealing and allowed recovery of emotional distress damages. . . .

We decline to follow the California court and to declare the mere bad-faith breach of an insurance indemnity contract an independent and separately actionable tort and to thereby open the door to recovery for mental pain and suffering caused by breach of a commercial contract.

Accordingly we affirm the decision of the Court of Appeals reversing the award for mental or emotional distress; we reverse the decision affirming the award of exemplary damages and set such award aside; and we affirm the decision of the Court of Appeals affirming the awards of $16,500 for breach of the disability insurance contract and $798.40 for breach of the companion life insurance policy.

WILLIAMS, J. (affirming in part and reversing in part).[7] Both as a matter of logic and persuasive case law, we find a disability insurance contract primarily personal rather than commercial in nature. Furthermore, it is common knowledge

---

7. *Editor's note:* This opinion is written as if it were the majority opinion, which it is not. It is interesting to speculate that it might have been the majority opinion at some point in the drafting process.

that disability insurance is obtained to promote peace of mind and avoid the insecurity and anguish of being disabled and without a paycheck to meet the normal demands of life. Consequently, that failure to provide such contracted-for peace of mind promotes emotional distress requires no argument. . . .

This dispute arose from defendant-insurer's failure to pay benefits pursuant to a disability income policy purchased by plaintiff from defendant on September 15, 1972. On December 2, 1972, plaintiff severely injured his right leg in a motorcycle accident. Plaintiff filed a claim for benefits. Defendant paid benefits for the first two months only after requiring that plaintiff provide extensive documentation as well as the filing of a separate claim for each month's benefits. Simultaneously, defendant allegedly conducted overt and covert investigations to determine the validity of plaintiff's claim. The first two months' benefits were not paid until some time after they were due. When the third month's payment was also late, plaintiff contacted defendant. In a May 2, 1973, phone conversation, an agreement was made whereby defendant would immediately pay three months' benefits in return for plaintiff's agreement to waive benefits for a six-month period, i.e., until October 1, 1973.

In November of 1973, plaintiff again requested claim forms for additional benefits, but never submitted a claim. Policy benefits remained unpaid through November of 1974 when plaintiff filed suit in the Genesee Circuit Court requesting the following relief in his complaint:

> Wherefore, this plaintiff claims damages, such as he may be entitled to under the law of this state, for violation of the various rights of the plaintiff by way of breach of contract, express or implied, misrepresentation and deceit, breach of a fiduciary duty, both express in amount as provided for in the policy and punitive in nature and in such amount to be determined by a jury, demand for which is hereby made by the plaintiff, in such amount in excess of ten thousand and no/100 ($10,000.00) dollars as may be assessed.

After the trial court ruled that plaintiff's complaint was sufficient without the necessity of amendment to permit the introduction of testimony regarding plaintiff's emotional distress damages claim, the following testimony was elicited from plaintiff on re-direct examination:

Q: Mr. Kewin, I just have a couple more questions and then I'm through. Can you recall whether there was any one conversation which was particularly distressful?

A: I don't remember the exact date, but there was one particular conversation that lasted 20 or 30 minutes where, at the end of that conversation, after I hung up the phone, I broke down to tears. I actually cried. And I haven't done that since I was a kid. I don't remember the last time I done that.

Q: How did you feel after that conversation? What was the effect of that on your emotional system?

A: Well, I was extremely upset, nervous, I didn't know where to go, what to do. They had all my answers, and I had absolutely nothing. I just—

Q: All right. Now, Mr. Kewin, one final question. In the entire proceeding, from the time you got hurt and filed your first claim after that accident of December 2nd, all the way up through the time they finally terminated you, and through the time you signed that May 2nd agreement, can you tell the jury, in your own words, what effect, if any, did all of this conduct that you claim the defendant engaged in, what effect did that have on you personally, . . . ?

A: I was extremely depressed, nervous, irritable, disillusioned, just—I was just a wreck.

After a lengthy trial, the jury was instructed as follows with respect to plaintiff's emotional distress claim:

> If you do make an award under the policy and if you find the plaintiff did suffer emotional distress as a result of the defendant's knowing, reckless, bad-faith conduct, then you must award a sum adequate to compensate the plaintiff for mental and emotional loss or injury, as you believe he was subjected to the effects caused by the defendant's conduct.

The court also instructed the jury that exemplary damages "are intended only as compensation for the supposed aggravation of an injury to the feelings of another by wanton or reckless acts of a defendant." . . .

Admittedly, disability contracts, much like other insurance contracts, involve a pecuniary element inasmuch as they are agreements to pay a sum of money upon the occurrence of a specified event. It is also true, however, that such contracts have as their central purpose certain highly personal ends, including: the elimination or minimization of financial hardship when a disability occurs, the protection of material security from the harsh consequences of disability, and the provision of emotional security through the insured's anticipation that he or she will be insulated from such financial disaster as well as the peace of mind the policy will provide when paid in the event of disability. Also, as in most insurance situations, it is elemental that an insured is basically contracting for both financial and emotional security in the event of loss. The primacy of emotional security is especially striking in the case of disability insurance contracts since the "very risks insured against presuppose that if and when a claim is made, the insured will be disabled and in strait financial circumstances and, therefore, particularly vulnerable. . . ." *Crisci v. Security Ins. Co.,* 426 P.2d 173 (Cal. 1967). "[Plaintiff] did not seek by the contract involved here to obtain a commercial advantage but to protect herself against the risks of accidental losses, including the mental distress which might follow from the losses. Among the considerations in purchasing liability insurance, as insurers are well aware, is the peace of mind and security it will provide in the event of an accidental loss. . . ." *Fletcher v. Western National Life Ins. Co.,* 89 Cal. Rptr. 78 (Cal. Ct. App. 1970). . . . [A] disability insurance contract is not primarily concerned with trade and commerce but with the peace of mind and security it will provide in the event of disability, not with profit but with the protection of policyholders against strait financial circumstances, not with pecuniary aggrandizement but with exemption from the inconvenience and annoyance of curtailed income.

The allowance of emotional distress damage will work no hardship on the insurer since, by the very nature of the risks insured against, a disability insurer must be presumed to have contemplated that emotional distress would accrue as a consequence of breach. Stated in terms of Hadley's objective standard, at the time of contract formation a hypothetical reasonable person in the position of the defaulting disability insurer, with the insurer's knowledge of the circumstances surrounding the disability insurance transaction, could reasonably have been expected to foresee or should have foreseen the disabled insured's emotional distress necessarily or reasonably resulting from the insurer's breach, had the insurer directed its attention to consideration of the matter. . . .

NOTES AND QUESTIONS

1. What do you think about the claim that emotional distress is not a sufficiently foreseeable consequence of the breach of a personal insurance contract? What are some insurance company advertising slogans and images that you remember? What are they selling? Rigorous adherence to a long, complicated document? Or the promise to "be there" in time of need? For an effort to use insurance company advertising to support the position of the dissent in *Kewin,* see Tom Baker, *Constructing the Insurance Relationship: Sales Stories, Claims Stories and Insurance Contract Damages,* 72 Tex. L. Rev. 1395 (1994). This same article also draws on the "common fund" doctrine to support including attorneys' fees and the costs of "aggravation and inconvenience" in insurance contract damages:

> [Insurance companies] stress that it is in the public interest to incur, and then to spread, the cost of challenging claims. Whether claims are denied because the written policy does not provide for payment, because the insurance company has a responsibility to future claimants, or because the claimants are undeserving, the [companies'] claims stories justify the denial by invoking the vision of the insurance company as guardian of the public trust, preserving the fund for the victims of tomorrow. The slogan "millions for defense, not one penny for tribute" may be honored in the breach, but it expresses a vision of the insurance company that permeates the claims stories.
>
> Yet, as the legal realists have explained, in enforcing the limits of a contract the courts also define those limits. While that lesson hardly seems revolutionary after cases like *Henningsen v. Bloomfield Motors, Inc.* and *C&J Fertilizer v. Allied Mutual Insurance Co.,* it adds an important gloss to the claims stories' vision of insurance as a public trust: The costs of insurance coverage litigation are appropriately borne by the insurance fund, not only because that litigation helps reject improper claims, but also because that litigation defines what is a proper claim.
>
> Courts cannot possibly resolve all disputed insurance claims, but they can, and do, through insurance coverage litigation, set standards for insurance companies' resolution of claims. Thus, the insurance companies' "millions" are not just for defense, they are also for the maintenance of the regulatory structure that makes the insurance enterprise possible. The millions spent by policyholders who prevail in insurance coverage litigation are no less essential to this structure.
>
> Put perhaps more concretely, an insured who prevails in a coverage case increases the value of the insurance company's promise to all its policyholders. Each of these other policyholders faces the risk of later being in the position of the insured in the coverage case. Thanks to the efforts of that insured, that position has become far stronger. The costs of successful insureds are appropriately borne by the premium-paying public because, as the claims stories stress, it is the members of that public who are the beneficiaries of the insurance contract constructed through this effort.

    Id. at 1429. Are you persuaded? Why or why not?

2. One of the few courts to adopt the position of the dissent in *Kewin* and to treat emotional distress as potentially recoverable consequential damages in *any* personal insurance case is the West Virginia Supreme Court. In the case of *Hayseeds, Inc. v. State Farm Fire & Cas.,* 352 S.E.2d 73, 78-79 (W. Va.

1986), the court agreed with the dissent in *Kewin* and made the following additional argument:

> There is no question that insureds do burn their own buildings from time to time and that other types of fraudulent claims are made with some regularity; and we are not unmindful that the dismal economic conditions in West Virginia today make arson an attractive expedient to more and more desperate people. Certainly it is not to the benefit of policyholders as a class for insurance companies to pay fraudulent claims. When an insurance company has reasonable grounds to believe that a claim is fraudulent in whole or in part, it is perfectly appropriate for the company to ask a court to decide the issue of the claim's legitimacy.
>
> Unfortunately, in the business of claims settlement we do not have simply two parties—the company that wishes to pay the lowest legitimate amount of money and the policyholder who wants maximum benefits under the policy. Between these two profit-maximizing, rational players, there is an entire corporate bureaucracy composed of agents, administrators, corporate counsel, and local litigating lawyers. This bureaucracy is neither inherently good nor inherently evil, and it performs a necessary function in the insurance industry. Nonetheless, the claims settlement bureaucracy is subject to the same dynamics as every other bureaucracy known to man: its natural tendency is to maximize upward mobility for middle management members of the bureaucracy and to augment the work that the bureaucracy is responsible for doing. In government, this phenomenon is often referred to as "turf protection." The extent to which pernicious dynamics prevail in any particular company's claims bureaucracy differs from company to company and from office to office within the same company. However, a policyholder who runs into an intransigent or unreasonable claims settlement bureaucracy is destined to be sorely put upon.
>
> Although the disparity of bargaining power between company and policyholder (often exacerbated by the dynamics of the settlement bureaucracy) make insurance contracts substantially different from other commercial contracts, efforts to provide greater balance have been halting at best, and have often depended upon fictions such as lack of "good faith" to circumvent general prohibitions against fee-shifting. . . .
>
> It is now the majority rule in American courts that when an insurer wrongfully withholds or unreasonably delays payment of an insured's claim, the insurer is liable for all foreseeable, consequential damages naturally flowing from the delay. *See* Annot. 47 A.L.R.3d 314 (1973). Unfortunately, awards of consequential damages currently turn on judicial interpretation of such malleable and easily manipulated concepts as "reasonable," "unreasonable," "wrongful," "good faith" and "bad faith." We believe that the interests of both the parties and the judicial system would be better served by the enunciation of a clear, bright line standard governing the availability of consequential damages in property damages insurance cases. Accordingly, we hold today that when a policyholder substantially prevails in a property damage suit against an insurer, the policyholder is entitled to damages for net economic loss caused by the delay in settlement, as well as an award for aggravation and inconvenience. . . .
>
> Our reading of the cases throughout the United States on bad faith settlement leads us to conclude that the result that we have just articulated concerning attorneys' fees and damages for economic loss and inconvenience are what many other courts have been trying to achieve by indirect means. But by achieving these desirable results through the ad hoc manipulation of highly subjective criteria, the rules have become unpredictable and confusing. Vol-

untary settlements (which are in everyone's interest) are best encouraged by the articulation of clear, concise, bright line rules.

3. Many states allow policyholders to recover emotional distress damages under a bad-faith tort claim when an insurer unreasonably refuses to pay a claim. *See, e.g., Goodson v. Am. Standard Ins. Co. of Wisconsin*, 89 P.3d 409, 415-17 (Colo. 2004) ("Non-economic losses recognized under the rubric of compensatory damages include emotional distress; pain and suffering; inconvenience; fear and anxiety; and impairment of the quality of life. . . .); *Ingalls v. Paul Revere Life Ins. Grp.*, 561 N.W.2d 273, 283 (N.D. 1997) ("[A] primary consideration in purchasing insurance is the peace of mind and security it will provide, an insured may recover for any emotional distress resulting from an insurer's bad faith."); *Bibeault v. Hanover Ins. Co.*, 417 A.2d 313, 319 (R.I. 1980) ("The duty of an insurer to deal fairly and in good faith with an insured is implied by law. Since violation of this duty sounds in contract as well as in tort, the insured may obtain consequential damages for economic loss and emotional distress and, when appropriate, punitive damages."); *Gruenberg v. Aetna Ins. Co.*, 510 P.2d 1032, 1035 (Cal. 1973) ("[P]laintiff has stated facts sufficient for the recovery of damages for mental distress whether or not these facts constitute 'extreme' or 'outrageous' conduct."); *Aetna Life Ins. Co. v. Lavoie*, 470 So. 2d 1060, 1073-74 (Ala. 1984) ("The tort of bad faith had as its genesis the very idea of providing a plaintiff who had been victimized by the intentional, wrongful handling of a claim by the insurer, the right to recover not only contract damages but for the loss occasioned by emotional suffering, humiliation, and embarrassment in addition to punitive damages."); *Nassen v. National States Ins. Co.*, 494 N.W.2d 231 (Iowa 1993) ("[T]he trauma visited upon elderly persons by having their worldly possessions dissipated by extended care costs that they believe should be covered by insurance . . . is a situation capable of producing severe mental suffering."); *Jacobsen v. Allstate Ins. Co.*, 215 P.3d 649, 664 (Mont. 2009).

Courts in other states have created heightened standards for recovery of emotional distress damages. *See, e.g., Universe Life Ins. Co. v. Giles*, 950 S.W.2d 48, 54 (Tex. 1997) ("In the context of bad faith actions, mental anguish damages will be limited to those cases in which the denial or delay in payment of a claim has seriously disrupted the insured's life."); *Pickett v. Lloyd's*, 621 A.2d 445, 455 (N.J. 1993) ("We agree with those courts that have held that absent egregious circumstances, no right to recover for emotional distress or punitive damages exists for an insurer's allegedly wrongful refusal to pay a first-party claim."); *Haagenson v. National Farmers Union Prop. & Cas. Co.*, 277 N.W.2d 648, 652 (Minn. 1979) (requiring egregious misconduct).

Still other jurisdictions require insureds to bring a separate cause of action for intentional infliction of emotional distress, an even higher standard. *See, e.g., Roper v. State Farm Mut. Auto. Ins. Co.*, 958 P.2d 1145, 1149 (Idaho 1998) ("Even though our opinion affirms the district court's dismissal of Roper's bad faith claims, nevertheless a separate cause of action for the tort of intentional infliction of emotional distress can be maintained, if all of the elements of the tort are proven. Although possibly supported by the same facts as the bad faith claims, the intentional infliction of emotional distress claim is a separate cause of action. . . ."); *Clark-Peterson Co. v. Indep. Ins. Associates*,

Ltd., 514 N.W.2d 912, 916 (Iowa 1994) ("Plaintiffs also claim severe emotional distress arose from defendants' various alleged breaches. To recover under such a theory, plaintiffs must show outrageous conduct that was 'so extreme in degree, as to go beyond all possible bounds of decency, and to be regarded as atrocious, and utterly intolerable in a civilized community.' . . . Plaintiffs also seek to recover for ordinary emotional distress, damages that are ordinarily unavailable in a breach-of-contract suit."); *Colford v. Chubb Life Ins. Co. of Am.*, 687 A.2d 609, 616 (Me. 1996). In other jurisdictions, an insured's right to recover damages for emotional distress is prescribed by statute. *See, e.g.*, Fla. Stat. Ann. §624.155 (permitting insured's to recover emotional distress damages in first-party bad-faith claims against health insurers; prior to the statute's enactment, recoverable damages were limited to breach of contract damages and attorneys' fees); *Time Ins. Co. v. Burger*, 712 So. 2d 389, 392 (Fla. 1998). The next section addresses bad-faith causes of action in greater detail.

4. You may remember from your contracts course the "American Rule," which says that, absent a statutory directive, the prevailing party in litigation is *not* entitled to recover attorneys' fees from the losing party. *Alyeska Pipeline Serv. Co. v. Wilderness Soc'y*, 421 U.S. 240, 247 (1975) ("In the United States, the prevailing litigant is ordinarily not entitled to collect a reasonable attorneys' fee from the loser."); *see also Hayseeds*, 352 S.E.2d at 78 ("In keeping with the American rule, it is generally held that, in the absence of a statutory or contractual provision providing for such recovery, attorneys' fees may not be recovered in an action on an insurance policy."). Most states, however, have created an exception by statute or judicial rule to the general American Rule and allow insureds to recover attorneys' fees for the action to enforce the insurance contract. Preliminary Draft Number 3 (PD3) of the RLLI describes the case law as follows:

> All but a very few jurisdictions allow courts to award attorneys' fees to a prevailing insured in designated circumstances. A substantial minority of states always award attorneys' fees to an insured who prevails in a liability insurance coverage action, whether or not the insurer breached the duty to defend. A somewhat larger plurality of states award attorneys' fees to a prevailing insured only if the insured proves that there was more than a simple breach, with most of those states requiring that the breach be in bad faith. A smaller number of states grant the court discretion to award fees to a prevailing insured, and it appears that courts in about half of those states routinely award attorneys' fees to insureds, while courts in the other half award attorneys' fees in more limited circumstances. . . .

PD3, Restatement of the Law of Liability Insurance §49, Comment C (September 2016).
   See, e.g., Del. Code Ann. tit. 18, §4102 ("The court . . . shall allow the plaintiff a reasonable sum as attorney's fees to be taxed as part of the costs."); Fla. Stat. Ann. §627.428 (awarding attorneys' fees when judgment is entered against an insurer); *Preferred Mut. Ins. Co. v. Gamache*, 686 N.E.2d 989, 993 (Mass. 1997) ("We hold, as an exception to our traditional rule disallowing attorney's fees and expenses, that an insured under a homeowner's policy, like Gamache, is entitled to the reasonable attorney's fees and expenses

incurred in successfully establishing the insurer's duty to defend under the policy"); *Hegler v. Gulf Ins. Co.*, 243 S.E.2d 443, 444 (S.C. 1978) ("[T]he legal fees incurred by appellant, in successfully asserting his rights against respondent's attempt in the declaratory judgment action to avoid its obligation to defend, were damages arising directly as a result of the breach of the contract."); *Blount v. Kennard,* 612 N.E.2d 1268, 1271 (Oh. Ct. App. 1992) ("When an insurer refuses to defend its insured as required by the policy, the insured may recover from the insurer attorney fees which the insured incurs in the action brought to enforce the duty to defend and in the defense of the claims for which the duty to defend exists."). But, *see Alliance Ins. Co. v. Reynolds*, 504 So. 2d 1215, 1216 (Ala. Civ. App. 1987) ("Alabama has long recognized that, absent a pertinent statute or contractual provision, an insured may not recover from his insurer attorney fees incurred in a declaratory judgement action to determine the existence of coverage under a liability policy."); *Aetna Cas. & Sur. Co. v. Com.*, 179 S.W.3d 830, 842 (Ky. 2005); *Shepard Marine Const. Co. v. Maryland Cas. Co.*, 250 N.W.2d 541, 543 (Mich. 1976).

5. Preliminary Draft 3 of the RLLI proposes a rule that provides insureds with "an award of a sum of money . . . for attorneys' fees and other costs incurred in a declaratory judgment action establishing the insured's rights under the policy." PD3, RLLI, §49. The RLLI offers the following rationale for this rule:

> The insured's right to attorneys' fees incurred in a declaratory judgment proceeding is most widely recognized in cases in which an insurer provides a defense under a reservation of rights and then files a declaratory judgment action seeking to terminate its defense duties. When the insured prevails in that declaratory judgment proceeding, courts require the insurer to pay the insured's attorneys' fees because policyholders purchase a liability insurance policy that includes the duty to defend or pay defense costs in order to receive a timely and effective legal defense, paid for by the insurer, so that the insured does not have to bear that burden alone. When an insurer brings a declaratory judgment action seeking to terminate its defense of a liability action, the insured is forced to hire a lawyer in order to preserve that defense, significantly frustrating that purpose. In that context, the insured's attorneys' fees can be understood to be part of the costs of the insured's defense. Once the insurer filed the action the insured could not as a practical matter continue to receive that defense unless it hired a lawyer and then prevailed in the declaratory judgment proceeding. Many courts also award attorneys' to an insured that initiates a declaratory judgment action as an application of a general rule awarding attorneys' fees to an insured who prevails in a liability insurance action.

PD3, RLLI, §49, Comment c.

A.   The Tort of Insurance Bad Faith

The following case is representative of those that reject the recovery of emotional distress and attorneys' fees as an element of contract damages but permit the recovery of those damages *in tort* if the policyholder proves that the insurance company breached the contract in bad faith.

ANDERSON v. CONTINENTAL INSURANCE CO.

Supreme Court of Wisconsin
271 N.W.2d 368 (1978)

HEFFERNAN, J. . . . The plaintiffs are Jacob R. Anderson and his wife, owners of a home in the City of Milwaukee. Effective October 1, 1973, they obtained a home-owner's insurance policy from the Continental Insurance Company, which, among other things, provided coverage for loss occasioned by fire, lightning, explosion, or smoke. While the policy was in effect, the plaintiffs, Anderson and wife, returned to their home on November 30, 1975, to discover that the walls, carpeting, furniture, draperies, and clothing in the house were covered with an oil and smoke residue, which allegedly was the result of a fire or an explosion in the furnace. On the following day, Continental Insurance Company was given notice of the damage.

It is alleged by the plaintiffs that the Underwriters Adjusting Company was delegated by Continental Insurance Company to handle the claim on behalf of Continental. Underwriters called in cleaners, who attempted to renovate and clean the premises and its contents. It nevertheless was necessary, according to the complaint, for the plaintiffs to repaint, clean, and restore the premises, and to replace carpets which shrank due to excessive cleaning ordered by Underwriters Adjusting Company. A pecuniary loss of $4,611.77 was alleged by the plaintiffs.

The Andersons attempted to negotiate with Underwriters as the agent for Continental Insurance Company, but all said negotiations were "to no avail."

It is alleged that Continental Insurance Company, Underwriters Adjusting Company, and Underwriters' manager in the area, Bernard A. Anderson, refused to negotiate in good faith concerning the amount of payment, and that each of them has submitted offers in settlement which were completely unrealistic and which had no relation to the damage incurred by the plaintiffs.

The plaintiff homeowners further recite that, when it became apparent that negotiations were not forthcoming or were to no avail, they retained an attorney to represent them in their claim against the insurance company. The complaint recites that counsel immediately filed a sworn proof of loss, which set forth in detail the inventory, the cost and the value, and the amount claimed in respect to the damages sustained. The proof of loss was filed within the time limit prescribed by the policy. On January 16, 1976, the proof of loss was transmitted to Underwriters Adjusting Company at Wauwatosa to the attention of B. A. Anderson. On January 23, 1976, the proof of loss was returned to plaintiffs' counsel by Underwriters' agent, B. A. Anderson, on behalf of Continental and Underwriters Adjusting Company. On January 28, 1976, the proof of loss was sent to Continental's home office in New York City. On February 3, 1976, plaintiffs' counsel was informed by Continental that the proof of loss had been referred to a Continental Vice President in charge of the Western Department of Continental. On February 19, 1976, plaintiffs' counsel made inquiry in respect to the disposition of the proof of loss; and on March 3, 1976, Roger S. Olson, Senior Vice President of Continental, informed plaintiffs' counsel that the matter had been turned over to Underwriters Adjusting Company and that B. A. Anderson, to whom counsel had sent the proof of loss on January 16, was authorized to handle any claims under the policy. After these peregrinations of the document, Continental again returned the proof of loss to plaintiffs' counsel.

The plaintiffs have alleged that the consistent refusal of Continental Insurance Company, Underwriters Adjusting Company, and B. A. Anderson to accept the sworn proof of loss and the refusal to negotiate in good faith were done with the knowledge and design of avoiding the obligations under the insurance contract. It is alleged that the conduct of each of the defendants was wi[l]lful, fraudulent, intentional, and in bad faith and for the purpose of discouraging, avoiding, or reducing the payment due under the terms of the policy. It is further alleged that each of the defendants acted maliciously and oppressively, with the design and intent to harass the plaintiffs maliciously and in an outrageous manner. Compensatory damages in the sum of $15,000 and punitive damages in the sum of $100,000 are demanded. . . .

By virtue of the relationship between the parties created by the contract, a special duty arises, the breach of which duty is a tort and is unrelated to contract damages. This tort of bad faith or malicious and intentional harassment by one party to a contract directed toward the other party, who seeks to assert his contract claim, has been referred to as a "tortious breach of contract." While that term may be a convenient shorthand method of denominating the intentional conduct of a contracting party when it acts in bad faith to avoid its contract obligations, it is confusing and inappropriate, because it could lead one to believe that the wrong done is the breach of the contract. It obscures the fact that bad faith conduct by one party to a contract toward another is a tort separate and apart from a breach of contract per se and it fails to emphasize the fact that separate damages may be recovered for the tort and for the contract breach.

When it is recognized that recovery is sought for the tort and not for the breach of contract, the clichés which are relied upon by the defendants—e.g., "Punitive damages are not allowed for a mere breach of contract" become irrelevant. The question whether punitive damages are permissible thus is not to be disposed of on grounds that what the plaintiffs assert is a breach-of-contract action, but rather must be considered under a discussion of whether the facts surrounding the tort of bad faith evidence such conduct that punitive or exemplary damages are permissible. This question will be discussed later in the opinion.

We emphasize at this juncture only that the tort of bad faith is not a tortious breach of contract. It is a separate intentional wrong, which results from a breach of duty imposed as a consequence of the relationship established by contract. This rationale had its origin in an opinion of this court. *Hilker v. Western Automobile Ins. Co.*, 235 N.W. 413 (Wis. 1931). In *Hilker,* the plaintiff asserted that the insurance company's bad faith conduct in failing to make an adequate investigation of an automobile accident, its failure to settle a case within the policy limits, and its indifference in respect to the insured's interests resulted in a judgment against the plaintiff in excess of his policy coverage. In a separate action brought against the insurer, Hilker sought recoupment of the overage [that] he was required to pay because of the defendant insurance company's conduct. The court acknowledged that the right asserted by Hilker against his insurance company could not be predicated upon any express provision of the contract. . . .

The rationale which recognizes an ancillary duty on an insurance company to exercise good faith in the settlement of third-party claims is equally applicable and of equal importance when the insured seeks payment of legitimate damages from his own insurance company. That such a duty arises out of the relationship between the contracting parties themselves cannot be doubted. As black letter law, Restatement, Law of Contracts 2d, sec. 231 (Tentative Drafts Nos. 1-7, Rev. and Edited, 1973), provides: "Every contract imposes upon each party a duty of good faith and fair dealing in its performance and its enforcement." . . .

Accepting as we do that an insured may state a claim for the tort of bad faith against its own insurer, the question remains: What elements or facts must be stated to assert a bad faith claim and did the Andersons allege such facts in their complaint. . . .

To show a claim for bad faith, a plaintiff must show the absence of a reasonable basis for denying benefits of the policy and the defendant's knowledge or reckless disregard of the lack of a reasonable basis for denying the claim. It is apparent, then, that the tort of bad faith is an intentional one. "Bad faith" by definition cannot be unintentional. "Bad faith" is defined as "Deceit; duplicity; insincerity." American Heritage Dictionary of the English Language 471 (1969). The same dictionary defines "deceit" as a "[stratagem]; trick; wile" (*id.* p. 342), and duplicity as "Deliberate deceptiveness in behavior or speech" (*id.* p. 405).

Hilker, supra, 235 N.W. 431, emphasizes that bad faith is the absence of honest, intelligent action or consideration based upon a knowledge of the facts and circumstances upon which a decision in respect to liability is predicated. While *Hilker* emphasizes the duty of ordinary care and reasonable diligence on the part of an insurer in handling claims, it is apparent from Hilker that the knowing failure to exercise an honest and informed judgment constitutes the tort of bad faith.

The tort of bad faith can be alleged only if the facts pleaded would, on the basis of an objective standard, show the absence of a reasonable basis for denying the claim, *i.e.,* would a reasonable insurer under the circumstances have denied or delayed payment of the claim under the facts and circumstances. *See, Hilker, supra,* and *Alt v. American Family Mut. Ins. Co.,* 237 N.W.2d 706 (Wis. 1976).

It is appropriate, in applying the test, to determine whether a claim was properly investigated and whether the results of the investigation were subjected to a reasonable evaluation and review. In the instant case, insofar as the complaint alleges, the insurer and the other defendants refused even to consider the nature and extent of the plaintiffs' damages, and specifically rejected and spurned the opportunity to evaluate and consider the submitted proof of loss. The pleading of the plaintiffs was sufficient in this respect. . . .

We are satisfied that the application of the test formulated above, which recognizes the intentional nature of the tort of bad faith and puts the test upon an objective basis, will minimize the fears expressed by the defendant insurance company that to permit claims for bad faith will result in extortionate lawsuits. Such result cannot follow when an insurance company in the exercise of ordinary care makes an investigation of the facts and law and concludes on a reasonable basis that the claim is at least debatable. . . .

It is apparent, however, that another aspect of the *in terrorem* nature of an action for bad faith arises because it is an intentional tort. Intentional torts may in some circumstances result in not only compensatory damages, but also punitive damages and damages for emotional injury.

In respect to a claim for emotional distress, we note that the plaintiffs herein alleged that each of the defendants acted "so as to maliciously and intentionally depress, distress and harass plaintiffs." Because the focus of all parties on this appeal was upon the question of the availability of the tort of bad faith, we do not determine whether damages for mental or emotional distress are allowable under the pleadings of this particular lawsuit. Some generalities in respect to damages for mental distress, we believe, are however appropriate. . . .

We conclude, however, . . . that in no circumstances may a plaintiff recover for emotional distress, even when there are other accompanying damages, unless the emotional distress is severe. A recovery for emotional distress caused by an insurer's bad faith refusal to pay an insured's claim should be allowed only when the distress is severe and substantial other damage is suffered apart from the loss of the contract benefits and the emotional distress. . . .

We do not conclude, however, that the proof of a bad faith cause of action necessarily makes punitive damages appropriate. Punitive damages are awarded to punish a wrongdoer and to serve as a deterrent. *Mid-Continent Refrigerator Co. v. Straka,* 178 N.W.2d 28, 32 (Wis. 1970). We pointed out in *Mid-Continent* that punitive damages are to be awarded "only where the wrong was inflicted 'under circumstances of aggravation, insult or cruelty, with vindictiveness or malice.' " *Mid-Continent Refrigerator Co.,* 178 N.W.2d at 32. We also stated therein that there is a distinction between the intent or malice necessary to maintain an action for intentional tort (such as bad faith) and the intent which must be shown to recover punitive damages. For punitive damages to be awarded in addition to compensatory damages for the tort, there must be a showing of an evil intent deserving of punishment or of something in the nature of special ill-will or wanton disregard of duty or gross or outrageous conduct. In the specific context of the intentional tort of bad faith, exemplary damages are not necessarily appropriate although the plaintiff be entitled to compensatory damages. For punitive damages to be awarded a defendant must not only intentionally have breached his duty of good faith, but in addition must have been guilty of oppression, fraud, or malice in the special sense defined by *Mid-Continent v. Straka. See also Silberg v. California Life Ins. Co. supra,* 521 P.2d 1103 (Cal. 1974). . . .

Order reversed and case remanded for trial.

NOTES AND QUESTIONS

1. What comes from creating a tort for the bad-faith breach of an insurance contract? What does using tort law accomplish that using contract law could not?

2. One difference between the tort and contract approaches is the usual standard of care. In a contract action, we typically do not ask why the defendant breached. Absent an act of God or some other truly extraordinary circumstance, *see, e.g., International Minerals & Chem. Corp. v. Llano, Inc.,* 770 F.2d 879 (10th Cir. 1985), *cert. denied,* 475 U.S. 1015 (1986) (releasing buyer from a requirements contract when it shut down a plant in response to new environmental regulations), the only question is "Did the defendant fulfill his or her promise?" If not, the plaintiff is entitled to expectation damages. When one person makes a legally binding promise to do something, he or she assumes the risk that future events will prevent him or her from keeping that promise—whether he or she is blameworthy or not. In contrast, such strict liability is rarely the relevant standard in tort law. Instead, tort law ordi-

narily starts with the premise that people are responsible for what happens to them, unless someone else negligently caused the harm. Nevertheless, there is no conceptual reason why contract law could not establish a quasi-negligence standard for what constitutes a bad faith breach of contract, as indeed the New Jersey Supreme Court did in *Pickett v. Lloyd's*, 621 A.2d 445 (N.J. 1993).

3. Look back at the brief excerpt from the *Hayseeds* opinion in the note following the *Kewin* case. The *Hayseeds* court claimed that tort standards cause more harm than they are worth, for two reasons. First, tort standards promote needless bickering over why the insurance company breached. Second, they lead too easily to punitive damages. What might the *Anderson* court respond? Is a tort of bad faith better than the ordinary contract approach of *Kewin*? Why or why not? Of course, as demonstrated by the New Jersey Supreme Court's decision to adopt the "tort" standard for the "contract" bad-faith action, it is not the label "tort" or "contract" that makes a difference, but rather the standard of care. *Hayseeds* prefers strict liability, whereas *Anderson* and *Pickett* prefer negligence (or, depending on your reading, perhaps negligence plus).

4. *Beck v. Farmers Insurance Exchange*, 701 P.2d 795 (Utah 1985), focused on the difference between bad faith in the first- and third-party insurance contexts. Third-party insurance (liability insurance) generally covers the cost of defending the policyholder, as well as any liability that he or she might have as a result of an accident. The Utah court concluded that tort was the appropriate doctrinal framework for third-party bad faith because the insurer and the policyholder are supposed to be on the same side (against the third-party claimant) and the insurer is, for that reason, a fiduciary. We will study this in the context of the "duty to settle" in Chapter 5. The Utah court did not want to extend the *tort* of bad faith to first-party insurance claims because it viewed that insurance relationship as inherently more adversarial. The Utah court reasoned that first-party insurance obliges an insurer to pay claims submitted by the insured in accordance with the contract; it does not create a fiduciary relationship of trust and reliance. Even though the *Beck* court wanted to limit bad-faith suits against first-party insurers to the contractual sphere, the court recognized that the insured may well suffer damages above and beyond the policy limits:

> An insured frequently faces catastrophic consequences if funds are not available within a reasonable period of time to cover an insured loss; damages for losses well in excess of the policy limits . . . may therefore be foreseeable and provable.

Id. at 802.

This could include bankruptcy or the peace of mind that the court recognized as part of the insurance agreement. Accordingly, the court reasoned that a jury could find that the insurer breached its duty of good faith by failing to adequately investigate and that the insured could potentially recover not only damages due to the breach itself but also those reasonably foreseeable at the time the contract was entered into. *Id.* at 802-803. Damages could therefore take into account the mental anguish suffered due to the rejection of the insured's claim. *Id.* at 801-802.

5. *Statutory bad faith.* The National Association of Insurance Commissioners adopted a Model Act relating to Unfair Methods of Competition and Unfair and Deceptive Practices in the Business of Insurance (1972) that has been adopted in many states. *See* William M. Shernoff et al., Insurance Bad Faith Litigation §6.03[2] (1984). The Act defines 14 acts that "if committed flagrantly and in conscious disregard of this Act" or "committed with such frequency to indicate a general business practice" constitute unfair settlement practices. *Id.* at §3. One of the enumerated acts is "[n]ot attempting in good faith to effectuate prompt, fair and equitable settlement of claims in which liability has become reasonably clear." Some states allow a private cause of action for violations of this act. *See, e.g.,* Fla. Stat. Ann. §624.155 (West 2005). Most states do not. *See, e.g., Rocanova v. Equitable Life Assurance Soc'y of the U.S.,* 634 N.E.2d 940 (N.Y. 1994). The state statutes that expressly permit a private cause of action typically do not require the policyholder or beneficiary to prove the "general business practice" required by the Model Act. *See, e.g., Terletsky v. Prudential Prop. & Cas. Ins. Co.,* 649 A.2d 680, 688-689 (Pa. Super. Ct. 1994) (stating that the standard of bad faith conduct under 42 Pa. Cons. Stat. Ann. §8371 (West 2007) is met by proof that the insurer "did not have a reasonable basis for denying benefits under the policy and knew or recklessly disregarded its lack of reasonable basis in denying the claim"). Courts in other states have held that the insurance statute establishes a standard of what constitutes an unfair or a deceptive trade practice, which is actionable through private cause of action in the state's general unfair and deceptive trade practice statute. *See, e.g. Mead v. Burns,* 509 A.2d 11 (Conn. 1986) (holding that the Connecticut Unfair Trade Practices Act permits a private cause of action to enforce violations of the Connecticut Unfair Insurance Practices Act). Statutory damages are typically less open-ended than those permitted under the bad faith tort. *See, e.g.,* Ga. Code Ann. §33-4-6 (West 2001) (providing for damages "in addition to the loss, not more than 50 percent of the liability of the insurer for the loss, or $5,000, whichever is greater, and all reasonable attorney's fees"); Mass. Gen. Laws ch. 93A, §9(3A) (2004) (providing that "damages may include double or treble damages, attorneys' fees and costs as herein provided"); *Whitney v. Continental Ins. Co.,* 595 F. Supp. 939 (D. Mass. 1984) (applying Mass. Gen. Laws ch. 93A, §9); *Van Dyke v. St. Paul Marine & Fire Ins. Co.,* 448 N.E.2d 357 (Mass. 1983) (noting that previously only a policyholder could assert a claim under Mass. Gen. Laws ch. 93A, §9; however, the legislature amended statute so it applies to "any person." Therefore, the statute applies to both first- and third-party claims or to any person who can demonstrate that he or she was adversely affected by a company's behavior).

6. Empirical research shows that the bad-faith cause of action does make a difference to insurance companies. *See* Mark J. Browne, Ellen S. Pryor & Bob Puelz, *The Effect of Bad-Faith Laws on First-Party Insurance Claims Decisions,* 33 J. Legal Stud. 355 (2004), which tested whether the existence of a bad-faith cause of action in a jurisdiction affected the amounts that insurance companies paid for uninsured and underinsured motorists insurance, using a database of 1992 claims that had been developed by the Insurance Research Council. This kind of insurance replaces (or supplements) the liability insurance of an uninsured (or underinsured) driver who is at fault in an auto accident. Controlling for a variety of claim and state-specific variables, the

authors compared the amounts paid in jurisdictions that recognized a tort cause of action (e.g., Wisconsin) with the amounts paid in jurisdictions that did not (e.g., Utah) or that capped the damages in first-party bad faith (e.g., Georgia). They found that the amounts paid for economic damages were 13.7 percent higher in the tort bad-faith states and that the amounts paid for noneconomic damages were 5.6 percent higher in the bad-faith states. *Id.* at 385, Table 7.

7. Deciding that "bad faith" is necessary for emotional distress damages (or, as in California or New York, for attorneys' fees) tells us only that something more than an "ordinary" breach of contract is required. Professor Roger Henderson concludes that most jurisdictions require the insured to show that the insurer's decision was at least reckless. *See* Roger C. Henderson, *The Tort of Bad Faith in First Party Insurance Transactions: Refining the Standard of Culpability and Reformulating the Remedies by Statute*, 26 U. Mich. J.L. Reform 1, §IV.D (1992). What else is required in Wisconsin after *Anderson?*

8. The recent Preliminary Draft of the RLLI articulates the standard for bad faith as follows: "An insurer is subject to liability for insurance bad faith when it fails to perform its duties under a liability insurance policy without a reasonable basis for its conduct and with knowledge or in reckless disregard of its obligation to perform." PD3, RLLI, §51. The rationale provided for this rule, which is consistent with the majority of jurisdictions, is as follows:

> Although jurisdictions differ widely in the verbal formulations used to describe the legal standard for insurance bad faith, the majority rule followed in this Section requires both an objective and a subjective element. This Section follows that approach, rather than the purely objective approach, because other liability insurance law rules provide sufficient incentive for insurers to make reasonable decisions. Thus, the stigma associated with a finding of liability insurance bad faith is appropriately limited to cases in which the insurer's culpability extends beyond negligence.
>
> The objective element is most commonly stated as the lack of a "reasonable" or a "fairly debatable" basis for the failure to perform. What these and other similar expressions of the objective element have in common is that the insurer must have a sufficient basis for any refusal to perform. An insurer has a sufficient basis if it takes a legal position that a reasonable insurer would take, or acts in a manner that a reasonable insurer would act in the circumstances. See also §19, Comment g. Because a reasonable insurer is knowledgeable about and follows liability insurance law, a coverage position that has no basis in the law of the jurisdiction—a determination that can be made by the court as a matter of law—would not be fairly debatable.
>
> The subjective element is most commonly stated as "with knowledge or in reckless disregard of" the obligation to perform. This means that the insurer failed to perform (a) when it knew was obligated to perform or (b) without regard to whether it had a reasonable basis for not performing, whether because of lack of investigation of the relevant facts, a failure to conduct the necessary state-specific legal research to evaluate the coverage position, or some other circumstance that placed the insurer on notice that it had not done what it needed to do in order to evaluate whether it had a reasonable basis for its position.

PD3, RLLI, §51, Comment b.

As you will see in chapters 3 and 4, the doctrine of insurance bad faith plays a somewhat different role in first-party insurance than it does in third-party or liability insurance. As will become clear, in the context of liability insurance, specialized rules regarding insurers' duties to provide a defense and to make reasonable settlement decisions have narrowed the scope of the general bad-faith remedy.

9. Professor Alan Sykes, who is critical of the bad-faith tort, maintains that *Anderson* sets out a negligence standard. Alan O. Sykes, *"Bad Faith" Breach of Contract by First-Party Insurers*, 25 J. Legal Stud. 405, 412-415 (1996). One reason why Sykes is critical of the bad-faith cause of action is his belief that insurers lack motivation to deny valid claims. Sykes argues that the time value of money does not motivate insurers to deny claims because (1) prejudgment interest is routinely awarded in breach of contract cases, (2) insureds will routinely challenge wrongful denials of coverage, and (3) a reputation for denying valid claims will lead to a loss of business. Think about these arguments as you read the next case.

B.   Punitive Damages

HANGARTER v. PROVIDENT LIFE & ACCIDENT INSURANCE CO.

United States Court of Appeals, Ninth Circuit
373 F.3d 998 (2004)

CLIFTON, Circuit Judge:

Joan Hangarter, a chiropractor who operated her own business, obtained an "own occupation" disability insurance policy in 1989 from Paul Revere Life Insurance Company. She filed a claim for total disability in July 1997 based on shoulder, elbow, and wrist pain. Paul Revere paid Hangarter benefits for an eleven-month period and then terminated her benefits based upon the opinion of its medical examiners and claim investigators that Hangarter was not "totally disabled" and continued to work and earn income, making her ineligible for benefits under the policy. Hangarter brought a diversity action alleging violation of Cal. Bus. & Prof. Code §17200 (the Unfair Competition Act, or UCA), breach of contract, breach of the covenant of good faith and fair dealing, and intentional misrepresentation against Paul Revere and its parent company, UnumProvident Corp. The jury returned a $7,670,849 verdict in Hangarter's favor, $5 million of which was for punitive damages. Raising a multitude of issues, Defendants appeal the district court's post-verdict denial of judgment as a matter of law (JMOL), the jury's award of damages, and a permanent injunction issued by the district court under the UCA.

We affirm the district court's denial of a JMOL and the jury's award of damages. We reverse the district court's permanent injunction under the UCA.

I.   BACKGROUND

Joan Hangarter owned her own chiropractic practice in Berkeley, California. On a typical day, she would treat between 30 and 50 patients. In 1989, Hangarter purchased an individual "own occupation" disability insurance policy from

Paul Revere. In 1993, Hangarter began to experience severe recurrent shoulder pain. She sought treatment from a chiropractor in her office, Dr. England, who adjusted her daily. In 1995 and 1996, Hangarter also saw an orthopedist, Dr. Isono. As a result of ongoing, severe pain in her shoulder, arm, and neck, Hangarter in 1997 started to see Dr. Linda Berry, a chiropractor, and to attend physical therapy sessions. Although Hangarter continued this treatment for approximately eight weeks, her pain was not alleviated. She filed a claim for benefits under her disability insurance policy in May 1997 and began receiving payments in October 1997. She was also in an auto accident in October 1997, which aggravated her pain.

Though she continued to be treated by Drs. Berry and Isono, Hangarter's condition did not improve. Between 1996 and 2000 Hangarter had 3 Magnetic Resonance Imaging studies (MRIs), which Dr. Isono interpreted as having abnormal findings. The third MRI in May 2000 showed her condition to be growing worse, despite treatment by Drs. Berry and Isono. Dr. Berry diagnosed Hangarter's symptoms as epicondylitis, cervical intervertebral disk syndrome, and tendinitis. Dr. Isono offered only surgery to correct the problem, which Hangarter rejected based on her past negative experience with post-surgery pain medication. Hangarter eventually discontinued seeing Dr. Isono and was treated solely by Dr. Berry, whose chiropractic manipulations gave her some pain relief.

In 1999, Paul Revere employed an "independent medical examiner" (IME), Dr. Aubrey Swartz, to examine Hangarter and her medical records. In contrast to the findings of Drs. Isono and Berry, Dr. Swartz concluded that Hangarter's condition was "normal" and that she would be able to see two chiropractic patients an hour. Dr. Edward Katz, an orthopedic surgeon, at the request of Hangarter's counsel, reviewed her medical records and examined her in July 2001, two years after Dr. Swartz. Dr. Katz disagreed with Dr. Swartz's conclusions. He found 75% range of motion in her neck, spasm and tenderness in the right trapezius muscle, and reduced grip strength in her arm. Dr. Katz also found evidence of cervical disk disease, a depressed biceps reflex on Hangarter's right side along with numbness and tingling of the middle finger of her right hand, an indicator of nerve root compression affecting the sensory portion of the nerve going down the arm. Dr. Katz reviewed the reports of the MRI scans of Hangarter's cervical spine taken in May 1997, finding mild to minimal central canal stenosis, a narrowing of the spinal canal which causes some compression on the spinal canal or the nerve roots. He concluded that Hangarter suffered from lateral epicondylitis, more commonly called tennis elbow, cervical disk disease, and rotator cuff tendinitis, and that her condition was worsening. Drs. Katz, Berry, and Isono testified that Hangarter could not maintain a normal, continuous chiropractic occupation.

While Hangarter was receiving benefits from her policy, she hired Dr. Parissa Peymani to adjust patients while she assisted with office management. Dr. Peymani testified that after she started working, Hangarter stopped seeing all but five to seven of her patients, which Dr. Berry had encouraged her to do to see if her condition was at all improving. Dr. Peymani testified that during the year-and-a-half she worked for her, Hangarter performed adjustments for only 5 out of over 9,000 patient visits. Hangarter ceased employing Dr. Peymani in May 1999, because she could no longer afford to pay her. She then sold her practice.

On May 21, 1999, Paul Revere terminated Hangarter's "total disability" bene-fits. The letter claimed that Hangarter was ineligible for benefits under the pol-icy as she was not "totally disabled" and was working and earning income. After Paul Revere terminated Hangarter's benefits, it attached her bank account for the insurance premiums, until the account was drained, at which point the com-pany cancelled her policy. Hangarter subsequently brought a diversity action against Defendants alleging violation of §17200 of the Unfair Competition Act, breach of contract, breach of the covenant of good faith and fair dealing, and intentional misrepresentation. After eleven days of trial, a jury of six returned a unanimous verdict for Hangarter. The total award was $7,670,849, including $5,000,000 for punitive damages, $1,520,849 for past and future unpaid ben-efits, $400,000 for emotional distress, and $750,000 for attorneys' fees. The dis-trict court also issued a permanent injunction under the UCA. Defendants filed a motion for a JMOL or for a new trial, which the district court denied. *See Hangarter v. Paul Revere Life Ins. Co.*, 236 F. Supp. 2d 1069 (N.D. Cal. 2002). This appeal followed.

II. DISCUSSION

A. TOTAL DISABILITY

1. *Jury Instruction*

. . . Defendants argue that the district court's jury instruction on the mean-ing of "total disability" was a misstatement of California law. The district court's instruction to the jury stated:

TOTAL DISABILITY

Plaintiff's policy defines "total disability" as follows:

"Total Disability" means that because of Injury or Sickness:

a. you are unable to perform the important duties of your Occupation; and
b. you are not engaged in any other gainful occupation; and
c. you are under the regular and personal care of a physician.

This means, according to the law in California, that plaintiff is eligible for benefits if she is unable to perform the substantial and material duties of her own occupa-tion in the usual and customary way with reasonable continuity.

The district court's jury instruction was based upon the California Supreme Court's holding in *Erreca v. Western States Life Ins. Co.*, 121 P.2d 689 (Cal. 1942), that "the term 'total disability' does not signify an absolute state of helplessness but means such a disability as renders the insured unable to perform the sub-stantial and material acts necessary to the prosecution of a business or occupa-tion in the usual or customary way." *Id.* at 695.

Defendants argue that because the "total disability" provision of Paul Revere policy was unambiguous, the district court's imposition of *Erreca's* definition of "total disability" was unwarranted under California law. Contrary to Defendants' position, California law *requires* courts to deviate from the explicit policy defini-tion of "total disability" in the occupational policy context where it is necessary to "offer protection to the insured when he is no longer able to carry out the substantial and material functions of *his* occupation." *Austero v. Nat'l Cas. Co.,* 148 Cal. Rptr. 653, 667 (Cal. Ct. App. 1978) (emphasis added), *overruled on other grounds by Egan v. Mut. of Omaha Ins. Co.,* 620 P.2d 141 (Cal. 1979). Indeed, "California courts oppose strict adherence to a highly limited definition of 'total disability' in both non-occupational and general occupational disability policies." *Id.; see also Moore v. American United Life Ins. Co.,* 197 Cal. Rptr. 878, 882-83 (Cal. Ct. App. 1984) (stating that the unambiguous "policy language *misstated* California law as it has existed since [*Erreca*]. When coverage provisions in general disability policies require total inability to perform 'any occupation,' the courts have assigned a common sense interpretation to the term 'total disability' " (emphasis added)).

The policy in this case defined "total disability" as being "unable to perform the important duties" of one's occupation and to not be "engaged in any other gainful occupation." As Defendants concede, Hangarter's policy was an occupational policy that insured Hangarter against the loss of her ability to perform *her* occupation as a chiropractor, not any other occupation. Given the occupational nature of the policy, the district court appropriately formulated a jury instruction that only referred to Hangarter's ability to perform the important duties of her own occupation. California courts have specifically upheld jury instructions in the occupational policy context that defined "total disability" as the inability to perform the substantial and material duties of one's *own* occupation. *See Austero,* 148 Cal. Rptr. at 665 (upholding the instruction if the "plaintiff was 'rendered unable to perform the substantial and material duties of *his* occupation in the usual and customary way,' that he was totally disabled" (emphasis added)). Additionally, for all practical purposes there is no difference between *Erreca's* use of the phrase "substantial and material duties" and the policy's use of the phrase "important duties."[8]

Defendants also contend that the imposition of *Erreca's* definition of total disability in this case obviated the policy's partial or residual disability provision.[9] This argument also disregards California law. In *Wright v. Prudential Ins. Co. of America,* 80 P.2d 752 (Cal. Dist. Ct. App. 1938), cited approvingly by the California Supreme Court in *Erreca,* the California District Court of Appeal specifically rejected the defendant's contention that the California judicial "rule [regarding 'total disability'] does not apply where the policy provides for 'various degrees of disability' ":

> No logical reason appears, however, why the same rule should not be applied where the policy provides for both total and partial disability in order to make the total disability clause "operative and to prevent a forfeiture" of the indemnity

---

8. Although the instruction eliminated the policy's requirement that Hangarter not be engaged in "any other gainful occupation" in order to receive "total disability" benefits, that appears proper under California law, even if the policy language seems unambiguous. *See Moore,* 197 Cal. Rptr. at 882-83, 892-93. Given that this case involved an occupational disability policy, the district court did not err in formulating a jury instruction that focused solely on Hangarter's ability to perform the substantial and material duties of her occupation, not any other occupation.

9. The policy provides residual disability benefits if the insured is unable to perform one or more of the important duties of her occupation; is unable to perform the important duties of her occupation for more than 80% of the time normally required to perform them; or her loss of earnings is equal to at least 20% of her former earnings while engaged in her occupation or another occupation; and she is under the regular and personal care of a physician.

provided by that clause. In either case a literal interpretation of the total disability clause would defeat the very purpose of insurance against total disability, because it rarely happens that an insured is so completely disabled that he can transact no business duty whatever. *The rule quoted has been applied in many cases where the policy in suit provided for both total and partial disability.* . . . The fact that the insured may do some work or transact some business duties during the time for which he claims indemnity for total disability or even the fact that he may be physically able to do so is not conclusive evidence that his disability is not total, if reasonable care and prudence require that he desist.

Id. at 761-62 (citations omitted) (emphasis added). The fact that the policy in this case contained a residual or partial disability clause does not make the district court's jury instruction inconsistent with California law. The district court therefore did not erroneously misstate California law in its jury instruction.

2. Jury's Total Disability Finding

"[T]he question of what amounts to total disability is one of fact. . . ." *Erreca,* 121 P.2d at 696. . . . The jury's special verdict made the specific finding that at the date her benefits were terminated by Defendant, "Plaintiff was unable to perform the substantial and material duties of her own occupation in the usual and customary way with reasonable continuity." Defendants argue that "undisputed evidence" demonstrates that Hangarter "continued to manage her business profitably" and engaged in a "gainful occupation" in violation of the precise terms of the policy. Given that the district court correctly applied California law in formulating its jury instruction for "total disability," our relevant inquiry is only whether the jury's factual finding of total disability, pursuant to the jury instruction, was supported by substantial evidence. The fact that some evidence might demonstrate that Hangarter violated the precise terms of the policy is immaterial.

There was sufficient evidence for the jury to find that Hangarter was totally disabled. Though there is conflicting evidence in the record regarding Hangarter's medical condition, the jury's determination that before the date of termination Hangarter was physically unable to perform "the substantial and material duties of her own occupation in the usual and customary way with reasonable continuity" is supported by substantial evidence. Three doctors testified that Hangarter could not maintain a continuous, normal chiropractic occupation. While Defendants note that Hangarter made a handful of attempts to perform chiropractic adjustments, futile attempts to return to one's previous occupation are insufficient to reverse the jury's determination of total disability under California law. *See Joyce,* 21 Cal. Rptr. at 368 ("[A] finding that the plaintiff was 'wholly and continuously disabled' is not precluded by the fact that he made two futile attempts to return to his job. Such finding must be upheld since the evidence shows that on each occasion of his return to work, he was unable to perform the duties of his occupation . . .").

Though Hangarter hired another chiropractor from 1997-1999 to treat her patients while she performed clerical tasks incidental to her primary occupation, this is insufficient to disqualify her from being "totally disabled" under California law. Hangarter had an *occupational* policy with Paul Revere, and was insured against losses stemming from her inability to perform her occupation as a chiropractor. Her occasional stints as an office manager do not constitute the occupational practice of chiropractic medicine. Under California law, the performance of tasks *incidental* to one's profession does not demonstrate that an individual is not "totally disabled." *See Culley v. New York Life Ins. Co.,* 163 P.2d 698, 701 (Cal. 1945) ("Recovery is not precluded under a total disability provision because the insured is able to perform sporadic tasks, or give attention to simple or inconsequential details incident to the conduct of business" (citations and quotation marks omitted)).

Similarly, the fact that Hangarter's enterprise possibly made a profit during this time period is also immaterial. As the California Supreme Court noted in *Erreca:*

> The insurer also stresses the magnitude of the respondent's enterprise and his income therefrom. Such matters have *no proper place* in the determination of whether respondent is totally disabled from performing remunerative work. Disability insurance is designed to provide a substitute for earnings when, because of bodily injury or disease, the insured is deprived of the capacity to earn his living. . . . *It does not insure against loss of income.* The respondent receives his income from his ranches as an owner or lessor; his labor contributes nothing toward it. The contention of the insurer would lead to the strange conclusion that a bedridden merchant is not totally disabled from performing gainful work because he receives a substantial income from a business, the management of which he has been forced to abandon to others.

Erreca, 121 P.2d at 695-96 (emphasis added).

Substantial evidence supports the jury's finding that Hangarter was unable to perform the substantial and material duties of her occupation as a chiropractor in a normal and continuous way. The district court therefore did not err in declining to disturb the jury's finding that Hangarter was totally disabled.

B.   JURY'S BAD FAITH DETERMINATION

A cause of action for breach of the implied covenant of good faith and fair dealing in the insurance context is characterized as insurance bad faith, for which a plaintiff may recover tort damages. "The key to a bad faith claim [under California law] is whether or not the insurer's denial of coverage was reasonable. . . . [T]he reasonableness of an insurer's claims-handling conduct is ordinarily a question of fact." *Amadeo v. Principal Mut. Life Ins. Co.,* 290 F.3d 1152, 1161 (9th Cir. 2002) (citations and quotation marks omitted). Where there is a genuine issue of an insurer's liability under a policy, a court can conclude that an insurer's actions in denying the claim were not unreasonable as a matter of law. *Chateau Chamberay Homeowners Ass'n v. Associated Int'l Ins. Co.,* 108 Cal. Rptr. 2d 776, 784 (Cal. Ct. App. 2001). "The genuine issue rule in the context of bad faith claims allows" a court to grant JMOL when "it is undisputed or indisputable that the basis for the insurer's denial of benefits was reasonable. . . . [A]n insurer is not entitled to judgment as a matter of law where, viewing the facts in the light most favorable to the plaintiff, a jury could conclude that the insurer acted unreasonably." *Amadeo,* 290 F.3d at 1161-62 (citations omitted).

Though the existence of a "genuine dispute" will generally immunize an insurer from liability, a jury's finding that an insurer's investigation of a claim was biased may preclude a finding that the insurer was engaged in a genuine dispute, even if the insurer advances expert opinions concerning its conduct. *See Chateau Chamberay,* 108 Cal. Rptr. 2d at 785 ("an [insurer] expert's testimony [demonstrating a genuine dispute as to liability] will not *automatically* insulate an insurer from a bad faith claim based on a biased investigation"); *see also Guebara v. Allstate Ins. Co.,* 237 F.3d 987, 996 (9th Cir. 2001) ("Our decision does not eliminate bad faith claims based on an insurer's allegedly biased investigation. Expert testimony does not automatically insulate insurers from bad faith claims based on biased investigations"). An insurer's bias may be shown through the following factors:

1. The insurer may have misrepresented the nature of the investigatory proceedings;
2. The insurer's employees lied in depositions or to the insured;
3. The insurer dishonestly selected its experts;
4. The insurer's experts were unreasonable; or
5. The insurer failed to conduct a thorough investigation.

Chateau Chamberay, 108 Cal. Rptr. 2d at 785; *cf. Sprague v. Equifax, Inc.,* 213 Cal. Rptr. 69, 79 (Cal. Ct. App. 1985) (fraudulent termination exists if insurer arranges "an inadequate medical examination, producing a false conclusion, which would form an apparently plausible basis for wrongfully terminating payments").

Substantial evidence was presented at trial that the jury could have relied upon in determining that Defendants engaged in a biased investigation. Frank Caliri testified that Paul Revere's letter terminating Hangarter's benefits was misleading, deceptive, and fell below industry standards as it incorrectly advised Hangarter about her rights under the policy. The letter claimed that Hangarter was "working," and therefore was in violation of the policy. This statement, as Paul Revere acknowledged in the same letter, was false because Hangarter had already sold her chiropractic business. Indeed, the letter went on to deny Hangarter any residual benefits, claiming that because she had "sold" her business and "was not working," she was ineligible for them. Moreover, the letter made no mention of recovery or rehabilitation benefits, and when Hangarter specifically asked about such benefits before the letter was issued, she was erroneously told that she was ineligible for them. Finally, the termination letter incorrectly stated that the policy was governed by ERISA. If true, this would have meant that Hangarter had no available remedies under state law, including punitive damages.[10]

Evidence was also presented that Defendants exhibited bias in selecting and retaining Dr. Swartz as the IME. Paul Revere used Dr. Swartz nineteen times from 1995 to 2000. Caliri testified that when an insurer "use[s] the same [IME] on a continual basis," the medical examiner becomes "biased" because they "lose their independence." Similarly, evidence showed that in thirteen out of thirteen cases involving claims for total disability, Dr. Swartz rejected the insured's

---

10. If an insurance policy is part of an employee welfare benefit plan governed by ERISA, then a plaintiff's state law claims relating to that policy are preempted and federal law applies to determine recovery. *See Pilot Life Ins. Co. v. Dedeaux,* 481 U.S. 41, 56-57 (1987); *Kanne v. Conn. Gen. Life Ins. Co.,* 867 F.2d 489, 493-94 (9th Cir. 1988) (per curiam) (holding that plaintiffs' "state statutory claims for compensatory and punitive damages" were preempted under *Pilot Life* even if the statute fell within ERISA's saving clause).

claim that he or she was totally disabled. Moreover, Defendants' letter retaining Dr. Swartz, written by an in-house medical consultant who had never examined Hangarter, claimed that there were no objective findings for a disabling injury. Caliri testified that this letter "bias[ed]" and "predispos[ed] the doctor" against finding disabling injuries by "telling him [Defendants'] opinion."

Additionally, Hangarter offered evidence that Defendants had developed and applied to her case file a comprehensive system for targeting and terminating expensive claims, such as those stemming from "own occupation" policies where the insured was a disabled professional who had been receiving benefits for months or years. Dr. William Feist testified that Defendants in the mid-to-late 1990s had instituted "unethical" policies such as "round table claim reviews" that were made with the goal of achieving a "net termination ratio" (the ratio of the value of terminated claims compared with new claims).[11] Caliri similarly testified that the round table process violated the insurance industry principle of looking at each policy claim objectively and on a case-by-case basis.

Viewing the evidence in Hangarter's favor, we conclude that the district court did not err in determining that the jury had substantial evidence before it to find that the Defendants engaged in a biased, and thus "bad faith," investigation.

[Discussion of future damages jury instruction omitted.]

D.   PUNITIVE DAMAGES

1.   *Availability under California Law*

Under California law Hangarter was entitled to punitive damages if she proved "by clear and convincing evidence that [Defendants] ha[ve] been guilty of oppression, fraud, or malice." Cal. Civ. Code §3294(a).

"Viewing the facts in a light most favorable to the judgment," we conclude that the jury's award of punitive damages was consistent with California law. California courts have upheld the awarding of punitive damages based on conduct nearly identical to that alleged of Defendants. In *Moore,* the court held that the fact that an insurance policy disregards applicable California law could serve as "[o]ne factor to consider in evaluating an award of punitive damages. . . . The jury could reasonably conclude that certain aspects of defendant's deceptive claims practices were particularly invidious because lay persons would be unlikely to discover the deception." *Moore,* 197 Cal. Rptr. at 895. Indeed, "lay persons would be unlikely to know that they had an established right under California law to have coverage determined using the broader *Erreca* standard rather than the explicit language of defendant's policy." *Id.* at 895-96.

Additionally, California courts have stated that biased medical examinations and claims targeting practices could serve as a basis for punitive liability under California law. *Id.* at 897. As the court in *Moore* held,

---

11. Caliri also testified, based on internal Provident documents, that Defendants set goals for terminating whole blocks of claims without reference to the merits of individual claims for benefits; e.g., a directive that each adjuster will maintain a list of ten claimants "where intensive effort will lead to successful resolution of the claim. As one drops off another name will be added." He referred to testimony by Ralph Mohney and Sandra Fryc that "resolution" of claims meant their "termination." Caliri testified that Hangarter's case file was taken to a round table on September 9, 1997.

[l]ooking at the record, as we must, in a light most favorable to the judgment, it appears the jury could properly have concluded the conduct of defendant in this case was highly reprehensible. The jury could conclude that defendant consciously pursued a practice or policy of cheating insureds out of benefits by obtaining incorrect opinions of total disability from treating physicians.

Id. (citations omitted). Moreover, the jury "could conclude that plaintiff's own treating physician was misled by defendant's systematic claims practices and that defendant acted in bad faith by summarily denying plaintiff's claim even though her treating physician had indicated she could not work at her regular occupation." *Id.*

Finally, California courts have held that punitive damages are warranted where the cumulative evidence "supports a finding of intent to injure, since [e]vidence establishing 'conscious disregard of another's rights' is evidence indicating that the defendant was aware of the probable consequences of his or her acts and willfully and deliberately failed to avoid those consequences." *Notrica v. State Comp. Ins. Fund,* 83 Cal. Rptr. 2d 89, 113 (Cal. Ct. App. 1999) (internal quotation marks omitted). The evidence proffered at trial that Defendants disregarded *Erreca's* definition of total disability, engaged in biased medical examinations, misinformed Hangarter regarding her potential benefits, and employed policies to achieve net termination ratios could support a jury's finding that Defendants had a "conscious course of conduct, firmly grounded in established company policy" that disregarded the rights of insureds. *Neal v. Farmers Ins. Exch.,* 582 P.2d 980, 987 (Cal. 1978).

The district court therefore did not err in concluding that the jury's award of punitive damages was consistent with California law.

2. Constitutional Due Process

Current Supreme Court jurisprudence instructs courts reviewing the constitutionality of punitive damages awards to consider the "reasonableness of a punitive damages award," of which the "most important indicium . . . is the degree of reprehensibility of the defendant's conduct." *BMW of North America, Inc. v. Gore,* 517 U.S. 559, 575 (1996). The Court in *Gore* laid out several important factors that are relevant in determining the reprehensibility of the defendant's conduct, including whether the harm caused was physical as opposed to economic; tortious conduct evinced an indifference to or a reckless disregard of the health or safety of others; the target of the conduct had financial vulnerability; the conduct involved repeated actions or was an isolated incident; and the harm was the result of intentional malice, trickery, or deceit, or mere accident. *Id.* at 576-77.

The jury's awarding of punitive damages in this case satisfies the general framework laid out in *Gore. See State Farm Mut. Auto. Ins. Co. v. Campbell,* 538 U.S. 408 (2003) ("While States enjoy considerable discretion in deducing when punitive damages are warranted, each award must comport with the principles set forth in *Gore.*"). The evidence, viewed in Hangarter's favor, can support the conclusion that Defendants' conduct was in reckless disregard of the rights and the physical well-being of Hangarter; was threatening to an individual who was economically vulnerable; was part of a general corporate policy and not an isolated incident; and caused harm in a deceitful manner.

Defendants argue that the Supreme Court's decision in *State Farm* compels the conclusion that, in order to be constitutional, punitive damages in this case should be limited to no more than $1,000,000. Defendants' argument is essentially that because their conduct in this case is less invidious than the defendant's conduct in *State Farm,* the 1:1 ratio of punitive damages to compensatory damages applied in that case should equally apply here. *State Farm's* 1:1 compensatory to punitive damages ratio is not binding, no matter how factually similar the cases may be.[12] Indeed, the Court in *Gore* stated that "we have *consistently rejected the notion* that the constitutional line is marked by a simple mathematical formula, even one that compares actual and potential damages to the punitive award. . . ." *Gore,* 517 U.S. at 582 (first emphasis added). Likewise, the Court in *State Farm* stated that "We decline again to impose a bright-line ratio which a punitive damages award cannot exceed." *Id.* at 1524 (citations omitted). "[B]ecause there are no rigid benchmarks that a punitive damages award may not surpass, ratios greater than those . . . previously upheld [by the Court] may comport with due process where a particularly egregious act has resulted in only a small amount of economic damages." *Id.* (citations and quotation marks omitted).

The ratio in this case is approximately 2.6:1, well within the Supreme Court's suggested range for constitutional punitive damages awards. *See id.* ("Single-digit multipliers are more likely to comport with due process, while still achieving the State's goals of deterrence and retribution. . . ."). Given that due process prohibits only a "grossly excessive" award, leaving to the states "*considerable flexibility* in determining" whether "the damages awarded [were] reasonably necessary to vindicate the State's legitimate interest in punishment and deterrence," the district court did not err in concluding that the jury's award of punitive damages was within constitutional parameters. *Gore,* 517 U.S. at 568 (emphasis added).

NOTES AND QUESTIONS

1. In economic terms, the court concludes that Unum/Provident was engaged in a routine practice of "opportunistic breach." Judge Richard Posner has written the following about opportunistic breach:

> It makes a difference in deciding which remedy to grant whether the breach was opportunistic. If a promissor breaks his promise merely to take advantage of the vulnerability of the promisee in a setting . . . where performance is sequential rather than simultaneous, we might as well throw the book at the

---

12. That said, there are important factual distinctions between *State Farm* and the case at bar. In *State Farm* the "compensatory damages for the injury suffered . . . likely were based on a component [emotional distress] which was duplicated in the punitive award." *State Farm,* 538 U.S. at 426-28. Indeed, the plaintiff in *State Farm* "suffered only minor economic injuries"; her award was primarily for emotional distress, the result of conduct which "it is a major role of punitive damages to condemn." *Id.* In contrast, Hangarter's damages for emotional distress were only one third of her pecuniary damages, suggesting that *State Farm's* concern over a duplicative award is not as strongly present here. Moreover, the defendant's out-of-state conduct in *State Farm,* which was legal in the jurisdiction where it occurred, bore little relation to the plaintiff's harm. *Id.* at 421-24. Here, Defendants do not assert that their alleged conduct is legal in any U.S. jurisdiction. Additionally, unlike in *State Farm,* a legally sufficient nexus existed between Defendant's allegedly widespread corporate policies and the termination of Hangarter's benefits. While the Court in *State Farm* noted that the conduct that harmed the plaintiffs was "scant," evidence presented in this case indicates that Defendants' challenged policies were company-wide. *Id.*

> promis[s]or. . . . Such conduct has no economic justification and ought simply to be deterred.

Richard A. Posner, Economic Analysis of Law §4.8 (5th ed. 1998). *See also* William S. Dodge, *The Case for Punitive Damages in Contracts,* 48 Duke L.J. 629, 652-655 (1999). Do you agree? If so, why are punitive damages needed to deter opportunistic breach? Most economists believe that compensatory damages alone ordinarily provide adequate deterrence in contract cases by requiring the breaching party to internalize the costs of the harm to the non-breaching party. What is different about insurance? Are insurance contracts particularly likely to present a problem of "opportunistic" breach? Why?

2. *Hangarter* is one of a number of cases assessing punitive damages against Unum/Provident companies for similar conduct. *See, e.g., Greenberg v. Paul Revere Life Ins.,* 91 Fed. Appx. 539 (9th Cir. 2004); *Leavey v. Unum/Provident Corp.,* 2006 WL 1515999, May 26, 2006 (D. Ariz.); *Shepard v. Unum/Provident Corp.,* 381 F. Supp. 2d 608 (E.D. Ky. 2005). Hangarter's attorney has written about Unum/Provident's systematic bad faith in Ray Bourhis, Insult to Injury: Insurance, Fraud, and the Big Business of Bad Faith (2005).

3. As we will study in Chapter 3, insurance benefits provided as part of an employment contract are governed by ERISA. Unum/Provident was correct that ERISA does not permit punitive damages. (Indeed, in the article that we will read in Chapter 3, Professor Langbein reports that this legal rule was a crucial part of the Unum/Provident plan.) But Hangarter purchased her disability insurance policy directly from Unum/Provident, and thus her rights were not affected by ERISA.

4. There are many cases awarding punitive damages against insurance companies. The following notes present some examples organized by type of insurance. As you read the examples, consider whether the opportunism they illustrate grows out of the dynamic addressed in the contract interpretation and estoppel cases (i.e., information imbalance at the point of sale), out of the dynamic addressed in the disproportionate forfeiture cases (i.e., opportunism at the point of claim), or out of something else entirely.

5. *Life insurance cases.* Note that the life insurance cases listed here involve deceptive sales practices. *See* Richard V. Ericson & Aaron Doyle, *The Institutionalization of Deceptive Sales in Life Insurance,* 46 Brit. J. Criminol. 993 (2006) (reporting results of their field research on the Canadian life insurance industry, authors conclude that "deceptive practices have long been institutionalized in life insurance sales").

   A. *Haggan v. Jackson Nat'l,* Case No. 96-0295 (Cir. Ct., Copiah Co., Miss. 1999). Three plaintiffs, Rev. Dolton Haggan, Mrs. Erma Myers, and Col. & Mrs. S.E. McDaniel, filed suit against Jackson National after they purchased life insurance policies from three different Jackson National agents and were told that their policies were "single premium" policies or else would be "paid in full" after only a few payments, so-called vanishing premium policies. The insurance company later informed the policyholders that additional payments, beyond what had been previously indicated, would be necessary to maintain their policies. The jury found that the policies were sold as part of an organized marketing plan conducted by the defendant from its home office and that the program was based on deceptive sales practices. Although the actual damages awarded were relatively low (approximately $7,000 per plaintiff), the jury awarded $32.5 million in punitive damages to the three collectively. According to the plaintiffs' lawyer, Smith Phillips, this case is significant in the area of "vanishing premium" insurance litigation because it was one of the first cases in which the defendant insurance company, Jackson National, was able to defeat class action certification on procedural grounds and chose instead to challenge the case of the plaintiffs, joined by the liberal joinder-of-claims rules of Mississippi. This was a strategic move to avoid the prodigious settlements that other insurance companies were facing in similar cases brought as class action suits. The arguments of the plaintiff regarding the amount of punitive damages were based on several factors: the harm that actually occurred, the potential harm that could have occurred had the practice not been arrested, and the absence of other punishments for the same conduct. The parties reached a confidential settlement before appeal. (Information obtained in a telephone conversation with Smith Phillips on March 1, 2002.)

B. *Aon Risk Servs. v. Mickles*, 96 Ark. App. 369 (2006). Aon denied life insurance policy proceeds due to an alleged misrepresentation on the policy. The plaintiff proved at trial that she had provided the correct information to the sales agent and that the sales agent had provided the correct information to the company (allowing the jury to conclude that the misrepresentation was made by an insurance company employee). The plaintiff also proved that the sales agent falsely represented that the policy would pay double indemnity in the event of an accidental death. The court upheld a jury award of $60,000 in insurance benefits and reduced the punitive damages award under the *Gore* factors from $2 million to $750,000.

6. *Health insurance cases.* As we will study in Chapter 3, most health insurance in the United States is provided as an employee benefit, and, as a result, the remedies available for failure to provide health benefits are governed by ERISA, which does not permit punitive damages. The following cases involved health insurance policies purchased through the individual health insurance market, not employment-based health insurance.

A. *Liberty Nat'l Life Ins. Co. v. McAllister*, 675 So. 2d 1292 (Ala. 1995). The insured, Edith McAllister, brought a fraudulent suppression action against her insurer, Liberty National Life Insurance Company (Liberty National), following her exchange of an older version of her cancer insurance policy for a newer, more expensive version that made sharp reductions or eliminated certain kinds of coverage, specifically, coverage for continued cancer treatments that had been covered by the older policy. The Alabama Supreme Court held that the jury's award of $100 million in punitive damages was warranted. During trial, evidence was presented showing that the insurer had instructed its agents to specifically mislead insureds that the newer policy provided better coverage when in fact it did not. A former Liberty National sales agent who himself conducted policy exchanges testified that:

> *A:* [agent]: We were showed just to highlight the benefits, the first occurrence benefits . . . we showed them what they were going to get but we never showed them what they were going to lose. . . .
>
> *Q:* Were you taught not to tell them what they were giving up?

> *A:* Yes, sir.
> *Q:* Who taught you that?
> *A:* Sales managers.

B. *Dardinger v. Anthem Blue Cross & Blue Shield*, 781 N.E.2d 121 (Ohio 2002). Three-quarters of the way through a cancer treatment that it had approved, the insurer refused to pay for any additional treatment costs and then put the patient, her family, and her doctors through a long and drawn-out internal appeal process. In affirming the finding that punitive damages were appropriate, the appellate court characterized the case as a "tragedy that evolved over months, as [the insurers] watched. They created hope, then snatched it away. They took a dignified death from Esther Dardinger and filled her last days with frustration, doubt, and desperation. And every minute of additional pain suffered by Esther Dardinger was a natural outgrowth of the defendants' practiced powerlessness, their active inactivity." The company reviewed the appeal but without the requisite urgency, given the insured's condition, and took almost 120 days. The company sent a coverage denial letter the day after the insured passed away. The court reduced the $49 million punitive damages to $30 million and ordered that the punitive damages award be divided between the estate ($10 million) and a cancer research center at a state university ($20 million).

7. *Auto insurance cases.*
   A. *Avery v. State Farm Mut. Auto. Ins. Co.*, 746 N.E.2d 1242 (Ill. App. Ct. 2001). The insureds brought a nationwide class action suit based on State Farm's failure to pay for original equipment manufacturer (OEM) parts used in policy-covered repairs. At trial State Farm presented evidence attempting to prove that non-OEM parts were the functional equivalent of OEM parts. The insureds presented evidence to the contrary in the form of State Farm's own documents and the testimony of current and former employees. The circuit court entered judgment in favor of the plaintiffs for $1.18 billion, $600 million of which consisted of punitive damages. The court found that State Farm had committed fraud by specifying non-OEM parts with the knowledge that they were inferior in terms of fit, quality, function, performance, corrosion resistance, appearance, and safety, and yet described the non-OEM parts to customers as "quality replacement parts" and suggested to insureds in brochures and through its agents that the non-OEM parts were equal to OEM parts in terms of quality. Furthermore, the court considered State Farm's claim that it would replace non-OEM parts at no cost to any unsatisfied customer fraudulent because often the customers would be responsible for contacting the parts manufacturer, most of which were located outside of the United States, and even this could occur only after a State Farm investigator approved the replacement. Finally, if the investigator approved the replacement, the customer had to purchase the part and then request an indemnity payment from State Farm. The appellate court reversed the lower court's award of disgorgement damages but affirmed the punitive damages award. The Supreme Court of Illinois weighed in on the issue, affirming the appellate court's decision

to deny equitable relief and reversing the grant of declaratory relief. *Avery v. State Farm Mut. Auto. Ins. Co.*, 835 N.E.2d 801 (Ill. 2005).

B. *Capstick v. Allstate Ins. Co.*, 998 F.2d 810 (10th Cir. 1993). Capstick's car caught fire and exploded. When Capstick reported the loss to Allstate, the claims representative classified it as a "suspicious loss" in the company's computer (apparently because Capstick's policy number could not be found at the time of the call, leading the agent who took the call to assume that the policy was new). Despite the fact that Capstick's policy number and past coverage by Allstate were confirmed in less than one-half hour after the report, Allstate continued to treat the claim as a suspicious loss. Allstate assigned the claim to an adjuster who was relatively inexperienced in fire loss claims. The adjuster reported that the car "looked burned up" and asserted that arson was probably involved. He interviewed Capstick and then filled out an affidavit for Capstick to sign. The affidavit left out most of the detailed information that Capstick had given about the circumstances leading up to the fire, perhaps most important the existence of several witnesses to the fire who might be able to testify as to its cause. Both the investigator and his supervisor decided not to interview these witnesses and rejected the conclusion of Allstate's mechanic that there were several plausible causes of the fire that were accidental. Allstate required Capstick to produce a large quantity of documents relating to his financial condition but then spent only a few minutes looking at them. Ultimately, the trial court found that Allstate had acted in bad faith by first failing to investigate Capstick's claim; by sending someone with questionable expertise to view the evidence of the incident completely out of context, without informing him of the actual circumstances of the fire; and by failing to conduct a legitimate investigation of the claim. The court concluded that Allstate had breached its duty of good faith and was guilty of conduct demonstrating "wanton or reckless disregard for the rights of the plaintiff" and awarded Capstick, among other damages, $1,500,000 in punitive damages. In affirming the judgment, the U.S. Court of Appeals for the Tenth Circuit pointed out that "[i]t is significant that Allstate specifically and repeatedly labeled Capstick as an arsonist and one who intended to pursue insurance fraud."

C. *Hollock v. Erie Ins. Exch.*, 842 A.2d 409 (Pa. Super. Ct. 2004). The trial court found that the insurer had engaged in "deliberate indifference and, in some cases, blatant dishonesty" in the handling of an uninsured motorists (UIM) claim. The appellate court stated:

> The court determined that Erie misrepresented the amount of Hollock's coverage, established an arbitrary reserve with "absolutely no relationship" to available documentation, discounted Hollock's projected wage loss projections without supporting medical or vocational evidence, refused to contact Hollock's employer to determine the extent of her inability to complete assigned tasks, and refused to pay Hollock's claim for UIM benefits although it had previously accepted and paid her first party claims from the same accident. . . . Ultimately the court characterized Erie as "a company run [amok]," whose supervisory personnel "sanction[ed] deceit" in the service of "a corporate belief that it is acceptable to tell a little lie so long as no one really gets hurt."

Id. at 419-420. The appellate court upheld a punitive damages award of $2.8 million, which represented a 10:1 multiple over the compensatory damages.

8. The recent Preliminary Draft of the RLLI provides that "punitive damages may be awarded for liability insurance bad faith if there is clear and convincing evidence that the insurer intentionally, maliciously, knowingly, wantonly, or with reckless disregard of its obligations, engaged in a course of outrageous or repeated conduct that disregarded the rights of the insured." PD3, RLLI, §53. The "clear and convincing" standard, which seems to be the prevailing rule, is justified as follows: "This more demanding standard reflects the understanding that the insured has already been compensated for the harm caused by the insurer's bad faith conduct and, thus, the usual balance of equities between a party that wrongly caused harm and a party that should not have suffered harm no longer applies. When seeking punitive damages, the plaintiff in a bad faith case becomes an instrument of public punishment, subject to the more demanding procedural requirements that commonly attend to matters of punishment." *Id.* at Comment b.

CHAPTER
3

First-Party Insurance:
Illustrative Lines and Issues

We now shift from contract doctrines and issues that cut across lines of insurance to those that arise in the context of specific lines. We begin with first-party insurance, which protects against damage to an insured's own property or person. The types of first-party insurance that we consider in this chapter are property, life, disability, and health insurance. The goal is not to make you an expert in the specialized details of these lines of insurance, but rather to expose you to the general nature of the coverage provided in selected kinds of first-party insurance. These units also provide a good opportunity for applying some of the general doctrines and concepts introduced in Chapters 1 and 2. We conclude with subrogation, an important topic that links first-party and third-party insurance.

I.   PROPERTY INSURANCE

Property insurance is the oldest form of commercial insurance, dating back to marine insurance sold in the late Middle Ages. From marine insurance, property insurance spread inland, first covering goods destined for a sea voyage against the possibility of fire in the warehouse, and then covering buildings and their contents against fire more broadly. The property insurance market in the United States expanded rapidly in the mid-nineteenth century, although the market suffered from periodic insolvencies until insurers recognized the importance of diversifying geographically, and state insurance regulators improved their ability to identify and prevent financial weakness.

The insurance policy that appears in Figure 3.1 is the ISO homeowners' insurance policy's version of the "standard form" homeowners' insurance policy drafted by an insurance industry committee under the auspices of the Insurance Services Office (ISO). The policy is the most recent version of what ISO calls an HO3 policy, or a "special form." In an HO3 policy, personal property is protected on a "named peril" basis, meaning that the property is protected from specified causes of loss (e.g., fire, windstorm, hail, explosion), while the dwelling and other structures are protected on an "all risk" basis. As you will see, the "declarations" part of the sample policy has a space to list additional policy forms and endorsements. If you were to deal with an actual policy, you would want to be sure that you had all of the forms and endorsements that formed the policy. Endorsements can change important aspects of the policy. For example, ISO has a standard "High Value Endorsement" that changes the coverage of personal property from "named peril" to the more desirable "all risk" coverage.

Homeowners' insurance includes both a liability insurance component and a property insurance component. Liability insurance is the topic of Chapters 4 and 5, but you might want to at least look at the liability insurance part of the HO3 form in Figure 3.1, so that you get a sense of how it compares to the property insurance part.

As you read through the policy, try to figure out which provisions would come into play in the scenarios listed below. In each case, imagine that you were confronting an insurance adjuster who insisted on denying every claim unless you could show exactly where in the policy it said that your loss was covered. Be sure to look for exclusions that might apply as well.

- An accidental kitchen fire damages the floor, walls, cabinets, and some of the appliances in the kitchen. How would your answer change, if at all, if the fire was due to the insured's failure to replace an aging appliance?
- A sewer backup floods the basement, causing damage to the drywall and carpeting.
- A fire destroys the garage and the car parked inside it.
- The policyholder's daughter, while attending college, had her laptop computer stolen from her apartment.

A. *The All Risk Concept, Causation, and Excluded Losses*

The "perils insured against" section of the homeowners policy reproduced in Figure 3.1 states, "We insure against risk of direct physical loss to property . . . except we do not cover any loss that results from a peril excluded or limited by this policy. . . ." This form of property insurance coverage is known as "all risk" property insurance. To obtain coverage under an all risk insurance policy, the policyholder has the burden of proving "physical loss to property." If the policyholder does so, the claim is covered unless the insurer demonstrates that the loss is excluded by the policy. To compare this form to other homeowners' insurance forms, see *http://doi.nv.gov/Consumers/Homeowners-Insurance/Policy-Forms/*.

As with all risk coverage generally, the homeowners' policy lists a number of perils that are excluded from coverage. It is this basic structure—all risks of physical loss are covered unless excluded—that distinguishes all risk coverage from the earlier "named peril" coverage. Under a named peril policy, a claim is covered only when the damage results from a specifically named peril (fire and explosion are the classic examples). Under an all risk policy, physical loss is covered unless it results from a specifically excluded peril (subject, of course, to the other terms and conditions of the policy). For an example of "named peril" coverage that still exists in the homeowners' policy, see the coverage for personal property on page 10 of the policy shown in Figure 3.1.

The first property insurance policies to be written on an all risk basis were marine insurance policies. "Perils of the sea" and "perils named and unnamed"

POLICY NUMBER:

HOMEOWNERS POLICY DECLARATIONS

Company Name:

Producer Name:

Named Insured:

Mailing Address:

The Residence Premises Is Located At The Above Address Unless Otherwise Stated:

Policy Period Year(s)	
Number Of Year(s):	
From:	12:01 AM standard time at the residence premises
To:	12:01 AM standard time at the residence premises

We will provide the insurance described in this policy in return for the premium and compliance with all applicable policy provisions.

Coverage is provided where a premium or limit of liability is shown for the coverage.

Section I – Coverages	Limit Of Liability	
A. Dwelling	$	
B. Other Structures	$	
C. Personal Property	$	
D. Loss Of Use	$	
Section II – Coverages		
E. Personal Liability	$	Each Occurrence
F. Medical Payments To Others	$	Each Person
	Premium	
Basic Policy Premium	$	
Additional Premium Charges Or Credits Related To Other Coverages Or Endorsements:		
	$	
	$	
	$	
Total Premium	$	

HO DS 01 05 11   © Insurance Services Office, Inc., 2010   **Page 1 of 3**

Figure 3.1 Sample Homeowners Policy

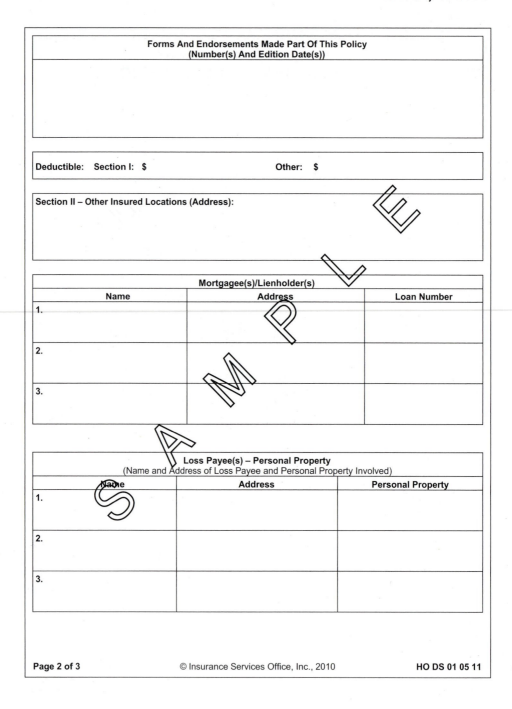

Forms And Endorsements Made Part Of This Policy
(Number(s) And Edition Date(s))

Deductible: Section I: $ Other: $

Section II – Other Insured Locations (Address):

Mortgagee(s)/Lienholder(s)

Name	Address	Loan Number
1.		
2.		
3.		

Loss Payee(s) – Personal Property
(Name and Address of Loss Payee and Personal Property Involved)

Name	Address	Personal Property
1.		
2.		
3.		

             © Insurance Services Office, Inc., 2010   HO DS 01 05 11

Countersignature Of Authorized Representative
Name:
Title:
Signature:
Date:

S A M P L E

HOMEOWNERS 3 – SPECIAL FORM

AGREEMENT

We will provide the insurance described in this policy in return for the premium and compliance with all applicable provisions of this policy.

DEFINITIONS

A. In this policy, "you" and "your" refer to the "named insured" shown in the Declarations and the spouse if a resident of the same household. "We", "us" and "our" refer to the Company providing this insurance.

B. In addition, certain words and phrases are defined as follows:

1. "Aircraft Liability", "Hovercraft Liability", "Motor Vehicle Liability" and "Watercraft Liability", subject to the provisions in **b.** below, mean the following:

   a. Liability for "bodily injury" or "property damage" arising out of the:

   (1) Ownership of such vehicle or craft by an "insured";

   (2) Maintenance, occupancy, operation, use, loading or unloading of such vehicle or craft by any person;

   (3) Entrustment of such vehicle or craft by an "insured" to any person;

   (4) Failure to supervise or negligent supervision of any person involving such vehicle or craft by an "insured"; or

   (5) Vicarious liability, whether or not imposed by law, for the actions of a child or minor involving such vehicle or craft.

   b. For the purpose of this definition:

   (1) Aircraft means any contrivance used or designed for flight except model or hobby aircraft not used or designed to carry people or cargo;

   (2) Hovercraft means a self-propelled motorized ground effect vehicle and includes, but is not limited to, flarecraft and air cushion vehicles;

   (3) Watercraft means a craft principally designed to be propelled on or in water by wind, engine power or electric motor; and

   (4) Motor vehicle means a "motor vehicle" as defined in **7.** below.

2. "Bodily injury" means bodily harm, sickness or disease, including required care, loss of services and death that results.

3. "Business" means:

   a. A trade, profession or occupation engaged in on a full-time, part-time or occasional basis; or

   b. Any other activity engaged in for money or other compensation, except the following:

   (1) One or more activities, not described in **(2)** through **(4)** below, for which no "insured" receives more than $2,000 in total compensation for the 12 months before the beginning of the policy period;

   (2) Volunteer activities for which no money is received other than payment for expenses incurred to perform the activity;

   (3) Providing home day care services for which no compensation is received, other than the mutual exchange of such services; or

   (4) The rendering of home day care services to a relative of an "insured".

4. "Employee" means an employee of an "insured", or an employee leased to an "insured" by a labor leasing firm under an agreement between an "insured" and the labor leasing firm, whose duties are other than those performed by a "residence employee".

5. "Insured" means:

   a. You and residents of your household who are:

   (1) Your relatives; or

   (2) Other persons under the age of 21 and in the care of any person named above;

   b. A student enrolled in school full time, as defined by the school, who was a resident of your household before moving out to attend school, provided the student is under the age of:

   (1) 24 and your relative; or

   (2) 21 and in your care or the care of a person described in **a.(1)** above; or

c. Under Section **II:**

(1) With respect to animals or watercraft to which this policy applies, any person or organization legally responsible for these animals or watercraft which are owned by you or any person included in **a.** or **b.** above. "Insured" does not mean a person or organization using or having custody of these animals or watercraft in the course of any "business" or without consent of the owner; or

(2) With respect to a "motor vehicle" to which this policy applies:

(a) Persons while engaged in your employ or that of any person included in **a.** or **b.** above; or

(b) Other persons using the vehicle on an "insured location" with your consent.

Under both Sections **I** and **II,** when the word an immediately precedes the word "insured", the words an "insured" together mean one or more "insureds".

6. "Insured location" means:

a. The "residence premises";

b. The part of other premises, other structures and grounds used by you as a residence; and

(1) Which is shown in the Declarations; or

(2) Which is acquired by you during the policy period for your use as a residence;

c. Any premises used by you in connection with a premises described in **a.** and **b.** above;

d. Any part of a premises:

(1) Not owned by an "insured"; and

(2) Where an "insured" is temporarily residing;

e. Vacant land, other than farm land, owned by or rented to an "insured";

f. Land owned by or rented to an "insured" on which a one, two, three or four family dwelling is being built as a residence for an "insured";

g. Individual or family cemetery plots or burial vaults of an "insured"; or

h. Any part of a premises occasionally rented to an "insured" for other than "business" use.

7. "Motor vehicle" means:

a. A self-propelled land or amphibious vehicle; or

b. Any trailer or semitrailer which is being carried on, towed by or hitched for towing by a vehicle described in **a.** above.

8. "Occurrence" means an accident, including continuous or repeated exposure to substantially the same general harmful conditions, which results, during the policy period, in:

a. "Bodily injury"; or

b. "Property damage".

9. "Property damage" means physical injury to, destruction of, or loss of use of tangible property.

10. "Residence employee" means:

a. An employee of an "insured", or an employee leased to an "insured" by a labor leasing firm under an agreement between an "insured" and the labor leasing firm, whose duties are related to the maintenance or use of the "residence premises", including household or domestic services; or

b. One who performs similar duties elsewhere not related to the "business" of an "insured".

A "residence employee" does not include a temporary employee who is furnished to an "insured" to substitute for a permanent "residence employee" on leave or to meet seasonal or short-term workload conditions.

11. "Residence premises" means:

a. The one family dwelling where you reside;

b. The two, three or four family dwelling where you reside in at least one of the family units; or

c. That part of any other building where you reside;

and which is shown as the "residence premises" in the Declarations.

"Residence premises" also includes other structures and grounds at that location.

 Copyright, Insurance Services Office, Inc., 1999 HO 00 03 10 00

DEDUCTIBLE

Unless otherwise noted in this policy, the following deductible provision applies:

Subject to the policy limits that apply, we will pay only that part of the total of all loss payable under Section **I** that exceeds the deductible amount shown in the Declarations.

SECTION I – PROPERTY COVERAGES

A. Coverage A – Dwelling

1. We cover:

   a. The dwelling on the "residence premises" shown in the Declarations, including structures attached to the dwelling; and

   b. Materials and supplies located on or next to the "residence premises" used to construct, alter or repair the dwelling or other structures on the "residence premises".

2. We do not cover land, including land on which the dwelling is located.

B. Coverage B – Other Structures

1. We cover other structures on the "residence premises" set apart from the dwelling by clear space. This includes structures connected to the dwelling by only a fence, utility line, or similar connection.

2. We do not cover:

   a. Land, including land on which the other structures are located;

   b. Other structures rented or held for rental to any person not a tenant of the dwelling, unless used solely as a private garage;

   c. Other structures from which any "business" is conducted; or

   d. Other structures used to store "business" property. However, we do cover a structure that contains "business" property solely owned by an "insured" or a tenant of the dwelling provided that "business" property does not include gaseous or liquid fuel, other than fuel in a permanently installed fuel tank of a vehicle or craft parked or stored in the structure.

3. The limit of liability for this coverage will not be more than 10% of the limit of liability that applies to Coverage **A**. Use of this coverage does not reduce the Coverage **A** limit of liability.

C. Coverage C – Personal Property

1. **Covered Property**

   We cover personal property owned or used by an "insured" while it is anywhere in the world. After a loss and at your request, we will cover personal property owned by:

   a. Others while the property is on the part of the "residence premises" occupied by an "insured"; or

   b. A guest or a "residence employee", while the property is in any residence occupied by an "insured".

2. **Limit For Property At Other Residences**

   Our limit of liability for personal property usually located at an "insured's" residence, other than the "residence premises", is 10% of the limit of liability for Coverage **C** or $1,000, whichever is greater. However, this limitation does not apply to personal property:

   a. Moved from the "residence premises" because it is being repaired, renovated or rebuilt and is not fit to live in or store property in; or

   b. In a newly acquired principal residence for 30 days from the time you begin to move the property there.

3. **Special Limits Of Liability**

   The special limit for each category shown below is the total limit for each loss for all property in that category. These special limits do not increase the Coverage **C** limit of liability.

   a. $200 on money, bank notes, bullion, gold other than goldware, silver other than silverware, platinum other than platinumware, coins, medals, scrip, stored value cards and smart cards.

   b. $1,500 on securities, accounts, deeds, evidences of debt, letters of credit, notes other than bank notes, manuscripts, personal records, passports, tickets and stamps. This dollar limit applies to these categories regardless of the medium (such as paper or computer software) on which the material exists.

   This limit includes the cost to research, replace or restore the information from the lost or damaged material.

c. $1,500 on watercraft of all types, including their trailers, furnishings, equipment and outboard engines or motors.

d. $1,500 on trailers or semitrailers not used with watercraft of all types.

e. $1,500 for loss by theft of jewelry, watches, furs, precious and semiprecious stones.

f. $2,500 for loss by theft of firearms and related equipment.

g. $2,500 for loss by theft of silverware, silver-plated ware, goldware, gold-plated ware, platinumware, platinum-plated ware and pewterware. This includes flatware, hollow-ware, tea sets, trays and trophies made of or including silver, gold or pewter.

h. $2,500 on property, on the "residence premises", used primarily for "business" purposes.

i. $500 on property, away from the "residence premises", used primarily for "business" purposes. However, this limit does not apply to loss to electronic apparatus and other property described in Categories **j.** and **k.** below.

j. $1,500 on electronic apparatus and accessories, while in or upon a "motor vehicle", but only if the apparatus is equipped to be operated by power from the "motor vehicle's" electrical system while still capable of being operated by other power sources.

Accessories include antennas, tapes, wires, records, discs or other media that can be used with any apparatus described in this Category **j.**

k. $1,500 on electronic apparatus and accessories used primarily for "business" while away from the "residence premises" and not in or upon a "motor vehicle". The apparatus must be equipped to be operated by power from the "motor vehicle's" electrical system while still capable of being operated by other power sources.

Accessories include antennas, tapes, wires, records, discs or other media that can be used with any apparatus described in this Category **k.**

4. Property Not Covered

We do not cover:

a. Articles separately described and specifically insured, regardless of the limit for which they are insured, in this or other insurance;

b. Animals, birds or fish;

c. "Motor vehicles".

(1) This includes:

(a) Their accessories, equipment and parts; or

(b) Electronic apparatus and accessories designed to be operated solely by power from the electrical system of the "motor vehicle". Accessories include antennas, tapes, wires, records, discs or other media that can be used with any apparatus described above.

The exclusion of property described in **(a)** and **(b)** above applies only while such property is in or upon the "motor vehicle".

(2) We do cover "motor vehicles" not required to be registered for use on public roads or property which are:

(a) Used solely to service an "insured's" residence; or

(b) Designed to assist the handicapped;

d. Aircraft meaning any contrivance used or designed for flight including any parts whether or not attached to the aircraft.

We do cover model or hobby aircraft not used or designed to carry people or cargo;

e. Hovercraft and parts. Hovercraft means a self-propelled motorized ground effect vehicle and includes, but is not limited to, flare-craft and air cushion vehicles;

f. Property of roomers, boarders and other tenants, except property of roomers and boarders related to an "insured";

g. Property in an apartment regularly rented or held for rental to others by an "insured", except as provided in **E.10.** Landlord's Furnishings under Section I – Property Coverages;

h. Property rented or held for rental to others off the "residence premises";

i. "Business" data, including such data stored in:

(1) Books of account, drawings or other paper records; or

(2) Computers and related equipment.

We do cover the cost of blank recording or storage media, and of prerecorded computer programs available on the retail market;

SAMPLE

 Copyright, Insurance Services Office, Inc., 1999 **HO 00 03 10 00**

j. Credit cards, electronic fund transfer cards or access devices used solely for deposit, withdrawal or transfer of funds except as provided in **E.6.** Credit Card, Electronic Fund Transfer Card Or Access Device, Forgery And Counterfeit Money under Section **I** – Property Coverages; or

k. Water or steam.

D. Coverage D – Loss Of Use

The limit of liability for Coverage **D** is the total limit for the coverages in **1.** Additional Living Expense, **2.** Fair Rental Value and **3.** Civil Authority Prohibits Use below.

1. Additional Living Expense

If a loss covered under Section **I** makes that part of the "residence premises" where you reside not fit to live in, we cover any necessary increase in living expenses incurred by you so that your household can maintain its normal standard of living.

Payment will be for the shortest time required to repair or replace the damage or, if you permanently relocate, the shortest time required for your household to settle elsewhere.

2. Fair Rental Value

If a loss covered under Section **I** makes that part of the "residence premises" rented to others or held for rental by you not fit to live in, we cover the fair rental value of such premises less any expenses that do not continue while it is not fit to live in.

Payment will be for the shortest time required to repair or replace such premises.

3. Civil Authority Prohibits Use

If a civil authority prohibits you from use of the "residence premises" as a result of direct damage to neighboring premises by a Peril Insured Against, we cover the loss as provided in **1.** Additional Living Expense and **2.** Fair Rental Value above for no more than two weeks.

4. Loss Or Expense Not Covered

We do not cover loss or expense due to cancellation of a lease or agreement.

The periods of time under **1.** Additional Living Expense, **2.** Fair Rental Value and **3.** Civil Authority Prohibits Use above are not limited by expiration of this policy.

E. Additional Coverages

1. Debris Removal

a. We will pay your reasonable expense for the removal of:

(1) Debris of covered property if a Peril Insured Against that applies to the damaged property causes the loss; or

(2) Ash, dust or particles from a volcanic eruption that has caused direct loss to a building or property contained in a building.

This expense is included in the limit of liability that applies to the damaged property. If the amount to be paid for the actual damage to the property plus the debris removal expense is more than the limit of liability for the damaged property, an additional 5% of that limit is available for such expense.

b. We will also pay your reasonable expense, up to $1,000, for the removal from the "residence premises" of:

(1) Your tree(s) felled by the peril of Windstorm or Hail or Weight of Ice, Snow or Sleet; or

(2) A neighbor's tree(s) felled by a Peril Insured Against under Coverage **C;**

provided the tree(s):

(3) Damage(s) a covered structure; or

(4) Does not damage a covered structure, but:

(a) Block(s) a driveway on the "residence premises" which prevent(s) a "motor vehicle", that is registered for use on public roads or property, from entering or leaving the "residence premises"; or

(b) Block(s) a ramp or other fixture designed to assist a handicapped person to enter or leave the dwelling building.

The $1,000 limit is the most we will pay in any one loss regardless of the number of fallen trees. No more than $500 of this limit will be paid for the removal of any one tree.

This coverage is additional insurance.

2. Reasonable Repairs

a. We will pay the reasonable cost incurred by you for the necessary measures taken solely to protect covered property that is damaged by a Peril Insured Against from further damage.

b. If the measures taken involve repair to other damaged property, we will only pay if that property is covered under this policy and the damage is caused by a Peril Insured Against. This coverage does not:

    (1) Increase the limit of liability that applies to the covered property; or

    (2) Relieve you of your duties, in case of a loss to covered property, described in **B.4.** under Section **I** – Conditions.

3. Trees, Shrubs And Other Plants

We cover trees, shrubs, plants or lawns, on the "residence premises", for loss caused by the following Perils Insured Against:

  a. Fire or Lightning;

  b. Explosion;

  c. Riot or Civil Commotion;

  d. Aircraft;

  e. Vehicles not owned or operated by a resident of the "residence premises";

  f. Vandalism or Malicious Mischief; or

  g. Theft.

We will pay up to 5% of the limit of liability that applies to the dwelling for all trees, shrubs, plants or lawns. No more than $500 of this limit will be paid for any one tree, shrub or plant. We do not cover property grown for "business" purposes.

This coverage is additional insurance.

4. Fire Department Service Charge

We will pay up to $500 for your liability assumed by contract or agreement for fire department charges incurred when the fire department is called to save or protect covered property from a Peril Insured Against. We do not cover fire department service charges if the property is located within the limits of the city, municipality or protection district furnishing the fire department response.

This coverage is additional insurance. No deductible applies to this coverage.

5. Property Removed

We insure covered property against direct loss from any cause while being removed from a premises endangered by a Peril Insured Against and for no more than 30 days while removed.

This coverage does not change the limit of liability that applies to the property being removed.

6. Credit Card, Electronic Fund Transfer Card Or Access Device, Forgery And Counterfeit Money

  a. We will pay up to $500 for:

    (1) The legal obligation of an "insured" to pay because of the theft or unauthorized use of credit cards issued to or registered in an "insured's" name;

    (2) Loss resulting from theft or unauthorized use of an electronic fund transfer card or access device used for deposit, withdrawal or transfer of funds, issued to or registered in an "insured's" name;

    (3) Loss to an "insured" caused by forgery or alteration of any check or negotiable instrument; and

    (4) Loss to an "insured" through acceptance in good faith of counterfeit United States or Canadian paper currency.

  All loss resulting from a series of acts committed by any one person or in which any one person is concerned or implicated is considered to be one loss.

  This coverage is additional insurance. No deductible applies to this coverage.

  b. We do not cover:

    (1) Use of a credit card, electronic fund transfer card or access device:

      (a) By a resident of your household;

      (b) By a person who has been entrusted with either type of card or access device; or

      (c) If an "insured" has not complied with all terms and conditions under which the cards are issued or the devices accessed; or

    (2) Loss arising out of "business" use or dishonesty of an "insured".

  c. If the coverage in **a.** above applies, the following defense provisions also apply:

    (1) We may investigate and settle any claim or suit that we decide is appropriate. Our duty to defend a claim or suit ends when the amount we pay for the loss equals our limit of liability.

    (2) If a suit is brought against an "insured" for liability under **a.(1)** or **(2)** above, we will provide a defense at our expense by counsel of our choice.

    (3) We have the option to defend at our expense an "insured" or an "insured's" bank against any suit for the enforcement of payment under **a.(3)** above.

Page 6 of 22   Copyright, Insurance Services Office, Inc., 1999   **HO 00 03 10 00**

7. Loss Assessment

a. We will pay up to $1,000 for your share of loss assessment charged during the policy period against you, as owner or tenant of the "residence premises", by a corporation or association of property owners. The assessment must be made as a result of direct loss to property, owned by all members collectively, of the type that would be covered by this policy if owned by you, caused by a Peril Insured Against under Coverage **A,** other than:

(1) Earthquake; or

(2) Land shock waves or tremors before, during or after a volcanic eruption.

The limit of $1,000 is the most we will pay with respect to any one loss, regardless of the number of assessments. We will only apply one deductible, per unit, to the total amount of any one loss to the property described above, regardless of the number of assessments.

b. We do not cover assessments charged against you or a corporation or association of property owners by any governmental body.

c. Paragraph **P.** Policy Period under Section **I** – Conditions does not apply to this coverage.

This coverage is additional insurance.

8. Collapse

a. With respect to this Additional Coverage:

(1) Collapse means an abrupt falling down or caving in of a building or any part of a building with the result that the building or part of the building cannot be occupied for its current intended purpose.

(2) A building or any part of a building that is in danger of falling down or caving in is not considered to be in a state of collapse.

(3) A part of a building that is standing is not considered to be in a state of collapse even if it has separated from another part of the building.

(4) A building or any part of a building that is standing is not considered to be in a state of collapse even if it shows evidence of cracking, bulging, sagging, bending, leaning, settling, shrinkage or expansion.

b. We insure for direct physical loss to covered property involving collapse of a building or any part of a building if the collapse was caused by one or more of the following:

(1) The Perils Insured Against named under Coverage **C;**

(2) Decay that is hidden from view, unless the presence of such decay is known to an "insured" prior to collapse;

(3) Insect or vermin damage that is hidden from view, unless the presence of such damage is known to an "insured" prior to collapse;

(4) Weight of contents, equipment, animals or people;

(5) Weight of rain which collects on a roof; or

(6) Use of defective material or methods in construction, remodeling or renovation if the collapse occurs during the course of the construction, remodeling or renovation.

c. Loss to an awning, fence, patio, deck, pavement, swimming pool, underground pipe, flue, drain, cesspool, septic tank, foundation, retaining wall, bulkhead, pier, wharf or dock is not included under **b.(2)** through **(6)** above, unless the loss is a direct result of the collapse of a building or any part of a building.

d. This coverage does not increase the limit of liability that applies to the damaged covered property.

9. Glass Or Safety Glazing Material

a. We cover:

(1) The breakage of glass or safety glazing material which is part of a covered building, storm door or storm window;

(2) The breakage of glass or safety glazing material which is part of a covered building, storm door or storm window when caused directly by earth movement; and

(3) The direct physical loss to covered property caused solely by the pieces, fragments or splinters of broken glass or safety glazing material which is part of a building, storm door or storm window.

b. This coverage does not include loss:

(1) To covered property which results because the glass or safety glazing material has been broken, except as provided in **a.(3)** above; or

(2) On the "residence premises" if the dwelling has been vacant for more than 60 consecutive days immediately before the loss, except when the breakage results directly from earth movement as provided in **a.(2)** above. A dwelling being constructed is not considered vacant.

c. This coverage does not increase the limit of liability that applies to the damaged property.

10. Landlord's Furnishings

We will pay up to $2,500 for your appliances, carpeting and other household furnishings, in each apartment on the "residence premises" regularly rented or held for rental to others by an "insured", for loss caused by a Peril Insured Against in Coverage **C**, other than Theft.

This limit is the most we will pay in any one loss regardless of the number of appliances, carpeting or other household furnishings involved in the loss.

This coverage does not increase the limit of liability applying to the damaged property.

11. Ordinance Or Law

a. You may use up to 10% of the limit of liability that applies to Coverage **A** for the increased costs you incur due to the enforcement of any ordinance or law which requires or regulates:

(1) The construction, demolition, remodeling, renovation or repair of that part of a covered building or other structure damaged by a Peril Insured Against;

(2) The demolition and reconstruction of the undamaged part of a covered building or other structure, when that building or other structure must be totally demolished because of damage by a Peril Insured Against to another part of that covered building or other structure; or

(3) The remodeling, removal or replacement of the portion of the undamaged part of a covered building or other structure necessary to complete the remodeling, repair or replacement of that part of the covered building or other structure damaged by a Peril Insured Against.

b. You may use all or part of this ordinance or law coverage to pay for the increased costs you incur to remove debris resulting from the construction, demolition, remodeling, renovation, repair or replacement of property as stated in **a.** above.

c. We do not cover:

(1) The loss in value to any covered building or other structure due to the requirements of any ordinance or law; or

(2) The costs to comply with any ordinance or law which requires any "insured" or others to test for, monitor, clean up, remove, contain, treat, detoxify or neutralize, or in any way respond to, or assess the effects of, pollutants in or on any covered building or other structure.

Pollutants means any solid, liquid, gaseous or thermal irritant or contaminant, including smoke, vapor, soot, fumes, acids, alkalis, chemicals and waste. Waste includes materials to be recycled, reconditioned or reclaimed.

This coverage is additional insurance.

12. Grave Markers

We will pay up to $5,000 for grave markers, including mausoleums, on or away from the "residence premises" for loss caused by a Peril Insured Against under Coverage **C.**

This coverage does not increase the limits of liability that apply to the damaged covered property.

SECTION I – PERILS INSURED AGAINST

A. Coverage A – Dwelling And Coverage B – Other Structures

1. We insure against risk of direct physical loss to property described in Coverages **A** and **B.**

2. We do not insure, however, for loss:

   a. Excluded under Section **I** – Exclusions;

   b. Involving collapse, except as provided in **E.8. Collapse** under Section **I** – Property Coverages; or

   c. Caused by:

   (1) Freezing of a plumbing, heating, air conditioning or automatic fire protective sprinkler system or of a household appliance, or by discharge, leakage or overflow from within the system or appliance caused by freezing. This provision does not apply if you have used reasonable care to:

   (a) Maintain heat in the building; or

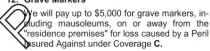

(b) Shut off the water supply and drain all systems and appliances of water.

However, if the building is protected by an automatic fire protective sprinkler system, you must use reasonable care to continue the water supply and maintain heat in the building for coverage to apply.

For purposes of this provision a plumbing system or household appliance does not include a sump, sump pump or related equipment or a roof drain, gutter, downspout or similar fixtures or equipment;

(2) Freezing, thawing, pressure or weight of water or ice, whether driven by wind or not, to a:

(a) Fence, pavement, patio or swimming pool;

(b) Footing, foundation, bulkhead, wall, or any other structure or device that supports all or part of a building, or other structure;

(c) Retaining wall or bulkhead that does not support all or part of a building or other structure; or

(d) Pier, wharf or dock;

(3) Theft in or to a dwelling under construction, or of materials and supplies for use in the construction until the dwelling is finished and occupied;

(4) Vandalism and malicious mischief, and any ensuing loss caused by any intentional and wrongful act committed in the course of the vandalism or malicious mischief, if the dwelling has been vacant for more than 60 consecutive days immediately before the loss. A dwelling being constructed is not considered vacant;

(5) Mold, fungus or wet rot. However, we do insure for loss caused by mold, fungus or wet rot that is hidden within the walls or ceilings or beneath the floors or above the ceilings of a structure if such loss results from the accidental discharge or overflow of water or steam from within:

(a) A plumbing, heating, air conditioning or automatic fire protective sprinkler system, or a household appliance, on the "residence premises"; or

(b) A storm drain, or water, steam or sewer pipes, off the "residence premises".

For purposes of this provision, a plumbing system or household appliance does not include a sump, sump pump or related equipment or a roof drain, gutter, downspout or similar fixtures or equipment; or

(6) Any of the following:

(a) Wear and tear, marring, deterioration;

(b) Mechanical breakdown, latent defect, inherent vice, or any quality in property that causes it to damage or destroy itself;

(c) Smog, rust or other corrosion, or dry rot;

(d) Smoke from agricultural smudging or industrial operations;

(e) Discharge, dispersal, seepage, migration, release or escape of pollutants unless the discharge, dispersal, seepage, migration, release or escape is itself caused by a Peril Insured Against named under Coverage **C**.

Pollutants means any solid, liquid, gaseous or thermal irritant or contaminant, including smoke, vapor, soot, fumes, acids, alkalis, chemicals and waste. Waste includes materials to be recycled, reconditioned or reclaimed;

(f) Settling, shrinking, bulging or expansion, including resultant cracking, of bulkheads, pavements, patios, footings, foundations, walls, floors, roofs or ceilings;

(g) Birds, vermin, rodents, or insects; or

(h) Animals owned or kept by an "insured".

Exception To c.(6)

Unless the loss is otherwise excluded, we cover loss to property covered under Coverage **A** or **B** resulting from an accidental discharge or overflow of water or steam from within a:

(i) Storm drain, or water, steam or sewer pipe, off the "residence premises"; or

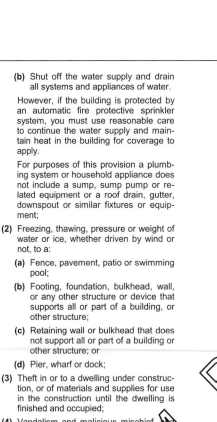

(ii) Plumbing, heating, air conditioning or automatic fire protective sprinkler system or household appliance on the "residence premises". This includes the cost to tear out and replace any part of a building, or other structure, on the "residence premises", but only when necessary to repair the system or appliance. However, such tear out and replacement coverage only applies to other structures if the water or steam causes actual damage to a building on the "residence premises".

We do not cover loss to the system or appliance from which this water or steam escaped.

For purposes of this provision, a plumbing system or household appliance does not include a sump, sump pump or related equipment or a roof drain, gutter, down spout or similar fixtures or equipment.

Section **I** – Exclusion **A.3.** Water Damage, Paragraphs **a.** and **c.** that apply to surface water and water below the surface of the ground do not apply to loss by water covered under **c.(5)** and **(6)** above.

Under **2.b.** and **c.** above, any ensuing loss to property described in Coverages **A** and **B** not precluded by any other provision in this policy is covered.

B. Coverage C – Personal Property

We insure for direct physical loss to the property described in Coverage **C** caused by any of the following perils unless the loss is excluded in Section **I** – Exclusions.

1. Fire Or Lightning

2. Windstorm Or Hail

This peril includes loss to watercraft of all types and their trailers, furnishings, equipment, and outboard engines or motors, only while inside a fully enclosed building.

This peril does not include loss to the property contained in a building caused by rain, snow, sleet, sand or dust unless the direct force of wind or hail damages the building causing an opening in a roof or wall and the rain, snow, sleet, sand or dust enters through this opening.

3. Explosion

4. Riot Or Civil Commotion

5. Aircraft

This peril includes self-propelled missiles and spacecraft.

6. Vehicles

7. Smoke

This peril means sudden and accidental damage from smoke, including the emission or puffback of smoke, soot, fumes or vapors from a boiler, furnace or related equipment.

This peril does not include loss caused by smoke from agricultural smudging or industrial operations.

8. Vandalism Or Malicious Mischief

9. Theft

a. This peril includes attempted theft and loss of property from a known place when it is likely that the property has been stolen.

b. This peril does not include loss caused by theft:

(1) Committed by an "insured";

(2) In or to a dwelling under construction, or of materials and supplies for use in the construction until the dwelling is finished and occupied;

(3) From that part of a "residence premises" rented by an "insured" to someone other than another "insured"; or

(4) That occurs off the "residence premises" of:

(a) Trailers, semitrailers and campers;

(b) Watercraft of all types, and their furnishings, equipment and outboard engines or motors; or

(c) Property while at any other residence owned by, rented to, or occupied by an "insured", except while an "insured" is temporarily living there. Property of an "insured" who is a student is covered while at the residence the student occupies to attend school as long as the student has been there at any time during the 60 days immediately before the loss.

10. Falling Objects

This peril does not include loss to property contained in a building unless the roof or an outside wall of the building is first damaged by a falling object. Damage to the falling object itself is not included.

11. Weight Of Ice, Snow Or Sleet

This peril means weight of ice, snow or sleet which causes damage to property contained in a building.

Copyright, Insurance Services Office, Inc., 1999

12. Accidental Discharge Or Overflow Of Water Or Steam

a. This peril means accidental discharge or overflow of water or steam from within a plumbing, heating, air conditioning or automatic fire protective sprinkler system or from within a household appliance.

b. This peril does not include loss:

(1) To the system or appliance from which the water or steam escaped;

(2) Caused by or resulting from freezing except as provided in Peril Insured Against **14.** Freezing;

(3) On the "residence premises" caused by accidental discharge or overflow which occurs off the "residence premises"; or

(4) Caused by mold, fungus or wet rot unless hidden within the walls or ceilings or beneath the floors or above the ceilings of a structure.

c. In this peril, a plumbing system or household appliance does not include a sump, sump pump or related equipment or a roof drain, gutter, downspout or similar fixtures or equipment.

d. Section I – Exclusion **A.3.** Water Damage, Paragraphs **a.** and **c.** that apply to surface water and water below the surface of the ground do not apply to loss by water covered under this peril.

13. Sudden And Accidental Tearing Apart, Cracking, Burning Or Bulging

This peril means sudden and accidental tearing apart, cracking, burning or bulging of a steam or hot water heating system, an air conditioning or automatic fire protective sprinkler system, or an appliance for heating water.

We do not cover loss caused by or resulting from freezing under this peril.

14. Freezing

a. This peril means freezing of a plumbing, heating, air conditioning or automatic fire protective sprinkler system or of a household appliance but only if you have used reasonable care to:

(1) Maintain heat in the building; or

(2) Shut off the water supply and drain all systems and appliances of water.

However, if the building is protected by an automatic fire protective sprinkler system, you must use reasonable care to continue the water supply and maintain heat in the building for coverage to apply.

b. In this peril, a plumbing system or household appliance does not include a sump, sump pump or related equipment or a roof drain, gutter, downspout or similar fixtures or equipment.

15. Sudden And Accidental Damage From Artificially Generated Electrical Current

This peril does not include loss to tubes, transistors, electronic components or circuitry that are a part of appliances, fixtures, computers, home entertainment units or other types of electronic apparatus.

16. Volcanic Eruption

This peril does not include loss caused by earthquake, land shock waves or tremors.

SECTION I – EXCLUSIONS

A. We do not insure for loss caused directly or indirectly by any of the following. Such loss is excluded regardless of any other cause or event contributing concurrently or in any sequence to the loss. These exclusions apply whether or not the loss event results in widespread damage or affects a substantial area.

1. Ordinance Or Law

Ordinance Or Law means any ordinance or law:

a. Requiring or regulating the construction, demolition, remodeling, renovation or repair of property, including removal of any resulting debris. This Exclusion **A.1.a.** does not apply to the amount of coverage that may be provided for in **E.11.** Ordinance Or Law under Section I – Property Coverages;

b. The requirements of which result in a loss in value to property; or

c. Requiring any "insured" or others to test for, monitor, clean up, remove, contain, treat, detoxify or neutralize, or in any way respond to, or assess the effects of, pollutants.

Pollutants means any solid, liquid, gaseous or thermal irritant or contaminant, including smoke, vapor, soot, fumes, acids, alkalis, chemicals and waste. Waste includes materials to be recycled, reconditioned or reclaimed.

This Exclusion **A.1.** applies whether or not the property has been physically damaged.

2. Earth Movement

Earth Movement means:

a. Earthquake, including land shock waves or tremors before, during or after a volcanic eruption;

 SAMPLE

    b. Landslide, mudslide or mudflow;

    c. Subsidence or sinkhole; or

    d. Any other earth movement including earth sinking, rising or shifting;

caused by or resulting from human or animal forces or any act of nature unless direct loss by fire or explosion ensues and then we will pay only for the ensuing loss.

This Exclusion **A.2.** does not apply to loss by theft.

3. Water Damage

Water Damage means:

    a. Flood, surface water, waves, tidal water, overflow of a body of water, or spray from any of these, whether or not driven by wind;

    b. Water or water-borne material which backs up through sewers or drains or which overflows or is discharged from a sump, sump pump or related equipment; or

    c. Water or water-borne material below the surface of the ground, including water which exerts pressure on or seeps or leaks through a building, sidewalk, driveway, foundation, swimming pool or other structure;

caused by or resulting from human or animal forces or any act of nature.

Direct loss by fire, explosion or theft resulting from water damage is covered.

4. Power Failure

Power Failure means the failure of power or other utility service if the failure takes place off the "residence premises". But if the failure results in a loss, from a Peril Insured Against on the "residence premises", we will pay for the loss caused by that peril.

5. Neglect

Neglect means neglect of an "insured" to use all reasonable means to save and preserve property at and after the time of a loss.

6. War

War includes the following and any consequence of any of the following:

    a. Undeclared war, civil war, insurrection, rebellion or revolution;

    b. Warlike act by a military force or military personnel; or

    c. Destruction, seizure or use for a military purpose.

Discharge of a nuclear weapon will be deemed a warlike act even if accidental.

7. Nuclear Hazard

This Exclusion **A.7.** pertains to Nuclear Hazard to the extent set forth in **M.** Nuclear Hazard Clause under Section **I** – Conditions.

8. Intentional Loss

Intentional Loss means any loss arising out of any act an "insured" commits or conspires to commit with the intent to cause a loss.

In the event of such loss, no "insured" is entitled to coverage, even "insureds" who did not commit or conspire to commit the act causing the loss.

9. Governmental Action

Governmental Action means the destruction, confiscation or seizure of property described in Coverage **A**, **B** or **C** by order of any governmental or public authority.

This exclusion does not apply to such acts ordered by any governmental or public authority that are taken at the time of a fire to prevent its spread, if the loss caused by fire would be covered under this policy.

B. We do not insure for loss to property described in Coverages **A** and **B** caused by any of the following. However, any ensuing loss to property described in Coverages **A** and **B** not precluded by any other provision in this policy is covered.

    1. Weather conditions. However, this exclusion only applies if weather conditions contribute in any way with a cause or event excluded in **A.** above to produce the loss.

    2. Acts or decisions, including the failure to act or decide, of any person, group, organization or governmental body.

    3. Faulty, inadequate or defective:

        a. Planning, zoning, development, surveying, siting;

        b. Design, specifications, workmanship, repair, construction, renovation, remodeling, grading, compaction;

        c. Materials used in repair, construction, renovation or remodeling; or

        d. Maintenance;

    of part or all of any property whether on or off the "residence premises".

SECTION I – CONDITIONS

A. Insurable Interest And Limit Of Liability

Even if more than one person has an insurable interest in the property covered, we will not be liable in any one loss:

1. To an "insured" for more than the amount of such "insured's" interest at the time of loss; or

2. For more than the applicable limit of liability.

B. Duties After Loss

In case of a loss to covered property, we have no duty to provide coverage under this policy if the failure to comply with the following duties is prejudicial to us. These duties must be performed either by you, an "insured" seeking coverage, or a representative of either:

1. Give prompt notice to us or our agent;

2. Notify the police in case of loss by theft;

3. Notify the credit card or electronic fund transfer card or access device company in case of loss as provided for in **E.6.** Credit Card, Electronic Fund Transfer Card Or Access Device, Forgery And Counterfeit Money under Section **I** – Property Coverages;

4. Protect the property from further damage. If repairs to the property are required, you must:

   a. Make reasonable and necessary repairs to protect the property; and

   b. Keep an accurate record of repair expenses;

5. Cooperate with us in the investigation of a claim;

6. Prepare an inventory of damaged personal property showing the quantity, description, actual cash value and amount of loss. Attach all bills, receipts and related documents that justify the figures in the inventory;

7. As often as we reasonably require:

   a. Show the damaged property;

   b. Provide us with records and documents we request and permit us to make copies; and

   c. Submit to examination under oath, while not in the presence of another "insured", and sign the same;

8. Send to us, within 60 days after our request, your signed, sworn proof of loss which sets forth, to the best of your knowledge and belief:

   a. The time and cause of loss;

   b. The interests of all "insureds" and all others in the property involved and all liens on the property;

   c. Other insurance which may cover the loss;

d. Changes in title or occupancy of the property during the term of the policy;

e. Specifications of damaged buildings and detailed repair estimates;

f. The inventory of damaged personal property described in **6.** above;

g. Receipts for additional living expenses incurred and records that support the fair rental value loss; and

h. Evidence or affidavit that supports a claim under **E.6.** Credit Card, Electronic Fund Transfer Card Or Access Device, Forgery And Counterfeit Money under Section **I** – Property Coverages, stating the amount and cause of loss.

C. Loss Settlement

In this Condition **C.**, the terms "cost to repair or replace" and "replacement cost" do not include the increased costs incurred to comply with the enforcement of any ordinance or law, except to the extent that coverage for these increased costs is provided in **E.11.** Ordinance Or Law under Section **I** – Property Coverages. Covered property losses are settled as follows:

1. Property of the following types:

   a. Personal property;

   b. Awnings, carpeting, household appliances, outdoor antennas and outdoor equipment, whether or not attached to buildings;

   c. Structures that are not buildings; and

   d. Grave markers, including mausoleums;

   at actual cash value at the time of loss but not more than the amount required to repair or replace.

2. Buildings covered under Coverage **A** or **B** at replacement cost without deduction for depreciation, subject to the following:

   a. If, at the time of loss, the amount of insurance in this policy on the damaged building is 80% or more of the full replacement cost of the building immediately before the loss, we will pay the cost to repair or replace, after application of any deductible and without deduction for depreciation, but not more than the least of the following amounts:

      (1) The limit of liability under this policy that applies to the building;

      (2) The replacement cost of that part of the building damaged with material of like kind and quality and for like use; or

      (3) The necessary amount actually spent to repair or replace the damaged building.

If the building is rebuilt at a new premises, the cost described in **(2)** above is limited to the cost which would have been incurred if the building had been built at the original premises.

b. If, at the time of loss, the amount of insurance in this policy on the damaged building is less than 80% of the full replacement cost of the building immediately before the loss, we will pay the greater of the following amounts, but not more than the limit of liability under this policy that applies to the building:

(1) The actual cash value of that part of the building damaged; or

(2) That proportion of the cost to repair or replace, after application of any deductible and without deduction for depreciation, that part of the building damaged, which the total amount of insurance in this policy on the damaged building bears to 80% of the replacement cost of the building.

c. To determine the amount of insurance required to equal 80% of the full replacement cost of the building immediately before the loss, do not include the value of:

(1) Excavations, footings, foundations, piers, or any other structures or devices that support all or part of the building, which are below the undersurface of the lowest basement floor;

(2) Those supports described in **(1)** above which are below the surface of the ground inside the foundation walls, if there is no basement; and

(3) Underground flues, pipes, wiring and drains.

d. We will pay no more than the actual cash value of the damage until actual repair or replacement is complete. Once actual repair or replacement is complete, we will settle the loss as noted in **2.a.** and **b.** above.

However, if the cost to repair or replace the damage is both:

(1) Less than 5% of the amount of insurance in this policy on the building; and

(2) Less than $2,500;

we will settle the loss as noted in **2.a.** and **b.** above whether or not actual repair or replacement is complete.

e. You may disregard the replacement cost loss settlement provisions and make claim under this policy for loss to buildings on an actual cash value basis. You may then make claim for any additional liability according to the provisions of this Condition **C.** Loss Settlement, provided you notify us of your intent to do so within 180 days after the date of loss.

D. Loss To A Pair Or Set

In case of loss to a pair or set we may elect to:

1. Repair or replace any part to restore the pair or set to its value before the loss; or

2. Pay the difference between actual cash value of the property before and after the loss.

E. Appraisal

If you and we fail to agree on the amount of loss, either may demand an appraisal of the loss. In this event, each party will choose a competent and impartial appraiser within 20 days after receiving a written request from the other. The two appraisers will choose an umpire. If they cannot agree upon an umpire within 15 days, you or we may request that the choice be made by a judge of a court of record in the state where the "residence premises" is located. The appraisers will separately set the amount of loss. If the appraisers submit a written report of an agreement to us, the amount agreed upon will be the amount of loss. If they fail to agree, they will submit their differences to the umpire. A decision agreed to by any two will set the amount of loss.

Each party will:

1. Pay its own appraiser; and

2. Bear the other expenses of the appraisal and umpire equally.

F. Other Insurance And Service Agreement

If a loss covered by this policy is also covered by:

1. Other insurance, we will pay only the proportion of the loss that the limit of liability that applies under this policy bears to the total amount of insurance covering the loss; or

2. A service agreement, this insurance is excess over any amounts payable under any such agreement. Service agreement means a service plan, property restoration plan, home warranty or other similar service warranty agreement, even if it is characterized as insurance.

G. Suit Against Us

No action can be brought against us unless there has been full compliance with all of the terms under Section **I** of this policy and the action is started within two years after the date of loss.

H. Our Option

If we give you written notice within 30 days after we receive your signed, sworn proof of loss, we may repair or replace any part of the damaged property with material or property of like kind and quality.

I. Loss Payment

We will adjust all losses with you. We will pay you unless some other person is named in the policy or is legally entitled to receive payment. Loss will be payable 60 days after we receive your proof of loss and:

1. Reach an agreement with you;
2. There is an entry of a final judgment; or
3. There is a filing of an appraisal award with us.

J. Abandonment Of Property

We need not accept any property abandoned by an "insured".

K. Mortgage Clause

1. If a mortgagee is named in this policy, any loss payable under Coverage **A** or **B** will be paid to the mortgagee and you, as interests appear. If more than one mortgagee is named, the order of payment will be the same as the order of precedence of the mortgages.

2. If we deny your claim, that denial will not apply to a valid claim of the mortgagee, if the mortgagee:

   a. Notifies us of any change in ownership, occupancy or substantial change in risk of which the mortgagee is aware;

   b. Pays any premium due under this policy on demand if you have neglected to pay the premium; and

   c. Submits a signed, sworn statement of loss within 60 days after receiving notice from us of your failure to do so. Paragraphs **E.** Appraisal, **G.** Suit Against Us and **I.** Loss Payment under Section I Conditions also apply to the mortgagee.

3. If we decide to cancel or not to renew this policy, the mortgagee will be notified at least 10 days before the date cancellation or nonrenewal takes effect.

4. If we pay the mortgagee for any loss and deny payment to you:

   a. We are subrogated to all the rights of the mortgagee granted under the mortgage on the property; or

   b. At our option, we may pay to the mortgagee the whole principal on the mortgage plus any accrued interest. In this event, we will receive a full assignment and transfer of the mortgage and all securities held as collateral to the mortgage debt.

5. Subrogation will not impair the right of the mortgagee to recover the full amount of the mortgagee's claim.

L. No Benefit To Bailee

We will not recognize any assignment or grant any coverage that benefits a person or organization holding, storing or moving property for a fee regardless of any other provision of this policy.

M. Nuclear Hazard Clause

1. "Nuclear Hazard" means any nuclear reaction, radiation, or radioactive contamination, all whether controlled or uncontrolled or however caused, or any consequence of any of these.

2. Loss caused by the nuclear hazard will not be considered loss caused by fire, explosion, or smoke, whether these perils are specifically named in or otherwise included within the Perils Insured Against.

3. This policy does not apply under Section I to loss caused directly or indirectly by nuclear hazard, except that direct loss by fire resulting from the nuclear hazard is covered.

N. Recovered Property

If you or we recover any property for which we have made payment under this policy, you or we will notify the other of the recovery. At your option, the property will be returned to or retained by you or it will become our property. If the recovered property is returned to or retained by you, the loss payment will be adjusted based on the amount you received for the recovered property.

O. Volcanic Eruption Period

One or more volcanic eruptions that occur within a 72 hour period will be considered as one volcanic eruption.

P. Policy Period

This policy applies only to loss which occurs during the policy period.

Q. Concealment Or Fraud

We provide coverage to no "insureds" under this policy if, whether before or after a loss, an "insured" has:

1. Intentionally concealed or misrepresented any material fact or circumstance;

2. Engaged in fraudulent conduct; or

3. Made false statements;

relating to this insurance.

R. Loss Payable Clause

If the Declarations show a loss payee for certain listed insured personal property, the definition of "insured" is changed to include that loss payee with respect to that property.

If we decide to cancel or not renew this policy, that loss payee will be notified in writing.

SECTION II – LIABILITY COVERAGES

A. Coverage E – Personal Liability

If a claim is made or a suit is brought against an "insured" for damages because of "bodily injury" or "property damage" caused by an "occurrence" to which this coverage applies, we will:

1. Pay up to our limit of liability for the damages for which an "insured" is legally liable. Damages include prejudgment interest awarded against an "insured"; and

2. Provide a defense at our expense by counsel of our choice, even if the suit is groundless, false or fraudulent. We may investigate and settle any claim or suit that we decide is appropriate. Our duty to settle or defend ends when our limit of liability for the "occurrence" has been exhausted by payment of a judgment or settlement.

B. Coverage F – Medical Payments To Others

We will pay the necessary medical expenses that are incurred or medically ascertained within three years from the date of an accident causing "bodily injury". Medical expenses means reasonable charges for medical, surgical, x-ray, dental, ambulance, hospital, professional nursing, prosthetic devices and funeral services. This coverage does not apply to you or regular residents of your household except "residence employees". As to others, this coverage applies only:

1. To a person on the "insured location" with the permission of an "insured"; or

2. To a person off the "insured location", if the "bodily injury":

a. Arises out of a condition on the "insured location" or the ways immediately adjoining;

b. Is caused by the activities of an "insured";

c. Is caused by a "residence employee" in the course of the "residence employee's" employment by an "insured"; or

d. Is caused by an animal owned by or in the care of an "insured".

SECTION II – EXCLUSIONS

A. "Motor Vehicle Liability"

1. Coverages **E** and **F** do not apply to any "motor vehicle liability" if, at the time and place of an "occurrence", the involved "motor vehicle":

a. Is registered for use on public roads or property;

b. Is not registered for use on public roads or property, but such registration is required by a law, or regulation issued by a government agency, for it to be used at the place of the "occurrence"; or

c. Is being:

(1) Operated in, or practicing for, any prearranged or organized race, speed contest or other competition;

(2) Rented to others;

(3) Used to carry persons or cargo for a charge; or

(4) Used for any "business" purpose except for a motorized golf cart while on a golfing facility.

2. If Exclusion **A.1.** does not apply, there is still no coverage for "motor vehicle liability" unless the "motor vehicle" is:

a. In dead storage on an "insured location";

b. Used solely to service an "insured's" residence;

c. Designed to assist the handicapped and, at the time of an "occurrence", it is:

(1) Being used to assist a handicapped person; or

(2) Parked on an "insured location";

d. Designed for recreational use off public roads and:

(1) Not owned by an "insured"; or

(2) Owned by an "insured" provided the "occurrence" takes place on an "insured location" as defined in Definitions **B. 6.a., b., d., e.** or **h.**; or

e. A motorized golf cart that is owned by an "insured", designed to carry up to 4 persons, not built or modified after manufacture to exceed a speed of 25 miles per hour on level ground and, at the time of an "occurrence", is within the legal boundaries of:

(1) A golfing facility and is parked or stored there, or being used by an "insured" to:

(a) Play the game of golf or for other recreational or leisure activity allowed by the facility;

Copyright, Insurance Services Office, Inc., 1999   HO 00 03 10 00

SAMPLE

(b) Travel to or from an area where "motor vehicles" or golf carts are parked or stored; or

(c) Cross public roads at designated points to access other parts of the golfing facility; or

(2) A private residential community, including its public roads upon which a motorized golf cart can legally travel, which is subject to the authority of a property owners association and contains an "insured's" residence.

B. "Watercraft Liability"

1. Coverages **E** and **F** do not apply to any "watercraft liability" if, at the time of an "occurrence", the involved watercraft is being:

a. Operated in, or practicing for, any prearranged or organized race, speed contest or other competition. This exclusion does not apply to a sailing vessel or a predicted log cruise;

b. Rented to others;

c. Used to carry persons or cargo for a charge; or

d. Used for any "business" purpose.

2. If Exclusion **B.1.** does not apply, there is still no coverage for "watercraft liability" unless, at the time of the "occurrence", the watercraft;

a. Is stored;

b. Is a sailing vessel, with or without auxiliary power, that is:

(1) Less than 26 feet in overall length; or

(2) 26 feet or more in overall length and not owned by or rented to an "insured"; or

c. Is not a sailing vessel and is powered by:

(1) An inboard or inboard-outdrive engine or motor, including those that power a water jet pump, of:

(a) 50 horsepower or less and not owned by an "insured"; or

(b) More than 50 horsepower and not owned by or rented to an "insured"; or

(2) One or more outboard engines or motors with:

(a) 25 total horsepower or less;

(b) More than 25 horsepower if the outboard engine or motor is not owned by an "insured";

(c) More than 25 horsepower if the outboard engine or motor is owned by an "insured" who acquired it during the policy period; or

(d) More than 25 horsepower if the outboard engine or motor is owned by an "insured" who acquired it before the policy period, but only if:

(i) You declare them at policy inception; or

(ii) Your intent to insure them is reported to us in writing within 45 days after you acquire them.

The coverages in **(c)** and **(d)** above apply for the policy period.

Horsepower means the maximum power rating assigned to the engine or motor by the manufacturer.

C. "Aircraft Liability"

This policy does not cover "aircraft liability".

D. "Hovercraft Liability"

This policy does not cover "hovercraft liability".

E. Coverage E – Personal Liability And Coverage F – Medical Payments To Others

Coverages **E** and **F** do not apply to the following:

1. Expected Or Intended Injury

"Bodily injury" or "property damage" which is expected or intended by an "insured" even if the resulting "bodily injury" or "property damage":

a. Is of a different kind, quality or degree than initially expected or intended; or

b. Is sustained by a different person, entity, real or personal property, than initially expected or intended.

However, this Exclusion **E.1.** does not apply to "bodily injury" resulting from the use of reasonable force by an "insured" to protect persons or property;

2. "Business"

a. "Bodily injury" or "property damage" arising out of or in connection with a "business" conducted from an "insured location" or engaged in by an "insured", whether or not the "business" is owned or operated by an "insured" or employs an "insured".

This Exclusion **E.2.** applies but is not limited to an act or omission, regardless of its nature or circumstance, involving a service or duty rendered, promised, owed, or implied to be provided because of the nature of the "business".

b. This Exclusion **E.2.** does not apply to:

(1) The rental or holding for rental of an "insured location";

SAMPLE

  (a) On an occasional basis if used only as a residence;

  (b) In part for use only as a residence, unless a single family unit is intended for use by the occupying family to lodge more than two roomers or boarders; or

  (c) In part, as an office, school, studio or private garage; and

 (2) An "insured" under the age of 21 years involved in a part-time or occasional, self-employed "business" with no employees;

3. Professional Services

"Bodily injury" or "property damage" arising out of the rendering of or failure to render professional services;

4. "Insured's" Premises Not An "Insured Location"

"Bodily injury" or "property damage" arising out of a premises:

 a. Owned by an "insured";

 b. Rented to an "insured"; or

 c. Rented to others by an "insured";

that is not an "insured location";

5. War

"Bodily injury" or "property damage" caused directly or indirectly by war, including the following and any consequence of any of the following:

 a. Undeclared war, civil war, insurrection, rebellion or revolution;

 b. Warlike act by a military force or military personnel; or

 c. Destruction, seizure or use for a military purpose.

Discharge of a nuclear weapon will be deemed a warlike act even if accidental;

6. Communicable Disease

"Bodily injury" or "property damage" which arises out of the transmission of a communicable disease by an "insured";

7. Sexual Molestation, Corporal Punishment Or Physical Or Mental Abuse

"Bodily injury" or "property damage" arising out of sexual molestation, corporal punishment or physical or mental abuse; or

8. Controlled Substance

"Bodily injury" or "property damage" arising out of the use, sale, manufacture, delivery, transfer or possession by any person of a Controlled Substance as defined by the Federal Food and Drug Law at 21 U.S.C.A. Sections 811 and 812. Controlled Substances include but are not limited to cocaine, LSD, marijuana and all narcotic drugs. However, this exclusion does not apply to the legitimate use of prescription drugs by a person following the orders of a licensed physician.

Exclusions **A.** "Motor Vehicle Liability", **B.** "Watercraft Liability", **C.** "Aircraft Liability", **D.** "Hovercraft Liability" and **E.4.** "Insured's" Premises Not An "Insured Location" do not apply to "bodily injury" to a "residence employee" arising out of and in the course of the "residence employee's" employment by an "insured".

F. Coverage E – Personal Liability

Coverage E does not apply to:

1. Liability:

 a. For any loss assessment charged against you as a member of an association, corporation or community of property owners, except as provided in **D.** Loss Assessment under Section **II** – Additional Coverages;

 b. Under any contract or agreement entered into by an "insured". However, this exclusion does not apply to written contracts:

  (1) That directly relate to the ownership, maintenance or use of an "insured location"; or

  (2) Where the liability of others is assumed by you prior to an "occurrence";

 unless excluded in **a.** above or elsewhere in this policy;

2. "Property damage" to property owned by an "insured". This includes costs or expenses incurred by an "insured" or others to repair, replace, enhance, restore or maintain such property to prevent injury to a person or damage to property of others, whether on or away from an "insured location";

3. "Property damage" to property rented to, occupied or used by or in the care of an "insured". This exclusion does not apply to "property damage" caused by fire, smoke or explosion;

4. "Bodily injury" to any person eligible to receive any benefits voluntarily provided or required to be provided by an "insured" under any:

 a. Workers' compensation law;

b. Non-occupational disability law; or

c. Occupational disease law;

5. "Bodily injury" or "property damage" for which an "insured" under this policy:

 a. Is also an insured under a nuclear energy liability policy issued by the:

  (1) Nuclear Energy Liability Insurance Association;

  (2) Mutual Atomic Energy Liability Underwriters;

  (3) Nuclear Insurance Association of Canada;

  or any of their successors; or

 b. Would be an insured under such a policy but for the exhaustion of its limit of liability; or

6. "Bodily injury" to you or an "insured" as defined under Definitions **5.a.** or **b.**

 This exclusion also applies to any claim made or suit brought against you or an "insured":

 a. To repay; or

 b. Share damages with;

 another person who may be obligated to pay damages because of "bodily injury" to an "insured".

G. Coverage F – Medical Payments To Others

 Coverage **F** does not apply to "bodily injury":

1. To a "residence employee" if the "bodily injury":

 a. Occurs off the "insured location"; and

 b. Does not arise out of or in the course of the "residence employee's" employment by an "insured";

2. To any person eligible to receive benefits voluntarily provided or required to be provided under any:

 a. Workers' compensation law;

 b. Non-occupational disability law; or

 c. Occupational disease law;

3. From any:

 a. Nuclear reaction;

 b. Nuclear radiation; or

 c. Radioactive contamination;

 all whether controlled or uncontrolled or however caused; or

 d. Any consequence of any of these; or

4. To any person, other than a "residence employee" of an "insured", regularly residing on any part of the "insured location".

SECTION II – ADDITIONAL COVERAGES

We cover the following in addition to the limits of liability:

A. Claim Expenses

 We pay:

1. Expenses we incur and costs taxed against an "insured" in any suit we defend;

2. Premiums on bonds required in a suit we defend, but not for bond amounts more than the Coverage **E** limit of liability. We need not apply for or furnish any bond;

3. Reasonable expenses incurred by an "insured" at our request, including actual loss of earnings (but not loss of other income) up to $250 per day, for assisting us in the investigation or defense of a claim or suit; and

4. Interest on the entire judgment which accrues after entry of the judgment and before we pay or tender, or deposit in court that part of the judgment which does not exceed the limit of liability that applies.

B. First Aid Expenses

 We will pay expenses for first aid to others incurred by an "insured" for "bodily injury" covered under this policy. We will not pay for first aid to an "insured".

C. Damage To Property Of Others

1. We will pay, at replacement cost, up to $1,000 per "occurrence" for "property damage" to property of others caused by an "insured".

2. We will not pay for "property damage":

 a. To the extent of any amount recoverable under Section **I**;

 b. Caused intentionally by an "insured" who is 13 years of age or older;

 c. To property owned by an "insured";

 d. To property owned by or rented to a tenant of an "insured" or a resident in your household; or

 e. Arising out of:

  (1) A "business" engaged in by an "insured";

  (2) Any act or omission in connection with a premises owned, rented or controlled by an "insured", other than the "insured location"; or

  (3) The ownership, maintenance, occupancy, operation, use, loading or unloading of aircraft, hovercraft, watercraft or "motor vehicles".

This exclusion **e.(3)** does not apply to a "motor vehicle" that:

(a) Is designed for recreational use off public roads;

(b) Is not owned by an "insured"; and

(c) At the time of the "occurrence", is not required by law, or regulation issued by a government agency, to have been registered for it to be used on public roads or property.

D. Loss Assessment

1. We will pay up to $1,000 for your share of loss assessment charged against you, as owner or tenant of the "residence premises", during the policy period by a corporation or association of property owners, when the assessment is made as a result of:

a. "Bodily injury" or "property damage" not excluded from coverage under Section II – Exclusions; or

b. Liability for an act of a director, officer or trustee in the capacity as a director, officer or trustee, provided such person:

(1) Is elected by the members of a corporation or association of property owners; and

(2) Serves without deriving any income from the exercise of duties which are solely on behalf of a corporation or association of property owners.

2. Paragraph I. Policy Period under Section II – Conditions does not apply to this Loss Assessment Coverage.

3. Regardless of the number of assessments, the limit of $1,000 is the most we will pay for loss arising out of:

a. One accident, including continuous or repeated exposure to substantially the same general harmful condition; or

b. A covered act of a director, officer or trustee. An act involving more than one director, officer or trustee is considered to be a single act.

4. We do not cover assessments charged against you or a corporation or association of property owners by any governmental body.

SECTION II – CONDITIONS

A. Limit Of Liability

Our total liability under Coverage **E** for all damages resulting from any one "occurrence" will not be more than the Coverage **E** limit of liability shown in the Declarations. This limit is the same regardless of the number of "insureds", claims made or persons injured. All "bodily injury" and "property damage" resulting from any one accident or from continuous or repeated exposure to substantially the same general harmful conditions shall be considered to be the result of one "occurrence".

Our total liability under Coverage **F** for all medical expense payable for "bodily injury" to one person as the result of one accident will not be more than the Coverage **F** limit of liability shown in the Declarations.

B. Severability Of Insurance

This insurance applies separately to each "insured". This condition will not increase our limit of liability for any one "occurrence".

C. Duties After "Occurrence"

In case of an "occurrence", you or another "insured" will perform the following duties that apply. We have no duty to provide coverage under this policy if your failure to comply with the following duties is prejudicial to us. You will help us by seeing that these duties are performed:

1. Give written notice to us or our agent as soon as is practical, which sets forth:

a. The identity of the policy and the "named insured" shown in the Declarations;

b. Reasonably available information on the time, place and circumstances of the "occurrence"; and

c. Names and addresses of any claimants and witnesses;

2. Cooperate with us in the investigation, settlement or defense of any claim or suit;

3. Promptly forward to us every notice, demand, summons or other process relating to the "occurrence";

4. At our request, help us:

a. To make settlement;

b. To enforce any right of contribution or indemnity against any person or organization who may be liable to an "insured";

 Copyright, Insurance Services Office, Inc., 1999 HO 00 03 10 00

    c. With the conduct of suits and attend hearings and trials; and

    d. To secure and give evidence and obtain the attendance of witnesses;

5. With respect to **C.** Damage To Property Of Others under Section **II** – Additional Coverages, submit to us within 60 days after the loss, a sworn statement of loss and show the damaged property, if in an "insured's" control;

6. No "insured" shall, except at such "insured's" own cost, voluntarily make payment, assume obligation or incur expense other than for first aid to others at the time of the "bodily injury".

D. Duties Of An Injured Person – Coverage F – Medical Payments To Others

1. The injured person or someone acting for the injured person will:

    a. Give us written proof of claim, under oath if required, as soon as is practical; and

    b. Authorize us to obtain copies of medical reports and records.

2. The injured person will submit to a physical exam by a doctor of our choice when and as often as we reasonably require.

E. Payment Of Claim – Coverage F – Medical Payments To Others

Payment under this coverage is not an admission of liability by an "insured" or us.

F. Suit Against Us

1. No action can be brought against us unless there has been full compliance with all of the terms under this Section **II**.

2. No one will have the right to join us as a party to any action against an "insured".

3. Also, no action with respect to Coverage **E** can be brought against us until the obligation of such "insured" has been determined by final judgment or agreement signed by us.

G. Bankruptcy Of An "Insured"

Bankruptcy or insolvency of an "insured" will not relieve us of our obligations under this policy.

H. Other Insurance

This insurance is excess over other valid and collectible insurance except insurance written specifically to cover as excess over the limits of liability that apply in this policy.

I. Policy Period

This policy applies only to "bodily injury" or "property damage" which occurs during the policy period.

J. Concealment Or Fraud

We do not provide coverage to an "insured" who, whether before or after a loss, has:

1. Intentionally concealed or misrepresented any material fact or circumstance;

2. Engaged in fraudulent conduct; or

3. Made false statements;

relating to this insurance.

SECTIONS I AND II – CONDITIONS

A. Liberalization Clause

If we make a change which broadens coverage under this edition of our policy without additional premium charge, that change will automatically apply to your insurance as of the date we implement the change in your state, provided that this implementation date falls within 60 days prior to or during the policy period stated in the Declarations.

This Liberalization Clause does not apply to changes implemented with a general program revision that includes both broadenings and restrictions in coverage, whether that general program revision is implemented through introduction of:

1. A subsequent edition of this policy; or

2. An amendatory endorsement.

B. Waiver Or Change Of Policy Provisions

A waiver or change of a provision of this policy must be in writing by us to be valid. Our request for an appraisal or examination will not waive any of our rights.

C. Cancellation

1. You may cancel this policy at any time by returning it to us or by letting us know in writing of the date cancellation is to take effect.

2. We may cancel this policy only for the reasons stated below by letting you know in writing of the date cancellation takes effect. This cancellation notice may be delivered to you, or mailed to you at your mailing address shown in the Declarations. Proof of mailing will be sufficient proof of notice.

    a. When you have not paid the premium, we may cancel at any time by letting you know at least 10 days before the date cancellation takes effect.

    b. When this policy has been in effect for less than 60 days and is not a renewal with us, we may cancel for any reason by letting you know at least 10 days before the date cancellation takes effect.

c. When this policy has been in effect for 60 days or more, or at any time if it is a renewal with us, we may cancel:

(1) If there has been a material misrepresentation of fact which if known to us would have caused us not to issue the policy; or

(2) If the risk has changed substantially since the policy was issued.

This can be done by letting you know at least 30 days before the date cancellation takes effect.

d. When this policy is written for a period of more than one year, we may cancel for any reason at anniversary by letting you know at least 30 days before the date cancellation takes effect.

3. When this policy is canceled, the premium for the period from the date of cancellation to the expiration date will be refunded pro rata.

4. If the return premium is not refunded with the notice of cancellation or when this policy is returned to us, we will refund it within a reasonable time after the date cancellation takes effect.

D. Nonrenewal

We may elect not to renew this policy. We may do so by delivering to you, or mailing to you at your mailing address shown in the Declarations, written notice at least 30 days before the expiration date of this policy. Proof of mailing will be sufficient proof of notice.

E. Assignment

Assignment of this policy will not be valid unless we give our written consent.

F. Subrogation

An "insured" may waive in writing before a loss all rights of recovery against any person. If not waived, we may require an assignment of rights of recovery for a loss to the extent that payment is made by us.

If an assignment is sought, an "insured" must sign and deliver all related papers and cooperate with us.

Subrogation does not apply to Coverage **F** or Paragraph **C.** Damage To Property Of Others under Section **II** – Additional Coverages.

G. Death

If any person named in the Declarations or the spouse, if a resident of the same household, dies, the following apply:

1. We insure the legal representative of the deceased but only with respect to the premises and property of the deceased covered under the policy at the time of death; and

2. "Insured" includes:

a. An "insured" who is a member of your household at the time of your death, but only while a resident of the "residence premises"; and

b. With respect to your property, the person having proper temporary custody of the property until appointment and qualification of a legal representative.

 Copyright, Insurance Services Office, Inc., 1999 **HO 00 03 10 00**

were early formulations of the all risk concept in the marine context. Property insurance coverage inland was much more restrictive. Nineteenth-century property insurance policies were called "fire insurance" policies for a reason — all they covered was damage by fire. To get coverage against other perils, one had to buy another insurance policy. Over time, property insurers began offering coverage against other perils. At the same time, marine insurers began extending their all risk concept inland, through "inland marine policies" offered to shipping companies and people shipping goods—by canal, rail, and eventually truck. As inland marine insurers gained market share, commercial property insurers responded by increasing the perils they were willing to cover to the point where, as a practical matter, the "all risk" coverage offered by the inland marine insurers and the "named peril" coverage offered by commercial property insurers was almost identical. At that point (approximately 1960 in the United States), the commercial property insurers did the logical thing and began to offer all risk coverage.

In switching from named peril to all risk insurance, the goal was not to dramatically expand the scope of coverage (that had already been accomplished), but to gain a marketing advantage and to change the burden of proof. Insurers accomplished their goal of maintaining the overall scope of property insurance coverage by drafting a series of exclusions (some borrowed from existing inland marine insurance policies) detailing the perils and damage that would not be insured.

The place where this history is most deeply embedded in property insurance policies is in the "ensuing loss" provisions of some property insurance exclusions. In drafting the new exclusions for the all risk form, insurers realized that there was a possibility that the exclusions would eliminate coverage that had been provided by the named peril policies. Named peril policies had provided very broad coverage for losses that resulted from the named perils, and insurers did not want that coverage reduced by the new exclusions. For example, more than a few fires surely had been caused by perils that would be excluded under the new all risk form, such as "wear and tear" (e.g., frayed wiring), "faulty materials" (e.g., defective fireproofing), and even "earth movement" (e.g., insurers had paid many losses following the San Francisco earthquake because of the fires that broke out).

To prevent the all risk policies from reducing the coverage previously provided against named perils, insurers leavened some of the new exclusions with "ensuing loss" provisions. For example, if you look in the right column on page 12 of Figure 3.1 in paragraph B you will see the following:

> However, any ensuing loss to property described in Coverages A and B not precluded by any other provision in this policy is covered.

The concept behind provisions of this sort is to preserve coverage in the event that an excluded peril causes a traditionally covered form of harm, as when "wear and tear" leads to a fire.

Ensuing loss provisions clarify how insurance policies respond to one variety of losses in which there are both excluded and covered causes of harm. Multiple causation cases come in many different varieties, however, and almost every variety has led to litigation. Inherent in the decision to exclude some perils is the need for courts to referee disputes about whether the insurance company is correctly drawing the line between covered and uncovered losses.

The line drawing tool that has produced the greatest amount of litigation is the doctrine of "proximate cause," which is sometimes called the doctrine of "efficient proximate cause" to distinguish the insurance law doctrine from the tort law doctrine of the same name. Like the analogous tort doctrine, the insurance law doctrine is a tool that courts use to distinguish between causes with legal significance and causes without legal significance. Just as there can be a "cause in fact" that is not a "proximate cause" of a harm for purposes of tort law, so too can there be a "but for" cause of a loss that is not an "efficient proximate cause" for purposes of property insurance law. For example, in a famous case involving property damage caused by the eruption of Mt. St. Helens, the Washington Supreme Court upheld a decision by the trial court that the jury should be asked to decide whether the efficient proximate cause of the loss was an "explosion"—which was covered by the policy—or "earth movement"—which was excluded. *See Graham v. Public Employees Mut. Ins. Co.*, 656 P.2d 1077 (Wash. 1983). Because it was the movement of earth that, in the end, actually destroyed the homes, earth movement was clearly a cause—and an excluded cause at that—of the loss. Yet the court held that a reasonable jury could find that earth movement was not an efficient proximate cause of the loss.

Some insurance companies were sufficiently upset by this and other decisions (which, in their view, required them to bear risks that they had attempted to exclude) that they attempted to rewrite their policies so that the efficient proximate cause doctrine would not apply. Whether they were successful is the question presented by the next case.

STATE FARM FIRE & CASUALTY CO. v. BONGEN

Supreme Court of Alaska
925 P.2d 1042 (1996)

COMPTON, C.J. Jerome Bongen and Elizabeth Bongen owned a home on Pillar Mountain in Kodiak. In the late 1980's, Kodiak Electric Association (KEA) clear-cut a right-of-way above the home to install transmission lines on City of Kodiak property. On October 31, 1991, following heavy rains, a mudslide destroyed the Bongen home. According to the Bongens' expert, the KEA transmission line project "contributed to or caused damage" to the Bongen home.

The Bongens filed a claim with their insurer, State Farm Fire and Casualty Company (State Farm). Their policy contained the following exclusion:

> We do not insure under any coverage for any loss which would not have occurred in the absence of one or more of the following excluded events. We do not insure for such loss regardless of: (a) the cause of the excluded event; or (b) other causes of the loss; or (c) whether other causes acted concurrently or in any sequence with the excluded event to produce the loss; or (d) whether the event occurs suddenly or gradually, involves isolated or widespread damage, arises from natural or external forces, or occurs as a result of any combination of these:
>
> . . . Earth Movement, meaning the sinking, rising, shifting, expanding or contracting of earth, all whether combined with water or not. Earth movement includes but is not limited to earthquake, landslide, mudflow, sinkhole, subsidence and erosion. Earth movement also includes volcanic explosion or lava flow. . . .

State Farm denied coverage based on this exclusion.

B.   The Earth Movement Exclusion Is Enforceable

The Bongens argue that, under the efficient proximate cause rule, the loss of their house is covered under the insurance policy. They claim that "the negligence of [KEA] and the City of Kodiak in undermining the soils above the homes" is a "covered event."

The Bongens' policy excluded from coverage any loss resulting from earth movement, regardless of the cause of the earth movement, and regardless of whether a non-excluded risk acted "concurrently or in any sequence with" earth movement. The superior court found that "both parties apparently agree that the policy terms as written exclude coverage in the present case." In holding that the earth movement exclusion was unenforceable, the superior court relied primarily on *Safeco Insurance Co. v. Hirschmann,* 773 P.2d 413 (Wash. 1989).

In *Hirschmann,* the Supreme Court of Washington held that an insurer is obligated to pay for damages resulting from a combination of covered and excluded perils if the efficient proximate cause is a covered peril, regardless of a policy exclusion stating the contrary. 773 P.2d at 416-17.

Most courts addressing the validity of exclusionary language actually or functionally identical to that found in the Bongens' policy have held that the exclusion is enforceable. In *Alf v. State Farm Fire & Casualty Co.,* 850 P.2d 1272 (Utah 1993), for example, the main waterline into the insureds' home ruptured, causing extensive flooding and erosion. *Id.* at 1273. The insureds argued that the earth movement exclusion—identical to the exclusion in the present case—should not apply because the efficient proximate cause of the damage was the burst waterline, a covered risk. The court rejected their argument, holding that under the exclusion, "coverage for damage resulting from earth movement [is excluded], despite the fact that the cause of the earth movement is a covered peril." *Id.* at 1275. The court concluded that "the proper path to follow is to recognize the efficient proximate cause rule only when the parties have not chosen freely to contract out of it." *Id.* at 1277.

Other courts are in accord with this position. *See, e.g., Front Row Theatre, Inc. v. American Mfrs. Mut. Ins. Co.,* 18 F.3d 1343, 1347 (6th Cir. 1994) ("When damage to an insured's property is caused by both a covered and an excluded event, coverage may be expressly precluded by language in the policy."); *Schroeder v. State Farm Fire & Cas. Co.,* 770 F. Supp. 558, 561 (D. Nev. 1991) ("The parties could, as they did, contract out of the efficient proximate cause doctrine without violating public policy"). . . . We favor the majority rule. . . . We can discern no sound policy reason for preventing the enforcement of the earth movement exclusion to which the parties in this case agreed. We therefore align ourselves with those courts holding that an insurer may expressly preclude coverage when damage to an insured's property is caused by both a covered and an excluded risk. The earth movement exclusion in the Bongens' policy is enforceable. . . .

D.   Application of the Earth Movement Exclusion Does Not Defeat the Reasonable Expectations of the Parties

. . . In order to determine the reasonable expectations of the parties, we look to 1) the language of the disputed policy provisions; 2) the language of other policy provisions; 3) relevant extrinsic evidence; and 4) case law interpreting similar provisions.

Given these four sources of guidance in interpreting the reasonable expectations of the insureds, we conclude that the Bongens could not have reasonably expected coverage for loss resulting from earth movement. The lead-in clause and the earth movement exclusion clearly exclude coverage for any loss in which earth movement was a concurrent cause. The Bongens have not pointed to any other provision in the policy which contradicts the exclusion. There is no relevant extrinsic evidence indicating that the Bongens, prior to the loss, expected coverage for a loss caused in part by earth movement. . . .

For all of these reasons, we conclude that it would not be reasonable for the Bongens to have expected that the efficient proximate cause rule would apply in Alaska, and that their loss would be covered despite the earth movement exclusion.

MATTHEWS, J., dissenting. I agree with the decision of the superior court and thus would remand this case for a jury determination of the efficient proximate cause of the loss of the Bongens' house. . . .

The question in this case is whether there is coverage in circumstances where there are covered and excluded perils in the chain of causation leading to a loss. In order to answer questions such as this[,] courts have developed the efficient proximate cause doctrine. Under this doctrine if the efficient, or dominant, cause of a loss is an insured peril, coverage exists even though an excluded peril also contributes to the loss. This is widely accepted. Appleman's Treatise on Insurance Law states the doctrine as follows:

> Where a peril specifically insured against sets other causes in motion which, in an unbroken sequence and connection between the act and final loss, produces the result for which recovery is sought, the insured peril is regarded as the proximate cause of the entire loss. It is not necessarily the last act in a chain of events which is, therefore, regarded as the proximate cause, but the efficient or predominant cause which sets into motion the chain of events producing the loss. An incidental peril outside the policy, contributing to the risk insured against, will not defeat recovery, nor may the insurer defend by showing that an earlier cause brought the loss within a peril insured against, where the insured peril was the last step prior to loss. In other words, it has been held that recovery may be allowed where the insured risk was the last step in the chain of causation set in motion by an uninsured peril, or where the insured risk itself set into operation a chain of causation in which the last step may have been an excepted risk.

5J. Appleman, Insurance Law and Practice §3083 at 309-311 (1970) (footnotes omitted). . . .

The issue, however, in this case, is not whether the efficient proximate cause doctrine is applicable in Alaska. It is whether, given the application of the doctrine and given that a covered peril is the efficient proximate cause of a loss, policy language can negate coverage where an excluded secondary peril also is present in the chain of causation. On this issue the courts are divided. . . .

I agree that the efficient proximate cause rule comports with the reasonable expectations of the insured. If an insured buys a policy seeking protection from a given peril, the insurer issuing the policy should not be able to avoid coverage because an excluded peril is also present in the chain of causation if the covered peril is the dominant cause of the loss. Numerous examples come to mind. A homeowner who acts negligently in the face of an approaching forest fire should not lose coverage because his negligence was a minor contributing factor to the loss of his house. A school district which, following a fire loss, must rebuild a school which is different from that which was destroyed because of the enforcement of an ordinance regulating construction should be covered under a replacement value fire policy. And a homeowner who is protected from damage by construction equipment should not lose coverage because a runaway bulldozer initiates an avalanche which damages his house, rather than directly running into it. The rule of efficient proximate cause was devised to prevent such counter-intuitive results.

In sum, I agree with the Washington and California authorities which hold that when an insurer issues a policy protecting against a peril, it cannot avoid coverage where the peril is the dominant cause of the loss merely because an excluded peril is also in the chain of causation operating on a secondary basis. The purpose of insurance is to insure and it is reasonable to expect coverage when an insured peril has, acting as a dominant force, brought about a loss.

In accordance with the foregoing, I would remand this case for a determination by the trier of fact as to whether a covered peril was the efficient proximate cause of the loss of the Bongens' home.

NOTES AND QUESTIONS

1. What would be the result under the HO3 policy reproduced in Figure 3.1? (See the earth movement exclusion on pages 11-12.) What lead-in language appears there? Does it express the same underwriting intent as the language in *Bongen*?

2. The history of the causation language in the exclusions section of standard property insurance cases is a classic example of the dynamic that Judge Clark described in his concurrence in *Gaunt, which is detailed in chapter 2.* The causation language in the earth movement exclusion in the HO3 form is the language that State Farm "improved on" using the language at issue in *Bongen*. The HO3 language replaced earlier standard form language that said:

> We do not insure for loss caused by, resulting from, contributed to or aggravated by any of the following.

See Michael Bragg, *Concurrent Causation and the Art of Policy Drafting: New Perils for Property Insurers,* 20 Forum 385, 396 (1985). Earlier standard form policies excluded, variously, loss "directly or indirectly from" excluded events (*see Stone v. Roy Ins. Co.,* 511 A.2d 717 (N.J. Super. Ct. App. Div. 1986)), "loss or damage caused directly or indirectly by" an excluded event (*see Edgarton & Sons, Inc. v. Minneapolis Fire & Marine Ins. Co.,* 116 A.2d 514, 516-517 (Conn. 1955)), or "loss caused wholly or in part by" an excluded event (*see Berry v. United Commercial Travelers,* 154 N.W. 598 (Iowa 1915)). Do these provisions seem to be intended to produce the "but for" causation test that the efficient proximate cause rule rejects? Because courts have been reluctant to make efficient proximate cause an immutable rule, insurance companies have continually gone back to the drafting room to make their "but for" intent ever more clear. State Farm's language is the latest step in that effort.

3. The case of *Safeco Insurance Co. of America v. Hirschmann,* 773 P.2d 413 (Wash. 1989), relied on by the trial court, concerned an insured who was forced to abandon his house when a "100-year" storm brought excessive rainfall and created a mudslide that damaged his house. Safeco denied coverage based on an earth movement exclusion that was preceded by the following new "lead-in" clause: "We do not cover loss caused by any of the following excluded perils, *whether occurring alone or in any sequence with a covered peril.*" *Id.* at 624-625. The court found that the new lead-in clause did not warrant circumvention of the efficient proximate cause rule announced in *Graham v. Public Employees Mutual Insurance Co.,* 656 P.2d 1077 (Wash. 1983). The court rejected the insurance company's argument that the language was sufficient to deny coverage for any excluded peril regardless of how insignificant the contribution from the excluded peril may have been. *Hirschmann,* 773 P.2d at 415. The court noted the deposition of Safeco's "vice president of personal lines-underwriting," who was asked the question, "doesn't [the language of your lead-in exclusionary clause] attempt to exclude a cause no matter how slight that cause may contribute to the loss?" He responded, "Yes, that's the intent." *Id.* at n.1.

4. The West Virginia court also rejected on public policy grounds State Farm's attempts to draft around the efficient proximate cause rule. The leading case is *Murray v. State Farm Fire & Casualty Co.,* 509 S.E.2d 1 (W. Va. 1998), a case involving facts that were strikingly similar to those in *Bongen.* The West Virginia court agreed with the Alaska Supreme Court that the lead-in language unambiguously meant that the loss was excluded. The court noted with approval the following observation:

> This [lead-in] clause, applied at face value, would clearly negate coverage in case of a concurring expected cause. The clause may clear up any ambiguities in the minds of insurance counsel, but whether it would do so for the insurance consumer is questionable. The change should have little impact on the objectively reasonable expectations of the insurance consumer. If anything, the clause is more confusing to the layman than was the old "contributed to, or aggravated by" exception. . . .

California has a statute requiring courts to follow essentially the same rule. Cal. Ins. Code §530 provides as follows: "An insurer is liable for a loss of which a peril insured against was the proximate cause, although a peril not contemplated by the contract may have been a remote cause of the loss; but he is not liable for a loss of which the peril insured against was only a remote cause." North Dakota also mandates the efficient proximate cause doctrine by statute. *See W. Nat. Mut. Ins. Co. v. Univ. of N. Dakota,* 643 N.W.2d 4, 13 (N.D. 2002) ("We conclude North Dakota has statutorily adopted the efficient proximate cause doctrine, and a property insurer may not contractually preclude coverage when the efficient proximate cause of a loss is a covered peril").

The West Virginia Supreme Court found five jurisdictions that enforce State Farm's earth movement policy language: Alaska, New York, Utah, Nevada, and Arizona. *See State Farm Fire & Cas. Co. v. Bongen,* 925 P.2d 1042 (Alaska 1996); *Kula v. State Farm Fire & Cas. Co.,* 212 A.D.2d 16 (N.Y.A.D.1995); *Alf v. State Farm Fire & Cas. Co.,* 850 P.2d 1272 (Utah 1993); *Schroeder v. State*

Farm Fire & Cas. Co., 770 F. Supp. 558 (D.Nev.1991); *Millar v. State Farm Fire & Cas. Co.*, 804 P.2d 822 (Ariz. 1990). Indeed, over the past 20 years courts in most jurisdictions have enforced State Farm's lead-in clause and earth movement policy language. *See, e.g. Duensing v. State Farm Fire & Cas. Co.*, 131 P.3d 127, 134 (Okla. Civ. App. 2005) ("[W]e conclude that the language of the lead-in clause to the earth movement exclusion is unambiguous. The only fair construction of that paragraph is that when more than one cause is involved in a loss which includes one of the excluded events named under the lead-in clause, in this case, earth movement, there is no coverage regardless of whether the causes acted concurrently or in any sequence with the excluded event."); *Chase v. State Farm Fire & Cas. Co.*, 780 A.2d 1123, 1130 (D.C. 2001) ("The causation language in the introduction to the earth movement exclusion is clearly intended to supplant the efficient proximate cause doctrine . . . This is a permissible outcome in the District of Columbia, as there is no statute or public policy requiring otherwise").

5.   Still, some courts allow recovery when an expected cause acts concurrently with a covered cause despite increasingly explicit exclusionary language. This approach seems likely to continue in at least some jurisdictions regardless of the insurance industry's persistent efforts to refine their policies. Courts appear to look at the exclusionary language only to determine which causes or events are covered and which are not, and pay little attention to surplus verbiage. This approach is most likely explained as a *sub silentio* application of the doctrine of reasonable expectations. *Id.* at 15 n.13, *citing* R. Fierce, *Insurance Law—Concurrent Causation: Examination of Alternative Approaches*, 1985 S. Ill. U. L.J. 527, 538 (1986).

The court criticized the jurisdictions that have enforced State Farm's language as follows:

> We question the holdings of these latter jurisdictions, as they found the earth movement policy language to be unambiguous and clear, and suggested that the policyholder's reasonable expectations were more in line with being a "fervent hope usually engendered by loss." *Millar,* 804 P.2d at 826. These latter jurisdictions also suggest that the policyholder and insurance company freely negotiated and defined the scope of coverage and intended to exclude the efficient proximate cause doctrine. Such a position is contrary to the position we have taken in our case law that "[i]nsurance contracts are notoriously complex . . . and border on the status of contracts of adhesion. Under this view insured and insurer do not stand in pari causa, and therefore, the insured's assent to the agreement lacks completeness in relation to that of the insurer." *Murray,* 509 S.E.2d at 15 n.14 (Citations omitted).

6.   Is there a simpler solution to these causation issues? At least one commentator believes so. In a recent article, Professor Christopher French argues that the "ensuing loss" clause found in most insurance policies requires insurers to indemnify their insureds whenever a covered peril contributes to the loss. *See* Christopher C. French, *The "Ensuing Loss" Clause In Insurance Policies: The Forgotten and Misunderstood Antidote to Anti-Concurrent Causation Exclusions,* 13 Nev. L.J. 215, 249 (2012) ("[T]he original purpose of the ensuing loss clause, the policy language in the clause, and the existing rules of policy interpretation all dictate that if a covered peril plays any role in the causation chain of events that leads to a loss, then the loss should be covered

regardless of whether the policy contains an anti-concurrent causation exclusion").

CAUSATION PROBLEMS

A. Due to an unusual combination of events, a kitchen fire in the Smiths' house caused a heating oil tank outside the house to explode. The Smiths' homeowners' insurer agreed to pay for the damage caused by the fire but not for the cost of cleaning up the oil-soaked soil in the backyard of the house. The insurance company stated that the cost of cleaning up the soil was excluded by the pollution exclusion in the policy. That exclusion read, in relevant part:

> We do not insure under any coverage for any loss which would not have occurred in the absence of one or more of the following excluded events. We do not insure for such loss regardless of: (a) the cause of the excluded event; or (b) other causes of the loss; or (c) whether other causes acted concurrently or in any sequence with the excluded event to produce the loss; or (d) whether the event occurs suddenly or gradually, involves isolated or widespread damage, arises from natural or external forces, or occurs as a result of any combination of these:

> Discharge, dispersal, seepage, migration, release or escape of pollutants. Pollutants means any solid, liquid, gaseous or thermal irritant or contaminant, including smoke, vapor, soot, fumes, acids, alkalis, chemicals, and waste.

Develop arguments for and against the insurance company's position. How would your analysis of coverage for this loss differ under the HO3 policy reproduced in Figure 3.1? Look at exclusion 7.e. on the right column of page 9 of the policy. How does it differ from the exclusion given above?

B. What would be the result under the language in A. if a kitchen fire was caused by nail polish remover (toluene) that was mistakenly spilled on a range? What result under the HO3 form?

C. The Miller family's home was located on the coast of Louisiana, just a few hundred yards away from the Gulf of Mexico, when Hurricane Katrina hit. As a result, the house was severely damaged by some combination of wind, rain, and storm surge. (*Storm surge* is defined as the abnormal rise of water generated by a storm over and above the predicted astronomical tides.) The Millers' homeowners' insurer took the position that it would pay only the damages resulting entirely from wind damage, and it further took the position that it was the policyholder's obligation to prove that the damage was exclusively caused by wind. The policy in question included the following exclusions:

> 1) We do not cover loss to any property resulting directly or indirectly from any of the following. Such a loss is excluded even if another peril or event contributed concurrently or in any sequence to cause the loss. . . .
> b) Water or damage caused by water-borne material. Loss resulting from water or water-borne material damage described below is not covered even if other perils contributed, directly or indirectly to cause the loss.
> Water and water-borne material damage means . . . flood, surface water, waves, tidal waves, overflow of a body of water, spray from these, whether or not driven by wind. . . .

Develop arguments for and against the insurance company's position. How would your analysis of coverage for this loss differ under the HO3 policy reproduced in Figure 3.1?

NOTES AND QUESTIONS

1. High-profile causation cases did in fact follow Hurricane Katrina, which hit the Gulf Coast, especially the coasts of Louisiana and Mississippi, in August 2005. As of the date of publication of this book, Katrina was the most costly natural disaster in U.S. history, with total property damage estimated at over $100 billion (in 2010 dollars), which is more than twice the damage sustained in the next most expensive hurricane, which was Andrew in 1992. In marked contrast to the experience following Andrew, private insurance recoveries after Katrina had not been sufficient to allow many people to rebuild their homes and businesses. *See* Tom Baker & Karen McElrath, *Whose Safety Net? Home Insurance and Inequality*, 21 Law & Soc. Inquiry 229 (1996) (reporting results of empirical research on Hurricane Andrew claims). In substantial part the difference between the Hurricane Katrina and Hurricane Andrew situations lies in the heavy flood losses that occurred during and immediately after Katrina. Much of the damage was caused by the massive storm surge. By contrast, most of the damage from hurricane Andrew was caused by wind. The reason this matters, of course, is that homeowners' policies typically contain an exclusion for any losses caused by flooding, even when the causal link is indirect or when flooding is only one of a number of concurrent causes.

2. What resulted following Katrina was a large amount of coverage litigation over the question whether damage from that storm was excluded by the flood exclusion. A significant amount of the insurance disputes and litigation is the unfortunate yet expected consequence of the public policy decision to provide flood coverage through a separate federal program, rather than through a federal program that made it possible for that coverage to be provided as part of the ordinary property insurance, as is the case for terrorism. Whenever an all risks insurance policy excludes coverage for one kind of risk and another kind of insurance provides coverage for that risk, a certain number of border skirmishes are to be expected, especially when the specialized insurance coverage is limited (as in the case of national flood insurance).

3. In one prominent Hurricane Katrina insurance case, federal district court Judge Duval ruled that the water exclusion in the standard ISO homeowners' insurance policies did not apply to homes that were damaged by the failure of the levees surrounding New Orleans when Katrina struck. *In re Canal Breaches Consolidated Litig.*, 466 F. Supp. 2d 729 (E.D. La. 2006). The ISO policy language is identical to that in the homeowners' policy reproduced in Figure 3.1. Judge Duval described the question presented as follows:

> Thus, the salient question becomes whether, in the context of an all-risk policy where coverage is provided for direct loss to property, these insurance provisions which exclude coverage for water damage caused by "flood" clearly and

unambiguously exclude from coverage damages caused by the alleged third party negligence of OLD which plaintiffs contend caused a section of the floodwall at the 17th Street Canal to break causing water to enter the streets of the City of New Orleans and homes of the plaintiffs in this suit. While words and phrases in insurance policies are to be construed using their plain, ordinary and generally prevailing meaning, unless the words have acquired a technical meaning, an ambiguity arises where a term is susceptible to two reasonable interpretations. Simply put, the question before the court is whether it is reasonable to find in the absence of further definition or provision in the ISO policy that there are two interpretations of the term "flood"—one which encompasses both a "flood" which occurs solely because of natural causes and a "flood" which occurs because of the negligent or intentional act of man and one which limits itself only to a flood which occurs solely because of natural causes.

Id. at 746. Based on a detailed review of dictionary definitions and prior decisions in Louisiana and elsewhere, Judge Duval decided that the term "flood" in the ISO policy meant naturally occurring events, not an "artificial" flood caused by the failure of a levee:

The fundamental argument made by the ISO insurers is that the word "flood" is all encompassing. They point out that the water damage which occurred to homes and businesses in New Orleans has been referred to as a "flood" in newspapers, general reports and many other sources. And thus, the water exclusion applies to the coverage sought by policy holders herein.

As demonstrated earlier, the word "flood" has numerous meanings. It is defined in virtually all dictionaries first as a noun then as a verb. In the policies being examined by the Court it is used as a noun. As noted, most of the definitions of the noun imply encroachment of water caused by an act of nature. Furthermore, this exclusion has been the subject of differing interpretations in the jurisprudence which further demonstrates that it is susceptible of two reasonable interpretations. As such, under Louisiana civilian principles and the *jurisprudence constant*, this Court finds the ISO Water Damage Exclusion ambiguous. . . .

It is the considered opinion of this Court that because the policies are all-risk, and because "flood" has numerous definitions, it reasonably could be limited to natural occurrences. Simply put, the language of the ISO Water Damage Exclusion chosen by the insurer is unclear. Indeed, the broad definition defendants seek to employ—that is that the term "flood" means the inundation of usually dry land by water—makes the remaining part of the exclusion superfluous. The ensuing words "waves, tidal water, overflow of a body of water or spray from any of these, whether or not driven by wind" all are instances relating to **natural** events which can cause inundation of usually dry land. Thus, to use the broadest definition of the term "flood" in interpreting this exclusion, would render the rest of the clause useless.

Id. at 756-757 (boldface in original). Relying on the different language in the State Farm policy, Judge Duval reached a different result with respect to the claims against State Farm. The relevant provision in the State Farm policy read as follows:

SECTION I — LOSSES NOT INSURED

2. We do not insure under any coverage for loss which would not have occurred in the absence of one or more of the following excluded events. We do not insure for such loss *regardless of: (a) the cause of the excluded event;* or (b) other causes of the loss; or (c) whether other causes acted concurrently or in any sequence with the excluded event to produce the loss; or (d) whether the event occurs suddenly or gradually, involves isolated or widespread damage, arises from natural or external forces, or occurs as a result of any combination of these:

c. (1) flood, surface water, waves, tidal water, overflow of a body of water, or spray from any of these all whether driven by wind or not;

Id. at 763 (emphasis added by the court).

Judge Duval found this difference to be decisive:

The State Farm policy does precisely what the ISO Water Exclusion Policy fails to do. It makes it clear that regardless of the **cause** of the flooding, there is no coverage provided for any flooding "regardless of the cause." Such language is clear to the Court and as such, the Court must find that the State Farm policy as written excludes coverage for all flooding.

Id. at 762-763 (boldface in original).

4.   The Fifth Circuit affirmed Judge Duval's ruling on the State Farm policy but reversed on the ISO policy. *See In re Katrina Canal Breaches Litig.,* 4 495 F.3d 191 (5th Cir. 2007). The court rejected the natural versus artificial distinction and ruled that the inundation was a "flood" within the meaning of the ISO and other policies at issue. The court noted, but did not rely on, the fact that policies issued under the National Flood Insurance Program would cover the losses in question (as long as the policyholders had purchased that coverage).

Finally, several defendants argue that in light of flood insurance available through the National Flood Insurance Program ("NFIP"), a reasonable policyholder would not expect homeowners policies to cover the flooding in this case. The defendants assert that we may consider the NFIP in interpreting "flood" because custom and industry usage is relevant under article 2053 of the [Louisiana] Civil Code. They contend that the NFIP's existence over many years has made it clear to property owners that standard all-risk policies do not cover flood damage, regardless of whether the cause of the flood is natural or non-natural, and that property owners who want flood coverage must purchase it through the NFIP; a reasonable policyholder thus would not expect the inundation of water in this case to be covered under a standard homeowners, renters, or commercial-property insurance policy.

The plaintiffs, in contrast, urge us not to consider the NFIP, contending that it has no bearing on this appeal. [And to] the extent the NFIP may be relevant, the plaintiffs argue that a reasonable policyholder would expect the NFIP to provide coverage for naturally occurring floods but that floods induced by negligence would be covered under standard all-risk policies.

We do not rely upon the NFIP to decide this appeal. Our decision is based instead upon our determination that the flood exclusions in the policies before us unambiguously preclude the plaintiffs' recovery. But to the extent that the NFIP's definition of "flood" is further evidence of the term's generally prevailing meaning, we note that it is consistent with our interpretation.

495 F.3d at 220-221.

5. Judge Duval's decision to treat the ISO and the State Farm policies differently, even if reversed on appeal, highlights a reality about the property insurance market that has until recently gone largely unnoticed: Although ISO policy forms provide standardized language that is adopted by many insurers, there are plenty of insurers who draft their own policy language. In *Reevaluating Standardized Insurance Policies*, 78 U. Chi. L. Rev. 1263 (2011), Professor Daniel Schwarcz, based on sampling of policies acquired from helpful state insurance regulators in six states, reports that many homeowners' insurers draft policy terms that diverge from the language in the ISO standard forms. And the divergence is usually not in a direction that favors policyholders. For example, Schwarcz found that some insurers include a longer list of excluded causes than the ISO policy does. Why would insurers do this? What is the potential disadvantage for policyholders? Are there any advantages to doing so? What more would we need to know to determine if such divergence from the ISO forms is better or worse for policyholders overall?

FLOOD INSURANCE NOTE AND QUESTIONS

As mentioned above, the conflicts that gave rise to the Katrina coverage litigation derive from the fact that coverage for flood damage and coverage for other types of damage to property are sold in different ways, through different policies. Homeowners' policies contain exclusions for damages causes by flood, with "damages caused by flood" being defined very (and increasingly) broadly, and thus coverage for hurricane-related risks being defined increasingly narrowly. This would not be a big problem if homeowners, in addition to homeowners' policies, purchased separate flood insurance policies. But they often do not. Why not? Some people forgo flood insurance because they underestimate the risk of flood or believe that they will sell their house and move before the next big flood hits (which is another way of saying they underestimate the risk). Some people (wrongly) believe that, if they do not have flood insurance, federal disaster relief will cover most of their losses. In fact, federal disaster relief, which is available only if a federal disaster is declared, comes mostly in the form of loans that have to be repaid with interest. Some people (also wrongly) believe that flood insurance is not available in their area.

While it is true that many mortgage insurers require homeowners to purchase flood insurance, that fact does not solve the problem of inadequate flood insurance coverage, for several reasons. First, many mortgage lenders do not require flood insurance if the property is located in low- to moderate-risk flood areas, even though roughly 25 percent of flood damage comes in precisely those areas. (Mortgage lenders are mandated by federal law only to require the purchase of flood policies in high-risk areas, known as "Special Flood Hazard Areas.") Second, many homes, especially those owned by older homeowners who have been living in the same place for many years, have no mortgages and thus no mortgage lenders to require the purchase of insurance. And finally, even when flood insurance is required by a lender, enforcement of the requirement is costly and imperfect. The result of all of this is the Katrina-type situation, where millions of homeowners end up being inadequately or entirely uninsured for flood damage to their homes.

Just as the *absence* of flood insurance can be a problem, the *presence* of flood insurance can be a problem when the coverage is not actuarially priced. Flood insurance is currently provided primarily through the NFIP, which is administered by the Federal Emergency Management Agency (FEMA). The NFIP policies are sold by regular insurance agents through private insurance companies, but the risk is underwritten by the federal government. Although premiums are charged to policyholders, those premiums are not based on actuarial predictions of expected risks. This is why the program regularly develops large deficits that require funds to be borrowed from the U.S. Treasury to pay claims. "Although in most years the NFIP collects enough premiums to cover each year's claims, a few catastrophic events more than wipe out the NFIP's reserves. As of 2014, the NFIP's debt exceeded $24 billion."[1] According to one recent Article,

> As a result of the [NFIP] discounts, people insured by the NFIP pay only a fraction of the full-risk premium. In 2006, FEMA estimated this fraction to be between 35% and 40%. The subsidy is, on average, close to two-thirds of the economic cost. An average premium charged by the NFIP was $721, but would cost between $1800 and $2060 if priced to cover full risk. In the areas with the highest risk of floods, the fraction of full risk paid by policyholders is even lower.[2]

In sum, the NFIP rates are not sufficient to cover all the risks associated with floods. As a result, the NFIP encourages building on floodplains beyond what would occur in the absence of this subsidy. It has been argued further that this distortion in the real estate market has led to increased building in areas near waterways and coastal zones that are especially ecologically sensitive.[3]

Similar cross-subsidies can be found within state-based government subsidies for wind insurance. While the federal government subsidizes flood insurance, it generally does not subsidize wind insurance. The U.S. government does provide ex post relief, through FEMA loans, for uninsured wind damage, but this relief is relatively meager, and there is no federal wind insurance program. (This is interesting, given that tornadoes and thunderstorms caused almost as much property damage in the aggregate as hurricanes.[4]) However, some coastal states provide subsidized coverage for wind losses. The largest program is the one provided by Citizens Property Insurance Corporation, the insurance company run by the state of Florida that specializes in wind policies and sinkhole policies. Ben-Shahar & Logue, *supra* at 590. Based on a study of Citizens' property insurance rate filings in 2012, Ben-Shahar and Logue determined that there was a substantial cross-subsidy built into Citizens homeowners' policies providing wind coverage, with homeowners whose property is located closest to the water in the most hurricane-prone areas of the state receiving the largest subsidies, funded by higher-than-actuarially fair rates charged to homeowners whose property was further inland. *Id.* Thus, putting together the NFIP cross-subsidies and state cross-subsidies, government-provided weather insurance has created a strong incentive for property owners to build on the coast.

Moreover, some have argued that this subsidy is not only inefficient but also distributively and geographically unfair. The *distributional* unfairness arises

---

1. Omri Ben-Shahar & Kyle D. Logue, *The Perverse Effects of Subsidized Weather Insurance*, 68 Stan. L. Rev. 571, 609 (2016).

2. Id. (citations omitted).

3. *See* J. Scott Holladay & Jason A. Schwartz, *Flooding the Market: The Distributional Consequences of the NFIP at 3 and 4* (N.Y.U. Sch. of Law, Inst. for Policy Integrity, Policy Brief No. 7, 2010), available online at *http://policyintegrity.org/documents/FloodingtheMarket.pdf*; and Ben-Shahar & Logue, *supra* at 611.

4. Lloyd's, Tornadoes: A Rising Risk? 4, 19 (2013).

because both the NFIP the NFIP subsidy tends to benefit the poorest communities and the wealthiest communities, the two groups that, pro rata, file the most and the largest claims, at the expense of middle-income communities, who file by far the fewest claims. It turns out that in many of these coastal and other floodplain areas, there are many poor homeowners and, closest to the water and the picturesque views available there, many rich homeowners. In addition, the premium structure has historically provided a subsidy to more expensive coastal homes, as those homes have disproportionately been grandfathered into the program at relatively low rates. The *geographic* unfairness derives from the fact that over 50 percent of the houses covered by the program are in Florida or Texas. And more generally, states along the Gulf and Atlantic coasts, where the hurricane risks are highest, tend to make much greater use of the NFIP than other regions of the country.[5] There is also strong evidence that Florida's subsidies for wind coverage tends to benefit the owners of relatively expensive coastal homes, at the expense of the owners of the relatively modest inland properties.[6]

The Biggert-Waters Flood Insurance Reform and Modernization Act of 2012 both extended the NFIP for five years and instituted some reforms aimed at dealing with some of the problems mentioned above. For example, the act calls for (1) phasing out subsidies for many properties and mandates premium increases on second homes (to allay some of the distributional concerns), (2) raising the cap on annual premium increases from 10 percent to 20 percent (to allow more realistic pricing and provide more stable funding for the program), and (3) imposing minimum deductibles for flood claims (to help deal with moral hazard concerns). The act generally pushes in the direction of increased use of actuarial pricing and increased use of private markets (for example, by reiterating FEMA's authority to purchase reinsurance to back the program). By most accounts, this change in the law was a move in the right direction because it would have brought some rationality to the pricing of flood insurance. The ultimate and eventual result of the 2012 act was that it was likely to enhance the efficiency of the signal in flood insurance pricing and was likely to reduce the regressive distributional effects of the old NFIP regime.

Unfortunately, the Biggert-Waters Act was not the last legislative word on the subject:

> [T]he backlash from property owners along coastal areas, where resulting premium increases were the greatest, was swift and effective. In some areas, there were reports of homeowners' premiums rising tenfold. The concern expressed by many lawmakers, on behalf of their angry constituents, was that unless Biggert-Waters was repealed or at least delayed, they wouldn't be able to remain in their homes or continue their small businesses. Thus, before Biggert-Waters was able to take effect, Congress passed the Homeowner Flood Insurance Affordability Act of 2014, which significantly weakened the changes made by Biggert-Waters. The political pressure to repeal Biggert-Waters was so successful that even Representative Maxine Waters voted in support of repealing her own bill. As a result, the 2014 Act imposed tighter limits on yearly premium increases, reinstated the NFIP grandfathering provision, and preserved the discounted premiums for properties even after being sold. The new law also called on FEMA to keep premiums at no more than one percent of the value of the coverage.[7]

5. Holladay & Schwartz, *supra.*
6. Ben-Shahar & Logue, *supra.*
7. Ben-Shahar & Logue, *supra,* at 589 (citations omitted).

Thus, Congress in 2014 undid most of the efficiency and distributional gains that Biggert-Waters promised.[8]

1. What do you make of the claim that the NFIP program encourages building in flood-prone areas? Can this practice be defended?
2. Is the fairness critique persuasive? If the NFIP regularly runs a deficit, which gets paid off by federal tax dollars (funded through the federal income tax system), does that make the NFIP regime more or less fair?
3. Do all of the same sorts of issues arise in connection with earthquake insurance? Note that there is currently no federal program of earthquake insurance comparable to the NFIP. There are, however, state-based programs, such as the California Earthquake Authority (CEA). Although coordinated through a state agency, the CEA provides earthquake policies that are largely privately funded, through actuarially priced premiums. Perhaps as a result, nearly 88 percent of California homeowners opt not to purchase earthquake insurance.
4. Consider the following proposals for dealing with the hurricane/flood underinsurance problem. What are the strengths and weaknesses of each?
    a. A federal law requiring all insurance companies who sell homeowners' insurance policies to provide coverage for damage caused by flooding; that is, a federal prohibition on the flood exclusion. Under this proposal, there would be no subsidies from the federal government to insurers. Also, the federal government would formally announce that it would not provide FEMA loans or grants to homeowners in a floodplain that did not have a private homeowners' insurance policy in place. The NFIP would be repealed. Subsidies could be provided by state and local governments to help homeowners pay for this insurance, but there would be no federal subsidies.
    b. A federal law requiring all insurance companies that sell homeowners' insurance policies to offer, in addition to their regular homeowners' policies that exclude flood coverage, "enhanced policies" that would include flood coverage on the same terms as are currently provided through NFIP policies; these would charge the same rates as those charged for the NFIP policies.
    c. A federal law requiring that homeowners purchase some type of flood insurance, either from the NFIP or from a private insurer.
    d. What if we expanded the proposals above and made them apply not only to floods but also to all natural disasters? How, if at all, would that change your analysis? What about human-made disasters?

B. Valuation

The most difficult part of most property insurance claims is establishing the value of the loss. In routine cases, valuation is often the only real issue. On the whole, valuation is a very fact-intensive question that does not produce much law of note. There are, however, some baseline questions about the basic approach

---

8. *See generally* Jennifer Wriggins, *Flood Money: The Challenge of U.S. Flood Insurance Reform in a Warming World,* 119 Penn. St. L. Rev. 361 (2014) (explaining the political context that resulted in the enactment of Biggert-Waters and the 2014 retrenchment, as well as arguing in favor of reduced cross-subsidies in the NFIP).

insurance companies should take in valuing a claim. The following Prohibition-era case from the New York Court of Appeals may well be the most influential of the cases setting the ground rules for valuing property insurance claims.

McANARNEY v. NEWARK FIRE INSURANCE CO.

Court of Appeals of New York
159 N.E. 902 (1928)

KELLOG, J. The plaintiff was the vendee of certain real estate, purchased in the year 1919 from the defendant Lembeck & Betz Eagle Brewing Company, under written contract, for the sum of $8,000. Seven large buildings, designed for the manufacture of malt, stood upon the premises. Malt had been extensively manufactured therein prior to the year 1918. Owing to the passage of the National Prohibition Act (27 USCA) its manufacture was discontinued in March of that year and thereafter the buildings ceased to be employed for any useful purpose. In January, 1920, policies of insurance insuring the plaintiff and the Lembeck & Betz Eagle Brewing Company, as their interest might appear, against loss of the buildings by fire, in the aggregate sum of $42,750, were taken out.

In April, 1920, the buildings were destroyed by fire. Subsequently the plaintiff served proofs of loss wherein he valued the buildings at approximately $60,000 and made claim for the total amount of the insurance. The defendant Newark Fire Insurance Company was one of the insuring companies. It had issued a policy insuring the plaintiff and the defendant Lembeck & Betz Eagle Brewing Company against fire loss in the amount of $2,500. The plaintiff demanded payment from it and, upon its refusal, brought this action to recover the sum of $2,500 promised by its policy. . . . The action was tried before a jury, to which the trial judge submitted the written question, "What was the intrinsic or depreciated structural value of the buildings burned?" The jury returned a verdict specifying the value to have been $55,000. The trial court, having ascertained that the plaintiff had paid to the Lembeck & Betz Eagle Brewing Company the full purchase price for the property, directed judgment in favor of the plaintiff against the Newark Fire Insurance Company for the amount of its policy, with interest.

Complaint is made that the trial court in the course of the trial committed a variety of errors in ruling upon the admissibility of proof offered by the defendant. It refused to receive proof that the plaintiff, when a director of the Lembeck & Betz Company, in the year 1919 reported to that company that he had been unable to obtain a purchaser for the property; that in the same year the corporation had directed the plaintiff to erect a sign upon the premises advertising the property for sale for the sum of $12,000. It refused to receive in evidence an affidavit made by the plaintiff in the year 1919 which was filed with the local board of assessors. In this affidavit the plaintiff had stated that the property had no value except for the production of malt; that the production of malt upon the premises had entirely ceased; that the owners would accept for the property the sum of $15,000; that the best offer which had been received was $6,000. To the rulings made, excluding such proof and proof of a similar nature, the defendant duly excepted. Complaint is also made of the court's charge to the jury and of its refusals to charge. The court said to the jury:

> "Your answer shall not be the market value—shall not be the sum that the buildings would sell for, but what it cost to build them—what it cost to build the structures, less depreciation proven in the case."

[The trial court] charged that the fact that the buildings, because of the passage of the National Prohibition Act, could no longer be used for the manufacture of malt, and the fact that the buildings could no longer be employed for any useful purpose, were wholly immaterial. It further charged that the value of the buildings destroyed was to be measured solely by the cost of replacement less deductions for physical deterioration. The defendant duly excepted to the charges made. It requested the court to charge several propositions of law which were the direct converse of the charges thus made, and, to its refusal, duly excepted.

The policy in suit contained the standard clause, applicable alike to fire losses whether of chattels or buildings, reading as follows:

> The insurance company does insure . . . and legal representatives to the extent of the actual cash value (ascertained with proper deductions for depreciation) of the property at the time of loss or damage, but not exceeding the amount which it would cost to repair or replace the same with material of like kind and quality within a reasonable time after such loss or damage.

We cannot agree with the defendant that, under this clause, the market value of the buildings destroyed was the exclusive measure of the plaintiff's loss. Insurance is thereby limited to "actual cash value (ascertained with proper deductions for depreciation) of the property at the time of loss or damage." Value ascertained by market price is necessarily expressive of a suitable deduction for depreciation. If "actual cash value" were synonymous with "market value," the words in parenthesis, to have force, would require depreciation to be twice subtracted. No such anomalous result could have been intended. In order that the parenthetical words should have force, therefore, "actual cash value" must be interpreted as having a broader significance than "market value." Moreover, if market value were the rule, property, for which there was no market, would possess no insurable value, a proposition which is clearly untenable. We think it manifest that the clause was not intended to restrict a recovery for this insurance loss to the market value of the insured buildings. We interpret "actual cash value" to have no other significance than "actual value" expressed in terms of money. For methods by which actual value may be ascertained, we must look beyond the terms of the policy to general principles of the law of damages.

No principle, obtaining in the law of damages, requires that the recovery be restricted to the market value of the buildings. True it is that articles of commerce destined for sale must be appraised, to measure loss through conversion or breach of contract, by the market prices at which such articles are bought and sold. The reason for the rule is this: The loser of the article, if awarded the prevailing price therefor, may enter the market and, with the sum awarded, replace the article lost with a substitute identical in kind and quality. Replacement in kind necessarily accomplishes complete indemnity. However, the rule presupposes the existence of a broad market with frequent trading in articles of an identical character with the article lost. It must be a market in which the loser "could have replaced the goods." It must show "what would be the value to a party if he wanted to get the same articles again." It must enable the loser to "supply himself with this article by going into the market and making his purchase at such price." It has been said that value does not inhere in the thing to be valued; that it is a subjective conception; that identity of belief, on the part of many traders, as indicated in a market, causes the conception to assume the objective quality of an established fact. Sedgwick on Damages §242. "Market value," as an exclusive measure of damages, necessarily involves identity of concept as disclosed by frequency of sale. "Proof of a single sale is not enough to establish a market value." Sedgwick, §244. Clearly, where no sales have been made, the opinion of an expert that the property in question "will sell" for a given sum does not establish "market value," in the sense of an exclusive criterion of value. "There cannot be an established market value for barges, boats, and other articles of that description, as in cases of grain, cotton, or stock. The value of such a boat depends upon the accidents of its form, age, and materials; and as these differ in each individual there could be no established market value." The Granite State, 3 Wall. 310, at p. 314 (18 L. Ed. 179). A luxurious private yacht of large dimensions, though marketable in the sense that she can be sold, in the true sense of the term has no market value. "She does not fall within the class of articles which are sold from day to day, so that frequent current market transactions will enable the owner, if he desires to sell, to obtain, within a reasonable time, a fair value, or, if he is compelled to replace, to replace at a like fair value." *The H. F. Dimock Metropolitan S.S. Co. v. Vanderbilt*, 77 F. 226 (1st Cir. 1896). The proposition that "if there be no market, in a restricted sense, yet if the commodity is the subject of sale and there is a selling price, the same rule obtains and proof of cost should be excluded," has not found approval in this court. *Todd v. Gamble*, [148 N.Y. 382 (1896)] Self-evidently, the buildings which are the subject of this action had no "market value" in a strict sense. In the first place, buildings, independently of the land upon which they stand, are never the subject of market sales. In the second place, no two buildings are alike in size, proportion, ornamentation, or otherwise. Doubtless no buildings, duplicating those destroyed, could be found the world over. They are incapable of replacement from any market whatsoever. Therefore, the strict rule that market value or market price is an exclusive measure of damage does not apply.

We do not agree with the plaintiff that, under the standard clause, the sole measure of damage was cost of reproduction less physical depreciation. The words "not exceeding the amount which it would cost to repair or replace the same with material of like kind and quality within a reasonable time after such loss or damage[]" afford no remedy to the assured. They merely express a privilege granted to the insurer. The insurer might, if it so elected, reconstruct the destroyed buildings upon their ancient pattern with materials of like kind and quality, or pay the assured the necessary cost of such reconstruction. If the insurer so elected, it could be allowed nothing for the difference between the value of the old and the new buildings. Wood on Fire Insurance, §472. The clause makes no allusion to depreciation, except as it provides for the recovery of "actual cash value" to be "ascertained with proper deductions for depreciation." This provision, while it doubtless comprehends cost of reproduction, does not restrict the field of investigation to such cost or provide that, with depreciation, it shall constitute an exclusive measure of recovery.

Indemnity is the basis and foundation of all insurance law. *Castellain v. Preston*, 11 Q.B.D. 380 (Cal. Ct. App. 1883); Richards on Insurance Law, p. 27; Wood on Fire Insurance, §471. "The contract of the insurer is not that, if the property is burned, he will pay its market value, but that he will indemnify the assured, that is, save him harmless or put him in as good a condition, so far as practicable, as he would have been in if no fire had occurred." *Washington Mills Mfg. Co. v.*

Weymouth Ins. Co., 135 Mass. 503 (1883). The insurer, in our case, in its contract with the plaintiff stipulated that it "does insure" the plaintiff "to the extent of the actual cash value." Under our interpretation of the phrase, the insurer "does insure" to the limit of actual value. To insure is "to guarantee or secure indemnity for future loss or damage." The Century Dictionary. Where insured buildings have been destroyed, the trier of fact may, and should, call to its aid, in order to effectuate complete indemnity, every fact and circumstance which would logically tend to the formation of a correct estimate of the loss. It may consider original cost and cost of reproduction; the opinions upon value given by qualified witnesses; the declarations against, interest which may have been made by the assured; the gainful uses to which the buildings might have been put; as well as any other fact reasonably tending to throw light upon the subject.

In the case at bar the trier of fact, in considering cost of reproduction, was required by the policy to make proper "deductions for depreciation." The word (depreciation) means, by derivation and common usage, a "fall in value; reduction of worth." *N.Y. Life Ins. Co. v. Anderson*, 263 F. at 529. It includes obsolescence. *Nashville, C. & St. L. R. Co. v. United States*, 269 F. 351, at 355. An obsolete thing is a thing no longer in use. In determining the extent to which these buildings had suffered from depreciation, the trier of fact should have been permitted to consider that, owing to the passage of the National Prohibition Act, they were no longer useful for the purposes to serve which they were erected. It should have been permitted to consider their adaptability or inadaptability to other commercial purposes. The law of damages distinguishes between marketable chattels possessed for purposes of sale and chattels possessed for the comfort and well-being of their owner. In the instance of the former it judges their value by the market price. In the instance of the latter it measures their loss, not by their value in a second-hand market, but by the value of their use to the owner who suffers from their deprivation. The latter measure is employed in the case of household furniture, family records, wearing apparel, personal effects, and family portraits. Doubtless the law should similarly discriminate between buildings used and usable for commercial purposes and buildings used and usable for residence purposes. "The considerations affecting the value of a family residence and of an apartment house or office building are not entirely the same." It might well be held that handsomely carved woodwork or other ornamental features, when found in a private home, have insurable value; whereas, when found in a factory, since they are not useful for factory purposes, they have no such value. However that may be, it is a self-evident proposition that factory buildings peculiarly adapted to the manufacture of malt must have depreciated in value when malt may no longer be manufactured; that buildings useful only for factory purposes have lost value when they are no longer used or usable for such purposes.

The foregoing discussion necessarily establishes that the trial judge committed reversible error in excluding the declarations against interest as to the value of the buildings, made by the plaintiff; in charging the jury that upon the question of value they must consider no other subject than cost of reproduction less depreciation; and in further charging that the obsolescence of the structures or their inutility for commercial or manufacturing purposes might not be considered. Accordingly, the judgment must be reversed.

The judgment should be reversed and a new trial granted, with costs to abide the event.

NOTES AND QUESTIONS

1. "Actual cash value" and other loss settlement provisions are directed at the problem of moral hazard. Insurance law embodies the concern about this aspect of moral hazard in the "indemnity principle," which Professor Robert Jerry describes as follows:

    > The goal of indemnity is to reimburse the insured for the loss sustained—and no more. The objective is to put the insured in the position the insured would have occupied had no loss occurred. The insured is not entitled to recover more than the damaged property is worth or more than its decline in value as a result of the damage.

    Understanding Insurance Law at 676 (3d ed. 1996).
    As reflected in the court's discussion of the indemnity principle, insurers are constantly on guard against the possibility that an insured might "gain" through a "loss." Can you articulate why? Of course, there are ways other than claims valuation provisions that insurance companies might prevent insureds from gaining through loss. What others can you find in the homeowners' form? What others can you think of? Think about the question this way: Suppose the court held the other way; what else could insurance companies do to control this moral hazard?

2. The circumstances surrounding the insurance policies and fire at issue in the *McAnarney* case are certainly suspicious, which might well explain the decision of the trial court. There undoubtedly are other cases in which a policyholder might legitimately complain that he or she was sold, and paid premiums for, a policy with a very high insured value and at the time of claim the insurance company was claiming that the property was worth only a fraction of the insured value. What incentive, if any, does the rule announced in the case give insurance companies to prevent agents from selling "too much" insurance on a given property? Why would an insurance agent have an incentive to engage in such overselling? Can you see the analogy between the overselling/claim valuation dynamic and the problem of post-claim underwriting discussed in the notes in the misrepresentation section (Section V) of Chapter 2?

3. The widespread belief that the actual cash value provision and insurance law's indemnity principle gave insurance companies the ability to have their cake and eat it too—collecting premiums on very high insured values and then settling claims on the basis of much lower "actual cash" values—led to the adoption of "valued policy laws" in many states around the turn of the twentieth century. A "valued policy law" obligates the insurance company to pay the full face value of the policy in the event of a total loss, regardless of the actual value of the insured property. How does this law change insurance companies' incentives with regard to overselling by insurance agents? For a recent valued policy case that cites the relevant literature, *see Seider v. O'Connell*, 612 N.W.2d 659 (Wis. 2000).

4. The actual cash value majority rule today is that reflected in the main case: Actual cash value is determined according to a broad evidence rule that includes consideration of depreciation and any other relevant factor. *See, e.g., Elberon Bathing Co. v. Ambassador*, 389 A.2d 439 (N.J. 1978); *Travelers Indem.*

Co. v. Armstrong, 442 N.E.2d 349 (Ind. 1982). Along with the Florida rule addressed below, competing standards to determining "actual cash value" include the "market value" approach, which has been adopted by California and Nebraska (*see, e.g., Erin Rancho Motels v. U.S. Fidelity & Guar. Co.,* 352 N.W.2d 561, 564 (Neb. 1984); *Jefferson Ins. Co. of N.Y. v. Superior Court,* 475 P.2d 880, 882 (Cal. 1970)), and a replacement cost minus depreciation rule that "used to be the majority rule." *Travelers Indem. Co. v. Armstrong,* 442 N.E.2d at 355. In contrast to *McAnarney,* some cases criticize the replacement cost minus depreciation approach as *under* compensating policyholders. *See Travelers Indem. Co. v. Armstrong,* 442 N.E.2d at 356 ("It . . . cannot always be said that the insured has been 'indemnified' if he is required to expend a substantial sum from his own pocket to restore his building, albeit to an improved condition, when it suited his purpose in its pre-loss condition").

5. Florida courts have held that, in cases of partial loss to dwellings, the "actual cash value" of the damage is "the cost of placing the building 'in as nearly as possible the same condition that it was before the loss, without allowing depreciation for the materials used.' " *Sperling v. Liberty Mutual Ins. Co.,* 281 So. 2d 297, 298 (Fla. 1973). *Sperling* followed the earlier *Glens Falls Ins. Co. v. Gulf Breeze Cottages* decision, which states:

> Bearing in mind that the purpose of the contract was to indemnify the owner against loss, we think the chancellor adopted a rule which was fair and just and that the property should have been placed in as nearly as possible the same condition that it was before the loss, without allowing depreciation for the materials used. Certainly it was not intended that the repairs should be made with materials which were not new. If depreciation were allowed, it would cast upon the owner an added expense which we do not believe was contemplated by the parties when they entered into the insurance contract.

Glens Falls Ins. Co. v. Gulf Breeze Cottages, 38 So. 2d 828, 830 (Fla. 1949). The Florida rule has won the support of the Supreme Court of Kansas, *see Thomas v. American Family Mut. Ins. Co.,* 666 P.2d 676, 679 (Kan. 1983) ("[W]e think the better rule, absent policy provisions to the contrary, is that set forth in *Sperling*"), and it is consistent with what may still be the rule in Pennsylvania. *See Fedas v. Ins. Co. of Pa.,* 151 A. 285 (Pa. 1930) (holding that "actual cash value" equals the "actual cost to replace": "[t]he actual cost of new material, with deduction for depreciation, which is not sufficient to replace the building as nearly as it could be as of the date of the fire, does not comply with the policy").

6. The Florida approach takes what Professor Kenneth Abraham refers to as a "functional conception" of indemnity, as distinguished from the "economic conception" reflected in the "replacement cost minus depreciation" rule. *See* Kenneth Abraham, Insurance Law & Regulation 262 (2d ed. 1995). The fact that consumers prefer functional to economic indemnity is demonstrated by the overwhelming success of "replacement cost" insurance policies.

7. *Doelger & Kirsten, Inc. v. National Union Fire Ins. Co. of Pittsburgh,* 167 N.W.2d 198 (Wis. 1969), presents a more likely to recur variation on *McAnarney.* In *Doelger & Kirsten,* a fire in a barn at a factory destroyed, among many other items, wooden forms for "alligator shears," an apparently obsolete form of

industrial equipment that the insured had moved out to the barn for storage in the event that the market for alligator shears ever returned. The Wisconsin court took the *McAnarney* approach and affirmed a trial court judgment that took their obsolescence into account. According to people in the insurance industry, many companies have obsolete pieces of equipment lying around their factories, and they never fail to try to get "replacement cost" for the equipment in the event of loss.

8. Today, policyholders typically have a choice between "replacement cost" and "actual cash value" coverage. Indeed, the difference between "replacement cost" and "actual cash value" may be one of the few aspects of property insurance coverage that is actually explained to consumers by insurance agents. Replacement cost policies pay what that term suggests, the full cost to replace damaged property, even if it is old or used. "New for old" is how some insurance agents explain it. As you can see from the loss settlement provision of the HO3 policy (beginning on the lower right-hand column of page 13 of Figure 3.1), the company promises to pay replacement cost only if the policyholder in fact replaces (or repairs) the damaged building; otherwise, the policy pays "actual cash value." What might be the reason for that limitation? Think about the incentives affecting the owner of an older building in a declining neighborhood if the policy provided otherwise.

9. The meaning of "replacement cost" has not led to as much litigation as has the meaning of "actual cash value." In deciding the actual cash value of property, insurance adjusters today typically use a replacement cost minus depreciation approach, unless that approach produces a result that is way out of line with the market value of the property. There are standard construction estimating texts that are prepared on a regional basis that make determining the replacement cost and depreciation a mechanical exercise. For a policyholder with a replacement cost policy who eventually replaces or rebuilds, the difference between the actual cash value and replacement cost is essentially irrelevant. For policyholders who decide not to rebuild, or who do not have a replacement cost policy, the difference can be quite significant, as the main case reflects. Does paying less than replacement cost conflict with the reasonable expectations of the average policyholder who purchased a replacement cost policy? After all, insurance companies sell their policies as "replacement cost" policies, not "replacement" policies. On the other hand, if a policyholder gets "replacement cost" whether he or she builds or not, what is the purpose of the replacement cost provision in the policy?

10. Replacement cost policies allow policyholders to replace "new for old," but policyholders often decide to improve or change their properties when they rebuild them. In that case, the law and practice is to calculate a "hypothetical replacement cost"—a fact-specific inquiry with substantial room to disagree, particularly when the property is unique. For example, calculation of the "hypothetical replacement cost" of the World Trade Center consumed enormous amounts of lawyer resources and did not finally end until the settlement of the insurance litigation in May 2007. *See SR Int'l Bus. Ins. Co. v. World Trade Center Props., LLC*, 445 F. Supp. 2d 320 (S.D.N.Y. 2006) (deciding a variety of technical issues relating to the valuation of the hypothetical replacement value of the World Trade Center); *SR Int'l Bus. Ins. Co. v. World Trade Center Props. LLC*, 2006 WL 3073220 (S.D.N.Y. Oct. 31, 2006) (later

decision ruling that the "the *most* the Insureds can recover on a replacement cost basis is the amount it would cost to reproduce the WTC beam-for-beam, pane-for-pane, as it stood early on the morning of September 11, 2001").

A NOTE ON VALUATION AND INSURANCE REDLINING

Not all homeowners are able to purchase replacement cost coverage. Some insurance companies have underwriting guidelines setting a minimum home value or maximum home age, or a minimum ratio between market value and replacement cost for homes to be eligible for replacement cost coverage. These and other underwriting guidelines have been challenged as a form of insurance "redlining" with a disparate impact on groups protected by the Fair Housing Act. *See, e.g.,* D.J. Powers, *The Discriminatory Effects of Homeowners Insurance Underwriting Guidelines,* in Insurance Redlining: Disinvestment, Reinvestment, and the Evolving Role of Financial Institutions 120 (Gregory D. Squires, ed., 1997). These guidelines can have a negative effect on neighborhoods because "actual cash value" coverage often does not provide people with enough money to replace their homes using the same quality construction after a fire or other catastrophe. As a result, the quality of the neighborhood declines with each fire or catastrophe because people either take the money to rebuild elsewhere, leaving an empty lot, or they rebuild a lower-quality, less attractive house on the old site.

Property insurance companies used for many years geographic guidelines that had an obvious discriminatory effect and in at least some instances apparently a discriminatory intent. *See* William H. Lynch, *NAACP v. American Family,* in Insurance Redlining at 157. The location of insurance agent offices — "the doughnut pattern of agent placement, in which agents locate in a suburban ring around a city while ignoring the inner-city core" — further exacerbated the resulting property insurance availability problems. Jay D. Schultz, *Homeowners Insurance Availability and Agent Location,* in Insurance Redlining at 83.

Minimum value and maximum age guidelines are sometimes defended on the grounds that it is more expensive to provide each dollar of coverage on a low value or older home than on a more typical home. What is the obvious answer to that defense? (Charge a higher price.) Minimum ratios between market value and replacement cost are sometimes defended on the grounds that a large disparity between (low) market value and (high) replacement cost provide an incentive for arson. Look at the "loss settlement" section on page 13 of the HO3 in Figure 3.1 to see what you think of that defense. If the house burns down and the owner decides to take the money rather than rebuild, how does the company value the loss? On a replacement cost basis?

THE AUTO VALUATION PROBLEM

A standard automobile insurance policy provides that the company will "pay for loss to your car," minus any deductible. The policy contains a provision limiting the insurer's liability to the lower of the actual cash value of the vehicle or the cost of repair or replacement, and a provision giving the insurer the right to settle a loss by paying up to the actual cash value of the car or paying "to repair or replace the property or part with like kind and quality."

Assume that whenever a car is involved in a serious collision the market value of the car after being repaired will be less than the market value of a similar car that had not been involved in an accident. Call this the "diminution in value." In a situation in which the insurer elects not to pay the "actual cash value" of the car but rather elects to pay to repair the car, should the insurer be required to pay to the insured the "diminution in value" resulting from the accident? *Compare State Farm Mut. Auto. Ins. Co. v. Mabry*, 556 S.E.2d 114 (Ga. 2001), *with Bickel v. Nationwide Mut. Ins. Co.*, 143 S.E.2d 903 (Va. 1965). *See generally* Thomas O. Farrish, *"Diminished Value" in Automobile Insurance: The Controversy and Its Lessons*, 12 Conn. Ins. L.J. 39 (2005-2006); L.S. Teller, *Measure of Recovery by Insured Under Automobile Collision Insurance Policy*, 43 A.L.R.2d 327 (2007). Some recent auto insurance policies explicitly exclude "loss . . . due to diminution in value." Does the absence of this exclusion in older policies mean that those policies obligate insurers to pay for diminution in value? How about the absence of this exclusion in recent policies?

C.   Business Interruption Insurance

With the growth of commercial fire insurance in the nineteenth century, insurers quickly realized that fire loss included not only the cost of rebuilding a damaged business, but also the lost income from the business during the period of restoration. That realization led to "use and occupancy" coverage, which eventually became known as "business interruption insurance." In the homeowners' insurance context, the analogous coverage is the "Coverage D - Loss of Use" coverage that appears on page 5 of the ISO homeowners' insurance policy shown in Figure 3.1.

The following case addresses a business interruption loss following the attack on the World Trade Center. In addition to introducing you to business interruption insurance, it provides an opportunity to introduce the topic of insurable interest.

ZURICH AMERICAN INSURANCE CO. v. ABM INDUSTRIES, INC.

United States Court of Appeals, Second Circuit
397 F.3d 158 (2005)

CARDAMONE, Circuit Judge. The terrorist attack on the World Trade Center complex in lower Manhattan on September 11, 2001, brought about a harvest of bitter distress and loss. Of the complex, one stone was not left on another; it was all thrown down, bringing about, in addition to human casualties, the loss and destruction of businesses. It is the loss of one business that is the focus of this appeal.

Appellant ABM Industries Incorporated (ABM, appellant, or insured), an engineering and janitorial service contractor, provided extensive services at the World Trade Center complex (WTC or complex). ABM was insured against business interruption by appellee Zurich American Insurance Company (Zurich, appellee, or insurer). Zurich, as plaintiff, initiated the instant litigation by bringing a declaratory judgment action in the United States District Court for the Southern District of New York (Rakoff, J.) against ABM, asking the court to determine the extent of its liability to ABM resulting from the loss of the WTC.

ABM had sought from Zurich business interruption (BI) insurance coverage for its losses.

ABM appeals from an order dated May 28, 2003 and final judgment entered on January 6, 2004 in the district court, denying its motion for partial summary judgment and granting such a motion in favor of Zurich. ABM contends the district court erred when it determined that, as a matter of law, ABM was not entitled to coverage under the Business Interruption provision, . . . of its insurance policy with Zurich. . . .

BACKGROUND

A.   ABM INDUSTRIES

ABM provided extensive janitorial, lighting, and engineering services at the World Trade Center. It operated the heating, ventilating, and air-conditioning (HVAC) systems for the entire WTC, essentially running the physical plant. ABM serviced the common areas of the complex pursuant to contracts with the owners Silverstein Properties and the Port Authority of New York and New Jersey.

Under these contracts ABM had office and storage space in the complex and had access to janitorial closets and slop sinks located on every floor of the WTC buildings. ABM also had effective control over the freight elevators. At the time of the attacks, it employed more than 800 people at the WTC, and its exclusive and significant presence at the complex allowed it to secure service contracts with nearly all of the WTC's tenants. ABM also had service contracts with various building owners and tenants at 34 other locations in lower Manhattan.

In order to handle these enormous responsibilities at the WTC, ABM created and manned a call center to which tenants reported problems. ABM's engineering department took complaints at the call center and dispatched its employees to remedy problems as they arose. Additionally, ABM developed complex preventative maintenance schedules through state-of-the-art software that tracked the equipment in the WTC. These procedures allowed ABM to repair equipment before it malfunctioned.

B.   THE INSURANCE POLICY

ABM procured insurance coverage from Zurich for properties serviced by ABM throughout North America. . . . The policy provides a blanket limit of $127,396,375, subject to various sublimits. Section 7.A(1) of the policy covers loss or damage to "real and personal property, including but not limited to property owned, controlled, used, leased, or intended for use by the Insured" (Insurable Interest provision). In addition to covering property damage, the policy also provides business interruption coverage under §7.B(1) by insuring against "loss resulting directly from the necessary interruption of business caused by direct physical loss or damage, not otherwise excluded, to insured property at an insured location" (Business Interruption or BI provision). The blanket limit of $127,396,375 is the only applicable limit to the BI provision. . . .

ABM's claims under the policy arise out of the complete destruction of the WTC by the terrorist attacks of September 11, 2001. ABM declares it has lost, as a result of these events, all income that it derived from its operations at the WTC. Specifically, it asserts that it should be compensated for its lost income resulting from the destruction of: (1) equipment it owned and used to perform its janitorial and maintenance services; (2) its offices and warehouses in which ABM operated and stored its supplies; (3) the on-site call center; (4) the freight elevators, janitorial closets and slop sinks to which it had exclusive access; (5) the common areas in the WTC; and (6) the spaces occupied by the tenants with whom ABM had contracts to provide services. . . .

C. PROCEEDINGS BELOW

In its complaint Zurich requested a declaration that ABM's business interruption losses were subject to a $10 million per-occurrence limit of liability. Zurich argued that this sublimit applied because ABM's claim arose from damage and destruction of the premises of ABM's customers and hence was encompassed by the policy's Contingent Business Interruption clause—a provision triggered by damage to properties "not operated by the Insured."

ABM contested the applicability of the CBI provision and insisted instead that the relevant provision, to which no sublimit applies, is the Business Interruption provision, invoked by ABM's extensive relationship with the World Trade Center complex.

On May 28, 2003 the district court granted Zurich's motion for partial summary judgment, finding the BI provision, as well as the other sources of coverage invoked by ABM, inapplicable to the majority of ABM's claims. The district court held that ABM could obtain BI coverage only for the income it lost resulting from "the destruction of the World Trade Center space that ABM itself occupied or caused by the destruction of ABM's own supplies and equipment located in the World Trade Center." *Zurich Am. Ins. Co. v. ABM Indus., Inc.*, 265 F. Supp. 2d 302, 305 (S.D.N.Y. 2003). The court reasoned that the policy restricts BI coverage to "insured property at an insured location," and that the common areas and the tenants' premises in the WTC did not constitute insured property as that term is defined in the policy. *Id.* Specifically, the court held that ABM neither "used" nor "controlled" these areas in a manner that sufficed for the creation of a "legally cognizable 'interest' in the property." *Id.* at 305-06. . . .

We . . . reverse its order granting summary judgment insofar as it held that ABM was not entitled to coverage under the Business Interruption clause of its insurance contract with Zurich. . . . We believe that ABM's activities at the World Trade Center created an insurable interest cognizable under New York law, and that this insurable interest falls within the scope of the policy's coverage. We thus grant summary judgment in favor of ABM on the issue of Business Interruption coverage, and remand that issue for determination of ABM's damages to the district court. . . .

II. BUSINESS INTERRUPTION COVERAGE

We think the district court failed to elucidate the natural and ordinary meanings of pertinent terms in the BI provision of the policy as they applied to all of the categories of property under which ABM is seeking BI coverage and thus erred in barring such coverage. We consider first the scope of BI coverage set out in §7.B of the policy, which covers loss resulting from the interruption of business caused by damage "to insured property at an insured location." The scope of the BI provision is effectively delineated by §7.A(1) of the policy, the Insurable Interest provision, which defines the scope of coverage as "[t]he interest of the

Insured in all real and personal property including but not limited to property owned, controlled, used, leased or intended for use by the Insured."

In construing §7.A(1), Zurich argues for application of the doctrine of *ejusdem generis,* a rule of statutory construction under which "general words are construed to embrace only objects similar in nature to those objects enumerated by the preceding specific words." *Circuit City Stores, Inc. v. Adams,* 532 U.S. 105, 114-15 (2001). Under this principle Zurich maintains that a property interest such as ownership or tenancy is necessary for coverage regardless of the level of "use" or "control." Such a reading would require us to ignore the phrase "but not limited to" as well as the disjunctive "or" in the provision. Moreover, if a property interest were required under the contract, the terms "controlled," "used," and "intended for use" would be superfluous. In interpreting an insurance contract under New York law, a court must strive to "give meaning to every sentence, clause, and word." *Travelers Cas. & Sur. Co. v. Certain Underwriters at Lloyd's of London,* 96 N.Y.2d 583, 594 (N.Y. 2001). Thus, we construe §7.A(1) to require only an "insurable interest," the outer boundaries of which we delineate below, rather than finding that a "property interest" is a predicate to coverage.

A.   COMMON AREAS, TENANTS' PREMISES, AND HVAC SYSTEM

Because ABM did not "own" or "lease" the common areas and the premises of the other tenants, whether they "controlled," "used," or "intended to use" these areas is the relevant inquiry. We believe ABM "used" the common areas and the premises of the other tenants in the WTC within the meaning of the Insurable Interest provision. Hence, summary judgment for ABM is appropriate on this issue.

The district court defined "use" as "to carry out a purpose or action by means of." *Zurich,* 265 F. Supp. 2d at 305 (*quoting* Webster's Third New Int'l Dictionary of the English Language (Unabridged) 2524 (2002)). The trial court concluded that ABM did not "use" the common areas and other tenants' premises in the WTC complex because it could accomplish its purpose of cleaning and earning income with "mop[s]" and "broom[s]." *Id.* Thus, according to the district court, the premises in question were "the locations of ABM's acts, not the means through which the acts were accomplished." *Id.*

We disagree with the district court's application of this definition. We think instead that the "plain meaning [of these words] unambiguously includes the actual situation for which coverage is sought." The existence and configuration of the common areas and tenants' premises were vital to the execution of ABM's business purpose. These areas and premises were the means by which ABM derived its income and were as essential to that function as ABM's cleaning tools. Following the definition cited by the trial court, ABM therefore "used" this property. Contrary to the district court's view, ABM's use of other items in accomplishing its purpose makes these areas of the complex no less important to ABM's tasks.

The conclusion reached by the court below that the common areas and leased premises in the WTC were merely the "locations" rather than the "means" of ABM's work not only overlooks the instrumentality of the property in ABM's processes, but categorically disfavors providers of physical labor. The furnishing of physical services usually entails entering the space of another. To deny ABM's loss-of-income coverage simply because its income is derived from labor that occurs outside of its own cubicles and offices artificially excludes service providers when the contract itself does not limit coverage in such a manner. The nature of ABM's business requires movement from its own leased spaces onto another's property.

To give an example, a reasonable person would not contest that a hypothetical accounting firm "uses" the offices it occupies. Such a person should also conclude a janitorial and electrical service provider "uses" the spaces it services because, in both situations, it is the space or property that engenders productivity. The district court erroneously held that ABM's usage was confined to the offices that ABM itself occupied. ABM, unlike the accounting firm, does not engage in predominantly mental labor and is thus prevented from working solely within the confines of its own offices. Its "usage" necessarily extends beyond those boundaries. It would be wrong to privilege the hypothetical accounting firm's relationship with the property, over ABM's, such that the former entity could be said to "use" the property while the latter would not. In other words, it makes no sense to deny that ABM "uses" these premises simply because they are also used by another when the nature of ABM's work compels this duality.

Further, even if ABM did not "carry out" their purpose of running a successful business through the common areas and leased offices in the complex, it can still be said that ABM "used" these areas following other common dictionary definitions of the term. Clearly, ABM "had recourse to" and "enjoyment of" these areas and indeed could avail itself of all areas of the World Trade Center where it performed operations. Webster's Third New Int'l Dictionary of the English Language (Unabridged) 2523 (2002). Additionally, ABM applied all areas of the WTC to its advantage, thus "put[ting]" the characteristics of the property "into action" and into its "service." *Id.* (defining the intransitive verb "use" as "to put into action or service: have recourse to or enjoyment of ").

B. PROPERTY OCCUPIED BY ABM

ABM also seeks BI coverage for income derived from property that it occupied, such as the "offices" and "warehouses" on site in which it stored equipment and conducted operations; its call center; and the freight elevators, janitorial closets, and slop sinks to which it had nearly exclusive access. Because ABM "used" and "controlled" the areas that it occupied as contemplated under the policy, we hold it is entitled to summary judgment on this issue of BI coverage.

ABM clearly availed itself of the property that it occupied to facilitate its income-producing activities and thus "used" this property. And while exclusive access to an area is not necessary to "control" that area, exclusivity strongly supports the conclusion that "control" exists. ABM's privileged relationship with, and management of, its offices, storage spaces, freight elevators, closets, and sinks indicates that it exerted power and directed influence over these premises. Therefore, ABM "controlled" its occupied properties. *See* Webster's Third New Int'l Dictionary of the English Language (Unabridged) 496 (2002) (defining the verb "control" as "to exercise restraining or directing influence over: . . . have power over").

Although ABM "used" and "controlled" this category of property, the district court held that it could not recover under the BI provision because "[t]he undisputed cause of the interruption here was the destruction of the World Trade Center, which would have totally interrupted the ABM business here in issue regardless of what happened to the freight elevators, loading docks, etc." *Zurich*, No. 01 Civ. 11200, slip op. at 2. We cannot agree with the

district court's approach to the causation issue because it artificially severs the
chain of events occurring on September 11. Since the destruction of the WTC
and the properties owned by ABM were obviously simultaneous, the destruction of ABM's occupied property was not "incidental to" the destruction of the
WTC, as concluded by the district court, because this property was *part of* the
complex. Accordingly, the ruination of the WTC, *including* the property at issue,
was the cause of ABM's business interruption. Contrary to the district court's
view, ABM's failure to have an interest in the entire WTC does not bar its claim
for lost income due to the destruction of a portion of the WTC. . . .

D. INSURABLE INTEREST

Given that, in our view, ABM "used" and "controlled" property in the WTC and
thereby acquired a BI claim, we next examine the district court's conclusion
that even if ABM "used" or "controlled" the common areas and the premises of
other tenants, its activities did not rise to the level necessary to create a "legally
cognizable 'interest'" in the property. *Zurich*, 265 F. Supp. 2d at 306. In light of
ABM's substantial influence over, and availment of, the WTC infrastructure to
develop its business, it is difficult to imagine what would constitute a "legally
cognizable 'interest' in the property," apart from ownership or tenancy. The
terms of the insurance policy, however, do not limit coverage to property owned
or leased by the insured. To the contrary, the policy's scope expressly includes
real or personal property that the insured "used," "controlled," or "intended
for use."

The district court's imposition of the "legally cognizable 'interest' in the
property" requirement is an impermissible hurdle to insurance coverage, contemplated by neither the parties nor the New York legislature. The only prerequisite to coverage mandated by New York law is that an entity have an "insurable
interest" in the property it insures. New York law embraces the *sui generis* nature
of an "insurable interest" and statutorily defines this term to include "any lawful and substantial economic interest in the safety or preservation of property
from loss, destruction or pecuniary damage." N.Y. Ins. Law §3401 (2002). ABM's
income stream is dependent upon the common areas and leased premises in
the WTC complex, and thus ABM meets New York's requirement of having an
"insurable interest" in that property.

The prophylactic function of the "insurable interest" requirement is not
destroyed by its breadth. Zurich asserts that extending ABM's insurable interest
to include the common areas and leased premises would mean that ABM has
direct damage coverage for these areas—"an absurd result." To the contrary,
ABM does not have and does not claim to have an insurable interest in these
properties for the purpose of direct damage coverage because it suffered no
direct pecuniary loss of asset value. The insurable interest requirement thus
avoids absurd results by protecting only that in which ABM has a financial
stake—its future stream of income.

Zurich further contends that ABM's interest is only derivative from the property, and that it does not constitute a direct interest in the property itself. In so
arguing, Zurich unsuccessfully seeks to amend the text of N.Y. Ins. Law §3401 by
narrowing the definition of an insurable interest. The outer reaches of an interest that can be insured clearly encompass an indirect economic interest in the
property. Such an interest can be insured if, as is the case here, it falls within the
definitional boundaries set by the insurance policy.

NOTES AND QUESTIONS

1. As with property insurance claims generally, the most difficult and hard-fought issues in business interruption insurance claims relate to valuation of the loss. Most of these issues are very fact intensive and, thus, not well suited to summary treatment in an appellate case or an introductory insurance law class.

2. The events of 9/11 resulted in a large number of insurance disputes, many of which included business interruption insurance issues. In *Abner, Herrman & Brock, Inc. v. Great Northern Insurance Co.*, 308 F. Supp. 2d 331 (S.D.N.Y. 2004), the court held that the covered business interruption losses were limited to the time required to restore access to the building, notwithstanding the fact that vehicular traffic in the area continued to be diverted. *See also Duane Reade, Inc. v. St. Paul Fire & Marine Ins. Co.*, 411 F.3d 384 (2d Cir. 2005) (holding that business interruption loss was limited to the length of time required to resume operations in another location reasonably equivalent to the former store at the World Trade Center, rather than the exact site of the store); *Children's Place Retail Stores, Inc. v. Federal Ins. Co.*, 829 N.Y.S.2d 500 (App. Div. 2007) (holding that business interruption loss was limited to the period it would have taken a reasonable retailer to resume operations in a different location); *Broad Street, LLC v. Gulf Ins. Co.*, 832 N.Y.S.2d 1 (App. Div. 2006) (holding that the covered loss of income loss was limited to the period that tenants were not permitted to return to the building).

3. In *United Air Lines, Inc. v. Insurance Co. of the State of Pennsylvania*, 439 F.3d 128 (2d Cir. 2006), United Air Lines sought recovery under the "Property Terrorism and Sabotage" policy, issued by ISOP, for the loss of revenue from the shutdown of air traffic following 9/11. The Second Circuit affirmed the trial court decision that such losses were not covered because they were not a "direct result" of damage to the airline's property. Rather, they were "caused by the nation-wide suspension of air service." United Air Lines tried to argue that it was entitled to coverage under a special provision of the policy relating to business loss attributable to damage to adjacent premises, reasoning that the Pentagon was adjacent to United's offices at Reagan National Airport, where United occupied lots of space and maintained equipment. The court affirmed the trial court's rejection of that argument:

> Ultimately, though, we need not resolve whether the Pentagon is "adjacent" to United's property. Even if it is, United cannot show that the Airport was shut down "as a direct result of damage to" the Pentagon. There was apparently a temporary halt of flights into and out of the Airport on 9/11 before the Pentagon was struck. The evidence also indicates, not surprisingly, that the government's subsequent decision to halt operations at the Airport indefinitely was based on fears of future attacks. The Airport was reopened when it was able to comply with more rigorous safety standards; the timetable had nothing to do with repairing, mitigating, or responding to the damage caused by the attack on the Pentagon.
>
> In other words, suppose American Airlines Flight 77 that day had missed the Pentagon and smashed into a private office building a mile beyond, or some other similar property not very far from the Airport but clearly not "adjacent" to it. In light of the hijacking of the other airplanes that morning and the successful attack on the World Trade Center, it can hardly be doubted that

the effect on subsequent flight operations generally, and United operations at the Airport in particular, would have been virtually identical. The interruption to United's business following the attacks was, therefore, not the "direct result" of damage to adjacent premises.

439 F.3d at 134. Note that the court conceded that United was entitled to recover for the lost profits attributable to its lost ticket office in the World Trade Center.

4. Litigation over the valuation of the World Trade Center loss continued until May 2007, when New York governor Elliot Spitzer announced the final settlement of the World Trade Center claims. *See* Charles Bagli, *Insurers Agree to Pay Billions at Ground Zero*, N.Y. Times, May 24, 2007, at A1 (reporting that the total insurance recovery for rebuilding the World Trade Center would be $4.55 billion, which represents "about half of the $9 billion cost of building five towers, retail space and possibly a hotel"). The *New York Times* reported:

    > As part of the deal, the Port Authority and Mr. Silverstein had to relinquish their claim that the companies owed more than $500 million in interest resulting from delays in making the payments. The insurers, in turn, abandoned their claim that they did not owe the money until the project was completed, in 2012. . . . Mr. Spitzer said the agreement, which ends all the litigation, was a collaborative effort on the part of many officials who had lost "patience with the ongoing fighting that didn't serve the public interest or the effort to rebuild."

    Id.

5. As might be expected, given the size and ramifications of 9/11, there was extensive insurance coverage litigation. Reported opinions issued in the cases addressed a wide variety of issues:

    A. Valuation of the property damage. *See SR Int'l Business Ins. Co., Ltd. v. World Trade Center Properties, LLC*, 445 F. Supp. 2d 320 (S.D.N.Y. 2006) (holding that the appraisal process, under the plain meaning of the contract, requires an estimate of replacement costs less depreciation to rebuild the covered buildings as they were prior to 9/11).

    B. The scope and valuation of the covered business interruption losses. *See United Air Lines, Inc. v. Insurance Co. of Pa.*, 439 F.3d 128 (2d Cir. 2006) (holding that the damage to insured's property must be "physical" to trigger the business interruption provision); *J&R Elecs. Inc. v. One Beacon Ins. Co.*, 825 N.Y.S.2d 462 (App. Div. 2006) (noting that the calculation of a company's lost business income pursuant to business interruption provision should take into account payments already made by insurer for damaged merchandise); *PMA Capital Ins. Co. v. US Airways, Inc.*, 262 S.E.2d 369 (Va. 2006) (finding compensation that US Airways received under the Air Stabilization Act to qualify as recoveries under the policy, and so amount due under the policy should be reduced accordingly).

    C. The applicability of the contamination exclusion. *See Parks Real Estate Purchasing Group v. St. Paul Fire & Marine Ins. Co.*, 472 F.3d 33 (2d Cir. 2006) (finding the term "contamination" to be ambiguous in the context of the policy).

D. Insurers' subrogation rights. *See In re Sept. 11 Prop. Damage & Business Loss Litig. v. Port Auth. of N.Y. & N.J.*, 468 F. Supp. 2d 508 (S.D.N.Y. 2006) (finding that waiver of an individual insurer's right to subrogation by insured, in a commercial lease, was valid because an insurer cannot recover from its own insured or from a third party who qualifies as an insured under the policy regardless); *Industrial Risk Insurers v. Port Auth. of N.Y. & N.J.*, 387 F. Supp. 2d 299 (S.D.N.Y. 2005) (noting that New York allows waiver of an insurer's subrogation rights in commercial leases because there is equal bargaining power and the claim did not arise out of gross negligence). For a discussion of subrogation doctrine, see Part VI of this chapter.

6. The insurable interest requirement alluded to in the *AMB Industries* case is common to both property and life insurance, though the details can be significantly different. (See Part II.b. below for a discussion of how the insurable interest doctrine applies to life insurance.) In essence, the insurable interest doctrine requires that, for an insurance policy to be enforceable (and to avoid being struck down as contrary to public policy), the person or organization that takes out the policy must have an insurable interest in the property or life being insured. In general what constitutes an insurable interest is some economic loss that will occur to the policyholder should the insured event take place. The details differ among jurisdictions. Some apply a "factual expectancy" test, which means only that the person seeking the insurance expects some economic gain if the property in question avoids harm. Other jurisdictions, however, apply a narrower definition of insurable interest, sometimes called the "legal interest" test, which is satisfied only if the policyholder has some legal interest—for example, a property right—in the property being insured. With property insurance, the rule typically is that the insured must have an insurable interest both at the time the policy is taken out and when the loss occurs. Different rules apply for life insurance. Although the insurable interest requirement arose as a matter of common law, statutory law now governs in many states.

7. The standard rationales offered for the insurable interest requirement are (a) a concern about moral hazard and (b) a concern about windfalls (i.e., gambling). Do these concerns provide a persuasive justification for the doctrine? Can you make an argument that, even in the absence of this doctrine, well-functioning insurance markets would likely produce a similar result: insurance policies being issued only if, and to the extent that, policyholders had an insurable interest in what is being insured? Is there some problem in insurance markets that suggest the need for the doctrine? What are the arguments for and against the two competing definitions of insurable interest?

8. The insurable interest doctrine is an example of the "principle of indemnity" in insurance law. This principle, mentioned in *ABM Industries* above, says that insureds should generally receive from their insurer an amount no greater than their full economic losses—not more than necessary to indemnify them. We will see this principle in action again, among other places, in the sections on coordination of benefits provisions (in Part III.B., dealing with disability insurance) and subrogation (in Part VI). This principle, and the provisions and doctrines that embody it, are typically justified on grounds similar to those articulated above for the insurable interest doctrine.

D.   Innocent Co-Insureds

For obvious reasons, property insurance policies exclude coverage for property loss caused intentionally by the beneficiary of the insurance policy. (What are these obvious reasons?) Indeed, even if an insurance policy did not explicitly exclude coverage in such a situation, an insurance company would have a very strong case for denying coverage on public policy grounds. (Why?)

Insured property often has more than one owner. Can an "innocent" owner recover when one owner intentionally destroys insured property? This question has important public policy overtones today because burning down the family home appears to be an unfortunately common form of separation assault. *See* Brief of Amici Curiae California Alliance Against Domestic Violence and Ad Hoc Committee of Law Professors Working on Domestic Violence in *Borman v. State Farm Fire & Cas. Co.*, 521 N.W.2d 266 (Mich. 1994). In some cases, this arson may be an attempt to physically injure the spouse. In other cases, it may simply be an attempt to destroy the most valuable family asset and thereby make it more difficult for a spouse who wants to leave to survive economically on his or her own.

WATSON v. UNITED SERVICES AUTOMOBILE ASSOCIATION
Supreme Court of Minnesota
566 N.W.2d 683 (1997)

ANDERSON, J. On the evening of January 13, 1994, a mobile home and its contents located at 569 East Gull River Road in Brainerd, Minnesota[,] were completely destroyed by fire. The Brainerd Fire Department investigated the fire and in its report listed the ignition factor as "undetermined."

At the time of the fire, the mobile home and the real estate on which it was located were being purchased by Elizabeth Watson and Keith Watson as joint tenants under the terms of a contract for deed. Elizabeth and Keith Watson lived in the mobile home together from 1986 until April 1991, when they separated and Elizabeth Watson moved out. Keith Watson continued to live in the home. After she left in 1991, Elizabeth Watson did not have a key to the home. Nonetheless, by Keith Watson's account, Elizabeth Watson "took care of" payment of real estate taxes on the property, while he paid the homeowner's insurance premiums. Elizabeth Watson petitioned to dissolve the parties' marital relationship and a marriage dissolution hearing was held on December 28, 1993, more than two weeks before the fire. At the hearing, a dissolution of the Watsons' marriage was granted, but the dissolution decree was not filed until January 31, 1994, 18 days after the fire. The record shows that both parties were experiencing some financial difficulties at the time of the fire.

Elizabeth and Keith Watson were named insureds on a homeowner's insurance policy issued by USAA, which policy covered the mobile home and its contents. The policy provided coverage of up to $27,800 for the dwelling, $27,800 for personal property, and $5,560 for loss of use. After the fire, the Watsons prepared a loss report. They provided the report to USAA on January 14, 1994. That same day, USAA inspected the loss site and advanced the Watsons $10,000 pursuant to the policy.

Elizabeth Watson subsequently submitted a claim to USAA for further insurance proceeds under the policy. USAA then conducted an investigation of the fire. As part of the investigation, USAA elicited two statements from Keith Watson in which he stated that he was in Aitkin, Minnesota[,] on a construction job during the time of the fire. He denied intentionally starting the fire or arranging to have the fire set. USAA, however, determined that the fire involved arson. USAA based its conclusion upon the elimination of all accidental sources of ignition, the pattern and progress of the fire, and the presence of kerosene in one of the carpet and padding samples taken from the living room of the home. Accordingly, USAA denied Elizabeth Watson's claim for insurance proceeds under two provisions in the policy which excluded coverage for intentional acts and concealment or fraud relating to the policy. The "intentional loss" provision contains the following language:

> Section I—Exclusions
>
> We do not insure for loss caused directly or indirectly by any of the following. Such loss is excluded regardless of any other cause or event contributing concurrently or in any sequence to the loss. . . .
>
> h. Intentional Loss, meaning any loss arising out of any act committed:
> (1) by or at the direction of an insured; and
> (2) with the intent to cause a loss.

The "concealment or fraud" provision of the policy contains the following language:

> Sections I and II—Conditions . . .
>
> 2. Concealment or Fraud. The entire policy will be void if an insured has:
>   a. before a loss, willfully; or
>   b. after a loss, willfully and with intent to defraud; concealed or misrepresented any material fact or circumstance relating to this insurance.

A jury trial was held from October 17 to 19, 1995. USAA presented the testimony of a specialist in fire debris analysis who had analyzed four samples of burned carpet and padding that were taken from the Watsons' mobile home. The specialist testified that of the four samples, only one revealed the presence of any ignitable liquid residue. The specialist recognized that residue as having the characteristics of burned kerosene. Elizabeth Watson also testified at trial, and stated that she was at her father's home in Nisswa at the time of the fire.

The jury returned a special verdict on October 19, 1995. The jury was asked to determine whether the fire at the Watsons' home was an incendiary fire (intentionally set), and found that the fire was incendiary in origin. The jury also found that Keith Watson had participated in, arranged for, or aided or abetted the setting of the fire. The jury further found that Keith Watson had willfully and with intent to defraud, concealed or misrepresented to USAA material facts or circumstances concerning this loss. The jury was not asked to decide whether Elizabeth Watson was an innocent insured.

. . . Based upon these findings, the court concluded that the USAA policy did not cover the Watsons' loss, and dismissed the action.

Elizabeth Watson appealed. The court of appeals agreed with the district court that the use of the term "an insured" in USAA's policy unambiguously denies coverage for an innocent insured when any other insured intentionally causes a loss or commits fraud. *Watson v. United Services Auto. Ass'n,* 551 N.W.2d 500, 502 (Minn. Ct. App. 1996). The court of appeals, however, reversed. *Id.* at 504. . . . The court of appeals observed that the Minnesota standard fire insurance policy contained in Minn. Stat. §65A.01 uses the term "the insured" instead of "an insured." *Id.* at 502. The court of appeals noted that this court has interpreted the term "the insured" as excluding coverage only for the particular insured who intentionally caused a loss or committed fraud and not for an innocent insured. *Id.* at 503 (*citing Hogs Unlimited v. Farm Bureau Mut. Ins. Co.,* 401 N.W.2d 381, 384 (Minn. 1987)). Accordingly, the court of appeals reformed USAA's policy to conform with the Minnesota standard fire insurance policy. *Id.* at 504. The court remanded to the district court for an order allowing Elizabeth Watson to recover her proportionate share of the insured loss. *Id.*

II

[The court first addressed USAA's argument that the appellate court decided the case based on a legal theory not raised at trial and then addressed the merits of that theory.]

A.   IS "AN INSURED" AMBIGUOUS?

In recent years, courts have looked to the language of the insurance policy to determine whether innocent co-insured spouses can recover insurance proceeds. The majority of courts use a contract-based theory which focuses on a contractual analysis of the insurance policy provisions. *See, e.g., Vance v. Pekin Ins. Co.,* 457 N.W.2d 589, 592 (Iowa 1990). Under this contract-based theory, if the policy language is ambiguous as to whether innocent co-insured spouses are excluded from coverage, courts will construe the policy to allow recovery by the innocent co-insured spouse. *See, e.g., Vance,* 457 N.W.2d at 592. USAA's insurance policy excludes from coverage a loss caused by the intentional acts of "an insured." In addition, under a second provision of USAA's policy, the fraudulent acts of "an insured" render the policy void.

Courts have generally found ambiguity in policies which exclude from coverage the intentional or fraudulent acts of "the insured." *See* Rachel R. Watkins Schoenig, *Property Insurance and the Innocent Co-Insured: Was it All Pay and No Gain for the Innocent Co-Insured?,* 43 Drake L. Rev. 893, 900 (1995) and cases cited therein.

. . . Courts have found no ambiguity, however, in policies which exclude from coverage the intentional or fraudulent acts of "you or any other insured," "any insured," and "an insured." *See Amick v. State Farm Fire and Cas. Co.,* 862 F.2d 704, 706 (8th Cir.1988) ("you or any other insured"). . . . Consistent with this line of cases, the court of appeals held in *Reitzner v. State Farm Fire and Cas. Co., Inc.* that a policy excluding coverage based on the intentional or fraudulent acts of "you or any other insured" unambiguously precluded an innocent coinsured assignee of the vendor of a contract for deed from recovering on the policy when the contract for deed vendee intentionally set fire to the property. *Reitzner,* 510 N.W.2d at 24. We conclude that the "an insured" language of USAA's policy unambiguously bars coverage for innocent co-insured spouses.

B.   STATUTE-BASED THEORY

But the conclusion that USAA's policy language is unambiguous does not end our inquiry. An emerging theory of recovery for innocent co-insured spouses, a statute-based theory, adds a second step to the contractual analysis. Under the statute-based theory, if an insurance policy provision unambiguously excludes coverage for innocent co-insured spouses, the court must then look to the state's statutory standard fire insurance policy. If the exclusion of coverage contained in the insurance policy conflicts with the level of protection provided in the statutory standard fire insurance policy, the court will hold the insurance policy unenforceable. To date, courts in Michigan, Louisiana, and Georgia have adopted this statute-based theory. The court of appeals also relied on this theory to invalidate USAA's intentional loss and concealment or fraud provisions. *Watson*, 551 N.W.2d at 502-504. Under the statute-based theory, courts have remedied a conflict between an insurance policy and the statutory standard fire insurance policy by reforming the insurance policy to provide at least the level of coverage provided for in the statute.

The Michigan courts provide an example of the statute-based theory in operation. In *Morgan v. Cincinnati Ins. Co.*, the Michigan Supreme Court contractually analyzed a provision of the Michigan standard fire insurance policy which stated that the policy shall be void if "the insured" commits fraud, and held that the statutory policy did not bar recovery for insureds who are innocent of fraud. 307 N.W.2d 53, 54-55 (Mich. 1981) (*citing* M.C.L.A. §500.2832). Subsequently, in *Ponder v. Allstate Ins. Co.*, 729 F. Supp. 60 (E.D. Mich. 1990) a United States District Court interpreting Michigan law held that an insurance policy's unambiguous concealment or fraud provision barring recovery as to "any insured" committing fraud must be reformed to conform with the fraud clause in the Michigan standard fire insurance policy. 729 F. Supp. at 61-62 (citing M.C.L.A. §500.2832). Thereafter, in *Borman v. State Farm Fire & Cas. Co.*, the Michigan Supreme Court held that a policy's intentional acts and concealment or fraud provisions using the language "you or any person insured" and "you [and/or] any other insured" were both in conflict with Michigan's standard fire insurance policy, and, therefore, were void. 521 N.W.2d at 267 n.4, 269 (*citing* M.C.L.A. §500.2832 (repealed 1990)). . . .

C.   MINNESOTA STANDARD FIRE INSURANCE POLICY

We turn, then, to the question of whether USAA's policy conflicts with the Minnesota standard fire insurance policy. The Minnesota standard fire insurance policy is contained in Minn. Stat. §65A.01. The statute was enacted to "do away with the evils arising from the insertion in policies of conditions ingeniously worded which restricted the liability of the insurer and gave the insured less protection than he might naturally suppose he was getting under his contract." *Heim v. American Alliance Ins. Co. of New York*, 180 N.W. 225, 226 (Minn. 1920). Because the statute has a remedial purpose, it must be broadly construed.

Minnesota Statutes section 65A.01 was intended to secure uniformity in fire insurance policies. *Id.* at 288, 180 N.W. at 227. Use of the statutory form is mandatory, and its provisions may not be omitted, changed, or waived. *Id.* This principle is reflected in the statute's "conformity clause," which states:

> No policy or contract of fire insurance shall be made, issued or delivered by any insurer . . . on any property in this state, unless it shall provide the specified

coverage and conform as to all provisions, stipulations, and conditions, with such form of policy, except as provided in . . . statutes containing specific requirements that are inconsistent with the form of this policy.

Minn. Stat. §65A.01, subd. 1. This court has held that when an insurance policy provision is in direct conflict with a statute regulating the insurance industry, the statute's conformity clause operates to substitute the statutory provisions for the policy provision. *Atwater Creamery Co. v. Western Nat. Mut. Ins. Co.,* 366 N.W.2d 271, 275 (Minn. 1985).

We agree with the court of appeals that the Minnesota standard fire insurance policy guarantees a minimum level of coverage that supersedes any attempt to limit coverage to less than the statutory minimum. *See Krueger v. State Farm Fire and Cas. Co.,* 510 N.W.2d 204, 209 (Minn. Ct. App. 1993). Insurance companies may, however, incorporate additional or different terms into their policies that offer more coverage than the statutory minimum. *See id.* The statute provides conditions under which insurance companies may incorporate additional or different terms into their policies:

> Any policy or contract . . . may be issued without incorporating the exact language of the Minnesota standard fire insurance policy, provided: Such policy or contract shall, with respect to the peril of fire, afford the insured all the rights and benefits of the Minnesota standard fire insurance policy and such additional benefits as the policy provides; . . . such policy is complete as to its terms of coverage; and, the commissioner is satisfied that such policy or contract complies with the provisions hereof.

Minn. Stat. §65A.01, subd. 1; *see also Fireman's Fund Ins. Co. v. Vermes Credit Jewelry,* 185 F.2d 142, 144 (8th Cir. 1950) (holding that any warranty, limitation, or condition which is not specifically authorized by Minnesota standard fire insurance policy or is not in harmony with the letter or spirit of the laws of Minnesota relating to fire insurance cannot be given effect).

USAA argues that Elizabeth Watson cannot recover under the USAA policy because the policy contains an "intentional loss" provision excluding coverage for any loss arising out of any act committed "by or at the direction of an insured," and Keith Watson, an insured, intentionally caused the loss. While the USAA insurance policy contains both an "intentional loss" provision and a "concealment or fraud" provision, in its brief to this court, USAA's arguments regarding the validity of its exclusion of coverage for innocent insureds solely concern the "intentional loss" provision. Because the Minnesota standard fire insurance policy does not contain a parallel "intentional loss" provision, USAA's "intentional loss" provision is an additional term. Therefore, we will uphold USAA's "intentional loss" provision only if it affords the insured all the rights and benefits of the Minnesota standard fire insurance policy or offers additional benefits which provide more coverage to the insured than the statutory minimum. We conclude that USAA's "intentional loss" provision, insofar as it excludes coverage for innocent co-insured spouses, is at odds with the rights and benefits of the Minnesota standard fire insurance policy.

Even though the Minnesota standard fire insurance policy does not contain a specific "intentional loss" provision, it does contain other provisions dealing with policy exclusions for intentional acts. For example, the "concealment or fraud provision" of the Minnesota standard fire insurance policy states:

> This entire policy shall be void if, whether before a loss, the insured has willfully, or after a loss, the insured has willfully and with intent to defraud, concealed or misrepresented any material fact or circumstance concerning this insurance or the subject thereof, or the interests of the insured therein.

Minn. Stat. §65A.01, subd. 3. It should be noted that USAA's concealment or fraud provision voids the policy if an insured has before a loss, willfully; or after a loss, willfully and with intent to defraud; concealed or misrepresented any material fact or circumstance relating to the insurance. Another provision states that the insurance company shall not be liable for a loss occurring "while the hazard is increased by any means within the control or knowledge of the insured. . . ." *Id.* We held in *Hogs Unlimited* that a policy containing the "standard fraud provision" using the "the insured" language of Minn. Stat. §65A.01, subd. 3, voids the policy only as to "guilty" insureds and not as to innocent co-insureds. *Hogs Unlimited*, 401 N.W.2d at 384-85. Thus, we conclude that the legislature's use of "the insured" in the Minnesota standard fire insurance policy evinces a general intent to compensate an innocent co-insured spouse despite the intentional acts of the other insured spouse.

Courts in other states have adopted similar reasoning. In *Borman*, the Michigan Supreme Court held that an insurance policy provision, which excluded coverage for the intentional acts of "you or any other insured," "cover[ed] the same subject matter, fraud on the insurer," as the concealment or fraud provision of the statutory standard policy. *Borman*, 521 N.W.2d at 267 n.4, 268-69. Similarly, in *Osbon*, the Louisiana Supreme Court determined that a policy's "intentional loss" provision did not conform to the Louisiana standard fire insurance policy even though the statute did not specifically contain an "intentional loss" provision. *Osbon*, 632 So.2d at 1159-61. The statute did, however, provide coverage for innocent co-insureds when "the insured" neglected to use all reasonable means to preserve the property after a loss, or when the hazard was increased by means within the control or knowledge of "the insured." *Id.* at 1159-60 (citing LSA-R.S. 22:691 F(2) (1995)).

III

USAA additionally argues that its insurance policy must be valid because the Commissioner of Commerce approved it. Minnesota Statutes section 65A.01, subdivision 1 does provide that approval of the commissioner is a prerequisite to the incorporation of additional or different terms into insurance policies. However, a provision in an insurance policy contrary to the Minnesota standard fire insurance policy cannot be permitted to stand even if the commissioner approved it. The commissioner is an administrative official with no power to alter the meaning and intention of the language of the legislature. We conclude that USAA's argument lacks merit. . . .

NOTES AND QUESTIONS

1. Courts in most jurisdictions have held that "*an* insured" means "*either* insured" and have enforced that meaning. Courts in a few states have found that the "an insured" language is ambiguous. *See, e.g., Michigan Millers Mut.*

Ins. Corp. v. Benfield, 140 F.3d 915 (11th Cir. 1998) (applying Florida law). Would an exclusion referring to intentional acts by "any insured" be clearer? Is the problem here really drafting? Think about Judge Clark's concurrence in *Gaunt*. Look at the intentional loss exclusion in the HO3 policy in Figure 3.1 (item 8, top right column, page 12 of policy). Is it clearer? Does it conflict with the statutory fire policy?

2. In a case that also relied on the statutory fire policy to find in favor of the innocent spouse, the Michigan Supreme Court noted the following public policy arguments made by amici on both sides of the issue:

> State Farm and amicus curiae Auto Club Group Insurance Company contend that barring recovery by innocent insureds is necessary to address the problems of affordability and cost control for the insurer and the consumer. State Farm asserts that when a home is destroyed by fire, State Farm usually incurs a net loss after the mortgage holder or loss payee is paid and any litigation is successfully defended. It contends that homeowner's insurance will become more affordable if the equity of innocent co-insureds is forfeited to fire insurers.
>
> *Amici curiae* on behalf of innocent co-insureds contend that many cases of homeowners' arson are related to domestic violence, and an inability of the innocent spouse to recover insurance proceeds may increase the guilty party's incentive to commit arson.

Borman v. State Farm Fire & Cas. Co., 521 N.W.2d 266, 270 (Mich. 1994). The court explained the latter amici's contentions as follows:

> It is contended that domestic violence is largely motivated by a desire of one spouse to control and dominate the other. That the abuser's desire to control is threatened when the abused partner attempts to leave the relationship, and the abuser may resort to threatening and actual conduct designed to constrain the abused partner to rejoin the abuser, and depriving the abused partner of a home for herself and her children may and has been part of the abuser's plans.

Id. at 270 n.17. *Cf.* Martha R. Mahoney, *Legal Images of Battered Women: Redefining the Issue of Separation*, 90 Mich. L. Rev. 1 (1991) (describing battering as a calculated struggle for power and control).

The brief filed in the case on behalf of the California Alliance Against Domestic Violence and Ad Hoc Committee of Law Professors Working On Domestic Violence argued that:

> Appellant, State Farm Insurance, argues that denying insurance coverage to "innocent" co-insureds will increase insurance arson. In fact, if appellant's effort succeeds, the result may be *more* arson, not less. This ironic result is possible for two related reasons: many cases of home owners' arson are domestic violence related, and, for many of those domestic violence related cases, the inability of the innocent spouse to recover insurance proceeds may actually *increase* the guilty party's incentive to commit arson. Doing away with the co-insured's right to insurance recovery will not deter the arson in these cases because the domestic violence arsonist is not motivated by the desire for personal financial gain. Rather, the purpose of the act of arson is frequently to force his estranged partner to return home or to punish her for having left.

Brief at 2. The court in *Borman* stated that it did not rely on any of these public policy arguments and, like the court in *Watson,* ruled for the innocent co-insured on the basis that the statutory fire policy treated co-insureds separately.

3. The courts' use of the statutory fire policy in these cases is an example of a general insurance law rule, which the Preliminary Draft Number 3 of the Restatement of the Law of Liability Insurance (RLLI) states as follows: "A liability insurance policy term or coverage that violates a statute, regulation, judicially declared public policy, or other mandatory legal rule is void." PD3, RLLI, §46(1).

4. In *Utah Farm Bureau Insurance Co. v. Crook*, 980 P.2d 685 (Utah 1999), the Utah Supreme Court narrowed an earlier case that appeared to establish a public policy in favor of granting recovery to innocent co-insureds. In *Crook,* Clinton Crook burned down a trailer he owned jointly with Rhonda Crook after she refused to leave a bar with him. The case turned on an analysis of the policy language, which contained an intentional loss exclusion with the "an insured" language present in the *Watson* policy. The court concluded that the exclusion unambiguously prevented Mrs. Crook from recovering her share of the value of the trailer. One judge concurred, writing:

> I believe the conclusion we have reached today, although legally correct, burdens Ms. Crook with an unjust result. I write to suggest that our legislature consider enacting legislation which would allow innocent co-insureds to recover under insurance policies despite the felonious intentional acts of spouses or other co-insureds. Many states have already created an "innocent spouse" rule of some variation. Nebraska, North Dakota, and Washington have recently enacted statutes which allow an "innocent spouse" to recover where the intentional act of a co-insured is part of a pattern of domestic abuse. See Neb. Rev. Stat. Ann. §44-7406(6) (1998); N.D. Cent. Code §26.1-32-04 (1995); Wash. Rev. Code §48.18.550 (1998).
>
> For example, the Washington statute cited above allows insurers to exclude coverage for losses caused by the intentional or fraudulent acts of any insured. However, that exclusion shall not apply to deny an insured's otherwise-covered property loss if the property loss is caused by an act of domestic abuse by another insured under the policy, the insured claiming property loss files a police report and cooperates with any law enforcement investigation relating to the act of domestic abuse, and the insured claiming property loss did not cooperate in or contribute to the creation of the property loss. *Id.* §48.18.550(3).

Id. at 689-690. For an extensive listing of other cases, see Larry D. Scheafer, *Annotation, Right of Innocent Insured to Recover Under Fire Policy Covering Property Intentionally Burned by Another Insured,* 11 A.L.R.4th 1228 (1999).

4. How effective do you think the Washington statute cited above would be in addressing the problem of battering-by-arson? Domestic violence is notoriously difficult to police, in part because women are afraid to cooperate. *See, e.g.,* Mahoney, *supra* note 2. The "law professors" brief in the *Borman* case criticized special rules for domestic violence cases, claiming that the rules would harm women who were unable to separate immediately after the assault by denying them the insurance proceeds that might enable them to leave at a future date. *See* Brief, *supra,* at 7.

5. Why should it take legislation to allow innocent spouses to recover? Why might insurance companies revise their policy language to switch from "the" to "an"? Should the ability of a vindictive spouse to succeed in destroying the family asset turn on the existence of a "the" or an "an" in a property insurance policy? What arguments might an insurance industry trade association mount in opposition to legislative reform of the sort referred to in note 3? Economic theory says that in a competitive market lower costs result in lower prices, which benefit consumers. Are there reasons to believe that the insurance market is not working here to produce a socially beneficial result? Why? Think here about the insurer-side adverse selection (the "lemons" problem) discussed in the first chapter and in connection with opportunism at the point of claim in Chapter 2.

6. If the insurer's denial of coverage in *Watson* is an example of insurer-side adverse selection, what would be wrong with a court refusing to enforce the "an" on public policy grounds? Could the doctrine of reasonable expectations be used to produce the same result? What is the significance of the statutory fire policy in the *Watson* and related cases? What is the insurer's argument in these cases for why the court should enforce the contractual language that diverges from the statutorily required language? Why is there nothing like *Chevron* deference by the court to the insurance regulator's decision to approve the language in the policy, despite the statutorily prescribed language?

7. Interestingly, the statutory fire policy on which the court based its decision dates back to the Standard Fire Policy enacted in New York and other jurisdictions in the late nineteenth century precisely because of this lemons problem. *See* Lester W. Zartman & William H. Price, Yale Readings in Insurance: Property Insurance 261-262 (1921). *Watson* suggests that the old form is still serving a useful function. The statutory form remains highly relevant also in relation to terrorism coverage. Following September 11, 2001, many states approved new terrorism exclusions for property insurance policies. (New York and California were prominent exceptions as of August 2002.) The statutory fire policy does not contain a terrorism exclusion and, thus, as long as property damage from a terrorist attack falls within the statutory fire insurance policy (e.g., the collapse of the World Trade Center as a result of the fire), the new terrorism exclusions should not have any effect on the loss in jurisdictions with the statutory policy.

8. In *Allstate Insurance Co. v. LaRandeau*, 622 N.W.2d 646 (Neb. 2001), the Nebraska Supreme Court endorsed Allstate Insurance Company's alternative, very sensible approach to the innocent spouse problem. Allstate paid the innocent spouse 50 percent of the value of the loss (notwithstanding the fact that the Allstate policy used the "any" version of the exclusion) and then brought a subrogation claim against the husband. (We will study subrogation at the end of this chapter). The court held:

> We conclude that Allstate may pursue its claim against LaRandeau, whose intentional act caused a loss not covered under the policy, to the detriment of an innocent coinsured. The rule against subrogation by an insurer should not preclude Allstate from asserting its subrogated claim against LaRandeau because the policy did not cover the risk at issue. With respect to the fire loss in question here, LaRandeau was not an innocent insured, but, rather, a wrong-

doer who intentionally caused the loss. Accordingly, recognition of Allstate's subrogation claim against him for the amounts which it paid to his wife, who *was* considered an innocent insured, serves the legitimate purpose of placing ultimate responsibility for the loss upon the intentional wrongdoer.

Id. at 651.

9. Express and implied arson exclusions have made property insurance claims departments into experts on the origins of fires. Indeed, there is an entire genre of mystery novels featuring insurance investigators and fires. One excellent example is Don Winslow's California Fire and Life (1999), which involves both separation assault and arson and contains a wealth of information about the art of arson investigation. Law students will be interested to note the role that an "insurance bad faith" case plays in developing the plot (though not pleased with either the portrayal or the fate of the lawyer who brings the case; remember what happened to the lawyer in Jurassic Park).

SITA'S INNOCENT CO-INSURED PROBLEM

The State of Superior has a statutory fire insurance policy that is identical to the statutory policy in Minnesota. Against the advice of their top lobbyist, the Superior Insurance Trade Association (SITA) drafted a bill that would prevent the Superior Supreme Court from following *Watson* or *Borman*. SITA persuaded a friendly member of the legislature's Insurance Committee to introduce the bill.

Sure enough, the introduction of the bill prompted the counteraction that the lobbyist predicted. The Superior Women's Advocacy Center drafted a bill that would prevent insurance companies from denying payment to innocent co-insureds in any claims in any property insurance policy (not just the fire losses addressed by the Superior Statutory Fire Insurance Policy), and the chair of the Superior legislature's Women's Caucus, who is also on the Insurance Committee, introduced the bill.

A. Try your hand at drafting both of the proposed bills.
B. Now try drafting a "compromise" statute along the lines of the Nebraska, North Dakota, and Washington statutes described in the excerpt from the Utah case in note 3 above.

Consider what arguments could be made in support of each of these three options. Can you think of another option—aside from killing both bills—that might restore the peace in the Insurance Committee?

II.   LIFE INSURANCE

Life insurance is one of the oldest forms of commercial insurance, dating back to at least seventeenth-century England. (Fraternal forms of life insurance are much older, tracing their history to ancient burial societies.) The origins of commercial life insurance lie in both what you would expect—prudence (i.e., providing for widows and orphans)—and in what you may find surprising—speculation (i.e., betting on the early death of a neighbor or public figure). *See* Geoffrey Clark, Betting on Lives: The Culture of Life Insurance in England 1695-1775 (1999). Insurance companies and reformers devoted tremendous efforts in the late eighteenth and nineteenth centuries to separating the "gambling" aspects of life insurance from its "thrift" components. *See* Robin Pearson, *Thrift or Dissipation? The Business of Life Assurance in the Early Nineteenth Century,* 43 Econ. Hist. Rev. 236 (1990). Arguably, with the recent rise in popularity of life insurance investment products linked to the performance of the stock market, we have come full circle. Stock indexed life insurance and annuities may have felt more like "prudence" than "speculation" during the 1990s, but the fact that they were sold by insurance companies rather than investment houses did not cushion the fall in the ensuing recession.

There are two basic types of individual life insurance sold in the United States today: term life insurance and savings-linked life insurance. "Term" life insurance is the simplest form of life insurance. It provides for a specified death benefit for as long as the premiums are paid. Typically, term life insurance is "guaranteed renewable," meaning that the insured has the option of deciding whether to continue paying premiums and thereby keeping the policy in force, and "natural premium," meaning that the premiums increase with advancing age according to the increased chance of death.

Savings-linked life insurance is our term for a wide variety of life insurance policies that contain both a savings and an insurance element. At one end of the spectrum is "traditional whole life" insurance, which typically is structured so that premiums remain constant over the projected course of the policy. In whole life insurance, the premiums paid in the early years of the policy exceed what is necessary to provide the term life insurance benefit, so the policy builds up a "reserve" that is applied to the term life insurance benefit later in life. If the policy is canceled early, the insured may be able to recover some of the reserve. The amount of the reserve payable on cancellation is called the "surrender value" of the policy. At the other end of the savings-linked life insurance spectrum is "universal" life insurance. With universal life insurance, the insured typically is able to pay, within limits, any amount of premiums in any given year, with the savings component of the policy being adjusted accordingly.

Two other very important insurance products sold by the life insurance industry are annuities and group life insurance. An annuity is, in a certain sense, the opposite of life insurance. With life insurance you pay premiums every year in return for the company's promise to write a very big check in the event you die. With annuities you pay a large sum up front in return for the company's promise to write you smaller checks every year for as long as you live. In terms that you may remember from first-year property class, an annuity provides a kind of "life estate," while simple term life insurance provides your heirs with a kind of "remainder." As with savings-linked life insurance, annuities have become very flexible savings vehicles in recent years.

Group life insurance is term life insurance sold through group contracts that typically are employment-based. Group life insurance has come to be seen as an expected employment benefit in "good" jobs. Often, employers will provide a certain amount of life insurance at no cost (a common face value of the death benefit is one year's salary). In addition, employees have the option of purchasing additional amounts of coverage. Because the costs associated with selling group insurance are reduced and because there is no individual underwriting, group life insurance provides for many people the most cost-effective form of life insurance coverage.

A.   Incontestability

METROPOLITAN LIFE INSURANCE CO. v. CONWAY

Court of Appeals of New York
169 N.E. 642 (1930)

CARDOZO, C.J. Metropolitan Life Insurance Company, the petitioner, applied to the Superintendent of Insurance, the predecessor of the present appellant, for his approval of a rider to be attached to its policies. The rider submitted was in the following form: 'Death as a result of service, travel or flight in any species of air craft, except as a fare-paying passenger, is a risk not assumed under this policy; but, if the insured shall die as a result, directly or indirectly, of such service, travel or flight, the company will pay to the beneficiary the reserve on this policy.' The Superintendent of Insurance refused his approval upon the ground that the proposed rider in his judgment was inconsistent with Insurance Law, section 101, subdivision 2 (Cons. Laws, ch. 28), which reads into every policy a provision that it 'shall be incontestable after it has been in force during the lifetime of the insured for a period of two years from its date of issue except for non-payment of premiums and except for violation of the conditions of the policy relating to military or naval service in time of war.' In certiorari proceedings to review this refusal, the Appellate Division found the conflict between rider and statute to be unreal, and reversed the determination.

The Insurance Law of this State prescribes certain terms, which must be embodied in every policy of life insurance, but does not otherwise limit the terms of the policy or of any rider to be attached to it except by the exaction that policy and rider shall be approved by the Superintendent of Insurance (Ins. Law, §101). The purpose of such approval is to avoid the risk of a departure from the terms of the statute with its enumerated restrictions[.] If approval is omitted, the policy or the rider is not invalid ipso facto unless in conflict with the provisions exacted by the statute. It is invalid even then to the extent of the conflict, and no farther. The statute reads itself into the contract, and displaces inconsistent terms.

We agree with the Appellate Division in its holding that rider and statute in this instance are consistent and harmonious. The provision that a policy shall be incontestable after it has been in force during the lifetime of the insured for a period of two years is not a mandate as to coverage, a definition of the hazards to be borne by the insurer. It means only this, that within the limits of the coverage, the policy shall stand, unaffected by any defense that it was invalid in its inception, or thereafter became invalid by reason of a condition broken. . . .

The meaning of the statute in that regard is not changed by its exceptions. A contest is prohibited in respect of the validity of a policy 'except for non-payment of premiums and except for violation of the conditions of the policy relating to military or naval service in time of war' (§101, subd. 2). Here again we must distinguish between a denial of coverage and a defense of invalidity. Provisions are not unusual that an insured entering the military or naval service shall forfeit his insurance. A condition of that order is more than a limitation of the risk. In the event of violation, the policy, at the election of the insurer, is avoided altogether, and this though the death is unrelated to the breach. No such result follows where there is a mere restriction as to coverage. The policy is still valid in respect of risks assumed.

Northwestern Mutual Life Ins. Co. v. Johnson, 254 U.S. 96 (1920), is not a decision to the contrary. The clause there in question was not a limitation as to coverage. It was a provision for a forfeiture. In case of the suicide of the insured, whether sane or insane, the policy was to be 'void.' This meant the forfeiture of the privilege to receive the surrender value of the policy or equivalent benefits, a privilege which would survive if there was merely a limitation of the hazards. Statutes there are indeed whereby the enjoyment of surrender values is preserved against forfeiture by the insurer for breach of a condition as to the payment of premiums (*see*[,] *e.g.,* N.Y. Ins. Law, §§88, 101, subd. 6), but not against conditions generally. What was said by Holmes, J., of the effect of the 'incontestable clause' must be read in the light of the question before him. It is true, as he says, that with such a clause the death of the insured coupled with the payment of the premiums, will sustain a recovery in the face of a forfeiting condition. It is quite another thing to say that the same facts will prevail against a refusal to assume the risk. Later cases in the Federal courts develop the distinction clearly. 'A provision for incontestability does not have the effect of converting a promise to pay on the happening of a stated contingency into a promise to pay whether such contingency does or does not happen' (*Sanders v. Jefferson Standard L. Ins. Co.,* 10 F2d 143, p. 144 (5th Cir 1925), citing and distinguishing *Northwestern Life Ins. Co. v. Johnson, supra*). Where there has been no assumption of the risk, there can be no liability (*Hearin v. Standard L. Ins. Co.,* 8 Fed. Rep. 2d 202; *Mack v. Connecticut Gen. L. Ins. Co.,* 12 Fed. Rep. 2d 416; [citations omitted]). The kind of insurance one has at the beginning, that, but no more, one retains until the end.

The order should be affirmed with costs.

NOTES AND QUESTIONS

1. The New York life insurance incontestability statute has been widely adopted. Even before such clauses were mandatory, some life insurance companies sold incontestable policies to assuage consumer mistrust. *See* Eric K. Fosaaen, Note, *AIDS and the Incontestability Clause,* 66 N.D. L. Rev. 267, 288 (1990). As Justice Holmes described in the *Northwestern Mutual Life* case cited by Judge Cardozo, the purpose of the clause "is plain and laudable—to create absolute assurance of the benefit, as free as may be from any dispute of the fact except the fact of death, and as soon as it reasonably can be done."

2. The insurance industry agreed so strongly with the holding in *Conway* that it drafted a model statute codifying that result:

    > A clause in any policy of life insurance providing that such policy shall be incontestable after a specified period shall preclude only a contest of the validity of the policy, and shall not preclude the assertion at any time of defenses based upon provisions in the policy which exclude or restrict coverage, whether or not such restrictions or exclusions are excepted in such clause.

See Fosaaen, *supra*, at 276. As of 1990, "27 states [had adopted] this or a similar, shorter statutory exception to the incontestability clause." *Id.* Professor Robert Works critically reviewed the history of the life insurance "orthodoxy" reflected in this statute in *Coverage Clauses and Incontestable Statutes: The Regulation of Post Claim Underwriting,* 1979 U. Ill. L. Forum 809. Professor Works argued that even the life insurance cases have hewed less closely to the distinction between "validity" and "coverage" defenses than a literal reading might suggest. He identified an "emerging" approach to life insurance incontestability clauses that addressed post-claim underwriting as "the evil addressed by the incontestable clause." *Id.* at 813. Think back to the post-claim underwriting discussion in the misrepresentation section (section V) in Chapter 2. Is the duty to investigate a common law cousin of the statutory incontestability requirement? How might the duty to investigate be developed to address the problems that animate incontestability laws? Are there benefits that an incontestability statute can provide that a more finely tuned common law rule might not?

3. The combination of AIDS and the incontestability provision posed a significant challenge to the insurance industry. Because of the long latency of AIDS, questions in a life insurance application could not protect insurers from AIDS-related adverse selection. In the early 1980s very little was known about the disease, other than that it was more prevalent in the gay community and among intravenous (IV) drug users than elsewhere. That correlation played into existing social stigma and led at least some life insurers to discriminate against people they identified (on the basis of stereotypes) as likely to be gay. *See generally* Deborah Stone, *The Rhetoric of Insurance Law: The Debate over AIDS Testing,* 15 Law & Soc. Inquiry 385 (1990). With the development of HIV testing, it became possible to know that one would quite likely develop AIDS long before there were any symptoms. This led to an understandable concern among insurance companies about adverse selection, and so they began requiring HIV tests for some life and disability insurance applicants. Insurers' use of HIV testing became a lightning rod for profound public anxiety about AIDS and predictive testing (the present-day example, which we study in Chapter 6, is genetic testing). The result was a very significant legislative effort to regulate AIDS testing. The first wave of legislation attempted to ban the use of tests or questions about tests by insurance companies. Subsequent legislation permitted the use of the tests but regulated, for example, how the results were communicated to applicants. *See, e.g.,* Fla. Stat. §627.429 (2003) (re: medical tests for HIV infection and AIDS for insurance purposes). Not a few people found out for the first time that they were HIV positive as a result of being denied life insurance. *See, e.g.,* Matthew Kredell, *When Cheers Became Tears; Magic's HIV-Forced Retirement from NBA Affected Entire World,* Daily News L.A., Nov. 7, 2001, at S1 (reporting that basketball star Magic Johnson learned in 1991 that he was HIV positive from a blood test taken in connection with a life insurance policy). Some courts have held, however, that insurance companies have no obligation to communicate the results of an HIV test to an applicant. *See Eaton v. Continental Gen. Ins. Co.,* 147 F. Supp. 2d 829 (N.D. Ohio 2001); *Petrosky v. Brasner,* 718 N.Y.S.2d 340 (App. Div. 2001).

ALLSTATE LIFE INSURANCE CO. v. MILLER
United States Court of Appeals, Eleventh Circuit
424 F.3d 1113 (2005)

BARKETT, Circuit Judge:

In this diversity insurance case, Appellant Allstate Life Insurance Company ("Allstate") appeals the summary judgment order granting to appellees Steve Miller and Nicholas Demetro ("the beneficiaries") the proceeds of a life insurance policy on the life of John Miller. Allstate argued below that the life insurance policy insuring the life of John Miller should be rescinded or declared void, alleging that the policy was obtained through the use of an imposter in Miller's place during the initial required medical examination. The district court rejected Allstate's attempts to rescind or void the life insurance policy at issue because: (i) the policy contained a clause—required by Florida statute—that rendered the policy incontestable after it was in force for two years during the life of the insured; and (ii) more than two years had passed since the policy was issued. Because we agree with the district court that Florida law recognizes no implied "imposter" exception to the two-year statutory incontestability period, summary judgment was properly granted and we affirm.

BACKGROUND

The Allstate life insurance policy on which this case centers went into effect on September 20, 2000, insuring the life of John Miller. The policy stated that if the insured died while the policy was in force, Allstate would pay a death benefit to the policy beneficiaries upon receiving proof of death. As required by Fla. Stat. §627.455, the policy further provided that it would become incontestable after remaining in force during the lifetime of the insured for a period of two years from its effective date.[9] On October 4, 2002, John Miller requested that the beneficiaries of the policy be changed, and named Steve Miller and Nicholas Demetro as beneficiaries. John Miller died on April 20, 2003—more than two years after the policy went into effect. The beneficiaries accordingly filed statements seeking to collect benefits under the policy.

Rather than disburse the benefits, Allstate sought a declaratory judgment that the policy was void ab initio, alleging that the policy application was completed using fraudulent information and that an imposter had appeared at the medical exam initially required by the insurance company in the place of John Miller. Allstate's complaint averred that this was the only possible conclusion that could be drawn from discrepancies between statements made on the policy application and the health of the individual examined before the policy was issued, as compared with the health conditions which ultimately led to John Miller's death. In response, the beneficiaries counter-claimed, alleging breach of contract based on Allstate's failure to pay benefits upon proof of death in accordance with the insurance policy's terms.

---

9. The text of the policy's incontestability clause reads: "This contract shall be incontestable after it has been in force during the lifetime of the insured for a period of two years from its start date except for nonpayment of premiums and expect as to provisions relative to benefits in event of disability and as to provisions which grant additional insurance specifically against death by accident or accidental death."

Although the district court permitted Allstate to engage in discovery to establish the factual predicate for its imposter argument, the district court ultimately granted the beneficiaries' motion for summary judgment, holding that because Allstate's claim was made after two years from the date of the policy's issue, it was barred by the policy's incontestability clause. The district court reasoned that Florida precedent has interpreted incontestability clauses as absolute bars to efforts by the insurer to rescind the policy after two years for any other reason than the articulated exceptions in the statute. Though Florida courts have not expressly rejected an insurer's attempt to bring an imposter-based fraud claim after the policy becomes incontestable, the district court found there to be no material difference between Allstate's imposter defense and the defenses of fraud and misrepresentation that Florida courts have expressly rejected once the two-year contestability period has expired. Allstate timely appealed. . . .

DISCUSSION

Florida law requires that "[e]very insurance contract shall provide that the policy shall be incontestable after it has been in force during the lifetime of the insured for a period of 2 years from its date of issue. . . ." Fla. Stat. §627.455.[10] Excepted from this statutory incontestability period are challenges based upon "nonpayment of premiums and . . . at the option of the insurer, [challenges] as to provisions relative to benefits in event of disability and as to provisions which grant additional insurance specifically against death by accident or accidental means." *Id.*

The Florida Supreme Court has explained that incontestability clauses, such as the one contained in §627.455, are "in the nature of, and serve[] a similar purpose as, a statute of limitations." *Prudential Ins. Co. of Am. v. Prescott,* 176 So. 875, 878 (Fla. 1937). As such, while incontestability clauses "recognize[] fraud and all other defenses, [they] provide[] a reasonable time in which they may be, but beyond which they cannot be, established." *Id.* The incontestability clause thus works to the mutual advantage of the insurer and the insured, "giv[ing] the insured a guaranty against expensive litigation to defeat his policy after the lapse of the time specified, and at the same time giv[ing] the company a reasonable time and opportunity to ascertain whether the [insurance] contract should remain in force." *Id.*

Accordingly, just as Florida courts would dismiss an otherwise-valid action once the statute of limitations on that claim had run, Florida's appellate courts have uniformly held that once the incontestability clause becomes effective, insurers are barred from attempting to rescind or cancel the insurance policy based on allegations that the insured engaged in fraud or misrepresentation. *See Kaufman v. Mut. of Omaha Ins. Co.,* 681 So. 2d 747, 750-53 (Fla. Dist. Ct. App. 1996) (rejecting insurer's attempt to rescind policy, based in part on insured's non-disclosure of preexisting conditions, where "the insurer's attempted rescission of the policy occurred over two years after the policy was issued, and consequently the attempted rescission was legally ineffective"); *see also, Bankers Sec.*

---

10. *Editor's note.* The Florida statute is in a section of the Florida insurance code that applies only to life insurance and annuities. Thus, this incontestability requirement does not apply to other kinds of insurance.

Life Ins. Soc. v. Kane, 885 F.2d 820, 821-22 (11th Cir. 1989) (refusing to create any court-created exception to the Florida incontestability statute and holding that the statutory incontestability clause barred efforts to rescind a policy based on alleged fraudulent misrepresentations made by the insured).

Under these cases, while an insurer may assert an imposter claim (or any number of other grounds) to rescind or void an insurance policy before the incontestability clause goes into effect, §627.455 prevents an insurer from doing so once the policy has been in effect for two years during the life of the insured, except on the three grounds enumerated in the statute. Accordingly, we find Allstate's arguments to the contrary unpersuasive.

First, Allstate argues that it is not contesting the policy in a manner prohibited by §627.455 because its suit is based upon a claim that the policy is void ab initio. Specifically, Allstate claims that its lack of knowledge as to John Miller's true medical condition meant that there was no meeting of the minds and no actual contract. However, Florida courts have already rejected claims by an insurer who sought to rescind an insurance policy because it would not have agreed to issue the policy had it known the true facts of the insured's medical history. *See* [*Prudential Ins. Co. of Am. v. Rhodriquez,* 285 So. 2d 689, 689-90 (Fla. Dist. Ct. App. 1973)].

Second, Allstate relies on the "weight of authority in other jurisdictions" to argue that we should recognize an imposter exception to the incontestability period. However, in diversity cases we are required to adhere to the decisions of the Florida appellate courts absent some persuasive indication that the Florida Supreme Court would decide the issue otherwise. As discussed above, the Florida appellate courts have uniformly and expressly held that the §627.455 incontestability clause bars an insurer from rescinding or contesting the policy based on alleged fraudulent misrepresentations the insured made in the policy application. We can discern no indication that the Florida Supreme Court would disagree. While Allstate argues that its so-called "imposter defense" is different in kind from the sorts of fraud and misrepresentation that Florida's appellate courts have rejected as a basis for obviating the statutory incontestability clause, we agree with the district court that the "imposter defense" is merely a species of fraud, indistinguishable from the use of an imposter for incontestability purposes. *Cf. Bradford Trust Co. v. Tex. Am. Bank-Houston,* 790 F.2d 407, 410 (5th Cir. 1986) (characterizing imposter scheme as species of fraud).

Finally, Allstate would have us rely on *Fioretti v. Massachusetts General Life Insurance Co.,* 892 F. Supp. 1492 (S.D. Fla. 1993), which distinguished an imposter defense from the fraudulent misrepresentations addressed by the Florida appellate courts. However, this court determined on appeal that it was New Jersey law which governed the insurance policy at issue. *See Fioretti,* 53 F.3d 1228, 1236 (11th Cir. 1995). Moreover, after *Fioretti,* the Fourth District Court of Appeal decided *Great Southern Life Insurance Co. v. Porcaro,* 869 So. 2d 585 (Fla. Dist. Ct. App. 2004). In *Porcaro,* the insured mysteriously disappeared. The insurer continued to accept premium payments, and more than two years after the policy was issued the representative of his estate obtained a probate court judgment declaring the insured to be dead. *Id.* at 586. The insurer refused to pay the policy proceeds, citing evidence that the insured *was not in fact dead,* but rather had fraudulently absconded in order to avoid prosecution. The trial court entered judgment for the estate in the amount of the policy, holding that the insurer was precluded from contesting the policy because of failure to do so within the two-year contestability window. *See id.* While the appeals court reversed and remanded because of a material issue of fact as to whether the insured died before the policy had been in effect for two years, its decision recognized that were a jury to determine that the insured lived for two years from the date the policy issued, the statutory incontestability clause would bar any defense of fraud based on the circumstances of the insured's disappearance. *See id.* at 587. If claims of potential fraud as to the fact of an insured's death—a fact most central to a life insurance contract—are subject to the statutory incontestability clause, Allstate's imposter claims cannot obviate §627.455 based on their importance in the contractual scheme. Furthermore, even if it could be argued that the alleged fraud in *Porcaro* prevented a meeting of the minds, as noted earlier, this rationale has been rejected by Florida courts. *See Rhodriquez*, 285 So. 2d at 689 (holding that statutory incontestability clause barred insurer's claim that had it known insured's true condition, it would not have agreed to issue the policy).

Because we agree with the district court that the statutory incontestability clause bars Allstate's efforts in this case to void the policy, we hold that summary judgment was properly granted.

NOTES AND QUESTIONS

1. The impersonation defense is rarely affirmed, and it usually applies only to cases where the named insured is never present at all, at the examination and the signing, so the impersonator ends up being the insured. *Ludwinska v. John Hancock Mut. Life Ins. Co.*, 178 A. 28, 29 (Pa. 1935), is one such case. The court described the key facts as follows:

    > Bertha Ludwinska applied for an industrial life insurance policy representing herself in the application as being thirteen years of age. She named her mother as beneficiary, and signed the application "Victoria Ludwinska," taking the physical examination for Victoria. The policy was delivered to her. Victoria was her sister, confined in an asylum as an imbecile, and had been so for four and a half years.

    The difference between *Miller* and *Ludwinska* is that the named party, Victoria, had not been able to authorize the impostor, Bertha, to contract with the insurer. Without authorization, there was still fraud but no contract, and the incontestability clause was never valid. The court found that the incontestability clause would have protected Victoria, if she had been able to consent. But the court treats insurance as personal and not transferable ("Insurance companies do not insure names. They insure lives. The name Victoria was not insured." *Id.* at 31). The insurer had intended to insure Bertha, no matter what name she wrote down. If Bertha died, would her mother be able to collect? If the insurance company figured out Bertha's clever ruse but had not said anything, preferring to insure the healthier daughter rather than Victoria, who would it actually have been insuring—the named insured or the impostor? *See also Maslin v. Columbian Nat'l Life Ins. Co.*, 3 F. Supp. 368 (S.D.N.Y. 1932) (a similar case ruling that the policy was void because there was an impostor at both the signing and the examination). In

Amex Life Assurance Co. v. Superior Ct., 930 P.2d 1264 (Cal. 1997), the California Supreme Court refused to recognize the impostor defense in a case in which an HIV-positive applicant sent someone else to the mandatory medical examination:

> In this case, Morales knew he was HIV (human immunodeficiency virus) positive when he applied for life insurance. He lied on the application form and sent an impostor to take the mandatory medical examination. With minimal effort, Amex could have discovered the fraud even before it issued the policy, but instead it collected the premiums for more than two years until Morales died. After the beneficiary filed a claim, Amex discovered from information long available that an impostor had taken the examination, and it denied the claim. Today, while recognizing that it is too late to contest coverage due to fraud, Amex urges us to adopt the so-called "impostor defense" that some states recognize. As generally applied, the defense provides that when a person applies for a life insurance policy and takes the medical examination but names another person as the insured, the policy does not insure the named person but, if anyone, the person who completed the application and took the examination.
>
> We need not decide whether to adopt the impostor defense because the facts of this case do not come within it. Here, the named insured, Morales, himself applied for the policy and did everything except take the medical examination. The policy insured him, not someone else. The fraud, though abhorrent and clearly justifying rescission of the policy during the two-year contestability period, is not qualitatively different from other types of fraud California courts have held may not be used to contest coverage once the contestability period has expired if the premiums have been paid. Therefore, Amex, which did nothing to protect its interests but collect premiums until Morales died after the contestability period, may no longer challenge coverage on the basis that an impostor took the medical examination.

Id. at 1265-1266.

2. Most states have adopted incontestability statutes for disability insurance as well. The California Supreme Court described the disability insurance statute as follows, in a very interesting case involving a policyholder disabled by AIDS, *Galanty v. Paul Revere Life Ins. Co.*, 1 P.3d 658 (Cal. 2000):

> The incontestability clause required in disability policies has very different language than the clause required in life insurance policies, and additional history. Section 10350.2, which governs disability policies, was based on the Uniform Individual Accident and Sickness Policy Provisions Law promulgated by the NAIC in 1950. Section 10350.2 was enacted in California the next year at the recommendation of the state's Insurance Commissioner, who had served on the NAIC committee responsible for the uniform law.
>
> Section 10350.2 offers a choice of two forms, labeled A and B, to insurers writing noncancellable policies of disability insurance, such as the policy Paul Revere issued to Galanty. The first paragraph of each form addresses challenges to the validity of the policy, but differs depending on the form. Form A expressly permits the insurer to defend claims based on fraudulent misstatements by the insured, in these words: "After two years from the date of issue of this policy no misstatements, *except fraudulent misstatements,* made by the applicant in the application for such policy shall be used to void the policy or to deny a claim for loss incurred or disability (as defined in the policy)

commencing after the expiration of such two-year period." §10350.2, form A, par. (a), italics added. Form A thus offers insurers greater protection against fraud by insureds than the incontestability clause required in life insurance policies. The latter does not permit the insurer, in most cases, to challenge the policy or its own liability on account of fraudulent statements by the insured in the application for insurance after the period of contestability has run.

Id. at 666-667. Form B states:

> a. After Your Policy has been in force for 2 years, excluding any time You are Disabled, We cannot contest the statements in the application.
> b. No claim for loss incurred or Disability that starts after 2 years from the Date of Issue will be reduced or denied because a sickness or physical condition not excluded by name or specific description before the date of loss had existed before the Date of Issue.

Id. at 663.

3. Should health insurance policies be incontestable as well? *See Button v. Connecticut Gen. Life Ins. Co.,* 847 F.2d 584 (9th Cir. 1988), for an example of a health insurance policy sold with an incontestability provision. What about automobile and homeowners' insurance? What are the relevant similarities and differences among these types of insurance?

4. Why might a disability insurer choose the broader incontestability provision at issue in *Galanty* (note 2 above) rather than the alternative provision that expressly reserved the fraud defense? It cannot be because insurance companies want to encourage consumers to lie on their insurance applications. Instead, it must reflect a judgment that the increased trust that consumers will have about the relationship outweighs whatever additional fraud results. What does that tell you about what disability insurance companies think that consumers think about insurance companies?

B.   Insurable Interest

The doctrine of "insurable interest" dates back to the eighteenth-century effort in England to separate "insurance" from "gambling." In 1746 for marine insurance and then in 1774 for life insurance, Parliament prohibited the sale of insurance to persons who have "no interest" in the person or object insured. *See generally* Robert H. Jerry II, Understanding Insurance Law §40 (3d ed. 2002). Prior to that time, it was common for people to speculate on the deaths of famous people by buying insurance on their lives. *See* Geoffrey Clark, Betting on Lives: The Culture of Life Insurance in England, 1695-1775 (1999).

GRIGSBY v. RUSSELL
United States Supreme Court
222 U.S. 149 (1911)

Justice HOLMES. This is a bill of interpleader brought by an insurance company to determine whether a policy of insurance issued to John C. Burchard, now deceased, upon his life, shall be paid to his administrators or to an assignee, the company having turned the amount into court. The material facts are that after he had paid two premiums and a third was overdue, Burchard, being in want and needing money for a surgical operation, asked Dr. Grigsby to buy the policy, and sold it to him in consideration of $100 and Grigsby's undertaking to pay the premiums due or to become due; and that Grigsby had no interest in the life of the assured. The circuit court of appeals, in deference to some intimations of this court, held the assignment valid only to the extent of the money actually given for it and the premiums subsequently paid.

Of course, the ground suggested for denying the validity of an assignment to a person having no interest in the life insured is the public policy that refuses to allow insurance to be taken out by such persons in the first place. A contract of insurance upon a life in which the insured has no interest is a pure wager that gives the insured a sinister counter interest in having the life come to an end. And although that counter interest always exists, as early was emphasized for England in the famous case of *Wainewright (Janus Weathercock)*[11], the chance that in some cases it may prove a sufficient motive for crime is greatly enhanced if the whole world of the unscrupulous are free to bet on what life they choose. The very meaning of an insurable interest is an interest in having the life continue, and so one that is opposed to crime. And what, perhaps, is more important, the existence of such an interest makes a roughly selected class of persons who, by their general relations with the person whose life is insured, are less likely than criminals at large to attempt to compass his death.

But when the question arises upon an assignment, it is assumed that the objection to the insurance as a wager is out of the case. In the present instance the policy was perfectly good. There was a faint suggestion in argument that it had become void by the failure of Burchard to pay the third premium *ad diem*, and that when Grisby paid, he was making a new contract. But a condition in a policy that it shall be void if premiums are not paid when due means only that it shall be voidable at the option of the company. *Knickerbocker L. Ins. Co. v. Norton*, 96 U.S. 234 (1877); *Oakes v. Manufacturers' F. & M. Ins. Co.*, 135 Mass. 248 (1883). The company waived the breach, if there was one, and the original contract with Burchard remained on foot. No question as to the character of that contract is before us. It has been performed and the money is in court. But this being so, not only does the objection to wagers disappear, but also the principle of public policy referred to, at least, in its most convincing form. The danger that might arise from a general license to all to insure whom they like does not exist. Obviously it is a very different thing from granting such a general license, to allow the holder of a valid insurance upon his own life to transfer it to one whom he, the party most concerned, is not afraid to trust. The law has no universal cynic fear of the temptation opened by a pecuniary benefit accruing upon a death. It shows no prejudice against remainders after life estates, even by the rule in Shelley's Case. Indeed, the ground of the objection to life insurance without interest in the earlier English cases was not the temptation to murder,

---

11. *Editor's note:* Janus Weathercock was the pen name of Thomas Griffiths Wainewright, who was accused of poisoning several people in order to collect life insurance. He was convicted of forgery (but not murder) and exiled to Australia in the mid-nineteenth century. His case was well known because of his association with Charles Lamb and the London Magazine. Both Charles Dickens and Edward Bulwer-Lytton are said to have modeled characters on Wainewright. Thus, Justice Holmes's reference would have been familiar to readers at the time, without the need for any citation. *See* Alexander Colin Campbell, Insurance and Crime, 223-238 (1902).

but the fact that such wagers came to be regarded as a mischievous kind of gaming. Stat. 14 George III., chap. 48.

On the other hand, life insurance has become in our days one of the best recognized forms of investment and self-compelled saving. So far as reasonable safety permits, it is desirable to give to life policies the ordinary characteristics of property. This is recognized by the bankruptcy law, §70, which provides that unless the cash surrender value of a policy like the one before us is secured to the trustee within thirty days after it has been stated, the policy shall pass to the trustee as assets. Of course the trustee may have no interest in the bankrupt's life. To deny the right to sell except to persons having such an interest is to diminish appreciably the value of the contract in the owner's hands. The collateral difficulty that arose from regarding life insurance as a contract of indemnity only (*Godsall v. Boldero*, 9 East, 72), long has disappeared (*Phoenix Mut. L. Ins. Co. v. Bailey*, 80 U.S. 616 (1871). And cases in which a person having an interest lends himself to one without any, as a cloak to what is, in its inception, a wager, have no similarity to those where an honest contract is sold in good faith.

Coming to the authorities in this court, it is true that there are intimations in favor of the result come to by the circuit court of appeals. But the case in which the strongest of them occur was one of the type just referred to, the policy having been taken out for the purpose of allowing a stranger association to pay the premiums and receive the greater part of the benefit, and having been assigned to it at once. *Warnock v. Davis*, 104 U.S. 775 (1881). On the other hand, it has been decided that a valid policy is not avoided by the cessation of the insurable interest, even as against the insurer, unless so provided by the policy itself. *Connecticut Mut. L. Ins. Co. v. Schaefer*, 94 U.S. 457 (1876). And expressions more or less in favor of the doctrine that we adopt are to be found also in *Aetna L. Ins. Co. v. France*, 94 U.S. 561 (1876); *Mutual L. Ins. Co. v. Armstrong*, 117 U.S. 591 (1886). It is enough to say that while the court below might hesitate to decide against the language of *Warnock v. Davis*, there has been no decision that precludes us from exercising our own judgment upon this much debated point. It is at least satisfactory to learn from the decision below that in Tennessee, where this assignment was made, although there has been much division of opinion, the supreme court of that state came to the conclusion that we adopt, in an unreported case, *Lewis v. Edwards*, December 14, 1903. The law in England and the preponderance of decisions in our state courts are on the same side.

Some reference was made to a clause in the policy that 'any claim against the company, arising under any assignment of the policy, shall be subject to proof on interest.' But it rightly was assumed below that if there was no rule of law to that effect, and the company saw fit to pay, the clause did not diminish the rights of Grigsby, as against the administrators of Burchard's estate.

Decree reversed.

NOTES AND QUESTIONS

1. *Grigsby* is the traditional U.S. citation for the proposition that insurable interest is determined at the time of the purchase of life insurance, not the time of death. In recent years this feature of insurance law facilitated the growth of a thriving secondary market in life insurance policies. This market first came to prominence in the wake of the AIDS outbreak. Before the

development of AIDS retroviral treatments, an HIV-positive diagnosis dramatically increased the value of any life insurance held by the HIV-positive individual. The "viatical settlement" industry emerged to facilitate the sale of these life insurance policies to investors, who would pay the premiums and, eventually, collect the death benefits. The development of retroviral treatments damped investors' enthusiasm for viatical settlements; the now-developed secondary industry expanded its scope to "life settlements" that were available to many different categories of people whose health status had changed dramatically for the worse since purchasing their life insurance.

2. The latest twist in the life settlements business involves organized investor groups that encourage the elderly to purchase life insurance policies in order to assign the policies to the investor groups. *See* Charles Duhigg, *Late in Life, Finding a Bonanza in Life Insurance*, N.Y. Times, Dec. 17, 2006, at 11; Holman W. Jenkins, Jr., *Business World: Life Insurers Face the Future, Grudgingly*, Wall St. J., Aug. 9, 2006, at A11; Liam Plevin & Rachel Emma Silverman, *Investors Seek Profits in Strangers' Deaths*, Wall St. J., May 2, 2006, at C1. Apparently the investors profit in two ways. First, there is the opportunity for tax deferral on the savings element within any cash value life insurance policy. *See* Kyle D. Logue, *The Current Life Insurance Crisis:* 32 Cumb. L. Rev. 1 (2001-2002). Second, because life insurance companies price their policies assuming that a certain percentage of the policyholders will stop paying their premiums and allow the policy to lapse (thereby reducing the amount of death benefits that the life insurance company will pay), the investor groups can beat the odds by keeping all the policies that they purchase. As long as their portfolio of policies is big enough to take care of the mortality risk, they are essentially certain to earn a (tax-free) positive return.

3. The origin of the insurable interest doctrine lies in efforts by courts, legislators, and some members of the emerging insurance industry to legitimate insurance as a respectable, moral industry not tainted with the sins of gambling. *See* Robert Merkin, *Gambling by Insurance—A Study of the Life Insurance Act of 1774*, 9 Anglo-Am. L. Rev. 331 (1980). It has been a long time since the life insurance industry has had to struggle with the morality of the enterprise as a whole. *See* Viviana Zelizer, Morals and Markets: The Development of Life Insurance in the United States (1979); Tom Baker, *On the Genealogy of Moral Hazard*, 75 Tex. L. Rev. 237 (1996); Mark J. Roe, *Foundations of Corporate Finance: The 1906 Pacification of the Insurance Industry*, 93 Colum. L. Rev. 639 (1993). For almost 100 years, the life insurance industry has succeeded, whether by luck or design, in displacing concerns about the legitimacy of life insurance into concerns about the behavior of life insurance agents. *See* on this topic fascinating work by a sociological research team and two provocative fictional first-person accounts of life insurance salesmen: Richard Ericson & Aaron Doyle, Uncertain Business (2005); Richard Ericson, Aaron Doyle & Dean Barry, Insurance as Governance (2003); Allan Gurganus, Blessed Assurance: A Moral Tale (1990) (also published in his collection of stories called White People); and Christopher Moore, Coyote Blue (1994).

The insurable interest doctrine, especially as it applies to life insurance, plays an important role in policing certain types of aggressive and often controversial investment strategies. The following case involves a recent investment strategy of this type. As you read the case, take some time to figure out exactly how this somewhat complex investment works. Who are the relevant parties? What the advantages to the investors of this particular investment vehicle? What are the advantages to the seller or promoter? Who is the promoter exactly? If we think of the insurable interest doctrine as a subspecies of the "public policy doctrine" more generally, who is the doctrine protecting here? What other forms of regulation might be used to provide that group with protection?

PHL VARIABLE INSURANCE CO. V. PRICE DAWE 2006 INSURANCE TRUST, ET AL.

Supreme Court of Delaware
28 A.3d 1059 (2011)

STEELE, C.J.:

This is a proceeding, under Article IV, Section 11(8) of the Delaware Constitution and Supreme Court Rule 41, on a question of law certified to, and accepted by us, from the United States District Court for the District of Delaware. The certified questions arise from two similar cases—*PHL Variable Insurance Co. v. Price Dawe 2006 Insurance Trust* (Dawe) and *Lincoln National Life Insurance Co. v. Joseph Schlanger 2006 Insurance Trust* (*Schlanger*). In both cases, an insurer sought a judicial declaration that a life insurance policy that lacked an insurable interest was void as an illegal contract wagering on human life. The district court denied both motions to dismiss and certified three questions to the Supreme Court of Delaware concerning the incontestability provision required under 18 *Del. C.* §2908 and the insurable interest requirement under 18 *Del. C.* §2704.

FACTUAL AND PROCEDURAL BACKGROUND

The Price Dawe 2006 Insurance Trust is a Delaware statutory trust that Price Dawe formed in December 2006 with a family trust as the beneficiary. Dawe was the beneficiary of the family trust. PHL Variable Insurance Co. (Phoenix) issued a $9 million Delaware life insurance policy on Dawe's life with an issue date of March 8, 2007. The Dawe Trust was the owner and beneficiary of the policy. The policy contains an incontestability provision stating that "[t]his policy shall be Incontestable after it has been in force for two years from the Issue Date, except for fraud, or any provision for reinstatement or policy change requiring evidence of insurability." Dawe died on March 3, 2010. On June 9, 2010, the Dawe Trust made a claim to Phoenix for the death benefit. Phoenix first contested the policy by filing this lawsuit on November 10, 2010, approximately 3½ years after the policy issue date. These facts are undisputed and constitute the official record for our purposes.

In its original complaint, Phoenix contended that Dawe did not qualify, and had no legitimate need, for a $9 million life insurance policy. The insurance company claims Dawe misrepresented his income and assets in his application and that he was financially induced into participating in the transaction as part of a stranger originated life insurance ("STOLI") scheme. Phoenix further alleges that Dawe never intended to retain the policy, and always intended that the policy would be immediately transferred to an unrelated third party investor, GIII, a private investing entity. Phoenix claims that the defendant Trust and Dawe were used as straw men to allow GIII, which had no insurable interest, to conceal a wager on Dawe's life. Phoenix more specifically contends that on or about May 14, 2007, less than two months after the policy went into force, GIII formally purchased the beneficial interest of the Dawe Trust from the Family Trust for $376,111, and did not file a change of ownership or change of beneficiary form with the company. After Dawe died, Phoenix received two competing claims for the death benefit, leading to an investigation that allegedly revealed the true nature of Dawe's life insurance transaction. Phoenix then filed suit in the United States District Court for the District of Delaware in order to obtain a declaration that the policy is void. After denying the defendant Trust's motion to dismiss, the district court certified three questions of Delaware law to this Court, which we accepted.

THE CERTIFIED QUESTIONS

The questions presented are issues of law which this Court decides *de novo.*

> 1) Does Delaware law permit an insurer to challenge the validity of a life insurance policy based on a lack of insurable interest after the expiration of the two-year contestability period required by 18 *Del.* C. §2908?

> 2) Does 18 *Del. C.* §2704(a) and (c)(5) prohibit an insured from procuring or effecting a policy on his or her own life and immediately transferring the policy, or a beneficial interest in a trust that owns and is the beneficiary of the policy, to a person without an insurable interest in the insured's life, if the insured did not ever intend to provide insurance protection for a person with an insurable interest in his or her life?

> 3) Does 18 *Del. C.* §2704(a) and (c)(5) confer upon the trustee of a Delaware trust established by an individual insured an insurable interest in the life of that individual when, at the time of the application for life insurance, the insured intends that the beneficial interest in the Delaware trust would be transferred to a third-party investor with no insurable interest in that individual's life following the issuance of the life insurance policy?

ANALYSIS

I. CERTIFIED QUESTION ONE: CONTESTABILITY

The first certified question, shared by both *Dawe* and *Schlanger,* concerns whether an insurer may claim that a life insurance policy never came into existence, on the basis of a lack of insurable interest, where the challenge occurs after the insurance contract's mandatory contestability period expires. As certified by the district court in *Dawe:*

> Does Delaware law permit an insurer to challenge the validity of a life insurance policy based on a lack of insurable interest after the expiration of the two-year contestability period required by 18 *Del. C.* §2908?

Our answer to question one is "**YES.**" That answer is consistent with that reached by the majority of courts; namely, that a life insurance policy lacking an insurable interest is void as against public policy and thus never comes into force, making the incontestability provision inapplicable.

Phoenix and *amicus curiae* American Council of Life Insurers argue that we should side with the majority of courts and hold that the expiration of a contractual contestability period mandated by the Delaware Insurance Code does not bar an insurer from contesting the validity of a life insurance policy based on a lack of insurable interest. They contend that under Delaware law, a life insurance policy without an insurable interest is nothing more than a wager on human life that is void as against public policy. As a result, the insurers assert, the incontestability provision does not bar their suits because the provision, which is only one component of the entire life insurance contract, never legally came into effect at all.

The defendant Dawe Trusts argues that we should side with the courts of New York and Michigan and hold that plaintiffs' suits are barred by the incontestability provision of each life insurance contract. They contend that the plain meaning of the pertinent provisions of the Insurance Code makes clear that these provisions bar all types of challenges to a life insurance policy's validity after the required contestability period expires. The defendants argue that the distinction between contracts void at the outset and those voidable at the option of the innocent party is irrelevant, and that life insurance policies in violation of Delaware's insurable interest requirement are not automatically void.

A. HISTORICAL BACKGROUND

An incontestability clause is a contractual provision wherein the insurer agrees that, after a policy has been in force for a given period of time, it will not contest the policy based on misrepresentations in the insurance application. The insurance industry has used incontestability clauses for more than 100 years to encourage customers to purchase insurance Originating in England in the mid-nineteenth century, incontestability clauses were created as a marketing device to increase public trust in insurance companies. Before incontestability clauses were introduced, insureds sometimes paid premiums for a long period of time only to have the insurer declare the contract void because of misrepresentations in the application. These misrepresentations were often innocent, but by that point the insured was deceased and unable to address the basis of the challenge. Insurance companies therefore created the incontestability clause in order to address consumer uncertainty.

Incontestability clauses provide security in financial planning for the insured, while also providing an insurer a reasonable opportunity to investigate any misrepresentations in the application. These provisions essentially serve the same function as statutes of limitation and repose. By the early twentieth century, life insurance policies included incontestability clauses as a matter of industry practice. Forty-three states have adopted mandatory contestable clauses relating to life insurance policies, while four states also have incontestability clauses relating to other types of insurance. Consequently, over the years, the clause has become a standard provision in most, if not all, life insurance contracts.

B. DELAWARE INSURANCE CODE

The Delaware Insurance Code requires that all life insurance policies include an incontestability clause. The applicable statute in relevant part provides:

> There shall be a provision that the policy shall be incontestable after it has been *in force* during the lifetime of the insured for a period of not more than 2 years

after its date of issue, except for (1) nonpayment of premiums, and (2) at the insurer's option, provisions relating to benefits in the event of total and permanent disability and provisions granting additional benefits specifically against death by accident or accidental means.

Section 2917 of the Insurance Code affirms the class of challenges that are covered by a mandatory incontestability provision, but also lists certain challenges that are not precluded by this language:

> A clause in any policy of life insurance providing that such policy shall be incontestable after a specified period shall preclude only a contest of the *validity of the policy* and shall not preclude the assertion at any time of defenses based upon provisions in the policy which exclude or restrict coverage, whether or not such restrictions or exclusions are excepted in such clause.

The defendant trusts argue that the plain language of section 2917 makes clear that an incontestability clause precludes any challenge to the enforceability of a life insurance contract after the two-year contestability period expires. This argument ignores the fact that the Delaware General Assembly chose to implement its goals through a mandatory *contractual* term, as distinguished from a direct ban on challenges to policy validity after a certain time. This creates an ambiguity in section 2917 on the meaning of the word "validity." We read the statute to be entirely subject to Delaware's existing law of contract formation. Put simply, under the Delaware statute, the incontestability provision should be treated like any other contract term. That reading is supported by the plain language of section 2908, which states that "[t]here shall be a provision that the policy shall be incontestable after it has been *in force* during the lifetime of the insured for a period of not more than 2 years." These words accordingly make the incontestability period *directly contingent* on the formation of a valid contract. That is the view of the majority of state courts that have considered this question.

C. DISTINGUISHING BETWEEN VOID AND VOIDABLE CONTRACTS

As with all contracts, fraud in the inducement renders a life insurance policy voidable at the election of the innocent party. Certain agreements, however, are so egregiously flawed that they are void at the outset. These arrangements are often referred to as void *ab initio,* Latin for "from the beginning." A court may never enforce agreements void *ab initio,* no matter what the intentions of the parties. The United States District Court for the District of Delaware succinctly explained this basic contract doctrine in the context of fraud:

> Under the common law of contracts, there is a distinction between fraud in the inducement and fraud in the "factum," or execution. Fraud in the factum occurs when a party makes a misrepresentation that is regarded as going to the very character of the proposed contract itself, as when one party induces the other to sign a document by falsely stating that it has no legal effect. If the misrepresentation is of this type, then there is no contract at all, or what is sometimes anomalously described as a void, as opposed to voidable, contract. If the fraud relates to the inducement to enter the contract, then the agreement is "voidable" at the option of the innocent party. The distinction is that if there is fraud in the inducement, the contract is enforceable against at least one party, while fraud in the factum means that at no time was there a contractual obligation between the parties.

Under Delaware common law, contracts that offend public policy or harm the public are deemed *void* as opposed to voidable.

D. A LIFE INSURANCE CONTRACT THAT LACKS AN INSURABLE INTEREST AT INCEPTION IS VOID AB INITIO

Under Delaware common law, if a life insurance policy lacks an insurable interest at inception, it is void *ab initio* because it violates Delaware's clear public policy against wagering. It follows, therefore, that if no insurance policy ever legally came into effect, then neither did any of its provisions, including the statutorily required incontestability clause. "[T]he incontestable clause is no less a part of the contract than any other provision of it." As a result, the incontestability provision does not bar an insurer from asserting a claim on the basis of a lack of insurable interest. We reject the contrary result reached in *New England Mut. Life Ins. Co. v. Caruso,* because in that case the New York court, unlike Delaware and most other jurisdictions, held that a policy lacking an insurable interest was *not* void at the outset.

Therefore, an insurer can challenge the enforceability of a life insurance contract after the incontestability period where a lack of insurable interest voids the contract. For this reason we answer Question one affirmatively.

II. CERTIFIED QUESTION TWO: INTENT TO TRANSFER

The second certified question concerns whether the statutory insurable interest requirement is violated where the insured procures a life insurance policy with the intent to immediately transfer the benefit to an individual or entity lacking an insurable interest:

> Does 18 *Del. C.* §2704(a) and (c)(5) prohibit an insured from procuring or effecting a policy on his or her own life and immediately transferring the policy, or a beneficial interest in a trust that owns and is the beneficiary of the policy, to a person without an insurable interest in the insured's life, if the insured did not ever intend to provide insurance protection for a person with an insurable interest in his or her life?

Our answer to question number two is "**NO**," so long as the insured procured or effected the policy and the policy is not a mere cover for a wager.

PHL and ACLI argue that the Dawe policy violates Delaware's insurable interest statute because Dawe procured the policy with the intent to transfer it immediately to an investor without an insurable interest. They argue that the insurable interest requirement is a substantive regulation that would be completely undermined by ignoring intent. The insurers assert that the opposite result is illogical because it would give a procedural loophole to STOLI scheme promoters.

The Dawe Trust counters that reading an intent requirement into the insurable interest statute is at odds with its plain language. The Trust accordingly urges this Court not to engraft an intent element onto the law because it would be at odds with our principles of statutory construction. More specifically, the Dawe Trust argues that insurable interest is determined only at the moment the life insurance contract becomes effective. According to the Dawe Trust, the Delaware Insurance Code abrogates older Delaware cases decided at common law, which looked beyond the initial beneficiary to the intent of the parties when determining insurable interest. The Trust also emphasizes that life insurance policies are freely assignable under Delaware law.

A. HISTORICAL BACKGROUND

Since the initial creation of life insurance during the sixteenth century, specula-tors have sought to use insurance to wager on the lives of strangers. In England, dead pools and the use of insurance to wager on strangers' lives actually became a popular pastime. In response, Parliament enacted the Life Assurance Act of 1774 which prohibited the use of insurance as a wagering contract unlinked to a demonstrated economic risk. Although the Act did not use the words "insurable interest," the concept was embedded in the Act. This principle eventually crossed the herring pond and became firmly rooted in the common law of every state in the Union. More than a century ago, the United States Supreme Court concisely articulated the public policy behind the insurable interest requirement:

> [T]here must be a reasonable ground, founded upon the relations of the parties to each other, either pecuniary or of blood or affinity, to expect some benefit or advantage from the continuance of the life of the assured. Otherwise the contract is a mere wage, by which the party taking the policy is directly interested in the early death of the assured. *Such policies have a tendency to create a desire for the event.* They are, therefore, independently of any statute on the subject, condemned, as being against public policy.

Over the last two decades, however, an active secondary market for life insur-ance, sometimes referred to as the life settlement industry, has emerged. This secondary market allows policy holders who no longer need life insurance to receive necessary cash during their lifetimes. The market provides a favorable alternative to allowing a policy to lapse, or receiving only the cash surrender value. The secondary market for life insurance is perfectly legal. Indeed, today it is highly regulated. In fact, most states have enacted statutes governing second-ary market transactions, and all jurisdictions permit the transfer or sale of legiti-mately procured life insurance policies. Virtually all jurisdictions, nevertheless, still prohibit third parties from creating life insurance policies for the benefit of those who have no relationship to the insured. These policies, commonly known as "stranger originated life insurance," or STOLI, lack an insurable inter-est and are thus an illegal wager on human life.

In approximately 2004, securitization emerged in the life settlement indus-try. Under this investment method, policies are pooled into an entity whose shares are then securitized and sold to investors. Securitization substantially increased the demand for life settlements, but did not affect the supply side, which remained constrained by a limited number of seniors who had unwanted policies of sufficiently high value. As a result, STOLI promoters sought to solve the supply problem by generating new, high value policies.

B. THE INSURABLE INTEREST STATUTE IS AMBIGUOUS

The plain language of 18 *Del. C.* §2704(a) is ambiguous because a literal read-ing of the statute would permit wagering contracts, which are prohibited by the Delaware Constitution. The rules of statutory construction are well settled. First, we must decide if the statute is ambiguous. A statute is ambiguous if it is susceptible of two reasonable interpretations or if a literal reading of its terms "would lead to an unreasonable or absurd result not contemplated by the leg-islature." If it is unambiguous, then there is no room for judicial interpretation and "the plain meaning of the statutory language controls." If, on the other hand, the statute is ambiguous, then we consider it as a whole and we read each section in light of all the others to produce a harmonious whole. Only when a statute is ambiguous do we look for guidance to its apparent purpose and place it as part of a broader statutory scheme. We also ascribe a purpose to the General Assembly's use of particular statutory language and construe it against surplusage if reasonably possible. Courts should, however, interpret statutory law consistently with pre-existing common law unless the legislature expresses a contrary intent. We accordingly must approach section 2704(a) with these principles of statutory construction in mind.

The Delaware Constitution prohibits all forms of gambling unless it falls within one of the enumerated exceptions. Nearly one hundred years ago, the United States Supreme Court explained, "[a] contract of insurance upon a life in which the insured has no interest is a pure wager. . . ." Accordingly, a life insurance policy procured or effected without an insurable interest is a wager on the life of the insured the Delaware Constitution prohibits. Because a literal reading of the statute creates an absurd result not contemplated by the General Assembly, we must interpret the statute in conformity with both Delaware law and the General Assembly's intent.

C. THE DELAWARE COMMON LAW REQUIRED AN INSURABLE INTEREST

Phoenix and ACLI argue that the statutory language prohibits entering into a life insurance contract with the intent immediately to transfer the policy to someone without an insurable interest. The United States District Court for the District of Delaware has reached the same conclusion. ACLI correctly points out that under Delaware common law, an assignment may not be used as a formalistic cover for what in substance amounts to a wager. Phoenix and ACLI also argue that ignoring intent would result in an illogical triumph of form over substance that would completely undermine the policy goals behind the insurable interest requirement. We agree.

For nearly one hundred years, Delaware law has required an insurable interest as a way to distinguish between insurance and wagering contracts. In *Baltimore Life Ins. Co. v. Floyd*, the court explained:

> [T]he legitimate scheme of life insurance is inclined to be distorted and to some it affords an invitation for a mischievous kind of gambling. To avoid this misuse of a most useful character of undertaking, in which a beneficiary may become interested in the early death of the insured, it is held that the insurance upon a life shall be effected and resorted to only for some benefit incident to or contemplated by the insured, and that insurance procured upon a life by one *or in favor of one under circumstances of speculation or hazard* amounts to a wager contract and is therefore void, upon the theory that it contravenes public policy.
>
> The presence of an insurable interest on the part of the beneficiary is urged as a request to avoid the appearance of a wager contract, holding that without such an interest, the interest in the beneficiary is speculative. An insurable interest of the beneficiary may be shown by proof of the fact of relationship between the beneficiary and the insured within certain degrees, and by proof of pecuniary interest, such as arise between partners and between debtors and creditors. Evidence of such an insurable interest is evidence that the contract is not a wager and is evidence of the contracts validity.

> If the beneficiary has an insurable interest *and the transaction is otherwise legal,* the policy is valid; if he has not such an interest the policy may be valid, if the transaction is bona fide and free from speculation.

In *Floyd,* the court analyzed the intricacies of the insurable interest requirement in detail, including the general rule that, where "the transaction is bona fide, a person may take insurance upon his own life for the benefit of one having no insurable interest in his life." This general rule is based upon "the theory that it is not reasonable to suppose that a person will insure his own life for the purpose of speculation." However, the identity of the contracting party is not dispositive to the determination of whether an insurance policy is bona fide.

One of the tests as to the validity of the contract is to determine by whom the premiums are to be paid. If the one taking the insurance pays the premiums, the transaction is generally upheld. But there is a strong, though not universal, tendency to condemn contracts in which the premiums are paid by the beneficiary [who holds no insurable interest].

In 1968, the General Assembly codified the insurable interest requirement, in a statute which essentially restated the substantive considerations of *Floyd.* When the General Assembly enacted section 2704 in 1968, it specified categories of persons who have an insurable interest in the life of the insured and who may "procure or cause to be procured" life insurance on the insured. These categories include anyone having a "lawful and substantial economic interest" in the insured's life, parties to a contract for the purchase or sale of a business interest, and any relatives having a "substantial interest engendered by love and affection."

D. THE GENERAL ASSEMBLY CODIFIED THE COMMON LAW INSURABLE INTEREST REQUIREMENT

The tenets of statutory construction require us to interpret statutes consistent with the common law unless the statutory language clearly and explicitly expresses an intent to abrogate the common law. Although the insurable interest requirement is originally a creature of both state and pre-*Erie* federal common law, it is now codified in the Delaware Insurance Code. In relevant part, the Insurance Code provides:

> Any individual of competent legal capacity may procure or effect an insurance contract upon his/her own life or body for the benefit of any person, but no person shall procure or cause to be procured any insurance contract upon the life or body of another individual unless the benefits under such contract are payable to the individual insured or his/her personal representatives or to a person having, at the time when such contract was made, an insurable interest in the individual insured.

Section 2704(a) has two parts. The first clause provides that a person may procure or effect insurance on *his own life* for the benefit of anyone. This clause has no limiting language concerning intent, or even requires the beneficiary to have an insurable interest in the life of the insured. Section 2704(a) provides that "[a]ny individual of competent legal capacity may procure or effect an insurance contract upon his/her own life or body for the benefit of *any person. . . .*" In contrast to the first clause, the remainder of the section concerns procuring insurance on the *life of another.* Under this language, policies "procure[d] or cause[d] to be procured" on the life of someone other than the person seeking

the insurance must be payable to the "insured or his/her personal representatives or to a person having, *at the time when such contract was made,* an insurable
interest in the individual insured."

Although the statute has been periodically updated, the substance of Delaware
law on insurable interest has remained the same. An insured is permitted to take
out an insurance policy on his own life, but the law prohibits persons other than
the insured from procuring or causing to be procured insurance, unless the
benefits are payable to one holding an insurable interest in the insured's life.

The insurable interest requirement serves the substantive goal of preventing
speculation on human life. For this reason, section 2704(a) requires more than
just technical compliance at the time of issuance. Indeed, the STOLI schemes
are created to feign technical compliance with insurable interest statutes. If a
third party procures life insurance on another person or causes the procurement of life insurance on another person—the beneficiary of that contract
must have an insurable interest in the life of the insured. At issue is whether
a third party having no insurable interest can use the insured as a means to
procure a life insurance policy that the statute would otherwise prohibit. Our
answer is no, because if that third party uses the insured as an instrumentality
to procure the policy, then the third party is actually causing the policy to be
procured, which the second clause of section 2704(a) proscribes.

The statute defines the moment in time the insurable interest requirement
applies—"the time when such contract was made," i.e., the moment the life
insurance contract becomes effective. Thus, the insurable interest requirement
does not place any restrictions on the subsequent sale or transfer of a bona
fide life insurance policy. Indeed, section 2720 of the Delaware Insurance Code
makes life insurance policies assignable to anyone, even a stranger, *subject to any
contractual restrictions in the policy.* Section 2720 comports with the United States
Supreme Court decision *Grigsby v. Russell* and does not abrogate the common
law as established in *Baltimore Life Ins. Co. v. Floyd.* Read this way, a life insurance
policy that is validly issued is assignable to anyone, with or without an insurable
interest, at any time. The key distinction is that a third party cannot use the
insured as a means or instrumentality to procure a policy that, when issued,
would otherwise lack an insurable interest.

Recently, the New York Court of Appeals answered a similar certified question, holding that an insured may procure insurance on his own life with the
intent to immediately assign it to another. We find *Kramer v. Phoenix Life Ins.
Co.* distinguishable because the insured purchased policies on his own life and
a provision of the New York insurance law that did not contain an insurable
interest requirement governed those policies. Moreover, *Kramer* was decided on
a narrow set of issues applying unique New York insurance statutes, which are
not applicable here. Notably, after *Kramer* the New York legislature revised the
state's insurance laws to prohibit STOLI transactions, limiting the precedential
value of *Kramer,* even in New York.

E. DETERMINING WHO PROCURED OR EFFECTED THE POLICY

The General Assembly did provide one specific exception to the insurable interest requirement, which allows issuance of a policy where the person paying
the premiums does not have an insurable interest in the insured's life. Under
that exception, the beneficiary must be a benevolent, educational or religious
institution and the payor be designated as the owner. The logical implication

of this exception is that in cases not covered, it would be impermissible if the person paying the premium had no insurable interest in the life of the insured or if the person paying the premiums were not the policy owner. For this reason, we must interpret section 2704 and section 2705 in harmony and not render the language of section 2705 superfluous.

"If the insured procures the policy at the behest of another, the policy may nevertheless lack a legally insurable interest." To determine who procured the policy, we look at who pays the premiums. Indeed, section 2704(a) and section 2705 read together require the insured to fund the premiums on the policy unless the payor is a charitable, benevolent, educational, or religious institution. Therefore, if a third party financially induces the insured to procure a life insurance contract with the intent to immediately transfer the policy to a third party, the contract lacks an insurable interest. Stated differently, if an insured procures a policy as a mere cover for a wager, then the insurable interest requirement is not satisfied.

An insured's right to take out a policy with the intent to immediately transfer the policy is not unqualified. That right is limited to bona fide sales of that policy taken out in good faith. A bona fide insurance policy sale or assignment requires that the insured take out the policy in good faith—not as a cover for a wagering contract. Certainly, if A cannot procure a life insurance policy on the life of B without having an insurable interest in B's life then A cannot induce B's procurement of a life insurance policy with the intent to allow A to immediately purchase the policy for a nominal sum. "If the first is a speculating and wagering policy so is the last." Thus, section 2704 requires courts to scrutinize the circumstances under which the policy was issued and determine who in fact procured or effected the policy.

Payment of the premiums by the insured, as opposed to someone with no insurable interest in the insured's life, provides strong evidence that the transaction is bona fide. Under section 2704(a), the insured is free to "procure or effect" a policy on his own life for the benefit of anyone. Life insurance policies, however, do not come into effect without premiums, so an insured cannot "procure or effect" a policy without actually paying the premiums. Notably, section 2708, which prohibits policies issued without the consent of the insured except in narrow situations not present here, utilizes the phrase "applies therefore or has consented thereto in writing." By implication, "procuring or effecting" a policy has to be something more than simply applying for a policy or providing written consent to the policy's issuance. Therefore, if a third party funds the premium payments by providing the insured the financial means to purchase the policy then the insured does not procure or affect the policy. Accordingly, third parties are prohibited from procuring or causing to be procured insurance contracts on the life of the insured unless the policy benefits are payable to someone with an insurable interest.

In summary, the insured's subjective intent for procuring a life insurance policy is not the relevant inquiry. The relevant inquiry is who procured the policy and whether or not that person meets the insurable interest requirements.

III. CERTIFIED QUESTION THREE: THE TRUST'S INTEREST

The third certified question concerns whether the relevant statutory provisions confer upon a trustee an insurable interest in the life of the individual insured who established the trust if the insured intends to transfer the beneficial interest in the trust to a third-party investor with no insurable interest. As certified by the district court:

> Does 18 *Del.* C. §2704(a) and (c)(5) confer upon the trustee of a Delaware trust established by an individual insured an insurable interest in the life of that individual when, at the time of the application for life insurance, the insured intends that the beneficial interest in the Delaware trust would be transferred to a third-party investor with no insurable interest in that individual's life following the issuance of the life insurance policy?

Our answer to question number three is "**YES,**" as long as the individual insured actually established the trust. If, however, the insured does not create and fund the trust then the relationship contemplated under section 2704(c)(5) is not satisfied.

Phoenix argues section 2704(c)(5) must be interpreted in the context of section 2704(a) and Delaware common law, which prohibit wagering contracts channeled through trusts. Dawe argues that section 2704(c)(5) recognizes a trust's right to own life insurance policies by conferring on a trustee a broad insurable interest in the life of the insured. Delaware statutory trusts did not exist at common law. The policy of the Delaware Statutory Trust Act is to give maximum effect to freedom of contract and the enforceability of governing instruments, and its provisions are to be construed broadly even if in derogation of the common law.

A. RECENT CHANGES TO SECTION 2704(C)(5)

Section 2704(c) describes categories of persons and entities having an insurable interest in the life of the insured. Section 2704(c)(5) confers on the trustee of a trust an insurable interest in the life of the person who established the trust.

On July 13, 2011, after the parties completed briefing, the Governor signed Senate Bill No. 83, an Act to amend Titles 10, 12, 18, and 25 of the Delaware Code relating to judicial procedure, fiduciary relations, insurance and property. Section 17 of that Act addresses 18 *Del.* C. §2704(c)(5).

At the time that the parties briefed the certified questions, section 2704(c)(5) provided in relevant part that:

> The trustee of a trust established by an individual has an insurable interest in the life of that individual and the same insurable interest in the life of any other individual as does any person who is treated as the owner of such trust for federal income tax purposes.

Section 2704(c)(5) now provides, in pertinent part, that:

> The trustee of a trust *created and initially funded* by an individual has an insurable interest in the life of that individual and the same insurable interest in the life of any other individual as does any person who is treated as the owner of such trust for federal income tax purposes *without regard to:*
>
> a. *The identity of the trust beneficiaries*
> b. *Whether the identity of the trust beneficiaries changes from time to time; and*
> c. *The means by which any trust beneficiary acquires a beneficial interest in the trust.*

Importantly, the prior statutory language did not limit who may be a trust beneficiary or require the beneficiary to have an independent insurable interest. The revised language expressly states that a trustee has an insurable interest "without regard to the identity of the trust beneficiaries, whether the [trust beneficiaries] change . . . , and the means by which any trust beneficiary acquires a beneficial interest in the trust." The Synopsis of Senate Bill 83 states the revisions were intended to "clarify the provisions of current law" concerning when a trust has an insurable interest, meaning the recent changes did not alter the earlier statute. Thus, a trust has an insurable interest in the life of the person who established—*created and initially funded*—the trust without regard to whether the beneficial interest in the trust is subsequently sold or transferred.

B. SECTION 2704(C)(5) MUST BE READ IN HARMONY WITH SECTION 2704(A)

As noted in Section IIC above, we must interpret section 2704(c) in light of section 2704(a) to create harmony within the statute. Section 2704(c)(5) requires more than just technical compliance with section 2704(a), otherwise section 2704(c)(5) would expressly authorize wagering contracts, so long as it was conducted through a trust for whom the insured was the settlor or grantor. And as explained in Question two, a life insurance policy procured or effected without an insurable interest is a wager on the life of the insured and is prohibited by the Delaware Constitution.

Section 2704(c)(5) only grants the trustee of a Delaware trust an insurable interest in the life of the individual insured if the trust is "established" by the individual insured. The insured, as settlor or grantor, must both create and initially fund the trust corpus. This requirement is not satisfied if the trust is created through nominal funding as a mere formality. If the funding is provided by a third party as part of a pre-negotiated agreement—then the substantive requirements of sections 2704(a) and 2704(c)(5) are not met.

Parties cannot use section 2704(c)(5) to do indirectly what 2704(a) clearly prohibits parties from doing directly. The general rule, as explained in Question two, "is that all persons have an insurable interest in their own life . . . and may . . . insure their life in good faith for the benefit of any person whom they see fit to name as the beneficiary, regardless of whether such person has an insurable interest in their life, provided it not be done by way of cover for a wagering policy." Thus, an individual insured can procure a policy and name his own trust as the owner and beneficiary of that validly procured life insurance policy, and the policy complies with the first clause of section 2704(a). Additionally, the individual insured can establish—create and initially fund—a trust for the purpose of procuring life insurance on the individual's own life and the trustee of that trust has an insurable interest under the second clause of section 2704(a) and section 2704(c)(5). In both scenarios, however, either the individual insured or the trustee must intend to purchase the policy for lawful insurance purposes, and not as a cover for a waging contract.

Where the individual insured creates a trust to hold a life insurance policy on his life and funds the trust with that policy or with money to pay its premiums then the trustee has the same insurable interest that the settlor has in his own life. Thus, we only inquire whether the owner (either the insured or the trust) has an insurable interest in the insured's life at the policy's inception and not whether the beneficiaries of the policy have an insurable interest. If the individual insured creates and initially funds the trust, then the trustee has an insurable interest without regard to how the trust beneficiaries obtained their interest.

Therefore, we answer Certified question three in the affirmative if the life insurance is procured for a legal purpose and not as a cover for an illegal wager contract. In cases where a third party either directly or indirectly funds the premium payments as part of a pre-negotiated arrangement with the insured to immediately transfer ownership, the policy fails at its inception for lack of an insurable interest.

Conclusion

For the above reasons, Certified Question one is answered in the affirmative, Certified Question two is answered in the negative and Certified Question three is answered in the affirmative.

NOTES AND QUESTIONS

1. Recall that the original purpose of the insurable interest requirement was to prevent gambling on individuals' lives. But if investor groups are able, with certainty, to "beat the odds" by pooling life insurance policies, are they really gambling? If not, should they still be subject to the insurable interest requirement? What other public policy reasons can you think of that would support imposing an insurable interest requirement on these investor groups when they pool individual life insurance policies?

2. Reread the incontestability clause in Dawe's policy: "[t]his policy shall be Incontestable after it has been in force for two years from the Issue Date, *except for fraud,* or any provision for reinstatement or policy change requiring evidence of insurability." *PHL Variable Ins. Co. v. Price Dawe*, 28 A.3d 1059, 1063 (Del. 2011) (emphasis added). Instead of finding the policy was void ab initio, could the court have reached the same outcome by following the incontestability clause as written? Why might the court not have chosen to take this approach?

3. The *Dawe* court defined an ambiguous statute as one that "would lead to an unreasonable or absurd result not contemplated by the legislature." 28 A.3d at 1070 (quoting *LeVan v. Indep. Mall, Inc.*, 940 A.2d 929, 933 (Del. 2007). What evidence does the court use to show that the General Assembly did not contemplate the result mandated by a literal reading of 18 Del. C. §2704(a)? In other words, what evidence does the court rely on in deriving the General Assembly's intent when passing the most recent text of the statute? What is more instructive on the legislature's intent than the statute's text? If the plain language of the statute is repugnant to the Delaware Constitution, should the court have struck the statute instead of rewriting the law?

4. Is there a meaningful difference between a person who acquires a life insurance policy with the intent to immediately transfer the policy and a person who is induced by another to purchase a policy for immediate transfer?

When determining who procured or effected the policy, Delaware courts must "scrutinize the circumstances under which the policy was issued and determine who in fact procured or effected the policy." The primary evidence considered by courts concerns who paid the policy's premium. 28 A.3d at 1075-76. Do you think that this is an effective way of determining whether the policy was purchased for the purpose of a wager? What other evidence might the court consider when reviewing the circumstance under which the policy was issued? (Remember that the original policyholder is necessarily deceased at this point in the inquiry.)

5. The court unequivocally states, "the insured's subjective intent for procuring a life insurance policy is not the relevant inquiry." *Id.* at 1076. However, the court also mandates that "[a]n insured's right to take out a policy with the intent to immediately transfer the policy is not unqualified. . . . [Person] A cannot induce B's procurement of a life insurance policy with the intent to allow A to immediately purchase the policy . . ." *Id.* at 1075-76. Can these two statements be reconciled? The court seems to be reasoning that in the latter example, it is actually Person A that purchased the policy. Is this correct? (Remember that the primary evidence used by the court in determining who purchased the policy is which person paid the premium.)

III.   DISABILITY INSURANCE

Disability insurance protects the income of the insured from loss due to disability. Of all the kinds of insurance that should form part of the safety net protecting Americans from misfortune, disability insurance is the most incomplete. *See* Kenneth Abraham & Lance Liebman, *Private Insurance, Social Insurance and Tort Reform: Toward a New Vision of Compensation for Illness and Injury*, 93 Colum. L. Rev. 75 (1993). Most people are much more likely to become disabled during their prime work years than they are to die, yet life insurance is much more common. The standard explanations for the disparity between the extent of life and disability insurance are the twin "information" problems of adverse selection and moral hazard. The adverse selection problem may an interesting example of selection on moral hazard. Different people have different tolerances or propensities to continue working in spite of health problems, regardless whether they have disability insurance or not. The idea of selection on moral hazard is that individuals know their propensity to change their behavior in response to insurance incentives. Insurance will be a "better deal" for people who are more likely to change their behavior in response to insurance. *Cf.* Liran Einav, Amy Finkelstein, Stephen P. Ryan, Paul Schrimpf, & Mark R. Cullen, *Selection on Moral Hazard in Health Insurance* (NBER Working Paper No. 16969, 2011).

This section begins by comparing the standards for disability under public insurance programs and the Americans with Disabilities Act and then examines two cases that discuss the meaning of "disability" in private disability insurance. We then explore the "coordination of benefits" among private disability insurance, workers' compensation, and Social Security Disability benefits. Section V below, on employment benefits, includes an important discussion of the standard of review under the Employment Retirement Income Security Act (ERISA) and the remedies available when an insurer wrongly refuses to pay a claim. That unit contains an excerpt from a recent article that argues that the Supreme Court's decisions on preemption and the standard of review facilitated the Unum/Provident disability insurance fraud addressed in *Hangarter v. Provident Life & Accident Insurance Co.*, 373 F.3d 998 (9th Cir. 2004), which we read in the punitive damages unit in Chapter 2.

A.   *The Meaning of Disability*

1. SOCIAL SECURITY

[T]he term "disability" means (A) inability to engage in any substantial gainful activity by reason of any medically determinable physical or mental impairment which can be expected to result in death or has lasted or can be expected to last for a continuous period of not less than 12 months, or (B) blindness. . . .

42 U.S.C. §416(i).

2. WORKERS' COMPENSATION

Compensable disability is generally defined as inability, as the result of a work-connected injury, to perform or obtain work suitable to claimant's qualifications and training.

From 7-81 Larson's Workers' Compensation Law §81.02 (2015).

3. AMERICANS WITH DISABILITIES ACT

Disability. The term "disability" means, with respect to an individual:

> (A) a physical or mental impairment that substantially limits one or more of the major life activities of such individual;
> (B) a record of such an impairment; or
> (C) being regarded as having such an impairment.

ADA §3(2).

As you read the following case, think about how the definitions of disability that the court discusses compare to the definitions above.

PRUDENCE LIFE INSURANCE CO. v. WOOLEY

Supreme Court of Mississippi
182 So. 2d 393 (1966)

JONES, Justice. This is an appeal from the Circuit Court of Smith County where appellee, plaintiff below, was awarded judgment against appellant, defendant below, on a health and accident insurance policy providing for disability. Because of error in an instruction given to plaintiff, the case is reversed and remanded for another trial.

On June 12, 1959, appellant issued its policy of insurance to appellee containing the disability clause hereinafter quoted. On June 2, 1960, appellee suffered a heart attack and was paid benefits for total disability under the quoted clause from that time through June 10, 1962. No payments have been made since that time, and appellee claimed that appellant owed him $5,260.00 as of the date of trial. The company denied that plaintiff was totally disabled within the meaning of the policy on June 10, 1962, and claimed that in May, 1963, the insured had ceased to be active in his business although he was not totally disabled, and the company had exercised its option to decline renewal of the policy under its provisions.

The policy contained the following definition of total disability,

> Complete loss of business time due to the inability of the insured to engage in his regular occupation or in any gainful occupation for which he is reasonably fitted by education, training or experience.

Appellee was fifty-four years of age and was and had been engaged in the occupation of farming and raising chickens. He is a high school graduate. Other than his experience as a farmer and broiler producer, he had worked as a carpenter, truck driver and equipment operator on construction jobs.

Evidence by the appellee, his wife and doctors was sufficient, though conflicting, to justify the jury's finding that he was totally disabled, and unable to perform acts required of him in his farming and chicken producing business, but there was evidence, if believed by the jury, to show he was not disabled from engaging "in any gainful occupation for which he is reasonably fitted by education, training or experience." The appellee requested and received an instruction which said if the jury believed from the evidence that plaintiff was prevented by his disease from performing the substantial acts required of him in his business, he was totally disabled within the meaning of the policy. The plaintiff's instruction said nothing about his ability or inability to engage in any other occupation as described in the policy's definition of disability. The appellant requested an instruction to the effect that "total disability" meant not only complete loss of time due to the inability of the insured to engage in his regular occupation, but also in any gainful occupation for which he is reasonably fitted by education, training or experience. This instruction was refused.

The question is therefore presented to us as to the construction of this particular disability provision of the policy involved. . . .

In 29A Am. Jur. Insurance §1518 at 622-3-4 (1960), it is said:

> The question whether there is a total disability when the insured, notwithstanding his injury, is able to work in other occupations, depends largely on the terms of the contract defining the disability. In the case of an "occupational disability" policy, inability to perform all the substantial and material acts necessary to the prosecution of the insured's business or occupation is sufficient to constitute total disability of the insured.
>
>   In the case of a "general disability" policy, the courts are in conflict as to the type of work which the insured must be unable to perform in order to be totally disabled within the meaning of the policy. Some courts refuse to distinguish between policies which relate specifically to disability in respect to a particular occupation and those which undertake to insure against disability from performing any sort of remunerative labor, holding that total disability occurs in either case if the insured

becomes unable to perform the duties of, or labor pertaining to, his particular occupation. According to this rule, recovery will not be prevented by the fact that the insured is able to perform all the substantial and material acts of some other business or occupation. At the other extreme, there is authority for the view that an insured person may not be regarded as totally disabled within a "general disability" clause until he is unable to follow any occupation whatsoever. Under this theory the liability of the insurer does not extend to cases where the insured is still capable of engaging in some occupation for profit. A majority of the courts, however, take the middle ground that it is not sufficient, in order to recover under the "general disability" clause, that the insured is disabled only from engaging in his usual business or occupation, but that he must also be unable to engage in any comparable occupation or employment for which he is fitted by education, experience, and physical condition. These cases proceed upon the theory that the term "total disability" as used in general disability clauses is a relative one depending in a large measure upon the character of the occupation or employment and the capabilities of the insured, and upon the circumstances of the particular case. While under this rule it is not sufficient, in order to recover under the disability clause, that the insured is disabled from engaging in his usual business or occupation, he need not be disabled from following any occupation whatsoever regardless of its character. The majority rule is particularly applicable where the plaintiff is insured as belonging to a particular group, such as railroad employees, and a general policy form is used. Under the majority rule, expressions such as "any occupation" and "any work," in the coverage clause, are converted into words of concrete significance and must be construed to mean the ordinary employment of the particular person insured, or such other employment, if any, approximating the same livelihood as the insured might fairly be expected to follow, in view of his station, circumstances, and physical and mental capabilities.

This policy is worded so as to bring it squarely within the rule of the majority of courts which took the middle ground as hereinbefore shown. The thinking of this Court was indicated by the statement in the Jones case. This provision is what may be termed a "double-barrel provision," which requires that disability be shown as inability to follow his regular occupation, or any other occupation for which the insured is reasonably fitted by education, training or experience. This provision is entirely different from any stated in the cases cited and brings it squarely within the majority rule announced in 29A Am. Jur., *supra*.

The instruction given for appellee, who was required to prove his case, should have required a finding in addition to that stated that he was disabled and incapable of performing any gainful occupation for which he was fitted by education, training or experience — or the substantial acts required thereby. . . .

NOTES AND QUESTIONS

1. What language in the policy at issue in *Wooley* identifies this as a "general" rather than an "occupational" disability insurance policy? Which would you expect would be more expensive: a general or an occupational disability insurance policy? How do the definitions of a general disability policy and an occupational disability policy differ from the definitions of "disability" in the Social Security and workers' compensation programs? How would you rank all these definitions in terms of the breadth of protection they provide?

2. Note that the Social Security, general, and occupational disability definitions all require a "total" disability, whereas workers' compensation allows for both total and partial disability. Why might Social Security not cover partial disability? Why might workers' compensation be different in this regard? Most observers agree that the market for private disability insurance is quite competitive. If so, why don't disability insurance companies sell coverage for partial disability? Can you understand "occupational" disability insurance as providing a kind of partial disability coverage? Think about that as you read the next case.

3. The definition of disability under the ADA is much more inclusive. Why? In an important article examining the role of disability in the social welfare system, Professor Matthew Diller wrote:

> Despite its appearance of medical objectivity, disability is a socially constructed status that can be defined in any number of ways. Definitions of disability both reflect and reinforce a series of normative values about the nature and extent of the social obligation to work. All disability benefit programs, like other public benefit programs, are created by a process of boundary drawing—a series of political, economic, and moral decisions that include some individuals in the category while excluding others.

Entitlement and Exclusion: The Role of Disability in the Social Welfare System, 44 U.C.L.A. L. Rev. 361, 363 (1996). Are Professor Diller's observations equally true about the boundaries drawn by private disability insurance? Professor Diller's observations about the "social obligation to work" help us see that the ADA definition of disability was conceived as a definition that would help people fulfill their "social obligation to work" rather than providing an exemption from that obligation. Under the ADA, being disabled means that an employer has to accommodate your needs so that you can work. Does this help explain the different approach to disability in the ADA and disability insurance?

4. The relationship between work and disability insurance and the role of disability insurance in the economy is poorly understood. The fact that disability insurance claims rise generally during recessions and rise in specific economic sectors during times of rapid change is usually treated as evidence of the moral hazard posed by disability insurance. Although that may be an accurate observation, does it tell us very much that is useful? As is so often the case, the label "moral hazard" can become a sophisticated form of victim blaming. *See generally* Tom Baker, *On the Genealogy of Moral Hazard,* 75 Tex. L. Rev. 237 (1996). Might there not be some benefit in providing a "soft landing" for the more vulnerable members of the workforce who are most likely to be squeezed out in difficult times? Since this is a well-recognized phenomenon, might insurance institutions be able to plan for it and adjust their premiums and assets accordingly?

5. Disability insurance can also provide a way for an employer to ease out an unhappy or unproductive worker or to "downsize" a workforce. Richard Ericson & Aaron Doyle, Uncertain Business: Insurance and the Limits of Knowledge (2004), illustrates these and other unofficial uses of disability insurance. To the extent that this externalizes the employer's costs onto the insurance pool, such a practice seems objectionable. But if the employer's premiums reflect this use of disability insurance as a human resources tool, is

there any objection? In connection with employer-provided disability insurance, it would be interesting to know what role employer preference plays in a disability insurance company's decision to deny a claim. This would be a worthy area of investigation for lawyers who represent disability insurance claimants. One human resources expert suggested in an interview that large private employers may have used disability insurance in this way during the era in which there was an implicit promise of lifetime employment, but that, with the end of that era, employers would rather simply terminate an employee and provide whatever severance benefits are owed. This same expert reported that this is especially the case when employers "self-insure" for the disability insurance benefits they provide to their employees.

6. One way of reducing the potential adverse selection in disability insurance is to provide the insurance through employment. Many employers in fact provide disability insurance benefits for their workers. Yet the income loss protection that these policies provide is much less complete than the health expenses protection that the employers provide for these same workers. Why? Why might an employer not want to provide good disability benefits? Why might an employer want to provide good disability benefits? How might the employer's interests in this regard conflict with those of the worker? Those of the insurance company?

7. Disability benefits are a politically charged issue in the United States. As part of its popular series *This American Life,* National Public Radio (NPR) broadcast a story in 2013 that analyzed the demographic makeup of Americans receiving disability payments from the federal government and the implications of its findings on the U.S. economy. *See* Chana Joffe-Walt, *Unfit for Work: The Startling Rise of Disability in America,* NPR (March 22, 2013), *http:// apps.npr.org/unfit-for-work/* ("The federal government spends more money each year on cash payments for disabled former workers than it spends on food stamps and welfare combined. . . . [T]he story of these programs — who goes on them, and why, and what happens after that — is, to a large extent, the story of the U.S. economy. It's the story not only of an aging workforce, but also of a hidden, increasingly expensive safety net"). The story was highly critical of what it called the "disability-industrial complex," which, according to the authors, has one goal: "push more people on disability." The authors reported that in some U.S. counties, nearly one in four working-age adults receive disability payments, and that "[t]he heath problems where there is most latitude for judgment — back pain, mental illness — are among the fastest growing causes of disability." *Id.* According to Joffe-Walt, the decision to place an individual on disability boils down to "a judgment call made in doctors' offices and courtrooms around the country." *Id.* The article suggests through innuendo that it is possible to game the system, and in tough economic times, displaced workers in fact are encouraged to do so.

These types of critiques against Social Security disability benefits are increasing in frequency. After the story was published, former high-ranking officials in the Social Security Administration were quick to respond. *See* Kenneth S. Apfel et al., *Open Letter from Eight Former Social Security Commissioners,* Social Security News (April 6, 2013), *http://socsecnews.blogspot. com/2013/04/open-letter-from-eight-former-social.html* ("[T]he series aired on NPR sensationalizes this growth [in disability payments] . . . We are deeply concerned that the series 'Unfit for Work' failed to tell the whole story and perpetuated dangerous myths about the Social Security disability programs and the people helped by this vital system"). The former commissioners noted that one in five Americans live with a disability "but only those with the most significant disabilities qualify for disability benefits. . . ." *Id.* This statement is exemplified by the fact that 15 to 20 percent of individuals placed on disability die within five years of receiving benefits. Contrary to the assertion that individuals on disability are lazy and do not want to work, 17 percent of individuals receiving disability payments work part time, albeit for very little. Countering the myth that anyone can be placed on disability with little proof, the former commissioners also explained that "less than one-third of initial DI and SI [disability and Social Security] applications are approved, and only about 40 percent of adult DI and SSI applicants receive benefits even after all levels of appeal." *Id.* They also attributed the rise in Social Security and disability to the aging of baby boomers and entering of women to the workforce, which were predicted as early as the 1990s.

HELLER v. EQUITABLE LIFE ASSURANCE SOCIETY

United States Court of Appeals, Seventh Circuit
833 F.2d 1253 (1987)

COFFEY, C.J. . . .

Dr. Stanley Heller, a physician, is licensed to practice medicine in the state of Illinois. Dr. Heller is a board-certified physician in the field of Cardiovascular Diseases and specializes in invasive cardiology. He was also the Director of the Cardiovascular Catheterization Laboratory at St. Joseph's Hospital, Chicago.

In early 1983 Dr. Heller met with Paul Berlin, an agent for The Equitable Life Assurance Society (Equitable) to discuss simplifying his existing professional disability insurance coverage. . . . Equitable's policy, issued the following month in April of 1983, provided that Dr. Heller would be paid the sum of $7,000 per month, after a 90-day elimination period, if and when he became totally disabled as defined in the policy. Dr. Heller, with the payment of an added premium, contracted for additional $1,200-per-month coverage while totally disabled under the policy for a period limited to one year with the same 90-day elimination period incorporated therein. . . .

During the latter quarter of 1983 Dr. Heller developed a painful and crippling condition in his left wrist and hand diagnosed as carpal tunnel syndrome. Dr. Heller testified that as he experienced the debilitating symptoms of the condition in his left wrist and into his hand, he was prevented from practicing in his specialty as an invasive cardiologist after March 20, 1984. Dr. Heller applied for benefit payments on his Equitable disability income policy in late March 1984. The policy issued to Dr. Heller defined "total disability" as follows:

> Total disability means the complete inability of the Insured, because of injury or sickness, to engage in the Insured's regular occupation, . . . provided, however, the total disability will not be considered to exist for any period during which the Insured is not under the regular care and attendance of a physician. . . .

Dr. Heller claimed that because he was unable to engage in his profession as an invasive cardiologist as a result of the carpal tunnel syndrome condition, and because he was under the regular care of a physician and had made timely premium payments, he was entitled to disability benefits under the policy. Initially, Equitable made payments pursuant to the disability income provisions, but terminated these payments after May 5, 1985, because he (Dr. Heller) refused to undergo carpal tunnel surgery upon Equitable's insistence. As a result of Equitable's refusal to continue payments under the contract, Dr. Heller initiated the present action.

Following a trial to the court, the trial judge found that if Dr. Heller were to undergo surgery to decompress the median nerve in his left wrist, he might very well be relieved of the carpal tunnel syndrome condition, thus allowing him to return to his practice. After reviewing Equitable's disability policy, the trial judge determined that Dr. Heller was not required to submit to elective surgery because Equitable failed to include the surgery requirement in its professional disability contract. The trial court ordered Equitable to reinstate disability payments. . . .

On appeal Equitable argues that because Dr. Heller refused to submit to surgery to relieve the debilitating and limiting effects of his carpal tunnel syndrome condition, the trial court erred in finding Dr. Heller to be totally disabled under the terms of the policy. . . .

II

Illinois law controls this case as Equitable issued the policy to Dr. Heller in Illinois, the state where Dr. Heller resided and practiced medicine. Our research reveals, and both parties agree, that the Illinois courts have not directly addressed the question of whether a disability income policy providing that the claimant must be "under the regular care and attendance of a physician" requires an insured to submit to surgical treatment for the condition causing the total disability in order to receive benefits. Thus, we rely on the traditional principles of insurance and contract law, long recognized by the Illinois courts as an appropriate basis for resolving whether the clause conditions coverage on the insured's undergoing surgery. Initially, Illinois courts apply the rule that any ambiguities in the provisions of an insurance policy will be construed against the drafter of the instrument, the insurer, and in favor of the insured. . . .

A reading of the Equitable disability policy discloses that it fails to set forth any requirement or limitation of coverage requiring an insured to submit to surgery for treatment of the condition causing the total disability. The policy provides coverage where (1) the insured is prevented from engaging in his or her regular occupation because of sickness or injury and is totally disabled; and (2) that the insured be under "the regular care and attendance of a physician." Equitable does not dispute that Dr. Heller is presently unable to practice as an invasive cardiologist but argues that his failure to submit to surgery for his disabling condition as recommended requires a finding by the Court that he is no longer "under the regular care and attendance of a physician." Therefore, Equitable asserts that Dr. Heller is no longer entitled to disability income benefits.

We reject Equitable's arguments because the language in the policy stating that the claimant must be "under the regular care and attendance of a physician" clearly does not include surgical procedures. Although the policy does not define the parameters of the clause "under the regular care and attendance of a physician," we refuse to add to and construe the policy beyond its clear and obvious language, to require the insured to submit to surgery, if and when surgery is recommended by the physician "rendering regular care and [in] attendance." The language is clear on its face to the average citizen and even more so to a member of the medical profession. We are convinced that under Illinois law the clause "under the regular care and attendance" means just what it says, namely, that the insured is obligated to periodically consult and be examined by his or her treating physician at intervals to be determined by the physician. Clearly the language does not condition disability payments on the insured's undergoing surgery if recommended by the physician rendering "regular care and [in] attendance." We refuse to indulge in judicial activism and condition coverage under the contract on the insured's undergoing surgery, when the insurer failed to provide such a conditional clause in the policy.

The clause, "under the regular care and attendance of a physician," was not intended to allow the insurer to scrutinize, determine, and direct the method of treatment the claimant receives. We are convinced that the purpose of the clause requiring the insured to be "under the regular care and attendance of a physician" is to determine that the claimant is actually disabled, *see, e.g., Russell v. Prudential Insurance Company of America*, 437 F.2d 602, 607 (5th Cir. 1971), is not malingering, and to prevent fraudulent claims.

The insurance industry by its very nature offers insurance coverage on a nonnegotiable basis, and consumers are unable to participate in the drafting of the language or the terms of the policy. Case law and fairness require that ambiguities in insurance policies be construed against the drafter of the policy, the insurance company.

In the absence of a clear, unequivocal and specific contractual requirement that the insured is obligated to undergo surgery to attempt to minimize his disability, we refuse to order the same. To hold otherwise and to impose such a requirement would, in effect, enlarge the terms of the policy beyond those clearly defined in the policy agreed to by the parties. Thus, under the terms of this disability policy, Dr. Heller is not required to undergo surgery for treatment of his carpal tunnel syndrome condition before he receives disability income payments. . . .

Lastly, Equitable argues that the "principle of fairness and good faith, a policy of motivating persons to correct rather than accept physical disabilities," necessitates that an insured suffering from causes that disabled him, avail himself of all reasonable means and remedies to relieve his disability, including surgery. Once again, we reject Equitable's argument. The record clearly establishes that Dr. Heller acted in good faith. Initially, Dr. Heller properly reported his disability to Equitable and consulted with and remained under the regular care of his physician as required under the policy. Further, at Equitable's request, Dr. Heller acquiesced to an examination performed by two specialists selected by Equitable, one a hand surgeon and the other a neurologist, at the Mayo Clinic in Rochester, Minnesota. Additionally, there is nothing in the record to establish that Dr. Heller failed to provide Equitable with any and/or all supplemental information required. The record further demonstrates that after Dr. Heller's condition was diagnosed and before he filed a claim for disability payments, Dr. Heller was forced to reduce his case load beginning in Dec. 1983 to March, 1984, and thereafter was forced to withdraw from practice. The trial court found that Dr. Heller fulfilled his obligations under the policy; we agree and hold that Dr. Heller did all that was required of him under the terms of the Equitable disability policy.

However, Equitable insists that the insured, as a party to an insurance contract, has a good faith "duty to cure his disability if he can do so without reasonable risk and pain to himself."[12] Equitable ignores the fact that many insureds, like the plaintiff-appellee, choose not to undergo surgery because of the accompanying risks of infection, transfusion (hepatitis), bleeding, motor enervation of the median nerve, adhesions, scar tissue, possible anesthetic shock, trauma, anxiety, and even reoccurrence of the carpal tunnel syndrome condition. We are convinced that under Illinois law an insured is not required to undergo these risks in the absence of a specific contractual requirement. Furthermore, it seems very evident that because of these risks and other risks in the majority of surgical procedures, courts have wisely adopted the doctrine of informed consent.

Although we might not choose to follow the same course of conduct and path of reasoning as Dr. Heller,[13] there is no moral, much less legal obligation or compelling reason, to second guess an insured's, and in this case Dr. Heller's, decision to forgo surgery. The insurance company seeking to condition coverage on its insureds' acquiescence to undergo surgery to minimize the extent of their disabilities, as well as the financial loss to the insurer, need only incorporate a specific requirement[14] to that effect in the policy, and we would not hesitate to enforce the same. On the other hand, insurers who fail to include this express surgical contractual requirement, and who refuse to cover an insured after entering into a binding and enforceable agreement after accepting substantial premiums, in circumstances such as those before us, cause problems not only for the insured, but for the insurance industry as well. Insurance companies,

---

12. Equitable asserts that:

> [t]he person, such as Dr. Heller, who "clings" to his disability must constantly guard against becoming better. He must always choose the cringing, somewhat masochistic method of dealing with the disability. These are not characteristics the law should encourage and reward.

App. Br. at 20. "Masochistic" can be defined as "a tendency to take pleasure in physical or mental suffering inflicted on one by oneself." Webster's Third New International Dictionary (1981). The record is barren of evidence that even indicates, much less establishes, that Dr. Heller's method of dealing with his disability was "masochistic," thus Equitable's assertion is necessarily inapt. Furthermore, Equitable never made this outrageous argument to the trial court. We point out that there is a substantial difference between (1) a self-inflicted injury, and (2) a disability not caused by the individual, but who simply refuses to endure the risk, trouble, expense and often trying experiences incident to medical treatment. In the case of a self-inflicted disability, the act itself is contrary to public policy, regardless of the existence of insurance. As we pointed out, Dr. Heller's course of conduct did not exhibit any trace of bad faith, much less indicate the injury was self-inflicted. We caution counsel that in the future it should refrain from inferring such ridiculous and malicious allegations of this nature without one scintilla of support.

13. We note that Dr. Heller has apparently abandoned his profession as a surgeon to pursue a new career in law.

14. For example, an insurance company might include a provision in the policy for submitting claims involving refusals to undergo surgical and medical procedures to a panel of experts. Each party could include a board-certified specialist in the relevant area of medical expertise required to sit on the panel, and the third panelist, also independent and board-certified, could be chosen by the Dean of a recognized medical school in the area. The specialists would be impaneled to determine the extent and the treatment of the disability and decide whether the insured should submit to surgery. The panel's decision would then be binding on the parties if so written into the contract with specificity.

members of a service industry, must recognize that, like their insureds, they have corresponding duties and obligations under the policy and must conduct themselves accordingly instead of attempting to rely on the courts to correct their own deficiencies in underwriting and/or careless policy drafting.

NOTES AND QUESTIONS

1. The court makes clear that the freedom to refuse surgery enunciated in this opinion is a default rather than an immutable rule. According to a leading insurance law treatise, the default rule in workers' compensation is the reverse: An injured worker will lose his or her workers' compensation benefits "if an employee refuses tendered surgery which is not especially dangerous and which, in all likelihood, would clear up or improve the condition causing the disability." Holmes' Appleman on Insurance §8A-4899. Why might the default rule for workers' compensation benefits be less favorable to the beneficiary than the default rule for private disability insurance? How do you think Dr. Heller would fare under the workers' compensation standard? What should be the rule under Social Security?

2. Suppose that the disability is based on a "mental" condition that can be treated by an antipsychotic or other mind-altering medicine. Should the insured be able to refuse the treatment and still receive disability benefits?

3. Suppose that Dr. Heller's insurance company had included a provision stating that "benefits will be paid for disability resulting from repetitive stress injuries only if the insured follows the medical treatment plan of the Company." Would Dr. Heller have succeeded in convincing the court to require the company to pay him the benefits nonetheless? Why don't insurance companies revise their forms to contain this language?

4. The court roundly rejected the company's "victim blaming" stance in this case. There is undoubtedly some degree of shamming and malingering among recipients of disability insurance benefits. *See* Richard Ericson & Aaron Doyle, Uncertain Business: Insurance and the Limits of Knowledge (2004). But another commonly overlooked problem is the highly variable and subjective nature of response to injury. Given that some extraordinary people are able to bounce back from almost anything, it is easy for an insurer with a vested interest in recovery to blame ordinary people who recover more slowly or not at all. For people whose powers of recovery are at the low end of the spectrum, the encounter with the disability insurance authorities (whether public or private) can be trying indeed.

5. The following is yet another example of a disability definition:

    > Because of sickness or injury you are unable to perform the material and substantial duties of your occupation, and are not engaged in any other occupation.

    See www.about-disability-insurance.com/totaldisability.html (visited Sept. 24, 2007). This is sometimes called an "income replacement" definition or "conduct" clause. How does it differ from the definition in *Heller*? Would Dr. Heller have qualified under this provision? What do you think about the incentives created by this definition? Suppose an insurer denied coverage in a case involving this exclusion and, in order to support her family, an insured who was unable to perform her own occupation took another job. Can the insurance company use the fact of that employment to justify its decision? *See Moots v. Bankers Life Co.*, 707 P.2d 1083 (Kan. Ct. App. 1985) (pointing out the unfairness of a legal rule through which "the insurer could simply terminate disability benefits, wait until the insured is driven by dire necessity to seek *any* kind of employment, and then justify the termination retrospectively based on the subsequent employment").

6. Some "own occupation" disability insurance policies have a limited period of "true" own occupation coverage (with a disability definition like that in *Heller*) and then a more extended period (typically to age 65) with the income replacement definition. *See* Jane Ann Schiltz, Counseling Professionals on Disability Insurance 14 (1997). Can you articulate a rationale for that form of coverage?

7. As disability insurance perhaps most graphically illustrates, insurance is a status maintenance technology. In other words, insurance helps people protect what they have. There is a huge difference between the status protection power of Social Security's disability insurance and that of Dr. Heller's own occupation disability insurance policy. What might explain the difference? Not adverse selection. (Why not?) Moral hazard? Yes and no. (Why and why not?) How about the ideal of equality? In his first public interview, Kenneth Feinberg, the Special Master of the September 11th Victim Compensation Fund, said, "I don't want a system that gives $6 million to the stockbroker on the 38th floor and $38,000 to the waiter at Windows on the World." Bob Van Noris, *Fund Boss Spurns Huge Payout Gaps in Interview, Says He'll Seek Fairness*, Nat'l L.J., Dec. 10, 2001, at A1. It is easy to see how Social Security disability benefit levels reflect a commitment to equality, because there is not a large gap between the highest amount that one can recover in SSD and the lowest amount (especially when compared to the huge differences in incomes). How does the Social Security definition of disability reflect this commitment?

8. Social Security requires applicants for disability insurance to submit to some forms of surgery as a condition for receiving benefits. *See Awad v. Secretary of Health & Human Servs.*, 734 F.2d 288 (6th Cir. 1984). In that case, the court relied on 20 C.F.R. §404.1530, which provides:

§404.1530   NEED TO FOLLOW PRESCRIBED TREATMENT.

(a) What treatment you must follow. In order to get benefits, you must follow treatment prescribed by your physician if this treatment can restore your ability to work.

(b) When you do not follow prescribed treatment. If you do not follow the prescribed treatment without a good reason, we will not find you disabled or, if you are already receiving benefits, we will stop paying you benefits.

(c) Acceptable reasons for failure to follow prescribed treatment. We will consider your physical, mental, educational, and linguistic limitations (including any lack of facility with the English language) when determining if you have an acceptable reason for failure to follow prescribed treatment. The following are examples of a good reason for not following treatment:

(1) The specific medical treatment is contrary to the established teaching and tenets of your religion.

(2) The prescribed treatment would be cataract surgery for one eye, when there is an impairment of the other eye resulting in a severe loss of vision and is not subject to improvement through treatment.

(3) Surgery was previously performed with unsuccessful results and the same surgery is again being recommended for the same impairment.

(4) The treatment because of its magnitude (e.g., open heart surgery), unusual nature (e.g., organ transplant), or other reason is very risky for you; or

(5) The treatment involves amputation of an extremity, or a major part of an extremity.

B. Coordination of Benefits

There are many circumstances in which a person may have more than one insurance policy covering a given loss. For example, consider the case of a person who becomes totally disabled as the result of a job-related accident. If she has a disability insurance policy, she may potentially be able to recover Social Security, workers' compensation, and disability insurance benefits. In the health and disability insurance contexts, issues involving overlapping insurance benefits are called "coordination of benefit" problems, and provisions in insurance policies addressing those situations are called "coordination of benefit" provisions. In the property and casualty insurance field, the corresponding terms are "other insurance" problems and clauses.

Disability insurance companies commonly insert coordination of benefit clauses in their contracts, ostensibly to address the adverse selection and moral hazard problems that could result from an individual who is able to earn "too much" income through the overlapping forms of disability insurance. The case that follows illustrates the operation of a common type of coordination of benefit clause in a group disability insurance policy.

CODY v. CONNECTICUT GENERAL LIFE INSURANCE CO.

Supreme Judicial Court of Massachusetts
439 N.E.2d 234 (1982)

ABRAMS, J. We granted the parties' applications for direct appellate review to determine whether the public policy of this Commonwealth permits coordination-of-benefits clauses in insurance contracts. We conclude that coordination-of-benefits clauses do not violate the public policy of this Commonwealth unless the company engaged in misleading marketing practices, or the insurance contract as a whole is without substantial economic value.

We summarize the facts. The defendant Connecticut General Life Insurance Co. entered into a group contract of insurance with Sun Oil Company (Sun Oil), effective January 1, 1970. Under the contract, the defendant agreed to pay eligible Sun Oil employees, who become totally disabled, fifty per cent of their base monthly earnings up to $5,000 a month. The contract also contained two coordination-of-benefits clauses. The first clause provided that the benefits under the contract would be reduced by certain other income benefits, including workers' compensation, and fifty per cent of the amount of the employee's primary Social Security benefits. The second clause stated that if the sum of the employee's benefits under the contract, other income benefits, and benefits from Social Security, exceed seventy-five per cent of the employee's base monthly earnings, the benefits under the contract would be reduced until the sum of all benefits equals seventy-five per cent of the employee's base monthly earnings.

The plaintiff William F. Cody, an employee of Sun Oil, elected to purchase the coverage provided by this group contract. Through payroll deductions, the plaintiff paid a portion of the monthly premium for this coverage. The plaintiff never saw a copy of the insurance contract. The defendant did not distribute copies of the insurance contract to the employee-beneficiaries. Instead, the defendant sent a copy of the contract to Sun Oil. Sun Oil then distributed to its employees a booklet describing the benefits provided under the contract. The plaintiff testified that after reading the booklet, he believed that he would receive seventy-five per cent of his base pay in the event of a long term disability.[15]

As an employee, the plaintiff trained new tractor-trailer drivers for Sun Oil. On March 1, 1971, a driver trainee hit an obstruction on Route 95 in Groveland and lost control of the truck he was driving. The plaintiff, a passenger in that truck, was severely injured as a result of this accident. From the date of the accident until April 15, 1981, the date of the trial, the plaintiff has not worked. The plaintiff received no benefits under the contract.

In February, 1977, the plaintiff sued the defendant in the Superior Court. The plaintiff alleged a breach of the insurance contract by the defendant's failure to pay him any benefits. At trial, the parties stipulated that the insurance contract controlled this action. The parties also stipulated that if the judge interpreted the contract to allow the defendant an offset for fifty per cent of the plaintiff's primary Social Security benefits, plus the full amount of workers' compensation payments received between September 1, 1971, and April 15, 1981, the plaintiff would not be entitled to any payments under the contract; if the judge interpreted the contract to allow the defendant to offset only fifty per cent of the plaintiff's primary Social Security benefits, the plaintiff would be entitled to $27,168.05 under the contract; if the judge interpreted the policy to allow no offsets at all, the plaintiff would be entitled to $52,402.70 under the contract.

The judge submitted to the jury two special verdict questions (1) whether the plaintiff was disabled at any time after September 1, 1973,[16] and (2) if so, during what period of time. The jury found that the plaintiff was totally disabled from September 1, 1973, until April 21, 1981, the date of the verdict.

Over the plaintiff's objection, the judge determined the amount of damages himself. The judge found that under the insurance contract the plaintiff was entitled to recover fifty per cent of his base monthly earnings reduced by his Massachusetts workers' compensation benefits and by fifty per cent of his primary Social Security benefits. Since these offsets reduced the plaintiff's benefits under the insurance contract to nothing, the judge entered judgment for the defendant. We affirm the judgment.

---

15. The plaintiff may have based this belief on the coordination-of-benefits clause that provided that if benefits from all sources exceed seventy-five per cent of the employee's base monthly earnings, the benefits under the contract will be reduced until benefits from all sources equal seventy-five per cent of the employee's base monthly earnings.

16. The defendant conceded that the plaintiff was disabled from the date of the accident until September 1, 1973.

The plaintiff appeals, claiming that the judge erred: (1) in failing to submit the issue of damages to the jury, and in entering judgment for the defendant; and (2) in enforcing the coordination-of-benefits clauses. We conclude that the judge correctly determined the question of damages himself. We also believe that the judge did not err in enforcing the coordination-of-benefits clauses contained in the contract. We add, however, that coordination-of-benefits clauses will no longer be enforced if they are misleading or if they render the insurance contract as a whole without substantial economic value.

1. Damages. The plaintiff claims that the judge erred in failing to submit the issue of damages to the jury, and in entering judgment for the defendant. We disagree.

. . . [T]he parties stipulated to the amount of damages that the plaintiff could receive under each possible interpretation of the contract. After this stipulation, the only disputed issues involved the plaintiff's disability. . . . Once the jury determined that the plaintiff had been totally disabled from September 1, 1973, to April 21, 1981, there were no other disputed factual issues for the jury to decide. Thereafter, the judge merely had to apply the law to the facts as found by the jury and as stipulated to by the parties. Specifically, he had to select, from the damage calculations to which the parties had stipulated that calculation which was consistent with his interpretation of the contract. In line with his construction of the contract, the judge determined that the plaintiff was entitled to nothing under the contract. We therefore conclude that the judge properly entered judgment for the defendant.

2. Coordination-of-benefits clauses. Relying on *Kates v. St. Paul Fire & Marine Ins. Co.,* 509 F. Supp. 477 (D. Mass. 1981), the plaintiff claims that the judge erred in enforcing the coordination-of-benefits clauses, because they violate public policy. We agree with the plaintiff that *Kates v. St. Paul Fire & Marine Ins. Co., supra* at 491, correctly states the public policy of this Commonwealth, that insurance contracts may not be misleading, and that coverages may not be "unrealistically limited" or so limited in scope as to be of no "substantial economic value." However, in this case, the insurance contract took effect, and the plaintiff's injury occurred, before the Legislature enacted the statutes that are the source of this public policy. We therefore believe that it would be unfair to apply this public policy in this case.

In the *Kates* case, *supra,* the judge correctly found one source of this public policy in G.L. c. 175 §110E,[17] Pursuant to G.L. c. 175 §110E, inserted by St. 1973, c. 1081, the Commissioner of Insurance may issue rules and regulations "to establish minimum standards of full and fair disclosure, for the form and content of policies of accident and sickness insurance which provide medical, surgical, or hospital expense benefits. . . ." Among the purposes of these rules and regulations are the "elimination of provisions which may be misleading . . . "; and the "elimination of coverages which are so limited in scope as to be of no substantial economic value." G.L. c. 175, §110E(b), (e). Although G.L. c. 175 §110E expressly does not cover "general" or "blanket" disability insurance contracts like that at issue in this case, the *Kates* decision properly determined that

---

17. There are other statutory sources for this policy. For example, G.L. c. 93A, §2, inserted by St. 1967, c. 813 §1, prohibits "unfair or deceptive acts or practices in the conduct of any trade or commerce," including insurance. *See Dodd v. Commercial Union Ins. Co.,* 373 Mass. 72, 75-76, 365 N.E.2d 802 (1977). In addition, the Commissioner of Insurance must make sure that insurance policies are readable. *See* G.L. c. 175, §2B, inserted by St. 1977, c. 801 §1.

the policies set out in that statute apply to such contracts. *Cf. Mailhot v. Travelers Ins. Co.,* 377 N.E.2d 681 (Mass. 1978); *Gaudette v. Webb,* 284 N.E.2d 222 (Mass. 1972). Since G.L. c. 175 §110E, was enacted after the effective date of the insurance contract at issue in this case, and after the injury giving rise to this claim, we believe it would be unfair to apply the public policy set out in that statute.

However, we think it is appropriate to elaborate on this policy for future cases. In the *Kates* case, the insurance contract clearly provided that payments on account of workers' compensation and Social Security would be deducted from the benefits provided by the policy. Nevertheless, the judge concluded that the contract was misleading. "In view of the marketing of this coverage through the workplace, employees electing to participate could reasonably expect to receive lifetime benefits if totally disabled from an injury sustained in their employment. Even though one who has all the relevant information about social security and worker compensation benefits could ascertain by close analysis of the coordination-of-benefits provisions that . . . [under the policy he would receive few benefits for on-the-job injuries], it would not be reasonable to expect that this fact would be discovered by a person who was considering whether to apply for participation."[18] *Id.* at 491-492. Thus, the *Kates* case demonstrates that a company's marketing techniques may make even a totally unambiguous insurance contract misleading. Since misleading insurance contracts violate the public policy of this Commonwealth, we believe that courts must limit the enforcement of these contracts to avoid unconscionable results.

If the insurance contract is not misleading, we think that the court must go on to decide whether the contract as a whole is without substantial economic value. The determination whether the contract is without substantial economic value is similar to an examination of the substantive unconscionability of a contract. A court must determine whether the contract terms are unreasonably favorable to one party. *See Zapatha v. Dairy Mart, Inc.,* 408 N.E.2d 1370 (Mass. 1980). Hence, a court should find that an insurance contract like that at issue in this case has substantial economic value as long as the premiums reflect the anticipated effect of any coordination-of-benefits clause.

Finally, we note that coordination-of-benefits clauses serve the public purpose of avoiding duplicate recoveries for the same injuries. *Mailhot v. Travelers Ins. Co.,* 377 N.E.2d 681 (Mass. 1978). These clauses enable insurance companies to charge lower premiums. We therefore conclude that unless the company engaged in misleading marketing practices, or the insurance contract as a whole is without substantial economic value, coordination-of-benefits clauses do not violate the public policy of this Commonwealth.

NOTES AND QUESTIONS

1. Review what you learned about insurance contract interpretation in Chapter 2 by deriving from common law principles the public policy that the court announces in this case. Begin by deciding what "substantial economic value" might mean. Does it mean that the price paid for the insurance pol-

---

18. To avoid a claim that an insurance contract like that at issue in this case is misleading, a company should specifically inform the consumer that because of the coordination-of-benefits clauses, he may not be entitled to any benefits under the policy for certain injuries. We emphasize that a clear warning prevents an insurance contract from being misleading.

icy must bear a fair relationship to the benefits provided? What common law principle of insurance contract interpretation might authorize courts to engage in this inquiry? How would a court determine whether the price was fair? Would this turn litigation over coordination of benefit clauses into hearings on insurance rates?

2. Might "substantial economic value" be determined, instead, in relation to what was promised? In other words, an insurance policy provides "substantial economic value" if the benefits provided bear a close relationship to the benefits that a reasonable policyholder would have understood the company was promising to pay. While this turns the "substantial economic value" test into the "reasonable expectations" test, it keeps courts out of the very difficult position of second-guessing consumer judgments. If "substantial economic value" means *any* economic value of substance, on the other hand, then it's difficult to see what the court accomplished. Any of the doctrines relied on in *C&J Fertilizer* creates a more exacting standard than that.

3. How would you describe the coverage provided by Cody's policy? Assuming for the moment that the coordination of benefits clause is enforceable, what benefit does the policy provide to workers who purchase it? In what circumstances will a worker collect disability insurance benefits? Is there a substantial economic benefit in that kind of coverage?

4. Was the company's marketing of the policy misleading? If you were advising Connecticut General following this case, how would you suggest that they describe the coverage provided by the policy in the future? What objections might you imagine being raised by the marketing department?

5. The coordination of benefit problems also comes up in the health insurance area. Perhaps the most common situation is when one member of a couple is covered by his or her own health insurance policy, as well as the health insurance policy of the other member of the couple. Another important health insurance coordination of benefit question concerns the relationship between Medicare benefits and employment-based health insurance benefits, a very important issue that often arises when someone continues working past the Medicare-eligible age of 65. *See* 42 C.F.R. §411.33 (stating that Medicare is a "secondary payer," meaning that, when there is other insurance available, Medicare will only pay the difference between the usual Medicare benefits minus the amount paid by the other insurance). For a conceptual overview of coordination of benefit problems, see Kenneth Abraham, Distributing Risk: Insurance, Legal Theory, and Public Policy 133 et seq. (1986).

6. *American Family Life Assurance Co. v. Blue Cross of Florida, Inc.*, 486 F.2d 225 (5th Cir. 1973), presents an interesting twist on coordination of benefit (COB) litigation. In that case, an insurer selling a cancer insurance policy claimed that another insurer that sold broad coverage health insurance engaged in an unlawful restraint on trade by including a COB clause in the broad coverage health insurance. The Blue Cross COB clause made Blue Cross "secondary" to the cancer policy, meaning that Blue Cross would pay for cancer treatments only once the benefits under the cancer policy were exhausted. Can you see why this COB clause would make it difficult for the cancer insurer to sell its policies? Professor Spencer Kimball notes that some insurance commissioners have tried to stop the sale of "dread disease"

policies. *See* Spencer Kimball, Cases and Materials on Insurance Law 461 (1992). Why? If broad coverage health insurance policies routinely include such COB clauses, do dread disease insurance policies provide a substantial economic benefit? If so, to whom?

MEGAMUTUAL'S HUMAN RESOURCES PROBLEM

MegaMutual's general counsel, Roberta Fernandez, has a human resources problem. One of her top lawyers, Paul Reed, was involved in an automobile accident a year ago while driving to a deposition. He returned from work six months after the accident and has not been able to perform at his former level. As a result of his absence and reduced productivity, work in the office has backed up. Other members of the staff are upset at the increase in their workload. Even worse, Fernandez has had to increase her use of outside counsel, leading the bean counters in finance to lean on her.

Everyone was willing to live with the problem so long as it seemed that Reed would get better, but now the consensus is that he will not. There has been permanent brain damage, nothing that anyone would notice in casual conversation, but his formerly extraordinary powers of abstract thinking and high-level reasoning are now merely ordinary, and that is not good enough for the demanding work in the general counsel's office. Reed could do much of the more routine work in the office, but Fernandez likes to use that work to train the newer lawyers, and she couldn't justify using such a highly compensated lawyer to do such simple work. If she were going to hire someone only to do that work, she would hire a paralegal.

A. Assume that Reed has a general disability policy (like the one in *Wooley*) through his employment at MegaMutual, that the accident was work related, and that he has a personal "own occupation" disability insurance policy with an "income replacement" prohibition like that discussed in note 5 after *Heller* ("because of sickness or injury, you are unable to perform the material and substantial duties of your occupation, *and are not engaged in any other occupation*"), which he purchased on his own through the state bar association. Assume also that, with some supervision, Reed could handle a law practice involving routine real estate conveyances, wills, and the like. Does Reed meet the standards for disability under Social Security and workers' compensation? Does Reed meet the standards for disability under the own occupation disability insurance policy? How about the general disability insurance policy?

B. Now assume that Reed's personal disability insurance policy contains a COB clause that is exactly like the one in *Cody,* that he is not eligible for Social Security benefits, that the maximum that he can receive from workers' compensation is $800 a month, and that the personal disability policy will replace up to 75 percent of his income (subject to the COB clause); note that his policy is more "generous" than the policy in Cody, which provided 51 percent of income replacement, subject to the COB clause. What is the maximum that he can collect from the personal disability policy? That, of course, depends on his income. Suppose that he makes $4,000 per month?

Suppose that he makes $8,000, or even $12,000? What does that tell you about the relative effect that disability insurance COB clauses have on people of different incomes? What happens to Reed's incentive to work once the income replacement coverage comes into effect? Suppose the disability insurance policy that he purchased through the state bar association provided own occupation disability protection for only five years and, thereafter, only general disability insurance coverage?

IV.   HEALTH INSURANCE

Of all the forms of insurance addressed in these materials, health insurance is the most certain to change significantly over the coming years. Annual expenditures on health care in the United States are over $2 trillion and rising. After an earlier period in which health care costs rose approximately at the general level of inflation, the last ten years have returned to a situation in which health care costs are rising faster than costs elsewhere in the economy. Two important reasons for this situation are the aging of the population and advances in medical technology.

Most health care expenses in the United States are paid by health insurance of one form or another. Indeed, there is no other comparably important sector of the U.S. economy in which so few of the people consuming the goods and services pay directly for those services. As a result, health insurance institutions play an absolutely central role in health care policy. When you combine the importance of health care, the enormous and rising costs, which amount to nearly 20 percent of gross domestic product (GDP), and the centrality of insurance to health care financing, you have a guaranteed recipe for continued change in health insurance institutions.

Because health insurance is commonly taught as part of a health law course, we have elected not to include any doctrinal material in this casebook. Instead, we include an excerpt of a law review article describing how the Affordable Care Act changed the health insurance landscape in the United States, along with a selection of provisions from the legislation. When health insurance is purchased from the individual market, the insurance law issues that arise are similar to those that arise under other first-party forms of insurance. When health insurance is provided as an employment benefit, however, the law that governs the interpretation of the contract and other matters is not insurance law, but rather employment law. The next section addresses two of the main differences that that makes.

HEALTH INSURANCE, RISK AND RESPONSIBILITY AFTER THE AFFORDABLE CARE ACT

Tom Baker

159 U. Pa. L. Rev. 1577 (2011)

With the passage of the Patient Protection and Affordable Care Act (PPACA) and the Health Care and Education Reconciliation Act of 2010 (HCERA), health insurance in the United States is on track to become a form of social insurance. While all insurance is social — so that "the loss lighteth rather easily upon many than heavily upon few" — to be considered social insurance in the traditional sense, the insurance must be compulsory and easily available, and the price must bear some relation to the ability to pay.

Parts of the U.S. health insurance system already meet those requirements: most significantly Medicare (for the elderly and formerly working disabled); Medicaid (for certain categories of the poor, including all children in low income families); and workers' compensation (for employment-related illness and injury). U.S. income tax and employment law strongly encourage the provision of general health benefits through employment, making employment-based health insurance a de facto obligation for most large employers and many small employers. But the legal choice to offer health insurance remains that of the employer, and individuals' only health insurance obligations are to pay Medicare taxes and to participate in the financing of Medicaid through the payment of their ordinary state and federal taxes. The Affordable Care Act will make large employers' obligations de jure starting in 2014, and it will create a legal obligation to obtain health insurance for employees' entire lifetime, not just for old age or in the event of total disability. . . . [T]he Affordable Care Act makes only incremental changes to Medicare, Medicaid, and the large-group insurance market (though the Medicaid change is historic in terms of U.S. social welfare policy). The Affordable Care Act dramatically reforms the individual and small-group insurance market. . . .

A.   MEDICARE

The Affordable Care Act made no fundamental changes to Medicare, which is the health insurance component of the Social Security program. Accordingly, health insurance for the eligible disabled (those who paid, or were dependents of someone who paid, Social Security taxes for forty quarters before becoming totally disabled) and seniors (who paid, or were married to someone who paid, Social Security taxes for forty quarters) will continue to consist of four parts:

- Part A, which covers inpatient care, hospice care, and some home health services and is financed entirely by a flat percentage tax on wages paid over the lifetime;
- Part B, which covers other medically necessary or preventive services and is funded in part by a flat percentage tax on wages paid over the lifetime (73%) and in part by premiums paid when enrolled (25%), that are based in part on income and are otherwise uniform regardless of age, health status, or any other factors;
- Part C, Medicare Advantage, which is a private-sector alternative to Parts A and B that allows individuals to obtain their health care benefits, typically including prescription drug benefits, from the health care financing companies active in the large-group market explained below and is funded in much the same way as parts A, B, and D; and
- Part D, which covers prescription drugs and is funded by premiums that vary according to the type of plan but are otherwise uniform regardless of age, health status, or any other factors.

The Affordable Care Act changes Medicare financing and risk distribution in three main ways:

- increasing the progressivity of Medicare financing by raising the wage tax on higher-income taxpayers, adding an income-based component to Part D premiums, and freezing the thresholds for income-based increments to Part B premiums;
- changing the cost-sharing formula for Part D so that individuals will gradually pay a smaller percentage of the costs of medication at the point of sale (meaning that a greater percentage of the costs will be paid in the form of Part D premiums); and
- reducing federal payments to Medicare Advantage plans, providing bonuses for quality ratings, and obligating these plans to maintain a medical-loss ratio of at least 85%.

In addition, the Act expands coverage for preventive health services and eliminates cost sharing for services designated as cost effective by the U.S. Preventive Services Task Force.

B.   MEDICAID

In form, the Act changed Medicaid only incrementally, but these changes are very significant in historical terms. The Act, for the first time in U.S. history, explicitly recognizes a national entitlement to health care for all of the poor—including able-bodied, working-age individuals—to be financed through general tax revenues. The Affordable Care Act thus abandons the concept of the "deserving poor" that has long been one of the main features of U.S. social welfare policy, including policies on access to health care. Starting in 2014, all lawful U.S. residents with family incomes of less than 133% of the federal poverty level (FPL) will be entitled to Medicaid.[19] Before the Act, Medicaid was available on a national basis only to pregnant women, children, parents of dependent children, and the elderly and disabled. These individuals had to meet state-determined income ceilings that varied by category, though there was a national floor for some categories: 100% of the index for the elderly, disabled, and children aged 7 to 19, and 133% of the index for pregnant women and children 6 years of age or younger. . . .

C.   THE INDIVIDUAL AND SMALL-GROUP MARKET

The Affordable Care Act makes the most dramatic changes to the individual and small-group insurance market, aiming to create:

- a single health insurance pool in each state;
- populated by all lawful residents in the state who do not have health benefits through a government program or a large employer;

---

19. *Editor's note.* The Supreme Court's health care decision made the expansion of Medicaid optional for the states. *National Federation of Independent Business v. Sebelius*, 567 U.S. __ (2012). The act, which famously mandates the purchase of health insurance, also contains penalties for failure to comply. Those penalties begin at $95 annually or 1 percent of an individual's income, whichever is higher, in 2014 and rise to $695 or 2.5 percent of income by 2016.

- serviced by health insurance plans that provide all essential health care benefits and compete on the basis of cost and quality; with
- guaranteed access and identical premiums for all, subject to a few narrowly tailored exceptions that do not include health status.

. . .

For present purposes, the key elements of the individual and small-group market reforms are the following:

- the mandates
- the subsidy
- minimum coverage requirements
- open enrollment and guaranteed renewal
- limits on individual risk-based pricing
- risk adjustments
- health exchanges

The paragraphs that follow briefly explain each of these elements. . . .

The Mandates. The Act obligates all lawful citizens to obtain "minimum essential coverage" and all large employers—i.e.[,] those with more than 50 employees—to start providing minimum essential coverage to their employees in 2014. The structure of these mandates makes obtaining coverage through the individual and small-group market the residual health care financing mechanism for people who do not qualify for a government health benefit program (Medicare, Medicaid, and Veterans benefits) or work for a large employer. The individual mandate is an important part of the solidarity equation because it requires everyone to be in the health insurance risk pool, addressing the adverse selection problem that would follow from other provisions of the Act that make it possible for high-risk people to enter the health insurance pool.

The Subsidies. The individual mandate obligates individuals to obtain a health plan. The subsidies encourage them to purchase a plan and reduce the likelihood that they will qualify for the hardship exceptions. Beginning in 2014, people with incomes up to 400% of the FPL will be eligible for financial assistance for coverage through the state health insurance exchanges: Those with incomes under 133% of the FPL will be covered under the newly expanded Medicaid program. Those with incomes up to 400% of the FPL will qualify for tax credits to reduce their premiums. They will also qualify for limited cost sharing under their plans to enable them to pay less out of pocket. Both the tax credits and reduction in cost sharing will apply on an income-based sliding scale and similarly will be structured to correspond to the actuarial categories of the plans. General federal revenues will fund the subsidies, which thus represent a major ability-to-pay component of the new health care social contract.

Minimum Essential Coverage Requirements. The minimum essential coverage requirements set a floor for contract quality standards on the health plans that may be offered in the individual and small-group market beginning in 2014. These standards have three primary components. First, plans must cover "essential health benefits," which are a package of benefits that the HHS Secretary will define. Second, the plan must limit annual cost sharing (e.g., deductibles and co-insurance) to the amount authorized under the Affordable Care Act's Health Savings Accounts (HSAs). In subsequent years, the limitation will be indexed to the annual limit on HSAs for self-only coverage and double that amount for any other plan. Third, the plan must meet one of four "actuarial value" requirements, which vary by level of coverage (bronze, silver, gold and platinum) and which set a percentage ceiling on the aggregate cost sharing of all the individuals in the plan. The "actuarial value" of a plan refers to the percentage of the total costs, to be paid by the plan, of covered services provided to all of the plan's participants, in the aggregate. For example, a silver-level plan must have an actuarial value of at least 70%, meaning that it cannot impose aggregate cost sharing of more than 30% of the total cost of covered benefits on the participants in the plan. In addition, the state-based exchanges appear to have discretion to include additional process and quality-related requirements based on their authority to determine whether "making available such [a] health plan through such [an] Exchange is in the interests of qualified individuals and qualified employers in the State or States in which such Exchange operates." . . .

Open Enrollment and Guaranteed Renewal. The open enrollment and guaranteed renewal requirements mean that all health insurance plans in the individual and small-group market must accept everyone who chooses to apply for or renew health insurance. These requirements eliminate the traditional authority of health insurance companies to choose whom they will insure — an authority that insurance companies have had no realistic choice to exercise in any way other than to exclude from the health insurance pool those people who most need to be in the pool. It is important to note that making it too easy for high-risk individuals to join the insurance pool actually poses a challenge to the solidarity equation by creating the possibility that people will violate the mandate unless and until they really need serious health treatment.

Limits on Individual Risk-Based Pricing. In the traditional, actuarial approach to private market insurance, insurance is understood as a series of bilateral contracts between insurance companies and their policyholders, and those contracts are understood as wagers, the odds (and therefore the price) of which should be set according to the likelihood that the policyholder will "win" by making a claim. If people have the choice whether to buy insurance or not, and if insurance companies have the authority to decide on an individual basis how much to charge for their products, then an insurance company that fails to set prices on this basis will not last long. The result is that those people who most need to be in the pool cannot afford to join the pool because their premiums will be too high. Accordingly, achieving health care solidarity through the private market requires limiting insurers' authority to decide on an individual basis how much to charge for their products.

The Act allows health plans in the individual and small-group market to vary their prices on the basis of only four factors: whether the applicant is an individual or family, the geographic region in which the applicant lives, age, and tobacco use. For the latter two factors, there are limits on the pricing differentials — 3 to 1 for age-based pricing differentials and 1.5 to 1 for tobacco-use pricing differentials — meaning that the price for the oldest group in the pool may not be more than three times the price for the youngest group and the price for the heaviest tobacco users may not be more than one-and-a-half times the price for comparable non-users. In addition, the Act permits the sale of special, high-deductible policies to people under the age of thirty, and, presumably, these policies will constitute a separate risk pool. (Such policies represent an example of risk classification by design explicitly permitted in the Act.) Finally, the Act authorizes wellness programs for small employer plans that may provide substantial rebates or other benefits to participants (up to 30% of the total premium, including the employer share, and potentially increasing to 50% at the discretion of the Secretaries of Labor, Health and Human Services, or the Treasury). The wellness programs have the potential to lead to de facto differential prices based on participation in the programs, but the programs may not be "a subterfuge for discriminating based on a health status factor." From a risk and responsibility perspective, these pricing factors and the wellness programs are among the most interesting aspects of the Act. . . .

Risk Adjustments. Risk adjustments are financial transfers among health plans based on the aggregate risk of the individuals who choose to participate in each plan. Plans that end up with a disproportionately high-risk membership are supposed to receive risk adjustment payments from plans that end up with a disproportionately low-risk membership so that the price that individuals pay for their insurance does not depend on their health risk, whether it is due to risk classification by design or to other sorting mechanisms that correlate with risk. The details of the risk adjustment mechanism are yet to be determined as of the date of this Edition, but the expectation is that the process will be similar to that for Medicare Advantage plans, which uses diagnosis and utilization data to make predictions about the risk level of the pool of people enrolled in each plan

The Exchanges. The exchanges are the marketplace through which individuals and small groups will purchase health care plans. Among other responsibilities, the exchanges must ensure that the plans listed on it comply with statutory requirements. The exchanges are also likely to be asked to administer the risk adjustments. Important, unanswered questions about the exchanges include how active exchanges should be in helping consumers make choices and whether states should exercise the option of allowing the federal government to create and operate the exchanges.

In summary, the changes to the individual and small-group market appear to be designed to make that market function as if all of the individuals who bought insurance in each exchange were the members of a very large single employment group with many choices for health benefits, analogous in many ways to the Federal Employee Health Benefit Program (FEHBP). . . .

D. THE LARGE-GROUP MARKET

The Act makes few changes to the large-group market, consistent with the belief that the market has been functioning acceptably well in providing health care access to most people working for large organizations. The large-group market is and will remain lightly regulated by the Department of Labor under the ERISA and HIPAA statutes. The main change introduced by the Act is that large employers—defined as an entity with more than [50] employees—must provide "minimum essential coverage" to their employees starting in 2014.

For large employers that already provide health care benefits (most already do), the new mandate will not impose much in the way of new obligations because—perhaps surprisingly—the Act exempts the large-group market from the "essential health benefits" requirements that will apply in the individual and small-group market. Large-group market plans do, however, have to meet the same annual cost-sharing limits as health plans in the small-group market, meaning that employees' out-of-pocket expenditures for covered health care expenses cannot exceed the maximum amount allowed for Health Savings Accounts and no more than $4000 of this cost sharing may be in the form of a deductible. In addition, large-group market plans will have to comply with some of the Affordable Care Act mandates such as the elimination of annual and aggregate limits on coverage, coverage for preventive services, dependent coverage, wellness programs, nondiscrimination on the basis of health status, and reporting.

The Act also regulates the content of large-group market plans indirectly. If an employer's plans are of such low quality that employees start to buy individual health plans on the exchanges, the employer will be penalized. In addition, states will have the option of giving large employers the choice to include plans offered through the exchanges as part of their employer-sponsored plan, allowing employees to use pretax dollars to buy health plans on the exchange. "Large" employers that are not very large are likely to encourage states to make that option available.

1.   **Selected Private Market Content Regulation in the Affordable Care Act**

The Affordable Care Act of 2010 is arguably the most significant federal private health insurance legislation of all time. The establishment of Medicare and Medicaid were more important in terms of expanding access to health care, but these were new government insurance programs. The Affordable Care Act recruited the private insurance market to expand access to health care. As reflected in the excerpt above, the ACA is an enormous piece of legislation that affected Medicaid and Medicare along with the private health insurance market. What follows are selected excerpts that affect the private market. We begin with the two sections that set the framework governing the contents of health insurance. Note that we have presented these portions of the ACA in thematic rather than numerical order. In each case, the section number corresponds to the section number in the ACA and the citations indicate where the section appears in the U.S. Code.

ACA: Overall Framework of Content Regulation

Sec. 2707 [42 U.S.C. §300gg–6]. Comprehensive Health Insurance Coverage.

(a) COVERAGE FOR ESSENTIAL HEALTH BENEFITS PACKAGE.—A health insurer that offers health insurance coverage in the individual or small group market shall ensure that such coverage includes the essential health benefits package required under section 1302(a) of the Patient Protection and Affordable Care Act.

(b) COST-SHARING UNDER GROUP HEALTH PLANS.—A group health plan shall ensure that any annual cost-sharing imposed under the plan does not exceed the limitations provided for under paragraphs (1) and (2) of section 1302(c).

Sec. 1201 [42 U.S.C. §300gg-3] Prohibition of Preexisting Condition Exclusions or Other Discrimination Based on Health Status

(a) In general

A group health plan and a health insurance issuer offering group or individual health insurance coverage may not impose any preexisting condition exclusion with respect to such plan or coverage.

[42 U.S. Code §300gg] Fair health insurance premiums

(a) Prohibiting discriminatory premium rates

(1) In general. With respect to the premium rate charged by a health insurance issuer for health insurance coverage offered in the individual or small group market—

(A) such rate shall vary with respect to the particular plan or coverage involved only by—

(i) whether such plan or coverage covers an individual or family;

(ii) rating area, as established in accordance with paragraph (2);

(iii) age, except that such rate shall not vary by more than 3 to 1 for adults (consistent with section 300gg–6(c) of this title); and

(iv) tobacco use, except that such rate shall not vary by more than 1.5 to 1; and

(B) such rate shall not vary with respect to the particular plan or coverage involved by any other factor not described in subparagraph (A).

(2) Rating area

(A) In general. Each State shall establish 1 or more rating areas within that State for purposes of applying the requirements of this subchapter.

(B) Secretarial review. The Secretary shall review the rating areas established by each State under subparagraph (A) to ensure the adequacy of such areas for purposes of carrying out the requirements of this subchapter. If the Secretary determines a State's rating areas are not adequate, or that a State does not establish such areas, the Secretary may establish rating areas for that State.

(3) Permissible age bands. The Secretary, in consultation with the National Association of Insurance Commissioners, shall define the permissible age bands for rating purposes under paragraph (1)(A)(iii).

(4) Application of variations based on age or tobacco use. With respect to family coverage under a group health plan or health insurance coverage, the rating variations permitted under clauses (iii) and (iv) of paragraph (1)(A) shall be applied based on the portion of the premium that is attributable to each family member covered under the plan or coverage.

Sec. 1302 [42 U.S.C. 18022]. Essential Health Benefits Requirements.

(a) ESSENTIAL HEALTH BENEFITS PACKAGE.—In this title, the term "essential health benefits package" means, with respect to any health plan, coverage that—

(1) provides for the essential health benefits defined by the Secretary under subsection (b);

(2) limits cost-sharing for such coverage in accordance with subsection (c); and

(3) subject to subsection (e), provides either the bronze, silver, gold, or platinum level of coverage described in subsection (d).

(b) ESSENTIAL HEALTH BENEFITS. —

(1) IN GENERAL. —Subject to paragraph (2), the Secretary shall define the essential health benefits, except that such benefits shall include at least the following general categories and the items and services covered within the categories:

(A) Ambulatory patient services.

(B) Emergency services.

(C) Hospitalization.

(D) Maternity and newborn care.

(E) Mental health and substance use disorder services, including behavioral health treatment.

(F) Prescription drugs.

(G) Rehabilitative and habilitative services and devices.

(H) Laboratory services.

(I) Preventive and wellness services and chronic disease management.

(J) Pediatric services, including oral and vision care.

. . .

(4) REQUIRED ELEMENTS FOR CONSIDERATION. —In defining the essential health benefits under paragraph (1), the Secretary shall—

(A) ensure that such essential health benefits reflect an appropriate balance among the categories described in such subsection, so that benefits are not unduly weighted toward any category;

(B) not make coverage decisions, determine reimbursement rates, establish incentive programs, or design benefits in ways that discriminate against individuals because of their age, disability, or expected length of life;

(C) take into account the health care needs of diverse segments of the population, including women, children, persons with disabilities, and other groups;

(D) ensure that health benefits established as essential not be subject to denial to individuals against their wishes on the basis of the individuals' age or expected length of life or of the individuals' present or predicted disability, degree of medical dependency, or quality of life;

(E) provide that a qualified health plan shall not be treated as providing coverage for the essential health benefits described in paragraph (1) unless the plan provides that—

(i) coverage for emergency department services will be provided without imposing any requirement under the plan for prior authorization of services or any limitation on coverage where the provider of services does not have a contractual relationship with the plan for the providing of services that is more restrictive than the requirements or limitations that apply to emergency department services received from providers who do have such a contractual relationship with the plan; and

(ii) if such services are provided out-of-network, the cost-sharing requirement (expressed as a copayment amount or coinsurance rate) is the same requirement that would apply if such services were provided in-network;

. . .

(5) RULE OF CONSTRUCTION. — Nothing in this title shall be construed to prohibit a health plan from providing benefits in excess of the essential health benefits described in this subsection.

(c) REQUIREMENTS RELATING TO COST-SHARING. —

(1) ANNUAL LIMITATION ON COST-SHARING. —

(A) 2014. — The cost-sharing incurred under a health plan with respect to self-only coverage or coverage other than self-only coverage for a plan year beginning in 2014 shall not exceed the dollar amounts in effect under section 223(c)(2)(A)(ii) of the Internal Revenue Code of 1986 for self-only and family coverage, respectively, for taxable years beginning in 2014.[20]

(B) 2015 AND LATER. — In the case of any plan year beginning in a calendar year after 2014, the limitation under this paragraph shall—

(i) in the case of self-only coverage, be equal to the dollar amount under subparagraph (A) for self-only coverage for plan years beginning in 2014, increased by an amount equal to the product of that amount and the premium adjustment percentage under paragraph (4) for the calendar year; and

(ii) in the case of other coverage, twice the amount in effect under clause (i). If the amount of any increase under clause (i) is not a multiple of $50, such increase shall be rounded to the next lowest multiple of $50.

(2) ANNUAL LIMITATION ON DEDUCTIBLES FOR EMPLOYER SPONSORED PLANS. —

(A) IN GENERAL. — In the case of a health plan offered in the small group market, the deductible under the plan shall not exceed—

(i) $2,000 in the case of a plan covering a single individual; and

(ii) $4,000 in the case of any other plan. The amounts under clauses (i) and (ii) may be increased by the maximum amount of reimbursement which is reasonably available to a participant under a flexible spending arrangement described in section 106(c)(2) of the Internal Revenue Code of 1986 (determined without regard to any salary reduction arrangement).

(B) INDEXING OF LIMITS. — In the case of any plan year beginning in a calendar year after 2014—

(i) the dollar amount under subparagraph (A)(i) shall be increased by an amount equal to the product of that amount and the premium adjustment percentage under paragraph (4) for the calendar year; and

(ii) the dollar amount under subparagraph (A)(ii) shall be increased to an amount equal to twice the amount in effect under subparagraph (A)(i) for plan years beginning in the calendar year, determined after application of clause (i). If the amount of any increase under clause (i) is not a multiple of $50, such increase shall be rounded to the next lowest multiple of $50.

---

20. *Editors' note:* This cross-reference is to the Internal Revenue Code section relating to Health Savings Accounts (HSAs), which are a special tax-preferred savings method for medical expenses. The cross reference links the permitted cost sharing to the amount that taxpayers are permitted to deposit into an HSA, thus making it possible for a taxpayer to fund all covered expenses using money that is excludable from income for purposes of the U.S. income tax.

(C) ACTUARIAL VALUE.—The limitation under this paragraph shall be applied in such a manner so as to not affect the actuarial value of any health plan, including a plan in the bronze level.

(D) COORDINATION WITH PREVENTIVE LIMITS.—Nothing in this paragraph shall be construed to allow a plan to have a deductible under the plan apply to benefits described in section 2713 of the Public Health Service Act.

(3) COST-SHARING.—In this title—

(A) IN GENERAL.—The term "cost-sharing" includes—

(i) deductibles, coinsurance, copayments, or similar charges; and

(ii) any other expenditure required of an insured individual which is a qualified medical expense (within the meaning of section 223(d)(2) of the Internal Revenue Code of 1986) with respect to essential health benefits covered under the plan.

(B) EXCEPTIONS.—Such term does not include premiums, balance billing amounts for non-network providers, or spending for non-covered services.

(4) PREMIUM ADJUSTMENT PERCENTAGE.—For purposes of paragraphs (1)(B)(i) and (2)(B)(i), the premium adjustment percentage for any calendar year is the percentage (if any) by which the average per capita premium for health insurance coverage in the United States for the preceding calendar year (as estimated by the Secretary no later than October 1 of such preceding calendar year) exceeds such average per capita premium for 2013 (as determined by the Secretary).

(d) LEVELS OF COVERAGE.—

(1) LEVELS OF COVERAGE DEFINED.—The levels of coverage described in this subsection are as follows:

(A) BRONZE LEVEL.—A plan in the bronze level shall provide a level of coverage that is designed to provide benefits that are actuarially equivalent to 60 percent of the full actuarial value of the benefits provided under the plan.

(B) SILVER LEVEL.—A plan in the silver level shall provide a level of coverage that is designed to provide benefits that are actuarially equivalent to 70 percent of the full actuarial value of the benefits provided under the plan.

(C) GOLD LEVEL.—A plan in the gold level shall provide a level of coverage that is designed to provide benefits that are actuarially equivalent to 80 percent of the full actuarial value of the benefits provided under the plan.

(D) PLATINUM LEVEL.—A plan in the platinum level shall provide a level of coverage that is designed to provide benefits that are actuarially equivalent to 90 percent of the full actuarial value of the benefits provided under the plan.

(2) ACTUARIAL VALUE.—

(A) IN GENERAL.—Under regulations issued by the Secretary, the level of coverage of a plan shall be determined on the basis that the essential health benefits described in subsection (b) shall be provided to a standard population (and without regard to the population the plan may actually provide benefits to).

(B) EMPLOYER CONTRIBUTIONS.—As revised by section 10104(b)(1) the Secretary shall issue regulations under which employer contributions to a health savings account (within the meaning of section 223 of the Internal Revenue Code of 1986) may be taken into account in determining the level of coverage for a plan of the employer. . . .

(3) ALLOWABLE VARIANCE.—The Secretary shall develop guidelines to provide for a de minimis variation in the actuarial valuations used in determining the level of coverage of a plan to account for differences in actuarial estimates. . . .

(e) CATASTROPHIC PLAN.—

(1) IN GENERAL.—A health plan not providing a bronze, silver, gold, or platinum level of coverage shall be treated as meeting the requirements of subsection (d) with respect to any plan year if—

(A) the only individuals who are eligible to enroll in the plan are individuals described in paragraph (2); and

(B) the plan provides—

(i) except as provided in clause (ii), the essential health benefits determined under subsection (b), except that the plan provides no benefits for any plan year until the individual has incurred cost-sharing expenses in an amount equal to the annual limitation in effect under subsection (c)(1) for the plan year (except as provided for in section 2713); and

(ii) coverage for at least three primary care visits.

(2) INDIVIDUALS ELIGIBLE FOR ENROLLMENT.—An individual is described in this paragraph for any plan year if the individual—

(A) has not attained the age of 30 before the beginning of the plan year; or

(B) has a certification in effect for any plan year under this title that the individual is exempt from the requirement under section 5000A of the Internal Revenue Code of 1986 by reason of—

(i) section 5000A(e)(1) of such Code (relating to individuals without affordable coverage); or

(ii) section 5000A(e)(5) of such Code (relating to individuals with hardships).

(3) RESTRICTION TO INDIVIDUAL MARKET.—If a health insurance issuer offers a health plan described in this subsection, the issuer may only offer the plan in the individual market. . . .

ACA: Selected Content Requirements

Sec. 2711 [42 U.S.C.A. §300gg-11]. No Lifetime or Annual Limits.

(a) PROHIBITION.—

(1) IN GENERAL.—A group health plan and a health insurance issuer offering group or individual health insurance coverage may not establish—

(A) lifetime limits on the dollar value of benefits for any participant or beneficiary; or

(B) except as provided in paragraph (2), annual limits on the dollar value of benefits for any participant or beneficiary.

(2) ANNUAL LIMITS PRIOR TO 2014.—With respect to plan years beginning prior to January 1, 2014, a group health plan and a health insurance

issuer offering group or individual health insurance coverage may only establish a restricted annual limit on the dollar value of benefits for any participant or beneficiary with respect to the scope of benefits that are essential health benefits under section 18022(b) of this title, as determined by the Secretary. In defining the term "restricted annual limit" for purposes of the preceding sentence, the Secretary shall ensure that access to needed services is made available with a minimal impact on premiums.

Sec. 2712 [U.S.C.A. §300gg-12]. Prohibition on Rescissions.

A group health plan and a health insurance issuer offering group or individual health insurance coverage shall not rescind such plan or coverage with respect to an enrollee once the enrollee is covered under such plan or coverage involved, except that this section shall not apply to a covered individual who has performed an act or practice that constitutes fraud or makes an intentional misrepresentation of material fact as prohibited by the terms of the plan or coverage. Such plan or coverage may not be cancelled except with prior notice to the enrollee, and only as permitted under section 300gg-2(b) or 300gg-42(b) of this title.

Sec. 2702 [42 U.S.C.A. §300gg-2]. Guaranteed Renewability of Coverage.

(b) GENERAL EXCEPTIONS.—A health insurance issuer may nonrenew or discontinue health insurance coverage offered in connection with a health insurance coverage offered in the group or individual market based only on one or more of the following:

(1) NONPAYMENT OF PREMIUMS.—The plan sponsor, or individual, as applicable, has failed to pay premiums or contributions in accordance with the terms of the health insurance coverage or the issuer has not received timely premium payments.

(2) FRAUD.—The plan sponsor, or individual, as applicable, has performed an act or practice that constitutes fraud or made an intentional misrepresentation of material fact under the terms of the coverage.

(3) VIOLATION OF PARTICIPATION OR CONTRIBUTION RATES.—In the case of a group health plan, the plan sponsor has failed to comply with a material plan provision relating to employer contribution or group participation rules, pursuant to applicable State law.

(4) TERMINATION OF COVERAGE.—The issuer is ceasing to offer coverage in such market in accordance with subsection (c) of this section and applicable State law.

(5) MOVEMENT OUTSIDE SERVICE AREA.—In the case of a health insurance issuer that offers health insurance coverage in the market through a network plan, there is no longer any enrollee in connection with such plan who lives, resides, or works in the service area of the issuer (or in the area for which the issuer is authorized to do business) and, in the case of the small group market, the issuer would deny enrollment with respect to such plan under section 2711(c)(1)(A).

(6) ASSOCIATION MEMBERSHIP CEASES.—In the case of health insurance coverage that is made available in the small or large group market (as the case may be) only through one or more bona fide associations, the membership of an employer in the association (on the basis of which the

coverage is provided) ceases but only if such coverage is terminated under this paragraph uniformly without regard to any health status-related factor relating to any covered individual.

42 U.S.C.A. §300gg-42. Guaranteed Renewability of Individual Health Insurance Coverage.

(b) GENERAL EXCEPTIONS.—A health insurance issuer may nonrenew or discontinue health insurance coverage of an individual in the individual market based only on one or more of the following:

(1) NONPAYMENT OF PREMIUMS.—The individual has failed to pay premiums or contributions in accordance with the terms of the health insurance coverage or the issuer has not received timely premium payments.

(2) FRAUD.—The individual has performed an act or practice that constitutes fraud or made an intentional misrepresentation of material fact under the terms of the coverage.

(3) TERMINATION OF PLAN.—The issuer is ceasing to offer coverage in the individual market in accordance with subsection (c) of this section and applicable State law.

(4) MOVEMENT OUTSIDE SERVICE AREA.—In the case of a health insurance issuer that offers health insurance coverage in the market through a network plan, the individual no longer resides, lives, or works in the service area (or in an area for which the issuer is authorized to do business) but only if such coverage is terminated under this paragraph uniformly without regard to any health status-related factor of covered individuals.

(5) ASSOCIATION MEMBERSHIP CEASES.—In the case of health insurance coverage that is made available in the individual market only through one or more bona fide associations, the membership of the individual in the association (on the basis of which the coverage is provided) ceases but only if such coverage is terminated under this paragraph uniformly without regard to any health status-related factor of covered individuals.

(c) REQUIREMENTS FOR UNIFORM TERMINATION OF COVERAGE.—

(1) PARTICULAR TYPE OF COVERAGE NOT OFFERED.—In any case in which an issuer decides to discontinue offering a particular type of health insurance coverage offered in the individual market, coverage of such type may be discontinued by the issuer only if—

(A) the issuer provides notice to each covered individual provided coverage of this type in such market of such discontinuation at least 90 days prior to the date of the discontinuation of such coverage;

(B) the issuer offers to each individual in the individual market provided coverage of this type, the option to purchase any other individual health insurance coverage currently being offered by the issuer for individuals in such market; and

(C) in exercising the option to discontinue coverage of this type and in offering the option of coverage under subparagraph (B), the issuer acts uniformly without regard to any health status-related factor of enrolled individuals or individuals who may become eligible for such coverage.

(2) DISCONTINUANCE OF ALL COVERAGE.—

(A) IN GENERAL.—Subject to subparagraph (C), in any case in which a health insurance issuer elects to discontinue offering all health insurance coverage in the individual market in a State, health insurance coverage may be discontinued by the issuer only if—

    (i) the issuer provides notice to the applicable State authority and to each individual of such discontinuation at least 180 days prior to the date of the expiration of such coverage, and

    (ii) all health insurance issued or delivered for issuance in the State in such market are discontinued and coverage under such health insurance coverage in such market is not renewed.

    (B) PROHIBITION ON MARKET REENTRY.—In the case of a discontinuation under subparagraph (A) in the individual market, the issuer may not provide for the issuance of any health insurance coverage in the market and State involved during the 5-year period beginning on the date of the discontinuation of the last health insurance coverage not so renewed.

   . . .

Sec. 2714 [42 U.S.C.A. §300gg-14]. Extension of Dependent Coverage.

    (A) IN GENERAL.—A group health plan and a health insurance issuer offering group or individual health insurance coverage that provides dependent coverage of children shall continue to make such coverage available for an adult child until the child turns 26 years of age. Nothing in this section shall require a health plan or a health insurance issuer described in the preceding sentence to make coverage available for a child of a child receiving dependent coverage. . . .

NOTES AND QUESTIONS

1. *Adverse selection.* The act allows open enrollment, prohibits insurance companies from discriminating against those with preexisting conditions, and disallows rescissions and lifetime and annual limits. To combat adverse selection, the act mandates, with some exceptions, individuals to enter the health insurance market. What are some issues with motivating individuals to enter the health insurance market? What are some solutions to motivate those without health insurance to purchase health insurance?

2. *Differential pricing.* The act allows for differential pricing based on only four factors: whether the applicant is an individual or family, the geographic region in which the applicant lives, age, and tobacco use. Do these factors seem reasonable? Should there be more? Fewer? Why these particular ones? How might an insurer rate geography (e.g., groups of states, groups of counties, regionally)? Additionally, these factors are given different pricing differentials. Should age have a higher differential than tobacco use, since tobacco use is optional? We address the general topic of insurance risk classification in Chapter 6.

3. *Essential health benefits.* The statute defining "essential health benefits" identifies several categories but is very broad in scope. What are the benefits to leaving "essential health benefits" broadly defined? Should these categories be more narrowly defined? Why or why not?

4. *Churn.* As noted above, the act mandates that noninsured individuals purchase insurance (subject to exceptions, most significantly, that the insur-

ance must be affordable). Some individuals will be able to use federal subsidies to aid in purchasing health insurance on the state exchanges. These subsidies, however, are tied to income level, which is prone to change. What are some potential issues with changing income-level and premium subsidies? If someone loses his job, how does this affect his subsidy amount? If he suddenly qualifies for Medicaid, how does this affect his health plan purchased using subsidy dollars? Policymakers are searching for ways to bridge health plans across income levels, most significantly the Medicaid/exchange border.

5. In response to the act, some employers have reduced employees' work hours so that the employees will not be regarded as sufficiently full time to be entitled to health benefits under the act. Is this rational behavior on the employers' part? Why or why not? Is this an issue that the act should have anticipated?

V. WHEN INSURANCE IS PROVIDED AS AN EMPLOYEE BENEFIT

Many people receive health, disability, and life insurance as part of their employee benefits. There are two main reasons for this. First, within limits that we will not explore, the value of first-party insurance provided to employees or paid for by employees through payroll deductions is excluded from taxable income. In effect, this tax rule allows employees to purchase insurance through their employer using pretax income, providing a very substantial incentive for obtaining insurance as an employee benefit, especially for higher-income workers.

Second, group insurance is generally cheaper than individual insurance because of lower administration costs and less risk of adverse selection. Administration costs are lower because the insurer gets to insure a whole group of people by selling the insurance to the employer. There is less risk of adverse selection because, on average, an employed person is healthier than an unemployed person and because the employer signs up the group as a whole. Even though individual employees generally have the choice not to take the insurance benefit, the fact that the employer pays all or most of the premium means that people generally take the benefit (except when someone is already getting health insurance from a family member's employer).

Employment benefit law is its own field, which is part of the larger field of employment law—one of the many fields related to insurance law. We are going to introduce you to just two important aspects of employment benefits law: (1) the rules governing preemption of state insurance law and the effect these rules have had on how employers provide "insurance" benefits to their employees, and (2) the rules governing the interpretation of ERISA plans, which are the documents that function like insurance policies in the employment benefit context.

Both of these aspects of employment law relate to the main federal law governing employee benefits—ERISA—which was enacted in 1974. As evidenced by the full name of ERISA—the Employment Retirement Income Security Act—pensions were the main focus of the reformers who pushed the statute through Congress. ERISA established an elaborate regulatory apparatus and guaranty system designed to ensure that employees receive the retirement benefits that they are promised. The insurance benefit provisions were added to ERISA at the last minute during the legislative process. Rather than establishing a true regulatory structure, however, the insurance benefit provisions in ERISA began a process of deregulating substantive regulation of employee health and disability benefits. *See* James A. Wooten, *The Most Glorious Story of Failure in the Business: The Studebaker-Packard Corporation and the Origins of ERISA*, 49 Buff. L. Rev. 683 (2001). As we will see, ERISA gave large employers the option of avoiding state insurance regulation entirely, without creating a federal regulatory structure that served the same purposes as state insurance regulation.

Arguably, such deregulation made sense in the context of the time. For qualified plans, ERISA replaced state insurance regulation with a version of trust law. Employment-based health insurance of that era was almost exclusively "indemnity" insurance, in which patients and their doctors made all the medical decisions and the health insurers simply covered a set percentage of the cost. The main regulatory issues were solvency and disclosure, both of which could be handled through a trust law approach. Whether that is still the case in an era of "managed care" is another question. As the role of health insurance in regulating health care becomes increasingly apparent, there is more widespread recognition that the hands-off approach of ERISA has the potential to undermine traditional state regulation in the field of health care. The Affordable Care Act largely maintained that hands-off approach.

A.   ERISA's Preemption of State Law

Until this part of the casebook, all of the law we have studied so far is state law. ERISA preempts state law in two ways. First, ERISA has an express preemption provision governing when ERISA preempts state law. Second, the Supreme Court has determined that ERISA preemption extends even further than the express preemption provision provides. Specifically, the Court has held that ERISA preempts state law related to remedies (including damages for bad-faith breach of an insurance contract) even though the express preemption provision does not say this. To understand precisely how ERISA preempts state insurance law with respect to employer provided health benefits, it is important to realize that ERISA uses trust law to govern the provision of health insurance benefits. When an employer decides to provide health benefits to its employees, the employer must set up what is called "an employee welfare benefit plan." This plan is formally a trust, which means that the parties operating the plan — the ones making decisions such as how to invest the plan's money or what counts as a covered benefit under the plan — are fiduciaries of the plan, with special legal obligations. Although ERISA does not require employers to provide health benefits to their employees, it does provide a federally mandated administrative apparatus that must be used if the employer decides to provide a health benefit plan.

Therefore, when determining what rules govern any employer-provided health benefit plan, a very important question is "*To what extent do state laws apply to the federally regulated plan?*" For example, if there is a state insurance law that requires all health insurance policies issued in that state to include a particular type of health insurance coverage, must an employer-provided ERISA-regulated plan comply with that requirement? Or is such a requirement preempted by ERISA? As will become clear, the answer to that question will depend critically on what type of health-benefit trust arrangement the employer has established.

There are two basic possibilities. Either the employer can create an "insured plan" or it can create a "self-insured plan." With an insured ERISA health benefit plan, the plan (or, more particularly, a party acting as a fiduciary of the plan) collects money from the employees (and perhaps from the employer as well) and uses that money to purchase a health insurance policy that provides health coverage to the employees. In such an arrangement, the health insurance company is both the insurer (in the sense that it is accepting the health risks of the employees, as defined in the policy, in exchange for the premiums) as well as the administrator of the plan (in the sense that the insurer actually decides which health claims are paid and administers payment). With a self-insured ERISA health benefit plan, however, the plan collects money from employees and/or the employer, but it does not purchase a risk-shifting health insurance policy. Rather, the plan invests the money itself, or through a plan administrator, and then uses those investments and the earnings on the investments to pay health benefit claims. Even under a self-insured ERISA plan, however, employers usually hire insurance companies to manage the trust and administer claims.

In sum, one way to think about all of this is as follows: When the employer sets up a trust that actually buys health insurance, the insurance company pays the providers out of a bank account owned by the insurance company. However, when the employer sets up a trust and hires the insurance company only to be the administrator, the insurance company pays the providers out of a bank account owned by the trust. There are (many) complicated details involved, but this explanation gets at the crucial difference.

How does all this affect the preemption question? Consider the following materials.

1. Express Preemption

The express preemption provisions appear in §514 of ERISA. Section 514 contains three parts that, in *Pilot Life Insurance Co. v. Dedeaux*, 481 U.S. 41, 44-5 (1987), Justice Sandra Day O'Connor referred to the "preemption clause," the "savings clause," and the "deemer clause." These labels have stuck. Here is the relevant language from §514:

> **1. The preemption clause:** "Except as provided in subsection (b) of this section [the saving clause], the provisions of this subchapter and subchapter III of this chapter shall supersede any and all State laws insofar as they may now or hereafter relate to any employee benefit plan. . . ." §514(a), as set forth in 29 U.S.C. §1144(a).
> **2. The savings clause:** "Except as provided in subparagraph (B) [the deemer clause], nothing in this subchapter shall be construed to exempt or relieve any person from any law of any State which regulates insurance, banking, or securities." §514(b)(2)(A), as set forth in 29 U.S.C. §1144(b)(2)(A).
> **3. The deemer clause:** "Neither an employee benefit plan . . . nor any trust established under such a plan, shall be deemed to be an insurance company

or other insurer, bank, trust company, or investment company or to be engaged in the business of insurance or banking for purposes of any law of any State purporting to regulate insurance companies, insurance contracts, banks, trust companies, or investment companies." §514(b)(2)(B), as set forth in 29 U.S.C. §1144(b)(2)(B).

Justice O'Connor summarized the "pure mechanics" of these three provisions as follows:

> If a state law "relate[s] to . . . employee benefit plan[s]," it is preempted. §514(a). The savings clause excepts from the preemption clause laws that "regulat[e] insurance." §514(b)(2)(A). The deemer clause makes clear that a state law that "purport[s] to regulate insurance" cannot deem an employee benefit plan to be an insurance company. §514(b)(2)(B). . . .

Id.

What does all of this mean? Remember that the issue is whether some state law requirement is preempted by ERISA. So, following Justice O'Connor's formula, assuming there is an employee health benefit plan involved (insured or self-insured), the first step in the analysis is to determine whether the state law "relates to" that plan. In general, the "relate to" phrase has been given a broad reading, which means that if a state law/regulation has any connection with or reference to the plan, it is considered to *relate to* the plan. That means that step one of preemption is relatively easy to trigger, although the Court has drawn some lines on how far the "relates to" preemption provision will reach.[21] Next is the savings clause: *If* the state law that relates to the employee plan happens to "regulate[] insurance," that state law is not preempted and must be complied with by the plan. However, in the third and final step, we see the importance of the insured/self-insured distinction. The deemer clause says that neither the plan, nor any trust established thereunder, may be "deemed" an insurance company. This phrase has been interpreted by the courts to mean that for the saving clause to apply, the plan must buy insurance. If the plan self-insures, then it is not bound by any state law that relates to it, because such a law is, again, preempted.

The implications of this analysis are profound. For one thing, lots of state insurance law can easily be preempted under section 514, provided that the employer self-insures the ERISA plan. And as it turns out, that is precisely what the vast majority of large employers who provide health coverage for their employees have done: They have established self-insured health benefit plans for their employees. Small employers are less able to self-insure their employees' health care expenses. And, of course, ERISA does not apply to health insurance purchased by individuals and not provided by their employer. As a result, the extent to which the health insurance an individual has will be affected by state laws regulating health insurance often depends on the size of the individual's employer.

---

21. *See, e.g., New York State Conference of Blue Cross & Blue Shield Plans v. Travelers Insurance Co.,* 514 U.S. 645 (1995), discussed further in the text below, which held that state laws imposing surcharges on some health insurers, but not others, did not "relate to" an employee benefit plan.

ERISA EXPRESS PREEMPTION PROBLEMS

Pilot Life addressed the question of whether ERISA preempted an insurance bad-faith action of the sort addressed in Chapter 2. The first question in *Pilot Life* was whether the common law that allows bad-faith damages for breach of an insurance contract comes within the §514 savings clause as a state law "which regulates . . . insurance." The Supreme Court held that it did not, because it was a general contract law rule, not an insurance law rule. That was news to many state supreme courts, but the Supreme Court gets to decide such things when interpreting federal statutes.

Consider whether the following state laws would be preempted by ERISA if (1) the health care benefits are provided through a group insurance policy purchased by an ERISA plan, and (2) the health care benefits are provided by a qualified ERISA trust administered by an insurance company:

1. A statute requiring that all health insurance sold in the state provides certain minimum benefits for contraceptives. *See Unum Life Ins. v. Ward,* 526 U.S. 358 (1999).
2. A statute prohibiting health maintenance organizations (HMOs) from excluding willing providers from their provider networks. *See Kentucky Ass'n of Health Plans, Inc. v. Miller,* 538 U.S. 329 (2003).
3. The common law "notice-prejudice rule" (discussed in *Aetna Casualty & Surety Co. v. Murphy* in Chapter 2), according to which noncompliance with filing or other deadlines in an insurance policy is grounds for refusal to pay only if the insurer can prove that the late notice prejudiced the insurer in some significant way. *See Unum Life Ins., supra.*

2.   "Complete" Preemption Under ERISA §502(a)

Pilot Life also considered whether Congress had intended to "completely" preempt state laws that affected the remedies available for breach of obligations under ERISA §502. Under this part of the court's analysis, the state's bad-faith remedies would be preempted even if they were enacted as a state law "which regulates . . . insurance" and therefore fell within the savings clause of §514. Section 502(a), as set forth in 29 U.S.C. §1132(a), provides:

> A civil action may be brought—
> (1) by a participant or beneficiary—
>   (A) for the relief provided for in subsection (c) of this section [concerning requests to the administrator for information], or
>   (B) to recover benefits due to him under the terms of his plan, to enforce his rights under the terms of the plan, or to clarify his rights to future benefits under the terms of the plan;
> (2) by the Secretary, or by a participant, beneficiary or fiduciary for appropriate relief under section 1109 of this title [breach of fiduciary duty];
> (3) by a participant, beneficiary, or fiduciary (A) to enjoin any act or practice which violates any provision of this subchapter or the terms of the plan, or (B) to obtain other appropriate equitable relief (i) to redress such violations or (ii) to enforce any provisions of this subchapter or the terms of the plan;
> (4) by the Secretary, or by a participant, or beneficiary for appropriate relief in the case of a violation of 1025(c) of this title [information to be furnished to participants];

(5) except as otherwise provided in subsection (b) of this subsection, by the Secretary

  (A) to enjoin any act or practice which violates any provision of this subchapter, or

  (B) to obtain other appropriate equitable relief

    (i) to redress such violation or

    (ii) to enforce any provision of this subchapter;

(6) by the Secretary to collect any civil penalty under subsection (i) of this section.

The *Pilot Life* Court held that Congress had intended that ERISA completely preempt any state law that expands the remedies available for a failure to provide plan benefits, even if that law regulates insurance. The relevant discussion from *Pilot Life* follows:

The Solicitor General, for the United States as amicus curiae, argues that Congress clearly expressed an intent that the civil enforcement provisions of ERISA §502(a) be the exclusive vehicle for actions by ERISA-plan participants and beneficiaries asserting improper processing of a claim for benefits, and that varying state causes of action for claims within the scope of §502(a) would pose an obstacle to the purposes and objectives of Congress. We agree. The conclusion that §502(a) was intended to be exclusive is supported, first, by the language and structure of the civil enforcement provisions, and second, by legislative history in which Congress declared that the preemptive force of §502(a) was modeled on the exclusive remedy provided by §301 of the Labor Management Relations Act, 1947 (LMRA), 61 Stat. 156, 29 U.S.C. §185.

The civil enforcement scheme of §502(a) is one of the essential tools for accomplishing the stated purposes of ERISA. . . . Under the civil enforcement provisions of §502(a), a plan participant or beneficiary may sue to recover benefits due under the plan, to enforce the participant's rights under the plan, or to clarify rights to future benefits. Relief may take the form of accrued benefits due, a declaratory judgment on entitlement to benefits, or an injunction against a plan administrator's improper refusal to pay benefits. A participant or beneficiary may also bring a cause of action for breach of fiduciary duty, and under this cause of action may seek removal of the fiduciary. §§502(a)(2), 409. In an action under these civil enforcement provisions, the court in its discretion may allow an award of attorney's fees to either party. §502(g). *See Massachusetts Mutual Life Ins. Co. v. Russell,* 473 U.S. 134, 147 (1985).

In *Russell,* we concluded that ERISA's breach of fiduciary duty provision, §409(a), 29 U.S.C. §1109(a), provided no express authority for an award of punitive damages to a beneficiary. Moreover, we declined to find an implied cause of action for punitive damages in that section, noting that "'the presumption that a remedy was deliberately omitted from a statute is strongest when Congress has enacted a comprehensive legislative scheme including an integrated system of procedures for enforcement.'" *Russell, supra,* at 147, quoting *Northwest Airlines, Inc. v. Transport Workers,* 451 U.S. 77, 97 (1981). Our examination of these provisions made us "reluctant to tamper with an enforcement scheme crafted with such evident care as the one in ERISA." *Russell, supra,* at 147.

In sum, the detailed provisions of §502(a) set forth a comprehensive civil enforcement scheme that represents a careful balancing of the need for prompt and fair claims settlement procedures against the public interest in encouraging the formation of employee benefit plans. The policy choices reflected in the inclusion of certain remedies and the exclusion of others under the federal scheme would be completely undermined if ERISA-plan participants and beneficiaries were free to obtain remedies under state law that Congress rejected in ERISA.

This means that the *Pilot Life* holding regarding preemption of state law remedies for bad-faith breach applies even if the employer decides not to create a trust and simply purchases traditional health insurance (or other forms of insurance) for its employees.

Given the *Pilot Life* decision, what are the implications of ERISA preemption for state health law in general? Taken to the logical extreme, quite a bit of state health law "relates to" an employee benefit plan, and most state health law would not be "saved" under the insurance savings clause of §514 if that law were to be found to be within the scope of the preemption clause of §514. *Pilot Life* itself left open how far ERISA would preempt the state regulation of medical care. The Supreme Court, however, did address that question indirectly in *New York State Conference of Blue Cross & Blue Shield Plans v. Travelers Insurance Co.,* 514 U.S. 645 (1995). *Travelers* involved a New York State statute that allowed hospitals to assess surcharges on the fees charged to some health insurers but not others. The Court wrote:

> If the common character of rate differentials even in the absence of state action renders it unlikely that ERISA preemption was meant to bar such indirect economic influences under state law, the existence of other common state action with indirect economic effects on a plan's costs leaves the intent to preempt even less likely. Quality standards, for example, set by the State in one subject area of hospital services but not another would affect the relative cost of providing those services over others and, so, of providing different packages of health insurance benefits. Even basic regulation of employment conditions will invariably affect the cost and price of services.
>
> Quality control and workplace regulation, to be sure, are presumably less likely to affect premium differentials among competing insurers, but that does not change the fact that such state regulation will indirectly affect what an ERISA or other plan can afford or get for its money. Thus, in the absence of a more exact guide to intended preemption than §514, it is fair to conclude that mandates for rate differentials would not be preempted unless other regulation with indirect effects on plan costs would be superseded as well. The bigger the package of regulation with indirect effects that would fall on the respondents' reading of §514, the less likely it is that federal regulation of benefit plans was intended to eliminate state regulation of health care costs.

Id. at 660-661.

This statement from the Court was widely understood to mean that ERISA would not preempt a malpractice action filed against an ERISA plan or a health insurer providing services through an ERISA plan. In combination, *Pilot Life* and the *Travelers* dicta produced a situation in which plaintiffs who are injured by health insurance company behavior can recover much more generous damages if they proceed on a medical malpractice cause of action than if they proceed under a denial of plan benefits cause of action.

Because of the *Pilot Life* case, people who are harmed by substandard medical care have a very significant incentive to argue that their harm resulted from medical malpractice rather than an improper insurance coverage determination. Yet when the alleged "malpractice" is the failure to provide a service and the entity that decided not to provide the service is the health insurance provider, one can reasonably wonder whether the distinction between medical malpractice and improper coverage determination makes sense.

In a world in which doctors of the patients' choosing make all the medical decisions and the health benefits question is limited to reimbursing the plaintiff for what the doctor ordered, the line between medical malpractice and denial of plan benefits seems clear. With the growth of managed health care, the line between health care financing and health care decision making has grown increasingly blurred. Legislators in some states thought that this situation presented an opening that would allow them to correct the incentive problem created by *Pilot Life*'s preemption of the bad faith cause of action. All that a state had to do was to create a malpractice-like cause of action that would apply to benefit denials that relied on medical decision making. The Supreme Court shut that opening down in the following case, making it clear that only Congress has the power to expand the remedies available for denial of ERISA plan benefits.

AETNA HEALTH INC. v. DAVILA

Supreme Court of the United States
542 U.S. 200 (2004)

Justice THOMAS. In these consolidated cases, two individuals sued their respective health maintenance organizations (HMOs) for alleged failures to exercise ordinary care in the handling of coverage decisions, in violation of a duty imposed by the Texas Health Care Liability Act (THCLA), Tex. Civ. Prac. & Rem. Code Ann. §§88.001-88.003. . . .

Respondent Juan Davila is a participant, and respondent Ruby Calad is a beneficiary, in ERISA-regulated employee benefit plans. Their respective plan sponsors had entered into agreements with petitioners, Aetna Health Inc. and CIGNA Healthcare of Texas, Inc., to administer the plans. Under Davila's plan, for instance, Aetna reviews requests for coverage and pays providers, such as doctors, hospitals, and nursing homes, which perform covered services for members; under Calad's plan sponsor's agreement, CIGNA is responsible for plan benefits and coverage decisions.

Respondents both suffered injuries allegedly arising from Aetna's and CIGNA's decisions not to provide coverage for certain treatment and services recommended by respondents' treating physicians. Davila's treating physician prescribed Vioxx to remedy Davila's arthritis pain, but Aetna refused to pay for it. Davila did not appeal or contest this decision, nor did he purchase Vioxx with his own resources and seek reimbursement. Instead, Davila began taking Naprosyn, from which he allegedly suffered a severe reaction that required extensive treatment and hospitalization. Calad underwent surgery, and although her treating physician recommended an extended hospital stay, a CIGNA discharge nurse determined that Calad did not meet the plan's criteria for a continued hospital stay. CIGNA consequently denied coverage for the extended hospital stay. Calad experienced postsurgery complications forcing her to return to the hospital. She alleges that these complications would not have occurred had CIGNA approved coverage for a longer hospital stay.

Respondents brought separate suits in Texas state court against petitioners. Invoking THCLA §88.002(a), respondents argued that petitioners' refusal to cover the requested services violated their "duty to exercise ordinary care when making health care treatment decisions," and that these refusals "proximately caused" their injuries. Petitioners removed the cases to Federal District Courts, arguing that respondents' causes of action fit within the scope of, and were therefore completely pre-empted by, ERISA §502(a). The respective District Courts agreed, and declined to remand the cases to state court. Because respondents refused to amend their complaints to bring explicit ERISA claims, the District Courts dismissed the complaints with prejudice.

Both Davila and Calad appealed the refusals to remand to state court. The United States Court of Appeals for the Fifth Circuit consolidated their cases with several others raising similar issues. The Court of Appeals recognized that state causes of action that "duplicat[e] or fal[l] within the scope of an ERISA §502(a) remedy" are completely pre-empted and hence removable to federal court. *Roark v. Humana, Inc.*, 307 F.3d 298, 305 (2002) (internal quotation marks and citations omitted). After examining the causes of action available under §502(a), the Court of Appeals determined that respondents' claims could possibly fall under only two: §502(a)(1)(B), which provides a cause of action for the recovery of wrongfully denied benefits, and §502(a)(2), which allows suit against a plan fiduciary for breaches of fiduciary duty to the plan.

Analyzing §502(a)(2) first, the Court of Appeals concluded that . . . respondents' claims did not fall within §502(a)(1)(B)'s scope. It found significant that respondents "assert tort claims," while §502(a)(1)(B) "creates a cause of action for breach of contract," *id.*, at 309, and also that respondents "are not seeking reimbursement for benefits denied them," but rather request "tort damages" arising from "an external, statutorily imposed duty of 'ordinary care.' " *Ibid.* From *Rush Prudential HMO, Inc. v. Moran,* 536 U.S. 355 (2002), the Court of Appeals derived the principle that complete pre-emption is limited to situations in which "States . . . duplicate the causes of action listed in ERISA §502(a)," and concluded that "[b]ecause the THCLA does not provide an action for collecting benefits," it fell outside the scope of §502(a)(1)(B). 307 F.3d at 310-311. . . .

Congress enacted ERISA to "protect . . . the interests of participants in employee benefit plans and their beneficiaries" by setting out substantive regulatory requirements for employee benefit plans and to "provid[e] for appropriate remedies, sanctions, and ready access to the Federal courts." 29 U.S.C. §1001(b). The purpose of ERISA is to provide a uniform regulatory regime over employee benefit plans. To this end, ERISA includes expansive pre-emption provisions which are intended to ensure that employee benefit plan regulation would be "exclusively a federal concern." *Alessi v. Raybestos-Manhattan, Inc.,* 451 U.S. 504, 523 (1981).

ERISA's "comprehensive legislative scheme" includes "an integrated system of procedures for enforcement." [*Massachusetts Mutual Life Ins. Co. v. Russell,* 473 U.S. 134,] 147. This integrated enforcement mechanism, ERISA §502(a), 29 U.S.C. §1132(a), is a distinctive feature of ERISA, and essential to accomplish Congress' purpose of creating a comprehensive statute for the regulation of employee benefit plans. . . . [A]ny state-law cause of action that duplicates, supplements, or supplants the ERISA civil enforcement remedy conflicts with the clear congressional intent to make the ERISA remedy exclusive and is therefore pre-empted.

The pre-emptive force of ERISA §502(a) is still stronger. In *Metropolitan Life Ins. Co. v. Taylor,* 481 U.S. 58, 65-66 (1987), the Court determined that the similarity of the language used in the Labor Management Relations Act, 1947 (LMRA), and ERISA, combined with the "clear intention" of Congress "to make §502(a)(1)(B) suits brought by participants or beneficiaries federal questions for the purposes of federal court jurisdiction in like manner as §301 of the LMRA," established that ERISA §502(a)(1)(B)'s pre-emptive force mirrored the pre-emptive force of LMRA §301. Since LMRA §301 converts state causes of action into federal ones for purposes of determining the propriety of removal, so too does ERISA §502(a)(1)(B). Thus, the ERISA civil enforcement mechanism is one of those provisions with such "extraordinary pre-emptive power" that it "converts an ordinary state common law complaint into one stating a federal claim for purposes of the well-pleaded complaint rule." *Metropolitan Life,* 481 U.S., at 65-66. Hence, "causes of action within the scope of the civil enforcement provisions of §502(a) [are] removable to federal court." *Id.* at 66. . . .

ERISA §502(a)(1)(B) provides:

> "A civil action may be brought—(1) by a participant or beneficiary — . . . (B) to recover benefits due to him under the terms of his plan, to enforce his rights under the terms of the plan, or to clarify his rights to future benefits under the terms of the plan."

29 U.S.C. §1132(a)(1)(B).

This provision is relatively straightforward. If a participant or beneficiary believes that benefits promised to him under the terms of the plan are not provided, he can bring suit seeking provision of those benefits. A participant or beneficiary can also bring suit generically to "enforce his rights" under the plan, or to clarify any of his rights to future benefits. . . .

To determine whether respondents' causes of action fall "within the scope" of ERISA §502(a)(1)(B), we must examine respondents' complaints, the statute on which their claims are based (the THCLA), and the various plan documents. Davila alleges that Aetna provides health coverage under his employer's health benefits plan. Davila also alleges that after his primary care physician prescribed Vioxx, Aetna refused to pay for it. The only action complained of was Aetna's refusal to approve payment for Davila's Vioxx prescription. Further, the only relationship Aetna had with Davila was its partial administration of Davila's employer's benefit plan.

Similarly, Calad alleges that she receives, as her husband's beneficiary under an ERISA-regulated benefit plan, health coverage from CIGNA. She alleges that she was informed by CIGNA, upon admittance into a hospital for major surgery, that she would be authorized to stay for only one day. She also alleges that CIGNA, acting through a discharge nurse, refused to authorize more than a single day despite the advice and recommendation of her treating physician. Calad contests only CIGNA's decision to refuse coverage for her hospital stay. And, as in Davila's case, the only connection between Calad and CIGNA is CIGNA's administration of portions of Calad's ERISA-regulated benefit plan.

It is clear, then, that respondents complain only about denials of coverage promised under the terms of ERISA-regulated employee benefit plans. Upon the denial of benefits, respondents could have paid for the treatment themselves and then sought reimbursement through a §502(a)(1)(B) action, or sought a preliminary injunction, see *Pryzbowski v. U.S. Healthcare, Inc.*, 245 F.3d 266, 274 (3d Cir. 2001) (giving examples where federal courts have issued such preliminary injunctions).

Respondents contend, however, that the complained-of actions violate legal duties that arise independently of ERISA or the terms of the employee benefit plans at issue in these cases. Both respondents brought suit specifically under the THCLA, alleging that petitioners "controlled, influenced, participated in and made decisions which affected the quality of the diagnosis, care, and treatment provided" in a manner that violated "the duty of ordinary care set forth in §§88.001 and 88.002." Respondents contend that this duty of ordinary care is an independent legal duty. . . . Because this duty of ordinary care arises independently of any duty imposed by ERISA or the plan terms, the argument goes, any civil action to enforce this duty is not within the scope of the ERISA civil enforcement mechanism.

The duties imposed by the THCLA in the context of these cases, however, do not arise independently of ERISA or the plan terms. The THCLA does impose a duty on managed care entities to "exercise ordinary care when making health care treatment decisions," and makes them liable for damages proximately caused by failures to abide by that duty. §88.002(a). However, if a managed care entity correctly concluded that, under the terms of the relevant plan, a particular treatment was not covered, the managed care entity's denial of coverage would not be a proximate cause of any injuries arising from the denial. Rather, the failure of the plan itself to cover the requested treatment would be the proximate cause. More significantly, the THCLA clearly states that "[t]he standards in Subsections (a) and (b) create no obligation on the part of the health insurance carrier, health maintenance organization, or other managed care entity to provide to an insured or enrollee treatment which is not covered by the health care plan of the entity." §88.002(d). Hence, a managed care entity could not be subject to liability under the THCLA if it denied coverage for any treatment not covered by the health care plan that it was administering. . . .

Hence, respondents bring suit only to rectify a wrongful denial of benefits promised under ERISA-regulated plans, and do not attempt to remedy any violation of a legal duty independent of ERISA. We hold that respondents' state causes of action fall "within the scope of" ERISA §502(a)(1)(B), *Metropolitan Life*, 481 U.S., at 66, and are therefore completely pre-empted by ERISA §502 and removable to federal district court. . . .

We hold that respondents' causes of action, brought to remedy only the denial of benefits under ERISA-regulated benefit plans, fall within the scope of, and are completely pre-empted by, ERISA §502(a)(1)(B), and thus removable to federal district court. The judgment of the Court of Appeals is reversed, and the cases are remanded for further proceedings consistent with this opinion.

It is so ordered.

Justice GINSBURG, with whom Justice BREYER joins, concurring.

The Court today holds that the claims respondents asserted under Texas law are totally preempted by §502(a) of the Employee Retirement Income Security Act of 1974 (ERISA or Act), 29 U.S.C. §1132(a). That decision is consistent with our governing case law on ERISA's preemptive scope. I therefore join the Court's opinion. But, with greater enthusiasm, as indicated by my dissenting opinion in *Great-West Life & Annuity Ins. Co. v. Knudson*, 534 U.S. 204 (2002), I also join "the rising judicial chorus urging that Congress and [this] Court revisit what is an unjust and increasingly tangled ERISA regime." *DiFelice v. Aetna U.S. Healthcare*, 346 F.3d 442, 453 (3d Cir. 2003) (Becker, J., concurring).

Because the Court has coupled an encompassing interpretation of ERISA's preemptive force with a cramped construction of the "equitable relief" allowable under §502(a)(3), a "regulatory vacuum" exists: "[V]irtually all state law remedies are preempted but very few federal substitutes are provided." *Id.*, at 456.

A series of the Court's decisions has yielded a host of situations in which persons adversely affected by ERISA-proscribed wrongdoing cannot gain make-whole relief. . . . As the array of lower court cases and opinions documents, fresh consideration of the availability of consequential damages under §502(a)(3) is plainly in order. *See* 321 F.3d at 106, 107 (Calabresi, J., dissenting in part) ("gaping wound" caused by the breadth of preemption and limited remedies under ERISA, as interpreted by this Court, will not be healed until the Court "start[s] over" or Congress "wipe[s] the slate clean"); *DiFelice*, 346 F.3d at 467 ("The vital thing . . . is that either Congress or the Court act quickly, because the current situation is plainly untenable."); John H. Langbein, *What ERISA Means by "Equitable": The Supreme Court's Trail of Error in* Russell, Mertens, *and* Great-West, 103 Colum. L. Rev. 1317, 1365 (2003) ("The Supreme Court needs to . . . realign ERISA remedy law with the trust remedial tradition that Congress intended [when it provided in §502(a)(3) for] 'appropriate equitable relief'"). . . .

NOTES AND QUESTIONS

1. The complete preemption of state law remedies for benefit denials means that states are free to mandate the benefits to be provided in health insurance policies, but not the remedies that may be granted for the failure to provide those benefits. The elimination of the state law remedies leaves ERISA plan beneficiaries vulnerable to opportunistic breach.

2. The Court has allowed states to establish procedural protections for health care beneficiaries. In *Rush Prudential HMO, Inc. v. Moran*, 536 U.S. 355 (2002), the Court held that ERISA did not preempt an Illinois statute that required HMOs to provide an independent medical review of benefit denials. The Court first held that that "savings" clause protected the Illinois statutes from express preemption:

> It is beyond serious dispute that under existing precedent §4-10 of the Illinois HMO Act "relates to" employee benefit plans within the meaning of §1144(a). The state law bears "indirectly but substantially on all insured benefit plans," *Metropolitan Life*, 471 U.S., at 739, by requiring them to submit to an extra layer of review for certain benefit denials if they purchase medical coverage from any of the common types of health care organizations covered by the state law's definition of HMO. As a law that "relates to" ERISA plans under §1144(a), §4-10 is saved from preemption only if it also "regulates insurance" under §1144(b)(2)(A). *Rush* insists that the Act is not such a law. . . .

In *Metropolitan Life,* we said that in deciding whether a law "regulates insurance" under ERISA's saving clause, we start with a "common-sense view of the matter," 471 U.S., at 740, under which "a law must not just have an impact on the insurance industry, but must be specifically directed toward that industry." The common-sense enquiry focuses on "primary elements of an insurance contract, [which] are the spreading and underwriting of a policyholder's risk." *Id.,* at 211. The Illinois statute addresses these elements by defining "health maintenance organization" by reference to the risk that it bears.

Rush contends that seeing an HMO as an insurer distorts the nature of an HMO, which is, after all, a health care provider, too. This, Rush argues, should determine its characterization, with the consequence that regulation of an HMO is not insurance regulation within the meaning of ERISA.

The answer to *Rush* is, of course, that an HMO is both: it provides health care, and it does so as an insurer. Nothing in the saving clause requires an either-or choice between health care and insurance in deciding a preemption question, and as long as providing insurance fairly accounts for the application of state law, the saving clause may apply. There is no serious question about that here, for it would ignore the whole purpose of the HMO-style of organization to conceive of HMOs (even in the traditional sense) without their insurance element. . . .

536 U.S. at 365-367.

The Court then explained that the Illinois statute was not subject to the complete preemption aspect of the *Pilot Life* analysis because the statute did not provide an additional or alternative remedy:

[T]his case addresses a state regulatory scheme that provides no new cause of action under state law and authorizes no new form of ultimate relief. While independent review under §4-10 may well settle the fate of a benefit claim under a particular contract, the state statute does not enlarge the claim beyond the benefits available in any action brought under §1132(a). And although the reviewer's determination would presumably replace that of the HMO as to what is "medically necessary" under this contract, the relief ultimately available would still be what ERISA authorizes in a suit for benefits under §1132(a). This case therefore does not involve the sort of additional claim or remedy exemplified in *Pilot Life, Russell,* and *Ingersoll-Rand,* but instead bears a resemblance to the claims-procedure rule that we sustained in *UNUM Life Ins. Co. of America v. Ward,* 526 U.S. 358 (1999), holding that a state law barring enforcement of a policy's time limitation on submitting claims did not conflict with §1132(a), even though the state "rule of decision," *id.,* at 377, could mean the difference between success and failure for a beneficiary. The procedure provided by §4-10 does not fall within *Pilot Life*'s categorical preemption.

536 U.S. at 379-380.

The Court concluded as follows:

In deciding what to make of these facts and conclusions, it helps to go back to where we started and recall the ways States regulate insurance in looking out for the welfare of their citizens. Illinois has chosen to regulate insurance as one way to regulate the practice of medicine, which we have previously held to be permissible under ERISA, *see Metropolitan Life,* 471 U.S., at 741. While the statute designed to do this undeniably eliminates whatever may have remained of a plan sponsor's option to minimize scrutiny of benefit denials, this effect of eliminating an insurer's autonomy to guarantee terms congenial to its own interests is the stuff of garden variety insurance regulation through the imposition of standard policy terms. *See id.,* at 742 ("State laws regulating the substantive terms of insurance contracts were commonplace well before the mid-70's"). It is therefore hard to imagine a reservation of state power to regulate insurance that would not be meant to cover restrictions of the insurer's advantage in this kind of way. And any lingering doubt about the reasonableness of §4-10 in affecting the application of §1132(a) [(ERISA's benefit enforcement provision)] may be put to rest by recalling that regulating insurance tied to what is medically necessary is probably inseparable from enforcing the quintessentially state-law standards of reasonable medical care. *See Pegram v. Herdrich,* 530 U.S., at 236. "In the field of health care, a subject of traditional state regulation, there is no ERISA preemption without clear manifestation of congressional purpose." *Id.,* at 237. To the extent that benefits litigation in some federal courts may have to account for the effects of §4-10, it would be an exaggeration to hold that the objectives of §1132(a) are undermined. The saving clause is entitled to prevail here, and we affirm the judgment.

536 U.S. at 387.

Justice Thomas dissented:

> Section 4-10 cannot be characterized as anything other than an alternative state-law remedy or vehicle for seeking benefits. In the first place, §4-10 comes into play only if the HMO and the claimant dispute the claimant's entitlement to benefits; the purpose of the review is to determine whether a claimant is entitled to benefits. Contrary to the majority's characterization of §4-10 as nothing more than a state law regarding medical standards, it is in fact a binding determination of whether benefits are due: "In the event that the reviewing physician determines the covered service to be medically necessary, the [HMO] *shall provide* the covered service." 215 Ill. Comp. Stat., ch. 125, §4-10 (2000) (emphasis added). Section 4-10 is thus most precisely characterized as an arbitration-like mechanism to settle benefits disputes.

536 U.S. at 394-395.

B.   *Interpretation of ERISA Plans*

One other important way that ERISA changes the traditional contract law framework is through the standard of review that courts apply to denial of benefit decisions. Under the contract law rules that we studied in Chapter 2, courts apply a "de novo" standard to questions of contract interpretation. The same de novo standard of review is the default rule for interpreting ERISA plans, but that default rule can be changed to a more deferential standard of review. *Firestone Tire & Rubber Co. v. Bruch,* 489 U.S. 101 (1989). John Langbein describes the ERISA approach and how it can interact with the preemption of bad faith damages, in the article excerpt that follows. The article provides additional background on the situation that led to the *Hangarter* punitive damages case in Chapter 2.

TRUST LAW AS REGULATORY LAW: THE UNUM/PROVIDENT SCANDAL AND JUDICIAL REVIEW OF BENEFIT DENIALS UNDER ERISA

John H. Langbein
101 Nw. U. L. Rev. 1315 (2007)

Authoritative evidence has come to light that for a period of some years, stretching from the mid-1990s into the present decade, Unum/Provident Corporation (Unum), the largest American insurer specializing in disability insurance, was engaged in a deliberate program of bad faith denial of meritorious benefit claims. . . .

The Unum/Provident scandal draws attention to a major failing in how the federal courts have understood their role in reviewing benefit denials under the Employee Retirement Income Security Act of 1974 ("ERISA"). Most disability insurance in the United States (apart from the Social Security program) is employer-provided, and hence ERISA-governed. Many, probably most, of the victims of the Unum/Provident scandal were participants and beneficiaries of ERISA-covered disability insurance plans. As regards Unum's ERISA-governed policies, Unum's program of bad faith benefit denials was all but invited by an ill-considered passage in an opinion of the United States Supreme Court, *Firestone Tire & Rubber Co. v. Bruch,* 489 U.S. 101 (1989), which allows ERISA plan sponsors to impose self-serving terms that severely restrict the ability of a reviewing court to correct a wrongful benefit denial. . . .

I. THE UNUM/PROVIDENT SCANDAL

Unum/Provident Corporation was assembled in the 1990s from several formerly separate companies. Unum and its various subsidiaries dominate the market for disability insurance. In 2003, Unum companies issued 40% of the individual disability policies and 25% of the group disability policies sold in the United States, covering more than 17 million persons.

Although most benefit claims arising under policies of disability insurance are processed routinely, a disability claim can give rise to a dispute about how impaired or how employable an insured actually is. Such cases are intrinsically factitious. The recurrent question is whether, on the facts regarding this worker's physical and occupational circumstances, he or she is unable to resume employment as defined in the policy. A reviewing court will not often find close guidance on such factual determinations from the policy terms, background rules of law, or prior cases. The amount at stake in a disability claim (an income stream that can endure for decades) can be quite large, even though the policy commonly integrates, and thus offsets, the insured's Social Security disability payments. The danger that an insured may exaggerate or falsify conditions of disability is ever present. Moral hazard dangers are more acute with disability insurance than with other forms of insurance, such as life insurance, in which it is more costly for the insured to qualify for the insurable event and harder to falsify it.

The growth of what became Unum was engineered by one J. Harold Chandler, who became CEO of a predecessor entity in 1993 and ran the merged companies until he was dismissed in 2003. Under Chandler, Unum instituted cost-containment measures that pressured claims-processing employees to deny valid claims. Pressures peaked in the last month of each quarter, called the "scrub months," when claims managers exhorted staff to deny enough claims to meet or surpass budget goals. Word of these practices began to emerge in lawsuits brought by former Unum claims-processing employees, and in investigative reports broadcast in 2002 by NBC's *Dateline* and CBS's *60 Minutes* news programs. Employees interviewed on the *Dateline* program disclosed that the claims that were "the most vulnerable" to pressures for bad faith termination were those involving "so-called subjective illnesses, illnesses that don't show up on x-rays or MRIs, like mental illness, chronic pain, migraines, or even Parkinsons." The *Dateline* story pointed to an internal company email cautioning a group of claims staff that they had one week remaining to "close," that is, deny, eighteen more claims in order to meet desired targets.

Some claims-processing employees who objected to these practices later contended that they had been intimidated into acquiescing, or dismissed for not complying. Several brought wrongful dismissal suits, which Unum defended on the ground that it had dismissed the dissidents for cause. The most prominent of the suits was that of Dr. Patrick McSharry, who had worked as a staff physician in Unum's claims review operations. He alleged that Unum made him review so many claims that he could not analyze them properly; that he was instructed "to use language . . . [to] support the denial of disability insurance"; that he was not allowed "to request further information or suggest additional medical tests"; and that he was "not supposed to help a claimant perfect a claim for disability insurance benefits."

Not all of Unum's bad faith benefit denial cases have arisen from policies issued under ERISA-covered plans, and the non-ERISA cases have escaped ERISA's various remedial disadvantages. Whereas ERISA has been interpreted to preclude the award of punitive damages, large punitive damage awards have been made against Unum/Provident companies for bad faith claim denials in several non-ERISA cases. In one such case, a federal judge sustained a $5 million award on the ground that the trial "jury heard more than enough evidence to conclude that Plaintiff was totally disabled and that Defendants in bad faith terminated her benefits and caused her damages."

Many federal courts have now commented on Unum's aggressive claims denial practices. Published opinions speak of "selective review of the administrative record," "lack of objectivity and an abuse of discretion by UNUM," misuse of "ambiguous test results," and claims evaluation practices that "defie[d] common sense" and "bordered on outright fraud." In a notable opinion in the district court in Massachusetts, Chief Judge Young collected citations to nearly twenty previous cases that he described as "reveal[ing] a disturbing pattern of erroneous and arbitrary benefits denials, bad faith contract misinterpretations, and other unscrupulous tactics." *Radford Trust v. First Unum Life Ins. Co.*, 321 F. Supp. 2d 226, 247 (D. Mass. 2004). He faulted Unum for behavior "entirely inconsistent with the company's public responsibilities and with its obligations under the [ERISA-covered disability] Policy" in the particular case.

As complaints, litigation, and media accounts multiplied, several state insurance commission staffs began investigating Unum's claims denial practices. In the view of the Georgia commissioner, Unum had been "looking for every technical legal way to avoid paying a claim." In 2003 and 2004, the Maine, Massachusetts, and Tennessee insurance regulators, acting on behalf of most other states, conducted a coordinated investigation and filed a report that accused Unum of systematic irregularities in obtaining and evaluating medical evidence of disability. Unum agreed to pay a $15 million fine, to reopen several years' worth of denied claims, and to make specified changes in its claims reviewing procedures and its corporate governance. In 2005 the California Department of Insurance settled separately with Unum, imposing an $8 million civil penalty. [Thirty-four] California regulators reported "violations of state law in nearly one-third of a random sample of about 1,000 claims handled by Unum/Provident." *Barron's*, the financial newspaper, reports that "[s]ince 2004, Unum has taken charge-offs of $135 million," including the multi-state and California fines, as a result of the investigations.

In the course of discovery proceedings in the lawsuits against Unum, there came to light a remarkable internal memorandum written in 1995 by a Unum executive. In it, he exults in the "enormous" advantages that ERISA, as interpreted by the courts, bestowed upon Unum in cases in which an insured sought judicial review of a benefit denial. "[S]tate law is preempted by federal law, there are no jury trials, there are no compensatory or punitive damages, relief is usually limited to the amount of benefit in question, and claims administrators may receive a deferential standard of review." The memorandum recounts that another Unum executive "identified 12 claim situations where we settled for $7.8 million in the aggregate. If these 12 cases had been covered by ERISA, our liability would have been between zero and $0.5 million." We see in this document Unum's keen understanding of how the deferential standard of review allowed under *Bruch* interacts with aspects of ERISA remedy law to facilitate aggressive claim denial practices.

Broadly speaking, there are two plausible interpretations of the Unum/Provident scandal. Unum could be such an outlier that the saga lacks legal policy implications. On this view, a rogue insurance company behaved exceptionally badly, it got caught and was sanctioned, and its fate should deter others. The other reading of these events is less sanguine: For reasons discussed below in Part III, conflicted plan decision-making is a structural feature of ERISA plan administration. The danger pervades the ERISA-plan world that a self-interested plan decision-maker will take advantage of its license under *Bruch* to line its own pockets by denying meritorious claims. Unum turns out to have been a clumsy villain, but in the hands of subtler operators such misbehavior is much harder to detect. . . .

III. ERISA'S CONFLICTED DECISIONMAKERS

A. PLAN ADMINISTRATION AS FIDUCIARY LAW

"In enacting ERISA," the Supreme Court has observed, "Congress' primary concern was with the mismanagement of funds accumulated to finance employee benefits and the failure to pay employees benefits from accumulated funds." This concern was an outgrowth of congressional investigations into labor union corruption, especially in the Teamsters Union, which uncovered evidence of looting, kickbacks, cronyism, and other serious maladministration in union-sponsored pension and benefit plans.

In ERISA Congress responded to these dangers by imposing fiduciary standards derived from private trust law for the administration of all employee benefit plans. ERISA's rule of mandatory trusteeship requires that "all assets of an employee benefit plan shall be held in trust. . . ." Moreover, ERISA treats all persons who administer a plan, in the sense of exercising material discretion over plan affairs, as ERISA fiduciaries. ERISA subjects these persons to its version of the core substantive rules of trust fiduciary law: the care norm, that is, the duty of prudent administration; and the loyalty rule, which requires plan fiduciaries to act "solely in the interest of the participants and beneficiaries and . . . for the exclusive purpose of . . . providing benefits to participants and their beneficiaries. . . ." ERISA's fiduciary law of plan administration governs claims administration as well as the administration of plan assets.

Although "ERISA abounds with the language and terminology of trust law, ERISA fiduciary law differs markedly from conventional trust law in one crucial respect. Trust law presupposes that the trustee who administers a trust will be disinterested, in the sense of having no personal stake in the trust assets, although the trust terms can make contrary provision. By contrast, ERISA fiduciaries are commonly aligned with the employer (or, in most plans that supply insurance benefits, with the insurance company to which the employer delegates administrative responsibilities for the particular plan). ERISA expressly authorizes the employer to use "an officer, employee, agent or other representative" as a fiduciary, thereby inviting the conflicts of interest that so trouble the law of benefit denials. This concession to employer interests, which departs notably from the trust tradition, was motivated by the concern that without it employers would be less likely to sponsor benefit plans. Because pension and welfare benefit plans entail major expenditures, the sponsor commonly prefers to have its own managers administering and monitoring plan operations for cost containment, a traditional management function.

B. DENIGRATING THE CONFLICT

The deferential standard of review allowed under *Bruch* heightens the dangers intrinsic to ERISA's authorization of conflicted plan decision-makers. We recall the Third Circuit's observation in *Bruch* that "every dollar saved by the [plan] administrator on behalf of his employer is a dollar in [the employer's] pocket." Not all courts have been adequately sensitive to the danger of conflicted decision-making in ERISA benefit denial cases. In particular, a notable string of Seventh Circuit cases has attempted to "apply[] a law-and-economics rationale to establish that no conflict exists." The reasoning in these opinions is deeply flawed.

1. Contrasting Gross Revenue. —Several of the Seventh Circuit cases belittle the danger of conflicts of interest by contrasting the gross revenue of the employer or the insurer with the amount of the disputed claim—asserting, for example, that "a corporation which generates revenues of nearly $6 billion annually . . . is . . . not likely to flinch at paying out $240,000." This reasoning improperly places wrongdoing beyond reproach so long as the benefit denied pales in comparison with the wrongdoer's gross revenue. Since virtually all plan benefit claims are "trivial" when so measured, the Seventh Circuit's rationale would wholly preclude a reviewing court from considering the role of conflict of interest in plan decision-making.

In light of what is now known about the Unum/Provident scandal, it is beyond conjecture that Judge Easterbrook erred when he asserted as late as December 2005 that "Unum is much too large to be affected by its resolution of any one benefits claim." However modest any one claim, if an insurer or other plan administrator denies enough claims, the aggregate savings can be quite significant. Unum reported paying $4.2 billion in disability benefits in 2004. To paraphrase Senator Dirksen (whose name adorns the Seventh Circuit's courthouse), $240,000 here, $240,000 there, pretty soon it's real money.

2. Reputation.—Another tack in the Seventh Circuit cases has been the claim that reputational incentives will adequately deter conflicted decision-makers from abuse. Judge Easterbrook has contended: "Large businesses . . . want to maintain a reputation for fair dealing with their employees. They offer fringe benefits such as disability plans to attract good workers, which they will be unable to do if promised benefits are not paid."

Reputational incentives may indeed constrain conflicted plan decision makers from abuse of authority, but competing considerations weaken that incentive. The danger of unfair treatment in a matter as remote as the denial of a future disability or other benefit claim seldom weighs heavily in an employee's thinking when accepting employment. It is a rare prospective employee who, if he or she has a choice of employers, undertakes to investigate the relative integrity of the benefit claims processes of those employers or their insurers. Because individual benefit denials are not publicized, and because many are quite justified on the merits, an underlying pattern of bias may be hard for the isolated employee to discern.

Moreover, the greater the prospective gain from denying a benefit claim, the greater the inclination to subordinate the risk of reputational injury. For example, as Judge Posner remarked in a pension case in which $125 million turned on the plan fiduciaries' decision about what compensation was covered under a benefit accrual formula, "a loss of reputation might be a price worth paying to avoid $125 million in unanticipated expense." Daniel Fischel and I have elsewhere pointed to the weakness of reputational incentives in severance plan cases that arise from corporate downsizings: "[T]he employer's reputational interest [is] not likely to be effective when the long term relationship [is] dissolving. . . . In these cases, the gains from self-interested action by non-neutral fiduciaries may outweigh the usual inhibiting future costs." Considerations of this sort suggest that labor markets lack the capital markets' efficiency in disseminating reputational information.

In a prominent case decided in 1987, *Van Boxel v. Journal Co. Employees' Pension Trust*, 836 F.2d 1048 (7th Cir. 1987), Judge Posner commented on the inadequacy of reputational incentives to prevent abusive plan administration. Speaking of a pension plan, he said that plan participants' rights "are too important these days for most employees to want to place them at the mercy of a biased tribunal subject only to a narrow form of 'arbitrary and capricious' review, relying on the company's interest in its reputation to prevent it from acting on its bias."

3. Confusing Contract with Fiduciary Obligation.—Judge Posner has recently gravitated toward his colleagues' apologetics for conflicted decision-making. In 2006 in *Rud v. Liberty Life Assurance Co.*, 438 F.3d 772 (7th Cir. 2006), he rejected the "argu[ment] that a conflict of interest exists because any money [that the insurer] pays to a claimant reduces its profits. The ubiquity of such a situation makes us hesitate to describe it as a conflict of interest." Seeking to explain why ubiquity should excuse an otherwise manifest conflict, Judge Posner analogized the ERISA benefit denial cases to the contractual relations of commercial parties, who "have a conflict of interest in the same severely attenuated sense, because each party wants to get as much out of the contract as possible."

In resorting to the language of contract to justify the self-serving behavior of an ERISA plan administrator who decides benefit claims, Judge Posner overlooks a profoundly important difference: ERISA requires the administrator (or an insurer exercising delegated powers of plan administration) to act in a fiduciary capacity. Under ERISA's duty of loyalty, the decision-maker must interpret and apply plan terms "solely in the interest of the participants and beneficiaries and . . . for the exclusive purpose of . . . providing benefits to participants and their beneficiaries. . . ." Judge Posner is, therefore, confusing a contract counterparty, who is allowed to act selfishly, with an ERISA fiduciary, who is forbidden to.

Although Judge Posner recognizes that "ERISA is a paternalistic statute in a number of respects, notably in its vesting rules," he fails to confront the reality that ERISA's fiduciary regime, which governs benefit denial cases, is also profoundly paternalistic. Precisely because ERISA subjects every employee benefit plan to ERISA's duties of loyalty, prudent administration, and "full and fair" internal review of benefit denials, we can be certain that Congress preferred these protective principles of ERISA fiduciary law over Judge Posner's concern about not making further "inroads into freedom of contract." To refute Judge Posner's 2006 opinion in *Rud* that the employment contract impliedly authorizes self-serving decision-making about plan benefits, one need look no further than Judge Posner's 1987 opinion in *Van Boxel*, in which he emphasized that plan participants' rights "are too important these days for most employees to want to place them at the mercy of a biased tribunal. . . ."

4. Experience Rating. —Judge Easterbrook has offered a pair of further rationalizations for deferring to conflicted decision-making. In a case involving denial of a benefit claim by Unum, decided before the Unum/Provident scandal became public, he pointed out that large group insurance policies are "retrospectively-rated," meaning "that the employer agrees to reimburse the insurer" for benefit payments and expenses. *Perlman v. Swiss Bank Comprehensive Disability Prot. Plan*, 195 F.3d 975, 981 (7th Cir. 1999). He reasoned that in such circumstances, because the employer rather than the insurer would bear the ultimate costs of approving claims, "we have no reason to think that the actual decision-makers at Unum approached their task any differently than do the decision-makers at the Social Security Administration," to whose decisions courts apply deferential review.

Judge Easterbrook's argument neglects a familiar commercial reality: Even when an insurance policy is experience-rated, the insurer still has a significant incentive to deny claims, because the market for insurance services is intensely competitive. Low-cost providers prevail over high-cost providers. The more effectively an insurer contains costs under an experience-rated policy, the better that insurer's chance of retaining the account and getting others. In a Third Circuit case, Judge Becker pointed to just this "active incentive to deny close claims in order to keep costs down" as "an economic consideration overlooked by the Seventh Circuit." *Pinto v. Reliance Standard Life Ins. Co.*, 214 F.3d 377, 388 (3d Cir. 2000).

5. Supposed Difficulties of Implementation. —Judge Easterbrook has also asserted, in a case involving Unum, that plan sponsors or their hirelings would be unable to get claims processing employees to misbehave, because getting employees to identify with the interests of their employer "is a daunting challenge for any corporation." There is indeed an economic literature, on which Judge Easterbrook drew, regarding the challenges of incentivizing employees. That literature does not, however, claim that employees cannot be incentivized; rather, the point is that overcoming such characteristic agency problems requires counter-incentives and more acute monitoring—just what Unum did to get its claims processing employees to engage for years in what Judge Young called a "pattern of erroneous and arbitrary benefits denials, bad faith contract misinterpretations, and other unscrupulous tactics." *Radford Trust v. First Unum Life Ins. Co.*, 321 F. Supp. 2d 226, 247 (D. Mass. 2004). The events in the Unum/Provident scandal demonstrate that the view advanced in the Seventh Circuit—that "applying a law and economics rationale . . . establish[es] that no conflict exists" in benefit denial cases involving conflicted decision-makers—is bad law and bad economics.

C. ANALOGIZING TO ADMINISTRATIVE LAW

In contending that courts have as much reason to be deferential to the decision-making of Unum as to that of the Social Security Administration, Judge Easterbrook was analogizing to administrative law. A prominent formulation of this analogy between ERISA plan decision-makers and governmental agencies appeared in a pre-*Bruch* opinion by Judge Wilkinson in the Fourth Circuit. He observed that although deferential review "is perhaps more commonly associated with appellate court review of administrative findings, deference is likewise due when a district court reviews the action of a private plan trustee." In both contexts, he reasoned, applying deferential review "ensure[s] that administrative responsibility rests with those whose experience is daily and continuous, not with judges whose exposure is episodic and occasional."

This analogy to the expertise of administrative agencies has been strongly resisted. In the Third Circuit opinion in *Bruch*, Judge Becker pointed out that a benefit denial case does not ordinarily "turn on information or experience which expertise as a claims administrator is likely to produce." In many circumstances, such a case will "turn on a question of law or contract interpretation. Courts have no reason to defer to private parties to obtain answers to these kinds of questions." He concluded that the "significant danger that the plan administrator will not be impartial [offsets] any remaining benefit which the administrator['s] expertise might be thought to produce."

Other courts have drawn attention to the significance of institutional and procedural differences between the two reviewing functions. The Eleventh Circuit has emphasized that "the individuals who occupy the position of ERISA fiduciaries are less well-insulated from outside pressures than are decision-makers at government agencies." This important ground of distinction, underscored so starkly in the Unum/Provident scandal, cuts strongly against Judge Easterbrook's contention that "[w]e have no reason to think that Unum's benefits staff is any more 'partial' against applicants than are federal judges when deciding benefits claims." The partiality of self-interested reviewers, long suspected in ERISA benefit denial practice, has now been documented in the Unum/Provident scandal.

In speaking of Social Security Administration (SSA) proceedings, which Judge Easterbrook equated with Unum's, Judge Posner has correctly observed that the SSA "is a public agency that denies benefits only after giving the applicant an opportunity for a full and fair adjudicative hearing. The procedural safeguards thus accorded, designed to assure a full and fair hearing, are missing from determinations by [ERISA] plan administrators."

D.   DEVELOPING BRUCH'S CONFLICT PROVISO

Bruch's conflict proviso, noticed above, made a potentially important concession to the hazards of conflicted decision-making. Even in a case in which the plan documents require deferential review, said the Supreme Court, if the "administrator or fiduciary . . . is operating under a conflict of interest, that conflict must be weighed as a 'facto[r] in determining whether there is an abuse of discretion.' " This slender passage has produced a large case law wrestling with the question of whether a plan decision-maker is conflicted, and if so, how much the reviewing court should temper its deference.

In an early post-*Bruch* decision, *Brown v. Blue Cross & Blue Shield of Alabama*, 898 F.2d 1556 (11th Cir. 1990), the Eleventh Circuit held that "when a plan beneficiary demonstrates a substantial conflict of interest on the part of the fiduciary responsible for benefits determinations, the burden shifts to the fiduciary to prove that its interpretation of plan provisions committed to its discretion was not tainted by self-interest." The Eleventh Circuit has adhered to this burden-shifting rule in later cases. This standard, if widely followed, would materially narrow the scope of deference that courts must grant to plan-dictated standards of review.

The other circuits have not, however, agreed. . . . The Supreme Court could, without confessing error in *Bruch*, materially reduce the scope of *Bruch*'s mischief by resolving this conflict among the circuits in favor of the position of the Eleventh Circuit, insisting on de novo review despite contrary plan terms in cases involving conflicted decision-making. That path is also open to any of the circuits that may find reason to reexamine the question. The suspicion is sometimes voiced in the ERISA plaintiffs' bar that part of what has motivated other circuits not to take advantage of their authority to resist plan-dictated deferential review clauses under *Bruch*'s conflict proviso is the fear that caseloads would increase. Deciding a case on the merits is indeed more time consuming than presuming the correctness of somebody else's self-serving decision. Because, however, Congress determined to subject ERISA plan benefit denials to federal judicial review, and because ERISA's draconian preemption provision suppresses the state-law causes of action that existed for many such cases before ERISA, the proper role of the federal courts is to decide these cases fairly, and not slough them off on biased decision-makers. The Unum/Provident scandal, showing just how serious the danger of conflicted plan decision-making really is, supplies a cogent justification for the lower courts to tighten the standard of review in such cases. For the Supreme Court, however, the better path would be to reconsider its misstep in *Bruch*. . . .

C.   PROTECTIVE PRINCIPLES FROM STATE INSURANCE LAW

The Unum/Provident scandal has provoked a concerted movement among state insurance commissioners to forbid terms in insurance policies that alter the standard of judicial review. The rationale for these interventions, in the words of the California provision, is that policy terms attempting to govern the standard of review deprive the insured of "the protections of California insurance law, including the covenant of good faith and fair dealing. . . ." The influential National Association of Insurance Commissioners is encouraging the states to take this position. The Hawaii Commissioner ruled in 2004 that "[a] 'discretionary clause' granting to a plan administrator discretionary authority so as to deprive the insured of a de novo appeal is an unfair or deceptive act or practice in the business of insurance and may not be used in health insurance contracts or plans in Hawaii." At that time such clauses were "prohibited by statute in Maine and Minnesota, and by Insurance Commissions in California, Illinois, Indiana, Montana, Nevada, New Jersey, Oregon, Texas, and Utah." In 2005, the Illinois regulations were further amended to forbid health or disability insurance contracts from "contain[ing] a provision purporting to reserve discretion to the [insurer] to interpret the terms of the contract, or to provide standards of interpretation or review that are inconsistent with the laws of th[e] State."

The question of whether such regulations, as applied to ERISA plans, will survive ERISA's preemption clause (under its exception for state insurance regulation) awaits resolution. As part of Unum's October 2005 settlement with the California regulators, the company agreed to cease using discretionary review clauses in insurance policies sold in that state. The principle that underlies the commissioners' initiative bears importantly on the question whether ERISA should continue to facilitate plan-dictated standard-of-review clauses. The commissioners contend that allowing an insurance policy to skew the standard of review against the insured interferes with the protective purpose of insurance regulatory law. Similarly, the view developed in this Essay is that allowing ERISA plan drafters to dictate the standard of judicial review of benefit denials undermines the regulatory purposes of ERISA. In the insurance commissioners' initiative against such plan terms there is a further demonstration that when conscientious policymakers think carefully about the issue, rather than toss it off in a hasty aside as the Supreme Court did in *Bruch*, they conclude that the standard of review of benefit denials ought not to be subject to self-serving alteration.

CONCLUSION

The Supreme Court in *Bruch* rightly interpreted ERISA to require non-deferential de novo review of plan decision-making, but in an ill-considered aside the Court allowed plan drafters to defeat that standard by requiring reviewing courts to defer to plan decision-making. The Unum/Provident scandal, by underscoring the dangers that arise when conflicted decision-makers deny claimed benefits, demonstrates that impartial judicial review in such cases is an essential safeguard against self-serving conduct.

The analogy to trust law on which the Court rested this branch of its decision in *Bruch* is unsound. Although the drafter of a private trust may indeed insist on greater judicial deference to trustee decision-making, the courts grant that deference on the premise that the purpose of trust law is to give maximum effect to the wishes of the transferor—that is, to private autonomy. In ERISA, by contrast, Congress employed trust law concepts for regulatory purposes, in order to limit private autonomy. Accordingly, the analogy to "general principles of trust law" on which the Court based its decision to allow plan drafters to defeat the otherwise applicable ERISA standard of review is a misapplication of trust law. When trust principles are transposed to regulatory purposes, as in ERISA, those purposes alter the normal balance in trust law between default and mandatory law. Like ERISA's substantive fiduciary norms of loyalty and prudence, ERISA's provision for judicial review of plan decision-making has an essentially protective purpose. Congress did not allow employers and other plan sponsors the option to decline to be subject to ERISA fiduciary law. For much the same reason, the Supreme Court was wrong to assume that ERISA meant to allow plan drafters to dictate reduced scrutiny for conflicted plan fiduciaries in contested benefit denial cases. The Court (or Congress) ought to learn from the Unum/Provident scandal and correct the mistake in *Bruch* before more ERISA plan participants and beneficiaries are victimized by more bad-faith benefit denials.

NOTES AND QUESTIONS

1. The complete preemption of state law remedies for benefit denials means that states are free to mandate the benefits to be provided in health insurance policies, but not the remedies that may be granted for the failure to provide those benefits. As the Unum/Provident scandal illustrates, the elimination of the state law remedies leaves ERISA plan beneficiaries vulnerable to opportunistic breach.

2. Professor Langbein focuses on a different aspect of ERISA that further reduces the ability of courts to police the conflicted loyalties of ERISA administrators: the standard for reviewing the denial of benefits. A pair of cases from the Ninth Circuit illustrates the significance of more deferential standard of review that Professor Langbein decries. *Day v. AT&T Disability Income Plan*, 685 F.3d 848 (9th Cir. 2012), and *Blankenship v. Liberty Life Assurance Co. of Boston*, 486 F.3d 620 (9th Cir. 2007), both addressed a somewhat complicated disability benefit question: the treatment of retirement benefits that a disabled former employee withdraws from the employer's retirement benefit plan and immediate rolls over into an Individual Retirement Account. In *Blankenship*, the court reviewed the administrator's decision under the traditional contract law de novo standard and found for the former employee. In *Day* the court affirmed the administrator's decision. Here is a short excerpt of the *Day* opinion that provides a good sense of the nature of the deferential standard:

> Because the Plan conferred full discretion on Sedgwick, unless Day's allegations of bias and misconduct are both true and warrant less deference, the district court correctly reviewed for an abuse of discretion. The district court did not err in finding no inherent or structural conflict of interest. The Plan is funded by AT&T and not Sedgwick, and administered by Sedgwick and not AT&T. Nor did the court err in rejecting Day's allegations of actual conflict of interest. Just because Sedgwick consulted with AT&T in responding to Day's concerns about his rolled over pension benefits being received by the IRA does not show that AT&T had any influence over Sedgwick's decision making process in this regard.
>
> Day's remaining contentions are likewise without foundation. Although he is correct that we generally apply de novo review when an administrator engages in "wholesale and flagrant violations of the procedural requirement of ERISA," and thus "fails to exercise discretion[,]" Day failed to present material or probative evidence in support of these bold assertions. At best he showed only that Sedgwick in its February 2009 and October 2009 letters elaborated on its initial reasons for rejecting his appeal, and that AT&T failed to provide him with copies of various documents that he was instead required to obtain from a separate AT&T office.
>
> Sedgwick's conclusion that Day received his pension benefits when he rolled them into an IRA was not an unreasonable interpretation. To "receive"

means to "take into possession or control." When a beneficiary rolls a pension into an IRA, he may not take possession of it, but he has control over the assets. For instance, he can choose the IRA and change it; and he can withdraw funds from it, albeit perhaps having to pay penalties for early withdrawal. It is therefore not unreasonable to say that he has received these benefits. . . .

Day contends this conclusion is in conflict with *Blankenship*. It is not, because our holding there is plainly distinguishable. We determined that a plan providing for an offset for pension benefits received by a beneficiary was ambiguous, because "receive" can mean either possession or control. Reviewing de novo and applying the doctrine of *contra proferentem*, we construed the ambiguity against the Plan and held that "receive" referred to funds actually coming into the possession of a beneficiary. Therefore, funds rolled over to an IRA were not to be used to offset disability benefits.

In rejecting *Blankenship* as controlling, Sedgwick correctly explained to Day that the case by its own terms does not apply here. As we acknowledged, *contra proferentem* applies when a plan does not grant a plan administrator discretion to interpret ambiguous plan terms; the doctrine does not apply when a plan "grants the administrator discretion to construe its terms." In the latter context, it is the administrator who resolves ambiguities in the plan's language. Because Sedgwick had discretion to interpret the Plan, the only question is whether Sedgwick's interpretation of "receive" to include Day's control of his IRA funds was unreasonable. It was not. The administrator therefore did not act unreasonably in concluding that Day had received pension benefits, and appropriately reduced his LTD benefits to account for the rollover.

3. As the opinion in *Day* indicates, there are exceptions to the deferential standard of review. While quite important to ERISA practice, these exceptions are too complicated to delve into here. For our purposes, it is sufficient to be aware that well-counseled employers can easily avoid these exceptions and, therefore, the dreaded (by employers) de novo standard of review. Not surprisingly, AT&T was well counseled, and *Day* is the result.

VI. SUBROGATION

The final topic in this chapter marks a transition in our consideration of the relationship between insurance and tort law. We touched on this relationship briefly in connection with the *Munroe* case noted in the misrepresentation unit in Chapter 2, and we mentioned it in this chapter in the context of the principle of indemnity. This part starts with an overview of the basic rules and functions of subrogation and then focuses on the role of subrogation in the settlement of suits. It concludes with a discussion of how to conceptualize the role of subrogation in the overall civil litigation system.

A.   The Basic Rules and Functions of Subrogation

Subrogation is the legal term for the right of an indemnitor (typically an insurance company) to obtain reimbursement for the amount it paid to indemnify another's loss from the person who is responsible for that loss. The indemnitor is sometimes referred to as the "subrogee" and the indemnitee as the "subrogor."

In the context of a tort claim, subrogation allows a first-party insurance company—a property or health insurer, for example—to "stand in the shoes" of its insured for purposes of collecting from a tort defendant what it paid on the insured's behalf. Since the insurance company only stands in the shoes of the policyholder, subrogation law usually provides the company no greater rights against the defendant than the plaintiff has.

Subrogation comes in three types: equitable, contractual, and statutory. Equitable subrogation, sometimes referred to (confusingly) as legal subrogation, applies in the absence of any contractual subrogation provision in the policy and in the absence of any governing statute. Contractual subrogation is what it sounds like: It is the subrogation expressly provided for in the insurance policy itself. Contractual subrogation provisions have long been included in property insurance policies and are included in virtually all such policies today. The inclusion of a subrogation term in accident, health, and disability policies began more recently, but it is now quite common as well. As will be discussed more fully below, subrogation has not generally been applied to life insurance. Statutory subrogation, of course, is provided by statute. Examples include the subrogation rights given to workers' compensation insurers by state workers' compensation statutes. In general, contractual subrogation, when the relevant policy language is clear, trumps rules of equitable subrogation, and statutory subrogation rules trump the other two if there is a conflict.

The primary functions of the subrogation doctrine are (1) to permit losses to be shifted to the party who is legally responsible for causing them and (2) thereby to prevent windfalls to the insured party. In the torts context, these functions of subrogation depend importantly on the existence and application of the traditional collateral source rule. To see how this works, consider the following highly stylized tort case: X's property is damaged by Y under circumstances that give X a tort claim against Y. Initially, X recovers for the damage to her property from her first-party property insurer. (For the sake of simplicity, assume that the loss is fully covered by insurance.) Upon indemnifying X's loss, the property insurer becomes subrogated to X's tort claim against Y. In the simplest case, it is the insurer that now brings the tort suit against Y, seeking to recoup the amounts paid out to cover X's losses. Assuming Y's responsibility to X is established (with, say, no defenses or reductions for comparative fault), and applying the traditional collateral source rule, the court would award the insurer, the full amount of the losses caused to X by Y—with no offset for the insurance proceeds paid to X. Thus, the traditional collateral source rule can be understood as a sort of collateral source non-offset rule. Working together, then, the collateral source "non-offset rule" and the subrogation doctrine result in (1) Y the tortfeasor being held responsible for the harm that he caused, and (2) X receiving full, but no more than full, compensation for her losses from her insurer.

The rationales for this complex arrangement should be familiar to any student of first-year torts. It is the same set of rationales that are provided for tort liability in general: namely, corrective justice (righting wrongfully caused losses) and/or efficient deterrence (shifting losses to the cheapest-cost avoider). Can you see how tort reform legislation that eliminates the traditional collateral source non-offset rule, replacing it with a collateral source offset rule, would change the role of tort law? How would such a reform affect the value of an insurer's subrogation claim?

For a long time, it was thought that life, disability, health, and accident insurers could not engage in any form of subrogation. The reason for this was the notion that these types of insurance, unlike property insurance, are not contracts of indemnity, and thus the principle of indemnity should not apply. With respect to accident, health, and disability insurance contracts, this notion has largely given way, and courts generally will enforce subrogation clauses in such policies. Moreover, as mentioned above, subrogation clauses are regularly found today in accident, health, and (somewhat less commonly) disability insurance policies.[22] Life insurance policies, however, are different. Not only does the doctrine of equitable subrogation not apply to life insurance, but also life insurance contracts do not contain subrogation clauses. The standard reason that is given for this difference is that life insurance has traditionally not been a contract of indemnity. Of course, life insurance contracts are in fact very much about indemnity, in the sense that the best argument for owning life insurance is replacing the income-earning power of a household breadwinner—much as commercial property insurance aims to replace income-generating property. Can you think of any good reasons why life insurance companies should not be given subrogation rights, at least contractually, just as all other insurers are? *See generally* Kenneth S. Abraham & Kyle D. Logue, *The Genie and the Bottle: Collateral Sources Under the September 11th Victim Compensation Fund*, 53 DePaul L. Rev. 591, 609-610 (2003) (suggesting the fact that most households have insufficient life insurance coverage as a possible rationale).

Following the attacks of September 11, 2001, Congress enacted the September 11th Victim Compensation Fund, which provided, among other things, a type of government-provided life insurance to the families of the victims. Two aspects of these awards are especially distinctive. First, the awards were unusually generous. The payments, which were designed to be a function of the victim's income, ranged from $250,000 to $7 million and averaged approximately $2 million per victim. And these were the amounts after reductions for collateral sources. That leads to the second distinctive aspect of the program: the collateral offset provision. The statute creating the fund provided that awards, after being calculated to replace income, would be reduced by "all collateral sources, including life insurance, pension funds, death benefit programs, and payments by Federal, State, or local governments related to the terrorist-related aircraft crashes of September 11, 2001." Air Transportation Safety and System Stabilization Act, §401(4). Why do you suppose that this form of government-provided life insurance was subject to collateral offsets? As between this rule and the alternative (a collateral non-offset rule), who would end up bearing the bulk of the costs of the September 11th Victim Compensation Fund? Notice that, although the fund treated various forms of private and government-provided life insurance as a collateral source to be offset, it did not treat a victim's savings account or charity received by the victim's family as a collateral source to be offset. Why not? If life insurance companies wanted to follow the collateral-offset precedent

---

22. Disability insurance policies are somewhat less likely to have a subrogation clause, but such clauses seem to be enforceable in disability insurance policies unless there is state legislation providing anything to the contrary. *Cf. Daughtry v. Union Cent. Life Ins. Co.*, 33 F. Supp. 2d 1174 (D. Ariz. 1999) (holding that ERISA preempts state law that prohibits subrogation—because the law was not specifically directed at insurance—and that ERISA plan documents provided that the disability insurer would be entitled to subrogate).

set by the September 11th Fund, how might they do it? *See generally* Abraham & Logue, *supra.*

Although the quintessential subrogation claim involves a first-party insurer bringing a tort action against the tortfeasor who is responsible for injuring the insured-tort victim, there are other types of insurance subrogation cases. One important example involves mortgage loans. When a party takes out a mortgage to purchase a piece of property, the borrower is sometimes referred to as the "mortgagor" and the lender (the party holding the mortgage on the property) as the "mortgagee." So long as there is an outstanding balance on the loan, the mortgagee faces some risk that the loan will not be repaid in the event the property that serves as security for the loan is destroyed. Therefore, the mortgagee will often take out an insurance policy on the property. If the property is destroyed, and the property insurer indemnifies the mortgagee, the property insurer then becomes subrogated to the mortgagee-lender's right to receive loan payments from the mortgagor.

B.   *Subrogation and Settlement*

Unless a statute gives a first-party insurer direct rights against the tortfeasor,[23] the subrogating insurer "stands in the shoes" of the plaintiff with respect to the tortfeasor. Thus, any defenses the tortfeasor has against the plaintiff are also valid against a subrogating insurer. This seems obvious with respect to substantive tort defenses like "no duty," "lack of proximate cause," "comparative negligence," and the like. (Why?) It may be less obvious, however, with respect to defenses like "settlement and release." Taken to its logical extreme, the "standing in the shoes" approach would allow an insured to collect from its insurance company and then make a settlement with the tort defendant that released the tort defendant and, in the process, cut out the insurance company.

Two well-accepted aspects of insurance law protect the insurance company in this situation. The first is the courts' decision to enforce conditions in first-party insurance policies that obligate policyholders to cooperate with their insurers in the protection of subrogation rights. These provisions mean that policyholders cannot, without their insurers' permission, do anything after a loss has already occurred to destroy the insurers' subrogation rights, on pain of losing the right to collect under the policy. For example, in *Allstate Insurance Co. v. Meeks*, 489 N.E.2d 530 (Ind. Ct. App. 1986), a policyholder who settled an auto accident claim with the tortfeasor first, releasing the tortfeasor from any further action in connection with the accident, and then attempted to collect from her own insurer for the damage to her car under the "comprehensive" coverage on her auto policy was held to have breached the cooperation clause and, therefore, was not entitled to payment under the policy.

This first aspect of insurance law protects the first-party insurer up to the point that it makes a payment under the policy. What protects the insurer once it has made the payment? The answer is an interesting feature of the common law of insurance. Provided that a tortfeasor has notice of subrogation rights

---

23. This is typically the case for workers' compensation for Medicare and Medicare benefits. *See* 42 U.S.C. §2651 (2001).

in connection with the tort claim, the common law grants the insurer rights directly against the tortfeasor, meaning that the plaintiff can no longer release those rights. *See, e.g., Leader Nat'l Ins. Co. v. Torres*, 779 P.2d 722 (Wash. 1989). This does not eliminate any substantive tort law defenses, only the defense of settlement and release. Thus, if a subrogating first-party insurer gives notice to the defendant of the existence of the subrogation claim, the subrogating insurer gets the right to assert that claim directly against the defendant in the event that the defendant settles with the plaintiff without the subrogating insurer's consent. *Id.* These principles make it very important for a first-party insurance company to promptly determine whether an insured loss took place in connection with a tort and, if so, to promptly give notice of the subrogation rights to all possible defendants and their liability insurance companies. As a result of these principles, well-counseled tort defendants and their liability insurance companies will not settle a case without the participation of any first-party insurers that have provided notice of subrogation rights. For a discussion of how this works in practice, see Tom Baker, *Blood Money, New Money, and the Moral Economy of Tort Law in Action,* 35 Law & Soc'y Rev. 275 (2001).

Note that these legal rules do not protect the insurer's subrogation rights in the event that the policyholder waives its rights against a third party before a loss. With limited exceptions, it is well established that such waivers are permissible and binding upon the insurer. *See generally* Randy J. Sutton, Annotation, *Validity, Construction, and Application of Contractual Waiver of Subrogation Provision,* 2006 A.L.R.6th 14 (2006).

Some of the knottiest questions in subrogation revolve around the relative rights of the tort victim and his or her first-party insurer to the proceeds of a tort judgment or settlement in a situation in which there is not enough money available to fully compensate both the victim and the first-party insurer. Before addressing this issue, however, consider the conceptually easier situation in which a tort victim has first-party insurance covering all or some of her loss and the tort defendant has adequate assets to cover all of that loss.

The following are three possible legal rules governing the "adequate asset" situation:

A. The victim gets to recover all of his or her loss from the tort defendant and also from the first-party insurer.
B. The victim's tort damages are reduced by the amount of his or her available first-party coverage and the tort defendant pays only for the uninsured components of the loss.
C. The tort defendant is required to pay for all of the loss, the first-party insurer is reimbursed for the amount that it paid on behalf of the victim, and the victim receives the remainder.

See generally Spencer L. Kimball & Don A. Davis, *The Extension of Insurance Subrogation,* 60 Mich. L. Rev. 841 (1962).

The first approach corresponds to the situation in which there is a collateral source rule in effect (meaning that collateral sources such as insurance are not deducted against the tort damages) and there is no right of subrogation. This approach can be justified on the grounds that the deterrence and retribution goals of tort law would be frustrated by reducing the defendant's responsibility, that the victim does not receive a windfall since he or she paid for the first-party benefits, and that the purported benefits of subrogation are outweighed by the administrative costs it imposes. *Cf. Id.* at 869-872.

The second approach corresponds to the situation in which there is no collateral source rule. This approach can be justified on the basis of the compensation goal of tort law. The plaintiff does not need to be compensated for financial harm that he or she did not in fact suffer. Many people believe that first-party insurance is a more efficient way to spread the cost of harm and that tort law does not really deter harm, especially with regard to automobile accidents (which represent the largest part of the tort "pie" in the United States and Britain). *See, e.g.,* P.S. Atiyah, The Damages Lottery (1997). Moreover, in the distressingly common situation in which the defendant does not have enough assets to fully compensate the victim, this approach will provide more complete compensation for the victim than any subrogation approach in which the first-party insurer is entitled to receive some of the payment. *See* Tom Baker, *Blood Money, New Money and the Moral Economy of Tort Law in Action,* 35 Law & Soc'y Rev. 275 (2001).

The third approach corresponds to the situation in which there is a collateral source rule and a right of subrogation. This approach can be justified on the grounds that the deterrence and retribution goals of tort law require that the defendant be fully responsible and that the indemnity principle of insurance law requires that the victim not be *overcompensated.* The victim in fact receives the insurance benefit that he or she was promised: prompt indemnification from the insurance company. If we assume that insurance is a competitive business, insurers will take subrogation recoveries into account in pricing their policies and, therefore, the insurance company is not in fact depriving consumers of anything that they have paid for.

The following two cases address the question of what happens under the third approach, when a case settles for an amount that does not cover all the plaintiff's damages.

RIMES v. STATE FARM MUTUAL AUTOMOBILE INSURANCE CO.

Supreme Court of Wisconsin
316 N.W.2d 348 (1982)

[Rimes was injured in an auto accident. State Farm, Rimes's auto insurer, paid approximately $10,000 of Rimes's medical bills under the "medical-pay" provisions of the auto policy. Rimes brought a tort action against the responsible parties. State Farm became a party to the extent of its subrogation interest. During the trial in that case, Rimes settled with the defendants for $125,000, an amount that he claimed represented substantially less than full compensation. State Farm demanded that it be repaid the $10,000 pursuant to its contractual subrogation rights:

> Upon payment . . . the company shall be subrogated to the extent of such payment to the proceeds of any settlement or judgment that may result from the exercise of any rights of recovery which the injured person . . . may have against any person . . . and such person shall execute and deliver instruments and papers and do whatever else is necessary to secure such rights. Such person shall do nothing after loss to prejudice such rights.

Rimes, State Farm, and the trial judge agreed to hold a mini-trial to the court to determine State Farm's rights to any of the settlement proceeds. The court found that Rimes's damages were in excess of $300,000, of which about $27,000 were for medical expenses, and that therefore the settlement did not make Rimes whole. As a result, the court held that State Farm was not entitled to any of the settlement. State Farm appealed to the court of appeals, which petitioned the supreme court to take the appeal directly.]

HEFFERNAN, J. The question presented is whether an automobile insurer, State Farm Mutual Automobile Insurance Company, which, under a subrogation agreement signed by its insured, Palmer H. Rimes, has made payment under the medical-pay provisions of its policy, has the right to recover those payments out of the monies received by its insured in a settlement with negligent third-party tortfeasors and their liability insurers, when, according to the findings and judgment of the circuit court, the settlement figure was less than the total damages sustained by the insured as the result of an automobile accident. . . .

In *Garrity v. Rural Mutual Insurance Company,* 253 N.W.2d 512 (Wis. 1977) the property owners were insured under a fire insurance policy with Rural Mutual Insurance Company. They suffered a fire loss to their barn and dairy when a negligently operated truck belonging to a feed mill burst into flames and caused the loss to the Garrity's property. The alleged fire loss exceeded the sum of the amount recovered under their fire policy and the policy limits on the vehicle driven by the negligent tortfeasor. The fire insurance company claimed, however, that it had a right of priority in any recovery of monies from the third-party tortfeasor up to the amount that it, the fire insurer, had paid on the fire loss. The subrogation agreement in *Garrity* provided that:

> This Company may require from the insured an assignment of all right of recovery against any party for loss to the extent that payment therefore is made by this Company.

Id. at 540.

The trial court in *Garrity* interpreted that subrogation agreement literally and, accordingly, permitted recovery by Rural Mutual up to the amount it paid on the fire loss. The subrogation agreement in the instant case between Rimes and State Farm is not significantly dissimilar and if literally interpreted would permit recovery by State Farm in the amount of medical payments made on behalf of Rimes. This court in *Garrity,* however, pointed out that the effect of "conventional subrogation" was the same as "legal subrogation,"[24] which arises by application of the principles of equity, and that, accordingly, the contractual terms of subrogation agreements in an insurance policy were to be applied according to the rules of equity. We said that:

> (In equitable subrogation) no right of subrogation against the insured exists upon the part of the insurer where the insured's actual loss exceeds the amount re-

---

24. "The creature of equity, strangely enough, is known as legal subrogation as opposed to conventional subrogation, which is the product of an agreement between the parties. Conventional subrogation most commonly appears in standard policy provisions or loan receipts, but the distinction is meaningless in terms of the policy justifications for the doctrine. The primary reason for the adoption of subrogation is the principle of indemnity." Denenberg, *Subrogation Recovery: Who is Made Whole,* FIC Quarterly 185, 186 (Winter 1979).

covered from both the insurer and the wrongdoer, after deducting costs and expenses. In other words, the insurer has no right as against the insured where the compensation received by the insured is less than his loss.

Id. at 543.

Wisconsin has long held . . . that the same rule applies to an insurer claiming subrogation under contract and that such insurer is to be allowed no share in the recovery from the tortfeasor if the total amount recovered by the insured from the insurer and the wrongdoer does not cover his entire loss. . . .

In the instant case, State Farm argues that *Garrity* is inapplicable because *Garrity* involved a property-damage fire case, where the total amount of damages is more easily determinable than the amount of damages sustained by plaintiff in a personal-injury action. While that is undoubtedly true, we see it as a distinction without a difference. The law of damages in personal-injury cases is premised upon the fact that the damages are reasonably ascertainable. The trial of a personal-injury action is based on that proposition, and we find the alleged difficulty of ascertainment of actual damages to be irrelevant to the merits of this case. Particularly, it is irrelevant when, in fact, the procedures adopted by the trial court were designed to determine with exactitude the actual damages sustained by Rimes. Whether the mini-trial procedure to the court which was utilized is appropriate to this purpose will be discussed further in this opinion. . . .

State Farm argues, however, that the fact that the plaintiffs gave a general release to the tortfeasors is "an affirmation by them that they have been made whole as required by law."

We think this overstates the characteristics of a release and settlement of a claim, particularly in a personal-injury case, where both the questions of liability and of damages prior to trial are to some degree in doubt. A pre-trial release in settlement is in fact usually appropriate only when such doubts exist. A release is merely the giving up of a right or claim, and it may or may not be for full consideration and may or may not make the grantor of the release whole. Moreover, a settlement is defined in Webster's Third New International Dictionary as "the satisfaction of a claim by agreement often with less than full payment."

Thus, it is apparent that the legal import urged by State Farm to be given to the settlement in this case is inappropriate. The most that can be said is that the plaintiffs gave up the right of action against the tortfeasors for consideration that may or may not have been sufficient to make them whole. No recital in any of the stipulations in this case evidences an acknowledgment by the plaintiffs that the settlement made them whole, and the very nature of settlements of personal-injury claims precludes a hypothesis that the grantor necessarily acknowledges full reimbursement for the wrong done. . . .

State Farm also argues that, had the case gone to a verdict before the jury and had the total damages returned been $125,000, which sum included the $9,649.90 for medical expenses incurred in the first year after the accident, State Farm would clearly have been entitled to recover the latter amount as its claim in subrogation. While that is undoubtedly true, that fact is irrelevant, because, had such been the result of the trial, we would be obliged to conclude that the damages found by the jury made the plaintiff whole. Rimes, unless he paid over the amount of State Farm's claim, would have reaped a double recovery. The medical payments were made long before trial; and were Rimes to keep all the proceeds of the judgment plus the medical payments, he would have been made whole plus the medical payments previously received. This he may not do under the equitable principles of subrogation. The verdict, under the facts hypothesized by State Farm, would have advised the trial court that the sum of $125,000 made the plaintiff whole. The parties here, however, by their stipulation determined to forego a jury verdict as the test of wholeness. It is clear then that a payment of $125,000, unless that sum had been arrived at by a jury whose intent was to make the plaintiff whole, was irrelevant. Under the facts of this case, the payment of $125,000 was the price that the defendant tortfeasors were willing to pay to avoid the risk of greater exposure; and it was the sum that Rimes was willing to accept. It has nothing to do with the determination of whether Rimes was made whole.

Under Wisconsin law the test of wholeness depends upon whether the insured has been completely compensated for all the elements of damages, not merely those damages for which the insurer has indemnified the insured. Thus the mere fact that the settlement figure of $125,000 exceeded the insurer's claim for subrogation is immaterial. The injured or aggrieved party is not made whole unless all his damages arising out of the tort have been fully compensated.

We pointed out in *Garrity* that the cause of action against a tortfeasor is indivisible. Accordingly, it is only when there has been full compensation for all the damage elements of the entire cause of action that the insured is made whole. Thus only where an injured party has received an award by judgment or otherwise which pays all of his elements of damages, including those for which he has already been indemnified by an insurer, is there any occasion for subrogation. As we said in *Garrity:*

> (W)here either the insurer or the insured must to some extent go unpaid, the loss should be borne by the insurer for that is a risk the insured has paid it to assume.

253 N.W.2d at 542.

COFFEY, J. (dissenting). I dissent because I believe that the case at bar is not controlled by the rule set forth in *Garrity v. Rural Mutual Insurance Company,* 253 N.W.2d 512 (Wis. 1977). Further, I believe that the majority's decision will not have a significant effect on the actual recoveries of injured plaintiffs while it will compel full-scale trials in cases where the plaintiff has already settled his principal claim and, thus, the decision is contrary to the policy interest in judicial economy. Finally, I dissent because the majority opinion places insurers in the embarrassing position of having to dispute the extent and validity of its own insured's case in order to exercise its statutorily permitted right to subrogation where the insured settles its case.

As the majority properly notes, the facts in *Garrity* differ from those presented in the instant case. I believe the critical distinction between this case and *Garrity* is the fact that in the case at bar, the plaintiffs voluntarily settled their entire claim for an amount less than the total limits of the available insurance monies, whereas, in *Garrity,* the plaintiff was seeking to recover all available insurance monies and it was assumed that that amount would be less than the total loss. This distinction is important because in the case at bar, had the plaintiffs fully litigated their case and had they received a favorable verdict, they would have undoubtedly been made whole and the insurer could have collected on its subrogation claim. The fact that there was a settlement of this case is a matter generally favored by the law, but a settlement should not be forced or so encouraged as to allow it to become a vehicle for impairing the rights of another; in this case, the rights of the subrogated insurer. The majority's expansion of the *Garrity* rule that a subrogated insurer cannot share in the insured's recovery until the insured is made whole allows the insured to effectively eliminate the insurer's statutory right of subrogation, where, as in the case at bar, the insureds settled their entire claim for an amount less than the total available insurance monies and less than their total damages. I believe this result is both erroneous and inequitable.

This court has consistently acknowledged that "the purpose of the doctrine (of subrogation) is to avoid unjust enrichment." *Id.* at 541. Preventing the insurer from exercising its subrogation rights where an insured settles for less than the amount of available insurance policy limits and for an amount less than the insured's total loss, effectively bars the subrogor from recovering his payment from the wrongdoer and, thus, unjustly enriches not only the wrongdoer but also the insured who has been reimbursed for his damages by the settlement. Thus, the majority's decision contravenes the very equitable principles upon which the doctrine of subrogation rests.

Under the majority's decision, the insurer is barred from recovering any part of the monies it paid from either the wrongdoer or the insureds, although it is obvious that some portion of settlement is intended to compensate the insureds for the damages for which they were indemnified by the insurer. The majority justifies this result by stating that the insureds must receive full compensation for all their damages before they are made whole as their damages are indivisible. But, in actuality, doesn't an insured impliedly concede that he is being made whole by accepting a payment in settlement of his claim, especially where the payment is less than the total monies available under the insurance contracts? In a personal injury case, both the valuation of compensatory damages and the determination of relative fault are inexact and always open to dispute. In light of that fact, I believe it is fair and reasonable to assume that a party is made whole by the amount for which he voluntarily settles his entire claim. Further, the majority's conclusion that the settling of insureds' damages is indivisible ignores the fact that in reality the injured parties' actual medical expenses are the most readily determined and often serve as a measuring stick for evaluating the plaintiffs' remaining compensatory damages. . . .

Because the majority's application of the equitable doctrine of subrogation in this case reaches the wholly unfair result of barring the insurer from exercising its subrogation rights even though the insureds voluntarily settled their claim, I believe the decision is erroneous. I dissent from the majority opinion for the additional reason that . . . in reality, the majority decision will not result in a greater recovery for a plaintiff-insured. This is because knowledgeable counsel will be aware that medical-pay coverage payments will not be recoverable by the subrogated insurer and, thus, they will view those payments as an offset in determining the settlement value of the case when the plaintiff-insured has received such payments. . . .

LUDWIG v. FARM BUREAU MUTUAL INSURANCE CO.

Iowa Supreme Court
393 N.W.2d 143 (1986)

LARSON, J. The plaintiff, Jeannette Ludwig, was insured under an automobile policy with Farm Bureau Mutual Insurance Company (hereinafter Farm Bureau) which provided coverage for medical expenses incurred by occupants of the insured vehicle. The policy also provided for subrogation for any medical payments made by it. In 1980, while the plaintiff was traveling in Kansas with her husband and mother-in-law, her car was involved in a collision with a truck. All three were injured, and Farm Bureau paid their medical expenses. The three occupants of the car then sued the truckline. Farm Bureau served notice of its subrogation rights on the trucker's insurance company.

The suit against the truckline was settled. A summary of the settlement showed a total amount of $45,000.00 received, with $13,223.26 allocated for subrogation claims for the three victims ($9380.97 for Farm Bureau and the balance for Blue Cross and Blue Shield, whose claim is not involved here). The balance of $31,776.72 was distributed to Jeannette Ludwig and the other two plaintiffs.

Farm Bureau was not involved in the settlement proceedings, however its subrogation interests were protected by the trucker's insurance company which issued a separate check for medical expenses, made payable jointly to Farm Bureau and Jeannette Ludwig. When a disagreement arose over who was entitled to this check, Ludwig filed suit . . . and the case proceeded to trial. . . . The district court, James L. McDonald, J., ruled that Farm Bureau was entitled to be reimbursed for its payments of medical expenses only if Ludwig had been "made whole" by the settlement with the truckline. The court concluded she had not been made whole and denied reimbursement. Farm Bureau appealed. We reverse and remand. . . .

The subrogation section of the policy provided:

> Upon payment under part II of this policy [the "medical protection" provision] the Company shall be subrogated to the extent of such payment to the proceeds of any settlement or judgment that may result from the exercise of any rights of recovery which the injured person or anyone receiving such payment may have against any person or organization and such person shall execute and deliver instruments and papers and do whatever else is necessary to secure such rights. Such person shall do nothing after loss to prejudice such rights.

Farm Bureau concedes that it cannot recover under this subrogation provision unless its insured has been "made whole" for her loss.

On the question of whether she had been made whole by her settlement with the trucker, the plaintiff proceeds from the premise that all settlements are by their nature compromises and necessarily result in less than full compensation. She testified that she had settled the case and accepted less than her actual losses because of the delay and mental stress inherent in a trial, not because her case was worth less than what she had demanded. She believed she would have received more if she had gone to trial. Under these circumstances, she argues, a presumption of inadequacy should be recognized.

Farm Bureau, on the other hand, argues that, when a settlement is made without the involvement of the subrogee, the insured is presumed to be "made whole." It argues that such rule is especially necessary where, as in this case, the insurance company's rights to proceed directly against the third party are effectively destroyed by the insured's general release of the third party. It also points to the language in the subrogation agreement which prohibits the insured from doing anything to prejudice its subrogation rights.

The district court did not adopt either of these presumptions, proceeding instead to make a determination from the evidence as to whether Ludwig had been fully compensated. It found that Ludwig's medical expenses, lost wages, expense of hired help, and car damage were established and attributed specific dollar amounts to those items. It noted that the plaintiff's medical expenses had been paid by Farm Bureau and that she had also been paid for them through the third-party settlement. It concluded, however, that she still had not been "made whole," because her claims for pain and suffering and disability had not been fully paid.

We believe this was error. An insured need not be paid in full for pain and suffering and disability before subrogation for medical expenses is allowed. Here the medical expenses advanced by Farm Bureau were made a specific item of settlement, and Jeannette Ludwig testified she knew at the time of the settlement that Farm Bureau and Blue Cross were to receive the amounts of their medical payments and that she was to get $20,000 for her other damages.

The plaintiff relies on the Wisconsin case of *Rimes v. State Farm Mutual Automobile Insurance Co.*, 316 N.W.2d 348 (Wis. 1982), which involved a similar fact situation. An insurance company, which had paid out under the medical-pay provisions of its automobile policy, attempted to recover a portion of the settlement proceeds from its insured. The district court there found, in a "mini-trial" on the subrogation claim, that the total damages to the insured parties was $300,433.54 and the settlement amount of $125,000.00 was therefore inadequate to make them whole. The Wisconsin Supreme Court, in a split decision, affirmed. . . .

In *Rimes*, there was no effort to isolate the settlement proceeds attributable to medical expenses because, under the court's approach, it would make no difference; if a third-party settlement left unsatisfied *any* elements of the claim, the insurer could not recover its medical payments. This ruling appears to stem from the Wisconsin court's view that the amounts of recovery for various elements of the third-party action cannot be separately identified. The court said that "the cause of action against a tort-feasor is indivisible. Accordingly, it is only where there has been full compensation for all the damage elements of the entire cause of action that the insured is made whole." *Id.*

A single negligent or wrongful act causing personal injury and property damage creates but one cause of action with separate items of damage. Often a subrogated amount is not coextensive with the claim against a third party; it usually involves only one element of damage as opposed to several. Nevertheless, the fact that the claims are not coextensive will not prevent recovery by a subrogated insurer. *See* 44 Am. Jur. 2d *Insurance* §1818, at 807.

> [T]he mere fact that the claim against the wrongdoer included a claim for losses not covered by insurance [and therefore not subrogated] does not prevent a release from rendering the insured liable to return the insurance money where the contract gives a right of subrogation. An insurance company which has paid a claim for property damage, for instance, to an insured automobile, has a right to share, under the principles of subrogation, in the proceeds of a recovery against or settlement with a tort-feasor in favor of the insured, who also suffered personal injuries in the same accident. In such a situation the burden of showing that the amount received by the insured represents the satisfaction of his claim for personal injuries, that is, the element of the cause of action with respect to which the insurer enjoys no right of subrogation, and not his claim for damages to the insured property, the element with respect to which the insurer may be subrogated, rests upon the insured, and in the absence of proof so showing, the recovery will be presumed to include the full amount of the property damage, and the insurer must be permitted to recover the full amount paid by it under the policy. . . .

Id. Exercising subrogation rights to some, but not all, of the claims is not considered to be a splitting of the cause of action. *Id.* §1812, at 801-02.

We disagree with the holding of the *Rimes* case. The amounts recovered against a third party for separate elements of a claim can be identified and credited toward subrogation claims, even though other elements of the third-party claim may not be fully satisfied. Allocation of the separate amounts could be done in the settlement documents, as in this case.[25] In the case of trial it could be done by special interrogatories, *Westendorf,* 330 N.W.2d at 702; *Dockendorf v. Lakie,* 61 N.W.2d 752, 756-57 (Minn. 1953), or by separate findings by the court in a nonjury case.

The purpose of subrogation is to prevent unjust enrichment of one party at the expense of another. *See* Restatement of Restitution §162, at 653 (1937); 73 Am. Jur. 2d *Subrogation* §4, at 601 (1974). When the total of the insured's recovery from a third party, and the insurance company's payments under the policy, still are less than the loss sustained, the insured has not been made whole, and the insurer may not recover against him. This principle is a salutary one; if any loss remains after reimbursement by the third party, it should be borne by the insurer who has been paid to assume such losses. Holding otherwise could result in a windfall to the insurer.

In this case, Farm Bureau's policy did not agree to indemnify Ludwig for pain and suffering or disability. Yet, denial of its claim for medical expenses because Ludwig had not also recovered for other elements of damage would have the effect of making Farm Bureau an insurer against those losses as well. This would be a windfall to an insured who has not paid for such protection.

An early Iowa case, *Chickasaw County Farmers' Mutual Fire Insurance Co. v. Weller,* 68 N.W. 443 (Iowa 1896), is analogous. There, a railroad company had caused a fire which burned a farmer's hay, pasture, and fences. The hay was insured, but the pasture and fences were not. The farmer settled with the railroad company, which paid for all of the farmer's losses, including the hay. The insurance company, which had also paid for the hay, sued the farmer for reimbursement under its subrogation clause. We held that, because the farmer's settlement with the railroad had earmarked a certain portion of it for damage to the hay, the insurer would be subrogated to that amount. This was so, even though the insured argued, as Ludwig does, that his total losses (those for the hay, pasture, and fences) exceeded his combined insurance and third-party recoveries. 68 N.W. at 444-45.

Cases from other jurisdictions have reached similar results. *See e.g. Mutual Hospitals Insurance, Inc. v. McGregor,* 368 N.E.2d 1376 (Ind. Ct. App. 1977) ($10,000 settlement; court determined approximately $5000 should be attributed to medical expenses, allowing insurance company's subrogation claim for medical expenses); *Voss v. Mike and Tony's Steakhouse,* 230 So. 2d 470 (La. Ct. App. 1969) (insurer subrogated on car damage claims; combined suit for

---

25. In the present case, the settlement amounts attributed to medical expenses were made clear by the settlement documents. In many cases, however, identification of specific amounts will be more difficult. A lump sum settlement might be made. Or the insured and the third party, perhaps being less than solicitous about the interests of a subrogee, might attempt to establish by agreement that the settlement included little or no reimbursement for medical expenses, thus increasing the insured's net recovery. *See Westendorf v. Stasson,* 330 N.W.2d 699, 702 (Minn. 1983). When the amount attributed to the subrogated claim cannot be determined by other means, a mini-trial, such as that used in *Rimes,* might be required.

property damage and personal injury settled; court segregated claims and held insured held car damage reimbursement in trust for insurer); *Davenport v. State Farm Mutual Auto Insurance Co.,* 404 P.2d 10 (Nev. 1965) (insurance company subrogated on payment of medical expense under automobile policy; settlement of $8000 for all items of damage without apportionment deems to include payment for medical expense; subrogation allowed); *Hamilton Fire Insurance Co. v. Greger,* 158 N.E. 60 (N.Y. 1927) (insured settled with third party for unsubrogated personal injury claim as well as claim for property damage, which was subrogated, without identification of amounts attributed to each; court said, if respective amounts could be identified, subrogation would be allowed); *Mattson v. Stone,* 648 P.2d 929 (Wash. Ct. App. 1982) (trial court found settlement with third party included payment for medical expense, making insured whole; insurer's subrogation claim allowed); *Transamerica Insurance Co. v. Barnes,* 505 P.2d 783 (Utah 1972) (subrogation for medical payment; summary judgment for insured reversed, case remanded for trial for determination of whether settlement had included medical expenses); *Scales v. Skagit County Medical Bureau,* 491 P.2d 1338 (Wash. Ct. App. 1971) (court apportioned part of verdict attributed to medical expense, based on percentage of verdict deemed to be collectible and gave subrogated insurance company credit accordingly). *See generally* Annot., 73 A.L.R.3d 1140 (1976); Annot., 51 A.L.R.2d 697 (1957).

We hold it was error to deny Farm Bureau's subrogation claim to the excess of Ludwig's recovery over and above her medical expenses. We remand for entry of judgment accordingly. On remand, the court shall consider whether Ludwig should be given credit for a portion of the attorney fees incurred in the collection of this amount from the third party. *See generally Skauge v. Mountain States Telephone Co.,* 565 P.2d 628 (Mont. 1977); *United Pacific Insurance Co. v. Boyd,* 661 P.2d 987 (Wash. Ct. App. 1983); *State Farm Mutual Auto Insurance Co. v. Geline,* 179 N.W.2d 815 (Wis. 1970); 6A Appleman, *supra,* §4096, at 287-88; 44 Am. Jur. 2d *Insurance* §1820, at 808. We express no view as to whether such allowance should be made.

NOTES AND QUESTIONS

1. In *Ludwig,* the settlement documents made clear how much of the settlement was paid for each of the elements of the damage. After *Ludwig,* do you expect settlement documents to be so clear? Why or why not?

2. Judge Posner addressed Wisconsin's "make-whole" rule in *Cutting v. Jerome Foods, Inc.,* 993 F.2d 1293 (7th Cir. 1993), an ERISA case involving a self-funded health plan that vested discretion over plan interpretation in the administrator:

    > [T]he "make-whole" issue is not about whether insurance subrogation is in general a good thing, as it doubtless is. A "make whole" rule does not enable the insured to gamble on double recovery, as he would be doing without subrogation. The rule comes into play only if without it the operation of the subrogation clause would, by making the insured in effect pay back the policy benefits with money he has received for another loss caused by the injury that gave rise to the policy claim, leave him with an uncompensated injury. That would be the consequence of subrogating Jerome Foods to Mrs. Cutting's tort

claim to the extent of the plan's medical benefits; the uncompensated non-medical costs that she incurred as a result of the accident would be $90,000 greater if subrogation is permitted. One can see why many state courts have thought that the inclusion of a boilerplate subrogation clause was not intended to have this effect—the effect, practically speaking, of curtailing coverage. To put this differently, rejection of "make whole" makes subrogation a lot like assignment. If insurance contracts required the insured to assign any tort claim he might have to the insurer, the price of the insurance would be lower but effective coverage would also be lower. The insured would recover only the policy limits, and not his full damages, even in a case in which a judgment had been secured against the tortfeasor, and collected, for those damages.

These arguments need not be thought decisive in favor of the make-whole rule. It is true that rejecting make whole would bring subrogation closer to assignment, but that would not necessarily be a bad thing. Assignment, by shifting the insured's tort rights to the insurance company, reduces the price of insurance and thus enables the insured to obtain more coverage, in effect trading an uncertain bundle of tort rights for a larger certain right, which is just the sort of trade that people seek through insurance. (The counter argument is that the make-whole rule is most likely to apply in a case of catastrophic loss, such as the present, where full insurance is rare.) It can also be argued against the make-whole rule that it is administratively more complex, requiring the medical insurer to calculate the insured's total medical and non-medical loss, and therefore that it makes insurance (or its equivalent in this case) more expensive to the insured—and makes it more expensive to him for the additional reason that he will have to pay for the additional coverage that the rule in effect provides. And no one's demand for insurance is unlimited. The counter argument on the administrative-complexity front is that subrogation (which the make-whole rule would eliminate in cases such as the present) involves an agency problem because of the insured's entitlement to any excess recovery that the insurer-subrogee obtains. The insurer, having no (or very little) interest in making money for the insured, may fail to press hard for an excess recovery. To which it can be replied that the make-whole rule simply shifts the disincentive to press hard from the insurer to the insured.

Fortunately we need not attempt to decide in this case whether the merits of the rule are sufficient on balance to warrant its use as a principle of interpretation of ERISA plans. Because, as the Cuttings concede, the make-whole rule is just a principle of interpretation, it can be overridden by clear language in the plan. Jerome Foods contends that the language is clear. The plan document does state rather flatly that the plan shall be subrogated to "all claims" by the covered individual against a third party to the extent of "any and all payments" made (or to be made) by the plan. But the language is no stronger than that in cases which have held that more was required to override the make-whole principle. And one of those cases (*Garrity*) is a Wisconsin case and Jerome Foods is a Wisconsin corporation (it both is incorporated in Wisconsin and has its principal place of business in that state), and this may be a clue to meaning, even though Wisconsin law does not govern the case. But at this point in the forensic badminton game the standard of judicial review becomes critical and decides the case in favor of Jerome Foods. For we cannot say that the company was unreasonable in interpreting this plan as disclaiming the make-whole principle. . . . This is as we have said a more limited form of insurance than is created by a make-whole provision, but Jerome Foods may not have been willing to provide—or the Cuttings to pay for—more generous coverage. We shall never know. We cannot say, however, that the administrator was unreasonable in concluding that the plan had disclaimed any obligation to make the Cuttings whole.

Id. at 1298-1299. Evaluate Posner's policy arguments for and against the make-whole rule. Which do you find most persuasive? Least persuasive? Why? If you were czar of the universe, which approach would you adopt: the make-whole rule or the "assignment" alternative? Why? Would you make this rule a "default" rule or an "immutable" rule (meaning that the parties could not vary it by contract)? Why? Would you prefer either of these approaches to the nonsubrogation alternatives introduced at the beginning of this section? Why? For a review of the various approaches that courts have taken to this question, see Elaine M. Rinaldi, *Apportionment of Recovery Between Insured and Insurer in a Subrogation Case,* 29 Tort & Ins. L.J. 803 (1994).

3. The rights of workers' compensation insurers to reimbursement are regulated by statute. A typical situation would be a delivery. If a truck driver is hit by a stranger while making a delivery, the truck driver would receive workers' compensation benefits because the accident happened while he was at work, but he would also be able to sue the person who caused the accident (so long as that person was not also working for the same employer at the same time). Many workers' compensation statutes provide that the workers' compensation carrier (or, if the employer "self-funds" workers' compensation benefits, the employer) is to be repaid *first* out of any settlement proceeds, precisely the opposite of the make-whole rule, while others provide that the injured worker and the workers' compensation carrier share the proceeds according to a set percentage. *See generally* Arthur Larson, Larson's Workers Compensation §117.01[1] (2001). For example, the Connecticut statute provides that the workers' compensation carrier be repaid first, while the Wisconsin statute allocates two-thirds of the recovery to the workers' compensation carrier (until the carrier is fully reimbursed). *Id.* The federal government has a similar statutory right to the first dollar of any tort payments for amounts it has paid for medical care (e.g., under Medicare). *See* 42 U.S.C.A. §2651 (2002). Why should workers' compensation and federal health benefits be treated differently than ordinary health or disability benefits?

   Empirical research suggests that, in practice, settlements are more favorable to injured victims and less favorable to workers' compensation carriers than the statutes provide. *See* Tom Baker, *Blood Money, New Money and the Moral Economy of Tort Law in Action,* 35 Law & Soc'y Rev. 275 (2001). For example, even though the Connecticut statute provides that the workers' compensation carrier is to be paid first, the standard practice in a situation in which the settlement provides less than complete compensation is the "rule of thirds," in which the plaintiff, the workers' compensation carrier, and the plaintiff's lawyer each get one-third of the settlement amount. *Id.* at 530-534. Why might the law in action be more generous to plaintiffs than the law on the books?

4. Professor Alan Sykes advanced an economics-based argument for the extension of the workers' compensation, insurer-gets-paid-first approach. *See* Alan O. Sykes, *Subrogation and Insolvency,* 30 J. Legal Stud. 383 (2001). Sykes observes that the tort goal of deterrence is unaffected by who gets paid first (can you see why?) and, thus, the decision about who gets paid first has to be resolved on the basis of some other principle. With deterrence out of the picture, the obvious goal is (efficient) compensation. (Within the dominant framework of law and economics, retribution is not regarded as a legiti-

mate goal of tort law.) In Sykes's view, each individual's choice among the available forms of first-party insurance reflects the optimal coverage for loss for that individual given the choices available in the market. From the perspective of victim compensation, tort damages are simply one more form of "coverage" for loss. Perhaps because it is very difficult to predict in advance whether there will be such tort "coverage" for loss, Sykes assumes that people do not take into account this form of coverage when choosing how much of what kinds of first-party insurance to buy. Given that assumption, the fact that a particular loss turns out to be "covered" by tort law is fortuitous from the perspective of the insured victim. If the efficient measure of compensation is what the insured victim was willing to pay for, any coverage the victim receives in excess of first-party insurance is a windfall. Between granting a larger windfall to victims or granting greater subrogation rights to insurers, the obviously better choice for Sykes is greater subrogation rights, because he believes that expanding subrogation rights will reduce the cost of first-party insurance, the clearly more efficient form of "coverage." How might putting retribution back into the picture affect this analysis?

5. Some tort observers have been wondering for years whether the benefits of subrogation outweigh the costs. It would take a fairly substantial belief in the moral hazard of tort windfalls to conclude that the amount of loss prevented by removing that windfall exceeds the additional costs imposed by subrogation. *See generally* Reuben Hasson, *Subrogation in Insurance Law—A Critical Evaluation,* 5 Oxford J. Legal Stud. 416 (1985). The standard construction contracts of the American Institute of Architects eliminate subrogation entirely for projects that use the forms. Professor Justin Sweet, who worked closely with the AIA in the development of these forms, defends that approach as follows:

> I recognize the classic arguments for subrogation, especially externalities and moral hazard. But I prefer the simplicity of the AIA approach. Subrogation claims are expensive to process. The insurer must show it is entitled to subrogation; then it must show negligence. The net recovery is not likely to be much. Usually only lawyers come out ahead.

Justin Sweet, Sweet on Construction Law 290 (1997).

CHAPTER
4

Liability Insurance

As discussed in Chapter 3, first-party insurance covers various types of risk to person or property. In some situations, however, those losses to person or property can be shifted from the injured parties—and from their first-party insurers—to the individuals or firms who are legally responsible for causing those losses. This is the realm of tort law, whose precise function is to shift losses from injured victims to legally responsible tortfeasors. Because of the presence of these potential tort claims, individuals and firms face a risk of being found liable or legally responsible for someone else's losses. This is a risk that can be (and often is) shifted to insurance companies through liability insurance policies. In sum, liability insurance covers various types of tort claims that are brought against individual and commercial policyholders.

Liability insurance can also cover other types of tort-like claims. For example, some courts have interpreted the commercial general liability (CGL) policy to cover Superfund cleanup costs imposed by the U.S. Environmental Protection Agency (EPA) on "potentially responsible parties" who are insureds. *Johnson Controls v. Employers Ins. Co. of Wausau*, 665 N.W.2d 257 (Wis. 2003) (holding, among other things, that environmental response costs are insured "damages" under the CGL policy). Liability insurance policies do not necessarily cover all claims for civil damages, however. Liability insurance policies, for example, often are interpreted not to cover run-of-the-mill breach of contract claims brought against insureds.

Liability insurance is also called "third-party insurance." Who the third party is depends on one's perspective. From the perspective of the covered liability claim, the two primary parties are the person bringing the claim and the insured defendant, and the third party is the defendant's liability insurance company. From the perspective of the liability insurance contract, the two main parties are the insurance company and the policyholder, and the third party is the person bringing the claim against the policyholder. As these two perspectives suggest, liability insurance implicates both tort law and contract law. Indeed, liability insurance is one of the most significant meeting points between these two legal fields.

This chapter is divided into three sections that correspond to the three most significant types of liability insurance: general liability insurance, auto liability insurance, and professional liability insurance. Liability insurance was invented in England in the late nineteenth century following the adoption of the employers' liability act. *See* Kenneth A. Abraham, The Liability Century (2008). The first policies were employers' liability policies that covered employers for claims arising under the act. When businesses got used to the idea of liability insurance they realized that they also could benefit from insurance against claims brought by the general public. The new liability insurance companies began offering "public liability" policies that, over time, became the general liability policies that we will study. Today's auto liability policies evolved from the teamster liability policies invented around the turn of the twentieth century. As we will see, professional liability insurance may be in the process of becoming a catchall category that would be more accurately described as errors and omissions or wrongful acts coverage. The "professional liability" label reflects the origins of the category in liability insurance sold to members of the historic professions: medicine and law.

I.   GENERAL LIABILITY INSURANCE

As the name "general liability insurance" suggests, this kind of liability insurance provides protection against a broad range of liability claims. There are stand-alone general liability insurance policies, and there are general liability coverage parts of package policies like homeowners' insurance, renters' insurance, landlords' insurance, and business owners' policies. When the term "general liability insurance" was first invented, the liability insurance protection provided by the policy probably covered all or most of the tort liabilities that a business enterprise faced, with the main exception of transportation-related liability claims, which were covered by auto and trucking policies. Perhaps for that reason, the liability insurance industry began calling these policies Comprehensive General Liability Insurance, an attractive name for marketing purposes that was replaced by the more accurate name "Commercial General Liability Insurance" in the mid-1980s, after the industry suffered from the consequences of the word "comprehensive" in asbestos insurance coverage litigation.

Like the property insurance policies that we studied in the last chapter, general liability insurance is an all risks form of insurance. There is a broad grant of coverage in the insuring agreement of the policy, followed by exclusions that narrow that grant of coverage, in addition to definitions and conditions that further limit the coverage and that establish notice, claims, and other procedures that the insurance company imposes on the purchaser.

We begin the general liability unit by examining the main technical problem addressed by the liability insurance contract: determining which claims are covered by which liability insurance policies. We start with an asbestos case that illustrates how difficult it can be to decide which insurance policy applies to a latent harm. We will then go through a series of simple problems that will acquaint you with how the insuring agreements in different kinds of liability insurance policies address the problem of specifying which liability insurance policies apply to a claim.

After exploring the insuring agreement, the general liability section addresses some important exclusions and conditions, some of which also appear in other forms of liability insurance. The culmination of the section is a set of materials addressing the problem of intentional harm. As with the coverage issues addressed in Chapter 3, the goal here is to teach you how to work with liability insurance policies and cases. It is difficult to predict the major liability insurance coverage issues of the future, but we can be certain that they will be decided using analytical approaches developed in resolving the major coverage issues of the past. Although of course it is important to understand the details involved in the cases, it is even more important to remember that the main goal is to develop a broader understanding of the dynamics of the liability insurance relationship.

A. *Understanding the Insuring Agreement*

This exploration of general liability insurance begins with cases and problems that address the interpretation of the "insuring agreement" of the standard general purpose liability policy. In the business market, this policy is called the CGL when it is sold as a separate liability policy and the liability coverage part when it is sold as part of a package policy. In the personal market, nearly identical provisions appear in the liability insurance part of the standard homeowner's, renter's, or condominium unit-owner's policy. Taken together, these liability insurance policies provide the basic non-automobile tort liability insurance coverage for most people and businesses in the United States.

Figure 4.1 (see pages 318-319) is a reproduction of the "Declarations" for CGL policies. Figure 4.2 (see pages 320-335) is a reproduction of a recent "occurrence" version of the CGL coverage form.

1. Trigger of Coverage

Our first liability insurance case explores the trigger of coverage in the context of asbestos bodily injury. As the court in that case succinctly explains, "trigger of coverage" is a "shorthand expression for identifying the events that must occur during a policy period to require coverage for losses sustained by the policyholder."

For the classic U.S. liability claim—the auto accident—trigger of coverage is almost never an issue. The auto policy covers "accidents" that take place during the policy period. Absent very unusual circumstances (such as an auto entering a skid at the stroke of midnight at the end of one policy period and colliding with a wall ten seconds into the next policy period), it is fairly straightforward to determine whether there was an "accident" during the "policy period."

In the past, general liability insurance policies also had an accident trigger, meaning that the policies would cover "accidents" that took place during the policy period. But a series of cases in the 1950s and 1960s revealed that what an accident isn't always as clear in the general liability context. Accidents are easy to identify when a cause and the resulting injury are both obvious and instantaneous (or nearly so). However, when either the cause or the injury takes place over time, there is a legitimate dispute about when the accident took place. Was it the cause or the injury? If it was the cause, was it the beginning of the cause or the whole period during which the causal events took place? Some insurance companies even took the position that something that took place over time was not an accident at all, because accidents, by definition, happen all at once.

POLICY NUMBER: **COMMERCIAL GENERAL LIABILITY**
                                                        CG DS 01 10 01

COMMERCIAL GENERAL LIABILITY DECLARATIONS

COMPANY NAME AREA	PRODUCER NAME AREA

NAMED INSURED: _____

MAILING ADDRESS: _____
_____

POLICY PERIOD: FROM _____ TO _____ AT 12:01 A.M. TIME AT
YOUR MAILING ADDRESS SHOWN ABOVE

**IN RETURN FOR THE PAYMENT OF THE PREMIUM, AND SUBJECT TO ALL THE TERMS OF THIS
POLICY, WE AGREE WITH YOU TO PROVIDE THE INSURANCE AS STATED IN THIS POLICY.**

LIMITS OF INSURANCE		
EACH OCCURRENCE LIMIT	$ _____	
DAMAGE TO PREMISES		
RENTED TO YOU LIMIT	$ _____	Any one premises
MEDICAL EXPENSE LIMIT	$ _____	Any one person
PERSONAL & ADVERTISING INJURY LIMIT	$ _____	Any one person or organization
GENERAL AGGREGATE LIMIT		$ _____
PRODUCTS/COMPLETED OPERATIONS AGGREGATE LIMIT		$ _____

RETROACTIVE DATE (CG 00 02 ONLY)
THIS INSURANCE DOES NOT APPLY TO "BODILY INJURY", "PROPERTY DAMAGE" OR "PERSONAL AND ADVERTISING INJURY" WHICH OCCURS BEFORE THE RETROACTIVE DATE, IF ANY, SHOWN BELOW. RETROACTIVE DATE: _____ (ENTER DATE OR "NONE" IF NO RETROACTIVE DATE APPLIES)

DESCRIPTION OF BUSINESS
FORM OF BUSINESS:

☐ INDIVIDUAL   ☐ PARTNERSHIP   ☐ JOINT VENTURE   ☐ TRUST

☐ LIMITED LIABILITY COMPANY   ☐ ORGANIZATION, INCLUDING A CORPORATION (BUT NOT IN-
                                CLUDING A PARTNERSHIP, JOINT VENTURE OR LIMITED LIABILITY
                                COMPANY)

BUSINESS DESCRIPTION: _____

CG DS 01 10 01   © ISO Properties, Inc., 2000   Page 1 of 2   ☐

Figure 4.1.   Commercial General Liability Declarations

ALL PREMISES YOU OWN, RENT OR OCCUPY	
LOCATION NUMBER	ADDRESS OF ALL PREMISES YOU OWN, RENT OR OCCUPY

CLASSIFICATION AND PREMIUM

LOCATION NUMBER	CLASSIFICATION	CODE NO.	PREMIUM BASE	RATE		ADVANCE PREMIUM	
				Prem/ Ops	Prod/Comp Ops	Prem/ Ops	Prod/Comp Ops
			$	$	$	$	$

	STATE TAX OR OTHER (if applicable)	$ _____
	TOTAL PREMIUM (SUBJECT TO AUDIT)	$ _____
PREMIUM SHOWN IS PAYABLE:	AT INCEPTION	$ _____
	AT EACH ANNIVERSARY	$ _____
	(IF POLICY PERIOD IS MORE THAN ONE YEAR AND PREMIUM IS PAID IN ANNUAL INSTALLMENTS)	

AUDIT PERIOD (IF APPLICABLE)	☐ ANNUALLY	☐ SEMI-ANNUALLY	☐ QUARTERLY	☐ MONTHLY

ENDORSEMENTS
ENDORSEMENTS ATTACHED TO THIS POLICY:
_____ _____ _____

THESE DECLARATIONS, TOGETHER WITH THE COMMON POLICY CONDITIONS AND COVERAGE FORM(S) AND ANY ENDORSEMENT(S), COMPLETE THE ABOVE NUMBERED POLICY.

Countersigned:	By:
(Date)	(Authorized Representative)

NOTE

OFFICERS' FACSIMILE SIGNATURES MAY BE INSERTED HERE, ON THE POLICY COVER OR ELSEWHERE AT THE COMPANY'S OPTION.

COMMERCIAL GENERAL LIABILITY COVERAGE FORM

Various provisions in this policy restrict coverage. Read the entire policy carefully to determine rights, duties and what is and is not covered.

Throughout this policy the words "you" and "your" refer to the Named Insured shown in the Declarations, and any other person or organization qualifying as a Named Insured under this policy. The words "we", "us" and "our" refer to the company providing this insurance.

The word "insured" means any person or organization qualifying as such under Section II – Who Is An Insured.

Other words and phrases that appear in quotation marks have special meaning. Refer to Section V – Definitions.

SECTION I – COVERAGES

COVERAGE A – BODILY INJURY AND PROPERTY DAMAGE LIABILITY

1. Insuring Agreement

   a. We will pay those sums that the insured becomes legally obligated to pay as damages because of "bodily injury" or "property damage" to which this insurance applies. We will have the right and duty to defend the insured against any "suit" seeking those damages. However, we will have no duty to defend the insured against any "suit" seeking damages for "bodily injury" or "property damage" to which this insurance does not apply. We may, at our discretion, investigate any "occurrence" and settle any claim or "suit" that may result. But:

     (1) The amount we will pay for damages is limited as described in Section III – Limits Of Insurance; and

     (2) Our right and duty to defend ends when we have used up the applicable limit of insurance in the payment of judgments or settlements under Coverages **A** or **B** or medical expenses under Coverage **C**.

     No other obligation or liability to pay sums or perform acts or services is covered unless explicitly provided for under Supplementary Payments – Coverages **A** and **B**.

   b. This insurance applies to "bodily injury" and "property damage" only if:

     (1) The "bodily injury" or "property damage" is caused by an "occurrence" that takes place in the "coverage territory";

     (2) The "bodily injury" or "property damage" occurs during the policy period; and

     (3) Prior to the policy period, no insured listed under Paragraph **1.** of Section II – Who Is An Insured and no "employee" authorized by you to give or receive notice of an "occurrence" or claim, knew that the "bodily injury" or "property damage" had occurred, in whole or in part. If such a listed insured or authorized "employee" knew, prior to the policy period, that the "bodily injury" or "property damage" occurred, then any continuation, change or resumption of such "bodily injury" or "property damage" during or after the policy period will be deemed to have been known prior to the policy period.

   c. "Bodily injury" or "property damage" which occurs during the policy period and was not, prior to the policy period, known to have occurred by any insured listed under Paragraph **1.** of Section II – Who Is An Insured or any "employee" authorized by you to give or receive notice of an "occurrence" or claim, includes any continuation, change or resumption of that "bodily injury" or "property damage" after the end of the policy period.

   d. "Bodily injury" or "property damage" will be deemed to have been known to have occurred at the earliest time when any insured listed under Paragraph **1.** of Section II – Who Is An Insured or any "employee" authorized by you to give or receive notice of an "occurrence" or claim:

     (1) Reports all, or any part, of the "bodily injury" or "property damage" to us or any other insurer;

     (2) Receives a written or verbal demand or claim for damages because of the "bodily injury" or "property damage"; or

     (3) Becomes aware by any other means that "bodily injury" or "property damage" has occurred or has begun to occur.

   e. Damages because of "bodily injury" include damages claimed by any person or organization for care, loss of services or death resulting at any time from the "bodily injury".

 © Insurance Services Office, Inc., 2012

Fig 4.2.   Commercial General Liability Coverage Form (Occurrence Version)

2. Exclusions

This insurance does not apply to:

a. Expected Or Intended Injury

"Bodily injury" or "property damage" expected or intended from the standpoint of the insured. This exclusion does not apply to "bodily injury" resulting from the use of reasonable force to protect persons or property.

b. Contractual Liability

"Bodily injury" or "property damage" for which the insured is obligated to pay damages by reason of the assumption of liability in a contract or agreement. This exclusion does not apply to liability for damages:

(1) That the insured would have in the absence of the contract or agreement; or

(2) Assumed in a contract or agreement that is an "insured contract", provided the "bodily injury" or "property damage" occurs subsequent to the execution of the contract or agreement. Solely for the purposes of liability assumed in an "insured contract", reasonable attorneys' fees and necessary litigation expenses incurred by or for a party other than an insured are deemed to be damages because of "bodily injury" or "property damage", provided:

(a) Liability to such party for, or for the cost of, that party's defense has also been assumed in the same "insured contract"; and

(b) Such attorneys' fees and litigation expenses are for defense of that party against a civil or alternative dispute resolution proceeding in which damages to which this insurance applies are alleged.

c. Liquor Liability

"Bodily injury" or "property damage" for which any insured may be held liable by reason of:

(1) Causing or contributing to the intoxication of any person;

(2) The furnishing of alcoholic beverages to a person under the legal drinking age or under the influence of alcohol; or

(3) Any statute, ordinance or regulation relating to the sale, gift, distribution or use of alcoholic beverages.

This exclusion applies even if the claims against any insured allege negligence or other wrongdoing in:

(a) The supervision, hiring, employment, training or monitoring of others by that insured; or

(b) Providing or failing to provide transportation with respect to any person that may be under the influence of alcohol;

if the "occurrence" which caused the "bodily injury" or "property damage", involved that which is described in Paragraph **(1)**, **(2)** or **(3)** above.

However, this exclusion applies only if you are in the business of manufacturing, distributing, selling, serving or furnishing alcoholic beverages. For the purposes of this exclusion, permitting a person to bring alcoholic beverages on your premises, for consumption on your premises, whether or not a fee is charged or a license is required for such activity, is not by itself considered the business of selling, serving or furnishing alcoholic beverages.

d. Workers' Compensation And Similar Laws

Any obligation of the insured under a workers' compensation, disability benefits or unemployment compensation law or any similar law.

e. Employer's Liability

"Bodily injury" to:

(1) An "employee" of the insured arising out of and in the course of:

(a) Employment by the insured; or

(b) Performing duties related to the conduct of the insured's business; or

(2) The spouse, child, parent, brother or sister of that "employee" as a consequence of Paragraph **(1)** above.

This exclusion applies whether the insured may be liable as an employer or in any other capacity and to any obligation to share damages with or repay someone else who must pay damages because of the injury.

This exclusion does not apply to liability assumed by the insured under an "insured contract".

f. Pollution

(1) "Bodily injury" or "property damage" arising out of the actual, alleged or threatened discharge, dispersal, seepage, migration, release or escape of "pollutants":

(a) At or from any premises, site or location which is or was at any time owned or occupied by, or rented or loaned to, any insured. However, this subparagraph does not apply to:

(i) "Bodily injury" if sustained within a building and caused by smoke, fumes, vapor or soot produced by or originating from equipment that is used to heat, cool or dehumidify the building, or equipment that is used to heat water for personal use, by the building's occupants or their guests;

(ii) "Bodily injury" or "property damage" for which you may be held liable, if you are a contractor and the owner or lessee of such premises, site or location has been added to your policy as an additional insured with respect to your ongoing operations performed for that additional insured at that premises, site or location and such premises, site or location is not and never was owned or occupied by, or rented or loaned to, any insured, other than that additional insured; or

(iii) "Bodily injury" or "property damage" arising out of heat, smoke or fumes from a "hostile fire";

(b) At or from any premises, site or location which is or was at any time used by or for any insured or others for the handling, storage, disposal, processing or treatment of waste;

(c) Which are or were at any time transported, handled, stored, treated, disposed of, or processed as waste by or for:

(i) Any insured; or

(ii) Any person or organization for whom you may be legally responsible; or

(d) At or from any premises, site or location on which any insured or any contractors or subcontractors working directly or indirectly on any insured's behalf are performing operations if the "pollutants" are brought on or to the premises, site or location in connection with such operations by such insured, contractor or subcontractor. However, this subparagraph does not apply to:

(i) "Bodily injury" or "property damage" arising out of the escape of fuels, lubricants or other operating fluids which are needed to perform the normal electrical, hydraulic or mechanical functions necessary for the operation of "mobile equipment" or its parts, if such fuels, lubricants or other operating fluids escape from a vehicle part designed to hold, store or receive them. This exception does not apply if the "bodily injury" or "property damage" arises out of the intentional discharge, dispersal or release of the fuels, lubricants or other operating fluids, or if such fuels, lubricants or other operating fluids are brought on or to the premises, site or location with the intent that they be discharged, dispersed or released as part of the operations being performed by such insured, contractor or subcontractor;

(ii) "Bodily injury" or "property damage" sustained within a building and caused by the release of gases, fumes or vapors from materials brought into that building in connection with operations being performed by you or on your behalf by a contractor or subcontractor; or

(iii) "Bodily injury" or "property damage" arising out of heat, smoke or fumes from a "hostile fire".

(e) At or from any premises, site or location on which any insured or any contractors or subcontractors working directly or indirectly on any insured's behalf are performing operations if the operations are to test for, monitor, clean up, remove, contain, treat, detoxify or neutralize, or in any way respond to, or assess the effects of, "pollutants".

(2) Any loss, cost or expense arising out of any:

(a) Request, demand, order or statutory or regulatory requirement that any insured or others test for, monitor, clean up, remove, contain, treat, detoxify or neutralize, or in any way respond to, or assess the effects of, "pollutants"; or

(b) Claim or suit by or on behalf of a governmental authority for damages because of testing for, monitoring, cleaning up, removing, containing, treating, detoxifying or neutralizing, or in any way responding to, or assessing the effects of, "pollutants".

However, this paragraph does not apply to liability for damages because of "property damage" that the insured would have in the absence of such request, demand, order or statutory or regulatory requirement, or such claim or "suit" by or on behalf of a governmental authority.

g. Aircraft, Auto Or Watercraft

"Bodily injury" or "property damage" arising out of the ownership, maintenance, use or entrustment to others of any aircraft, "auto" or watercraft owned or operated by or rented or loaned to any insured. Use includes operation and "loading or unloading".

This exclusion applies even if the claims against any insured allege negligence or other wrongdoing in the supervision, hiring, employment, training or monitoring of others by that insured, if the "occurrence" which caused the "bodily injury" or "property damage" involved the ownership, maintenance, use or entrustment to others of any aircraft, "auto" or watercraft that is owned or operated by or rented or loaned to any insured.

This exclusion does not apply to:

(1) A watercraft while ashore on premises you own or rent;

(2) A watercraft you do not own that is:

(a) Less than 26 feet long; and

(b) Not being used to carry persons or property for a charge;

(3) Parking an "auto" on, or on the ways next to, premises you own or rent, provided the "auto" is not owned by or rented or loaned to you or the insured;

(4) Liability assumed under any "insured contract" for the ownership, maintenance or use of aircraft or watercraft; or

(5) "Bodily injury" or "property damage" arising out of:

(a) The operation of machinery or equipment that is attached to, or part of, a land vehicle that would qualify under the definition of "mobile equipment" if it were not subject to a compulsory or financial responsibility law or other motor vehicle insurance law where it is licensed or principally garaged; or

(b) The operation of any of the machinery or equipment listed in Paragraph **f.(2)** or **f.(3)** of the definition of "mobile equipment".

h. Mobile Equipment

"Bodily injury" or "property damage" arising out of:

(1) The transportation of "mobile equipment" by an "auto" owned or operated by or rented or loaned to any insured; or

(2) The use of "mobile equipment" in, or while in practice for, or while being prepared for, any prearranged racing, speed, demolition, or stunting activity.

i. War

"Bodily injury" or "property damage", however caused, arising, directly or indirectly, out of:

(1) War, including undeclared or civil war;

(2) Warlike action by a military force, including action in hindering or defending against an actual or expected attack, by any government, sovereign or other authority using military personnel or other agents; or

(3) Insurrection, rebellion, revolution, usurped power, or action taken by governmental authority in hindering or defending against any of these.

j. Damage To Property

"Property damage" to:

(1) Property you own, rent, or occupy, including any costs or expenses incurred by you, or any other person, organization or entity, for repair, replacement, enhancement, restoration or maintenance of such property for any reason, including prevention of injury to a person or damage to another's property;

(2) Premises you sell, give away or abandon, if the "property damage" arises out of any part of those premises;

(3) Property loaned to you;

© Insurance Services Office, Inc., 2012

(4) Personal property in the care, custody or control of the insured;

(5) That particular part of real property on which you or any contractors or subcontractors working directly or indirectly on your behalf are performing operations, if the "property damage" arises out of those operations; or

(6) That particular part of any property that must be restored, repaired or replaced because "your work" was incorrectly performed on it.

Paragraphs **(1)**, **(3)** and **(4)** of this exclusion do not apply to "property damage" (other than damage by fire) to premises, including the contents of such premises, rented to you for a period of seven or fewer consecutive days. A separate limit of insurance applies to Damage To Premises Rented To You as described in Section **III** – Limits Of Insurance.

Paragraph **(2)** of this exclusion does not apply if the premises are "your work" and were never occupied, rented or held for rental by you.

Paragraphs **(3)**, **(4)**, **(5)** and **(6)** of this exclusion do not apply to liability assumed under a sidetrack agreement.

Paragraph **(6)** of this exclusion does not apply to "property damage" included in the "products-completed operations hazard".

k. Damage To Your Product

"Property damage" to "your product" arising out of it or any part of it.

l. Damage To Your Work

"Property damage" to "your work" arising out of it or any part of it and included in the "products-completed operations hazard".

This exclusion does not apply if the damaged work or the work out of which the damage arises was performed on your behalf by a subcontractor.

m. Damage To Impaired Property Or Property Not Physically Injured

"Property damage" to "impaired property" or property that has not been physically injured, arising out of:

(1) A defect, deficiency, inadequacy or dangerous condition in "your product" or "your work"; or

(2) A delay or failure by you or anyone acting on your behalf to perform a contract or agreement in accordance with its terms.

This exclusion does not apply to the loss of use of other property arising out of sudden and accidental physical injury to "your product" or "your work" after it has been put to its intended use.

n. Recall Of Products, Work Or Impaired Property

Damages claimed for any loss, cost or expense incurred by you or others for the loss of use, withdrawal, recall, inspection, repair, replacement, adjustment, removal or disposal of:

(1) "Your product";

(2) "Your work"; or

(3) "Impaired property";

if such product, work, or property is withdrawn or recalled from the market or from use by any person or organization because of a known or suspected defect, deficiency, inadequacy or dangerous condition in it.

o. Personal And Advertising Injury

"Bodily injury" arising out of "personal and advertising injury".

p. Electronic Data

Damages arising out of the loss of, loss of use of, damage to, corruption of, inability to access, or inability to manipulate electronic data.

However, this exclusion does not apply to liability for damages because of "bodily injury".

As used in this exclusion, electronic data means information, facts or programs stored as or on, created or used on, or transmitted to or from computer software, including systems and applications software, hard or floppy disks, CD-ROMs, tapes, drives, cells, data processing devices or any other media which are used with electronically controlled equipment.

q. Recording And Distribution Of Material Or Information In Violation Of Law

"Bodily injury" or "property damage" arising directly or indirectly out of any action or omission that violates or is alleged to violate:

(1) The Telephone Consumer Protection Act (TCPA), including any amendment of or addition to such law;

(2) The CAN-SPAM Act of 2003, including any amendment of or addition to such law;

(3) The Fair Credit Reporting Act (FCRA), and any amendment of or addition to such law, including the Fair and Accurate Credit Transactions Act (FACTA); or

(4) Any federal, state or local statute, ordinance or regulation, other than the TCPA, CAN-SPAM Act of 2003 or FCRA and their amendments and additions, that addresses, prohibits, or limits the printing, dissemination, disposal, collecting, recording, sending, transmitting, communicating or distribution of material or information.

Exclusions **c.** through **n.** do not apply to damage by fire to premises while rented to you or temporarily occupied by you with permission of the owner. A separate limit of insurance applies to this coverage as described in Section **III** – Limits Of Insurance.

COVERAGE B – PERSONAL AND ADVERTISING INJURY LIABILITY

1. Insuring Agreement

a. We will pay those sums that the insured becomes legally obligated to pay as damages because of "personal and advertising injury" to which this insurance applies. We will have the right and duty to defend the insured against any "suit" seeking those damages. However, we will have no duty to defend the insured against any "suit" seeking damages for "personal and advertising injury" to which this insurance does not apply. We may, at our discretion, investigate any offense and settle any claim or "suit" that may result. But:

(1) The amount we will pay for damages is limited as described in Section **III** – Limits Of Insurance; and

(2) Our right and duty to defend end when we have used up the applicable limit of insurance in the payment of judgments or settlements under Coverages **A** or **B** or medical expenses under Coverage **C**.

No other obligation or liability to pay sums or perform acts or services is covered unless explicitly provided for under Supplementary Payments – Coverages **A** and **B**.

b. This insurance applies to "personal and advertising injury" caused by an offense arising out of your business but only if the offense was committed in the "coverage territory" during the policy period.

2. Exclusions

This insurance does not apply to:

a. Knowing Violation Of Rights Of Another

"Personal and advertising injury" caused by or at the direction of the insured with the knowledge that the act would violate the rights of another and would inflict "personal and advertising injury".

b. Material Published With Knowledge Of Falsity

"Personal and advertising injury" arising out of oral or written publication, in any manner, of material, if done by or at the direction of the insured with knowledge of its falsity.

c. Material Published Prior To Policy Period

"Personal and advertising injury" arising out of oral or written publication, in any manner, of material whose first publication took place before the beginning of the policy period.

d. Criminal Acts

"Personal and advertising injury" arising out of a criminal act committed by or at the direction of the insured.

e. Contractual Liability

"Personal and advertising injury" for which the insured has assumed liability in a contract or agreement. This exclusion does not apply to liability for damages that the insured would have in the absence of the contract or agreement.

f. Breach Of Contract

"Personal and advertising injury" arising out of a breach of contract, except an implied contract to use another's advertising idea in your "advertisement".

g. Quality Or Performance Of Goods – Failure To Conform To Statements

"Personal and advertising injury" arising out of the failure of goods, products or services to conform with any statement of quality or performance made in your "advertisement".

h. Wrong Description Of Prices

"Personal and advertising injury" arising out of the wrong description of the price of goods, products or services stated in your "advertisement".

© Insurance Services Office, Inc., 2012
CG 00 01 04 13

i. **Infringement Of Copyright, Patent, Trademark Or Trade Secret**

"Personal and advertising injury" arising out of the infringement of copyright, patent, trademark, trade secret or other intellectual property rights. Under this exclusion, such other intellectual property rights do not include the use of another's advertising idea in your "advertisement".

However, this exclusion does not apply to infringement, in your "advertisement", of copyright, trade dress or slogan.

j. **Insureds In Media And Internet Type Businesses**

"Personal and advertising injury" committed by an insured whose business is:

(1) Advertising, broadcasting, publishing or telecasting;

(2) Designing or determining content of web sites for others; or

(3) An Internet search, access, content or service provider.

However, this exclusion does not apply to Paragraphs **14.a., b.** and **c.** of "personal and advertising injury" under the Definitions section.

For the purposes of this exclusion, the placing of frames, borders or links, or advertising, for you or others anywhere on the Internet, is not by itself, considered the business of advertising, broadcasting, publishing or telecasting.

k. **Electronic Chatrooms Or Bulletin Boards**

"Personal and advertising injury" arising out of an electronic chatroom or bulletin board the insured hosts, owns, or over which the insured exercises control.

l. **Unauthorized Use Of Another's Name Or Product**

"Personal and advertising injury" arising out of the unauthorized use of another's name or product in your e-mail address, domain name or metatag, or any other similar tactics to mislead another's potential customers.

m. **Pollution**

"Personal and advertising injury" arising out of the actual, alleged or threatened discharge, dispersal, seepage, migration, release or escape of "pollutants" at any time.

n. **Pollution-related**

Any loss, cost or expense arising out of any:

(1) Request, demand, order or statutory or regulatory requirement that any insured or others test for, monitor, clean up, remove, contain, treat, detoxify or neutralize, or in any way respond to, or assess the effects of, "pollutants"; or

(2) Claim or suit by or on behalf of a governmental authority for damages because of testing for, monitoring, cleaning up, removing, containing, treating, detoxifying or neutralizing, or in any way responding to, or assessing the effects of, "pollutants".

o. **War**

"Personal and advertising injury", however caused, arising, directly or indirectly, out of:

(1) War, including undeclared or civil war;

(2) Warlike action by a military force, including action in hindering or defending against an actual or expected attack, by any government, sovereign or other authority using military personnel or other agents; or

(3) Insurrection, rebellion, revolution, usurped power, or action taken by governmental authority in hindering or defending against any of these.

p. **Recording And Distribution Of Material Or Information In Violation Of Law**

"Personal and advertising injury" arising directly or indirectly out of any action or omission that violates or is alleged to violate:

(1) The Telephone Consumer Protection Act (TCPA), including any amendment of or addition to such law;

(2) The CAN-SPAM Act of 2003, including any amendment of or addition to such law;

(3) The Fair Credit Reporting Act (FCRA), and any amendment of or addition to such law, including the Fair and Accurate Credit Transactions Act (FACTA); or

(4) Any federal, state or local statute, ordinance or regulation, other than the TCPA, CAN-SPAM Act of 2003 or FCRA and their amendments and additions, that addresses, prohibits, or limits the printing, dissemination, disposal, collecting, recording, sending, transmitting, communicating or distribution of material or information.

COVERAGE C – MEDICAL PAYMENTS

1. Insuring Agreement

  a. We will pay medical expenses as described below for "bodily injury" caused by an accident:

    (1) On premises you own or rent;

    (2) On ways next to premises you own or rent; or

    (3) Because of your operations;

    provided that:

      (a) The accident takes place in the "coverage territory" and during the policy period;

      (b) The expenses are incurred and reported to us within one year of the date of the accident; and

      (c) The injured person submits to examination, at our expense, by physicians of our choice as often as we reasonably require.

  b. We will make these payments regardless of fault. These payments will not exceed the applicable limit of insurance. We will pay reasonable expenses for:

    (1) First aid administered at the time of an accident;

    (2) Necessary medical, surgical, X-ray and dental services, including prosthetic devices; and

    (3) Necessary ambulance, hospital, professional nursing and funeral services.

2. Exclusions

We will not pay expenses for "bodily injury":

  a. Any Insured

    To any insured, except "volunteer workers".

  b. Hired Person

    To a person hired to do work for or on behalf of any insured or a tenant of any insured.

  c. Injury On Normally Occupied Premises

    To a person injured on that part of premises you own or rent that the person normally occupies.

  d. Workers' Compensation And Similar Laws

    To a person, whether or not an "employee" of any insured, if benefits for the "bodily injury" are payable or must be provided under a workers' compensation or disability benefits law or a similar law.

  e. Athletics Activities

    To a person injured while practicing, instructing or participating in any physical exercises or games, sports, or athletic contests.

  f. Products-Completed Operations Hazard

    Included within the "products-completed operations hazard".

  g. Coverage A Exclusions

    Excluded under Coverage **A**.

SUPPLEMENTARY PAYMENTS – COVERAGES A AND B

1. We will pay, with respect to any claim we investigate or settle, or any "suit" against an insured we defend:

  a. All expenses we incur.

  b. Up to $250 for cost of bail bonds required because of accidents or traffic law violations arising out of the use of any vehicle to which the Bodily Injury Liability Coverage applies. We do not have to furnish these bonds.

  c. The cost of bonds to release attachments, but only for bond amounts within the applicable limit of insurance. We do not have to furnish these bonds.

  d. All reasonable expenses incurred by the insured at our request to assist us in the investigation or defense of the claim or "suit", including actual loss of earnings up to $250 a day because of time off from work.

  e. All court costs taxed against the insured in the "suit". However, these payments do not include attorneys' fees or attorneys' expenses taxed against the insured.

  f. Prejudgment interest awarded against the insured on that part of the judgment we pay. If we make an offer to pay the applicable limit of insurance, we will not pay any prejudgment interest based on that period of time after the offer.

 © Insurance Services Office, Inc., 2012 CG 00 01 04 13

g. All interest on the full amount of any judgment that accrues after entry of the judgment and before we have paid, offered to pay, or deposited in court the part of the judgment that is within the applicable limit of insurance.

These payments will not reduce the limits of insurance.

2. If we defend an insured against a "suit" and an indemnitee of the insured is also named as a party to the "suit", we will defend that indemnitee if all of the following conditions are met:

a. The "suit" against the indemnitee seeks damages for which the insured has assumed the liability of the indemnitee in a contract or agreement that is an "insured contract";

b. This insurance applies to such liability assumed by the insured;

c. The obligation to defend, or the cost of the defense of, that indemnitee, has also been assumed by the insured in the same "insured contract";

d. The allegations in the "suit" and the information we know about the "occurrence" are such that no conflict appears to exist between the interests of the insured and the interests of the indemnitee;

e. The indemnitee and the insured ask us to conduct and control the defense of that indemnitee against such "suit" and agree that we can assign the same counsel to defend the insured and the indemnitee; and

f. The indemnitee:

(1) Agrees in writing to:

(a) Cooperate with us in the investigation, settlement or defense of the "suit";

(b) Immediately send us copies of any demands, notices, summonses or legal papers received in connection with the "suit";

(c) Notify any other insurer whose coverage is available to the indemnitee; and

(d) Cooperate with us with respect to coordinating other applicable insurance available to the indemnitee; and

(2) Provides us with written authorization to:

(a) Obtain records and other information related to the "suit"; and

(b) Conduct and control the defense of the indemnitee in such "suit".

So long as the above conditions are met, attorneys' fees incurred by us in the defense of that indemnitee, necessary litigation expenses incurred by us and necessary litigation expenses incurred by the indemnitee at our request will be paid as Supplementary Payments. Notwithstanding the provisions of Paragraph **2.b.(2)** of Section **I** – Coverage **A** – Bodily Injury And Property Damage Liability, such payments will not be deemed to be damages for "bodily injury" and "property damage" and will not reduce the limits of insurance.

Our obligation to defend an insured's indemnitee and to pay for attorneys' fees and necessary litigation expenses as Supplementary Payments ends when we have used up the applicable limit of insurance in the payment of judgments or settlements or the conditions set forth above, or the terms of the agreement described in Paragraph **f.** above, are no longer met.

SECTION II – WHO IS AN INSURED

1. If you are designated in the Declarations as:

a. An individual, you and your spouse are insureds, but only with respect to the conduct of a business of which you are the sole owner.

b. A partnership or joint venture, you are an insured. Your members, your partners, and their spouses are also insureds, but only with respect to the conduct of your business.

c. A limited liability company, you are an insured. Your members are also insureds, but only with respect to the conduct of your business. Your managers are insureds, but only with respect to their duties as your managers.

d. An organization other than a partnership, joint venture or limited liability company, you are an insured. Your "executive officers" and directors are insureds, but only with respect to their duties as your officers or directors. Your stockholders are also insureds, but only with respect to their liability as stockholders.

e. A trust, you are an insured. Your trustees are also insureds, but only with respect to their duties as trustees.

2. Each of the following is also an insured:

a. Your "volunteer workers" only while performing duties related to the conduct of your business, or your "employees", other than either your "executive officers" (if you are an organization other than a partnership, joint venture or limited liability company) or your managers (if you are a limited liability company), but only for acts within the scope of their employment by you or while performing duties related to the conduct of your business. However, none of these "employees" or "volunteer workers" are insureds for:

(1) "Bodily injury" or "personal and advertising injury":

(a) To you, to your partners or members (if you are a partnership or joint venture), to your members (if you are a limited liability company), to a co-"employee" while in the course of his or her employment or performing duties related to the conduct of your business, or to your other "volunteer workers" while performing duties related to the conduct of your business;

(b) To the spouse, child, parent, brother or sister of that co-"employee" or "volunteer worker" as a consequence of Paragraph **(1)(a)** above;

(c) For which there is any obligation to share damages with or repay someone else who must pay damages because of the injury described in Paragraph **(1)(a)** or **(b)** above; or

(d) Arising out of his or her providing or failing to provide professional health care services.

(2) "Property damage" to property:

(a) Owned, occupied or used by;

(b) Rented to, in the care, custody or control of, or over which physical control is being exercised for any purpose by;

you, any of your "employees", "volunteer workers", any partner or member (if you are a partnership or joint venture), or any member (if you are a limited liability company).

b. Any person (other than your "employee" or "volunteer worker"), or any organization while acting as your real estate manager.

c. Any person or organization having proper temporary custody of your property if you die, but only:

(1) With respect to liability arising out of the maintenance or use of that property; and

(2) Until your legal representative has been appointed.

d. Your legal representative if you die, but only with respect to duties as such. That representative will have all your rights and duties under this Coverage Part.

3. Any organization you newly acquire or form, other than a partnership, joint venture or limited liability company, and over which you maintain ownership or majority interest, will qualify as a Named Insured if there is no other similar insurance available to that organization. However:

a. Coverage under this provision is afforded only until the 90th day after you acquire or form the organization or the end of the policy period, whichever is earlier;

b. Coverage **A** does not apply to "bodily injury" or "property damage" that occurred before you acquired or formed the organization; and

c. Coverage **B** does not apply to "personal and advertising injury" arising out of an offense committed before you acquired or formed the organization.

No person or organization is an insured with respect to the conduct of any current or past partnership, joint venture or limited liability company that is not shown as a Named Insured in the Declarations.

SECTION III – LIMITS OF INSURANCE

1. The Limits of Insurance shown in the Declarations and the rules below fix the most we will pay regardless of the number of:

a. Insureds;

b. Claims made or "suits" brought; or

c. Persons or organizations making claims or bringing "suits".

2. The General Aggregate Limit is the most we will pay for the sum of:

a. Medical expenses under Coverage **C;**

b. Damages under Coverage **A,** except damages because of "bodily injury" or "property damage" included in the "products-completed operations hazard"; and

c. Damages under Coverage **B.**

3. The Products-Completed Operations Aggregate Limit is the most we will pay under Coverage **A** for damages because of "bodily injury" and "property damage" included in the "products-completed operations hazard".

4. Subject to Paragraph **2.** above, the Personal And Advertising Injury Limit is the most we will pay under Coverage **B** for the sum of all damages because of all "personal and advertising injury" sustained by any one person or organization.

5. Subject to Paragraph **2.** or **3.** above, whichever applies, the Each Occurrence Limit is the most we will pay for the sum of:

   a. Damages under Coverage **A**; and

   b. Medical expenses under Coverage **C**

   because of all "bodily injury" and "property damage" arising out of any one "occurrence".

6. Subject to Paragraph **5.** above, the Damage To Premises Rented To You Limit is the most we will pay under Coverage **A** for damages because of "property damage" to any one premises, while rented to you, or in the case of damage by fire, while rented to you or temporarily occupied by you with permission of the owner.

7. Subject to Paragraph **5.** above, the Medical Expense Limit is the most we will pay under Coverage **C** for all medical expenses because of "bodily injury" sustained by any one person.

The Limits of Insurance of this Coverage Part apply separately to each consecutive annual period and to any remaining period of less than 12 months, starting with the beginning of the policy period shown in the Declarations, unless the policy period is extended after issuance for an additional period of less than 12 months. In that case, the additional period will be deemed part of the last preceding period for purposes of determining the Limits of Insurance.

SECTION IV – COMMERCIAL GENERAL LIABILITY CONDITIONS

1. Bankruptcy

Bankruptcy or insolvency of the insured or of the insured's estate will not relieve us of our obligations under this Coverage Part.

2. Duties In The Event Of Occurrence, Offense, Claim Or Suit

a. You must see to it that we are notified as soon as practicable of an "occurrence" or an offense which may result in a claim. To the extent possible, notice should include:

   (1) How, when and where the "occurrence" or offense took place;

   (2) The names and addresses of any injured persons and witnesses; and

   (3) The nature and location of any injury or damage arising out of the "occurrence" or offense.

b. If a claim is made or "suit" is brought against any insured, you must:

   (1) Immediately record the specifics of the claim or "suit" and the date received; and

   (2) Notify us as soon as practicable.

   You must see to it that we receive written notice of the claim or "suit" as soon as practicable.

c. You and any other involved insured must:

   (1) Immediately send us copies of any demands, notices, summonses or legal papers received in connection with the claim or "suit";

   (2) Authorize us to obtain records and other information;

   (3) Cooperate with us in the investigation or settlement of the claim or defense against the "suit"; and

   (4) Assist us, upon our request, in the enforcement of any right against any person or organization which may be liable to the insured because of injury or damage to which this insurance may also apply.

d. No insured will, except at that insured's own cost, voluntarily make a payment, assume any obligation, or incur any expense, other than for first aid, without our consent.

3. Legal Action Against Us

No person or organization has a right under this Coverage Part:

a. To join us as a party or otherwise bring us into a "suit" asking for damages from an insured; or

b. To sue us on this Coverage Part unless all of its terms have been fully complied with.

A person or organization may sue us to recover on an agreed settlement or on a final judgment against an insured; but we will not be liable for damages that are not payable under the terms of this Coverage Part or that are in excess of the applicable limit of insurance. An agreed settlement means a settlement and release of liability signed by us, the insured and the claimant or the claimant's legal representative.

4. Other Insurance

If other valid and collectible insurance is available to the insured for a loss we cover under Coverages **A** or **B** of this Coverage Part, our obligations are limited as follows:

a. Primary Insurance

This insurance is primary except when Paragraph **b.** below applies. If this insurance is primary, our obligations are not affected unless any of the other insurance is also primary. Then, we will share with all that other insurance by the method described in Paragraph **c.** below.

b. Excess Insurance

(1) This insurance is excess over:

(a) Any of the other insurance, whether primary, excess, contingent or on any other basis:

(i) That is Fire, Extended Coverage, Builder's Risk, Installation Risk or similar coverage for "your work";

(ii) That is Fire insurance for premises rented to you or temporarily occupied by you with permission of the owner;

(iii) That is insurance purchased by you to cover your liability as a tenant for "property damage" to premises rented to you or temporarily occupied by you with permission of the owner; or

(iv) If the loss arises out of the maintenance or use of aircraft, "autos" or watercraft to the extent not subject to Exclusion **g.** of Section **I** – Coverage **A** – Bodily Injury And Property Damage Liability.

(b) Any other primary insurance available to you covering liability for damages arising out of the premises or operations, or the products and completed operations, for which you have been added as an additional insured.

(2) When this insurance is excess, we will have no duty under Coverages **A** or **B** to defend the insured against any "suit" if any other insurer has a duty to defend the insured against that "suit". If no other insurer defends, we will undertake to do so, but we will be entitled to the insured's rights against all those other insurers.

(3) When this insurance is excess over other insurance, we will pay only our share of the amount of the loss, if any, that exceeds the sum of:

(a) The total amount that all such other insurance would pay for the loss in the absence of this insurance; and

(b) The total of all deductible and self-insured amounts under all that other insurance.

(4) We will share the remaining loss, if any, with any other insurance that is not described in this Excess Insurance provision and was not bought specifically to apply in excess of the Limits of Insurance shown in the Declarations of this Coverage Part.

c. Method Of Sharing

If all of the other insurance permits contribution by equal shares, we will follow this method also. Under this approach each insurer contributes equal amounts until it has paid its applicable limit of insurance or none of the loss remains, whichever comes first.

If any of the other insurance does not permit contribution by equal shares, we will contribute by limits. Under this method, each insurer's share is based on the ratio of its applicable limit of insurance to the total applicable limits of insurance of all insurers.

5. Premium Audit

a. We will compute all premiums for this Coverage Part in accordance with our rules and rates.

b. Premium shown in this Coverage Part as advance premium is a deposit premium only. At the close of each audit period we will compute the earned premium for that period and send notice to the first Named Insured. The due date for audit and retrospective premiums is the date shown as the due date on the bill. If the sum of the advance and audit premiums paid for the policy period is greater than the earned premium, we will return the excess to the first Named Insured.

c. The first Named Insured must keep records of the information we need for premium computation, and send us copies at such times as we may request.

6. Representations

By accepting this policy, you agree:

a. The statements in the Declarations are accurate and complete;

© Insurance Services Office, Inc., 2012

b. Those statements are based upon representations you made to us; and

c. We have issued this policy in reliance upon your representations.

7. Separation Of Insureds

Except with respect to the Limits of Insurance, and any rights or duties specifically assigned in this Coverage Part to the first Named Insured, this insurance applies:

a. As if each Named Insured were the only Named Insured; and

b. Separately to each insured against whom claim is made or "suit" is brought.

8. Transfer Of Rights Of Recovery Against Others To Us

If the insured has rights to recover all or part of any payment we have made under this Coverage Part, those rights are transferred to us. The insured must do nothing after loss to impair them. At our request, the insured will bring "suit" or transfer those rights to us and help us enforce them.

9. When We Do Not Renew

If we decide not to renew this Coverage Part, we will mail or deliver to the first Named Insured shown in the Declarations written notice of the nonrenewal not less than 30 days before the expiration date.

If notice is mailed, proof of mailing will be sufficient proof of notice.

SECTION V – DEFINITIONS

1. "Advertisement" means a notice that is broadcast or published to the general public or specific market segments about your goods, products or services for the purpose of attracting customers or supporters. For the purposes of this definition:

a. Notices that are published include material placed on the Internet or on similar electronic means of communication; and

b. Regarding web sites, only that part of a web site that is about your goods, products or services for the purposes of attracting customers or supporters is considered an advertisement.

2. "Auto" means:

a. A land motor vehicle, trailer or semitrailer designed for travel on public roads, including any attached machinery or equipment; or

b. Any other land vehicle that is subject to a compulsory or financial responsibility law or other motor vehicle insurance law where it is licensed or principally garaged.

However, "auto" does not include "mobile equipment".

3. "Bodily injury" means bodily injury, sickness or disease sustained by a person, including death resulting from any of these at any time.

4. "Coverage territory" means:

a. The United States of America (including its territories and possessions), Puerto Rico and Canada;

b. International waters or airspace, but only if the injury or damage occurs in the course of travel or transportation between any places included in Paragraph **a.** above; or

c. All other parts of the world if the injury or damage arises out of:

(1) Goods or products made or sold by you in the territory described in Paragraph **a.** above;

(2) The activities of a person whose home is in the territory described in Paragraph **a.** above, but is away for a short time on your business; or

(3) "Personal and advertising injury" offenses that take place through the Internet or similar electronic means of communication;

provided the insured's responsibility to pay damages is determined in a "suit" on the merits, in the territory described in Paragraph **a.** above or in a settlement we agree to.

5. "Employee" includes a "leased worker". "Employee" does not include a "temporary worker".

6. "Executive officer" means a person holding any of the officer positions created by your charter, constitution, bylaws or any other similar governing document.

7. "Hostile fire" means one which becomes uncontrollable or breaks out from where it was intended to be.

8. "Impaired property" means tangible property, other than "your product" or "your work", that cannot be used or is less useful because:

a. It incorporates "your product" or "your work" that is known or thought to be defective, deficient, inadequate or dangerous; or

b. You have failed to fulfill the terms of a contract or agreement;

if such property can be restored to use by the repair, replacement, adjustment or removal of "your product" or "your work" or your fulfilling the terms of the contract or agreement.

9. "Insured contract" means:

   a. A contract for a lease of premises. However, that portion of the contract for a lease of premises that indemnifies any person or organization for damage by fire to premises while rented to you or temporarily occupied by you with permission of the owner is not an "insured contract";

   b. A sidetrack agreement;

   c. Any easement or license agreement, except in connection with construction or demolition operations on or within 50 feet of a railroad;

   d. An obligation, as required by ordinance, to indemnify a municipality, except in connection with work for a municipality;

   e. An elevator maintenance agreement;

   f. That part of any other contract or agreement pertaining to your business (including an indemnification of a municipality in connection with work performed for a municipality) under which you assume the tort liability of another party to pay for "bodily injury" or "property damage" to a third person or organization. Tort liability means a liability that would be imposed by law in the absence of any contract or agreement.

      Paragraph **f.** does not include that part of any contract or agreement:

      (1) That indemnifies a railroad for "bodily injury" or "property damage" arising out of construction or demolition operations, within 50 feet of any railroad property and affecting any railroad bridge or trestle, tracks, road-beds, tunnel, underpass or crossing;

      (2) That indemnifies an architect, engineer or surveyor for injury or damage arising out of:

         (a) Preparing, approving, or failing to prepare or approve, maps, shop drawings, opinions, reports, surveys, field orders, change orders or drawings and specifications; or

         (b) Giving directions or instructions, or failing to give them, if that is the primary cause of the injury or damage; or

      (3) Under which the insured, if an architect, engineer or surveyor, assumes liability for an injury or damage arising out of the insured's rendering or failure to render professional services, including those listed in **(2)** above and supervisory, inspection, architectural or engineering activities.

10. "Leased worker" means a person leased to you by a labor leasing firm under an agreement between you and the labor leasing firm, to perform duties related to the conduct of your business. "Leased worker" does not include a "temporary worker".

11. "Loading or unloading" means the handling of property:

    a. After it is moved from the place where it is accepted for movement into or onto an aircraft, watercraft or "auto";

    b. While it is in or on an aircraft, watercraft or "auto"; or

    c. While it is being moved from an aircraft, watercraft or "auto" to the place where it is finally delivered;

    but "loading or unloading" does not include the movement of property by means of a mechanical device, other than a hand truck, that is not attached to the aircraft, watercraft or "auto".

12. "Mobile equipment" means any of the following types of land vehicles, including any attached machinery or equipment:

    a. Bulldozers, farm machinery, forklifts and other vehicles designed for use principally off public roads;

    b. Vehicles maintained for use solely on or next to premises you own or rent;

    c. Vehicles that travel on crawler treads;

    d. Vehicles, whether self-propelled or not, maintained primarily to provide mobility to permanently mounted:

       (1) Power cranes, shovels, loaders, diggers or drills; or

       (2) Road construction or resurfacing equipment such as graders, scrapers or rollers;

    e. Vehicles not described in Paragraph **a., b., c.** or **d.** above that are not self-propelled and are maintained primarily to provide mobility to permanently attached equipment of the following types:

       (1) Air compressors, pumps and generators, including spraying, welding, building cleaning, geophysical exploration, lighting and well servicing equipment; or

       (2) Cherry pickers and similar devices used to raise or lower workers;

    f. Vehicles not described in Paragraph **a., b., c.** or **d.** above maintained primarily for purposes other than the transportation of persons or cargo.

 © Insurance Services Office, Inc., 2012 CG 00 01 04 13

However, self-propelled vehicles with the following types of permanently attached equipment are not "mobile equipment" but will be considered "autos":

(1) Equipment designed primarily for:

  (a) Snow removal;

  (b) Road maintenance, but not construction or resurfacing; or

  (c) Street cleaning;

(2) Cherry pickers and similar devices mounted on automobile or truck chassis and used to raise or lower workers; and

(3) Air compressors, pumps and generators, including spraying, welding, building cleaning, geophysical exploration, lighting and well servicing equipment.

However, "mobile equipment" does not include any land vehicles that are subject to a compulsory or financial responsibility law or other motor vehicle insurance law where it is licensed or principally garaged. Land vehicles subject to a compulsory or financial responsibility law or other motor vehicle insurance law are considered "autos".

13. "Occurrence" means an accident, including continuous or repeated exposure to substantially the same general harmful conditions.

14. "Personal and advertising injury" means injury, including consequential "bodily injury", arising out of one or more of the following offenses:

a. False arrest, detention or imprisonment;

b. Malicious prosecution;

c. The wrongful eviction from, wrongful entry into, or invasion of the right of private occupancy of a room, dwelling or premises that a person occupies, committed by or on behalf of its owner, landlord or lessor;

d. Oral or written publication, in any manner, of material that slanders or libels a person or organization or disparages a person's or organization's goods, products or services;

e. Oral or written publication, in any manner, of material that violates a person's right of privacy;

f. The use of another's advertising idea in your "advertisement"; or

g. Infringing upon another's copyright, trade dress or slogan in your "advertisement".

15. "Pollutants" mean any solid, liquid, gaseous or thermal irritant or contaminant, including smoke, vapor, soot, fumes, acids, alkalis, chemicals and waste. Waste includes materials to be recycled, reconditioned or reclaimed.

16. "Products-completed operations hazard":

a. Includes all "bodily injury" and "property damage" occurring away from premises you own or rent and arising out of "your product" or "your work" except:

(1) Products that are still in your physical possession; or

(2) Work that has not yet been completed or abandoned. However, "your work" will be deemed completed at the earliest of the following times:

  (a) When all of the work called for in your contract has been completed.

  (b) When all of the work to be done at the job site has been completed if your contract calls for work at more than one job site.

  (c) When that part of the work done at a job site has been put to its intended use by any person or organization other than another contractor or subcontractor working on the same project.

Work that may need service, maintenance, correction, repair or replacement, but which is otherwise complete, will be treated as completed.

b. Does not include "bodily injury" or "property damage" arising out of:

(1) The transportation of property, unless the injury or damage arises out of a condition in or on a vehicle not owned or operated by you, and that condition was created by the "loading or unloading" of that vehicle by any insured;

(2) The existence of tools, uninstalled equipment or abandoned or unused materials; or

(3) Products or operations for which the classification, listed in the Declarations or in a policy Schedule, states that products-completed operations are subject to the General Aggregate Limit.

17. "Property damage" means:

a. Physical injury to tangible property, including all resulting loss of use of that property. All such loss of use shall be deemed to occur at the time of the physical injury that caused it; or

b. Loss of use of tangible property that is not physically injured. All such loss of use shall be deemed to occur at the time of the "occurrence" that caused it.

For the purposes of this insurance, electronic data is not tangible property.

As used in this definition, electronic data means information, facts or programs stored as or on, created or used on, or transmitted to or from computer software, including systems and applications software, hard or floppy disks, CD-ROMs, tapes, drives, cells, data processing devices or any other media which are used with electronically controlled equipment.

18. "Suit" means a civil proceeding in which damages because of "bodily injury", "property damage" or "personal and advertising injury" to which this insurance applies are alleged. "Suit" includes:

a. An arbitration proceeding in which such damages are claimed and to which the insured must submit or does submit with our consent; or

b. Any other alternative dispute resolution proceeding in which such damages are claimed and to which the insured submits with our consent.

19. "Temporary worker" means a person who is furnished to you to substitute for a permanent "employee" on leave or to meet seasonal or short-term workload conditions.

20. "Volunteer worker" means a person who is not your "employee", and who donates his or her work and acts at the direction of and within the scope of duties determined by you, and is not paid a fee, salary or other compensation by you or anyone else for their work performed for you.

21. "Your product":

a. Means:

(1) Any goods or products, other than real property, manufactured, sold, handled, distributed or disposed of by:

(a) You;

(b) Others trading under your name; or

(c) A person or organization whose business or assets you have acquired; and

(2) Containers (other than vehicles), materials, parts or equipment furnished in connection with such goods or products.

b. Includes:

(1) Warranties or representations made at any time with respect to the fitness, quality, durability, performance or use of "your product"; and

(2) The providing of or failure to provide warnings or instructions.

c. Does not include vending machines or other property rented to or located for the use of others but not sold.

22. "Your work":

a. Means:

(1) Work or operations performed by you or on your behalf; and

(2) Materials, parts or equipment furnished in connection with such work or operations.

b. Includes:

(1) Warranties or representations made at any time with respect to the fitness, quality, durability, performance or use of "your work"; and

(2) The providing of or failure to provide warnings or instructions.

 © Insurance Services Office, Inc., 2012 CG 00 01 04 13

After courts in many jurisdictions largely rejected insurers' attempts to narrowly define the term "accident," the industry decided to give up on the accident trigger for general liability coverage. In the mid-1960s, the predecessors to the Insurance Services Office redrafted the standard general liability form to replace the accident policy with what came to be known as an "occurrence" policy. The CGL policy in Figure 4.2 is an occurrence policy.

OWENS-ILLINOIS, INC. v. UNITED INSURANCE CO.

Supreme Court of New Jersey
650 A.2d 974 (1994)

O'HERN, J. This appeal involves . . . a dispute between a manufacturer of an asbestos product and its insurers concerning . . . "trigger of coverage" [which is] a shorthand expression for identifying the events that must occur during a policy period to require coverage for losses sustained by the policyholder. . . .

The most salient feature of this case is that it concerns a decades-old manufacturing activity. From 1948 to 1958, O-I manufactured and distributed Kaylo, a thermal insulation product containing approximately fifteen percent asbestos. Between 1948 and 1963, O-I was self-insured; it maintained no insurance to cover its products-liability losses but bore that risk itself. Products-liability law was at that time in its early stages. From September 1, 1963, to September 1, 1977, O-I was insured under excess indemnity (umbrella) insurance policies issued by the Aetna Casualty and Surety Company (Aetna). [From 1977 to 1985 O-I was insured by a group of companies that are referred to in this opinion as the "Insurance Companies."] . . .

Toward the end of 1977, O-I's in-house legal department became aware of a number of asbestos-related lawsuits involving the Kaylo product. Early in 1978, O-I gave notice of those claims to Aetna. . . . Aetna took the position, with which O-I originally agreed, that the cases should be reported on a manifestation basis, that is, the policy in effect when the disease manifested itself should respond to the claim. Because most statutes of limitations were of at least several years in duration, O-I assumed that Aetna would be the responsible carrier. As a precaution, O-I also informed the Insurance Companies of the asbestos claims.

. . . As claims continued to mount, O-I recognized that the claims were no longer the exclusive responsibility of Aetna because the manifestation dates were now presumed to be after September 1, 1977. Accordingly, in 1980 O-I gave formal notice to the Insurance Companies of the pendency of those asbestos claims. The Insurance Companies . . . maintained, however, that the trigger of coverage was the exposure to the product and not the manifestation of the disease. Because the exposures had presumably predated the issuance of [their] policies, the Insurance Companies declined coverage.

By January 1980, O-I had established a $3 million reserve for general legal expenses, substantially generated by its growing number of asbestos cases. . . . The economic realities of this litigation are stark. By 1991, when O-I filed its Appellate Division briefs, it had settled 43,000 bodily-injury lawsuits. More than 90,000 bodily-injury and sixty-three property-damage cases were pending in all states and some territories. With bodily-injury lawsuits accumulating at the rate of 1700 per month, O-I's unreimbursed costs of defending and settling those cases had by then exceeded $95 million. O-I had already spent close to $10 million in defense and settlement costs associated with the property-damage cases. The questions raised here concern which of the insurance policies issued from 1977 to 1985 provide indemnity to O-I and to what extent. . . .

THE POLICY LANGUAGE

The source of any duty on the part of the Insurance Companies to defend actions or to pay any judgments is obviously in the contract of insurance. The . . . policy language pertinent to the trigger-of-coverage issue is as follows:

> The [insurance] company will pay on behalf of the insured all sums which the insured shall become legally obligated to pay, either by adjudication or settlement, as damages because of personal injury or property damage . . . to which this insurance applies, caused by an occurrence and the [insurance] company shall indemnify the insured for costs associated with the defense of any suit or claim against the insured seeking damages on account of such personal injury or property damage. . . .

The policies do not refer to a "trigger"; "the term 'trigger' is merely a label for the event or events that under the terms of the insurance policy determines whether a policy must respond to a claim in a given set of circumstances." . . .

To place the issues in context, we shall use an example to which most of us can relate. (The example is intended not to suggest that workers might in fact contract disease in the manner as stated but only to simplify our analysis.) Assume that a group of workers occupied an office building for nine years under the following circumstances. For the first three years, the building owners had no liability insurance, assuming any risk of loss. During each of the middle three years, the owners were insured under a CGL policy with the Trustworthy Insurance Company for $5,000,000 per occurrence. For the remaining three years of the period, the owners were again uninsured. Assume, too, that during the first three years the building occupants were exposed to asbestos fibers in the ceilings and insulation but that all asbestos products were removed at the end of the third year. During the first three years, no occupants of the building manifested any symptoms of disease. During the fourth, fifth, and sixth years, there was "exposure in residence," that is, some building occupants began to develop breathing problems, but no disease was diagnosable. In the final three years, some of the building's occupants were diagnosed with asbestos-related diseases.

In the tenth year the owners received claims from thirty people who had worked in the building during the entire nine years asserting that they were suffering from asbestos-related disease as a result of their work environment. The owners, when presented with the claims, no longer had insurance. They sought coverage, however, for all the claims from the Trustworthy Insurance Company, which had insured the owners for three of the nine years—years when the building contained no asbestos. Must Trustworthy respond to the claims? If so, to what extent?

Trustworthy's CGL policy is as broad as those in this case. The policy promised that the company would pay all sums that the insured should become legally obligated to pay as damages for bodily injury caused by an occurrence during the policy period. Each of the thirty claimants in our hypothetical might recover from the owners a large sum, let us say $500,000, for a total of $15,000,000 in damages. Was there an occurrence during the fourth, fifth, and sixth years that calls for full indemnity? The owners contend that the fibers once inhaled by the building occupants continued to cause injury to the occupants during those middle years, and that they paid premiums to cover their risk of liability for injury during those three years even if caused by earlier exposure. The owners seek indemnity to the extent of the full $5,000,000 for each year of coverage, for a total of $15,000,000. The first question is: Were the policies issued in the middle years "triggered"?

TRIGGER OF COVERAGE

Not surprisingly, the answer to the trigger-of-coverage question varies by jurisdiction. The most frequently offered theories for the trigger of coverage are (1) the exposure theory, (2) the manifestation theory, and (3) the continuous-trigger theory. A concise summary of these approaches is contained in a law review article cited by the respected Judge Jack B. Weinstein of the Eastern District of New York in *Uniroyal, Inc. v. Home Insurance Co.*, 707 F. Supp. 1368, 1387 (1988), a case concerning coverage for toxic-induced disease related to Agent Orange:

> Fixing the date of an injurious occurrence is crucial to determining which of the several insurers in a company's history must bear the liability for an environmental incident. Injuries from toxic wastes usually evolve slowly, and thus it is difficult to define the date on which an occurrence triggers liability for insurance purposes. Many years may pass from the time a toxin enters the body until the time the toxin's presence manifests itself in the form of a disease. The word "occurrence" itself is ambiguous because the injury process is not a definite, discrete event. Courts have set the time of occurrence in three ways: at the date of exposure, at the date of manifestation, and over the continuous period from exposure to manifestation (the "continuous trigger" rule).
>
> The exposure theory holds that the date of occurrence is the date on which the injury-producing agent first contacts the body. The leading case espousing this view is the Sixth Circuit's decision in *Insurance Co. of North America v. Forty-Eight Insulations, Inc.* [633 F.2d 1212 (6th Cir. 1980), *clarified in part*, 657 F.2d 814 (6th Cir.), *cert. denied*, 454 U.S. 1109 (1981)]. The court in *Forty-Eight* found that the occurrence was the immediate contact of an asbestos fiber with the lungs, even though the disease took some time to develop. The court's central purpose was to maximize coverage: it chose the exposure theory because the plaintiff was effectively uninsured after 1976, and any other theory would have put the date of occurrence after 1976. In most toxic waste cases, however, when exposure is not discoverable until many years after the fact, the exposure rule will not provide a feasible method for insurers to monitor risks and charge appropriate premiums.
>
> Courts have similarly adopted the manifestation theory for its expedience in maximizing coverage. In *Eagle-Picher Industries v. Liberty Mutual Insurance Co.* [682 F.2d 12 (1st Cir. 1982), *cert. denied*, 460 U.S. 1028 (1983)], the First Circuit argued that the injury resulting from inhalation of asbestos fibers did not "occur" until the disease manifested itself. The court took note of the *Forty-Eight* opinion but distinguished it on the ground that, given the particular facts before the court, the manifestation rule would maximize coverage. In most cases, however, a manifestation rule would reduce coverage: insurers would refuse to write new insurance for the insured when it became apparent that the period of manifestations, and hence

a flood of claims, was approaching. The insured would be left without coverage for victims whose diseases were not yet manifested.

The continuous trigger theory has also been justified by its ability to maximize coverage in particular cases. In *Keene Corp. v. Insurance Co. of North America* [667 F.2d 1034 (D.C. Cir. 1981), *cert. denied*, 455 U.S. 1007 (1982)], the District of Columbia Circuit held that because asbestos related disease develops slowly, the date of the occurrence should be the continuous period from exposure to manifestation. It held all the insurers over that period liable for the continuous development of the disease. Again, the court relied on the presumption of maximizing coverage. Because it avoids the dangers of the manifestation rule, and because it encourages all insurers to monitor risks and charge appropriate premiums, the continuous trigger rule appears to be the most efficient doctrine for toxic waste cases.

Developments in the Law—Toxic Waste Litigation, 99 Harv. L. Rev. 1458, 1579–81 (1986) (footnotes omitted).

The conceptual underpinning of the continuous-trigger theory, then, is that injury occurs during each phase of environmental contamination—exposure, exposure in residence (defined as further progression of injury even after exposure has ceased), and manifestation of disease.

At least two other less-frequently followed theories exist. One is the "injury-in-fact" (or "damages-in-fact") approach, which holds that coverage is triggered by a showing of actual injury or damage-producing event. *See, e.g., American Home Prods. Corp. v. Liberty Mut. Ins. Co.*, 565 F. Supp. 1485 (S.D.N.Y. 1983), *aff'd as modified*, 748 F.2d 760 (2d Cir. 1984). Under that theory, coverage is triggered by "a real but undiscovered injury, proved in retrospect to have existed at the relevant time . . . irrespective of the time the injury became manifest." *Id.* at 1497. "That is, after an injury has been diagnosed, it may be inferred, from the nature of the gestation period and from the stage of the illness, that the harm actually began sometime earlier." *Armstrong World Indus., Inc. v. Aetna Casualty & Sur. Co.*, 26 Cal. Rptr. 2d 35, 52 (Ct. App. 1993), *review granted sub nom. In re Asbestos Ins. Coverage Cases*, 866 P.2d 1311 (Cal. Ct. App. 1994).

Finally, the "double-trigger" theory holds that injury occurs at the time of exposure and the time of manifestation, but not necessarily during the intervening period. *E.g., Zurich Ins. Co. v. Raymark Indus., Inc.*, 514 N.E.2d 150, 161 (Ill. 1987).

The court in *Keene Corp. v. Insurance Co. of North America*, 667 F.2d 1034, 1041, 1048-49 (D.C. Cir. 1981), *cert. denied*, 455 U.S. 1007 (1982), relied on the presumption of maximizing coverage, but that appears an uneven principle in this setting. To return to our example of the office building: Had we adopted the manifestation theory in an earlier effort to maximize coverage, the building owners in our hypothetical would be uncovered. Had we adopted, for the same reason, the exposure theory, the owners would be similarly uncovered. A rule of law premised on nothing more than the result-oriented goal of maximizing coverage has been described as "judicial legislation." *American Home Prods., supra*, 565 F. Supp. at 1512. A more consistent principle is required. . . .

The Insurance Companies insist that the record in this case is incomplete because it does not contain "medical testimony that the inhalation of asbestos causes immediate tissue damage." *Ibid.* However, Judge Keefe, the judge presiding over the early phase of this matter in the Chancery Division, had an extraordinary understanding of the nature of asbestos-induced disease. He was at that time presiding over the unified statewide administration of all asbestos trials, and had conducted many asbestos trials. He found

> absolutely no basis for discovery on the issue of the nature of asbestos disease. I think the courts of this state, not only the trial and appellate level, but the Supreme Court level, have acknowledged the fact that asbestos disease is a progressive disease, and that there is insult to tissue upon inhalation, and the insult continues during the residency, and obviously bodily injury occurs during the entire period of time, up to and including the date of manifestation of the disease.

The "overwhelming weight of authority" elsewhere acknowledges the progressive nature of asbestos-induced disease, and affirms that "'bodily injury' occurs when asbestos is inhaled and retained in the lungs." *Lloyd E. Mitchell, Inc. v. Maryland Casualty Co.*, 595 A.2d 469, 478 (Md. 1991). Generalities about asbestos may be overblown. Still, we are satisfied, like most American jurisdictions, that medical science confirms that some injury to body tissue occurs on the inhalation of asbestos fibers, and that once lodged, the fibers pose an increased likelihood of causing or contributing to disease. *Lloyd E. Mitchell, Inc., supra*, 595 A.2d at 478–81. . . .

Accepting that inhalation of asbestos fibers causes some injury to tissue, does that injury trigger coverage under a CGL policy? Many courts have answered that question by finding ambiguity in the language of the policy and construing the policy in favor of the policyholders. . . . However, . . . we do not find ambiguity in the language of the "occurrence" clause. The words are all familiar and easily understandable. . . .

What is not so easily understandable is the point at which the law will say that injury requires indemnity. In that sense, the concept of injury, like the related concepts of duty and causation, is an instrument of policy. After all, the air we breathe and the water we drink contain trace elements of toxic substances. The law decides when an invasion of the body constitutes an injury entitling one to damages. . . .

Our own law has drawn the line on liability to indemnify for injury in different ways in different contexts. In *Ayers v. Township of Jackson*, 525 A.2d 287 (N.J. 1987), we concluded that absent diagnosed disease, the ingestion of toxic substances that enhanced the risk of progressive growth of cancer did not constitute a legal injury warranting compensation. In *Mauro v. Raymark Industries, Inc.*, 561 A.2d 257 (N.J. 1989), we held that even when the body suffered diagnosable injury due to asbestos exposure (thickening of chest walls and calcification of diaphragm), the injury was insufficient to allow recovery for the enhanced risk of contracting cancer.

What we did, however, in the face of doubtful scientific premises was to adapt our law to the uncertainties of medical causation. In *Ayers, supra*, we held that even when there is no bodily injury (or none that can be found), "the public health interest may justify judicial intervention even when the risk of disease is problematic." 525 A.2d at 287. We said that "mass-exposure toxic-tort cases involve public interests not present in conventional tort litigation." *Id.* at 287. We thus allowed tort recovery for medical-surveillance damages even without evidence of physical injury. *Id.* at 287. In *Mauro* we relaxed our statute of limitations and single-controversy doctrines to allow victims to assert later claims when the foreshadowed disease eventually occurs. In candor, we "acknowledge[d] that our resolution of [that] issue [was] imperfect." 561 A.2d at 257.

So too here, our resolution of the issues is necessarily imperfect. Our concepts of legal causation were developed in an age of Newtonian physics, not of molecular biology. Were it possible to know when a toxic substance clicks on a switch that alters irrevocably the composition of the body and before which no change has "occurred," we might be more confident that occurrence-causing damages had taken place during a particular policy period. The limitations of science in that respect only compound the limitations of law. . . .

NOTES AND QUESTIONS

1. Can you tell which trigger approach the court will adopt? Do you have an opinion about which approach the court *should* adopt? On what might that depend? Consider the following potential considerations: the "plain meaning" of the insurance policy, the "reasonable expectations" of commercial policyholders, compensation of injured workers, and stable and predictable insurance rates.

2. Asbestos claims have been a watershed event for the property and casualty insurance industry, which has struggled to spread the enormous losses suffered by workers and their families. For a vivid description of asbestos litigation, *see* Paul Brodeur, Outrageous Misconduct (1985). Asbestos claims played a significant role in the financial problems that led to the reorganization of the venerable Lloyd's of London, and they placed severe strains on the U.S. property casualty insurance industry in the 1980s. Indeed, were it not for the economic expansion of the 1990s (which dramatically increased the value of the insurance companies' investment portfolios), asbestos claims might have affected some U.S. property casualty insurers similarly. From an actuarial perspective, the main problem presented by the asbestos claims is that insurers did not accurately predict the cost of claims of this sort when they priced their CGL policies.

3. The economic impact of the asbestos cases made them significant to the insurance industry. What makes them significant to insurance law is their status as the first mass tort cases that really pushed the boundaries of liability insurance coverage. The sheer volume of litigation and the enormous sums of money at stake meant that almost every issue that could be litigated was in fact litigated. The asbestos insurance cases broke new ground on trigger, allocation of damages between insurers, the meaning of many liability insurance exclusions, and the standard of proof regarding lost insurance policies (since asbestos had such a long latency period, companies sometimes could not locate copies of potentially triggered policies), along with many other issues. Jeffrey W. Stempel, *Assessing the Coverage Carnage: Asbestos Liability and Insurance Three Decades After Dispute*, 12 Conn. Ins. L.J. 349, 464-66 (2006) (describing adoption of the asbestos exclusion in comprehensive general liability insurance policies from 1986 and later).

4. Insurance analysts have often predicted that the industry would soon see the light at the end of the asbestos litigation tunnel. A famous industry memo from the mid-1970s predicted that the litigation would burn out by the early 1980s—precisely when in fact the litigation began to threaten the solvency of the asbestos manufacturers. When the asbestos insurance coverage litigation reached its peak in the late 1980s, some analysts predicted that asbestos litigation would soon decline. Indeed, many insurance coverage

lawyers believed well into the mid-1990s that environmental liability claims were and would remain more significant than asbestos claims. Yet, at the turn of the twenty-first century, it was environmental litigation that declined significantly, while asbestos litigation continued to push major manufacturers into bankruptcy and to threaten the profitability of the property casualty industry. *See* Queena Sook Kim, *Firms Hit by Asbestos Litigation Take Bankruptcy Route*, Wall St. J., December 21, 2000. Some significant insurers made efforts to "wall off" the profitable parts of their businesses from the asbestos claims. *See* Liability-Based Restructuring Working Group of the NAIC Financial Condition (EX4) Subcommittee, Liability-Based Restructuring White Paper §VII.A, (1997). Richard E. Stewart and Steven E. Sigalow, *How Lloyd's Saved Itself*, 37 The Ins. Forum 9 (2010); Judy Greenwald, *Pennsylvania Lets ACE Complete Sale of Runoff Reinsurers; Several Cedents Fought Move*, Bus. Ins., July 10, 2006, at 4.

A NOTE ON THE "SCOPE" OR "ALLOCATION" OF COVERAGE ISSUE [1]

The *Owens-Illinois* court eventually announced that it would adopt a continuous trigger, but first the court discussed the "allocation" rule that would apply. An "allocation" or "scope of coverage" question (the two terms are used interchangeably) arises whenever more than one liability insurance policy is triggered by a claim. In *Owens-Illinois* (OI), for example, the court faced the problem of deciding how the responsibility for paying the OI claims would be divided up among OI and its insurers. Recall that with a continuous trigger, all the policies on the risk from the time of a plaintiff's initial exposure to the date of death are "triggered" by the plaintiff's claim. If OI had purchased the same amount of insurance every year from the same insurance company, and if none of those insurance policies had exclusions that applied to asbestos claims, the allocation rule would not matter to OI. All the costs from all the claims would be the insurance company's responsibility, subject to the applicable deductibles and the combined policy limits. How the insurance company decided to assign responsibility among the various policies it sold Owens-Illinois over the years would make no difference to OI.

OI's actual situation was much more complicated, so the allocation rule made a great deal of difference to OI and its insurers. OI had purchased different amounts of coverage from different sets of insurers in different years. In some years, OI had chosen to be "self-insured" to a significant extent (meaning that it had a very high "self-insured retention," a fancy term for a very high deductible). In other years, OI had purchased some of its insurance from companies that were insolvent and, therefore, not able to pay. Finally, after asbestos claims had begun to mount in the 1980s, the insurance industry had inserted asbestos

---

1. Like "trigger," "allocation" and "scope of coverage" are not terms in standard liability insurance policies. Instead, they are shorthand terms for specific types of insurance policy interpretation questions. "Allocation" and "scope of coverage" are two different terms for the same problem. "Allocation" is the more widely used term, but some policyholder advocates prefer the term "scope of coverage" because they believe that that term better emphasizes the breadth of the insurance company's promise to pay, while the term "allocation" predisposes courts to limit that promise.

exclusions in the liability policies of OI and other asbestos defendants, with the result that OI's coverage for asbestos claims ended long before the damage from asbestos was over.

OI took the position that any triggered policy was obligated to pay in full for a claim. In OI's view, the obligation of the triggered policies was "joint and several," and, as with joint and several liability in tort law, the plaintiff can decide which defendant has to pay a claim, leaving it to the defendants to work out afterward how they will share that burden. This approach would allow OI to choose how to go through its coverage, with the result that OI could exhaust almost all the limits of all its solvent carriers before it was responsible for paying more than the applicable deductibles.

OI's insurance carriers, on the other hand, took the position that the responsibility for paying for each claim should be divided equally among the potentially responsible parties—including OI—according to the time on the risk. In effect, they would divide the total cost of a given claim by the total number of years between the first exposure and death, and assign the resulting amount as the separate (not joint) responsibility of the carrier on the risk in each year. If there was no carrier on the risk, OI would then be responsible. Especially because OI was self-insured in some years, and then lost all its coverage for asbestos injuries in the 1980s, this approach would mean that OI would bear a large percentage of the asbestos costs from almost every claim, increasingly so the farther that 1980 receded into history.

Although the *Owens-Illinois* court did not adopt the position of either party, the decision that it did adopt was closer to the carriers' than OI's, so the continuous trigger decision was much less valuable to OI than might otherwise be thought:

> At least in the context of asbestos-related personal injury and property damage, the rules that we adopt will attempt to relate the theory of a continuous trigger causing indivisible injury to the degree of risk transferred or retained in each of the years of repeated exposure to injurious conditions. In the absence of a satisfactory measure of allocation, we believe that straight annual progression is not an appropriate measure of allocation. The degree of risk transferred or retained in the early years of an enterprise like O-I's obviously was not at all comparable to that sought to be insured in later years. Hence, any allocation should be in proportion to the degree of the risks transferred or retained during the years of exposure. We believe that measure of allocation is more consistent with the economic realities of risk retention or risk transfer. That later insurers might need to respond to pre-policy occurrences is not unfair. "These are 'occurrence' policies which, by their nature, provide coverage for pre-policy occurrences (acts) which cause injury or damage during the policy period." [citation omitted] In this case, the year-by-year increase in policy limits must have reflected an increasing awareness of the escalating nature of the risks sought to be transferred. We believe that a better formula (putting aside for a moment the problem of periods of self-insurance) is that developed in California. In [*Armstrong World Industries v. Aetna Cas. & Sur. Co.,* 26 Cal. Rptr. 2d 35, 57 (Cal. App. 1 1993)], the court allocated the losses among the carriers on the basis of the extent of the risk assumed, *i.e.,* proration on the basis of policy limits, multiplied by years of coverage.

> To explain the concept, we return to our example of the office-building workers. If we were to accept the constant levels of the policy limits as evidence of constant risks assumed over the nine-year span from exposure to manifestation (in the case of disease manifested in the ninth year), the carriers on the risk in

years four, five, and six would each pay one-ninth of the loss, or collectively thirty-three percent. If the facts of coverage had been otherwise — let us say policies had been in effect for years one through three in the amount of two million per year and in years four through six at three million per year — we might assess the risk assumed in years seven through nine at four million per year. Carriers during the first three years would bear roughly twenty-two percent (6/27ths); carriers covering the middle three years would bear thirty-three percent (9/27ths); and the building owners would bear forty-four percent of the risk (12/27ths). Of course, policy limits and exclusions must be taken into account. We recognize that such even mathematical proportions will not occur, and so we must repose a substantial measure of discretion in a master who must develop the formula that fairly reflects the risks assumed or transferred.

We realize that many complexities encumber the solution that we suggest involving, as it does, proration by time and degree of risk assumed — for example, determining how primary and excess coverage is to be taken into account or the order in which policies are triggered. The parties did not focus on those issues. Still, we do not believe that the issues are unmanageable. Constructing the model for analysis of the self-insurance portion of the risk assumed by O-I is difficult but not impossible. We recognize the difficulties of apportioning costs with any scientific certainty. However, the legal system "frequently resolves issues involving considerable uncertainty." [citation omitted]

On remand, coincident with resolving the other coverage issues, the court shall appoint a master, one skilled in the economics of insurance, to create a model for allocating the claims. Above all, the master should develop a workable system for efficient assignment and administration of the claims. Because the defendants refused to involve themselves in the defense of the claims as presented, they should be bound by the facts set forth in the plaintiff's own records with respect to the dates of exposure and with respect to the amounts of settlements and defense costs. Those losses for indemnity and defense costs should be allocated promptly among the companies in accordance with the mathematical model developed, subject to policy limits and exclusions. We stress that there can be no re-litigation of those settled claims. Exact dates of exposure may not now be available. Available data should enable the master to grasp the generality of the underlying claims and the exposures involved. (Even under the *Keene* formula exposure dates were necessary to determine contribution.)

. . . In future cases, insurers aware of their responsibility under the continuing-trigger theory might minimize their costs by assuming responsibility for or involving themselves in the defense of the actions with the ultimate allocation of costs to be determined in accordance with the same general formulas. If, after experience, we are convinced that our solution is inefficient or unrealistic, we will not hesitate to revisit the issue.

. . . To recapitulate, we hold that when progressive indivisible injury or damage results from exposure to injurious conditions for which civil liability may be imposed, courts may reasonably treat the progressive injury or damage as an occurrence within each of the years of a CGL policy. That is the continuous-trigger theory for activating the insurers' obligation to respond under the policies. . . . Because multiple policies of insurance are triggered under the continuous-trigger theory, it becomes necessary to determine the extent to which each triggered policy shall provide indemnity. "Other insurance" clauses in standard CGL policies were not intended to resolve that question. A fair method of allocation appears to be one that is related to both the time on the risk and the degree of risk assumed. When periods of no insurance reflect a decision by an actor to assume or retain a risk, as opposed to periods when coverage for a risk is not available, to expect the risk-bearer to share in the allocation is reasonable. Estimating the degree of risk assumed is difficult but not impossible.

Owens-Illinois, 650 A.2d at 984-994.

The opinion that follows addresses a related trigger of coverage question in a property damage context. How might the policy considerations that Judge Posner identifies affect the resolution of the trigger question in the asbestos bodily injury context?

ELJER MANUFACTURING INC. v. LIBERTY MUTUAL INSURANCE CO.

United States Court of Appeals, Seventh Circuit
972 F.2d 805 (1992)

POSNER, Circuit Judge. . . . If a manufacturer sells a defective product or component for installation in the real or personal property of the buyer, but the defect does not cause any tangible change in the buyer's property until years later, can the installation itself nonetheless be considered a "physical injury" to that property? The defective product or component in such a case is like a time bomb placed in an airplane luggage compartment: harmless until it explodes. . . . Or like a defective pacemaker which is working fine now but will stop working in an hour. Is the person or property in which the defective product is implanted or installed physically injured at the moment of implantation or installation — in a word, incorporation — or not until the latent harm becomes actual?

The product at issue is a plumbing system, called "Qest," that appellant Eljer's U.S. Brass subsidiary manufactured and sold to plumbing contractors all over the United States between 1979 and 1986 (some have continued to be sold for installation in mobile homes, but we can ignore that detail). Between a half million and three-quarters of a million Qest systems were installed in houses and apartments, invariably behind walls or below floors or above ceilings, so that the repair or replacement of the unit requires breaking into walls, floors, or ceilings. Within a year after the first units were sold and installed, complaints about leaks began coming in and the first products-liability lawsuit was brought against U.S. Brass in 1982. By 1990 several hundred additional suits had been filed, some of them class actions, involving altogether almost 17,000 of the systems; and it is estimated that ultimately 5 percent of the total number of Qest systems ever sold will have failed in circumstances likely to provoke a tort suit. Eljer reckons U.S. Brass's potential tort liability in the hundreds of millions of dollars, most of which Eljer hopes to recover from insurers — but only if it wins this case. . . .

Liberty Mutual, the principal defendant, issued a series of annual Comprehensive General Liability Insurance policies[2] to Eljer covering the years 1979 through 1988. Travelers, the other defendant, provided excess coverage for Eljer between 1982 and 1986. The policies cover liability for "property damage" accidentally caused by Eljer or its subsidiaries, defined as

> (1) physical injury to or destruction of tangible property which occurs during the policy period, including the loss of use thereof at any time resulting therefrom, or

---

2. *Editor's note:* The CGL policy in these materials is called a "commercial general liability" policy. Such policies were formerly known as "comprehensive general liability" policies. The insurance industry apparently changed the name to avoid creating the misleading impression that the coverage afforded was "comprehensive," i.e., protected the insured against all liability claims.

(2) loss of use of tangible property which has not been physically injured or destroyed provided such loss of use is caused by an occurrence [defined, so far as relevant here, as an accident, including continuous or repeated exposure to conditions] during the policy period.

This language was changed in the last three policies (covering 1986 through 1988), but, the parties agree, not materially.

Eljer brought this declaratory judgment suit to establish that the physical injury to the property of the buyer of a Qest system occurs when the system is installed in the buyer's house or apartment, not when it begins to leak or is replaced or is recognized to have reduced the value of the buyer's property. If this is right, essentially all the "property damage" inflicted by the defective systems occurred during the years in which Liberty's insurance policies were in force, because those were the years in which the systems were sold and installed. Liberty, however, contends that with respect to Eljer's liability. . . .

Many of the leaks upon which tort claims against Eljer are based did not occur until after the expiration of Liberty's last insurance policy at the end of 1988. And many people did not realize till then that their Qest systems were potentially defective and reducing the value of their homes. . . . So if the insurance companies' arguments prevail, Eljer will not be able to shift a substantial part of the burden of the tort claims against it to Liberty—or to Travelers, whose coverage expired even sooner.

The district judge agreed with the insurance companies that property damage within the meaning of the Comprehensive General Liability Insurance form contract does not occur upon installation of the defective system. . . . In the case of claims that arise from leaks, property damage occurs, in the district judge's view, when the leak occurs, while in the case of claims for the cost of repair or replacement incurred in anticipation of a leak it occurs at the time of repair or replacement. Eljer challenges these rulings. . . .

The central issue in the case—when if ever the incorporation of one product into another can be said to cause physical injury—pivots on a conflict between the connotations of the term "physical injury" and the objective of insurance. The central meaning of the term as it is used in everyday English—the image it would conjure up in the mind of a person unschooled in the subtleties of insurance law—is of a harmful change in appearance, shape, composition, or some other physical dimension of the "injured" person or thing. If water leaks from a pipe and discolors a carpet or rots a beam, that is physical injury, perhaps beginning with the very earliest sign of rot—the initial contamination (an important question in asbestos cases, as we shall see). The ticking time bomb, in contrast, does not injure the structure in which it is placed, in the sense of altering the structure in a harmful, or for that matter in any way—until it explodes. But these nice, physicalist, "realistic" (in the philosophical sense) distinctions have little to do with the objectives of parties to insurance contracts. The purpose of insurance is to spread risks and by spreading cancel them. Most people (including most corporate executives) are risk averse, and will therefore pay a premium to avoid a small probability of a large loss. Once a risk becomes a certainty—once the large loss occurs—insurance has no function. The last point at which a Qest plumbing system has an insurable risk of being defective and causing harm is when it is installed. When it starts to leak is too late; the risk has turned into a certainty and cannot be spread by being insured. It may also be too late when so many other Qest systems have failed that the unknowable risk has become a statistical certainty (or nearly so). For the individual homeowner there is still uncertainty as to whether and when his Qest will leak, so he may still be able to buy insurance against such an eventuality, though the premium will be very high because the risk is very great. For Eljer, however, which is liable for all the leaks traceable to the defectiveness of the system (as distinct from mistakes in installation, or other causes for which Eljer is not responsible), the pooling of the risks of the individual homeowners has produced a near certainty of a loss in excess of $100 million. How much in excess no one yet knows, and this leaves some room for insurance. But we are told that Eljer has had no primary liability coverage since the last Liberty policy expired at the end of 1988 and no excess coverage since the last Travelers policy expired at the end of 1986.

It would be an overstatement to say that the insurance policies which Eljer bought from the defendants had *no* value unless property damage is deemed to occur in the policy year in which the system is installed rather than in the policy year—more likely post-policy year—in which it fails or is so likely to fail that the prudent homeowner replaces it (perhaps vacating the home until it is replaced) or the market writes down the value of the home to reflect the risk of the system's failing and causing water damage and loss of use. Some systems malfunctioned in the year of installation; there has therefore been some payout under the insurance policies. And, because of limited liability, corporations have less incentive to buy insurance than private individuals do, David Mayers & Clifford W. Smith, Jr., *On the Corporate Demand for Insurance*, 55 J. Bus. 281 (1982); maybe limited coverage for modest premiums was all Eljer wanted or bought. But the defendants make nothing of the special character of the corporate insurance market—nor is it clear just how special it is, given risk aversion by executives and other employees, and the costs of bankruptcy (*id.* at 283-85)—instead treating this case as if Eljer had been an individual who had been seeking liability insurance. In these circumstances we should not be quick to assume that the standard general liability policy issued by the American insurance industry provides what to an outsider at any rate appears to be largely though not completely illusory coverage in an important class of cases.

Nor are literal interpretations, which assume that words or phrases are always used in their ordinary-language sense, regardless of context, the only plausible interpretations of contractual language, especially when the contract is between sophisticated business entities. We should at least ask what function "physical injury" might have been intended to perform in a comprehensive general liability policy beyond just drawing a commonsensical, lay person's, ordinary-language distinction between physical injury and physical noninjury.

Apparently the term was intended to distinguish between *physical* and *non-physical* injuries rather than to distinguish between *injuries* and *noninjuries*. The 1966 version of the General Comprehensive Liability Insurance policy form had defined "property damage" as "injury to or destruction of tangible property." Most courts, in apparent harmony with the drafters' intentions, gave the term "injury" in the new definition a broad interpretation. Some, however, excluded injuries in which there was no physical contact between the injurer and the property injured by him. (*Sola Basic Industries, Inc. v. United States Fidelity & Guaranty Co.*, 280 N.W.2d 211 (Wis. 1979), reviews the case law.) For example, if a manufacturer of construction cranes sold a defective crane which collapsed in front of a restaurant, blocking access to it and thereby impairing the restaurateur's income, and the restaurateur sued the manufacturer and recovered a judgment, the manufacturer's liability insurer might not have to pay, because the blocking of access might not be considered an injury to tangible property. To allay doubts on this score by sharpening the aim of the 1966 definition, the insurance industry's committee charged with updating the Comprehensive General Liability Insurance policy form redid the definition in 1973, producing the two-part definition that we quoted earlier from Liberty's policies. The second part, which is new, explicitly covers the injury inflicted by our hypothetical crane manufacturer—a "loss of use of tangible property which has not been physically injured or destroyed." The first part of the new definition is the old definition with "physical" prefixed to "injury" to distinguish the two parts. Both cover injury, but the second part covers injury which is not "physical" because there is no physical touching of the tort victim's property. There was no intent to curtail liability in a case of physical touching, as where a defective water system is installed in a house.

We can now see more clearly that two senses of "physical injury" are competing for our support. One, which the insurers want us to adopt, is an injury that causes a harmful physical alteration in the thing injured. The other, which is what the draftsmen of the Comprehensive General Liability Insurance policy apparently intended and what rational parties to such a policy would intend in order to make the policy's coverage real and not illusory, is a loss that results from physical contact, physical linkage, as when a potentially dangerous product is incorporated into another and, because it is incorporated and not merely contained (as a piece of furniture is contained in a house but can be removed without damage to the house), must be removed, at some cost, in order to prevent the danger from materializing. There is an analogy to fixtures in the law of real and personal property—improvements to property that cannot be removed without damaging it. In effect we are being asked to choose between "*physical* injury" and "physical *injury*."

Human beings give structure to their experience—cut the world of perception up into usable slices—through language, in accordance with the needs and interests of the moment. For many purposes the distinction between touching and altering is important; if two automobiles collide, it makes a big difference whether they merely touch each other or dent each other. For other purposes, other distinctions are more important, such as that between harms from touching, whether or not some harmful physical change ensues, and harms from other interferences with valued interests. Battery is a tort of touching, and, provided the touching is not permitted and offensive, the fact that the victim was not bruised or wounded goes only to the issue of damages. Assault is not a tort of touching—it becomes battery if the assailant touches his victim, as distinct from making a merely threatening gesture. Physical contact, not physical injury in the layman's sense, distinguishes the two torts.

Within the class of unintentional torts, too, the distinction between touching and not touching is often made. Under traditional tort law, if you hit a bridge and put it out of commission, you are liable to the owner of the bridge but not to merchants who lose business because customers cannot reach them with the bridge down. You have not touched the merchants or their property. The doctrine of "economic loss," illustrated by the *Rickards* case makes touching a prerequisite to tort liability for damage to property and thus rules out loss-of-use claims by persons with whose property the tortfeasor had made no physical contact.

The evolution of the bipartite structure of the Comprehensive General Liability Policy may have been shaped by this distinction between physical and economic loss (a poor choice of words—all the losses for which tort victims sue are economic). At first the distinction was so ingrained in tort law that there was little demand for liability insurance on the part of injurers who had not physically touched their victims, because such an injurer would have no liability against which to insure. The bar to this sort of liability weakened—though gradually, haltingly, and only in some jurisdictions—through an increasing recognition of exceptions. The demand for insurance against liability for loss of use unaccompanied by physical injury in the traditional sense rose concomitantly. It is not surprising that a new definition of property damage—a definition that encompassed two forms of injury, one physical and one not—emerged, and that coverage was extended to the second. . . .

All this may seem an aside, since these appeals (we have held) do not involve loss of use, but only physical injury. The significance of the loss of use provision, however, lies in what it tells us about the meaning of the physical injury provision. Whatever the precise function of the loss of use provision—whatever its precise relation to the economic loss doctrine—it was not added, and injury redescribed as physical injury, in order to curtail the preexisting insurance coverage for injury to tangible property. That coverage was and remains broad. Not promiscuously so. We do not think that every time a component part fails, the resulting injury can be backdated to the date of installation or incorporation. The expected failure rate must be sufficiently high to mark the product as defective—sufficiently high, as is alleged to be the case regarding the Qest plumbing system, to induce a rational owner to replace it before it fails, so likely is it to fail. That condition was satisfied. We believe that the coverage provided by Comprehensive General Liability Insurance encompassed (loss of use to one side) the tort claims against [Eljer].

NOTES AND QUESTIONS

1. Judge Posner decides on an "installation" trigger in part because he concludes that these kinds of claims would otherwise be uninsurable. In other words, he interprets the insurance policy to promote the underlying purpose of risk spreading. Of course, that underlying purpose always favors the policyholder, so consider how useful it really is. If the trigger is "manifestation," manufacturers will be unable to obtain coverage because once the losses become manifest, insurance companies will surely refuse to issue additional insurance.

2. An Illinois intermediate appellate court addressed coverage under excess insurance policies for claims arising from the Qest system in the case of *Travelers v. Eljer Mfg., Inc.*, 718 N.E.2d 1032 (Ill. App. Ct. 1999). The Illinois court disagreed with Judge Posner's analysis, writing:

In the context of a declaratory judgment action involving insurance coverage for claims made by reason of the failure of the Qest System at issue in this case, the *Eljer* court undertook to interpret the same definition of property damage that appears in the Post-1981 policies; namely, "physical injury to . . . tangible property." After noting a perceived conflict between "the connotations of the term 'physical injury' and the objective of [CGL] insurance" (*Eljer*, 972 F.2d at 808) and rejecting the notion that words or phrases used in insurance policies are always to be interpreted in their ordinary-language sense, the *Eljer* majority construed the phrase "physical injury" to include the installation of a Qest System because its expected failure rate is sufficiently high that a rational owner would be induced to replace it before it fails. In arriving at its construction of the phrase "physical injury," the majority relied almost exclusively upon its determination of the function that the phrase was intended to perform in a CGL policy. *See Eljer*, 972 F.2d at 806-14. However, as the dissenting judge in *Eljer* points out:

> The majority believes that interpreting the phrase is all a matter of emphasis — '*physical* injury' versus 'physical *injury*.' In my view, the phrase must be interpreted as '*physical injury*,' with both words given effect. The majority's account cannot give both words meaning at the same time.

Eljer, 972 F.2d at 814 (Cudahy, J., dissenting).

In interpreting the meaning of "physical injury," the majority in *Eljer* ignored the plain meaning of the phrase and adopted a construction which, as the dissenting judge points out, fails to give effect to both words at the same time. . . .

The word "physical" modifies injury in the definition of property damage as contained in the Post-1981 Policies and, thus, restricts recovery for intangible losses. Under the plain and unambiguous language of these policies, some physical injury to tangible property must be shown in order to trigger coverage. Purely economic losses, such as damages for inadequate value, costs of repair or replacement, and diminution in value, . . . resulting from a product's inferior quality or its failure to perform for the general purposes for which it was manufactured and sold, do not trigger coverage under the Post-1981 Policies absent physical injury to tangible property. *Diamond State*, 611 N.E.2d 1083, 1088-1090 (Ill. App. Ct. 1993); see also *Bituminous Casualty Corp. v. Gust K. Newberg Construction Co.*, 578 N.E.2d 1003, 1007 (Ill. App. Ct. 1991).

Nothing in the evidentiary material submitted to the trial court even suggests that any physical injury was caused to a structure or a mobile home at the time that a Qest System was installed. To the contrary, the only reasonable inference to be drawn from the parties' submissions is that a Qest System functions upon installation but is prone to developing leaks prematurely due to a progressive process of deterioration. . . .

Eljer, 718 N.E.2d at 1038-1041. The Illinois Supreme Court affirmed in part and reversed in part the appellate court's opinion. The decision expressly overruled the intermediate appellate court decision that Judge Posner had relied on to determine Illinois law, holding that the diminution of value to homes because of the installation of the Qest system was not "physical injury to tangible property within the meaning of the insurance policies issued post-1981." *Travelers v. Eljer*, 757 N.E.2d 481 (Ill. 2001).

CLAIMS-MADE VS. OCCURRENCE

Figure 4.2 above is one of the most commonly used "occurrence-based" general liability policies purchased by businesses. Figure 4.3 below shows the insuring agreement portion of the claims-made version of the CGL coverage form. Compare this insuring agreement with that in the occurrence version of the policy reproduced in Figure 4.2. The rest of the CGL claims-made form is identical in most respects to that occurrence version. If *Eljer* had purchased claims-made" CGL policies, which policies would have been triggered? The asbestos cases led the insurance industry to attempt to shift to claims-made insurance, but they were unsuccessful in the commercial general liability market because commercial buyers strongly preferred the occurrence form. Some of this history is recounted in *Hartford Fire Insurance Co. v. California*, 509 U.S. 764 (1993), which addressed the question whether actions taken by four large domestic liability insurers, in concert with several domestic and foreign reinsurers, to change the CGL policy in several ways (including from occurrence-based structure to a claims-made structure) was exempt from federal antitrust laws because of the McCarran-Ferguson Act or rather fell under the "boycott" carve out to the McCarran-Ferguson examption. It is possible to buy claims-made CGL coverage, but it is a small market when compared to sales of the occurrence coverage. Even pharmaceutical companies and medical device manufacturers have been able to purchase a hybrid form of coverage that provides many of the benefits of the occurrence form. *See* Richard Jacobs, Lorelie S. Masters, & Paul Stanley, Liability Insurance in International Arbitration: The Bermuda Form (2006).

Does the presence of a market for claims-made insurance policies undercut Judge Posner's reasoning in *Eljer?* Think back to the *Eljer* and OI cases and imagine that they had involved CGL policies with this claims-made insuring agreement. How would that have affected the amount of insurance that they would have had for their claims, and which insurance policies would have applied to which claims? These questions might be easier for you to answer after working through the problems that follow.

The one area in which the insurance industry successfully shifted into claims-made insurance is professional liability insurance, beginning with medical liability insurance in the mid-1970s. *See generally* Bob Works, *Excusing Nonoccurrence of Insurance Policy Conditions in Order to Avoid Disproportionate Forfeiture: Claims Made Formats as a Test Case*, 5 Conn. Ins. L.J. 505 (1998-1999). We will explore some of the consequences of that shift in the professional liability unit in this chapter.

COVERAGE A   BODILY INJURY AND PROPERTY DAMAGE LIABILITY

1. Insuring Agreement
    a. We will pay those sums that the insured becomes legally obligated
        to pay as damages because of "bodily injury" or "property damage"
        to which this insurance applies. We will have the right and duty to
        defend the insured against any "suit" seeking those damages. How-
        ever, we will have no duty to defend the insured against any "suit"
        seeking damages for "bodily injury" or "property damage" to which
        this insurance does not apply. We may, at our discretion, investigate
        any "occurrence" and settle any claim or "suit" that may result. . . .

    b. This insurance applies to "bodily injury" and "property damage" only
        if:
        (1) The "bodily injury" or "property damage" is caused by an "occur-
             rence" that takes place within the "coverage territory";
        (2) The "bodily injury" or "property damage" did not occur before the
             Retroactive Date, if any, shown in the Declarations or after the
             end of the policy period; and
        (3) A claim for damages because of the "bodily injury" or "property
             damage" is first made against any insured, in accordance with
             paragraph **c.** below, during the policy period or any Extended
             Reporting Period we provide under Section V — Extended Re-
             porting Periods.

    c. A claim by a person or organization seeking damages will be deemed
        to have been made at the earlier of the following times:
        (1) When notice of such claim is received and recorded by any in-
             sured or by us, whichever comes first; or
        (2) When we make settlement in accordance with Paragraph **1.a.**
             above. . . .

Copyright ISO 2003, reproduced by permission.

Figure 4.3.   CGL Claims-Made Form (excerpt from the insuring agreement only)

PROBLEM: THE CASES AGAINST DR. BILL

Dr. Bill plays three roles in this hypothetical: he is a physician, a business
owner, and an officer in Medical Imaging Company. In each of these roles, he
did something dumb that resulted in some type of loss to Ms. Q.

Here are all the dumb things that Dr. Bill did, all of which happened in year 1:

- **In his role as doctor**: During an operation to remove Ms. Q's appendix, Dr.
  Bill left a sponge in her abdomen.
- **In his role as business owner**: He forgot to repair the broken front step at
  his medical office. As a result, Ms. Q, while visiting the office for a checkup,
  fell and broke her kneecap.
- **In his role as officer of the company**: He unknowingly but negligently
  signed fraudulent checks for a large sum of money on behalf of Medical
  Imaging Company. It turns out that Ms. Q is a shareholder in the company.

For each of these separate harms, Ms. Q files suit in year 3. Now answer the following questions:

1. Assuming that Dr. Bill had a CGL occurrence policy (like the one in Figure 4.2) for each of the three years, which, if any, of those policies (i.e., year 1, year 2, or year 3) would be triggered by these incidents? Which of the three incidents would be the trigger? What additional information, if any, do you need to answer these questions?

2. Assuming instead that Dr. Bill had a CGL *claims-made* policy (like the one in Figure 4.3) for each of the three years, which, if any, of those policies would be triggered? Which of the three incidents would be the trigger? What additional information if any do you need to answer these questions?

3. Assuming that Medical Imaging Company had a directors' and officers' policy (like the one in Figure 4.4) for each of the three years, which, if any, of those policies would be triggered by the facts above? Which of the three incidents would be the trigger? What additional information, if any, do you need to answer these questions?

PROBLEM: DR. MARY'S CHOICE

A. In years 1-5, Dr. Mary had a series of CGL occurrence policies. In the middle of year 5, Dr. Mary learned that she could buy a CGL claims-made policy for year 6 at a much lower premium than a CGL occurrence policy.

Questions (you might want to review your answers to these question after answering the questions in C below):

1. Why is the claims-made policy for year 6 less expensive?

2. What "retroactive date" does Dr. Mary need?

3. What retroactive date and extended reporting period combination would make the coverage provided by a CGL claims-made policy for year 6 the same as the coverage provided by a CGL occurrence policy for year 6?

4. All other things being equal, if Dr. Mary switches to claims-made policies, what do you expect will happen to her premiums over time?

5. If Dr. Mary switches to a claims-made policy, what problems might she have later switching back to occurrence coverage?

INSURING AGREEMENT

The Underwriter will pay, on behalf of the **Insured Persons, Loss** from **Claims** first made during the **Policy Period,** except to the extent that such **Loss** is paid by any other insurance or as indemnification from any source.

DEFINITIONS

"**Claim**" means (1) written notice received by any **Insured Person** or the **Company** that any person or entity intends to hold an **Insured Person** responsible for a **Wrongful Act,** including but not limited to a legal, injunctive, or administrative proceeding against an **Insured Person** for a **Wrongful Act,** or (2) a legal, injunctive or administrative proceeding against an **Insured Person** solely by reason of his or her status as a director or officer of the **Company.**

"**Wrongful Act**" means any actual or alleged act, error, omission, misstatement, misleading statement or breach of duty by an **Insured Person** in his or her capacity as:

(1)   a director or officer of the **Company,** or
(2)   a director or officer of an **Outside Entity,** but only during such time that such service is at the specific written request of the **Company.**

Copyright 2001 Chubb Executive Risk. Reproduced by permission.

Figure 4.4.   Director's and Officers' Liability Form (selected provisions)*

* This specimen policy is provided for illustrative purposes only. The precise coverage afforded by any policy is subject to the terms and conditions of the policy as issued.

B. Dr. Mary decided to switch to the CGL claims-made policies, which she bought each year in years 6-10. In year 10, she decided that she would retire in year 11.

Questions (you might also want to review your answers to these questions after answering the questions in C):

1. Does Dr. Mary need new insurance policies when she is retired? Why?
2. What offers better coverage for a retired doctor: claims-made or occurrence policies? Does it depend on what kind of coverage the doctor has had? Why?
3. For how long does a retired doctor need malpractice insurance? Or, how long should the extended reporting period be?

C. Consider a claim alleging that Dr. Mary misdiagnosed a hip disorder in Jimmy D, leading to permanent partial disability (assume that there is no applicable statute of limitations). Potentially relevant facts include the following:

*   Jimmy visited Dr. Mary for annual checkups during years 1, 2, and 3.
*   The complaint alleges that diagnosing the disorder during any of these visits would have reduced the plaintiff's disability.
*   Another doctor discovered the disorder in year 9.
*   Dr. Mary learns Jimmy's parents have consulted a lawyer in year 10.
*   Jimmy and his parents file suit in year 11.

Question: Which of Dr. Mary's policies cover the claim? If you can't determine that, what questions do you need answered for you to know? Assume a reasonable answer to those questions (be sure to think through how you would answer those questions in a real case) and then decide.

D. Suppose that, instead of the CGL policies described above, during years 1-10, Dr. Mary had bought a medical malpractice policy with an insuring agreement like the one reproduced below.

Insuring Agreement:

The company will pay on behalf of the insured all sums which the insured shall be legally obligated to pay as damages because of injury arising out of the rendering of or failure to render, during the policy period, professional services in the practice of the named insured's profession as a physician or surgeon by the named insured or by any person for whose acts or omissions the named insured is legally responsible except as a member of a partnership or as an officer, director, or shareholder of a medical corporation, and the company shall have the right and duty to defend any suit against the insured seeking damages, even if any of the allegations of the suit are groundless, false, or fraudulent, and may make such investigation and such settlement of any claim or suit as it deems expedient, but the company shall not be obligated to pay any claim or judgment or defend any suit after the applicable limit of the company's liability has been exhausted by payment of judgments or settlements.

Figure 4.5.   Medical Malpractice Liability Form (selected provisions)

QUESTIONS

1. Which years' policies would be triggered by the claim in C?
2. Is this question easier to answer with the medical malpractice policy than with the CGL policies?
3. Does the "professional services" trigger provide any benefit to a doctor in retirement? Would it provide the same benefit if the medical malpractice policy was a claims-made policy? (We will explore the definition of "professional services" in Section III of this chapter.)

2.   What Is Bodily Injury?

The preceding cases addressed the question of *when* bodily injury or property damage takes place. The next two cases, decided by the New Jersey Supreme Court the same day, address a conceptually related question: *What* is bodily injury? The first case involves a claim brought by a schoolteacher against a parent for defamation and emotional distress. The second case involves a claim brought by a former employee against his former employer for wrongful discharge. In both cases, there was no physical contact between the plaintiff and the defendant, and the primary harm was emotional.

VOORHEES v. PREFERRED MUTUAL INSURANCE CO.

Supreme Court of New Jersey
607 A.2d 1255 (1992)

GARIBALDI, J.: The primary issue in this appeal is whether a homeowner's insurance policy providing coverage for bodily injuries caused by the insured will cover liability for emotional distress accompanied by physical manifestations. We hold that it will. . . .

In the underlying suit, filed in 1985, Eileen Voorhees was sued by her child's teacher for her comments questioning the teacher's competency and fitness. The complaint against Voorhees indicates that Voorhees and other parents had expressed their concern about the teacher at an open school-board meeting and had requested that their children be removed from her class. The school board decided to relieve the teacher of her teaching duties pending the results of a psychiatric examination. . . . The teacher alleged that the parents' accusations and the school system's response caused her extreme emotional distress. Medical evidence generated in response to interrogatories revealed that the emotional distress associated with the events had resulted in "an undue amount of physical complaints," including "headaches, stomach pains, nausea, . . . [and] body pains. . . ."

Voorhees' homeowner's-insurance policy requires Preferred Mutual to defend her against any suits alleging "bodily injury," defined as "bodily harm, sickness or disease." Authorities dispute whether emotional-distress injuries are covered under bodily-injury insurance policies.

The terms of that dispute focus on two primary considerations: (1) whether the term "bodily injury" is ambiguous and should thus be construed against the insurer; and (2) whether finding coverage for emotional distress under a bodily-injury policy would conflate the coverage provided by bodily-injury policies with the broader coverage traditionally provided by personal-injury policies.

Many of the courts addressing the ambiguity of the phrase "bodily injury" in light of claims for emotional distress have done so in all-or-nothing terms, ignoring the specific nature of the injuries alleged and the context in which they occurred. We believe that one cannot evaluate the "ambiguity" of a phrase like "bodily injury" in a vacuum. Whether the term is ambiguous depends on the context in which it is being used.

In the present case, the schoolteacher's alleged emotional injuries resulted in certain physical consequences, including nausea, headaches, and the like. This case thus requires us to address the "ambiguity" of the phrase "bodily injury" in the context of emotional injuries that have led to physical consequences. We thus reserve the discussion of its ambiguity when emotional distress does not result in physical consequence for our companion case, *SL Industries, Inc. v. American Motorists Insurance Co.,* 607 A.2d 1266 (N.J. 1992)....

We conclude that the term "bodily injury" is ambiguous as it relates to emotional distress accompanied by physical manifestations. That ambiguity should be resolved in favor of the insured. Moreover, we find such an interpretation to be in accord with the insured's objectively-reasonable expectations. That "emotional distress can and often does have a direct effect on other bodily functions" is well recognized. An insured who is sued on account of an injury involving physical symptoms could reasonably expect an insurance policy for liability for bodily injuries to provide coverage....

We conclude, therefore, that "bodily injury" encompasses emotional injuries accompanied by physical manifestations. Here the injured party's emotional distress resulted in physical manifestations. Attached to the schoolteacher's answers to interrogatories was a medical report by a psychiatrist who had examined the teacher. In his report the doctor states that the teacher had informed him that she suffered from "headaches, stomach pains, nausea, depression, and body pains." The doctor found such physical complaints "real" and consistent with the teacher's emotional distress allegations. We note that the physical manifestations necessary to trigger coverage under a "bodily injury" policy do not, per se, demonstrate the severe emotional distress necessary to sustain a claim for the infliction of emotional distress. We are defining the term "bodily injury" under insurance law, not tort law.

Because the teacher demonstrated that she was suing Voorhees for bodily injuries incurred as a result of her emotional distress, Preferred Mutual was obligated to defend her unless and until the physical ailments were disproved or the underlying allegations were dismissed....

SL INDUSTRIES, INC. v. AMERICAN MOTORISTS INSURANCE CO.

Supreme Court of New Jersey
607 A.2d 1266 (1992)

[Editor's Note: This case concerned American Motorists' obligation to defend a claim brought against SL Industries for wrongful discharge and age discrimination by a plaintiff, Mr. Whitcomb.]

GARIBALDI, J. . . .

A.   Coverage Under the Bodily-Injury Policy

SL Industries' General Liability Policy obligated American to defend the company for liability for "bodily injury," defined as "bodily injury, sickness or disease." In *Voorhees v. Preferred Mutual*, [607 A.2d 1255 (N.J. 1992)], we concluded that when emotional distress results in physical manifestations the term "bodily injury" is ambiguous, and must therefore be construed in favor of the insured. We noted that such an interpretation accords with an insured's objectively-reasonable expectations.

Here Whitcomb, through his response to interrogatories, indicated that he had "suffered loss of sleep, loss of self-esteem, humiliation, and irritability." The final pretrial Stipulation and Order indicated that Whitcomb was seeking damages for "physical and mental pain and suffering, including humiliation, loss of self-esteem, irritability and sleeplessness."

We must determine whether Whitcomb's symptoms constitute physical injuries resulting from emotional distress. The only symptom that might remotely be considered a physical injury is his alleged sleeplessness. Although we recognize that there is no litmus test for determining where to draw the line between emotional and physical injuries, we nonetheless believe that such a distinction exists. Even acknowledging that it is not unusual for emotional distress to cause physical symptoms, see *Voorhees, supra,* not all emotional distress is physically manifested. In evaluating whether sleeplessness is an emotional or physical condition, we conclude that it is, at base, emotional in nature. To designate sleeplessness a physical injury would be tantamount to conceding that emotional and physical injuries are indistinguishable. In contrast, the headaches, stomach pains, nausea, body pains, and medically-diagnosed "undue amount of physical complaints" that resulted from emotional distress in our companion case, *Voorhees,* do fall on the side of physical injuries. As in *Voorhees, supra,* we note that our evaluation of what constitutes a "bodily injury" triggering insurance coverage is not intended to define the term "bodily injury" with respect to an emotional-distress claim under tort law.

The question next presented is whether emotional distress unaccompanied by physical injuries can be deemed within the coverage of an insurance policy protecting against liability for bodily injuries. As we noted in *Voorhees,* whether a policy phrase is ambiguous depends on the factual context in which it is applied. . . .

We hold that in the context of purely emotional distress, without physical manifestations, the phrase "bodily injury" is not ambiguous. Its ordinary meaning connotes some sort of physical problem.

Many jurisdictions agree that the term "bodily injury" is not ambiguous in its requirement that an injury have some physical component in order to be considered "bodily." We find unpersuasive the case law construing "bodily injuries" to include emotional injuries without physical manifestations. First, some courts are unpersuasive because their conclusory holdings are largely unexplained. Second, other courts have concluded that the impossibility of separating physical from mental symptoms justifies the conclusion that both mental and physical injuries are bodily injuries. We recognize that the difficulty in distinguishing between mental and physical injuries may justify characterizing "bodily injury" to be ambiguous in some circumstances. *See, e.g., Voorhees, supra.* Nonetheless, that occasional difficulty does not justify holding the term "bodily injury" to be ambiguous with respect to all types of emotional injuries. The phrase should be analyzed on a case-by-case basis to determine whether the alleged injuries are sufficiently akin to physical injuries to render the term "bodily injury" ambiguous. . . . [S]uch an examination in this case discloses that Whitcomb's alleged injuries do not qualify as bodily injuries.

Nor are we persuaded by the argument that we should find emotional-distress claims within the coverage of a bodily-injury policy because insurance coverage ought to conform to developments in tort law. When the standard insurance language was developed, it was designed to cover insureds against the type of suits most likely to be brought against them—suits claiming bodily injuries. Now that tort law has expanded to recognize claims for emotional distress, both with and without physical manifestations, the argument is that an insured would reasonably expect coverage to be extended to those suits. We disagree. Tort law and insurance law are not coextensive. When tort law changes, courts should not presume whether, and to what degree, the parties would want those developments reflected in the contract. Regardless of changes in tort law, an insured does not reasonably expect the policy to be interpreted in ways that contravene the contract's language.

Moreover, this case does not present a situation in which an insured's objectively-reasonable expectations are so contrary to the policy's ordinary meaning that they should overcome that meaning. Most insureds understand that the coverage of their "bodily injury" policies is limited to injuries involving some sort of connection with a physical problem.

In sum, we conclude that in the context of purely emotional injuries, without physical manifestations, the phrase "bodily injury" is not ambiguous. Its ordinary meaning connotes a physical problem. Because Whitcomb's emotional claims lacked physical manifestations, SL Industries will not be able to recover for its liability to Whitcomb under the bodily-injury policy.

NOTES AND QUESTIONS

1. The court concludes that the term "bodily injury," which is the same term in both policies, is ambiguous in the *Voorhees* case but unambiguous in the *SL Industries* case. How does it reconcile those seemingly incongruous results? Is the court's approach to interpreting that term in the policies consistent with the approaches to interpretation discussed at the beginning of Chapter 2? How does it compare with the American Law Institute (ALI) approach to interpretation (discussed in Section II of Chapter 2) in particular?

2. These cases, especially the *SL Industries* case, illustrate the fact that liability insurance policies are sometimes interpreted not to provide coverage for particular types of tort or tort-like causes of action. These two cases address the relationship between tort and insurance law. The cases reflect an "insurance as contract" understanding in which insurance contracts are voluntary undertakings by insurance companies to assume specifically enumerated financial obligations imposed by tort rules. We might also understand liability insurance as the financing mechanism for tort compensation. From this perspective, promoting victim compensation may be a legitimate goal in interpreting liability insurance contracts. What cases have you read that reflect the latter understanding?

3. Risk distribution is one of the main justifications for products liability, and for that reason insurability is an important factor in some states in deciding the scope of products liability. Insurance has also played an important role in the abrogation of common law immunities such as charitable immunity and interfamily immunity. If courts are going to take insurability into ac-

count, should they consider whether something theoretically is insurable, whether there in fact is insurance in the market, or whether the particular defendant in fact has insurance? *See, e.g., Ard v. Ard,* 414 So. 2d 1066 (Fla. 1982) (ruling that parental immunity is waived to the extent of the applicable liability insurance coverage).

The frequency and magnitude of cyber-security breaches at private corporations, as well as government institutions, seems to be growing with every passing year.[3] From the large retail establishments, such as Target, to established financial institutions, such as JPMorgan Chase, to the U.S. government's Office of Personnel Management, tech-savvy criminals have found ways either to create or exploit existing loopholes in even the most sophisticated cyber-security systems, creating the possibility that the sensitive personal and financial information of millions of individuals may be compromised. Further, as the Internet of Things expands to include mechanical devices that potentially give the most malicious hackers the capacity to cause property damage and bodily injury on a vast scale—from utility infrastructure to autonomous vehicles—the scope of cyber-risk seems to be expanding.

For this reason, organizations increasingly seek to find coverage for cyber-risks either in their existing property and liability policies or in the newer, specialized cyber-risk policies offered by many insurers.[4] Most major insurers now offer policies that, in the event of a data breach, provide both first-party coverage (e.g., for the cost of investigating and correcting any security breach and dealing with the negative publicity, as well as business-interruption losses) and third-party coverages (e.g., for the cost of defending and indemnifying claims for the unauthorized disclosure of customers' private information). Some insurers even offer coverage for cyber-extortion, a sort of data kidnapping in which hackers threaten to release a virus into an organization's (or individual's) computer system unless a ransom is paid.

Because of the relatively new nature of cyber-risk, the number of published judicial opinions involving cyber-risk policies is relatively small. The following cyber-risk case does not involve intentional hacking, but rather an accidental disclosure of what was meant to be private information. Consider closely the language of the policy in question. Also, as you read the case, think about whether there would be liability coverage here under the CGL policy shown in Figure 4.2.

TRAVELERS INDEMNITY COMPANY OF AMERICA
v.
PORTAL HEALTHCARE SOLUTIONS, LLC

35 F. Supp. 3d 765
(U.S. Dist. Ct., E.D. Virginia, 2014)

LEE, District Judge.

This matter is before the Court on Plaintiff Travelers Indemnity Company of America's ("Travelers") and Defendant Portal Healthcare Solutions, LLC ("Portal")'s Cross–Motions for Summary Judgment. (Docs. 20, 22). The parties

---

3. Indeed, there is good evidence that this is so. *http://www.informationisbeautiful.net/visualizations/worlds-biggest-data-breaches-hacks/* (graphically illustrating the increasing number and increasingly large—in terms of numbers of records stolen—hacks over the past ten years).

4. For a useful summary of the legal issues related to cyber-risk insurance, *see generally* Bert Wells, Rukesh Korde, & Teresa Lew, 4-29 New Appleman on Insurance Law Library Edition §29.01 (2015).

dispute whether Travelers has a duty to defend Portal against class-action allegations that Portal posted confidential medical records on the internet, making the records available to anyone who searched for a patient's name and clicked on the first result.

The issue before the Court is whether Portal's insurance policies with Travelers cover the conduct alleged in the underlying class action. The Court holds that the insurance policies do cover the conduct alleged because exposing confidential medical records to online searching is "publication" giving "unreasonable publicity" to, or "disclos[ing]" information about, a person's private life. Thus, Travelers has a duty to defend Portal against the underlying class action. Accordingly, the Court denies Travelers' Motion for Summary Judgment and grants Portal's Motion for Summary Judgment.

I. Background

This case involves two policies that Travelers issued to Portal covering the electronic publication of certain materials. Travelers is an insurance provider and Portal is a business specializing in the electronic safekeeping of medical records for hospitals, clinics, and other medical providers. Travelers issued to Portal two substantially identical insurance policies (collectively the "Policies"): the first policy was effective from January 31, 2012 to January 31, 2013 (hereinafter the "2012 Policy"), and the second policy was effective from January 31, 2013 to January 31, 2014 (hereinafter the "2013 Policy").

The 2012 and 2013 Policies obligate Travelers to pay sums Portal becomes legally obligated to pay as damages because of injury arising from (1) the "electronic publication of material that . . . gives unreasonable publicity to a person's private life" (the language found in the 2012 Policy) or (2) the "electronic publication of material that . . . discloses information about a person's private life" (the language found in the 2013 Policy). (*See* Doc. 1, at 5–6.)

On April 18, 2013, a class-action suit was filed in New York state court alleging that Portal failed to safeguard the confidential medical records of patients at Glen Falls Hospital ("Glen Falls"), posting those records on the internet and causing those records to become publicly accessible on the internet. Glen Falls had contracted with Portal for the electronic storage and maintenance of its patients' confidential medical records, and either Glen Falls or Portal contracted with Carpathia Hosting, Inc. to host those records on an electronic server. The class-action suit brings claims for negligence or gross negligence, breach of warranty, breach of contract, and injunctive relief.

Two patients of Glen Falls, Dara Halliday and Teresa Green, discovered that when they conducted a "Google" search of their respective names, the first link that appeared was a direct link to their respective Glen Falls medical records. The class-action suit alleges that patients' confidential medical records were accessible, viewable, copyable, printable, and downloadable from the internet by unauthorized persons without security restriction from November 2, 2012 to March 14, 2013.

On April 3, 2014, Travelers filed a Motion for Summary Judgment seeking a declaration that it does not have a duty to defend Portal in the class action suit. On the same day, Portal also filed a Motion for Summary Judgment seeking an order compelling Travelers to defend it against the underlying class action.

II. [Editor's Note: Discussion of summary judgment standard
of review omitted]

III. ANALYSIS

The Court grants Portal's Motion for Summary Judgment and denies Travelers'
Motion for Summary Judgment because exposing confidential medical records
to public online searching placed highly sensitive, personal information before
the public. Thus, the conduct falls within the Policies' coverage for "publication" giving "unreasonable publicity" to, or "disclos[ing]" information about, a
person's private life, triggering Travelers' duty to defend.

. . .

The Policies contain two relevant prerequisites to coverage. First, the Policies
require an electronic "publication" of material. Second, the 2012 and 2013
Policies respectively require that the published material give "unreasonable
publicity" to, or "disclose" information about, a person's private life. Using this
framework, the Court's analysis is divided into, first, an analysis of how Portal's
alleged conduct constitutes a "publication" of electronic material, and second,
an analysis of how the "publication" gave "unreasonable publicity" to, and
"disclose[d]" information about, patients' private lives.

A. MAKING CONFIDENTIAL MEDICAL RECORDS PUBLICLY
ACCESSIBLE VIA AN INTERNET SEARCH DOES FALL WITHIN
THE PLAIN MEANING OF "PUBLICATION."

First, the Court finds that exposing material to the online searching of a patient's name does constitute a "publication" of electronic material, satisfying the
Policies' first prerequisite to coverage.

The term "publication" is not defined in the 2012 or 2013 Policies. Because the
term is undefined, "general rules of contract interpretation, and specifically insurance contract interpretation, require" that the term "be given its plain and ordinary
meaning." *Solers, Inc. v. Hartford Cas. Ins. Co.*, 146 F. Supp. 2d 785, 792 (E.D. Va.
2001). Virginia courts customarily turn to dictionaries for help in deciphering a
term's plain meaning. *See e.g., Sheets v. Castle*, 263 Va. 407, 559 S.E.2d 616, 620 (2002)
(turning to *Black's Law Dictionary* for the plain meaning of "prevailing party"). . . .

Here, Travelers has provided the Court with a definition of "publication"
from *Webster's Third New International Dictionary* as "to place before the public (as
through a mass medium)." Exposing medical records to the online searching
of a patient's name, followed by a click on the first result, at least "potentially
or arguably" places those records before the public. Any member of the public
could retrieve the records of a Glen Falls patient, whether he or she was actively
seeking those records or searching a patient's name for other purposes, like a
background check. Because medical records were placed before the public, the
Court finds that Portal's conduct falls within the plain meaning of "publication."

Travelers raises two arguments for why Portal's conduct did not effect a "publication." The Court finds neither argument persuasive. First, Travelers suggests
that because "the entire purpose of the services Portal provided was to keep the
medical records private and confidential," there cannot have been a publication. But the issue cannot be whether Portal intentionally exposed the records
to public viewing since the definition of "publication" does not hinge on the

would-be publisher's intent. Rather, it hinges on whether the information was placed before the public. Because an unintentional publication is still a publication, the Court rejects Travelers' intent-based argument.

Travelers' second argument is that Portal's conduct did not effect a "publication" because no third party is alleged to have viewed the information. Rather, the patients accessed their own records and only alleged that the information was available for view by a third party. But again, the issue is not whether a third party accessed the information because the definition of "publication" does not hinge on third-party access.

Publication occurs when information is "placed before the public," not when a member of the public reads the information placed before it. By Travelers' logic, a book that is bound and placed on the shelves of Barnes & Noble is not "published" until a customer takes the book off the shelf and reads it. Travelers' understanding of the term "publication" does not comport with the term's plain meaning, and the medical records were published the moment they became accessible to the public via an online search.

Lastly, Travelers cites to nonbinding law distinguishable from the present case. Two of the cases involve plaintiffs—and only the plaintiffs—being handed paper receipts bearing their personal credit card information. *See Creative Hospitality Ventures, Inc. v. U.S. Liability Ins. Co.*, 444 Fed. Appx. 370 (11th Cir. 2011); *Whole Enchilada, Inc. v. Travelers Prop. Cas. Co. of Am.*, 581 F. Supp. 2d 677 (W.D. Pa. 2008). These cases are distinguishable because, here, the confidential medical records were not given to the patients directly but were posted publicly online. Thus, the medical records were given not only to the patients but to anyone with a computer and internet access.

Travelers cites to a third case involving the loss of computer tapes containing personal data. *See Recall Total Info. Mgmt. Inc. v. Fed. Ins. Co.*, 147 Conn. App. 450, 83 A.3d 664 (2013). Specifically, the computer tapes fell out of the back of a van, were taken by an unknown person, and were never recovered. *Id.* at 667. This case is distinguishable because, here, the information was posted on the internet and thus, was given not just to a single thief but to anyone with a computer and internet access.

For these reasons, the Court finds that the facts and circumstances alleged in the class-action complaint at least "potentially or arguably" constitute a "publication" within the meaning of the Policies.

B. POSTING CONFIDENTIAL MEDICAL RECORDS ONLINE WITHOUT SECURITY RESTRICTION GIVES "UNREASONABLE PUBLICITY" TO, AND "DISCLOSURE" OF INFORMATION ABOUT, PATIENTS' PRIVATE LIVES.

Next, the Court finds that the public availability of a patient's confidential medical records gave "unreasonable publicity" to that patient's private life and "disclose[d]" information about that patient's private life, satisfying the Policies' second prerequisite to coverage.

Here, Travelers provides a definition of "publicity" from *Merriam Webster's Collegiate Dictionary* as "the quality or state of being obvious or exposed to the general view." There can be no question that posting medical records online without security restriction exposes the records to the general view and thus, gives the records "publicity" since, quite literally, any member of the public can view, download, or copy those records.

Travelers argues that no "publicity" occurred when Portal posted the records because "Portal did not take steps *designed* to attract public interest or gain public attention or support." This argument focuses on the second definition of "publicity" as "an act or device designed to attract public interest." That, however, is only one definition of "publicity." That Portal's conduct falls within the broader and primary definition of "publicity" suffices to establish that Portal gave unreasonable publicity to patients' private lives when it posted their medical records online without security restriction.

Travelers also provides a definition of "disclosure" from *Black's Law Dictionary* as meaning "[t]he act or process of making known something that was previously unknown; a revelation of facts." Here, there can be no question that the unrestricted posting of medical records on the internet made something known that previously had been unknown. Specifically, it made medical records previously known only to the patient suddenly known to the public at large.

Travelers argues that Portal's conduct did not "disclose" patients' private lives because the patients in the class-action suit only viewed their own records and, of course, the patients already had knowledge of those records. However, under the plain meaning of "disclosure," the records were disclosed the moment they were posted publicly online, regardless of whether a third party viewed them. Travelers' own definition of "disclosure" refers to the "[t]he act or *process* of making known something that was previously unknown." (*See id.* (emphasis added)). What Portal did by posting the records was engage in the *process* of making previously unknown records suddenly known to the public at large.

For these reasons, the Court finds that the facts and circumstances alleged in the class-action complaint gave "unreasonable publicity" to, and "disclose[d]" information about, patients' private lives within the meaning of the Policies.

IV. CONCLUSION

For the reasons above, Travelers' Motion for Summary Judgment is DENIED as to Traveler's duty to defend Portal in the underlying class action, Portal's Motion for Summary Judgment is GRANTED as to the duty to defend, and the Court DIRECTS Travelers to provide a defense for Portal against the underlying class action.

NOTES

Scholars are beginning to examine the roles that cyber-risk insurance and cyber-risk insurers play in the way that companies do business in the modern (digital) world. *See,* e.g., Shauhin Talesh, *Data Breach, Privacy, and Cyber Liability Insurance: How Insurance Companies Act as "Compliance Managers" for Businesses,* LAW & SOCIAL INQUIRY (under review). The abstract to Professor Talesh's paper describes his research as follows:

> Through participant observation at cyber liability insurance conferences, interviews, and content analysis of insurer loss prevention manuals and risk management services, my study bridges these two literatures and highlights how the insurance field acts as a compliance manager for organizations dealing with cyber security threats. Well beyond pooling and transferring risk, insurance companies offer cyber liability insurance and a series of unique risk-management services that influence the form of compliance of organizations dealing

with privacy laws. My data reveal that while prior empirical research suggests that human resource officials, managers, and in-house counsel influence the meaning of compliance by communicating an altered ideology of what laws mean that is shaped by managerial values, insurance institutions—and the risk management services that accompany cyber liability insurance—play an important role in shaping the way organizations deal with cyber threats and comply with privacy laws.

3.   The Application of Limits and Deductibles: The "Number of Occurrences" Issue

As you may know from examining your own insurance policies, insurance companies limit the risks that they assume through the use of deductibles and policy limits. A "deductible" is the amount that the policyholder must pay for a given claim before the insurance company has to pay. The basic idea behind a deductible is to give the policyholder a stake in the claim (addressing moral hazard) and to avoid insurance company involvement in very small claims (for which it makes little sense for people to buy insurance). Insurance companies offer a range of deductibles that allow policyholders to trade off certainty and price. Homeowners' and personal automobile insurance policies can have deductibles as low as $100. Commercial liability policies can have deductibles as high as many millions of dollars. A very high deductible is sometimes called a "self-insured retention" in the commercial context.

Particularly in the mass tort context, the application of deductibles can have a very significant impact. For example, OI had a $100,000 per occurrence self-insured retention until 1970 and $250,000 after that. Deciding the nature of the asbestos "occurrence" would make an enormous difference to OI and its insurers. If each separate claim is a separate "occurrence," OI essentially would have no insurance coverage for the claims (because OI would have to contribute $100,000 or $250,000 for each claim for each triggered policy period). On the other hand, if the decision to manufacture asbestos is the "occurrence," OI would have a great deal of insurance coverage. *Compare Owens-Illinois v. United Ins. Co.,* 625 A.2d 1 (N.J. Super. 1993) (holding that claims against OI arose out of a "series of interrelated acts" that "should be treated as a single occurrence for purpose of calculating the deductible") *with Metropolitan Life Ins. Co. v. Aetna Cas. & Sur. Co.,* 765 A.2d 891 (Conn. 2001) (holding that each individual claim arises from a separate occurrence, with the result in that case that the excess insurers did not have to pay for any asbestos claims against Met Life). People on both sides of coverage litigation have claimed that courts are unusually results-oriented in deciding the number of occurrences.

If the "deductible" determines the point at which the insurance company must begin to pay claims, the policy "limit" determines the point when the insurance company can stop paying claims.[5] A policy limit defines the maximum that the insurance company is obligated to pay (unless there are consequential or punitive damages, as explored in Section VII in Chapter 2). Like deductibles,

---

5. When we get to the "duty to defend" in Chapter 5, we will see that in most liability insurance policies, the costs of defense do not count against the limits and that the insurance company generally has a duty to defend a particular claim until the end of the litigation, even if it is willing to pay the entire policy limits to settle the claim.

limits are commonly written on a per occurrence basis. In addition, a policy may have an "aggregate" limit, which represents the total amount that the company promises to pay for all occurrences covered by a particular policy.

TRANSPORT INSURANCE CO. v. LEE WAY MOTOR FREIGHT, INC.

**United States District Court for the Northern
District of Texas, Dallas Division
487 F. Supp. 1325 (1980)**

SANDERS, J. . . .

In a previous suit, *United States v. Lee Way,* Lee Way was found to have engaged in a pattern and practice of race discrimination and ordered to pay over $1.8 million in damages to individual discriminatees. In the present case Transport asks this Court to determine whether the liability imposed upon Lee Way in the previous suit resulted from a single occurrence, a separate occurrence as to each of the four terminal locations involved, or a separate occurrence as to each of the individual discriminatees.

The Court finds and concludes that the pattern and practice of discrimination found by the court in *United States v. Lee Way* constitutes "one occurrence" as that term is used in the insurance policies. . . .

I.   BACKGROUND

A.   UNITED STATES V. LEE WAY

In June of 1972, the United States filed suit against Lee Way and two labor unions, alleging that they had engaged in and were engaging in a pattern and practice of discrimination in employment. *United States v. Lee Way Motor Freight, Inc., et al.,* W.D. Okla., Civil Action No. 72–445. Following several months of trial, the district court issued its findings and conclusions on December 27, 1973, in which it found and concluded that Lee Way had engaged in a pattern and practice of employment discrimination. The court determined that Lee Way had discriminated on the grounds of race in its hiring practices and in its promotion and transfer policies, all of which operated to restrict black employees to the poorest paying and least desirable jobs.[6] The court noted that certain practices, although neutral on their face, operated to freeze the status quo of prior discriminatory practices and thus could not be lawfully maintained.

After referring the case to a special master for determination of individual entitlement to relief, the trial court entered its final judgment October 11, 1977, wherein it ordered Lee Way to pay the sum of $1,818,191.33 as damages in the form of forty-seven individual back-pay awards, ranging from $3,000 to $138,000. . . .

---

6. The Court found that Lee Way discriminated against blacks in hiring and job placement and specifically found that Lee Way's no-transfer policy, which was neutral in its face, operated discriminatorily. (Findings 34–37 and Conclusions 9–11). It was company policy that no employee would transfer between job classifications covered by different bargaining units. The policy's effect "froze" blacks into menial and lower-paying positions which they traditionally had held and prevented placement in more desirable higher-paying jobs. Even though this policy had been found to be unlawful in *Jones v. Lee Way Motor Freight, Inc.,* 431 F.2d 245 (10th Cir. 1970), Lee Way had continued to enforce a similar policy which provided that anyone who transferred could not carry over his seniority for bidding and layoff purposes. It, too, was found to be unlawful by the district court (Conclusion 10).

B.   THE INSURANCE POLICIES

For many years prior to the filing of *United States v. Lee Way*, Lee Way had purchased all its insurance coverage from Transport. In January 1967, Lee Way purchased from Transport additional insurance in the form of a series of eight excess umbrella insurance policies which afforded substantially higher limits of liability and broader coverages than the underlying Transport policies. This excess umbrella coverage (in the form of annually renewed policies) was in effect from January 1, 1967, through early 1978. The first five policies (those in effect from January 1, 1967, until mid-1972) expressly provided coverage for discrimination. However, in late August or early September 1972, Transport rewrote the umbrella policy then in effect with an endorsement excluding any future coverage for discrimination. Consequently, in this action the Court is only concerned with the five umbrella policies which were in effect from January 1, 1967, through late August or early September, 1972.

The general coverage provision [in the policies at issue] says that Transport will indemnify Lee Way

> for all sums which (Lee Way) shall be obligated to pay by reason of the liability imposed upon (Lee Way) by law . . . for damages, . . . on account of personal injuries . . . caused by or arising out of each occurrence happening anywhere in the world.

The term "personal injuries" is separately defined and includes discrimination as one kind of personal injury. . . .

The declarations of the policies in question provide for a deductible amount to be borne by Lee Way of $25,000 per occurrence. Thus, if Lee Way's discriminatory conduct constituted one occurrence, then Lee Way bears only one $25,000 deductible amount. If Lee Way's conduct as to each individual discriminatee constituted a separate occurrence as to each, then Lee Way must bear the first $25,000 of each back-pay award.

II.   SINGLE VS. MULTIPLE OCCURRENCE

The Court is unable to find another case that has addressed this precise issue. The question of what constitutes a single "accident" or "occurrence," as the terms are used within liability policies to limit an insurer's liability to a specified amount, has been addressed in numerous cases and is the subject of one annotation. 55 A.L.R.2d 1300. The cases indicate that a court should "examine the policies in light of the business purposes sought to be achieved by the parties and the plain meaning of the words chosen by them to effect those purposes." *Champion International Corp. v. Continental Cas. Co.*, 546 F.2d 502, 505 (2nd Cir. 1976); *see also, Union Carbide Corp. v. Travelers Indem. Co.*, 399 F. Supp. 12, 17 (W.D. Pa. 1975). The district court in *Union Carbide v. Travelers, supra,* explained that a term such as "occurrence" should be construed in the light of the hazard insured against. *Id.*

In this case the hazard insured against is discrimination. In the prior litigation, Lee Way was found to have engaged in a "pattern and practice" of discrimination. "Pattern and practice" actions have the following characteristics:

1. A pattern and practice of discrimination exists only where the defendant routinely follows generalized policies, procedures or practices which have a discriminatory effect. Individual instances of discrimination are not a pattern and practice.

2. A pattern and practice of discrimination is ordinarily proven through the use of statistics and other evidence of a general nature. Proof of individual instances of discrimination alone is not proof of a pattern and practice.

3. In a pattern and practice case, the cause of action belongs to the Government and not to the individuals affected. However, once the defendant's liability is established, the Government can obtain equitable relief (including back pay) for those specific individuals found to have been affected by the pattern and practice.

4. Intent to discriminate is irrelevant in a pattern and practice case. Instead, the Government must merely show that the defendant's policies, procedures or practices were not accidental or inadvertent.

5. In a pattern and practice case, the defendant's policies, procedures and practices need not themselves be discriminatory. Rather, if they are facially neutral but have the effect of perpetuating past discrimination, the defendant is nevertheless liable.

The findings and conclusions of the district court in *United States v. Lee Way* indicate that these same characteristics existed at Lee Way. The court concluded that Lee Way discriminated on a "system-wide basis" which was found to be "corporate policy." The government presented statistical evidence establishing a prima facie showing of discrimination as well as evidence of individual instances serving as "examples" which "confirmed" the Court's findings of system-wide discrimination. Furthermore, the court found that evidence of the company's discriminatory reputation was relevant and admissible in proving a pattern or practice of racial discrimination. The judgment established clearly that the discrimination suffered by Lee Way's minority employees resulted from a uniform, system-wide policy.

When the language of the Transport policies is construed in light of the particular hazard insured against, the inevitable conclusion is that the discrimination suffered by Lee Way's employees constituted a single "occurrence" as that term is used in the policies.

The definition of "occurrence" is broad in its scope:

> The term "occurrence" means an accident or a happening or event or a continuous or repeated exposure to conditions which . . . result in personal injury . . . during the policy period. All such exposure to substantially the same general conditions existing at or emanating from one premises location shall be deemed one occurrence.

The first sentence of the definition standing alone indicates that the discrimination here constituted one "occurrence." Lee Way's employees were subject to a "continuous or repeated exposure to conditions," viz., company-wide discriminatory policies and practices, which resulted in "personal injury," i.e., discrimination. The prior judgment (as well as relevant case law) shows that the pattern and practice of discrimination found to have occurred consisted of generalized discriminatory policies routinely followed. Minority employees suffered a "continuous or repeated exposure" to such discriminatory conditions and thus there was only "one occurrence."

The last sentence of the quoted definition establishes clearly that the pattern and practice of discrimination constituted "one occurrence." It states, that all exposure "to substantially the same general conditions" shall be deemed "one occurrence." The individual discriminatees were exposed to the same system-wide corporate policy of discrimination, albeit at different times and places. Yet, the language is clear in its intent that all exposure to the same conditions is deemed one occurrence. It follows that all exposure to the pattern and practice of discrimination (i.e., "substantially the same general conditions") must be deemed "one occurrence."

The fact that Lee Way operated four separate trucking terminals (Oklahoma City, Los Angeles, Houston, and San Antonio) is no reason for dividing Lee Way's liability into four separate occurrences—one occurrence at each of the four terminal locations. Exposure to the same general conditions "existing at or *emanating* from one premises location" constitutes a single "occurrence." (emphasis added) The court in *United States v. Lee Way* concluded that the pattern and practice of discrimination was a continuous company-wide policy traceable to the decisions and procedures made at Lee Way's headquarters terminal in Oklahoma City. Lee Way's discriminatory policies originated in Oklahoma City and emanated from its headquarters there; the discriminatory policies thus emanated from one location; it would gild the lily to say more.

The fact that the parties provided for a "per occurrence" deductible, as opposed to a "per claim" deductible, is further indication that the parties intended that Lee Way's discriminatory practices would be deemed a single occurrence. The $25,000 deductible "per occurrence" suggests that the policy was not intended to define coverage on the basis of individual instances of discrimination. In a case involving very similar policy language, the Second Circuit affirmed a district court's holding that the continuous and repeated distribution of defective products constituted but a single "occurrence," even though there were 1400 different claims arising from individual ultimate users. *Champion International Corp. v. Continental Cas. Co.*, 546 F.2d 502, *supra*. The appellate court considered the insured's selection of a "per occurrence" deduction to be important in interpreting "occurrence." *Id.* at 505. It regarded the insured's distribution of defective vinyl-covered paneling as one "occurrence" out of which 1400 "claims" arose. *Id.* at 506. In the instant case, each individual award of back pay should be regarded as a different "claim" arising out of but one "occurrence," viz., the continuous and repeated exposure to discriminatory employment conditions.

Transport could have limited the meaning and scope of discrimination to single, individual acts of discrimination and excluded from coverage a pattern and practice of discrimination; it did not do so. Discrimination is included without qualification in the definition of "personal injury," and "personal injury" is used in the expansive definition of "occurrence." . . .

Finally, although the plain language of the policy alone supports the Court's "single occurrence" conclusion, the analogous case law also upholds this result. The rationale underlying the various decisions which have held that particular events constituted but a single occurrence has been that courts generally look to the cause as opposed to the effect of such events. The great majority of courts have adopted a "cause" analysis, *American Casualty Co. v. Heary*, 432 F. Supp. 995, 997, holding that where a single event, process or condition results in injuries, it will be deemed a single occurrence even though the injuries may be widespread in both time and place and may affect a multitude of individuals. *See St. Paul-Mercury Indemnity Co. v. Rutland*, 225 F.2d 689 (5th Cir. 1955) (derailment resulting in injury to sixteen freight cars single occurrence); *Haerens v.*

Commercial Cas. Ins. Co., 279 P.2d 211 (Cal. App. Dep't Super. Ct. 1955) (several panes of glass broken while working on house single occurrence); *Barrett v. Iowa National Mut. Ins. Co.*, 264 F.2d 224 (9th Cir. 1959) (fire damage to contents of different apartments single occurrence); *Weissblum v. Glens Falls Ins. Co.*, 219 N.Y.S.2d 711, *rev'd on other grounds*, 244 N.Y.S.2d 689 (N.Y. 1961) (numerous lights broken at different times by different persons during construction work single occurrence); *Wilkinson & Son, Inc. v. Providence*, 307 A.2d 639 (N.J. Super. Ct. Law Div. 1973) (contractor damaged several apartments by tracking paint on carpets single occurrence). But *see Elston-Richards Storage Co. v. Indemnity Ins. Co. of North America*, 194 F. Supp. 673 (W.D. Mich. 1960), *aff'd* 291 F.2d 627 (6th Cir. 1961). The judgment in *United States v. Lee Way* clearly establishes that the individual discriminatees were harmed by a single, continuous cause: company-wide discriminatory employment policies. . . .

NOTES AND QUESTIONS

1. Two later cases also held that multiple acts of discrimination or police brutality were one occurrence for the purposes of applying deductibles. *See Appalachian Ins. Co. v. Liberty Mutual Ins. Corp.*, 507 F. Supp. 59 (W.D. Pa. 1981), *aff'd*, 676 F.2d 56 (3d Cir. 1982) (gender discrimination); *Mead Reinsurance v. Granite State Ins. Co.*, 873 F.2d 1185 (9th Cir. 1989) (police brutality). In these cases and *Lee Way*, the decision favored the policyholders by reducing the number of deductibles that the policyholders were required to pay. Suppose that the interests of the parties were reversed, because the deductible amount was very low and the policies in question had relatively low per occurrence and aggregate limits. Should that change the result?

2. One high-profile "number of occurrences" case involved contaminated feed that led to the tragic destruction of tens of thousands of farm animals in 1973 and 1974. Apparently, the feed was contaminated after Michigan Chemical mistakenly shipped a toxic flame retardant, rather than a magnesium oxide feed supplement, to a feed company. *See Michigan Chem. Corp. v. American Home Assur. Co.*, 728 F.2d 374 (6th Cir. 1984). The destruction of the animals was "property damage" covered by Michigan Chemical's liability insurance policies. In the litigation over who was responsible for how much of the damage, Michigan Chemical and one of the insurance companies took the position that each claim filed against Michigan Chemical was a separate occurrence, while other insurers took the position that the mistaken shipment(s) of flame retardant was one occurrence. The district court found that "occurrence" was ambiguous and, applying the rule of *contra proferentem*, ruled that each claim was a separate occurrence (because that maximized coverage for Michigan Chemical). On appeal, the court applied the "cause" discussed in *Lee Way* and held that the shipment of the flame retardant was the occurrence. The court remanded to the district court to determine how many shipments there had been.

3. If there was only one shipment of flame retardant in the *Michigan Chemical* situation, but it caused damage in two policy years, must the insurance company pay a full "occurrence" policy limit for each year? Why or why not? The opinion in *Michigan Chemical* suggests that the court understood that a

single occurrence decision would limit the insurance companies' obligation to a single per occurrence limit, even though the property damage took place in two years. For a contrary view *see* Thomas Baker & Eva Orlebeke, *The Application of Per Occurrence Limits from Successive Policies,* 3 Envtl. Claims J. 411 (1991).

4. Of course, the most high-profile "number of occurrences" case in 2002 was a property insurance case: *World Trade Center Properties v. Travelers Indemnity Co.,* 2002 U.S. Dist. Lexis 9863 (S.D.N.Y. June 5, 2002), which is included at the beginning of Chapter 2. As reflected in the decision by Judge Martin, the policyholders in that case claimed that each plane crash was a separate "occurrence" under the property insurance policies covering the World Trade Center, while the insurance companies claimed that the two planes were part of a coordinated attack on a single location and, therefore, they should be obligated to pay no more than one "occurrence" limit.

   Should "occurrence" mean the same thing in property and liability insurance? Consider, for example, whether the equities of coverage maximization are the same in both situations. In a property insurance case, any shortfall between the amount of the damage and the insurance that is available results from the policyholder's decision to underinsure. In most property insurance "number of occurrence" cases, the policyholder purchased enough insurance to cover the full value of the property, so the policyholder is attempting to *reduce* the number of occurrences to reduce the number of deductibles. The main thing that makes the World Trade Center case different in that regard is the fact that the policyholder chose not to insure the full value of the property.

   The concept of "insuring to value" also distinguishes property and liability insurance. What would it mean to "insure to value" in the liability insurance context? What would be "full insurance" for liability insurance? In a liability insurance case, the real beneficiaries of a coverage maximization approach may well be the tort victims, who had no control over the amount of insurance the tort defendant purchased. Thus, even if we could determine whether the policyholder had purchased, in some abstract sense, "enough" liability insurance, the main harm following from a decision to underinsure would likely fall on the tort victim. Does victim protection explain some courts' efforts to maximize coverage? Is that appropriate?

5. The number-of-occurrences issue is addressed in §41 of the Restatement of the Law of Liability Insurance (RLLI) (TD1) and the accompanying comments as follows:

   > §41. Number of Accidents or Occurrences
   > For liability insurance policies that have per-accident or per-occurrence policy limits, retentions, or deductibles, the number of accidents or occurrences is determined by reference to the cause(s) of the bodily injury, property damage, or other harm that forms the basis for the claim, unless otherwise stated in the policy.
   >
   > *Comment:*
   >
   > *a. Determining the number of accidents and occurrences.* Liability insurance policies that contain per-accident or per-occurrence policy limits, deductibles, or

self-insured retentions can give rise to controversies regarding the number of accidents or occurrences that have taken place during a particular policy period. The number of accidents or occurrences can have large implications for the total amount of coverage available. Arguably the most famous number-of-occurrences example is the attack on the World Trade Center in 2001. With roughly $3.6 billion at stake in that situation, insureds argued that there were at least two occurrences (two planes, two buildings), and insurers argued that there was no more than a single occurrence (one terror plot). The World Trade Center case involved first-party property insurance, but the same issue arises in connection with liability insurance, which also uses per-occurrence limits. As in many cases that raise the number-of-occurrences question, the result in the World Trade Center case turned on the relevant language in the contract. The court determined that the plain meaning of the language in one policy provided for a single occurrence and the relevant language in another policy was ambiguous, with the result that in the case of the latter policy the two-occurrence interpretation that favored the non-drafting insured was applied.

The term "occurrence" itself is typically defined within a general liability insurance policy to mean "an accident, including continuous or repeated exposure to substantially the same general harmful conditions." Determining the number of accidents or occurrences that have taken place during the policy period is notoriously difficult. From the perspective of the policy limits, the more occurrences there are, the better the result will be for the insured because the larger the total amount of coverage will be. However, the opposite is true from the perspective of deductibles or retentions: all else equal, the fewer the occurrences, the better the result for the insured will be because the smaller will be the share of a covered claim that must be borne by the insured. Unfortunately, the question of how many "accidents" there were and the question of whether all the losses at issue in a given claim were the result of "continuous or repeated exposure to substantially the same general harmful conditions" often has no clear answer. As a result, courts have developed two general doctrinal tests for determining the number of accidents or occurrences for purposes of calculating both the number of policy limits and the number of deductibles or retentions that will apply: the "effects test" and the "cause test."

b. The effects test. Under the effects test, each injured individual or piece of damaged property tends to be regarded as a separate occurrence. The "effects test" is a relatively old rule that has fallen out of favor with the courts. Most of the courts that originally adopted this approach have abandoned it, because treating each separate injured person or damaged property as a separate occurrence effectively converts a "per occurrence" policy into a "per claim" policy, which runs counter to the language of occurrence-based coverage. This effects test also conflicts with the reasonable expectations of the contracting parties, who would expect "an occurrence" to mean something akin to "an accident," expanded of course to also include "continuous or repeated exposure to substantially the same general harmful conditions." Considering, for example, the case of an explosion that injures many bystanders, the ordinary understanding of "accident" would refer to the explosion, not to each of the individual injuries.

c. The cause test(s). Consistent with the explosion example, a substantial majority of courts that have addressed the number-of-accidents-or-occurrences issue look to the cause of the loss rather than the effect. Under the "cause test," courts determine the number of accidents or occurrences by asking how many "causes," "liability-triggering events," or "unfortunate events" produced the injury or damage. If there is one cause, there is one accident or occurrence, and hence one per-accident or -occurrence policy limit (and, if applicable, one deductible or retention) under each of the policies that is triggered. If there are five causes, there are five accidents or occurrences and five per-accident or occurrence policy limits, subject to any applicable aggregate limit (and, if applicable, five deductibles or retentions). Courts have concluded that the cause test fits more closely than the effects test with the language of the policies and also with the expectations of the parties. Application of the cause test tends to result in fewer occurrences than the effects test, all else equal.

The cause test itself takes a number of forms. Some courts and commentators have helpfully organized the various versions of the cause test into two different subtests: the "proximate-cause" or "immediate-cause" test, on the one hand, and the "liability-event" test on the other. Under the proximate- or immediate-cause test, the court looks to the significant causal actions or events that are most proximate—closest in time and/or space—to the harm to determine the number of occurrences. By contrast, the liability-events test focuses on the cause that is within the control of the insured: the act or omission on the part of the insured that would constitute an alleged breach of a duty and thus give rise to a potential tort action. These two versions of the cause test often result in the same number of occurrences because the alleged negligence of the insured will often also be the most proximate (immediate) cause of the harm.

Although a majority of courts have adopted some version of the cause test for determining the number of occurrences, no single version of that test seems clearly to dominate. Moreover, no version of the cause test generates precise and predictable outcomes across the entire range of cases. Nevertheless, the cause test is generally considered more consistent than the effects test with the reasonable expectations of both insurers and insureds. As with other issues related to the application of insurance policy language to specific cases, if there are disputed facts, such questions will typically be decided by a jury. If the facts are not in dispute, the court can make as-a-matter-of-law determinations of the number of causes and thus the number of per-occurrence or per-accident policy limits or deductibles to apply in a given case. In making such determinations, courts may take into account the structure of the overall insurance program to determine what number of causes is most consistent with the intent of the parties. In such cases, the court should follow the ordinary rules of insurance-policy interpretation, assuming that the policy contains standard-form terms, and, to the extent that the policy is ambiguous as applied to the claim at issue, should choose the interpretation that favors the insured unless the insurer persuades the court that this interpretation is unreasonable. See §3.

Illustrations:

1. A retail store owner has a commercial general-liability insurance policy with a per-occurrence policy limit of $1 million, a deductible of $50,000 per occurrence, and no aggregate limit. Wrongly believing that the store is being robbed, the owner takes out a gun and fires a shot over the head of each of the three individuals who the owner believes are involved in the robbery. Because the owner is a poor shot, each of the bullets strikes the individuals in question, who turn out not to be involved in any robbery at all. Each of the three individuals files suit against the owner, alleging three separate

negligence actions. There are three occurrences, corresponding to the three alleged acts of negligence by the owner. The maximum amount of potential coverage in this case is $2,850,000: ($3 million policy limits) – ($150,000 deductibles).

2. A retail store owner has a commercial general-liability insurance policy with a per-occurrence policy limit of $1 million, a deductible of $50,000 per occurrence, and no aggregate limit. An employee of the store comes into the store with a gun and shoots eight customers before being apprehended by the police. The victims each file suit against the owner, alleging negligent supervision and negligent hiring. With respect to the owner's potential liability, there is one occurrence, corresponding to the alleged negligent failure to exercise reasonable care in the hiring and supervision of the employee in relation to this single violent episode. The maximum amount of potential coverage in this case is $950,000: a $1 million policy limit and $50,000 deductible.

3. The insured is a manufacturer of both cattle feed and a form of chemical flame retardant that is poisonous if eaten. The insured distributes the two products in nearly identical brown bags, with only a small, similar-appearing label distinguishing the two. The insured mistakenly ships four loads of the chemical flame retardant to four different cattle-food retailers, one shipment to each retailer. Each of the four retailers then ships the bags of the flame retardant to 25 different farmers. Each of those 100 farmers feeds the flame retardant to 200 cows. All 20,000 of the infected cows become sick from the flame retardant and eventually have to be destroyed. The insured has a standard general-liability insurance policy with coverage for product-liability claims that applies to the year in question, with a per-occurrence policy limit of $10 million, an aggregate limit of $50 million, and a deductible of $500,000 per occurrence. The policy defines an occurrence as "an accident, including continuous or repeated exposure to substantially the same general harmful conditions."

There are two reasonable conclusions regarding the number of occurrences. First, one could reasonably conclude that there were four occurrences, corresponding to four acts of negligence: the four shipments of flame retardant. Under this interpretation, the losses associated with each of the four shipments would be aggregated, and the insured would have $38 million of coverage: (4 x $10 million per-occurrence limit) – (4 x $500,000 per-occurrence deductible). Second, one could also reasonably conclude that there was one occurrence, corresponding to the negligent decision to package and distribute such dangerously different products in nearly identical bags. Under this interpretation, the insured would have $9.5 million of coverage: $10 million – $500,000. Because either of these interpretations is reasonable, the occurrence limit is ambiguous as applied. Therefore, in the absence of extrinsic evidence that persuades the court that the four-occurrence interpretation is unreasonable, the court should interpret the policy to identify four occurrences in this case.

The illustrations that are contained in the comments of a Restatement of the Law are intended to show how the rule in question would apply in easy cases. Are the cases in the illustrations above, from RLLI (TD1), "easy cases"? How would the illustrations come out using an "effects test"?

B.   *Environmental Liability Insurance Coverage Issues*

Over the last 30 years, environmental claims have been almost as significant to the property casualty insurance industry as asbestos claims. As reflected by the environmental coverage problem that follows the case and notes below, environmental claims raise many of the same issues as asbestos claims: trigger of coverage, number of occurrences, and allocation. The case below addresses an issue that is unique to environmental claims: the application of the pollution exclusion to claims involving toxic chemicals. As the *Peace* case describes, the pollution exclusion has evolved over time. In a classic illustration of the dynamic described by Judge Clark in *Gaunt,* insurers have reacted to what they perceived as unduly narrow interpretations of the exclusion by redrafting the exclusion to make more and more clear their intent to exclude coverage for environmental claims. In the process, they have drafted the exclusions so broadly that some courts have concluded that insurers have overstepped. As with *Gaunt* and *C&J Fertilizer* in Chapter 2, the majority and dissenting opinions in *Peace* nicely showcase different approaches to insurance contract interpretation.

PEACE v. NORTHWESTERN NATIONAL INSURANCE CO.

Supreme Court of Wisconsin
596 N.W.2d 429 (1999)

DAVID T. PROSSER, J. Djukic owned an apartment building. Kevin Peace lived with his mother in an apartment in that building. Peace's guardian ad litem sued Peace's landlord, Djukic Enterprises, for lead poisoning. Djukic's liability policy contained the following exclusion:

2. EXCLUSIONS.
This insurance does not apply to:
     f.(1) "Bodily injury" or "property damage" arising out of the actual, alleged or threatened discharge, dispersal, release, or escape of pollutants:
          (a) At or from premises you own, rent or occupy;
          (b) At or from any site or location used by or for you or others for the handling, storage, disposal, processing or treatment of waste;
          (c) Which are at any time transported, handled, stored, treated, disposed of, or processed as waste by or for you or any person or organization for whom you may be legally responsible; or
          (d) At or from any site or location on which you or any contractors or subcontractors working directly or indirectly on your behalf are performing operations:
               (i) if the pollutants are brought on or to the site or location in connection with such operations; or
               (ii) if the operations are to test for, monitor, clean up, remove, contain, treat, detoxify or neutralize the pollutants.
     (2) Any loss, cost, or expense arising out of any governmental direction or request that you test for, monitor, clean up, remove, contain, treat, detoxify or neutralize pollutants.

Northwestern refused to defend Djukic and filed a summary judgment motion in the tort proceeding seeking a declaration that it had no duty to defend. The trial court granted the motion and stayed the tort claim[,] pending resolution of the appeal of the summary judgment. The court of appeals affirmed the trial court. The Wisconsin Supreme Court vacated that decision and remanded the case to the court of appeals for reconsideration in light of *Donaldson v. Urban Land Interests, Inc.*, 564 N.W.2d 728 (Wis. 1997) (holding that the absolute pollution exclusion did not apply to a claim involving a buildup of carbon monoxide from human respiration inside a building). The court of appeals then reversed the trial court's summary judgment and Northwestern appealed.

The question before us is whether the circuit court properly granted summary judgment to Northwestern by concluding that the policy Djukic purchased did not provide coverage for bodily injury claims arising from ingestion of lead derived from lead-based paint that has chipped, flaked, or deteriorated into dust within a residence. To answer this question, we first consider whether lead present in paint is a pollutant under the plain meaning of Northwestern's pollution exclusion clause. If it is, we then consider whether, when lead-based paint chips, flakes, or deteriorates into dust or fumes, that action constitutes a discharge, dispersal, release, or escape under the policy. Both inquiries must be answered in the affirmative for the pollution exclusion clause to preclude coverage, and for us to affirm the circuit court's grant of summary judgment. *See Donaldson*, 564 N.W.2d 728. . . .

The term "pollutants" is defined in the policy. "Pollutants means any solid, liquid, gaseous or thermal irritant or contaminant, including smoke, vapor, soot, fumes, acids, alkalis, chemicals and waste. Waste includes materials to be recycled, reconditioned or reclaimed." . . .

A number of words within the definition of "pollutants" are not defined in the policy. When determining the ordinary meaning of these words, it is appropriate to look to the definitions in a non-legal dictionary.

A "contaminant" is defined as one that contaminates. American Heritage Dictionary of the English Language 406 (3d ed. 1992). "Contaminate" is defined as "1. To make impure or unclean by contact or mixture." *Id.* at 406.

An "irritant" is defined as the source of irritation, especially physical irritation. *Id.* at 954. "Irritation" is defined, in the sense of pathology, as "A condition of inflammation, soreness, or irritability of a bodily organ or part." *Id.* at 954.

"Chemical," one of the examples of contaminants or irritants included in the policy's definition of "pollutants," is defined as "A substance with a distinct molecular composition that is produced by or used in a chemical process." *Id.* at 327. The dictionary also defines "chemistry" as "The science of the composition, structure, properties, and reactions of matter, especially of atomic and molecular systems. 2. The composition, structure, properties, and reactions of a substance." *Id.* at 328.

"Lead" is also defined in the dictionary. Lead is a "soft, malleable, ductile, bluish-white dense metallic element, extracted chiefly from galena and used in containers and pipes for corrosives, solder and type metal, bullets, radiation shielding, paints, and antiknock compounds." *Id.* at 1023.

"Lead" is a chemical element with particular properties. It may be "used in a chemical process." It clearly fits within the definition of "chemical."

"Lead paint," which is composed of lead and other chemicals, starts out as a liquid and becomes a solid after it is applied and dries. Over time, lead paint may chip and flake[,] becoming solid "waste." When it begins to deteriorate, it may give off "fumes." When it begins to disintegrate, it becomes dust—fine, dry particles of matter which, like smoke and soot, can float in the air[,] affecting human respiration until it eventually settles on the ground.

Lead poisoning from paint at residential properties is generally caused by the inhalation of lead-contaminated dust particles or toxic lead fumes through res-piration or the ingestion of lead-based paint chips by mouth. The consequences can be disastrous for children. . . .

Lead is a solid contaminant. Lead paint either is or threatens to be a solid or liquid contaminant. Lead paint chips are a solid contaminant. Lead paint fumes are a gaseous irritant or contaminant. Lead paint dust is a solid (although some-times an airborne) irritant or contaminant. There is little doubt that lead derived from lead paint chips, flakes, or dust is an irritant or serious contaminant. . . .

II

The second issue is whether Peace's injuries arose out of the "discharge, disper-sal, release, or escape of pollutants. . . ."

The words "discharge," "dispersal," "release," and "escape" are not defined in the policy, but they appear to describe the entire range of actions by which something moves from a contained condition to an uncontained condition. "Release" is a transitive verb. "Discharge," "disperse," and "escape" are verbs that can be either transitive or intransitive. This implies that the movement from a contained condition to an uncontained condition can be either intentional and purposeful or accidental and involuntary. In its transitive form, the verb "discharge" is defined: "To release, as from confinement. . . ." In its intransitive form, the verb "discharge" is defined, in part, as "To pour forth, emit, or release contents." The American Heritage Dictionary of the English Language 530 (3d ed.). "Escape" is defined, in part, as "1. To break loose from confinement. . . . 2. To issue from confinement or an enclosure; leak or seep out. . . ." *Id.* at 625. . . .

We believe the plain language of the policy covers the release of paint con-taining lead from a wall or ceiling into the air or onto the floor. "Common sense tells us that lead paint that never leaves a wall or ceiling does not cause harm. Implicit in the Negligence Complaint . . . must be an allegation that the lead paint somehow separated from the wall or ceiling, and entered the air, or fell on the floor, furniture or fixtures in the apartment." *Lefrak Organization, Inc. v. Chubb Custom Ins. Co.,* 942 F. Supp. 949, 954 (S.D.N.Y. 1996). . . .

Our decision in *Donaldson v. Urban Land Interests, Inc.,* 564 N.W.2d 728 (Wis. 1997), is not inconsistent with this conclusion. *Donaldson* was a "sick building" case in which Hanover Insurance Company attempted to exclude liability for the consequences of an inadequate air exchange system in a building. The building defect caused an excessive accumulation of carbon dioxide in the work area. Hanover attempted to categorize exhaled carbon dioxide as a pollutant, justifying its invocation of the pollution exclusion clause. This court disagreed. We approved the analysis of Judge Daniel Anderson of the court of appeals, who dissented, saying that "a reasonable insured would not expect [the clause] to include the avoidance of liability for the accumulation of carbon dioxide in an office because provisions were not made for introducing fresh air into the office." *Id.* at 728 (citation omitted).

This court found the pollution exclusion clause did not apply to the particular facts of that case. . . . The court contrasted exhaled carbon dioxide with the nonexhaustive list of pollutants in the pollution exclusion clause and observed that exhaled carbon dioxide is universally present and generally harmless in all but the most unusual circumstances. *Id.* at 728. The same cannot be said for lead paint chips, flakes, and dust. They are widely, if not universally, understood to be dangerous and capable of producing lead poisoning. The toxic effects of lead have been recognized for centuries. Reasonable owners of rental property understand their obligation to deal with the problem of lead paint. . . .

Throughout the country, injured parties and insured parties have resorted to the history of the pollution exclusion clause in an effort to show that it was intended to apply to industrial pollution and that the terms "discharge," "dispersal," "release," and "escape" are environmental terms of art.

In *Sphere Drake Ins. Co. v. Y.L. Realty Co.*, 990 F. Supp. 240, 243 (S.D.N.Y. 1997), the court summarized its view of the law as follows:

> Several courts recently have interpreted pollution exclusion clauses similar to the one at issue here. The overwhelming trend in these cases has been to hold that such clauses do not exclude contaminants such as lead paint poisoning. . . . These courts have held, and this Court agrees, that pollution exclusion clauses refer only to industrial and environmental pollution. . . . The language of the exclusion clause supports this interpretation. The clause discusses injuries caused by "discharge, dispersal, release, or escape of pollutants." These are terms of art in environmental law, generally used to describe the improper disposal or containment of hazardous waste.

The problem in dealing with this argument is that it calls for construction of the pollution exclusion clause based on materials outside the four corners of the policy. In most jurisdictions, courts interpreting insurance contracts do not go outside the four corners of the policy unless and until they find ambiguity in the policy's terms. However, once a court finds ambiguity in the policy, it almost automatically rules against the insurer. The Catch-22 in insurance cases is that once ambiguity has been found, the insurer will lose even if the insurer has the better argument about how to construe its clause based on evidence outside the insurance contract.

Because we conclude that the clause is not ambiguous, we have no duty to explore materials outside the policy. Nonetheless, in the interest of intellectual integrity, the argument deserves response. . . .

In 1966, comprehensive general liability (CGL) insurance policies contained a broad coverage clause reading:

> The company will pay on behalf of the insured all sums which the insured shall become legally obligated to pay as damages because of bodily injury or property damage caused by accident.

In 1970, the standard CGL policy was revised to include a Qualified Pollution Exclusion, which excluded coverage for claims:

> Arising out of the discharge, dispersal, release, or escape of smoke, vapors, soot, fumes, acids, alkalis, toxic chemicals, liquids or gases, waste materials, or other irritants, contaminants or pollutants *into or upon the land, the atmosphere or any water course or body of water but this exclusion does not apply if such discharge, dispersal, release, or escape is sudden and accidental.*

In 1985, an Absolute Pollution Exclusion clause replaced the Qualified Pollution Exclusion clause. The words of the new model clause are nearly identical to the clause in the Northwestern policy. The Absolute Pollution Exclusion (1) dropped the phrase "but this exclusion does not apply if such discharge, dispersal, release, or escape is sudden and accidental"; (2) dropped the phrase "into or upon the land, the atmosphere or any water course or body of water"; (3) restructured the exclusion and added four conditional phrases including the key phrase "at or from premises you own, rent or occupy"; and (4) dropped the adjective "toxic" before the word "chemicals." . . . [T]he 1985 revision substantially broadened the pollution exclusion and made it applicable to premises owned, rented, or occupied by the insured. Removing the adjective "toxic" before the noun "chemical" had the effect of expanding the number of chemicals regarded as pollutants. We find these undisputed changes in the clause inconsistent with the proposition that the clause, after revision, was intended to apply solely to industrial pollution. We agree with the court in *Oates by Oates v. New York*, 597 N.Y.S.2d 550, 553 (N.Y. Ct. Cl. 1993), when it said: "In all candor, we cannot imagine a more unambiguous statement of intent than, after being told by the courts that 'land, atmosphere and water course' imply industrial pollution, to replace such language with 'premises you own, rent or occupy.'" . . .

The final contention is that it is unreasonable to apply the pollution exclusion clause to routine incidents such as paint peeling off a wall. . . .

We do not believe it is necessary to detail all the articles in professional journals as well as newspapers, popular magazines, and business publications, and all the government reports and regulations, to support our conclusion that by the mid-1980s, an ordinary property owner could not reasonably expect to purchase a standard liability insurance policy with a pollution exclusion clause, and thereby shift to the insurer liability for personal injuries arising from a person's ingestion of lead in chipped or flaked paint or dust at or from the insured premises. The phrase "at or from premises you own, rent, or occupy" directly counters the notion that the policy is confined to industrial pollution, for there is not much familiarity with industrial pollution from rented apartments. . . .

The decision of the court of appeals is reversed and the cause remanded.

SHIRLEY S. ABRAHAMSON, Chief Justice (dissenting). As the majority opinion carefully documents, courts around the country have divided over the proper interpretation of the pollution exclusion clause. When numerous courts disagree about the meaning of language, the language cannot be characterized as having a plain meaning. Rather, the language is ambiguous; it is capable of being understood in two or more different senses by reasonably well-informed persons even though one interpretation might on careful analysis seem more suitable to this court. . . .

N. PATRICK CROOKS, J. (dissenting). The result of the majority opinion is to deprive young Kevin Peace, and, in many instances, other child victims of lead poisoning, of an effective remedy for their harm. By stripping landlords who may have been negligent concerning lead-based paint of insurance coverage, the majority guarantees that, frequently, no damages will ever be collected for such children. In reaching its conclusion, the majority fails to apply the proper method for analyzing whether an insurer has a duty to defend, disregards this court's two-year-old decision in *Donaldson v. Urban Land Interests, Inc.*, 564 N.W.2d

728 (Wis. 1997), and ignores the well-established principle that insurance policies are to be interpreted from the perspective of the reasonable insured with any ambiguities construed in the insured's favor. . . .

Based on our determination that the scope of the pollution exclusion clause is restricted to reasonable applications, we did not focus in *Donaldson* on the broad terms of the pollution exclusion clause, such as "irritant," "contaminant," and "chemicals." Instead, in considering whether carbon dioxide was unambiguously included within the clause, we carefully evaluated the expectations of the reasonable insured. *See id.* at 728. We stressed the "common sense" approach taken by courts in determining when the pollution exclusion clause is applicable. *Id.* at 728 (quoting *Pipefitters*, 976 F.2d at 1043-44). Because a reasonable insured would not necessarily understand carbon dioxide to be a "pollutant," we determined that the carbon dioxide was not unambiguously included within the definition of "pollutant" in the pollution exclusion clause. *Id.* at 728. . . .

The majority misses the point of *Donaldson* and ignores its plain applicability in this case. It is clear from our decision in the wake of *Donaldson* to vacate the court of appeals' original opinion in this case that we felt that our holding in *Donaldson* affected the outcome of this case, yet the majority today reaches the very same conclusion as that reached by the court of appeals in the opinion we vacated! . . .

"Pollutant" is a term which generally conjures up images of industrial smokestacks and heavy machinery in the mind of a reasonable lay person. Dirty lakes, chemical-laden streams, and thick layers of smog typify the items which immediately occur to a person upon hearing the word "pollution." The pollution exclusion clause does not refer to "lead," "paint," or any other comparable term which might give a hint to a reasonable insured that common materials which are benign in normal circumstances could qualify as "pollutants."

Dictionary definitions likewise do not indicate that the term "pollutant" might encompass lead in paint. "Pollutant" is defined in the *American Heritage Dictionary* as, "Something that pollutes, especially a waste material that contaminates air, soil, or water." American Heritage Dictionary 1402 (3d ed. 1992). The relevant definitions of "pollute" are: "1. To make unfit for or harmful to living things, especially by the addition of waste matter. . . . 2. To make less suitable for an activity, especially by the introduction of unwanted factors: The stadium lights polluted the sky around the observatory. 3. To render impure or morally harmful; corrupt." American Heritage Dictionary 1402 (3d ed. 1992).

The lead in paint does not fit within these common definitions. Lead was not "waste matter" added to the paint in this case, and it was not an "unwanted factor" in the paint. On the contrary, lead was intentionally included as one of the desired ingredients in the paint at the time of the paint's original manufacture. For this reason, a reasonable lay person would not necessarily view the lead in paint as a "pollutant." As one court explained:

> A common understanding of a pollutant is a substance that "pollutes" or renders impure a previously unpolluted object, as when chemical wastes leach into a clean water supply. Here the lead did not pollute the paint: it was purposefully incorporated into the paint from the start. The paint was intentionally applied to the premises. At the time, the paint was legal. It was considered neither impure nor unwanted.

Insurance Co. of Ill. v. Stringfield, 685 N.E.2d 980, 983–84 (Ill. App. Ct. 1997). . . .

The majority also provides a lengthy recitation of the history of the pollution exclusion clause, concluding that it does not support the conclusion that the terms "discharge," "dispersal," "release," and "escape" in the clause are terms of art in environmental law. *See* majority op. at 444-46. Because I find that the first condition required for the pollution exclusion clause to apply is not met in this case, I need not discuss the second condition (whether there was a "discharge, dispersal, etc." under the terms of the policy). *See Donaldson,* 564 N.W.2d 728. It is significant, however, that several courts have concluded that the pollution exclusion clause is aimed at dealing with industrial and environmental pollution. Pointing out that no language has ever been added to the clause to specifically address lead or lead-based paint, these courts have concluded that amendments to the clause have failed to include lead or lead-based paint unambiguously in the definition of "pollutant," and thus, have not altered the historical purpose of the clause to exclude environmental and industrial pollution. . . .

NOTES AND QUESTIONS

1. As reflected by the authority cited in the majority and the dissent, the courts are split on the applicability of pollution exclusions in liability insurance policies to "nontraditional" pollution. For a recent case, see Judge Posner's opinion in *Scottsdale Indem. Co. v. Village of Crestwood,* 673 F.3d 715 (7th Cir. 2012). What about Justice Abrahamson's position? Does this split of authority indicate that the plaintiff's position is, at the least, reasonable? When language is ambiguous—either on its face or in application—the *contra proferentem* rule makes the policyholder the winner so long as there is a reasonable argument in the policyholder's favor. Neither the majority nor the dissent responded to her argument. How might they have responded?

2. There was an enormous amount of litigation in the 1980s and 1990s regarding the application of the sudden and accidental pollution exclusion. The controversy largely focused on the question whether there should be a temporal limitation on the "sudden and accidental" exception contained at the end of the pollution exclusion. If so, the exclusion would apply to pollution claims unless the "discharge, dispersal, or release" resulted from an abrupt event. Perhaps the most complicating features of this dispute were disclosures filed by representatives of the insurance industry in state insurance departments in 1970 in connection with the use of the then-brand-new pollution exclusion. At the very least the disclosures strongly implied that the exclusion did not cut back on the coverage provided by the policy, but rather clarified insurers' intent not to cover intentional pollution. Policyholders successfully argued in some courts that the disclosures demonstrate that "sudden and accidental" really means "unexpected and unintended." *See, e.g., Claussen v. Aetna Cas. & Sur. Co.,* 380 S.E.2d 686 (Ga. 1989). The New Jersey Supreme Court was sufficiently disturbed by the lack of candor in the pollution exclusion filings to apply the doctrine of "regulatory estoppel" to hold that insurers are estopped from applying the sudden and accidental pollution exclusion more broadly than is consistent with the 1970 regulatory disclosures. *See Morton Int'l, Inc. v. General Accident Ins. Co. of Am.,* 629 A.2d 831 (N.J. 1993). Other courts took a "plain meaning" approach to the pollution exclusion and gave it the temporal meaning the industry requested.

3. In 1992, the Alaska Supreme Court summarized the state of litigation over the sudden and accidental pollution exclusion as follows:

> We have never had occasion to interpret the standard language of the pollution exclusion, nor do we deem it necessary to do so now. However, many other courts have done so.
>
> Most courts which have interpreted the pollution exclusion consider the phrase "sudden and accidental" to be ambiguous and thus construe it against the insurer to mean "unexpected or unintended." *But see United States Fidelity & Guar. Co. v. Star Fire Coals, Inc.*, 856 F.2d 31, 34 (6th Cir. 1988) ("sudden and accidental" is clear and plain language which "only a lawyer's ingenuity could make ambiguous"). As the Supreme Court of Georgia noted
>
>> it is, indeed, difficult, to think of "sudden" without a temporal connotation: a sudden flash, a sudden burst of speed, a sudden bang. But, on reflection one realizes that, even in its popular usage, "sudden" does not usually describe the duration of the event, but rather its unexpectedness: a sudden storm, a sudden turn in the road, sudden death. Even when used to describe the onset of an event, the word has an elastic temporal connotation that varies with expectations: Suddenly, its spring.
>
> *Claussen v. Aetna Casualty & Surety Co.*, 380 S.E.2d 686, 688 (Ga. 1989). A discharge of sewage over several days or a few weeks, as occurred in the present case, can easily be seen as "sudden" when compared to the seven or eight years of coal dust discharge that occurred in *Star Fire Coals*, 856 F.2d at 35, but may not be considered sudden when compared to an instantaneous spill.
>
> Some cases say that the pollution exclusion "was solely meant to deprive active polluters of coverage." *See, e.g., United Pacific Ins. v. Van's Westlake Union*, 664 P.2d 1262, 1266 (Wash. App. 1983) (quoting *Niagara Cty. v. Utica Mut. Ins. Co.*, 427 N.Y.S.2d 171 (N.Y. Sup. Ct. 1980)). *See also Star Fire Coals*, 856 F.2d at 35 ("such pollution exclusion clauses apply to the release of wastes and pollutants taking place on a regular basis or in the ordinary course of business"). This interpretation is lent further support by the fact that new pollution exclusion language was drafted in 1985 which eliminated the "sudden and accidental" language and "shifts the emphasis to industrial sites." 1 W. Freedman, Richards on the Law of Insurance §5:2[d] (6th ed. Supp. 1991). Though we do not decide this issue, this interpretation would preclude application of the pollution exclusion to Gross as a matter of law.

Sauer v. The Home Indemnity Co., 841 P.2d 176 n.8 (Alaska 1992).

4. Another liability insurance exclusion that has been very important in many environmental cases is the "own property" exclusion. Based on that exclusion, insurance companies have refused to use liability insurance policies to pay for the costs of cleaning up the policyholder's own property. The underlying rationale is that liability insurance is intended to protect the policyholder against claims for damage to the person or property of others. In a sense, the "own property" exclusion is another kind of market segmentation exclusion: It excludes from the liability insurance policy coverage that is at least theoretically available in the first-party property insurance market. As with the pollution exclusion, courts have varied widely in their application of the own property exclusion. Perhaps the most pro-policyholder position is that adopted by Judge Posner in *Patz v. St. Paul Fire & Marine Ins. Co.*, 15 F.3d 699 (7th Cir. 1994), in which the Seventh Circuit held that the exclusion does not apply so long as the reason for the cleanup is to prevent

damage to others. A more pro-insurer position is represented by *State v. Signo Trading Int'l, Inc.*, 612 A.2d 932 (N.J. 1992), which held that there must be actual damage to third-party property before the insurance company is obligated to pay.

Suppose that a company voluntarily cleans up its property to avoid what it regards as certain liability in the future. Would the costs that it incurs to avoid this liability be "damages" within the meaning of the Insuring Agreement in the CGL policy?

ENVIRONMENTAL COVERAGE PROBLEM

Consider the application of the "sudden and accidental" and "absolute" pollution exclusions to the following situations (the text of the sudden and accidental exclusion appears near the end of the majority opinion in *Peace*):

1. An EPA Superfund order to clean up chemicals leaking from barrels that Company X buried on its property. The barrels began leaking gradually when they became rusted from contact with groundwater over a period of years.
2. An EPA Superfund order to clean up chemicals leaking from an "evaporation pond" that Company Y maintained on its property. Company Y piped liquid waste into the pond, which was lined with concrete. After the liquid evaporated, Company Y scraped up the toxic residue and disposed of it off site. The concrete became cracked very early after the pond was constructed, and chemicals leaked into the earth from beneath the pond whenever there was liquid in the pond.
3. Bodily injury claims filed by workers in Company ABC's furniture-finishing plant. The workers allege that they were injured by physical contact with furniture-finishing chemicals and by breathing fumes. They allege that Company ABC was negligent in not requiring them to wear protective clothing (especially gloves) and in not providing adequate ventilation.

C.   The Problem of Intentional Harm

As with other forms of "all risk" insurance, the CGL policy provides a very broad grant of coverage in the Insuring Agreement section of the policy, but then lists a significant number of exclusions that carve out exceptions to this broad grant of coverage. It is not possible to cover all the exclusions in an introductory course. This section focuses on intentional harm exclusions. At the end of the Section II Auto Liability Insurance unit, we will address a second important category of exclusions that appears in general liability insurance policies: market segmentation exclusions.

The problem of intentional harm is covered in detail here for two main reasons. First, it raises very interesting public policy issues regarding the nature of insurance and the relationship between liability insurance and tort law. Second, the problem of intentional harm brings to the surface some of the tensions in the liability insurance relationship that we will discuss in Chapter 5.

1.   Defining "Expected or Intended"

The "expected or intended from the standpoint of the insured" language that presently appears in the first exclusion in the CGL policy reproduced at the beginning of this chapter has appeared in different places in earlier versions of the CGL policy. The following case is decided under the 1973 version of the CGL policy, in which the "expected or intended" language appeared in the definition of "occurrence."

CARTER LAKE v. AETNA CASUALTY & SURETY CO.

United States Court of Appeals, Eighth Circuit
604 F.2d 1052 (1979)

STEPHENSON, C.J., This is a diversity case initiated by appellant City of Carter Lake, Iowa, alleging that its comprehensive general liability insurance policy issued by the appellee, The Aetna Casualty and Surety Company, provided coverage for the negligent actions of Carter Lake's personnel which resulted in six separate incidents of sewage backup into the basement of a Carter Lake residence owned by William and Kesano Mecseji. . . . The court held that the policy only covered the first incident of sewage backup. . . . *City of Carter Lake v. Aetna Cas. & Sur. Co.*, 454 F. Supp. 47 (D. Neb. 1978). We agree. . . .

On February 26, 1975, the basement of one William Mecseji's house was flooded with raw sewage. The (city's) sewage pump had overloaded and had shut off. The sewage began to back up into the system and flooded the lowest area in the drainage system in the Carter Lake area, which happened to be the Mecseji basement. The city maintenance personnel reset the pump[,] and the basement began to drain. Mr. Mecseji filed a claim against the City for his damages in the amount of $418.12. The City referred this claim to Aetna who initially denied the claim on the basis that the City was not negligent.

Due to repeated, identical failures of the sewage pump, the Mecseji basement was flooded again on July 14, 1975, August 2, 1975, and August 21, 1975. The Mecsejis filed suit against Carter Lake on August 26, 1975, alleging that the damage to their property was the result of Carter Lake's negligence. Their complaint was subsequently amended in January, 1976, to include two additional incidents of flooding on December 16, 1975, and December 18, 1975, again due to failure of the sewage pump. By letter of February 26, 1976, Aetna notified Carter Lake that it would defend the City in the lawsuit but that Aetna would not pay for any damages incurred subsequent to the first flooding, February 26, 1975. The City hired additional counsel for the trial and was represented by both private counsel and Aetna's counsel. Following trial the jury returned a verdict in favor of the Mecsejis in the amount of $11,404.14. The Mecsejis have since garnished this sum, plus interest ($12,533.78 total), from Carter Lake's account.

Carter Lake then brought this action against Aetna to recover not only the amount paid to the Mecsejis, but also the attorney fees which it incurred in appealing the adverse decision in state court after Aetna refused to appeal, and for the attorney fees incurred in bringing this action. . . .

An examination of Iowa case law does reveal certain broad principles which are used for interpretation of insurance contracts. . . .

With these principles in mind, we examine the policy provisions in question. In the coverage part of the policy it is stated that: "The company will pay on behalf of the insured all sums which the insured shall become legally obliged to pay as damages because of bodily injury or property damage to which this insurance applies, caused by an occurrence. . . ." In a separate part of the policy labeled "Definitions," "occurrence" is defined as "an accident, including continuous or repeated exposure to conditions, which results in bodily injury or property damage neither expected nor intended from the standpoint of the Insured(.)" The term "accident" is not further defined in the policy.

Carter Lake contends that the policy should be construed by ascertaining the meaning of the word "occurrence[]" rather than the word "accident." We disagree. It is true that "occurrence" has a broader meaning than "accident" as those words are generally understood. However, when all of the provisions of the policy are considered as a whole, there is no ambiguity as to the intention of the parties to give the word "occurrence" the restricted meaning of an accident, including continuous repeated exposure to conditions, which results in bodily injury or property damage neither expected nor intended from the standpoint of the insured. *See* R. Keeton, Basic Text on Insurance Law §5.4(c), at 300 (1971) (use of word "occurrence" rather than "accidents" broadens coverage by including losses from the continuing operation as well as a sudden event, but does not change coverage with relation to degree of expectability of the loss). *But see Grand River Lime Co. v. Ohio Cas. Ins. Co.*, 289 N.E.2d 360, 365 (Ohio Ct. App. 1972) (use of occurrence broadens coverage).

It is beyond dispute that Carter Lake did not intend to cause the sewage backups. Thus, the exclusion for intentional acts is not applicable even though the underlying acts and omissions of Carter Lake were intentional. Nevertheless, Aetna maintains that the backups subsequent to February 25, 1976, were not occurrences or accidents as those terms are used in the policy because the subsequent backups were "expected." Aetna attempts to equate expected with reasonable foreseeability. In arguing for such an interpretation, Aetna primarily relies on the cases of *City of Aurora v. Trinity Universal Ins. Co.*, 326 F.2d 905 (10th Cir. 1964), *Gassaway v. Travelers Ins. Co.*, 439 S.W.2d 605 (Tenn. 1969), and *Town of Tieton v. General Ins. Co.*, 380 P.2d 127 (Wash. 1963).

In *City of Aurora v. Trinity Universal Ins. Co., supra*, the policy provided coverage for losses "caused by accident." The question before the Tenth Circuit was whether a sewage backup was caused by accident. The city had absorbed the sewage system of a newly annexed area, and later discovered that it was inadequate. To prevent flooding of a lift station in this area, a small pump at the station was intermittently operated, increasing the discharge of water into the main. The combination of rainfall and the operation of the pump caused sewage and water to back up from the main into several residences. In holding that the loss was not caused by accident, the court stated that:

> (A) loss which is the natural and probable consequence of a negligent act is not "caused by accident," within the meaning of policies of this kind. . . . At the same time, we have been careful to recognize that negligently caused loss may be accidental, within the meaning of the policy, if in fact an immediate or concurrent cause of the loss is an unprecedented or unforeseeable event. In these circumstances, the loss is not the natural and probable consequence of the negligent act, and is hence caused by accident.

Id. at 906 (citations omitted).

In *Gassaway v. Travelers Ins. Co., supra,* a suit was brought by homeowners against the insurer of a corporation which had owned a lot and installed a drainage facility which discharged water underneath the house. The corporation had not disclosed the existence of the drainage facilities. The issue before the Tennessee Supreme Court was whether the corporation was insured under a policy which insured against liability caused by "accident." The court found that the corporation had not intended to cause the damage and had been guilty of only ordinary negligence. The court held that although the policy covered some acts of negligence, it did not cover all such acts. The court approved the following definition: "Accident as used in insurance liability policies (is) an event not reasonably to be foreseen, unexpected and fortuitous." *Id.,* 439 S.W.2d at 608. The court further stated:

> The element of foreseeability cannot be ignored. The Circuit Court determined V & M Homes knew these drainage facilities created a risk and under these facts we think V & M Homes could reasonably foresee that what did occur could occur. When a reasonably foreseeable event does occur, it cannot be said to be a result that was unforeseen and unexpected or fortuitous.

Id. 439 S.W.2d at 608-09.

In *Town of Tieton v. General Ins. Co., supra,* the town constructed a sewage lagoon adjacent to the property of David and Jean Pugsley. As a result of the operation of the sewage facility, the Pugsleys' well became contaminated and they recovered a judgment from the town. The record indicated that seepage is a normal and expected result of this type of sewage facility, and that prior to the construction of the lagoon the town had been advised by health officials of the possibility of the lagoon contaminating the Pugsleys' well. In holding that the damage to the Pugsleys' property was not caused by accident, the Washington Supreme Court stated:

> No one contends that the contamination of the well was intended. Yet, the lack of such intent does not by itself compel us to conclude that such result was "caused by accident." The element of foreseeability cannot be ignored. . . .
>
> The evidence most favorable to respondent supports no more than a finding that respondent took a calculated business risk that the Pugsley property would not be damaged. From a business standpoint, it may have been wise to have taken this calculated risk and to have proceeded with the construction of the lagoon without first condemning the Pugsley property or arranging to supply water to it by means other than their well. But, when, under the facts of this case, the possibility of contamination became a reality, it cannot be said that the result was "unusual, unexpected, and unforeseen."

Id. 380 P.2d at 130-31.

The opinions in these cases paint with too broad a brush and apparently represent a minority view. See 7A J. Appleman, Insurance Law and Practice §4492 (1962). Cases from other jurisdictions view the problem from a different perspective. *See, e.g., Cross v. Zurich Gen. Accident & Liab. Ins. Co.,* 184 F.2d 609 (7th Cir. 1950); *N.W. Elec. Power Coop., Inc. v. American Motorists Ins. Co.,* 451 S.W.2d [356,] 361-64 [(Mo. Ct. App. 1969)]; *McGroarty v. Great American Ins. Co.,* 329 N.E.2d 172 (N.Y. 1975), *aff'g* 351 N.Y.S.2d 428 (App. Div. 1974);

Orkin Exterminating Co. v. Massachusetts Bonding & Ins. Co., 400 S.W.2d 20, 26-27 (Tex. Civ. App. 1965). These cases, which involve policy clauses which provide coverage for losses "caused by accident," generally take the approach that if the damage was not intentionally caused, it was caused by accident. Whether the damage was expected is not considered. A somewhat typical example is *Cross v. Zurich Gen. Accident & Liab. Ins. Co., supra.* In *Cross*, while the plaintiffs were engaged in the cleaning of an exterior of a building several windows were damaged by the cleaning solution. In holding that the damage was caused by accident the court stated:

> Plaintiffs may have been negligent in not keeping sufficient water on the windows, but the very fact that water was applied to each window negatives any idea that plaintiff intended to damage same. And lacking such intent, the damage was accidental, even though caused by negligence.

Id. at 611.

In the present case, after the first incident of flooding the Mecsejis presented a claim to the city for their actual damages of $418.12. After examination of the claim the city's attorney recommended that it be paid, and it was forwarded to Aetna. Aetna responded in a letter to the Mecsejis denying liability. The letter stated in part: "In order for us to be legally responsible, our insured must be guilty of negligence." Aetna is now in effect claiming that because the city was negligent, i.e., the injury was reasonably foreseeable, there is no coverage.

To adopt Aetna's interpretation that an injury is not caused by accident because the injury is reasonably foreseeable would mean that only in a rare instance would the comprehensive general liability policy be of any benefit to Carter Lake. Enforcement of the policy in this manner would afford such minimal coverage as to be patently disproportionate to the premiums paid and would be inconsistent with the reasonable expectations of an insured purchasing the policy. Under Aetna's construction of the policy language if the damage was foreseeable then the insured is liable, but there is no coverage, and if the damage is not foreseeable, there is coverage, but the insured is not liable. This is not the law. The function of an insurance company is more than that of premium receiver.

An interpretation of the word "accident" as used in this type of comprehensive general liability policy which is consistent with the results reached in most of the cases confronting the issue, if not the broad language sometimes employed, is to look at the question of whether a result is "expected" as a matter of probability. We reject the argument that a result is expected as that term is used in insurance policies simply because it was reasonably foreseeable. The reasonable expectation of an insured in securing a comprehensive general liability policy is that it will cover some negligent acts. It does not follow, however, that because the policy covers some negligent acts it must cover all negligent acts. An insured need not know to a virtual certainty that a result will follow its acts or omissions for the result to be expected. *But see State Farm Fire & Cas. Co. v. Muth*, 207 N.W.2d 364 (Neb. 1973). Rather, each case must be determined by examination of the totality of the circumstances. For the purposes of an exclusionary clause in an insurance policy the word "expected" denotes that the actor knew or should have known that there was a substantial probability that certain consequences will result from his actions. If the insured knew or should have

known that there was a substantial probability that certain results would follow his acts or omissions then there has not been an occurrence or accident
as defined in this type of policy when such results actually come to pass. The
results cease to be expected and coverage is present as the probability that the
consequences will follow decreases and becomes less than a substantial probability. *See* R. Keeton, Basic Text on Insurance Law §5.4(c), at 298-300 (1971).

After the first backup, the probability of an identical equipment failure and
consequential flooding of the Mecsejis' basement on a particular day was relatively slight, about 2% [w]ith hindsight. However, there was clearly a substantial probability of another backup at some time caused by an identical equipment failure if the equipment was not replaced or an alarm system installed.
Nevertheless, Carter Lake took the calculated risk that such backup would not
occur, and elected to continue operations without correcting its methods. Once
the city was alerted to the problem, its cause, and the likelihood of reoccurrence, it could not ignore the problem and then look to Aetna to reimburse it
for the liability incurred by reason of such inaction. Accordingly, the floodings
subsequent to the February 26, 1975, incident were not unexpected and thus
were not accidents or occurrences as those terms were used in the insurance
policy.

PHYSICIANS INSURANCE CO. OF OHIO v. SWANSON

Supreme Court of Ohio
569 N.E.2d 906 (1991)

SYLLABUS OF THE COURT

In order to avoid coverage on the basis of an exclusion for expected or intentional injuries, the insurer must demonstrate that the injury itself was expected
or intended.

On July 29, 1987, two groups of teenage children were playing near a small
lake commonly referred to as the Turkeyfoot Heights swimming area. One
group consisted of William Swanson, Mark Jogerst, and Joseph Jogerst. The
other group was composed of Todd Baker, Robert Will, Mark Peridon, Shawna
Wagler, and Shawna's brother and sister. Both groups of children had been
swimming prior to their initial encounter. After Bill Swanson and his friends
got out of the water and began to dry off on a nearby dock, someone in the
other group insulted them. As a result, as they were leaving the area one of
Bill Swanson's friends made an obscene gesture directed at the other group of
children. Robert Will and Mark Peridon began to chase after Bill Swanson and
his friends. Having no success at catching the other boys, both Robert and Mark
returned to their group, which by then was resting at a picnic table close to the
water's edge.

Meanwhile, Bill Swanson and the Jogerst brothers went to Bill's house. After
a short time, Bill went up to his parents' bedroom, and while there, he saw and
decided to take his father's BB gun. Bill and the two brothers went back toward
the swimming area. They positioned themselves behind a shed approximately
seventy to one hundred feet from the picnic table. Still upset over the previous
encounter, Bill aimed the BB gun in the direction of the group at the picnic
table, and shot three times. According to his testimony, Bill was aiming at a sign
on a tree some ten to fifteen feet from the picnic table. His purpose in shooting
at the sign was to scare the members of the group. Bill testified that because of

the distance between the picnic table and the sign, he did not believe he would hit any of the children at the picnic table.

Shawna Wagler testified that while she and other members of her group were sitting around the picnic table, she felt a sting on her thigh. At first, Shawna did not know what had happened and initially blamed the sting on someone in her group. However, after glancing around the area, Shawna saw Bill standing behind the shed and pointing the BB gun in her direction. Shawna pointed towards Bill and said "There he is." With that, Todd Baker, who was lying on his stomach on top of the picnic table, looked up and turned his head in the direction of Bill Swanson. At that moment, Todd was struck in the eye with a BB. As a result of this injury, Todd lost his right eye.

Todd Baker's parents filed a civil complaint on behalf of Todd and themselves against the Swansons, appellants herein. The Swansons had two insurance policies in effect at the time: one was issued by the Physicians Insurance Company of Ohio ("PICO"), while the other policy was issued by the Cincinnati Insurance Company ("Cincinnati"). The insurance companies filed a declaratory judgment action against the Swansons and the Bakers, seeking a declaration of their obligations under their respective contracts of insurance. Specifically, PICO and Cincinnati sought a ruling that the policies' exclusionary provisions exempted them from the duty to defend and indemnify the Swansons against the Bakers' lawsuit.

The trial court heard the declaratory judgment action on January 5, 1989. After making findings of fact and conclusions of law, the court held that Bill Swanson did not intentionally injure Todd Baker: "The evidence does not support a finding that William Swanson shot the BB gun with the intent to injure anybody or with the belief that such injury was substantially certain to occur." The trial court concluded that Todd was injured by reason of an accident. Because both insurance policies excluded only expected or intentional injuries, the trial court determined that both PICO and Cincinnati had a duty to defend and indemnify. Both insurance companies appealed.

The court of appeals found our decision in *Preferred Risk Ins. Co. v. Gill*, 507 N.E.2d 1118 (Ohio 1987), to be controlling. After noting the similarity of the language in the two policies at bar and the policy in *Gill*, the appellate court reasoned "that it is the intentional nature of the act of the insured, rather than the result of such an act, such as the specific injury to Todd's right eye, which determines whether coverage will apply." Upon reviewing the trial court's findings and applying the above reasoning, the court of appeals reversed.

Finding its decision to conflict with that of the Eleventh District Court of Appeals in *Motorists Ins. Co. v. Dadisman*, 1988 WL 232960 (Ohio App. 1988), the court certified the record of the case to this court for review and final determination.

ALICE ROBIE RESNICK, J. The issue presented in this case is the application of a provision in a contract of insurance excluding coverage for injuries expected or intended by the insured. We begin our analysis by reviewing the language of the two provisions involved.

The PICO insurance policy issued to appellants contains the following:

"Part I, Exclusions to Part G and Part H
"1. Part G, Personal Liability Coverage and Part H, Medical Payments to Others
does [*sic*] not apply to bodily injury or property damage:
    "a) which is expected or intended by the insured[.]"

Appellants' policy with Cincinnati states as follows:

> "PART I-DEFINITIONS
> "1. Personal Injury means:
>   "A. bodily harm . . . to others caused by an accident;
>   "3. Accident means an event or series of unrelated events that unexpectedly, unintentionally and suddenly causes personal injury or property damage during the policy period.
>
> "PART IV - WHAT IS NOT COVERED - EXCLUSIONS
>   "8. We will not cover Personal Injury or Property Damage caused intentionally."

I

While the insurance policy issued by Cincinnati contains language different from that in the PICO policy, both policies are the same in effect: neither policy provides coverage for intentional or expected personal injuries caused by the insured. The difference is that one policy achieves this result by way of an express exclusion for such injuries (PICO), whereas the other policy does so by way of definition and an exclusion (Cincinnati). Since the effect of both policies is the same, we will treat the respective policy provisions in like manner.

Relying heavily on our decision in *Gill, supra,* the court of appeals concluded that both policies excluded coverage for the injury suffered by Todd Baker. When construing these policy provisions, the appellate court read *Gill* as focusing on the intentional nature of the act, rather than the result of the act, *i.e.,* the injury. The court of appeals went on to note that the trial court specifically found that Bill intentionally fired the gun in the direction of Todd and the others at the picnic table. Thus, applying the above standard to the trial court's findings of fact and conclusions of law, the court of appeals held that the exclusions applied because the insured had acted intentionally.

In *Gill,* we held that "the insurer has no duty to defend or indemnify its insured where the insurer demonstrates in good faith in the declaratory judgment action that the act of the insured was intentional and therefore outside the policy coverage." *Id.* at paragraph two of the syllabus. However, the fact pattern in *Gill* is markedly different from that of the present case. The insured in *Gill* had pleaded guilty to aggravated murder with specifications for killing an eleven-year-old girl. While applying a policy exclusion nearly identical to that in the PICO policy to that fact pattern, we stated, ". . . where the conduct which prompted the underlying wrongful death suit is so indisputably outside coverage, we discern no basis for requiring the insurance company to defend or indemnify its insured. . . ." *Id.* 507 N.E.2d at 1123. After noting that an essential element of aggravated murder is that the perpetrator intend to cause death, the *Gill* court concluded that "Kerri's death was clearly 'expected or intended by the insured' and therefore the policy does not provide coverage for whatever personal liability Gill [the insured] may have." *Id.* 507 N.E.2d at 1124.

Thus, our holding that there was no coverage in *Gill* was premised on the facts that the insured *intended to cause the injury* of another person, and that this intent was conclusively established by the insured's plea of guilty to aggravated murder. Stated otherwise, our decision was based on a finding that the insured intended to cause an injury, *i.e.,* the death of an eleven-year-old girl. While *Gill* used language regarding the intentional act or conduct of the insured, *Gill* actually stands for the proposition that it is the resultant *injury* which must be intended for the exclusion to apply to deny coverage. ✳

II

Provisions contained in an insurance policy excluding intentional or expected injuries have been the subject of an extensive body of case law. *See* 12 Couch, Insurance 184-193, §44A:133 (2d ed. 1981); Annotation, Construction and Application of Provision of Liability Insurance Policy Expressly Excluding Injuries Intended or Expected By Insured, 31 A.L.R.4th 957 (1984). Our current interpretation of *Gill* is consistent with the majority rule that has emerged from the case law on this issue in other jurisdictions. In *State Farm Mut. Auto. Ins. Co. v. Worthington*, 405 F.2d 683 (8th Cir. 1968), the insured had fatally wounded a young boy who he thought had tried to steal his watermelons. The insured had fired a .22 caliber rifle in an attempt to scare the young man. In holding that an intentional injury exclusion did not preclude coverage, the court stated that "[t]he preponderance of the evidence in this case indicates that while the discharge of the firearm was intentional the fatal wounding . . . was not intentional but accidental." *Id.* at 686. The court went on to note that "[a]lmost all acts are intentional in one sense or another but many unintended results flow from intentional acts." *Id.* at 688.

While interpreting an exclusion for "property damage caused intentionally by or at the direction of the insured," the Supreme Court of Pennsylvania stated that "the vast majority of courts which have considered such a provision have reached the conclusion that before the insurer may disclaim liability, it must be shown that the insured intended by his act to produce the damage which did in fact occur. Annot., 2 A.L.R.3d 1238 (1965). We subscribe to such a view. There is a very real distinction between intending an act and intending a result and the policy exclusion addresses itself quite clearly to the latter." *Eisenman v. Hornberger*, 264 A.2d 673, 674 (Pa. 1970). The court concluded that while the insured intentionally had broken into the home of another to steal liquor, there was no evidence that a fire caused by the insured had been intentional. The insured minor boy had been using matches to see, and had dropped them as they burnt down to the stem. The court held that absent evidence of an intent to cause the resulting damage (in that case a fire), the exclusion was not applicable. . . .

In *Colonial Penn Ins. Co. v. Hart*, 291 S.E.2d 410 (Ga. App. 1982), the evidence presented at trial showed that the insured had fired at a vandal in an attempt to frighten him. The court framed the issue as follows: ". . . the issue in the instant case was not whether Mr. Rice intentionally fired the shotgun. This fact is uncontroverted. Rather, '[t]he *only* issue . . . was whether the [bodily injury] was "either expected or intended from the standpoint of [Mr. Rice]". . .' *Transamerica Ins. Co. v. Thrift-Mart*, 285 S.E.2d 566 (Ga. App. 1981)." (Emphasis sic.) *Id.* 291 S.E.2d at 412. The court upheld the jury's finding that the injury to the vandal was not intentional, and thus the exclusion was inapplicable. . . .

From the above case law, it can be seen that other jurisdictions require that in order for an exclusion of this nature to apply, an insurer must demonstrate not only that the insured intended the act, but also that he intended to cause harm or injury. The rationale for this rule of law is twofold. First, the plain language of the policy is in terms of an intentional or expected *injury,* not an intentional or expected *act.* Were we to allow the argument that only an intentional act is required, we would in effect be rewriting the policy. Second, as the courts above have noted, many injuries result from intentional acts, although the injuries themselves are wholly unintentional.

III

In the case at bar, the trial court found that while the insured intentionally fired a BB gun in the direction of the injured person, the injury itself was neither intended nor substantially certain to occur. Rather, the finder of fact conclusively found that the injury was accidental. Based on our interpretation of *Gill, supra,* and the persuasive reasoning of the courts in other jurisdictions, we find the court of appeals erred by requiring that only the act of the insured need be shown to have been intentional.

Therefore, we hold that in order to avoid coverage on the basis of an exclusion for expected or intentional injuries, the insurer must demonstrate that the injury itself was expected or intended. It is not sufficient to show merely that the act was intentional. In this case the exclusion is inapplicable because the trial court's determination that Todd Baker's injury was not intentionally inflicted or substantially certain to occur is supported by competent, credible evidence. Therefore, the insurers are obligated to defend and indemnify the appellants. The decision of the court of appeals is reversed.

Judgment reversed.

WRIGHT, J., dissenting.

I must respectfully but vigorously dissent from today's majority opinion, which holds that an insurer cannot deny coverage to its insured who commits an intentional tort intended or expected to cause injury, yet who merely underestimates the precise extent of harm that results from the tortfeasor's intentional conduct. It is clear to me that this holding misconstrues the plain language of the pertinent insurance policies in this case. It is also clear that this holding flies in the face of long-stated public policy which precludes insuring against intentional torts. . . .

In order to properly review the court of appeals' analysis, it is illustrative to first examine several noteworthy facts and circumstances which surrounded Todd Baker's unfortunate injury and which were before the trial court. There was extensive trial testimony to indicate that the tortfeasor, Bill Swanson, had considerable experience in using the gun in question and had a keen awareness of its destructive potential. Swanson admitted on the stand that he had been shooting with his father numerous times and that his father had warned him that the gun was dangerous and could inflict injury. The tortfeasor admitted that he knew the gun could inflict injury and confirmed that he had previously used the gun to kill a squirrel. He also stated that he had used the gun to hit tin cans twenty to thirty feet away.

Additionally, the court heard testimony indicating that Bill Swanson aimed and shot at a group of four teenagers who were in proximity to one another around a picnic table. Shawna Wagler, whom Swanson shot in the thigh immediately prior to shooting Todd Baker in the eye, testified that she was within a foot or two of Todd Baker during the course of these tragic events. Further testimony from Wagler and from Robert Will indicated that Swanson deliberately and directly aimed at this group of young people.

Testimony also revealed that there were few, if any, visual obstructions to block or interfere with Swanson's line of sight. Wagler testified that she could clearly see the upper half of the tortfeasor's body as he fired upon the group. Joseph Jogerst, who accompanied Swanson when Swanson fired upon the group, stated that nothing obstructed their view except a little tree. Finally, Joseph Jogerst testified that he heard two screams seconds after shots were fired. It would have been possible for the trial court to conclude from that testimony that the tortfeasor could have heard Shawna Wagler scream before he fired the shot that partially blinded Todd Baker. Thus, Swanson could have heard as well as seen evidence of the physical injuries his assault was inflicting. The trial court obviously disbelieved Swanson's testimony (highlighted by the majority) that he was aiming at a sign ten to fifteen feet away from the victims.

From these facts and circumstances the trial court reasonably found that "... William Swanson ... intentionally shot ... [and] intentionally fired in the direction of Todd C. Baker and three of his teenage friends. ...". ...

I find it more reasonable to state that *Gill* stands for the proposition clearly enunciated in the opinion that where an insurance policy employs such intentional tort coverage exclusions, the court construing the terms of the policy may infer intent to harm as a matter of law, when the insured could reasonably expect that his or her *conduct* would result in bodily injuries which are a natural and probable result of that conduct. It troubles me that the majority implies that only a few states follow such a position. By my count, at least seventeen states follow such a viewpoint. *See* Annotation, Construction and Application of Provision of Liability Insurance Policy Expressly Excluding Injuries Intended or Expected by Insured, 31 A.L.R.4th 957 (1984 & Supp. 1989). ...

Keeping in mind then that the trial court *specifically* found that the tortfeasor, Swanson, intentionally shot his rifle and intentionally aimed at the unfortunate group of teenagers, I will now conduct a brief review of some pertinent holdings and analyses from other jurisdictions construing policy language similar to that in this case.

In *Transamerica Ins. Group v. Meere*, 694 P.2d 181 (Ariz. 1984), the Arizona Supreme Court was required to review a policy exclusion for personal injury "which is expected or intended by the insured" in the context of an exchange of physical blows in a fight. The court stated, "... if the trier of fact determines that ... [the insured] was the aggressor and acted wrongfully by striking ... [the alleged victim] without legal justification, the basic intent to injure will be presumed and the exclusion will apply. ..." *Id.* 694 P.2d at 189. Recently, in reviewing an employer's sexual harassment of an employee, the Arizona Supreme Court opined that "[t]he conduct of ... [the insured] was so certain to cause injury to ... [the victim] that his intent to cause harm is inferred as a matter of law, despite his statements to the contrary that all he intended was to provide pleasure and satisfaction. ..." *Continental Ins. Co. v. McDaniel*, 772 P.2d 6, 8 (Ariz. 1988).

Federal courts construing California law have also subscribed to this viewpoint. For instance, the United States Court of Appeals for the Ninth Circuit found, in construing California law in a sexual molestation case, that "... there is an irrebuttable presumption of an intent to harm in child molestation cases, regardless of whether the defendant was convicted of a general or specific intent crime. For such conduct to be excluded from insurance coverage, all that must be shown is the intent to commit the acts constituting the molestation. Therefore, the only issue in the instant case is whether there was sufficient evidence that . . . [the tortfeasor] did not form the intent to *act* to withstand a motion for summary judgment." (Emphasis *sic*.) *State Farm Fire Ins. & Cas. Co. v. Abraio*, 874 F.2d 619, 623 (9th Cir. 1989).

When reviewing the intent of a tortfeasor who kicked his victim in the face, an Illinois appellate court implicitly endorsed determinations from other jurisdictions ". . . that a similar policy exclusion applies regardless of whether the tort defendant intended the specific injury as long as that defendant intended to injure the particular victim. . . ." *Mid America Fire Co. v. Smith*, 441 N.E.2d 949, 950-951 (Ill. App. 4 1982).

Indiana appeals courts have consistently followed the position I advocate herein. The court in *Heshelman v. Nationwide Mut. Fire Ins. Co.*, 412 N.E.2d 301, 302 (Ind. Ct. App. 1980), examined the intent involved when physical blows were exchanged during union picketing and held, "'. . . The latter intent [to cause injury] may be established either by showing an actual intent to injure, or by showing the nature and character of the act to be such that intent to cause harm to the other party must be inferred as a matter of law.'" *See, also, Indiana Lumbermens Mut. Ins. Co. v. Brandum*, 419 N.E.2d 246, 248 (Ind. Ct. App. 1981), involving a wrongful death action in which the driver of one car in a fit of jealous rage deliberately rammed a second car containing a driver and the tortfeasor's fiancée. There, the appeals court stated, ". . . It is possible to infer the intent to harm the injured party from the nature of the insured's acts. . . ." *Id.* at 248.

An appeals court in Kansas conducted an analysis quite similar to that of the court of appeals in this case in *Cas. Reciprocal Exchange v. Thomas*, 647 P.2d 1361 (Kan. Ct. App. 1982). There, the trial court had found that the tortfeasor pointed a gun at the victim and fired, injuring the victim. The court further found that the tortfeasor did not bump or touch anything to jar his trigger finger prior to the gun's firing. The appellate court declared, ". . . to say that the act of aiming and firing the gun was intentional, but the injury was not, draws too fine a distinction. The better rule is . . . that where an intentional act results in injuries which are a natural and probable result of the act, the injuries are intentional." *Id.* at 1364, citing *Prosser, Law of Torts* §8 (4th ed. 1971), and *Restatement of the Law 2d, Torts* §8A Comment b (1965).

In *Auto-Owners Ins. Co. v. Gardipey*, 434 N.W.2d 220 (Mich. Ct. App. 1988), a Michigan appellate court, construing an exclusionary provision as applied to assault with intent to commit criminal sexual conduct, held ". . . [t]he intent to injure or harm can be inferred as a matter of law from the alleged sexual penetration. . . ." *Id.* 434 N.W.2d at 222.

The Minnesota Supreme Court, in *Continental Western Ins. Co. v. Toal*, 244 N.W.2d 121 (Minn. 1976), considered the nature of a tortfeasor's intent during the course of an armed robbery. In that oft-cited case, a robber shot and killed a victim and that victim's estate later brought a wrongful death suit against all the participants in the robbery, including one who was present and armed during the shooting, and another who was the "chief planner" of the crime and who drove the getaway car. Both of these men testified that they did not intend to injure anyone, but that the shooting did not come as a surprise. The court explained ". . . that an injury is 'expected or intended' from the standpoint of the insured if a reason for an insured's act is to inflict bodily injury *or* 'when the character of the act is such that an intention to inflict an injury can be inferred' as a matter of law." (Emphasis *sic*.) *Id.* 244 N.W.2d at 125. The Minnesota Supreme Court reaffirmed this holding in *Fireman's Fund Ins. Co. v. Hill*, 314 N.W.2d 834 (Minn. 1982). *See, also, Truck Ins. Exchange v. Pickering*, 642 S.W.2d 113, 116 (Mo. Ct. App. 1982), citing and approving the holding in *Toal, supra.*

The Nebraska Supreme Court had before it in *State Farm Fire & Cas. Co. v. Victor*, 442 N.W.2d 880 (Neb. 1989), the shooting death of a person who was alleged to have taken money from purses at a party and at whom the insured fired a shot in retaliation when he saw his silhouette in a doorway. The court reiterated the rule:

> "' . . . [A]n injury is "expected or intended" from the standpoint of the insured if a reason for an insured's act is to inflict bodily injury *or if the character of the act is such that an intention to inflict an injury can be inferred as a matter of law.*' "

(Emphasis *sic;* citations omitted.) *Id.* at 882-883, quoting *Jones v. Norval*, 279 N.W.2d 388, 391 (Neb. 1979). The court went on to state:

> "'To hold that under such circumstances the testimony of the insured that he did not intend to injure the plaintiff is sufficient to permit the fact finder to find that no harm to the injured party was intended, simply ignores reality. Any reasonable analysis requires the conclusion that from the very nature of the act harm must have been intended.' "

Id. 442 N.E.2d at 883, quoting *Jones, supra.*

In *Snyder v. Nelson*, 564 P.2d 681 (Or. 1977), a man angered by a woman's rejection of his advances rammed into the woman's automobile causing personal injury and property damage. There, the Oregon Supreme Court averred that the trier of fact may infer from the natural and probable results of a tortfeasor's actions that the tortfeasor intentionally injured the victim and damaged her property.

The Vermont Supreme Court reviewed a case in which a sheriff mistakenly sold a mobile home at a sheriff's sale. *State v. Glens Falls Ins. Co.*, 404 A.2d 101 (Vt. 1979). While holding that the sheriff's conduct was not "intentional" in this case, the court averred ". . . where the circumstances indicate the insured knew his act would damage the injured party he must be taken to have intended it despite subjective testimony to the contrary. . . ." *Id.* at 104.

A Washington appellate court availed itself of the opportunity to determine the applicability of insurance exclusionary language in a case involving non-consensual intercourse in *Western Natl. Assur. Co. v. Hecker*, 719 P.2d 954 (Wash. Ct. App. 1986). It opined that " . . . intent may be actual or may be inferred by the nature of the act and the accompanying reasonable foreseeability of harm. . . ." *Id.* at 960.

Finally, a Wisconsin appellate court recently held in a case involving sexual molestation of a minor that certain acts ". . . are so certain to result in injury to . . . [the victim] that the law will infer an intent to injure on behalf of the actor without regard to his or her claimed intent. . . ." *K.A.G. v. Stanford*, 434 N.W.2d 790, 793 (Wis. Ct. App. 1988).

I close by constructing a scenario which I believe might actually be forthcoming under the analysis and holding the majority presents today. Imagine, if you will, an arsonist who "unintentionally" kills a tenant in an apartment building that the arsonist intentionally sets on fire. Thereafter, the estate of the victim brings a wrongful death suit against the arsonist tortfeasor seeking to recover for the tenant's death. Under today's holding, the insurance company, whose policy provides coverage for personal injuries caused by the arsonist, would be responsible for paying the wrongful death claim. For the insurance company to avoid paying the claim, it would have to show that the arsonist specifically intended to kill the victim when he burned the building.

Lest I be accused of taking today's holding to an illogical extreme, I point to the holding of the New Jersey Supreme Court in *Ambassador Ins. Co. v. Montes*, 388 A.2d 603 (N.J. 1978). That court subscribed to the majority's viewpoint and held that an arsonist's insurer was indeed responsible for paying the wrongful death claim of the arsonist's victim, in a case that duplicates exactly the scenario I posit above. Clearly, to hold insurance companies responsible for paying claims for an insured's homicidal behavior shocks one's conscience, yet such a holding is the logical result of today's holding.

Accordingly, and for the reasons stated above, I would affirm the judgment of the court of appeals and exclude this tortfeasor from the protection of the coverage in question, which by the deliberate and intentional nature of his conduct he does not deserve.

NOTES AND QUESTIONS

1. *City of Carter Lake* and the majority and dissent in *Swanson* represent three distinct approaches to the expected or intended exclusion. Which makes the most sense to you? Why?

2. Iowa courts have adopted the rule preferred by the dissent in *Swanson*—namely, that the exclusion applies whenever the policyholder intends to cause some harm, even if a different kind or degree of harm results. That rule can lead to results that are difficult to take. For example, the Iowa Supreme Court did not follow the rule in a case where an 11-year-old defendant killed his friend by throwing a baseball at him after an argument. *See Amco Ins. Co. v. Haht*, 490 N.W.2d 843 (Iowa 1992). The boy intended to cause some harm, but because there was a significant difference between the harm intended and the harm that resulted, and the defendant was so young, the court created an exception. Might Bill Swanson's age partly explain the result in *Swanson* as well? Is there a difference between throwing a baseball and shooting a BB gun? Is there a difference between the harm that one would expect to result from each action?

3. Should mistakes of ownership or identity matter to the application of the expected or intended exclusion? Consider *Tennessee Farmers Mut. Ins. Co. v. Evans*, 814 S.W.2d 49 (Tenn. 1991) (finding no coverage because even though the policyholder, who burned $186,000, believed that the money belonged to her husband, it in fact did not; her action to burn the money was intentional, regardless of her mistaking the identity of the owner, and so fell within the expected or intended exclusion); *American Family Mut. Ins. Co. v.*

Johnson, 816 P.2d 952 (Colo. 1991) (finding that a policyholder intended to kick a woman, even though his action was based on the mistaken belief that the woman was his wife, as she left the bar with another man; therefore, his action was excluded). Do you think that rule would apply in all cases? Suppose a parent mistakenly spanked another person's child?

4. Inferred intent is frequently used to preclude coverage in sexual molestation cases. Courts often disregard the requirement for a showing of a subjective intent to injure on the grounds that the intent is inherent in the sexual act. Because the intent to injure is presumed, coverage is excluded by the expected or intended exception in CGL policies. Consider *Standard Fire Ins. Co. v. Blakeslee*, 771 P.2d 1172 (Wash. Ct. App. 1989) (finding no coverage, under either the CGL or the professional liability policy, for a dentist who sexually molested a patient). The *Berdella* case discussed in the excerpt at the beginning of the criminal act unit is an exception to this practice. What is at stake when a court presumes the intent to injure? What are the policy reasons for doing so? Against?

5. The *Swanson* dissent referred to the New Jersey case of *Ambassador v. Montes*, which is our next case. As you read that case, consider whether the *Swanson* dissent accurately characterized it, or whether the result might turn on an important factual distinction that the dissent leaves out—namely, the lack of either an expected or intended exclusion or an accident requirement in the insurance policy at issue in *Ambassador v. Montes*.

2.   The Public Policy Issue

As we saw in *Watson v. United Services Automobile Association*, 566 N.W.2d 683 (Minn. 1997), in Chapter 3, express and implied exclusions for intentional harm can raise knotty questions. As reflected by the fact that courts are willing to *imply* an intentional harm exclusion in an insurance policy, there are strong public policy reasons in favor of limiting coverage in the case of some intentional harm. From an efficiency perspective, the problem is one of moral hazard. From a corrective justice perspective, the problem is the immorality of insulating a person from the consequences of very wrongful behavior. Even more than other insurance coverage issues, the problem of intentional harm requires us to be especially attuned to the public policy consequences of the options before us.

The case that follows presents an unusual and insightful analysis that challenges us to think "outside the box" with regard to intentional harm and liability insurance.

AMBASSADOR INSURANCE CO. v. MONTES
Supreme Court of New Jersey
388 A.2d 603 (1978)

SCHREIBER, J. . . . The assured Joseph Satkin owned, among other properties, two old wooden tenement buildings in Passaic, one at 78 Washington Place, and the other at 80-82 Washington Place. The building at 80-82 Washington Place was a two-and-a-half story duplex four-family house in which 11 to 14 persons resided. The building was in a dangerous condition and had been scheduled for demolition. In the early morning hours of May 11, 1973, a fire broke out in the stairwell of 82 Washington Place. The Passaic Fire Department was alerted at 3:27 a.m. and promptly responded. However, the fire spread rapidly due to an open air draft and took four lives.

Joseph Satkin was tried and convicted of arson, conspiracy to commit arson, and felony murder for having intentionally caused the fire. Rafael Montes, as administrator ad prosequendum and as general administrator, instituted an action against Satkin for the death and injuries of Marilyn Ortega Perez, an infant who perished in the fire. Plaintiff Ambassador Insurance Company refused to defend that action, which has been placed on the inactive trial calendar pending final disposition of this action. In this declaratory judgment proceeding, [regarding the insurer's obligations under Satkin's liability insurance policy] the plaintiff insurance company has joined Satkin and Rafael Montes, as administrator, as defendants.

At the conclusion of the trial the trial court found that Satkin intended to burn the building. Because of the early morning hour at which the fire was started, nature of the structure, and surrounding facts, the court held it was reasonable to expect that people in the building might be injured. The court concluded that in causing such a fire the defendant Satkin had completely disregarded the safety of the inhabitants and found that the death and injury were the intended result of an intended act. Therefore coverage under the policy was denied.

The Appellate Division, noting that the plaintiff's liability policy did not contain an express exclusion for the consequences of an intentional wrongdoing, held that such omission was immaterial because public policy prohibits indemnity for the civil consequences of one's intentional wrongdoing. It opined that the guidelines for determining the nonexistence of coverage were either that the insured had a specific intent to inflict the injuries that occurred or that he knew the injuries were substantially certain to follow the performance of the intentional act. The Appellate Division reasoned that since Satkin did not intend to injure or kill anyone, though his act was in wanton and reckless disregard for the safety of those living in the building, the criteria were not met and there was coverage. We agree with the result reached, but not for the reasons stated.

The plaintiff's policy which was placed in evidence as a joint exhibit provided that:

> The company will pay on behalf of the Insured all sums which the Insured shall become legally obligated to pay as damages because of
> Coverage A, bodily injury or
> Coverage B, property damage
> to which this Insurance applies, caused by an occurrence and the company shall have the right and duty to defend any suit against the Insured seeking damages on account of such bodily injury or property damage, even if any of the allegations of the suit are groundless, false or fraudulent. . . .

The insurance policy in evidence did not contain a definition of "occurrence," nor a provision which excluded coverage for intentional acts. Both parties have agreed that the factual record is so limited. . . .

On the face of the policy, plaintiff's obligation to defend the action and pay on behalf of its insured any amount up to the announced limits due on account of the injuries suffered and the death of Marilyn Ortega Perez is obvious. The plaintiff concedes as much for it does not rely upon any exclusionary clause or other pertinent limitation in the policy.[7] Its only defense is that public policy prohibits insurance indemnity for the civil consequences of an insured's intentional wrongdoing.

It has been said that indemnification of a person for a loss or damage incurred as a result of his willful wrongdoing in violation of a criminal statute is contrary to public policy. 7 Appleman, Insurance Law and Practice §4252 at 5 (1962). Were a person able to insure himself against the economic consequences of his intentional wrongdoing, the deterrence attributable to financial responsibility would be missing. Further, as a matter of moral principle no person should be permitted to allege his own turpitude as a ground for recovery. Accordingly, we have accepted the general principle that an insurer may not contract to indemnify an insured against the civil consequences of his own willful criminal act.

However, this principle is not to be applied under all circumstances. Certainly it should not come into play when the wrongdoer is not benefited and an innocent third person receives the protection afforded by the insurance. Recovery has been allowed to cover losses occasioned by an intentional act of the insured. In *Fidelity-Phoenix Fire Ins. Co. v. Queen City Bus & Transfer Co.*, 3 F.2d 784 (4th Cir. 1925), the president of a corporation, who owned 25% of the issued and outstanding capital stock, intentionally set fire to a motor bus owned by the corporation and on which he held a mortgage. The fire insurance company was compelled to pay the fire insurance to the corporation to be used for creditors and stockholders other than the wrongdoer. *See* Annotation, "Fire insurance on corporate property as affected by its intentional destruction by a corporate officer, employee or stockholder," 37 A.L.R.3d 1385 (1971). In another situation a husband and wife owned property as tenants by the entirety and had fire insurance covering the property. The husband intentionally set fire to the property and then committed suicide. It was held that his act of arson did not bar the innocent wife's recovery under the fire insurance policy. *Howell v. Ohio Casualty Ins. Co.*, 327 A.2d 240 (N.J. Super. Ct. App. Div. 1974).

When the insurance company has contracted to pay an innocent person monetary damages due to any liability of the insured, such payment when ascribable to a criminal event should be made so long as the benefit there of does not [i]nure to the assured. In furtherance of that justifiable end, under most circumstances it is equitable and just that the insurer be indemnified by the insured for the payment to the injured party. In subrogating the insurer to the injured person's rights so that the insurer may be reimbursed for its payment of the insured's debt to the injured person, the public policy principle to which we adhere, that the assured may not be relieved of financial responsibility arising out of his criminal act, is honored. The insurer's discharge of its contractual obligations by payment to an innocent injured third person will further the public interest in compensating the victim. *See Burd v. Sussex Mutual Ins. Co.*, 267 A.2d 7 (N.J. 1970).

This application of subrogation is consonant with its traditional usage as an equitable mechanism to force the ultimate satisfaction of an obligation by the

---

7. We note that our dissenting Brother refers to a definition of "occurrence" which is not before us. The plaintiff insurance carrier does not raise any issue as to the word "occurrence" including the specific incident involved. . . .

person who in good conscience should pay. In *Camden Trust Co. v. Cramer*, 40 A.2d 601 (N.J. 1945), Justice Heher described the principle in the following manner:

> Subrogation is a doctrine of purely equitable origin and nature, although it is a right that is now considered as within the cognizance of courts of law in certain circumstances. Since it is an equity, it is subject to the rules governing equities; and it is axiomatic that it will not be enforced where it would be inequitable so to do. It will not be allowed to work injustice to others having equal or superior equities. The right of subrogation must be founded upon an equity just and reasonable according to general principles, an equity that will accomplish complete justice between the parties to the controversy. . . . Subrogation is a device adopted by equity to compel the ultimate discharge of an obligation by him who in good conscience ought to pay it. [citation omitted] The process is analogous to the creation of a constructive trust, the creditor being compelled to hold his rights against the principal debtor, and his securities, in trust for the subrogee.

Id. at 603. . . .

In the casualty insurance field subrogation is most often found when the insurer who has indemnified the insured for its damage or loss is subrogated to any rights that the insured may have against a third party. In the absence of subrogation either the insured would collect twice and be unjustly enriched, or, if the insured were not entitled to double recovery, the third party wrongdoer would go free. *Standard Accident Ins. Co. v. Pellecchia*, 104 A.2d 288 (N.J. 1954).

Insurers have also been permitted to recover from their insureds. Appleman has declared that "[t]he right of subrogation, or more properly called indemnification where sought from its own insured, is enforced where it would be inequitable to deny such remedy." 8 Appleman, *supra* §4935 at 461 (1973). The same thought was expressed in *Malanga v. Manufacturers Cas. Ins. Co.*, 146 A.2d 105 (N.J. 1958). The defendant insurance company had issued a comprehensive liability insurance policy to a partnership, the named insured. Under the terms of the policy the individual partners were also covered. The policy excluded coverage for damages resulting from an assault and battery committed by the insured. Alfred Malanga, a partner, committed an assault and battery in the course of the partnership business. The injured third party recovered a verdict against the partnership. The partnership, having paid the judgment, sought reimbursement from the insurance company. The court concluded that the partnership was covered and the insurance company was obligated to reimburse the partnership. However, it was held "[o]f course, Alfred Malanga should not individually benefit by our determination in this case. The issue of his liability to the defendant insurer under its right of subrogation is not in any way affected." *Id.* at 110.

Here the comprehensive general liability insurance policy expressly and clearly obligated the plaintiff insurance company to pay on Satkin's behalf those sums which Satkin was legally indebted to pay as damages because of personal injury to and the death of Marilyn Ortega Perez. The plaintiff insurance company cannot and should not escape from that duty on the ground that the damages were due to its assured's criminal act. However, Satkin should not receive or be entitled to the benefit of the insurer's payment and the insurer's right of subrogation should accomplish that end. . . .

PASHMAN, J., concurring. I concur in the result reached by the majority. The conclusion is sound that where a liability insurance policy facially provides coverage for an insured intentional wrongdoer, such coverage should extend to an injured third party, with the insurer subsequently being subrogated to the rights of the third party against the insured. As Justice Schreiber aptly points out, sound public policy is furthered where injured parties are reimbursed, so long as no benefit is received by the tortfeasor. My concurrence is based on uneasiness over whether the majority opinion demonstrates coverage under the policy, given the definition of "occurrence." My conclusion is that there is coverage in spite of that definition.

By the terms of the policy, coverage exists if the insured is liable for damages arising out of an "occurrence," defined as "an accident . . . which results in bodily injury or property damage neither expected nor intended from the standpoint of the insured." I find coverage because Satkin did not *intend* to injure the decedent under a proper definition of that term.

The major problem with this case is that the Appellate Division selected an improper standard of intent, and then erroneously applied that standard. The Appellate Division followed *Hanover Insurance Group v. Cameron,* 298 A.2d 715 (N.J. Super. Ct. Ch. Div. 1973), in adopting the definition of intent as used in Restatement, Torts 2d, §8A (1965). 371 A.2d 292 (N.J. Super. Ct. App. Div. 1977).

§8A. INTENT

The word "intent" is used throughout the Restatement of this Subject to denote that the actor desires to cause consequences of his act, or that he believes that the consequences are substantially certain to result from it.

The Appellate Division also cited the following part of Restatement, Torts 2d §8A, comment b:

If the actor knows that the consequences are certain or substantially certain, to result from his act, and still goes ahead, he is treated by the law as if he had in fact desired to produce the result.

If I believed that this were indeed a proper definition of intent in the context of liability insurance, my conclusion would be that the injuries resulting from Satkin's arson were intentional and not an occurrence under this policy. Surely, one who starts a fire in an old multi-storied wood frame building at 3 a.m., directly under the main stairwell, without warning any of the inhabitants, should be held to be substantially certain that some of these persons would be seriously injured or killed. The Appellate Division's conclusion that Satkin's act did not meet the objective standard of intent inherent in the *Restatement* strains credulity.

Moreover, the trial court found as a matter of fact that Satkin could not have said in his mind, as he did this act, "[T]hey'll all get out; there's a fire escape."

. . . The finding that Satkin knew with substantial certainty that his act of arson would injure his tenants is amply supported by the evidence, and is unassailable. Under a principled application of the Restatement standard, the Appellate Division could do nothing but affirm the denial of coverage at trial.

However, I reject the Restatement standard as a definition of intent in the liability insurance field. It is really no different from the rule that a tortfeasor intends the natural and probable consequences of his acts, a standard which has been roundly rejected in liability insurance policy cases.

The proper standard of intent for liability insurance cases was announced in *Lyons v. Hartford Insurance Group,* 310 A.2d 485 (N.J. Super. Ct. App. Div. 1973), *cert. denied,* 315 A.2d 411 (N.J. 1974), as whether the injury was the intended result of an intentional act. In *Lyons,* an off-duty police officer whose conduct after a long drinking bout caused him to be assaulted, shot and killed a man. He claimed that he merely wanted to fire a warning shot and that the revolver went off prematurely.

The policy had an exclusion clause which prevents coverage for an injury expected or intended from the standpoint of the insured. The Appellate Division injected this clause into the case for the first time, and reversed the trial court's dismissal of the insured's declaratory judgment action concerning coverage. The Appellate Division used the following test to determine coverage:

> Thus, the distinction between intended and unintended results of intentional acts is well recognized. The trial court did not apply this principle. The oral opinion below can be construed as holding that if Lyons intended to fire without any specific intent to cause death or bodily harm, coverage did not exist. Such a principle is at war with the authorities discussed here. The short of it is, if Lyons intended to maim or kill Berger he has no coverage. If his intent was, as he says, to fire a warning shot, but he unintentionally fired prematurely, coverage exists.

Lyons v. Hartford Insurance Group, supra at 489

Under *Lyons,* Satkin should be charged with intent to injure his tenants only if that was his subjective desire. This is the correct standard for liability insurance cases. Since one purpose of such insurance is to protect injured third parties, as between the liability insurer of a culpable actor and an innocent third party it is the better policy to place the risk of loss with the insurer where intent to injure is unclear.

Moreover, the standard which I advocate is the prevailing one.

> The courts have generally held that injury or damage is "caused intentionally" within the meaning of an "intentional injury exclusion clause" if the insured has acted with the specific intent to cause harm to a third party, with the result that the insurer will not be relieved of its obligations under a liability policy containing such an exclusion unless the insured has acted with such specific intent. Under this view, it is not sufficient that the insured's intentional, albeit wrongful, act has resulted in unintended harm to a third person; it is the harm itself that must be intended before the exclusion will apply. There is, however, some authority for the proposition that such a clause will operate to relieve a liability insurer of its duty to indemnify an insured whose intentional act has caused harm to a third person where the nature or character of the act is such that an intent to cause harm is thereby inferred as a matter of law.

Annotation, *Liability Insurance: Specific Exclusion of Liability for Injury Intentionally Caused by Insured,* 2 A.L.R.3d 1238, §2 at 1241 (1965).

The leading decision for the majority view is *Lumbermens Mutual Insurance Co. v. Blackburn,* [477 P.2d 62, 66 (Okl.1970)], where the Court held that the intentional throwing of a hard object by insured's son, which injured plaintiff, was not within a policy exclusion where the trial court found that no injury was actually intended. In *Caspersen v. Webber,* 213 N.W.2d 327 (Minn. 1973), the court also held that an injury was not caused intentionally within the meaning of an intentional injury exclusion clause. The insured had deliberately pushed aside plaintiff in entering a coat checkroom but did not desire or intend her resulting fall and back injury. To the same effect is *Hawkeye Sec. Insurance Co. v. Shields,* 187 N.W.2d 894, 901 (Mich. Ct. App. 1971), which held that the insurer will only avoid liability if the insured not only intended the act which led to the injury[] but also intended to cause bodily injury to the injured party. *See also Putnam v. Zeluff,* 127 N.W.2d 374 (Mich. 1964); *Smith v. Moran,* 209 N.E.2d 18 (Ill. Ct. App. 1965) (insurer is liable for the unintended result of an intentional act). The holding in *Lyons, supra,* can be most readily interpreted as following these cases. . . .

For a tortfeasor to be charged with intent to injure for purposes of a liability insurance policy, the majority rule requires that he have an actual subjective desire to injure a party. It is apparent that this rule cannot be harmonized with the Restatement test. . . .

The whole purpose behind Satkin's act of arson was to defraud the insurance company and obtain payment for the value of his property. He never desired that his tenants suffer injury or death. While he certainly displayed a callous disregard for their safety, he did not want to see them harmed by his act. Thus, Satkin did not "expect or intend" the deaths of his tenants in the subjective sense that is required for his act to be excluded from the definition of "occurrence." He was covered for the injuries caused by his despicable act, but is also liable to the insurer as the subrogee of an injured third party.

While the issue need not be reached here, it is my opinion that the so-called public policy against covering an insured for his intentional torts should be reexamined. This is particularly so where, as here, a subrogation theory exists so that the tortfeasor can in no way profit from his intentional wrongful act. With the prospect of criminal sanction and the spectre of civil liability despite coverage facing any wrongdoer, there is little reason to deny coverage which would protect the innocent injured party.

CLIFFORD, J., dissenting. By making the proceeds of a comprehensive general liability insurance policy available to compensate the estate and next-of-kin of a murder victim who perished in an intentionally set fire, the Court has devised a way to reach the "deep pockets." In achieving this remarkable result the majority obligates other insured property owners to bear the losses intentionally inflicted by a criminal merely because that criminal likewise happened to carry liability insurance on his property. In so doing the Court has disregarded the specific provisions of the policy in question as well as long-established public policy considerations. The law of insurance has thereby been turned on its head. I dissent.

On May 11, 1973 Marilyn Ortega Perez and three others died in a fire on Washington Place, Passaic. The owner of the property, defendant Joseph Satkin, was convicted of felony-murder on an indictment charging him with having intentionally caused the fire. Suit was instituted against Satkin for Ms. Perez's injuries and damages occasioned by the fire and the resultant pecuniary loss of her next-of-kin. Ambassador Insurance Company, Satkin's liability insurance carrier on this and at least forty-nine other pieces of his income-producing property, refused to defend Satkin and denied coverage. This declaratory judgment action tests the company's decision in that regard.

In finding coverage the Court reasons that on the face of the policy the company's obligation to defend and pay on behalf of its insured is "obvious"; that the policy contains no exclusion for the insured's intentional wrongdoing, and in fact constitutes an undertaking "to pay an innocent person monetary damages due to any liability of the insured, whether or not resulting from the insured's willful criminal act," *ante* at 606; and that the public policy principle against insurance coverage for intentional wrongdoing is vindicated by enforcing the carrier's payment to the injured party and permitting the insurer there after to be subrogated to the injured person's rights against the insured. On each supporting ground this reasoning fails.

First, the policy does not, on its face, provide coverage. In setting forth the policy provisions, *ante* at 605, the majority has quoted only so much of the insurance contract as spells out an obligation on the part of the company to "pay on behalf of the Insured all sums which the Insured shall become legally obligated to pay as damages because of (bodily injury or property damage) . . . caused by an *occurrence* . . ." (emphasis added). Conspicuously absent from the majority's analysis, however, is any discussion of the definition of "occurrence," which the policy defines as "an accident . . . which results in bodily injury or property damage neither expected nor intended from the standpoint of the insured. . . ."[8] That the fire in question was not, under any meaning of the word, an accident, seems beyond question. Nor is there any doubt that the bodily injury resulting here was "intended." The Restatement (Second) of Torts §8A (1965) provides that

> [t]he word "intend" is used throughout the Restatement of this subject to denote that the actor desires to cause consequences of his act, Or that he believes that the consequences are substantially certain to result from it (emphasis supplied).

Applying this definition in the instant case, there can be little question that Satkin "intended" to cause the victim's bodily injuries. By burning one of his rented dwelling houses at three o'clock in the morning, Satkin undoubtedly knew that injuries were substantially certain to follow his intentional act. So while there is no specific exclusion for the insured's intentional acts, neither is there coverage for Satkin's satanic conduct in this case. . . .

But it is on the third ground asserted by the Court in support of its conclusion—the public policy dimension—that today's decision so plainly departs from established law. The Court concedes that as a general rule it would violate public policy to allow indemnification of a person for loss or damage resulting from his willful wrongdoing in violation of a criminal statute, reasoning however

---

8. In complying with the trial court's request for a copy of the policy issued by Ambassador to Satkin, counsel for the carrier failed to include the page containing "definitions"; therefore, the trial court did not have the benefit of the entire policy. Likewise, counsel ha[s] not presented [an] argument based on the definition of "occurrence." At oral argument we inquired about the policy's definition of "occurrence," and specifically requested and thereafter received the complete policy. While the Court chooses to ignore the definition section, and counsel for Ambassador, after submitting the full policy, asks (inexplicably) that we "disregard the policy forwarded" to us after oral argument, I do not understand how we can properly or intelligently decide this case without application of the policy's definition of "occurrence." I would accept as part of the record so much of the insuring agreement filed with us as contains the definitions of terms used elsewhere in the policy, see R. 2:5-4(a), or at the very least give the attorneys the opportunity to present any argument relating to the definition of occurrence as they might wish to make. See Dresner v. Carrara, 353 A.2d 505 (N.J. 1976). Cf. U.S. Trust Co. of N.Y. v. State, 353 A.2d 514 (N.J. 1976), rev'd on other grounds, 431 U.S. 1 (1977).

that this principle is inapplicable when ". . . the wrongdoer is not benefited and an innocent third person receives the protection afforded by the insurance." *Ante* at 606. In support of this proposition, the Court relies on *Fidelity-Phoenix Fire Insurance Co. v. Queen City Bus & Transfer Co.,* 3 F.2d 784 (4th Cir. 1925) and *Howell v. Ohio Casualty Insurance Co.,* 327 A.2d 240 (N.J. Super. Ct. App. Div. 1974). Those cases are clearly distinguishable and afford no support whatsoever for the majority's position, inasmuch as in each the party recovering from the insurance carrier was an Express beneficiary of a fire insurance policy issued to the injured party. These cases were rightly decided and reflect a sound judicial approach: there is unquestionably no public policy reason to prevent a person from obtaining fire insurance protection against the consequences of the intentional criminal acts of third parties.

The instant case, however, does not represent an attempt by a victim of an intentional wrongdoer to recover the proceeds of a fire and accident policy *issued* to the victim and providing coverage against the intentional criminal acts of third parties. Rather, it involves an effort by a victim to recover the proceeds of a liability policy *issued to an insured* (the wrongdoer) and providing coverage for the consequences of his actions. . . .

NOTES AND QUESTIONS

1.   How do you think the case would have come out if the insurance company's counsel had not neglected to introduce the complete insurance policy into the trial record? Why? The New Jersey Supreme Court later addressed this question in *Allstate Insurance Co. v. Malec,* 514 A.2d 832 (N.J. 1986), which addressed an intentional harm exclusion in an automobile policy. The court wrote:

> That brings us to the fourth principle: a specific exclusion for intentional wrongful acts is valid and consistent with public policy. The question whether that principle retains its vitality is of some importance to the automobile insurance industry. We are told by amici that 180 of their 700 member companies write motor vehicle liability insurance in New Jersey and that those companies write about 80 percent, by premium volume, of that insurance in this state. Moreover, "all or virtually all" of the policies written for that coverage contain exclusions of liability coverage for harm intentionally caused by the insured. Both counsel acknowledged at oral argument that neither of them had seen an automobile liability policy that did not contain the exclusion that is the subject of this appeal.
>
> The most recent direct statement of this Court on the question of whether public policy can tolerate indemnifying, by the insurance mechanism, a wrongdoer for the civil consequences of his intentional acts is found in *Ambassador Ins. Co. v. Montes, supra,* 388 A.2d 603, which involved a comprehensive general liability insurance policy. *Id.* at 604. There the named insured intentionally set fire to the covered property. Four people died in the fire. In the ensuing civil action for the wrongful death of one of the victims, Ambassador Insurance Company refused to defend its insured, and thereafter brought an action for a declaratory judgment of its obligation under the policy. The trial court denied coverage on the ground that the decedent's injuries and death were the "intended result of an intended act." *Id.* at 604. The Appellate Division reversed. It noted that the Ambassador policy "did not contain an express

exclusion for the consequences of an intentional wrongdoing," *id.* at 604, but concluded that the omission of such an exclusion was "immaterial because public policy prohibits indemnity for the civil consequences of one's intentional wrongdoing." *Ibid.* It held, however, that because the insured did not intend to injure or kill anyone, there was coverage. *Ibid.* This Court affirmed the judgment, but on a different basis.

In the course of its opinion the Court acknowledged—significantly for today's purposes—the general proposition that "public policy prohibits insurance indemnity for the civil consequences of an insured's intentional wrongdoing." *Id.* at 605. As the opinion states:

> It has been said that indemnification of a person for a loss or damage incurred as a result of his willful wrongdoing in violation of a criminal statute is contrary to public policy. Were a person able to insure himself against the economic consequences of his intentional wrongdoing, the deterrence attributable to financial responsibility would be missing. Further, as a matter of moral principle no person to allege his own turpitude as a ground for recovery. Accordingly, we have accepted the general principle that an insurer may not contract to indemnify an insured against the civil consequences of his own willful criminal act.

[*Id.* at 482-483, 388 A.2d 603 (citations omitted).]

The Court added, however, that the stated principle was "not to be applied under all circumstances." *Id.* at 605. The circumstances that led the Court to find coverage in *Ambassador* were that (1) the policy provided on its face for coverage, (2) there was no exclusionary clause or other pertinent limitation in the policy, (3) payment of the policy proceeds would protect an innocent third person without benefiting the wrongdoer-insured, and (4) the insurer could indemnify itself by being subrogated to the third party's rights against the insured-tortfeasor. *Id.* at 605-07.

Ambassador has been read, correctly, as having "modified the prior-settled rule that indemnification by liability insurance of a person for a loss incurred as a result of his own willful wrongdoing in violation of a criminal statute is contrary to public policy. . . ." *New Jersey Mfrs. Ins. Co. v. Brower,* 391 A.2d 923 (N.J. Super. Ct. App. Div. 1978). The Ambassador holding has been held not to apply, however, where, as in this case, the policy contains a specific clause excluding liability coverage for the insured's intentional wrongful act. *Ibid.*

Ambassador was decided by a divided Court. The appeal produced three opinions. Neither time nor the opportunity for further deliberation has altered the conscientiously held views of the remaining members who participated in *Ambassador.* The Court is therefore not of one mind on the broad policy question of whether, in the absence of a specific exclusion, a liability insurer can nevertheless be called on to indemnify a wrongdoer for his intentional misconduct that results in liability to an innocent third party.

But we need not revisit *Ambassador.* "We need not even count heads . . . or display our ardor for, or aversion to, the respective contesting viewpoints"; see *Green v. Sterling Extruder Corp.,* 471 A.2d 15 (N.J. 1984). We are content to give *Ambassador* a narrow reading and to limit today's decision to no more than the circumstances require. We therefore adopt the view of *New Jersey Mfrs. Ins. Co. v. Brower, supra,* 391 A.2d at 927, that *Ambassador* is distinguishable on its facts from this case and does not stand in the way of our declaring that a specific exclusion, in an automobile liability insurance policy, from coverage for the insured's liability caused by his intentional wrongful acts does not violate either public policy or, as we have held, *supra* at 835-837, the statutory scheme.

This is particularly so where, as here and doubtless in the vast majority of automobile cases, there are available to the claimant other sources of recovery, such as personal independence payment (PIP) benefits, uninsured motorist coverage, and workers' compensation benefits.

2. *Ambassador* is an unusual case, and the pay and then subrogate rule that it applies definitely does not represent the majority rule. Yet there is much to recommend in the approach of the court in that case. If liability insurance is the instrument that makes tort liability into a risk-spreading system, what is wrong about the approach in *Ambassador?* From a corrective justice perspective, isn't there something anomalous when the victim of an intentional wrong is less likely to receive compensation than the victim of a negligent wrong? How about from an efficiency perspective? As the court in *Ambassador* noted, insurance for intentional harm presents a public policy problem when the insured benefits from that insurance. In economic terms, insurance for intentional harm presents a moral hazard problem. But when the victim, not the insured, benefits, and the insurance company is permitted to subrogate against the insured, it is difficult to see how a moral hazard is created (except, perhaps, in the always complicated situation in which the victim and the tortfeasor are related; but this seems no more complicated in liability claims than in arson claims of the sort discussed in Chapter 3).

3. If the *Ambassador* approach makes such good sense, why aren't liability insurance policies drafted to produce that result? If you had a choice between a standard liability insurance policy and one that was drafted to produce the result in *Ambassador,* which would you buy? Which would be more expensive? Which would better protect your interests? As this thought experiment should demonstrate, we cannot expect the market to produce liability insurance policies that are optimal from a victim compensation perspective. Whether we think that victims are the "real" beneficiaries of liability insurance or not, they do not get to choose the liability insurance policies that their tortfeasors purchase. Should courts take that into account in interpreting liability insurance policies? How? Is it too far-fetched to think of something like the reasonable expectations of victims?

4. Section 47 of Preliminary Draft 3 of RLLI addresses the issues raised in *Ambassador.* Read that section and the accompanying comments, excerpted below, and compare the result under that section with the result in *Ambassor.* Which do you prefer?

§47 Insurance of Liabilities Involving Aggravated Fault[9]

. . .

(2) Except as barred by public policy, a liability insurer may provide insurance against civil liability for criminal acts, expected or intentionally caused harm, fraud, or other conduct involving aggravated fault.

Comment:

a. Scope. This Section addresses the insurability of defense costs and damages incurred in legal actions involving aggravated fault. This Section does not address the question whether a particular insurance policy contains terms

---

9. This section was approved as amended at the May 2016 Annual Meeting of the RLLI. At that time, it was numbered Section 34 of the RLLI.

that would provide such coverage. This latter question is one of interpretation that is addressed using the rules of insurance-contract interpretation set forth in §§3 and 4. The rules in this Section apply only if the application of the ordinary rules of insurance-contract interpretation determines that the insurance policy provides the coverage in question. A term in an insurance policy excluding such coverage is enforceable.

. . .

c. Defense coverage for uninsurable civil liabilities. Courts also generally enforce liability insurance defense coverage for uninsurable civil actions. The public-policy objections to insurance for certain liabilities are based upon the premise that the insured is liable for the wrong upon which the remedy is based. Defense coverage provides the means for the insured to contest liability, not to avoid the financial consequences of liability actually assessed. Although there are no public-policy-based restrictions on such defense coverage under prevailing insurance law, this Section recognizes that such restrictions could be imposed by statute or regulation. See §46.

. . .

e. Insurability of vicarious liability. Courts generally permit insurance coverage of liabilities that are assessed vicariously, even in situations in which the liability of the primary actor would be uninsurable in the jurisdiction, for example liability for punitive damages.

f. Insurability of liabilities based on morally offensive acts. There is some old legal authority supporting the proposition that liability insurance law should limit coverage for morally offensive acts, without regard to the presence of applicable exclusions or absence of incentive effects created by insurance, but recent authority is to the contrary. Such a prohibition would have the unfortunate consequence that the victims of some of the most offensive wrongs would be least likely to be able to obtain redress for those wrongs. That such a situation presently obtains for certain liabilities because of exclusions in liability insurance policies (exclusions for certain sexual-molestation suits provide a ready example) does not provide a basis for a common-law prohibition of such coverage.

g. Insurability of liability for intentional harm. Insurance law recognizes the potentially deleterious consequences that could result from the incentives created by liability insurance for intentional harm. Because intentional harm is ordinarily under the conscious control of the insured, and because such harm may even be part of the objective of the insured's wrongful act, insurance for the liabilities arising out of those wrongful acts poses a potential threat to the deterrence and retribution purposes of liability law. Nevertheless, these deterrence- and retribution-based concerns do not support a blanket prohibition on insurance of all liabilities arising out of intentional injuries. In many cases the presence or absence of insurance has no effect on the behavior of the wrongdoer. The case of an assault that occurs in the heat of passion is an obvious example, but many wrongs are committed without regard for the consequences or the presence or absence of insurance covering the potential liability. Moreover, the presence of liability insurance can promote, rather than hinder, the objectives of tort law, by providing compensation for the victim as well as the means to employ the civil-justice system to name, blame, and shame the defendant. Although there are some state statutes and judicial options that state that intentional injuries are not insurable, those statutes and decisions have generally not been tested in relation to liability insurance policies that explicitly provide coverage for intentional torts as described in Comment h.

h. *Insurance coverage of liability for intentional harm.* The contemporary liability insurance market includes a variety of policy forms that cover intentional common law or statutory torts, for example: defamation, disparagement, trademark infringement, unfair competition, false imprisonment, employment discrimination, wrongful termination, malicious prosecution, invasion of privacy, and certain statutory violations. Courts regularly enforce insurers' promises to provide these coverages, even in cases involving intentional injuries, typically without any mention of the tension between these coverages and the traditional public-policy-based concern about insurance for intentional harm. Those relatively few cases that do discuss the insurability issue generally resolve that issue by explaining that providing liability insurance (a) does not undercut the purpose of the underlying liability and (b) promotes the compensation purpose of that liability. Cases enforcing the "final adjudication" clause in certain intentional harm or misconduct exclusions also result in coverage for liabilities involving intentional harm. The final adjudication clause in such exclusions generally states that the exclusion only applies to a legal action if there has been final adjudication of the designated misconduct in that legal action. The practical impact of the clause is that even a post-trial settlement of the underlying legal action prevents the exclusion from being applied, because the settlement means that there was no "final adjudication" of the misconduct.

i. *Insurability of liability for punitive damages.* There is a split in the authority regarding the insurability of liability for punitive damages. The courts in the majority of states that have considered the issue have held that liability for punitive damages is insurable, leaving the question of whether a liability insurance policy provides coverage for punitive damages to the interpretation of the insurance policy. Courts in nearly as many states have held that liability insurance for directly assessed punitive damages contravenes the public policy of the state.

Courts that prohibit insurance for direct punitive damages provide both deterrence- and retribution-based justifications for this decision. As with insurance of liabilities arising out of intentional injuries, these justifications do not apply with equal force in all cases involving punitive damages. Under the deterrence justification, punitive damages are sometimes necessary to create incentives for parties to take reasonable care to avoid accidents, and insurance could dampen the incentive effect of such awards. However, punitive damages can be assessed in situations in which there is little or no reason to believe that the presence of liability insurance for punitive damages will have any effect on behavior, for example in the drunk-driving context or other contexts in which there are widely known criminal penalties. Under the retributivist justification, punitive damages represent a consequence for highly wrongful conduct, and insurance lessens the sting of that consequence. However, the availability of insurance for punitive damages may promote the retributive objectives of punitive damages, especially when defendants cannot be made to pay a substantial punitive-damages judgment. The availability of insurance against liability for punitive damages helps to motivate the plaintiff to bring an action against the wrongful actor and thereby express the public commitment to the value of persons that is one of the core principles of retribution.

Moreover, a declaration that insuring against liability for punitive damages violates public policy of a state often turns out to have little or no effect, other than to lead insureds to find the coverage elsewhere. Specifically, large organizations and wealthy individuals are able to procure, and regularly do procure, insurance that covers direct punitive damages even when those damages are assessed in jurisdictions in which courts have declared that such insurance violates the public policy of the state. Policyholders obtain such insurance by purchasing insurance issued with insurance-policy forms that contain favorable choice-of-law and venue clauses and, often, arbitration clauses. Sometimes this insurance is purchased in offshore jurisdictions. This means that a prohibition against insurance for punitive damages awards primarily affects legal actions brought against individuals and small- to medium-sized businesses, significant numbers of which are likely to be, for practical purposes, judgment proof and, thus, unaffected by whatever incentive effects might in theory result from that insurance.

   j. *Subrogation against the insured as an alternative to a public-policy based prohibition.* Subrogation against the insured provides an alternative to a public-policy based prohibition of insurance for certain liabilities. Under this approach, which has been recognized by some courts, the insurer's obligations are determined based solely upon the interpretation of the liability insurance policy. If insulating the insured from the financial consequences of a particular covered liability would contravene the public purpose of the imposition of that liability, the insurer may seek indemnification from the insured. This alternative more closely tailors the liability insurance rule to the underlying deterrence and retribution objectives than a general prohibition of insurance coverage for such liabilities. If the insured has the financial capacity, the insurer's right to indemnification will place the financial responsibility on the insured. If the insured does not have the financial capacity, the availability of the insurance will make it possible for the underlying tort action to proceed.

   This indemnification right is an exception to the general rule that an insurer may not subrogate against its insured. The two most widely accepted purposes for the anti-subrogation rule are to prevent the insurer from using the right of subrogation to, in effect, avoid providing coverage to the insured and to avoid conflicts of interest between insurer and insured. In these exceptional cases, the first purpose gives way to the public policy against providing financial protection for the insured. Moreover, the second purpose does not apply, because both of the potential rules – an implied-in-law exclusion of coverage and a right of indemnification against the insured – create similar conflicts of interest between the insurer and the insured.

3. "Intent" at the Borders of Tort Law, Criminal Law, and Insurance Law

STATE FARM FIRE & CASUALTY CO. v. WICKA

Supreme Court of Minnesota
474 N.W.2d 324 (1991)

GARDEBRING, J. This case raises two issues, the first legal and the second evidentiary, involving whether an intentional act exclusion of a homeowner's liability policy applies to the conduct of an insured who, because of mental illness, may lack the capacity to form the intent to injure. In light of public policy favoring coverage where the injury threatens the general public, we construe the policy language as providing coverage where, because of mental illness, the insured's act is the product of a failure of the insured's volitional or cognitive capacities.

   On the early morning of December 31, 1982, Stephen B. Kintop stormed into the living room of his ex-girlfriend, Colleen Hughes, smashing through the front door with a pistol in his hand. Standing in Hughes' living room was Paul R.

Peterson, an acquaintance of Kintop's who was then dating Hughes. Upon seeing the gun brandished by Kintop, Peterson fled through the back door into the street outside. Kintop pursued. Firing as he chased the fleeing Peterson, Kintop shot Peterson several times, wounding him in the hip and head. Collapsing but still conscious, Peterson heard Kintop whimper as he reloaded and approached. Kintop then killed himself. . . .

Despite severe injuries caused by multiple gunshot wounds, Peterson survived to sue Kintop's estate for damages. Defense of the suit was tendered to State Farm Fire & Casualty Company (State Farm), the homeowner's carrier for Kintop's parents. . . . State Farm commenced the present declaratory judgment action, disputing coverage based on the policy's "intentional act" exclusion, which provides:

> 1. Coverage L—Personal Liability and Coverage M—Medical Payments To Others Do Not Apply To:
>   (a) bodily injury or property damage which is expected or intended by the insured; . . .

[Editor's Note: The lengthy procedural discussion is omitted here. This case is an appeal from a summary judgment in favor of State Farm. The plaintiffs claimed that intent was a question of fact and that testimony by a psychiatrist would show that Kintop was incapable of forming the necessary intent.]

The law and society have always approached a person's claimed mental illness with a degree of skepticism and disbelief. This societal mistrust stems, in part, from the fear that mental illness is feigned with ease and frequency. *See United States v. Trapnell*, 495 F.2d 22, 24 (2d Cir.), *cert. denied*, 419 U.S. 851, (1974). Stronger skepticism arises when a putatively mentally ill person has a "normal appearance" or "doesn't look sick." Perlin, *Psychodynamics and the Insanity Defense: "Ordinary Common Sense" and Heuristic Reasoning*, 69 Neb. L. Rev. 3, 23 (1990). Despite these inherent suspicions, the concept that the mentally ill person should be relieved from responsibility for certain acts has existed for at least the past millennium. Within the area of insurance law, an extensive debate has occurred as to whether and when an insured's mental illness prevents the application of an intentional act exclusion to the acts of an insured. Two lines of authority have emerged, which agree that mental illness may affect the application of an intentional act exclusion, but disagree as to when that occurs.

The first line of cases holds, as a matter of law, that the intentional act exclusion does not apply if the injury results from an insane act. Beyond this general premise, however, the cases diverge and articulate varying standards for judging the insured's capacity to act intentionally. Some courts have adopted what amounts to a "civil insanity" standard, applying coverage where the insured suffered from derangement of intellect that deprived the insured of the capacity to govern conduct in accordance with reason. The necessary degree of impairment in other jurisdictions is less apparent.

By contrast, the opposing, more narrow view, holds that injury caused by a mentally ill insured is intentional where the insured understands the physical nature of the consequences of the acts and intends to cause injury, though being incapable of distinguishing right from wrong. Using the insured's ability to understand the nature and consequences of his actions as the benchmark for establishing whether an act was intentional, the narrow view maintains that an insane person may "intend" an act even though the person cannot appreciate the wrongfulness of that conduct. Many of these jurisdictions also adhere to an objective standard for determining intent.

Although we reject the formulations advanced under both the liberal and narrow views, we agree that an insured's mental illness can defeat the application of the intentional act exclusion. The question in need of answer remains, however: When and under what circumstances does an insured's mental illness defeat the application of the intentional act exclusion? To answer the question presented in this case of first impression, we examine the existing principles of law in this state regarding insurance and the application of intentional act exclusions.

As it applies to sane individuals, the law in Minnesota is well-settled: an intentional act exclusion applies only where the insured acts with the specific intent to cause bodily injury. The requisite intent demands that the insured intended the harm itself, not that the insured intended to act. . . .

It is axiomatic that before an insured can be held liable the insured must have been able to entertain the proscribed intent to cause bodily injury and must have, in fact, done so. In *Woida v. North Star Mutual Ins. Co.,* 306 N.W.2d 570, 573 (Minn. 1981), this court inferred an intent to cause bodily injury where the insured, after planning the action with others, fired several shots from a high-powered rifle at a truck knowing that the truck was occupied. Similarly in Stone, we held that the insured demonstrated an intent to cause bodily injury when, after agreeing to settle a dispute by fighting, the insured wrapped his fist with his belt and struck the other combatant. [*Iowa Kemper Ins. v. Stone,* 269 N.W.2d 885, 886-87 (Minn.1978)]. Finally, in *Continental Western Ins. Co. v. Toal,* 244 N.W.2d 121 (Minn. 1976), this court inferred an intent to cause bodily injury where the insureds had planned an armed robbery, knowing their weapons were loaded and that someone might be killed or injured. *Id.* at 125-26. While mental capacity was not at issue, the inference of an intent to cause bodily injury in *Woida, Stone,* and *Toal* follows because the insureds understood the obvious nature of their respective actions and the foreseeability of harm flowing from those actions. Had these insureds not understood the nature of their acts, no inference could ensue. While our cases demonstrate that an insured's cognitive capacity is presumed, the cognitive capacity requirement parallels the cognitive capacity test in our criminal law.

Under the criminal presumption of cognitive capacity, the law presumes sanity and places the burden of proving incapacity on the party asserting it. While a strict standard is justified before relieving criminal responsibility, we believe the [criminal standard] provides but a partial answer when dealing within the realm of insurance law. An intent to cause bodily injury requires not only that the insured appreciate the nature and wrongfulness of his actions, but the requisite intent also demands that the insured's actions be voluntary, originating from insured's own free will.

The law rests on a postulate of free will — that all persons of sound mind are presumed capable of conforming their conduct to the requirements of the law, and when any person freely chooses to violate the law or intrude upon another's rights, that person may justly be held responsible. . . .

This court held in *Farmers Ins. Exch. v. Sipple,* 225 N.W.2d 373, 376-77 (Minn. 1977) that the submission of the intent issue to the jury was warranted where the facts were in dispute and suggested that the insured acted instinctively in the form of a reflex when the insured struck a farmer during a heated exchange.

Similarly, in *Brown v. State Automobile & Casualty Underwriters*, 293 N.W.2d 822, 824-25 (Minn. 1980) we held denial of summary judgment proper where the insured argued he acted reflexively when he struck a baggage clerk after a tug-of-war over some luggage caused a deep cut in the insured's finger. Finally, we rejected an insured's claims of self-defense and reflexive action in *Smith v. Sent.* 313 N.W.2d 202, 203-04 (Minn. 1981), where the insured's own action escalated the violence of a barroom fray. Each of these cases demonstrates that the insured's ability to choose the particular action is as much a part of the intent formulation as the insured's ability to appreciate the choice he has made. Moreover, intent becomes a question for the trier of fact when the evidence suggests that the insured was not the master of his own will.

The law in Minnesota strikes a delicate balance between societal and individual interests when dealing with the rights and responsibilities of the mentally ill. As our cases show, an intent to cause bodily injury requires that the insured possess both cognitive and volitional capacities, either of which may be affected by an insured's mental illness. We hold, therefore, that for the purposes of applying an intentional act exclusion contained in a homeowner's insurance policy, an insured's acts are deemed unintentional where, because of mental illness or defect, the insured does not know the nature or wrongfulness of an act, or where, because of mental illness or defect, the insured is deprived of the ability to control his conduct regardless of any understanding of the nature of the act or its wrongfulness.

This rule not only addresses the cognitive and volitional components already existing in the law concerning intentional act exclusions, but the rule also construes the insurance policy in accordance with the reasonable expectations of the insured. The purpose of the intentional act exclusion is to deny the insured a license to commit wanton and malicious acts. Both insurer and insured expect coverage will lie for unintentional injuries caused by the insured, regardless of the insured's mental condition. Given these expectations, we see no discernable difference between injuries caused by a mentally ill insured, who lacks the ability to formulate an intent to injure, and the insured who acts out of reflex or self-defense. Nor do we believe any financial disincentive would sway those persons who, because of mental illness, lack the capacity to conform conduct to the law. In foreclosing insureds from manipulating their insurance coverage through the voluntary use of intoxicants, we stated:

> [W]e are not inclined to create a situation where the more drunk an insured can prove himself to be, the more likely he will have insurance coverage.

Peterson, 405 N.W.2d at 422. Unlike intoxication, mental illness is hardly voluntary and not laden with the potential for abuse or fraud. . . .

NOTES AND QUESTIONS

1. This is the second case in this book addressing the problem of domestic violence. The first case was *Watson v. United Services Automobile Association* in Chapter 3. For an insightful analysis of the significance of insurance to victims of domestic violence, *see* Jennifer Wriggins, *Domestic Violence Torts* 75 S. Cal. L. Rev. 121 (2001). Given the prevalence of domestic violence, it is no

exaggeration to say that victims of domestic violence are among the people most affected by intentional harm exclusions in personal lines liability insurance. Pointing to cases like these and to the attempt of some life and health insurance companies to keep battered women out of their insurance pools (as we will discuss in the risk classification unit in Chapter 6), feminists claim that the insurance industry has an unhappy history regarding victims of domestic violence. Those who have a strong belief in the ultimate fairness of the market may see this criticism as an attempt to place upon insurance companies the burden of subsidizing risky people. Those who are more sympathetic to the feminist criticism may see insurance company efforts to avoid coverage for the costs of domestic violence as an example of insurer-side adverse selection. What do you think? Why?

2. Allstate and some other insurance companies have been unsatisfied with the results of cases like *Wicka* and, in response, have added "criminal acts" exclusions to their policies. For example, Allstate has added the following exclusion to its homeowners insurance policies:

LOSSES WE DO NOT COVER UNDER COVERAGE X:

   1. **We** do not cover any **bodily injury** or **property damage** intended by, or which may reasonably be expected to result from the intentional or criminal acts or omissions of, any **insured person**. This exclusion applies even if:
   a) such **insured person** lacks the mental capacity to govern his or her conduct.

See, e.g., Wright v. Allstate Cas. Co.,, 797 N.W.2d 531 (Wis. App. 2011) (finding that the mental capacity clause in Allstate's intentional act exclusion bars coverage). As you read the excerpt and case that follow, think about whether these exclusions support or inhibit the compensatory, deterrence, and retributive goals of tort law.

4. The Criminal Acts Exclusion

HOME LIABILITY COVERAGE: DOES THE CRIMINAL ACTS EXCLUSION WORK WHERE THE "EXPECTED OR INTENDED" EXCLUSION FAILED?

Daniel C. Eidsmore & Pamela K. Edwards
5 Conn. Ins. L.J. 707

The axiom that bad facts make bad law could not have been any truer than in the case of Robert A. Berdella. In 1984, Berdella, a Kansas City, Missouri area resident went on a four-year torture and killing spree. Over that period of time Berdella killed at least six men, all in gruesome fashion. The seventh potential victim was able to escape from Berdella's home and call police after breaking free from a bed in which his hands and feet were tied for a period of five days.

When police investigated Berdella's home, they found human skulls, photographs of men being sodomized and tortured, and journal notes describing the torture. In 1988, Berdella pled guilty to six counts of murder and was sentenced to life in prison without parole.

During the plea stage of the criminal proceeding, Berdella pled guilty to first-degree murder for three of the murders, in the other three, to those of Todd Stoops, Jerry Howell, and James Ferris[,] he pled guilty to second-degree murder. With the first-degree murder pleas, Berdella admitted that he intended to kill the victims. In the second-degree murder cases Berdella did not admit that he intended to kill Stoops, Howell, or Ferris. Instead, he only admitted that he intended to torture them physically and sexually. He maintained that their deaths were unintentional.

The criminal record indicated that Berdella injected the victims with drugs and kept them alive for his "perverted desires." The victims died as a result of drug injection, asphyxiation from being gagged, bleeding, or infection. Berdella died in prison one year after his guilty plea.

Civil suits were filed against Berdella's estate by the [victims'] families for wrongful death. Although Berdella had only $63,000 in personal assets, he did have a homeowner's insurance policy with $100,000 per occurrence limits (arguably each murder could have been a separate occurrence). Berdella was insured by Economy Fire and Casualty Company (Economy). In the wrongful death actions, the plaintiffs attempted to trigger coverage by alleging that Berdella's actions amounted to negligence. In response, Economy filed a separate declaratory judgment action, citing its common policy language found in all home liability policies (in one form or another) that excludes liability coverage for bodily injury or property damage "expected or intended" from the standpoint of the insured.

In the declaratory judgment action, the trial court agreed with Economy's Motion for Summary Judgment finding that the exclusionary language did bar coverage for the allegations made in the wrongful death action. The victims' families appealed. The Western District of Missouri Court of Appeals granted the appeal.

In its unanimous opinion, the Court of Appeals reversed the trial court's findings as to the claims of Stoops, Howell, and Ferris. The Court of Appeals ruled that the mere fact that Berdella pled guilty to three counts of second-degree murder did not establish that he intended to kill the three men for purposes of the civil or the declaratory actions. The court stated: "The record does establish that Berdella intended to harm these individuals, but it does not establish, without genuine issue of material fact, that Berdella . . . expected or intended the result (the deaths) which occurred."

By finding that Berdella intended to torture his victims but did not expect or intend to kill them, the court handed the case back to the jury. This decision also placed the case back into the realm of potential coverage under Economy's homeowner's policy.

The rest is history. The resulting jury verdict in the civil case, one year after the Court of Appeals ruling on the declaratory judgment action still stands today as the highest compensatory award in United States legal history. The livid jurors awarded the Stoops family $5 billion ($2.5 billion for wrongful death and $2.5 billion for "aggravating circumstances"). Although Economy had planned to appeal the verdict, its policy of insurance also covered pre- and post-judgment interest on the entire judgment. The interest on $5 billion amounted to $600,000 a day! Economy was forced to settle the claim rather than appeal and risk insolvency on the outcome of one appeal. Economy paid the Stoops family

$2.5 million. The death claims presented by the Howell and Ferris families were settled out of court for undisclosed sums. This decision, although sensational, serves as a blueprint of what can go wrong when an insurer asserts the expected or intended coverage defense. Generally, the expected or intended exclusion is a good coverage defense in the absence of any other grounds upon which to deny coverage. But in the numerous instances where the exclusion is not enforced it can be very costly for the insurer. Missouri is not the only jurisdiction to struggle with a criminal conviction by an insured and still fail to determine that the harm arising out of the act in question was not excluded by the expected or intended exclusion of the homeowner's policy.

NOTES AND QUESTIONS

1. This excerpt highlights the intersection between criminal, tort, and insurance law. All three use words like "intent" and "intentional" to draw doctrinal lines. Should these words have the same meaning in all three areas of the law? Criminal, tort, and insurance law all have different purposes, histories, and institutions. Should those differences be reflected in different understandings of what it means to "intend" an act? This issue nicely illustrates Nietzsche's point that words are "pockets" into which we put different meanings in different times and places. It is easy to see this pocket-like character when dealing with words, like "consideration," whose legal meaning is so divorced from everyday meaning. It is harder, and thus more important, to see this when dealing with other words, like "intend," that we use on an everyday basis in a way that approximates how they are used in law. Of course, recognizing that it might be appropriate for criminal, tort, and insurance law to use different standards of intent does not tell us what those standards should be. Recognizing the unique usage of the word "intent" in each legal context is helpful in understanding both the intentional harm and criminal acts exclusions.

2. The court in the *Berdella* coverage case, *Economy Fire & Casualty Co. v. Haste*, 824 S.W.2d 41 (Mo. Ct. App. 1991) held that, although Berdella had intended to harm his victims, the insurance company had not proved on summary judgment that he intended to kill them. Thus, the court remanded for a trial on coverage for the wrongful death claims (but not for the harm done to the victims before they were killed).

3. Is the *Berdella* case one of moral hazard? Put another way, was the existence of the liability insurance likely to have affected Berdella's behavior? Should courts take into account the economics of moral hazard in making decisions like this?

4. In thinking about the relationship among tort law, deterrence, and insurance, consider the following: Under prevailing insurance law doctrine, the more depraved the defendant, the less likely the plaintiff will be able to recover. Is that good public policy? Are there significant insurance-based reasons for that result? How you feel about this and other related questions depends on your view of liability insurance. If it exists to protect defendants, the *Berdella* case is an outrage. If it exists to compensate victims, the criminal act exclusion companies have drafted in reaction to cases like *Berdella* might present the greater concern.

5. For a discussion of these and other issues, *see generally* Tom Baker, *Liability Insurance at the Tort-Crime Boundary, in* Fault Lines: Tort Law as Cultural Practice (David M. Engel & Michael McCann, eds., 2009):

> This essay explores how liability insurance mediates the boundary between torts and crime. Liability insurance sometimes separates these two legal fields, for example through the application of standard insurance contract provisions that exclude insurance coverage for some crimes that are also torts. Perhaps less obviously, liability insurance also can draw parts of the tort and criminal fields together. For example, professional liability insurance civilizes the criminal law experience for some crimes that are also torts by providing defendants with an insurance-paid criminal defense that provides more than ordinary means to contest the state's accusations. The crime-tort separation in liability insurance cannot be explained by economic incentives, alone. Morality matters, too. The fact that liability insurance sometimes provides coverage for criminal defense costs suggests that liability insurance institutions could cover a broader swath of crime torts than they do, providing further support for the claim that consequentialist reasoning, alone, cannot explain the observed relationship between liability insurance, torts, and crime. The tort-crime separation reflects and reinforces a concept of liability insurance as protection for defendants, rather than as a fund for victims. In turn, this concept of insurance reflects and reinforces an understanding of tort claims as encounters between particular plaintiffs and defendants, rather than as a price setting or loss spreading insurance mechanism. . . .

> The *Berdella* case is just one, particularly graphic example from an entire genre of moral monster stories that have emerged in the insurance case law out of the effort to enforce the crime-tort separation. These stories feature drunken brawlers, wife batterers, child molesters, doctors, and dentists who rape sedated patients, and other moral monsters who commit a second crime by asking the insurance company to pay for their first one. Among published opinions, the *Berdella* case is unusual principally in the fact that the insurance company lost. For that reason, it played an important, "never again" role in the subsequent effort to include a criminal acts exclusion in some homeowners' insurance policies. It is easy to see these moral monster stories as a result of the crime-tort separation, but they also reproduce that separation. They allow insurance companies to occupy the moral high ground while refusing to pay victims who indisputably deserve compensation. The stories place the spotlight of attention on the moral monster, not the deserving victim, and they appropriate the victim's wrong for the insurance company. In the process, they legitimate a crime-tort separation that makes the outrage in the *Berdella* insurance case the fact that Berdella's insurance company had to pay, rather than the fact that the company for years refused to pay the victims' families. . . .

> At a more general level, the crime-tort separation in liability insurance and the accompanying moral monster stories also reflect and reproduce an understanding of a tort claim as an encounter between a specific plaintiff and a specific defendant, rather than as the price setting or loss spreading mechanism that a social engineer might describe. There are, of course, other institutions that promote this individualized, corrective justice understanding of tort law, but the crime-tort separation in liability insurance is special because it operates within an institution—insurance—that, in so many other ways, promotes the price setting and loss spreading approaches. Thanks in part to the crime-tort separation, a liability insurance claims file is not just an administrative record classifying the nature and economic value of bodily injury or other harm. Instead, the claims file is also an inquiry into the state of mind of the

defendant. Like every other aspect of the claims-handling process, this inquiry undoubtedly becomes routinized and subject to rules of thumb that reduce the individualized nature of the inquiry. Nevertheless, the crime-tort separation provides an additional fault-line, beyond those provided by tort law, along which the bureaucratic claims handling process can break down, releasing the individualized drama of litigation.

The following is an early case addressing the criminal acts exclusion. Note that it is unclear in this case whether the exclusion at issue includes the "mental capacity" clause referenced in note 2 following the *Wicka* case. That clause would not have been relevant in this case, so it is possible that the court simply did not reference that section of the exclusion.

ALLSTATE INSURANCE CO. v. PEASLEY

Supreme Court of Washington
932 P.2d 1244 (1997)

DOLLIVER, J.—An insurance company asks for a declaration that a criminal acts exclusion in its homeowner's insurance policy precludes insurance coverage to a guest who was shot by the homeowner, when the shooting constituted the crime of reckless endangerment. We find the criminal acts exclusion applies to the facts of this case.

While a guest in James Peasley's house, Ardis Parker was shot in the stomach by James Peasley. Parker sustained serious but nonfatal injuries. Both Peasley and Parker maintain the shooting was accidental.

After reviewing the facts surrounding the shooting and interviewing Peasley's neighbors who had heard a loud argument from Peasley's house at the time of the shooting, the local prosecutor charged Peasley with second degree assault. Peasley was tried and convicted, but the Court of Appeals reversed the conviction because of an erroneous jury instruction. *State v. Peasley*, No. 29919–1-I (Wash. Ct. App. 1993). Peasley then bargained with the prosecutor and pleaded guilty to second degree reckless endangerment in exchange for the prosecutor's recommendation of a suspended sentence.

Ardis Parker sued Peasley for damages arising from her injuries. Peasley was insured by Allstate Insurance Company (Allstate). When Allstate learned of Parker's lawsuit, Allstate brought this summary judgment against both Peasley and Parker seeking a declaration that a criminal acts exclusion in the Peasley's homeowner's insurance policy (Policy) excluded coverage for Parker's injuries because they were the result of Peasley's criminal acts. The trial court granted summary judgment for Allstate, and the Court of Appeals affirmed. We also affirm.

Summary judgment in this case is appropriate because the interpretation of language in an insurance policy is a matter of law. The insurance contract must be viewed in its entirety; a phrase cannot be interpreted in isolation. When construing the policy, the court should attempt to give effect to each provision in the policy. . . .

[W]e must look to the exclusion at issue in Peasley's Policy:

LOSSES WE DO NOT COVER:
1. **We** do not cover any **bodily injury** which may reasonably be expected to result from the intentional or criminal acts of an **insured person** or which are in fact intended by an **insured person.**

Clerk's Papers at 23.

Peasley claims the phrase "criminal acts" is ambiguous. He acknowledges Allstate's reading of the phrase, but he argues a reasonable person could understand the phrase as denoting only *intentional* crimes. If the phrase is subject to more than one reasonable interpretation, the interpretation most favorable to the insured will be applied. If the phrase is unambiguous on its face, then it must be applied as written. The Court of Appeals held the phrase clearly and unambiguously includes both intentional and unintentional criminal acts.

Before addressing Peasley's claim of ambiguity, we must break down the exclusion clause. Because the disjunctive conjunction "or" separates "intentional" from "criminal," we can break the clause down into the following order:

> Allstate does not cover
> A. any bodily injury which may reasonably be expected to result from the
>   1. intentional acts of an insured person, or
>   2. criminal acts of an insured person, or
> B. injuries which are in fact intended by an insured.

As used in the clause, the word "intentional" clearly denotes its own category of acts—acts which are intentional, whether or not they are criminal. Likewise, the word "criminal" denotes its own category of acts—acts which are criminal, *presumably* whether or not they are intentional. We say presumably because Peasley claims the phrase criminal acts can be read by the ordinary person as denoting *only* intentional criminal acts.

Since Peasley's Policy appears to leave the phrase "criminal acts" undefined, we turn to the dictionary to determine the common meaning of the words. *Boeing Co. v. Aetna Casualty & Surety Co.*, 784 P.2d 507 (Wash. 1990); *see also Kish v. Insurance Co. of N. America*, 883 P.2d 308, 312 (Wash. 1994) (looking to the dictionary to define "flood" as used in an exclusionary clause). The definitions for the adjective "criminal" include the following:

> 1 : involving or being a crime 2 : relating to crime or its punishment—distinguished from *civil* 3 : guilty of crime or serious offense 4a: REPREHENSIBLE, BLAMEWORTHY, DISGRACEFUL b : EXCESSIVE, EXTORTIONATE 5 : of or suitable to a criminal 6: concerned with crime or criminal law[.]

Webster's Third New International Dictionary 536 (1986) (examples of usage omitted). Peasley's claimed ambiguity is not supported by the dictionary. None of the definitions of criminal include intent as part of the adjective's meaning. To the contrary, the dictionary gives the suggestion "criminal carelessness" as an example under the first definition.

Most of the definitions for criminal refer the reader to the noun, "crime," so the definition of crime is relevant to the analysis.

> crime . . . 1a: . . . an offense against public law (as a misdemeanor, felony, or act of treason) providing a penalty against the offender but not including a petty violation of municipal regulation . . . b: an offense against the social order or a violation of the mores that is dealt with by community action rather than by an individual or kinship group 2 [obsolete] . . . 3a: a gross violation of law—distinguished from *misdemeanor; trespass* b : a grave or aggravated offense against or departure from moral rectitude 4 : criminal activity: conduct in violation of the law 5a: an evil act : SIN : a violation of divine law; *esp* : a grievous sin b : sinful conduct: WRONGDOING 6: something reprehensible, foolish, indiscreet, or disgraceful . . . [.]

Webster's at 536 (examples of usage omitted). The third and fifth definitions offer more restrictive uses than the other definitions, suggesting the word crime could be used to indicate only *serious* wrongful acts. Even those restrictive definitions do not include *intent* as a necessary component. The dictionary fails to support Peasley's claim that the phrase criminal acts could be read as denoting only intentional criminal acts.

Peasley supports his argument by citing *Van Riper v. Constitutional Gov't League*, 96 P.2d 588 (Wash. 1939). *Van Riper* concerned a death benefit certificate which a wife sought to enforce after her husband died in a car accident. The certificate provided the payment of benefits would be

> incontestable and absolutely free from any conditions as to residence, travel, place or manner of death, except suicide or death due to acts committed in criminal violation of law, including picketing, or the use of intoxicating liquor or narcotics.

Van Riper, 96 P.2d at 589. The husband's death was caused by his own negligent driving—driving which, the court found, violated numerous traffic laws and constituted a criminal misdemeanor. *Van Riper*, 96 P.2d at 589. The defendant argued it was excused from paying benefits on the certificate because the decedent's death was caused by his criminal driving. The court disagreed.

In analyzing the exclusion, *Van Riper* first looked to the phrase[] "violation of law[]" and cited numerous cases from other jurisdictions where traffic violations qualified as violations of law. *Van Riper*, 96 P.2d at 590. The court found the adjective "criminal" worked to modify the violation of law phrase, thereby creating a new phrase that was more restrictive. *Van Riper*, 96 P.2d at 590. After quoting multiple definitions of criminal, the court declared the layperson would read the phrase "criminal violation of law" as signifying acts done "with malicious intent, from evil nature, or with a wrongful disposition to harm or injure other persons or property." *Van Riper*, 96 P.2d at 591. Negligent driving did not trigger the exclusion.

Van Riper's holding fails to support Peasley's reading of the Allstate exclusion in this case. *Van Riper's* analysis was context specific, and it is not controlling on how this court interprets the use of the word "criminal" in the context of Allstate's exclusionary clause. More importantly, *Van Riper's* holding did not rest upon the intentional/unintentional distinction as argued by Peasley. Rather, the court's[] holding rested upon a distinction between *serious* crimes and nonserious crimes. The court held a traffic violation, although a misdemeanor, was not a serious crime. Other jurisdictions have cited *Van Riper* as standing for this exact rule of law. *See, e.g., Sledge v. Continental Casualty Co.*, 639 So. 2d 805, 813 (La. Ct. App. 1994) (citing *Van Riper* for the rule: "'violation of law' exclusion in life insurance policy applied only to criminal acts of a serious nature"); see also *Trevathan v. Mutual Life Ins. Co.*, 113 P.2d 621, 625 (Or. 1941). This holding is still current, reflected by the fact that most traffic offenses are no longer part of the criminal code. *See* RCW 46.63.020. *Van Riper* fails to support Peasley's argument that the adjective "criminal" denotes intentional criminal acts.

As discussed above, *none* of the definitions for crime or criminal include intent as a necessary element. The more restrictive, third definition of crime in *Webster's Dictionary* focuses on *serious* violations of law, but seriousness does not equate intent, and Peasley has not urged this court to restrict Allstate's criminal acts exclusion to *serious* crimes.

Even if we did restrict the exclusion to serious crimes, a reading supported by *Van Riper,* the exclusion would still encompass the criminal act to which Peasley pleaded guilty. Reckless endangerment in the second degree is defined as reckless conduct "which creates a substantial risk of death or serious physical injury to another person." RCW 9A.36.050(1). A reckless act creating a substantial risk of death or serious injury is undeniably a serious act and a serious crime. Reading Allstate's criminal acts exclusion to encompass Peasley's criminal act is consistent with *Van Riper.*

Peasley's claimed ambiguity does not exist. As used in Allstate's exclusionary clause, the phrase "criminal acts" does not distinguish between intentional and unintentional crimes. The language is unambiguous, and it clearly encompasses Peasley's criminal act of reckless endangerment. This court must enforce the Policy as written.

Reading "criminal acts" as including unintentional crimes is supported by the rule of construction which states a policy should be construed so as to give effect to each provision. The exclusionary clause first excludes injuries which result from the "intentional . . . acts of an insured. . . ." This clause explicitly encompasses all intentional acts, whether they are criminal or not. If we restricted the meaning of "criminal acts" to just *intentional* criminal acts, we would thereby render the "criminal acts" phrase meaningless and superfluous since other language in the exclusionary clause already encompasses all intentional acts. . . .

Peasley also attacks the phrase "injury which may reasonably be expected to result" as ambiguous. He argues the phrase could be read as requiring the insured's subjective expectation that the injury could result. Implicit in this argument is the position that Peasley *did* not subjectively expect Parker's injuries to result from his recklessness. The Court of Appeals applied an objective standard of expectation.

The exclusion applies to injuries "which may reasonably be expected to result" from certain acts of the insured. Although the phrase does not indicate whose reasonable expectations are at issue, the use of "reasonably" implies a removed observer, looking at the facts from a neutral, "reasonable" perspective.

Additionally, if we were to read "may reasonably be expected" as requiring a subjective standard, this would create another redundancy in the exclusion. The last phrase in the exclusion denies coverage for any injury which is "in fact intended by an **insured person**." This last phrase plainly encompasses a subjective standard. *See Rodriguez v. Williams,* 729 P.2d 627 (Wash. 1986) (the phrase, "expected or intended by the insured," denotes a subjective standard). Since a different phrase in the exclusion already addresses injuries subjectively intended by the insured, it would be redundant to read "may reasonably be expected" as setting a subjective standard.

Peasley's conduct and the resulting injury to Parker clearly satisfy the objective standard of reasonable expectation. As stated by the Court of Appeals, the elements of reckless endangerment meet the objective standard. Conduct is reckless when one knows of and disregards a substantial risk that a wrongful act may occur and his disregard of such substantial risk is a gross deviation from conduct that a reasonable man would exercise in the same situation. RCW 9A.08.010(1)(c). By definition of the crime to which Peasley pleaded guilty, Parker's serious physical injuries were reasonably expected to result from Peasley's reckless act.

Peasley argues public policy is violated by allowing an insurer to exclude coverage for injuries resulting from non-intent criminal acts of the insured. Peasley admits the public policy concerns against coverage exclusions in automobile insurance cases have not been applied in the context of homeowner's insurance cases, but he claims the same policy considerations should apply. We rejected the same argument in *State Farm Gen. Ins. Co. v. Emerson*, 687 P.2d 1139 (Wash. 1984).

Emerson involved a homeowner's insurance policy that excluded liability coverage for injuries to family members of the insured. Emerson claimed the exclusion violated public policy by leaving victims without financial compensation. This court responded:

> While we are not unmindful that serious and costly accidents occur in the home, and that innocent victims may be left without meaningful compensation in the absence of insurance, we do not perceive the same level of concern for financial compensation by negligent homeowners as exists for negligent automobile owners and users.
>
>   Absent prior expression of public policy from either the Legislature or prior court decisions, our inquiry as to whether the family exclusion clause clearly offends the public good must be answered in the negative. "The term 'public policy,' ... embraces all acts or contracts which tend clearly to injure the public health, the public morals, the public confidence in the purity of the administration of the law, or to undermine that sense of security for individual rights, whether of personal liberty or of private property, which any citizen ought to feel." (Italics omitted.) [*LaPoint v. Richards*, 403 P.2d 889 (Wash. 1965).]

Such a showing has not been made here. We shall not invoke public policy to override an otherwise proper contract even though its terms may be harsh and its necessity doubtful. . . .

NOTES AND QUESTIONS

1. One reported decision construing the criminal acts exclusion that found for the policyholder is *Allstate Ins. Co. v. Zuk*, 574 N.E.2d 1035 (N.Y. 1991). In *Zuk*, the policyholder pled guilty to recklessly causing the death of his friend after a gun that he was cleaning went off accidentally. The court of appeals reversed an intermediate appellate court decision granting summary judgment in favor of Allstate. The court of appeals held that whether the death could "reasonably be expected to result" from the criminal acts was a factual question. The court agreed with Allstate that the guilty plea "established that Smith's death was caused by a criminal act." The court reasoned further as follows:

    > Under the terms of Allstate's exclusionary clause, however, the inquiry does not stop with the determination that the loss resulted from a criminal act. In order for the exclusion to contradict coverage, the loss must be one that could "reasonably be expected to result" from the criminal act, a phrase subject to a variety of different meanings in a civil versus criminal elision.
    >
    >   Zuk's conviction of second degree manslaughter was necessarily based on a finding that he recklessly caused Smith's death (Penal Law §125.15 [1]). A person acts recklessly, in a criminal context, when that person is aware of and consciously disregards a substantial and unjustifiable risk of a result, where the risk is of such a nature and degree that to disregard it constitutes a gross

deviation from the standard of conduct of a reasonable person (Penal Law §15.05 [3]).

While an almost metaphysical argument can be mounted that disregarding a known risk of death—the criminal standard—is equivalent to reasonably expecting that death will occur as a result of the action taken—the standard expressed in the policy—the particular matrix of this policy clause and factual context allow at least one other reasonable, and therefore disqualifying, syllogism. A person may engage in behavior that involves a calculated risk *without expecting*—no less reasonably—that an accident will occur. Such behavior, which may be reckless for criminal responsibility purposes, does not necessarily mean that the actor reasonably expected the accident to result. People classically seek insurance coverage for just such circumstances. That the accidental discharge of the shotgun Zuk was cleaning actually resulted in Smith's death, and that his conviction for manslaughter by statutory definition requires the result of death as an element of the crime, do not establish as a matter of law that Zuk reasonably expected Smith's death to result from his actions. Under the terms of this exclusion clause, whether a result is reasonably expected should be gauged as of the time and circumstances of the conduct engaged in by the particular actors, not attributed in hindsight based on an eventual criminal conviction, if any.

In sum, the issue whether Smith's death could "reasonably be expected to result" from Zuk's acts was not necessarily determined in the criminal proceeding and was not identical to the issues that were determined there. Thus, Allstate should not be permitted to use collateral estoppel to deprive the Zuks of their only opportunity to determine the effect, if any, of the conviction with its distinctively defined elements on the applicability of the exclusion clause.

Can you reconcile the results in the two *Allstate* criminal acts exclusion cases? Suppose that the New York Court of Appeals faced a case exactly like *Peasley*. How would you persuade the court to find for Peasley as well?

2. Suppose there had been a criminal acts exclusion in the *Berdella* case? Berdella pled guilty to murder in the second degree. The relevant Missouri statute defined that crime as follows:

> 1. A person commits the crime of murder in the second degree if he: Commits or attempts to commit any felony, and in the perpetration or the attempted perpetration of such felony or in the flight from the perpetration or attempted perpetration of such felony, another person is killed as a result of the perpetration or attempted perpetration of such felony or immediate flight from the perpetration of such felony or attempted perpetration of such felony.

The felonies that formed the basis of Berdella's felony murder plea appear to have been illegally restraining the victims (who were bound, gagged, and sedated) and torturing them. Does *Zuk* provide any room for coverage? Does *Peasley?*

3. What do you think about the public policy implications of criminal acts exclusions? Should such exclusions be permitted in auto insurance policies? If there was such an exclusion in an auto policy, would someone convicted of drunk driving in connection with an accident have coverage for that accident? Do you feel differently about the first-party property component of the auto insurance coverage than the liability component?

4. Some jurisdictions allow insurers to submit criminal verdicts as evidence of intent. *See Thornton v. Paul*, 384 N.E.2d 335 (Ill. 1978) (an assault and

battery conviction is allowed as evidence in determining the application of an assault and battery exclusion). *But see Thurmond v. Monroe,* 601 N.E.2d 1048 (Ill. App. Ct. 1992) (declining to extend *Thornton*'s rule where a lower court allowed a conviction for driving too fast as evidence in a wrongful death suit).

5. Defense lawyers report that "more and more, prosecutors in the United States and elsewhere are mounting criminal proceedings in traditional tort situations." Richard M. Dunn, David R. Hazouri, & Julie Rannik, *Criminalization of Negligent Acts by Employees of U.S. and Foreign Corporations,* Defense Couns. J. 17, Jan. 2002, 401. It has long been recognized that liability insurance policies generally do not require the insurance company to defend the policyholder against criminal prosecution (because prosecutions are not "suits seeking damages"). *See, e.g., Shelter Mut. Ins. Co. v. Bailey,* 513 N.E.2d 490 (Ill. App. Ct. 1987). Should the existence of a parallel criminal proceeding in a traditional tort setting relieve the insurer of the duty to defend the tort case as well? This is a question that you will be better able to answer after we study the duty to defend in Chapter 5. For now, it is enough to consider the potential scope of a criminal acts exclusion at a time when U.S. society seems to be shifting toward criminalizing more and more behavior.

THE PROSECUTOR'S PROBLEM

Assume that Stephen Kintop survived the altercation reported in the *Wicka* case. You are the prosecutor responsible for deciding whether to charge him with violating the criminal statutes below.

Alternative A: Assume for the moment that a criminal conviction can be used as the basis for an offensive collateral estoppel in an insurance coverage case. Would a guilty plea by Kintop to either of the charges below threaten insurance coverage for Kintop's victim?

A person commits battery if he:

(a) Actually and intentionally touches or strikes another person against the will of the other; or
(b) intentionally causes bodily harm to an individual.

A person commits aggravated battery who, in committing battery:

(1) intentionally or knowingly causes great bodily harm, permanent disability, or permanent disfigurement; or
(2) uses a deadly weapon.

Alternative B: Suppose that Kintop goes to trial, uses an insanity defense, and is convicted of aggravated battery. What effect should that have on State Farm's expected or intended defense? Should you consider whether a criminal prosecution will affect the availability of insurance money for injured victims?

Alternative C: Kintop is insured under a policy with the criminal act exclusion quoted in *Allstate v. Peasley.* Consider the same questions.

II. AUTOMOBILE LIABILITY INSURANCE[10]

Auto insurance arrangements and requirements in the United States vary from state to state, largely in detail rather than in fundamental respect. The core insurance aspects of the insurance business are regulated exclusively at the state level, but auto insurance is to a significant extent advertised and sold in a national market. Moreover, there are national organizations that actively promote their auto liability and insurance agendas in legislatures and insurance departments across the country. As a result, there is a national pattern to auto liability and insurance.

Auto liability insurance is mandatory in all but a very few states. In the vast majority of states, the relevant auto accident and insurance system involves traditional negligence liability and liability insurance combined with uninsured motorists' insurance. The scope of the required auto insurance policy is very broad. Auto insurance covers essentially all bodily injuries that an at-fault driver causes to other people, so long as any one of the following participants in the accident has an insurance policy: the at-fault driver, the owner of that driver's car, the injured person, or the owner of the car that the injured person occupied. Of course, there are some exceptions to coverage, but none of them seem likely to leave defendants without insurance in a large number of cases. *See generally* Irvin E. Schermer & William J. Schermer, Automobile Liability Insurance §§6:1-6:24 (4th ed. 2004) (reviewing and collecting cases regarding standard exclusions in auto insurance policies). The standard auto insurance policy provides liability protection for an insured person when he or she drives any car, and it provides liability protection for any authorized driver of an insured car. In addition, it provides uninsured and underinsured motorists' protection for an at-fault injury whenever there is no other insurance covering the defendant (uninsured protection) or the amount of the auto insurance covering the defendant is less than the victim's auto insurance (underinsured protection). In that case, the uninsured motorists' protection of the injured person (or the owner of the car in which that person was riding) functions like the missing or inadequate liability insurance of the driver who caused the accident. That is, uninsured motorist coverage provides the injured party what amounts to the recovery that would be available in tort against the at-fault driver, if that driver were available and adequately insured.

Notwithstanding the very broad *scope* of the required auto liability insurance policy, the legally mandated *amount* of insurance is quite low relative to the losses that can result from a serious auto accident. A typical "mandatory minimum" amount of auto bodily injury liability coverage for individuals is $25,000 per person injured in an accident and $50,000 maximum per accident, and some states permit even lower amounts of insurance. *See* Robert H. Joost, Automobile Insurance and No Fault Law Table 4-3 at 492 (2d ed. 2002) (listing mandatory liability insurance limits in U.S. jurisdictions without no-fault laws). The practical effect of these low limits is exacerbated in many states by the interaction of the "collateral source rule" (which allows plaintiffs to include

10. The introductory paragraphs are adapted from Tom Baker, *Liability Insurance, Moral Luck, and Auto Accidents*, 9 Theoretical Inquiries in Law 165 (2008).

in their damages losses covered by first-party insurance such as health insurance and workers' compensation) and subrogation doctrine. See Section VI, "Subrogation," in Chapter 3. As a result, depending on the subrogation rules that apply, the injured plaintiff sometimes has to share the inadequate liability insurance money with a workers' compensation or health insurance company.

Much higher amounts of auto liability insurance coverage are available on the market, and many people buy additional coverage. Bodily injury liability limits of $100,000 per person and $300,000 per accident have become a middle-class norm, in part because auto-leasing companies require their clients to purchase at least that amount of coverage. Additional, "umbrella" bodily injury limits of $1 million or more are increasingly common among upper-income drivers.

The bureaucratization of the automobile insurance claims adjustment process means that the vast majority of automobile liability claims are settled, typically without formal admission of fault (although the insurance company's record of the settlement will be treated as an admission of fault for purposes of future liability insurance purchases), and many of those claims are settled without a lawsuit or other public record of the claim. Except in serious injury cases in which a large insurance policy is available to pay the damages, adjusters' and plaintiffs' lawyers settle these cases according to "rules of thumb"—simplified approximations of what they believe would be the result on average were the cases actually to go to trial. The sociologist H. Laurence Ross put it this way:

> Adjustment of insurance claims compromises the legal mandate for individualized treatment with the need of a bureaucratic system for efficient processing of cases. This compromise can be observed at many points in the processes of investigation and evaluation. Investigation is vastly simplified, for instance, by presumptions as to liability based on the physical facts of the accident. Accidents are thus seldom individualized to an insurance adjuster or a claims attorney. Rather, they are rear-enders, red-light cases, stop sign cases, and the like, and the placement of an accident into one of these categories ordinarily satisfies the requirements for investigation of liability. . . .

H. Laurence Ross, Settled Out of Court: The Social Process of Insurance Claims Adjustment 135 (1970). He also observed, "An injury situation that can qualify a claim as a 'big case' may receive something of the individualized treatment envisaged by the appellate courts." *Id.*

A.   The Omnibus Clause

ODOLECKI v. HARTFORD ACCIDENT & INDEMNITY CO.

Supreme Court of New Jersey
264 A.2d 38 (1970)

PROCTOR, J. This case concerns the question of coverage under the omnibus clause of an automobile liability insurance policy. The policy was issued by the defendant, Hartford Accident & Indemnity Company (Hartford) to Mrs. Kathryn Zylka, and covered her automobile which was involved in a collision on July 7, 1964. The omnibus clause was of standard form and provided in pertinent part that coverage under the policy was extended to the named insured, her spouse, and "any person while using the automobile provided the actual use of the automobile is by the named insured or such spouse or with the permission of either."

The facts are not in material dispute. Mrs. Zylka, the owner of the insured vehicle, gave her teenage son, Michael, general permission to use the car when he returned home from college for his summer vacation. She also told him not to let anyone else drive the car. This admonition was repeated on several occasions when he used the car. On the night of July 7, 1964, Michael was using the car for a social visit to a neighbor's house. While there he permitted his friend, the plaintiff, Douglas Odolecki, to borrow the car in order that the latter might pick up his girl friend. On his way to a hospital where the girl worked, Odolecki was involved in an accident with another car which resulted in the filing of several personal injury actions against him.

After receiving notice of the accident, the defendant-insurer informed the plaintiff that he was not covered by the policy issued to Mrs. Zylka since he was not operating the vehicle with the 'permission' of the named insured or her spouse as required by the policy. The plaintiff filed the present action to have himself declared an additional insured. Sitting without a jury, the trial court held that the Zylka policy did not cover the plaintiff as an additional insured because Mrs. Zylka had never given him permission to use the car, because she had expressly prohibited her son from giving permission to others to use the car, and because the use of the car was not within the use granted by Mrs. Zylka to her son. In denying plaintiff relief the trial judge relied principally on this Court's decision in *Baesler v. Globe Indemnity Co.*, 162 A.2d 854 (N.J. 1960). Plaintiff appealed to the Appellate Division, and pending argument there, we granted certification on our own motion.

Baesler, upon which the trial court relied, is virtually identical with the present case. There, the named insured bought a car for the exclusive use of his nephew with the stipulation that the car not be used by others. Despite this admonition, the nephew permitted a friend to use the automobile for a social engagement, and while the friend was driving he had an accident in which his passenger was injured. The passenger recovered a judgment for personal injuries against the friend-driver, and the latter, claiming to be an additional insured, sued the insurer of the named insured to recover the amount of the judgment. In a four to three decision, this Court held that the plaintiff was not covered by the policy which the defendant had issued. The Court noted the general rule that, ordinarily, a permittee is not authorized to allow another to use an insured vehicle on the basis of his own permission to use it and that therefore there could be no coverage under the standard omnibus clause. *Id.* at 854. Since we adhered to this rule at that time, it followed, a fortiori, that when there was an express prohibition by the named insured, and no other countervailing factor, the second permittee could not claim a greater right than he could in the absence of such a prohibition. The plaintiff concedes that under *Baesler* he is not entitled to qualify as an additional insured, but he argues that our decisions since *Baesler* have eroded the holding in that case to the point where it no longer represents the law of this state. The validity of this contention depends upon an analysis of these post-*Baesler* decisions.

In the term of court following *Baesler*, we decided *Matits v. Nationwide Mutual Ins. Co.*, 166 A.2d 345 (N.J. 1960). There we dealt with the related question of whether the original permittee was an additional insured when she substantially deviated from the scope of the named insured's permission. In that case the husband of the named insured lent his wife's car to a neighbor so that the latter could visit her sick mother in a nearby town. After the visit, the permittee drove in a direction away from the named insured's home and alternately visited two bars over a period of several hours. On the way home, she was involved in a collision with another car.

We were called upon to decide whether the permittee's deviation vitiated the named insured's initial permission so as to deprive her of coverage under the standard omnibus clause of the policy issued by the defendant insurer. The law of New Jersey pertaining to coverage when a permittee deviated from the scope of permission was then unclear. *See Rikowski v. Fidelity & Casualty Co.,* 189 A. 102 (N.J. 1937). Other jurisdictions had adopted one of three views. The first is the liberal or 'initial permission' rule which allows coverage if a person has permission to use the automobile irrespective of any deviations from the scope of permission so long as it remains in his possession. The second view, the moderate or 'minor deviation' rule, allows coverage only where the deviation from the scope of the permissive use does not constitute a gross violation. Finally, the strict or 'conversion' rule denies coverage for any deviation from the time, place, or purpose specified. 166 A.2d at 345. For a discussion of these rules, see generally 7 Appleman, Insurance Law and Practice, §§4366, 4367, 4368, and cases cited therein.

In *Matits,* we adopted the initial permission rule. It was our view that the minor deviation and conversion rules, which made coverage turn on the scope of permission given in the first instance, rendered coverage uncertain, fostered unnecessary litigation, and did not comport with New Jersey's legislative policy of assuring an available fund for the innocent victims of automobile accidents. *See* Motor Vehicle Security-Responsibility Law, N.J.S.A. 39:6-23 to 60; Unsatisfied Claim and Judgment Fund Law, N.J.S.A. 39:6-61 to 91; Motor Vehicle Liability Security Fund Act, N.J.S.A. 39:6-92 to 104. Accordingly, we held that if a person is given permission to use a motor vehicle in the first instance, any subsequent use short of an unlawful taking while it remains in his possession, is a permissive use within the standard omnibus clause in an automobile liability insurance policy regardless of any restrictions given by the named insured. Therefore, the permittee was an additional insured under the policy issued by the defendant insurer. 166 A.2d at 345.

In a dissenting opinion, Justice Hall contended that the minor deviation rule was the only sound approach to the problem. He expressed the belief, however, that the Court's adoption of the initial permission rule undermined the holding of *Baesler* since it rendered irrelevant any actions by a permittee subsequent to the grant of original permission. He reasoned that the majority's holding made it impossible for an insured to restrict a grant of permission, and therefore that the result in *Baesler* was irreconcilable with that in *Matits*.

Our holding in *Matits* has since been reaffirmed in *Small v. Schuncke,* 201 A.2d 56 (N.J. 1964), and *Selected Risks Insurance Co. v. Zullo,* 225 A.2d 570 (N.J. 1966). Now we must decide whether initial permission is unrestrictable in terms of second permittees as well as in terms of scope of deviations.

We had already indicated in *Baesler* that in certain circumstances a prohibition of a loan to a second permittee could be ineffective regarding insurance coverage. There we noted that if, for example, a father gave his son the use of the family car for a social engagement and the son turned over the wheel to a fellow occupant despite his father's admonitions to the contrary, there might be coverage. 162 A.2d at 854. This dictum later became our holding in *Indemnity Ins. Co., etc. v. Metropolitan Cas. Ins. Co. of N.Y.,* 166 A.2d 355 (N.J. 1960), decided the same day in *Matits.* There the named insured lent her car to an employee for the purpose of driving several customers on a business inspection. The employee was specifically instructed not to let anyone else drive the car. While returning from the inspection the employee allowed a passenger to drive and the car was involved in an accident. We held that the passenger-second permittee was covered since the car was being used for the purpose permitted by the named insured. 166 A.2d at 355. Thus, it was possible for a second permittee to qualify as an additional insured notwithstanding the original permittee's violation of the named insured's instructions.

In *Matits,* and the subsequent cases in which we continued to follow the initial permission rule, we emphasized the importance of minimizing litigation of omnibus clause coverage. We were concerned with the continuing problem of determining factually the scope of permission given by the named insured. In order to alleviate the problem we adopted the rule that once permission was given to use a car on the highways, the person giving permission could not bar coverage by restricting the time, place, or purpose for which the car could be used. Clearly, the same kind of litigation results from a rule which inquires into the named insured's permission regarding the use of the car by persons other than his initial permittee. The question again depends upon the scope of the permission. Instead of what the named insured said regarding the time, place, and purpose of the permissive use, a court must examine what was said regarding other drivers. This kind of inquiry is precisely what we sought to avoid in *Matits.*

Thus, *Baesler* is not consistent with our announced policy of limiting litigation which turns on petty factual distinctions, particularly where these distinctions bear so little relationship to the subject of insurance coverage in the named insured's own mind. A named insured's admonitions to his permittee regarding the use of the vehicle by other drivers is rarely if ever intended to restrict the scope of insurance coverage. Moreover, as Chief Justice Weintraub pointed out in his dissent in *Baesler:* 'A named insured untutored in law and fearful that his consent might lead to his own liability for damages in excess of the policy limits (indeed by statute in some jurisdictions he would be so liable) may well be tempted to invent a claim that he prohibited others to drive or to convert a precatory request into a binding prohibition.' 162 A.2d at 860-861. We add that the fear of insurance policy cancellations might well have the same effect.

A second and more important policy is that of assuring that all persons wrongfully injured have financially responsible persons to look to for damages. *Matits,* 166 A.2d at 345. In other words, a liability insurance contract is for the benefit of the public as well as for the benefit of the named or additional insured. The Legislature's desire to implement this policy is demonstrated by our financial responsibility laws cited above. In *Zullo,* we discussed the importance of these statutes and held that an insurer could not depart from the omnibus coverage described in N.J.S.A. 39:6-46(a) which contained substantially the same language we construed in *Matits.* 225 A.2d 570. Thus, insurers were required to draw policies which conformed with the initial permission rule.

Although the above policy considerations would seem to dictate a departure from *Baesler,* we are urged that the language of the omnibus clause precludes coverage for a prohibited second permittee. More specifically, defendant argues that the words "provided the actual use of the automobile is by the named insured or with (her) permission" could not include use by Odolecki since Mrs. Zylka had told her son not to let anyone else drive the car. We fail, however, to see the distinction between a case where a first permittee exceeds the scope of permission in terms of time, place, or purpose, and a case where he exceeds the scope of permission in terms of use of the vehicle by another. Once an owner voluntarily hands over the keys to his car, the extent of permission he actually grants is as irrelevant in the one case as in the other. And, as *Matits* and its progeny indicate restrictions are irrelevant in scope cases. The spurious nature of this distinction was pointed out by Cohen & Cohen in their article, '*Automobile Liability Insurance: Public Policy and the Omnibus Clause in New Jersey,*' 15 Rutgers L. Rev. 155, 168 (1961). We think that once the initial permission has been given by the named insured, coverage is fixed, barring theft or the like. *Matits,* 166 A.2d at 345. There is no claim of such an unlawful taking in the present case.

Accordingly, we hold that plaintiff was an additional insured within the terms of the policy issued to Mrs. Zylka by the defendant insurer. *Baesler v. Globe Indemnity Co.* is no longer the law of this state. Reversed.

NOTES AND QUESTIONS

1. In *Odolecki,* the court lays out three different rules about how the court can see permission: the "initial permission rule," the "strict rule," and a middle ground varying from "minor variation" to "gross deviation."
2. The strict rule reflects an "insurance as contract" approach that protects the person who purchased the policy, not the third-party victim. Given the financial responsibility objective of mandatory automobile insurance, it's not surprising that the strict approach has not found much favor. Is there an argument that the strict approach might not even be consistent with a reasonable expectations approach to contract interpretation? Do people reasonably expect that household rules about when a car can be used might have ramifications outside the house? Would a parent threaten a child, "be back before dark or you won't be covered"?
3. The initial permission rule is sometimes referred to as the "hell or high water rule" because once permission has been given, it continues to exist, "come hell or high water." Practicing Law Institute, Personal Injury Law and Technique Course Handbook, Automobile Insurance Problems 20 (1968). *Universal Underwriters Insurance Co. v. Taylor,* 408 S.E.2d 358 (W. Va. 1991), presents an extreme example. A car dealer permitted Taylor to test-drive a black 1986 Camaro. He did not come back, so the dealer reported the car as stolen. Then, 16 days later, Taylor got in an accident that killed the other driver, and the car dealer's insurance company was obligated to pay. Do you think that *Taylor* pushes the initial permission rule too far? Who should be responsible for the damage caused by a former permittee driving a stolen car? Should it be the policyholder, who might have been a better judge of character? Or the victim, who should be covered under his or her own uninsured motorist coverage? Should it matter whether the victim has uninsured motorists' insurance? Would your answer to this question differ depending on whether the victim lived in a household without a car (and thus did not have the opportunity to purchase uninsured motorists' insurance)?

4. The "minor variation" or "gross deviation" rule allows a permitted driver to deviate from the permitted use of the vehicle, but only to a limited degree. Is going out drinking a minor deviation from permission to take a company car straight home? If we understand liability insurance as benefiting drivers, then going out drinking might seem to be a gross deviation. One way to protect the accident victim would be to understand "minor" and "gross" in terms of likelihood. Given the unfortunate prevalence of drinking and driving, however, stopping at a bar on the way home would seem to be a foreseeable deviation. *See generally* Joseph Gusfield, The Culture of Public Problems: Drinking-Driving and the Symbolic Order (1984); H. Laurence Ross, Confronting Drunk Driving: Social Policy for Saving Lives (1992).

B. The Family Member Exclusion

STATE FARM MUTUAL AUTOMOBILE INSURANCE CO. v. BALLARD

Supreme Court of New Mexico
54 P.3d 537 (2002)

SERNA, C.J. This case involves a single vehicle accident that occurred within New Mexico. Plaintiff State Farm Insurance Company seeks a declaration in the United States District Court for the District of New Mexico that the Georgia policy it issued to Defendant Carol Ballard limits liability coverage to $50,000. This Court accepted certification from Judge Leslie C. Smith on the question of whether New Mexico law appl[ies] to interpret a step down provision in a Georgia automobile liability insurance policy . . . where the non-resident insureds are injured in a one-vehicle accident in New Mexico through no fault of any New Mexico citizen and where the insureds receive significant medical care in New Mexico paid for by the county Indigent Hospital and County Health Care Act. *See* NMSA 1978, §39-7-4 (1997) ("The supreme court of this state may answer a question of law certified to it by a court of the United States . . . if the answer may be determinative of an issue in pending litigation in the certifying court and there is no controlling appellate decision, constitutional provision or statute of this state."). We conclude that New Mexico law applies in this case and that, under New Mexico law, the family exclusion step down provision contained in the Georgia policy is invalid.

I. FACTS AND BACKGROUND

Carol Ballard and two of her children, Carla and Chaz, were injured in a single vehicle accident on August 11, 1998, in Luna County, New Mexico. Her third child, Erika Ballard, and the driver, Robert Evans, a family friend, died as a result of this accident. These individuals were not residents of this state, and no New Mexicans were involved in the accident.

Carol and Eric Ballard, the parents of the three children, divorced in March of 1998 in California. Prior to the divorce, they purchased automobile insurance from State Farm. About one month after the divorce, Carol Ballard moved to Georgia with her two daughters while her son remained with Eric Ballard. She purchased automobile insurance from a State Farm agent in Georgia, stating that she wanted the same coverage which she had in California.

The Georgia policy contained limits of $100,000/300,000 for liability and $100,000/300,000 for uninsured motorist coverage. The policy does not include a choice of law provision. The policy contains a family exclusion step down provision:

> THERE IS NO COVERAGE: . . .
>   2. FOR ANY BODILY INJURY TO:
>   c. ANY INSURED OR ANY MEMBER OF AN INSURED'S FAMILY RESIDING IN THE INSURED'S HOUSEHOLD:
>   (1) IF INTRA-FAMILIAL TORT IMMUNITY APPLIES; OR
>   (2) TO THE EXTENT THE LIMITS OF LIABILITY OF THIS COVERAGE EXCEED THE LIMITS OF LIABILITY REQUIRED BY LAW IF INTRA-FAMILIAL TORT IMMUNITY DOES NOT APPLY.

The Ballards' son expressed his desire to join his mother in Georgia a few months later; as a result, Carol Ballard, her two daughters, and Robert Evans drove to California to bring the child to Georgia. While returning to Georgia, the accident occurred. Carla Ballard was seriously injured and required treatment for several months at a hospital in Las Cruces, New Mexico, as well as outpatient care until June of 2000. The hospital costs were apparently paid by the Dona Ana County indigent funds. Carol Ballard lived in Las Cruces from August 1998 until July 2000 for her daughter's care, while working as a medical transcriptionist for her Georgia employer. Plaintiff State Farm paid her approximately $17,000 for medical benefits as well as liability coverage of $50,000.

Plaintiff argues that Georgia law applies and that its liability under the policy is limited to the $50,000 amount required under the New Mexico Mandatory Financial Responsibility Act, NMSA 1978, §§66-5-201 to -239 (1983, as amended through 2001) (NMMFRA), by operation of the step down provision contained in the policy exclusion. Defendants argue that New Mexico law applies and that coverage is not limited to $50,000 because the familial exclusion provision is invalid under New Mexico law.

II.   DISCUSSION

"[T]he rights and liabilities of persons injured in automobile accidents are determined under the laws of the state where the accident happened." *State Farm Auto. Ins. Co. v. Ovitz*, 873 P.2d 979, 981 (N.M. 1994). The parties agree that New Mexico law therefore applies to the issues of tort liability and damages. Plaintiff recognizes that intra-familial tort immunity is invalid in New Mexico and thus argues that, under the step down provision, the coverage limits of $100,000/300,000 "should be reduced so as not to 'exceed the limits of liability required by law,'" or $25,000/50,000 of the NMMFRA. Defendants argue that the step down provision is unenforceable. "[T]he policy of New Mexico is to interpret insurance contracts according to the law of the place where the contract was executed," which is referred to as *lex loci contractus. Shope v. State Farm Ins. Co.*, 925 P.2d 515 (N.M. 1996); *State Farm Auto. Ins. Co. v. Ovitz*, 873 P.2d 979, 981 (N.M. 1994). Under the facts of this case, applying the *lex loci contractus* rule, we would rely on Georgia law to interpret the policy.

Defendants argue that Georgia law would not support enforcement of the provision based upon ambiguities in the policy and Carol Ballard's reasonable expectations. We disagree. Georgia appellate courts have held that step down provisions similar to the one at issue in this case are valid. *E.g., Cotton States Mut. Ins. Co. v. Coleman,* 530 S.E.2d 229, 230-31 (Ga. Ct. App. 2000). However, our recognition of Georgia law regarding familial exclusion does not end the inquiry. Defendants argue that application of Georgia's law, which would limit their recovery under the step down provision, is precluded by New Mexico law.

"To overcome the rule favoring the place where a contract is executed, there must be a countervailing interest that is fundamental and separate from general policies of contract interpretation." *Shope v. State Farm Ins. Co.,* 925 P.2d 515 (N.M. 1996). Application of the rule must result in a violation of "fundamental principles of justice" in order to apply New Mexico law rather than the law of the jurisdiction where the contract was signed. *Shope v. State Farm Ins. Co.,* 925 P.2d 515 (N.M. 1996); *see Reagan v. McGee Drilling Corp.,* 933 P.2d 867 (N.M. Ct. App. 1997) ("The threshold . . . is whether giving effect to another state's policies would 'violate some fundamental principle of justice, some prevalent conception of good morals, some deep-rooted tradition of the common weal' of the forum state.") (quoted authority omitted).

In *Shope,* this Court addressed stacking of insurance coverage, which was specifically precluded under the insurance contract in accordance with Virginia law, where the policy was purchased. 925 P.2d at 515. We explained that, "[w]hile New Mexico public policy does favor the stacking of coverage in underinsured motorist cases, our rationale in establishing this policy did not concern fundamental principles of justice, but focused on the expectations of the insured." *Id.* (citation omitted). We concluded that, "[w]hile we interpret New Mexico insurance contracts to avoid repugnancy in clauses that prohibit stacking of coverages for which separate premiums have been paid, this rule is one of contract interpretation that does not rise to the level of a fundamental principle of justice." *Id.* Thus, in the present case, we address whether giving effect to Plaintiff's step down provision limiting Defendants' recovery by applying Georgia's familial exclusion law violates fundamental principles of justice, warranting application of New Mexico law despite the fact that the contract at issue was executed in Georgia. In contrast to the issue presented in *Shope,* Plaintiff's step down provision is more than a matter of contract interpretation; we determine that the reduction in coverage for a discrete group of individuals in this context, based solely on their familial relationship to the insured, implicates a fundamental principle of justice.

This Court has held that exclusion of coverage for insureds and family members violates the requirements of the NMMFRA as well as our precedent, and that such exclusions are thus contrary to New Mexico public policy. *Estep v. State Farm Mut. Auto Ins. Co.,* 703 P.2d 882, 884-88 (N.M. 1985). In *Estep,* we reiterated the abandonment of the common law rule of interspousal immunity: "New Mexico has established that interspousal immunity is an 'archaic precept' out of tune with and contrary to public policy. *Maestas v. Overton,* 531 P.2d 947 (N.M. 1975)." *Id.* at 885.

Since a wife in this jurisdiction has a cause of action for injuries suffered because of her husband's negligence, it is difficult to discern how a fundamental public policy purpose of the Financial Responsibility Act—*i.e.,* to provide financial protection to those who sustain injury through the negligence of motor vehicle owners or operators—is served, or how the requirement of the Act—*i.e.,* to provide proof of financial responsibility for losses from liability imposed by law which arise from the use of an insured motor vehicle—is observed, when the family exclusion clause in the policy specifically carves out from coverage a considerable segment of the class of individuals the NMMFRA is designed to protect. *Id.* We held that "State Farm's inclusion of a restriction against coverage for household members is . . . a violation of the requirements of the [NMMFRA] and a repudiation of New Mexico's public policy." *Id.* at 886.

Plaintiff argues that "[t]he *Estep* Court did not find that the exclusion violated any public policy other than that expressed by the" NMMFRA. We disagree. While *Estep* discussed and rejected interspousal immunity in the context of the NMMFRA, the analysis was directed to familial exclusion as contrary to protecting innocent accident victims. *See id.* at 886. As this Court expressed in *Maestas,* "the rule [of interspousal immunity] is not one made or sanctioned by the legislature, but rather is one that depends for its origins and continued viability upon the common law." 531 P.2d at 948 (quoted authority omitted). Familial exclusion, whether in relation to insurance contracts, as in *Estep,* or tort law, as in *Maestas,* is an anachronism, not simply because it conflicts with the NMMFRA, but because "the reasons for the rule are no longer valid." *Flores v. Flores,* 506 P.2d 345, 347 (N.M. Ct. App. 1973) (rejecting interspousal immunity for intentional torts), *cited with approval in Maestas,* 531 P.2d at 948.

This Court, in *Estep,* rejected the insurer's argument that the potential for fraudulent or collusive claims justified a family exclusion clause: "denial of negligence actions to an entire class of persons—here, all family members—cannot be tolerated simply because some undefined portions of that class might instigate fraudulent lawsuits." 703 P.2d at 886. We also rejected the insurer's argument that freedom of contract supported such exclusions, noting that the effect of the policy's exclusion on third parties who are or may be ignorant of the insurance arrangements and unable or incompetent to contract for coverage for themselves, illustrates the fragility of any assertion that the terms of this or similar insurance policies truly are the product of conscious bargaining between the parties. *Id.* at 886-87. "In either case, [whether a named insured or the family of the insured,] an innocent accident victim may suffer financial hardship if such clauses are validated. Consequently, we find that such an exclusion also violates public policy and the statutes, and is therefore void." *Id.* at 887 (quoting *Hughes v. State Farm Mut. Auto Ins. Co.,* 236 N.W.2d 870, 886 (N.D. 1975)). We take this opportunity to reaffirm that a restriction of this type limiting coverage for household members violates New Mexico law and is a repudiation of our public policy.

Plaintiff asserts that the rationale of the step down clause in its policy "is that liability coverage is designed to protect insureds from liability they may incur to third parties, not to protect the insureds for their own injuries," thus resulting in an ability to provide liability coverage at a reduced cost. Plaintiff argues that the NMMFRA "requires a minimal amount of coverage to avoid catastrophic financial hardship and its purpose should not be extended," and that there is "no public policy in New Mexico that compels application of New Mexico law." We disagree. Carol Ballard did not purchase the minimum amount of insurance required by law; she purchased liability coverage of $100,000/$300,000. The step down provision and the fact that Carla Ballard is her daughter and resides with her limits her recovery under the policy to the $25,000/50,000 amount. As a matter of public policy, Carla Ballard is as much an "innocent victim" of the accident as an unrelated individual would be under the policy. Thus, while the step down provision does not implicate the policy underlying the minimum insurance required by law because it provides that minimum amount, it does implicate the NMMFRA's broader protection of innocent accident victims. Once Plaintiff sold Carol Ballard insurance that exceeded the "limits required by law," this coverage applies equally to all accident victims, whether the victim is a family member or not, as a matter of New Mexico public policy.

Plaintiff points out that Georgia has also rejected a familial exclusion provision that resulted in elimination of all coverage as against public policy. *See Stepho v. Allstate Ins. Co.,* 383 S.E.2d 887, 888-89 (Ga. 1989). Plaintiff argues that *Estep* is distinguishable based on the fact that *Estep* addressed a provision which excluded all liability coverage, rather than limiting the recovery to the amount defined within the NMMFRA, as Plaintiff is attempting with the policy in the present case. We disagree. Our Court of Appeals has addressed an almost identical household exclusion provision that limited coverage which "exceeds the limits of liability required by the New Mexico Financial Responsibility law." *Martinez v. Allstate Ins. Co.,* 946 P.2d 240 (N.M. Ct. App. 1997). In *Martinez v. Allstate Ins. Co.,* 946 P.2d 240 (N.M. Ct. App. 1997), the Court of Appeals concluded that this household exclusion provision, which the insurance company used to reduce benefits otherwise due for underinsured motorist coverage, was invalid. The Court of Appeals held that this limiting provision violated the policies underlying the uninsured motorist statute, despite the fact that the limiting provision applied only to amounts exceeding the statutory minimum of the NMMFRA. *See id.* Like *Martinez,* the policy of protecting innocent accident victims within the NMMFRA and the policy against familial exclusion or limitation extend beyond the minimum amount of coverage required by law. Thus, in New Mexico, family exclusion provisions such as Plaintiff's, whether limiting or completely excluding benefits based on familial status, violate public policy and fundamental principles of justice.

Plaintiff argues that *Martinez* is inapplicable because it addressed an uninsured motorist policy rather than liability insurance, and that uninsured motorist coverage is distinguishable because it creates a legal entitlement to recovery. As support for its argument, Plaintiff relies upon *State Farm Mutual Automobile Insurance Co. v. Progressive Specialty Insurance Co.,* 35 P.3d 309 (N.M. Ct. App. 2001), which held that the NMMFRA, as compared to the uninsured motorist statutes, does not require coverage for punitive damages. We reject Plaintiff's argument. *Progressive* is inapplicable; in the present case, Defendants are attempting to recover compensatory, not punitive, damages. *See id.* ("'Financial hardship,' whether catastrophic or otherwise, is far less evident from unrequited punitive damages."); *Torres v. El Paso Elec. Co.,* 987 P.2d 386 (N.M. 1999) (discussing the purposes of punitive damages as punishing a wrongdoer and deterring future tortious conduct). Unlike punitive damages, compensatory damages protect innocent accident victims consistent with the "fundamental public policy purpose of the Financial Responsibility Act." *Estep,* at 885.

We note that Plaintiff's argument does have support from other jurisdictions. *See, e.g., Allstate Ins. Co. v. Hart,* 611 A.2d 100, 104 (Md. 1992) (holding that, "in light of the limited nature of Maryland's public policy against household exclusion clauses and the express statutory permissibility of household exclusion clauses under some circumstances, we cannot conclude that there is a sufficiently strong Maryland public policy against household exclusion clauses that would justify disregarding the *lex loci contractus* principle under the facts of this case") (citation omitted). However, in *Hart,* relied upon by Plaintiff, the Court of Appeals of Maryland noted that the state policy disapproving household exclusions was based solely on statutory interpretation and that household exclusions above the minimum statutory amount are valid in Maryland. *Id.* at 103. The court concluded that, "[e]ven if [the law of the state where the vehicle was registered] were not applied, under the circumstances of this case the household exclusion clause would appear to be valid under Maryland law." *Id.* at 103-04. As discussed above, our Court of Appeals has held that even household exclusions above a statutory minimum are invalid in this State. *See Martinez,* 946 P.2d at 240.

Based upon our established disapproval of family exclusion clauses, we conclude that it is inappropriate to apply the *lex loci contractus* rule under the facts of this case and instruct the United States District Court to apply New Mexico law rather than Georgia law. Because we answer the certified question on this basis, we need not address the parties' other contentions.

III. CONCLUSION

We conclude that the *lex loci contractus* rule does not apply under the facts of this case, and thus, Georgia law does not determine whether the provision is valid. We reaffirm our rejection of family exclusion provisions as offensive to New Mexico public policy. Therefore, we answer the certified question affirmatively: New Mexico law should apply to interpret the step down provision in the Georgia automobile liability insurance policy.

It is so ordered.

NOTES AND QUESTIONS

1. Interspousal immunity was founded on the outdated notion that spouses should be seen as one person by the law and that people cannot sue themselves. Some courts have preserved the doctrine on the grounds that it maintains harmony in the household and avoids collusion and fraud against insurance companies. One has to wonder about the harmony justification: What would disrupt the "[d]omestic tranquility, peace, and harmony in the family unit" more, an uninsured injury or a suit to recover damages that would, in reality, be paid by an insurance company? Florida presents an interesting example of a gradual reduction in the scope of the immunity that takes explicit account of insurance. *See Ard v. Ard,* 414 So. 2d 1066 (Fla. 1982) (holding that the common law rule against interfamily lawsuits does not apply when the family member has insurance that covers the liability). *See also Sturiano v. Brooks,* 523 So. 2d 1126 (Fla. 1988) (holding that the death of a spouse also voided the rationale for interspousal immunity). Florida enforces family member exclusions in auto insurance policies [*see Florida Farm Bureau Ins. Co. v. Gov. Employees Ins. Co.,* 387 So. 2d 932 (Fla. 1980)], with the result that the individual chooses whether to subject himself or herself to potential interfamily liability when he or she purchases insurance. Do you prefer the approach of the New Mexico or the Florida courts? Why?

2. The doctrine of *lex loci contractus* provides that the law of the state where the contract was signed should be the law that applies. Many jurisdictions have

rejected this approach in favor of the "significant relationships" test. *See, e.g., Wood Bros. Homes, Inc. v. Walker Adjustment Bureau,* 601 P.2d 1369 (Colo. 1979); *Sturiano,* 523 So. 2d at 1129; *Champagnie v. W.E. O'Neil Constr. Co.,* 395 N.E.2d 990 (Ill. App. Ct. 1979); *Choate, Hall & Stewart v. SCA Servs., Inc.,* 392 N.E.2d 1045 (Mass. 1979); *State Farm Mut. Auto. Ins. Co. v. Simmons's Est.,* 417 A.2d 488 (N.J. 1980); *Auten v. Auten,* 124 N.E.2d 99 (N.Y. 1954). According to the Restatement (Second) of Conflict of Laws §188 (2007), this test provides that:

> (1) The rights and duties of the parties with respect to an issue in contract are determined by the local law of the state that, with respect to that issue, has the most significant relationship to the transaction and the parties under the principles states in §6.
> (2) In the absence of an effective choice of law by the parties, the contacts to be taken into account in applying the principles of §6 to determine the law applicable to an issue include:
>> (a) the place of contracting,
>> (b) the place of negotiation of the contract,
>> (c) the place of performance,
>> (d) the location of the subject matter of the contract, and
>> (e) the domicile, residence, nationality, place of incorporation, and place of business of the parties.
> These contacts are to be evaluated according to their relative importance with respect to the particular issue.
> (3) If the place of negotiating the contract and the place of performance are in the same state, the local law of this state will usually be applied. . . .[9]

C. Arising Out of the Use of an Automobile

FARM BUREAU MUTUAL INSURANCE CO. v. EVANS

Court of Appeals of Kansas
637 P.2d 491 (1981)

ABBOTT, J. This is an appeal by two automobile liability insurance carriers from an order granting summary judgment against them holding that the respective policies issued by them provided coverage for the accident in question.

The determinative issue in this case is whether liability for bodily injury caused by the throwing of a lighted firecracker (M-80) from the rear of a parked station wagon "arose out of the use of an automobile" so as to be covered under the automobile liability insurance policies in issue.

On April 28, 1979, a going-away party was being held for David and Karen Evans. The party was held in a large, open field. Several bonfires were going; keg beer was available. It started to rain and turn[ed] cold. Damon Rose (not a party to this action), at his wife's request, parked the Roses' station wagon so that the back seat was facing a bonfire. The Rose station wagon has three seats,

---

9. The Restatement (Third) Conflict of Laws is currently being drafted. The reporter, Kermit Roosevelt, occupies the office immediately adjacent to one of this book's authors. As of the time of publication of this edition, he had not yet turned his attention to conflict of law in insurance. Stay tuned for updates.

the back one of which faces the rear of the station wagon. The tailgate was open. Mike Ehinger was sitting in the middle of the back seat facing the fire. Kathy Rose and Danny Ireland were beside him. It is alleged that Ehinger, with the aid of Rose and Ireland, lit an explosive device known as an M-80 and threw it out of the rear of the station wagon. It landed in a glass of beer held by Karen Evans. When it exploded, Karen Evans received extensive damage to her hand and a number of puncture wounds to her body from the shattered glass.

The Evanses are plaintiffs in a personal injury action brought against Kathy Rose, Mike Ehinger and Danny Ireland for Karen's personal injuries sustained as a result of the explosion. Farm Bureau Mutual Insurance Company, Inc., insures the Rose automobile[,] and Farmers Insurance Company, Inc., insures an automobile owned by Mike Ehinger. Both policies provide coverage for bodily injury "arising out of the ownership, maintenance or use" of the insured vehicle.

The question before the trial court was whether the two policies provided coverage for Mike Ehinger, Danny Ireland and Kathy Rose, or any of them, with regard to claims made against them by the Evanses. The trial court determined that there was coverage because the automobile was being used as shelter, a reasonable incident of its use and one reasonably contemplated by the parties to the insurance contract.

The policy provision in question is mandated by the legislature. K.S.A. 1980 Supp. 40-3107(b). As an automobile liability coverage clause, it is to be interpreted broadly to afford the greatest possible protection to the insured. *United States Fidelity & Guar. Co. v. Farm Bureau Mut. Ins. Co.*, 584 P.2d 1264 (Kan. Ct. App. 1978). In the case before us, the trial court found the vehicle was being "used" within the meaning of the coverage clause because of its use as a shelter. But mere use of a vehicle, standing alone, is not sufficient to trigger coverage. Thus, even though the vehicle was being used within the meaning of the automobile liability policies, the question remains whether that use is so remote from the negligent act that it can be said there was no causal relationship between the use of the car and the injuries sustained.

Kansas has construed the word "use" in connection with automobile liability policies on three occasions: *Alliance Mutual Casualty Co. v. Boston Insurance Co.*, 411 P.2d 616 (Kan. 1966); *Esfeld Trucking, Inc. v. Metropolitan Insurance Co.*, 392 P.2d 107 (Kan. 1964); *United States Fidelity & Guar. Co. v. Farm Bureau Mut. Ins. Co.*, 584 P.2d 1264 (Kan. Ct. App. 1978). None of these cases is exactly in point, but language found in *Esfeld* indicates Kansas follows the majority rule that there must be some causal connection between the use of the insured vehicle and the injury. In *Esfeld*, the court stated:

> In determining the coverage of a policy such as our present one a court must consider whether the injury sustained was a natural and reasonable incident or consequence of the use of the vehicle involved for the purposes shown by the declarations of the policy though not foreseen or expected.

392 P.2d at 107.

The general rule in other jurisdictions is that "arising out of the use" of a vehicle requires the finding of some causal connection or relation between the use of the vehicle and the injury. *E.g., Richland Knox Mutual Insurance Company v. Kallen*, 376 F.2d 360 (6th Cir. 1967). Stated another way, an injury does not arise out of the "use" of a vehicle within the meaning of the coverage clause of an automobile liability policy if it is caused by some intervening cause not identifiable with normal ownership, maintenance and use of the insured vehicle and the injury complained of. *Kangas v. Aetna Casualty Co.*, 235 N.W.2d 42 (Mich. Ct. App. 1975). The provision, however, imparts a more liberal concept of a causation than "proximate cause" in its traditional, legal sense. *Watson v. Watson*, 326 So. 2d 48 (Fla. Dist. Ct. App. 1976).

We need not decide whether a different result might be reached if the vehicle had been in motion at the time. Some courts have held that if a vehicle is moving and the speed of the car contributed to the impact of a thrown missile, such would be a sufficient causal connection. Likewise, the mere throwing of the contents of an ashtray or other trash normally found in a vehicle could constitute a use. The throwing of an explosive device from a car, however, has generally been held to be so remotely connected with the use of the vehicle that it is not causally related to the injury. *Kraus v. Allstate Insurance Company*, 379 F.2d 443 (3d Cir. 1967).

The use of the Roses' vehicle did not causally contribute to Karen's injuries anymore than it would have if one of the occupants under the facts present in this case had shot her with a firearm. The fact that the M-80 was lit inside the vehicle and the defendants might have had difficulty lighting it if no shelter had been available is so remote that it does not furnish the necessary causal relationship between the use of the car and her injuries. We see no more difference in the use of the vehicle here under the facts present than if the owner of the vehicle had been outside the car and in order to avoid the rain had held the device under the car or stood on the "leeward" side of it to light the device.

Having concluded the trial court erred in determining that the insurance policies in question provided coverage, we deem the remaining issues moot. Reversed with directions to enter judgment for the insurance carriers on their motions for summary judgment.

NOTES AND QUESTIONS

1. In *McKenzie v. Auto Club Insurance Association*, 580 N.W.2d 424 (Mich. 1998), McKenzie was living in his car and was partially asphyxiated by carbon monoxide from his car while he was sleeping in a camper attached to his pickup truck. The court found that the car was being used for shelter and not "as a motor vehicle." Do you think that the carbon monoxide poisoning created a relationship because it is a risk normally associated with cars rather than other kinds of shelter? Or do you believe that since the car was not being "used or maintained" as a car, there should be no coverage? How is this case similar to *Evans?*

2. What about cars and violence? If the presence of the car triggered the assault, either because of road rage or alcohol, it might be covered. *See, e.g., Foss v. Cignarella*, 482 A.2d 954 (N.J. Super. Ct. Law Div. 1984). After a minor accident, an inebriated Cignarella left his car and stabbed Foss in the chest. Because the attack was provoked by the accident, there was a nexus between the car and the violence. While treating the facts as presenting a close case, the court ruled that the claim was not covered by the auto policy. Courts have been also been hesitant to cover carjackings. Should the result depend

on how close the assault was to the car? What if the cost of the car was a motivating factor in the assault? *See, e.g., Blish v. Atlanta Cas. Co.*, 736 So. 2d 1151 (Fla. 1999).

D. *Market Segmentation Exclusions*

"Market segmentation exclusions" are exclusions contained in one type of insurance policy (or one part of an insurance policy) that correspond to the coverage offered by another type of insurance policy (or another part of an insurance policy). The classic market segmentation exclusion is the automobile liability exclusion in a homeowner's insurance policy. Market segmentation exclusions do just what that name implies: They segment the insurance market, typically according to the kind of risk that is covered. From the insurance companies' perspective, the goal of market segmentation exclusions is to eliminate overlapping or double coverage so that, for example, if a claim is covered by an auto policy, it would not also be covered by a homeowners' policy. Other examples include the "business pursuits" exclusion in a homeowners' policy (see the *Economy Fire & Casualty* case discussed in Chapter 2), the professional services exclusion in a general liability policy, and flood exclusions in property insurance policies. As this last property insurance example illustrates, market segmentation exclusions are a feature of first-party insurance policies, as well as liability insurance policies. As this example also illustrates, an exclusion may not start out as a "market segmentation" exclusion. It may start out simply as an ordinary exclusion. But the absence of the coverage may stimulate others to provide that coverage, as happened with flood exclusions and national flood insurance.

"Market segmentation exclusion" is a term that one of this book's authors has coined, and courts and commentators have not necessarily looked at these exclusions as members of a common class. Nevertheless, these exclusions all share a fundamental feature: The coverage that they exclude is available elsewhere in the insurance market, and thus, with respect to these exclusions, insurance companies have the strongest possible claim that the policyholder "chose" not to obtain that coverage (or chose to purchase it elsewhere). Should that "strongest possible claim" place insurance companies in a stronger position to strictly enforce these exclusions than other types of exclusions? From an "insurance as contract" position, what difference does it make whether coverage for an excluded peril is available elsewhere in the insurance market?

STATE FARM FIRE & CASUALTY v. CAMARA
Court of Appeal of California, Third District
133 Cal. Rptr. 600 (1976)

PARAS, J. Plaintiff, injured in an automobile accident, seeks to obtain coverage under the general liability coverage provisions of the defendant-driver's "homeowner's" insurance policy. The injured party, Cheryl DeBoer (herein referred to as "plaintiff," although she is a defendant in this action for declaratory relief filed by the insurer, State Farm Fire & Casualty Company), appeals from a judgment declaring that the policy did not afford coverage for the accident. We affirm.

Plaintiff was injured while a passenger in a 1970 Volkswagen Dune Buggy, California license No. 672 BCB, operated by her brother-in-law, Frank Camara, during a deer hunting trip. She filed suit against Camara, alleging that he drove off a fire protection road "upon a very steep hillside at a point which was used to skid logs down hill," and a "collision" ensued, proximately causing her injuries. In the third cause of action, admittedly in an effort to obtain coverage on Camara's homeowner's policy, she alleged that Camara so negligently "designed, constructed, and assembled the vehicle as to proximately cause the vehicle to overturn." No evidence was presented at the trial, the parties having agreed that the issue is whether this allegation designates a risk covered by the State Farm homeowner's policy.[8] . . .

[I]n *State Farm Mut. Auto. Ins. Co. v. Partridge*, 514 P.2d 123 (Cal. 1973), the Supreme Court was confronted with a related, but actually different question. The plaintiff was accidentally shot by the defendant while riding in the latter's automobile. Defendant had filed the trigger mechanism of his .357 Magnum pistol to give it "hair trigger action." While defendant was shooting at jackrabbits out the window of the moving vehicle, the vehicle hit a bump and the gun accidentally discharged, injuring plaintiff. Plaintiff sought coverage under both defendant's automobile insurance policy and his homeowner's policy. The insurer conceded the obvious, that if the gun had accidentally fired while the insured was walking down the street or running through the woods, any resultant damage would be covered by the homeowner's policy; but it contended that coverage could not apply to damages sustained while riding in an automobile because the policy excluded injuries, "arising out of the . . . use . . . of a motor vehicle." The Supreme Court ruled that the injury was *jointly* caused by negligent driving (an excluded risk) and negligent filing of the trigger mechanism (an included risk); since therefore the liability of the insured arose in part from negligent conduct unrelated to the automobile (the filing of the trigger mechanism) and existed independently of the automobile's use, the homeowner's policy provided coverage.

. . . [The court held in *Partridge* that] where coverage of a risk is reasonably contemplated by the parties and such risk is independent of the "ownership, maintenance, operation, use, loading, or unloading" of a vehicle, the risk will be covered under a homeowner's policy even if the injury also arises out of the ownership, maintenance, etc. of the vehicle.

Two later cases have considered *Partridge*. The first was *United Services Automobile Assn. v. United States Fire Ins. Co.*, 111 Cal. Rptr. 595 (Ct. App. 1973), in which the named insured's son was attempting to start a friend's car at the friend's house, and was pouring gasoline into the carburetor. The carburetor backfired, igniting the gasoline. The son wildly threw the burning can, which injured his friend. The Court of Appeal held that the injuries arose out of the "use" of a non-owned automobile, and hence were covered under the insured's automobile policy. . . . The second was *Glens Falls Ins. Co. v. Rich*, 122 Cal. Rptr. 696 (Ct. App. 1975), which, like *Partridge*, involved the accidental discharge of a gun on a hunting trip. Defendant stopped his vehicle on a logging road to shoot a squirrel, and reached under the seat for his shotgun as he opened the car door. The shotgun discharged, injuring his passenger. The court held as follows:

8 Camara's automobile insurance liability limit was $100,000, the full amount of which was paid to plaintiff in settlement. Plaintiff claims damages greater than this, resulting in this attempt to obtain the additional $50,000 of the homeowner's policy coverage.

The rationale of *Partridge* is applicable to the instant case. The undisputed facts establish that DuBay placed a loaded gun under the front seat of his vehicle and that the gun fired when he reached for the gun. Such an act, if found to be negligent and a proximate cause of Rich's injury, would make DuBay liable to Rich for his injuries. Accordingly, DuBay's homeowner's policy would provide coverage for Rich's claim. The trial court's determination that there was a causal connection between DuBay's use of the vehicle does not affect the coverage under the homeowner's policy. We perceive that under the holding of *Partridge,* Rich may recover if the accident arose from a cause not involving the use of the vehicle or from a cause concurrent with any cause arising from the use of the vehicle.

49 Cal. App. 3d at 394-395.

II

We now advert to the instant case. Coverage E of defendant's homeowner's policy, entitled "Personal Liability," states that coverage is provided for damages "caused by an occurrence." "Occurrence" is broadly defined as "an accident, including injurious exposure to conditions, which results, during the policy term, in bodily injury or property damage." However, the policy contains an exclusion which states that coverage does not apply:

> (a) [to] bodily injury or property damage arising out of the ownership, maintenance, operation, use, loading, or unloading of: . . . (2) [any] motor vehicle owned or operated by, or rented, or loaned to any insured; . . .

Thus we come to the crucial question. When Camara started with a 1970 Volkswagen and "designed, constructed, and assembled" it into a dune buggy (which activity caused or contributed as a cause to the injury), did such activity arise out of the "ownership, maintenance, operation, use, loading, or unloading" of the vehicle? If so, . . . such activity is excluded. It is undisputed that the vehicle was at all times owned by Camara; hence the work of design, construction and assembly necessarily arose out of its "ownership." Most certainly such work arose out of the vehicle's "use." "The term is not confined to motion on the highway, but extends to any activity in utilizing the insured vehicle in the manner intended or contemplated by the insured." Since the question is therefore answered in the affirmative, there is no coverage.[11]

III

Even if we conceived of the work on the dune buggy as not involving its ownership, maintenance, etc., the result would not be different. Two distinct activities must be considered: first, that which is asserted to be the negligent cause of the injury (construction and assembly of the dune buggy), and second, that which more directly brought the injury about (the accident on the steep hillside).

---

11. We are not unmindful of the rule of construction that uncertainties in policy language are construed in favor of imposing liability on the insurer. *Pacific Indem. Co. v. Truck Ins. Exch.,* 74 Cal. Rptr. 793 (Ct. App. 1969). But the activity of reconstruction of a vehicle so as to convert it into a dune buggy is so clearly a use thereof by its owner under the cited authorities as to admit of no other conclusion.

Both such activities are included within the meaning of the exclusionary phrase "bodily injury . . . *arising out* of the ownership, maintenance, operation, use, loading, or unloading of . . . any motor vehicle" (emphasis added); if *either* arose out of the ownership, etc. of the vehicle, coverage for the injury is excluded. We have thus far considered the first; now we turn to the second.

In contrast to *Partridge,* . . . the injury in the instant case did not involve an instrumentality other than and separate from the vehicle itself. Under the undisputed facts, the accident would not have happened *but for* the defendant's design and construction of the dune buggy. But it does not follow that the accident did not *arise out of the operation or use* of a motor vehicle. The facts show the contrary. As Partridge held, the nonvehicle-related cause must be independent of the vehicle-related cause in order for the liability to be covered by the homeowner's policy. Although the operation or use of the dune buggy was not the sole cause of the accident, any contributing *design* cause was dependent upon such operation or use, such that any liability for negligent design necessarily arose out of the operation or use of the motor vehicle.

In other words, the *only* way in which plaintiff could have been exposed to the claimed design risk was through the operation or use of the motor vehicle. Under such circumstances defendant's asserted liability could not but arise out of the ownership, maintenance, operation or use of the vehicle; it was therefore excluded. This result ineluctably accords with the reasonable expectations of Camara. As a reasonable person who purchased both the automobile policy and the homeowner's policy, he could not expect the homeowner's policy to indemnify him against a claim arising out of such facts.

NOTES AND QUESTIONS

1. Note that Camara's auto insurance policy paid the claim (although the limits of that policy were less than the damages at issue). Suppose that Camara didn't have any auto insurance. Would that affect your analysis of the issue? Should it?

2. Another market segmentation exclusion that has generated a great deal of litigation is the "products-completed operations hazard" exclusion in the commercial general liability policy (see page 334, definition 16 in Figure 4.2). This exclusion segments the products/operations hazard into two parts: risks arising while the work is in progress, which is covered under the "ordinary" limits of the CGL; and risks arising from products placed into the market or completed operations, which are covered through the purchase of a separate limit for "products and completed operations coverage."

GUNS AND TRUCKS AND OTHER PROBLEMS AT THE AUTO-GENERAL LIABILITY BORDER

1. At an outdoor picnic, a group of boys were playing in and around the parked cars and pickup trucks. One truck was locked, with the window rolled halfway down. While crawling into the truck through the window, a boy bumped into a shotgun that was on the gun rack above the rear window of the cab of the truck. The gun discharged, seriously injuring a girl seated in the cab of

an adjacent truck. The girl sued the boy and the owner of the pickup truck. The boy is an insured under his parents' homeowners' insurance policy. The owner of the pickup truck (who is not a member of the boy's family) has a homeowners' insurance policy and an automobile insurance policy. In the complaint, the girl alleged that the boy negligently discharged the gun, and that the owner of the truck was negligent in leaving the window of the truck half open and the gun loaded. "Upon information and belief," she alleged also that the trigger of the gun was unusually sensitive and that the owner of the truck knew that to be the case. Assume that the homeowners' policies at issue contain the same auto exclusion as in the *State Farm v. Camara* case, and that the auto policy applies only to liability "arising out of the ownership, maintenance, operation, and use of the insured vehicle." *See Mid-Century Ins. Co. of Tex. v. Lindsey*, 997 S.W.2d 153 (Tex. 1999). Which policies provide coverage for the claim?

2. Consider whether claims against the owner of a vehicle (based on negligent entrustment of the vehicle to another person) arising out of the following situations would be covered by automobile insurance, general liability insurance, or both:

   - A passenger struck in the eye by car keys tossed out of an apartment window. *See State Auto. & Cas. Underwriters v. Beeson*, 516 P.2d 623 (Colo. 1973).
   - A dog, locked in a parked car, bites a person through the rolled-down window. *See American States Ins. Co. v. Allstate Ins. Co.*, 484 So. 2d 1363 (Fla. Dist. Ct. App. 1986).
   - A car or truck is negligently used as a landscaping tool or to drag debris. *See Cawthon v. State Farm Fire & Cas. Co.*, 965 F. Supp. 1262 (W.D. Mo. 1997).
   - The rape of a student on a school bus by a bus driver. *See Roe v. Lawn*, 615 N.E.2d 944 (Mass. App. Ct. 1993). *But see Aetna Cas. & Sur. Co. v. U.S. Fidelity & Guar. Co.*, 806 F.2d 302 (1st Cir. 1986).
   - A "drive-by" shooting. *See Nationwide Gen. Ins. Co. v. Royal*, 700 A.2d 130 (Del. 1997).
   - A car bombing. *See Mayer v. State Farm Mut. Auto. Ins. Co.*, 944 P.2d 288 (Okla. 1997).
   - The death of an infant after being left unattended in a car on a hot summer day. *See St. Paul Mercury Ins. Co. v. Chilton-Shelby Mental Health Center*, 595 So. 2d 1375 (Ala. 1992).

In all these cases, should it make a difference whether the claim is covered by another form of insurance?

III. PROFESSIONAL LIABILITY INSURANCE

A. *The Definition of "Professional Services"*

Many CGL policies exclude coverage for property loss or injury caused by professional services. Unlike the intentional act exclusions we have read about, professional services are not excluded for public policy reasons. Rather, the insurance industry has segmented the market and created separate policies to cover the risk. The following case explores the definition of "professional services." Consider why the court settles on the definition that it does.

MEDICAL RECORDS ASSOCS., INC. v. AM. EMPIRE SURPLUS LINES INS. CO.

United States Court of Appeals, First Circuit
142 F.3d 512 (1998)

LYNCH J. This diversity case requires us to determine whether setting fees for copies of medical records is, under Massachusetts law, part of the "professional service" provided by a medical records processing company, thus putting it within the coverage of a professional errors and omissions insurance policy. The appellee, American Empire Surplus Lines Insurance Co. (American Empire), refused to defend and indemnify the appellant, Medical Records Associates, Inc. (MRA), in connection with a claim of overcharging. The district court concluded that the insurer acted properly because its policy does not cover billing practices. We agree, and therefore affirm the dismissal of Medical Records' case.

I. BACKGROUND

Appellant MRA is a medical records processing business. It contracts with Massachusetts hospitals and medical centers to carry out the medical facilities' statutory obligation to provide patients or their attorneys with copies of the patients' medical records upon request. *See* Mass. Gen. L. ch. 111, §§70, 70E(g). MRA charges a fee, which is paid by the recipient of the records.

In August 1993, MRA received a demand letter on behalf of the law firm Lubin & Meyer, P.C., and others similarly situated, claiming that MRA had overcharged for copies and also may have included improper charges on its bills, in violation of Mass. Gen. L. ch. 93A and other state statutes. MRA referred the claim to American Empire, with whom it had an errors & omissions (E & O) policy providing defense and indemnification for claims based on the company's professional activities. American Empire declined coverage based on several policy exclusions, and MRA thereafter settled the case for an unspecified sum. The company then demanded that American Empire reimburse attorney's fees and settlement costs, but the insurer again refused. This breach of contract action followed.

The district court concluded that the Lubin & Meyer claim fell outside the coverage provided by the American Empire policy because the alleged overbilling was not part of MRA's professional service as a medical records processing company. It viewed billing as a "ministerial act," or "routine aftereffect," associated with, but not part of, the professional service performed by MRA. It therefore granted American Empire's motion to dismiss the complaint. . . .

II. DISCUSSION

A professional errors and omissions insurance policy provides limited coverage, usually as a supplement to a general comprehensive liability (CGL) policy, for conduct undertaken in performing or rendering professional acts or services.

Whether the American Empire policy provides coverage is determined by comparing the allegations of the underlying claim—in this case, those contained in the Lubin & Meyer demand letter—with the policy provisions. The duty to defend arises if those allegations are "reasonably susceptible" of an interpretation that they state a covered claim, but there is no duty to defend or indemnify if the allegations fall "expressly outside" the policy provisions. [Citations omitted.]

The policy at issue here states that American Empire's duty to defend attaches when a suit alleges "damages from, or connected with negligent acts, errors, omissions" within the scope of the policy's coverage. The nature of the insurance afforded by the policy is described in the indemnity provision, which states that the insurer will cover:

> Loss which the Insured shall become legally obligated to pay . . . by reason of any actual or alleged negligent act, error or omission committed in the rendering or failure to render the Professional Services stated in the Declarations.

The Declarations attachment identifies the professional services as "Medical Records Processor," but contains no elaboration of that term.

The policy thus requires American Empire to provide a defense and coverage for any claim that MRA improperly "render[ed] or fail[ed] to render the Professional Services" of a medical records processor. The question for us is whether the conduct that is the subject of the demand letter—fee setting and billing—is among those services. Guided by the relevant cases and, as the case-law directs, "ordinary experience and common sense," we conclude that it is not.

A widely accepted description of the coverage provided by a professional E & O policy, framed by the Nebraska Supreme Court and endorsed repeatedly by Massachusetts courts, limits the scope of such policies to activity involving "specialized" knowledge or skill:

> The term "professional" in the context used in the policy provision means something more than mere proficiency in the performance of a task and implies intellectual skill as contrasted with that used in an occupation for production or sale of commodities. A "professional" act or service is one arising out of a vocation, calling, occupation, or employment involving specialized knowledge, labor, or skill, and the labor or skill involved is predominantly mental or intellectual, rather than physical or manual. . . . In determining whether a particular act is of a professional nature or a "professional service" we must look not to the title or character of the party performing the act, but to the act itself.

Marx v. Hartford Acc. & Indem. Co., 157 N.W.2d 870, 872 (Neb. 1968), *quoted in Roe*, 587 N.E.2d at 217 (noting that this standard has been "widely accepted"). Thus, even tasks performed by a professional are not covered if they are "ordinary" activities "achievable by those lacking the relevant professional training and expertise," *Jefferson Ins.*, 677 N.E.2d at 230.

In *Jefferson Ins.*, the alleged negligent conduct involved delay by the insured company's ambulance in responding to a medical emergency. The court concluded that the basis for the delay—miscommunication between the ambulance company's radio dispatcher and the ambulance attendants about an address—did not constitute professional services. The court explained:

It was rather in the nature of non-specialized, clerical or administrative activity requiring neither special learning, intellectual skill, nor professional judgment. Nothing in the record suggests that specialized training, skill, or knowledge, beyond the normal intelligence of the ordinary prudent person, is required: to receive messages from the police, to relay those messages or otherwise supply ambulances with the information necessary for emergency medical technicians to render emergency services, to follow directions, or to locate and drive to specified addresses. To the contrary, ordinary experience and common sense . . . indicate that such activities require only the everyday, practical abilities of the average adult, not the art of the adept.

Id. at 102, 677 N.E.2d at 231. In another of the few Massachusetts cases tackling the "professional services" issue, *Camp Dresser & McKee, Inc. v. Home Ins. Co.,* 568 N.E.2d 631, 635 (Mass. App. Ct. 1991), the inquiry concerned the failure of a consulting company to warn employees working on a project of certain job hazards. In deciding that an exclusion in a CGL policy for damages arising out of professional services did not apply, the court concluded that the challenged activities properly were viewed as "management tasks" of a nonprofessional nature. In *Roe,* too, application of the *Marx* standard led to a holding that the challenged conduct was nonprofessional; a dental malpractice policy was found inapplicable to damages caused by a dentist's improper sexual relationship with a patient. 587 N.E.2d at 218.

These cases do not paint an unwavering line of demarcation between "professional" and "nonprofessional" activities. While the conduct in *Roe* was entirely outside the provision of dental services, in both *Jefferson* and *Camp Dresser,* the alleged negligence occurred during the performance—or non-performance—of tasks that are "inherent in the practice of the insured's profession," *see USM Corp. v. First State Ins. Co.,* 652 N.E.2d 613, 614 (Mass. 1995). In those cases, it was the unskilled nature of the specific task—not the absence of a professional endeavor—that rendered the professional services exclusion inapplicable. It is perhaps of some significance that the latter two cases involved *exclusions* to CGL policies—removing professional services from the policies' otherwise comprehensive coverage—rather than professional E & O policies, in light of the well established canon that insurance policies are to be construed in favor of the insured. A court applying that maxim might well be inclined to find certain conduct to be both covered by a professional E & O policy but not excluded by a CGL policy's professional liability exclusion.

We think the bottom line, however, is that "professional services" as covered by an E & O policy in Massachusetts embrace those activities that distinguish a particular occupation from other occupations—as evidenced by the need for specialized learning or training—and from the ordinary activities of life and business. In this case, MRA has made a valiant effort to depict its fee-setting activity as an integral part of the service it provides to medical patients and their representatives. Because MRA is required by statute to charge a "reasonable" fee for the copies it provides, and because a high cost for copies could impact the statutorily guaranteed patient access to records, MRA makes the argument that billing is a crucial component of its professional activity—distinguishing it in that respect from other types of businesses.

Accepting the premise that MRA's billing practices are distinctively important because of the public policy concerns reflected by the state laws governing them does not, however, lead inevitably to the conclusion that they fall within the category of professional services. Simply because a task is regulated does not make it "professional." And, while knowing how to access a patient's file, determining whether a medical file is complete, and judging who is a proper recipient of medical records are activities that reasonably may be viewed to require particularized knowledge, we fail to see how setting a price for photocopies and producing accurate invoices are other than generic business practices.[12]

In addition, at oral argument on appeal, MRA acknowledged that the hospitals could have chosen to meet their statutory obligation of providing access to patient records by paying Medical Records directly, rather than imposing the cost on the requestors. And, before the district court, Medical Records conceded that "it could retrieve, copy and provide medical records without billing for the service." These assertions reinforce our view that the billing is most sensibly seen as either a separate service provided by Medical Records for the hospitals or, as the district court found, an incidental part of the business—but not the profession—of medical records processing. As in most other businesses, the bill is an effect of the service provided, not part of the service itself.

MRA suggests that characterizing the fee-setting component of its business as non-professional, because it does not satisfy the standard of "special learning acquired through considerable rigorous intellectual training," *see Roe*, 587 N.E.2d at 217, would lead to exclusion of all of its services since any error committed by MRA could be traced to a ministerial act, *e.g.*, searching the wrong hospital's records, omitting an important report from a medical record, or retrieving the wrong patient's file. The upshot, says MRA, is that a professional E & O policy such as the one it paid for would be worthless to a medical records business.

We disagree that classifying some of MRA's work as nonprofessional would cast all of it into that category. For example, in an age when privacy concerns are fundamental, judgments about who may have access to medical information are both significant and, it seems to us, not always easily made. The ability to make such decisions arguably depends on "special learning" and "intellectual skill," and the risks associated with release of records to unauthorized individuals appear substantial. Even if some aspects of record-processing, such as the copying of files or setting of fees, are deemed ministerial or "ordinary," that characterization does not negate the professional nature of its core functions.

Also unavailing is MRA's reliance on two attorney's fee cases, *Continental Cas. Co. v. Cole*, 809 F.2d 891 (D.C. Cir. 1987), and *Lyons v. American Home Assur. Co.*, 354 N.W.2d 892 (Minn. Ct. App. 1984), neither of which involved a dispute over the amount charged for a professional service. In *Cole*, a referring attorney filed suit for breach of contract and fiduciary duty against a law firm that had not, as promised, obtained his consent to a settlement, and did not share the fees it received. In *Lyons*, partners of a lawyer, Lyons, sued, *inter alia*, for breach of

12 Further support for the conclusion that the policy did not include billing or fee-setting among the services for which coverage was provided is found in the policy application itself. The application asked MRA to "[d]escribe in detail the profession and professional services for which coverage is desired." MRA did not include billing or fee-setting in its response. It listed only the hands-on tasks associated with obtaining and providing copies of the medical records themselves: "Process Medical Record requests for Hospitals; Photocopy said records and forward to requestors; Provide other medical record consultative and management services, as required." We note that not all of the activities listed would, in fact, qualify as professional services. Photocopying, for example, would quite clearly not satisfy the *Marx* standard.

fiduciary duty when Lyons forewent, without consulting them, a one-third contingency fee in favor of a smaller amount. Both cases, therefore, were attorney vs. attorney actions involving judgments in dealing with clients, not client disputes centering on the administrative procedures of setting fees or generating invoices.

MRA also relies heavily on *Jefferson Ins. Co.*, 677 N.E.2d at 225, in which both a CGL insurer and an E & O insurer claimed the other was responsible for covering their common insured, an ambulance company. The allegedly negligent conduct was the delay in arriving at the home of a stricken individual who later died; the delay, as noted above, resulted from miscommunication of an address. The trial court allocated the loss solely to the E & O insurer, ruling that the CGL policy's professional services exclusion relieved that insurer of responsibility. On appeal, the only issue raised was whether the CGL policy *also* covered the loss. The appeals court held that it did, concluding that "the negligent conduct complained of did not constitute professional services," *id.* at 230-31, and thus was not within the professional liability exclusion. Because there was no appeal from the ruling that the exclusion for professional services applied, the odd result was that both insurers were held liable.

MRA argues that *Jefferson* supports its position because the professional liability policy there was deemed applicable even though the alleged negligent conduct did not involve medical services or any activity or treatment typically thought of as "professional." Other than at that superficial level, however, *Jefferson* provides little support for MRA. First, the appeals court never considered whether the E & O policy provided coverage for the dispatcher/driver miscommunication, as the E & O insurer's liability was not challenged on appeal. Second, although the appeals court did explicitly recognize that the two policies overlapped in coverage in the circumstances of that case, *see id.* at 103 n. 18, 677 N.E.2d at 231 n. 18, it did not interpret the E & O policy. Rather, it noted the trial judge's reliance on deposition testimony from the E & O insurer's underwriting manager that the policy covered "any employee acting within the scope of his duties," and the judge's view that "the essential injury alleged in the complaint arose out of the failure to render (timely) emergency care services." *Id.* at 228 n. 9. The E & O insurer's concession of coverage therefore played a significant role in *Jefferson*.

Third, on the continuum of professional services, we think an ambulance company's failure to find the correct address quickly is much closer to the core of the emergency care profession than fee-setting is to the central function of the medical records profession. Indeed, setting a price for services and sending bills are functions of every business, and not ones inherent in the processing of medical records.

In sum, we are persuaded that the district court properly found that the allegedly improper conduct challenged in the Lubin & Meyer letter is not within the coverage of MRA's E & O policy. The judgment of the district court is therefore affirmed.

NOTES AND QUESTIONS

1. The insurance policy at issue in this case is a Miscellaneous Professional Liability (MPL) policy. Unlike other professional liability policies, MPL policies contain a blank space in the declarations form where the insurance company inserts a special definition of "professional services" for each

policyholder. Consider whether the narrow definition that the *Medical Records* court borrows from the *Marx* case makes sense in the context of an MPL policy.

2. *Marx* represents the majority view regarding the definition of "professional services." The court defined a professional act or service as one "arising out of a vocation, calling, occupation, or employment involving specialized knowledge, labor, or skill, and the labor or skill involved is predominantly mental or intellectual, rather than physical or manual." *Marx v. Hartford Accident & Indem. Co.*, 157 N.W.2d 870, 872 (Neb. 1968). Is this a helpful definition? Would an insured know that he was not covered for management tasks or routine activities? *See Marx*, 157 N.W.2d at 872 (noting that the boiling of water for sterilization purposes did not require professional skill or knowledge and therefore was beyond the scope of coverage of the professional liability policy). If routine business activities are not covered by a professional liability policy, how can a professional protect herself from those types of mistakes or accidents?

3. In *Medical Records* and *Marx,* the courts make a distinction based on whether the activity in question was professional or an ordinary, routine activity requiring no specialized skill. Is this distinction helpful? Other courts have made a commercial versus professional distinction. *Harad v. Aetna Cas. & Surety Co.*, 839 F.2d 979 (3d Cir. 1988) (defining "commercial" as relating to the running of a business, activities that everyone, regardless of occupation, must engage in). Does this distinction provide more clarity then the professional/nonprofessional discussion in *Medical Records?* The court in *Medical Records* acknowledges that such a distinction has exceptions and notes that a person may be engaged in a professional service, but the action resulting in liability may be one that required no specialized skill. *Medical Records*, 142 F.3d at 515. Could you argue in dissent that billing by a records company is in fact a professional service? Consider also whether an argument can be made on the basis of reasonable expectations or *contra proferentem.*

4. As mentioned, there are various types of professional liability policies for just about every profession that you can think of: architect, real estate agent, technicians, and so on. The following are cases regarding varying occupations and a court's application of the professional services definition.

   a. Medical Liability Policy
      i. *St. Paul Fire & Marine Ins. Co. v. Jacobson*, 48 F.3d 778 (4th Cir. 1995) (finding that an infertility specialist who utilized his own sperm to impregnate patients was covered by his professional liability policy because the insemination of patients required medical knowledge and special skill).
      ii. *Records v. Aetna Life & Cas. Ins.*, 683 A.2d 834 (N.J. Super. Ct. App. Div. 1996) (finding the definition of "professional services" to encompass an altercation between a doctor and a nurse, during which the doctor struck the nurse, regarding the transfer of a patient).
      iii. *St. Paul Fire & Marine Ins. Co. v. U.S. Fire Ins. Co.*, 655 F.2d 521 (3d Cir. 1981) (finding slanderous statements made by one physician against another during a committee meeting and regarding the upgrade of hospital facilities were covered by the professional liability policy).

    b. Miscellaneous Liability Policy

       i. *American Motorists Ins. Co. v. Republic Ins. Co.*, 830 P.2d 785 (Alaska 1992) (holding that an architect's competitive bid was a professional service).

      ii. *Bancroft v. Indemnity Ins. Co. of N. Am.*, 203 F. Supp. 49 (D.C. La. 1962) (holding that an accountant's advice regarding IRS regulations fell within his professional liability policy).

     iii. *St. Paul Mercury Ins. Co. v. Chilton-Shelby Mental Health Center,* 595 So. 2d 1375 (Ala. 1992) (holding that a day care center was providing a professional service in transporting children, and therefore the death of a child who was inadvertently left within a van was covered).

    c. Lawyers' Liability Policy

       i. *Passanante v. Yormark,* 350 A.2d 497 (N.J. Super. Ct. App. Div. 1975) (finding that an attorney's failure to file claim within the statute of limitations period constituted negligence and required coverage).

      ii. *Harad v. Aetna Cas. & Surety Co.*, 839 F.2d 979 (3d Cir. 1988) (finding that drafting a complaint requires specialized skill and knowledge and is therefore covered by the policy).

     iii. In cases where a lawyer is acting as a fiduciary or providing investment advice, courts have been less consistent. See *Continental Cas. Co. v. Burton,* 795 F.2d 1187 (4th Cir. 1986) (embezzling a client's funds is considered within the realm of professional services because the attorney was acting as a fiduciary); *General Accident Ins. Co. v. Namesnik,* 790 F.2d 1397 (9th Cir. 1986) (a tax attorney's advice regarding a client's investments were found not to constitute a professional service).

     iv. Other cases where coverage was not found: *Elliot v. Continental Cas. Co.*, 949 So. 2d 1247 (La. 2007) (the policy did not cover the attorney's fraudulent acts); *Fanaras Enters., Inc. v. Doane,* 666 N.E.2d 1003 (Mass. 1996) (the attorney's failure to repay loans given to him by the client was not covered because at the time there was no attorney-client relationship); *Ross v. Home Ins. Co.,* 773 A.2d 654 (N.H. 2001) (the policy did not cover rape of a client).

5. Often there is a CGL policy in play as well as a professional liability policy. Might this affect a court's coverage decision? How so? In *Medical Records,* the court discusses the *Jefferson* case, in which both the CGL and professional liability policy were found to provide coverage. Given market segmentation and the professional services exclusion in most CGL policies, how is this possible? If it is possible for both policies to provide coverage, is it also possible that neither policy could be found to provide coverage? *See Bohreer v. Erie Ins. Group,* 475 F. Supp. 2d 578 (E.D. Va. 2007) (holding that the professional services exclusion in CGL applied and that the funeral director's professional liability endorsement did not provide coverage for crematory services, but rather only those arising out of a funeral director's services); *Visiting Nurse Ass'n of Greater Philadelphia v. St. Paul Fire & Marine Ins. Co.,* 65 F.3d 1097 (3d Cir. 1995) [finding that the professional services exclusion in CGL applied, but that professional liability policy did not provide coverage because the case was brought by a competitor for Racketeer-Influenced and Corrupt Organizations (RICO) act violations]. What decision rule should a

court apply in circumstances in which a policyholder has both a CGL policy that contains an exclusion for professional services and a professional services policy? Does your answer depend on whether the CGL or the professional services policy has a higher policy limit or lower deductible?

6. Kevin LaCroix has frequently criticized insurers' treatment of the professional services exclusion in his widely read and influential D&O Diary Blog, http://www.dandodiary.com/. An excerpt from one post appears below. Note that he addresses his remarks to brokers and insurance company personnel—specifically, the people who draft directors' and officers' liability (D&O) insurance policies and who handle claims—not to courts or insurance regulators. That reflects the dominant role of insurance professionals in insurance law in action. Formerly a partner in the insurance coverage practice group of a Washington, D.C., law firm, and later the chief executive officer of a D&O insurance company owned by Berkshire Hathaway, LaCroix now works in a wholesale insurance brokerage company. A wholesale broker works with retail brokers to place specialized or hard-to-find coverage. Among other benefits of working through a wholesale broker can be the ability to obtain favorable coverage terms. For example, the evolving set of endorsements that a private company working through LaCroix's company typically can obtain is many pages long and significantly broadens coverage, as opposed to the standard D&O insurance policies offered by the companies with whom he places the coverage.

Most private company D&O insurance policies typically have a professional services exclusion. All too often these exclusions are worded with the broad "based upon, arising out of" preamble. An exclusion with the broad preamble would be worded something like this: "The insurer shall not be liable to make any payment for Loss in connection with any Claim made against any Insurer alleging, arising out of, based upon, or attributable to the Organization's or any Insured's performance of or any failure to perform professional services for others, or any act(s), errors or omission(s) relating thereto."

The purpose of this exclusion is similar to the purpose of several other exclusions in private company D&O insurance policies, and that is to make sure that claims stay in their proper lane. For example, an ERISA exclusion in a D&O insurance policy ensures that the D&O insurance policy is not called upon to address a fiduciary liability claim that properly should be addressed by the policyholder's fiduciary liability policy. Similarly, the D&O insurance policy's BI/PD exclusion properly ensures that the D&O insurance is not called upon to address claims for bodily injury or property damage as those claims properly should be addressed by the policyholder's CGL policy. The exclusions avoid overlapping coverages between the policyholder's various policies.

The purpose of the professional services exclusion in the D&O insurance policy is to avoid overlapping coverages between the D&O policy and the policyholder's E&O insurance policy – that is, to ensure that the D&O policy is not called upon to address claims that properly should be addressed by the E&O policy. Because this is the purpose of the professional services exclusion, in my view the appropriate wording to be used in the exclusion is the narrower "for" wording. I have always felt that the use of the broad "based upon, arising out of" preamble sweeps far too broadly for the exclusion's purpose and threatens to extend the exclusion's preclusive effect beyond the exclusion's purpose of keeping the various liability claims in the appropriate insurance lane.

The broad wording is a problem for all types of policyholders, but it is particularly inappropriate for policyholders in service industries. Basically, everything a policyholder does in a service industry arises out of their performance of professional services. An exclusion with this wording threatens coverage for the most likely claims the policyholder could encounter. The problem is that for a services business all likely claims will arise out of or relate in some way to the company's services.

And unfortunately, all too often, I see private company D&O insurance claim adjusters trying to rely on this kind of exclusion in order to deny coverage for a claim, even though the claim does not involve an E&O claim but merely because it involves in some way the services of a service company policyholder. In prior blog posts, I have written (most recently here) about cases in which the insurer has successfully relied on a professional services exclusion to preclude coverage for claims, even though the claim is not an E&O claim. Indeed, it is becoming a far too regular occurrence in my own portfolio as well. The problem with the way that the insurers are trying to apply the exclusion in reliance on the broad preamble is that it threatens to render the policy meaningless and the supposed coverage under the policy illusory.

The solution to this problem is that the D&O insurers should change their policies to use the narrow "for" wording rather than the broad "based upon, arising out of" wording. Unfortunately, there are some carriers that will not agree to make this change. The fact is that in light of the exclusion's purpose—that is, to keep the D&O policy properly aligned with the policyholder's E&O coverage—there is absolutely no reason whatsoever for the carrier to use the broader wording. With the narrow "for" wording, the D&O insurer has all the protection it needs to ensure that the D&O policy is not called upon to address claims that properly should be addressed in the policyholders' E&O policy.

I have made this argument before, too. I am raising this argument again here for the same reason I made the prior argument with respect to the contractual liability exclusion. That is, I want to appeal to carriers to make this change on their own, and I want to rally my fellow professionals on the policyholder side to press the insurers on this issue.

There is one more point I want to make on this issue. That is that the underwriters who are working on policies with the broadly worded professional services exclusion need to see how broadly their colleagues on the claims side are trying to apply this exclusion. The extent to which some claims adjusters stretch to try to apply this exclusion to preclude coverage is truly appalling; the underwriters need to see that their claims adjuster colleagues are applying the exclusion so broadly that there is literally nothing left of the policy's purported coverage. If these claims adjusters' position with the exclusion is correct, there is absolutely no reason why anybody would ever even think of buying the insurance. The underwriters need to reconsider their position on this issue and to allow the "for" wording on the professional services exclusion, so that that their policies are not irrelevant and pointless.

See http://www.dandodiary.com/2016/05/articles/d-o-insurance/two-things-do-insurers-regularly-get-wrong/.

GUARANTY NATIONAL INS. CO. v. NORTH RIVER INSURANCE CO.

United States Court of Appeals, Fifth Circuit
909 F.2d 133 (1990)

JERRE S. WILLIAMS, C.J. This case arises out of a psychiatric patient's suicide at Texarkana, Texas, Memorial Hospital. The hospital's liability is established. The district court resolved a dispute between the hospital's primary insurers and the hospital's excess liability insurers by holding that an exclusion in the hospital's primary comprehensive general liability policy did not apply to preclude coverage under that policy and that the single claim limit of liability in the hospital's primary professional malpractice policy applied. We affirm.

I

On September 13, 1983, Margaret Wagner was admitted to Texarkana Memorial Hospital for psychiatric care with directions that she be placed in the hospital's "closed" unit.[13] The closed unit, however, was full. Hospital staff decided, therefore, to place Wagner in the less secure, "open" unit. On September 14, 1983, Wagner jumped to her death from the window of her fourth floor hospital room.

The administrator of Wagner's estate sued the hospital on behalf of Wagner's survivors. A jury found the hospital negligent in three respects:

(1) failure to monitor and to observe Wagner properly;
(2) failure to maintain the windows in Wagner's room in a proper manner to prevent escape or suicide; and
(3) failure to maintain an adequate staff of properly trained personnel in the psychiatric unit.

Each of these negligent acts was found to be a proximate cause of Wagner's death. The jury awarded Wagner's survivors $968,985.82 in damages. This judgment is final.

When Wagner died, the hospital was insured under four policies. First, a primary comprehensive general liability insurance policy issued by North River Insurance Company provided up to $500,000 coverage for each occurrence resulting in bodily injury liability. The North River policy contained an exclusion for liability arising from medical malpractice and professional services. The second policy, issued by United States Fire Insurance Company, provided primary hospital professional liability coverage. Coverage under this policy was limited to $200,000 for "each claim" and $600,000 "aggregate." The third policy, issued by Guaranty National Insurance Company, provided the first layer of excess liability coverage. This policy provided up to $500,000 of coverage per occurrence above the general liability coverage. It also provided coverage of $500,000 for "each claim" or $1,000,000 "aggregate" above the hospital's professional liability insurance. Finally, Ranger Insurance Company issued a policy that established a second layer of excess liability insurance. This second layer provided coverage of up to $25,000,000 in excess of all underlying insurance.

In partial satisfaction of the judgment, U.S. Fire paid $200,000 plus interest. U.S. Fire claimed $200,000 was the limit of its liability under the primary professional liability policy. North River paid nothing, claiming that the professional services exclusion in the comprehensive general liability policy excluded any coverage for Wagner's death. Guaranty and Ranger paid the remainder of the judgment.

---

13. Access to the closed unit is restricted. Also, this unit has window screens that prevent patients from escaping through the windows.

Guaranty and Ranger filed the present lawsuit against North River. Guaranty and Ranger claimed that under the terms of the North River policy, North River was liable for a portion of the original judgment. . . . Each party filed a motion for summary judgment. The district court granted Guaranty's and Ranger's motions for summary judgment against North River, holding that under the comprehensive general liability policy North River was liable under the original judgment. . . . North River appeals. . . .

III

The North River policy provides, in pertinent part, that North River will "pay on behalf of [the hospital] all sums which [the hospital] shall become legally obligated to pay as damages because of . . . bodily injury . . . to which this insurance applies. . . ." The policy also contains a malpractice and professional services exclusion that excludes coverage for bodily injury that occurs "due to . . . the rendering of or failure to render . . . any service or treatment conducive to health or of a professional nature. . . ." North River claims this exclusion exempts North River from any responsibility for the judgment against the hospital. Guaranty and Ranger, however, assert that North River cannot avoid liability under this exclusion, because the hospital's liability was founded, in part, on the hospital's failure to safeguard Wagner's window and the hospital's failure adequately to staff the psychiatric ward. Guaranty and Ranger claim that these errors did not involve professional services excluded under the professional services provision.

We interpret the North River exclusion to avoid coverage only for actions taken on behalf of a patient that are based on professional, medical judgment. The hospital's liability in this case, however, was founded, in part, on its negligent failure to maintain Wagner's window in such a manner as to prevent her from committing suicide through the window. The hospital's error was not that it decided as a matter of professional judgment not to protect the open unit patients from the perils posed by the windows. Instead, the error was that once the hospital decided to provide such protection, it did not do so adequately. Testimony at the original trial revealed that a psychiatric patient previously had escaped from the open unit through an opened window. The hospital then placed screws in the window sashes to prevent the windows from being opened more than a few inches. This protection, however, proved to be inadequate to prevent Wagner's death.[14] The decision to protect the open unit patients through screws in the window sashes rather than through fixed, protective screens over the windows was an administrative, business decision and was not a professional, medical decision. We conclude, therefore, that the professional services exclusion in the North River policy does not reach the error for which the hospital was found to be liable.

The cases that come closest to the facts of this case support our interpretation of the North River exclusion. At least two cases specifically address hospitals' failures to safeguard their patients' safety. For example, in *Duke University v. St. Paul Fire & Marine Ins. Co.*, 386 S.E.2d 762 (N.C. Ct. App.), *review denied*, 393 S.E.2d 876 (1990), a hospital patient was injured when she attempted to get

---

14. Wagner apparently jumped through the window without first opening it.

out of a specially designed dialysis chair that was equipped with casters. The accident occurred because the hospital's employees negligently failed to lock the casters so that the chair would not move. The hospital was insured under a general liability policy that excluded coverage for liability "arising out of the providing or failure to provide professional services. . . ." The court held that the exclusion precluded coverage only for "those services for which professional training is a prerequisite to performance." Since no professional training was required as a prerequisite properly to operate the dialysis chair, the exclusion did not prevent coverage for the patient's injuries.

Our conclusion also is supported by *D'Antoni v. Sara Mayo Hospital*, 144 So. 2d 643 (La. Ct. App. 1962). In *D'Antoni,* an elderly patient fell out of her bed because of the hospital's employees' negligent failure to raise the side rail on her bed. The hospital's comprehensive general liability insurer claimed this failure was an act of malpractice that was excluded under the policy's professional services exclusion. The court, however, held that the failure to raise the protective side rail was not a professional service because:

> [t]he raising of the side rail was purely a mechanical act which any unskilled person could perform. It certainly requires no professional training or knowledge. The side rails were not a part of the patient's treatment per se since she could have recovered without them. They were simply a safeguard to provide her with a safe place to stay and were not a "service or treatment conducive to health" anymore than a safe floor to walk on would be. Neither was the maintaining of the rails a nursing service since the placing of the rails could be performed by anyone without the slightest nurses' training. While the initial decision to attach the side rails to the bed may have involved professional judgment, once the attending physician issued the order the professional aspect of it was complete. The placing and maintaining the rails in position was purely mechanical.

Id. at 646-47 (citations omitted).

We recognize that some courts have construed professional services exclusions broadly in holding that the exclusions precluded coverage. For example, in *Antles v. Aetna Casualty and Sur. Co.*, 34 Cal. Rptr. 508 (Ct. App. 1963), the court held that a professional services exclusion precluded coverage under a chiropractor's general liability policy. The chiropractor's liability stemmed from an accident in which a negligently-mounted heat lamp fell on a patient. The court held that the failure of the heat lamp occurred during professional services and therefore was within the terms of the exclusion. We are convinced, however, that the better authority supports our interpretation of the North River exclusion.

The distinction between professional services and non-professional services has been defined by this Court, in a case which clearly does not control but does support, by contrast, our holding in the instant case. In *Big Town Nursing Homes, Inc. v. Reserve Ins. Co.*, 492 F.2d 523 (5th Cir. 1974), a man who voluntarily entered a hospital for an alcoholism treatment program physically was restrained from quitting the program. The patient was restrained pursuant to a hospital policy that directed the nurses physically to restrain patients the nurses evaluated as irrational. The patient sued the hospital for false imprisonment. The hospital called upon its insurance company, claiming coverage under a malpractice rider that created coverage for liability arising from "error or mistake

. . . in rendering or failing to render . . . medical, surgical, dental, or nursing care. . . ." The Court, called upon to determine whether the claim was covered, held that the hospital's errors occurred in the course of "rendering . . . medical . . . or nursing care. . . ." The Court explained that the nurses' restraint of the patient was not "a purely physical action in response to a business determination, but rather [was] the exercise of a trained nursing judgment in obedience to an established medical policy." *Id.* at 525.

In the present case, the hospital's failure to maintain Wagner's window was not an "exercise of a trained . . . judgment in obedience to an established medical policy." To the contrary, the hospital's decision to safeguard Wagner's window through screws in the window sashes rather than through fixed, protective screens was an administrative decision. Consequently, the malpractice and professional services exclusion in the North River policy does not avoid coverage for liability that occurred due to the hospital's failure to maintain Wagner's window in a manner to prevent her escape.

Our conclusion that the North River policy provides coverage at least for the failure to maintain security as to the windows raises a second issue: can North River be liable for a judgment that is founded in part on a covered action and in part on an excluded action (the hospital's failure to observe properly)? The answer clearly is yes. In Texas, an insurer is not liable only when a covered peril and an excluded peril concurrently cause a loss. *Cagle v. Commercial Standard Ins. Co.*, 427 S.W.2d 939, 944 (Tex. App. 1968) (no writ). Where a loss, however, is caused by a covered peril and an excluded peril that are independent causes of the loss, the insurer is liable. *Id.* The failure to maintain the window and the failure to observe properly were independent causes, because the jury found that each of the hospital's acts of negligence separately was a proximate cause of Wagner's death. We conclude, therefore, that North River is liable under its policy, notwithstanding that the loss was caused, in part, by an excluded loss. . . .

GEE, C. J., dissenting in part:

The majority holds that the medical malpractice exclusion clause in North River's liability insurance policy does not apply to the hospital's failure to maintain the windows near a mentally ill patient in such a manner as to prevent her suicide because the decision about how to maintain them is a "purely administrative" one. My abiding conviction is that only a medical professional is equipped to assess the degree and character of restraint needful for the safety of a given psychotic patient and that, therefore, such a decision involves a professional judgment—the recognition and weighing of medical, not administrative, risks. I therefore respectfully dissent.

The stipulated facts of the case tell us that the hospital decided to secure the windows with screws rather than to provide the additional protection that screens or other measures could have offered. That decision proved to be wrong, not because a screwed-shut window presents a risk in the way that a slippery wet floor or an inadequately lighted stairwell present a risk, but because a medical professional should have recognized that a closed window would be an insufficient deterrent to a seriously mentally ill patient bent on suicide. Only a medical professional, not an administrator or a maintenance person, could recognize the particular risk to this patient presented by unscreened windows. To require an "administrator" to do so would be to hold him, not to a standard of ordinary care, but to the level of care of one possessing medical knowledge of the risks associated with the treatment of such a person as Ms. Wagner.

Our opinion in *Big Town Nursing Homes, Inc. v. Reserve Ins. Co., Inc.,* 492 F.2d 523 (5th Cir. 1974), adds credence to this view. There we held that an insurance policy which provided malpractice coverage included liability for the unlawful restraint of a patient because the restraint was the exercise of "a trained nursing judgment in obedience to an established medical policy" and not "a purely physical action in response to a business determination." Likewise, the record before us shows no business motivation for screwing the windows shut, but only a medical one stemming from the treatment of a mentally ill patient.

The cases cited by the majority involve the negligence of non-medical personnel in failing to follow established hospital policy—such things as a failure to engage the brakes on a dialysis chair and the failure to raise a patient's bedrail. In today's case, it was not the negligence of non-medical personnel that caused the harm—as it might have been had the window been improperly screwed shut and then opened by the patient—it was the inadequacy of the medical judgment itself. . . .

NOTES AND QUESTIONS

1. The court draws a line between professional and nonprofessional services to determine the existence of coverage under the CGL policy. How persuasive is the argument that the failure to maintain a window properly in a psychiatric patient's room was "purely administrative"? What role does proximate cause play?

2. In *Records v. Aetna Life & Casualty Insurance,* 683 A.2d 834 (N.J. Super. Ct. App. Div. 1996), the court found that a physical altercation between a doctor and nurse over the transfer of a nursing home patient was covered under the professional liability policy. The court reasoned that the altercation arose out the rendering of the physician's services and could be viewed as an effort to prevent the patient's transfer. *Id.* at 836-837. Therefore, because the injury arose out of the doctor's professional services, it was covered under the policy:

   > The liability sections of the Aetna homeowners policy include a series of exclusions, one of which is for any bodily injury "arising out of the rendering or failing to render professional services." The language of this exclusion is nearly identical to the basic coverage provision of the MIIX medical malpractice policy. The evident intent of such a provision in a homeowners policy is to exclude coverage for claims that ordinarily would be covered by professional malpractice insurance. *See Frankenmuth Mut. Ins. Co. v. Kompus,* 354 N.W.2d 303, 311-12 (Mich. Ct. App. 1984); *Fire Ins. Exchange v. Alsop,* 709 P.2d 389, 390 (Utah 1985). Since we have previously concluded that Koch's claim against plaintiff is such a claim, it comes within the "professional services" exclusion of the Aetna policy.

   Id. at 838-839. The court treated the CGL and professional liability policies as complements and, without much reasoning, concluded that the claim cannot be covered by both. Can this decision be reconciled with the majority in *Guaranty National?* With the dissent?

WOO v. FIREMAN'S FUND INSURANCE CO.

Supreme Court of Washington
164 P.3d 454 (2007)

FAIRHURST, J. This case arises from a practical joke that an oral surgeon, Dr. Robert C. Woo, played on an employee, Tina Alberts, while he was performing a dental procedure on her. . . .

I. STATEMENT OF THE CASE

Alberts worked for Woo as a dental surgical assistant for about five years. Her family raised potbellied pigs, and she often talked about them at work. She claims that over the course of her employment, Woo made several offensive comments about her pigs. Woo claims his comments about Alberts' pigs were part of a "friendly working environment" he encouraged in the office.

The event that precipitated this case occurred during a procedure Woo agreed to perform for Alberts to replace two of her teeth with implants. The procedure required Woo to install temporary partial bridges called "flippers" as spacers until permanent implants could be installed. When he ordered the flippers for Alberts' procedure, Woo also ordered a second set of flippers shaped like boar tusks to play a practical joke on Alberts.[15] While Alberts was under anesthesia, Woo and his staff removed Alberts' oxygen mask, inserted the boar tusk flippers in her mouth and took photographs of her, some with her eyes pried open. After taking the photographs, Woo completed the planned procedure and inserted the normal flippers.

Woo subsequently had the photographs developed but claims that when he saw them he concluded they were ugly and should not be shown to Alberts. He also claims he told another surgical assistant he thought the photographs were ugly. He claims that he did not expect his staff to give them to Alberts before talking with him. However, about a month later, Woo's staff gave Alberts the photographs at a gathering to celebrate her birthday. Stunned, Alberts proceeded to assist in a dental surgery procedure after receiving the photographs, but after that procedure, she went home and never returned to her job. Woo called Alberts several times and wrote to apologize, but Alberts did not respond.

Shortly thereafter, Alberts filed suit against Woo alleging outrage, battery, invasion of privacy, false light, public disclosure of private acts, nonpayment of overtime wages, retaliation for requesting payment of overtime wages, medical negligence, lack of informed consent, and negligent infliction of emotional distress. . . . About five months after Alberts filed suit, Fireman's notified Woo that his policy did not cover the claims asserted in Alberts' suit and declined to fund his defense.

Fireman's refused to defend under the professional liability provision on the grounds that the acts alleged in Alberts' complaint did not arise out of the

---

15. Woo claims he was originally planning to show the boar tusk flippers to Alberts at the time of the procedure while she was under local anesthetic. He claims, however, that because Alberts asked for a general anesthetic the morning of the procedure, he decided instead to put them in her mouth while she was under general anesthesia, take photographs, and show the photographs to her afterward.

provision of dental services. . . . It refused to defend under the general liability provision on the grounds that the alleged practical joke was intentional and was not considered a "business activity."

Because Fireman's refused to defend him, Woo paid attorney John Versnel to defend him against Alberts' suit and settled with Alberts just prior to trial for $250,000. Woo then brought suit against Fireman's alleging breach of duty to defend under the professional, employment practices, and general liability provisions of Woo's insurance policy, bad faith, and violation of the CPA [(the Consumer Protection Act (CPA), chapter 19.86 RCW)]. He further alleged that Fireman's was estopped from denying coverage under the policy as a result of its breach of the duty to defend.

The parties submitted cross motions for summary judgment. The trial court granted Woo's motion for partial summary judgment holding that Fireman's breached its duty to defend.

Following trial on the bad faith and CPA issues, a jury found that Fireman's failed to act in good faith, violated the CPA, and awarded Woo damages in the amount of $750,000. The trial court entered judgment against Fireman's and awarded damages under the jury verdict, attorney fees and costs pursuant to *Olympic Steamship Co. v. Centennial Insurance Co.,* 811 P.2d 673 (Wash. 1991), and recovery of the $250,000 settlement Woo negotiated with Alberts.

Fireman's appealed to the Court of Appeals, Division One. *Woo v. Fireman's Fund Ins. Co.,* 114 P.3d 681 (Wash. Ct. App. 2005). The Court of Appeals reversed the trial court's summary judgment order regarding duty to defend and instructed the trial court to vacate the jury's verdict and dismiss the case. The Court of Appeals did not reach Fireman's remaining issues on appeal. *Id.* at 681. Woo petitioned this court for review, which we accepted. *Woo v. Fireman's Fund Ins. Co.,* 134 P.3d 1171 (Wash. 2006). Woo also requests attorney fees and costs on appeal. . . .

1.   PROFESSIONAL LIABILITY PROVISION

Woo makes [two] basic arguments with regard to Fireman's duty to defend under the professional liability provision. First, he argues that the insertion of boar tusk flippers in Alberts' mouth constituted the practice of dentistry as defined in his policy and RCW 18.32.020. Second, he argues that the Court of Appeals improperly extended the "sexual misconduct" rule from *Standard Fire Insurance Co. v. Blakeslee,* 771 P.2d 1172 (Wash. Ct. App. 1989) in concluding that Woo's actions did not constitute the practice of dentistry. . . .

a.   Conduct Falling within the Definition of the Practice of Dentistry

The professional liability provision states that Fireman's will defend any claim brought against the insured "even if the allegations of the claim are groundless, false or fraudulent." NSW at 000080. It defines "dental services" as "all services which are performed in the practice of the dentistry profession as defined in the business and professional codes of the state where you are licensed." NSW at 000102. RCW 18.32.020 defines the practice of dentistry and states:

> A person practices dentistry, within the meaning of this chapter, who (1) represents himself as being able to diagnose, treat, remove stains and concretions from teeth, operate or prescribe for any disease, pain, injury, deficiency, deformity, or physical condition of the human teeth, alveolar process, gums, or jaw, or (2) offers or undertakes by any means or methods to diagnose, treat, remove stains or

concretions from teeth, operate or prescribe for any disease, pain, injury, deficiency, deformity, or physical condition of the same, or take impressions of the teeth or jaw, or (3) owns, maintains or operates an office for the practice of dentistry, or (4) engages in any of the practices included in the curricula of recognized and approved dental schools or colleges, or (5) professes to the public by any method to furnish, supply, construct, reproduce, or repair any prosthetic denture, bridge, appliance, or other structure to be worn in the human mouth.

Woo argues that the Court of Appeals erred in concluding the insertion of boar tusk flippers in Alberts' mouth did not constitute the practice of dentistry as defined in RCW 18.32.020. He claims the joke was "intertwined with employee and patient relationships, areas of Woo's ownership and operation of the dental office." Suppl. Br. of Pet'r Woo at 5. Fireman's responds that the allegations in Alberts' complaint unambiguously establish that Woo's practical joke was not connected to treating Alberts' condition. It asserts the boar tusk flippers were not intended to replace Alberts' teeth—they were intended only as a practical joke. Fireman's also asserts that insertion of the boar tusk flippers was not covered under the professional liability provision because Woo "interrupted his rendering of dental services."

The Court of Appeals based its conclusion that Fireman's had no duty to defend Woo under the professional liability provision on two flawed premises. First, it concluded, "[n]o reasonable person could believe that a dentist would diagnose or treat a dental problem by placing boar tusks in the mouth while the patient was under anesthesia in order to take pictures with which to ridicule the patient." *Woo,* 114 P.3d at 681. [W]hat a reasonable patient would believe a dentist would do is irrelevant to our determination of whether Fireman's had a duty to defend under the professional liability provision. Rather, the rule requires us to determine whether the complaint alleged facts that were conceivably covered under the insurance policy.

Second, the Court of Appeals erred in concluding Fireman's had no duty to defend Woo under the professional liability provision because Woo's actions "could not conceivably be considered a means or method 'to diagnose, treat, remove stains and concretions from teeth, operate or prescribe for any disease, pain, injury, deficiency, deformity, or physical condition.'" *Woo,* 114 P.3d at 681 (quoting RCW 18.32.020). The court's definition of what Woo's policy conceivably covers was overly constrained. In addition to covering the rendering of dental services, the professional liability provision covers ownership, maintenance, or operation of an office for the practice of dentistry and Alberts' complaint alleged Woo's practical joke took place while Woo was conducting his dental practice. The insertion of the boar tusk flippers was also intertwined with Woo's dental practice because it involved an interaction with an employee. In fact, that employee interaction was as much a part of his dental practice as the rendering of dental services to his patients.

Moreover, Woo's practical joke did not interrupt the dental surgery procedure, as Fireman's argues. After administering anesthesia and preparing Alberts for surgery, Woo inserted the boar tusk flippers, took photographs, removed the boar tusk flippers, and inserted another set of flippers. The acts that comprised the practical joke were integrated into and inseparable from the overall procedure.

In sum, Alberts' complaint alleges that Woo inserted a flipper, albeit oddly shaped, during a dental surgery procedure while he was operating an office for the practice of dentistry. The rule for determining whether an insurer has a duty to defend only requires the complaint to allege facts that could impose liability on the insurer. *Truck Ins.,* 58 P.3d at 276. Because RCW 18.32.020 defines the practice of dentistry so broadly, the fact that his acts occurred during the operation of a dental practice conceivably brought his actions within the professional liability provision of his insurance policy.

We conclude that Fireman's had a duty to defend under Woo's professional liability provision because the insertion of boar tusk flippers in Alberts' mouth conceivably fell within the policy's broad definition of the practice of dentistry.

b.   *Extension of* Blakeslee

Woo next argues that in concluding that his practical joke did not constitute the practice of dentistry, the Court of Appeals improperly extended *Blakeslee* to include more than just sexual assault. He argues that *Blakeslee* should apply only in a sexual assault context because sexual contact during dental treatment presumes intent to injure whereas the same does not hold true for "an innocently conceived group joke." Fireman's counters that *Blakeslee* merely stands for the general proposition that an insured should not expect insurance coverage to apply to problems that fall outside the policy coverage. It also claims the court did not apply the "intent to injure" rule of sexual assault cases with regard to the professional liability provision—it only applied settled law to a unique set of facts.

Blakeslee involved a dentist accused of sexually assaulting a patient during a dental procedure while the patient was under the influence of nitrous oxide. 771 P.2d at 1172. The court noted that medical malpractice insurance policies do not cover a physician's sexual contact with a patient. *Id.* at 1172 (citing *Wash. Ins. Guar. Ass'n v. Hicks,* 744 P.2d 625 (Wash. Ct. App. 1987) (a gynecologist's sexual assault of a patient)). It concluded, therefore, that because there could be *no legitimate course of treatment* involving sexual contact between a dentist and a patient, the dentist's insurance policy did not cover his actions. *Id.* at 625.

The Court of Appeals analogized the facts of this case to *Blakeslee* by noting that, like Blakeslee, Woo took advantage of Alberts' anesthetized state for his own purposes. *Woo,* 114 P.3d at 681. It also analogized this case to *Blakeslee* on the grounds that the professional services that Woo rendered were not the proximate cause of Alberts' injuries. *Id.*

We conclude the Court of Appeals improperly analyzed the significance of the act at issue by focusing only on the facts that Woo inserted the boar tusk flippers for his own purposes and the injuries did not arise from the treatment Alberts requested. It ignored the fact that application of *Blakeslee* to other contexts could inappropriately narrow the duty to defend. It also failed to consider that sexual contact is never an appropriate component of dental treatment whereas other actions could conceivably fall within the broad definition set out in the insurance policy and RCW 18.32.020.[16]

---

16. *Blakeslee* expressly recognized a distinction between factual situations in which sexual contact is necessitated by the treatment being provided and those in which it is not, citing a case involving improper sexual contact by a gynecologist. *Blakeslee,* 771 P.2d at 1172 (citing *St. Paul Fire & Marine Ins. Co. v. Asbury,* 720 P.2d 540 (Ariz. Ct. App. 1986)). The *Asbury* court concluded that because the improper sexual contact was "intertwined with and inseparable from" a gynecologist's services, it fell within the gynecologist's professional liability policy. *Id.* Although the *Blakeslee* court rejected *Asbury,* we note that the facts here are more analogous to those in *Asbury* than they are to *Blakeslee.* Woo's insertion of the boar tusk flippers was intertwined with and inseparable from the real treatment he performed on Alberts, whereas the sexual contact by the dentist in *Blakeslee* was not.

Additionally, the Court of Appeals failed to recognize that the *Blakeslee* analysis was based on the duty to indemnify, not the duty to defend. *Woo,* 114 P.3d at 681. The insurer in *Blakeslee* properly defended under a reservation of rights and sought a declaratory judgment. *Blakeslee,* 771 P.2d at 1172. *Blakeslee*'s analysis, therefore, focused on whether the insurance policy actually provided coverage. In contrast, our focus in this case is whether the facts alleged in the complaint conceivably triggered a duty on the part of Fireman's to defend. Thus, *Blakeslee* does not even provide the proper framework for our analysis.

We conclude that the Court of Appeals improperly extended *Blakeslee* to a nonsexual assault context. . . .

C. JOHNSON, J. (dissenting).

The duty to defend arises when a complaint against the insured, construed liberally, alleges facts which could, if proved, impose liability upon the insured within the policy's coverage. In her complaint, Tina Alberts alleged that Robert Woo devised a scheme to humiliate her, ordered the boar tusks, placed them in her mouth when she was unconscious, took pictures, had them developed, and told Alberts that she had a trophy to take home. . . .

Because I would simply affirm the Court of Appeals' commonsense ruling in this case, I do not reach some of the arguments analyzed by the majority. However, I wish to emphasize at the outset that awarding three quarters of a million dollars in damages to Woo based only on his self-interested testimony, without any expert testimony support whatsoever, is separately egregious. . . .

More important, perhaps, is that the majority's reward of Dr. Woo's unethical and intentional behavior will likely be perceived as an abuse of the tort system. The insurance company must pay Dr. Woo $750,000 in damages, additional attorney fees, and also reimburse the $250,000 that Dr. Woo paid to the real victim. In total, Dr. Woo (and his attorneys) will receive a million dollars more than the amount that his traumatized ex-employee was compensated for this cruel "joke." Ultimately, patients in Washington will pay for Woo's malfeasance through their doctors' higher costs and insurance premiums.

FACTS

Tina Alberts (Ms. Alberts) worked as a surgical assistant for Dr. Woo. She informed Woo that she cared for abandoned pot-bellied pigs and had even named one "Walter." *Id.* Woo had made remarks such as, "I am going to hunt Walter down and kill him," "I am going to barbecue him," and "I will find him and eat him." Woo went boar hunting and brought photographs of a dead boar into the office to show Ms. Alberts, as well as a picture of himself in front of a skinned pig hanging on a hook. *Woo v. Fireman's Fund Ins. Co.,* 114 P.3d 681 (Wash. Ct. App. 2005). Without a trace of irony, Woo claims his comments about pigs were part of a "friendly working environment" he encouraged in his office.

Ms. Alberts had two baby teeth that had never been replaced by permanent teeth. Woo told Ms. Alberts that he would replace the baby teeth with permanent implants. *Woo,* 114 P.3d at 681. On the day of the procedure, Ms. Alberts was given general anesthesia ostensibly so that her baby teeth could be removed. *Id.*

However, Woo had prepared a pair of artificial boar tusks without Ms. Alberts' knowledge or consent. While Ms. Alberts was anesthetized and sleeping, Woo removed the oxygen mask, inserted the boar tusks in her mouth, and took mocking photographs, some with her eyes pried open. *Id.* (Because of the anesthesia he had administered, she remained unconscious throughout.) Woo then took out the boar tusks and resumed the dental procedure.

Woo had the pictures developed and prints made at a public photo shop. A few days later, Ms. Alberts was given one wrapped package as a birthday present. Upon opening the package, Ms. Alberts saw the pair of shaped boar tusks "flippers." Moments later, Dr. Woo's assistants gave Ms. Alberts another envelope. This envelope contained pictures of Ms. Alberts, while under anesthesia, with the boar tusks protruding from her mouth while her lips and eyes were pried open. She was stunned. Woo exhibited no remorse at the time, telling Ms. Alberts she "had a trophy to take home." Ms. Alberts suffered severe emotional distress as a result of the experience, left the office, and never returned to work. . . .

This court has clearly held that "'[t]he contract should be given a practical and reasonable rather than a literal interpretation; it should not be given a strained or forced construction which would lead to an extension or restriction of the policy beyond what is fairly within its terms, or which would lead to an absurd conclusion, or render the policy nonsensical or ineffective.'" *E-Z Loader Boat Trailers, Inc. v. Travelers Indem. Co.,* 726 P.2d 439 (Wash. 1986).

The Court of Appeals unambiguously applied this reasonable expectation of coverage test. Under this standard, Dr. Woo's actions are not covered by his insurance. The Court of Appeals referred to the dental services definitional statute, RCW 18.32.020, and applied the correct *reasonable person* standard to interpret the policy. The court noted, "*No reasonable person* could believe that a dentist would diagnose or treat a dental problem by placing boar tusks in the mouth while the patient was under anesthesia in order to take pictures with which to ridicule the patient." (emphasis added). This court must also apply the average reasonable person standard to determine if a claim is "clearly not covered by the policy." In sum, we must determine if Woo's actions are within the scope of covered claims, as reasonably understood by the average insurance purchaser. Using this test, we now proceed at more length to analyze Woo's several claims under sections of the policy.

PROFESSIONAL LIABILITY

Woo contends that the professional liability provision protects him from any claims that allege faulty dental services. He argues that creating the boar tusks and inserting them in Ms. Alberts' mouth was the practice of dentistry. *See* RCW 18.32.020. Based on a commonsense reading of the relevant provisions and Washington statutes, I strongly disagree.

In his briefing to this court, Woo specifically argues that his invasion of Ms. Alberts' privacy was "dentistry," as defined by subsections (1), (3) and (5) of the statute. However, the grotesque invasion of privacy perpetrated by Woo is not covered by the statutory definition of dentistry as reasonably construed. Clearly, the actionable behavior was the unauthorized porcine "joke," not the eventual and separate proper replacement of Ms. Alberts' teeth.

Woo was not practicing dentistry within the statutory definition when he placed boar tusks in Ms. Alberts' mouth, then pried her eyes open, and took distasteful photographs (which also had no dentistry function, unlike earlier x-rays or impressions).[17] Clearly, the placement of the foreign tusks in Ms. Alberts' mouth was not intended to treat any "disease, pain, injury, deficiency, deformity, or physical condition," and Woo did not represent that the tusks had any therapeutic or cosmetic value. Indeed, he did not tell the patient about these actions. In short, just because Woo is a dentist, does not mean that every act he perpetrates in his office is dentistry.

Next, Woo argues that his joke is covered under RCW 18.32.020(3) because it was "intertwined with employee and patient relationships," although he admits that the actual plan was "ill-conceived in hind-sight." The average person would agree that such relationships require a baseline level of respect for personal and social boundaries. Here, Woo ignored his employee and patient relationships by violating the victim's trust and committing an intentional tort. Woo's stunt was not intertwined with employee relationships, but it perpetrated in spite of them, as an attempt to satisfy his own odd sense of humor. We should reject Woo's strained reasoning as an effort to rewrite an insurance policy to avoid his own responsibility. An average, reasonable person would not consider this unauthorized temporary tusk implantation as "employee relations" or "business operation aspects."

Finally, Woo asserts that faux boar tusks are covered under the statutory definition as a "prosthetic denture, bridge, appliance, or other structure to be worn in the human mouth." RCW 18.32.020(5). The Court of Appeals unanimously rejected this rationale, correctly in my view. The court clearly stated:

> While Dr. Woo was clearly rendering dental services when he administered anesthesia, removed Alberts' teeth, and put in the proper flippers, we conclude as a matter of law that when he placed the boar tusks in her mouth and took pictures, he was not rendering professional services.

Again, the statutory and commonsense definition refers to devices that aid patient's oral health and could include cosmetic devices that are consensually installed. Neither definition applies to the tusks. The mere fact that the boar tusks were produced with dental techniques does not place them within the scope of the statute.

The majority's conclusion that Woo's insertion of faux boar tusks into an unsuspecting patient and prying her eyes open for a series of humiliating photographs was "integrated into and inseparable from the overall procedure" is an improper construction of "dental services" under the insurance policy and our case law. Such reasoning erroneously converts our mandate of broad insurance coverage into total coverage. Under the majority's analysis, no act is outside the scope of the policy, no matter how tortious, as long as the victim is anesthetized and sitting in a dentist's chair. Such reasoning belies the fundamental principles of insurance underwriting where inconceivable; tortious activity must be

---

17. *See* Resp'ts' Suppl. Citation of Authorities from Oral Argument, Ex. A at 545-46:
Q: And the reason why the mouth was opened, the eyes were propped open, took pictures is because that was part of the practical joke that you were going to show Tina later.
A: As far as the eye goes it could be. I don't know why. Could be we checking the eye, could be the staff thought it would be more funny so they do that. . . .
Question: Her eyes would ordinarily be closed at this point in the anesthesia?
Answer: Yes, yes.

excluded from coverage. I would hold that there is no statutory basis for coverage under any section of RCW 18.32.020.

Next, the majority asserts that *Blakeslee* was improperly applied to the instant case by the Court of Appeals. *See Standard Fire Ins. Co. v. Blakeslee*, 771 P.2d 1172 (Wash. 1989). *Blakeslee* stands for the proposition that when defining "professional liability insurance coverage in cases involving sexual misconduct during dental or medical procedures, 'courts look to the act itself, rather than the title of the party performing the act or the place where the act occurred.'" In my view, the Court of Appeals properly applied the *Blakeslee* rationale to the instant case, holding that the mere fact the "joke" took place within a dental office is not sufficient. *Id*. Further, Woo's behavior was not a "legitimate course of treatment" merely because it occurred in a dentist's chair.

Blakeslee held that the insurer had no duty to indemnify the insured dentist in a suit alleging that the dentist lifted his patient's shirt, fondled her while she was anesthetized, and then proceeded to fill her cavities. 771 P.2d at 1172. Similarly, Woo may have begun a dental procedure, but he stopped providing dental services and began his intentional "practical joke," inserting tusks and taking crass pictures. Only later did Woo resume legitimate dental services by installing replacement teeth. Inserting boar tusks into an unwitting patient is not a "legitimate course of treatment," even if Woo's intent was not to physically injure but only to humiliate. *Id*. at 1172.

The majority attempts to limit *Blakeslee*'s significance by asserting "that application of *Blakeslee* to other contexts could inappropriately narrow the duty to defend." I disagree. Applying *Blakeslee* in the instant case does not narrow the duty to defend; it merely affirms the commonsense conclusion that the duty to defend extends only to "legitimate courses of treatment" and not to intentional tortious activities.

Clearly, the personal privacy concerns inherent in the *Blakeslee* decision are also present in the nonsexual humiliation of an anesthetized patient. *See Woo*, 114 P.3d at 681 ("like *Blakeslee*, Dr. Woo took advantage of his patient's anesthetized state to take actions for his own purposes rather than for her treatment"). Ms. Alberts' injuries do not arise from the practice of dentistry or any legitimate course of treatment, but from an unauthorized stunt performed on an unconscious employee. This legal issue is not "fairly debatable" and Fireman's correctly relied on *Blakeslee*'s general proposition that our inquiry is focused only on the act, not the profession of the actor.

In sum, Woo's "joke" is easily separated from the legitimate course of treatment (the permanent replacement of two baby teeth). Under *Blakeslee*, and under a commonsense interpretation of the insurance policy, these separate actions do not fall under any covered provision of Woo's professional liability policy. . . .

NOTES AND QUESTIONS

1. Do you find the majority or the dissent more persuasive? What public policy reasons support their conclusions? Is the dissent correct in asserting that insurance premiums will escalate for innocent doctors and, therefore, that health care costs will increase for patients?

2.   *Woo* refers to a topic that has produced an enormous amount of profession-
     al liability coverage litigation: sexual misconduct. Under the professional/
     nonprofessional distinction set forth in *Marx*, sexual misconduct typically
     is precluded from coverage unless, as in *Woo*, the court can find that the
     act was integrated into the professional service. *See, e.g., St. Paul Fire & Ma-
     rine Ins. Co. v. Shernow*, 610 A.2d 1281 (Conn. 1992) (claim arising out of a
     dentist's repeated administration of nitrous oxide, which permanently dam-
     aged plaintiff's lung capacity, was covered despite the fact that the dentist
     did this to continue molesting the patient). Liability for sexual acts in cases
     involving mental health professionals typically is covered under this ap-
     proach because of the known risk of transference and counter-transference
     in mental health treatment. *See St. Paul Fire & Marine Ins. Co. v. D.H.L.*, 459
     N.W.2d 704 (Minn. 1990); *Cox v. Executive Risk Indem. Inc.*, 59 P.3d 721 (Wy.
     2002). Some policies sold to mental health professionals contain sexual acts
     exclusions, however, which typically are enforced. *See, e.g., Chicago Ins. Co.
     v. Manterola*, 955 P.2d 982 (Ariz. Ct. App. 1998). Why do you think insur-
     ance companies have sexual act exclusions? Who benefits? Who is harmed?
     Is there any profession where you think a policyholder would specifically
     request coverage for sexual acts? Remember, the insurance company has a
     duty to defend against false accusations as well as legitimate ones.

3.   In *St. Paul Fire & Marine Ins. Co. v. Asbury*, 720 P.2d 540 (Ariz. Ct. App. 1986),
     the Arizona Court of Appeals took a different approach, holding that sexual
     misconduct during the course of treatment is inseparable from the profes-
     sional service rendered because the doctor's treatment of patients provides
     the opportunity for the misconduct. Similarly, in *Princeton Insurance Co. v.
     Chunmang*, 698 A.2d 9 (N.J. 1997), the New Jersey Supreme Court adopted
     a "substantial nexus" approach, holding that there was a substantial nexus
     of time and place between a gynecologist's improper behavior during a gy-
     necological exam and the practice of medicine. As with almost all liability
     insurance coverage issues, the question is whom the court is trying to pro-
     tect: the insured defendant or the innocent victim. *See generally* David M.
     Lang, Commentary, *Sexual Malpractice and Professional Liability: Some Things
     They Don't Teach in Medical School—A Critical Examination of the Formative Case
     Law*, 6 Conn. Ins. L.J. 151 (1999-2000).

4.   We will revisit *Woo* in Section I, "The Duty to Defend," in Chapter 5. If you
     can't wait, turn to the column by Adam Scales, *Can This Pig Fly? How a Dentist
     Assaulted a Patient and Made a Million Dollars*, near the beginning of Chap-
     ter 5.

B.   *Directors' and Officers' Liability Insurance*[18]

Directors' and officers' (D&O) liability insurance protects corporate directors and officers and the corporation itself from liabilities arising as a result
of the conduct of directors and officers in their official capacities. For private

18. Introduction adapted from Tom Baker and Sean Griffith, Predicting Corporate Governance
Risk: Evidence from the Directors' and Officers' Liability Insurance Market, 74 Chi. L. Rev. 487
(2007).

or nonprofit corporations, employment-related claims are the most common source of D&O liabilities. For public corporations, the dominant source of D&O risk, both in terms of claims brought and liability exposure, is shareholder litigation.

D&O liability insurance coverage evolved from basic corporate liability policies but was not commonly purchased by U.S. corporations until the early to mid-1960s. Although it was initially unclear whether corporations would be legally permitted to insure directors and officers against losses that the corporation could not legally indemnify, the question was settled when state legislatures enacted statutes expressly permitting D&O insurance regardless of whether the loss was one that the corporation itself could indemnify. For example, Delaware General Corporation Law §145(g) provides:

> A corporation shall have power to purchase and maintain insurance on behalf of any person who is or was a director, officer, employee or agent of the corporation . . . against any liability asserted against such person and incurred by such person in any such capacity, or arising out of such person's status as such, whether or not the corporation would have the power to indemnify such person against such liability under this section.

Del. Code Ann. tit. 8, §145(g) (2007).

A typical D&O policy sold to a publicly traded corporation contains three different types of coverage. First, there is coverage to protect individual managers from the risk of shareholder litigation. This type of coverage is typically referred to by industry professionals as "Side A" coverage, and it is what most nonspecialists think of as D&O insurance. However, D&O policies also contain two other, less widely known types of coverage. The second type, referred to within the industry as "Side B" coverage, reimburses the corporation for its indemnification payments to officers and directors. The third, "Side C" coverage, protects the corporation from the risk of shareholder litigation to which the corporate entity itself is a party. Covered losses include compensatory damages, settlement amounts, and legal fees incurred in defense of claims arising as a result of the official acts of directors and officers. The first case in this section highlights the very interesting fact that the covered defense costs include the costs of defending against criminal prosecution.

D&O policies have three principal exclusions: (1) the Fraud exclusion for claims involving actual fraud or personal enrichment, (2) the Prior Claims exclusion for claims either noticed or pending prior to the commencement of the policy period, and (3) the Insured v. Insured exclusion for litigation between insured persons. The Fraud exclusion prevents insureds from receiving insurance benefits when they have actually committed a wrongful act, often defined as a "dishonest or fraudulent act or omission or any criminal act or omission or any willful violation of any statute, rule or law." Whether an act comes within the Fraud exclusion depends upon the wording of the policy, which may require "final adjudication" of the fraudulent act or merely evidence that the fraudulent act has "in fact" occurred. We will address this exclusion in this section.

The Prior Claims exclusion carves out any claims noticed or pending prior to the commencement of the current policy, which ordinarily would be covered under a prior policy. Finally, the Insured v. Insured exclusion withholds insurance proceeds for losses stemming from litigation between insured parties, such as directors suing the corporation or the officers or the corporation suing an officer or director. Other common exclusions remove peripheral claims—such as environmental claims, ERISA claims, claims alleging bodily injury or emotional distress, and claims arising from service to other organizations—from the scope of coverage, leaving shareholder litigation as the principal covered risk.

As a result of D&O insurance, liability insurers bankroll shareholder litigation in the United States. Nearly all public corporations purchase D&O policies, and nearly all shareholder litigation settles within the limits of these policies. As a result, the D&O insurer serves as an intermediary between injured shareholders and the managers who harmed them.

FLINTKOTE CO. v. LLOYD'S UNDERWRITERS

Supreme Court of New York, New York County
1976 WL 16591, *aff'd*, 391 N.Y.S.2d 1005 (1977)

ASCH, J. Plaintiff, The Flintkote Company ('Flintkote'), has moved for an order granting summary judgment on the first cause of action in plaintiff's complaint against defendant Lloyd's Underwriters ('Lloyd's') and partial summary judgment on the second cause of action on the issue of the coverage of Lloyd's Insurance Contract (the 'Insurance Contract').

On May 11, 1971, Flintkote and Lloyd's entered into the Insurance Contract in suit. The relevant provisions of the Insurance Contract are found in Paragraph 1, the 'Insuring Clause,' which sets forth the extent of coverage; and in Paragraph 2(c), wherein the term 'loss' is defined. The Insuring Clause provides:

'1. Insuring Clause
This policy shall, subject to its terms, conditions and limitations as hereinafter provided, pay on behalf of the Company loss (as hereinafter defined) arising from any claim or claims which may be made during the policy period against each and every person, jointly or severally, who was or now is or may hereafter be a Director or Officer of the Company who is included in the meaning of those terms as defined in Clause 2(a) of this policy (who are hereinafter individually or collectively sometimes called the 'Directors'), by reason of any Wrongful Act (as hereinafter defined) in their respective capacities of Directors or Officers of the Company, but only when the Company shall be required or permitted to indemnify the Directors for damages, judgments, settlements, costs, charges or expenses incurred in connection with the defense of any action, suit or proceeding to which the Directors may be a party or with which they may be threatened or in connection with any appeal therefrom, pursuant to the law, common or statutory, or the Charter or By-Laws of the Company duly effective under law, which determines and defines such rights of indemnity.'

The term 'loss' is defined in Paragraph 2(c) as follows:

'. . . (c) The term 'loss' shall mean any amount the Company [Flintkote] is required or permitted to pay to the Directors as indemnity for a claim or claims against him arising out of those matters set forth in the Insuring Clause above, whether actual or asserted and, subject to the applicable limits and conditions of this policy, shall include damages, judgments, settlements and costs, charges and expenses, incurred in the defense of actions, suits or proceedings and appeals therefrom for which payment by the Company may be required or permitted according to applicable law, common or statutory, or under provisions of the Company's Charter or By-Laws effective pursuant to law; provided always that such subject of loss shall not include fines or penalties imposed by law or other matters which may be deemed uninsurable under the law pursuant to which this policy shall be construed.'

Flintkote has continuously carried directors' and officers' indemnification insurance with defendant Lloyd's since 1958. Prior to August 1967, insurance coverage was limited to reimbursement against loss arising solely from civil claims. In August 1967, at Lloyd's initiative and at a substantially increased premium, coverage under the Insurance Contract was expanded by Lloyd's to include the cost of defending criminal proceedings to which directors or officers were named as defendants.

On Dec. 27, 1973, a federal grand jury in Pittsburgh returned a criminal misdemeanor indictment charging the nation's six major gypsum producers, including Flintkote, with violating Section 1 of the Sherman Anti-trust Act (15 U.S.C. etc. 1), Cr. No. 73-347 (U.S.D.W.D. Pa.). In addition to the six companies named in the indictment, the grand jury also indicted the top ranking corporate officials from each of the six companies. Included amongst the individuals indicted were George J. Pecaro, then Flintkote's Chairman of the Board, and James D. Moran, then Flintkote's President. The indictment identified Messrs. Pecaro and Moran as directors and officers of Flintkote, and charged them with individually conspiring with the other defendants to fix prices of gypsum products.

Flintkote's Chairman and President incurred legal fees, costs, charges and other expenses in connection with their defense of the indictment. Pursuant to Section 67 of the Massachusetts Business Corporation Law and in accord with Flintkote's by-laws, Flintkote granted the individual defendants first interim and later final indemnification for the legal fees, costs, charges and other expenses incurred by them in their defense. The propriety of granting indemnification to the individual defendants has never been disputed by Lloyd's.

Subsequent to the filing of the indictment, Flintkote and the individual defend[an]ts contested the charges. Thereafter, on Jan. 16, 1975, Flintkote, and the individual defendants together with a number of other corporate and individual defendants, pleaded *nolo contendere*. Their pleas were accepted by the court, each was fined and they were dismissed as defendants from the action. The fines were paid by each individual defendant from his own assets and no claim was made against Flintkote for indemnification of the fines. Manifestly, the sums sought in this action relate only to legal fees and related expenses and do not include any fines or penalties.

In its answer, Lloyd's contends that the claims made herein are 'legally uninsurable.' Lloyd's bases this defense on the theory that as a matter of federal public policy corporations which plead *nolo contendere* to antitrust charges should be denied the contractual benefits of a Lloyd's insurance policy. This defense raised only issues of law.

The position Flintkote takes on this motion is simply that no such public policy exists and the insurance contract clearly provides for payment of this claim. Federal public policy imposes no penalties upon those who plead *nolo contendere* (other than a sentence in the specific case). It urges that the public policy of Massachusetts (where Flintkote is incorporated) as well as the public policy of

New York recognizes and, indeed expressly *by statute*, encourages the propriety of insuring directors, officers and corporations for the expenses incurred in that defense of criminal actions without regard to the result of the criminal proceeding.

It is accepted law that an insurance contract should be construed according to its terms[.] Moreover, where any doubt or ambiguity exists as to the meaning of the Insurance Contract, it is to be construed against the insurance company, its draftsman.

The Insurance Contract provides that Flintkote is insured against the risk that it may be required or permitted to indemnify its directors and officers for their criminal defense expenses. There is no limitation set forth in the policy dealing with the situation in which Flintkote itself is also charged with the same offense. In August 1967, Lloyd's unilaterally offered to amend its form of insurance contract specifically to include the defense of criminal actions, if the insured agreed to pay a markedly increased premium. Flintkote agreed to the changed form of contract and the increased premium resulting in the issuance to it by Lloyd's of the Insurance Contract of the type in suit here.

If Lloyd's in drafting its policy had intended to deny coverage in cases where the corporation was charged together with its directors and officers, it could easily have provided that coverage would be denied in all cases involving criminal charges against individual directors or officers if the insured corporation is charged with the same offense and fails to defeat the charges. Lloyd's failure to limit clearly the extent of its undertaking by such a specific exclusion is fatal to its position on this motion. . . .

The insurance contract specifically provides for recovery of defense expenses even though the insured's directors or officers are *convicted* of criminal charges. Paragraph 2(c) of the Insurance Contract specifically excludes reimbursement of criminal fines and penalties which, of course, can only be levied in cases in which convictions occur. The failure to exclude defense expenses in cases where the directors or officers receive fines and penalties must be construed as recognition of the propriety of payment of such defense expenses regardless of the outcome of the criminal case. Lloyd's claim thus boils down to the improbable assertion that the Insurance Contract expressly allows a corporation to recover the costs of indemnifying defense expenses of convicted directors or officers but bars recovery by the insured following such indemnification because the insured was convicted of the same offense.

In its reasoning Lloyd's argument is identical with the claims which were rejected in *Messersmith v. American Fidelity Co.*, 175 N.Y.S. 169 (N.Y. App. Div. 1919), *aff'd* 133 N.E. 432 (N.Y. 1921). *Messersmith* involved an insurer's refusal to indemnify its insured against a personal injury judgment under an automobile liability policy because the insured had permitted his minor son, an unlicensed driver, to operate the auto. In language exactly applicable to the instant case the Appellate Division held:

> '. . . [I]f the insurance policy in question undertook by its express terms to indemnify the plaintiff against damages resulting to him because of his violation of a criminal statute he could not recover. In such a case the contract on its face would be illegal and void and to prove his cause of action the plaintiff would have to prove his contract and that, being void and illegal on its face, could not be enforced.

'It seems to me, however, that there is a great difference between such a case and the case at bar.

'Here the contract on its face is perfectly legal. It does not purport to indemnify the plaintiff against damages growing out of the performance of an illegal act. The insurance policy, as drawn, had been approved by the State and was issued for a valid consideration. The plaintiff in this case to make out his cause of action was not required to prove any unlawful act.'

(187 App. Div. at 36).

"An obligation will be enforced, though indirectly connected with an illegal transaction, if it is supported by an independent consideration, so that the plaintiff does not require the aid of the illegal transaction to make out his case" (*Armstrong v. American Exchange Bank*, 133 U.S. 433, 469). *Messersmith* distinguishes between insurance contracts which are illegal on their face because they would immunize a wrongdoer against the prescribed penalties for his criminal conduct, and those which provide coverage against financial exposure which may be incurred incidentally as the consequence of criminal conduct. The Insurance Contract and undisputed facts of this case place it squarely in the latter category. Federal public policy favors reimbursement of criminal defense expenses whether or not the defendant is found guilty. An argument similar to the one made by Lloyd's was rejected by the United States Supreme Court in *Commissioner v. Tellier*, 383 U.S. 687 (1966). In *Tellier*, a taxpayer sought to deduct legal expenses incurred in defense of a securities fraud indictment as to which he was found guilty. The United States Supreme Court drew the distinction between the defendant's criminal conduct and his right to obtain a legal defense. In responding to the contention that allowing the taxpayer a deduction for his legal fees would frustrate "public policy," the court held:

"*No public policy is offended* when a man faced with serious criminal charges employs a lawyer to help in his defense. This is not 'proscribed conduct.' *It is his constitutional right*"(*Chandler v. Freta[g]*, 348 U.S. 3 (1954); *see Gideon v. Wainwright*, 372 U.S. 335 (1963)).

In an adversary system of criminal justice, it is a basic of our public policy that a defendant in a criminal case have counsel to represent him.

'Congress has authorized the imposition of severe punishment upon those found guilty of the serious criminal offenses with which the respondent was charged and of which he was convicted. But we can find no warrant for attaching to that punishment an additional financial burden that Congress has neither expressly nor implicitly directed' (*Id.* at 694).

Similarly, in *Central Coat, Apron & Linen Services, Inc. v. United States*, 298 F. Supp. 1201 (S.D.N.Y. 1969), the court applied the same reasoning to antitrust cases and permitted a corporation, which had indemnified its convicted president for antitrust criminal defense expenses, to deduct the cost on counsel fees paid in the antitrust suits deduction taken by the taxpayer for all counsel fees paid in the antitrust suits should have been allowed. . . .

Congress has also dealt with the public policy arguments made here by Lloyd's. In 1969, Congress added Section 162(g) to the Internal Revenue Code which permits a tax deduction for the non-punitive portion of judgments in certain antitrust treble damage cases. Congress did not however decide to punish antitrust offenders by denying them a tax deduction for their legal defense expenses. Congress did not wish to create any public policy against granting individuals convicted of violating the antitrust laws the financial assistance of paying legal defense costs to which they were otherwise entitled. Lloyd's has failed to show that any federal public policy with respect to the Sherman Act or otherwise provides for forfeitures of a corporation's contractual right to insurance against the high cost of antitrust defense expenses for its directors and officers. The antitrust laws provide criminal penalties and treble damage recoveries but do not bar recovery of legal defense expenses pursuant to a valid contract of insurance. The public policy expressed in Section 67 of the Massachusetts Business Corporation Law ('Massachusetts BCL'), (the law under which *Flintkote* granted indemnification) and Sections 723 and 727 of the New York Business Corporation Law ('New York BCL'), (the state of Flintkote's principal place of business and where the Insurance Contract was purchased) favors indemnification of directors and officers for legal defense expenses. Both New York and Massachusetts passed indemnification laws to encourage the best people to serve as corporate directors and officers by providing them with protection against the hazard of being forced to incur the sometimes staggering expense burden of defending difficult and complicated cases. Neither state draws a distinction between the corporation's power to indemnify for either civil or criminal cases. Both states permit a corporation to obtain insurance to fund the cost of indemnification expenses for criminal defense proceedings.

While there is little legislative history regarding the more recent Massachusetts statute, the legislative history with respect to the earlier adopted New York statute makes it clear that indemnification is authorized in cases in which a plea of *nolo contendere* was entered. The New York Legislature adopted Section 723 of the New York BCL, in response to the holding of *Schwarz v. General Aniline & Film Corp.*, 113 N.E.2d 533 (N.Y. 1953). In *Schwarz*, the Court of Appeals held that a corporate director or officer who was indicted for alleged violations of the Sherman Act and who pleaded *nolo contendere* to the indictment, could not be reimbursed by the corporation for his defense expenses. The New York Legislature reacted by overruling that *Schwarz* decision. The official comment to Section 723 succinctly states:

> 'The purpose of this section is to codify the common law principle that directors or officers are reimbursable by the corporation for expenses incurred and amounts paid in the defense of actions or proceedings other than derivative actions. To the extent that the corporation may be required to indemnify directors and officers for the defense of criminal actions or proceedings, *Schwartz [sic] v. General Aniline & Film Corp.*, 113 N.E.2d 533 (N.Y. 1953) has been overruled.'

(Section 723, New York BCL Legislative Studies and Reports, McKinney's at p. 937 [1963]).

With respect to the question of whether public policy favors the spreading of the risk of corporate indemnification through the use of insurance (such as that involved here) this court need look no further than to Section 727 of the New York BCL, adopted in 1969, two years prior to the issuance of the Insurance Contract. Section 727 of the New York BCL permits a corporation to purchase and maintain insurance to indemnify the *corporation* for any obligation which it incurs as a result of the indemnification of directors and officers for the cost of their defense of a criminal indictment. In this regard Section 727(e) expressly states:

> 'This section is the public policy of this state to spread the risk of corporate management, notwithstanding any other general or special law of this state or any other jurisdiction *including the federal government.*' (Emphasis added.)

Section 67 of the Massachusetts BCL also permits a corporation to purchase insurance to cover the costs of indemnifying its directors and officers.

Our legal system[,] which has been the handmaiden of the free enterprise system, is not always available to pass legal judgment on the moral derelictions which are incurred in the earning of corporate profits.

NOTES AND QUESTIONS

1. *Flintkote* expresses the prevailing view on what kinds of losses corporations are permitted to insure against. Punitive damages may be the leading exception, at least in jurisdictions in which punitive damages are uninsurable. For corporations with access to the Bermuda insurance market, even that limit on insurability can be avoided through a "difference in conditions" or "wrap" policy that provides insurance against losses that are insurable in Bermuda but not insurable somewhere else. We will address insurance for punitive damages in the duty to settle unit in Chapter 5.

2. The RLLI follows the Flintkote approach to insurance for defense costs. Section 47 of PD No. 3 provides as follows:[10]

> Except as barred by public policy, a liability insurance policy may cover defense costs incurred in connection with any legal action, including but not limited to: a criminal prosecution; an action seeking fines, penalties, or punitive damages; and an action alleging criminal acts, expected or intentionally caused harm, fraud, or other conduct involving aggravated fault.

Comments *b* and *c* explain as follows:

> *b. Defense coverage for criminal proceedings.* Payment of the costs of defending criminal proceedings brought against an insured is among the forms of defense coverage that are permissible for liability insurers to provide. Whether such defense costs are insured under any particular liability insurance policy is a question of interpretation. Although there are no public-policy-based restrictions on such defense coverage under prevailing insurance law, this Section recognizes that such restrictions could be imposed by statute or regulation. See §46. Courts generally hold that such coverage does not violate public policy, among other reasons because such insurance promotes the presumption of innocence and other constitutionally protected aspects of a criminal defense.
>
> *c. Defense coverage for uninsurable civil liabilities.* Courts also generally enforce liability insurance defense coverage for uninsurable civil actions. The public-

---

10. This provision was approved by the ALI at the May 2016 annual meeting.

policy objections to insurance for certain liabilities are based upon the premise that the insured is liable for the wrong upon which the remedy is based. Defense coverage provides the means for the insured to contest liability, not to avoid the financial consequences of liability actually assessed. Although there are no public-policy-based restrictions on such defense coverage under prevailing insurance law, this Section recognizes that such restrictions could be imposed by statute or regulation. . . .

3. Some professional liability insurance policies sold to doctors and lawyers also provide coverage for criminal defense costs, but the liability insurance policies sold in the personal lines market (e.g., auto, homeowners, umbrella) do not. For middle-class individuals, drunk driving is the offense that is most likely to put them in contact with the criminal justice system. Given the relatively low threshold for a driving under the influence (DUI) offense, the near-complete dependence on the auto as a means for transportation in most areas of the United States, and the widespread use of alcohol, a DUI charge is a real risk, and an experienced criminal defense lawyer is bound to be helpful in navigating that situation. Thus, there would seem to be a substantial demand for the inclusion of DUI criminal defense coverage in a standard auto or homeowners' policy. Yet those policies do not include that coverage. Why might that be so? Why do you think that doctors' and lawyers' professional liability insurance policies do provide criminal defense coverage?

4. Whether shareholders should want corporations to purchase D&O insurance (or any other kind of insurance) is an interesting question. Insurance for individual directors and officers is easily explained by risk aversion. But insurance for the corporation itself is not so easily explained, at least not if we understand the corporation as the agent of the shareholders. *See* David Mayers & Clifford W. Smith, Jr., *On the Corporate Demand for Insurance*, 55 J. Bus. 281, 294 (1982). Arguably, a fully diversified investor already is protected against the kind of firm specific losses for which insurance is available. For that reason, economists traditionally have concluded that the real reason that corporations purchase insurance is not to spread risk, but rather to obtain other services, such as (1) tax benefits, (2) reduced bankruptcy transaction costs, (3) reduced credit costs, (4) access to contingent external capital at the price of internal capital, and (5) monitoring services. *See* Kenneth A. Froot, David S. Scharfstein, & Jeremy C. Stein, *Risk Management: Coordinating Corporate Investment and Financing Policies*, J. Fin., Dec. 1993, at 1629; Mayers & Smith, *supra.* This is a complicated matter that is better addressed in a corporate finance class. For present purposes it is enough to be aware that there are doubts about whether the corporate protection aspect of D&O insurance (and, by extension, some other kinds of insurance) actually benefits shareholders or, instead, whether it represents a kind of agency cost, similar to excessive management compensation. *See* Tom Baker & Sean Griffith, Ensuring Corporate Misconduct: How Liability Insurance Undermines Shareholder Litigation (U. Chicago P. 2010).

In the next case, Judge Posner identifies one potential public policy limit on the scope of directors' and officers' liability insurance.

LEVEL 3 COMMUNICATIONS, INC. v. FEDERAL INSURANCE CO.

United States Court of Appeals, Seventh Circuit
272 F.3d 908 (2001)

POSNER, C.J. This appeal comes in a diversity suit seeking damages from a pair of insurance companies (a primary carrier, Federal, and an excess carrier that's no longer a party) that refused to pay on a policy of directors' and officers' liability insurance, a "D&O" policy, as it's known. Despite its name, such a policy insures not only officers and directors themselves but also their corporation if, as happened here, the corporation indemnifies them for their liability. This is known as "company reimbursement coverage," as distinct from "direct" coverage of the directors and officers.

[Level 3 settled a securities fraud lawsuit for $11.8 million. The district court held that $10 million of that amount was covered by the Federal policy.

Federal has appealed, arguing that the settlement, though an outlay by the insured, was not a "loss" within the meaning of the insurance policy, defined as "the total amount which any Insured Person becomes legally obligated to pay . . . including, but not limited to . . . settlements," because the relief sought in the suit against Level 3 was restitutionary in nature. The plaintiffs had sold shares in their corporation to Level 3 and charged that they had done so because of fraudulent representations that Level 3 had made. In effect, Level 3 was accused of having obtained the plaintiffs' company by false pretenses; and the plaintiffs' suit sought to rescind the transaction and recover their shares, or rather the monetary value of the shares because their company can no longer be reconstituted. It's as if, Federal argues, Level 3 had stolen cash from the other shareholders and had been forced to return it and were now asking the insurance company to pick up the tab. Federal continues that a D&O policy is designed to cover only losses that injure the insured, not ones that result from returning stolen property, and that if such an insurance policy did insure a thief against the cost to him of disgorging the proceeds of the theft it would be against public policy and so would be unenforceable. . . .

The interpretive principle for which Federal contends—that a "loss" within the meaning of an insurance contract does not include the restoration of an ill-gotten gain—is clearly right. [Citations omitted.] The two cases on which Level 3 relies, *International Ins. Co. v. Johns*, 874 F.2d 1447, 1454-55 (11th Cir. 1989), and *Limelight Productions, Inc. v. Limelite Studios, Inc.*, 60 F.3d 767, 769 (11th Cir. 1995), are distinguishable, though *Limelight* only tenuously. The facts were similar to those in the present case, but the operative term in the insurance policy was "damages" rather than "loss," and so was broader. *In re Estate of Corriea*, 719 A.2d 1234, 1240-41 (D.C. 1998), is similar.

As the interpretive principle controls this case, we need not consider the issue of enforceability, though the two issues are intertwined, since obviously an insurance policy wouldn't be presumed to have been drafted in such a way as to make it unenforceable.

It is true, as Level 3 emphasizes, that the plaintiffs in the underlying suit were not seeking either the return of the shares that Level 3 had allegedly winkled them out of or the value of the shares on the date they were purchased. They were seeking the difference between the value of the stock at the time of trial and the price they had received for the stock from Level 3. That is standard damages relief in a securities-fraud case. But it is restitutionary in character.

It seeks to divest the defendant of the present value of the property obtained by fraud, minus the cost to the defendant of obtaining the property. In other words, it seeks to deprive the defendant of the net benefit of the unlawful act, the value of the unlawfully obtained stock minus the cost to the defendant of obtaining the stock. It is equivalent to seeking to impress a constructive trust on the property in favor of the rightful owner. How the claim or judgment order or settlement is worded is irrelevant. An insured incurs no loss within the meaning of the insurance contract by being compelled to return property that it had stolen, even if a more polite word than "stolen" is used to characterize the claim for the property's return.

We can imagine situations in which there would be a covered loss; this is important as showing that the D&O policy would not be rendered illusory by the acceptance of Federal's interpretation. An example would be a fraudulent statement by a corporate officer that inflated the price of the corporation's stock without conferring any measurable benefit on the corporation. Or suppose that unbeknownst to Level 3 the officer had stolen property for its benefit and, not knowing this, Level 3 defended against a suit seeking the return of the property and incurred heavy legal expenses in that defense. Those expenses would be a loss to the company not offset by any benefit to it, unlike the "expense" that consists simply of the value of the stolen property, a wash. All that the plaintiffs in the underlying suit obtained was the amount they received in settlement of their claim against Level 3, and that amount was part of Level 3's gain from its officers' misbehavior. [Citations omitted.]

Level 3 acknowledges that if a judgment had been entered in the suit against it on the basis of a judicial determination that it had engaged in fraud, Federal would win; the policy so provides. It couples this acknowledgment with the inconsistent assertion that almost the entire purpose of D&O policies is to insure corporations and their officers and directors against claims of fraud. Pressed at argument concerning this inconsistency, it argued that the line runs between judgments and settlements. As long as the case is settled before entry of judgment, the insured is covered regardless of the nature of the claim against it. That can't be right. *Reliance Group Holdings, Inc. v. National Union Fire Ins. Co.,* 594 N.Y.S.2d 20, 25 (N.Y. App. Div., 1st Dept. 1993) ("determination of this appeal should not hinge on the circumstance that Reliance made restitution by way of settlement instead of in satisfaction of a judgment after trial"). It would mean, as Level 3's lawyer confirmed at argument, that if Level 3, seeing the handwriting on the wall, had agreed to pay the plaintiffs in the fraud suit all they were asking for (a very large amount—almost $70 million), which they surely would not have done had there been no evidence of fraud (no rational defendant settles a nuisance suit for the full amount demanded in the complaint, unless the amount is trivial), Federal would still be obligated to reimburse Level 3 for that amount. And that would enable Level 3 to retain the profit it had made from a fraud. In fact Level 3 settled with the plaintiffs in the fraud suit for the not inconsiderable amount of $12 million after the trial had begun and much of the expense of defending the suit had therefore already been incurred. It is not surprising, therefore, that Level 3 has made no attempt to show that the fraud suit was groundless and the settlement merely an effort to avoid the expense of defending a nuisance suit.

If Level 3 *had* shown that the fraud suit was groundless, that there was no ill-gotten gain that insurance would enable it to keep, would the $12 million be a "loss" within the meaning of the policy? Federal argues no, that all that matters is that the payment by the insured for which reimbursement is sought be in respect of a claim of fraudulent appropriation. Level 3 denies this. We need not decide; and prudence is definitely the better part of valor here, since we can find no guidance on the point from cases or other materials.

NOTES AND QUESTIONS

1. The question of which shareholder liability claims fall within the *Level 3* restitutionary principle is a hot topic in D&O coverage litigation. *See, e.g., CNL Hotels & Resorts, Inc. v. Houston Cas. Co.*, 2007 WL 788361 (M.D. Fla. Mar. 14, 2007) (holding on summary judgment that the settlement paid in satisfaction of a class action brought under Section 11 of the Securities Act of 1933 was an uninsurable disgorgement of money wrongly taken).

2. The settlement/judgment line to which Judge Posner referred in *Level 3* comes from the "final adjudication" language that commonly appears in the Fraud exclusion in D&O insurance policies. The final adjudication provision obligates the insurer to fund the criminal and civil defense of directors or officers unless and until the fraud is finally adjudicated in the proceeding for which coverage is sought. *See* John H. Mathias, Jr., et al., Directors and Officers Liability: Prevention, Insurance, and Indemnification §8.04 (4th ed. 2003) (collecting cases holding that "[i]f the exclusion requires a final adjudication, that adjudication must take place in the underlying action for which coverage is sought"); *see also Little v. MGIC Indem. Corp.*, 836 F.2d 789, 794 (3d Cir. 1987) (noting that the final adjudication language requires an insurance company to "pay loss as the insured incurs legal obligation for such loss, subject to the requirement that the insured reimburse any monies received if it is subsequently determined in a judicial proceeding that he engaged in active and deliberate dishonesty."). Because shareholder litigation is almost always settled—and, therefore, not adjudicated in the proceeding for which coverage is sought—the Fraud exclusion has not had the impact that a simple reading of the D&O insurance policy might suggest. Mathias et al., *supra* (noting that the application of the final adjudication provision "drastically diminishes the force and effect of the [actual fraud] exclusion"). Some more recent policies contain broader Fraud exclusions, but these exclusions have not yet been tested. *Id.*

3. Is *Level 3* consistent with *Flintkote*? Why is hedging against the possibility of having to pay millions of dollars to settle a disputed civil securities fraud claim more offensive than hedging against the probability of having to pay millions of dollars to defend a criminal fraud prosecution? For cases holding that the applicability of the disgorgement rule to a securities fraud claim or settlement is a question of fact not susceptible to summary judgment, *see Unified Western Grocers, Inc. v. Twin City Fire Insurance Co.*, 457 F.3d 1106 (9th Cir. 2006) (stating that the insurance law rule is narrow and limited to situations in which "[t]he defendant is asked to return something he wrongfully received; he is not asked to compensate the plaintiff for injury suffered as a result of his conduct"); *Pan Pacific Retail Properties, Inc. v. Gulf Ins. Co.*, 471 F.3d 961 (9th Cir. 2006). *Cf. Limelight Prods., Inc. v. Limelite Studios, Inc.*, 60

F.3d 767 (11th Cir. 1995) (holding that "ill gotten gains" paid as damages under the Lanham Act are insurable under Florida law).

4. Judge Posner has recently doubled down on his view, taking (in dicta) the broad position in *Ryerson Inc. v. Federal Ins. Co.*, 676 F.3d 610 (7th Cir. 2012), that claims seeking restitution are uninsurable:

> Whether a claim for restitution is based on fraud or on some other deliberate tortious or criminal act, or at the other extreme of the restitution spectrum merely on an innocent mistake or the rendition of a service for which compensation is expected but contracting is infeasible (as when a physician ministers to a person who collapses unconscious on the street); and whether the plaintiff is seeking the return of property or the profits that the defendant made from appropriating it, a claim for restitution is a claim that the defendant has something that belongs of right not to him but to the plaintiff. A claim for "damages" in the proper sense of the word is different. If a car driven negligently hits and injures a pedestrian, the pedestrian will sue the driver for the monetary equivalent of the harm done to him, not for the "profit" that the accident generated for the driver. It generated no profit; it gave him nothing.

For a recent critical analysis, see Christopher French, *The Insurability of Claims for Restitution*, 18 U. Pa. J. Bus. L. 599 (2016). While there is an undeniable appeal to avoiding coverage for a big claim, we cannot help wondering whether the D&O insurance industry really wants courts to set boundaries on what they can insure, particularly in light of the wide array of hedging devices available through the financial services markets. *See* Tom Baker, *Insurance Liability Risks,* 29 Geneva Papers on Risk and Insurance 128, 147 (2004) ("if established liability insurance companies walk away from substantial risks, economic actors will find alternative ways to transfer those risks, which is not in the long-term interests of existing liability insurers").

C. Late Notice Under a Claims-Made Policy

The notice provision is one of the most litigated conditions in liability insurance policies of all kinds. As we saw in the *Aetna v. Murphy* case used to introduce the doctrine of disproportionate forfeiture in Chapter 2, courts in many states have adopted a "prejudice" requirement for late notice claims under occurrence and accident policies. One of the ways that claims-made policies differ from occurrence policies is the location of the notice requirement in the policy form. Claims-made policies incorporate a notice requirement directly into the trigger provisions, for example, by stating that coverage is provided for claims reported during the policy period. If you haven't already worked through the Dr. Bill and Dr. Mary problems earlier in this chapter, which illustrate the difference between occurrence and claims-made triggers, now is the time to do that.

Courts have struggled to determine whether moving the notice requirement from the "conditions" portion of the insurance policy into a trigger provision allows insurance companies to avoid the prejudice requirement. This is the issue addressed in the following case. If you are a careful reader, you will be able to predict the outcome of the *Gulf* case from the way that the court characterizes the issue in the very first paragraph of the opinion. As you read the opinion, consider how the insured might have characterized the case so that it would have appeared more susceptible to the *Aetna v. Murphy* disproportionate forfeiture analysis.

GULF INSURANCE CO. v. DOLAN, FERTIG & CURTIS

Supreme Court of Florida
433 So. 2d 512 (1983)

EHRLICH, Justice. This is a case of first impression in Florida. The issue is whether the Court can engraft upon an unambiguous claims-made insurance policy a reasonable additional period of time after the policy period expires for reporting claims that arise late in the contract term.

Respondent (Dolan) is a law firm. It contracted with petitioner (Gulf) for a claims-made insurance policy for the period November 20, 1978 to November 20, 1979. Gulf's policy with Dolan required Gulf to pay all sums on behalf of the insured that the insured should become legally obligated to pay as damages for any claim arising out of professional legal services first made against the insured during the policy period. The policy required that the claim arise for services performed during the policy period; that the claim be known to or made against the insured during said period; and that the insured notify the insurer thereof during said period.

Dolan did not renew the Gulf policy but instead contracted with Lawyers Professional Liability Insurance Company (LPLIC) for a claims-made policy effective for the period November 20, 1979 to November 20, 1980. That policy contained a retroactive provision extending back to 1977, except for claims arising out of any occurrence prior to the effective date of the policy if the insured knew of it prior to the policy period.

On November 19, 1979, the Gulf policy's final day, Dolan received a letter from a client advising it that it no longer represented the client, suggesting that Dolan was grossly negligent in its professional performance, and requesting that Dolan place its malpractice carrier on notice.

Dolan notified LPLIC on or about December 6, 1979 of the existence of this claim. LPLIC informed Dolan [o]n January 16, 1980 that the claim would not be covered because the claim had been known to Dolan before the LPLIC policy was issued. Dolan then contacted Gulf in writing on February 12, 1980 concerning the malpractice claim. Gulf denied coverage, stating it was not notified during the policy period as expressly required in the contract.

Meanwhile, the aggrieved client sued Dolan and received a judgment in excess of $50,000. Dolan then commenced a suit for declaratory relief seeking a determination of whether Gulf or LPLIC or both were liable for the damages award. LPLIC's motion for summary judgment was denied; Gulf's was granted. Dolan appealed the granting of Gulf's motion for summary judgment to the district court. That court, in *Dolan, Fertig & Curtis v. Gulf Insurance Co.*, 419 So. 2d 1108 (Fla. Dist. Ct. App. 1982), reversed Gulf's summary judgment. It held that the contract was not ambiguous and that claims-made policies were not against public policy. However, "in order to make the contract fair," 419 So. 2d at 1110, the district court held that there should be a reasonable time after the policy period expires for reporting claims that are discovered late in the policy period, even though that time extends beyond the termination of the policy. On Petition for Rehearing, the district court certified the following question to us:

> As a matter of policy may the court require that "claims made" professional liability policies should (*sic*) be subjected to a reasonable additional period beyond the termination date of the policy for reporting claims that arise late in the contract term?

419 So. 2d at 1111. We have jurisdiction pursuant to article V, section 3(b)(4), Florida Constitution. We answer the certified question in the negative and quash the opinion of the district court.

The liability insurance policy at issue in this case is referred to as a claims-made policy (sometimes called a discovery policy) as distinct from an occurrence policy. An occurrence policy is a policy in which the coverage is effective if the negligent act or omission occurs within the policy period, regardless of the date of discovery or the date the claim is made or asserted. Initially, all professional liability policies were occurrence policies but because of numerous difficulties with this type of coverage, claims-made policies were initiated and the present trend is toward the latter type. Kroll, *The "Claims Made" Dilemma in Professional Liability Insurance*, 22 U.C.L.A. L. Rev. 925, 926 (1975). A claims-made policy is a policy "wherein the coverage is effective if the negligent or omitted act is discovered and brought to the attention of the insurer within the policy term." 7A Appleman 312. The essence, then, of a claims-made policy is notice to the carrier within the policy period.

Respondent has argued to this Court that we should strike down all claims-made liability insurance policies as being inequitable agreements and thus in violation of public policy. This we decline to do. Consistent with the views of numerous of our sister courts, we believe that claims-made policies are not "patently offensive or inimical to the public welfare . . . [nor do they] have a clear capacity to support or encourage conduct which is deleterious, anti-social or unlawful." *Rotwein v. General Accident Group*, 247 A.2d 370, 376 (N.J. Super. Ct. Law Div. 1968).

> Courts . . . should be guided by the rule of extreme caution when called upon to declare transactions void as contrary to public policy and should refuse to strike down contracts involving private relationships on this ground, unless it be made clearly to appear that there has been some great prejudice to the dominant public interest sufficient to overthrow the fundamental public policy of the right to freedom of contract between parties sui juris.

Bituminous Casualty Corp v. Williams, 17 So. 2d 98, 101 (Fla. 1944) (citations omitted). The great prejudice to the dominant public interest has not been clearly shown; we hold, therefore, that claims-made liability contracts, in general, are not against our public policy.

The district court, in the decision below, certified its question of great public importance on the basis of a contract having "no express provision fixing a *reasonable* time after the policy period expires for reporting claims that are discovered late in the policy period. . . ." 419 So. 2d at 1111 (emphasis supplied). We believe that the district court at this juncture has misapplied the concept of a "reasonable time" as it relates to a claims-made policy. Both claims-made and occurrence policies generally have provisions written into the contract that require, as a condition of the policy, that the insured give notice of the claim to the insurance carrier "immediately," "promptly," "as soon as practicable," or "within a reasonable time." This is bottomed on the premise of prejudice to the insurer who, because of a client's delayed notice to it, has, for example, lost the opportunity of making a timely investigation, forming an estimate of its rights and liabilities, or preventing fraud upon it.

Notice within an occurrence policy is not the critical and distinguishing feature of that policy type. Occurrence policies are built around an insurer who is liable for the insured's malpractice, no matter when discovered, so long as the malpractice occurred within the time confines of the policy period. Coverage depends on when the negligent act or omission occurred and not when the claim was asserted. The occurrence insurer, then, is faced with a "tail" that extends beyond the policy period itself. This "tail" is the lapse of time between the date of the error (within the policy period) and the time when a claim is made against the insured. The giving of notice is only a condition of the policy, and in no manner is it an extension of coverage itself. It does not matter when the insurer is notified of the claim by the insured, so long as the notification is within a reasonable time and so long as the negligent act or omission occurred within the policy period itself.

Claims-made policies, likewise, require that notification to the insurer be within a reasonable time. Critically, however, claims-made policies require that notice be given *during the policy period* itself. When an insured becomes aware of any event that could result in liability, then it must give notice to the insurer, and that notice must be given "within a reasonable time" or "as soon as practicable"—at all times, however, during the policy period.

With claims-made policies, the very act of giving an extension of reporting time after the expiration of the policy period, as the district court proposes, negates the inherent difference between the two contract types. Coverage depends on the claim being made and reported to the insurer during the policy period. Claims-made or discovery policies are essentially *reporting* policies. If the claim is reported to the insurer during the policy period, then the carrier is legally obligated to pay; if the claim is not reported during the policy period, no liability attaches. If a court were to allow an extension of reporting time after the end of the policy period, such is tantamount to an *extension of coverage* to the insured gratis, something for which the insurer has not bargained. This extension of coverage, by the court, so very different from a mere condition of the policy, in effect rewrites the contract between the two parties. This we cannot and will not do.[20]

As one commentator has noted:

> An underwriter who is secure in the fact that claims will not arise under the subject policy . . . after its termination or expiration can underwrite a risk and compute

---

20. The district court posed the following factual situation:

> A time comes at the end of the policy period when it may well be *impossible* for the insured to notify the company of a claim. The extreme case would involve the receipt of a claim by the insured minutes before the midnight expiration of the term on the last day thereof.

419 So. 2d at 1110. Without deciding the issue at this time, we believe that under the circumstances a "reasonable time" would not be germane to a claims-made contract; instead, if an impossibility prevented notice being given to an insurer at the very end of the policy period, it may well be that an insured would be relieved of giving notice during the period of such impossibility. In most instances, this would be measurably shorter than a "reasonable" period of time. That issue is not before us, however, and we decline to fully address it.

premiums with greater certainty. The insurer can establish his reserves without having to consider the possibilities of inflation beyond the policy period, upward-spiraling jury awards, or later changes in the definition and application of negligence.

Kroll at 928 (footnote omitted). This theoretically results in lower premiums for an insured since there is no open-ended "tail" after the expiration date of the policy. In fact, there can be no "tail" unless, of course, an extended reporting period is written into the claims-made policy itself. Some claims-made policies do provide that claims made against the insured during the policy period may be reported to the insurer during a specified period after the end of the policy period. *See James & Hackworth v. Continental Casualty Co.*, 522 F. Supp. 785 (N.D. Ala. 1980); *Gereboff v. Home Indemnity Co.*, 383 A.2d 1024 (R.I. 1978) (one year specified in the policy). The liability policy in this case did not so provide. However, it contained a provision[21] which gave the insured, in consideration of an additional premium, the right, which need be exercised by written notice not later than 30 days after the termination date of the policy, to have issued an endorsement providing an extended discovery period within which claims otherwise covered by the policy may be reported to the insurer after the end of the policy period. This extended discovery endorsement would thus have permitted Dolan to report the claim in question to Gulf at a point in time after the termination date of the policy period. Dolan, however, declined to avail itself of this quasi-"tail" provision.[22] "[T]he insured received what [it] paid for by the present policy, with premiums presumably reduced to reflect the limited coverage." *Livingston Parish School Board v. Fireman's Fund Am. Ins. Co.*, 282 So. 2d 478, 483 (La. 1973). Dolan cannot now be heard to complain. . . .

NOTES AND QUESTIONS

1. Dolan's claim against LPLIC eventually came to a similar end. That claim was denied based on the following exclusion in the LPLIC policy:

> This policy does not apply:
> . . . i) to any claim arising out of any acts or omissions occurring prior to the effective date of this policy if the insured at the effective date knew or could have reasonably foreseen that such acts or omissions might be expected to be the basis of a claim or suit.

---

21. That section reads:

In the event of termination of insurance either by non-renewal or cancellation of this policy, or termination of an extended discovery period, the Named Insured shall have the right upon payment of an additional premium (to be computed in accordance with the Company's rules, rates, rating plans and premiums applicable on the effective date of the endorsement) to have issued an endorsement(s) providing additional EXTENDED DISCOVERY PERIOD(S) in which claims otherwise covered by this policy may be reported. The limits of liability at the time this insurance is terminated shall be the limits applicable to each extended discovery period. Such right hereunder must, however, be exercised by the Named Insured by written notice not later than thirty (30) days after such termination date.

22. This right was available to Dolan at the time it notified LPLIC of the claim in question on December 6, 1979 and for a period of two weeks thereafter.

After losing the Gulf claim before the Florida Supreme Court, the Dolan firm obtained a summary judgment against LPLIC in Florida trial court. On appeal, the Florida Court of Appeal summarily reversed, stating:

> It is without dispute that prior to the effective date of the policy, Dolan had received notice from a former client, Charter Life Insurance Company, of the client's claim for malpractice arising out of acts or omissions which had occurred during the retroactive period (which claim in due course resulted in a judgment in favor of Charter against Dolan). Dolan's knowledge, prior to the effective date of the policy, of Charter's claim for malpractice falls squarely within the clear and unambiguous language of the exclusion.

LPLIC v. Dolan, 524 So. 2d 677, 678 (Fla. Dist. Ct. App. 1988). Does this mean that when switching claims-made policies, policyholders should always purchase the extended reporting period? Does that make sense?

2.   Professor Works has argued that courts and commentators have fundamentally misunderstood the late notice problem in claims-made policies and that the doctrine of disproportionate forfeiture should be available to relieve policyholders with claims-made policies, as well as those with occurrence policies. *See* Bob Works, *Excusing Nonoccurrence of Insurance Policy Conditions in Order to Avoid Disproportionate Forfeiture: Claims Made Formats as a Test Case,* 5 Conn. Ins. L.J. 505 (1998-1999). How might the insured have used the doctrine of disproportionate forfeiture in *Gulf v. Dolan?* Is the fact that notice was part of the claims-made "trigger" in the Gulf policy a distinguishing feature between *Dolan* and *Aetna v. Murphy?* Should that distinction make the difference that it did?

3.   In addition to the "forfeiture risk" that claims-made triggers have introduced into the liability insurance market (as illustrated in the Gulf case), claims-made triggers have increased the "classification risk" borne by policyholders. *Classification risk* is the risk that the insured's risk status will change so that the insured cannot get coverage for harm that it has already created. Professor Works describes classification risk as resulting from "triggers that fall so late in the tort liability sequence that the insurer knows of the potential claim before any policy has been triggered." Works, *supra*, at 632. This is likely to be particularly true in the "bet the company" products liability context. Typically, insurance companies insert claim-specific exclusions (sometimes called "laser" exclusions in light of their narrow focus) into an insurance policy as soon as it becomes clear that an insured will face a large number of claims. This has happened with asbestos, silicone breast implants, and toxic shock syndrome claims, among many others. Do you see why the insured bears more "classification risk" under a claims-made policy than an occurrence policy?

ROOT v. AMERICAN EQUITY SPECIALTY INSURANCE CO.

Court of Appeal of California, Fourth District, Division 3
30 Cal. Rptr. 3d 631 (2005)

SILLS, P.J. This case involves one of the worst nightmares faced by most every attorney, doctor, accountant or other professional covered by a malpractice insurance policy: the possibility of no malpractice coverage under a "claims made and reported" policy where a claim is made very late in the policy period and the insured learns of the claim under highly ambiguous circumstances, so the claim is not reported until there is confirmation of that claim, which is shortly after the policy has expired.

As we will now show, the reporting requirement in this case is such a condition that may be equitably excused under the particular circumstances of this case. Accordingly, we reverse the judgment obtained by the malpractice insurer on a summary judgment motion.

However, we emphasize the narrowness of today's decision. We will take great pains to show that by no means do we blanketly apply a blunderbuss "notice-prejudice" rule to this, or any other claims made and reported malpractice policy. (The notice-prejudice rule holds that "[u]nless an insurer can demonstrate actual prejudice from late notice, the insured's failure to provide timely notice will not defeat coverage." *See* Croskey, Heeseman & Johnson, Cal. Practice Guide: Insurance Litigation ¶3:168, p. 3-377 (The Rutter Group 2004).) In fact, we will devote some space to explaining why the notice-prejudice rule sweeps much too broadly in the context of claims made and reported policies and should not be applied here. (On this point we will thus agree with existing case law.) Even so, there are at least a few times when the established common law of contracts (bearing on when the non-occurrence of a condition precedent works a forfeiture) may operate to excuse the non-occurrence of a condition, and this case is one of them.

II.   FACTS

A.   THE CLAIM

Plaintiff Walter Root had a legal malpractice insurance policy with defendant American Equity Specialty Insurance Company. The policy period ran from February 28, 1998 to midnight, Sunday February 28, 1999. Afterwards, Root had legal malpractice insurance with another insurer, not otherwise disclosed in the record.

On Thursday, February 25, 1999, a former client of Root's, Farideh Jalali, filed a malpractice suit against Root. Jalali did not, however, serve notice of the suit until after February 28, 1999, i.e., into the policy period of Root's subsequent insurer. However, on February 25, i.e., with three days left on the American Equity malpractice policy, someone at a "legal journal" apparently got wind of the suit, because Root received a phone call from a person who identified herself as an employee of a "legal journal." (The record does not say *which* legal journal it was.) The caller sought Root's reaction to the filing of Jalali's suit.

Root thought that the call was a "possible prank," and in any event thought the reporter's call was nothing more than mere "hearsay regarding a potential claim."[23]

---

23. Here is the exact language from Root's declaration in opposition to the American Equity's eventual summary judgment motion: "Approximately one year later, on February 25, 1999, I received a telephone call from a person who identified herself as an employee of a legal journal who was seeking my reaction to the alleged filing of a lawsuit by Jalali accusing me of legal malpractice. At that time, I was a sole practitioner and I had never been sued by a client after more than 20 years of practicing law. I regarded the call as a possible prank and, in the middle of a typically busy day, did not immediately stop to think about when my professional liability policy expired, what its reporting requirements were, whether third party hearsay regarding a potential claim constituted a reportable event, or any of the other myriad implications of the call."

As it would turn out, the Jalali malpractice suit arose out of a settlement of a discrimination case in which Root had obtained a whopping $2.75 million for his client. This court would later, in reversing a judgment for malpractice obtained by Jalali (and before this court was ever aware of the instant coverage case), hold that Root had done "a very good job." *See Jalali v. Root,* 1 Cal. Rptr. 3d 689 (Cal. Ct. App. 2003). As we showed in that opinion, Jalali didn't even attempt to argue that her underlying discrimination case was worth anything more than the $2.75 million Root had obtained for her. He had drained the case for all it was worth.

Root left for a weekend vacation on Saturday, February 27, returning Tuesday, March 2. On that day Root read an article in the same "legal journal" describing Jalali's lawsuit.

Apparently, the call wasn't a prank after all. Root *immediately* notified American Equity of the claim.

American Equity denied any coverage under the policy because Root had not reported the claim during the policy period. Root defended the Jalali claim on his own (his own firm representing him) and eventually sued American Equity for breach of contract, seeking, essentially, fees incurred in defending (ultimately successfully) the Jalali action. As it turned out later in this appeal, Root also notified his subsequent insurer of the Jalali action, but that insurer denied coverage on the theory that the reporter's telephone call gave Root had a "basis" to believe that his representation of Jalali would lead to a claim.

In the coverage litigation with his first insurer, American Equity obtained a summary judgment based on the lack of any report during the policy period. It is from that judgment that Root has brought this appeal.

B.   THE CONTRACT TERMS

Now let us quote the relevant parts of the American Equity insurance contract. (Original bold emphasis omitted, original capitalization modified to regular type.)

First, there is a notice on the cover page which concerns the need for a claim to be both made in and reported by the insured during the policy period:

> This is a "Claims Made" policy. The coverage afforded by this policy is limited to claims arising from the performance of Professional Services which are first made against the Insured and reported in writing to the Company while the policy is in force. Please review the policy carefully and discuss the coverage thereunder with your insurance agent, broker or other representative.

Second, the insuring agreement, in pertinent part, obligates the insurer to indemnify the insured for

> all sums in excess of the Deductible stated in the Declarations which the Insured shall become legally obligated to pay as Damages as a result of claims first made against the insured during the policy period and reported in writing to the company during the policy period by reason of any act, error or omission. . . .

(This is set forth on ISO form LPL100-S.)

Third, there is a "claims" portion of the policy, which also addresses the time frame for reporting a claim—basically as "soon as practicable during the Policy Period." It reads:

As a condition precedent the Insured's right to the protection afforded by this insurance:

(a) the Insured shall, as soon as practicable during the Policy Period, give to the Company written notice of any Claim against the Insured which might be covered hereby, together with the fullest information obtainable. If the Claim is made or suit is brought against the Insured, the Insured shall immediately forward to the Company every demand, notice, summons or other process received by him or his representative; and

(b) if during the Policy Period the Insured shall first become aware of one or more specific acts, errors or omissions with respect to which no Claim has been made but which could reasonably be expected to form the basis of a Claim which might be covered hereby, the Insured shall, within the Policy Period, give the Company written notice of:

(i) the specific act, error or omission;

(ii) the injury or damage which has or may result from such act, error or omission; and

(iii) the circumstance by which the Insured first became aware of such act, error or omission.

However, this notice requirement has an interesting clause following it, which provides that, in essence, a *report* to the company during the policy period will be deemed *a claim* even if no actual demand has yet been made on the insured:

> If the insured strictly complies with the foregoing notice requirements, any Claim that may subsequently be made against the Insured arising out of such act, error or omission shall be deemed for the purposes of this insurance to have been made and reported in writing on the date such notice is received by the Company.

Next, there is the definition of "claim," which is quite short:

> "Claim" means: a demand, including service of suit or institution of arbitration proceedings, for money against an Insured.

There is also an exclusion for claims arising out of prior acts under circumstances the insured was reasonably aware would "be expected" to be the basis of a claim:

> This policy does not apply: . . .
> To any of the following described claims arising out of any circumstance, act, error or omission occurring prior to the initial Company coverage date: . . .
>
> (b) Any Claim against any Individual Insured who, on or before the Initial Company Coverage Date, knew, should reasonably have known, or had any basis to believe that any such circumstance, act, error or omission might reasonably be expected to be the basis of a Claim.

Finally, we should take note of what the policy does not have—an extended reporting period endorsement. In fact, on the record before us, we must accept as true Root's declaration that American Equity never offered him the chance to buy such an endorsement.

An extended reporting period endorsement would have given Root a set amount of extra time to report claims—which would be useful in cases, such as his, where the insured learns of a claim under arguably ambiguous circumstances. In the reported cases, such extended periods have typically been for 60 days. *See Gulf Ins. Co. v. Dolan, Fertig & Curtis*, 433 So. 2d 512, 516 (Fla. 1983) ("*Dolan, Fertig*").

III.   DISCUSSION

As we will now show, there is much uncharted territory involving the problem of the "last minute claim" in a claims made and reported policy[.] The case closest on point of which we are aware is the Florida Supreme Court's decision in *Gulf Ins. Co. v. Dolan, Fertig & Curtis*, 433 So. 2d at 512. In *Dolan, Fertig*, the policyholder (a law firm) became aware of a claim on the day before the policy expired—November 19 in a case where the policy expired November 20. The firm then reported the claim to its subsequent insurer—the one who, to use the insurance industry expression, "came on the risk" after November 20. However, that subsequent insurer denied the claim in January, and it wasn't until mid-February (February 12 to be exact) that the law firm reported the claim to its initial insurer—the one "on the risk" until November 20. The coverage litigation with its initial insurer made its way to the Florida Supreme Court.

In the Florida Supreme Court, however, the law firm could not resist the temptation to swing for the bleachers—nothing so modest as the law of condition precedent and disproportionate forfeiture. The law firm, after all, had missed the reporting deadline by almost three months. So the law firm went for the broadest possible ruling from the Florida high court, going even beyond reliance on the notice-prejudice rule. The firm asked the Florida Supreme Court to "strike down all claims-made liability insurance policies as being inequitable agreements and thus in violation of public policy." *Dolan, Fertig*, 433 So. 2d at 514.

Rather than succeeding in having the court strike down all claims-made policies, the law firm struck out. Its position was rejected for basically the same reason the notice-prejudice rule would be rejected—the fundamental principle that courts ought not to be handing out insurance coverage for claims that the insurer never bargained to pay and the insured never paid premiums for. *Dolan Fertig*, 433 So. 2d at 515 ("If a court were to allow an extension of reporting time after the end of the policy period, such is tantamount to an *extension of coverage* to the insured gratis, something for which the insurer has not bargained.").

But it also pays to read footnotes. If one only reads the text of the *Dolan, Fertig* opinion, one might gather the idea that even the tiniest, slightest extra time to report a claim after the policy period had expired was absolutely, 100 percent, never a possibility under a claims made and reported policy. *See Dolan, Fertig*, 433 So. 2d at 515. The *Dolan, Fertig* court was, however, not willing to go that far. In fact, when confronted with the hard hypothetical situation of a very, very late claim, made minutes before the expiration of the policy, posed by the intermediate Florida Court of Appeal, the Florida Supreme Court wilted. It could not bring itself to say that there was no possibility that a late claim might ever be excused:

The district court posed the following factual situation:

> A time comes at the end of the policy period when it may be *impossible* for the insured to notify the company of a claim. The extreme case would involve the receipt of a claim by the insured minutes before the midnight expiration of the term on the last day thereof. [Citation to appellate court's opinion.]

> Without deciding the issue at this time, we believe that under the circumstances a "reasonable time" would not be germane to a claims-made contract; instead, if an impossibility prevented notice being given to an insurer at the very end of the policy period, it may well be that an insured would be relieved of giving notice during the period of such impossibility. In most instances, this would be measurably shorter than a "reasonable" period of time. That issue is not before us, however, and we decline to fully address it.

Dolan, Fertig, 433 So. 2d at 516 n.1, original emphasis.

We need only note that the *Dolan, Fertig* court did not need to address the problem of the extremely late claim, because the notice that was ultimately tendered to the first insurer was late by about three months. Moreover, the insured law firm had been given the opportunity to purchase a 60-day "tail," which itself would have alleviated the late-claim hypothetical. *See Dolan, Fertig*, 433 So. 2d at 516.

We are thus aware of no case, such as the one before us, where the late report was made a de minimis time after the expiration of the policy and where the insured had not been given the opportunity to be protected under an extended claim reporting endorsement.

a. *The Problem*

The central issue in this case, then, is whether the policy period reporting requirement is a condition precedent of coverage that may be equitably excused when it works a forfeiture. The complicating factor is that the reporting requirement here is found in the insuring clause, and therefore at least *looks* as if it is an element of the defining scope of coverage rather than just a mere "condition." As we will now show, the reporting condition in Root's policy here does *not* go to basic coverage but quacks, walks, looks and functions like a condition, not an element of the fundamental risk insured.

b. *As a Matter of Textual Exegesis*

The first reason to conclude that the policy period reporting requirement is a condition is simple. The policy tells us it is.

Besides being in the insuring clause, the reporting condition is also repeated in the "claims" section of the policy: "*As a condition precedent* the Insured's right to the protection afforded by this insurance: [¶] (a) the Insured shall, as soon as practicable *during the Policy Period*, give to the Company written notice of any Claim against the Insured which might be covered hereby, together with the fullest information obtainable." Italics added.

It might be supposed that this particular language is a separate reporting condition, i.e., there is a reporting requirement as an element of coverage in the insuring clause which operates without regard to a need to give notice "as soon as practicable" and another, separate reporting requirement which is contained in the conditions section of the policy which makes the need to report "as soon as practicable" a condition of coverage. The problem with that line of reasoning, though, is that at least insofar as the policy seeks to put the onus on the insured to report a claim during the policy period, the two reporting requirements are identical. And by making the identical need to report during the policy period part of the insuring clause and an express condition, the policy becomes ambiguous (in fact, practically enigmatic!) as to whether the requirement to report during the policy period is an element of coverage, a condition, or both. One of the alternative interpretations of that ambiguity is that there is really one requirement to report during the policy period, announced in the insuring clause and further delineated in the conditions, and that one basic requirement is indeed a condition. Superfluity does not vitiate, and in fact there are occasions when it defines.

c.   As a Matter of Commercial Reality

But even if the policy did not contain the seeds of its own cognitive dissonance on the problem of whether the policy period reporting requirement is an element of coverage or condition, an examination of the commercial reality behind the reporting requirement provides ample proof that it is, fundamentally, a condition.

To do that, we must first examine the reason why insurers changed from "occurrence" to "claims made" (and then "claims made and reported") policies in the first place. It is a little more complex than it has been made out in some of the cases.

The key is the pricing of premiums. The core idea behind the move to claims made insurance policies was to *close the gap* between the time when the insurer *prices* a risk and the time when the insurer may incur an obligation to *pay on* that risk.[24]

On reflection, of course, the idea of closing the pricing gap is unremarkable. Pretty much everybody who has the slightest acquaintance with insurance law knows that the longer the gap between the time the insurer takes the premiums and the time when the insurer pays out on the risk, the more likely the insurer is to get burned. *See Pacific Employers,* 270 Cal. Rptr. at 779. ("In an effort to reduce their exposure to an unpredictable and lengthy 'tail' of lawsuits filed years after the occurrence they agreed to protect against, underwriters shifted to the 'claims made' policy.") Insurers, like all businesses in a free market, have the fundamental problem of making decisions now that depend on future events, and their survival depends on guessing right often enough to be profitable.

Perhaps the most striking example of insurers charging low premiums to insure against occurrences that would later come back to cost them dearly has been in the area of pollution liability and toxic torts, where claims were made

---

24. *See* Works, *Excusing Nonoccurrence of Insurance Policy Conditions in Order to Avoid Disproportionate Forfeiture: Claims-Made Formats as a Test Case,* 5 Conn. Ins. L.J. at 516:

> Other things being equal, the insurer's financial people will want to employ a policy trigger that falls later in the sequence than earlier, in order to shorten the time between when a policy obligation is priced and when the extent of the obligation is determined. Statistical models of insurance pools that help inform insurance underwriting and pricing decisions depend in part on the quality of the loss frequency and severity estimations they employ. Consequently, the longer the period for which one must "develop" immature historical loss data in order to estimate ultimate loss costs for policies written in the past, and the longer into the future one must peer in an effort to trend those estimates of past loss costs in order to make predictions about future loss costs for new policies, the greater the likelihood for error.

in the 1980's and 1990's against policies which were priced in the 1950's and 1960's. *See, e.g., Aerojet-General Corp. v. Transport Indemnity Co.,* 948 P.2d 909 (Cal. 1997) (pollution claims brought in late 1970's and early 1980's involved policies "incepting as early as 1950"); *Dart Industries, Inc. v. Commercial Union Ins. Co.,* 52 P.3d 79 (Cal. 2002) (toxic drug claims made against drug company from 1970's onward involved policies going back as early as 1946).

Professional malpractice insurance underwriting is likewise particularly vulnerable to gaps between the time of pricing and the time of obligation. *See Pacific Employers,* 270 Cal. Rptr. at 779 ("Underwriters soon realized, however, that 'occurrence' policies were unrealistic in the context of professional malpractice because the injury and the negligence that caused it were often not discoverable until years after the delictual act or omission.").

From the foregoing, we can deduce that the length of time between premium pricing and the surfacing of insurer obligation to pay can become a risk in itself. Now, with traditional "occurrence" policies, the risk of a claim surfacing at some future date after the policy period has expired is borne by the insurer. With pure "claims made" policies, that risk is shifted to the insured, who pays present dollars for protection against claims that will themselves be paid in those same dollars, that is, without regard to inflation and at a time relatively close to the insurer's pricing decision. There is no disproportion, as there can be in occurrence policies, between premiums paid to the insurer and outgo from the insurer.

But what *risk,* we must ask, does the addition of the reporting requirement in claims made and reported policies actually shift from the insurer to the insured? The basic risk of the late-surfacing claim—whether surfacing two days or 20 years after the policy period has expired—has already been addressed by going to claims made coverage. Since the claim must still be made during the policy period, and the prosecution of that claim is independent of any report of it by the insured to the insurer,[25] no additional pricing risk is shifted by the reporting requirement.

So what is shifted by the reporting requirement? Two things.

The first, and most important, is the administrative convenience of *monitoring* potential payouts. In a word, a reporting requirement gives the insurer administrative "closure" and that is surely worth something, at least to the insurer, which is passed on to the insured in the form of lower premiums. Anyone who has ever dealt with insurers and their claims adjusters knows that they tend to put at least a little value on simply being able to close a file. Perhaps more importantly, a policy period reporting requirement facilitates the quicker accumulation of loss history. By the end of the policy period the insurer definitely knows whether X risk generated any claims in Y period, and it knows it quicker (but only slightly quicker) with a claims made and reported policy than it knows it with a pure claims made policy. (However, even this bit of information is of only limited value: While the reporting requirement means that the insurer may

---

25. Thus, for example, suppose that a suit is filed against the insured during the policy period but not served (and the insured has no knowledge of the suit otherwise) until well after the policy period has expired. And then the malpractice suit is prosecuted, in due course. Note that the *pricing risk* which engendered the move to claims made policies in the first place is no different whether the policy is written on a pure claims made or a claims made and reported basis. The report has no effect on what the insurer would ordinarily pay out in the normal course of the prosecution of the claim.

know *whether* any claims were filed, it is unlikely to know *how much* it will have to pay out on any late made but timely reported claims.)

The second shift is the risk of claims which would—and this is important—*otherwise* be within the scope of basic coverage of the policy, but which the insurer need not pay because of an action the *insured* does not take. As such, it operates as a simple forfeiture clause: Don't report in the policy period, and lose coverage you otherwise would have had.

It should be apparent that considered either way—either as a shift of administrative monitoring costs or as a naked forfeiture clause—the reporting requirement functions as a condition precedent to coverage, not as a definition of coverage. Put it this way: Assuming timely report by the insured, the risk borne by the insurer on the insured's behalf is exactly the same as in pure claims made coverage. The addition of a reporting requirement therefore doesn't go to risk of a claim against the insured (i.e., what sort of claim might fall within the ambit of the costs the insurer promises to cover), but to the logically independent risk that the insured simply will not report the claim in time.

The Equitable Excuse of a Condition Is Not Adoption of the Notice-Prejudice Rule

The general rule is an equitable one, which basically allows the court to excuse a condition when it results in a forfeiture. We must now hasten to add that this mere possibility is considerably different from the notice-prejudice rule which the courts rejected in *Dolan, Fertig.*

The notice-prejudice rule is, ironically enough, a fairly inflexible instrument. Prejudice is hard to show under the rule. In the *Flack* case, for example, the court read *Campbell v. Allstate*, 384 P.2d at 155, for the proposition that the burden is on the insurer to show that it has been prejudiced by any delay, and further that mere passage of time does not even establish a presumption or inference of prejudice. *See Flack*, 85 Cal. Rptr. at 693. Thus even though the insurer claimed that it had been deprived of the chance to settle a case for a small sum early in the proceedings, or of having its own counsel represent it, that was not enough. *See id.* at 693.

Given that inflexibility, it is no wonder why [the] *Dolan, Fertig* court [was] loathe to agree with the insureds that the notice-prejudice rule could be applied to the case. To do so would have effectively obliterated the "and reported" part of the "claims made and reported" policy. . . .

We agree with that analysis. Consider the inflexible breadth of the notice-prejudice rule: It can apply to cases involving delays many months, perhaps even years, after the expiration of the policy period, and it puts the burden on the insurer to show prejudice from even long delays in reporting. Application of the rule thus fundamentally rewrites the claims made and reported contract into a pure claims made contract.

But the possible equitable excuse of a condition precedent is much more flexible and nuanced, and does no violence to the claims made and reported nature of the policy.

First of all, it is not a bright-line test. Equities vary with the peculiar facts of each case. Sometimes—indeed most of the time—it will not be equitable to excuse the non-occurrence of the condition, so it is not excused. Granted, the factually intense nature of the inquiry may make summary judgment more difficult for insurers to obtain in certain cases (like this one), but that is a result that comes with California's common law rule that conditions can be excused if equity requires it.

For example, in the present case, the fact that the insurer did not give the insured the opportunity to buy an extended reporting endorsement which would (if it was anything like the ones in the reported cases) have given him an extra 60 days to report any claims may be of significance. Had Root been given that opportunity, for example, equity might not require excuse of the condition, because its excuse would, in effect, be to give Root the benefit of something that he had the opportunity to buy and passed up. The same might be said if Root had had sufficient time to conduct an investigation as to whether a claim had indeed been made against him,[26] or had delayed reporting the claim beyond the day on which he received confirmation of the claim. But given this record the facts are sufficient to support the equitable excuse of the reporting condition, so summary judgment should not have been granted. Given these facts it would be "most inequitable" to enforce the condition precedent of a report during the policy period.

The judgment is reversed with directions for the trial court to conduct further proceedings not inconsistent with this opinion.

NOTES AND QUESTIONS

1. This case presents an opportunity to revisit the disproportionate forfeiture doctrine introduced in Chapter 2. This is the first case in the book since *Aetna v. Murphy* in which a court has explicitly used that doctrine. When you sit down to review the materials for your final exam, it would be useful to consider whether there are other cases in which disproportionate forfeiture could have been used, or in which the underlying intuition—that insurance companies shouldn't be able to avoid a claim based on a technicality—might explain the result.

2. In an unpublished opinion issued soon after *Root,* the same California court found for the insurance company in a case involving the following facts:

Factual Timeline:

- Nov. 1, 2000 to Nov. 1, 2001: policy period 1
- Oct. 1, 2001: insured receives letter announcing plaintiffs' intention to file suit.
- Oct. 16, 2001: lawsuit filed
- Nov. 1, 2001 to Nov. 2, 2002: policy period 2 (same insurer)

---

26. For example, the question arises: Why couldn't Root, on the Thursday when he received the call ostensibly from a reporter at a legal journal, have simply faxed or emailed what he had learned, and easily protected himself? The answer is that Root didn't learn of "the claim" that Thursday; at most he learned of the *possibility* of a claim against him in a case where he had every objective reason to think there would be no claim. Given that circumstance, Root was not free simply to report the claim to his insurer on the theory that it would do no harm to make the report. It might very well have harmed him to make such a report. To do so would have been to prejudice his chances of being able to report the claim to his second insurer. By making a report in the policy period of insurer one, most lawyers know that insurer two will pounce on the fact of that report to argue that the claim did not occur in its policy period. (As it turned out, though, his forbearance ultimately didn't do him any good.) The point is, given information that only raises a bare possibility of a claim, an insured must do some investigating. And here, while it may not have been impracticable to simply fax over notice to American Equity, it surely was impracticable, during the last two business days remaining on the policy, to investigate whether Jalali had, indeed, sued him. Depending on the court, for example, even sending over an attorney service to obtain a copy of the complaint might not work. Clerks records might not be up to the latest minute and a copy of the complaint might not be readily obtainable. Moreover, since we are dealing with a case that proceeds from a summary judgment motion, all reasonable inferences must be resolved in favor of the responding party, including the inference that any investigation necessary to ascertain whether there really was a claim against him could not have been completed by the close of business Friday.

- Nov. 6, 2001: lawsuit served
- Dec. 11, 2001: insured provides notice to insurer

Policies 1 & 2:

- Both issued by the same insurer
- Both issued on a claims made and reported form similar to the policies in *Root.*
- Policy 1 had the following claim reporting provision: "if a claim is made against any Insured you must . . . notify us as soon as practicable, but in no event later than 30 days after the end of the policy period.
- Policy 2 had a reasonably foreseeable claim exclusion analogous to exclusion in Root's later policy

See Goings & Goings, Inc. v. U.S. Risk, Inc., 2005 WL 3320863 (Cal. Ct. App. Dec. 8, 2005). How are these facts different from those in *Root?* Should the fact that both policies were issued by the same insurer affect the result? Would it make a difference to know that the insurer had made no claims under Policy 1? Suppose the policyholder had already filed claims under Policy 1 that had the potential to exhaust the aggregate limits of that policy?

3. In *Root,* the California court goes to great lengths to distinguish *Dolan, Fertig.* Are you persuaded? Suppose the *Root* case had come first. How might the lawyers for the Dolan, Fertig law firm have used *Root* to obtain insurance coverage for its clients?

This is a revised version of the Section contained in TD No. 1. We included the entire comments from this Section in this casebook because they provide a good opportunity to review the difference between occurrence and claims made coverage. Once you understand the pricing and reserving points in comments d and e, you'll understand claims made insurance better than most practicing lawyers.

Restatement of the Law Liability Insurance

Preliminary Draft No. 3

§36. Notice and Reporting Conditions[27]

(1) The failure of the insured to satisfy a notice-of-claim condition excuses an insurer from performance of its obligations under a liability insurance policy only if the insurer demonstrates that it was prejudiced as a result.

---

27. The Reporters' Memorandum to PD No. 3 says the following about this Section:

PD No. 3 includes a completely revised subsection (2) that explicitly adopts the "no prejudice" rule for claim reporting conditions while including an exception to that rule that is more closely tailored to the disproportionate forfeiture concern that led us to draft the former §37 (2). Note that we received some comments in advance of the Annual Meeting that led us to conclude that the draft of §37 included in TD No. 1 was conceptually flawed and, thus, we requested that it not be voted upon at the Meeting.

Section 37 in TD No. 1 provided as follows:

§37. Notice-of-Claim Conditions

(1) The failure of the insured to satisfy a notice-of-claim condition excuses an insurer from performance of its obligations under a liability insurance policy only if the insurer demonstrates that it was prejudiced as a result, except as stated in subsection (2).

(2) The rule stated in subsection (1) does not apply when a claim is first reported to the insurer after the end of the reporting period of a claims-made-and-reported policy, provided that the insured was afforded a reasonable time in which to report the claim.

(2) With respect to claims first reported after the conclusion of the claim-reporting period in a claims-made-and-reported policy, the failure of the insured to satisfy the claim-reporting condition in the policy excuses an insurer from performance under the policy without regard to prejudice, except when all of the following requirements are met:

(A) The policy does not contain a reasonable extended reporting period;

(B) The claim at issue is made too close to the end of the policy period to allow the insured a reasonable time to satisfy the condition; and

(C) The insured reports the claim to the insurer within a reasonable time.

Comment:

a. Notice-of-claim conditions. Liability insurance policies commonly contain terms that condition coverage on the timely provision by the insured of a notice of claim. The purpose of such conditions is to allow insurers to obtain the information that they need to investigate and defend legal actions. Notice-of-claim conditions are the most frequently excused conditions in liability insurance policies. The vast majority of jurisdictions have recognized the notice-prejudice rule followed in this Section. When applying a prejudice requirement, courts generally take a case-by-case approach to evaluating the substantiality of the asserted harm. What is required is that the failure to satisfy the condition prevented the insurer from protecting its interests in a significant way. See §34, Comment *d.* The insurer bears the burden of proving prejudice. See §34, Comment *e.*

b. Reasons for the notice-prejudice rule. The notice-prejudice rule addresses several problems with strict enforcement of notice-of-claim conditions. First, strict enforcement exposes insureds to a substantial risk of disproportionate forfeiture of insurance coverage, because the value of the coverage to the insured often substantially exceeds the harm to the insurer from the breach of the notice condition. The notice-prejudice rule allows the insurer to avoid coverage if, in fact, the delay caused significant harm, while preserving coverage for the insured in those cases in which the delay did not. Second, strict enforcement of notice-of-claim conditions rewards insurers whose policies contain unreasonable, difficult-to-satisfy conditions, thereby encouraging the drafting of such conditions. The notice-prejudice rule allows the insurer to avoid coverage only when the delay caused significant harm, thereby providing no encouragement for unreasonable notice conditions. Third, strict enforcement of the condition interferes with the objectives of the underlying liability regime, which depend in many instances on the presence of liability insurance. See §34, Comment *g.* Because the notice-prejudice rule is more closely tailored to the objective of the notice condition—access to the information needed to investigate and defend legal actions—it interferes less with the objectives of the liability regime than a strict-condition approach.

Illustrations

1. Insured Driver hits Pedestrian, causing serious injuries that lead to more than $100,000 in medical expenses. Police arrive at the scene and charge Driver with Driving Under the Influence. Pedestrian sues Driver. Driver ignores the suit and never provides notice to Insurer. Two years later, Pedestrian obtains a default judgment against Driver and, for the first time, notifies Insurer, seeking payment of the applicable $100,000 limit of coverage under the automobile

insurance policy Insurer issued to Driver that was in force at the time of the accident. Insurer denies coverage based on Driver's failure to satisfy the notice condition in the policy. Insurer cannot show that it was prejudiced by the extensive delay in receiving notice because Driver was plainly at fault and Pedestrian's damages exceeded the policy limits and, thus, Insurer would have had to pay the full policy limits even if it had received prompt notice of the accident. Driver's failure to satisfy the notice condition in the policy does not excuse Insurer's obligation to cover the suit.

2. Insured Driver 1 is in an accident with Driver 2 at an intersection. The accident causes serious injuries to Driver 2, leading to more than $25,000 in medical expenses. There is a witness at the scene who reported to a police officer that Driver 1 was proceeding through the intersection at a modest speed, with a green light, and that Driver 2 was running a red light. Driver 2 files a lawsuit against Driver 1. Driver 1 ignores the suit and never provides notice to Insurer. Two years later Driver 2 obtains a default judgment against Driver 1 and, for the first time, notifies Insurer seeking payment of the applicable $25,000 limit of coverage under the automobile liability insurance policy Insurer issued to Driver 1 that was in force at the time of the accident. Insurer denies coverage based on Driver's failure to satisfy the notice condition in the policy. Even if Insurer would be able to set aside the default judgment, it was prejudiced by the extensive delay in receiving notice because it cannot now locate the witness, despite making reasonable efforts, and there is no other evidence that conclusively demonstrates that Driver 1 was not at fault. Thus, Driver 1's failure to satisfy the notice condition in the policy excuses Insurer's obligation to cover the suit.

c. Claim-reporting conditions in claims-made-and-reported policies. A claims-made-and-reported policy is a claims-made policy that includes a term in the insuring agreement section of the policy that conditions coverage on the insured reporting the claim within a specified period. Courts have referred to such conditions in a claims-made-and-reported policy as "claim-reporting conditions," to distinguish them from the notice-of-claim conditions referred to in subsection (1) and Comments *a* and *b* of this Section. Courts generally conclude that putting the reporting requirement in the insuring agreement of a claims-made policy makes that condition sufficiently material to the contract that the ordinary notice-prejudice rule does not apply. This conclusion is based on a determination that a claim-reporting condition in a claims-made-and-reported policy has additional purposes beyond the traditional claims-management purpose of a notice-of-claim condition. These additional purposes are: (a) simplifying insurers' reserving practices and (b) reducing the amount of uncertainty in insurance pricing.

Typically, the claim-reporting condition in contemporary claims-made-and-reported policies requires the claim to be reported before the end of what is known as an "extended-reporting period," which is the period between the end of the policy period and the deadline for reporting claims, although there are still some claims-made-and-reported policies sold in which the claim-reporting deadline is the end of the policy period. Claims-made-and-reported policies typically also contain a second, traditional notice-of-claim condition in the policy. A claims-made policy that contains only the traditional notice condition, and not the claim-reporting condition in the insuring agreement, is not a claims-made-and-reported policy and, thus, only the ordinary notice-prejudice rule would apply to such a policy.

d. The reserving justification for strict enforcement of the claim-reporting condition. A claim-reporting condition in a claims-made policy has the potential to affect liability insurance reserving practices more significantly than a notice-of-claim condition in an occurrence policy. A "reserve" is an accounting entry in the financial statements of an insurer that represents the insurer's estimate of the losses that it will have to pay in the future for a defined set of claims or under a defined set of policies. Insurance accounting distinguishes between "case reserves"—which are reserves for specific claims that have been reported to the insurer—and reserves for losses that are "incurred but not reported (IBNR)". An insurer's IBNR loss reserve is supposed to reflect the insurer's best estimate of the amounts that it will have to pay on claims that have not yet been reported under the class of policies for which the insurer is setting the IBNR loss reserve. If there is a date certain after which no new claims can be reported under a group of policies issued during a specific time, the insurer would be able to set a zero-dollar IBNR reserve at that time for that group of policies. A claim-reporting condition that sets an outside limit on the date by which all claims under a policy must be reported allows the insurer to have a date certain on which it can reduce its IBNR reserves on that policy to zero.

It is not possible for an insurer to use a notice-of-claim condition to achieve a zero-dollar IBNR reserve goal under an occurrence policy. Occurrence policies are triggered by harms or activities that take place during the policy period, and there is the possibility of claims being reported many months or even years after the policy period. With the passage of time, the likelihood of new claims generally declines, but asbestos liability under commercial general-liability insurance policies serves as the cautionary counter-example. This means that strict application of a notice-of-claim condition in occurrence or accident policies could not have as material an effect on insurers' IBNR reserving practice as could the strict application of a claim-reporting condition in claims-made policies.

The significance of this IBNR difference can be overstated, however. The uncertainty attendant to liability insurance reserving is not eliminated when the insurer is able to set a zero-dollar IBNR reserve. There is ample room for uncertainty with regard to the case reserves set on the claims for which the insurer has received the required report. Moreover, modest extensions of the time before the insurer can set the zero-dollar IBNR reserve are unlikely to have a material impact on the insurer's financial condition. Put another way, it is the ability of the insurer to set an enforceable deadline on when a claim may be reported that can be material to the insurer's financial reports, not the precise date of the deadline. Moreover, there is no particular reason that the deadline needs to be coterminous with the end of the policy period, especially because setting that deadline at the end of the policy period would lead to a disproportionate forfeiture in cases in which the insured learns of the claim too close to the end of the policy period to allow the insured a reasonable time to report that claim to the insurer by the deadline.

e. The pricing-uncertainty justification for strict enforcement of the claim-reporting condition. The second justification for the claims-made-and-reported policy exception to the notice-prejudice rule is the potential increase in pricing uncertainty that could result from allowing claims to be reported too long after the end of the policy period. All other things being equal, the further into the future the insurer needs to estimate its losses, the more uncertainty there will be in that estimate. Because occurrence policies expose insurers to potential claims quite far into the future, even extensive delay in receiving notice of claims is unlikely to materially increase the uncertainty involved in pricing an occurrence policy. By contrast, because one of the main objectives of the claims-made form of coverage was to shorten the period between the payment of premiums for a policy and the payment of claims under that policy in order to reduce that uncertainty, a delay in receiving notices under claims-made policies that regularly goes well beyond the end of the policy period could lead to a meaningful increase in pricing uncertainty for those claims-made policies.

It is important to note, however, that this potential increase in pricing uncertainty also does not provide adequate justification for strict enforcement of a claim-reporting condition in all cases in which a claim is first close to the end of the policy period. As with the reserving benefit, the reduction in pricing uncertainty comes from the presence of an enforceable deadline on receiving claim reports. The insurer receives substantially the same reduction in pricing uncertainty from a claim-reporting condition that provides the insured with a reasonable time to report a claim. Accordingly, the application of a deadline for reporting a claim to a claim that the policyholder cannot reasonably report by that deadline would create a disproportionate forfeiture.

f. A reasonable extended reporting period. Contemporary claims-made-and-reported policies commonly provide for an additional period of time, after the end of the policy period, during which the insured may report a claim that was first made during the policy period. This additional period of time is generally referred to as an "extended reporting period." Typically, claims-made-and-reported policies include an extended reporting period of at least 60 days, often longer. Whether a 60 day extended reporting period is a "reasonable extended reporting period" in all cases is beyond the scope of this Restatement, although it should be noted that some states have statutes requiring the inclusion of such an extended reporting period in a claims-made-and-reported policy and such statutes could be regarded as a legislative determination that 60 days is reasonable.

g. When the policy does not contain a reasonable extended reporting period. Published opinions rarely address the situation in which an insured did not have a reasonable time in which to report a claim. The vast majority of published opinions that strictly enforce claims-reporting conditions in claims-made-and-reported policies involve claims in which the policy contained an extended-reporting period or the insured reported the claim unreasonably long after the end of the policy period. Published opinions often describe claims that are reported over a year after the policy period ended, and there are few published opinions, especially in recent years, that involve claims that are reported less than three months after the end of the policy period. This is likely the result of the fact that most insurers wisely choose not to press to judgment denials of coverage that are based on claim-reporting requirements that an insured could not reasonably comply with in the circumstances. Among the few published opinions to address this situation, the majority strictly enforce the claim-reporting condition, but recent, more persuasive authority concludes that the loss of coverage due to the failure of the insurer to provide the insured with a reasonable time to report the claim in the circumstances is a disproportionate forfeiture. That is the approach followed in this Section.

Relaxing the requirement that a claim must be reported during the policy period, by requiring that the insured must have had a reasonable time to satisfy the condition, does not pose a material increase in risk to the insurer. An insurer that grants the insured a reasonable time to report a claim receives all of the legitimate benefits of strict enforcement of a claim-reporting condition that is included in the insuring agreement of a claims-made policy. While there are undoubted benefits to prompt reporting, the modest delay needed to allow the insured a reasonable time to report a claim should rarely, if ever, harm the insurer. And, if the delay does harm the insurer, the ordinary prejudice rule would protect the insurer. The only additional benefit that an insurer receives when it fails to grant the insured a reasonable time to provide notice is an illegitimate one: cost savings attributable to non-payment of claims that are forfeited by insureds because there was insufficient time to report those claims.

i. Prejudice is required when notice is late but given before the end of the reporting period. The notice-prejudice rule applies to claims reported before the end of the reporting period under the policy because the justifications for the claims-made-and-reported exception to the notice-prejudice rule do not apply until that period is over. Until that time, the insurer remains subject to additional claims and, thus, subject to uncertainty about the number and severity of the claims that will be reported under the policy as well as the IBNR reserve.

Illustrations

3. Attorney is insured under a claims-made-and-reported lawyers' professional liability insurance (LPL) policy issued by Insurer with no extended reporting period, meaning that the reporting period is coterminous with the policy period, which ends on midnight, December 31, Year 1. On the morning of Christmas Eve day (December 24), Attorney receives a voice mail from a reporter asking for a comment about a lawsuit that Attorney's former client is said to be preparing to file against Attorney. Under the terms of the Attorney's LPL policy, this voice mail constitutes the making of a claim on December 24. Attorney does not respond to the reporter's call, planning to address the issue, if there is one, after the holidays. As of midnight December 31, Insurer A issues Attorney a new LPL policy with a policy period from December 31, Year 1, to December 31, Year 2. The new LPL policy provides coverage only for claims first made during Year 2. On January 6 Attorney is served with a complaint filed by the former client alleging malpractice. Attorney immediately sends the complaint to Insurer. Attorney's failure to satisfy the claim-reporting condition in the Year 1 policy is excused because the claim was made too close to the end of the policy period to allow Attorney a reasonable time to satisfy the condition in the circumstances and Attorney reported the claim to Insurer within a reasonable time.

4. Same facts as Illustration 1, except that the LPL policy contains a statutorily mandated 60-day extended reporting period, which ends on March 1, Year 2, and Attorney does not report the claim to Insurer until April 1, Year 2. Based on the statute mandating the 60-day extended reporting period and the extensive publicity within the Bar regarding the nature of claims-made-and-reported LPL insurance, a 60-day extended reporting period is a reasonable extended reporting period. Thus, Attorney's failure to satisfy the claim-reporting condition in the Year 1 policy is not excused, without regard to whether in these specific

circumstances, the claim was made too close to the end of the policy period to allow Attorney a reasonable time to satisfy the condition in the circumstances, or whether Attorney reported the claim to the insurer within a reasonable time.

5. Attorney is insured under an LPL policy issued by Insurer with a one-year policy period and a 180-day extended-reporting period. Halfway through the policy period Attorney receives a letter from a former client alleging that Attorney committed malpractice. Under the terms of the Attorney's LPL policy, this letter constitutes the making of a claim that must be reported "as soon as practicable" and before the end of the extended-reporting period. For many months, Attorney unsuccessfully attempts to resolve the matter with the former client. Shortly before the 180-day-extended-reporting period is over, Attorney reports the matter to Insurer as a claim under the LPL policy. Insurer reserves the right to contest coverage based on Attorney's failure to comply with the requirement in the policy that the claim be reported "as soon as practicable." Because Attorney reported the claim within the reporting period specified in the LPL policy, Attorney's failure to satisfy the "as soon as practicable" condition excuses Insurer from its obligations under the policy only if Insurer can demonstrate that it was prejudiced as a result of the delay.

MARCELLA DEMOYNE'S LATE NOTICE PROBLEM

This problem offers a preview of some of the conflict of interest issues addressed in Chapter 5. Please do not focus at this point on the merits of the malpractice claim. You'll be in a better position to evaluate that claim after completing Chapter 5. For the moment, focus simply on the late notice and claims-made issues.

Marcella DeMoyne is the partner in her law firm responsible for working with the firm's broker, Able Insurance, to purchase insurance coverage for the firm. Traditionally, the firm has purchased its claims-made malpractice insurance from Lawyers Ltd.

In the summer of 2010, one of the Able brokers told Marcella that Attorneys' Assurance was offering very competitive premiums for law firms like hers. Marcella authorized Able to solicit a quote from Attorneys' Assurance, and, sure enough, the quote came in significantly below the renewal premium that Lawyers Ltd. quoted for the firm, with the same retroactive date (January 1, 1990) and other policy provisions as the Lawyers Ltd. policy. Marcella and her partners decided to make the switch at the renewal date of December 31, 2010.

Following the recommendation of Able, Marcella sent out a memo to her partners one month before the renewal date, informing them that whenever law firms switch from one malpractice carrier to another disputes can arise over which carrier is responsible for which claims, particularly when claims arise around the time of the switch. In the memo, Marcella asked her partners to inform her of any situations that could potentially result in a claim, so that she could put Lawyers Ltd. on notice before the policy expired.

In response to her memo, Marcella received a call from her partner, Roger Fischer, informing her that he had recently defended a bar fight case in which his client had been the subject of a verdict in excess of the policy limits. The liability insurance carrier in the case had so far refused to pay the claim, and the plaintiffs in the case had stated that they would not accept a post-trial assignment of rights in settlement of the claim. Roger said that he was not sure that the case would result in a suit against the firm, but that there was a real possibility that it would. The plaintiffs' lawyer in the case was known to be very aggressive. Roger had heard that the lawyer had said in a bar association meeting: "My job is to get the maximum recovery for my client. When I get an excess verdict, the first place I look is the defendant's liability carrier. The second place I look is the defense lawyer's malpractice carrier."

On December 15, 2010, Marcella wrote a letter to Lawyers Ltd. informing the company that she was placing it on notice of a claim against the firm arising out of Roger's defense of the bar fight case. Lawyer Ltd. immediately wrote back, stating that it would not open a file on the case because there was not yet a claim.

On February 1, 2011, Roger received a letter from the plaintiffs' lawyer in the bar fight case, inviting Roger to attend a settlement meeting with his client's liability insurance company. The letter stated that Max should obtain a new defense lawyer because, in the plaintiffs' lawyer's view, Roger had committed malpractice in the defense of the case by not attempting to settle the case on terms that would have protected the client's assets; and, therefore, Roger should put his malpractice carrier on notice and make sure that a representative of the malpractice carrier attended the settlement meeting as well.

Marcella discussed the letter with her Able broker, who suggested that she notify both Lawyers Ltd. and Attorneys' Assurance of the claim. She did so. Lawyers Ltd. denied coverage for the potential malpractice claim on the grounds that, if a claim had been made at all, it was first made after the end of the policy period. Attorneys' Assurance denied coverage on the grounds that the claim arose out of circumstances that Marcella's firm knew or should have known would result in a claim before the inception of the policy period.

The Lawyers Ltd. and Attorneys' Assurance policies each contained the following relevant provisions:

> The Underwriter will pay, on behalf of the Insured Persons, Loss from claims first made during the policy period arising out of the rendering or failure to render professional services to which this insurance applies, except to the extent that such Loss is paid by any other insurance or as indemnification from any source.
>
> This insurance applies only if the rendering of or failure to render professional services did not occur before the Retroactive Date, if any, shown in the Declarations or after the end of the policy period.
>
> A claim by a person or organization seeking damages will be deemed to have been made at the earlier of the following times:
>
> When notice of such claim is received and recorded by any insured or by us, whichever comes first; or
>
> When we make settlement. . . .

Analyze the potential for coverage under the two policies. Is it possible that there is no coverage for the claim? How might you distinguish this case from the *Dolan* case?

CHAPTER
5

Liability Insurance Relationship Issues

In Chapter 4, we examined the coverage provided by standard liability insurance policies without focusing in any detail on the complicating effects of an actual or potential tort lawsuit against the insured (the "underlying claim"). The existence of an underlying claim means that there are both claim-paying and defense aspects to liability insurance coverage. These two aspects are often referred to in shorthand as *indemnity coverage* and *defense coverage*. Although it is not always possible to draw a clear line between the two, indemnity coverage generally is the protection that the carrier provides against the insured having to pay a judgment, whereas defense coverage is the protection that the carrier provides against the insured having to pay the costs of defending the underlying claim. (To illustrate why it is not always possible to draw a clear line, think about whether amounts paid to settle a claim in advance of trial implicate indemnity coverage, defense coverage, or both.)

Due to the high costs of defending a claim, the value of the defense coverage is considerable. Few ordinary people can easily afford the cost of defending a tort claim, nor are they likely to be able to identify and choose a skilled defense lawyer or monitor their defense. This explains why it is that people would want to purchase defense as well as indemnity coverage. In addition to the convenience of one-stop shopping, can you imagine why it is that indemnity and defense coverage are typically sold as a package?[1]

Douglas Richmond, a former insurance defense and coverage lawyer who is also a prolific author, describes the reasons that insurance companies insist on the right to defend as follows:

> It is easy to see how liability insurers benefit from exercising their right to defend. By controlling their insured's defense, insurers are able to choose defense counsel. The selection of counsel is important to insurers first because it allows them to select proven and capable counsel, and second because it best positions them to negotiate favorable compensation terms with the attorneys. By controlling the defense, insurers are also able to seize settlement opportunities and to control

---

1. The explanation for large corporate purchases of insurance is more complicated. Can you think why? For a large business, the mix of indemnity and defense coverage that it purchases (at least for claims of a manageable size) is just another example of the "make or buy" decision that businesses routinely face. Unless a business faces truly unique risks or a high claims volume, it may well decide that it is more cost effective to purchase defense services from an insurance company than to hire the lawyers. One important determination of liability insurers' preferences with regard to the mix of indemnity and defense coverage is the level of risk retained by the insured. In general, the larger the deductible or self-insured retention, the more comfortable liability insurers are with the insured retaining significant responsibility for the defense of the claim. Can you see why?

settlement negotiations and terms to the extent possible. Insurers' control of the defense allows them to participate in strategic decisions that might otherwise be made solely by counsel or their insureds. Defense control in a broader sense allows insurers to defeat baseless claims, to expose and defeat overstated claims, to discourage or minimize future litigation against their insureds by defending aggressively and thus becoming known as a tough adversary or unappealing target, and to prevent collusion between claimants and insureds.

Liability Insurer's Right to Defend Their Insureds, 35 Creighton L. Rev. 115, 116 (2001).

Traditionally, only amounts paid to settle a claim or satisfy a judgment have counted against the limits of the policy, so that the value of the defense coverage is in addition to the limits of the policy. In recent years, some insurers have begun to sell policies in which the costs of defense count against the limits of the policy. Some defense lawyers call these policies "burning candle" or "wasting" policies. Can you see why? We will not be studying any cases in which the defense costs count against the limit, but it would be a good test of your understanding of the materials to think about how the relationship of the defense costs to the limits would affect your analysis of the issues that we address.

We will explore the liability insurance relationship by examining cases that develop three distinct sets of duties: the insurance company's duty to defend, the insurance company's duty to settle, and the policyholder's duty to cooperate in the defense and settlement of a claim. The scope and limits of these duties are not set out in any detail in liability insurance policies. Instead, they have developed through common law adjudication, occasionally modified by statute, as lawyers, insurance companies, policyholders, and sometimes tort claimants have struggled to understand and define the obligations that they owe to each other in the crucible of tort litigation.

I. THE DUTY TO DEFEND

The first liability insurance relationship issue that we explore here is the insurance company's duty to defend. Examine the insuring agreement in the sample commercial general liability (CGL) policy in Chapter 4 (see Figure 4.2). What does it say about the insurance company's duty to defend? If your answer is "not much," you're on the right track. Nevertheless, the policy is not completely silent. The insuring agreement says that the company has "the right and duty to defend the insured against any suit seeking those damages."

Notice that the company has not only the "duty" to defend, but also the "right" to defend. The duty protects the policyholder, and the right protects the company. Why does the company want such a right? In what kinds of situations might it matter?

Now notice that the duty and right attach to suits "seeking those damages." What are "*those* damages"? Answering that question requires you to think hard about how the indemnity and defense obligations fit together. If that seems too difficult at the moment, come back to the question after reading the next case.

A. ***The Basic Duty***

GRAY v. ZURICH INSURANCE CO.

Supreme Court of California
419 P.2d 168 (1966)

TOBRINER, J. This is an action by an insured against his insurer for failure to defend an action filed against him which stemmed from a complaint alleging that he had committed an assault. The main issue turns on the argument of the insurer that an exclusionary clause of the policy excuses its defense of an action in which a plaintiff alleges that the insured intentionally caused the bodily injury. . . .

Plaintiff, Dr. Vernon D. Gray, is the named insured under an insurance policy issued by defendant. A "Comprehensive Personal Liability Endorsement" in the policy states, under a paragraph designated "Coverage L," that the insurer agrees "[T]o pay on behalf of the insured all sums which the insured shall become legally obligated to pay as damages because of bodily injury or property damage, and the company shall defend any suit against the insured alleging such bodily injury or property damage and seeking damages which are payable under the terms of this endorsement, even if any of the allegations are groundless, false or fraudulent; but the company may make such investigation and settlement of any claim or suit as it deems expedient." The policy contains a provision that "[T]his endorsement does not apply" to a series of specified exclusions set forth under separate headings, including a paragraph (c) which reads, "under coverages L and M, to bodily injury or property damages caused intentionally by or at the direction of the insured."

The suit which Dr. Gray contends Zurich should have defended arose out of an altercation between him and a Mr. John R. Jones.[2] Jones filed a complaint in Missouri alleging that Dr. Gray "willfully, maliciously, brutally and intentionally assaulted" him; he prayed for actual damages of $50,000 and punitive damages of $50,000. Dr. Gray notified defendant of the suit, stating that he had acted in self-defense, and requested that the company defend. Defendant refused on the ground that the complaint alleged an intentional tort which fell outside the coverage of the policy. Dr. Gray thereafter unsuccessfully defended on the theory of self-defense; he suffered a judgment of $6,000 actual damages although the jury refused to award punitive damages.

Dr. Gray then filed the instant action, charging defendant with breach of its duty to defend. Defendant answered, admitting the execution of the policy but denying any such obligation. . . . [T]he court rendered judgment in favor of defendant. . . .

Defendant argues that it need not defend an action in which the complaint reveals on its face that the claimed bodily injury does not fall within

---

2. Immediately preceding the altercation Dr. Gray had been driving an automobile on a residential street when another automobile narrowly missed colliding with his car. Jones, the driver of the other car, left his vehicle, approached Dr. Gray's car in a menacing manner and jerked open the door. At that point Dr. Gray, fearing physical harm to himself and his passengers, rose from his seat and struck Jones. [Editor's Note: *As in previous chapters, the footnotes in this chapter are sequential, and do not use the numbers from the original sources.*]

the indemnification coverage; that here the Jones complaint alleged that the insured committed an assault, which fell outside such coverage. Defendant urges, as a second answer to plaintiff's contention, that the contract, if construed to require defense of the insured, would violate the public policy of the state and that, indeed, the judgment in the third party suit upholding the claim of an intentional bodily injury operates to estop the insured from recovery. Defendant thirdly contends that any requirement that it defend the Jones suit would embroil it in a hopeless conflict of interest. Finally it submits that, even if it should have defended the third party suit, the damages against it should encompass only the insured's expenses of defense and not the judgment against him.

We shall explain our reasons for concluding that defendant was obligated to defend the Jones suit, and our grounds for rejecting defendant's remaining propositions. Since the policy sets forth the duty to defend as a primary one and since the insurer attempts to avoid it only by an unclear exclusionary clause, the insured would reasonably expect, and is legally entitled to, such protection. As an alternative but secondary ground for our ruling we accept, for purposes of argument, defendant's contention that the duty to defend arises only if the third party suit involves a liability for which the insurer would be required to indemnify the insured, and, even upon this basis, we find a duty to defend.

In interpreting an insurance policy we apply the general principle that doubts as to meaning must be resolved against the insurer and that any exception to the performance of the basic underlying obligation must be so stated as clearly to apprise the insured of its effect. . . .

When we test the instant policy by these principles we find that its provisions as to the obligation to defend are uncertain and undefined; in the light of the reasonable expectation of the insured, they require the performance of that duty. At the threshold we note that the nature of the obligation to defend is itself necessarily uncertain. Although insurers have often insisted that the duty arises only if the insurer is bound to indemnify the insured, this very contention creates a dilemma. No one can determine whether the third party suit does or does not fall within the indemnification coverage of the policy until that suit is resolved; in the instant case, the determination of whether the insured engaged in intentional, negligent or even wrongful conduct depended upon the judgment in the Jones suit, and, indeed, even after that judgment, no one could be positive whether it rested upon a finding of plaintiff's negligent or his intentional conduct. The carrier's obligation to indemnify inevitably will not be defined until the adjudication of the very action which it should have defended. Hence the policy contains its own seeds of uncertainty; the insurer has held out a promise that by its very nature is ambiguous.

Although this uncertainty in the performance of the duty to defend could have been clarified by the language of the policy we find no such specificity here. An examination of the policy discloses that the broadly stated promise to defend is not conspicuously or clearly conditioned solely on a nonintentional bodily injury; instead, the insured could reasonably expect such protection.

The policy is a "comprehensive personal liability" contract; the designation in itself connotes general protection for alleged bodily injury caused by the insured. The insurer makes two wide promises: "To pay on behalf of the insured all sums which the insured shall become legally obligated to pay as damages because of bodily injury or property damage, and the company shall defend any suit against the insured alleging such bodily injury or property damage and seeking damages which are payable under the terms of this endorsement, even if any of the allegations of the suit are groundless, false, or fraudulent": clearly these promises, without further clarification, would lead the insured reasonably to expect the insurer to defend him against suits seeking damages for bodily injury, whatever the alleged cause of the injury, whether intentional or inadvertent.

But the insurer argues that the third party suit must seek "damages which are *payable* under the terms of this endorsement"; it contends that this limitation *modifies* the general duty to defend by confining the duty only to actions seeking damages within the primary coverage of the policy. Under "Exclusions" the policy provides that it "does not apply . . . under coverage L and M to bodily injury . . . caused intentionally by . . . the insured."

The very first paragraph as to coverage, however, provides that "the company shall defend any such suit against the insured alleging such bodily injury" although the allegations of the suit are groundless, false or fraudulent. This language, in its broad sweep, would lead the insured reasonably to expect defense of *any* suit regardless of merit or cause. The relation of the exclusionary clause to this basic promise is anything but clear. The basic promise would support the insured's reasonable expectation that he had bought the rendition of legal services to defend against a suit for bodily injury which alleged he had caused it, negligently, nonintentionally, intentionally or in any other manner. The doctrines and cases we have set forth tell us that the exclusionary clause must be "conspicuous, plain and clear." *Steven v. Fidelity & Casualty Co.*, 58 Cal. 2d 862, 878 [(1962)]. This clause is not "conspicuous" since it appears only after a long and complicated page of fine print, and is itself in fine print; its relation to the remaining clauses of the policy and its effect are surely not "plain and clear."

A further uncertainty lurks in the exclusionary clause itself. It alludes to damage caused "intentionally by or at the direction of the insured." Yet an act of the insured may carry out his "intention" and also cause unintended harm. When set next to the words "at the direction of the insured" the word "intentionally" might mean to the layman collusive, willful or planned action beyond the classical notion of intentional tort. This built-in ambiguity has caused debate and refined definition in many courts; in any event, the word surely cannot be "plain and clear" to the layman.

The insured is unhappily surrounded by concentric circles of uncertainty: the first, the unascertainable nature of the insurer's duty to defend; the second, the unknown effect of the provision that the insurer must defend even a groundless, false or fraudulent claim; the third, the uncertain extent of the indemnification coverage. Since we must resolve uncertainties in favor of the insured and interpret the policy provisions according to the layman's reasonable expectations, and since the effect of the exclusionary clause is neither conspicuous, plain, nor clear, we hold that in the present case the policy provides for an obligation to defend and that such obligation is independent of the indemnification coverage.

The insurer counters with the contention that this position would compel an insurer "issuing a policy covering liability of the insured for maintenance, use or operation of an automobile . . . to defend the insured in an action for damages for negligently maintaining a stairway and thereby allegedly causing injury to another — because the insured claims that the suit for damages was false or groundless." The "groundless, false, or fraudulent" clause, however, does not extend the obligation to defend without limits; it includes only defense to those actions of the nature and kind covered by the policy. Here the policy insures against "damages because of bodily injury." As we have pointed out, in view of the language of the policy, the insured would reasonably expect protection in an action involving alleged bodily injury. On the other hand the insured could not reasonably expect protection under an automobile insurance policy for injury which occurs from defect in a stairway. Similarly an insured would not expect a defense for an injury involving an automobile under a general comprehensive policy which excluded automobile coverage. We look to the nature and kind of risk covered by the policy as a limitation upon the duty to defend; we cannot absolve the carrier from the duty to defend an insured for loss of the nature and kind against which it insured.

Our holding that the insurer bore the obligation to defend because the policy led plaintiff reasonably to expect such defense, and because the insurer's exclusionary clause did not exonerate it, cuts across defendant's answering contention that the duty arises only if the pleadings disclose a cause of action for which the insurer must indemnify the insured. Defendant would equate the duty to defend with the complaint that pleaded a liability for which the insurer was bound to indemnify the insured. Yet even if we accept defendant's premises, and define the duty to defend by measuring the allegations in the Jones case against the carrier's liability to indemnify, defendant's position still fails. We proceed to discuss this alternative ground of liability of the insurer, accepting for such purpose the insurer's argument that we must test the third party suit against the indemnification coverage of the policy. We point out that the carrier must defend a suit which *potentially* seeks damages within the coverage of the policy; the Jones action was such a suit.

Defendant cannot construct a formal fortress of the third party's pleadings and retreat behind its walls. The pleadings are malleable, changeable and amendable. Although an earlier decision reads: "In determining whether or not the appellant was bound to defend . . . the language of its contract must first be looked to, and next, the allegations of the complaints . . . " (*Lamb v. Belt Casualty Co.*, 3 Cal. App. 2d 624, 630 [(1935)]), courts do not examine only the pleaded word but the potential liability created by the suit. Since the instant action presented the potentiality of a judgment based upon nonintentional conduct, and since liability for such conduct would fall within the indemnification coverage, the duty to defend became manifest at the outset.

To restrict the defense obligation of the insurer to the precise language of the pleading would not only ignore the thrust of the cases but would create an anomaly for the insured. Obviously, as *Ritchie v. Anchor Casualty Co.*, 135 Cal. App. 2d 245 [(1955)], points out, the complainant in the third party action drafts his complaint in the broadest terms; he may very well stretch the action which lies in only nonintentional conduct to the dramatic complaint that alleges intentional misconduct. In light of the likely overstatement of the complaint and of the plasticity of modern pleading, we should hardly designate the third party as the arbiter of the policy's coverage.

Since modern procedural rules focus on the facts of a case rather than the theory of recovery in the complaint, the duty to defend should be fixed by the facts which the insurer learns from the complaint, the insured, or other sources. An insurer, therefore, bears a duty to defend its insured whenever it ascertains facts which give rise to the potential of liability under the policy. In the instant case the complaint itself, as well as the facts known to the insurer, sufficiently apprised the insurer of these possibilities; hence we need not set out when and upon what other occasions the duty of the insurer to ascertain such possibilities otherwise arises.

Jones' complaint clearly presented the possibility that he might obtain damages that were covered by the indemnity provisions of the policy. Even conduct that is traditionally classified as "intentional" or "willful" has been held to fall within indemnification coverage. Moreover, despite Jones' pleading of intentional and willful conduct, he could have amended his complaint to allege merely negligent conduct. Further, plaintiff might have been able to show that in physically defending himself, even if he exceeded the reasonable bounds of self-defense, he did not commit willful and intended injury, but engaged only in nonintentional tortious conduct. Thus, even accepting the insurer's premise that it had no obligation to defend actions seeking damages not within the indemnification coverage, we find, upon proper measurement of the third party action against the insurer's liability to indemnify, it should have defended because the loss could have fallen within that liability.

We turn to the insurer's second major contention that the contract cannot be read to require the insurer to defend an action seeking damages for an intentional wrong because such an obligation would violate public policy. In support of this argument it relies upon Insurance Code §533 and Civil Code §1668.

The contention fails on two grounds. In the first place, the statutes forbid only contracts which indemnify for "*loss*" or "*responsibility*" resulting from willful wrongdoing. Here we deal with a contract which provides for *legal defense* against an action charging such conduct; the contract does not call for indemnification of the insured if the third party plaintiff prevails. In the second place, as we pointed out in *Tomerlin v. Canadian Indemnity Co.*, 394 P.2d 571 (Cal. 1964), the statutes "establish a public policy to prevent insurance coverage from encouragement of willful tort." Thus *Tomerlin* held that if an insurer's obligation to pay a judgment based on willful conduct results from an estoppel *after* the conduct, the obligation could not have previously encouraged the conduct. Similarly, the present contract does not offend the statute; a contract to defend an assured upon mere accusation of a willful tort does not encourage such willful conduct.

Nor can we accept defendant's argument that the duty to defend dissolves simply because the insured is unsuccessful in his defense and because the injured party recovers on the basis of a finding of the assured's willful conduct. Citing *Abbott v. Western Nat. Indem. Co.*, 331 P.2d 997 (Cal. App. 1958), the insurer urges that if the judgment in a third party suit goes against the insured it operates as "res judicata or collateral estoppel in the insured's action or proceeding against the insurer."

We have explained that the insured would reasonably expect a defense by the insurer in all personal injury actions against him. If he is to be required to finance his own defense and then, only if successful, hold the insurer to its promise by means of a second suit for reimbursement, we defeat the basic reason for the purchase of the insurance. In purchasing his insurance the insured would reasonably expect that he would stand a better chance of vindication if supported by the resources and expertise of his insurer than if compelled to handle and finance the presentation of his case. He would, moreover, expect to be able to avoid the time, uncertainty and capital outlay in finding and retaining an attorney of his own. "The courts will not sanction a construction of the insurer's language that will defeat the very purpose or object of the insurance." (*Ritchie v. Anchor Casualty Co., supra,* 135 Cal. App. 2d 245, 257.)

Similarly, we find no merit in the insurer's third contention that our holding will embroil it in a conflict of interests. According to the insurer our ruling will require defense of an action in which the interests of insurer and insured are so opposed as to nullify the insurer's fulfillment of its duty of defense and of the protection of its own interests. For example, the argument goes, if defendant had defended against the Jones suit it would have sought to establish either that the insured was free from any liability or that such liability rested on intentional conduct. The insured, of course, would also seek a verdict holding him not liable but, if found liable, would attempt to obtain a ruling that such liability emanated from the nonintentional conduct within his insurance coverage. Thus, defendant contends, an insurer, if obligated to defend in this situation, faces an insoluble ethical problem.

Since, however, the court in the third party suit does not adjudicate the issue of coverage, the insurer's argument collapses. The only question there litigated is the insured's *liability.* The alleged victim does not concern himself with the theory of liability; he desires only the largest possible judgment. Similarly, the insured and insurer seek only to avoid, or at least to minimize, the judgment. As we have noted, modern procedural rules focus on whether, on a given set of facts, the plaintiff, regardless of the theory, may recover. Thus the question of whether or not the insured engaged in intentional conduct does not normally formulate an issue which is resolved in that litigation.[3]

In any event, if the insurer adequately reserves its right to assert the noncoverage defense later, it will not be bound by the judgment. If the injured party prevails, that party or the insured will assert his claim against the insurer. At this time the insurer can raise the noncoverage defense previously reserved. In this manner the interests of insured and insurer in defending against the injured party's primary suit will be identical; the insurer will not face the suggested dilemma.

Finally, defendant urges that our holding should require only the reimbursement of the insured's expenses in defending the third party action but not the payment of the judgment. Defendant acknowledges the general rule that an insurer that wrongfully refuses to defend is liable on the judgment against the insured. (*Arenson v. National Automobile & Cas. Ins. Co.,* 286 P.2d 816 (Cal. 1955); Civ. Code, §2778.) Defendant argues, however, that the instant situation should be distinguished from that case because here the judgment has not necessarily been rendered on a theory within the policy coverage. Thus defendant would limit the insured's recovery to the expenses of the third party suit.

We rejected a similar proposal in *Tomerlin v. Canadian Indemnity Co., supra,* 61 Cal. 2d 638, 649-650. In that case, as we have noted, the insurer's obligation to defend arose out of estoppel. The insurer contended that we should apply a "tort" theory of damages to its wrongful refusal to defend. Such a theory, we explained, would impose upon the insured "the impossible burden" of proving

---

3. In rare cases the issue of punitive damages or a special verdict might present a potential conflict of interests, but such a possibility does not outweigh the advantages of the general rule. Even in such cases, however, the insurer will be still bound, ethically and legally, to litigate in the interests of the insured.

the extent of the loss caused by the insurer's breach. As this court said in an analogous situation in *Arenson v. National Auto. & Cas. Ins. Co.*, 310 P.2d 961 (Cal. 1957): "Having defaulted such agreement the company is manifestly bound to reimburse its insured for the full amount of any obligation reasonably incurred by him. It will not be allowed to defeat or whittle down its obligation on the theory that plaintiff himself was of such limited financial ability that he could not afford to employ able counsel, or to present every reasonable defense, or to carry his cause to the highest court having jurisdiction. . . . Sustaining such a theory . . . would tend . . . to encourage insurance companies to similar disavowals of responsibility with everything to gain and nothing to lose."

In summary, the individual consumer in the highly organized and integrated society of today must necessarily rely upon institutions devoted to the public service to perform the basic functions which they undertake. At the same time the consumer does not occupy a sufficiently strong economic position to bargain with such institutions as to specific clauses of their contracts of performance, and, in any event, piecemeal negotiation would sacrifice the advantage of uniformity. Hence the courts in the field of insurance contracts have tended to require that the insurer render the basic insurance protection which it has held out to the insured. This obligation becomes especially manifest in the case in which the insurer has attempted to limit the principal coverage by an unclear exclusionary clause. We test the alleged limitation in the light of the insured's reasonable expectation of coverage; that test compels the indicated outcome of the present litigation.

The judgment is reversed and the trial court instructed to take evidence solely on the issue of damages alleged in plaintiff's complaint including the amount of the judgment in the Jones suit, and the costs, expenses and attorney's fees incurred in defending such suit.

NOTES AND QUESTIONS

1. Note that the court provides two independent grounds for ruling that the insurer breached the duty to defend. Arguably, more careful drafting of the insurance policy could defeat the reasonable expectations ground. Are the newer policies better drafted in this regard? If Dr. Gray's policy had contained the duty to defend and expected or intended provisions contained in the CGL policy reproduced at the beginning of Chapter 4 or the homeowners' policy reproduced in Chapter 3, would he reasonably expect a defense against an intentional tort suit?

2. The second ground for decision is the more influential and widely followed. Under this ground, Dr. Gray gets a defense because it is clear from the facts that there is a negligence claim lurking in the background. The court holds that the insurer has an obligation to consider all the facts, not just the facts alleged in the complaint. Most courts—California courts included—direct insurers to begin answering the duty to defend question by examining the allegations of the complaint. If the complaint sets out allegations that, if true, would obligate the insurance company to pay the claim, the insurance company has the obligation to defend the claim. This rule is variously referred to as the "complaint allegation" rule, the "four corners" rule (named for the "four corners" of the complaint that define the underlying claim),

or the "eight corners" rule (named for the four corners of the complaint plus the four corners of the insurance policy). In terms of the language of the CGL policy, the complaint allegation rule makes the complaint the presumptive determinant of whether a suit seeks "those damages." Although courts and commentators universally agree that the complaint is the place to start when deciding whether a claim is covered, they part company with regard to two important related issues: (1) the strength of the presumption that follows from the analysis of the complaint and (2) the procedure that the policyholder or the company has to follow to rebut the presumption. Consider the following possibilities:

A. The allegations of the complaint are dispositive, meaning that they create an irrefutable presumption regarding the nature of the claim. Insurance carriers have no obligation to defend a claim unless and until a complaint sets out a potentially covered cause of action.

B. The allegations of the complaint create a strong presumption that can be rebutted only through facts proven in a declaratory judgment proceeding on the duty to defend. If the complaint sets out a potentially covered cause of action, the carrier must defend until it proves in court that it has a valid defense to coverage.

C. The allegations of the complaint create a presumption that can be rebutted by the discovery of contrary facts during the litigation. If the insurance company discovers that there are potentially covered aspects of the claim that are not mentioned in the complaint, the duty to defend is triggered. Likewise, if the insurance company discovers that it has a valid defense to coverage, it can withdraw from the defense. In either case, any subsequent litigation over whether the insurance company breached the duty to defend will turn on the "real" facts about the underlying case as they are developed in litigation, not the words set out in the complaint in the underlying case.

D. The allegations in the complaint create a presumption that can be rebutted in the policyholder's favor by the discovery of contrary facts during the litigation and that can be rebutted in the carrier's favor only through facts proven in a declaratory judgment proceeding.

3. Courts commonly relax the complaint allegation rule when doing so favors the policyholder. *See generally* James M. Fischer, *Broadening the Insurer's Duty to Defend: How* Gray v. Zurich Insurance Co. *Transformed Liability Insurance into Litigation Insurance*, 25 U.C. Davis L. Rev. 141 (1991). If the insurer knows of facts not included in the complaint that bring the case within coverage, the insurer must defend. *See, e.g., Fitzpatrick v. American Honda Motor Co.*, 575 N.E.2d 90, 93 (N.Y. 1991) (an insurer must "provide a defense when it has actual knowledge of facts establishing a reasonable possibility of coverage"). Professor Robert Jerry terms this exception to the complaint allegation rule as a counter rule—the "potentiality" rule. *See* Robert Jerry II, *The Insurer's Right to Reimbursement of Defense Costs*, 42 Ariz. L. Rev. 13, 22-23 (2002). The dissent in *Fitzpatrick* argued that the potentiality rule was an unnecessary complication. If there is a claim that is potentially covered, the plaintiff's lawyer can be counted upon to amend the complaint, because without a liability insurance company in the case, he or she is unlikely to be paid. What do you think about that argument? Should the defendant's right to a

defense be linked to the skill or self-interest of the plaintiffs' lawyer? Some cases have gone further and held the insurer responsible for breach of the duty to defend in situations in which a reasonable investigation would have revealed facts extrinsic to the complaint that indicated that the claim was potentially covered. *See Fitzpatrick* at 93 n.2 (collecting cases).

4. Some courts have created other exceptions to the complaint allegation rule: when "incontrovertible and indisputable facts . . . confirmed by its own insured, demonstrate that there never was any insurance coverage for the casualty alleged in the first place," *Rowell v. Hodges,* 434 F.2d 926, 929-930 (5th Cir. 1970); when there are actual facts relating to "such ancillary matters as whether the insured paid the premiums or whether he is the proper insured under the policy," *State Farm Fire & Cas. Co. v. Shelton,* 531 N.E.2d 913, 919 (Ill. App. Ct. 1988); where the claim is "patently outside of the risks covered by the policy," *Liberty Mut. Ins. Co. v. Metzler,* 586 N.E.2d 897, 901 (Ind. Ct. App. 1992); or where a "complaint has been drafted in bad faith and designed only to bring an insurer into a case," *State Farm Ins. Co. v. Trezza,* 469 N.Y.S.2d 1008, 1012 (N.Y. Sup. Ct. 1983). Why might these situations be treated differently from other kinds of defenses?

5. Professor Susan Randall has argued that the complaint allegation rule should be jettisoned entirely. *Redefining the Insurer's Duty to Defend,* 2 Conn. Ins. L.J. 221 (1997). In her view, the duty to defend should depend on all the facts and circumstances. Requiring an insurance company to defend a claim that its adjusters think is not covered sets up an inevitable conflict of interest that, in her view, creates problems for more insureds than it helps. In addition, the complaint allegation rule encourages plaintiffs' lawyers to shade the facts in the drafting of complaints. What do you think of these criticisms? How does the California Supreme Court address them?

6. The complaint allegation rule is commonly understood to mean that an insurance company has the obligation to defend an entire lawsuit, so long as there is at least one potentially covered cause of action. An extreme example of this is described in *Buss v. Superior Court,* 939 P.2d 766 (Cal. 1997), which concerned an insurer's obligations with respect to a 27-count complaint against Jerry Buss, the owner of the Los Angeles Lakers, only one of which was potentially covered by the liability insurance policy. The California Supreme Court confirmed the insurer's duty to defend the entire suit, but it allowed the insurer to recoup from the insured at the end of the lawsuit the costs of defense attributable to noncovered claims. How much protection does this provide a liability insurance carrier in situations involving homeowners' or small business liability insurance policies? *See generally* Jerry, *supra* note 3. What might be the reasons for obligating the insurance company to defend the entire lawsuit, not simply the covered portion?

7. Notice that the court rules that an insurer that breaches the duty to defend must pay the underlying tort judgment even if that judgment was based on a cause of action that is excluded by the policy. Why? Think carefully about whether this result can be explained under the ordinary expectation damages rule of contract law (or, for that matter, under a tort approach to damages). What policy considerations justify requiring an insurer to pay a judgment that it would not have had to pay had it provided the policyholder with a lawyer?

The ALI's Restatement of the Law of Liability Insurance (RLLI) deals at length with the duty to defend. As you read the following sections of those principles—the black letter rules and the accompanying comments—think about how those rules respond to the sorts of concerns raised in the notes and questions above.

RESTATEMENT OF THE LAW LIABILITY INSURANCE
American Law Institute (Tent. Draft No. 1, Approved May 2016)

§13. Conditions Under Which the Insurer Must Defend

(1) An insurer that has issued an insurance policy that includes a duty to defend must defend any legal action brought against an insured that is based in whole or in part on any allegations that, if proven, would be covered by the policy, without regard to the merits of those allegations.

(2) For the purpose of determining whether an insurer must defend, the legal action is deemed to be based on:

(a) Any allegation contained in the complaint or comparable document stating the legal action; and

(b) Any additional allegation, not contained in the complaint or comparable document stating the legal action, that a reasonable insurer would regard as an actual or potential basis for all or part of the action.

(3) The insurer must defend until its duty to defend is terminated under §18, unless undisputed facts establish as a matter of law that:

(a) The defendant in the action is not an insured under the insurance policy pursuant to which the duty to defend is asserted;

(b) The automobile involved in the accident is not a covered automobile under the policy pursuant to which the duty to defend is owed and the defendant is not otherwise entitled to a defense; or

(c) The claim was reported late under a claims-made-and-reported policy in circumstances that qualify under the rule stated in §36(2).

. . .

Comment:

a. The duty to defend and the complaint-allegation rule. When evaluating whether to defend a legal action that is brought against an insured, the insurer must take as true all of the facts alleged in the complaint or comparable document that favor coverage. An allegation in a complaint that, if proven, would subject the insured to a covered liability conclusively establishes that the insurer has a duty to defend, subject only to the exception permitted by subsection (3) (which allows an insurer to avoid the duty to defend without filing a declaratory-judgment action in narrowly defined circumstances). This widely accepted rule is variously known as the "four corners," "eight corners," or "complaint-allegation" rule. The "four corners" label refers to the four corners of the complaint, reflecting that the insurer must defend based on the allegations in the complaint even if facts outside the complaint would demonstrate that those allegations are false. The "eight corners" label refers to the four corners of the complaint plus the four corners of the insurance policy, reflecting that, as long as the complaint contains an allegation that would be covered by the policy, parties and judges can make the duty-to-defend determination simply by reference to the complaint and the policy.

When an insurer has the duty to defend, it must do so until that duty terminates in one of the ways enumerated in §18. Typically, this means the insurer must defend the legal action all the way through final adjudication of the action, unless the action is settled or the insurer prevails in a declaratory-judgment action establishing that the action is not covered by the liability insurance policy.

b. The potential for coverage. If the insurer knows or reasonably should know of information that, under flexible modern pleading rules, could reasonably be expected to be added as an allegation, and that, if so added, would require the insurer to defend, then the insurer has a duty to defend the action. Except as provided in subsection (3), the consideration of facts outside the complaint works in one direction only: facts or circumstances not alleged in the complaint or comparable document generally may not be used to justify a refusal or failure to defend. Such information may be used, however, in a declaratory-judgment action brought by the insurer seeking to terminate its duty to defend an action that it is defending under a reservation of rights. See §18, Comment *j*. This is the majority rule.

. . .

c. Coverage questions that turn on facts not at issue in the legal action against the insured. The general rule is that insurers may not use facts outside the complaint as the basis for refusing to defend, with the result that even an insurer with a strong factual basis for contesting coverage must defend under a reservation of rights and then file a declaratory-judgment action in order to avoid the duty to defend. Nevertheless, courts have identified three specific exceptions to this rule: (1) when undisputed facts demonstrate that the defendant in the action is not an insured under the insurance policy pursuant to which the duty to defend is asserted, (2) when undisputed facts demonstrate that the automobile involved in the accident at issue was not a covered automobile under the policy pursuant to which the duty to defend is asserted, and (3) when undisputed facts demonstrate that a claim was reported late under a claims-made-and-reported policy in circumstances in which the notice-prejudice rule does not apply. In these circumstances, courts have allowed insurers to refuse to defend even when the elements of the complaint-allegation rule are otherwise met. Whether courts should recognize other narrow exceptions to this rule should be determined on a case-by-case basis that gives due regard for the importance of judicial supervision of the decision to refuse to provide a defense in circumstances that meet the requirements of the complaint allegation rule.

§14. Duty to Defend: Basic Obligations

When an insurance policy obligates an insurer to defend a legal action:

(1) Subject to the insurer's right to terminate the defense under §18, the duty to defend the action includes the obligation to provide a defense of the action that:

    (a) Makes reasonable efforts to defend the insured from all of the causes of action and remedies sought in the action, including those not covered by the liability insurance policy; and

    (b) Requires defense counsel to protect from disclosure to the insurer any information of the insured that is protected by attorney-client privilege, work-product immunity, or a defense lawyer's duty of confidentiality under rules of professional conduct, if that information could be used to benefit the insurer at the expense of the insured;

(2) The insurer may fulfill the duty to defend using its own employees, except when an independent defense is required; and

(3) Unless otherwise stated in the policy, the costs of the defense of the action are borne by the insurer in addition to the policy limits.

Comment:

. . .

b. *The duty to defend the whole action.* It is often said that the insurer has a duty to defend the "whole claim." This Section states that rule more precisely: the insurer's duty is to defend the insured from all of the causes of action and remedies sought in a suit or other proceeding that the insurer has the duty to defend. This way of stating the duty distinguishes between judgment risks and non-judgment risks. Judgment risks are the potential direct legal consequences of the legal action to the insured: the entry of judgment and the associated obligation to pay damages or provide other remedies. Those risks are sometimes not fully insured because the damages may exceed the policy limits, some of the remedies sought may be of a type that is not insured by the policy, or the insurer may have a ground for contesting coverage. The insurer's duty to defend includes the obligation to provide a defense of the legal action that makes reasonable efforts to defend the insured from all of the judgment risks, whether they are insured or not, as long as there is one actual or potential cause of action that is covered. Non-judgment risks are the other possible consequences of the legal action, such as loss of reputation or goodwill. Such risks typically are not insured. In defending the insured against judgment risks, insurers as a practical matter do protect insureds against non-judgment risks, but courts have not identified specific obligations regarding non-judgment risks. Thus, the insurer's duties with regard to non-judgment risks are subject only to the obligations it agrees to assume as well as the general duty of good faith and fair dealing.

. . .

§19. Consequences of Breach of the Duty to Defend

(1) An insurer that breaches the duty to defend a legal action loses the right to assert any control over the defense or settlement of the action.

(2) An insurer that breaches the duty to defend without a reasonable basis for its conduct must provide coverage for the legal action for which the defense was sought, notwithstanding any grounds for contesting coverage that the insurer could have preserved by providing a proper defense under a reservation of rights pursuant to §15.

Comment:

a. *The importance of defense coverage.* The rules in this Section identify additional consequences, beyond ordinary contract damages, for breach of the duty to defend. These rules reflect the importance of the defense coverage provided by traditional liability insurance policies, which promise to pay for the defense of any potentially covered claim and, in most cases, also to select the defense lawyer and manage the defense. Liability insurance defense coverage provides the access to civil justice for defendants that corresponds to the access to civil justice that contingent-fee arrangements make possible for plaintiffs. Without an insurer-funded defense lawyer, many if not most consumers and small businesses would be deprived of an adequate defense. Other defendants with access to greater resources would not be as defenseless, but when such defendants choose to purchase insurance that promises to provide them with a defense, as opposed to the after-the-fact reimbursement of their own defense costs, they are deserving of the benefits of that protection.

b. Providing an incentive to fulfill the duty to defend. The rule in subsection (2) encourages insurers to fulfill their duty to defend by providing a consequence for a wrongful breach of that duty that corrects the misalignment of incentives that might otherwise lead a rational insurer to abandon its insured in some cases. Ordinary contract damages may not provide an adequate incentive for insurers to defend in cases in which the insurer believes that the coverage-relevant facts ultimately will be resolved in its favor, notwithstanding the insurer's clear duty to defend. Thus, the rule in subsection (2) is a corollary to the complaint-allegation rule, which requires insurers to resolve all factual uncertainty in favor of coverage when deciding whether to defend. See §13, Comment *a*.

An insurer that could abandon the defense whenever it concludes that the coverage-relevant facts are in its favor, without significant risk of having to pay a judgment or settlement of the action, would have an incentive to do so. That incentive would be especially strong if the insured did not have the resources to pay for an effective defense. In that situation, the costs of the defense for which the breaching insurer would be obligated to reimburse the insured, at some uncertain point in the future and only if the insured brings a breach-of-contract action, may be less than what the insurer would have to pay for an adequate defense on a real-time basis. As a result, the insurer could be better off by wrongly refusing to defend. The rule in subsection (2) changes that calculus by exposing the insurer to the risk of having to pay the full claim, thereby encouraging the insurer to fulfill its duty.

. . .

j. Damages for breach of the duty to defend. Chapter 4 will address the general topic of damages for breach of the liability insurance contract. In general, the damages include the foreseeable consequences of a breach of the insurer's contractual obligations. When an insurer breaches the duty to defend, those consequences include the reasonable costs of defense, any amount by which a non-covered settlement or judgment entered in the case is larger than it otherwise would have been as a result of the breach of the duty to defend, and any other damages recoverable for breach of a liability insurance contract. The insurer is also obligated to pay any covered judgment or the reasonable amount of any covered settlement, subject to the policy limits, but that obligation is part of the insurer's ordinary duty to pay covered claims, not part of the damages for breach of the duty to defend. A breach of the duty to defend does not ordinarily obligate the insurer to indemnify the insured for amounts in excess of the policy limit, unless the insured can demonstrate that the breach caused that excess verdict. Otherwise, an insurer that breaches the duty to defend may become obligated to pay amounts in excess of the policy limit only because of the breach of some other obligation, such as the duty to make reasonable settlement decisions.

The following entertaining and informative column by Professor Scales considers the duty to defend aspects of the *Woo* case covered in Section III of Chapter 4 ("Professional Liability Insurance").

CAN THIS PIG FLY? HOW A DENTIST ASSAULTED A PATIENT AND MADE A MILLION DOLLARS

Adam Scales
FindLaw August 15, 2007

http://writ.news.findlaw.com/commentary/20070815_scales.html

In yesterday's column I discussed the facts of a remarkable insurance law case [*Woo v. Fireman's Fund Ins. Co.*]. A dentist, Dr. Woo, took advantage of the fact that his patient and former assistant, Ms. Alberts, was under sedation for a procedure to play an ugly practical joke on her.

More specifically, Woo gave Alberts temporary implants crafted specially to resemble boar's teeth, and photographed her while she was unconscious and had her mouth open to display the implants. When his insurer failed to defend the case on the ground that Woo's tort was not covered, Woo and his attorney quickly settled with Alberts—then sued his insurer, Fireman's, for failing to defend him.

In this column, I'll explain why and how he won that case.

WE THOUGHT HE WAS KIDDING

Fireman's had agreed to defend Dr. Woo against claims arising from the practice of dentistry. Washington law defines "dentistry" very broadly, covering almost every conceivable variation of dental care. Because the claim arose from Woo's implantation of temporary teeth—albeit teeth shaped like boar tusks—Woo argued that the policy applied.

This sounds like a stretch, but Fireman's misstep resulted in Woo getting the maximum benefit of the doubt. Insurers have systematic advantages over policyholders, and courts have accordingly tilted the playing field *against* insurers. Thus, an insurer must defend its policyholder if there is any possible basis for coverage. An insurer must defend even if the claim is fraudulent or groundless. The duty extends to cases involving interrelated claims that will certainly not be covered (such as a premeditated murder). Accordingly, plaintiffs' lawyers are careful to sprinkle throughout their complaints rather abstract allegations that are sure to look like covered claims. As I teach my Insurance Law students, every complaint has at least two counts. Count One says, "The defendant intentionally shot me." Count Two says, "The defendant negligently shot me." And Alberts's complaint dutifully recited a number of claims that facially fell within coverage, such as medical malpractice, and her lack of informed consent to his "joke."

Insurers often must defend claims for which, in a perfect legal system where I personally decided every coverage question, they would not actually have to pay. This is called the "Four Corners," or "Eight Corners," rule. After comparing the complaint with the insurance policy, if *any* part of the complaint potentially falls within *any* of the policy provisions (we're up to eight corners now), the insurer must defend, even if a full picture would show that the claim isn't really covered.

It's easy to criticize this rule when we understand all the facts. But typically, neither the insurer nor the policyholder knows all the facts when a complaint is filed. The policyholder can't wait for a full investigation before beginning his defense; the litigation process *is* the investigation. Insurers often believe that when the facts emerge, they will favor a no-coverage position. But insurers have an obvious incentive to err on the side of their own interests. The Four Corners rule requires them to err on the side of coverage.

The *Woo* court added a gloss to this rule. Unsurprisingly, caselaw on coverage for inserting boar tusks into anesthetized patients is rather thin. Fireman's pointed to a line of cases denying coverage where physicians had sexually assaulted drugged patients. Those decisions held that such assaults had no conceivable relationship to medical treatment, and therefore, did not trigger a "professional services" liability policy. The court of appeals thought this disposed of Woo's case, but the Washington Supreme Court held that an insurer must *also* give the benefit of any *legal* uncertainty to the policyholder.

Thus, insurers must construe *both* the factual allegations of an underlying complaint (e.g., whether the conduct was negligent or intentional) *and* the existing law of insurance coverage (e.g., whether practical jokes are akin to sexual assault) in the policyholder's favor. Abstractly, this is probably the correct answer, given the legal system's comprehensive allocation of uncertainties against insurers, but it puts insurers in an awkward position.

NO CONTROLLING LEGAL AUTHORITY

Fireman's had obtained an attorney's "opinion letter" advising that it had no duty to defend. Opinion letters are generally worthless, and this was no exception. The letter carefully noted the unsettled reach of the "sexual assault exception," but concluded there was no duty here. The Washington Supreme Court found that Fireman's had thus given itself, rather than its policyholder, the benefit of the doubt.

This explicit extension of the Four Corners rule to legal uncertainty is very interesting, and I'm going to label it the "Four Corners and the Magic Eight Ball Rule": The insurer must defend whenever the body of insurance law does not unequivocally establish noncoverage. If, upon peering into Ball, an insurer's $300/hour oracles report the situation "hazy" or "outlook not so good," it must defend.

This rule is appealing, but it has real costs. An insurer faithfully applying it will end up defending cases where the likelihood of coverage is remote, but detectable. Very few legal issues permit slam-dunk, no-judge-in-his-right-mind-could-hold-otherwise answers. Moreover, it is often impractical for insurers to defend a case the policyholder is certain to lose (a sadistic dentist, for example), while still avoiding payment because they think the claim isn't covered. Smart plaintiffs' lawyers invariably put settlement offers on the table. These force insurers to weigh the risks of walking away, thus inviting a large settlement by the policyholder (who is free to act once the insurer has left the room), or taking a losing case to trial, thus inviting a catastrophic award from an angry jury. Either scenario creates an opportunity for a bad faith claim. Thus, an insurer that refuses to defend or settle a claim risks far more than the value of the policy unless its lawyer can guarantee victory on the question of coverage.

Ultimately, while policyholders who are being sued may benefit from the Washington Supreme Court's rule, other policyholders will bear the cost—passed on by their insurers—of the incorrect payouts that inevitably arise from the imperfect machinery of litigation. That tradeoff may be worth-while, but I am not so sure.

SMILE! THANKS, NOW I'M COVERED

Unfortunately, the court went further than it needed to, and determined that Dr. Woo's perversions constituted the practice of dentistry, and thus were *actually* covered, rather than *potentially* covered. According to the 5-4 ruling, the stunt "did not interrupt the dental surgery procedure." Rather, "Woo's insertion of the boar tusk flippers was intertwined with and inseparable from the real treatment he performed on Alberts[.]"

A quick search for the precise legal term that describes these conclusions reveals that "stupid" falls most readily to hand. According to the uncontested account accepted by the court, Woo did indeed interrupt the scheduled procedure. The majority opinion offers nothing to explain how boar tusks, pried eyelids, and amateur photography contributed to the treatment of Alberts. As a vigorous dissent noted, the majority's approach leaves a doctor covered for any misconduct "as long as the victim is anesthetized and sitting in a dentist's chair."

In partial defense of the result, such cases do present a genuine dilemma. It is precisely because Dr. Woo *was* using his medical training and skills that his violation of trust was so grave. Had he taped a pair of tusks to Alberts's mouth while she was passed out after an office cocktail party, most people would have a somewhat different reaction; it would not obviously impugn him as a *physician*, though it might be in poor taste.

The court should have considered a more functional approach to distinguishing between medical treatment that merely goes seriously awry, and the misuse of medical skill to achieve unlawful ends. Imagine that two gynecologist brothers are insane. They decide that the best way to help pregnant women would be to kidnap and operate on them using special obstetrical tools they have designed. Undoubtedly, such bloody efforts would fall within the definition of the practice of medicine. But it is odd to think that the very instrument of wrongdoing — their medical training — would insulate them from the liability consequences of that instrument's misuse.

On the other hand, assigning to professional liability insurers responsibility for all harms related to one's professional station might be the most effective way to combat misbehavior. In abuse cases of all kinds, we frequently question why the relevant licensing authority or employer didn't act more quickly when warning signs first appeared. It is interesting to note that Woo is still practicing dentistry. If he were deemed uninsurable because of his extracurricular hobbies, that might be a more effective deterrent to abuse than the unpredictable lightning strike of crushing tort liability.

Finally, the court examined the question of intent. Readers with a background in torts and some familiarity with insurance may wonder why Woo's coverage wasn't denied under the standard exclusion for "expected or intended injury." The short answer is that many courts require that the resulting *harm* be intended in order for this exclusion to operate.

The term "accident," which is the touchstone of insurance coverage, has historically had a number of somewhat confused definitions. Believe me, one could write a book-length treatment of this deceptively simple word.[4] Indeed, in several well-known cases, policyholders committed arson and were convicted of murder. But they retained liability coverage because they intended only to destroy property or collect insurance money, and thought nothing of the victims who perished! Because Woo likely did not intend harm, but merely acted without regard to Alberts's dignity, the court found her injuries "accidental," and the exclusion did not apply.

THOSE AREN'T CAVITIES, THEY'RE ZEROES

The rest is destined that place in legal history reserved for hot coffee lawsuits and false advertising claims against the makers of *The Neverending Story*. Because his insurer should have defended him, Dr. Woo recovered the $250,000 he had paid Alberts. But he also claimed emotional distress due to his insurer's abandonment. Despite "the absence of any medical, psychiatric, or expert testimony" attesting these injuries, a jury awarded him $750,000, which suggests the rather even quality of justice throughout the judicial system of Washington State. And naturally, Fireman's had to pay for Dr. Woo's legal costs.

Woo will surely become an insurance casebook classic. I have only been able to touch on a few of the important issues it raises. Is *Woo* all wrong? I wish it were. There is not a single page of the majority opinion—including the facts, the supremely unpersuasive leaps of reasoning, and the payoff at the end—that does not infuriate. I suspect that Fireman's counted on that very reaction; it must have been stunned to see Woo emerging throughout as a sympathetic victim of a well-intended practical joke gone awry! Students of legal rhetoric would do well to study this case; one merely has to contrast the tone of the majority opinion with that of the dissent (and the lower appellate opinion, now reversed) to see the impact of framing an issue. Perhaps if the judges had seen an "assault," rather than a "practical joke," they might have hesitated before bending the supple law of insurance coverage in Woo's favor.

My judgment is that *Woo* is a profoundly distasteful application of a seemingly worthy rule. I have to believe that insurance law is capable of doing better in unusual cases like this. But if it isn't, then we ought to rethink how comfortable we are with the costs of its presently creaky administration, and what practical alternatives exist. Most of the time, I think the legal system is correct to allocate doubts against insurers, but this is the rare case in which the result is plainly unjust. Perhaps the court didn't mean everything it said; some later passages equivocate on the issue of "conceivable vs. actual" coverage.

I'm reminded of the one argument I find convincing in favor of the "exclusionary rule," which frees the guilty criminal in order to vindicate the rights of the innocent. In law school, my Criminal Law professor observed that the usual alternative—punishing rights-violating police officers—wouldn't actually result in more convictions. The police would simply avoid the bad behavior thought necessary to catch the criminals. The only difference between that system and the current one is that now, we have to watch the crook smirking as

---

4. See Adam F. Scales, Man, God and the Serbonian Bog: The Evolution of Accidental Death Insurance, 86 Iowa L. Rev. 173 (2000).

he walks out of court a free man. Perhaps that is how one should feel about the *Woo* case.

Dr. Woo's attorney describes his client as a "kindhearted, fun-loving man." Perhaps if he had it to do all over again, he would instead present Alberts with a birthday cake while singing "Spider Pig." But then, he wouldn't be a rich man today. Woo's attorney also believes that the decision will send a message to insurers that they should think twice before abandoning their policyholders. He is probably correct. But I wonder whether the residents of Washington will get that message. Most people don't particularly like going to the dentist, and this perverse outcome is unlikely to help. Perhaps that's the real legacy of Dr. Woo: the next time a patient squirms in the dentist's chair and wonders, "Is it safe?", the answer will be no.

B. The Reservation of Rights, Terminating the Duty to Defend, and Dealing with Conflicts of Interest

The complaint allegation rule inevitably requires liability insurers to defend claims that are, in at least some sense, not covered. The typical understanding is that the insurer can avoid defending a claim that meets the complaint allegation rule only by bringing a declaratory judgment action (except in the limited circumstances explored in the notes above). As discussed in the following case, there are some circumstances in which the liability insurance company is not permitted to bring a declaratory judgment action and thus must defend a case that it believes is not covered all the way to trial. As the court in the next case recognizes, these circumstances exacerbate the conflict of interest between the liability insurer and the insured with regard to the defense of the case. The solution the court suggests was novel at the time, but it has become very common.

EMPLOYERS' FIRE INSURANCE CO. v. BEALS

Supreme Court of Rhode Island
240 A.2d 397 (1968)

KELLEHER, J. . . . The incident which gave rise to this action occurred in Providence on May 24, 1965, at St. Dunstan's Day School. On that day, John Marzocchi and one Chester K. Beals, Jr., both of whom were third-grade pupils, were in attendance at their class. The usual classroom routine was suddenly interrupted when John, for some reason not evident in this record, struck Chester in the right eye with a lead pencil. As a result of this tragic circumstance, Chester suffered grave injury and is reported to be permanently deprived of vision in his stricken eye.

The policy in which John is an insured defines under Insuring Agreements the insurer's obligation as follows:

(a) Liability: To pay on behalf of the Insured all sums which the Insured shall become legally obligated to pay as damages because of bodily injury or property damage, and the Company shall defend any suit against the Insured alleging such bodily injury or property damage and seeking damages which are payable under the terms of this policy, even if any of the allegations of the suit are groundless, false or fraudulent. . . .

The policy, however, contains under Special Exclusions a clause which provides that no coverage is afforded if the " . . . bodily injury or property damage [was] caused intentionally by or at the direction of the Insured. . . ."

The insurer in the instant action has joined as defendants John, Chester and Chester's parents. In its complaint, the insurer alleges that John "intentionally struck" Chester with a pencil and therefore, by operation of its exclusionary clause referred to above, it disclaims any obligation to defend John or indemnify him against any damages which he might be obligated to pay as a consequence of the injury he inflicted on Chester.

The superior court appointed a guardian ad litem for each of the minor defendants. John's guardian denies that his ward intentionally injured his schoolmate.

Some two and one-half months after the filing of the insurer's complaint, Chester and his parents on March 27, 1967 commenced a civil action against John, his parents, St. Dunstan's Day School and the third-grade teacher. The complaint consists of six counts. In each count, Chester seeks to recover $250,000 for his injuries while his parents seek the sum of $50,000 for their consequential damages. That part of the complaint relative to the present action contains an allegation which declares that John Marzocchi "negligently and carelessly, or willfully or maliciously" caused the pencil to strike Chester.

In dismissing the insurer's complaint, the trial justice observed that the uniform declaratory judgments act (G.L. 1956, chap. 30 of title 9) was not designed to compel an injured person, himself not being a party to the insurance contract, to litigate issues in a declaratory judgment action which would otherwise be tried in the pending tort suit. In short, to use the words of the trial justice, the declaratory judgment should not be used to force the parties to have "a dress rehearsal" of an important issue expected to be tried in the injury suit. . . .

The insurer maintains that the facts in the present controversy present it with a perplexing dilemma which can only be resolved by a declaratory judgment. It seeks to have decided by a declaratory proceeding whether or not the injury complained of by Chester was intentionally inflicted by John or was in the alternative the result of an accident. If this issue were decided, insurer's obligation to defend and indemnify would be clearly settled and all the parties would presumably act in accordance with its determination. The insurer further asserts that a failure to have this issue resolved before the trial on the injury causes a sharp conflict of interest to arise between itself and the insured. This conflict can be concisely described as follows: the prime interests of the insurer would best be served by an adjudication that the injury to Chester was caused intentionally, for in such an event insurer owes no duty to defend or indemnify insureds; contrariwise, the prime interests of the insured would best be served by either an adjudication that the injury to Chester was the result of a pure accident—for in such an event the insurer clearly owes a duty to defend—or alternatively was the result of the negligent conduct of defendant, in which case insurer would be obliged to defend and indemnify insured up to the extent of its policy limits. Moreover, if the insurer attempts to exculpate itself from obligations under the policy by a showing that the injury to Chester was intentionally caused, it would expose the insured to greater personal liability and a possible award of punitive damages. This polarization of interest, argues the insurer, makes it imperative that the above issue be disposed of before the principal tort suit, otherwise attorneys designated to represent the insured by the insurer would be asked to represent simultaneously two different parties with irreconcilable interests.

The narrow issue raised by this appeal is whether or not the trial justice in denying insurer's request for a declaratory judgment so abused his discretion as to warrant a reversal of his actions. For the reasons which follow, we think he acted with propriety and accordingly uphold his decision.

Initially we wish to point out that . . . [the] declaratory judgments act is concerned with a remedy, the granting of which is purely discretionary. This discretionary power remains intact despite the technical sufficiency of the complaint to withstand a 12(b)(6) motion or its apparent efficacy to invoke the court's jurisdiction. Thus, even if the complaint contains a set of facts which bring it within the scope of our declaratory judgments act, there is no duty imposed thereby on the court to grant such relief, but rather the court is free to decide in the exercise of its discretion whether or not to award the relief asked for. We point out, however, that this discretion is not absolute and its exercise is subject to appropriate appellate review.

The utility of a declaratory judgment action in liability insurance cases cannot be denied, for it is a remedy readily adaptable to controversies in which there is a hassle over the coverage offered by a policy as applied to a crystallized set of facts. Oftentimes it is the most expeditious and fairest method by which an insurer can secure an advance determination as to its contractual duty to defend or indemnify one of its policyholders. 6A Moore, Federal Practice para. 57:19, at 3111 (2d ed.). Use of a declaratory action can be effectively summoned to resolve a wide variety of legal and factual issues which are peculiarly common to insurance cases; for example, it can be employed to dispose of issues relating to policy liability limits, waiver of rights, forfeiture of rights for alleged nonpayment of premiums and ownership, assignment or beneficiary rights. 3 Barron & Holtzoff, Federal Practice and Procedure, §1264, ¶282-86. Thus when uncertainty exists as to the precise obligations and rights flowing between an insurer and an insured by reason of a contract of insurance, a declaratory action could well provide the much needed source of enlightenment and clarification in order that both parties can proceed to litigate issues fully aware of the responsibilities and duties, if any, each may owe to the other.

Although there may be a recognized need for a declaration of rights emanating from an insurance contract, it is nonetheless proper for a court in the exercise of its discretion to refuse to grant a declaratory judgment under certain circumstances. Certainly before such a judgment is awarded, the court must carefully examine and weigh all relevant factors which bear on the propriety of granting this type of relief in order to be assured that no rights of any interested party will be abused in the process. Among the factors considered by courts in this regard are the inconvenience and burden to respective litigants and the inequitable conduct on the part of the individual seeking the relief. 3 Barron & Holtzoff, *supra*, §1265 at 299. Courts have, for example, not infrequently admonished insurance attorneys against the unfair use of declaratory judgments as a procedural fencing technique to influence unduly the choice of a forum, to wrest control of litigation from injured parties, or to cause a confusing alteration of the burden of proof or the burden of going forward with evidence. 6A Moore, *supra*, at 3113; Note, *Availability of a Declaratory Judgment When Another Suit Is Pending*, 51 Yale L.J. 511, 515 [(1942)]. If it appears that a declaratory judgment would work such resultant injustice upon any interested party, courts have uniformly rebuffed its attempted invocation.

In addition, it is most important for courts in considering whether or not to award a declaratory judgment to examine the issues sought to be resolved by the insurer. If the troublesome issue giving rise to insurer's dilemma is one which is separable from the issues awaiting to be litigated in the principal tort suit, a declaratory judgment should be liberally awarded. Advance determination of such issues is of great assistance to all the parties; and an early resolution of questions of this type, generally speaking, does not adversely affect the interest of the injured party. Thus, declaratory judgment proceedings are ideally suited for preliminary disposition of such issues as whether or not lack of timely notice or failure to cooperate on the part of the insured absolves the insurer of its obligation to defend or indemnify.

On the other hand, if the vexatious issue giving rise to the conflict of interests between the insured and the insurer is inextricably related to those issues which will ultimately determine the insured's liability to the injured party in the tort suit, courts normally and justifiably deny the application for a declaratory judgment. *Nationwide Mut. Ins. Co. v. Dennis*, 217 N.Y.S.2d 680 (N.Y. App. Div. 1961). To award a declaratory judgment in such an event would doubtlessly clear up the insurer's obligation to the insured under their insurance contract, but, in our opinion, it would do so at the harsh expense of the injured party. We are of the belief that to allow insurance companies to litigate issues which are identical with ones to be tried later during the injury suit would be tantamount to permitting insurance companies to assume unfairly the control and command of the tort litigation. To do otherwise would surely jeopardize the injured party's right to direct, control and manage the course of his injury suit.

The insurer in this case plainly seeks to have adjudicated in its declaratory action the causation of the injury to the Beals youth; this same issue is a vital one to be resolved in the ensuing damage action brought by Beals against its insured, John Marzocchi; accordingly, notwithstanding the penumbra of uncertainty which obscures the insurer's duty under its policy to the insured, the trial justice, in our opinion, acted with due propriety in declining to award a declaratory judgment in the instant matter.

Having concluded that the trial justice correctly dismissed the insurer's complaint, we deem it appropriate at this point to direct a comment relative to the duty owed by an insurer to the insured when performance of such a duty raises a serious conflict of interests question for an attorney designated to represent both the insurer and the insured at the trial of the injury suit. . . .

While the insurer makes much of the alleged conflict of interests, it overlooks the fact that if John's guardian appreciates the conflict of interests which arises for attorneys who are asked by the insurance company to provide a defense for John in this action and nonetheless expresses willingness to accept the services of the insurance attorneys in his defense, the significance of the conflict of interests issue dissolves. An examination of Canon 6 of the professional ethics of the Rhode Island Bar Association discloses that an attorney may represent conflicting interests after a full disclosure of the pertinent facts has been made to the parties involved and they have expressly consented to his retention as counsel. In the instant case, if the insurance company can acquire the assent of John's guardian, it will resolve all doubts as to the propriety of a defense undertaken on John's behalf by the insurer's attorney.

If, however, an insured, after having been apprised of the conflicting interests existing between him and his insurer, declines to be represented by the insurer's attorney, we have a different situation. Concerned as we are that the public's trust in the judicial processes be maintained, this court cannot stand idly by in such circumstances. We are as conscious of an insurer's concern that it control the defense of any action brought against one of its insureds as we are of an insured's expectations that his rights will be properly protected. In our opinion, however, an insured, when faced with the quandary posited by the facts of the instant case, has a legitimate right to refuse to accept the offer of a defense counsel appointed by the insurance company; and when an insured elects to exercise this prerogative, the insurer's desire to control the defense must yield to its obligation to defend its policyholder.

There is, therefore, a discernible need to discover a solution to this dilemma which will, at the same time, be mutually protective and satisfactory to the parties. Our search of the case law and scholarly works dealing with this particular problem plainly indicates to us that no unanimity exists as to any single answer. *See* Keeton, *Ancillary Rights of the Insured Against His Liability Insurer,* 28 Ins. Counsel J. 395 [1961]; Appleman, *Conflicts in Injury Defenses,* 1957 Ins. L.J. 545; Keeton, *Liability Insurance and Responsibility for Settlement,* 67 Harv. L. Rev. 1136 [(1954)].

One novel solution to the problem posed, has been proposed by the New York Court of Appeals. In *Prashker v. United States Guarantee Co.,* 136 N.E.2d 871 (N.Y. 1956), it was suggested that where a conflict of interests has arisen between an insurer and its insured, the attorney to defend the insured in the tort suit should be selected by the insured and the reasonable value of the professional services rendered should be assumed by the insurer. While this suggestion seemingly would afford full protection to the insured's interests, we note that insurers may well be reluctant to endorse it since they feel that their right to rely on a policy's exclusionary clause may be jeopardized.

Another possible solution to the problem under consideration would be to have the insured and the insurer represented by two different attorneys, each of whom is pledged to promote and protect the prime interests of the client he represents. In this way it appears that the deleterious conflict of interests imposed on an attorney who attempts the difficult task of representing both parties is also averted.

Because the insurer has a legitimate interest in seeing that any recovery based on finding of negligence on the part of its insured is kept within reasonable bounds, and since the total expense of this defense is to be assumed by the insurer under its promise to defend, we believe that in each of the above two suggestions the engagement of an independent counsel to represent the insured should be approved by the insurer. Such approval, however, should not be unreasonably withheld.

While an insurer may be dismayed in its having to pay the cost of two attorneys for one civil suit, we are cognizant that the necessity for this action stems from its failure to provide within any degree of clarity for this contingency when it placed the exclusionary clause in its insured's contract. The insurer, being the draftsman, should have set forth its provisions in such clear and distinct language as would have avoided any doubt relative to the extent of its duty to defend. Under a well-established principle, the words of an insurance contract are construed against the insurer. 4 Williston, Contracts, §621, pp. 764-65 (3d ed. Jaeger). Accordingly, the insurance company is bound by the terms of its own contract.

We wish to make it plainly understood that the above two suggested procedures for avoiding the conflict of interests in cases similar to the one now before us, are not to be taken as the only avenues by which an attorney can act with due propriety in these cases. The decision as to which of these alternatives or as to any others which may be proposed in the future is of course to be made conjunctively by the insured, the insurer and the attorneys involved. . . .

NOTES AND QUESTIONS

1. The conflict of interest in this case is, at least in part, a product of the complaint allegation rule. If the insurance company could simply refuse to defend, without concern that it would be estopped from contesting coverage as a result, there would be no conflict of interest. Of course, there would also be no insurer-paid defense, and it is possible that, in the absence of something like the complaint allegation rule, at least some insurers would refuse to defend legitimately covered claims when they judged that the insured defendant would be unlikely to take any action against them as a result. And defendants might be unlikely to take action in a great many cases because, if there is no insurance to collect, plaintiffs may well abandon their claims. As this suggests, the complaint allegation rule in part protects plaintiffs, and thus living with the conflicts of interest that the rule creates may be necessary to promote the compensation and other goals of tort law. As this brief discussion demonstrates, seemingly obscure and definitely arcane legal rules regarding the liability insurers' duty to defend have a real impact on tort law in action.

2. One of the concerns that the court uses as a basis for affirming the trial court's dismissal of the declaratory judgment action is that the declaratory judgment action would determine facts that ought to be determined in the underlying tort case. One alternative to forbidding the declaratory judgment action would be a rule that the facts determined in the declaratory judgment proceeding would not be preclusive in the underlying tort case. For an excellent analysis of these and related issues, see generally Ellen S. Pryor, *The Tort Liability Regime and the Duty to Defend,* 58 Md. L. Rev. 1 (1999). Not all courts have precluded insurers from bringing declaratory judgment actions in which the facts of the underlying tort case will be determined. *See, e.g., Preferred Risk Ins. Co. v. Gill,* 507 N.E.2d 1118 (Ohio 1987). Is the risk that the insured will lose "control and command of the tort litigation" outweighed by the potential efficiency inherent in a declaratory judgment?

3. For an insightful student note arguing that simultaneous declaratory judgment proceedings should be allowed even in "overlap" cases (i.e., cases in which the same facts are relevant to both liability and coverage, as in *Beals*), provided that the insured is not collaterally estopped in the tort case by the result in the coverage case, see Gregor J. Schwinghammer, Jr., Comment, *Insurance Litigation in Florida: Declaratory Judgments and the Duty to Defend,* 50 U. Miami L. Rev. 945 (1996). What might be some of the practical differences between the litigation behavior of parties in tort actions in jurisdictions that permit simultaneous declaratory judgment actions and jurisdictions that do not?

4. Notwithstanding the fact that New York, Rhode Island, and Illinois (*see Maryland Casualty Co. v. Peppers*, 355 N.E.2d 24 (Ill. 1976)) arrived at the "independent counsel" solution to the conflict of interest first, independent defense counsel are widely called "*Cumis* counsel" after the first California appellate court decision to adopt this approach. *See San Diego Navy Fed. Credit Union v. Cumis Ins. Soc'y, Inc.*, 208 Cal. Rptr. 494 (Ct. App. 1984). The California legislature subsequently enacted a statute, Cal. Civ. Code §2860 (West 2001), clarifying the *Cumis* obligation:

§2860.   Provision of Independent Counsel to Insured; Conflicts of Interest; Selection of Counsel; Waiver of Right to Counsel

(a) If the provisions of a policy of insurance impose a duty to defend upon an insurer and a conflict of interest arises which creates a duty on the part of the insurer to provide independent counsel to the insured, the insurer shall provide independent counsel to represent the insured unless, at the time the insured is informed that a possible conflict may arise or does exist, the insured expressly waives, in writing, the right to independent counsel. An insurance contract may contain a provision which sets forth the method of selecting that counsel consistent with this section.

(b) For purposes of this section, a conflict of interest does not exist as to allegations or facts in the litigation for which the insurer denies coverage; however, when an insurer reserves its rights on a given issue and the outcome of that coverage issue can be controlled by counsel first retained by the insurer for the defense of the claim, a conflict of interest may exist. No conflict of interest shall be deemed to exist as to allegations of punitive damages or be deemed to exist solely because an insured is sued for an amount in excess of the insurance policy limits.

(c) When the insured has selected independent counsel to represent him or her, the insurer may exercise its right to require that the counsel selected by the insured possess certain minimum qualifications which may include that the selected counsel have (1) at least five years of civil litigation practice which includes substantial defense experience in the subject at issue in the litigation, and (2) errors and omissions coverage. The insurer's obligation to pay fees to the independent counsel selected by the insured is limited to the rates which are actually paid by the insurer to attorneys retained by it in the ordinary course of business in the defense of similar actions in the community where the claim arose or is being defended. This subdivision does not invalidate other different or additional policy provisions pertaining to attorney's fees or providing for methods of settlement of disputes concerning those fees. Any dispute concerning attorney's fees not resolved by these methods shall be resolved by final and binding arbitration by a single neutral arbitrator selected by the parties to the dispute.

(d) When independent counsel has been selected by the insured, it shall be the duty of that counsel and the insured to disclose to the insurer all information concerning the action except privileged materials relevant to coverage disputes, and timely to inform and consult with the insurer on all matters relating to the action. Any claim of privilege asserted is subject to in camera review in the appropriate law and motion department of the superior court. Any information disclosed by the insured or by independent counsel is not a waiver of the privilege as to any other party.

(e) The insured may waive its right to select independent counsel by signing the following statement: "I have been advised and informed of my right to select independent counsel to represent me in this lawsuit. I have considered this matter fully and freely waive my right to select independent counsel at this time. I authorize my insurer to select a defense attorney to represent me in this lawsuit."

(f) Where the insured selects independent counsel pursuant to the provisions of this section, both the counsel provided by the insurer and independent counsel selected by the insured shall be allowed to participate in all aspects of the litigation. Counsel shall cooperate fully in the exchange of information that is consistent with each counsel's ethical and legal obligation to the insured. Nothing in this section shall relieve the insured of his or her duty to cooperate with the insurer under the terms of the insurance contract.

5. The *Cumis* statute appears to contemplate that the insured is entitled to choose the independent counsel. The *Beals* court also contemplates that the insured is entitled to choose the counsel, but the insurer should "approve" the counsel, with the proviso that such approval "shall not be unreasonably withheld." What problems can you foresee in permitting the insurance company to choose the counsel? *Cf. United States Fid. & Guar. Co. v. Lewis A. Roser Co.,* 585 F.2d 932, 938 n.5 (8th Cir. 1978) ("Even the most optimistic view of human nature requires us to realize that an attorney employed by an insurance company will slant his efforts, perhaps unconsciously, in the interest of his real client—the one who is paying his fee and from whom he hopes to receive future business—the insurance company."). What problems can you see in giving the insurance company authority to refuse to approve the counsel?

Consider how the RLLI sections excerpted below address the issues raised in the *Beals* case and in the notes above. Specifically, under what circumstances must a liability insurer provide an independent counsel to defend the insured against a claim? In such cases, what obligations are imposed on the independent counsel? For a reservation of rights to be effective, what must be included in the letter to the insured? If an insurer agrees to defend the insured's claim under a reservation of rights, under what circumstances can the insurer later withdraw from the defense without losing its right to contest coverage?

RESTATEMENT OF THE LAW LIABILITY INSURANCE

American Law Institute (Tent. Draft No. 1, May 2016)

§15.   Reserving the Right to Contest Coverage

(1) An insurer that undertakes the defense of a claim may later contest coverage for the claim only if it provides notice to the insured, before undertaking the defense, of any ground for contesting coverage of which it knows or should know.

(2) If an insurer already defending a legal action learns of information that provides a ground for contesting coverage for that action, the insurer must give notice of that ground to the insured within a reasonable time in order to reserve the right to contest coverage for the action on that ground.

(3) Notice to the insured of a ground for contesting coverage must include a written explanation of the ground, including the specific insurance-policy terms and facts upon which the potential ground for contesting coverage is based, in language that is understandable by a reasonable person in the position of the insured.

(4) When an insurer reasonably cannot complete its investigation before undertaking the defense of a legal action, the insurer may temporarily reserve its right to contest coverage for the action by providing to the insured an initial, general notice of reservation of rights, in language that is understandable by a reasonable person in the position of the insured, but to preserve that reservation of rights the insurer must pursue that investigation with reasonable diligence and must provide the detailed notice stated in subsection (3) within a reasonable time.

Comment:

a. The basis for the reservation-of-rights requirement. The rule requiring insurers to provide timely notice in order to preserve the right to contest coverage was originally grounded in estoppel. The underlying idea is that insureds' expectations about their liability insurance protection are formed in relation to a full-coverage case. In a full-coverage case, the insurer faces substantially all of the risk, and a rational insured not only can safely concede full control over the defense to the insurer, but also can choose to engage with the defense at the minimal level required to satisfy the duty to cooperate. Once there is the possibility that the insurer may refuse to pay a judgment, however, the insured faces a very different calculus. Now the insurer asserts that it does not face substantially all of the risk. That leads to potential conflicts of interest regarding the scope and direction of the defense and settlement strategy. If insureds do not receive notice of the possibility that the insurer may later deny coverage, they are deprived of the opportunity to engage with the defense at a level appropriate to the risk, and they may not realize, for example, that they have the right to independent counsel.

This situation may meet the requirements of estoppel in many cases. For example, the insurer's provision of a defense of an action without providing notice of the potential ground for contesting coverage can be understood as a promise to pay the settlement or judgment that may result. The insured's passive acceptance of, rather than active engagement in, the defense can be treated as reasonable and detrimental reliance on the insurer's promise. There are two problems with grounding this rule entirely in estoppel, however. First, the rule is now so well established that an insurer that does not raise a ground for contesting coverage should be understood to have waived its right to contest coverage in nearly all cases. Second, there are situations in which it would be very difficult for the insured to demonstrate detrimental reliance, particularly in the consumer context. For these reasons, among others, courts in practice have dispensed with the need to explicitly satisfy the requirements of estoppel in the reservation-of-rights context. This Section recognizes that practical reality by stating a simple-to-apply, straightforward rule that requires an insurer to inform the insured about the insurer's possible defenses to coverage at the outset of the defense of a claim, or, pursuant to subsection (4), within a reasonable time thereafter. Insurers that do not timely reserve their rights to contest coverage lose those rights. . . .

e. No right to reject the defense. This Section does not follow a minority rule that gives an insured the option to "reject the defense" under a reservation of rights issued pursuant to a liability insurance policy that does not explicitly grant the insured this option. Under this "reject the defense" rule, an insurer, in effect, gives up the right to defend whenever it provides notice to the insured of a potential ground for contesting coverage: the insured may choose to allow the insurer to continue defending under a reservation of rights, but it has the option of hiring and paying the lawyer directly and later seeking reimbursement from the insurer. This rule has been justified on the grounds of protecting insureds from conflicts of interest. Yet, managing conflicts of interest does not require the insurer to relinquish the right to defend in every case in which the insurer reserves the right to contest coverage. A reservation of rights undeniably reduces the alignment of interest between insurer and insured from that of a full-coverage case, but other rules governing the duty to defend and the duty to make reasonable settlement decisions better protect the insured than a rule that gives the insured the option of self-funding its own defense and then seeking reimbursement.

In some cases, the independent-defense requirement of §16 provides better protection to insureds than the "reject-the-defense" rule, because the insurer is required to pay for an independent defense on an ongoing basis. In other cases, insureds are protected by the rule stated in §14 requiring the insurer to provide a defense that makes reasonable efforts to protect them from all of the judgment risks posed by the legal action and the rule stated in §25(3) authorizing them to settle without the insurer's consent unless the insurer waives any grounds for coverage. Moreover, a reject-the-defense approach would be meaningless in many, if not most, cases involving consumer insureds, as such insureds are unlikely to have the resources to self-fund the defense of a legal action.

Nevertheless, the rules stated in this Section do not prohibit parties from entering into insurance contracts that provide the insured the right to reject the defense. In addition, insureds that wish to have the option to reject the defense may also contract for that right through a claims-handling agreement, which is a common form of contract entered into as part of a liability insurance program assembled by commercial policyholders.

. . .

§16. The Obligation to Provide an Independent Defense

When an insurer with the duty to defend provides the insured notice of a ground for contesting coverage under §15 and there are facts at issue that are common to the legal action for which the defense is due and to the coverage dispute, such that the action could be defended in a manner that would benefit the insurer at the expense of the insured, the insurer must provide an independent defense of the action.

Comment:

a. Common facts at issue in the legal action and the coverage dispute. When there are facts that are common to the claimant's allegations in the legal action for which a defense is sought and to the insurer's asserted ground for contesting coverage, there is the risk that the defense of the action may be handled in a manner that advantages the insurer in contesting coverage. This risk exists even if facts adjudicated in the coverage proceeding are not binding in the underlying legal action brought against the insured, because the knowledge gained in the underlying proceeding could be used in the coverage proceeding. Leaving the management of this conflict of interest to the professional judgment of the defense lawyer selected by the insurer may in fact be adequate to protect insureds in most situations, but there are enough examples of mistakes having been made at the insured's expense to justify a structural, rather than a disciplinary and malpractice-liability, solution. The structural solution stated in this Section—requiring an independent defense—provides better protection to insureds and also increases the legitimacy of liability insurance and defense lawyers within the civil-justice system. This approach is consistent with Restatement Third, The Law Governing Lawyers, which recognizes the potential for conflicts of interest whenever there is a question about insurance coverage for a legal action. See §134 (Compensation or Direction of a Lawyer by a Third Person), Comment *f* (representing an insured).

Illustrations:

1. When investigating a serious but otherwise routine "slip and fall" involving a repairman at the home of an insured with adequate liability insurance for the resulting suit, the insurer discovers information indicating that the insured has been conducting business at the home, despite having answered "no" to a question in the policy application regarding business at the home. The insurer reserves the right to contest coverage for the suit on the grounds of misrepresentation. Because the facts that will determine the outcome of the misrepresentation defense are different than the facts that will determine the outcome of the slip-and-fall claim, the insurer is not obligated to provide an independent defense.

2. Following a legal separation in an abusive marriage, the insured regularly stalks his wife. One evening, in a drunken rage, the insured shoots his wife's boyfriend and then himself. Both survive. The boyfriend files suit against the insured, who requests a defense from his homeowners' insurer asserting that he lacked the mental capacity to form the intent needed for the intentional-harm exclusion in the liability insurance policy to apply. The insurer agrees to defend the suit but reserves the right to contest coverage based on the intentional-harm exclusion. The insurer must provide an independent defense because the intent of the insured is a fact that may affect liability and damages in the suit against the insured as well as the potential coverage contest, thereby creating a risk that the defense of the suit may be handled in a manner that increases the likelihood that the insurer will be able to avoid coverage through the application of the intentional-harm exclusion.

b. Benefit the insurer in contesting coverage. Any reservation of rights creates a divergence between the interests of the insured and the insurer. As long as there is a possibility that the insurer will be able to avoid coverage for the legal action, the insurer has less incentive to defeat that action and, thus, more reason to underinvest in the defense of the action. Liability insurance law protects insureds from insurer underinvestment through the ordinary duty-to-defend requirements (including liability for failure to provide an adequate defense), the ability of insureds to settle without consent under §25(3), and the potential for bad-faith liability. This independent-counsel requirement is directed at a problem that is qualitatively different than the more routine underinvestment incentive. The independent-counsel requirement addresses the possibility that an insurer may actively manage the defense to avoid coverage for the legal action. While labels, alone, are not sufficient to convey the distinction, the independent-counsel requirement addresses the risk of sabotage, not underinvestment.

. . .

§18. Terminating the Duty to Defend a Legal Action

An insurer's duty to defend a legal action terminates only upon the occurrence of one or more of the following events:

(1) An explicit waiver by the insured of its right to a defense of the action;

(2) Final adjudication of the action;

(3) Final adjudication or dismissal of part of the action that eliminates any basis for coverage of any remaining components of the action;

(4) Settlement of the action that fully and finally resolves the entire action;

(5) Partial settlement of the action, entered into with the consent of the insured, that eliminates any basis for coverage of any remaining components of the action;

(6) If so stated in the insurance policy, exhaustion of the applicable policy limit;

(7) A correct determination by the insurer based on undisputed facts not at issue or potentially at issue in the legal action for which the defense is sought, as permitted under §13(3); or

(8) Final adjudication that the insurer does not have a duty to defend the action.

. . .

PROBLEM: CAROL GREEN'S FALL

Carol Green sued Tom Brown because of a slip and fall she suffered at his house. The complaint alleges that Carol visited a house owned by Tom, that she fell and was injured during the visit, and that the injuries were caused by Tom's negligence. Tom tendered the suit to Good Neighbor Insurance. Good Neighbor believes that it has a defense to coverage.

Consider the following possible coverage defenses in light of all the ALI Principles excerpted so far in this chapter. For each defense, consider whether that defense would relieve Good Neighbor from the obligation to defend the lawsuit and, if not, if there is a way that Good Neighbor could eventually be relieved of the obligation to defend. Consider also whether Tom should be entitled to "independent counsel" for his defense.

A. The claim is not covered because Tom is not a named insured under the Good Neighbor policy.

B. The claim is not covered because Tom failed to pay his premiums and Good Neighbor followed the statutorily mandated procedures for canceling the policy.

C. The claim is not covered because Tom lied to the insurance agent about the number of people who lived in the house. He said that he lived alone, but in reality, this is a group house occupied by eight students, one of whom was the person that Carol was visiting at the time she fell. Good Neighbor does not insure group houses under standard homeowners' insurance policies such as the one issued to Tom.

D. The claim is not covered because it is excluded under the "business pursuits" exclusion. Carol Green was a patient coming for an appointment in Tom Brown's home office.

E. The claim is not covered because Tom breached the notice requirement under the policy. He failed to notify Good Neighbor until there was a default judgment entered against him in the underlying case, and he now wants Good Neighbor to try to have the judgment set aside and the case reopened.

F. The claim is not covered because Tom breached the duty to cooperate. He lied to the adjuster who investigated the claim, and he refused to show up for his deposition. As a result, Good Neighbor wishes to withdraw from its defense of the claim.

G. The claim is not covered because it is excluded under the intentional act exclusion in the policy. Tom intentionally pushed Carol down the stairs during an argument.

After you have decided for each possible coverage defense what the insurer's legal obligations would be, consider how the following factors might affect what the insurer actually does in defending the claim:

A. The strength of the coverage defense—that is, whether the insurer is 100 percent certain that the coverage defense will stand up in court. Consider, for example, how an insurer might behave differently if it seemed that the coverage defense was only somewhat more likely than not to be upheld.

B. The strength of the plaintiff's underlying claim. Consider whether the insurer might treat a weak claim differently than a strong claim.

C. The dollar value of the plaintiff's underlying claim (for the time being, assume that the limits of the policy exceed the plaintiff's demand).

D. The wealth of the policyholder. Consider how the risks facing the insurer vary according to the wealth of the policyholder, and why. For example, think about how the incentives of the underlying plaintiff and the policyholder differ in a situation in which the policyholder is an ordinary middle-class person whose assets will be very difficult to collect as compared to a situation in which the policyholder is a solvent corporation or wealthy individual.

II.   THE DUTY TO SETTLE

Typically, liability insurance policies provide that the insurance company has the "discretion" to settle a claim, but they say nothing about any duty to settle. Look at the insuring agreement in the sample CGL policy (see Figure 4.2), for example. Why might insurance companies want their policies to clearly state that the company has the discretion to settle a claim?

Despite the absence of policy language regarding the duty to settle, the duty is almost as old as mass market liability insurance itself. The primary reason why courts have imposed the duty is perhaps best encapsulated in the explanation that the duty prevents insurers from gambling with their policyholders' money. A simple example illustrates what that explanation means.

Consider a situation in which an insured bought the statutory minimum amount of automobile liability insurance and is then involved in a serious accident that badly injures another person. The exact dollars at issue are not important, but a common statutory minimum level of automobile bodily injury liability coverage is $20,000 per person and $40,000 per accident, an amount of money that cannot begin to cover the medical expenses, lost wages, and pain and suffering of a seriously injured person.

If the insured defendant's liability is clear, just about any insurance company will immediately offer to pay the policy limits to settle the claim, regardless of whether there is a duty to settle, if only to avoid the cost of defending the claim. If the insured defendant has a possible defense to the claim, however, the insurance company's incentives in this situation could change dramatically, depending on whether the policy limit caps the insurance company's exposure. If the insurance company's possible liability is capped at the policy limits (plus the costs of defense), the insurance company's incentives to settle the case are much less than they would be if the insurance company's potential liability included the entire damages to the plaintiff.

A simple numerical example should make this clear. Suppose that there is a factual dispute about whether it was the injured plaintiff or the insured defendant who ran a red light and therefore was at fault for the accident. Suppose further that the insurance company's claims supervisor in charge of the case believes that there is a 20 percent chance that the jury will find the defendant liable. Assume also that, if the jury does find the defendant liable the likely verdict will be in the range of $50,000 and that there is an 80 percent chance of a defense verdict of no liability. Suppose, finally, that the policy limit is $20,000 and the bare bones cost of taking the case to trial is $5,000. What all of this means is that, if the case were to go to trial and result in a $50,000 plaintiff's verdict, the insurer would be on the hook for only the $20,000 policy limit in addition to the cost of trying the case, while the insured would be responsible for the amount of the award in excess of the policy limit — that is, the insured would be responsible for paying the $30,000 "excess judgment" owed to the tort plaintiff.

This situation — giving the insurer total discretion over settlement decisions in situations in which there is a claim against the insured that is potentially in excess of the policy limit — creates a conflict of interest. The insurer will prefer to take some cases to trial that the insured would prefer to settle. This is because the insurer's expected cost of going to trial is, under some conditions, lower than the insured's expected cost of going to trial. The duty to settle is a response to this divergence of interests.

To see this point using the numbers from the example above, note that the expected cost to the insurer of going to trial can be calculated as follows:

> (20% chance of losing the tort suit against the insured x $20,000 policy limit)
> + (80% chance of winning the tort suit against the insured x $0)
> + ($5,000 defense costs, which the policy makes the responsibility of the insurer)

     $9,000

What this means is that, if the insurer received a settlement demand of, say $12,000, the insurer would have an incentive to reject the offer and take the case to trial, preferring to risk the $50,000 judgment—of which, again, only $20,000 would be the insurer's responsibility. Indeed, the insurer would reject any settlement demand greater than $9,000, assuming that the insurer is risk neutral (i.e., it is indifferent between paying $9,000 with certainty or taking a risky bet with an expected value of $9,000), which seems a reasonable starting assumption, and assuming that the insurer is not overly concerned about earning a bad reputation for exploiting this conflict of interest.

The insured has a very different set of incentives. The insured, at least at this point in the case, would prefer that the insurer accept *any* settlement demand that is equal to or less than the policy limit of $20,000. This is because such a settlement would be fully covered by the insurer, as provided in the policy. (We are ignoring the possibility of deductibles, which would admittedly complicated the picture.) Thus, in the example above, the insured would obviously want the insurer to accept the $12,000 settlement demand.

As this example shows, capping the insurance company's liability at the policy limits allows the insurance company to use its control over settlement to gamble with the policyholder's money. The insurance company is rolling the dice, but it is the policyholder who will have to pay if the wrong number comes up. For a similar explanation in Judge Easterbrook's characteristically pithy language, see *Transport Insurance Co. v. Post Express Co.*, 138 F.3d 1189 (7th Cir. 1998). This basic conflict of interest has long been recognized by the courts.

The following case was the first in which the California Supreme Court held that a liability insurance company had a duty, under certain circumstances, to settle a covered claim within the limits of the policy. When you look at the dollars at issue in the case, keep in mind that the accident took place in the 1950s. Also, as you read the case, begin to think about what the legal rule should be. Specifically, do we want a rule that says insurers must accept any settlement demand within the policy limits? Or do we want a rule that requires insurers to accept only "reasonable" settlement demands? What would the standard for a reasonable settlement demand be? We will return to these questions after the case.

COMUNALE v. TRADERS & GENERAL INSURANCE CO.

Supreme Court of California
328 P.2d 198 (1958)

GIBSON, C.J. Mr. and Mrs. Comunale were struck in a marked pedestrian crosswalk by a truck driven by Percy Sloan. Mr. Comunale was seriously injured, and his wife suffered minor injuries. Sloan was insured by defendant Traders and General Insurance Company under a policy that contained limits of liability in the sum of $10,000 for each person injured and $20,000 for each accident. He notified Traders of the accident and was told that the policy did not provide coverage because he was driving a truck that did not belong to him. When the Comunales filed suit against Sloan, Traders refused to defend the action, and Sloan employed competent counsel to represent him. On the second day of the trial Sloan informed Traders that the Comunales would compromise the case for $4,000, that he did not have enough money to effect the settlement, and that it was highly probable the jury would return a verdict in excess of the policy limits. Traders was obligated to defend any personal injury suit covered by the policy, but it was given the right to make such settlement as it might deem expedient. Sloan demanded that Traders assume the defense and settlement of the case. Traders refused, and the trial proceeded to judgment in favor of Mr. Comunale for $25,000 and Mrs. Comunale for $1,250.

Sloan did not pay the judgment, and the Comunales sued Traders under a provision in the policy that permitted an injured party to maintain an action after obtaining judgment against the insured. (*See* Ins. Code, §11580, subd. (b)(2).) In that suit judgment was rendered in favor of Mr. Comunale for $10,000 and in favor of Mrs. Comunale for $1,250. This judgment was satisfied by Traders after it was affirmed.

Comunale obtained an assignment of all of Sloan's rights against Traders and then commenced the present action to recover from Traders the portion of his judgment against Sloan which was in excess of the policy limits. The jury returned a verdict in Comunale's favor, but the trial court entered a judgment for Traders notwithstanding the verdict. . . .

LIABILITY IN EXCESS OF THE POLICY LIMITS

In determining whether Traders is liable for the portion of the judgment against Sloan in excess of the policy limits, we must take into consideration the fact that Traders not only wrongfully refused to defend the action against Sloan but also refused to accept an offer of settlement within the policy limits. It is not claimed the settlement offer was unreasonable in view of the extent of the injuries and the probability that Sloan would be found liable, and Traders' only reason for refusing to settle was its claim that the accident was not covered by the policy. Because of its wrongful denial of coverage, Traders failed to consider Sloan's interest in having the suit against him compromised by a settlement within the policy limits.

There is an implied covenant of good faith and fair dealing in every contract that neither party will do anything which will injure the right of the other to receive the benefits of the agreement. This principle is applicable to policies of insurance. *Hilker v. Western Automobile Ins. Co.*, 231 N.W. 257, 258 (Wis. 1930), *aff'd on rehg.*, 235 N.W. 413 (Wis. 1931). In the *Hilker* case it is pointed out that the rights of the insured "go deeper than the mere surface of the contract written for him by defendant" and that implied obligations are imposed "based upon those principles of fair dealing which enter into every contract." 231 N.W. at 258. It is common knowledge that a large percentage of the claims covered by insurance are settled without litigation and that this is one of the usual methods by which the insured receives protection. Under these circumstances the implied obligation of good faith and fair dealing requires the insurer to settle in an appropriate case although the express terms of the policy do not impose such a duty.

The insurer, in deciding whether a claim should be compromised, must take into account the interest of the insured and give it at least as much consideration as it does to its own interest. When there is great risk of a recovery beyond the policy limits so that the most reasonable manner of disposing of the claim is a settlement which can be made within those limits, a consideration in good faith of the insured's interest requires the insurer to settle the claim. Its unwarranted refusal to do so constitutes a breach of the implied covenant of good faith and fair dealing.

There is an important difference between the liability of an insurer who performs its obligations and that of an insurer who breaches its contract. The policy limits restrict only the amount the insurer may have to pay in the performance of the contract as compensation to a third person for personal injuries caused by the insured; they do not restrict the damages recoverable by the insured for a breach of contract by the insurer.

The decisive factor in fixing the extent of Traders' liability is not the refusal to defend; it is the refusal to accept an offer of settlement within the policy limits. Where there is no opportunity to compromise the claim and the only wrongful act of the insurer is the refusal to defend, the liability of the insurer is ordinarily limited to the amount of the policy plus attorneys' fees and costs.

In such a case it is reasoned that, if the insured has employed competent counsel to represent him, there is no ground for concluding that the judgment would have been for a lesser sum had the defense been conducted by insurer's counsel, and therefore it cannot be said that the detriment suffered by the insured as the result of a judgment in excess of the policy limits was proximately caused by the insurer's refusal to defend. This reasoning, however, does not apply where the insurer wrongfully refuses to accept a reasonable settlement within the policy limits.

Most of the cases dealing with the insurer's failure to settle involve an insurer who had assumed the defense of the action against the insured. It is generally held that since the insurer has reserved control over the litigation and settlement it is liable for the entire amount of a judgment against the insured, including any portion in excess of the policy limits, if in the exercise of such control it is guilty of bad faith in refusing a settlement. Those cases are, of course, factually distinguishable from the present one since Traders never assumed control over the defense. However, the reason Traders was not in control of the litigation is that it wrongfully refused to defend Sloan, and the breach of its express obligation to defend did not release it from its implied duty to consider Sloan's interest in the settlement.

We do not agree with the cases that hold there is no liability in excess of the policy limits where the insurer, believing there is no coverage, wrongfully refuses to defend and without justification refuses to settle the claim. An insurer who denies coverage does so at its own risk, and, although its position may not have been entirely groundless, if the denial is found to be wrongful it is liable for the full amount which will compensate the insured for all the detriment caused by the insurer's breach of the express and implied obligations of the contract. Certainly an insurer who not only rejected a reasonable offer of settlement but also wrongfully refused to defend should be in no better position than if it had assumed the defense and then declined to settle. The insurer should not be permitted to profit by its own wrong.

A breach which prevents the making of an advantageous settlement when there is a great risk of liability in excess of the policy limits will, in the ordinary course of things, result in a judgment against the insured in excess of those limits. Section 3300 of the Civil Code provides that the measure of damages for a breach of contract is the amount which will compensate the party aggrieved for all the detriment proximately caused by the breach, or which, in the ordinary course of things, would be likely to result from it. . . .

It follows from what we have said that an insurer, who wrongfully declines to defend and who refuses to accept a reasonable settlement within the policy limits in violation of its duty to consider in good faith the interest of the insured in the settlement, is liable for the entire judgment against the insured even if it exceeds the policy limits.

NOTES AND QUESTIONS

1. It is important to point out that much of the California Code, applied in the *Comunale* decisions above, is a codification of California common law, which is not materially different in any systematic sense from the common law of other jurisdictions on this issue. The question resolved in this case under the California Civil Code would be resolved similarly under the common law of most other jurisdictions (though the standard of care for breach of the "duty to settle" does differ somewhat from jurisdiction to jurisdiction). *See generally* Kent Syverud, *The Duty to Settle*, 76 Va. L. Rev. 1113 (1990). What is the doctrinal source of the duty to settle? If breaching the duty to settle breaches the contract, and the contract caps the liability of the insurance company at the policy limit, how is it that the damages for breach of the contract include an amount in excess of that policy limit? The court provides clear answers to these questions. It is important that you understand them.

2. Unfortunately, some courts and commentators have referred to damages in excess of the policy limits as "extracontractual" damages. In the literal sense, this label is accurate: The policyholder gets some *extra* damages because the insurance company breached the *contractual* duty to settle. However, the label has led to muddied thinking. In combination with the liberal use of the term "bad faith" to describe the breach of the duty of good faith that provides the doctrinal foundation for the duty to settle (dating from the first duty to settle case, *Hilker v. Western Automobile Insurance Co.*, 231 N.W. 257 (Wis. 1930)), the term "extracontractual damages" has led many students, and not a few courts and lawyers (and even some law professors!), to misperceive "extracontractual" to mean *beyond contract*, in the sense that the damages being awarded are damages that are somehow not grounded in contract doctrine. As we saw in Chapter 2, damages in excess of the policy limits can be awarded as consequential damages for breach of the insurance contract. Is the recovery in *Comunale* based on tort or contract principles?

3. What is the standard for deciding whether an insurance company breached the duty to settle in this case? What is the difference between a strict liability standard and a negligence standard in this context? What are the pros and cons of each? What is the risk being allocated here? How does the standard of care affect the allocation of that risk? Does or should the intent of the insurance company matter in deciding whether the duty to settle has been breached? Consider these questions again after reading the following note.

A NOTE ON THE STANDARD IN DUTY TO SETTLE CASES

Many courts deciding duty to settle cases apply a version of the negligence standard that is sometimes called the "disregard the limits" rule. The idea, which was first articulated by Professor Robert Keeton in 1954, is simple enough to state: "With respect to the decision whether to settle or try the case, the insurer, acting through its representatives, must use such care as would have been used by an ordinarily prudent insurer with no policy limit applicable to the claim." Robert E. Keeton, *Liability Insurance and Responsibility for Settlement,* 67 Harv. L. Rev. 1136, 1147 (1954). The Supreme Court of California adopted Keeton's articulation in *Crisci v. Sec. Ins. Co.,* 426 P.3d 173, 176 (Cal. 1967), and the "disregard the limits" rule has since become the most common standard in duty to settle cases. *Crisci,* 426 P.3d at 176 ("In determining whether an insurer has given consideration to the interests of the insured, the test is whether a prudent insurer without policy limits would have accepted the settlement offer"); *see also* Paul E. B. Glad et al., 3 New Appleman on Insurance Law Library Ed. §16.06[4][a] ("The most widely used test is typically formulated as 'whether a prudent insurer without policy limits would have accepted the settlement offer'") *quoting Crisci,* 426 P.2d at 176; Kenneth S. Abraham, Insurance Law and Regulation 664-665 (5th ed. 2010) ("The *Crisci* rule is standard law in most jurisdictions . . ."); Syverud, 76 Va. L. Rev. at 1122 & n.23 (noting that at least 16 states have adopted Keeton's standard, which had "gained its most prominent endorsement from the California Supreme Court" in *Crisci*); David R. Anderson & John W. Dunfee, *No Harm, No Foul: Why a Bad Faith Claim Should Fail When the Insurer Pays the Excess Verdict,* 33 Tort & Ins. L.J. 1001, 1004 (1994) (writing that, in most jurisdictions, "an insurer should accept a below-limits settlement demand only if the circumstances are such that a reasonable prudent insurer would settle, or if failure to settle would unreasonable risk a judgment in excess of the policy limits"); Jeffrey W. Stempel, 1 Stempel on Insurance Contracts, §9.05[B], 9-153 ("Many courts require the insurer to behave as if it had no policy limits when making settlement determinations").

The ALI's RLLI adopts a version of this negligence standard for the duty to settle, which it articulates as a "duty to make reasonable settlement decisions" as follows:

§24. The Insurer's Duty to Make Reasonable Settlement Decisions[5]

(1) When an insurer has the authority to settle a legal action brought against the insured, or the authority to settle the action rests with the insured but the insurer's prior consent is required for any settlement to be payable by the insurer, and there is a potential for a judgment in excess of the applicable policy limit, the insurer has a duty to the insured to make reasonable settlement decisions.

(2) A reasonable settlement decision is one that would be made by a reasonable insurer who bears the sole financial responsibility for the full amount of the potential judgment.

(3) An insurer's duty to make reasonable settlement decisions includes the duty to make its policy limits available to the insured for the settlement of a covered legal action that exceeds those policy limits if a reasonable insurer would do so in the circumstances.

---

5. Editor's note: This Section was approved as part of TD. No. 1 in May 2016. This version is from the January 2017 Council Draft No. 2, which differs from that in T.D. No. 1 in two respects: (a) the replacement of the word "insurer" for "person" in subsection (2) and (b) the comments regarding the application of the reasonableness standard.

Comment:

a. A duty to make reasonable settlement decisions rather than the "duty to settle." The duty set forth in this Section is a longstanding rule of insurance law that is frequently referred to in shorthand by commentators and some courts as the "duty to settle." This Section uses a more accurate term, the "duty to make reasonable settlement decisions," to emphasize that the insurer's duty is not to settle every legal action, but rather to protect the insured from unreasonable exposure to a judgment in excess of the limits of the liability insurance policy. Although a strict-liability standard of the sort that might be suggested by the label "duty to settle" would eliminate the need for the reasonableness evaluation, a strict-liability standard has not found favor in the courts. Moreover, the reasonableness standard followed in this Section is more closely tailored to the conflict of interest that underlies the legal duty.

The insurer's duty to make reasonable settlement decisions arose as a special application of the general contract-law duty of good faith and fair dealing in the context of insurance policies that granted the insurer discretion over the settlement of an insured liability action. As courts early recognized, when the insured faces a potential judgment in excess of the policy limit (an "excess judgment"), the insurer may have an incentive to undervalue the possibility of a loss at trial, since a portion of that loss will be borne by the insured rather than by the insurer, absent a legal rule assigning the risk of excess judgment to the insurer. . . .

The duty to make reasonable settlement decisions creates an incentive for insurers to take into account this risk to insureds and excess insurers. Because the purpose of the duty to make reasonable settlement decisions is to align the interests of insurer and insured in cases that expose the insured to damages in excess of the policy limits, the duty is owed only with respect to the exposure to such excess damages. With respect to liability for damages within the policy limits, the insurer's contractual liability for those damages already provides an incentive for the insurer to make reasonable settlement decisions.

b. Equal consideration and the "disregard the limits" rule. In the insurance context, the general duty of good faith and fair dealing is often described as requiring the insurer to give equal consideration to the interests of its insured. The duty to make reasonable settlement decisions can be similarly described as requiring the insurer to give equal consideration to the insured's exposure in excess of the policy limits. When there is the potential for a judgment in excess of the policy limit, equal consideration requires managing the litigation and settlement process in a manner that neutralizes, to the extent possible, the conflict of interest described in Comment *a.* Courts and commentators use a variety of verbal formulas to articulate that requirement more precisely. The standard stated in subsection (2) implements the equal-consideration requirement in actionable terms. A reasonable settlement offer is one that would be accepted or made by a reasonable insurer that bears the sole financial responsibility for the full amount of the potential judgment. Courts and commentators sometimes refer to this formulation of the standard as the "disregard the limits" rule, because it requires the insurer to evaluate the reasonableness of a settlement offer without regard to the policy limits, or, to put it in another way, in a manner that "disregards the limits" of the policy.

c. Relationship to the duty of good faith and fair dealing. Because of its origins in the duty of good faith and fair dealing, courts in some jurisdictions refer to the standard for breach of the duty in the settlement context as one of "bad faith." That formulation suggests the need to prove some bad intent on the part of the insurer that goes beyond the reasonableness standard stated in this Section, and some courts do require such a showing. In most breach-of-settlement-duty cases, however, even those that invoke the language of bad faith, the ultimate test of liability is whether the insurer's conduct was reasonable under the circumstances. To make clear that an insurer's settlement duty is grounded in commercial reasonableness, this Section does not use the term "bad faith" to describe the insurer's breach of the duty to make reasonable settlement decisions. Under the rule followed in this Restatement, an insurer is subject to liability for insurance bad faith only when it fails to perform its duties under a liability insurance policy without a reasonable basis for its conduct and with knowledge or in reckless disregard of its obligation to perform. See §51. . . .

d. Applying the reasonableness standard. The "reasonable insurer" referred to here is a legal construct, similar to that of the "reasonable person" in tort law. As such, it can be understood as an average or ordinary insurer that sells liability insurance of the kind and in the amounts of the liability insurance policy at issue. The duty to make reasonable settlement decisions includes the duty to accept a settlement offer that a reasonable insurer would accept and to make an offer to settle when a reasonable insurer would do so, if that reasonable insurer had sold an insurance policy with limits that were sufficient to cover any likely outcome of the legal action. . . .

In evaluating the reasonableness of an insurer's settlement decisions, the trier of fact may consider, among other evidence, expert testimony as well as testimony from the lawyers and others involved in the underlying insured liability claim. The reasonableness of settlement offers may also take into account other facts, such as the amount of time that is given to evaluate an offer and the jurisdiction in which the case would be tried. It is also appropriate for the trier of fact to consider the procedural factors addressed in Comment *e*. It is important to note that this standard takes into account only the interests of the parties in relation to the legal action at issue, not the insurer's interest in minimizing the overall size of the losses in its portfolio of claims. Otherwise, the insurer would not be giving equal consideration to the interests of the insured.

The effect of this rule is that, once a claimant has made a settlement offer in the underlying litigation that a reasonable insurer would have accepted, an insurer that rejects that offer thereafter bears the risk of an excess judgment against the insured at trial. One practical effect of this rule is to give claimants an incentive during the pretrial phase to make reasonable settlement offers within the policy limits, since the insurer's rejection of such an offer sets the stage for a subsequent breach-of-settlement-duty lawsuit in the event of a verdict that produces an excess judgment that is covered by the policy. In that subsequent lawsuit, it will not be sufficient for the policyholder to simply demonstrate that the amount of the was reasonable; the policyholder must also demonstrate that a reasonable insurer would have accepted the offer. Nevertheless, evidence that the amount of the offer was reasonable would ordinarily be enough to make the reasonableness of the insurer's decision to reject the offer a question of fact. . . .

e. Procedural factors may be considered. The reasonableness standard requires the trier of fact in the breach-of-settlement-duty suit to evaluate the expected value of the underlying legal action at the time of the failed settlement negotiations. That inquiry may be complex and difficult in some cases. Because of the difficulty of determining, in hindsight, whether a settlement offer was reasonable, it is appropriate for the trier of fact to consider procedural factors that affected the quality of the insurer's decisionmaking or that deprived the insured of evidence that would have been available if the insurer had behaved reasonably. Factors that may affect the quality of the insurer's decisionmaking include a failure to conduct a reasonable investigation, and a failure to conduct negotiations in a reasonable manner or to follow the recommendation of its adjuster or chosen defense lawyer or to fail to seek the defense lawyer's recommendation. Factors that may deprive the insured of evidence include a failure to conduct a reasonable investigation, a failure to follow the insurer's claims-handling procedures, a failure to keep the insured informed of within-limits offers or the risk of excess judgment, and the provision of misleading information to the insured.

Such factors are not enough to transform a plainly unreasonable settlement offer into a reasonable offer, but they can make the difference in a close case by allowing the jury to draw a negative inference from the lack of information that reasonably should have been available or from the low quality of the insurer's decisionmaking and fact-gathering processes. Just as reasonable investigation and settlement procedures cannot guarantee that an insurer will make a decision that is substantively reasonable, however, the failure to employ reasonable procedures does not necessarily mean that the insurer's decision was substantively unreasonable. In breach-of-settlement-duty cases in which the facts do not make clear that the insurer's settlement decision was substantively reasonable, the factfinder may decide based on these other procedural factors that the settlement decision was unreasonable. . . .

g. The causation difference between rejecting a settlement offer and choosing not to make an offer. An insurer's decision to reject a reasonable settlement offer made by a claimant potentially has different consequences than an insurer's decision not to make its own reasonable settlement offer, even in those situations in which a reasonable insurer would have made such an offer. The difference comes from the causation requirement in an action for breach of the duty. When an insurer breaches the duty by failing to accept a settlement offer (in situations in which failing to make such an offer constitutes a breach of the duty), and the case goes to trial resulting in an excess judgment against the insured, the causation requirement is satisfied: had the insurer accepted the settlement offer, there would have been no trial and no possibility of an excess judgment. By contrast, when the insurer breaches the duty by failing to make its own settlement offer (in situations in which failing to make its own settlement offer constitutes a breach of the duty), and the case goes to trial and an excess judgment ensues, causation remains in question. The insurer's failure to make an offer caused the excess judgment only if the claimant would have accepted a reasonable offer from the insurer. Proving causation is difficult. Before the trial, the claimant would have been in the best position to answer the question whether he or she would have accepted the settlement offer, but after the trial the claimant's interests will often be too closely aligned with those of the insured defendant to be objective. Other good sources of objective evidence on the matter will be scarce. Nevertheless, a trier of fact may conclude that an insurer's decision not to make a settlement offer or counteroffer constitutes an unreasonable settlement decision.

————————————

Now we are ready to discuss the question of what constitutes a "reasonable settlement decision." Let's return to our hypothetical settlement negotiation from above. There has been an auto accident involving an injury to a tort claimant; the insured/tort-defendant has an auto liability policy with a $20,000 limit (no deductible); and, as assessed by the experienced trial lawyer hired by the insurer to assess and, if necessary, defend the case, there is a 20 percent probability that, if the case is taken to trial, the plaintiff will win an award of $50,000. On the other hand, there is also an 80 percent chance of a defense verdict of no liability. As noted above, in the absence of a duty to settle, there is a conflict of interest. If we assume estimated litigation costs to be about $5,000 (and ignore the possibility of risk aversion), the insurer would accept only settlement demands less than or equal to its expected cost of taking the case to trial, which is, according to these numbers, $9,000. The insured, by contrast, would be happy with any settlement less than or equal to the policy limits of $20,000.

Is either position reasonable? We have already noted that the insurer has an incentive to completely ignore the cost to the insured of going to trial — the risk of the $30,000 excess judgment. However, requiring the insurer to accept any and all settlement demands seems unreasonable as well — and, frankly, expensive. That is, if the rule required insurers to accept any and all settlement demands, such that insurers could *never* insist on taking a case to trial, the result would be higher overall settlement payouts to tort claimants, which might eventually translate into higher liability insurance premiums for all insurance purchasers. So how do we decide what is a reasonable approach to settlements? The rule adopted by the ALI, based on Keeton's "disregard the limits" rule, suggests an answer: What settlement decision would a reasonable person that bears the sole financial responsibility for the full amount of the potential judgment — in our example, the full $50,000 — make? The answer, if we put risk aversion to one side for the moment, is that such a person would be willing to accept a settlement demand that is substantially less than, but not be willing to accept a settlement demand that is substantially greater than, the *expected total cost of trying the case.* In our hypothetical, that amount is around $15,000, if you take into account defense costs.[6] From this perspective, settlement offers substantially greater than $15,000 would be considered unreasonable (and may be rejected by the insurer without breaching the duty to settle); and settlement offers substantially less than $15,000 would be considered reasonable (and thus

6. As stated earlier in this chapter, that figure is determined as follows: (20 percent chance of losing the tort suit x $50,000 potential trial judgment) + (80 percent chance of winning the tort suit x $0) + $5,000 expected trial costs. In our example here, we add in defense costs because those are part of the costs of going to trial, and because a reasonable insurer should take them into account. Courts adopting the disregard the limits rule, however, generally (for reasons that are not entirely clear) do not include, or do not expressly include, defense costs. *See* generally §24 RLLI, comments a-d (explaining the duty to make reasonable settlement decisions).

rejection of those offers by an insurer would be unreasonable). Thus, imagine the following timeline, again using the facts of our hypothetical:

1. At some point after the tort suit is filed against the insured, the tort plaintiff offers to settle the case for $12,000.
2. The insurer, ignoring its duty to make reasonable settlement decisions (and opting to gamble with the insured's money), decides instead to take the case to trial.
3. The trial ensues, and in fact, the bad thing (from the insured's perspective) happens: there is a plaintiff's verdict of $50,000, whereupon the insurer then agrees to pay its $20,000 policy limit, leaving the insured on the hook for the remaining $30,000 excess judgment.
4. Now the insured brings a suit against the insurer, alleging that the insurer, by rejecting the clearly reasonable settlement demand, breached the duty to make reasonable settlement decisions (or, as often happens, the insurer assigns the right to bring that suit to the tort claimant, who then brings the suit against the insurer).
5. The court, after hearing evidence on what the likely outcome of going to trial was at the time that the settlement demand was received, determines that the insurer was unreasonable to have rejected the $12,000 settlement demand, which was significantly less than the total expected cost of going to trial. As a result, the insurer must pay, in addition to the policy limits, the $30,000 excess judgment. (Whether the court might also award additional consequential damages, or even punitive damages, depends on the circumstances, as discussed in the materials below.)

While some courts do in fact apply the disregard the limits rule in a fashion similar to what was just described, the description is somewhat of an oversimplification. Many courts hearing duty to settle cases also consider factors beyond the expected cost of going to trial. For example, some courts take into account whether the insurer has kept the insured informed of settlement demands. Also, if an insurer completely refuses to negotiate with a tort claimant, never offering any settlement proposals of its own when the claimant fails to make an offer, that fact might be taken into account in deciding whether the insurer overall acted reasonably in taking the case to trial.

For a discussion of the other factors that courts sometimes take into account in duty to settle cases, see §24 RLLI, TD1, comment e, and accompanying reporters' note. *See also* Kenneth S. Abraham, *The Natural History of the Insurer's Liability for Bad Faith*, 72 Tex. L. Rev. 1295, 1302-1306 (1994) (describing factors that courts take into account in duty-to-settle analysis); and Douglas R. Richmond, *Bad Insurance Bad Faith Law*, 39 Tort Trial & Ins. Prac. L.J. 1, 5 (2003) (same). For examples of courts applying the disregard the limits rule, see, *e.g., Archdale v. American Internat. Specialty Lines Ins. Co.*, 64 Cal. Rptr. 3d 632, 645 (Cal. App. 2d Dist. 2007) (citing *Johansen*, 538 P.2d at 748) ("the only permissible consideration in evaluating the reasonableness of the settlement offer becomes whether, in light of the victim's injuries and the probable liability of the insured, the ultimate judgment is likely to exceed the amount of the settlement offer"); *Jackson v. Am. Equity Ins. Co.*, 90 P.3d 136, 142 (Alaska 2004) ("When there is a great risk of a recovery beyond the policy limits so that the most reasonable manner of disposing of the claim is a settlement which can be made within those limits, a consideration in good faith of the insured's interest requires the insurer to settle the claim."); and *Rupp v. Transcon. Ins. Co.*, 627 F. Supp. 2d 1304, 1320 (D. Utah 2008) (deciding that, although "the Utah Supreme Court has not addressed whether breach of the duty to accept reasonable settlement offers releases the insured from complying with a legal action limitation provision," the Court likely would find the insured released).

Some complain that the disregard the limits rule is unfair to insurers and harms insureds because it does not permit the lawyer hired by the insurer to represent the insured to engage in strategic negotiations with the tort plaintiff. For example, it is sometimes argued that, under the disregard the limits rule, if the claimant makes a reasonable settlement demand, the insurer is required to accept it, even though it might be possible for the insurer, by playing hardball and rejecting that initial offer, to negotiate for a more favorable settlement. Is this right? Does the disregard the limits rule *require* the insurer to accept any reasonable settlement offer? Or does it merely impose on the insurer the risk of an excess judgment if it rejects such an offer and the case then goes to trial?

Another criticism of the duty to make reasonable settlement decisions is that it lets policyholders off the hook for their own decision to underinsure. *See, e.g.*, Alan O. Sykes, *Judicial Limitations on the Discretion of Liability Insurers to Settle or Litigate: An Economic Critique*, 72 Tex. L. Rev. 1345 (1994) (raising this and other interesting criticisms of the rule). One response to the critics, suggested by the reasonable expectations argument, is that their analysis assumes that in purchasing low-limit policies, policyholders are making a conscious decision to allow insurance companies to gamble with their money. The court in *Comunale* didn't think so, however. A second, more substantive, response is that the rule comes into play most often in the automobile insurance context, where many people will buy the statutory minimum coverage regardless of the existence of a duty to settle or not, and the duty to settle serves the valuable function in that context of making more money available for automobile accident victims. Since the existence of the duty is of long standing, automobile insurance policy premiums surely have taken it into account. Can you see how the duty to settle makes a low-limit insurance policy much more valuable, and thus more expensive? If the increased value of the policy is reflected in higher premiums, in what sense are the policyholders "let off the hook," as Professor Sykes suggests?

Research suggests that plaintiffs' personal injury lawyers very rarely collect real money from real people and that the prevailing norm in the personal injury bar is that the goal in ordinary negligence cases is collecting as much of the available insurance money as possible but leaving the defendant's assets alone (unless the defendant is a wealthy corporation or individual). *See* Tom Baker, *Blood Money, New Money, and the Moral Economy of Tort Law in Action*, 35 Law & Soc'y Rev. 275 (2001). Can you see how the duty to settle might play a role in maintaining that no "blood money" norm? What do you think about that norm? Should an insurance company be able to avoid paying a verdict in excess of the policy limits by arguing that the plaintiff never would have been able to collect that money from the defendant and, thus, the defendant was not in fact harmed to that extent? What are some theoretical and practical objections to that defense? What might it do to the blood money norm?

Courts in Michigan have limited the damages payable for breach of the duty to settle to the value of the assets the plaintiff could have collected from the defendant. *See Frankenmuth Mut. Ins. Co. v. Keeley*, 461 N.W.2d 666 (Mich. 1990), *rev'g on reh'g,* 447 N.W.2d 691 (Mich. 1989) (limiting the insurance company's liability to the lesser of (a) the verdict in the underlying tort case or (b) the policy limits plus the assets of the insured). This "Michigan rule" is discussed in Kyle Logue, *Solving the Judgment Proof Problem,* 72 Tex. L. Rev. 1375 (1994), and Seth Chandler, *Reconsidering the Duty to Settle,* 42 Drake L. Rev. 741, 782-783 (1993). Chandler describes the Michigan rule as "functionally equivalent to a third party beneficiary contract that a potential tortfeasor enters into with an insurer for the benefit of a prospective victim." *Id.* at n.65. In contrast to the Michigan rule, the majority rule allows the plaintiff in a duty to settle case to recover the full amount of the excess judgment, even if that excess judgment exceeds the insured defendant's available assets. Which rule—Michigan or majority—would be more likely to encourage the purchase of liability insurance with adequate policy limits?

In jurisdictions that apply some version of the negligence or reasonableness standard discussed above, a judgment against the insured in excess of the policy limits will not necessarily lead to "excess" liability for the insurance company. To recover in an action for breach of the duty to settle, the insured will have to prove that a reasonable insurance company would have settled within the policy limits. Litigating that question involves the same kind of evidence that was presented at the trial in the underlying tort claim plus expert testimony, either by experienced trial lawyers or insurance claims personnel. Perhaps because hindsight is always 20/20, personal injury lawyers report that such excess verdict cases almost always are settled in advance of trial in the duty to settle action, with the insurance company paying all or a large part of the excess verdict. As a result, many personal injury lawyers regard a carrier's refusal to settle a case within the policy limits as, in effect, lifting the policy limits for the case. *See* Tom Baker, *Blood Money, New Money, and the Moral Economy of Tort Law in Action,* 35 Law & Soc'y Rev. 275, 292 (2001). If this is true, then even under the de jure negligence standard for evaluating breaches of the duty to settle there is a de facto strict liability rule. What are the advantages of such a rule, as compared with a negligence rule? What would be the effect on liability insurance premiums? Is that result a good or a bad thing?

Perhaps because the de facto rule seems to be strict liability in many jurisdictions, given how the disregard the limits rule is applied in practice, some jurisdictions have considered adopting an explicit strict liability approach to the duty to settle, in which the carrier would be liable for the amount in excess of the policy limits any time it had the possibility of settling within those limits. *See* Robert Jerry II, Understanding Insurance Law 901-902 (3d ed. 2002). Professor Jerry reports that no court has actually taken that step, but the West Virginia Supreme Court came close in *Shamblin v. Nationwide Mutual Insurance Co.,* 396 S.E.2d 766 (W. Va. 1990). The court articulated the following "hybrid" negligence/strict liability standard:

> We believe that wherever there is a failure on the part of an insurer to settle within policy limits where there exists the opportunity to so settle and where such settlement within policy limits would release the insured from any and all personal liability, that the insurer has prima facie failed to act in its insured's best interest and that such failure to so settle prima facie constitutes bad faith towards its insured.
>
> In other words, it will be the insurer's burden to prove by clear and convincing evidence that it attempted in good faith to negotiate a settlement, that any failure to enter into a settlement where the opportunity to do so existed was

based on reasonable and substantial grounds, and that it accorded the interests and rights of the insured at least as great a respect as its own. Whether an insurer demonstrates that it comported with this very strong obligation of good faith to its insured must necessarily turn on the facts of each case, as the factual scenarios are as varied and endless as the imagination. In assessing whether an insurer is liable to its insured for personal liability in excess of policy limits, the proper test to be applied is whether the reasonably prudent insurer would have refused to settle within policy limits under the facts and circumstances of the case, bearing in mind always its duty of good faith and fair dealing with its insured. Further, in determining whether the efforts of the insurer to reach settlement and to secure a release for its insured as to personal liability are reasonable, the trial court should consider whether there was an appropriate investigation and evaluation of the claim based upon objective and cogent information; whether the insurer had a reasonable basis to conclude that there was a genuine and substantial issue as to liability of its insured; and whether there was potential for substantial recovery of an excess verdict against its insured. Not one of these factors may be considered to the exclusion of the others. For instance, an insurer might have a genuine and reasonable issue as to its insured's liability, but if the settlement offer can be considered fair when cast against the possibility of a substantial excess verdict against the insured, the liability issue in and of itself may not be sufficient grounds for the insurer to have refused to settle. Likewise, it is the insurer's burden to act in good faith in actively seeking settlement and a release of its insured from personal liability, as opposed to the obligation being solely that of the injured party, his attorney, or the insured. Nor is this list of factors to be considered in any way exhaustive. Any salient fact or circumstance regarding the reasonableness of the insurer's actions, and its concern or lack of concern for the protection of its insured, may be considered in determining whether the insurer is liable to its insured for any judgment obtained against him in excess of policy limits.

Id. at 776.

Notice the other factors that the *Shamblin* court lists that should be taken into account by a court in doing the duty to settle reasonableness analysis — procedural factors such as whether there was an appropriate investigation by the insurer. This is a common approach. Because of the difficulty of determining, in hindsight, whether a settlement demand or offer was reasonable, many courts hold that it is appropriate for the trier of fact to consider procedural factors that affected the quality of the insurer's decision making or that deprived the insured of evidence that would have been available if the insurer had behaved reasonably. Such factors should not be considered enough to transform a plainly unreasonable settlement demand into a reasonable demand, but they can make the difference in a close case by allowing the jury to draw a negative inference from the lack of information that reasonably should have been available or from the low quality of the insurer's decision-making and fact-gathering processes. For a general discussion of the multiple factors that courts take into account in the duty to settle analysis, *see* Kenneth S. Abraham, *The Natural History of the Insurer's Liability for Bad Faith*, 72 Tex. L. Rev. 1295, 1302-1306 (1994) (describing factors that courts take into account in duty to settle analysis); *and* Douglas R. Richmond, *Bad Insurance Bad Faith Law*, 39 Tort Trial & Ins. Prac. L.J. 1, 5 (2003) (same).

The following problem raises two questions: (1) If an insured attempts to mitigate damages by contributing to a pretrial settlement, can the insured later recover that amount from the insurer through a duty to settle action? and (2)

Does the liability insurer's duty to settle exist when the insurer has a good-faith coverage dispute?

PROBLEM: BMC V. TRUSTWORTHY

Bob Jones was injured while unloading a truck operated by TruckinCo. Bob Jones sued TruckinCo, and TruckinCo filed a third-party complaint against BMC, which owned the truck. BMC tendered the claim to Trustworthy Insurance. Trustworthy assumed the defense under protest, observing that BMC had not notified it until two years after the accident, when Jones filed suit, despite a clause in the contract providing the following:

> You must promptly notify us or our agent of any accident or loss. You must tell us how, when, and where the accident or loss happened. You must assist in obtaining the names and addresses of any injured persons and witnesses.

During the litigation, Jones settled with TruckinCo and offered to settle the case against BMC for the Trustworthy policy limits of $1 million. Trustworthy refused to settle.

Scenario A

As the trial approached, the defense lawyer that Trustworthy hired to defend BMC became increasingly concerned about the likely outcome of the trial. Jones's condition had taken a turn for the worse and, as a result of the settlement, TruckinCo employees were now cooperating with Jones. In the defense lawyer's view, BMC was certain to be held liable, and the damages would be at least $1.5 million, and possibly well over $2 million. As a result of this analysis, Trustworthy offered to settle the case for the policy limits. Jones refused. BMC offered to "top off" the $1 million with $200,000, and Jones agreed.

Trustworthy paid Jones the $1 million policy limits. BMC paid Jones the additional $200,000 and immediately sued Trustworthy for breach of the duty to make a reasonable settlement decision. Trustworthy defended on the grounds that breach of the duty to make a reasonable settlement decision is not actionable unless it results in a *verdict* in excess of the policy limits. The trial court agreed and granted summary judgment for Trustworthy. BMC has appealed. *Cf. Twin City Fire Ins. Co. v. Country Mut. Ins. Co.*, 23 F.3d 1175 (7th Cir. 1994). Develop the arguments for and against the appeal.

Scenario B

The case did not settle. At trial, Jones obtained a verdict of $2 million against BMC. Trustworthy immediately sought a declaratory judgment that the claim was not covered. BMC counterclaimed for breach of the policy and for breach of the duty to settle the case within the policy limits. The trial court in the coverage case concluded after a bench trial that BMC had not breached the notice clause but that the late notice defense was "fairly debatable" and thus Trustworthy had not breached any duties by refusing to settle the case within the policy limits. BMC appealed. *Cf. Transport Ins. Co. v. Post Express Co.*, 138 F.3d 1189 (7th Cir. 1998); *Mowry v. Badger State Mut. Cas. Co.*, 385 N.W.2d 171, 175-185 (Wis. 1986). Develop the arguments for and against the appeal.

Consider how Scenario B would be handled under the ALI approach:

§25 The Effect of a Reservation of Rights on Settlement Rights and Duties

(1) A reservation of the right to contest coverage does not relieve an insurer of the duty to make reasonable settlement decisions stated in §24.

(2) Unless otherwise stated in a liability insurance policy or agreed to by the insured, an insurer may not settle a claim and thereafter demand reimbursement of the settlement amount from the insured on the grounds that the claim was not covered.

. . .

Comment:

a. Reservation of rights does not eliminate the duty to make reasonable settlement decisions, but there is no such duty for noncovered actions. Under the rule set forth in this subsection (1), an insurer is subject to the duty to make reasonable settlement decisions even if that insurer reasonably believes that the policy at issue does not cover the legal action. What this means in practice is that, if an insurer that is defending a legal action against an insured under a reservation of rights rejects a reasonable settlement demand (a settlement demand that a reasonable insurer facing the entire potential liability would accept), or otherwise makes an unreasonable settlement decision as defined in §24, the insurer will be responsible for any excess judgment that results at the trial of the legal action along with other appropriate damages, provided that the action is determined to be covered. If the action is determined not to be covered, the insurer will of course not be liable for any of the judgment. An insurer has no duty to settle noncovered legal actions. Thus, an insurer that reserves the right to contest coverage and then receives a settlement offer within the policy limits must choose whether to accept the settlement (and bear the cost of the settlement above the deductible) or to reject the settlement and risk the possibility of facing liability for an excess judgment against the insured if the action turns out to be covered.

This widely adopted rule allocates to the insurer a portion of the risk associated with reasonable but mistaken beliefs on the part of the insurer regarding coverage and discourages insurers from delaying settlement negotiations in the underlying lawsuit while potential coverage disputes with the insured are being resolved. A few jurisdictions, however, follow an alternative rule, which permits the insurer to take into account its doubts about coverage when deciding whether to accept a settlement demand. In other words, under the minority rule, the insurer may, when calculating the maximum reasonable settlement that it will accept, discount the expected value of the case further by the probability that there will be no coverage and thus no requirement that the insurer contribute to the settlement. This alternative approach places the risk of the insurer's mistaken coverage decisions upon the insured, increasing the likelihood of substantial uninsured excess judgments. This is because there will be a broader range of litigated cases that potentially will produce trials and fewer settlements, because insurers, in reservation-of-rights cases, will be willing to contribute less to a settlement than is the case under the majority rule. The majority rule is superior because it places the risk of mistaken coverage decisions upon the party best able to reduce and spread that risk.

Illustration:

1. A claimant files a tort suit against the insured seeking damages of $500,000. The insured has a duty-to-defend liability insurance policy that has policy limits of $100,000 and that assigns settlement discretion to the insurer. The insured tenders the defense of the suit to the insurer, which agrees to defend under a reservation of rights. The insurer reasonably believes that it has a ground for contesting coverage that relieves it from any duty to indemnify the insured for the suit. As the case approaches trial, the claimant makes a reasonable settlement demand of $80,000. The insurer rejects the settlement demand. The suit then goes to trial, resulting in a $500,000 verdict against the insured. If the coverage dispute is resolved in the insured's favor, the insurer is liable for its coverage limit plus the excess judgment of $400,000, along with other reasonably foreseeable consequential damages. If the coverage dispute is resolved in the insurer's favor, the insurer is not liable to the insured for any damages.

b. When a legal action has both covered and noncovered components. Some legal actions brought against a liability insured will have both covered and noncovered components. In such a situation, the reasonableness of the insurer's settlement decisions is to be evaluated based on the valuation of the covered component(s) of the action. That is, if the settlement demand is reasonable, taking into account the covered components alone (that is, as a settlement of only the covered cause(s) of action), then rejection of the settlement demand will constitute a breach of the duty to make reasonable settlement decisions. If, however, the settlement demand is outside of the range of reasonableness for settlement of the covered component alone, then the insurer's rejection of the settlement will not by itself be considered a breach of the duty to make reasonable settlement decisions. In such a case, whether the insurer has breached its settlement duty will depend on other factors that bear on the question of insurer reasonableness, such as the procedural factors addressed in Comment *e* of §24. For example, where a legal action involves both a covered component and a noncovered component (such as punitive damages where such damages are expressly excluded from coverage under the policy or the law in the jurisdiction treats such coverage as a violation of public policy), the duty to make reasonable settlement decisions would include a duty on the part of the insurer to investigate the facts relevant to both the covered and noncovered components and to convey that information to the insured. The insurer would also have an obligation to inform the insured of the amount it (the insurer) would be willing to contribute to an overall settlement. However, the control of the settlement of the noncovered components of the legal action would rest with the insured, or, if appropriate, with the excess insurer or insurers.

The next two cases address the damages to which a duty to settle plaintiff is entitled.

PPG INDUSTRIES, INC. v. TRANSAMERICA INSURANCE CO.

Supreme Court of California
975 P.2d 652 (1999)

KENNARD, J. . . . Plaintiff PPG Industries, Inc. (PPG) is the successor in interest to Solaglas California, Inc. (Solaglas). Solaglas was a distributor and installer of replacement windshields for cars and trucks. On July 17, 1982, in Colorado,

George Miller was driving a truck manufactured by General Motors Corporation (GMC) when another vehicle collided with the left rear of the truck, causing it to jump a curb and strike a metal light pole. The truck's windshield, which had been installed by a Solaglas facility in Colorado, "popped out" and Miller was ejected through the opening. The resulting injuries rendered Miller a quadriplegic.

Miller sued Solaglas in Colorado, seeking both compensatory and punitive damages. Solaglas tendered the defense to its liability carrier, Transamerica Insurance Company (Transamerica), which had issued policies totaling $1.5 million. Transamerica agreed to defend Solaglas, but it informed Solaglas that the insurance policies did not provide indemnity coverage for punitive damages.

Settlement efforts were unsuccessful, and a jury trial in Colorado resulted in a judgment for Solaglas, but this judgment was reversed on appeal. Miller then offered to settle for an amount within the limits of Solaglas's liability coverage. Transamerica turned down Solaglas's requests to accept the settlement offer. Thereafter, a second jury trial resulted in a judgment against Solaglas for $6.1 million ($5.1 million in compensatory damages and $1 million in punitive damages). Solagas appealed. . . .

Transamerica paid the policy limits of $1.5 million plus $1,277,094.88 as costs and interest on the judgment against Solaglas in the Miller lawsuit. Industrial Indemnity Company, which had insured Solaglas for $9 million in excess liability coverage, paid the remaining $3.6 million in compensatory damages, leaving PPG, Solaglas's successor in interest, to pay the $1 million in punitive damages.

In June 1994, PPG sued Transamerica in Los Angeles, California, for breach of the covenant of good faith and fair dealing implied in each of Transamerica's policies. PPG alleged that Transamerica had breached the covenant by unreasonably refusing to settle the Miller lawsuit; PPG sought to recover from Transamerica as compensatory damages the $1 million it had been ordered to pay as punitive damages in the Miller lawsuit.

The trial court granted summary judgment for Transamerica, relying on the well-established rule prohibiting indemnity coverage for punitive damages awarded against the insured. The Court of Appeal affirmed the judgment.

II

Implied in every contract is a covenant of good faith and fair dealing that neither party will injure the right of the other to receive the benefits of the agreement. This covenant imposes a number of obligations upon insurance companies, including an obligation to accept a reasonable offer of settlement. An insurer's breach of the implied covenant of good faith and fair dealing "will provide the basis for an action in tort." Because breach of the implied covenant is actionable as a tort, the measure of damages for tort actions applies, and the insurance company generally is liable for "any damages which are the proximate result of that breach."

Here, PPG contends it is entitled to recover from its insurance company any monetary award, including punitive damages, that it became legally obligated to pay in the Miller lawsuit. According to PPG, settlement would have terminated that lawsuit, thus precluding any punitive damage liability, and therefore the insurer's failure to settle the lawsuit was a proximate cause of the award of punitive damages. Not so. As we shall explain, Transamerica's failure to settle the Miller lawsuit was a cause in fact but not a *proximate cause* of the award of punitive damages.

Proximate cause involves *two* elements. One is *cause in fact*. An act is a cause in fact if it is a necessary antecedent of an event. Here, there were at least *two* causes in fact of the insured's liability for punitive damages in the third party lawsuit: the insured's own intentional and egregious misconduct in installing the windshield on the truck, and the insurance company's alleged negligence in failing to settle the third party lawsuit, on the theory that settlement would not have exposed PPG to liability for punitive damages.

To simply say, however, that the defendant's conduct was a necessary antecedent of the injury does not resolve the question of whether the defendant should be liable. In the words of Prosser and Keeton: "[T]he consequences of an act go forward to eternity, and the causes of an event go back to the dawn of human events, and beyond. But any attempt to impose responsibility upon such a basis would result in infinite liability for all wrongful acts, and would 'set society on edge and fill the courts with endless litigation.'" (Prosser & Keeton on Torts, *supra*, §41, at 264, quoting *North v. Johnson,* 58 Minn. 242 (1894).) Therefore, the law must impose limitations on liability other than simple causality. These additional limitations are related not only to the degree of connection between the conduct and the injury, but also with public policy. As Justice Traynor observed, proximate cause "is ordinarily concerned, not with the fact of causation, but with the various considerations of policy that limit an actor's responsibility for the consequences of his conduct." *Mosley v. Arden Farms Co.,* 157 P.2d 372 (Cal. 1945) (conc. opn. of Traynor, J.).

In this case, there are at least three policy considerations that strongly militate against allowing the insured, the morally culpable wrongdoer in the third party lawsuit, to shift to its insurance company the obligation to pay punitive damages resulting from the insured's egregious misconduct in that lawsuit.

First, there is the policy of not allowing liability for intentional wrongdoing to be offset or reduced by the negligence of another. In both Colorado and California, punitive damages may be awarded only if it is proven that the defendant engaged in conduct intended to cause injury or engaged in despicable conduct with a conscious disregard of the rights or safety of others. . . . By contrast, the action that the insured, PPG, then brought against its insurance company, Transamerica, was based on Transamerica's alleged negligent failure to settle the third party lawsuit against the insured in Colorado. . . . Thus, allowing PPG to shift to Transamerica its responsibility to pay the punitive damages in the third party action would violate the public policy against reducing or offsetting liability for intentional wrongdoing by the negligence of another.

Second, the purposes of punitive damages, in both California and Colorado, are to punish the defendant and to deter future misconduct by making an example of the defendant. If we were to allow the intentional wrongdoer, here the insured, to shift responsibility for its morally culpable behavior to the insurance company, which surely will pass to the public its higher cost of doing business, we would defeat the public policies of punishing the intentional wrongdoer for its own outrageous conduct and deterring it and others from engaging in such conduct in the future.[7] As we explained in a previous case: "'The policy considerations in a state where, as in [California], punitive damages are awarded for punishment and deterrence, would seem to require that the damages rest ultimately as well as nominally on the party actually responsible for the wrong. If that person were permitted to shift the burden to an insurance company, punitive damages would serve no useful purpose. Such damages do not compensate the plaintiff for his injury, since compensatory damages already have made the plaintiff whole.'" *Peterson v. Superior Court*, 642 P.2d 1305 (Cal. 1982).

Third, our public policy prohibits indemnification for punitive damages. *See, e.g.*, Ins. Code, §533; *Peterson v. Superior Court, supra*, 31 Cal. 3d at 157; *City Products Corp. v. Globe Indemnity Co.*, 88 Cal. App. 3d [31,] 39-41 [(1979)]. . . .

MOSK, J. I dissent. . . . The insurer's duty to defend its insured, which arises at tender, is of no lesser significance as a legal matter than its duty to indemnify it, which arises after establishment of liability. Neither is it of any lesser significance as a practical matter. It has been stated: "The insured's desire to secure the right to call on the insurer's superior resources for the defense of . . . claims is, in all likelihood, typically as significant a motive for the purchase of insurance as is the wish to obtain indemnity for possible liability." . . .

Pursuant to the covenant of good faith and fair dealing, which is implied by law in every liability insurance policy the insurer has a duty to make reasonable efforts to settle a claim against its insured by the insured's victim—which accords with the public policy favoring settlement. The insurer's duty to settle arises from its interrelated duty to defend. In discharging its duty to settle, the insurer must give at least as much weight to its insured's interests as to its own, and must act as though it alone would have to bear any ensuing judgment. In effecting a settlement, the insurer is not prohibited from offering a sum to avoid punitive damages as well as compensatory damages. Nor could it be. Otherwise, it would effectively be prohibited from offering any sum whatsoever for many claims. That is because many claims seek punitive damages as well as compensatory damages. For it is easy to allege oppressive, fraudulent, or malicious conduct. It may indeed be difficult to prove such conduct. But it is also difficult to predict with any confidence what any given trier of fact may find in the premises.

If the insurer breaches its duty to settle the claim of its insured's victim, it commits a tort against its insured, at least if its breach is "wrongful." *Comunale v. Traders & General Ins. Co., supra*, 50 Cal. 2d at 663; accord, e.g., *Crisci v. Security Ins. Co., supra*, 66 Cal. 2d at 432-433. And if it commits such a tort, it is liable to it for damages to compensate for all the detriment that it proximately caused. Such detriment includes—but is not limited to—any sums that its insured became legally obligated to pay its victim as damages for its claim. The damages for which the insurer is liable are not affected in their amount by any limits

---

7. We recognize that a settlement of the underlying action would relieve the insured of personal liability for its own acts of intentional egregious conduct giving rise to a claim for punitive damages. As the highest court of the State of New York has observed: "Our system of civil justice may be organized so as to allow a wrongdoer to escape the punitive consequences of his own malfeasance in order that the injured plaintiff may enjoy the advantages of a swift and certain pretrial settlement. However, the benefit that a morally culpable wrongdoer obtains as a result of this system, i.e., being released from exposure to liability for punitive damages, is no more than a necessary incident of this process." *Soto v. State Farm Ins. Co.*, 635 N.E.2d 1222, 1225 (N.Y. 1994).

on indemnification specified in any liability insurance policy. That is because they do not constitute indemnification, which, as *section 2772* of the Civil Code makes plain, comprises payment that is required under the terms of a liability insurance policy itself. Rather, as the very name declares, they are damages, which comprise payment that is compelled by law. . . .

Inasmuch as the insurer is liable to its insured for damages to compensate for *all* the detriment that it proximately caused by its tortious breach of its duty to settle the claim of the insured's victim, and inasmuch as such detriment includes *any* sums that its insured became legally obligated to pay *its* victim as damages for its claim, it follows that the insurer is liable to the insured for damages to compensate for detriment in the form of the sum that its insured became legally obligated to pay *its* victim as *punitive damages* as well as *compensatory damages*. Otherwise, for the wrong the insured suffered at its insurer's hands, there would not be a remedy, or at least not a complete remedy. . . .

The majority's conclusion *against the insured as such* rests on the familiar notion of proximate cause, which they import from the law of negligence. They quote the observation of then Justice Traynor, that proximate cause "is ordinarily concerned, not with the fact of causation, but with the various considerations of [public] policy that limit an actor's responsibility for the consequences of his conduct." *Mosley v. Arden Farms Co.*, 157 P.2d 372 (Cal. 1945) (conc. opn. of Traynor, J.). But they fail to quote Witkin, that such considerations are those that would make it "*unjust* to hold" the actor "legally responsible." 6 Witkin, Summary of Cal. Law, Torts, §968, p. 359, italics added. Considerations of this sort are altogether absent here. For it is hardly unjust to hold the insurer legally responsible for *all* damages to its insured. That is because *no* damages would have arisen had it not tortiously breached its duty to settle.

In support of their conclusion against the insured as such, the majority present three points. None, as will appear, proves to bear any persuasive force.

First, the majority assert that to recognize the insurer's liability to its insured for punitive damages "would . . . violate the public policy against permitting liability for intentional wrongdoing to be offset or reduced by the negligence of another. . . ." It would not. Indeed, it would not even implicate it at all. The identified public policy operates by comparing the relative culpability of the plaintiff and the defendant within a single action—for example, the culpability of the insured's victim vis-à-vis the culpability of the insured itself in an action brought by the former against the latter for bodily injury and property damage. It does not operate, however, by comparing the relative culpability of the defendants in two separate actions—for example, the culpability of the insured in an action brought against it by its victim for bodily injury and property damage vis-à-vis the culpability of the insurer in an action brought against it by its insured for tortious breach of its duty to settle. As stated, section 3523 of the Civil Code declares that "[f]or *every* wrong there is a remedy." (Italics added.) That means for the insured's wrong against its victim. And also for the insurer's wrong against its insured.

Second, the majority assert that to recognize the insurer's liability to its insured for punitive damages "would . . . defeat the purposes of" such damages, "which are to punish and deter the wrongdoer. . . ." It would not. Such liability would not be inconsistent with deterrence. Surely, it is inconceivable that the insured would be enticed to engage in oppressive, fraudulent, or malicious conduct on the speculation that its insurer might perhaps tortiously breach its duty to settle, and then might perhaps be held liable to it for damages therefor.

In addition, such liability would not be inconsistent with punishment. It would cover only the insured's out-of-pocket costs attributable to the payment of punitive damages. It would not reach various related opportunity and transaction costs, which are always real in fact if not certain in law. Opportunity costs are often substantial. Time passes, usually several years, between the insured's payment of punitive damages to its victim and its insurer's payment of damages to the insured itself compensating therefor. Often substantial as well are transaction costs. "[A]ny litigation involves transaction costs," which "are not limited to the monetary costs of the litigation" itself, "but also include the toll the litigation takes" on the insured. Litigation that threatens the insured with punitive damages and ultimately makes good on the threat involves transaction costs greater still. In light of such opportunity and transaction costs, punishment and deterrence perdures. In any event, a payment in settlement avoids punitive damages at the outset. By doing so, it may be said to "defeat the purposes of punitive damages" even more completely, since it obviates any and all opportunity and transaction costs that would subsequently be incurred by the "wrongdoer." Nevertheless, as the majority themselves admit, it is not prohibited.

Third, the majority assert that to recognize the insurer's liability to its insured for punitive damages "would . . . violate the public policy against indemnification for" such damages. It would not. Indeed, it would not even implicate it at all—and certainly no more so than the public policy favoring settlement of the underlying claim. The insurer's payment to its insured is not *indemnification,* inasmuch as it is not required under the terms of any liability insurance policy. It is rather *damages,* inasmuch as it is compelled by law. To be sure, a payment of this sort *makes up* for punitive damages. But, as stated, a payment in settlement *avoids* such damages at the outset. The latter is not prohibited. Neither is the former. . . .

NOTES AND QUESTIONS

1. From the insured's perspective, what is the difference between an excess compensatory damages verdict and a punitive damages verdict? As the court acknowledges (and as research makes clear — *see* Tom Baker, *Transforming Punishment into Compensation: In the Shadow of Punitive Damages,* 1998 Wis. L. Rev. 211), insurance companies in fact pay a premium to settle punitive damages claims all the time, even in jurisdictions in which insurance for punitive damages is against public policy. These settlements are not denominated "punitive damages" payments, but they are based on the same aggravated fault that produces punitive damages.

2. One formal difference between an excess verdict and punitive damages is the following: In the excess verdict situation, the insurance company most likely would have been willing to sell the insured the additional coverage that the duty to settle, in effect, imposes on the insurance company. In the punitive damages context, the insurance company would have been prohibited from selling that insurance in some jurisdictions.

3. What are the likely practical consequences of the result of this case? All other things being equal, would the settlement value of a punitive damages case be higher under the rule announced in this case or under the rule preferred by the dissent? On what might that depend?

4.   Notice that California treats the duty to settle as a tort duty and uses the doctrine of proximate cause to limit the insurance company's obligation. Suppose that a court treated the duty as a contractual duty. What contract doctrine could be used to limit the insurer's duty correspondingly?

5.   Insurance for punitive damages is a controversial topic. Most states permit insurance for punitive damages that are assessed vicariously, but only slightly more than half the states permit insurance for punitive damages assessed directly against a wrongdoer. *See* Catherine M. Sharkey, *Revisiting the Noninsurable Costs of Accidents*, 64 Md. L. Rev. 409 (2005). The policy reasons for this rule against insuring punitive damages are those set out in the main case. The main arguments for permitting insurance for punitive damages are pragmatic. Insurance for punitive damages does not undercut the deterrent objectives of tort law as much as commonly assumed because insurance companies have an incentive to police the problem of moral hazard. Insurance for punitive damages does not undercut the retributive objectives of tort law as much as commonly assumed because insurance and tort law in action calibrate the sting of a tort action according to the defendant's culpability and the ability to pay off. Moreover, insurance underwriting practices reduce the ability of repeat offenders to use insurance to insulate themselves from the retributive aims of tort law. Finally, as a practical matter, insurance for punitive damages in fact is available to corporate defendants as a result of offshore insurance policies issued in places like Bermuda. Thus, the prohibition almost surely has no practical effect on the loss-causing behavior of insureds at either end of the wealth spectrum: The average individual defendant is highly unlikely to ever be required to pay anything substantial out of his or her own pocket, and whether the high-end corporate defendant has to pay out of its own coffers depends on whether the corporation's risk managers chose to buy the offshore insurance or not. *See generally* Tom Baker, *Reconsidering Insurance for Punitive Damages*, 1998 Wis. L. Rev. 101.

6.   The RLLI states the rule with respect to duty to settle damages as follows:

> An insurer that breaches the duty to make reasonable settlement decisions is subject to liability for the full amount of damages assessed against the insured in the underlying suit, without regard to the policy limits, as well as for any other foreseeable harm caused by the insurer's breach of duty.

RLLI §27. Does this approach sound more like the position of the majority or the dissent in *PPG Industries?* Comment *d* to the RLLI states:

> *d. When the underlying suit results in punitive damages.* When the underlying suit against the insured results in the award of punitive damages, a difficult question arises regarding the appropriate measure of compensatory damages in the subsequent breach-of-settlement-duty case. If the insurer is found to have breached the duty to make reasonable settlement decisions, the insured or its assignee is entitled to recover for any and all reasonably foreseeable consequences of the breach of the duty. Under the rule stated in this Section, such reasonably foreseeable consequences include the full excess judgment, including any punitive damages awarded at the underlying trial. This rule is unproblematic in a jurisdiction in which punitive damages are insurable.
>
> In jurisdictions in which insurance for punitive damages is contrary to public policy, however, there is tension between a rule forbidding the sale of liability insurance against punitive damages and a rule that requires an

insurer to indemnify the insured for such damages when the insurer has breached the duty to make reasonable settlement decisions. Although most courts have not addressed this issue, the very few state courts that have addressed it have resolved the tension in favor of the public policy against insurance for punitive damages, typically in divided judgments with strong dissents, indicating that there is considerable uncertainty regarding the direction insurance law should take. This Section follows the approach of the dissenting judges in those cases for two reasons. First, this approach furthers the public policy in favor of encouraging reasonable settlement decisions by insurers. Second, the contrary approach would create a conflict of interest in the defense of the claim that would increase the frequency of cases in which independent counsel would be required under §16. See §16, Comment *d.* Third, the incentive argument in favor of the contrary approach is implausible.

THE BIRTH CENTER v. ST. PAUL COS., INC.

Supreme Court of Pennsylvania
787 A.2d 376 (2001)

NEWMAN, J. . . .

THE UNDERLYING ACTION — NORRIS V. THE BIRTH CENTER

This claim arose out of St. Paul's bad faith refusal to engage in settlement negotiations in the underlying action, *Norris.* In that case, Gerald and Denise Norris ("Parents") filed suit on November 16, 1986 against Birth Center alleging that its negligence during the birth of their daughter Lindsey[] caused her to suffer severe physical injury and permanent brain damage. After service of the complaint, The Birth Center turned to St. Paul, its professional liability insurance carrier, for its legal defense. St. Paul hired counsel to defend The Birth Center and undertook an investigation of the Parents' claim.

On August 2, 1991, the Parents proposed, on behalf of Lindsey, to settle the case within the limits of The Birth Center's professional liability insurance policy with St. Paul. The Birth Center notified St. Paul that it was making a firm demand to settle the case within its policy limits. On August 7, 1991, St. Paul refused to settle or to even make an offer of settlement.

During the course of an August 8, 1991 pre-trial conference, the presiding judge recommended settlement of *Norris* within the limits of The Birth Center's insurance policy. Again, St. Paul refused. At a second pre-trial conference, a second judge assigned to the case also recommended settlement within Birth Center's policy limits. The Birth Center demanded settlement in accordance with the judge's recommendation; but St. Paul refused to negotiate or offer any money.

In January of 1992, St. Paul requested the defense attorneys for The Birth Center and one of the doctors involved in Lindsey's delivery to prepare pretrial reports for St. Paul's consideration. In her report to St. Paul, defense counsel for The Birth Center stated that The Birth Center had, at best, a fifty-percent chance of successfully defending the lawsuit at trial. Furthermore, she advised that the jury verdict could range from $1,250,000.00 to $1,500,000.00. The doctor's defense counsel advised St. Paul that he believed that The Birth Center had a thirty-five percent chance of winning at trial and predicted a jury verdict of $5,000,000.00 to $6,000,000.00.

On January 27, 1992, the executive director of The Birth Center put St. Paul on written notice of the potential for compensatory damages and expressed her deep concerns regarding the possibility of a verdict in excess of Birth Center's policy limits. She explained that such a verdict would have devastating effects upon The Birth Center and could risk its continued existence. When expressing the same concerns to the St. Paul claims representative assigned to the case, the claims representative informed her that St. Paul tries "all of these bad baby cases, and we're going to trial." (N.T. 5/6/96 at 16).

Before the commencement of the Norris trial, a third judge, who ultimately presided over that trial, held another conference and recommended settlement within The Birth Center's policy limits. St. Paul refused to make any offer whatsoever. Then, on February 12, 1993, the Parents made a high/low offer of settlement, in which St. Paul would pay a non-refundable $300,000.00 amount regardless of the verdict. If, however, the jury returned a verdict in excess of Birth Center's policy limits, the Parents agreed to accept the policy limits as total satisfaction of the verdict. Finally, the settlement offer provided that if the jury returned a verdict lower than The Birth Center's maximum coverage[] but higher than the low figure of $300,000.00, then the Parents would accept such verdict as full satisfaction of The Birth Center's liability. St. Paul refused this offer of settlement and made no counter-offer.

On February 16, 1993, the day of trial, a final pre-trial conference took place in the robing room of the trial judge. At this time, the Parents reasserted their high/low offer of settlement. The Birth Center expressed its desire that St. Paul agree to the Parents' proposal; but, a representative of St. Paul, present during the discussion in the robing room, rejected the high/low offer of settlement on the record. Following St. Paul's rejection, the judge stated that he believed that St. Paul's actions were in bad faith and that it was putting its interests ahead of those of its insured.

The Norris trial ensued. After the start of the trial, but before the jury returned a verdict, the trial judge instructed defense counsel for The Birth Center to contact St. Paul to see if it intended to make any offer of settlement. When counsel returned from her telephone conversation with St. Paul, she stated to those present in the robing room: "They must be crazy. They're not offering a dime. They won't give me authority to offer any money in this case, you know I can't believe it."

On March 4, 1993, the jury returned a verdict in favor of the Parents for $4,500,000.00, with The Birth Center liable for sixty percent of that amount. The final verdict was molded to include delay damages and interest and totaled $7,196,238. The Birth Center's ultimate liability amounted to $4,317,743.00. St. Paul agreed to indemnify The Birth Center for the entire verdict and the parties settled the case for $5,000,000. Before St. Paul paid the excess verdict, it requested that The Birth Center sign a release in exchange for the payment, but The Birth Center refused to sign the release. St. Paul paid on September 20, 1993.

THE BIRTH CENTER V. ST. PAUL — THE BAD FAITH ACTION

On June 3, 1994, The Birth Center sued St. Paul, alleging that St. Paul breached its fiduciary duty to The Birth Center, its implied covenant of good faith, and its contract. The Birth Center also claimed that St. Paul's failure to settle Norris within its policy limits constituted negligence, reckless disregard for the rights of Birth Center, willful and wanton behavior and bad faith pursuant to the Bad Faith Statute, 42 Pa. C.S.A. §8371.

On May 3, 1996, the trial began. The Birth Center claimed that St. Paul's refusal to engage in reasonable settlement negotiations damaged "its business, reputation and credit." Appellee's Br. at 11. After the trial, the jury found, by clear and convincing evidence, that St. Paul acted in bad faith and that its actions were a substantial factor in bringing about harm to The Birth Center totaling, $700,000.00 in compensatory damages. The jury did not award punitive damages.

St. Paul moved for judgment notwithstanding the verdict. On February 7, 1997, the trial court granted St. Paul's motion. The trial court concluded that St. Paul's payment of the excess verdict nullified The Birth Center's bad faith claim, that compensatory damages are not available pursuant to 42 Pa. C.S.A. §8371, and that, because it believed that it had not charged the jury on the breach of contract claim, that The Birth Center could not recover compensatory damages based on that theory. . . .

On appeal, the Superior Court determined that the payment of the excess verdict did not preclude the award of compensatory damages and that the trial court had charged the jury on breach of contract. Therefore, it reversed the decision of the trial court, reinstated the jury award, and remanded the case for a determination of The Birth Center's entitlement to interest, attorney's fees and costs pursuant to 42 Pa. C.S.A. §8371.

St. Paul appealed the Superior Court's decision to this Court.

DISCUSSION

A. PAYMENT OF THE EXCESS VERDICT

Next, we address St. Paul's arguments that the trial court properly granted its motion for a judgment notwithstanding the verdict because of its contentions that: (1) an insurer's payment of an excess verdict precludes all bad faith claims, and (2) allowing The Birth Center to recover additional compensatory damages would discourage insurance companies from satisfying excess verdicts. St. Paul states:

> The effect of the Superior Court's holding is to discourage insurance companies from satisfying excess verdicts unless they are required to do so. If an insurance company can still be exposed to a bad faith suit even after voluntarily satisfying an excess verdict, the company has no incentive to pay the excess.
> If it remains exposed to the bad faith claim and punitive damages anyway, the obvious course for the insurance company is to stand its ground, defend the bad faith claim, and leave its insured to its own devices.

Appellant's Br. at 15.

While St. Paul's argument has facial appeal, it does not stand up to closer examination. St. Paul did not pay the excess verdict out of the goodness of its heart. It had reason to believe that The Birth Center was going to sue for bad faith and it knew that if it were found to have acted in bad faith, it would be liable for punitive damages as well as the amount of the excess verdict. 42 Pa C.S.A. §8371. It, therefore, appears that St. Paul paid the excess in an attempt to avoid a punitive damages award.

The purpose of damages in contract actions is to return the parties to the position they would have been in but for the breach. *Gedeon v. State Farm Mut. Auto. Ins. Co.*, 188 A.2d 320, 322 n.5 (Pa.). The relationship and dispute between The Birth Center and St. Paul flow from their contract. *Gray v. Nationwide Mut. Ins. Co.*, 223 A.2d 8, 12 (Pa. 1966). "Breach of . . . [the] obligation [to act in good faith] constitutes a breach of the insurance contract for which an action in assumpsit will lie." *Id.* Therefore, where an insurer acts in bad faith, the insured is entitled to recover such damages sufficient to return it to the position it would have been in but for the breach. St. Paul's payment of the excess verdict does not bar The Birth Center's claim for compensatory damages because The Birth Center was able to prove that St. Paul's bad faith conduct was a substantial factor in The Birth Center suffering damages in addition to the excess verdict.

Furthermore, there is no reason to limit damages to the amount of the verdict where the insured can show that the insurer's bad faith conduct caused it additional damages. The insurer's conduct is not the subject of the underlying court action against the insured and, except for the amount of the excess verdict, damages stemming from the insurer's bad faith conduct are not resolved by the action against the insured. Where, as here, the insured can prove that it sustained damages in excess of the verdict, the insurer's payment of the excess has little to do with the insured's damages. Accordingly, the insurer's payment of the excess should not free it from other known or foreseeable damages it has caused its insured to incur.

Requiring insurers, who act in bad faith, to pay excess verdicts protects insured from liability that, absent the insurer's bad faith conduct, the insured would not have incurred. The insured's liability for an excess verdict is a type of compensatory damage for which this court has allowed recovery. Therefore, when an insurer breaches its insurance contract by a bad faith refusal to settle a case, it is appropriate to require it to pay other damages that it knew or should have known the insured would incur because of the bad faith conduct.

The dissent would hold that an insurer's bad faith refusal to settle a claim against its insured does not give rise to a contract cause of action. For the reasons set forth in this opinion, we respectfully disagree. However, we respond to point out that the characterization of the claim by the dissent has no bearing on the outcome of this particular case. Whether Birth Center's cause of action sounds in contract or in tort, the jury found by clear and convincing evidence that St. Paul acted in bad faith and that its actions were a substantial factor in bringing about harm to the Birth Center totaling $700,000.00 in compensatory damages. In appropriate circumstances, compensatory damages are available in both contract and tort causes of action. Indeed, generally, compensatory damages are easier to recover in tort actions than in contract actions. Consequently, in this case, which does not involve a statute of limitations issue, the dissent's assertion that the claim should sound in tort instead of contract is irrelevant. . . .

NOTES AND QUESTIONS

1. How does the court address St. Paul's argument that allowing a recovery in this case will reduce liability insurers' incentive to pay an excess verdict without litigation? Can you develop an argument that the result in this case would actually increase liability insurer's incentive to pay an excess verdict without litigation?

2. Are the *PPG* and *Birth Center* cases consistent? Both cases differ from the typical duty to settle case, in that the harm that resulted from the breach of the duty to settle is a kind of harm that was not insurable.

3. This case highlights the liability insurer's status as a "repeat player" in the tort litigation arena. For St. Paul, the Norris claim was simply one of many "bad baby" cases, while for the Birth Center it was a very particular and threatening attack on its competence. (For a fascinating and accurate inside view of the dynamics of one "bad baby" case, see Barry Werth, Damages (1998).) St. Paul hoped that its tough litigation stance would demonstrate that it was not a pushover. Presumably company officials also believed that there was a sufficient chance that it would obtain a defense verdict that it was willing to risk paying an excess verdict in the hope that a good result in this case would reduce the settlement costs in future cases. The Birth Center's reputational interests, of course, ran in the other direction. We will address this and other conflicts of interest in more detail later in the chapter. For the moment, it is sufficient to understand the incentives that create the conflict and to understand the duty to settle as a legal invention that attempts to resolve the conflict in the insured's favor. At the same time, the duty to settle also makes more money available to tort victims, which necessarily raises the cost of liability insurance.

4. What result if St. Paul had waived the policy limits following the August 8, 1991 pretrial conference? Would it have breached the duty to make a reasonable settlement decision? If not, would the Birth Center be entitled to compensation for the $700,000 in compensatory damages? Consider the following comments to §51 of the RLLI, as appears on PD No. 3 (September 2016):

> *e. Avoiding liability for bad faith breach of the duty to make reasonable settlement decisions.* For insurers who are concerned about their ability to accurately predict whether a future jury would regard their reason as a good one in the circumstances, there is a safe harbor approach to avoiding liability for bad faith: when the insurer rejects the settlement offer it can notify the insured that it has waived the policy limit in the case. Such a waiver provides the insurer with a safe harbor because, as stated in Comment *a* to §24, the insurer's duty to make reasonable settlement decisions is owed to the insured only in cases that expose the insured to a risk of a judgment in excess of the policy limit. A waiver that eliminates that risk satisfies the legal duty to protect the insured from that risk.

III.   LIABILITY INSURANCE CONFLICTS OF INTEREST

Liability insurance conflicts of interest follow from the limited nature of liability insurance coverage. Reflecting on the liability insurance cases studied so far, we can see that there are two broad categories of limits on the liability insurance coverage, one of which can be further subdivided for purposes of analyzing conflicts of interest.

The first category is dollar limits on the amount of coverage. As we have seen, the dollar limit on the amount of coverage creates a conflict of interest that may encourage an insurance company to gamble with the insured's money. This "dollar limit" conflict is addressed by the duty to settle.

The second category is verbal limits on the nature of the coverage. There are three kinds of verbal limits, each of which creates a conceptually different kind of conflict. The first of these "verbal limit" conflicts follows from *limits on the kinds of harm to tort victims* that are covered by the policy. For example, intentional harm is not covered. This first kind of verbal limit produces the conflict explored in *Beals*. The second follows from *limits on the kinds of harm to the policyholder* that are covered by the policy. For example, in at least some states punitive damages are not covered. This second kind of verbal limit produces the conflict that led to the concerns Justice Mosk articulated in his dissent in *Transamerica*. The third follows from the possibility that the policyholder may lose coverage as a result of a breach of its obligations to the insurance company under the policy, such as the duty to disclose information in the application process and the duty to cooperate, which we explore in the final unit in this chapter.

If an insured could transfer to the insurance company all the risk associated with a particular claim, there would be no concern about the insurance company taking advantage of the insured. This would not mean that there would be no conflict of interest — only that the conflict of interest would not work to the disadvantage of the insured. If the insurance company bears all the risk, the insured would have little incentive to cooperate with the insurance company in the defense of the claim. Insurance companies address this kind of conflict of interest through the duty to cooperate. The duty to cooperate is a verbal limit that itself can create a conflict of interest in a case in which the insurance company asserts a breach of the duty as a defense.

As a result of the duty to cooperate and the other verbal and dollar limits on liability insurance coverage, there are no liability insurance claims in which there is not at least the potential for the insurance company to engage in strategic behavior at the expense of the insured.

In all these conflict situations, the insurance company and the insured share the risk of a bad outcome in the underlying tort case, but—at least according to the language of the standard form policy—only the insurance company controls the defense and settlement of the case. Thus, there is an opportunity for the insurance company to advance its own interests at the expense of the insured—an example of the potential for opportunistic behavior that insurance law is designed to police.

A. Pattern Conflict Cases

The following hypothetical cases illustrate each of the four kinds of conflict situations that we have explored. For each case, be sure that you can describe the nature of the conflict and that you can identify specific decisions that may have to be made by the defense lawyer or the insurance company that would directly implicate the competing interests of the insurance company and the insured defendant.

1. Dollar Limits

The Low Limits Case

An individual insured with a $100,000 limit liability insurance policy cut off a stranger's foot with a lawn mower. The stranger filed suit seeking $1 million and then offered to settle the case for $100,000.

The Multiple Victim Case

An insured family with an automobile liability insurance policy with a $300,000-per-accident limit caused a multiple-car accident. Three family members seriously injured in one of the cars filed suit before any of the other victims. The three immediately offer to settle for $300,000.

2. Verbal Limits on the Covered Harm to Victims

The Separation Assault

Following a legal separation in an abusive marriage, the insured regularly stalked his wife. One evening, in a drunken rage, the insured shot his wife's boyfriend and then himself. Both survived. The boyfriend filed suit against the insured, who requested a defense from his homeowners' insurance company. The company agreed to defend the case but reserved the right to contest its obligation to pay any judgment on the grounds that the insured intended the harm.

The Softball Case

The company hired a lawyer to defend what seemed to be a routine negligence claim filed by a spectator injured at a high school softball game. During informal interviews, two potential witnesses told the defense lawyer that the insured had deliberately thrown her bat at the plaintiff, who had been heckling the insured. The lawyer talked to the insured, who denied the story. When the lawyer next talked to the two potential witnesses, they said they had since spoken to the plaintiff's lawyer, who told them that the plaintiff would prefer to treat the incident as an accident and that they would not be needed as witnesses in the case.

3. Verbal Limits on the Covered Harm to Policyholders

The Food Poisoning Case

An insured restaurant faces a food poisoning claim. The company's claims manager believes that the plaintiff's case is weak on causation grounds. The restaurant owner believes that litigation of the case would cause negative publicity that would decrease sales. The plaintiff offers a presuit settlement of the claim for an amount that is greater than what the claims manager reasonably believes to be the present value of the expected judgment in the case (adjusted for the plaintiff's probability of success) but less than what the restaurant owner reasonably believes to be the sum of that present value plus the reputational harm that the plaintiff can cause the restaurant.

The Punitive Damages Case

After leaving a bar at closing, an insured driver drove through a red light and hit a pedestrian in a crosswalk. The driver stopped, backed up, drove around the victim (now lying badly injured in the street), and proceeded to an after-hours club, where he was later arrested and charged with driving while intoxicated and leaving the scene of an accident. The victim survived to bring a compensatory and punitive damages claim. Punitive damages are not insurable in the jurisdiction.

4. Verbal Limits Relating to Policyholders' Obligations

The Misrepresentation Case

In investigating a serious but otherwise routine slip and fall involving a repairman at the home of an insured with adequate liability insurance for the resulting claim, the company discovered that the insured had been conducting business at the home, despite having answered "no" to a question in the policy application regarding business at the home. The company undertook the defense of the insured but reserved the right to contest its obligation to pay any judgment on misrepresentation grounds.

B. *The Defense Lawyer's Responsibilities in a Conflict Case*

Whether the insured defendant is the defense lawyer's "sole," "primary," or "coequal" (with the insurance company) client is a controversial issue. Professional responsibility specialists traditionally have understood that the insurance defense lawyer's "client" is the insured defendant, while the liability insurance company is a "third-party payer" and not a client. Indeed, this understanding of the professional obligations informed the tentative draft of the Restatement (Third) of the Law Governing Lawyers. *See* Robert H. Jerry II, Understanding Insurance Law 811 (2d ed. 1996). When the time came to approve the draft, the third-party payer characterization of insurance companies produced a firestorm of protest within the American Law Institute (ALI).

The excerpts that follow are from the Restatement as adopted by the ALI. What position on the status of the liability insurance company did the ALI adopt?

RESTATEMENT (THIRD) OF THE LAW GOVERNING LAWYERS

§121.   Basic Prohibition of Conflict of Interest

Unless all affected clients and other necessary persons consent to the representation under the limitations and conditions provided in §122, a lawyer may not represent a client if the representation would involve a conflict of interest. A conflict of interest is involved if there is a substantial risk that the lawyer's representation of the client would be materially and adversely affected by the lawyer's own interests or by the lawyer's duties to another current client, a former client, or a third person.

§122.   Client Consent to a Conflict of Interest

(1) A lawyer may represent a client notwithstanding a conflict of interest prohibited by §121 if each affected client or former client gives informed consent to the lawyer's representation. Informed consent requires that the client or former client have reasonably adequate information about the material risks of such representation to that client or former client.

(2) Notwithstanding the informed consent of each affected client or former client, a lawyer may not represent a client if:

(a) the representation is prohibited by law;

(b) one client will assert a claim against the other in the same litigation; or

(c) in the circumstances, it is not reasonably likely that the lawyer will be able to provide adequate representation to one or more of the client.

§134. Compensation or Direction of a Lawyer by a Third Person

(1) A lawyer may not represent a client if someone other than the client will wholly or partly compensate the lawyer for the representation, unless the client consents under the limitations and conditions provided in §122 and knows the circumstances and conditions of the payments.

(2) A lawyer's professional conduct on behalf of a client may be directed by someone other than the client if:

(a) the direction does not interfere with the lawyer's independence of professional judgment;

(b) the direction is reasonable in scope and character, such as by reflecting obligations borne by the person directing the lawyer; and

(c) the client consents to the direction under the limitations and conditions provided in §122.

Comment "d":

When the conditions of the Subsection are satisfied, the client has, in effect, transferred to the designated third person the client's prerogatives of directing the lawyer's activities. . . . The third person's directions must allow for effective representation of the client and the client must give informed consent to the exercise of the power of direction by the third person. The direction must be reasonable in scope and character, such as by reflecting the obligation borne by the person directing the lawyer. Such directions are reasonable in scope and character if, for example, the third party will pay any judgment against the client and making a decision that defense costs beyond those designated by the third party would not significantly change the likely outcome. Informed client consent may be effective with respect to many forms of direction, ranging from the informed consent to particular instances of direction, such as in a representation in which the client otherwise directs the lawyer, to informed consent to general direction of the lawyer by another, such as an insurer or indemnitor on whom the client has contractually conferred the power of direction.

Comment "f":

 . . . Certain practices of designated insurance-defense counsel have become customary and, in any event, involve primarily standardized protection afforded by a regulated entity in recurring situations. Thus a particular practice permissible under this Section may not be permissible for a lawyer in non-insurance arrangements with significantly different characteristics.

It is clear in an insurance situation that a lawyer designated to defend the insured has a client-lawyer relationship with the insured. The insurer is not, simply by the fact that it designates the lawyer, a client to the lawyer. . . . With respect to client consent . . . in insurance representations, when there appears to be no substantial risk that a claim against a client insured will not be fully covered by an insurance policy pursuant to which the lawyer is appointed and is to be paid, consent in the form of the acquiescence of the client-insured to an informative letter should be all that is required. The lawyer should either withdraw or consult with the client-insured when a substantial risk that the client-insured will not be fully covered is apparent. . . .

When there is a question whether a claim against the insured is within the coverage of the policy, a lawyer designated to defend the insured may not reveal adverse confidential client information of the insured to the insurer concerning that question without explicit informed consent of the insured. That follows whether or not the lawyer also represents the insurer as a co-client and whether or not the insurer has asserted a "reservation of rights" with respect to its defense of the insured.

With respect to events or information that create a conflict of interest between the insured and insurer, the lawyer must proceed in the best interests of the insured. . . . If the designated lawyer finds it impossible to proceed, the lawyer must withdraw. . . .

NOTES AND QUESTIONS

1. *Silver and Syverud.* Professor Charles Silver was one of the people who led the protest against the Restatement drafters' initial single client position. *See, e.g.,* Charles Silver & Michael Sean Quinn, *Are Liability Carriers Second-Class Clients? No, But They May Be Soon — A Call to Arms Against the Restatement (Third) of the Law Governing Lawyers,* Coverage, Mar./Apr. 1996, at 21. Professor Silver's earlier controversial article with Dean Kent Syverud launched an extended round of scholarship reexamining the professional responsibilities of defense lawyers. *See* Charles Silver & Kent Syverud, *The Professional Responsibilities of Insurance Defense Lawyers,* 45 Duke L.J. 255 (1995). Silver and Syverud concluded that the insured defendant and the liability insurance company are co-equal clients of the insurance defense lawyer and that, as a result, the lawyer cannot privilege the interests of the individual client over the insurance company. Their analysis contradicted the conventional wisdom among professional responsibility scholars, as well as most insurance defense lawyers. Indeed, in their article, Silver and Syverud are careful to acknowledge that most of the insurance defense lawyers that they spoke to in the course of their project believed that the insured defendant is their primary (or even only) client. Silver and Syverud report that it took some work to convince the insurance defense lawyers who sponsored their project (the International Association of Insurance Defense Lawyers) to accept their dual client conclusion.

2. *Bar Associations and Courts.* Notwithstanding the controversy over the adoption of the Restatement (Third) of the Law Governing Lawyers, bar associations and courts that have considered the issue subsequently have concluded that the defense lawyer's primary obligations are owed to the insured defendant and that, in the event of a conflict between the interests of the insurance company and the defendant, the defense lawyer is obligated to defer to the interests of the insured defendant. *See, e.g., In the Matter of the Rules of Professional Conduct and Insurer Imposed Billing Rules and Procedures,* 2 P.3d 806 (Mont. 2000); Submission of Legal Bills to Auditor Company Hired by Insurer, CT Informal Op. 00-20 (2000); Ill. Bar Assn. Advisory Op. 98-08 (1998) ("the insured is, at a minimum, the defense lawyer's primary client").

3. The Softball Case described in the pattern conflict cases presents a very practical illustration of the difference that the professional obligation makes. If the insured is the only or primary client, then the defense lawyer can in good conscience withhold information about the intentional harm possibility from the insurance company. If the insured and the insurance company are co-equal clients, the defense lawyer faces a conflict. Silver and Syverud conclude that the defense lawyer must tell the insured that the lawyer is obligated to provide the information to the company, but that the

insured can instruct the lawyer not to do so. If the insured so instructs, the lawyer must withdraw from the defense and notify the insurance company that there is a conflict of interest that requires the withdrawal, without telling the insurance company of the nature of the conflict. What position does California's *Cumis* statute take on this question? What position does the Restatement (Third) of the Law Governing Lawyers take? For criticism of the Silver and Syverud analysis by a professional responsibility scholar, see Steven Pepper, *Applying the Fundamentals of Lawyers' Ethics to Insurance Defense Practice*, 4 Conn. Ins. L.J. 27 (1997-1998). For criticism from an insurance law perspective, see Tom Baker, *Liability Insurance Contracts and Defense Lawyers: From Triangles to Tetrahedrons*, 4 Conn. Ins. L.J. 101 (1997-1998). Both of these articles were part of a symposium prompted by the Silver and Syverud analysis. Together with Professor Ellen Pryor, Professor Silver has continued to extend the application of his dual client analysis. *See* Ellen Smith Pryor & Charles Silver, *Defense Lawyers' Professional Responsibilities: Part I—Excess Exposure Cases*, 78 Tex. L. Rev. 599 (2000); Ellen Smith Pryor & Charles Silver, *Defense Lawyers' Professional Responsibilities: Part II—Contested Coverage Cases*, 15 Geo. J. Legal Ethics 29 (2001).

4. The work of Silver et al. may have more impact in the long run than suggested by the chilly reception of the Montana Supreme Court in the opinion referenced in note 2 above. A casual and entirely unscientific review of insurance company pleadings, insurance trade literature, and conversations among defense lawyers and insurance claims professionals suggests that, as a result of their analysis, lawyers are increasingly likely to employ the "dual client" framework. This means that courts will have ample opportunity in the years ahead to reconsider the traditional primary client rule.

5. What are some of the problems created by the dual client rule that are absent in the case of a third-party payer or primary client rule? What are some of the problems created by the third-party payer or primary client rule that are absent in the case of a dual client rule? Given that liability insurance dates back to the end of the nineteenth century, and that mass market auto and homeowners' liability insurance became a significant factor in tort litigation as early as World War II, does it seem strange to you that such a fundamental issue is still open? Does this suggest that the conflicts of interest are of greater theoretical and analytical interest than practical interest? Many torts lawyers think so.

CONFLICTS PROBLEMS

1. A New Jersey insured with a typical homeowners' policy is quoted in the press as saying that her daughter's teacher is incompetent. The teacher sues, alleging defamation and negligent infliction of emotional distress. The complaint alleges that the teacher has suffered "loss of esteem, humiliation, irritability, sleeplessness, and an undue amount of physical complaints" as a result of the insured's statement. Recall that the New Jersey Supreme Court held in *Voorhees v. Preferred Mutual Insurance Co.*, 607 A.2d 1255 (N.J. 1992) that the term "bodily injury" in a liability policy includes "emotional distress with accompanying physical manifestations."

The liability insurance claims supervisor believes that the emotional distress claim has no merit and, therefore, that the case is not "really" a covered case. The supervisor instructs the insurance defense lawyer to file a motion to dismiss the count. If the motion to dismiss is granted, the company will refuse to provide a further defense on the grounds that the only remaining count, defamation, does not seek covered damages. What should the lawyer do? If you conclude that the lawyer cannot file the motion, how should the insurance company proceed? What can the teacher do to protect her interests?

As you think about this hypothetical, consider the following statement from *Voorhees*, which was not included in the excerpt in Chapter 4: "When an emotional distress claim is not supported factually, the insurer can and should move to dismiss the meritless claims."

2. Mrs. Garcia was driving her husband to work when the car went off the road and struck a tree, injuring her husband. Mr. Garcia brought a lawsuit against Mrs. Garcia, the dealership that sold them the car, and the manufacturer of the car. The claim against the dealership and the manufacturer was based on an alleged "blowout" of a tire that caused the car to leave the road. The claim against Mrs. Garcia was based on her negligence in not avoiding the accident. The Garcias' automobile liability insurer defended Mrs. Garcia in the lawsuit. In her deposition, Mrs. Garcia testified that she heard and felt the tire blow out while she was driving on the road and that the blowout caused her to lose control of the car. Shortly before trial, Mr. Garcia settled his action against the dealer and the manufacturer. At the *Garcia v. Garcia* trial, Mrs. Garcia testified as follows on direct examination by her counsel:

> *Q:* Okay. Around the time the accident happened, did you hear any unusual sounds around your car?
> *A:* Yes.
> *Q:* What did you hear?
> *A:* A small explosion.
> *Q:* Okay. And where did the small explosion seem to be coming from?
> *A:* I can't say for sure, because at the time of the explosion, I was already in the woods.
> *Q:* Did you hear any sounds while you were on Moss Mill Road that were unusual to you?
> *A:* No.

The defense lawyer immediately asked for a recess. In the recess, the lawyer explained to the judge that this testimony was directly contrary to Mrs. Garcia's testimony in her deposition, that this new version of events was also contrary to Mrs. Garcia's interest as a defendant in the case, and that, if believed, it would almost certainly result in a judgment against her. The lawyer asked the court for permission to treat his client as a hostile witness and to impeach her testimony by playing the deposition testimony and arguing to the jury that the new version of events seemed to be an effort by Mrs. Garcia to help her husband obtain a handsome verdict. Should the judge permit this course of action? Should the defense lawyer have requested it?

Suppose that the judge allows the defense lawyer to go ahead. Assuming that that course of action is a breach of the defense lawyer's obligations to Mrs. Garcia, what remedy should she be entitled to? *See Montanez v. Irizarry-Rodriguez*, 641 A.2d 1079 (N.J. Super. Ct. App. Div. 1994).

3. Cars driven by Jones and Smith collide, causing $5,000 in personal injury and property damage to Jones and $2,000 in personal injury and property damage to Smith. Jones sues Smith, who counterclaims against Jones. Smith is represented in the suit by defense counsel hired by Good Neighbor Insurance. A jury finds both drivers equally negligent in the collision, and accordingly awards $2,500 to Jones on her claim against Smith, and $1,000 to Smith on his counterclaim against Jones.

   Both Smith and Jones are insured, so if the judgment is entered $2,500 for Jones and $1,000 for Smith, each will collect that amount from the other's insurer. The Comparative Negligence Act in the relevant jurisdiction provides:

   > When two claimants are liable to each other in damages, the claimant who is liable for the greater amount is entitled to a credit toward his liability in the amount of damages owed by him by the other claimant.

   Smith, the party who would be entitled to the credit under the act, instructs his lawyer to forgo the credit and to move for entry of judgment of $2,500 for Jones and $1,000 for Smith. Good Neighbor instructs the insurance defense lawyer to argue that the credit is mandatory and that judgment must be entered for Jones, only, in the amount of $1,500, with the result that Smith will collect nothing. Should the defense lawyer follow that instruction? If not, what should Good Neighbor do to protect its interests? Assume that there are good-faith arguments for the position that credit is mandatory and for the position that it can be waived.

4. A products manufacturer faces a series of products liability suits involving an alleged failure to warn. An important element of a failure to warn action is proof that the manufacturer knew of the allegedly dangerous potential of the product.

   A. The manufacturer's insurance carrier has a potential concealment defense that would require proving the same knowledge that the plaintiffs in the underlying failure to warn action need to prove. The carrier files a declaratory judgment action raising the concealment defense.

   B. A jury in a failure to warn case found that the manufacturer had the requisite knowledge. So far no underlying plaintiffs have been able to convince other courts to apply that finding (on an offensive collateral estoppel basis) in other actions. The carrier files an offensive collateral estoppel motion seeking to apply that finding in the declaratory judgment action.

   C. The carrier's insurance coverage counsel meets with the plaintiffs' counsel from underlying actions and exchanges information obtained from third parties (not the insured) in return for information from the plaintiffs' counsel about trial strategy, etc.

   First, articulate how these actions illustrate a conflict of interest. Second, consider whether these actions should be considered a breach of the insurance company's duty of good faith and fair dealing. In considering this second question, think about how else the insurance company could achieve the legitimate end of avoiding coverage on the basis of conceal-ment or intentional harm. Are there ways to structure the litigation of these defenses so that they do not harm the insured in the underlying tort actions? Should the insurance company be obligated to do so? With respect to each of these issues, what role should the insurance defense law-yer have in informing the insured or the insurance company of its rights and obligations?

The following case presents one example of how an insurance defense lawyer managed the various conflicts and potential conflicts inherent in a low-limit case. As you read the case, consider whether Judge Posner is correct in conclud-ing that the defense lawyer's mistake did not harm the policyholder. Should there be a "no harm, no foul" rule here? Be sure to consider the strategic con-siderations that led the various parties to the tort lawsuit to behave in the ways that they did.

STEELE v. THE HARTFORD FIRE INSURANCE CO.

United States Court of Appeals, Seventh Circuit
788 F.2d 441 (1986)

POSNER, J. The common law of Illinois makes it a civil wrong for a liability insur-er to refuse, in bad faith, to settle litigation against the insured, thereby expos-ing the insured to a judgment in excess of the policy limits. We must consider the meaning of "bad faith" in the factual setting of this case.

The story begins with a lawnmower accident in 1974 to Charles E. Steele, Jr., who was five years old at the time. His grandfather, Hershel Bauman, was using a mower manufactured by Arctic Enterprises Inc. to cut the grass at the home of Harry Tjardes, a neighbor, who paid Bauman for this service. Charles was riding on the back of the mower. He fell off, and Bauman accidentally backed the mower over Charles's foot; the resulting injury was so serious that the foot had to be amputated. Bauman and his wife had a homeowners' policy, issued by the Hartford Fire Insurance Company, which provided liability coverage of $25,000 for bodily injury. The policy provided, "This Company shall not be obli-gated to pay any claim or judgment or to defend any suit after the applicable limit of this Company's liability has been exhausted by payment of judgments or settlements."

The Hartford offered Charles's father $25,000, the full policy limits, in exchange for a general release of liability. The settlement had to be approved by an Illinois court, which appointed James Walker as the boy's guardian *ad litem* and then on Walker's recommendation rejected the settlement. By giving a general release, Walker would have given up the right to sue on Charles's behalf both Harry Tjardes — the owner of the property on which the accident had occurred and therefore arguably the employer *pro tem.* of Bauman and if so lia-ble for Bauman's negligence under the principle of respondeat superior — and Arctic Enterprises, which would be liable on the ground of products liability if the lawnmower had been defective or unreasonably dangerous.

The settlement having fallen through, the Hartford hired a local lawyer, Guy Fraker, to defend against Charles's claim. Walker wrote Fraker offering to settle with the Hartford for $25,000 plus a covenant not to sue Bauman, explaining, "The nature of the injury makes it clear that [if the claim were prosecuted to a jury verdict] the verdict would exceed the policy coverage of $25,000 and thus create a judgment against Mr. Bauman in excess of the insurance coverage. However, it is not the desire of the guardian to invade the personal assets of Mr. Bauman if the claim can be promptly settled for the amount of insurance coverage. . . ." Upon receipt of this letter Fraker wrote the Baumans to explain the situation, and in particular that if they settled for just a covenant not to sue rather than a general release, "There is a real possibility that either of these parties [Tjardes and Arctic] would turn around and sue you, seeking indemnity." He added, "This is a fairly complex problem and one which I would strongly urge you to discuss with your own personal attorney of your choice."

The Baumans replied that they had no personal attorney and wanted to discuss the matter with Fraker. They met at Fraker's office for more than an hour and he explained to them with the aid of a diagram the difference between a general release and a covenant not to sue. Fraker testified that at the end of the conference the Baumans told him "that this thing had been a real tragedy for them. They wanted the injured party to have the money, but they also wanted this to be at an end, and they did not wish to have continued exposure on their own part to a lawsuit." Fraker wrote a confirmatory letter to the Baumans, summarizing the conference in some detail. Again he explained that if Walker refused to give a general release, "This would leave them [i.e., the Steeles and Walker] in a position where they could make claim against either the manufacturer of the lawn mower or the owner of the property. There is a distinct possibility then that either of these parties would sue you and seek indemnity from you. If the Hartford pays the $25,000.00 and does not obtain a Release, your personal assets would then be exposed out over by either of these parties. . . . You indicated to me that as far as you were concerned you did not want the Hartford to settle the case and pay the policy limits unless they could obtain a Release, fully clearing you of further potential liability."

Walker remained adamant in his refusal to settle the case with the Hartford in exchange for a general release and in 1976 he brought a suit in state court on Charles's behalf against Bauman, Tjardes, and Arctic. The Hartford retained Fraker to defend the claim against Bauman. Tjardes moved unsuccessfully to obtain summary judgment on Walker's claim against him, but then agreed with Fraker to waive any right to seek indemnity from Bauman in the event that Walker obtained a judgment against Tjardes, provided that Fraker settled Walker's claim against Bauman. Apparently Tjardes's lawyer thought that a settlement of Walker's claim against Bauman would operate as a release of Walker's claim against Tjardes as well. Armed with this agreement, and knowing that under Illinois law as it then stood a manufacturer sued for products liability could not get indemnity from a joint tortfeasor (though the law was in flux, and the risk of such an action could not be entirely discounted), Fraker now offered to settle the suit against Bauman for the policy limits plus a covenant not to sue. Before Walker responded to this offer the Illinois Supreme Court changed its mind about indemnity, see *Skinner v. Reed-Prentice Division Package Machinery Co.*, 374 N.E.2d 437 (Ill. 1977), and Arctic promptly filed a third-party claim against Bauman for indemnity of any damages that it might be ordered to pay in Walker's suit. Fraker thereupon withdrew the offer to Walker, and this removed the premise of the deal with Tjardes. A few weeks later the Illinois Supreme Court decided not to apply its new rule on indemnity to pending cases. *See id.* at 444 (1978).

Settlement efforts having failed, Walker's case against the three defendants proceeded to trial. At the start of the trial Walker offered to settle with Tjardes for $25,000 plus an agreement not to seek indemnity against Bauman. This offer was consistent with Walker's earlier assurance to Fraker that he would not seek to collect a judgment out of Bauman's personal assets. The record contains no evidence of what those assets might be; the district judge's statement that Bauman was "impecunious" has no basis in the record.

Tjardes now counteroffered $10,000 (and the covenant), but Walker refused. Walker settled with Arctic for $25,000. Fraker then offered to pay the full policy limits in exchange for just a covenant not to sue Bauman, but Walker refused; the offer, he said, had come too late. The case came on for trial against Tjardes and Bauman. The trial judge granted a directed verdict for Tjardes. The jury brought in a verdict against Bauman of $135,000 for Charles and $30,000 for his father. The Hartford paid $25,000, the policy limits, in partial satisfaction of the judgment.

Walker brought a supplementary proceeding against Bauman to collect the unpaid balance of the judgment. That proceeding was settled by Bauman's assigning to the Steeles his right to sue the Hartford for bad faith. The Steeles then brought this suit against the Hartford, which removed the case to federal district court. [Discussion of diversity jurisdiction omitted.] . . .

After a three-day bench trial, the district judge awarded judgment for the Steeles in the amount of the excess judgment against Bauman, and the Hartford has appealed.

We may assume without having to decide that whether the insurance company acted in bad faith in not advising the Baumans to settle Walker's claim for the policy limits plus a covenant not to sue is a question of fact within the meaning of Rule 52(a) of the Federal Rules of Civil Procedure. The cases assume this without discussion. *See, e.g., Bailey v. Prudence Mutual Casualty Co., supra,* 429 F.2d at 1390. The issue of bad faith is similar in character to that of negligence, especially since, as we are about to see, negligence may be deemed bad faith in a refusal-to-settle case such as this. These "mixed questions of law and fact" as they are sometimes called—it would be more informative to describe them as questions of the application of law to fact—sometimes are reviewed under the clearly-erroneous standard applicable to questions classified as factual, sometimes receive plenary appellate review like pure issues of law, and sometimes are reviewed under an intermediate standard. The standard most favorable to the appellees would of course be the clearly-erroneous standard, and as the appellant doesn't challenge it[,] we shall apply it.

But this does not carry the day for the appellees. We think the district court's determination that Fraker and the Hartford were guilty of bad faith was clearly erroneous, for our review of the record leaves us with a strong conviction that the insurance company acted throughout in perfectly good faith. The company incurred significant expenses (Fraker's fees) in an effort to protect its insured from an excess judgment, and it kept the insured fully advised of its strategy all the way.

The company, acting as it was required to do as the perfectly loyal and reasonably intelligent agent of its insured, had to balance two risks. The first was that if it held out for a general release Walker would refuse to settle, would go on to victory in the courtroom, would obtain a judgment in excess of the policy limits, and would then levy on Bauman's personal assets. This risk was not great. Because the Baumans were Mrs. Steele's parents and Charles's grand-parents, the Steeles did not want to levy on Mr. Bauman's personal assets; and although Charles's suit was not in the control of the Steeles, the guardian *ad litem,* Walker, had assured Fraker that he would not levy against the Baumans. There is no suggestion that Bauman is a man of wealth (the low policy lim-its suggest he is not); and it is hardly likely that Mrs. Steele, imitating King Lear's bad daughters, would turn Charles's grandparents out of their home in order to satisfy a judgment in excess of the policy limits. Fraker could therefore reasonably believe that Walker would not press the matter to a trial against Bauman. A somewhat greater danger was that Walker would obtain damages against Tjardes and Arctic, one or both of whom would turn around and seek indemnity against Bauman; no family relationship would inhibit either of them from trying to collect a judgment out of Bauman's personal assets. This risk may have been rather slight also. Bauman might not have sufficient liquid assets to be worth suing, and anyway Walker's claim against Tjardes was tenu-ous, depending as it did on successfully characterizing Bauman as an employee rather than independent contractor of Tjardes. Since, as it turned out, Bauman had supplied the mower and Tjardes had not supervised Bauman's mowing, the latter characterization was by far the more plausible. Finally, Arctic, except for a brief interval during the settlement negotiations, seemed not to have a legal right to indemnity.

The weakness of Walker's claim against Tjardes is a two-edged sword. It reduced the threat of a third-party claim against Bauman but increased the likelihood that Walker would in the end agree to give Bauman a general release. An additional reason why Walker might ultimately yield on the issue of the release would be the Steeles' desire not to collect a judgment out of Bauman's personal assets. They would be doing this indirectly if they got judg-ments against Tjardes and Arctic, either of whom turned around and got a judgment for indemnity against Bauman; and Fraker could reasonably believe that an awareness of this possibility might influence Walker in negotiating the issue of the general release, though in the end it did not. Moreover, weak as it appears to have been, Walker's claim against Tjardes was strong enough to induce Tjardes (actually his insurance company) to offer $10,000 to settle it. If the offer had been accepted Tjardes could have turned around and sued Bauman for indemnity, which is conventionally available where an employer is held liable for his employee's tort under the doctrine of respondeat superior (the ground for the action against Tjardes). Prosser and Keeton on the Law of Torts §51, at p. 341 and n.6 (5th ed. 1984). Though not wealthy, Bauman might be good for $10,000, or a sufficient fraction of that amount to make suit worthwhile. Evidently Arctic, which did sue Bauman, thought so. To prevent the risk of an indemnity action from materializing, Fraker wanted to hold out for a general release from Walker; but the problem was that by giving it to him Walker would be giving up a chance to get some additional damages, from Tjardes or Arctic or both.

Fraker's best strategy might have been to work out a three-cornered arrange-ment among himself, Walker, and Tjardes, whereby both Walker and Tjardes would agree not to sue Bauman; and to take his chances with Arctic. But in fact he tried this approach. By November 1977 the elements of such a deal were in hand, but it fell apart the next month when the risk materialized. Later, when Fraker tried to resurrect the deal, Tjardes balked at the amount demanded by

Walker; and by the time Arctic had fallen out of the picture again, Walker was no longer willing to settle the case on his original terms.

The fact that Fraker let the reins slip from his hands would not establish bad faith in any common meaning of the term. Nevertheless there is authority in Illinois for extending the term to include a negligent failure to settle within the policy limits; see in particular *Browning v. Heritage Ins. Co.*, 338 N.E.2d 912, 916 (Ill. App. Ct. 1975). The idea behind this extension (an idea nowhere expressed, and just a guess on our part) may be that the insurance policy implicitly commits the insurer to use due care to protect the insured from an excess judgment. Why an insurer should be thought voluntarily to assume a duty whose faithful fulfillment can only encourage people to underinsure is not clear to us. Generally it has been thought that more than simple negligence is required. *See, e.g., Voccio v. Reliance Insurance Cos.*, 703 F.2d 1, 2 (1st Cir. 1983). In the absence of any holding by the Illinois Supreme Court, and any explanation in the decisions of the lower courts of Illinois, we are entitled to doubt that simple negligence is enough under Illinois law. . . . But we need not resolve our doubts; we can assume without having to decide that negligence is enough; for we do not think that a reasonable factfinder could deem Fraker's representation even negligent, let alone in bad faith in some stronger sense. Mistake is not negligence; the duty of good faith does not make the insurance company an insurer against the uncertainties inherent in the settlement process. Indeed, "mistake" may be the wrong word. The proper perspective for judging Fraker is *ex ante* (before the fact) rather than *ex post*. If Fraker chose the correct course on the basis of what he knew, he should not be called mistaken because of unavoidable uncertainty about whether the course would succeed.

Fraker demonstrated good faith in the ordinary sense of these words by protecting the insured's interests at the expense of the insurance company's. If he had gotten Bauman to settle on the terms originally offered by Walker, the insurance company would have been off the hook; the policy allowed it to walk away as soon as it settled for the full policy limits. Instead it hung around (in the person of its agent, Fraker), vainly trying to defend Bauman against an excess judgment—vainly trying to obtain a release from Tjardes—and incurred legal expenses in these endeavors. We do not suggest that this was altruism, for we know what would have happened if the company had settled on Walker's original terms. If and when Tjardes and Arctic filed claims for indemnity against Bauman (Arctic actually did file such a claim, as we said), Bauman would have accused the insurance company of having settled prematurely with Walker in order to avoid the expense of defending the third-party claims. It seems, then, that whatever Fraker did he would be exposing the Hartford to a claim of bad faith. It cannot be the law that every excess judgment must be paid by the insurance company, so that in effect liability insurance policies have no limits. Such a strange result would not even help policyholders in the long run; insurance companies would have to charge much higher prices, especially for policies with low limits.

The principal evidence of bad faith on which the district court relied was, first, the Baumans' deposition testimony that they didn't understand the complex legal fix they were in, and, second, a letter Fraker wrote the Hartford early on explaining what he conceived to be a potential conflict of interest between the Baumans and the Hartford. The first piece of evidence is of very slight relevance. The duty to represent the insured in good faith includes a duty to explain clearly and simply the legal choices facing the insured; it is not an absolute duty to enlighten where enlightenment may be impossible because of the insured's refusal to listen or his incapacity to understand the most patient and lucid explanation. Uncontradicted evidence consisting of Fraker's letters and diagram shows that he explained the legal situation to the Baumans with great care. If they didn't understand, it was not his fault. He advised them to consult their own lawyer, and they refused. He couldn't make them, and is not chargeable with their misunderstanding. His letters to them are in fact models of how to explain law to laymen. Although he can be criticized for having exaggerated the danger of a suit for indemnity by Arctic as Illinois law then stood, in fact he was prophetic, for Illinois law changed in the course of the litigation. Only the fact that the Illinois Supreme Court decided to make the change prospective spared the Baumans the acute danger of being forced to indemnify Arctic (unless Walker gave Bauman a general release) as Fraker feared.

Fraker's letter to the insurance company is the "smoking gun." But it is smoke without fire. The letter said:

> The question is, of course, do we have to take less than a full release in order to remain in good faith to our insured. There are two reasons we would want to obtain a full release. One is consistent with the interest of our insured, one is not. There is the obvious possibility here of third party action. In the event there is an action against other potential defendants, this would expose the personal assets of the insured to such an action. Here, our interests are consistent. The other is that it would expose the Hartford to costs of defense which the Hartford should be concerned about, but the insured should not be and accordingly, the conflict. To refuse this settlement for the latter reason would be bad faith.

If the policy had required the Hartford to bear all legal expenses arising out of an insured event, the dilemma identified by Fraker would have been a real one. But the policy states in language that could not be clearer that once the Hartford paid the full policy limits in settlement of a claim against the insured it would have no further obligation to defend him. The Steeles argue that maybe the term "settlement" as used in the insurance policy excludes a covenant not to sue, but that is nonsense. A covenant not to sue is a common form of settlement, and is certainly within the contemplation as well as literal terms of the policy. It is apparent that Fraker was not familiar with the policy; more surprising is why no one at the Hartford straightened him out.

Even if there was no actual conflict of interest between the Baumans and the Hartford—no way in which the Hartford could have been made worse off by settling with Walker in exchange for a covenant not to sue Bauman rather than a general release—if Fraker, mistakenly thinking there was a conflict, had tried to push the Baumans to hold out for a general release, he and therefore his principal would have been guilty of bad faith. But there is no evidence of that either. He advised them to get their own lawyer. He told the Baumans as accurately as he could what he perceived the tradeoffs to be between the alternative courses of action. True, he did not tell them that the median jury verdict for the loss of a foot was $175,000, but this was not a material omission. The Baumans knew they faced the risk of an excess judgment and faced it either way—in a suit by the Steeles and in an indemnity action by Tjardes and (less probably) Arctic. If the Steeles got a $175,000 judgment against Bauman he would be personally liable for $150,000 (the difference between the judgment and the policy limits). If they got a judgment for $150,000 against Tjardes ($175,000 minus the amount that they would have received from his joint tortfeasor, Bauman, by virtue of the insurance policy), Tjardes would have a claim for $150,000 against Bauman. Although the Steeles were likelier to win a judgment against Bauman than against Tjardes because Tjardes's liability was more doubtful than Bauman's, Tjardes was likelier actually to levy on Bauman's assets than the Steeles were, so that the choice of which risk the Baumans should run was a close one. These risks came from the fact that the Baumans had bought a policy with such low limits. Maybe they could afford no more; but it was not the Hartford's fault that they faced an inescapable dilemma. Fraker laid out the relevant considerations to the Baumans as clearly as it was possible to do and they made their choice. The Steeles say that Fraker should have advised the Baumans of his imagined conflict of interest. But if he had told them, erroneously, that the insurance company would be better off holding out for a general release, this would not, so far as appears, have altered their decision—a decision motivated by their perception of their own self-interest.

Fraker's mistake, even if negligent in some sense—even if a breach of ethical duty to the Baumans, whose lawyer he was as well as the Hartford's—cannot impose liability on the Hartford, because the mistake did not cause him to subordinate the Baumans' interests to that of the Hartford. The only relevant bad faith is that which causes the insurance company to act otherwise than it would do if acting in perfect good faith. Without proof of causation, there can be no recovery of damages. *Voccio v. Reliance Ins. Cos., supra,* 703 F.2d at 3-4. Fraker only had to give the Baumans' interests equal weight; for whatever reason he gave their interest paramount weight. To press for a general release could only help the Baumans, since (unlike the otherwise somewhat similar case of *Stoner v. State Farm Mutual Automobile Ins. Co.,* 780 F.2d 1414, 1418-19 (8th Cir. 1986)) the Hartford would have been off the hook by settling for the full policy limits in exchange merely for a covenant not to sue. The policy expense to the Hartford would have been the same, its legal expense (Fraker's fees) lower. Maybe Fraker pressed as hard as he did for the release because he mistakenly thought it would benefit the Hartford as well as the Baumans, but the only thing that matters is that he followed a course of action objectively consistent only with his giving primacy to the insured's interest. The insurance company cannot be punished just because its lawyer exceeded the call of duty to the insured. The law does not punish one for doing the right thing for the wrong reason.

Granted, Fraker did not inquire into the strength of the Steeles' case against Tjardes, which was material to the menace of a suit by Tjardes against Bauman for indemnity. But this omission was not the basis of the district court's decision, and does not by itself create liability. For there is (once again) no suggestion that the investigation would have altered Fraker's advice. We know the claim against Tjardes had some colorable merit because Tjardes offered $10,000 in settlement and the Steeles refused, evidently thinking they could do better at trial, though in the event they did worse. Had they accepted the settlement or won at trial Tjardes would probably have sought indemnity from Bauman. Fraker was not unreasonable to think this a greater threat than the threat (which never materialized) of the Steeles' collecting a judgment against Bauman after assuring him (via Walker's letter) that they would not do so.

We note finally the anomaly of the district court's awarding the Steeles more than $100,000 when there is no evidence that they would or could have collected any of this money from Bauman. The potential harm to the Baumans from the alleged bad faith of the insurance company came from exposing Mr. Bauman to a judgment in excess of the policy limits. But that could hurt the Baumans only to the extent that the excess was collected out of his assets. Suppose he had no assets, present or prospective (the significance of this qualification will become apparent in a moment). Then the Baumans were not damaged at all and the damage claim they assigned to the Steeles should have been worth nothing. Or suppose they had assets, but, consistently with Walker's assurance, the Steeles would not have tried to levy on them (apparently all the Steeles wanted from the Baumans was the assignment of this cause of action); again it would be impossible to see how the Baumans had lost $140,000 ($135,000 + $30,000 – $25,000) because of the excess judgment. It is true that Illinois is usually classed with those states which hold that an insured can recover an excess judgment caused by the insurer's failure to settle the litigation in good faith even without proof that the insured would or could have paid the judgment. *See* Annot., 63 A.L.R.3d 627, 641 (1975), *citing Wolfberg v. Prudence Mutual Casualty Co.,* 240 N.E.2d 176 (Ill. App. Ct. 1968). Actually the picture is more complicated. *Wolfberg* holds only that the fact of having a judgment entered against you causes harm, even if the judgment is not collected. . . .

The fact that an excess judgment cannot be fully executed does not excuse the insurer from liability or show that the insured has incurred no damages at all, because even an unexecuted judgment can cause an injury, present or future, that can be monetized. But the damages need not be exactly equal to the amount of the excess judgment they could be more or less. Here it seems plain that they were less—maybe zero (which if true is further evidence that Fraker had the Baumans' best interests at heart). Since the insurance company has not argued the point we do not rely on it but merely note it for future reference. We rest our decision entirely on the absence of evidence that the insurance company represented Bauman in bad faith. . . .

NOTES AND QUESTIONS

1. As Judge Posner recognizes, insurance defense lawyers' duties have to be understood in the context of the strategic interests of the plaintiff, as well as of the insurance company and the insured.

2. Do you agree with Judge Posner that the lawyer's "let[ting] the reins slip from his hands" did not harm the defendants? Can you imagine a situation in which it would?

3. What does Judge Posner's discussion of the assets of the defendants suggest that he would think about the Michigan rule regarding the duty to settle discussed following the *Comunale* case? (Recall that the Michigan rule is that, in a breach of the duty to settle a case, the liability insurance company's liability is limited to the lesser of (a) the verdict or (b) the policy limits plus the insured defendant's assets.) What do you think of the dicta suggesting that there should, in effect, be no liability for breach of the duty to settle unless the plaintiff would really have tried to collect from the defendant? What effect might that have on the tradition against collecting from the defendants' personal assets in an ordinary negligence case? Is the answer likely to be the same in intrafamily lawsuits and stranger lawsuits? Consider whether

the result in the *Steele* case might reflect the traditional judicial hostility to intrafamily lawsuits.

IV.   THE DUTY TO COOPERATE

The final liability insurance relationship issue that we discuss here is the duty to cooperate. Professor Jerry states the following about the duty to cooperate:

> The primary obligation that the insured owes the insurer in third party litigation (apart from paying the premium when due) is the duty of cooperation. The duty to cooperate is essentially the flipside of the insurer's duty to defend. The insurer promises in the liability policy to provide the insured with a defense, but the insured simultaneously commits to cooperate with the insurer in making settlements, providing evidence, enforcing subrogation rights, and attending hearings, trials, and depositions. Also, the insured commits not to take any action that would adversely affect the insurer's handling of the claim.

Robert H. Jerry II, Understanding Insurance Law 845 (3d ed. 2002). Like the insurance company's *right* to defend and *discretion* to settle, the core idea behind the insured's duty to cooperate seems to be controlling the moral hazard that can result from the insurance company's obligation to defend and pay the claim. Can you see why this is so?

A.   The Basic Duty

The first case that we examine next addresses the basic outlines of the duty to cooperate. The second set of cases addresses the very interesting questions of whether, when, and how liability insurance conflicts of interest relieve the insured of the duty to cooperate. As you read the first case, consider whether moral hazard is an adequate explanation for the application of the duty to cooperate in this situation. If not, what is? What does this case suggest about the nature of the duty to cooperate that is not captured by the simple economic explanation?

WILDRICK v. NORTH RIVER INSURANCE CO.

United States Court of Appeals, Eighth Circuit
75 F.3d 432 (1996)

MORRIS SHEPPARD ARNOLD, J. Lonnie Kent Wildrick sued North River Insurance Company in 1992, claiming that North River breached its contract by withdrawing its defense of Phillips, P.C., a professional corporation earlier sued by Mr. Wildrick for negligence in the performance of accounting services. Mr. Wildrick asserted that claim as both a third-party beneficiary of Phillips's professional liability insurance policy and as Phillips's assignee for claims against North River relative to Phillips's defense in the professional negligence action (which resulted in a state court judgment against Phillips for approximately $427,500). Mr.

Wildrick also asserted claims for breach of fiduciary duty, breach of an implied covenant of good faith and fair dealing, and bad faith.

On motion by North River, the district court dismissed the third-party beneficiary claim in late 1992 for failure to state a claim. On motion by North River, the district court granted summary judgment to North River in late 1994 on the remaining claims, holding, as a matter of law, that Phillips had failed to cooperate in the professional negligence case. Mr. Wildrick appeals. We affirm the rulings of the district court.

I

Robert Phillips was the principal in a professional corporation that performed accounting services between 1983 and 1986 for an Iowa company owned by Lonnie Kent Wildrick (for simplicity's sake, we call the professional corporation "Phillips" in this opinion; we refer to Robert Phillips himself as "Robert Phillips" or "Mr. Phillips"). In late 1986, in preparation for the sale of his company, Mr. Wildrick requested an independent audit of the company's finances. As a result of the independent audit, Mr. Wildrick learned that financial statements prepared by Phillips for the company overstated the company's accounts receivable by at least $100,000.

In late 1988, Mr. Wildrick sued Phillips in Iowa state court, alleging conversion, breach of contract, and professional negligence in accounting services—all three counts based on payments alleged to have been improperly made to Phillips, to Robert Phillips, or to another entity in which Phillips's principal, Robert Phillips, was also the principal. The allegedly improper payments were exactly the same in each count. (Mr. Wildrick also sued Robert Phillips, individually, but Mr. Phillips's subsequent petition for bankruptcy stayed any action against him personally.) Phillips notified the company that had issued Phillips's professional liability insurance policy, North River Insurance Company. The insurance company advised Phillips, in response, that North River would provide "a complete defense to all allegations" of the complaint. North River called to Phillips's attention, however, that North River was reserving its rights to limit the defense provided to only those claims covered by the policy.

The professional liability insurance policy issued by North River covered claims made against Phillips between late 1988 and late 1989 and contained three provisions relevant to this case. First, the policy excluded from coverage any claims "arising out of any dishonest, fraudulent, criminal or malicious act or omission" of Phillips and any claims "arising out of [Phillips's] gaining in fact any personal profit or advantage to which [Phillips] was not legally entitled." Second, the policy stated that in "any legal proceedings" against Phillips involving a claim arguably covered by the policy, Phillips was required to "cooperate with [North River] and upon [North River's] request [to] attend hearings and trials and [to] assist in effecting settlements, securing and giving evidence, . . . and in the conduct of suits"; Phillips was also required "not [to] . . . admit any liability." Finally, the policy provided that North River was not liable for claims against Phillips arguably covered by the policy unless Phillips "shall have fully complied with all the terms" of the policy.

North River hired a lawyer to defend Phillips in the state court action. From late 1988 until early 1991, according to an affidavit, a deposition, and subsequent trial testimony from that lawyer in a related action, Robert Phillips "represented . . . that [Mr. Wildrick's lawsuit] came as a complete shock to him and that the allegations . . . that he converted funds to his own use were completely untrue." During that period, according to the lawyer, Mr. Phillips "vehemently and vigorously denied to [the lawyer] that he, or to his knowledge anyone at Phillips, P.C., had ever converted or misappropriated funds entrusted to him." In addition, Mr. Phillips "represented to [the lawyer] that there were appropriate explanations for all of the funds paid to him, his professional corporation, and [the other entity in which Mr. Phillips was the principal]."

Specifically, according to the lawyer, Robert Phillips asserted that "he was to receive a yearly salary of $30,000 for his accounting work" (as business manager) for Mr. Wildrick's company and that some of the payments reflected reimbursement to Mr. Phillips of advances that he made to Mr. Wildrick's company to pay bills. Mr. Phillips also contended, with respect to the other entity in which he was also the principal, first, that Mr. Wildrick had asked Mr. Phillips to deposit a $25,000 check to the credit of that entity in order to "prevent others in the business and Mr. Wildrick's wife from knowing how profitable [Mr. Wildrick's company] was" and, second, that "checks and cash had been paid back to Mr. Wildrick." In early January, 1991, in preparation for a settlement conference, the lawyer hired by North River advised the state court, with respect to Phillips's defense, that "Mr. Phillips generally denies that he improperly made any payments from [Mr. Wildrick's company] to either himself, his firm or [the other entity in which Mr. Phillips was a principal]. . . . It is [Phillips's] position that all such payments were proper."

Just two days later, however, a second lawyer, hired by Robert Phillips himself, advised the state court and the lawyer hired by North River that Mr. Phillips had been "in contact with . . . the office of the United States Attorney . . . to present his admission of misappropriation of funds entrusted to him." (It later became known that Mr. Phillips first went to law enforcement authorities in mid-December, 1990, approximately three weeks before the second lawyer's letter.) The second lawyer stated that the lawyer hired by North River "had no knowledge" of that contact.

Four days after the second lawyer's letter to the state court, a front-page article appeared in the local newspaper stating that Robert Phillips had "told federal investigators [that] he stole more than $1 million from some of his clients." . . . The settlement conference in the state court action took place on that same day. At that conference, Mr. Wildrick evidently advised the state court that he intended to drop the claims for breach of contract and for conversion, and that a professional negligence claim would be the only issue for trial. Mr. Wildrick did amend his complaint to that effect at a pretrial conference in early February, 1991, four days before the state trial.

Only hours after the pretrial conference, [held in early February 1991, four days before trial] North River informed Phillips that North River was withdrawing its defense of Phillips. North River gave as its reason Robert Phillips's failure to cooperate, as required by the terms of Phillips's professional liability insurance policy. . . .

Although North River advised both Phillips and the lawyer hired by North River to defend Phillips that it would pay no more expenses associated with the professional negligence action (and did not), the lawyer appeared at trial nonetheless. He cross-examined witnesses offered by Mr. Wildrick but offered no witnesses or evidence himself. That trial, which was held to the court rather than to a jury, resulted in a state court judgment of approximately $427,500 against Phillips. North River refused to pay the judgment. Phillips subsequently assigned to Mr. Wildrick any claims that Phillips had against North River relative to Phillips's defense in the professional negligence action.

Mr. Wildrick sued North River in 1992, alleging breach of contract and other claims related to North River's withdrawal of its defense of Phillips in the state court action. . . .

The district court granted summary judgment to North River, holding, first, that because Robert Phillips "repeatedly lied to and concealed facts from his defense counsel" in the state court action, Phillips failed to cooperate with North River, as a matter of law, and, second, that North River was actually prejudiced by that failure to cooperate. On appeal, Mr. Wildrick argues that Mr. Phillips's conduct did not amount to a failure to cooperate, as a matter of law; that because North River knew or should have known of Mr. Phillips's deception, North River waived the use of any failure to cooperate as a defense to payment under the professional liability insurance policy; and, further, that a genuine issue of material fact exists with respect to whether North River was actually prejudiced by Mr. Phillips's conduct. . . .

II

We consider first the question of whether Robert Phillips failed to cooperate, as a matter of law. "The purpose of a cooperation clause is to protect insurers and prevent collusion between insureds and injured parties." *American Guarantee and Liability Insurance Co. v. Chandler Manufacturing Co.,* 467 N.W.2d 226, 229 (Iowa 1991). "The kind of cooperation required . . . is honest cooperation. Honest cooperation involves telling the truth. It cannot be based on persistent falsehood going to the very essence of the problem." *Western Mutual Insurance Co. v. Baldwin,* 137 N.W.2d 918, 924 (Iowa 1965) (*en banc*).

It is undisputed that, less than four months after the state court judgment was rendered, Robert Phillips pleaded guilty in federal court to two counts of mail fraud and, in doing so, stipulated that he had embezzled approximately $294,700 from Mr. Wildrick's company between 1983 and 1985. Basically, North River contends that by asserting, during the period preceding the state trial on the professional negligence claim, that legitimate reasons existed for every payment to Phillips, to himself, or to the other entity in which he was also the principal, Mr. Phillips "actively misled" the lawyer hired by North River in a way that went to the "very essence of the problem," *Western Mutual,* 137 N.W.2d at 924, presented in the professional negligence action—in other words, in a way that was not only substantial but also material. In response, Mr. Wildrick argues that a "refusal to divulge all known facts is not sufficient, in and of itself, to establish a failure to cooperat[e]," as a matter of law.

Mr. Wildrick cites as authority for his argument a case that did not involve a cooperation clause of the scope present in Mr. Wildrick's case. *See Glade v. General Mutual Insurance Association,* 246 N.W. 794, 795-96 (Iowa 1933), overruled in part on different issue, *Western Mutual,* 137 N.W.2d at 925-26. That case, moreover, turned not on whether the insured failed to cooperate, as a matter of law, but on the questions of waiver by, and prejudice to, the insurance company. *See id.,* 246 N.W. at 796-98. In that case, furthermore, the court concluded that the insured had admitted to the insurance company that he was at fault in the vehicle accident in question and had not "declined to state the facts" to the insurance company; it was only at the trial for damages from the vehicle accident that the insured "declined to divulge the details of the accident." *Id.* at 796. Indeed, the court stated, the insured in that case "paid the judgment rendered against him" in the trial for damages and "acted in perfect good faith and under the belief that [the plaintiff in the trial for damages] had a valid cause of action against him for damages." *Id.* The facts in Mr. Wildrick's case are in no way comparable, or analogous, to those in *Glade*.

Nor do we find the three other cases cited by Mr. Wildrick to be of any avail to him. In *American Guarantee,* 467 N.W.2d at 230, the insurance company failed to use "reasonable diligence" to gather the facts from its insured—the insurance company only wrote letters to its insured and did not personally contact him, take a statement or deposition from him, or attempt to make him testify. In Mr. Wildrick's case, however, it is clear from Robert Phillips's own deposition and subsequent trial testimony in a related action that the lawyer hired by North River to defend Phillips met numerous times with Mr. Phillips and that Mr. Phillips's criminal lawyer asserted shortly before the state trial on the professional negligence claim that Mr. Phillips would invoke his fifth amendment privilege against self-incrimination if called to testify at that trial. In Mr. Wildrick's case, we see no issue present of North River's failure to use reasonable diligence to obtain Mr. Phillips's cooperation.

In *Farm and City Insurance Co. v. Hassel,* 197 N.W.2d 360, 363 (Iowa 1972) (*en banc*), overruled in part on different issue, *Ideal Mutual Insurance Co. v. Winker,* 319 N.W.2d 289, 296 (Iowa 1982), the court specifically referred to other cases in which the circumstances established, as a matter of law, a failure to cooperate. In one of those cases, the insured "advanced four separate versions" of the events in question (and thus "misled" the insurance company) and refused to explain to the insurance company why he decided to plead guilty to charges associated with a vehicle accident. *Id.* In another of those cases, the insured "made false statements" as to whether he was drinking before the vehicle accident and as to "other facts pertinent to the inquiry" (and thus "obviously misled" the insurance company). *Id.* The cases described by that court as establishing, as a matter of law, a failure to cooperate involved facts that are much closer to the facts in Mr. Wildrick's case than to the facts involved in *Farm and City* itself (an insured who admitted all along that he had been drinking but denied that he had been intoxicated, and who pleaded guilty to a misdemeanor in order to avoid felony charges, *id.* at 361-62; the court held that the insured's conduct was not a failure to cooperate, *id.* at 362-63).

In *Western Mutual,* 137 N.W.2d at 924, the insured "lied repeatedly to escape responsibility for his own acts," which amounted to "a clear, intentional and serious breach" of the duty to cooperate with the insurance company (insured first lied to insurance company about starting fire, then admitted to injured party that he started fire but did not tell insurance company until three and a half months later—after settlement negotiations—that he had confessed to injured party and had reached agreement with injured party to restrict his own exposure to damages, *id.* at 920-25). The court in that case specifically held that "[s]ecrecy for that long is not in accord with good faith." *Id.* at 926. In Mr. Wildrick's case, Robert Phillips lied to the lawyer hired by North River for over two years. . . .

The district court was thus quite correct in holding, as a matter of law, that Robert Phillips failed to cooperate with the insurance company. Unless North River waived the use of any failure to cooperate as a defense to payment under the professional liability insurance policy, that failure gives rise to a rebuttable presumption of prejudice suffered by North River. We turn, then, to the question of waiver.

III

Mr. Wildrick argues that North River waived the use of any failure to cooperate as a defense to payment under the professional liability insurance policy by acknowledging, early on, that Phillips was likely to be found liable for professional negligence. Mr. Wildrick also argues that because North River knew or should have known, at least six months before the state trial in the professional negligence action, of serious and questionable gaps and irregularities in Phillips's records, yet waited to withdraw its defense of Phillips until four days before that trial, North River waived its right to use any failure to cooperate as a defense to payment under the professional liability insurance policy. Those arguments actually address the question of prejudice more than waiver; we nonetheless consider the issue of waiver by itself at this point.

North River offered an affidavit, a deposition, and subsequent trial testimony in a related action by the lawyer whom it hired to defend Phillips in the professional negligence action. North River also offered letters from itself to Robert Phillips. All of that evidence shows that immediately after North River learned of the professional negligence action in late 1988, North River asserted its intention to reserve its rights to limit the defense provided to only those claims covered by the policy. North River reaffirmed that reservation of rights three months later and, again, four and a half months before the state trial.

It is true that the letters directed Robert Phillips's attention particularly to various specific exclusions from coverage—claims arising from "dishonest, fraudulent, [or] criminal" acts, claims arising from "personal profit or advantage" to which the insured "was not legally entitled," and claims arising from accounting services provided to any company in which the insured was a manager or shareholder. The letters also specifically stated, however, that North River's agreement to provide a defense "should not be construed by [Mr. Phillips] as a waiver of any of" its rights under the policy. One of those rights was the right to insist that Phillips comply with other conditions of the policy, including the cooperation clause. Under these circumstances, we see no waiver by North River of the use of Mr. Phillips's failure to cooperate as a defense to payment under the professional liability insurance policy.

IV

The real focus of Mr. Wildrick's arguments is that, as a matter of law, North River was not prejudiced by Robert Phillips's failure to cooperate. As noted above,

Mr. Wildrick offers two primary bases for that conclusion on his part. First, Mr. Wildrick cites the acknowledgment of the lawyer hired by North River, early in the professional negligence action, that Phillips was likely to be found liable. Second, Mr. Wildrick points to the fact that, until the week before the state trial, North River was apparently ready to go to trial, despite its knowledge of, or the obviousness of, serious and questionable gaps and irregularities in Phillips's records. In the alternative, Mr. Wildrick contends that, at the very least, a genuine issue of material fact exists with respect to whether North River was prejudiced.

Specifically, Mr. Wildrick notes that the conversion count was not dropped until shortly before trial and, therefore, that North River had the opportunity to, and in fact did, examine Phillips's records with respect to Mr. Wildrick's company. As of August, 1990, that examination showed at least $80,000 entirely unaccounted for. As of that same time, Mr. Wildrick also notes, the lawyer hired by North River to defend Phillips concluded that damages of $200,000 to $250,000 were likely to be awarded. In spite of those facts, Mr. Wildrick argues, North River made no settlement offer until just before trial, when North River evidently offered only a negligible amount. Essentially, Mr. Wildrick contends, North River suffered no prejudice from Robert Phillips's denial of the conversion charges, because North River already knew, and evidently accepted, that it was likely to be found liable for substantial damages in the professional negligence action.

In response, North River alleges a "waste of time, effort and expense" occasioned by Robert Phillips's two-year denial of wrongdoing. Specifically, North River notes that it hired an accountant to search Phillips's records for legitimate payments to Mr. Phillips, or to entities that he controlled, from Mr. Wildrick's company—legitimate payments that in fact did not exist. North River also suggests that it might have attempted settlement much earlier if it had known the truth about Mr. Phillips's conduct. We observe, in addition, that North River would have saved on fees paid to the lawyer hired to defend Phillips if the truth about Mr. Phillips's conduct had been revealed earlier.

This is not a case where the insurance company "was fully advised as to all of the facts . . . and was [therefore] at all times in a position to negotiate [a] settlement[]." *Farm and City Insurance Co. v. Hassel*, 197 N.W.2d 360, 363 (Iowa 1972) (*en banc*) overruled in part on different issue, *Ideal Mutual Insurance Co. v. Winker*, 319 N.W.2d 289, 296 (Iowa 1982). Rather, in this case, North River "acted upon the misrepresentation [and] concealment of its insured," *id.*, and incurred "extra and unnecessary expense," *Western Mutual*, 137 N.W.2d at 925, in doing so. We need not know, or be able to determine, the exact amount of that expense in order to hold that Mr. Wildrick has failed to establish a genuine issue of material fact on the question of prejudice to North River. *Id.* at 926-27. Because that expense was clearly "more than minimal or inconsequential," North River was prejudiced, as a matter of law. *Id.* at 927. . . .

NOTES AND QUESTIONS

1. This case raises fascinating issues about the relationship between the duty to cooperate and the duty to defend. Recall that the complaint allegation rule ordinarily requires an insurance company to defend the insured until

the claim is confined outside of coverage. Surely Phillips was entitled to a defense under that rule. In *Continental Insurance Co. v. Bayless & Roberts, Inc.*, 608 P.2d 281 (Alaska 1980), the Alaska Supreme Court held that the complaint allegation rule applies to a noncooperation defense and, moreover, that noncooperation raises such profound conflicts of interest that the policyholder can demand an independent counsel paid for by the insurance company. Did North River breach the duty to defend in this case by abandoning the defense four days before trial after it learned of the—at the time only alleged—noncooperation?

2. Now consider the actions of Phillips's defense lawyer. Did that lawyer fulfill his professional responsibilities? One wonders whether the "related action" referred to in the opinion was a malpractice action. While we clearly do not have all the relevant facts, the case highlights the perilous position of an insurance defense counsel when an insurance company abandons the defense. As this case illustrates, the lawyer's professional responsibilities are not necessarily coextensive with the insurance company's obligations to defend the insured. Can you craft an argument that would make the insurance company's defense obligations coextensive with the defense lawyer's professional responsibilities? Should they be? Why or why not?

3. Examine carefully the evidence that the court gives in support of the conclusion that Phillips failed to cooperate "as a matter of law." One element is the statement by Phillips's criminal defense lawyer that Phillips would invoke his Fifth Amendment privilege against self-incrimination if called to testify in the upcoming civil trial. Should insurance law require a policyholder to abandon that privilege as a condition of receiving a defense? A second element is the fact that Phillips lied to his lawyer about the fraud. Based on the experience of one of the authors of this casebook as a prosecutor, as well as conversations with other prosecutors, we believe that people who commit fraud almost always lie to their lawyers. *Cf.* Tom Cruise's statement in *Minority Report*: "They always run. You know, they always run." Indeed, the lies that defendants tell their lawyers in these situations rarely are half as fabulous as the lies that they tell their families and themselves. If lying to the insurance defense lawyer in a civil fraud case is a breach of the duty to cooperate, how valuable are errors and omissions insurance, directors' and officers' (D&O) insurance, and other kinds of insurance that supposedly provide protection against fraud claims? Is this another example of a fundamental flaw in the tort liability insurance civil justice system? Is this yet another situation in which the greater the moral responsibility of the defendant, the less likely the victim will receive compensation?

4. *Coburn v. Fox*, 389 N.W.2d 424 (Mich. 1986), addressed the duty to cooperate in the context of mandatory automobile insurance. The defendant (Fox) failed to appear for deposition or trial, despite vigorous efforts on the part of his liability insurance company (certified letters, phone calls, and even visits to his house). The insurance carrier refused to pay the resulting judgment based on the insured's failure to cooperate. In an action to recover the proceeds of the policy, the trial court granted summary judgment for the carrier. The court found that the carrier had made diligent efforts to obtain the cooperation of the insured and that the noncooperation prejudiced the carrier because there was some evidence that the plaintiff (Coburn) was negligent. The Michigan

Court of Appeals reversed, arguing that "[w]here insurance coverage is mandatory, the risk of non-recovery should be placed on the insurance company and not on the victim." *Coburn v. Fox*, 350 N.W.2d 852 (Mich. Ct. App. 1984). The court of appeals explained that this "decision does not invalidate non-cooperation clauses," because the insurer was not liable to the insured under the contract, and the insurer may sue the insured for breach of contract. The Michigan Supreme Court affirmed, explaining:

> The decision by the Legislature to make residual liability coverage compulsory under the no-fault act is critical. Before 1973, motorists purchased insurance to protect themselves. Under the no-fault act, the Legislature requires PIP [personal injury protection] and liability insurance to protect the members of the public at large from the ravages of automobile accidents. While a noncooperation clause may be valid where the insurance was optional, the general rule where an injured third person seeks recovery under a compulsory liability policy is that the failure of the insured to cooperate with the insurer is not a valid defense:
>
>> "In cases involving required insurance, the insurer may not assert noncooperation as a defense to an action or garnishment proceedings brought by an injured member of the public within the class sought to be protected by the applicable financial responsibility statute."
>> Long, Liability Insurance, §14.19, pp. 14-52.
>>
>> "[M]ost of the cases . . . recognize that failure to give notice of an accident, or other lack of cooperation on the part of the insured, does not constitute a defense to an action by an injured member of the public to recover from the insurer, where the policy or bond was procured in compliance with a general compulsory liability or financial responsibility insurance statute, such statutes being for the benefit of members of the public, and not of the insured." Anno: Failure to give notice, or other lack of cooperation by insured, as defense to action against compulsory liability insurer by injured member of the public, 31 A.L.R.2d 645, 647.

What do you think of this argument? Should the principle be applied more broadly to types of liability insurance other than liability insurance, which is required by law? How does this approach to noncooperation by the insured fit with our theories of the function(s) of the tort system?

RESTATEMENT OF THE LAW LIABILITY INSURANCE

American Law Institute (Tent. Draft No. 1, Approved May 2016)

§29. The Insured's Duty to Cooperate

When an insured seeks liability insurance coverage from an insurer, the insured has a duty to cooperate with the insurer. The duty to cooperate includes the obligation to provide reasonable assistance to the insurer:

(1) In the investigation and settlement of the legal action for which the insured seeks coverage;

(2) If the insurer is providing a defense, in the insurer's defense of the action; and

(3) If the insurer has the right to associate in the defense of the action, in the insurer's exercise of the right to associate.

Comment:

a. Purpose of the duty to cooperate. Like much of the law governing the management of potentially insured legal actions, the duty to cooperate serves to align the incentives of insurer and insured. The duty to cooperate primarily addresses the incentives of the insured. In a full-coverage liability action, in which a liability insurance policy shifts all or most of the important legal risks of a legal action to the insurer, the insured may lack adequate incentives to assist the insurer in managing the defense. In some cases, the insured may even have an incentive to collude with the claimant, for example because of a prior relationship with the claimant or simply to avoid the aggravation and inconvenience of a fully adversarial suit. The duty to cooperate addresses this problem by encouraging insured defendants to give an insured legal action the same attention that they would give to an uninsured legal action that puts their own assets at risk. In addition, the duty to cooperate obligates the insured to provide information that the insurer needs to investigate whether the legal action is covered, subject to the rule protecting confidential information stated in §11(2). . . .

§30. Consequences of the Breach of the Duty to Cooperate

(1) An insured's breach of the duty to cooperate relieves an insurer of its obligations under an insurance policy only if the insurer demonstrates that the failure caused or will cause prejudice to the insurer.

(2) If an insured's collusion with a claimant is discovered before prejudice has occurred, the prejudice requirement is satisfied as long as the collusion would have caused prejudice to the insurer had it not been discovered.

Comment:

a. Relationship to existing law. Existing duty-to-cooperate law follows two main approaches. A minority of jurisdictions follow a strict-condition rule, in which any material breach of the duty to cooperate relieves the insurer of its obligations, whether or not that breach causes prejudice to the insurer in regard to the legal action, as long as the duty to cooperate is stated in the insurance policy as a condition. Consistent with the approach taken in this Section, the majority of jurisdictions impose a prejudice requirement, regardless of the language of the insurance policy, such that a breach of the duty to cooperate relieves the insurer of its obligations only if that breach prejudices the insurer in regard to the legal action. Commentators agree that the prejudice standard in the duty-to-cooperate context is difficult for insurers to satisfy. One reason is the traditional concern of liability insurance law not to interfere with the objectives of the underlying liability regime, which may depend on the presence of liability insurance. In that regard, some courts do not enforce the duty to cooperate in automobile liability insurance cases in a way that would compromise the statutory mandatory-minimum coverage, because of the state's public policy in favor of compensation embodied in the state's automobile financial-responsibility statute. . . .

   d. Objections to a strong-condition approach. There are a number of problems with a strong-condition approach, regardless of whether it employs the strict-condition rule or an undemanding-prejudice standard. First, these rules expose insureds to a substantial risk of disproportionate forfeiture of insurance coverage, because the value of the coverage to the insured very often substantially exceeds the harm to the insurer from the breach of the duty to cooperate. Second, these rules interfere more than is necessary with the objectives of the underlying liability regime, which depend in many instances on the presence of liability insurance. Third, by holding out the possibility that the insurer can avoid coverage altogether in more cases, these rules may discourage insurers from moving quickly to resolve claims. Finally, the strict-condition approach may create an incentive for insurers to increase the demands on insureds to cooperate, beyond what is truly necessary, in order to increase the possibility that the insured will fail to cooperate. The purpose of the duty to cooperate is to align the incentives of insurer and insured defendants, so that defendants give insured legal actions the kind of attention that they would give to an uninsured legal action that risked their own assets. The rule stated in this Section achieves that purpose without creating the risk of disproportionate forfeiture, interfering as fully with the underlying liability regime, slowing down the resolution of insured liability actions, or creating perverse incentives.

   It is worth noting that the objections to the strong-condition approach do not apply with as much force when the insured breaches the duty to cooperate by colluding with the plaintiff. Collusion with a plaintiff significantly interferes with the underlying liability regime, which presumes an adversarial relationship between plaintiff and defendant. Moreover, allowing plaintiffs to attempt to collude with the defendant in order to recover significantly larger amounts from the insurance company would create perverse incentives for both plaintiffs and defendants. Because the object of such collusion is to collect additional money from the insurer, an insurer that proves collusion will almost certainly satisfy the prejudice requirement. If the collusion is discovered before substantial harm has already occurred, the prejudice requirement is satisfied as long as the collusion would have prejudiced the insurer if the collusion had not been discovered. . . .

   e. The disproportionate-forfeiture principle. The rule stated in this Section is an application of the disproportionate-forfeiture principle in liability insurance law. Under this principle, a small and minimally blameworthy breach of a condition by an insured does not excuse the insurer from performance, because the harm to the insurer from the breach is so much less than the value of the coverage to the insured. There are both efficiency and fairness rationales for the disproportionate-forfeiture principle. The principle is efficient in the sense that it applies contract terms in a manner that most insureds would bargain for, if they had the information and bargaining power, because the principle protects insureds from the precise kinds of risks for which they purchase liability insurance: their own negligence. The principle is fair because it is consistent with widely accepted proportionality norms, as well as the public policy in favor of compensation of the underlying claimants. . . .

   f. Ordinary procedure for contesting coverage. When a breach of the duty to cooperate provides a defense to coverage, the ordinary procedural rules for contesting coverage apply. The insurer must reserve its rights under §15 and, if it wishes to withdraw from the defense of the action, it must seek adjudication that it does not have a duty to defend. See §18.

B.   Settlements and the Duty to Cooperate

In a "full coverage" case in which the insurance limits are adequate for the claim at hand and the insurance company is defending the case without a reservation of rights, the insurance company arguably needs the duty to cooperate to make sure that the insured doesn't abandon the case. When there is not enough coverage, or when the insurance company has reserved its rights, the insured may worry that the insurance company will use the duty to cooperate as a weapon (for example, by not allowing the insured to settle the case). That fear can lead the insured to take matters into his or her own hands, as happened in the following case.

MILLER v. SHUGART

Supreme Court of Minnesota
316 N.W.2d 729 (1982)

SIMONETT, Justice. . . .

   Plaintiff Lynette Miller was injured in an automobile accident on June 19, 1976, when a car owned by defendant Barbara Locoshonas and driven by defendant Mark Shugart, in which Lynette was a passenger, struck a tree. Locoshonas had an auto liability policy with Milbank Mutual Insurance Company. Milbank, however, contended Shugart, the driver of the car, was not an agent of the owner and thus not covered under the policy. To determine this coverage question, Milbank, shortly after the accident, commenced a declaratory judgment action. Milbank provided separate counsel at its expense to represent the insured and the driver.

   On January 8, 1979, judgment was entered in the declaratory judgment action adjudging that Milbank's policy afforded coverage to both Locoshonas and Shugart. On January 31, 1979, plaintiff Lynette Miller commenced her personal injury action against Locoshonas and Shugart. In April 1979 Milbank appealed the declaratory judgment decision to this court, and in April 1980 we summarily affirmed.

   Twice while the appeal was pending, counsel for Locoshonas and Shugart advised Milbank they were negotiating a settlement with plaintiff's attorney and invited Milbank to participate in the negotiations. Milbank refused, pointing out it could not do so while the coverage question was unresolved.

   In September 1979, plaintiff and the two defendants signed a stipulation for settlement of plaintiff's claims in which defendants confessed judgment in the amount of $100,000, which was twice the limit of Milbank's policy. The stipulated judgment further provided that it could be collected only from proceeds of any applicable insurance with no personal liability to defendants. Milbank was advised of the stipulation. Judgment on the stipulation was entered on November 15, 1979.

In May 1980, following this court's summary affirmance on the coverage issue, plaintiff Miller served a garnishment summons on Milbank. Milbank interposed an answer to the supplemental complaint setting out the history of the litigation and alleging that the confession of judgment was in violation of its policy and that Milbank was thus not bound by the judgment. Plaintiff then moved for summary judgment in her favor for $50,000, the policy limits, plus interest and costs. Milbank countered with its own motion for summary judgment, claiming defendants had breached the cooperation clause of the policy . . . and that the confessed judgment was invalid. The trial court granted plaintiff's motion, adjudging plaintiff was entitled to recover the $50,000 limits plus interest on $100,000. . . .

The main question is whether the judgment stipulated to by the plaintiff and the defendant insureds is the kind of liability the insurer has agreed under its policy to pay. This involves an inquiry into whether the judgment is the product of fraud or collusion perpetrated on the insurer and whether the judgment reflects a reasonable and prudent settlement.

A

We first must deal with a threshold issue. Milbank argues the indemnity agreement of its policy has been voided because the insureds breached their duty under the policy to cooperate.[8] We disagree.

Under the auto liability policy, Milbank has a duty to defend and indemnify its insureds, and the insureds have a reciprocal duty to cooperate with their insurer in the management of the claim. Plaintiff contends that defendants were relieved from their duty to cooperate because Milbank breached its duty to defend. We would put the issue differently. Milbank has never abandoned its insureds nor, by seeking a determination of its coverage, has it repudiated its policy obligations. Milbank had a right to determine if its policy afforded coverage for the accident claim, and here Milbank did exactly as we suggested in *Prahm v. Rupp Construction Co.*, 277 N.W.2d 389, 391 (1979), where we said a conflict of interest might be avoided by bringing a declaratory judgment action on the coverage issue prior to trial. This is the route Milbank followed, appropriately providing another set of attorneys to defend the insureds in the declaratory judgment action.

On the other hand, while Milbank did not abandon its insureds neither did it accept responsibility for the insureds' liability exposure. What we have, then, is a question of how should the respective rights and duties of the parties to an insurance contract be enforced during the time period that application of the insurance contract itself is being questioned. Viewed in this context, Milbank's position, really, is that it has a superior right to have

---

8. The insurance policy provides in pertinent part:

The insured shall cooperate with the company and, upon the company's request, assist in making settlements. . . . The insured shall not, except at his own cost, voluntarily make any payment, assume any obligation or incur any expense other than for first aid for others at the time of the accident.

the coverage question resolved before the plaintiff's personal injury action is disposed of either by trial or settlement. It is unlikely plaintiff could have forced defendants to trial before the coverage issue was decided. Put this way, the question becomes: Did the insureds breach their duty to cooperate by not waiting to settle until after the policy coverage had been decided? In our view, the insureds did not have to wait and, therefore, did not breach their duty to cooperate.

While the defendant insureds have a duty to cooperate with the insurer, they also have a right to protect themselves against plaintiff's claim. The attorneys hired by Milbank to represent them owe their allegiance to their clients, the insureds, to best represent their interests. If, as here, the insureds are offered a settlement that effectively relieves them of any personal liability, at a time when their insurance coverage is in doubt, surely it cannot be said that it is not in their best interest to accept the offer. Nor, do we think, can the insurer who is disputing coverage compel the insureds to forego a settlement which is in their best interests.

On the facts of this case we hold, therefore, that the insureds did not breach their duty to cooperate with the insurer, which was then contesting coverage, by settling directly with the plaintiff.

B

The next issue is whether Milbank may avoid the stipulated judgment on the grounds of fraud or collusion. We hold as a matter of law that the judgment was not obtained by fraud or collusion.

We start with the general proposition that a money judgment confessed to by an insured is not binding on the insurer if obtained through fraud or collusion. *Coblentz v. American Security Co. of New York*, 416 F.2d 1059 (5th Cir. 1969). In this case, however, Milbank has not made any showing of fraud or collusion. . . .

As we understand Milbank's argument, it is that the fraud and collusion consist of the defendant insureds settling the claims over Milbank's objections and contrary to the insurer's best interests, and in confessing judgment for a sum twice the amount of the policy limits. This conduct, however, need be neither fraudulent nor collusive. As we have just held, the defendant insureds had a right to make a settlement relieving them of liability. They also advised Milbank of what they were doing. Moreover, they waited to settle until after the district court had found coverage to exist. We see nothing improper in defendants' conduct. Nor is there anything wrong with the insureds' confessing judgment in an amount double the policy limits, since plaintiff, in her motion for summary judgment, has recognized Milbank's coverage is only $50,000 and seeks to recover no more than that sum from Milbank.[9] The interest question will be addressed separately.

This is not to say that Milbank's position is enviable. As the trial court observed, it had "serious doubts about the propriety of the procedure whereby the insurer

---

9. If plaintiff had sought to recover more than the policy limits from Milbank, an issue of fraud or collusion might present itself. Nor, on the other hand, have the defendant insureds any claim for a bad-faith excess claim against Milbank, since the insureds are not personally harmed by Milbank's failure to pay the amount of the judgment in excess of the policy limits.

is placed in a 'no-win' situation as was done here." If the insurer ignores the "invitation" to participate in the settlement negotiations, it may run the risk of being required to pay, even within its policy limits, an inflated judgment. On the other hand, if the insurer decides to participate in the settlement discussions, ordinarily it can hardly do so meaningfully without abandoning its policy defense. Nevertheless, it seems to us, if a risk is to be borne, it is better to have the insurer who makes the decision to contest coverage bear the risk. Of course, the insurer escapes the risk if it should be successful on the coverage issue, and, in that event, it is plaintiff who loses.

We hold, as a matter of law, on the showing made on plaintiff's motion for summary judgment, that the stipulated judgment against the defendant insureds was not obtained by fraud or collusion.

C

Although having found that the stipulated judgment is untainted by fraud or collusion, our inquiry is not at an end. It seems to us there must also be a showing that the settlement on which the stipulated judgment is based was reasonable and prudent.

The settlement stipulation recites that defendants confess judgment in favor of plaintiff in the amount of $100,000 "upon the condition that plaintiff agree that her judgment may be satisfied only from liability insurance policies in force at the time . . . and that this judgment is not satisfiable nor may it be a lien upon any other assets of defendants. . . ." Defendants agreed judgment could be entered *ex parte* adjudging the driver Shugart negligent although the parties further agreed, somewhat inconsistently, that the stipulation "does not constitute an admission by either defendant of his or her negligence," and it was also agreed the stipulation and judgment could not be used as an admission by the defendants in any other lawsuit.

Plainly, the "judgment" does not purport to be an adjudication on the merits; it only reflects the settlement agreement. It is also evident that, in arriving at the settlement terms, the defendants would have been quite willing to agree to anything as long as plaintiff promised them full immunity. The effect of the settlement was to substitute the claimant for the insureds in a claim against the insurer. Thus on this appeal we see only the plaintiff claimant and the defendants' insurer in dispute, with the insureds taking a passive, disinterested role. Moreover, it is a misnomer for the parties to call plaintiff's judgment a "confessed" judgment. If this were truly a confessed judgment or even a default judgment, it is doubtful that it could stand. It seems more accurate to refer to the judgment as a judgment on a stipulation.

In these circumstances, while the judgment is binding and valid as between the stipulating parties, it is not conclusive on the insurer. The burden of proof is on the claimant, the plaintiff judgment creditor, to show that the settlement is reasonable and prudent. The test as to whether the settlement is reasonable and prudent is what a reasonably prudent person in the position of the defendant would have settled for on the merits of plaintiff's claim. This involves a consideration of the facts bearing on the liability and damage aspects of plaintiff's claim, as well as the risks of going to trial. This can be compared with the somewhat analogous situation in which a joint tortfeasor seeking contribution from a co-tortfeasor must prove the settlement made was reasonable. *See, e.g.,* *Samuelson v. Chicago, Rock Island & Pacific R. Co.,* 178 N.W.2d 620 (Minn. 1970).

It may be instructive to point out how this case differs from *Butler Brothers v. American Fidelity Co.,* 139 N.W. 355 (Minn. 1913). In *Butler* we held that a stipulated judgment, while not conclusive on the insurer, was presumptively so, and that the burden was on the insurer to show the settlement was unreasonable. In *Butler,* however, the insured entered into a settlement with the plaintiff in the course of a "real trial" while defending itself after being abandoned by its insurer. Thus the *Butler* settlement had quite different bona fides than the settlement made here. Here we think it appropriate, and so hold, that the burden of proving reasonableness is on the plaintiff claimant.

This leaves us with the question of what to do in this case. The trial court granted plaintiff summary judgment against Milbank for its policy limits of $50,000. The question is whether the record shows, as a matter of law, that the stipulated judgment, to the extent of $50,000, was reasonable and prudent. Not much proof was submitted to the trial court on this issue at the hearing on the motions for summary judgment. Nonetheless, it does appear, without dispute, that this was a one-car accident, with the plaintiff as passenger, in which the car left the road and hit a tree. As to damages, the settlement stipulation recites, and it is undisputed by Milbank, that plaintiff suffered "severe and disfiguring personal injuries," that no-fault benefits in excess of $20,000 were paid and that the no-fault benefits were likely to total $35,000 or more. The trial court states in its memo that Mr. Forsythe, retained by Milbank to represent the insureds, had reviewed the liability and damage aspects of the claim and had concluded "there was a substantial likelihood that ultimately judgment would be entered against his clients . . . for more than any possible insurance coverage. . . ." On this showing, not disputed, we conclude the trial court did not err in granting summary judgment in favor of plaintiff and against Milbank to the extent of $50,000. . . .

NOTES AND QUESTIONS

1. The Arizona Supreme Court in *Arizona Property & Casualty Insurance Guaranty Fund v. Helme,* 735 P.2d 451 (Ariz. 1987), also faced a similar question regarding a breach of the duty to cooperate. The court agreed with the result in *Miller v. Shugart,* on the grounds that the carrier had committed an anticipatory breach of the insurance contract. The relevant portion of the opinion appears below:

> A cooperation clause such as Imperial's is used to protect the insurer's right to a fair adjudication of the insured's liability and to prevent collusion between the insured and the injured person. Ordinarily, an insured's breach of the cooperation clause relieves a prejudiced insurer of liability under the policy. Insurance policies, however, are governed by the basic contract law principle that if one party to a contract breaches the agreement, the other party is no longer obligated to perform his or her contractual obligations. Throughout this litigation, survivors have claimed that the doctors were justified in settling the claims against them because the Fund had breached the material obligations of the insurance contract first. Survivors suggest that the

Fund "abandoned" its insureds by breaching both its express duties to defend and indemnify, and its implied duty of good faith. Because we find as a matter of law that the Fund anticipatorily repudiated its duty to indemnify, we need not address the other breaches raised by survivors. . . .

The Fund interpreted the statutes and the Imperial policy as obligating it to pay a maximum of $99,900, no matter what amount of damages were found at trial. The Fund admits that it told its insureds that it would pay only one covered claim. This contraction of coverage was based on the Fund's erroneous interpretation of the policy's "occurrence" definition. We recently stated that a party which repudiates its contract obligations on the basis of an incorrect interpretation of a contract has committed an anticipatory breach. *Snow v. Western Savings & Loan Association,* 730 P.2d 204, 210-11 (Ariz. 1986). The Fund, therefore, anticipatorily breached its contractual and statutory obligations as a matter of law.

As a general matter, insurance carriers owe their insureds three duties, two express and one implied. These are the duties to indemnify, the duty to defend, and the duty to treat settlement proposals with equal consideration. Any breach, actual or anticipatory, of these duties deprives the insured of the security that he has purchased because the breach leaves him exposed to personal judgment and damage which may not be covered or may exceed the policy limits. Accordingly, when such a breach occurs, the insured is generally held to be freed from his obligations under the cooperation clause. *Damron v. Sledge,* 460 P.2d 997 (Ariz. 1969).

Although the insurers in Damron and Paynter breached by refusing to defend, the principle of those cases remains the same: once an insurer breaches any duty to its insured, the insured is no longer fully bound by the cooperation clause. No other rule is sensible. The insured exposed by his insurer "to the sharp thrust of personal liability . . . need not indulge in financial masochism. . . ." *Damron,* 460 P.2d at 999, quoting *Critz v. Farmers Insurance Group,* 41 Cal. Rptr. 401, 408 (Cal. Ct. App. 1964).

Helme, 735 P.2d at 458-459. Notice that the court wrote that "the insured is no longer *fully* bound by the cooperation clause" (emphasis added). That suggests that there is still some duty to cooperate. What might the insured still be obligated to do?

2. Does the rule announced in *Miller v. Shugart* and *Helme* increase or decrease transaction costs in tort litigation? One argument that it decreases transaction costs goes as follows: The rule promotes settlement of the underlying tort case and discourages carriers from raising weak coverage defenses. (How?) This means that carriers will generally raise only stronger coverage defenses. In cases in which there is a reasonably strong coverage defense, the coverage litigation is the "real" litigation, so that a rule that quickly disposes of the tort case and leaves the coverage case to be litigated will more quickly focus judicial resources on the "real" dispute. What counterarguments do you see?

3. If *Miller v. Shugart* settlements are enforceable in a given jurisdiction, should a defense lawyer have an ethical obligation to suggest them? Would that be possible under the "two co-equal clients" approach of Silver et al.?

4. §25 of the RLLI follows the *Miller v. Shugart* rule, specifying the following procedural requirements:

(3) When an insurer has reserved the right to contest coverage for a legal action, the insured may settle the action without the consent of the insurer and without violating the duty to cooperate or other restrictions on the insured's settlement rights contained in the policy, provided the following requirements are met:

(a) The insurer is given the opportunity to participate in the settlement process;

(b) The insurer declines to withdraw its reservation of rights after receiving prior notice of the proposed settlement;

(c) It would be reasonable for a person who bears the sole financial responsibility for the full amount of the potential covered judgment to accept the settlement; and

(d) If the settlement includes payments for damages that are not covered by the liability insurance policy, the portion of the settlement allocated to the insured component of the action is reasonable.

Comment *e* to §25 explains as follows:

> Courts have reached different conclusions about whether an insured may protect its interests by accepting a settlement within the limits of the policy in circumstances in which an insurer that has not accepted coverage refuses to withdraw either its coverage contest or its control over settlement. While perhaps not yet the majority rule, an increasingly large number of states permit the insured to settle without the consent of the insurer under the conditions stated in subsection (3). This rule allows the insured to protect itself against the risk of a large, uncovered verdict while preserving the insurer's right to contest both coverage and the reasonableness of the settlement.
>
> The effect of the rule is to give an insurer that is disputing coverage for a legal action the choice between (a) accepting the coverage obligation and retaining control of the defense and settlement of the legal action or (b) preserving the right to contest coverage and permitting the insured to settle the legal action. The rule encourages insurers to drop a weak ground for contesting coverage in order to maintain control over settlement of the legal action because it is primarily the insurer's money at stake in that action when its grounds for contesting coverage are weak. The rule encourages insurers with strong grounds for contesting coverage to grant control over settlement to the insured. Granting the insured control over settlement in such cases is appropriate: because of the strong grounds for contesting coverage, it is primarily the insured's money at stake.

In the next case, the Supreme Court of Texas disagrees vigorously with the Arizona and Minnesota courts, but not on the basis of the duty to cooperate. As you read the case, consider the following:

- Can *Miller v. Shugart, Helme,* and *State Farm v. Gandy* be reconciled?
- What might distinguish the facts of the Texas case from the Arizona and Minnesota cases?
- Does the Texas court's reasoning leave open the possibility of such fact-based distinctions?
- Is this an example of bad facts making bad law, or are there generic objections to "Miller-Shugart" agreements that the Arizona and Minnesota courts ignored?
- What are the practical consequences of the two competing approaches in day-to-day insurance defense litigation?

STATE FARM FIRE & CASUALTY CO. v. GANDY

Supreme Court of Texas
925 S.W.2d 696 (1996)

[This case concerns rights under a liability insurance policy in connection with a claim of sexual abuse brought by a young woman, Julie Gandy, against her stepfather, Ted Pearce. Pearce had a homeowners' insurance policy issued by State Farm. State Farm agreed to defend the Gandy claim under a reservation of rights that asserted as potential coverage defenses the expected or intended exclusion and the possible lapse of the policy. After a series of missteps in the defense of the case, Pearce's lawyer agreed to a "courthouse steps" settlement offer, under which Pearce would confess judgment and assign to Gandy all his rights under the State Farm policy and Gandy would give up the right to collect the judgment from Pearce himself.

Gandy then brought this action against State Farm as Pearce's assignee on two alternative theories. The first theory was a straightforward *Miller v. Shugart* claim that alleged that the claim was covered and she should be entitled to collect the settlement amount. The second theory provided a basis for recovery even if the claim was not covered. This alternative theory alleged that Pearce was injured because State Farm had failed to properly conduct his defense. Had State Farm properly defended Pearce, the damage award assessed him would have been far less, or so Gandy alleged.

The trial court found that there was no coverage for the claim, holding that sexual abuse was intentional conduct not covered by the policy, thereby rejecting her first theory. The court also found, however, that State Farm had in fact breached its obligation to conduct Pearce's defense properly and ruled for Gandy on her alternative theory. The appellate court readily affirmed the trial court's decision on the first theory and reluctantly affirmed on the second theory, writing an opinion criticizing the Texas Supreme Court decisions that the court believed obligated it to affirm. On further appeal, the Texas Supreme Court affirmed the appellate court's ruling on the first theory and addressed the second theory as follows:]

. . . State Farm argues that Pearce's assignment to Gandy should not be given effect. We agree. . . . In reaching this conclusion, we begin with a brief history of the law of alienability of choses in action. . . .

II

Alienability of choses in action[10] has its roots in equity, not law. At early common law, a chose in action could not be assigned. Dean Ames referred to this rule as being one "of the widest application" and "a principle of universal law." Two principal bases have been suggested for the rule. One is that the rule precluded litigation like that already prohibited by champerty and maintenance. An early proponent of this explanation was the great Lord Coke, who declared "the aversion of the 'sages and founders of our law' to the 'multiplying of contentions and suits.'" The second basis offered for the rule is that the common law regarded

---

10. A "chose in action" is a legal claim such as the breach of contract claim of Pearce against State Farm. The settlement between Pearce and Gandy involved the assignment of Pearce's chose in action to Gandy.

rights as personal. Expounding on this view, Holmes argued that rights at common law (and in most early legal systems) were perceived to be relational and situational—that is, determined by the identity of the particular individuals involved and their transaction or circumstances. A claim or cause of action was part of a right of redress that was personal to the holder by virtue of the injury suffered and thus incapable of transfer. To separate a cause of action from a particular plaintiff's right of redress was to risk unjust prosecution of claims. A right or obligation could not be enforced apart from its context without risking distortion.

As early as the fifteenth century the common-law rule against alienability of choses in action began to give way to the demand of commerce that assigned debts be enforceable. What law courts would not oblige, chancery courts would. For a long period of time, assignments of some debts conveyed equitable rights of enforcement but no legal rights. . . .

The only remnants of the rule against alienability of choses in action to survive passage of the common law to America were those pertaining to some torts. In Texas, the merger of law and equity allowed assigned rights to be enforced as fully as they would have been in chancery court. Only five days after the Congress of the Republic of Texas adopted the common law, it provided by statute for assignment of both negotiable and non-negotiable written instruments. But even contract rights not covered by the statute could be assigned.

In some jurisdictions the rule expanded to include claims *ex delicto* as well as *ex contractu*. An 1895 Texas statute provided that personal injury claims survived to the heirs and legal representatives of the injured party. On the theory that assignability of a chose in action depended on whether it survived the owner's death, personal injury claims thus became assignable in Texas.

Practicalities of the modern world have made free alienation of choses in action the general rule, but they have not entirely dispelled the common law's reservations to alienability, or displaced the role of equity or policy in shaping the rule. Even today, the general rule is that a contractual assignment may be "inoperative on grounds of public policy." Restatement (Second) of Contracts §317(2)(b) (1981). The Restatement notes numerous limitations on alienation of choses in action. *Id.* ch. 15, introductory note. The increase in litigation caused by assignments, noted by Lord Coke, remains a matter of concern. So does the effect of alienability on the parties and circumstances in the original transaction or occurrence. As Holmes succinctly summarized, "the history of early law everywhere shows that the difficulty of transferring a mere right was greatly felt when the situation of fact from which it sprung could not also be transferred. Analysis shows that the difficulty is real." . . .

The common law's concerns about alienability of choses in action, voiced by Lord Coke and Holmes, echo in our own decisions. In widely different contexts we have invalidated assignments of choses in action that tend to increase and distort litigation. We have never upheld assignments in the face of those concerns. With these things in mind, we turn to the assignment in this case, and others like it.

A

First, Pearce's settlement with Gandy did not end the litigation, nor could there have been any reasonable contemplation that it would. Once Gandy attempted to enforce against State Farm a $6 million agreed judgment against Pearce for sexual abuse, the likelihood of a negotiated end to the litigation was virtually nil. Even after the district court held as a matter of law that State Farm's policy did not cover Gandy's claims, and that State Farm was never obliged to defend Pearce, the litigation forged on. Had the coverage issue been resolved early on in Gandy's litigation against Pearce, it is doubtful that Gandy would have proposed settlement with Pearce on the terms she did. An assignment of Pearce's actions against State Farm for mishandling Gandy's non-covered claim would have been of no value to Gandy.

The point of this settlement was not to end the litigation but to prolong it. Had it ended simply with a judgment against Pearce, Gandy would have had little hope of ever recovering anything at all, given Pearce's impecunious circumstances. Obviously, as Gandy's counsel freely testified, the entire purpose of the arrangement was to find a way to recover against State Farm.

Second, Pearce's settlement with Gandy greatly distorted the litigation that followed. In her suit against Pearce, Gandy alleged that he sexually abused her for three and one-half years. From the beginning she claimed to be entitled to recover at least $1 million actual damages, as well as punitive damages. Her sworn statements to the district attorney and her deposition testimony consistently assert a despicable, egregious pattern of sexual abuse by her stepfather over a number of years. Gandy testified that she suffered damages of $50,000 on each occasion. When Gandy's lawyer prepared an agreed judgment, he concluded that it was unrealistic to expect the district court to render judgment for an amount equal to $50,000 per occurrence—well over $15 million in actual damages alone. His opinion as an experienced litigator in the area was that a finding of 325 separate incidents of abuse and actual damages of $12,500 per incident was "a fair evaluation of what the scope and extent of her injuries were." Had Gandy's lawyer remained of that opinion when this action against State Farm was tried, there would have been no apparent injury to Pearce. If Pearce indeed got exactly what was coming to him in the agreed judgment, then he was not damaged by his alleged lack of competent counsel. The difference between the agreed judgment rendered against Pearce and the judgment that should have been rendered against him would be zero.

Instead, however, Gandy's position in this case is—as it must be for her to succeed—that Pearce would never have been found liable for so large an amount of damages had State Farm handled his defense properly. Even if her lawyer had testified that his "fair evaluation" of Gandy's damages was much higher than it would have been had Pearce had competent counsel, Gandy cannot avoid shifting positions. In her suit against Pearce, her incentive, fueled by belief in her cause, was to obtain as large a judgment as possible. In her suit as Pearce's assignee against State Farm, her incentive, driven by the economic realities of obtaining a judgment against a solvent defendant, is to argue that Pearce was not as liable as she earlier asserted. Inevitably, Gandy's settlement with Pearce forced her to take inconsistent positions if she was to have any hope of actually recovering anything.

Gandy was not the only party moved to alter positions. Pearce at first steadfastly denied that he abused Gandy, ever. Then, he pleaded nolo contendere to criminal abuse charges and agreed to a judgment reciting that he had abused Gandy 325 times in two years. He agreed to a judgment against himself for more than $6 million, knowing that it could not be rendered without his agreement. In the present case he returned to his prior position: he never abused Gandy.

And he claims he would have been able to establish his total innocence if only State Farm had provided competent counsel to represent him. In Gandy's suit against him, Pearce opposed her as hard as he could. In Gandy's suit against State Farm, he agreed to cooperate with her.

Parties often take inconsistent positions in lawsuits. Generally the law permits this, but the situation here is different. Here the parties took positions that appeared contrary to their natural interests for no other reason than to obtain a judgment against State Farm. Gandy and Pearce arranged for an agreed judgment to be rendered without notice to State Farm, even though State Farm had contacted Pearce's attorneys repeatedly and had instructed them to send their fee statements for payment. Gandy and Pearce obviously attempted to take advantage of State Farm. The court of appeals did not exaggerate when it called Gandy's agreed judgment against Pearce "a sham", or when it stated that the judgment "perpetrates a fraud" and "an untruth". The agreed judgment was an essential element of the settlement allowing Gandy to prosecute Pearce's claim against State Farm. Without the assignment and covenant not to execute, the agreed judgment would never have been rendered. In these circumstances, we have no hesitation in holding that the assignment was invalid.

B

Settlement arrangements like the one here are not unusual in cases in which plaintiffs' claims are arguably covered by defendants' insurance. They are also used in other contexts. We first discuss the cases involving insurance.

Typically in such cases, a plaintiff, P, asserts a claim against a defendant, D, who requests his insurer, I, to provide a defense and coverage under a policy of insurance. I ordinarily has three options: to accept coverage of P's claim and provide D a defense, to provide a defense but reserve the right to contest coverage, or to deny coverage and refuse a defense. D may accept a defense tendered with a reservation of rights, or he may insist that I first accept coverage. D may become concerned about the prospect of personal liability to P if I denies coverage, or the coverage issue remains unresolved, or I mishandles the defense, or I refuses P's offer to settle the claim within policy limits. The principal justification for a settlement arrangement like the one in this case is that it provides D a means of avoiding personal liability by assigning P his claims against I for coverage, negligent defense, and refusal to settle. In return, P agrees to limit D's personal liability. The arrangement is especially attractive to P when his claim against D is weak, or when his chances of full recovery against D are small.

The principal problem with the arrangement, as the present case illustrates, is that once it is made, D no longer has any incentive to oppose P. If the agreement is struck prior to a trial of P's claims, D may agree to a judgment against himself, as in the present case, or may allow P to take a judgment after a brief evidentiary hearing in which D's participation, if any, is minimal. In a subsequent action by P against I, P's damages are measured by the value of his claim against D. If the issue is coverage, P may be entitled to recover from I what it should have recovered against D. If the issue is refusal to settle, P may be entitled to recover his damages in excess of I's policy limits. If the issue is mishandling of the defense, P, as D's assignee, may be entitled to recover from I the difference between the judgment rendered against D and the judgment that would have been rendered but for *I*'s misconduct. In any case, the value of *P*'s claim against *D* is material in the second action.

If *P* and *D* settle after an adversarial trial, the value of *P*'s claim can be taken to be the amount of the judgment obtained. But if settlement is before such a trial, an evaluation of *P*'s claims becomes very difficult. Appraisal of a chose in action, never an easy task because of the lack of any objective measure or market, is all the harder when *D* ceases to oppose *P*. It is difficult enough to try to determine what *P* would have recovered had he gone to trial against *D;* the determination is even more difficult when *D*'s opposing position must be reconstructed and its merits assessed without *D*'s cooperation.

The effort to make this determination produces a trial like the one in this case, in which the parties' positions are confused and distorted because of the settlement arrangement. Pearce swore that he never molested Gandy in any way, despite the fact that he agreed to a judgment that he sexually abused her 325 times. Gandy's lawyer swore that $4,062,500 was a fair evaluation of Gandy's damages, but Gandy's expert testified that if Pearce had been competently represented Gandy would have recovered less than half that much. While the courts favor settlement of disputes and incline to enforcing parties' agreements toward that end, we do not do so when . . . the result is worse than if the parties had not settled. The settlement arrangement in the present case did not resolve the parties' disputes but prolonged and confused them. Such an arrangement is invalid.

Not every settlement involving an assignment of rights in exchange for a covenant to limit the assignor's liability has the problems we have described. For example, as we have said, if the settlement follows an adversarial trial, the difficulties in evaluating *P*'s claim are no longer present. That value has been fairly determined. We should not invalidate a settlement that is free from this difficulty simply because it is structured like one that is not.

Moreover, the difficulty in evaluating *P*'s claim is not the only consideration. It must be balanced against the advantage to *D* of having a means of avoiding personal liability to *P*. But *D* does not need this advantage when the prospect of personal liability can be determined beforehand. For example, when issues of coverage and the duty to defend arise, it is not unusual for *I* or *D* or both to attempt to adjudicate them before *P*'s claim is adjudicated. Disputes between *I* and *D* can often be expeditiously resolved in an action for declaratory judgment while *P*'s claim is pending. If successful, *D* should be entitled to recover attorney fees. Tex. Civ. Prac. & Rem. Code §37.009; Tex. Ins. Code art. 21.55, §6. *D* may also be entitled to recover a penalty against *I* equal to eighteen percent of the claim. Tex. Ins. Code art. 21.55, §6. We recognize that prosecution of a declaratory judgment action may be burdensome to *D*, but often *I* will assume the burden of having the issues resolved. A plaintiff who thinks a defendant should be covered by insurance may be willing to await or even assist in obtaining an adjudication of the insurer's responsibility.

Balancing the various considerations we have mentioned, we hold that a defendant's assignment of his claims against his insurer to a plaintiff is invalid if (1) it is made prior to an adjudication of plaintiff's claim against defendant in a fully adversarial trial, (2) defendant's insurer has tendered a defense, and (3) either (a) defendant's insurer has accepted coverage, or (b) defendant's insurer has made a good faith effort to adjudicate coverage issues prior to the adjudication of plaintiff's claim. We do not address whether an assignment is also invalid if one or more of these elements is lacking. In no event, however, is a judgment for plaintiff against defendant, rendered without a fully adversarial trial, binding on defendant's insurer or admissible as evidence of damages in an action against defendant's insurer by plaintiff as defendant's assignee. . . .

We believe this balancing of interests minimizes any hardship on an insured defendant. Determining an insurer's obligations before its insured incurs liability benefits both the insurer and the insured by removing that uncertainty. An insurer has ample disincentives to deny coverage or a defense without good reason: it will be liable for its own attorney fees in litigating the dispute and may be liable for the insured's attorney fees, a statutory penalty, and even bad faith damages. The significance of the disincentives to denying coverage and a defense without clear justification is apparent in this case. Although Pearce's sexual abuse of Gandy was clearly intentional conduct excluded from coverage under Pearce's homeowner's policy, State Farm nevertheless volunteered to pay for counsel to defend him and his wife against Gandy's claims. Pearce may have been confused about State Farm's offers to him, but there can be no question about what State Farm intended, given its defense of Gandy's mother. . . .

There may be other circumstances in which an assignment of a chose in action to an opposing litigant in settlement of that litigant's claim does not necessitate more, and more complex, litigation. We are not able to foresee all such situations. When the considerations are those we have described here, however, we believe the assignment must be held invalid.

NOTES AND QUESTIONS

1. What was the nature of the flip-flop that the court found objectionable in *Gandy*? Were there comparable flip-flops in *Miller v. Shugart*? Compare the claims that the defendant assigned to the plaintiff in the two cases: breach of the duty to settle in *Miller v. Shugart* and, in effect, ineffective defense in *Gandy*. Might the differences in those claims be a basis for distinguishing between the two cases? Yet the Texas court, at least in dicta, treats all such settle and assign agreements alike. Why might the Texas court have objected to all such agreements, not simply those that then attack the underlying settlement as a sham?

2. In *Miller v. Shugart*, the conflict of interest that justified the settle and assign agreement grew out of a coverage defense. Would the same reasoning apply to conflicts that result from inadequate insurance limits? Why or why not? How does a settlement that is prompted by a fear of no coverage differ from a settlement that is prompted by a fear of inadequate coverage? How do both differ from a settlement prompted by a negligent defense? The Texas court suggests that all three kinds of settlements "increase and distort litigation" because the defendant and the plaintiff are no longer adverse once they settle. Is this alignment of interests so unusual? Plaintiffs and defendants are, in many ways, not adverse in almost any "full coverage case." Indeed, the common interest between the plaintiff and the defendant is one of the reasons for the duty to cooperate.

3. Notice that the court suggests that the conflicts in a *Gandy* situation can be addressed by litigating coverage first. How does that suggestion fit with the concerns that motivate other courts to stay declaratory judgment actions in

cases in which the facts in the underlying tort action overlap with the facts in the coverage case?

4. Would you expect to see a *Miller v. Shugart* agreement in a case in which the defendant is solvent? What would motivate a plaintiff to accept that kind of a deal with a solvent defendant? Would that give you cause for concern about the reasonableness of the settlement? Why?

V.   THE IMPACT OF LIABILITY INSURANCE ON TORT LAW[11]

Having completed our study of liability insurance, now would be a good time to step back and consider the relationship between liability insurance and tort liability. In his important book, The Liability Century: Insurance and Tort Law from the Progressive Era to 9/11 (2008), Professor Kenneth Abraham describes tort law and liability insurance as a binary star that expanded over the course of the twentieth century. Without tort law or some analogous statutory rights, there would be no demand for liability insurance. Less obviously to some people (but surely not to students who have made it to this point in the semester), without liability insurance, there would be less demand for tort law.

Leaving tort doctrine aside,[12] liability insurance has at least the following seven impacts on tort law:

- For claims against all but the wealthiest individuals and organizations, liability insurance is a de facto element of tort liability.
- Liability insurance limits are a de facto cap on tort damages.
- Tort claims are shaped to match the available liability insurance, with the result that liability insurance policy exclusions become de facto limits on tort liability.
- Liability insurance makes lawsuits against ordinary individuals and small organizations into "repeat player" lawsuits on the defense side, making tort law in action less focused on the fault of individual defendants and more focused on managing aggregate costs.
- Liability insurance personnel transform complex tort rules into simple "rules of thumb," also with the result that tort law in action is less concerned with the fault of individual defendants than tort law on the books.
- Negotiations over the boundaries of liability insurance coverage (which appears nowhere in tort law on the books) drive tort law in action.
- The periodic "insurance crises" caused by the ups and downs of the liability insurance underwriting cycle drive the movement for restrictive tort reform.

11. This section is adapted from Tom Baker, *Liability Insurance as Tort Regulation: Six Ways That Liability Insurance Shapes Tort Law in Action*, 12 Conn. Ins. L.J. 1 (2006), and *Medical Malpractice and the Insurance Underwriting Cycle*, 54 DePaul L. Rev. 393 (2005).

12. Whether liability insurance has had any effect on tort doctrine is a controversial question. *See generally* Liability in Tort and Liability Insurance (Gerhard Wagner ed., 2005). The abrogation of traditional immunities (charitable, intrafamily, and governmental) presents the strongest case for those who argue that liability insurance has affected tort doctrine. Liability insurance may have allowed lawmakers to believe that inserting tort law into the domain of the family, the state, and the church would be less disruptive than might otherwise be supposed. (Try telling that to the Catholic Church today, though.) Liability insurance also may have encouraged some defendants to attempt to abandon their immunity in order to force their liability insurers to compensate their victims.

The paragraphs that follow briefly describe each.

A. In Practice, Liability Insurance Is an Element of Tort Liability

The legal elements of tort liability are well known. The defendant must have a legal duty to avoid harm to the plaintiff. The defendant must have breached the standard of care that applies in the particular situation, and that breach must have caused damage to the plaintiff. For a lawyer considering whether to take a particular case on a contingency basis, however, or for a litigant considering whether to finance a claim on some other basis, these legal elements are only a starting point. Liability by itself is not enough. The defendant must have the ability to pay.

Given the extent of consumer debt, the availability of bankruptcy to discharge civil liabilities, and the existence of limited but important exceptions to the assets that must be liquidated in a bankruptcy proceeding, the practical reality of tort litigation in the United States is that liability insurance is the only asset that plaintiffs can count on collecting. *See* Steven G. Gilles, *The Judgment-Proof Society*, 63 Wash. Lee L. Rev. 603 (2006). There is some evidence that this is also the case in many commercial disputes. Professor Lynn Lopucki has advanced and defended the controversial but plausible thesis that corporate groups increasingly locate risk in entities with no assets and place assets in entities with no risk, with the result that the liability insurance of the risky entity is all that is available for victims if and when the risk matures into harm. *See* Lynn Lopucki, *The Death of Liability*, 106 Yale L.J. 1 (1996). He may well have overstated the case for ordinary tort litigation, but for mass tort claims he is not far from the mark. The increasing use of corporate bankruptcy as a mass tort litigation risk management tool makes liability insurance the asset that matters for mass tort victims as well. *See* Alan N. Resnick, *Bankruptcy as a Vehicle for Resolving Enterprise-Threatening Mass Tort Liabilities*, 148 U. Pa. L. Rev. 2045 (2000).

If liability insurance is a de facto element of tort liability, then people without liability insurance will not be subject to tort liability. In practice, people in the United States are required, either by law or contract, to purchase liability insurance in a wide variety of settings (a fact showing that lawmakers and strong contracting parties understand that liability insurance is a practical predicate for tort liability). But people are not required to purchase liability insurance in all settings. For example, people who rent their homes in the United States are rarely required to purchase liability insurance and rarely do so voluntarily. The only liability insurance that most renters purchase is automobile liability insurance. As a result, most renters are, as a practical matter, immune from civil suit in the United States, except in the case of an automobile accident.

B. Liability Insurance Policy Limits Are De Facto Caps on Tort Damages

Liability insurance policies in the United States are sold with limits on the amount of money that the liability insurer is obligated to pay for a particular claim or event, even if the damages owed by the insured are much larger. For example, the limit on the mandatory automobile liability insurance policy in the state of Connecticut is $20,000 per person, $40,000 per accident, meaning that the maximum amount that the liability insurer must pay any one person is

$20,000 and the maximum amount that the insurer must pay all victims from any one accident is $40,000. Of course, many people voluntarily purchase automobile liability insurance policies with limits that are much higher, but many people do not.

For defendants who would not be sued in the absence of liability insurance, the fact that the insurance policy limit functions as a de facto "cap" on the defendants' tort liability is obvious. What may not be quite so obvious is that the policy limit more often than not functions as a cap even for defendants who have other assets. There is good evidence that payments in excess of the policy limits are extraordinarily rare in cases involving individual defendants and nearly as rare in cases involving commercial defendants.[13]

In our view, this situation results from a combination of factors: the existence of a cause of action for breach of the insurer's duty to settle, the anchoring effect of the policy limit during settlement negotiations, the liability insurer's power to control settlements within the policy limits but not beyond the policy limits, and the related development of settlement norms within the tort litigation bar. But the reasons that liability insurance policy limits function as a cap on tort damages do not matter for present purposes. What matters is the consequence: Even tort litigation against wealthy individuals and large organizations has become, in all but the unusual case, an exercise in recovering money from liability insurance companies, and only from those companies.

C.   Tort Claims Are Shaped to Match the Available Liability Insurance

This next effect of liability insurance on tort law in action is a corollary to the first two. If only people with insurance are sued, and if the suits are targeted at recovering insurance money, then claims that fit into one of the exclusions in the applicable liability insurance policy (and thus would not be covered by the policy) are not worth bringing. Of course, there are exceptions. Some defendants have enough assets that insurance does not matter. And some plaintiffs have the interest and the means to bring a lawsuit even when the defendant is not able to pay the damages. But the existence of these exceptions does not change the effect that the general rule has on the shape of tort law in action: Exclusions in liability insurance policies create, in effect, remote islands of tort liability that lawyers and law professors know about, but almost no one goes to visit. Both legal rules and professional norms require defense lawyers to place the interests of the insured defendant ahead of the interests of the insurance

---

13. *See* Kathryn Zeiler et al., *Physicians' Insurance Limits and Malpractice Payments: Evidence from Texas Closed Claims, 1990-2003*, J. Legal Stud. (forthcoming 2007) (reporting that doctors almost never have to pay their own money in a medical malpractice case); Bernard S. Black, Brian R. Cheffins, & Michael Klausner, *Outside Director Liability*, 58 Stan. L. Rev. 1055 (2006) (reporting that directors and officers of corporations do not as a practical matter face any individual liability in securities fraud actions because claims are virtually always settled within the limits of their D&O insurance policies); Tom Baker, *Blood Money, New Money, and the Moral Economy of Tort Law in Action*, 35 Law & Soc'y Rev. 275 (2001). *See also* Texas Department of Insurance, 2002 Texas Liability Insurance Closed Claim Annual Report 2, *available at http://www.tdi.state.tx.us/reports/pdf/taccar2002 .pdf* (reporting that there was a payment in excess of policy limits in only 31 out of 9,723 liability insurance paid claims in 2002 and that the total amount paid above the limits in those cases was $9 million, as compared to $1.8 billion in total liability payments in Texas in 2002; by comparison settlements by commercial insured within their deductible totaled $41 million in Texas in 2002).

company that pays the defense costs. As a result, defense lawyers in the United States to some extent cooperate with the plaintiffs' lawyers in shaping claims to fit the available coverage.

D.   Liability Insurers Are the Ultimate "Repeat Players"

Tort doctrine treats tort liability as the responsibility of a particular defendant to a particular plaintiff for a particular wrong. Liability insurance shifts the liability of the particular defendant to an entity for which that liability is simply one among an enormous portfolio of contingent financial obligations. Legal norms obligate the insurance company, and to a greater extent the lawyer employed by the insurance company, to handle the liability claim so that the interests of the particular defendant are paramount, and in my experience insurance companies largely attempt to honor that norm (though we have studied contrary cases).

But insurance companies also recognize and act on the fact that they hold a portfolio of claims. This means that the results in one case can affect the results in another. As a result, liability insurers have an interest in the development of tort law rules and settlement norms that goes far beyond the interests of any ordinary defendant. In the terms of Mark Galanter's classic study, liability insurers are the ultimate "repeat players." Mark Galanter, *Why the "Haves" Come Out Ahead: Speculations on the Limits of Legal Change*, 9 Law & Soc'y Rev. 95 (1974). The "repeat player" phenomenon makes tort law in action less focused on the fault of individual defendants and more focused on managing aggregate costs.

Many liability insurance company executives would assert that their "repeat player" advantage is more than outweighed by the bias of judges and juries. Judges and juries know that defendants have insurance, and as a result they are more likely to award the plaintiff damages, or so the argument goes. Interestingly, empirical research on jury behavior suggests that juries are at least as concerned with the health and other first-party insurance held by the plaintiffs, and with making sure that the plaintiffs do not get a double recovery. *See* Shari S. Diamond & Neil Vidmar, *Jury Room Ruminations on Forbidden Topics*, 87 Va. L. Rev. 1857 (2001). But the direction of the bias is less important than the widespread belief that it exists. Since cases are settled in the "shadow of the law" based on the parties' predictions about what will happen in court, a widespread belief that juries act in certain ways has the same effect whether juries in fact act in that way or not.

Liability insurance helps transform tort litigation into a multiplayer iterative game that develops and transmits beliefs and norms that become part of the rules of that game. Those beliefs and norms constitute the real tort law for far more people than does the tort law on the books.

E.   Liability Insurance Transforms Tort Rules into Simple "Rules of Thumb"

Ross's classic study of automobile accident claims handling provides the most extended account of the way that insurance adjusters transform complex tort rules into simpler and more easily administered rules of thumb. *See* H. Laurence

Ross, Settled Out of Court: The Social Process of Insurance Claims Adjustment (1970). In an important sense, this effect of liability insurance on tort law in action is simply an instance of the "repeat player" effect just described. But the practical implications of insurance adjustment are worth special mention. Otherwise, one might be misled into thinking that the "repeat player" status of the liability insurance company primarily affects only the development of tort law on the books.

One of Ross's best examples is the rear-end collision—an automobile accident in which one car hits another car from behind. According to the formal tort law rule, liability depends on a careful and case-specific analysis of the accident and a consideration of whether the drivers exercised the degree of care that a reasonable person would ordinarily exercise in that situation. Ross's adjusters applied a simpler, easier-to-administer rule that probably had the same result as the formal rule in most situations. Their rule was that the driver of the car in back was liable in all cases. Such rules are not universally applied. The greater the stakes, the more likely that the rules of thumb will give way to the particularized assessments that formal tort doctrine requires. But, in the aggregate they combine to make tort law in action less focused on the individual fault of individual defendants than tort law on the books.

Ross generalized from this example as follows:

> Adjustment of insurance claims compromises the legal mandate for individualized treatment with the need of a bureaucratic system for efficient processing of cases. This compromise can be observed at many points in the processes of investigation and evaluation. Investigation is vastly simplified, for instance, by presumptions as to liability based on the physical facts of the accident. Accidents are thus seldom individualized to an insurance adjuster or a claims attorney. Rather, they are rear-enders, red-light cases, stop sign cases, and the like, and the placement of an accident into one of these categories ordinarily satisfies the requirements for investigation of liability. . . .
>
> These observations are not meant as criticism of the good faith of the insurance industry or other parties associated in the handling of claims. Rather they are meant to put claims handling into proper context; to show that here as elsewhere—for example in handling pleas to criminal charges, or in making decisions as to whether a mental condition merits institutional commitment—a large-scale society proceeds by routinizing and simplifying inherently complex and difficult procedures. This is how the work of the world is done. This is the law, as it is experienced by its clients rather than by its philosophers. Perhaps in the light of some kinds of legal philosophy it is bad law. In my opinion, such legal philosophy has lost contact with the reality of modern society.

Id. at 135.

F.   *Negotiations over Insurance Boundaries Drive Tort Law in Action*

This next way that liability insurance shapes tort law is a bit harder to describe. The main idea here is a corollary of impacts one, two, and three taken as a whole. As you may recall, those three are (1) liability insurance is a de facto element of tort law, (2) liability insurance limits are de facto caps on tort damages, and (3) tort claims are shaped to match the available liability insurance coverage. Each of these, of course, overstates the case. There are exceptions.

Each of these impacts calls attention to a different kind of liability insurance boundary: who has liability insurance, for how much, and with regard to what kinds of liabilities. Each of these kinds of boundaries exerts a shaping force on tort law. As a philosophical and doctrinal matter, tort liability certainly could exist outside the boundaries of liability insurance coverage, but we are not going to go through the effort of establishing liability "out there" very often because there is no return in it. This suggests that liability insurance coverage establishes to some extent the boundaries of tort law itself, or at the very least the boundaries of tort law in action.

Alternatively, we might say that uninsured individuals are "outlaws" with regard to tort law and that liability insurance industry practices have the effect of making people "outlaws" with regard to tort liabilities. The kinds of practices that turn people into tort law outlaws include exclusions in liability insurance policies, marketing practices that leave populations uninsured (e.g., "redlining"), and the practice in the United States of bundling liability insurance with some kinds of property insurance but not others.

As this suggests, negotiations over who gets insurance, for how much, and against which kinds of liabilities drive tort law in action. These negotiations occur in legislatures debating what kinds of liability insurance to require and when; in administrative agencies debating how much effort to devote to enforcement of the insurance mandate; within large organizations debating whether to include an insurance clause in a standard form contract, how to word the clause, and whether to allow waivers; among contracting parties negotiating whether to include insurance requirements in their deals; and in the many places in which liability insurers establish and apply rules regarding who gets insurance, for how much, and against which kinds of liabilities. These kinds of negotiations establish the boundaries of liability insurance coverage. They mark the frontier between the domesticated, insurance purchasing tort law citizen and the tort law outlaw, as well as the frontier between the lawed and unlawed activities of that domesticated, insurance purchasing tort law citizen.

A second kind of negotiation over boundaries takes place within the context of tort claims. These are negotiations over whether this particular defendant has insurance, whether the insurance is sufficient to cover the amounts claimed as damages, and whether the particular liabilities at issue are covered by the defendant's insurance policy. Because of the profoundly practical effect of these negotiations — among other things, they determine whether and how much the plaintiffs' lawyers will get paid — it is not surprising that they have spawned a host of secondary legal rules and professional norms, some of which we have studied. These secondary rules and norms define the boundaries of liability insurance coverage, so that a reasonably complete understanding of tort law in action requires not only an appreciation of the formal liability rules and the shape and extent of liability insurance coverage but also the rules and norms that govern the resolution of questions regarding people and liabilities that lie in close proximity to the liability insurance boundaries.

G.   *Insurance Crises Drive the Movement for Restrictive Tort Reform*

This final effect of insurance on tort law takes some work to understand, but the effort is worth it for any law student who wants to develop an informed view about tort reform. Baker studied this phenomenon most closely in the medical malpractice context, so that is the example that we will use here.

As your professor may remember, medical malpractice insurance premiums went up rapidly during the 2002-2004 period, and doctors, hospitals, and insurance companies blamed lawyers, judges, and juries for this situation. The doctors' refrain was "The tort system is out of control." The TV or newspaper image that anchored that refrain in the public mind is a throng of doctors in white coats massed on the steps of the state capital demanding tort reform. It was not crazy for doctors and many other people to think that malpractice lawsuits were the reason for the insurance premium hikes. Few people really understand how insurance companies work, but most people do know this: Over the long run, an insurance company works something like a bank. The amount of money going in has to equal the amount of money going out. So many people think that big increases in the amount of money coming in the front door—the malpractice insurance premiums—must reflect a big increase in the amount of money going out the back door—payments for medical malpractice cases.

Unfortunately, the liability insurance business is not that simple. The liability insurance industry goes through a boom-and-bust cycle—the insurance underwriting cycle—that is especially pronounced in medical liability insurance. In the insurance market, there are alternating periods in which insurance is priced below cost (a "soft" market) and periods in which insurance is priced above cost (a "hard" market). Notably, coverage is plentiful and nonprice terms are favorable to policyholders when the insurance is sold below cost, while coverage is restricted and nonprice terms are unfavorable to policyholders when the insurance is priced above cost. This cycle presents a puzzle to industry insiders and outsiders alike, who all wonder why the "good stuff" is sold cheaply one year, becomes hard to get at almost any price one or two years later, is widely and cheaply available just a few years after that, and then is almost certain to disappear once again at some uncertain point in the future.

"Cost" is the most important word in the previous paragraph, and it is the key to understanding the insurance underwriting cycle. The meaning of insurance cost implied in this definition involves a retrospective perspective that insurers cannot adopt when setting prices. At the time that insurers set their prices, most of the costs of the insurance coverage can be known with certainty only once all the claims under the policies have been paid. As a result, insurers constantly have to imagine the future to decide how to price their insurance policies today. This situation creates a remarkably high degree of uncertainty in insurance pricing, especially as compared to products like potato chips, automobiles, and sneakers, and even as compared to most other services. This uncertainty about insurance costs is the fuel that drives the underwriting cycle. The details are complicated; if you would like to learn more, see Tom Baker, *Medical Malpractice and the Insurance Underwriting Cycle*, 54 DePaul L. Rev. 393 (2005), and Sean M. Fitzpatrick, *Fear Is the Key: A Behavioral Guide to Underwriting Cycles*, 10 Conn. Ins. L.J. 255, 257 (2004).

The bottom line is that the underwriting cycle creates insurance crises, not changes in tort law or claiming behavior. In the long run, liability insurance prices must bear a reasonable relationship to claim costs, or else insurers will not be able to pay claims as they become due. But there is ample room for big, short-term price changes that have nothing to do with claim costs. Litigation behavior and malpractice claim payments did not change in any significant, systemic sense between 1970 and 1975, between 1981 and 1986, or between 1996 and 2001. What changed, instead, were insurance market conditions and the investment and cost projections that the insurance market built into medical malpractice insurance premiums over those periods. Insurers that had offered low prices based on rosy scenarios in 1970, 1981, and 1996 switched to high prices based on pessimistic scenarios in 1975, 1986, and 2001.

Hard markets are a trigger for legislative efforts to limit tort remedies. Nothing concentrates the minds of legislators on the alleged excesses of malpractice liability more than doctors who are angry about skyrocketing insurance premiums, and the immediate driver of those skyrocketing premiums invariably is a turn in the underwriting cycle. It is no coincidence that California's Medical Injury Compensation Reform Act (the original legislation capping noneconomic damages)[14] came during the hard market of the 1970s, the largest round of tort reform came during the hard market of the 1980s, and the recent round of tort reform came during the hard market that began in late 2001. The public attention given to insurance availability during the hard market phases of the medical malpractice underwriting cycle helped shift the development of tort law from courts to legislatures.

This shift has a structural impact on the development of tort law. In legislatures, tort reform advocates are able to frame certain classes of defendants as "victims" of tort law in a way that simply cannot be done in the courtroom. In the courtroom, tort law grows through an encounter between individuals, not factions or interest groups. The aspects of medical malpractice liability that tort reformers find most objectionable—noneconomic damages and to a lesser extent joint and several liability—come into play only once the jury or judge has decided that the defendant is responsible for the plaintiff's harm. At that point, the only "victim" is the plaintiff. The defendant is a perpetrator. The situation in the legislature is very different. Doctors as a class, especially those in high-risk specialties like obstetrics, can easily be framed as the "victims" of sudden, very large increases in insurance premiums.

The underwriting cycle affects not only the timing and location of efforts to limit tort law remedies, but also the content of those efforts. Tort reform efforts have focused most intensely on aspects of tort law that make claims more difficult to value, such as joint and several liability and noneconomic damages, and thus contribute to the uncertainty that is the basic fuel of the underwriting cycle.

We will conclude with a metaphor that may help to illustrate the power that liability insurance has to shape the development of tort law. Imagine a network of streams and rivers carrying water through the countryside to the sea. Water represents claims for relief. Tort law is the network of streams, rivers, and lakes through which the water flows into the sea. Water that makes it into the sea represents the successful requests for tort law relief (whether by settlement,

---

14. Medical Injury Compensation Reform Act of 1975 (MICRA) (codified at Cal. Bus. & Prof. Code §6146 (West 2003), Cal. Civ. Code §3333 (West 1997), Cal. Civ. Proc. Code §§ 340.5, 1295 (West 1982).

which is much more likely, or adjudication). Within this metaphor, insurance is an invisible force that affects how much it rains and where, erects dams in some places, and sends huge torrents of water into others. Insurance is a force that turns some small tort rivulets into streams and some tort streams into wide, straight rivers of tort liability.

Studying a snapshot of the landscape, we would see how the tort law streams and rivers channel the flow of requests for relief, but we would miss the channeling force of liability insurance. Anyone who goes out and lives in the countryside would soon notice the strange pattern of rainfall and the odd placement of dams. Observing the landscape over time, she might even start to wonder what, exactly, is channeling what. Does the network of tort law streams and rivers channel the requests for relief, or do those requests channel the streams and rivers? And what explains why it rains so heavily on that hillside, while this other one is dry?

CHAPTER
6

Insurance Regulation

The previous chapters of this book examined some of the ways that contract and related fields of law regulate insurance arrangements. This chapter addresses issues relating to the regulation of insurance arrangements by administrative agencies. Although most industries are subject to some agency-based government regulation (think of all of the sectors of the economy that are regulated by the various federal agencies, including the Food and Drug Administration, the Environmental Protection Agency, the Securities and Exchange Commission (SEC), and so on), few sectors of the U.S. economy are more heavily regulated than insurance.

What is striking about insurance, however, is that, among the more heavily regulated industries, insurance is the only one in this country that is regulated almost exclusively at the state level. Although proposals have recently been made to allow insurance companies the option of forming under a federal charter, and thereby becoming subject to federal rather than state regulation, no such reform has yet been adopted. Thus, it continues to be the case that, instead of having a single agency that is responsible for regulating the insurance industry, we have 51, including all 50 U.S. states and the District of Columbia, each tasked with interpreting and applying its own jurisdiction's insurance code.

As this chapter will show, the fact that insurance regulation is mostly state regulation affects the types of regulations that are promulgated. To varying degrees, states coordinate their efforts through the National Association of Insurance Commissioners (NAIC). The NAIC is addressed further in the unit on insurance federalism in Section II of this chapter. Insurance regulation is a broad field that cannot be covered in detail in an introductory insurance course. The purpose of these materials is to provide a sense of the issues involved in traditional insurance regulation and an understanding of the unique federal-state framework that governs the insurance field.

I.   OVERVIEW

There are many possible ways to describe insurance regulation. We begin with a brief overview categorizing insurance regulation according to *function*. Then we present an excerpt from a white paper that one of us prepared in 2011 with lawyers from the former insurance regulatory powerhouse firm of Dewey Lebouef in 2011 for the National Insurance Office of the Treasury Department. That excerpt discusses the justifications for insurance regulation in theoretical terms.

A.   Functional Divisions of Insurance Regulation

First, let's consider the types of insurance regulation that exist in all of the 51 jurisdictions. There are six main functional divisions of insurance regulation: (1) licensing (of insurance companies and intermediaries), (2) taxation, (3) solvency, (4) rates, (5) forms, (6) access and availability, and (7) market conduct.

Licensing is the oldest form of insurance regulation, dating back to the process of granting charters to enter the insurance business. Although the process has become more formalized over the years, the basic idea remains the same. To become licensed to do business in a jurisdiction, an insurance company must demonstrate the experience and abilities of its management team, as well as its financial soundness. These licensing powers also come into play when one insurance company, or a group of investors, seeks to gain control over an insurance company currently operating in a jurisdiction. This facet of insurance licensing makes insurance mergers and acquisitions a very lawyer-intensive enterprise.

Today, licensing requirements are also directed at insurance intermediaries: agents, brokers, adjusters, and "third-party administrators" (entities that administer trusts that perform insurance-like functions, such as self-funded workers' compensation or employee benefit trusts). Typically, there is an educational requirement, an exam, and a division of the insurance department responsible for investigating intermediary malfeasance. An alternative approach to insurance intermediary regulation (which no state insurance department has adopted) would be to make insurance companies responsible for all the activities of the intermediaries they use. This approach would give insurance companies greater incentive to supervise intermediaries and would allow regulators to focus more of their attention on the control procedures of the insurance companies.

Taxation of insurance premiums is nearly as old as regulation through licensing. Indeed, one of the main purposes of licensing was to provide states with the opportunity to tax insurance entrepreneurs. The main function of these taxes was not so much to regulate the behavior of insurance companies, but to provide a source of revenue for the states. Although we do not consider taxation issues in this text, readers should be aware that federal income tax law has played an enormous role in shaping contemporary insurance arrangements. For example, as we discussed in Section III of Chapter 3, the connection between employment and insurance has been strongly reinforced by the tax law rule that fringe benefits are not taxable income to employees, and the recent growth in life insurance investment products is almost entirely attributable to tax law.

Solvency regulation in the United States dates to the mid-nineteenth century, when a rash of insurance company insolvencies threatened the legitimacy of the fledgling insurance industry. Individual insurers recognized that it was not enough to attempt on their own to ensure that they had adequate reserves to meet their promises. They had to work together to minimize the number of insurance insolvencies so that the public would have confidence that their premium dollars would not be wasted. This collective action was necessary for two reasons. First, the insolvency of one company threatened the public trust in other companies because people were (and are) quite aware of their inability to be sure that the company they do business with is financially sound. Second, at least some of the insolvencies resulted from overly optimistic, or overly competitive, companies that charged premiums that were too low. The low prices charged by these "bad" companies threatened the ability of the "good" to charge adequate premiums. (Both of these reasons are examples of the insurer-side adverse selection, or the "lemons problem" or "race-to-the-bottom problem," which was introduced in Chapter 1.) As a result, responsible insurers petitioned their state legislatures to begin regulating the financial soundness of insurance companies.

There are numerous regulatory tools directed at solvency. Some of the most important are capital requirements, financial reporting and accounting requirements (which are considerably more conservative from a solvency perspective than the "generally accepted accounting principles" that inform financial reporting elsewhere in the economy), limits on the kinds and concentration of investments insurance companies can make with the funds that they hold in reserve to pay claims, and requirements that insurance companies justify their insurance rates (although the solvency component of rate regulation does not receive much attention today). In addition, states have created "guaranty funds" that will pay many types of insurance claims in the event that an insurance company becomes insolvent. These guaranty funds, covered in more detail in Section III of this chapter, protect consumer confidence directly by providing the means to pay claims in the event of an insolvency and indirectly by providing an incentive for financially healthy insurance companies to take over and assume the financial obligations of insurance companies that are heading toward insolvency. Traditionally, solvency regulation has been the most important function of state insurance regulation. Nearly everything in the insurance field depends on the insurance company having the ability to honor its commitments.

Rate regulation, as just suggested, began as a solvency tool. Because of the concern of excessive competition (or excessive optimism) among insurance companies, insurance regulators monitored rates to be sure that they were "adequate." Over time, regulators expanded their concerns to address "excessive" and "discriminatory" rates as well. The standard statute authorizing rate regulation in most states provides that insurance rates must be "adequate, not excessive and nondiscriminatory." How insurance departments have implemented these rate-regulation goals has varied widely over time and place. One model, which formerly was employed to the fullest extent in automobile insurance in Massachusetts, envisions insurance companies as a kind of public utility and the state insurance department as the entity charged with setting insurance rates based on the underlying costs of providing the insurance and the need for investors to earn a return on their capital. The other extreme is to rely entirely on the market and to permit insurance companies to charge whatever people are willing to pay.[1]

In recent years, states have gravitated toward a market approach, especially with regard to whether rates are "adequate" and "not excessive" and especially with regard to commercial lines of insurance. Nevertheless, the concern over excessive rates remains strong in many states, particularly in the workers' compensation and auto insurance fields and, to a lesser extent, homeowners' insurance. There is little evidence that auto, workers' compensation, or homeowners'

---

1. Part of the explanation for why state insurance regulators have been given the role of guarding against excessive rates derives from two facts about the industry: (1) insurers have a history of coordinating in setting rates in ways that would generally be considered violations of federal antitrust laws and (2) the insurance industry has been explicitly exempted from those laws. See the discussion below of the history and application of the McCarran-Ferguson Act. These facts help to explain the Massachusetts public-utility approach to rate regulation.

insurance are less competitive than other lines of insurance. The more persuasive explanation for the increased attention paid those lines of insurance is political salience. Auto and workers' compensation insurance are mandatory *de jure,* and homeowners' insurance is mandatory *de facto* (because of the insurance clauses in standard mortgage notes), and all three lines of insurance are very visible to consumers and small business owners.

Rate regulation also includes restrictions on the types of risk classification that insurers can engage in. As discussed in Chapter 1, insurers classify risks so that they can charge premiums that approximate, as accurately as possible, each insured's expected costs. This practice helps insurers to maximize profits. Aggressive risk classification by insurers can be a sign of a competitive insurance market, as insurers compete for relatively low risk insureds, and it can have beneficial effects on insureds' incentives to reduce risks. (Recall the discussion in Chapter 1 of insurance as regulation.) As we discuss at greater length below, however, there are a number of reasons why allowing insurers to engage in unfettered risk classification may not always produce the fairest or even the most efficient outcomes. These fairness and efficiency objections to certain types of risk classification help to explain why government regulators sometimes impose restrictions on the types of risk classification that insurers may engage in.

Form regulation dates to the statutory enactment of the standard fire insurance policy in the late nineteenth century. With limited exceptions, all states require that all insurance policies sold in the state be on forms approved by the state insurance departments. In many states and with many lines of insurance, forms are deemed "approved" if they are filed with the state insurance department and not explicitly disapproved within a certain time period. The degree of scrutiny given to forms varies considerably, along lines that should be intuitively obvious. With the exception of workers' compensation insurance—the terms of which are set by statute—commercial insurance forms typically receive less scrutiny than personal lines of insurance. New forms that grant broader coverage are generally approved as a matter of course. The degree of scrutiny given to forms that narrow coverage varies according to the salience of the coverage at issue. For example, terrorism exclusions received much greater scrutiny in the period following September 11, 2001, than they might have a year earlier.

Access and availability regulation is a relatively new feature on the insurance regulatory landscape. As the name suggests, these regulations are directed at ensuring that insurance is available and that people have access both to insurance and to the goods and services for which insurance is required.

Perhaps the most important type of access and availability regulations are those that establish "residual market mechanisms." Residual market mechanisms establish "insurers of last resort," a means for people to purchase insurance when there is no other insurer willing to provide it to them. The policies sold in the residual market often have lower limits and are priced higher than those sold in the regular market, although the prices that are charged in the residual markets are typically less than the expected costs of the applicant for the residual policy. The shortfall between the premiums charged and the payouts made to residual insured is usually covered by a tax imposed on all insurers doing business in the state in the relevant line of insurance. That tax is then passed on through premium increases to policyholders in the regular insurance markets. Residual market mechanisms are most common in areas in which there is mandatory insurance—auto and workers' compensation—but many states also have residual market mechanisms for property and health insurance.

Without a residual market mechanism, insurance companies effectively control access to many of the goods and services that require insurance. This is one of the regulatory powers of insurance that social scientists have begun to examine. *See, e.g.,* Carol A. Heimer, *Insuring More, Ensuring Less: The Costs and Benefits of Private Regulation through Insurance, in* Embracing Risk 116 (Tom Baker & Jonathan Simon eds., 2002).

Other examples of access and availability regulation are limits on risk classification (discussed further below), requirements that certain kinds of coverage be included in policies, and requirements designed to ensure widespread marketing of insurance. Prohibiting certain kinds of classification makes insurance available to people who would be excluded, or charged a prohibitively high price, as a result of these classifications. Requiring that certain kinds of coverage be included in policies distributes the costs of those benefits across a broader population and therefore makes them more available to those who need them, provided of course that the requirements do not make the coverage so expensive that people choose not to buy insurance. Finally, regulations directed at insurance marketing prevent insurance companies from using targeted marketing efforts to exclude people that they would not legally be able to exclude through more direct means.

Market conduct regulation is a catch-all term for a wide variety of efforts to ensure that insurance companies live up to their promises. One of the most important market conduct statutes is the NAIC Model Unfair and Deceptive Trade Practices Act, covered in the unit on risk classification in Section III of this chapter, below. Market conduct regulation addresses claims practices, advertising and other marketing, and underwriting. State insurance departments regularly conduct market conduct examinations in which regulators go on-site to insurance company offices to review files. *See* Robert W. Klein & James W. Schacht, *An Assessment of Insurance Market Conduct Surveillance,* 20 J. Ins. Reg. 51 (2001). *Cf.* William C. Whitford & Spencer L. Kimball, *Why Process Consumer Complaints? A Case Study of the Office of the Commissioner of Insurance of Wisconsin,* 1974 Wis. L. Rev. 639.

Most states have antitrust laws that regulate price-fixing and other anticompetitive behavior. New York's antitrust law was one of the tools included in the litigation strategy that Eliot Spitzer used as New York's attorney general to force changes in insurance brokerage practices. Like the famous Armstrong Investigations in the early twentieth century, Spitzer's investigations propelled him briefly into the New York governor's mansion, evidencing a long-running public concern about the power of the insurance industry. Sean Fitzpatrick, *The Small Laws: Eliot Spitzer and the Way to Insurance Market Reform,* 74 Fordham L. Rev. 3041 (2006).

B. *Theoretical Justifications of Insurance Regulation*

MODERNIZING INSURANCE REGULATION IN THE UNITED STATES

L. Charles Landgraf, John S. Pruit, and Tom Baker

Insurance regulation long predates the rise of a centralized administrative state at the national level. Insurance regulation grew up at the state level out of necessity as only the states had the governmental resources at the time. At least until the late 19th century (and in many cases long after), insurers and insurance producers were largely state-specific or regional businesses. Thus, there was not the demand for strong national coordination that might have pushed the federal government to develop the necessary administrative capacity, as occurred in the transportation and banking sectors.

Moreover, it is important to recognize that insurance regulation has developed in response to specific problems, shaped by the then-prevailing political and economic understandings and opportunities, all of which evolved over more than two hundred years. There was no grand design, nor even a consistent understanding of the purposes and possibilities of insurance itself or of insurance regulation.

Nevertheless, it is possible to identify a small set of widely accepted objectives and categories of insurance regulation that can serve as a starting point for considering what can and should be done to modernize and improve the system of insurance regulation in the United States. That is the goal of this part of our report. We begin with the *objectives*, drawing from the conceptual vocabulary of social science and with the benefit of the history that gave rise to the system of regulation currently in place.

A.   Objectives of Insurance Regulation

We start from the premise that there is a broad consensus that insurance regulation should rely on the private market to promote the efficient and fair delivery of insurance services, though recognizing that there is considerable disagreement about the best way to do so. These very general objectives—efficiency and fairness—provide the beginnings of a useful conceptual framework because they point toward bodies of knowledge in law and social science. The efficiency objective draws on economics and psychology and related approaches to law and regulation. The fairness objective draws on moral philosophy and psychology and related approaches to law and regulation.

1.   PROMOTING THE EFFICIENT DELIVERY OF INSURANCE THROUGH THE MARKET

The concept of efficiency points toward the utilitarian objective of the greatest good for the greatest number. In the insurance context, this means spreading the most risk at the lowest cost. Social science research and insurance history have taught that there are three main obstacles that inhibit private insurance markets from achieving this objective in the absence of robust insurance regulation.

These three obstacles are: (i) the difficult-to-observe quality of insurance; (ii) the "positive externalities" of insurance; and (iii) the perceived cognitive and behavioral limits of individuals in relation to a complex product like insurance. This vocabulary and way of understanding insurance markets are relatively new, especially in the context of two hundred years of insurance regulation. Nevertheless, they provide a useful explanation for the existence of most of the core aspects of insurance regulation.

a.   The difficult-to-observe quality of insurance

For markets to work, people need to have confidence in the products for sale. People also need to be able to distinguish among the quality and features of competing products, so that they can make an informed choice about how best to spend their money. Insurance poses tremendous problems in these regards. Many of the most important aspects of the quality of insurance are not easily observable by ordinary people. That makes insurance what economists call a "credence good," meaning that people have to trust in the quality of the product even though they do not have the capacity to evaluate that quality when they buy it. Other kinds of credence goods include medicine, many kinds of food, and most financial services. Governments in all advanced societies regulate credence goods to make them worthy of the trust needed to make markets in these goods possible.

The unobservable aspects of insurance product quality include the financial solidity of the insurance company, the details of the insurance contracts and the claims servicing practices of the insurance company. Some of these aspects of insurance product quality are not completely unobservable. For example, the written terms of an insurance contract appear in black and white on the insurance policy form (assuming that the insurance company is willing to provide the policy in advance, which is not always the case). But it is so time consuming and expensive to evaluate the terms of the contract or, indeed, most of the other observable aspects of quality, that no individual person or company would rationally make that effort. Other aspects of quality, such as past claims servicing practices or current financial conditions, might be observable in theory, but observation would require the disclosure of information that the insurer prefers to keep private.

Finally, some aspects of insurance product quality are completely unobservable by anyone at the time of purchase because they depend on what happens in the future. Insurance consists fundamentally of the promise to pay money in the future, sometimes very far in the future. No one can observe today the financial condition and claims paying practices of an insurance company in the future.

Much of insurance regulation can be understood as protecting the quality of insurance organizations and insurance contracts. When properly designed and implemented, solvency regulation, market conduct regulation and the licensing of insurance companies and intermediaries all promote the consumer trust in insurance products needed to make the insurance market function.

b.   *The positive externalities of insurance*

Sound insurance institutions are both evidence of, and preconditions for, a stable, productive society. Sound insurance institutions provide benefits to neighborhoods, communities and other social groups that exceed the aggregate value of the benefits to the individuals in the group. These "positive externalities" of insurance are an additional reason why an unregulated private insurance market will not supply as much insurance as would be optimal. Much of insurance regulation helps promote the growth in insurance markets that captures the positive externalities of insurance. Access and availability regulation is especially important in this regard. When properly designed and implemented, access and availability regulation brings insurance to individuals and entities that would not otherwise be adequately served.

The positive externalities also help explain why the costs of insurance regulation should not be imposed entirely on insurance institutions. By supporting insurance markets, insurance regulation benefits the broader society and, thus, should be supported by society at large, not just by those who purchase insurance through taxes on insurance premiums or cross subsidies within insurance pools.

c.   *The cognitive and behavioral limits of individuals*

Psychologists and behavioral economists are only beginning to carefully study some of the limits on human decision making that may affect consumer behavior in the purchase of insurance and that explain some aspects of consumer protection regulation. Insurance is a complex product that requires people to make commitments, today, to protect themselves against things that may or may not happen, sometimes very far in the future. Cognitive and behavior limits that may discourage people from purchasing insurance appropriate to their circumstances include hyperbolic discounting (an exaggerated preference for money today rather than tomorrow), complexity aversion and procrastination. At the same time, there are other limits that encourage people to purchase some kinds of insurance that are very expensive relative to the benefit provided, such as very low deductibles, extended product warranties for relatively low cost goods and special purpose insurance against highly feared risks that could be more cheaply insured through more general purpose insurance.

A perception that individuals will not make the right decisions because of these limitations and that insurers will take advantage of this to the individuals' detriment, rightly or wrongly, is the reason behind a significant portion of product regulation. The legislature or regulator decides whether a product or contract term is suitable or not suitable rather than leaving it to be sorted out among insurers and consumers participating in a free market. A more modern approach may be to design systems that foster allowing consumers to make appropriate choices, rather than making choices for consumers by writing rules that prevent the sale of designated products or mandate specified terms and conditions.

2.   PROMOTING FAIRNESS IN AND THROUGH INSURANCE

Fairness is an elusive but important concept that helps to explain some aspects of insurance regulation that cannot be explained as efforts to promote the efficient delivery of insurance through the private market. Insurance operates through "routine, mundane transactions that nevertheless define the contours of individual and social responsibility," with the result that "[i]nsurance, then, not only distributes risk . . . it also distributes responsibility." So understood, it is easy to see that insurance arrangements implicate the kinds of questions about distributional and procedural justice that people think through in a common-sense way in terms of fairness.

Who can be part of the risk pool? What losses are covered? How completely? Who has to pay how much for the privilege of joining the risk pool? What restrictions can the group place on the conduct of its members? What inquiries can the group make as a condition of membership or of paying a claim? What hurdles can it erect? What hoops may people be made to jump through to qualify for insurance or to make a claim?

It is not surprising that society does not leave such matters entirely to the discretion of insurance institutions or to the operation of the insurance market, no matter how much faith people have in markets. Moreover, the fact that insurance markets need some kind of regulation in order to meet the objective of promoting efficiency as just described practically guarantees that concepts of fairness will play an important role, if only because fairness provides a more effective rallying point for popular support for insurance regulation than efficiency.

In that context, the concept of "actuarial fairness" has played an important role in debates about the scope and function of insurance regulation. Among other things, actuarial fairness calls for "each insured [to] pay according to the quality of his risk," thus justifying on the basis of fairness the approach to insurance pricing and other matters that efficiency typically would call for. While this approach to fairness has been subject to sustained attack, both the concept and the attack support a larger point. Whether to regulate insurance on the basis of fairness is not in question. What is in question is what is fair in what context.

As the example of actuarial fairness suggests, the efficiency-promoting aspects of insurance regulation generally can be recast in terms of fairness. For example, is it fair for someone to pay insurance premiums for years only to find that the company doesn't have the money to pay her claim? Similarly, is it fair for insurance companies to use agents who mislead or otherwise take advantage of consumers? Few states compile and retain detailed legislative materials leading to the enactment of state laws, making it impracticable to conduct a comprehensive review of the legislative history of state insurance laws. Were we able to do so, however, we suspect that we would find many more references to fairness than efficiency and, where widely accepted notions of fairness and efficiency conflict, we would expect to see fairness prevail.

To a degree, conflicts between efficiency and fairness in relation to insurance regulation arise out of disagreements about the extent to which private insurance markets should participate in the reproduction of inequality. In part because insurance organizations have emphasized the non-commercial, altruistic and social aspects of insurance, there is a longstanding tradition in insurance thought and regulation that regards insurance arrangements as instruments for ameliorating misfortune, with misfortune understood in much broader terms than the realization of the contingencies specified in an ordinary property casualty or life insurance contract.

In philosophical terms, this disagreement reflects different intuitions about moral entitlements and the role of insurance arrangements in relation to those entitlements. In one approach, people are morally entitled to everything that they have, even those things over which they had no control and for which they might appear to have no responsibility for obtaining. In this view, people are entitled to the fruits of their health status even when it results from genetics and people are entitled to the fruits of the stability of their local economy whether they chose to live there or not. Taken to an extreme, this approach could lead to the rejection of insurance entirely. More commonly, however, this approach regards insurance as a means to protect entitlements from loss and encourages insurance on that basis.

In another approach, people have a strong moral entitlement only to things that they deserve, and not to the outcomes of morally arbitrary events or matters, such as genetic endowment, economic conditions or childhood upbringing. In this view, people are not entitled to the fruits of their health status, except as it results from their efforts, and people are not entitled to the fruits of the stability of their local economy, except to extent that they chose on a nonarbitrary basis to live there and contributed to that stability. Taken to an extreme, this approach easily could regard most of the distribution of resources in society as morally arbitrary and, on that basis, employ insurance as an institution for very significant redistribution of resources. More commonly, however, this approach regards private insurance as a means for rounding just some of the hard corners of life and looks to progressive taxation and social insurance as the appropriate institutions for reducing inequality more broadly. Some of the questions of insurance regulation on which these two approaches tend to diverge include limits on the discretion of insurance companies to define risk categories that are used for pricing and underwriting and limits on the discretion of insurance companies to vary premiums on the basis of those categories.

II. MARKING THE BOUNDARIES OF STATE AND FEDERAL AUTHORITY

A. *What Is Insurance Under State Law?*

Whatever the content of insurance regulation, there is a need to determine the range of economic activity to which that regulation applies. Typically, state insurance codes make it unlawful to engage in the sale of "insurance" without a license from the state insurance department. The codes also impose a variety of obligations on those engaged in the sale of insurance and empower state insurance departments to enforce those obligations. Thus, the definition of the term "insurance" is central to determining the jurisdiction of state "insurance" departments.

The following two statutory provisions are examples of the most common state statutory definitions of insurance. Consider how much economic activity that most people would not otherwise think of as insurance would be classified as such under a literal reading of these definitions.

WEST VIRGINIA CODE §33-1-1

"Insurance" is a contract whereby one undertakes to indemnify another or pay a specified amount upon determinable contingencies.

NEW MEXICO STAT. §59A-1-5

"Insurance" is a contract whereby one undertakes to pay or indemnify another as to loss from certain specified contingencies or perils, or to pay or grant a specified amount or determinable benefit in connection with ascertained risk contingencies, or to act as a surety.

Wisconsin has one of the more interesting definitions, which is to be expected since Professor Spencer Kimball, one of the leading insurance scholars of the twentieth century, was the reporter for the committee that redrafted the Wisconsin Insurance Code. In keeping with Professor Kimball's view that "[t]here is no good definition of 'insurance' for any purpose" (the opening sentence in his insurance casebook!), the Wisconsin statutes do not provide a general definition of "insurance":

WIS. STAT. §600.03(25)(A)

"Insurance" includes any of the following:
   1. Risk distributing arrangements providing for compensation of damages or loss through the provision of services or benefits in kind rather than indemnity in money.
   2. Contracts of guaranty or suretyship entered into by the guarantor or surety as a business and not as merely incidental to a business transaction. . . .
      (b) "Insurance" does not include a continuing care contract, as defined in §647.01(2).

What do you think might explain this definitional provision? What does it accomplish that the other definitions do not?
   Consider how useful these statutes would be to address the issue in the following case.

GRIFFIN SYSTEMS, INC. v. OHIO DEPARTMENT OF INSURANCE
Supreme Court of Ohio
575 N.E.2d 803 (1991)

[This case concerns Ohio Department of Insurance (ODI) jurisdiction over "vehicle protection plans (VPPs)" sold by Griffin Systems. The plans promise to repair or replace any of the covered units and parts of the motor vehicle when those units or parts break down due to a defect. The plans specifically exclude coverage for repairs necessitated by weather-related damage, collisions, vandalism, negligence, or failure to perform required service maintenance.]
   SWEENEY. The determinative issue presented in this appeal is whether appellant's vehicle protection plans are contracts "substantially amounting to insurance" within the meaning of R.C. 3905.42. . . . R.C. 3905.42 provides as follows:

   No company, corporation, or association, whether organized in this state or elsewhere, shall engage either directly or indirectly in this state in the business of insurance, or enter into any contracts substantially amounting to insurance, . . . unless it is expressly authorized by the laws of this state, and the laws regulating it and applicable thereto, have been complied with.

Appellee ODI argues that the vehicle protection plans offered and sold by appellant are "contracts substantially amounting to insurance," and, thus, should be subject to the full array of insurance regulations within R.C. Title 39.

ODI contends, and the court of appeals below agreed, that the key element that subjects appellant's protection plans to insurance laws and regulations is that appellant is neither the seller nor the manufacturer of the product it purports to warrant. ODI essentially asserts that extended warranties offered by sellers and manufacturers are part of the inducement process of making the product more desirable to the prospective buyer. Since appellant is an independent third party to the transaction, ODI submits that the claimed warranty appellant offers and sells is in reality a contract "substantially amounting to insurance."

The appellant, on the other hand, citing *State, ex rel. Duffy, v. Western Auto Supply Co.*, 16 N.E.2d 256 (Ohio 1938), and *State, ex rel. Herbert, v. Standard Oil Co.*, 35 N.E.2d 437 (Ohio 1941), contends that since its vehicle protection plans cover only those repairs necessitated by mechanical breakdown of defective parts, the protection plans constitute warranties and not contracts of insurance. Appellant relies on *Duffy, supra,* and argues that the instant vehicle protection plans limit reimbursement to loss due to defects in the product, and do not promise to reimburse loss or damage resulting from perils outside of and unrelated to defects in the product itself. Appellant submits that the issue of whether the seller or manufacturer (as opposed to an independent third party) offers or sells the type of contract in issue is wholly irrelevant.

In *Duffy, supra,* this court was asked to determine whether written guarantees issued by Western Auto covering tires it sold constituted contracts "substantially amounting to insurance" under G.C. 665. The language of one of the Western Auto guarantees stated that it protected the tires "'against blowouts, cuts, bruises, rim-cuts, under-inflation, wheels out of alignment, faulty brakes or other road hazards that may render the tire unfit for further service (except fire and theft).' It then provided that 'In the event that the tire becomes unserviceable from the above conditions, we will (at our option) repair it free of charge, or replace it with a new tire of the same make at any of our stores, charging __th of our current price for each month which has elapsed since the date of purchase. The new tire will be fully covered by our regular guarantee in effect at time of adjustment. Furthermore: every tire is guaranteed against defects in material or workmanship without limit as to time, mileage or service.'" *Id.,* at 257.

In finding that the Western Auto guarantees were contracts substantially amounting to insurance, this court held in *Duffy, supra,* at paragraphs three and four of the syllabus:

> A warranty promises indemnity against defects in an article sold, while insurance indemnifies against loss or damage resulting from perils outside of and unrelated to defects in the article itself.
>
> A contract whereby the vendor of automobile tires undertakes to guarantee the tires sold against defects in material or workmanship without limit as to time, mileage or service, and further expressly guarantees them for a specified period against "blowouts, cuts, bruises, rim-cuts, under-inflation, wheels out of alignment, faulty brakes or other road hazards that may render the tire unfit for further service (except fire or theft)," or contracts to indemnify the purchaser "should the tire fail within the replacement period" specified, without limitation as to cause of such "failure," is a contract "substantially amounting to insurance" within the provisions of Section 665, General Code, which requires such guarantor or insurer to comply with the laws of the state authorizing and regulating the business of insurance.

The foregoing syllabus language clearly indicates that the "guarantees" in *Duffy* were found to be contracts substantially amounting to insurance because such guarantees promised to indemnify for losses or damages to the product outside of and unrelated to defects inherent in the product itself.

Several years later, in *Herbert, supra,* this court was faced with another tire warranty/guarantee that was challenged by the Attorney General of Ohio. Therein, the tire warranty offered by Standard Oil promised repair or replacement for a limited period under certain conditions and provided in pertinent part:

> This Warranty and Adjustment Agreement does not cover punctures, tires ruined in running flat, tires injured or destroyed by fire, wrecks or collisions, tires cut by chains, or by obstruction on vehicle, theft, clincher tires, tubes used in any form, or tires used in taxicab or common carrier bus service.
>
>   This Warranty and Adjustment Agreement does not cover consequential damages.

Id., 35 N.E.2d at 439.

In finding that the Standard Oil tire warranty was indeed a warranty, and not a contract substantially amounting to insurance, this court held in paragraphs four and five of the syllabus as follows:

> A warranty or guaranty issued to a purchaser in connection with the sale of goods containing an agreement to indemnify against loss or damage resulting from perils outside of and unrelated to inherent weaknesses in the goods themselves, constitutes a contract substantially amounting to insurance within the purview of Section 665, General Code.
>
>   A written warranty delivered to a purchaser, representing that the articles sold are so well and carefully manufactured that they will give satisfactory service under ordinary usage for a specified length of time, and providing for an adjustment in the event of failure from faulty construction or materials, but expressly excluding happenings not connected with imperfections in the articles themselves, is not a contract substantially amounting to insurance within the meaning of Section 665, General Code.

In summarizing the law enunciated in both *Duffy* and *Herbert* it is readily apparent that a contract "substantially amounting to insurance" in this context is one that promises to cover losses or damages over and above, or unrelated to, defects within the product itself.

A careful review of the instant vehicle protection plans indicates that losses or damages sustained by the purchaser of the product which are unrelated to defects within the product itself are specifically excluded from coverage. Thus, it would appear that under both *Duffy* and *Herbert,* the instant vehicle protection plans are indeed warranties, and are not contracts substantially amounting to insurance.

However, as mentioned before, ODI asserts that the crucial distinction, as noted by the court of appeals below, is that warranties not sold by either the vendor or manufacturer of the product are not made to induce a purchase of the product, and therefore constitute contracts substantially amounting to insurance. While the foregoing assertion may appear to be facially valid, we find it to be unpersuasive. Obviously, the distinction made in this vein was of no apparent consequence in *Duffy, supra,* inasmuch as it was the *seller* of the product therein who issued the "warranty" that this court found to be a contract substantially amounting to insurance.

In our view, the crucial factor in determining whether a contract is a warranty or something substantially amounting to insurance is not the status of the party offering or selling the warranty, but rather the type of coverage promised within the four corners of the contract itself. Under the rule of law announced in both *Duffy* and *Herbert*, it is clear that warranties that cover only defects within the product itself are properly characterized as warranties (as was the case in *Herbert, supra*), whereas warranties promising to cover damages or losses unrelated to defects within the product itself are, by definition, contracts substantially amounting to insurance (as was the case in *Duffy, supra*).

The fact that appellant herein is not the manufacturer, supplier, or seller of the products it purports to warrant is, in our view, of little or no consequence in determining whether its protection plans are subject to R.C. Title 39. Common experience in today's marketplace indicates that a large number of consumer products carry a short-term warranty, but that agreements that extend the warranty beyond the period of time offered by the manufacturer may often be purchased for additional consideration. Certainly, it can be safely surmised that most people are not induced to buy a specific product based upon an extended warranty agreement that may be purchased at an extra cost. Carrying ODI's arguments to their logical extreme, however, a seller of consumer products can offer such extended warranties to cover losses or damages, while independent third parties would be subject to insurance regulations even if the extended warranties specifically exclude losses or damages unrelated to defects in the product. Under such circumstances, we reject the status-determinative approach urged by ODI and adopted by the appellate court below, in favor of the substance-of-the-contract approach urged by appellant. . . .

Therefore, based on all the foregoing, we hold that a motor vehicle service agreement which promises to compensate the promisee for repairs necessitated by mechanical breakdown resulting exclusively from failure due to defects in the motor vehicle parts does not constitute a contract "substantially amounting to insurance" within the purview of R.C. 3905.42.

Accordingly, the judgment of the court of appeals is hereby reversed.

WRIGHT, dissenting. . . .

During the last twenty years, factory and dealer warranties on various consumer goods have proliferated, particularly in the automobile business. In recent years, a much more comprehensive warranty has been offered by various dealers covering almost every aspect of the future functioning of the automobiles sold and the component parts thereof. This sort of warranty has proved attractive to the buyer and highly profitable to the dealer. In this instance, Griffin had no relationship with the consumer whatsoever until after the consumer had purchased the automobile, at which point Griffin directly solicited the consumer by mail for sale of its VPP. Having signed up the consumer, Griffin reinsured its business with the Great Plains Insurance Company, a Nebraska corporation, which is a wholly owned subsidiary of Griffin and is unlicensed to sell insurance in the state of Ohio. Therefore, without considering whether the VPPs before us here insure against contingencies other than product defects, we have a contract that is totally distinguishable from the warranty we found in *Herbert*. It is perfectly apparent that the VPP is not a warranty proposed by a manufacturer-seller *and* used for the purpose of inducing or increasing sales of the product in question. In a word, we have a case of first impression here which is certainly not controlled by either *Herbert* or *Duffy*. Indeed, the *Duffy* case seems to directly support the holding of the court of appeals. . . .

The Ohio General Assembly has given ODI the broadest authority to regulate *all* forms of insurance by way of R.C. 3905.42, which states in pertinent part: "No company . . . shall engage . . . in the business of insurance, or enter into any contracts substantially amounting to insurance, or in any manner aid therein, or engage in the business of guaranteeing against liability, loss, or damage, . . . unless it is expressly authorized by the laws of this state, and the laws regulating it and applicable thereto, have been complied with." In the Duffy case, we "'[b]roadly defined insurance . . . [as] a contract by which one party, for a compensation called the premium, assumes particular risks of the other party and promises to pay to him or his nominee a certain or ascertainable sum of money on a specified contingency. As regards property and liability insurance, it is a contract by which one party promises on a consideration to compensate or reimburse the other if he shall suffer loss from a specified cause, or to guarantee or indemnify or secure him against loss from that cause.' . . ." *Id.* at 258-259. In my view, the VPPs offered by Griffin are within this definition.

The appellee herein cites Vance, The Law of Insurance §1, p. 2 (3 Ed. 1951), which lists the following five elements as distinguishing characteristics of insurance: (1) the insured possesses an insurable interest; (2) the insured is subject to loss through the destruction or impairment of that interest by the happening of some designated peril; (3) the insurer assumes the risk of loss; (4) such assumption is part of the general scheme to distribute actual losses among a large group of persons bearing similar risks; and (5) the insured pays a premium as consideration for the promise. There is no question that each of the above-described elements is present under Griffin's VPP.

Griffin can hardly be likened to a manufacturer, supplier or seller offering an extended warranty on one of its products. As stated above, Griffin is clearly not involved in the manufacture or sale of automobiles, and has no control over the risk of defects in those products. It is an independent, for-profit entity offering a contract insuring against the risk of mechanical breakdown of a motor vehicle—an insurable interest. Griffin, for consideration of a stated premium from the policyholder, assumes the risk of certain specified losses and presumably distributes that risk among a larger group of persons bearing similar risks. This case does not involve a warranty because a warranty is a statement or representation made by the seller or manufacturer of goods contemporaneously with and as a part of the contract of sale.

Appellee has drawn our attention to opinions from out of state and under federal law in support of its position. *Griffin Systems, Inc. v. Washburn*, 505 N.E.2d 1121 (Ill. App. Ct. 1987), examined the same VPPs at issue in this case and concluded that they are insurance contracts. That opinion distinguished Griffin's VPPs from a warranty or service contract. The court stated, ". . . the distinguishing feature which sets . . . [manufacturer's or seller's service contracts and warranties] apart from an insurance policy is the fact that the respective compan[ies] *manufacture or sell the products which they agreed to repair or replace.* No third parties are involved nor is there a risk accepted which the company, because of its expertise, is unaware of. . . ." (Emphasis *sic*.) *Id.* at 1124. . . .

Griffin urges this court to focus on whether it would "make sense" to apply the insurance statutes and regulations to its VPPs. The real issue, however, is whether each VPP contains the requisite elements of insurance such that it is a contract that "substantially amount[s] to insurance." As shown above, Griffin's VPP contains those elements and is, therefore, insurance. Because it is insurance, under R.C. 3905.42, ODI has the authority to regulate it. . . .

NOTES AND QUESTIONS

1. The courts in most states that have considered the question posed in *Griffin* have taken the approach of the dissent, holding that extended warranties offered by manufacturers and sellers are not subject to insurance regulation but that extended warranties offered by independent third parties are subject to insurance regulation. *See, e.g., GAF Corp. v. County Sch. Bd. of Washington County,* 629 F.2d 981 (4th Cir. 1980) (manufacturer's extended warranty is not insurance); *Rayos v. Chrysler Credit Corp.,* 683 S.W.2d 546 (Tex. App. 1985); *Guaranteed Warranty Corp. v. Humphrey,* 533 P.2d 87 (Ariz. Ct. App. 1975) (third-party extended warranty is insurance). What do you think? How might your answers differ under the three approaches set out in the following note?

2. Eric M. Holmes's Appleman on Insurance (2d ed.) (1996) describes three different approaches to the "What is insurance?" question. The first, the "substantial control" test, is that set forth in the quotation from Vance cited by the dissent in *Griffin*. The second is the "principal object or ancillary test" that lies behind the distinction between extended warranties offered in connection with a sale and separate from that sale. One source commonly cited for this approach is Keeton on Insurance:

    > [I]nsurance regulatory laws are not properly construed as aimed at an absolute prohibition against the inclusion of any risk-transferring-and-distributing provisions in contracts for services or for the sale or rental of goods. In short, the presence of a small element of insurance, if one wishes to call it that, closely associated with the predominant element of the transaction — the element that gives the transaction its distinctive character — does not conclusively demonstrate that the transaction is within the reach of insurance regulation.

    Keeton on Insurance §8.2(c) (1971).

    The final approach, which is that advocated by Professor Holmes, is the "regulatory value" test:

    > Courts should examine each commercial transaction to determine if the discrete transaction ought to be regulated in the public interest as the business of insurance. Obviously, neither "roof leak insurance" nor "tire insurance" is a viable insurance business and so affected with a public interest to merit state regulation. Such enterprises do not support an independent book of insurance business and ought not to be subject to the expense of complying with state insurance regulatory laws. But the same cannot be said for vehicle protection plans (VPP), collision damage

waivers (CDW), homeowner's warranty (HOW), AAA (providing sundry services such as towing, bail bonds, and so on), various prepaid service plans (prepaid medical services, legal services, funeral services, etc.) and similar contractual provisions that have a "public interest" insurance element. Should it be outcome determinative if such promises are held to be beyond the promisor's control but incidental and thus not insurance? It simply does not follow from that determination that such promises should not be regulated. . . . Pursuant to this supplemental test, courts should minimally make the following inquiries.

(1) What is the private interest sought to be protected in the commercial transaction? (Matters, such as insurable interest and risk of harm to that interest, under traditional definitions are evaluated here.)

(2) Who is the party assuming the risk transferred? Is the protected interest indigenous to that party? (Arguably, there is more need for regulation if the assuming party is an independent, for-profit entity promising indemnity against certain risks to the insurable interest.)

(3) Is the protected interest indigenous to the state and all its citizens? (Manifestly, a state and its citizens have a common indigenous interest in safety and health, including the delivery and quality of medical care, safe cars, well-built homes, and the like. Other interests may not be indigenous.)

(4) Does the value of the indigenous interest invoke the purposes and policies of state insurance regulation for all its citizens? (Many reasons justify state insurance regulation, for example: to assure solvency, to assure fairness in rates and rating classifications, and to prevent contractual over-reaching. These concerns are addressed in this final question.)

Holmes's Appleman on Insurance §1.4 (2d ed.) (1996). Consider how each of these tests, and the definitions in the statutes that preceded *Griffin*, would classify the contractual arrangements set out in the problems that follow.

PROBLEMS IN STATE JURISDICTION OVER "INSURANCE" ACTIVITY

1. A trucking company entered into a contract with a truck maintenance company to provide all the required maintenance and repairs for its trucks for the year at a flat price. Is this an insurance contract? *See Transportation Guarantee Co. v. Jellins,* 174 P.2d 625 (Cal. 1946).

2. An automobile dealer offered flat-priced "service contracts" to purchasers of new cars, pursuant to which the dealer promised to repair or replace a specified set of automobile components at no additional charge during the service contract period. Is this an insurance contract? *See Jim Click Ford v. City of Tucson,* 739 P.2d 1365 (Ariz. Ct. App. 1987).

3. An insurance company is considering selling "home service contracts" to consumers. The contracts would obligate the company to repair or replace specified home appliances and components (e.g., heating systems) during the service contract period. Is this insurance?

4. Auto rental companies are required in many states to provide "minimum financial responsibility (MFR)" protection to their renters as part of the auto rental package. This MFR protection covers the renter to approximately

the same extent as would the mandatory minimum auto insurance policy. Does providing this protection put auto rental companies in the insurance business? Auto rental companies also offer a number of optional protection contracts in connection with car rentals. They sell "collision damage waivers," which protect the renter from responsibility for damage to the rental car. They sell "liability protection contracts," which protect the renter from responsibility for damage to third parties (up to a specified limit). Does offering these optional protections put auto rental companies in the insurance business?

5. If the liability protection contracts in question 4 are not insurance, would similar long-term protection contracts sold by auto insurance dealers in connection with the sale of an auto be insurance? Can you draw a line between these two kinds of contracts that would address the factors enunciated by Vance and Keeton?

6. In connection with issuing loans, a bank decided to offer a "debt forgiveness" option at an additional charge. If the borrower elected to pay the additional fee, the bank would completely forgive the debt in the event of the borrower's death and temporarily waive the requirement of making payments during any period of disability. Is this insurance? Would it matter whether the fees for the debt forgiveness were calculated on an actuarial basis (i.e., in a similar fashion to life and disability insurance premiums)? Would it matter whether the bank itself purchased insurance to cover its obligation to forgive the loan payments? *See First Nat'l Bank v. Taylor*, 907 F.2d 775 (8th Cir. 1990).

7. Catastrophe bonds are financial instruments that insurance companies use to hedge their property insurance risks. A "cat bond" will pay the bondholder one interest rate if the number or cost of catastrophes in a given year is below a given threshold and another, lesser interest rate if the number or cost of catastrophes is above a given threshold. Cat bonds can be thought of as substitutes for reinsurance. (Reinsurance is insurance for insurance companies.) Are cat bonds "insurance"?

8. The widespread use of credit default swap (CDS) contracts was notoriously at the center of the financial crisis of 2008. In its most basic form, a CDS is a contract that provides lenders with protection against the risk of a defaulting borrower. The lender pays a premium to a third-party seller who promises in return that, in the event of a default on the loan by the borrower, it will indemnify the lender for its loss, usually in the amount of the unpaid balance of the loan. This version of the CDS looks very much like an insurance contract, with one party shifting a risk to another for a premium under circumstances in which the purchaser of the contract has what looks like an insurable interest in the underlying property interest being insured—here, the loan principal. In fact, however, CDS contracts were not limited to this sort of insurance function; rather, many investors used CDS contracts to speculate, in effect to gamble, on the possibility that a borrower might fall on hard times and not be able to pay its debts. As a result, when the market for mortgage-backed securities began to collapse in 2007 and 2008, the problem was made much worse because it triggered payouts on numerous large CDS contracts, which put an enormous strain on the large financial intermediaries who had sold many such contracts and whose financial health, it turns out, is crucial to the functioning of

overall global financial system. Some have argued that if CDS contracts had been regulated as insurance, the financial crisis of 2008 would not have happened, or at least it would have been substantially less severe. Indeed, the New York State Insurance Department at the time went so far as to announce plans to regulate credit derivatives as insurance, to prevent such financial disasters from happening in the future. *See* Circular Letter No. 19 (2008). This regulatory change never came to pass, however. Can you think of arguments for and against treating CDS contracts as insurance for state regulatory purposes? *Contrast* Arthur Kimball-Stanley, *Insurance and Credit Default Swaps: Should Like Things Be Treated Alike?*, 15 Conn. Ins. L. J. 241 (2008) (arguing that CDS contracts should be regulated as insurance because they create same moral hazard regulatory concern that traditional insurance contracts do) *with* M. Todd Henderson, *Credit Derivatives Are Not "Insurance,"* 16 Conn. Ins. L. J. 1 (2009) (arguing that CDS contracts should not be regulated as insurance for a long list of reasons, including (1) unlike the purchasers of most insurance contracts, the purchasers of CDS contracts tend to be knowledgeable and sophisticated; (2) because many CDS contracts are not meant to reduce risk but are instead pure speculation, they should not be regulated as insurance; (3) CDS contracts do not always involve risk pooling in the way that insurance contracts do; and (4) CDS contracts cannot be distinguished from countless other contracts that also involve risk shifting).

B. Insurance Federalism

Among the financial services industries, all of which are heavily regulated, insurance is unique in being almost exclusively regulated at the state level. This is at least in part the result of a long history of state regulation dating to the mid-nineteenth century, a time when the institutions of national government were arguably not up to the task of regulation, combined with the insurance industry later having successfully weathered the Depression era financial reverses that led to the federal regulation of the banking and securities industries. Traditionally, most insurance industry leaders have preferred state regulation to federal regulation.

Recently, however, there appears to be substantial support for establishing an optional federal insurance regulatory framework that insurance companies can invoke by obtaining a federal charter. For example, the National Insurance Act of 2006, S. 2509, 109th Cong., 2d Sess. (April 5, 2006), introduced into the U.S. Senate, would have created a "comprehensive system of Federal chartering, licensing, regulation, and supervision" of insurance companies and agents. That bill, however, did not pass. The most recent expansions of federal involvement in insurance regulation can be found in the Patient Protection and Affordable Care Act (PPACA), which somewhat alters the landscape for health insurance regulation (and is discussed more fully in chapter 3), and the Dodd-Frank Wall Street Reform and Consumer Protection Act ("Dodd-Frank"), Pub. L. 111-203, 124. Stat. 1376 (2010).

Dodd-Frank established a new Federal Insurance Office (FIO) within the U.S. Department of Treasury. The FIO is authorized under the statute to collect data on the insurance industry, including the affordability of insurance for traditionally underserved communities; recommend that an insurance company be subject to regulation as a nonbank financial company supervised by the [Dodd-Frank] Board of Governors; assist in negotiating "covered agreements" between the United States and foreign entities; and determine whether state insurance measures are preempted by such agreements.

In December 2013, FIO published its first major report in which it proposed reforms to both state and federal oversight and regulation of the insurance industry. The report including the following recommendations:

FIO believes that, in the short term, the U.S. system of insurance regulation can be modernized and improved by a combination of steps by the states and certain actions by the federal government. The recommendations are as follows.

Areas of Near-Term Reform for the States

Capital Adequacy and Safety/Soundness

1) For material solvency oversight decisions of a discretionary nature, states should develop and implement a process that obligates the appropriate state regulator to first obtain the consent of regulators from other states in which the subject insurer operates.

2) To improve consistency of solvency oversight, states should establish an independent, third-party review mechanism for the National Association of Insurance Commissioners Financial Regulation Standards Accreditation Program.

3) States should develop a uniform and transparent solvency oversight regime for the transfer of risk to reinsurance captives.

4) State-based solvency oversight and capital adequacy regimes should converge toward best practices and uniform standards.

5) States should move forward cautiously with the implementation of principles-based reserving and condition it upon: (1) the establishment of consistent, binding guidelines to govern regulatory practices that determine whether a domestic insurer complies with accounting and solvency requirements; and (2) attracting and retaining supervisory resources and developing uniform guidelines to monitor supervisory review of principles-based reserving.

6) States should develop corporate governance principles that impose character and fitness expectations on directors and officers appropriate to the size and complexity of the insurer.

7) In the absence of direct federal authority over an insurance group holding company, states should continue to develop approaches to group supervision and address the shortcomings of solo entity supervision.

8) State regulators should build toward effective group supervision by continued attention to supervisory colleges.

Reform of Insurer Resolution Practices

9) States should: (1) adopt a uniform approach to address the closing out and netting of qualified contracts with counterparties; and (2) develop requirements for transparent financial reporting regarding the administration of a receivership estate.

10) States should adopt and implement uniform policyholder recovery rules so that policyholders, irrespective of where they reside, receive the same maximum benefits from guaranty funds.

Marketplace Regulation

11) States should assess whether or in what manner marital status is an appropriate underwriting or rating consideration.

12) State-based insurance product approval processes should be improved by securing the participation of every state in the Interstate Insurance Product Regulation Commission (IIPRC) and by expanding the products subject to approval by the IIPRC. State regulators should pursue the development of nationally standardized forms and terms, or an interstate compact, to further streamline and improve the regulation of commercial lines.

13) In order to fairly protect consumers in all parts of the United States, every state should adopt and enforce the National Association of Insurance Commissioners Suitability in Annuities Transactions Model Regulation.

14) States should reform market conduct examination and oversight practices and: (1) require state regulators to perform market conduct examinations consistent with the National Association of Insurance Commissioners Market Regulation Handbook; (2) seek information from other regulators before issuing a request to an insurer; (3) develop standards and protocols for contract market conduct examiners; and (4) develop a list of approved contract examiners based on objective qualification standards.

15) States should monitor the impact of different rate regulation regimes on various markets in order to identify rate-related regulatory practices that best foster competitive markets for personal lines insurance consumers.

16) States should develop standards for the appropriate use of data for the pricing of personal lines insurance.

17) States should extend regulatory oversight to vendors that provide insurance score products to insurers.

18) States should identify, adopt, and implement best practices to mitigate losses from natural catastrophes.

Areas for Direct Federal Involvement in Regulation

1) Federal standards and oversight for mortgage insurers should be developed and implemented.

2) To afford nationally uniform treatment of reinsurers, FIO recommends that Treasury and the United States Trade Representative pursue a covered agreement for reinsurance collateral requirements based on the National Association of Insurance Commissioners Credit for Reinsurance Model Law and Regulation.

3) FIO should engage in supervisory colleges to monitor financial stability and identify issues or gaps in the regulation of large national and internationally active insurers.

4) The National Association of Registered Agents and Brokers Reform Act of 2013 should be adopted and its implementation monitored by FIO.

5) FIO will convene and work with federal agencies, state regulators, and other interested parties to develop personal auto insurance policies for U.S. military personnel enforceable across state lines.

6) FIO will work with state regulators to establish pilot programs for rate regulation that seek to maximize the number of insurers offering personal lines products.

7) FIO will study and report on the manner in which personal information is used for insurance pricing and coverage purposes.

8) FIO will consult with Tribal leaders to identify alternatives to improve the accessibility and affordability of insurance on sovereign Native American and Tribal lands.

9) FIO will continue to monitor state progress on implementation of Sub-title B of Title V of the Dodd-Frank Act, which requires states to simplify the collection of surplus lines taxes, and determine whether federal action may be warranted in the near term.

Federal Insurance Office, U.S. Department of the Treasury, How to Modernize and Improve the System of Insurance Regulation in the United States (December 2013).[2]

To understand these recommendations, it is necessary first to understand the context of the historically state-based regulation system of the insurance industry. Why is the insurance industry, unlike the banking industry, regulated primarily at the state level in the first place? What is the "National Association of Insurance Commissioners" (NAIC) referenced by the FIO report, and what role does it currently play? The following article excerpt provides a brief history of the NAIC and describes the unique approach to federalism in the area of insurance regulation. After reading the excerpt, return to the FIO recommendations and examine the extent to which—at least in the view of the federal regulators—the NAIC is living up to its promise.

INSURANCE REGULATION IN THE UNITED STATES: REGULATORY FEDERALISM AND THE NATIONAL ASSOCIATION OF INSURANCE COMMISSIONERS

Susan Randall
26 Fla. St. U. L. Rev. 625 (1999)

THE NATIONAL ASSOCIATION OF INSURANCE COMMISSIONERS

The NAIC is a voluntary association of the insurance commissioners from each of the fifty states, the District of Columbia, and the U.S. territories. Shortly after the 1868 Supreme Court decision in *Paul v. Virginia,* which established state supremacy over insurance, state regulators formed the NAIC to further what they viewed as necessary uniformity in insurance regulation. The history of the NAIC, from its beginning in 1871 to the present, illuminates the tension between state-level regulation and an acknowledged need for uniformity. The NAIC's central role in the United States system of insurance regulation demonstrates that, for the most part, the states' regulatory apparatus has been unable to function appropriately as individual units because of the complex national and international nature of the insurance industry.

PAUL V. VIRGINIA: INSURANCE IS SUBJECT TO STATE REGULATION

Organized regulation of the insurance industry by the states began in the mid-1800s. Faced with the need to supervise a burgeoning industry, several state legislatures created independent administrative agencies to supervise insurance within their borders. As insurance operations extended across states lines, the

2. This report is available at *https://www.treasury.gov/initiatives/fio/reports-and-notices/Documents/How%20to%20Modernize%20and%20Improve%20the%20System%20of%20Insurance%20Regulation%20in%20the%20United%20States.pdf.*

industry sought federal regulation to avoid burdensome multiple state regulations, preferring what it presumed would be weak federal regulation to sometimes aggressive state oversight.

Hoping to supplant state authority, several New York-based insurance companies hired Samuel Paul to represent them as an agent in Virginia but refused to deposit the licensing bond required by Virginia law. Paul was consequently denied a license to sell insurance. He sold policies, nonetheless, and was convicted of violating the Virginia statute. The Virginia Supreme Court affirmed the conviction, and insurance companies, led by the National Board of Fire Underwriters, used the case to challenge state regulation of insurance in the U.S. Supreme Court. Paul argued that Virginia's laws violated the Privileges and Immunities Clause by requiring additional security for foreign insurers and that the power to regulate insurance resided in the federal government under the Commerce Clause. The Supreme Court held that the insurers were not protected as "citizens" within the meaning of the Privileges and Immunities Clause and that "[i]ssuing a policy of insurance was not a transaction of commerce." Thus, the Supreme Court's decision placed the burden of insurance regulation squarely on the states, to the industry's disappointment. Further efforts also proved unsuccessful: the Supreme Court maintained its position that insurance was not subject to federal oversight, and attempts to amend the Constitution to permit the federal government to regulate insurance failed. . . .

In 1871 the New York superintendent of insurance, George W. Miller, asked the insurance commissioners in each of the thirty-six states to attend a meeting to discuss insurance regulation. Representatives of nineteen states attended, marking the beginning of what was then known as the National Insurance Convention. A contemporary account of the meeting emphasized the need for uniformity in protective regulation:

> In a session "remarkable for its harmony," the commissioners are now "fully prepared to go before their various legislative committees with recommendations for a system of insurance law which shall be the same in all states—not reciprocal, but identical; not retaliatory, but uniform. That repeated consultation and future concert of action will eventuate in the removal of discriminating and oppressive statutes which now disgrace our codes, and that the companies and the public will both be largely benefited, we have no manner of doubt."

Thirty states attended the next meeting that same year.

THE DEVELOPMENT OF STATE REGULATION

For three-quarters of a century after the Supreme Court decision in *Paul*, state authority over insurance regulation was unquestioned. By the 1940s, state regulation was fairly comprehensive, with the exception of rate regulation. Most states had adopted some form of rate regulation, but its scope and enforcement varied widely. For practical purposes, "insurance rate making was as yet largely uncontrolled in the United States."

In Missouri, however, the situation was different. Missouri's superintendent of insurance resisted rate increases and was sued by 139 insurance companies in 137 lawsuits brought to enjoin the prevention of rate increases. The court granted a temporary injunction permitting the increase but required that the difference between the old and new rates be deposited in the court until final disposition. Negotiations took place for several years, and in the late 1930s, the Missouri Superintendent of Insurance, Emmett O'Malley, a member of the Kansas City political machine, negotiated a settlement with the industry in exchange for substantial payoffs from 134 fire insurance companies. The insurers would receive higher future rates and eighty percent of the fund; the state would retain twenty percent. The Missouri attorney general, Roy McKittrick, filed suit against the companies contributing to the bribe, charging them with conspiracy to defraud the state and the policyholders and later with conspiracy to fix prices and limit competition. Because the conspiracy involved out-of-state insurers acting through multi-state rate-making bureaus, McKittrick took the matter to the U.S. Department of Justice.

In late 1942, a grand jury indicted South-Eastern Underwriters Association (SEUA), its officers, and the 198-member companies for violations of the Sherman Act, charging conspiracy to fix rates and the monopolization of trade in fire insurance. The district court, relying on *Paul,* dismissed the indictment. In 1944 the Supreme Court in *United States v. South-Eastern Underwriters Ass'n*, 322 U.S. 533 (1944) reversed its earlier decision in *Paul* and in a four-to-three decision held that insurance is interstate commerce subject to federal regulation under the Commerce Clause.

The decision was viewed as an assault on state regulatory and tax authority over the insurance industry, and the NAIC's response was swift. The NAIC proposed a bill that was introduced with revisions by Senators Pat McCarran (D-Nev.) and Warren Ferguson (R-Mich.), and signed into law by President Franklin Roosevelt on March 9, 1945. The McCarran-Ferguson Act declares that the business of insurance will be subject to state law:

> Congress hereby declares that the continued regulation and taxation by the several States of the business of insurance is in the public interest, and that silence on the part of the Congress shall not be construed to impose any barrier to the regulation or taxation of such business by the several States.

Under the Act, federal law supersedes state insurance regulation only if it specifically relates to "the business of insurance." If, however, the states do not regulate the business of insurance, the Sherman and Clayton Acts, as well the Federal Trade Commission Act, still apply.

Again, the NAIC responded quickly. In cooperation with the All-Industry Committee, a group of industry representatives organized by the NAIC, the NAIC drafted model laws to demonstrate that the states were regulating insurance and to preclude federal intervention. By the early 1950s, most of the states had enacted these laws.

NAIC GOALS AND FUNCTIONS

This history demonstrates the inconsistent dual commitment to uniformity of regulation and preservation of state regulation. The NAIC's constitution also reflects this tension. The NAIC's current constitution, adopted in 1980, articulates the basic goals of insurance regulation—to ensure the solvency of insurers and to protect policyholders—but includes a commitment to the preservation of state regulation and not, incidentally, to the preservation of the NAIC. The constitution provides:

> The objective of this body is to serve the public by assisting the several State insurance supervisory officials, individually and collectively, in achieving the following fundamental insurance regulatory objectives:
> (1) Maintenance and improvement of state regulation of insurance in a responsive and efficient manner;
> (2) Reliability of the insurance institution as to financial solidity and guaranty against loss;
> (3) Fair, just and equitable treatment of policyholders and claimants.

Prior to the adoption of its new constitution in 1980, the NAIC's stated objectives more clearly indicated its conflicting commitments to both centralized regulation and the preservation of regulation by the states. For more than a century, between its inception in 1871 until the adoption of the 1980 NAIC constitution, the NAIC stated its purposes in this way:

> The object of this association shall be to promote uniformity in legislation affecting insurance; to encourage uniformity in departmental rulings under the insurance laws of the several states; to disseminate information of value to insurance supervisory officials in the performance of their duties; to establish ways and means of fully protecting the interest of insurance policyholders of the various states, territories and insular possessions of the United States; and to preserve to the several states the regulation of the business of insurance.

Elsewhere, the NAIC stated a goal of creating a "national" regulatory system.

The tension among the NAIC's various organizational goals is evident: the goal of uniform, nationalized regulation is facially inconsistent with the preservation of autonomous regulation by the states. To preserve state regulation, the NAIC has increasingly assumed a national role, centralizing many basic regulatory functions and operating as a quasi-federal agency by attempting to enforce national standards.

The growth of the NAIC illustrates the states' increasing reliance on the NAIC to regulate what has become a national industry. In 1987 the NAIC's staff numbered about seventy and its budget was approximately $5.9 million. Its staff currently numbers at least 300, and its budget exceeds $40 million. Its complex organizational structure demonstrates the breadth and diversity of its tasks. As of April 1998, the NAIC had more than 115 different committees, subcommittees, task forces, and working groups. Its headquarters are located in Kansas City, Missouri, with a specialized office for uniform securities valuation in New York, and an office in Washington, D.C., to deal with legislative and policy issues.

The tasks performed by the NAIC also illustrate the increasing nationalization of insurance regulation. In addition to performing basic regulatory functions itself, the NAIC supports, coordinates, and, on some occasions, even directs state regulators. The NAIC performs centralized duties that mirror those of federal regulators in other industries, including the prescription of standard forms for insurance company annual financial statements; the coordination of regional financial examinations of insurance companies; the creation and maintenance of an extensive system of national databases to facilitate state monitoring of insurers and insurance agents; the rating of non-U.S. insurers for the states; the periodic review and accreditation of state insurance departments; the drafting of model laws and regulations, many of which have been adopted by state legislatures; the valuation of insurance company investments; training of state insurance regulators; the preparation of statistical reports for state regulators; the assistance to state regulators with technical financial analysis; and the assistance to U.S. officials negotiating international trade agreements that concern insurance issues.

In the midst of this expansion of its activities, staff, and funding, the NAIC has suffered something of an identity crisis. In 1995 the NAIC officially defined itself as a private trade organization. Around the same time, Robert M. Willis, District of Columbia insurance commissioner, described the NAIC as a "trade organization" and distinguished his role as a public official from his role as a member of the NAIC. Similarly, in a 1994 opinion, U.S. District Judge Peter Leisure stated that the NAIC was not a government body but "a private trade association composed of government regulators from different states."

None of these self-definitions squared with the NAIC's active and central role in the processes of state insurance regulation. In 1995, at the urging of some NAIC members, and in particular James Schacht, acting Illinois insurance commissioner, an NAIC working group prepared a written report discussing the NAIC's status. The group split over whether the NAIC was "a group of public officials imbued with the public trust" or "an instrumentality of the states." The membership of the NAIC ultimately concluded that it had characteristics of both. Schacht stated, "At least we know we are not a trade organization."

Regardless of the NAIC's difficulties defining itself, it is clear that the NAIC is a private rather than a governmental entity. This status carries two important implications: first, the NAIC has no power to compel the states or the industry, and second, the NAIC is a completely self-governing entity, neither accountable to voters nor subject to government oversight. Thus, although the NAIC has assumed a central and national role in insurance regulation, acting in many ways as a federal agency, it cannot sanction regulators or insurers, and it is not subject to various mechanisms designed to ensure fair and open regulatory policy making and processes, including the Administrative Procedure Act of 1966, the Federal Advisory Committee Act, the Freedom of Information Act (FOIA), the Government in the Sunshine Act, the Paperwork Reduction Act of 1980, or the state law analogues.

As a result, the NAIC is closely identified with the insurance industry. Capture of regulatory agencies by the regulated industry is a much-described and much-discussed phenomenon. However, the problem of capture as it exists in other regulatory contexts is minimal when compared to the problem in the insurance industry. The industry directly funds the NAIC. Each year the NAIC assesses insurance companies a fee, based on premium volume, to file information in its centralized databases. In recent years, database fees account for approximately half of the NAIC's revenues. In contrast, state assessments account for less than five percent of revenues. As a result, members of the industry view the NAIC as part of the industry[3] and accountable to the industry. Furthermore, much of the NAIC's work often appears to be in direct response to the industry. . . .

---

3. Spencer L. Kimball, writing in the late 1960s, observed:

> The insurance regulator is conceived by far too many insurance executives, and too often he conceives himself, as a part of the industry, existing to serve the industry. Indeed, I have heard life insurance men express the notion that it would be useful to have a national regulator to "represent" the industry in the executive branch of the national government. Nothing unsavory was intended—whatever else one may say about the insurance business, it is a business run by honorable men. However, the notion that a regulator should "represent" the industry is a subtly corrupted point of view.

In addition to creating the FIO, Dodd-Frank created the Financial Stability Oversight Council (FSOC) and gave it broad authority to identify, monitor, and regulate large financial institutions—including insurance companies—whose failure could cause another financial crisis similar to the one in 2008. The FSOC has exercised this authority to designate three large insurance companies—MetLife, Inc., American International Group, Inc., and Prudential Financial, Inc.—as "systemically important" financial institutions, a designation that subjects those companies to greater oversight and enhanced capital requirements. MetLife challenged its designation in federal court, arguing, among other things, that the FSOC arbitrarily and capriciously failed to take into account the costs to the company of this designation. The federal district court in the District of Columbia agreed with Metlife. *MetLife v. Financial Stability Oversight Council,* 2016 WL 1391569 (March 30, 2016). That decision is currently under appeal.

Following is the text of the McCarran-Ferguson Act (MFA), discussed in Professor Randall's article above. For decades, the MFA has been the "quasiconstitutional" basis for the division between federal and state authority for regulation of insurance. Read the text of the statute very carefully, and then take some time to read the small sample of the many, many cases that apply the MFA in various contexts.

THE McCARRAN-FERGUSON ACT

15 U.S.C. §1011.   Declaration of Policy

The Congress hereby declares that the continued regulation and taxation by the several States of the business of insurance is in the public interest, and that silence on the part of the Congress shall not be construed to impose any barrier to the regulation or taxation of such business by the several States.

15 U.S.C. §1012.   Regulation by State Law; Federal Law Relating Specifically to Insurance; Applicability of Certain Federal Laws After June 30, 1948

(a) State regulation. The business of insurance, and every person engaged therein, shall be subject to the laws of the several States which relate to the regulation or taxation of such business.

(b) Federal regulation. No Act of Congress shall be construed to invalidate, impair, or supersede any law enacted by any State for the purpose of regulating the business of insurance, or which imposes a fee or tax upon such business, unless such Act specifically relates to the business of insurance: Provided, That after June 30, 1948, the Act of July 2, 1890, as amended, known as the Sherman Act, and the Act of October 15, 1914, as amended, known as the Clayton Act, and the Act of September 26, 1914, known as the Federal Trade Commission Act, as amended, shall be applicable to the business of insurance to the extent that such business is not regulated by State law.

Spencer Kimball, *The Case for State Regulation of Insurance, in* Insurance, Government, and Social Policy: Studies in Insurance Regulation 411, 432 (Spencer L. Kimball & Herbert S. Denenberg eds., 1969).

15 U.S.C. §1013. Suspension until June 30, 1948, of Application of Certain Federal Laws; Sherman Act Applicable to Agreements to, or Acts of, Boycott, Coercion, or Intimidation

(a) Until June 30, 1948, the Act of July 2, 1890, as amended, known as the Sherman Act, and the Act of October 15, 1914, as amended, known as the Clayton Act and the Act of September 26, 1914, known as the Federal Trade Commission Act, as amended, and the Act of June 19, 1936, known as the Robinson-Patman Antidiscrimination Act, shall not apply to the business of insurance or to acts in the conduct thereof.

(b) Nothing contained in this Act shall render the said Sherman Act inapplicable to any agreement to boycott, coerce, or intimidate, or act of boycott, coercion, or intimidation.

The U.S. Supreme Court has addressed the boundaries of McCarran-Ferguson's reverse preemption in an important series of cases that we will sample below. The first case addresses the power of the SEC to regulate variable annuities. In the process, the opinion limits the definition of "insurance" under the act. To understand the court's reasoning, you'll need to pay careful attention to the difference between a traditional (or fixed) annuity and a variable annuity. For our purposes, it is not important for you to understand what a "security" is, other than to accept that the statutory definition is broad enough to include both traditional and variable annuities.

SECURITIES & EXCHANGE COMMISSION v. VARIABLE ANNUITY LIFE INSURANCE CO.

Supreme Court of the United States
359 U.S. 65 (1959)

Mr. Justice DOUGLAS delivered the opinion of the Court.

This is an action instituted by the Securities and Exchange Commission to enjoin respondents from offering their annuity contracts to the public without registering them under the Securities Act of 1933, 48 Stat. 74, 15 U.S.C. §77a, and complying with the Investment Company Act of 1940, 54 Stat. 789, 15 U.S.C. §80a. . . .

Respondents are regulated under the insurance laws of the District of Columbia and several other States. It is argued that that fact brings into play the provisions of the McCarran-Ferguson Act, 59 Stat. 33, 15 U.S.C. §1011, §2(b) of which provides that "No Act of Congress shall be construed to invalidate, impair or supersede any law enacted by any State for the purpose of regulating the business of insurance. . . ." It is said that the conditions under which that law is applicable are satisfied here. The District of Columbia and some of the States are "regulating" these annuity contracts and, if the Commission is right, the Federal Acts would at least to a degree "supersede" the state regulations since the Federal Acts prescribe their own peculiar requirements. Moreover, "insurance" or "annuity" contracts are exempt from the Securities Act when "subject to the supervision of the insurance commissioner . . . of any State. . . ." Respondents are also exempt from the Investment Company Act if they are "organized as an insurance company, whose primary and predominant business activity is the writing of insurance . . . and which is subject to supervision by the insurance commissioner . . . of a State. . . ." While the term "security" as defined in the Securities Act[4] is broad enough to include any "annuity" contract, and the term "investment company" as defined in the Investment Company Act[5] would embrace an "insurance company," the scheme of the exemptions lifts pro tanto the requirements of those two Federal Acts to the extent that respondents are actually regulated by the States as insurance companies, *if indeed they are such.* The question common to the exemption provisions of the Securities Act and the Investment Company Act and to §2(b) of the McCarran-Ferguson Act is whether respondents are issuing contracts of insurance.

We start with a reluctance to disturb the state regulatory schemes that are in actual effect, either by displacing them or by superimposing federal requirements on transactions that are tailored to meet state requirements. When the States speak in the field of "insurance," they speak with the authority of a long tradition. For the regulation of "insurance," though within the ambit of federal power (*United States v. South-Eastern Underwriters Assn.,* 322 U.S. 533 (1944)), has traditionally been under the control of the States. We deal, however, with federal statutes where the words "insurance" and "annuity" are federal terms. Congress was legislating concerning a concept which had taken on its coloration and meaning largely from state law, from state practice, from state usage. Some States deny these "annuity" contracts any status as "insurance." Others accept them under their "insurance" statutes. It is apparent that there is no uniformity in the rulings of the States on the nature of these "annuity" contracts. In any event how the States may have ruled is not decisive. For, as we have said, the meaning of "insurance" or "annuity" under these Federal Acts is a federal question.

While all the States regulate "annuities" under their "insurance" laws, traditionally and customarily they have been fixed annuities, offering the annuitant specified and definite amounts beginning with a certain year of his or her life. The standards for investment of funds underlying these annuities have been conservative. The variable annuity introduced two new features. First, premiums

---

4. Section 2(1) provides:

When used in this title, unless the context otherwise requires—

(1) The term "security" means any note, stock, treasury stock, bond, debenture, evidence of indebtedness, certificate of interest or participation in any profit-sharing agreement, collateral-trust certificate, preorganization certificate or subscription, transferable share, investment contract, voting-trust certificate, certificate of deposit for a security, fractional undivided interest in oil, gas, or other mineral rights, or, in general, any interest or instrument commonly known as a "security," or any certificate of interest or participation in, temporary or interim certificate for, receipt for, guarantee of, or warrant or right to subscribe to or purchase, any of the foregoing.

15 U.S.C. §77(b)(1).

5. Section 3(a) provides in part:

When used in this title, "investment company" means any issuer which—

(1) is or holds itself out as being engaged primarily, or proposes to engage primarily, in the business of investing, reinvesting, or trading in securities; . . .

(3) is engaged or proposes to engage in the business of investing, reinvesting, owning, holding, or trading in securities, and owns or proposes to acquire investment securities having a value exceeding 40 per centum of the value of such issuer's total assets (exclusive of Government securities and cash items) on an unconsolidated basis.

collected are invested to a greater degree in common stocks and other equities. Second, benefit payments vary with the success of the investment policy. The first variable annuity apparently appeared in this country about 1952 when New York created the College Retirement Equities Fund to provide annuities for teachers. It came into existence as a result of a search for a device that would avoid paying annuitants in depreciated dollars. The theory was that returns from investments in common stocks would over the long run tend to compensate for the mounting inflation. The holder of a variable annuity cannot look forward to a fixed monthly or yearly amount in his advancing years. It may be greater or less, depending on the wisdom of the investment policy. In some respects the variable annuity has the characteristics of the fixed and conventional annuity: payments are made periodically; they continue until the annuitant's death or in case other options are chosen until the end of a fixed term or until the death of the last of two persons; payments are made both from principal and income; and the amounts vary according to the age and sex of the annuitant. Moreover, actuarially both the fixed-dollar annuity and the variable annuity are calculated by identical principles. Each issuer assumes the risk of mortality from the moment the contract is issued. That risk is an actuarial prognostication that a certain number of annuitants will survive to specified ages. Even if a substantial number live beyond their predicted demise, the company issuing the annuity—whether it be fixed or variable—is obligated to make the annuity payments on the basis of the mortality prediction reflected in the contract. This is the mortality risk assumed both by respondents and by those who issue fixed annuities. It is this feature, common to both, that respondents stress when they urge that this is basically an insurance device.

The difficulty is that, absent some guarantee of fixed income, the variable annuity places all the investment risks on the annuitant, none on the company. The holder gets only a *pro rata* share of what the portfolio of equity interests reflects—which may be a lot, a little, or nothing. We realize that life insurance is an evolving institution. Common knowledge tells us that the forms have greatly changed even in a generation. And we would not undertake to freeze the concepts of "insurance" or "annuity" into the mold they fitted when these Federal Acts were passed. But we conclude that the concept of "insurance" involves some investment risk-taking on the part of the company. The risk of mortality, assumed here, gives these variable annuities an aspect of insurance. Yet it is apparent, not real; superficial, not substantial. In hard reality the issuer of a variable annuity that has no element of a fixed return assumes no true risk in the insurance sense. It is no answer to say that the risk of declining returns in times of depression is the reciprocal of the fixed-dollar annuitant's risk of loss of purchasing power when prices are high and gain of purchasing power when they are low. We deal with a more conventional concept of risk-bearing when we speak of "insurance." For in common understanding "insurance" involves a guarantee that at least some fraction of the benefits will be payable in fixed amounts. *See Spellacy v. American Life Ins. Ass'n*, 131 A.2d 834, 839 (Conn. 1957); 1 Couch, Cyclopedia of Insurance Law, §25; 1 Richards, Law of Insurance, §27; 1 Appleman, Insurance Law and Practice, §81. The companies that issue these annuities take the risk of failure. But they guarantee nothing to the annuitant except an interest in a portfolio of common stocks or other equities—an interest that has a ceiling but no floor. There is no true underwriting of risks, the one earmark of insurance as it has commonly been conceived of in popular understanding and usage. Reversed.

Mr. Justice HARLAN, whom Mr. Justice FRANKFURTER, Mr. Justice CLARK, and Mr. Justice WHITTAKER join, dissenting. . . .

The characteristics of a typical variable annuity contract have been adumbrated by the majority. It is sufficient to note here that, as the majority concludes, as the two lower courts found, and as the SEC itself recognizes, it may fairly be said that variable annuity contracts contain both "insurance" and "securities" features. It is certainly beyond question that the "mortality" aspect of these annuities—that is the assumption by the company of the entire risk of longevity—involves nothing other than classic insurance concepts and procedures, and I do not understand how that feature can be said to be "not substantial," determining as it does, apart from options, the commencement and duration of annuity payments to the policyholder. On the other hand it cannot be denied that the investment policies underlying these annuities, and the stake of the annuitants in their success or failure, place the insurance company in a position closely resembling that of a company issuing certificates in a periodic payment investment plan. Even so, analysis by fragmentization is at best a hazardous business, and in this instance has, in my opinion, led the Court to unsound legal conclusions. It is important to keep in mind that these are not cases where the label "annuity" has simply been attached to a securities scheme, or where the offering companies are traveling under false colors, in an effort to avoid federal regulation. The *bona fides* of this new development in the field of insurance is beyond dispute.

The Court's holding that these two companies are subject to SEC regulation stems from its preoccupation with a constricted "color matching" approach to the construction of the relevant federal statutes which fails to take adequate account of the historic congressional policy of leaving regulation of the business of insurance entirely to the States. It would be carrying coals to Newcastle to reexamine here the history of that policy which was fully canvassed in the several opinions of the Justices in *United States v. South-Eastern Underwriters Assn.*, 322 U.S. 533 (1944), . . . Suffice it to say that in consequence of this Court's decision 90 years ago in *Paul v. Virginia*, 75 U.S. 168 (1968), and the many cases following it, there had come to be "widespread doubt" prior to the time the Securities and Investment Company Acts were passed "that the Federal Government could enter the field [of insurance regulation] at all." *Wilburn Boat Co. v. Fireman's Fund Ins. Co.*, 348 U.S. 310, 318 (1955). . . .

In 1944, this Court removed the supposed constitutional basis for exemption of insurance by holding, in *United States v. South-Eastern Underwriters Assn.*, *supra*, that the business of insurance was subject to federal regulation under the commerce power. Congress was quick to respond. It forthwith enacted the McCarran Act, 59 Stat. 33, 15 U.S.C. §§1011-1015, which on its face demonstrates the purpose "broadly to give support to the existing and future state systems for regulating and taxing the business of insurance," *Prudential Ins. Co. v. Benjamin*, 328 U.S. 408, 429 (1946) and "to assure that existing state power to regulate insurance would continue." *Wilburn Boat Co. v. Fireman's Fund Ins. Co.*, *supra*, at 319. Thus, rather than encouraging Congress to enter the field of insurance, the *South-Eastern* decision spurred reiteration of its undeviating policy of abstention.

In this framework of history the course for us in these cases seems to me plain. We should decline to admit the SEC into this traditionally state regulatory domain.

Admittedly the variable annuity was not in the picture when the Securities and Investment Company Acts were passed. It is a new development combining both substantial insurance and securities features in an experiment designed to accommodate annuity insurance coverage to contingencies of the present day economic climate. This, however, should not be allowed to obscure the fact that Congress intended when it enacted these statutes to leave the future regulation of the business of insurance wholly with the States. This intent, repeatedly expressed in a history of which the Securities and Investment Company Acts were only a part, in my view demands that *bona fide* experiments in the insurance field, even though a particular development may also have securities aspects, be classed within the federal exemption of insurance, and not within the federal regulation of securities. Certainly these statutes breathe no notion of concurrent regulation by the SEC and state insurance authorities. The fact that they do not serves to reinforce the view that the congressional exemption of insurance was but another manifestation of the historic federal policy leaving regulation of the business of insurance exclusively to the States. . . .

NOTES AND QUESTIONS

1. Would variable annuities be "insurance" under the state law approaches set out in the preceding section? If the McCarran-Ferguson Act was designed to maintain state primacy in the field of insurance regulation, should the state courts' views on the definition of insurance be given deference by the federal courts? Why not?

2. Kimball and Heaney have criticized the *Variable Annuity Life Insurance Co.* (*VALIC*) opinion for overstating the difference between traditional and variable annuities, on the grounds that "the conservative interest assumptions made by the insurance company make the assumption of investment risk almost illusory. . . . The crucial risk assumed by the insurer, the mortality risk, has been equally assumed in both cases and the investment risk, while not assumed at all by the insurer in the one case [variable annuities] is scarcely more than nominally assumed by the insurer in the other." Spencer L. Kimball & Barbara P. Heaney, Federalism and Insurance Regulation: Basic Source Materials 71 (1995). By the same reasoning, would the reliability of mortality tables make the assumption of the mortality risk equally "almost illusory" from the perspective of the insurance company (although certainly hot from that of the insured)? Think back to the law of large numbers in the first chapter. So long as the insurer has a large enough pool, the mortality risk is just as illusory as the investment risk in a traditional annuity.

3. One of the main things that is at stake here is who gets to sell annuities. If annuities have to be registered under the Securities Act, the seller must be licensed by the National Association of Securities Dealers. If annuities are "insurance," exempt from the act, the seller must be a licensed insurance agent. Today, many financial advisors hold both sets of licenses, but that

was not the case historically. More recently, the status of annuities became an issue in the competition between banks and insurance companies. In the early 1990s, national banks petitioned the Comptroller of the Currency to declare that national banks are authorized to sell both traditional and variable annuities because the sales are "incidental" to the "business of banking" under the National Bank Act, which explicitly permits national banks to purchase and sell "securities and stock without recourse, solely upon the order, and for the account of, its customers," and explicitly prohibits "underwrit[ing] any issue of securities or stock." The comptroller agreed with the banks. *VALIC* challenged the comptroller's decision, which eventually reached the Supreme Court. The Court agreed with the comptroller, holding that "for the purpose at hand, annuities are properly classified as investments, not 'insurance.'" *NationsBank v. Variable Annuity Life Ins. Co.*, 513 U.S. 251 (1995). The *NationsBank* Court did not cite *SEC v. VALIC* or make any attempt to rationalize the results in the two *VALIC* cases. Can you?

4. In an influential article that made a persuasive case for thinking about insurance regulation in comparison to other forms of financial regulation, Professor Howell Jackson explained why insurance regulation is, in general, more intrusive than other forms of financial services regulation, such as securities and banking regulation. *See* Howell E. Jackson, *Regulation in a Multisectored Financial Services Industry,* 77 Wash. U. L.Q. 319 (1999). Both insurance and banking are more risky than selling securities because banks and insurance companies bear investment risk (at least when they are engaged in "traditional" banking and insurance activities). Insurance is more risky than banking, however, because the conditions that affect whether and how much an insurance company has to pay to a particular customer are more uncertain. Jackson explained that the greater insolvency risk leads to more intrusive regulation and, therefore, an incentive for companies to engage in what Jackson called "regulatory arbitrage": attempting to have financial products classified into a category with less intrusive regulation. According to this logic, we would expect companies to argue that variable annuities are "securities," not "insurance," in order to take advantage of the less intrusive federal securities regulatory regime.

5. This case illustrates a federalism dynamic that complicates Professor Jackson's observations. For insurance companies, which already operate under insurance regulation and presumably have become comfortable with that regulation, the McCarran-Ferguson Act provides an incentive to offer other kinds of financial arrangements under the label "insurance" so that the regulatory regimes governing those other kinds of financial arrangements do not apply to the insurance company. Comparing securities and insurance regulation, we can see that securities regulation in fact is less intrusive. Although of course there are exceptions, the governing principle in securities regulation is *disclosure*. Insurance regulation contains disclosure-oriented elements, along with others. The most important other elements are those directed at protecting the solvency of the insurance company. Why should variable annuities be subject to the (on the whole) less protective securities regulatory regime? Should insurance companies offering variable annuities be subject to overlapping regulatory regimes?

SEMI-ANNIE'S VARIABLE ANNUITY PROBLEM

Following the Supreme Court decision in *VALIC,* an insurance entrepreneur incorporated Semi-Annie, Inc., under the laws of the State of Superior and obtained a license from the State of Superior to issue annuities. The annuities differed from the variable annuities at issue in *VALIC* in two ways. First, they guaranteed a minimum 1 percent annual return. Second, in return for that guaranteed return, the "upside" potential was limited, such that the maximum return that the policyholders would earn in any particular year was 3 percentage points less than the return earned in Semi-Annie's underlying investment account. So, for example, if Semi-Annie's investment account earned 10 percent in a given year, the policyholders annuity accounts would earn only 7 percent for that year. On the other hand, if Semi-Annie's investment account lost 50 percent in a given year, the policyholders' accounts would nevertheless earn a 1 percent return for the year. Are Semi-Annie's semivariable annuities contracts of insurance within the meaning of the federal securities laws addressed in *VALIC?*

The next case addresses the power of the SEC to regulate insurance companies' communications with their shareholders. The opinion limits the definition of "business of insurance" under the Act. Consider how the results in this case square with the definitions of insurance explored in the "What is insurance?" unit of this chapter. What might explain the narrower approach to "insurance" in the federal opinions as compared to that in the state opinions?

SECURITIES & EXCHANGE COMMISSION v. NATIONAL SECURITIES, INC.

Supreme Court of the United States
393 U.S. 453 (1969)

Mr. Justice MARSHALL delivered the opinion of the Court.

This case raises some complex questions about the Securities and Exchange Commission's power to regulate the activities of insurance companies and of persons engaged in the insurance business. The Commission originally brought suit in the United States District Court for the District of Arizona, pursuant to §21(e) of the Securities Exchange Act of 1934, 48 Stat. 900, as amended, 15 U.S.C. §78u(e). . . . According to the amended complaint, National Securities and various persons associated with it had contrived a fraudulent scheme centering on a contemplated merger between National Life & Casualty Insurance Co. (National Life), a firm controlled by National Securities, and Producers Life Insurance Co. (Producers). The details of the alleged scheme are not important here. . . . In plain language, Producers' shareholders were not told that they were going to pay part of the cost of National Securities' acquisition of control in their company.

The Commission was denied temporary relief, and shortly thereafter Producers' shareholders and the Arizona Director of Insurance approved the merger. The two companies were formally consolidated into National Producers Life Insurance Co. on July 9, 1965. . . .

Respondents contend that [the McCarran-Ferguson] Act bars the present suit since the Arizona Director of Insurance found that the merger was not "inequitable to the stockholders of any domestic insurer" and not otherwise "contrary to law," as he was required to do under the state insurance laws. Ariz. Rev.

Stat. Ann. §20-731 (Supp. 1969). If the Securities Exchange Act were applied, respondents argue, these laws would be "superseded." The SEC sees no conflict between state and federal law; it contends that the applicable Arizona statutes did not give the State Insurance Director the power to determine whether respondents had made full disclosure in connection with the solicitation of proxies. Although respondents disagree, we do not find it necessary to inquire into this state-law dispute. The first question posed by this case is whether the relevant Arizona statute is a "law enacted . . . for the purpose of regulating the business of insurance" within the meaning of the McCarran-Ferguson Act. Even accepting respondents' view of Arizona law, we do not believe that a state statute aimed at protecting the interests of those who own stock in insurance companies comes within the sweep of the McCarran-Ferguson Act. Such a statute is not a state attempt to regulate "the business of insurance," as that phrase was used in the Act. . . .

The question here is whether state laws aimed at protecting the interests of those who own securities in insurance companies are the type of laws referred to in the 1945 enactment. The legislative history of the McCarran-Ferguson Act offers no real assistance. Congress was mainly concerned with the relationship between insurance ratemaking and the antitrust laws, and with the power of the States to tax insurance companies. *See, e.g.,* 91 Cong. Rec. 1087-1088 (remarks of Congressmen Hancock and Celler). The debates centered on these issues, and the Committee reports shed little light on the meaning of the words "business of insurance." *See* S. Rep. No. 20, 79th Cong., 1st Sess. (1945); H. R. Rep. No. 143, 79th Cong., 1st Sess. (1945). In context, however, it is relatively clear what problems Congress was dealing with. Under the regime of *Paul v. Virginia, supra,* States had a free hand in regulating the dealings between insurers and their policyholders. Their negotiations, and the contract which resulted, were not considered commerce and were, therefore, left to state regulation. The *South-Eastern Underwriters* decision threatened the continued supremacy of the States in this area. The McCarran-Ferguson Act was an attempt to turn back the clock, to assure that the activities of insurance companies in dealing with their policyholders would remain subject to state regulation. As the House Report makes clear, "it [was] not the intention of Congress in the enactment of this legislation to clothe the States with any power to regulate or tax the business of insurance beyond that which they had been held to possess prior to the decision of the United States Supreme Court in the *Southeastern Underwriters Association* case." H. R. Rep. No. 143, 79th Cong., 1st Sess., 3 (1945).

Given this history, the language of the statute takes on a different coloration. The statute did not purport to make the States supreme in regulating all the activities of insurance *companies;* its language refers not to the persons or companies who are subject to state regulation, but to laws "regulating the *business* of insurance." Insurance companies may do many things which are subject to paramount federal regulation; only when they are engaged in the "business of insurance" does the statute apply. Certainly the fixing of rates is part of this business; that is what *South-Eastern Underwriters* was all about. The selling and advertising of policies, *FTC v. National Casualty Co.,* 357 U.S. 560 (1958), and the licensing of companies and their agents, cf. *Robertson v. California,* 328 U.S. 440 (1946), are also within the scope of the statute. Congress was concerned with the type of state regulation that centers around the contract of insurance, the transaction which *Paul v. Virginia* held was not "commerce." The relationship between insurer and insured, the type of policy which could be issued, its reliability, interpretation, and enforcement—these were the core of the "business of insurance." Undoubtedly, other activities of insurance companies relate so closely to their status as reliable insurers that they too must be placed in the same class. But whatever the exact scope of the statutory term, it is clear where the focus was—it was on the relationship between the insurance company and the policyholder. Statutes aimed at protecting or regulating this relationship, directly or indirectly, are laws regulating the "business of insurance."

In this case, Arizona is concerning itself with a markedly different set of problems. It is attempting to regulate not the "insurance" relationship, but the relationship between a stockholder and the company in which he owns stock. This is not insurance regulation, but securities regulation. It is true that the state statute applies only to insurance companies. But mere matters of form need not detain us. The crucial point is that here the State has focused its attention on stockholder protection; it is not attempting to secure the interests of those purchasing insurance policies. Such regulation is not within the scope of the McCarran-Ferguson Act. . . .

NOTES AND QUESTIONS

1. In a decision that has important implications for the application of a broad range of federal civil rights and consumer protection statutes, the Supreme Court addressed the application of RICO—the Racketeer-Influenced and Corrupt Organizations Act—to insurance activity. *Humana Inc. v. Forsyth*, 525 U.S. 299 (1999). RICO does not "specifically relate to the business of insurance." Nevertheless, the Court permitted the application of RICO in an insurance fraud case because there was no state insurance law that RICO would "invalidate, impair, or supersede." The Court adopted the following formulation of the "invalidate, impair, or supersede" test:

    > When federal law does not directly conflict with state regulation, and when application of the federal law would not frustrate any declared state policy or interfere with a State's administrative regime, the McCarran-Ferguson Act does not preclude its application.

    The Court noted that this formulation was proposed by the NAIC in an amicus brief. *Id.* at 307.

2. The common thread that links all or most of the Supreme Court's McCarran-Ferguson Act cases is the preservation of traditional federal authority even when that authority affects insurance companies. We find state law decisions that take an expansive view of insurance to ensure that the public obtains the benefits of insurance regulation in a broad range of activities. And we find federal law decisions that take a narrow view of insurance to ensure that the public obtains the benefits of a wide variety of federal statutes. The one place where this dynamic breaks down is the Employee Retirement Income Security Act (ERISA). As we saw in Chapter 3, ERISA preempts state regulation of health and disability insurance without providing anything in its place. In the McCarran-Ferguson Act cases, defining insurance narrowly generally protects the public by allowing room for federal enforcement.

But in the ERISA context, defining insurance narrowly leaves employees exposed to an unregulated health care benefits market.

3. The next case applies *Humana* to an effort to obtain redress for the apparent Unum/Provident disability insurance fraud that Professor John Langbein described in "Trust Law as Regulatory Law: The Unum/Provident Scandal and Judicial Review of Benefit Denials Under ERISA," the Northwestern Law Review article excerpted in Section V of Chapter 3. In this case, one of the Unum/Provident companies is attempting to use the McCarran-Ferguson Act to avoid a RICO claim.

WEISS v. FIRST UNUM LIFE INSURANCE CO.

United States Court of Appeals, Third Circuit
482 F.3d 254 (2007)

RENDELL, Circuit Judge.

Richard Weiss brought suit under the Racketeer Influenced and Corrupt Organizations Act ("RICO"), 18 U.S.C. §§1961-1968, against his insurer, First Unum Life Insurance Co. ("First Unum"), claiming that First Unum discontinued payment of his disability benefits as part of First Unum's racketeering scheme involving an intentional and illegal policy of rejecting expensive payouts to disabled insureds. The District Court dismissed his claim, believing that the allowance of such a RICO claim would interfere with New Jersey's statutory regulation of insurers, and thus run afoul of the McCarran-Ferguson Act. We disagree and will reverse.

FACTUAL AND PROCEDURAL HISTORY

The facts of the underlying RICO suit are straightforward. From July 1997 to August 2001, Weiss was employed by Tucker Anthony Sutro as an investment banker. He was insured by First Unum through a group insurance policy with Tucker Anthony Sutro. The policy provided long-term disability benefits when the insured is "'limited from performing the material and substantial duties of [his] regular occupation due to . . . sickness or injury.'" On January 2, 2001, Weiss suffered an acute heart attack requiring an emergency angioplasty. On June 25, 2001, he was hospitalized again due to ventricular tachycardia. Weiss continues to suffer from severe left ventricular dysfunction and extremely low blood pressure, resulting in frequent lightheadedness, weakness, and shortness of breath. After suffering the initial attack, Weiss filed a claim in May 2001 stating that he was totally disabled and seeking long-term disability benefits under the group disability plan issued by First Unum to Tucker. First Unum approved the claim and paid Weiss the maximum short-term disability benefit available under the plan from January 2, 2001 (the date of the infarction) to July 1, 2001. Weiss applied for and was paid long-term disability benefits from July 26, 2001, to October 23, 2001, at which point First Unum discontinued Weiss's benefits. The reason First Unum did so is at the heart of Weiss's federal RICO challenge. . . .

On November 26, 2002, Weiss filed claims based on violations of RICO and conspiracy to violate RICO; violation of New Jersey's state RICO Act; conspiracy to violate New Jersey's RICO Act; wrongful termination of insurance benefits; negligent and intentional infliction of emotional distress; and violation of New

Jersey's Consumer Fraud Act ("CFA"), N.J. Stat. Ann. §56:8-1-20. Specifically, Weiss alleges that his claim was targeted for termination because it exceeded $11,000 per month. He alleges that on October 3, 2001, defendants David Gilbert, Paul Keenan, George DiDonna, Lucy-Baird Stoddard, and others conspired at a roundtable meeting to terminate Weiss's benefits and devise a rationalization for doing so. Weiss claims that DiDonna did not receive or examine his hospital records until the termination decision was reached, and that tests that would make clear the severity of his injury were purposely never ordered. He avers not merely a bad-faith denial of benefits limited to his case, but rather that his denial is one instance in a pattern of fraudulent activity by First Unum aimed at depriving its insureds with large disability payouts of their contractual benefits. . . .

DISCUSSION

In order to determine whether the District Court was correct, we must first explicate the purpose and contours of the McCarran-Ferguson Act. The McCarran-Ferguson Act, was enacted in 1945 in response to the decision in *United States v. South-Eastern Underwriters Association,* 322 U.S. 533 (1944), which held that Congress could regulate the business of insurance with its Commerce Clause authority. Section 1 of the Act, codified at 15 U.S.C. §1011, expressed Congress's "Declaration of Policy."

> The Congress hereby declares that the continued regulation and taxation by the several States of the business of insurance is in the public interest, and that silence on the part of the Congress shall not be construed to impose any barrier to the regulation or taxation of such business by the several States.

Section 2 of the Act, codified at 15 U.S.C. §1012, set forth Congress's attempt to explain the federal-state balance that was intended:

> (a) State regulation. The business of insurance, and every person engaged therein, shall be subject to the laws of the several States which relate to the regulation or taxation of such business.
> (b) Federal regulation. No Act of Congress shall be construed to invalidate, impair, or supersede any law enacted by any State for the purpose of regulating the business of insurance, or which imposes a fee or tax upon such business, unless such Act specifically relates to the business of insurance: Provided, That after June 30, 1948, the Act of July 2, 1890, as amended, known as the Sherman Act, and the Act of October 15, 1914, as amended, known as the Clayton Act, and the Act of September 26, 1914, known as the Federal Trade Commission Act, as amended, shall be applicable to the business of insurance to the extent that such business is not regulated by State law.

Thereafter, in *Prudential Insurance Co. v. Benjamin,* 328 U.S. 408 (1946), the Supreme Court explained the legislative intent behind the statute. It wrote that Congress's purpose

> was broadly to give support to the existing and future state systems for regulating and taxing the business of insurance. This was done in two ways. One was by

removing obstructions which might be thought to flow from its own power, whether dormant or exercised, except as otherwise provided in the Act itself or in future legislation. The other was by declaring expressly and affirmatively that continued state regulation and taxation of this business is in the public interest and that the business and all who engage in it "shall be subject to" the laws of the several states in these respects.

Id. at 429-430.

Years later in the comprehensive opinion in *Sabo v. Metropolitan Life Insurance Co.,* 137 F.3d 185 (3d Cir. 1998), a case involving the relationship between RICO and Pennsylvania's Unfair Insurance Practices Act ("UIPA"), 40 Pa. Cons. Stat. Ann. §§1171.1-.15 (1999), we canvassed the different features of the Act and parsed the terms of Section 2(b), including what constituted the "business of insurance." There, as here, the case turned on the initial portion of Section 2(b) — "No Act of Congress shall be construed to invalidate, impair, or supersede any law enacted by any State for the purpose of regulating the business of insurance. . . ." — as RICO clearly is not a law "specifically relating to the business of insurance." In *Sabo* we noted that the "phrase 'invalidate, impair, or supersede' is not defined anywhere in the Act," and we were thus "faced with the considerable task of grappling with its construction." *Sabo,* 137 F.3d at 193. . . .

One year later, the Supreme Court in *Humana Inc. v. Forsyth,* 525 U.S. 299 (1999), provided an authoritative explanation of the phrase "invalidate, impair, or supersede," as once again RICO was the basis for a McCarran-Ferguson Act challenge. At issue in *Humana* was the impact civil RICO would have on the Nevada state insurance system. The Court noted that in Section 2(b) of the Act Congress was attempting to control the interplay between the federal and state laws not yet written. "In §2(b) of the Act . . . Congress ensured that federal statutes not identified in the Act or not yet enacted would not automatically override state insurance regulation. Section 2(b) provides that when Congress enacts a law specifically relating to the business of insurance, that law controls." *Id.* at 307. In charting the scope of Section 2(b), the Court rejected the view that "Congress intended to cede the field of insurance regulation to the States, saving only instances in which Congress expressly orders otherwise." *Id.* at 308. At the same time that it rejected any notion of field preemption, it also rejected "the polar opposite of that view, i.e., that Congress intended a green light for federal regulation whenever the federal law does not collide head on with state regulation." *Id.* at 309. With those extremes rejected, the Supreme Court established the following formulation for applying §1012(b): "When federal law does not directly conflict with state regulation, and when application of the federal law would not frustrate any declared state policy or interfere with a State's administrative regime, the McCarran-Ferguson Act does not preclude its application." *Id.* at 310.

Noting that there was no direct conflict with Nevada's state regulation, the Supreme Court then examined a variety of factors to assess the impact of RICO. The Court began by noting that "Nevada provides both statutory and common-law remedies to check insurance fraud." *Humana,* 525 U.S. at 311. In addition to the administrative penalties that could be imposed on violators, "[v]ictims of insurance fraud may also pursue private actions under Nevada law." *Id.* at 312. "Moreover, the Act is not hermetically sealed; it does not exclude application of other state laws, statutory or decisional. Specifically, Nevada law provides that an insurer is under a common-law duty to negotiate with its insureds in good faith and to deal with them fairly." *Id.* at 312 (quotations omitted).

The Supreme Court also cited both the availability of punitive damages, *id.* at 313, and the scope of those damages. The Court noted that "plaintiffs seeking relief under Nevada law may be eligible for damages exceeding the treble damages available under RICO." *Id.* Concluding, the Court wrote that it saw

> no frustration of state policy in the RICO litigation at issue here. RICO's private right of action and treble damages provision appears to complement Nevada's statutory and common-law claims for relief. In this regard, we note that Nevada filed no brief at any stage of this lawsuit urging that application of RICO to the alleged conduct would frustrate any state policy, or interfere with the State's administrative regime. We further note that insurers, too, have relied on the statute when they were the fraud victims.

Id. (citation omitted).

In sum, the *Humana* analysis explored the specific interplay between RICO and the state insurance scheme. As described above, the non-exclusive list of factors the Court examined in *Humana* included the following: (1) the availability of a private right of action under state statute; (2) the availability of a common law right of action; (3) the possibility that other state laws provided grounds for suit; (4) the availability of punitive damages; (5) the fact that the damages available (in the case of Nevada, punitive damages) could exceed the amount recoverable under RICO, even taking into account RICO's treble damages provision; (6) the absence of a position by the State as to any interest in any state policy or their administrative regime; and (7) the fact that insurers have relied on RICO to eradicate insurance fraud. *Humana,* 525 U.S. at 311-314. . . .

With this background and these principles in mind, we turn now to the case before us. The District Court concluded that the New Jersey scheme was far more limited than the Nevada scheme that the Supreme Court had found compatible with RICO in *Humana,* and accordingly held that the RICO claims were barred by Section 2(b). The District Court reviewed the New Jersey regulatory scheme and found several reasons why RICO would "frustrate . . . declared state policy or interfere with [New Jersey's] administrative regime." *Weiss v. First Unum Life Ins. Co.,* 416 F. Supp. 2d 298, 301 (D.N.J. 2005). New Jersey's Insurance Trade Practices Act ("ITPA") regulates the business of insurance in New Jersey, and ITPA has no private right of action for insureds. Nor does ITPA provide for punitive damages. . . .

Weiss urges on appeal that the District Court erred as a matter of law in failing to recognize that New Jersey has "long favored and approved cumulative private and public remedies to combat unfair insurance practices and insurance fraud." Appellant's Br. 14. Weiss argues that there is no state policy mandating the exclusivity of the ITPA as a remedy for insurance frauds, and that the absence of a statutory right of action is not dispositive under *Humana.* Moreover he argues that ITPA is complemented, not impaired, by the presence of civil RICO. . . .

First Unum urges that allowing RICO claims such as Weiss's would frustrate New Jersey's comprehensive system of laws regulating the insurance industry. First Unum's reading of *Humana* is that the "McCarran-Ferguson Act precludes a RICO action in a case such as this unless the applicable state insurance law permits an aggrieved policy holder or beneficiary to seek recovery of damages similar in nature to those permitted under RICO." Respondents' Br. 19-20.

Similarly it argues that McCarran-Ferguson "precludes a Federal RICO action unless the law of the state in which the RICO action is filed provides for recovery of damages analogous to those provided by RICO," Respondents' Br. 14, and that analogous damages are not available in New Jersey.

We review the District Court's decision de novo, and we must assess the impact of the federal law in question in light of the *Humana* factors. . . . We begin with an overview of ITPA, and will examine the component parts of the New Jersey regulatory scheme as they relate to claims such as this.

ITPA empowers a Commissioner to "examine and investigate into the affairs of every person engaged in the business of insurance in this State in order to determine whether such person has been or is engaged in any unfair method of competition or in any unfair or deceptive act or practice prohibited by . . . this act." N.J. Stat. §17:29B-5. This includes unfair claim-settlement practices, such as "[r]efusing to pay claims without conducting a reasonable investigation based upon all available information," §17:29B-4(9)(d), and "[n]ot attempting in good faith to effectuate prompt, fair and equitable settlements of claims in which liability has become reasonably clear," N.J. Stat. §17:29B-4(9)(f). If after conducting a hearing the commissioner concludes that the business practice violates ITPA's provisions, the commissioner "shall make his findings in writing and shall issue and cause to be served upon the person charged with the violation an order requiring such person to cease and desist from engaging in such method of competition, act or practice." §17:29B-7(a). The commissioner may also "order payment of a penalty not to exceed $1,000.00 for each and every act or violation unless the person knew or reasonably should have known he was in violation of this chapter, in which case the penalty shall be not more than $5,000.00 for every act or violation." *Id.*

The powers to investigate violations are not entirely within the Commissioner's discretion. "A person aggrieved by a violation of this act may file a complaint with the Commissioner of Banking and Insurance. Upon receipt of the complaint, the commissioner *shall* investigate an insurer to determine whether the insurer has violated any provision of this act." §17:29B-18 (emphasis added). After such investigation, the Commissioner may "order an insurer that is in violation to pay a monetary penalty of $5,000 for each violation," §17:29B-18b(1), "order the insurer to make restitution to the aggrieved person," §17:29B-18b(2), or "obtain equitable relief in a State or federal court of competent jurisdiction against an insurer, as well as the costs of suit, attorney's fees and expert witness fees," §17:29B-18b(3). Aside from these forms of relief available, ITPA explicitly notes that its penalties are not intended to be exclusive. "The powers vested in the commissioner by this act shall be additional to any other powers to enforce any penalties, fines or forfeitures authorized by law with respect to the methods, acts and practices hereby declared to be unfair or deceptive." §17:29B-12. In sum, the New Jersey system is best seen as limited, regulating without setting forth private remedies yet not explicitly or implicitly excluding other remedies.

(1) STATUTORY PRIVATE RIGHT OF ACTION

The parties agree that there is no private right of action under ITPA, but differ as to the implications of this conclusion. First Unum urges that this absence is the legislature's intention; Weiss urges that the lack of the provision is simply the product of a legislative impasse. (The New Jersey Supreme Court in *Pickett v. Lloyd's,* 621 A.2d 445 (1993), noted that "on the score of whether we should recognize a [common law] remedy for the wrong, we realize that legislation has been proposed to provide such a remedy, but has not yet passed." 621 A.2d at 452 (citing New Jersey legislative record)). The parties do agree, however, that the "absence of a private cause of action under the ITPA does not end the inquiry," Respondents' Br. 43, and First Unum acknowledges that ITPA itself conceives of its penalties working in tandem with others. *See* §17:29B-12 ("The powers vested in the commissioner by this act shall be additional to any other powers to enforce any penalties, fines or forfeitures authorized by law with respect to the methods, acts and practices hereby declared to be unfair or deceptive"). Accordingly, we view the absence of a private right of action in ITPA as an obstacle to Weiss's claim, but by no means an insurmountable one.

(2) COMMON LAW RIGHT

The parties agree that New Jersey provides a common law right of action against insurers for the recoupment of wrongly withheld benefits. In *Pickett v. Lloyd's,* 621 A.2d 445 (N.J. 1993), the New Jersey Supreme Court "recognize[d] a remedy for bad-faith refusal" of benefits, despite the absence of New Jersey statutory law that would provide such a remedy. *Id.* at 452. The fact that this is one of the few recognized methods for recoupment of benefits outside the administrative apparatus is urged by the parties as pointing to opposite conclusions. Weiss claims this shows that RICO would not disturb the administrative regime, while First Unum argues that the legislature's decision not to enact a statutory right of action after *Pickett* reflects a desire for a limited remedial scheme. Nevertheless, it is undisputed that a common-law right of recovery is available in New Jersey.

(3) OTHER STATE LAWS

We noted in *Sabo* that treble damages were available under other Pennsylvania statutes, and that this undercut the argument that the insurance scheme was intended to be exclusive. "Pennsylvania courts have held that the state's general consumer protection statute . . . provides a private remedy and treble damages for victims of insurance fraud. This certainly undercuts any purported balance struck by the Pennsylvania legislature favoring administrative enforcement to the exclusion of private damages actions and we see no reason why a federal private right of action cannot coexist with the UIPA in these circumstances." *Sabo,* 137 F.3d at 195 (citation omitted).

Similarly, the New Jersey Consumer Fraud Act (CFA) makes treble damages available to redress violations. By its terms, the CFA prohibits:

> The act, use or employment by any person of any unconscionable commercial practice, deception, fraud, false promise, misrepresentation, or the knowing concealment, suppression, or omission of any material fact with intent that others rely upon such concealment, suppression or omission, *in connection with the sale or advertisement of any merchandise or real estate, or with the subsequent performance of such person as aforesaid,* whether or not any person has in fact been misled, deceived or damaged thereby. . . .

N.J. Stat. Ann. §56:8-2 (emphasis added). . . .

(4)-(5) AVAILABILITY OF PUNITIVE DAMAGES AND SCOPE
OF POSSIBLE DAMAGES

New Jersey law also appears to be unclear as to whether punitive damages are available against insurance companies on facts such as these. Weiss contends that *Pickett* left the door open for punitive damages to be awarded in a suit based on common law. While *Pickett* stated that "wrongful withholding of benefits . . . does not thereby give rise to a claim for punitive damages," 621 A.2d at 455, it nonetheless indicated that on some fact patterns a cause of action independent from the bad-faith denial of benefits could be sustained: "Carriers are not insulated from liability for independent torts in the conduct of their business. For example, '[d]eliberate, overt and dishonest dealings,' insult and personal abuse constitute torts entirely distinct from the bad-faith claim." *Id.* Further, the *Pickett* Court added that "in order to sustain a claim for punitive damages, a plaintiff would have to show something other than a breach of the good-faith obligation as we have defined it." *Id.* The parties have argued whether a racketeering scheme constitutes conduct so wrongful as to warrant punitive damages. We think it is at the very least arguable that a racketeering scheme by an insurer against its insureds would constitute a distinct and egregious tort under New Jersey law.

(6) PRESENCE OR ABSENCE OF STATE BRIEF

Although the State of New Jersey has not informed us of any "declared state policy," the District Court found a limiting policy implicit in the structure of the New Jersey scheme, and found it would be frustrated and impaired by RICO. First Unum, taking a cue from the District Court, argues that the decision by the state legislature not to amend the ITPA to provide a statutory right of action after *Pickett* was decided weighs against allowing the RICO suit. "The absence of such a [statutory] claim . . . is the product of a reasoned and declared public policy of the state of New Jersey." Respondents' Br. 24 (citing *Pickett*). We conclude that the inferences to be drawn from legislative action (and inaction) are not so clear. Further, one would have assumed that such a "reasoned and declared public policy" would have led to New Jersey's voicing its interest at every stage of the instant litigation. That has not happened. The fact that ITPA was not amended after *Pickett* could mean that the state legislature believed the common law remedy adequate; it could also mean that it assumed that RICO would apply and therefore that remedy was adequate as well. Or, other legislative priorities could have taken precedence. In short, there is no "declared state policy" conspicuous from the structure of New Jersey law or the pattern of legislative history. We can draw no specific conclusion from New Jersey's silence; if anything, it weighs against First Unum.

(7) RELIANCE BY STATE INSURERS

There is no evidence in the record as to the reliance by state insurers on federal civil RICO provisions in New Jersey. But it is logical to assume, as the Supreme Court did in *Humana*, that deeming federal civil RICO suits to be unavailable because they would impair the state scheme would deprive insurers of an important weapon of self-defense. *See Humana*, 525 U.S. at 314 ("We further note that insurers, too, have relied on the statute when they were the fraud victims."); *see also* Eric Beal, Note, *It's Better to Have Twelve Monkeys Chasing You Than One Gorilla:* Humana Inc. v. Forsyth, *The McCarran-Ferguson Act, RICO, and Deterrence,* 5 Conn. Ins. L.J. 751, 776 (1998-1999) ("Paradoxically, if Humana Inc. had prevailed [insurers] might have hampered the insurance industry's ability via RICO to 'fight back' against fraud committed by policyholders[]. RICO has been described as being 'the single most valuable tool available to insurers through the American jurisprudence system.' Insurers have brought RICO actions for fraud against policyholders, attorneys, and other insurance companies.") (citations and footnotes omitted). We find that depriving all players in the New Jersey insurance scheme of the right to sue under RICO is not part of the state's declared insurance policy, and we cannot simply presume such an atypical legislative aim from the structure of New Jersey's insurance laws.

Examining the above factors in this case as compared to *Humana,* it is clear that the aspects of the Nevada scheme presented a clearer case, and it might even be said that the finding by the unanimous Court that the two schemes "complement[ed]" each other, *Humana,* 525 U.S. at 313, was not subject to serious debate. Here, the allowance of treble damages, or punitive damages analogous to the treble damages available under RICO, is not as clear. The issue, then, is whether the absence of extensive legislative regulation of claims against insurers or provision of remedies, coupled with judicial sanctioning of certain remedies for bad faith denials of benefits, indicates that RICO would impair the state regulatory scheme. We think not. There is nothing in the regulatory scheme that indicates that allowing other remedies as part of its regulation of insurance would frustrate or interfere with New Jersey's insurance regime. To the contrary, the legislation permits additional remedies, *see* §17:29B-12, and the New Jersey courts have felt free to fashion them. Moreover, the New Jersey Supreme Court's reasoning in *Lemelledo* [*Lemelledo v. Beneficial Management Corp. of Amer.,* 150 N.J. 255 (1997)] in connection with the CFA points to encouraging, rather than limiting, other remedies in this area.

Furthermore, RICO embodies federal policies of an expansive nature. *See Sedima v. Imrex Co.,* 473 U.S. 479, 498 (1985) ("RICO was an aggressive initiative to supplement old remedies and develop new methods for fighting crime"). The need for this type of regulation was not contemplated when McCarran-Ferguson was enacted. We should be wary of underestimating the significance of these federal policies and should not go out of our way to find impairment of a state scheme when such impairment is not clear. . . .

After canvassing the *Humana* factors, we are left with the firm conviction that RICO does not and will not impair New Jersey's state insurance scheme. Though RICO is a powerful tool, we conclude as the Supreme Court did in *Humana* that "we see no frustration of state policy in the RICO litigation at issue here." 525 U.S. at 313. Indeed, in light of the common law and statutory remedies available, we do not read New Jersey's scheme as intended to be exclusive. Nor do we find that RICO will disturb or interfere with New Jersey's state insurance regime. RICO's provisions supplement the statutory and common-law claims for relief available under New Jersey law. We conclude that RICO augments New Jersey's insurance regime; it does not impair it.

The previous McCarran-Ferguson Act cases examined the scope of the act's reverse preemption. 42 U.S.C. §1013 contains an exception to the reverse preemption rule for Sherman Act antitrust claims involving "an agreement to boycott, coerce, or intimidate, or an act of boycott, coercion, or intimidation." The following case discusses the application of that exception. In the process, it presents a fascinating picture of the relationship between primary insurers and reinsurers during the mid-1980s, when some powerful members of the industry wished to shift the commercial general liability (CGL) market to a claims-made form of coverage.

This case presents an opportunity for you to review some of the topics covered in Chapter 4 and introduces the concept of reinsurance, which is a form of insurance that insurance companies buy to transfer some of the risk that they assume when they sell insurance. In the first edition of this casebook, the insurance regulation chapter was Chapter 3. One of the main reasons for moving insurance regulation to the end of the book was to make sure that students would have the liability background necessary to understand this very interesting case.

HARTFORD FIRE INSURANCE CO. v. CALIFORNIA

Supreme Court of the United States
509 U.S. 764 (1993)

Justice SOUTER. . . .

The Sherman Act makes every contract, combination, or conspiracy in unreasonable restraint of interstate or foreign commerce illegal. 26 Stat. 209, as amended, 15 U.S.C. §1. These consolidated cases present questions about the application of that Act to the insurance industry, both here and abroad. The plaintiffs (respondents here) allege that both domestic and foreign defendants (petitioners here) violated the Sherman Act by engaging in various conspiracies to affect the American insurance market. A group of domestic defendants argues that the McCarran-Ferguson Act, 59 Stat. 33, as amended, 15 U.S.C. §1011 *et seq.*, precludes application of the Sherman Act to the conduct alleged. . . . We hold that most of the domestic defendants' alleged conduct is not immunized from antitrust liability by the McCarran-Ferguson Act. . . .

I

The two petitions before us stem from consolidated litigation comprising the complaints of 19 States and many private plaintiffs alleging that the defendants, members of the insurance industry, conspired in violation of §1 of the Sherman Act to restrict the terms of coverage of commercial general liability (CGL) insurance available in the United States. Because the cases come to us on motions to dismiss, we take the allegations of the complaints as true.

A

According to the complaints, the object of the conspiracies was to force certain primary insurers (insurers who sell insurance directly to consumers) to change the terms of their standard CGL insurance policies to conform with the policies the defendant insurers wanted to sell. The defendants wanted four changes.

First, CGL insurance has traditionally been sold in the United States on an "occurrence" basis, through a policy obligating the insurer "to pay or defend claims, whenever made, resulting from an accident or 'injurious exposure to conditions' that occurred during the [specific time] period the policy was in effect." App. 22 (Cal. Complaint P52). In place of this traditional "occurrence" trigger of coverage, the defendants wanted a "claims-made" trigger, obligating the insurer to pay or defend only those claims made during the policy period. Such a policy has the distinct advantage for the insurer that when the policy period ends without a claim having been made, the insurer can be certain that the policy will not expose it to any further liability. Second, the defendants wanted the "claims-made" policy to have a "retroactive date" provision, which would further restrict coverage to claims based on incidents that occurred after a certain date. Such a provision eliminates the risk that an insurer, by issuing a claims-made policy, would assume liability arising from incidents that occurred before the policy's effective date, but remained undiscovered or caused no immediate harm. Third, CGL insurance has traditionally covered "sudden and accidental" pollution; the defendants wanted to eliminate that coverage. Finally, CGL insurance has traditionally provided that the insurer would bear the legal costs of defending covered claims against the insured without regard to the policy's stated limits of coverage; the defendants wanted legal defense costs to be counted against the stated limits (providing a "legal defense cost cap").

To understand how the defendants are alleged to have pressured the targeted primary insurers to make these changes, one must be aware of two important features of the insurance industry. First, most primary insurers rely on certain outside support services for the type of insurance coverage they wish to sell. Defendant Insurance Services Office, Inc. (ISO), an association of approximately 1,400 domestic property and casualty insurers (including the primary insurer defendants, Hartford Fire Insurance Company, Allstate Insurance Company, CIGNA Corporation, and Aetna Casualty and Surety Company), is the almost exclusive source of support services in this country for CGL insurance. ISO develops standard policy forms and files or lodges them with each State's insurance regulators; most CGL insurance written in the United States is written on these forms. All of the "traditional" features of CGL insurance relevant to this litigation were embodied in the ISO standard CGL insurance form that had been in use since 1973 (1973 ISO CGL form). For each of its standard policy forms, ISO also supplies actuarial and rating information: it collects, aggregates, interprets, and distributes data on the premiums charged, claims filed and paid, and defense costs expended with respect to each form, and on the basis of these data it predicts future loss trends and calculates advisory premium rates. Most ISO members cannot afford to continue to use a form if ISO withdraws these support services.

Second, primary insurers themselves usually purchase insurance to cover a portion of the risk they assume from the consumer. This so-called "reinsurance" may serve at least two purposes, protecting the primary insurer from catastrophic loss, and allowing the primary insurer to sell more insurance than its own financial capacity might otherwise permit. Thus, "the availability of reinsurance affects the ability and willingness of primary insurers to provide insurance to their customers." Insurers who sell reinsurance themselves often purchase insurance to cover part of the risk they assume from the primary insurer; such "retrocessional reinsurance" does for reinsurers what reinsurance does for primary insurers. Many of the defendants here are reinsurers or reinsurance brokers, or play some other specialized role in the reinsurance business; defendant Reinsurance Association of America (RAA) is a trade association of domestic reinsurers.

B

The prehistory of events claimed to give rise to liability starts in 1977, when ISO began the process of revising its 1973 CGL form. For the first time, it proposed two CGL forms (1984 ISO CGL forms), one the traditional "occurrence" type, the other "with a new 'claims-made' trigger." The "claims-made" form did not have a retroactive date provision, however, and both 1984 forms covered "'sudden and accidental' pollution" damage and provided for unlimited coverage of legal defense costs by the insurer. Within the ISO, defendant Hartford Fire Insurance Company objected to the proposed 1984 forms; it desired elimination of the "occurrence" form, a retroactive date provision on the "claims-made" form, elimination of sudden and accidental pollution coverage, and a legal defense cost cap. Defendant Allstate Insurance Company also expressed its desire for a retroactive date provision on the "claims-made" form. Majorities in the relevant ISO committees, however, supported the proposed 1984 CGL forms and rejected the changes proposed by Hartford and Allstate. In December 1983, the ISO Board of Directors approved the proposed 1984 forms, and ISO filed or lodged the forms with state regulators in March 1984.

Dissatisfied with this state of affairs, the defendants began to take other steps to force a change in the terms of coverage of CGL insurance generally available, steps that, the plaintiffs allege, implemented a series of conspiracies in violation of §1 of the Sherman Act. . . .

The [plaintiffs] charge the four domestic primary insurer defendants and varying groups of domestic and foreign reinsurers, brokers, and associations with conspiracies to manipulate the ISO CGL forms. In March 1984, primary insurer Hartford persuaded General Reinsurance Corporation (General Re), the largest American reinsurer, to take steps either to procure desired changes in the ISO CGL forms, or "failing that, [to] 'derail' the entire ISO CGL forms program." General Re took up the matter with its trade association, RAA, which created a special committee that met and agreed to "boycott" the 1984 ISO CGL forms unless a retroactive-date provision was added to the claims-made form, and a pollution exclusion and defense cost cap were added to both forms. RAA then sent a letter to ISO "announcing that its members would not provide reinsurance for coverages written on the 1984 CGL forms," and Hartford and General Re enlisted a domestic reinsurance broker to give a speech to the ISO Board of Directors, in which he stated that no reinsurers would "break ranks" to reinsure the 1984 ISO CGL forms.

The four primary insurer defendants (Hartford, Aetna, CIGNA, and Allstate) also encouraged key actors in the London reinsurance market, an important provider of reinsurance for North American risks, to withhold reinsurance for coverages written on the 1984 ISO CGL forms. As a consequence, many London-based underwriters, syndicates, brokers, and reinsurance companies informed ISO of their intention to withhold reinsurance on the 1984 forms, and at least some of them told ISO that they would withhold reinsurance until ISO incorporated all four desired changes into the ISO CGL forms.

For the first time ever, ISO invited representatives of the domestic and foreign reinsurance markets to speak at an ISO Executive Committee meeting. At that meeting, the reinsurers "presented their agreed upon positions that there would be changes in the CGL forms or no reinsurance." The ISO Executive Committee then voted to include a retroactive-date provision in the claims-made form, and to exclude all pollution coverage from both new forms. (But it neither eliminated the occurrence form, nor added a legal defense cost cap.) The 1984 ISO CGL forms were then withdrawn from the marketplace, and replaced with forms (1986 ISO CGL forms) containing the new provisions. After ISO got regulatory approval of the 1986 forms in most States where approval was needed, it eliminated its support services for the 1973 CGL form, thus rendering it impossible for most ISO members to continue to use the form. . . .

C

Nineteen States and a number of private plaintiffs filed 36 complaints against the insurers involved in this course of events, charging that the conspiracies described above violated §1 of the Sherman Act, 15 U.S.C. §1. After the actions had been consolidated for litigation in the Northern District of California, the defendants moved to dismiss for failure to state a cause of action, or, in the alternative, for summary judgment. The District Court granted the motions to dismiss. *In re Insurance Antitrust Litigation,* 723 F. Supp. 464 (1989). It held that the conduct alleged fell within the grant of antitrust immunity contained in §2(b) of the McCarran-Ferguson Act, 15 U.S.C. §1012(b), because it amounted to "the business of insurance" and was "regulated by State Law" within the meaning of that section; none of the conduct, in the District Court's view, amounted to a "boycott" within the meaning of the §3(b) exception to that grant of immunity. 15 U.S.C. §1013(b).

The Court of Appeals reversed. *In re Insurance Antitrust Litigation,* 938 F.2d 919 (9th Cir. 1991). Although it held the conduct involved to be "the business of insurance" within the meaning of §2(b), it concluded that the defendants could not claim McCarran-Ferguson Act antitrust immunity . . . [because] the conduct alleged . . . fell within the §3(b) exception for "act[s] of boycott, coercion, or intimidation." . . .

II

The petition in No. 91-1111 touches on the interaction of two important pieces of economic legislation. The Sherman Act declares "every contract, combination in the form of trust or otherwise, or conspiracy, in restraint of trade or commerce among the several States, or with foreign nations, . . . to be illegal." 15 U.S.C. §1. The McCarran-Ferguson Act provides that regulation of the insurance industry is generally a matter for the States, 15 U.S.C. §1012(a), and (again, generally) that "no Act of Congress shall be construed to invalidate, impair, or supersede any law enacted by any State for the purpose of regulating the business of insurance," §1012(b). Section 2(b) of the McCarran-Ferguson Act makes it clear nonetheless that the Sherman Act applies "to the business of insurance to the extent that such business is not regulated by State Law," §1012(b), and §3(b) provides that nothing in the McCarran-Ferguson Act "shall render the . . . Sherman Act inapplicable to any agreement to boycott, coerce, or intimidate, or act of boycott, coercion, or intimidation," §1013(b). . . .

Justice SCALIA delivered the opinion of the Court. . . .

Determining proper application of §3(b) of the McCarran-Ferguson Act to the present cases requires precise definition of the word "boycott." It is a relatively new word, little more than a century old. It was first used in 1880, to describe the collective action taken against Captain Charles Boycott, an English agent managing various estates in Ireland. The Land League, an Irish organization formed the previous year, had demanded that landlords reduce their rents and had urged tenants to avoid dealing with those who failed to do so. Boycott did not bend to the demand and instead ordered evictions. In retaliation, the tenants "sent Captain Boycott to Coventry in a very thorough manner." J. McCarthy, England Under Gladstone 108 (1886). "The population of the region for miles round resolved not to have anything to do with him, and, as far as they could prevent it, not to allow any one else to have anything to do with him. . . . The awful sentence of excommunication could hardly have rendered him more helplessly alone for a time. No one would work for him; no one would supply him with food." *Id.,* at 108-109. Thus, the verb made from the unfortunate Captain's name has had from the outset the meaning it continues to carry today. To "boycott" means "to combine in refusing to hold relations of any kind, social or commercial, public or private, with (a neighbor), on account of political or other differences, so as to punish him for the position he has taken up, or coerce him into abandoning it." 2 Oxford English Dictionary 468 (2d ed. 1989).

Petitioners have suggested that a boycott ordinarily requires "an absolute refusal to deal on any terms," which was concededly not the case here. We think not. As the definition just recited provides, the refusal may be imposed "to punish [the target] for the position he has taken up, or *coerce him into abandoning it.*" The refusal to deal may, in other words, be *conditional,* offering its target the incentive of renewed dealing if and when he mends his ways. This is often the case—and indeed seems to have been the case with the original Boycott boycott. *Cf.* McCarthy, *supra,* at 109 (noting that the Captain later lived "at peace" with his neighbors). Furthermore, other dictionary definitions extend the term to include a *partial* boycott—a refusal to engage in some, but not all, transactions with the target. *See* Webster's New International Dictionary 321 (2d ed. 1950) (defining "boycott" as "to withhold, wholly *or in part,* social or business intercourse from, as an expression of disapproval or means of coercion" (emphasis added)).

It is, however, important—and crucial in the present cases—to distinguish between a conditional boycott and a concerted agreement to seek particular terms in particular transactions. A concerted agreement to terms (a "cartelization") is "a way of obtaining and exercising market power by concertedly exacting terms like those which a monopolist might exact." L. Sullivan, Law of Antitrust 257 (1977). The parties to such an agreement (the members of a cartel) are not engaging in a boycott. . . .

Thus, if Captain Boycott's tenants had agreed among themselves that they would refuse to renew their leases unless he reduced his rents, that would have been a concerted agreement on the terms of the leases, but not a boycott. The tenants, of course, did more than that; they refused to engage in other, unrelated transactions with Boycott—*e.g.,* selling him food—unless he agreed to

662 6 Insurance Regulation

their terms on rents. It is this expansion of the refusal to deal beyond the targeted transaction that gives great coercive force to a commercial boycott: unrelated transactions are used as leverage to achieve the terms desired. . . .

In addition to its use in the antitrust field, the concept of "boycott" frequently appears in labor law, and in this context as well there is a clear distinction between boycotts and concerted agreements seeking terms. The ordinary strike seeking better contract terms is a "refusal to deal" —*i.e.,* union members refuse to sell their labor until the employer capitulates to their contract demands. But no one would call this a boycott, because the conditions of the "refusal to deal" relate directly to the terms of the refused transaction (the employment contract). A refusal to work changes from strike to boycott only when it seeks to obtain action from the employer unrelated to the employment contract. This distinction is well illustrated by the famous boycott of Pullman cars by Eugene Debs' American Railway Union in 1894. The incident began when workers at the Pullman Palace Car Company called a strike, but the "boycott" occurred only when other members of the American Railway Union, not Pullman employees, supported the strikers by refusing to work on any train drawing a Pullman car. See *In re Debs,* 158 U.S. 564, 566-567 (1895) (statement of the case). The refusal to handle Pullman cars had nothing to do with Pullman cars themselves (working on Pullman cars was no more difficult or dangerous than working on other cars); rather, it was in furtherance of the collateral objective of obtaining better employment terms for the Pullman workers. In other labor cases as well, the term "boycott" invariably holds the meaning that we ascribe to it: Its goal is to alter, not the terms of the refused transaction, but the terms of workers' employment.

The one case in which we have found an activity to constitute a "boycott" within the meaning of the McCarran-Ferguson Act is *St. Paul Fire & Marine Ins. Co. v. Barry,* 438 U.S. 531 (1978). There the plaintiffs were licensed physicians and their patients, and the defendant (St. Paul) was a malpractice insurer that had refused to renew the physicians' policies on an "occurrence" basis, but insisted upon a "claims made" basis. The allegation was that, at the instance of St. Paul, the three other malpractice insurers in the State had collectively refused to write insurance for St. Paul's customers, thus forcing them to accept St. Paul's renewal terms. Unsurprisingly, we held the allegation sufficient to state a cause of action. The insisted upon condition of the boycott (not being a former St. Paul policyholder) was "artificial": it bore no relationship (or an "artificial" relationship) to the proposed contracts of insurance that the physicians wished to conclude with St. Paul's competitors.

Under the standard described, it is obviously not a "boycott" for the reinsurers to "refuse to reinsure coverages written on the ISO CGL forms until the desired changes were made," because the terms of the primary coverages are central elements of the reinsurance contract—they are *what* is reinsured. The "primary policies are . . . the basis of the losses that are shared in the reinsurance agreements." 1 B. Webb, H. Anderson, J. Cookman, & P. Kensicki, Principles of Reinsurance 87 (1990). Indeed, reinsurance is so closely tied to the terms of the primary insurance contract that one of the two categories of reinsurance (assumption reinsurance) substitutes the reinsurer for the primary or "ceding" insurer and places the reinsurer into contractual privity with the primary insurer's policyholders. And in the other category of reinsurance (indemnity reinsurance), either the terms of the underlying insurance policy are incorporated by reference (if the reinsurance is written under a facultative agreement), or (if the reinsurance is conducted on a treaty basis) the reinsurer will require full disclosure of the terms of the underlying insurance policies and usually require that the primary insurer not vary those terms without prior approval.

Justice Souter simply disregards this integral relationship between the terms of the primary insurance form and the contract of reinsurance. He describes the reinsurers as "individuals and entities who were not members of ISO, and who would not ordinarily be parties to an agreement setting the terms of primary insurance, not being in the business of selling it." *Ante,* at 788. While this factual assumption is crucial to Justice Souter's reasoning (because otherwise he would not be able to distinguish permissible agreements among primary insurers), he offers no support for the statement. But even if it happens to be true, he does not explain why it *must* be true—that is, why the law must exclude reinsurers from full membership and participation. The realities of the industry may make explanation difficult:

> Reinsurers also benefit from the services by ISO and other rating or service organizations. The underlying rates and policy forms are the basis for many reinsurance contracts. Reinsurers may also subscribe to various services. For example, a facultative reinsurer may subscribe to the rating service, so that they have the rating manuals available, or purchase optional services, such as a sprinkler report for a specific property location.

2 R. Reinarz, J. Schloss, G. Patrik, & P. Kensicki, Reinsurance Practices 18 (1990).

Justice Souter also describes reinsurers as being outside the primary insurance industry. That is technically true (to the extent the two symbiotic industries can be separated) but quite irrelevant. What matters is that the scope and predictability of the risks assumed in a reinsurance contract depend entirely upon the terms of the primary policies that are reinsured. The terms of the primary policies are the "subject-matter insured" by reinsurance, Carter, *supra,* at 4, so that to insist upon certain primary-insurance terms as a condition of writing reinsurance is in no way "artificial"; and hence for a number of reinsurers to insist upon such terms jointly is in no way a "boycott."[6]. . .

Justice Souter suggests that we have somehow mistakenly "posited . . . autonomy on the part of the reinsurers." We do not understand this. Nothing in the complaints alleges that the reinsurers were deprived of their "autonomy," which we take to mean that they were coerced by the primary insurers. (Given the sheer size of the Lloyd's market, such an allegation would be laughable.) That is not to say that we disagree with Justice Souter's contention that, according to the allegations, the reinsurers would not "have taken exactly the same course of action without the intense efforts of the four primary insurers." But the same could be said of the participants in virtually all conspiracies: If they had not been enlisted by the "intense efforts" of the leaders, their actions would not have been the same. If this factor renders otherwise lawful conspiracies (under McCarran-Ferguson) illegal, then the Act would have a narrow scope indeed. . . .

Under the test set forth above, there are sufficient allegations of a "boycott" to sustain the relevant counts of complaint against a motion to dismiss. For example, the complaints allege that some of the defendant reinsurers threatened to "withdraw entirely from the business of reinsuring primary U.S. insurers who wrote on the occurrence form." Construed most favorably to respondents, that allegation claims that primary insurers who wrote insurance on disfavored forms would be refused all reinsurance, *even* as to risks written on *other forms*. If that were the case, the reinsurers might have been engaging in a boycott—they would, that is, unless the primary insurers' other business were relevant to the proposed reinsurance contract (for example, if the reinsurer bears greater risk where the primary insurer engages in riskier businesses). Other allegations in the complaints could be similarly construed. For example, the complaints also allege that the reinsurers "threatened a boycott of North American CGL risks," not just CGL risks containing dissatisfactory terms, that "the foreign and domestic reinsurer representatives presented their agreed upon positions that there would be changes in the CGL forms or no reinsurance," that some of the defendant insurers and reinsurers told "groups of insurance brokers and agents . . . that a reinsurance boycott, and thus loss of income to the agents and brokers who would be unable to find available markets for their customers, would ensue if the [revised] ISO forms were not approved."

Many other allegations in the complaints describe conduct that may amount to a boycott if the plaintiffs can prove certain additional facts. For example, General Re, the largest American reinsurer, is alleged to have "agreed to either coerce ISO to adopt [the defendants'] demands or, failing that, 'derail' the entire CGL forms program." If this means that General Re intended to withhold all reinsurance on all CGL forms—even forms having no objectionable terms—that might amount to a "boycott." Also, General Re and several other domestic reinsurers are alleged to have "agreed to boycott the 1984 ISO forms unless a retroactive date was added to the claims-made form, and a pollution exclusion and a defense cost cap were added to both [the occurrence and claims made] forms." Liberally construed, this allegation may mean that the defendants had linked their demands so that they would continue to refuse to do business on *either* form until *both* were changed to their liking. Again, that might amount to a boycott. . . .

III. TOPICS IN SUBSTANTIVE INSURANCE REGULATION

Having surveyed the forms of and justifications for insurance regulation, and having explored the boundary between state and federal jurisdictional issues, we now consider three specific substantive topics in insurance regulation in greater detail: insurance guaranty funds, residual market mechanisms, and limits on insurance risk classification. Each of these topics raises interesting distributional questions. The goals of this section are to convince you that insurance regulation raises important questions about individual and social responsibility, and to alert you to the complexities inherent in using private market institutions to achieve egalitarian ends.

---

6. After remand, the case was settled for an amount that seemed to many observers (this one included) to be a very small amount in light of the allegations. One explanation may be that the alleged conspiracy was unsuccessful. Real claims-made coverage is still rare in the CGL market. Even pharmaceutical companies and medical device manufacturers have been able to purchase a hybrid form of coverage that provides many of the benefits of the occurrence form. *See* Richard Jacobs, Lorelie S. Masters, & Paul Stanley, Liability Insurance in International Arbitration: The Bermuda Form (2006).

A.   *Insurance Guaranty Funds*

Insurance guaranty funds are an emergency measure that requires surviving insurers to provide funds to cover an insolvent insurer's claims. They provide a backstop to private insurance arrangements. First introduced in New York for workers' compensation insurance in 1935, insurance guaranty funds did not become widespread until the 1960s. *See generally* David Moss, When All Else Fails 264-281 (2002). One of the goals of solvency regulation is to prevent insurance companies from failing. When companies do fail, guaranty funds protect consumers by paying all or a portion of the insolvent insurer's claims.

Some critics of state insolvency regulation argue that insurance regulators work *too* hard to prevent insolvencies, and that in a healthy insurance market, some insurance companies will—and should—fail. How might insurance guaranty funds encourage some state insurance regulators to allow companies to fail? How might those same funds encourage other state regulators to try too hard to save a failing company (and, thus, increase the total losses when the company finally is declared insolvent)?

The following provisions are selected portions of a model law establishing a guaranty association for property and casualty insurers. This model law is one of many model laws drafted by the NAIC.

Read the model law so that you decide whether, and if so how, the law answers the following questions:

1. How is the guaranty association funded?
2. What is the maximum amount that a company can be required to pay to the fund?
3. What is the maximum amount the fund will pay per claim?
4. Which of the insureds of an insolvent company are not eligible to file a claim with the fund?
5. Can the fund assess an auto insurance company in the event a homeowners' insurance company goes insolvent?
6. Who decides when an insurer is insolvent? What are the criteria?

POST-ASSESSMENT PROPERTY AND LIABILITY INSURANCE GUARANTY ASSOCIATION MODEL ACT

2.   Purpose

The purpose of this Act is to provide a mechanism for the payment of covered claims under certain insurance policies, to avoid excessive delay in payment and to the extent provided in this Act minimize financial loss to claimants or policyholders because of the insolvency of an insurer, and to provide an association to assess the cost of such protection among insurers.

3.   Scope

This Act shall apply to all kinds of direct insurance, but shall not be applicable to the following:

A. Life, annuity, health or disability insurance;

B. Mortgage guaranty, financial guaranty or other forms of insurance offering protection against investment risks;

C. Fidelity or surety bonds, or any other bonding obligations;

D. Credit insurance, vendors' single interest insurance, or collateral protection insurance or any similar insurance protecting the interests of a creditor arising out of a creditor-debtor transaction.

E. Insurance of warranties or service contracts including insurance that provides for the repair, replacement or service of goods or property, indemnification for repair, replacement or service for the operational or structural failure of the goods or property due to a defect in materials, workmanship or normal wear and tear, or provides reimbursement for the liability incurred by the issuer of agreements or service contracts that provide such benefits;

F. Title insurance;

G. Ocean marine insurance;

H. Any transaction or combination of transactions between a person (including affiliates of such person) and an insurer (including affiliates of such insurer) which involves the transfer of investment or credit risk unaccompanied by transfer of insurance risk; or

I. Any insurance provided by or guaranteed by government. . . .

5.   Definitions

As used in this Act:

A. "Affiliate" means a person who directly, or indirectly, through one or more intermediaries, controls, is controlled by, or is under common control with an insolvent insurer on December 31 of the year immediately preceding the date the insurer becomes an insolvent insurer.

B. "Association" means the [state] Insurance Guaranty Association created under Section 6.

C. "Claimant" means any insured making a first party claim or any person instituting a liability claim, provided that no person who is an affiliate of the insolvent insurer may be a claimant.

D. "Commissioner" means the Commissioner of Insurance of this state.

F. "Covered claim" means an unpaid claim, including one for unearned premiums, submitted by a claimant, which arises out of and is within the coverage and is subject to the applicable limits of an insurance policy to which this Act applies issued by an insurer, if the insurer becomes an insolvent insurer after the effective date of this Act and:

(1) The claimant or insured is a resident of this state at the time of the insured event, provided that for entities other than an individual, the residence of a claimant, insured or policyholder is the state in which its principal place of business is located at the time of the insured event; or

(2) The claim is a first party claim for damage to property with a permanent location in this state.

(3) "Covered claim" shall not include:

(a) Any amount awarded as punitive or exemplary damages;

(b) Any amount sought as a return of premium under any retrospective rating plan;

(c) Any amount due any reinsurer, insurer, insurance pool or underwriting association as subrogation recoveries, reinsurance recoveries, contribution, indemnification or otherwise. No claim for any amount due any reinsurer, insurer, insurance pool or underwriting association may be asserted against a person insured under a policy issued by an insolvent insurer other than to the extent the claim exceeds the association obligation limitations set forth in Section 8 of this Act;

(d) Any first party claims by an insured whose net worth exceeds $25 million on December 31 of the year prior to the year in which the insurer becomes an insolvent insurer; provided that an insured's net worth on that date shall be deemed to include the aggregate net worth of the insured and all of its subsidiaries as calculated on a consolidated basis; or

(e) Any first party claims by an insured which is an affiliate of the insolvent insurer.

G. "Insolvent insurer" means an insurer licensed to transact insurance in this state, either at the time the policy was issued or when the insured event occurred, and against whom a final order of liquidation has been entered after the effective date of this Act with a finding of insolvency by a court of competent jurisdiction in the insurer's state of domicile.

H. (1) "Member insurer" means any person who:

(a) Writes any kind of insurance to which this Act applies under Section 3, including the exchange of reciprocal or inter-insurance contracts; and

(b) Is licensed to transact insurance in this state (except at the option of the state).

(2) An insurer shall cease to be a member insurer effective on the day following the termination or expiration of its license to transact the kinds of insurance to which this Act applies, however, the insurer shall remain liable as a member insurer for any and all obligations, including obligations for assessments levied prior to the termination or expiration of the insurer's license and assessments levied after the termination or expiration, with respect to any insurer that became an insolvent insurer prior to the termination or expiration of the insurer's license.

6. Creation of the Association

There is created a nonprofit unincorporated legal entity to be known as the [state] Insurance Guaranty Association. All insurers defined as member insurers in Section 5H shall be and remain members of the association as a condition of their authority to transact insurance in this state. . . .

8. Powers and Duties of the Association

A. The association shall:

(1) (a) Be obligated to pay covered claims existing prior to the order of liquidation, arising within thirty (30) days after the order of liquidation, or before the policy expiration date if less than thirty (30) days after the order of liquidation, or before the insured replaces the policy or causes its cancellation, if the insured does so within thirty (30) days of the order of liquidation. The obligation shall be satisfied by paying to the claimant an amount as follows:

(i) The full amount of a covered claim for benefits under a workers' compensation insurance coverage;

(ii) An amount not exceeding $10,000 per policy for a covered claim for the return of unearned premium;

(iii) An amount not exceeding $500,000 per claimant for all other covered claims.

(2) Be deemed the insurer to the extent of its obligation on the covered claims and to that extent shall have all rights, duties and obligations of the insolvent insurer as if the insurer had not become insolvent, including but not limited to, the right to pursue and retain salvage and subrogation recoverable on covered claim obligations to the extent paid by the association.

(3) Assess insurers amounts necessary to pay the obligations of the association under Section 8A(1) subsequent to an insolvency, the expenses of handling covered claims subsequent to an insolvency, and other expenses authorized by this Act. The assessments of each member insurer shall be in the proportion that the net direct written premiums of the member insurer for the calendar year preceding the assessment bears to the net direct written premiums of all member insurers for the calendar year preceding the assessment. Each member insurer shall be notified of the assessment not later than thirty (30) days before it is due. A member insurer may not be assessed in any year an amount greater than two percent (2%) of that member insurer's net direct written premiums for the calendar year preceding the assessment. If the maximum assessment, together with the other assets of the association, does not provide in any one year an amount sufficient to make all necessary payments, the funds available shall be prorated and the unpaid portion shall be paid as soon as funds become available. The association shall pay claims in any order that it may deem reasonable, including the payment of claims as they are received from the claimants or in groups or categories of claims. The association may exempt or defer, in whole or in part, the assessment of a member insurer, if the assessment would cause the member insurer's financial statement to reflect amounts of capital or surplus less than the minimum amounts required for a certificate of authority by a jurisdiction in which the member insurer is authorized to transact insurance.

NOTES AND QUESTIONS

1. The Federal Deposit Insurance Corporation (FDIC) guarantees deposits up to $250,000 per individual in federally chartered banks. Two of the most significant differences between the FDIC and insurance guaranty funds are that the FDIC is prefunded by bank insurance premiums and banks are permitted to advertise that deposits are federally insured, whereas guaranty funds are not prefunded and the model guaranty fund acts prohibit insurers from advertising that their obligations are similarly guaranteed.

    These guarantees and other aspects of banking regulation commonly are justified on the grounds that consumer confidence protects the banking system as a whole. If consumers are not confident in the ability of a bank to give them their deposits on demand, they may start a "run" on a bank whenever there is bad news. Like other financial institutions, banks make money by investing the money that they hold on people's behalf. If too many people ask for their money back all at once (that's what a "run" on a bank is), even a solvent bank won't be able to honor those requests. Most insurance companies aren't subject to a run of this sort, because policyholders are not entitled to get their money back on demand (except for some forms of life insurance and annuities that are investment products). Nevertheless, an insurance company is subject to a slow-motion run. If people are concerned about an insurance company's ability to pay claims, they will buy insurance from other companies. The reduction in premiums will place pressure on the company's cash flow and may require it to liquidate some of its assets at a loss to keep operations going. Just as with the (faster) run on a bank, the belief that an insurance company is in financial trouble can be self-fulfilling. As a result, consumer confidence is just as important to the long-term viability of insurance as of banking.

Should insurance companies be permitted to advertise their guarantees? Why might insurance companies be opposed to such advertisements? Might the resulting pressure on state legislatures to increase the amount guaranteed, which would increase the exposure of insurance companies to assessments, be part of the explanation?

2. There is a separate model act for life and health insurance. Like the Property and Casualty Act, the NAIC Life and Health Model Act limits the amount that the guaranty fund will pay. The life and health limiting provision is as follows:

3. C. The benefits that the Association may become obligated to cover shall in no event exceed the lesser of:

(1) The contractual obligations for which the insurer is liable or would have been liable if it were not an impaired or insolvent insurer, or

(2) (a) With respect to one life, regardless of the number of policies or contracts:

(i) $300,000 in life insurance death benefits, but not more than $100,000 in net cash surrender and net cash withdrawal values for life insurance;

(ii) In health insurance benefits:

(I) $100,000 for coverages not defined as disability insurance or basic hospital, medical and surgical insurance or major medical insurance including any net cash surrender and net cash withdrawal values;

(II) $300,000 for disability insurance;

(III) $500,000 for basic hospital medical and surgical insurance or major medical insurance; or

(iii) $100,000 in the present value of annuity benefits, including net cash surrender and net cash withdrawal values;

(b) With respect to each individual participating in a governmental retirement benefit plan established under Section 401, 403 (b) or 457 of the U.S. Internal Revenue Code covered by an unallocated annuity contract or the beneficiaries of each such individual if deceased, in the aggregate, $100,000 in present value annuity benefits, including net cash surrender and net cash withdrawal values;

(c) With respect to each payee of a structured settlement annuity (or beneficiary or beneficiaries of the payee if deceased), $100,000 in present value annuity benefits, in the aggregate, including net cash surrender and net cash withdrawal values, if any;

(d) However, in no event shall the Association be obligated to cover more than (i) an aggregate of $300,000 in benefits with respect to any one life under Paragraphs 2(a), 2(b) and 2(c) of this subsection except with respect to benefits for basic hospital, medical and surgical insurance and major medical insurance under Paragraph 2(a)(ii) of this subsection, in which case the aggregate liability of the Association shall not exceed $500,000 with respect to any one individual, or (ii) with respect to one owner of multiple non-group policies of life insurance, whether the policy owner is an individual, firm, corporation or other person, and whether the persons insured are officers, managers, employees or other persons, more than $5,000,000 in benefits, regardless of the number of policies and contracts held by the owner.

Do these amounts seem enough to you? Do the amounts protected by the property and casualty act seem enough to you? How should we think about how much is "enough" in this context? Should the amounts differ by location? Note that there is no limit on the amount of workers' compensation benefits protected by the property and casualty act. Is that consistent with the limit on the health insurance protection in the Life and Health Act? What might explain the difference? Might the fact that employers remain responsible for workers' compensation benefits when workers' compensation carriers go insolvent be relevant? Should employers have the same obligation for health benefits?

3. The NAIC Life and Health Insurance Guaranty Fund Model Act differs from the Property Casualty Model Act most significantly in that the association established by the life and health act has the responsibility of continuing the coverage provided by insolvent insurers. Can you see why that would be more important for life and health insurance than for property and casualty insurance? The comment to Section 1 of the Life and Health Act states:

> The basic purpose of this model act is to protect policy owners, insureds, beneficiaries, annuitants, payees and assignees against losses (both in terms of paying claims and continuing coverage) which might otherwise occur due to an impairment or insolvency of an insurer. Unlike the property and liability lines of business, life and annuity contracts in particular are long-term arrangements for security. An insured may have impaired health or be at an advanced age so as to be unable to obtain new and similar coverage from other insurers. The payment of cash values alone does not adequately meet such needs. Thus it is essential that coverage be continued. In like manner, an insured may be unable to obtain new health insurance or, at least, he may lose protection for prior illness.

4. David Moss explains that the assessment approach was justified in part as providing an incentive for the insurance industry to press for strict regulation: "A prefunded FDIC-style system . . . would invite regulatory laxity by making insurance bailouts seem relatively painless." When All Else Fails 272 (2002). How might the assessment model encourage companies to press for strict enforcement of solvency regulation?

5. Critics of the model act approach to guaranty funds argue that the assessment approach encourages insurance commissioners to delay declaring that an insurance company is insolvent. One alternative approach would be to establish guaranty funds that work more like traditional insurance mechanisms, where companies would pay premiums (based on their risk) that would fund the guaranty fund *in advance. See, e.g.,* William R. Feldhaus & Paul M. Kazenski, *Risk-Based Guaranty Fund Assessments: An Allocation*

Alternative for Funding Insurance Insolvencies, 17 J. Ins. Reg. 42 (1998). Would this take care of the problem of commissioner inaction? How would this be different from mandatory reinsurance? Under this alternative approach, would you want the same regulator that is charged with declaring that a company is insolvent to set the premiums? Why or why not?

6. What alternative approaches can you suggest to address the problem of commissioner inaction? What might be the problem with a commissioner pulling the insolvency trigger too easily? The National Conference of Insurance Guaranty Funds (NCIGF), the organization for state property-casualty guaranty funds, reported in 2014 that its member guaranty funds had paid more than $27 billion to claimants since 1976. With respect to life and health insurers, the National Organization of Life and Health Insurance Guaranty Associations (NOLHGA) reported that its members had made claims payments to more than 2.5 million consumers in roughly 100 multistate insolvency cases. NOLHGA reported that no new insolvencies requiring guaranty fund obligations were triggered in 2014. Why do you suppose that there have been so many more property/casualty insurance company insolvencies than life and health company insolvencies? Does the fact that there have been relatively few payouts for life and health insurance company insolvencies over the years give you confidence that large life insurance companies, such as MetLife, are currently safe from insolvency in the event of a system-wide shock of the sort that we saw in 2008?

NEW MEXICO LIFE INSURANCE GUARANTY ASSOCIATION
v. MOORE

Supreme Court of New Mexico
596 P.2d 260 (1979)

[This was an action brought against New Mexico Blue Cross and Blue Shield and two HMOs to require them to make payments to the life and health insurance guaranty fund organized according to New Mexico's version of the NAIC model life and health insurance guaranty act.]

The [New Mexico Life Insurance Guaranty] Association is organized pursuant to the Guaranty Act, §§59-22-1 to 17, N.M.S.A. 1978. . . . Section 59-22-3 provides that the Guaranty Act applies to

all direct life insurance policies, health insurance policies, annuity contracts and contracts supplemental to life and health insurance policies and annuity contracts. It also applies to reinsurance of such contracts which does not provide for liability without diminution because of the insolvency of the ceding company.

All insurers are required to be members of the Association as a condition of their authority to transact insurance business covered by the Act. §59-22-5. . . . When a "member insurer" becomes insolvent, the Association guarantees or reinsures all the covered policies of the insolvent insurer and provides money, notes, guarantees or other means to assure payment of the contractual obligations of the insolvent insurer. §59-22-7. . . .

The question we address in this appeal is whether defendants are engaged in the "kind of insurance to which the . . . Guaranty Act applies." The difficulty in answering this question arises because the Act does not define the terms "insurance" or "health insurance." This is a case of first impression in New Mexico. . . .

Hospital Service, Inc., was incorporated by the Board of Directors of what was then the Presbyterian Hospital. The purpose of Hospital Service was to

> furnish hospital care to Subscribers or such of the public as shall become Subscribers; to provide for such hospitalization in hospitals or hospital with which this Corporation has a contract; to operate as a nonprofit corporation in order to secure hospital protection at a minimum cost to its Subscribers. . . .

Concurrent with the development of Hospital Service, the New Mexico Medical Society developed a physician prepayment plan known as the New Mexico Physicians Service. The plan existed independently of any enabling legislation. The New Mexico Legislature enacted the Physicians Service Plans Act in 1947. *See* N.M. Laws 1947, ch. 157, §1. Surgical Service, Inc. was formed in October 1947. Its purpose was to

> establish, maintain, and operate a voluntary, nonprofit medical-surgical plan . . . whereby the services of any Doctor of Medicine are provided, at the expense of the Corporation, in the manner specified in the contract with Subscribers. Such medical and surgical care, may be provided in their entirety or in part as the Corporation may determine and as set out and as set forth in such contracts.

In 1960, Surgical Service became an approved Blue Shield Plan and began using the Blue Shield symbol. It contracted with doctors to accept payment from Surgical Service as payment in full for covered services. . . .

We note that Blue Cross has approximately 200,000 members who are eligible for various benefits. . . .

Insurance usually involves a contract whereby the insurer, for an adequate consideration, undertakes to indemnify the insured against loss arising from specified perils, or to reimburse him for all or part of an obligation he has incurred. *Barkin v. Board of Optometry*, 75 Cal. Rptr. 337 (Ct. App. 1969). *See also* 43 Am. Jur. 2d *Insurance* §1 (1969).

Webster's Third New International Dictionary of the English Language 1173 (unabr. ed. 1976) defines "insurance" as:

> the action or process of insuring or the state of being insured usu. against loss or damage by a contingent event (as death, fire, accident or sickness) . . . coverage by contract whereby for a stipulated consideration one party undertakes to indemnify or guarantee another against loss by a specified contingency or peril. . . .

The United States Supreme Court has recently stated that

> [t]he primary elements of an insurance contract are the spreading and underwriting of a policyholder's risk.

Group Life & Health Insurance Co. v. Royal Drug Co., 440 U.S. 205, 211 (1979).

Generally, a nonprofit corporation which provides members of a group with medical services and hospitalization is considered not engaged in insurance and thus not subject to insurance laws. In *Hospital Service Corp. of R.I. v. Pennsylvania Ins. Co.*, 227 A.2d 105 (R.I. 1967), the Rhode Island Supreme Court upheld as valid a provision in a hospitalization policy that the company would be subrogated and succeed to the subscriber's right to recover. The court stated its opinion that Blue Cross "is not engaged in the insurance business and is therefore not an 'insurer.'" *Id.* at 111. Indeed, Blue Cross and Blue Shield organizations have historically taken the position that they are not insurance companies. *See* Denenberg, *The Legal Definitions of Insurance,* 30 J. Ins. 319 (1963).

In *Group Life, supra,* the Supreme Court cited *Jordan v. Group Health Ass'n,* 107 F.2d 239 (D.C. Cir. 1939), as "illustrative of the contemporary view of health care plans." 440 U.S. at 227. Like defendants in the case at bar, Group Health was a nonprofit corporation organized to provide members who had paid a fixed annual premium with various medical services and supplies. Group Health contracted with physicians and hospitals to provide those services. The D.C. Court of Appeals held that Group Health was not engaged in the business of insurance. The court stated:

> Although Group Health's activities may be considered in one aspect as creating security against loss from illness or accident, more truly they constitute the quantity purchase of well-rounded, continuous medical service by its members. Group Health is in fact and in function a consumer cooperative. The functions of such an organization are not identical with those of insurance or indemnity companies. The latter are concerned primarily, if not exclusively, with risk. . . . On the other hand, the cooperative is concerned principally with *getting service rendered* to its members and doing so at lower prices made possible by quantity purchasing and economies in operation. Its primary purpose is to reduce the cost rather than the risk of medical care; to broaden the service to the individual in kind and quantity; to enlarge the number receiving it; . . . (Footnotes omitted.)

107 F.2d at 247.

In *California Physicians' Service v. Garrison,* 172 P.2d 4 (Cal. 1946), California Physicians' Service sought a declaratory judgment that it was not engaged in the business of insurance within the meaning of California's regulatory statutes. The Insurance Commissioner appealed from judgment for plaintiff. The California Supreme Court affirmed the trial court's judgment that Physicians' Service was not engaged in the business of insurance. The court stated:

> There is another and more compelling reason for holding that the Service is not engaged in the insurance business. Absence or presence of assumption of risk or peril is not the sole test to be applied in determining its status. The question, more broadly, is whether, looking at the plan of operation as a whole, "service" rather than "indemnity" is its principal object and purpose. [Citations omitted.] Certainly the objects and purposes of the corporation organized and maintained by the California physicians have a wide scope in the field of social service. Probably there is no more impelling need than that of adequate medical care on a voluntary, low-cost basis for persons of small income. The medical profession unitedly is endeavoring to meet that need. Unquestionably this is "service" of a high order and not "indemnity."

172 P.2d at 16. . . .

The Association asserts that because defendant health plans are subject to the Insurance Company Insolvency Act, N.M.S.A. §§59-6-31 to 35 (1978) and the Unfair Insurance Practices Act, N.M.S.A. §§59-11-9 to 22 (1978), it follows that they are also subject to the Guaranty Act. Section 59-6-32 provides that an insurance company includes "mutual nonprofit hospital service corporations" and "nonprofit medical service corporations." Section 59-11-11 states that "[f]or purposes of the Unfair Insurance Practices Act, health care plans shall be deemed to be engaged in the business of insurance[.]" We note that there is no specific mention in the Guaranty Act of nonprofit medical or hospital service corporations. Rather, the Legislature has elected to apply the Act only to "insurers" and "health insurance policies." We find that legislation impacting on health care plans requires specific reference to health plans or amendment of the Guaranty Act and Nonprofit Health Care Plan Act.

We conclude that defendants are not "member insurers" within the meaning of the Guaranty Act and that they are not engaged in "any kind of insurance" to which the Act applies. Our conclusion is based on the fact that defendant health plans are service benefit organizations, as distinguished from the indemnity benefit nature of commercial insurers.

NOTES AND QUESTIONS

1. Do health maintenance organizations (HMOs) and service benefit health care plans "spread and underwrite risk"? Consider whether the defendants would be regarded as insurers under the statutory and other definitions addressed in the "What is insurance?" unit in Section IIA of this chapter.
2. Given that it is so easy to counter the argument that HMOs and service benefit plans are not "insurance," what might explain the court's reluctance to subject the defendants to the Guaranty Act? If an HMO is not covered by the guaranty fund, what happens to its members in the event of insolvency? Do HMO subscribers need less protection than people who purchase traditional health insurance?

PROBLEM: GUARANTY FUNDS FOR RISK-BEARING HEALTH CARE PROVIDERS?

A recent trend in the health care marketplace is for groups of physicians or other health care providers to form large organizations that are capable of taking on risk. For example, a primary care physician organization may contract with a health care financing organization to provide primary care services for a given group for a given period of time at a flat fee. Should the risk-bearing provider groups be covered by guaranty funds? Consider whether these groups offer health care "insurance." How are they like HMOs? How are they unlike HMOs? If they are not covered by guaranty funds, how are their patients protected?

B. Residual Market Mechanisms

Residual market mechanisms are statutory arrangements that are designed to provide insurance for people who are unable to purchase insurance in the "open" market. In effect, residual market mechanisms create a ceiling on the price that an insurer can charge high-risk customers. If an insurer charges a higher price, a rational consumer would prefer to purchase the insurance through the residual market. The following is an excerpt from a background paper on residual markets prepared by the industry's Insurance Information Institute.

RESIDUAL MARKETS

Insurance Information Institute Insurance Issues Update **(2015)**

Insurance is a mechanism through which individuals and businesses can transfer risk to another entity: an insurance company. Many different programs have been established to assure that insurance is available to individuals and businesses having difficulty obtaining coverage in the "voluntary market," that is the risk that insurers voluntarily assume. The business that insurers do not voluntarily assume is called the residual market. Residual markets may also be called "shared," because the profits and losses of each type of residual market are shared by all insurers in the state selling that type of insurance, or involuntary, because insurers do not choose to underwrite the business, in contrast to the regular voluntary market.

The Automobile Residual Market

The first of the residual market mechanisms for automobile coverage was established in New Hampshire in 1938. As states began to pass laws requiring drivers to furnish proof of insurance, having auto liability insurance became a prerequisite for driving a car. Today, all 50 states and the District of Columbia use one of four systems to guarantee that auto insurance is available to those who need it. All four systems are commonly known as assigned risk plans, although the term technically applies only to the first type of plan, where each insurer is required to assume its share of residual market policyholders or "risks." (The term "risk" is used in the insurance industry to denote the policyholder or property insured as well as the chance of loss.) Commercial auto insurance is also available through the residual market.

Automobile Insurance Plans: The assigned risk plan, the most common type, currently found in 43 states and the District of Columbia, generally is administered through an office created or supported by the state and governed by a board representing insurance companies licensed in the state. Massachusetts was the last state to adopt an assigned risk plan. It began a three-year change-over process from a reinsurance facility in April 2008.

When agents or company representatives are unable to obtain auto insurance for an applicant in the voluntary market, they submit the application to the assigned risk plan office. These applications are distributed randomly by the automobile insurance plan to all insurance companies that offer automobile liability coverage in the state in proportion to the amount of their voluntary business. Thus, if on a given day the plan receives 100 applications from agents around the state, a company with 10 percent of that state's regular private passenger automobile insurance business will be assigned 10 of those applicants and will be responsible for all associated losses.

Generally, each insurer services the policyholders assigned to it just as it would the policyholders it insures in the voluntary market. However, there are exceptions. For example, five states have set up a service center to carry out all administrative and service functions, except handling claims. In many jurisdictions, companies that prefer not to service the policies of policyholders assigned to them can make arrangements for a fee to have them serviced by others, either by the Plan or by "servicing companies," insurers that service other companies' business as well as their own. A few states allow such service arrangements in the commercial auto residual market, especially large commercial accounts such as taxis and corporate-owned fleets.

Assigned risk policies usually are more restricted in the coverage they can provide and have lower limits than voluntary market policies. In addition, premiums for assigned risk policies usually are significantly higher, although not always sufficiently high enough to cover the increased costs of insuring high-risk drivers.

Joint Underwriting Associations (JUAs): Automobile JUAs, found in four states, Florida, Hawaii, Michigan and Missouri, are state-mandated pooling mechanisms through which all companies doing business in the state share the premiums of business outside the voluntary market as well as the profits or losses and expenses incurred. To simplify the policyholder distribution process, insurance agents and company representatives are generally assigned one of several servicing carriers (companies that have agreed for a fee to issue and service JUA policies). They submit applications to that company, which then issues the JUA policy. In Michigan, however, agents submit applications directly to the JUA office, which then distributes them to the servicing carriers. Coverages offered by JUAs generally are the same as those offered in the voluntary market but the limits may be lower. Although rates may be higher than in the voluntary market, they may not be sufficient for the JUA to be self-sustaining. State statutes setting up the JUA generally permit it to recoup losses by surcharging policyholders or deducting losses from state premium taxes. (JUAs may be set up for other lines of insurance, including homeowners insurance. JUAs for commercial insurance coverage, such as medical malpractice and liquor liability, may operate somewhat differently in some states, see below.)

Reinsurance Facilities: Reinsurance facilities exist in North Carolina and New Hampshire. An automobile reinsurance facility is an unincorporated, nonprofit entity, through which auto insurers provide coverage and service claims. After issuing a policy, an insurer decides whether to handle the policy as part of its regular "voluntary business" or transfer it to the reinsurance facility or pool. An insurer is permitted to transfer or "cede" to the pool a percentage of its policies. Premiums for this portion of business are sent to the pool and companies bill the pool for claims payments and expenses. Profits or losses are shared by all auto insurers licensed in the state.

State Fund: One state, Maryland, has a residual market mechanism for auto insurance which is administered by the state. It was created in 1973. Private insurers do not participate directly in the Maryland Automobile Insurance Fund (MAIF) but are required by law to subsidize any losses from the operation, with the cost being charged back against their own policyholders. In years that the fund has a loss, all Maryland insured drivers, including MAIF drivers, help offset the deficit through an assessment mechanism.

Size of the Auto Insurance Market: Together, residual market programs insured 1.87 million cars in 2012, about 1.0 percent of the total market, according to the AIPSO, which tracks such data. In 1990 the residual market served 6.3 percent of the total market. In 2012, in a major change from much of the 1990s, only one state, North Carolina, had more than a million cars insured through the residual market. In South Carolina, which enacted sweeping reforms in 1998, the residual market dropped from 38 percent of all insured cars in 1996 to zero in 2012.

The North Carolina residual auto insurance market is unusual in that the laws governing the North Carolina Reinsurance Facility, the state's auto insurance residual market pool, have produced a complex system of subsidies that keeps the pool's population high. Drivers with traffic violation points on their record and inexperienced drivers in the pool do pay higher rates, but some of those in the pool, because of some lesser risk, pay the same as the highest rate charged good drivers. All rates are highly regulated.

Voluntary market rates in North Carolina are kept low. As a result, auto insurers send business that is not expected to be profitable to the pool and the pool loses money each year. This shortfall is offset by surcharges incorporated into premiums, spreading the loss across all drivers. Supporters of the system say the subsidy system makes it easier for more people to buy insurance—North Carolina is among the states with the lowest percentage of uninsured drivers. Critics say that good drivers should not have to pay more so that others can get a good deal.

Other states have seen their residual market fluctuate, depending on conditions in the voluntary market such as the regulatory environment and rate adequacy. For example, in 1987, close to 1.8 million drivers were insured in the New Jersey shared market, compared with about 97,300 in 1993. But gradually, this number crept up again as insurers began to withdraw from the state because of the overly harsh regulatory system. Market reforms passed in New Jersey in recent years have brought more auto insurance companies into the market, increasing competition and reducing the need for drivers to seek coverage in the residual market. A 2004 study of residual markets by the Property Casualty Insurers Association of America found that in states where competition is the primary regulator of price, the residual market tends to be small.

. . .

OTHER RESIDUAL MARKET ENTITIES

JUAs for Other Lines of Insurance: JUAs are not limited to automobile insurance. At various times, there have been JUAs for residential insurance. Florida's residential JUA became part of its Citizens Property Insurance Corporation in 2002. Florida also has a workers compensation JUA, which was established in 1993. A number of states have medical malpractice JUAs, most of which were set up in the 1970s or 1980s when the line was beset by high losses. However, in the 1990s, the market for medical malpractice insurance softened, as in other commercial sectors, and several JUAs were dissolved. Some states have provided extra protection in the form of a state-subsidized layer of "excess" medical malpractice coverage in addition to the JUA or separately, either to reduce the cost of additional coverage or to make it more readily available. In a number of states rising costs in the early 2000s forced several insurers to leave the medical malpractice marketplace, which in turn diminished the amount of medical malpractice coverage available. Some of the excess programs set up by states were short-term solutions to the most recent crisis and have sunset clauses. These require the entity to cease operations unless conditions warrant its continued existence.

In some states, medical malpractice JUAs operate in a fashion similar to JUAs for automobile insurance, through servicing insurers. In others, such as South Carolina, the medical malpractice JUA serves as an insurance company, collecting premiums, issuing policies in its own name and adjusting losses. Depending on the state, if the medical malpractice JUA runs into financial difficulties, the shortfall is picked up by the state's insurance companies, its medical care providers or some form of financing that ultimately is paid for by taxpayers. When the insurance industry is assessed, assessments are spread over as broad a base as possible, sometimes the entire liability insurance market. Each company contributes in proportion to its share of the liability market, which may include personal and commercial automobile liability, general and professional liability and, in some states, workers compensation as well.

In many states, the insurance commissioner has been given standby authority to set up a JUA whenever marketplace conditions for any type of insurance require such a move. When it became obvious that insurance was becoming more difficult to obtain in parts of Florida, following the disastrous hurricane seasons of 2004 and 2005, the state set up a statewide commercial JUA to provide commercial property insurance.

Market Assistance Plans (MAPs): A MAP is a temporary, voluntary clearinghouse and referral system designed to put people looking for insurance in touch with insurance companies. They are organized when something happens to cause insurance companies to cut back on the amount of insurance they are willing to provide. MAPs are generally administered by agents' associations, which assign insurance applications to a group of insurers doing business in a state. These companies have agreed to take their share of applicants on a rotating basis. In the mid-1980s, MAPs were set up for liability insurance. At that time, some businesses like ski resorts and bars, as well as municipalities, were having trouble finding liability insurance because of the increase in lawsuits filed against them. When the liability insurance market eventually adjusted and liability insurance became readily available once again, most liability insurance MAPs were dismantled.

Increasingly, MAPs are being created to deal with property insurance problems. In New Jersey, for example, where insurers are concerned about potential storm losses, the insurance department established a MAP in the 1990s, known as WindMAP. Insurers representing 70 percent of the state's homeowners insurance market participate. Some 20,000 residents in 92 ZIP codes are eligible to apply to the plan for coverage.

MAPs may be organized for a single line of insurance, such as daycare liability or homeowners insurance, or for a broad range of liability coverages. Homeowners insurance MAPs have been formed in several East Coast states, including Connecticut and in Texas, and medical malpractice MAPs were created in states such as Washington, when the medical community had difficulty finding malpractice insurance.

WORKERS COMPENSATION

Workers Compensation Assigned Risk Plans and Pools: The mechanism used to handle the residual market varies from state to state. In the four remaining states with a monopolistic state workers compensation fund (West Virginia switched to a competitive market in July 2008), all businesses are insured through that fund. In most states with a competitive state fund (an entity that competes for business with private insurers), the fund accepts all risks rejected by the voluntary market, thus eliminating the need for assigned risk plans. In states without a competitive fund, insurers may be assigned applicants based on their market share and service those employers as they would employers that came to them through the voluntary market, through a system known as direct assignment. They may also participate in the residual market through a reinsurance pooling arrangement.

. . .

OTHER POOLING ARRANGEMENTS

Nuclear Energy and Other Voluntary Pools: The use of nuclear fission for peaceful purposes brought with it a demand for limits of liability insurance significantly higher than individual companies alone were able to provide. Originally three nuclear energy pools were voluntarily organized in the United States by the insurance industry in response to this demand. Now there is one. American Nuclear Insurers provides liability and property damage coverage for nuclear reactors and fabricators and transporters of reactor fuels. The pool purchases reinsurance from Lloyd's and other insurers not domiciled in the United States. Policies are issued in the name of the pool, showing each member company's participation.

Reinsurance Pools: There are two basic types of reinsurance pools. In the first, an individual member company underwrites the risks and issues the policy to the policyholder. The member then automatically reinsures the risk with the pool in accordance with the pooling agreement. In the second type, the pool functions as a general reinsurer, underwriting reinsurance policies for primary companies regardless of whether they are members of the pool. Examples of reinsurance pools include the Registered Mail Insurance Association, which covers currency, securities and other valuables transported by registered and first-class mail, and shippers of property transported by armored cars; and the Excess Bond Reinsurance Association, which offers fidelity coverage (protection against employee fraud) to commercial banks.

Unsatisfied Judgement Funds: Unsatisfied Judgment Funds exist in three states—Michigan, New York and North Dakota—to compensate victims of auto accidents (with the exception of uninsured vehicle owners) who cannot collect the damages awarded them, generally because the defendant had no insurance or assets with which to pay the judgment.

Unsatisfied Judgment Funds are administered differently, depending on the state. In two states—Michigan and South Dakota—they are administered by the state and in New York by insurers alone. New Jersey began to phase out its fund in 2003. Like residual markets, these funds are partially subsidized or totally paid for through assessments against insurance companies. To be eligible for state funds, accident victims must be residents of the state and have been injured in an accident that occurred within state boundaries. Out-of-state residents usually are eligible if their home state provides a similar program. There are few standard provisions. Each state has its own set of rules which determine deductibles, maximum compensation available, minimum size of losses covered, coverage for property damage and so on.

The following case is a facial constitutional challenge to a New Jersey statute that taxed automobile insurers in New Jersey to raise funds to pay off the accumulated debt of an automobile residual market mechanism in the state. The insurers strenuously objected to the tax because the statute prohibited them from raising their rates to cover the costs of the tax. As a result, the insurers claimed that they would not be able to earn the "fair and adequate return" to which they were entitled.

In many ways, automobile insurance rate litigation of this sort is a throwback to an earlier era, in which government agencies set prices for a wide variety of "public services." Government price setting raises interesting and complex legal and economic issues, most of which are beyond the scope of an introductory insurance law text. When reading the case, focus on the following issues:

1. The differences between the "assigned risk" and "joint underwriting association" approaches tried in New Jersey
2. The specific steps the New Jersey legislature took to address the accumulated debt of the JUA
3. How the New Jersey Department of Insurance and the court made the "square peg" of the reform statute fit into the "round hole" of the fair and adequate return requirement

As always, the goal here is not to make you an instant expert on automobile insurance rate litigation, but rather to sensitize you to the kinds of issues presented when the government sets up a residual market mechanism.

STATE FARM MUTUAL AUTOMOBILE INSURANCE COMPANY v. NEW JERSEY

Supreme Court of New Jersey
590 A.2d 191 (1991)

HANDLER, J. . . . For years, New Jersey's system of automobile insurance regulation, like those of many other states, has faced an intractable problem of providing coverage for high-risk drivers. Prior to 1983, drivers who could not obtain coverage directly from insurers in the voluntary market were insured through an Assigned Risk Plan, under which the Commissioner of Insurance apportioned high-risk drivers among all auto insurers doing business in New Jersey. In 1983, the Automobile Full Insurance Availability Act replaced the assigned-risk system with the New Jersey Automobile Full Insurance Underwriting Association, commonly known as the Joint Underwriting Association or JUA.

All insurers licensed to write automobile insurance in New Jersey were required to be members of the JUA. The objective of the new scheme was to create a more extensive system of allocating high-risk drivers to carriers, and through the JUA, to provide such drivers with coverage at rates equivalent to those charged in the voluntary market. . . .

Because the JUA insured high-risk drivers but also required that their rates be the same as voluntary-market rates, it was anticipated that premium revenues would not cover costs of claims against JUA policies. Therefore, in addition to normal premium income, the JUA was also given income from Department of Motor Vehicle surcharges for moving violations and drunken driving convictions, policy "flat charges," and "residual market equalization charges," or

RMECs, to be added to policy rates for voluntary-market insureds. Thus, the JUA was a system in which the insurance costs of high-risk drivers were subsidized by the imposition of fees on segments of the general population of motorists. The JUA was supposed to be operated on a no-profit, no-loss basis, with RMECs increased or decreased as needed to accomplish that result.

However one may view the objectives of the JUA, the system did not achieve its goals. More and more drivers became unable to procure voluntary-market coverage, until by 1988 over 50% of New Jersey drivers had to be insured through the JUA. Claims against JUA insureds were sizeable and greatly exceeded the JUA's available income. Despite the imposition of substantial RMECs from 1988 through 1990, the JUA nonetheless accumulated a deficit of over $3.3 billion in unpaid claims and other losses.

Automobile insurance reform, including the reduction of the cost of insurance, and particularly some plan for eliminating the unwieldy JUA, repaying its debt, and replacing it with a more workable distribution of the automobile insurance market, became a priority for the Legislature and the executive branch in 1990. By March of that year the Fair Automobile Insurance Reform Act had been adopted.

The principal goals of the Reform Act were to reduce insurance costs for most New Jersey drivers, to depopulate the JUA by switching insureds to the voluntary market, and to create a funding mechanism to pay off the JUA debt. To these ends, the Act provided that the JUA would cease writing or renewing policies as of October 1, 1990. The "depopulation" of the JUA would be accomplished by classifying insured drivers into three categories: (1) high-risk drivers in the (revived) Assigned Risk Plan (10% of the market); (2) "non-standard" risk drivers, who would be insured by private insurers directly, but who could be charged rates up to 135% of those of standard risks (15% of the market); and (3) standard-risk, voluntary-market insureds covered at prevailing rates (the remaining 75% of the market). Presumably, the higher rates now to be charged high-risk and "non-standard" risk drivers should bring the premium income on such coverage in line with actual costs, and this coverage would no longer be subsidized.

There remains, however, the problem of how to pay off the JUA's prior accumulated debt of over $3.3 billion; this, too, is addressed by the Reform Act. The Act creates the New Jersey Automobile Insurance Guaranty Fund (Auto Fund), a separate fund within the State Treasury, to collect and disburse the various payments designed to pay off the JUA debt. Reform Act, §23; N.J.S.A. 17:33B-5. The Act assigns to the Auto Fund certain sources of income that under the prior scheme went to the JUA, e.g., surcharges for driving violations and drunken driving convictions. It also creates new sources of revenue for the Auto Fund, e.g., fees on lawyers, doctors, and auto body repair businesses, higher automobile registration fees, and, most significant in the context of this litigation, the imposition of additional assessments and surtaxes on insurers.

The assessments imposed on insurance carriers are collected through the Property Liability Insurance Guaranty Association (PLIGA). . . . Section 75 of the Reform Act addresses recoupment from policyholders of PLIGA assessments both for insolvencies and for the JUA bailout. Insurers have always been permitted to pass through the insolvency assessments to policyholders. . . . However, the Act expressly prohibits such surcharges to recover the new assessments for the JUA bailout. Section 75b states:

> No member insurer shall impose a surcharge on the premiums of any policy to recoup assessments paid pursuant to [the provision requiring assessments to be loaned to the Auto Fund].

N.J.S.A. 17:30A-16b.

In addition to the new assessments, the Reform Act, §76, imposes a special surtax on insurers to go toward the JUA bailout. This surtax is a greater amount, 5% of net premiums, but is imposed for a shorter period (only three years, 1990, 1991 and 1992), than the assessments. . . . The Reform Act, §78, addresses the question of whether the additional surtaxes can be charged to consumers:

> The Commissioner of Insurance shall take such action as is necessary to ensure that private passenger automobile insurance policyholders shall not pay for the surtax imposed pursuant to section 76.

N.J.S.A. 17:33B-51.

The insurers argue that because of the passthrough prohibitions of Sections 75 and 78, it is impossible for the Commissioner of Insurance to grant any rate relief to counteract the substantial loss of net income that will result from the new assessments and surtaxes. The insurers further claim that the assessments and surtaxes will necessarily cause them to operate at a loss, and they will thus be deprived of a constitutionally adequate rate of return. . . .

The primary bases of the insurers' challenges to the Reform Act are the takings clause of the fifth amendment to the United States Constitution (as applicable to state action through the fourteenth amendment), the due process clause of the fourteenth amendment, and analogous provisions of the New Jersey Constitution. Although the takings and due process claims are factually interrelated and are ordinarily brought in tandem in challenges to governmental rate or price-control regulations, each is actually a distinct basis for challenge.

Of the two pertinent constitutional issues, the courts have developed more definite and clearer standards for substantive due process claims than for takings claims. This Court has chosen to apply the same standards developed by the United States Supreme Court under the federal Constitution for resolving due process claims under the New Jersey Constitution. Courts have, of course, long been reluctant to interfere with the states' regulation of their internal economic affairs. Thus, the United States Supreme Court's 1934 decision of *Nebbia v. New York*, 291 U.S. 502, 525, upholding the constitutionality of a state system of price supports for milk, set the basic standard for validity under the due process clause: "the guaranty of due process . . . demands only that the law shall not be unreasonable, arbitrary or capricious, and that the means selected shall have a real and substantial relation to the object sought to be attained." . . .

The standards for the constitutionality of government rate or price controls under the takings clause were set by the United States Supreme Court's 1944 decision in [*Federal Power Commission v. Hope Natural Gas Co.*, 320 U.S. 591 (1944)]. There, the Court made clear that participants in a regulated industry are entitled to something more than mere survival:

> From the investor or company point of view it is important that there be enough revenue not only for operating expenses but also for the capital costs of the business. These include service on the debt and dividends on the stock. . . . By that standard the return to the equity owner should be commensurate with returns on

investments in other enterprises having corresponding risks. That return, more-over, should be sufficient to assure confidence in the financial integrity of the enterprise, so as to maintain its credit and to attract capital. . . .

Id., 320 U.S. at 603. . . . We have posited a like standard: to avoid confiscatory results under the takings clause, "the return should be one which is generally commensurate with returns on investments in other enterprises having compa-rable risks." [*Hutton Park Gardens v. Town Council of Town of West Orange,* 68 N.J. 543, 570 (1975).] . . .

However, the constitutional requirement that a business be permitted a return sufficient to assure its financial health does not necessarily require any particu-lar level of profit above what is adequate to attract and retain invested capi-tal. . . . In sum, while government regulation cannot wreak too great an inter-ference with "distinct investment-backed expectations," *Penn Cent. Transp. Co. v. City of New York,* 438 U.S. 104, 124 (1978), a participant in a highly regulated industry must anticipate that its profit levels can be capped or even reduced by changes in government regulation. There is no constitutional entitlement to maximum profits. . . .

The facial constitutionality of the Reform Act depends on whether the new burdens on the insurers, the surtaxes and assessments, necessarily preclude a fair rate of return. That determination in turn requires the resolution of two questions—first, do Sections 75 and 78 of the statute absolutely bar cost passthroughs to offset the impact of the assessments and surtaxes; and second, if one or both of those new costs cannot be recovered through standard rate relief, does the Reform Act nonetheless permit the Commissioner otherwise to set rates that would provide a fair rate of return . . . ?

In determining whether Sections 75 and 78 absolutely prohibit passthroughs, there is no real room for doubt that the mandatory terms of Section 78 dem-onstrate the Legislature's intent to preclude entirely any consideration of the surtaxes in standard ratemaking: "The Commissioner . . . *shall* take such action . . . to *ensure* that . . . policyholders *shall not pay for the surtax.*" (Emphasis added.) While Section 75 is less absolute in tone, its terms were evidently influ-enced by the surcharges for insolvency assessments that insurers historically have been permitted to add directly to policyholders' premiums. We believe that it is consistent both with the more obvious prohibition of Section 78, and with the use of surcharges as the only recognized method for passing along insolvency assessments, to construe Section 75's prohibition of "surcharges . . . to recoup assessments" as absolute. The idiosyncratic language of Section 75, in context, indicates that the Legislature intended to foreclose the only existing means by which costs of the assessments could be shifted directly to consumers.

If we were remitted only to the terms of Sections 75 and 78, we would be con-strained to rule that those provisions standing alone do not allow any recovery of the assessments and surtaxes through rate increases. However, while Sections 75 and 78 foreclose relief in standard ratemaking, Section 2g implicitly grants the Commissioner overriding authority to guarantee insurers a fair rate of return by some means other than direct passthrough. Thus, Section 2g does not contradict the prohibition, under Sections 75 and 78, of direct passthroughs of the costs of the surtaxes and assessments. Section 2g expressly acknowledges that "automobile insurers are *entitled* to earn an adequate rate of return through the *ratemaking process.*" N.J.S.A. 17:33B-2g (emphasis added). The statute should be liberally construed as giving the Commissioner ample authority to follow that directive and achieve the legislative objective.

The State further asserts that various provisions of the Act provide additional or supplementary means for the insurers to obtain relief from inadequate rates, despite the direct passthrough prohibitions of Sections 75 and 78. In particular, if an insurer is at risk because of an "unsafe or unsound financial condition," the Commissioner may suspend (1) its obligation to accept the allocation of risks under an Assigned Risk Plan, *see* Reform Act, Sections 91 and 92; (2) its obligation to issue or renew automobile policies, Reform Act, Sections 93 and 94; (3) its obligation to pay PLIGA assessments, Reform Act, Sections 95 and 96; and (4) its obligation to pay the premiums surtax, Reform Act, Sections 98 and 99. The State also points out that carriers can increase their income through available "flex rate" increases, which permit insurers to raise rates by amounts related to increases in certain components of the Consumer Price Index without prior regulatory approval. N.J.S.A. 17:29A-44. Further, the Act contains various "cost-saving" provisions, which the State contends are likely to decrease insurers' costs and thus increase profitability. These include provisions that cap personal-injury benefits, allow an insured to select a health insurer as the primary carrier for personal-injury benefits, establish fee limits on health-care providers, require inspection of automobiles prior to providing physical-damage coverage, establish an anti-fraud program, and provide limits on towing and storage charges. The insurers, with considerable vigor, argue that the cost "savings" that the State attributes to the foregoing provisions are problematic and unrealistic. Nevertheless, while the "cost-saving" and other statutory provisions may not individually or collectively assure a fair rate of return for insurers, as the State stresses, they do increase the possibility of avoiding confiscatory rates. . . .

Recently-adopted regulations of the Department of Insurance governing when and how rate relief may be available to offset the surtaxes and assessments corroborate the legislative meaning suggested by the statutory text and history, *i.e.,* that a fair rate of return is to be assured under the Reform Act despite the specific prohibitions of Sections 75 and 78. That administrative understanding is persuasive evidence of the intent of the Legislature in enacting the regulatory scheme.

On November 26, 1990, the Commissioner issued "emergency regulations" to implement the Reform Act; those regulations, with certain amendments, were permanently adopted on January 25, 1991. The regulations and their implications for the constitutional validity of the Reform Act were addressed by the parties on appeal. The Insurance Department's summary of the regulations governing rate filings emphasizes the Act's prohibition of passthroughs. It also explains that the regulations establish a special, separate rate-increase filing procedure for any insurer who believes that the effect of the surtaxes and assessments, in its particular case, is to preclude a constitutionally adequate rate of return:

> N.J.A.C. 11:3-16.10 is amended to confirm that the Property-Liability Insurance Guaranty Association assessment and the surtax imposed by sections 74 and 76 of the Act, respectively, may not be incorporated into the expense base for determining rates. This implements sections 75 and 78 of the Act which prohibit direct pass-through of the assessment or surtax to policyholders. The Act and the Constitution of the United States, however, provide that insurers are entitled to earn an adequate rate of return through the ratemaking process. An insurer may thus

request rate relief if it is unable to earn an adequate rate of return due to imposition of the assessment or surtax. Accordingly, the Department is proposing a new rule, N.J.A.C. 11:3-16.11, which sets forth the filing requirements for an insurer desiring to modify its rates to reflect the assessment or surtax. The data filed will enable the Commissioner to evaluate the insurer's experience on all lines of business in New Jersey; the insurer's operational efficiency; the insurer's method of allocation of expenses; and the synergistic effect of mandated private passenger automobile insurance on the profitability of other lines of business.

[Rate Filing Requirements, supra, pp. 6-7]. . . .

To that end, the regulations provide a new procedure for separate rate increase filings by insurers who can demonstrate that payment of the surtaxes and assessments has denied them a fair rate of return. . . .

Thus, the Department of Insurance interprets the Reform Act as authorizing consideration of the economic effect of the surtaxes and assessments in addressing an insurer's claim that it is being deprived of a constitutionally adequate return. Further, the Department apparently intends that in such circumstances, it will take the surtaxes and assessments into account in ratemaking despite the Act's directive that insurers cannot obtain a direct passthrough or include those costs as expense-side items in standard rate-increase filings. . . .

Because we find that the Act is facially valid, it will be appropriate for the Commissioner to render determinations on individual insurers' rate-increase applications in the first instance, before challenges to the constitutionality of the application of the statute and regulations are brought. The Department of Insurance has the particular expertise necessary to develop the detailed record of an insurer's financial performance that must form the basis for any as-applied challenge.

The plaintiffs here, or any other affected insurers, are free to institute as-applied challenges to the Reform Act in the event that the relief afforded to them under N.J.A.C. 11:3-16.11 is either substantively or procedurally inadequate to assure a constitutionally fair rate of return. We imply no view on whether the statute and regulations will pass constitutional muster in the event of an as-applied challenge.

NOTES AND QUESTIONS

1. The larger the subsidies that are built into a residual market mechanism, the larger the population will be in that residual market. The failure of the New Jersey JUA resulted from a combination of many political factors, but the economics were fairly straightforward. First, the rates charged to people in the JUA were too low relative to the rates charged in the voluntary market, with the result that the population in the JUA grew much larger than anticipated in the design of the JUA. Second, the "residual market equalization charges (RMECs)" and the fines and fees that were supposed to allow the JUA to operate on a break-even basis were not in fact adequate to the job.

    There is no reason in theory why the JUA could not have operated on a break-even basis. The problem is that it would have required much larger RMECs than the Department of Insurance was politically able to assess the insurers in the voluntary market. So, the costs of insuring high-risk drivers were pushed off into the future. When the future finally came, the legislature attempted to wish the costs away.

2. In a concurring opinion, Justice Garibaldi cautioned the Department of Insurance as follows:

> Current economic conditions compound my concerns. In the past, insurance companies, like banks, were always considered financial bulwarks. That is no longer true. Although the size of the accumulated unpaid debt of the Joint Underwriting Association is deplorable, the failure or withdrawal of insurance companies providing coverage in this state would prove even more damaging. Therefore, it is imperative that insurance companies actually receive a "fair and adequate rate of return" within a reasonable period of time.
>
> Neither the insurance company nor this state's insurance market will be adequately protected by the pyrrhic discovery after it has ceased doing business here (and perhaps elsewhere) that it deserved a rate increase five years ago.

3. If automobile insurers are prohibited from raising their rates to recover the new charges, where will they get the money to pay the new charges? Why might an insurer be willing to make very little money on automobile insurance in New Jersey?

4. In what other ways might the New Jersey legislature have addressed the JUA debt? What are the politics of those other approaches?

5. After the New Jersey Department of Insurance regulations and the New Jersey Supreme Court decision, what is left of the New Jersey legislature's prohibition on passing through to automobile insurance consumers the accumulated debt of the JUA?

LEGAL MALPRACTICE RESIDUAL MARKETS PROBLEM

With the rise of legal malpractice claims in the United States, there has come the recognition that unless the lawyers have malpractice insurance, the victims of legal malpractice will not receive compensation. As a result, some state legislators have proposed that lawyers be required to carry a mandatory minimum amount of legal malpractice insurance.

The legislature in the State of Superior is considering such a proposal. Currently, the legal malpractice market in Superior is entirely voluntary, rates are set on a competitive basis (meaning that the State Insurance Department approves whatever rates insurers submit), and there are three types of insurers active in the market: (1) a small group of major property and casualty insurers that provide legal malpractice insurance as one of their "specialty lines," (2) a nonprofit insurer organized by the state bar association, and (3) a nonprofit insurer organized by large national law firms that insures only large law firms that are willing to abide by its loss prevention guidelines.

1. Should legal malpractice insurance be mandatory?
2. Should there be a residual market mechanism?
3. If there is, should it be a JUA, an assigned risk plan, or something else?

4. If it is a JUA, how should the JUA rates be set and the shortfalls funded?
5. If it is an assigned risk plan, how should risks be assigned?
6. Should legal malpractice insurers be members of the P&C Guaranty Fund?
7. Should there be a separate guaranty fund?
8. How do your answers to items 2 through 7 affect your answer to item 1?

Consider these questions from the perspectives of each of the categories of insurers, the Superior Insurance Department, the Superior Bar Association (which is dominated by small and medium-sized "general practice" firms), the Superior Trial Lawyers Association (whose members typically represent plaintiffs in personal injury litigation), the Superior Defense Lawyers Association (whose members typically represent defendants and insurers in personal injury litigation), the "bishops" (the informal name for the managing partners of the large Superior City law firms, who meet for breakfast twice a year to discuss issues of common concern), and legislators.

C. Insurance Risk Classification

1. Introduction

Risk classification is the generic insurance term for treating people differently according to predictions about the frequency and size of the future claims that they will make against their policies. Two examples of insurance risk classification are charging smokers higher premiums for life insurance than nonsmokers and charging teenage boys higher premiums for automobile insurance than teenage girls. Insurance risk classification applies judgments about the future, claiming the behavior of a group to the individuals who are classed within that group.

A traditional economic justification for insurers' practice of risk classification is the problem of adverse selection, which we discussed in Chapter 1, Section II. In brief, the basic idea is that, in a voluntary insurance market, if everyone is charged the same price for insurance, low-risk people are less likely to buy insurance than are high-risk people. *See* Michael Rothschild & Joseph Stiglitz, *Equilibrium in Competitive Insurance Markets: An Essay on the Economics of Imperfect Information,* 90 Q.J. Econ. 629 (1976). Thus, if an insurer can charge premiums that closely approximate an insured's particular expected costs, the incentive for adverse selection is reduced. Risk classification can also help to reduce problems of moral hazard. For example, if a homeowners' insurance company charges lower premiums to individuals who install smoke detectors and who make use of a particular type of storm-resistant roofing tile, such a premium discount can induce insureds to make smart investments in risk reduction. Omri Ben-Shahar & Kyle D. Logue, *Outsourcing Regulation: How Insurance Reduces Moral Hazard,* 111 Mich. L. Rev. 1, 224 & 230 (2012).

More generally, it is easy to see why insurers in a competitive market would have an incentive to classify applicants according to the risk that they pose. Risk classification is one of the most potent competitive tools. If one insurer develops a new way of separating relatively low-risk insureds from high-risk insureds, that insurer has a competitive advantage; it can attract the low-risk insureds away from other insurers whose underwriting techniques are less accurate. In addition, assuming the people the innovative insurer rejects get insurance elsewhere, it increases the average risk of the less innovative competitors. Moreover, the innovative insurer can attract low-risk insureds who have opted not to buy insurance (because prices were too high) back into the market in a way that the other insurers cannot. This dynamic gives all insurers an incentive to research and develop cost-effective ways of classifying risks. As discussed in Chapter 1, insofar as these risk classification techniques actually induce insureds to take steps to reduce their risks, risk classification acts as a form of private regulation of risk and can enhance overall efficiency.

Risk classification by insurers can be justified not only on efficiency grounds but also on fairness grounds. In insurance circles, a private insurance arrangement is "fair" if it is "actuarially fair," and actuarial fairness is usually understood to mean that the premium and coverage differences are actuarially accurate — that is, they correspond accurately to differences in expected losses. Thus, according to Professor Spencer Kimball, the goal of "fair" insurance discrimination is "to measure as accurately as is practicable the burden shifted to the insurance fund by the policy holder and to charge exactly for it, no more and no less." Spencer L. Kimball, *Reverse Sex Discrimination: Manhart*, 1979 American Bar Found. Res. J. 83, 105. The idea is that it is generally fair to charge premiums equal to expected costs, because we are doing nothing more than making people "cover their own costs" or "carry their own weight." This is a widely held view, even outside the insurance industry. Note that the argument for the use of actuarially fair insurance premiums is very similar to the argument for the use of "benefit taxation" among public finance scholars. Under a benefit tax, individual taxpayers are taxed according to the benefit they receive from the public expenditure being funded by the tax. *See* James R. Hines Jr., *What Is Benefit Taxation?*, 75 J. Pub. Econ. 483, 483 (2000).

On this view, in a market economy, people choose and pay for the goods and services that they consume. Insurance is one of those services, and relatively high-risk people consume "more" insurance, so they should pay more. In addition, we have a strong principle of treating like people alike, a principle that is violated by charging low-risk people the same price as high-risk people. This vision of insurance is especially attractive to Americans because of our individualist cultural history and values. In addition, at least some forms of risk classification have been framed as protecting "decent" "good" people from "moral hazards," who pose a threat to the solvency of the insurance pool, and other forms of risk classification as providing an incentive for "responsible" behavior.

Although risk classification by insurers can be socially efficient and can be regarded as fair, the reverse can also be true. Risk classification can both socially inefficient and unfair. Risk classification can be inefficient, for example, when adverse selection and moral hazard are not significant problems and yet insurers still invest expensive resources in classifying risks. Some insurance markets are naturally resistant to adverse selection, perhaps because insureds lack the information necessary to engage in it, or have other constraints on adverse selection, such as insurance mandates imposed by law. *See, e.g.,* Peter Siegelman, *Adverse Selection in Insurance Markets: An Exaggerated Threat*, 113 Yale L.J. 1223, 1224 (2004); *and* Tom Baker, *Containing the Promise of Insurance: Adverse Selection and Risk Classification, in* Moral Risks (Richard Ericson & Aaron Doyle eds., 2003). Where this is true, any resources spent by insurers on classifying risks is socially wasteful, and can amount to a type of unnecessary "arms race." In such situations, insurers can be seen as spending resources to "skim" the best risks for themselves while trying to stick their competitors with the worst risks, and such risk classification provides little or no value to society.

Risk classification can also be inefficient if the particular classifications used by insurers turn out not to be so accurate or closely correlated with differences in expected losses. Insofar as insureds receive signals from and respond behaviorally to differences in insurance premiums, risk classifications that are actuarially inaccurate reward socially inefficient (i.e., risk-increasing) behavior. One might wonder why insurance companies, with all of their risk-related sophistication and with the incentives created by competition, would ever classify inaccurately. But it can happen. For example, insurers can simply become stuck in their ways through path dependence. As a result, insurers who have collected risk information based on risk categories chosen in the past may have a tendency to continue using those categories after they have lost their utility. Or there may be better risk indicators than those insurers have used, yet that cannot be known without the information that is developed only once insurers decide to classify risk on the basis of those indications. *See* Kenneth S. Abraham, Distributing Risk (1986).

Risk classification can also be unfair. Indeed, when governments seek to restrict insurers' use of particular characteristics, it is typically fairness-related arguments that take center stage. When is insurer risk classification unfair? First, as noted above, it is possible for particular risk classifications to be actuarially unfair, in the sense of being statistically inaccurate or unreliable. Or maybe the average risk within a given category is accurate, but the variance within the category is vast, imposing huge amounts of unjustified cross subsidization within the insurance pool. Almost everyone would agree that there is a potential fairness concern in these cases. Charging people different rates based on factors that are either irrelevant or only barely relevant to expected costs, in the absence of some countervailing fairness or efficiency rationale, seems wrong. That is presumably why many states have laws that impose limitations on the use of various characteristics in the underwriting process unless the insurer can show that the characteristic in fact correlates with expected losses. *See generally* Ronen Avraham, Kyle D. Logue & Daniel Schwarcz, *Understanding Insurance Anti-Discrimination Laws*, 87 S. Cal. L. Rev. 195 (2014).

Even actuarially fair insurance classifications can be considered unfair or unjust. *See generally* Kenneth S. Abraham, Distributing Risk: Insurance, Legal Theory, and Public Policy (1986); Regina Austin, *The Insurance Classification Controversy*, 131 U. Pa. L. Rev. 517 (1983). For example, some might argue that, for a particular risk category to be fair, it should be simple enough to be understood by the parties who are affected by it. Some regard risk classifications that are based on pure correlation between a particular characteristic and higher expected costs, and that have no clear causal link, as an unfair basis for drawing distinctions. In addition, many would object on fairness grounds to any use by insurers of certain historically suspect classifications, such as race, religion, or national origin, whether or not those characteristics turned out empirically to correlate with differences in expected costs. In the same way, there may be fairness objections to other risk categories that are not explicitly about historically suspect classifications but may be considered a proxy for such classifications.

Two final fairness-based rationales for regulating insurers' ability to use particular characteristics in classifying risks involve the concepts of social solidarity and distributional equality. The principle of social solidarity—which is much stronger in Europe than in the United States—holds that insurance exists for the benefit of the group and therefore it should be structured to promote the broadest possible risk distribution, an idea that is consistent with placing limits on insurers' ability to classify risks. In addition, the principle of distributional equality suggests that society should seek to eliminate or at least reduce certain arbitrary differences in opportunities or economic well-being that exist between individuals, especially where those differences are not the result of voluntary, informed choices but rather are the result of "brute luck." *See generally* Ronald Dworkin, *What Is Equality? Part 1: Equality of Welfare,* 10 Phil. & Pub. Affairs 185 (1981); and *What Is Equality? Part 2: Equality of Resources,* 10 Phil. & Pub. Affairs 283 (1981). Reducing such arbitrary inequality has long been a justification for redistributive taxation and for social welfare programs. The same type of rationale can be used to enact laws that limit insurers from taking into account characteristics that correlate with differences in expected costs *and* that are utterly beyond the control of the insureds. Such laws can also be understood as providing an alternative, and surprisingly efficient, system of redistributing resources from the better off to the less well off. Kyle Logue & Ronen Avraham, *Redistributing Optimally: Of Tax Rules, Legal Rules, and Insurance,* 56 Tax L. Rev. 147 (2002).

NOTES AND QUESTIONS

1. If actuarially accurate risk classification is fair, why is social insurance not funded through risk-adjusted premiums? How is social insurance typically funded? Why do all the members of an employment group pay the same price for health insurance? Why does no one object when a life insurance company decides not to sell life insurance to a victim of tobacco companies' teenage marketing strategy, but a health insurance company's decision not to offer health insurance to a victim of domestic abuse prompts a wave of legislation? *See* Deborah Hellman, *Is Actuarially Fair Insurance Pricing Actually Fair? A Case Study in Insuring Battered Women,* 32 Harv. C.R.-C.L. L. Rev. 355 (1997). *See also* Tom Baker, *Containing the Promise of Insurance: Adverse Selection and Risk Classification,* 9 Conn. Ins. L.J. 371 (2003); Leah Wortham, *Insurance Classification: Too Important to Be Left to Actuaries,* 19 U. Mich. J.L. Reform 349 (1986); Leah Wortham, *The Economics of Insurance Classification: The Sound of One Invisible Hand Clapping,* 47 Ohio St. L.J. 835 (1986).

2. Jonathan Simon has criticized some forms of insurance risk classification and other examples of what he terms "actuarial practices" on the grounds that they do not correspond to subjective identity. *See* Jonathan Simon, *The Ideological Effects of Actuarial Practices,* 22 Law & Soc'y Rev. 771 (1988). Other examples of actuarial practices include standardized testing (e.g., the Law School Admission Test (LSAT)), targeted marketing, and poll-driven political campaigns. What all these practices have in common is the sophisticated use of social statistics, a form of knowledge that flowered earliest in the insurance field.

Professor Simon is concerned that these actuarial groupings will undercut the traditional social categories around which people have organized their lives, reducing the capacity to mobilize action in a democratic society. Does this ring true? As Regina Austin has observed, "[h]owever much the companies plead happenstance, insurance 'risk' classifications correlate with a fairly simplistic and static notion of social stratification that is familiar to everyone." 131 U. Pa. L. Rev. at 534. The 'risk' classification categories she examined were occupation, age, sex, marital status, and neighborhood. Why might insurance companies choose those categories? How does the use of these categories fit with Professor Simon's concern?

3.   Professor Hellman's case study in insuring battered women demonstrates the power of creating new social groups or labels. "Battered women" was a new social category created in the late twentieth century by social workers and criminal defense lawyers attempting to create a new defense in criminal law, so that women who killed husbands who regularly beat them would not spend their lives in prison. *Cf.* Martha R. Mahoney, *Legal Images of Battered Women: Redefining the Issue of Separation,* 90 Mich. L. Rev. 1 (1991). This effort in social categorization was successful in criminal law and in broader social consciousness, with the result that insurance companies began to use it as an underwriting tool. As this suggests, "actuarial practices" typically are not conjured up out of thin air. Instead, they are derivative of existing social categories. In part, it has been the resistance to the use of existing social categories—such as race and gender—that has driven insurance companies to innovate in their risk classifications. As you may recall, we have explored two other insurance law issues that affect battered women: the "innocent insured" exception to the arson exclusion in property insurance policies and the meaning of "intent" for purposes of the intentional act exclusion to liability insurance policies.

4.   One of the most recent developments in personal lines risk classification is the use of credit scores. Credit scores are developed on the basis of credit information maintained by the large consumer credit data aggregation agencies, which consider such things as frequency of late payments, size and number of loans, and other factors that go into the "credit history" of consumers. Although insurers defend credit scores on the grounds that they reward responsibility and that they are an actuarially sound measurement of risk, some states have been limiting the use of credit scores because of their disturbing correlation to race and a feeling of unfairness as people can be stuck with bad credit scores from the same periods of disability or need that insurance is supposed to mitigate against. Because of the actuarial accuracy of credit scores, they have withstood disparate impact challenges. *See, e.g., Dehoyos v. Allstate Corp.,* 345 F.3d 290 (5th Cir. 2003); *Dehoyos v. Allstate Corp.,* 240 F.R.D. 269 (W.D. Tx. 2007); *Owens v. Nationwide Mut. Ins. Co.,* No. Civ. 3:03-CV-1184-H, 2005 WL 1837959 (N.D. Tex. Aug. 2, 2005). There has been more progress in state legislation, as a majority of states prohibit or in some way regulate the use of credit scores. Ronen Avraham, Kyle D. Logue, & Daniel Schwarcz, *Understanding Insurance Anti-Discrimination Laws,* 87 S. Cal. L. Rev. 195, 265 (2014). Interestingly, a handful of states have laws expressly permitting the use of credit scores in insurance underwriting. *Id. See also* Frank M. Fitzgerald, The Use of Insurance Credit Scoring in

Automobile and Homeowners Insurance (2002) (an influential study conducted for the Michigan legislature about the use of credit scores).

2. Legal Limits on Risk Classification by Insurers

In the previous section, we discussed the efficiency and fairness reasons why it makes sense that insurers should generally be permitted to classify risks—to charge different premiums based on differences in insureds' risk profiles—and why it is sensible to place some legal limits on insurers' risk classification practices. That leads to another interesting question: What legal limits in fact exist on the risk classification practices of insurance companies?[6] You may be surprised to learn that there are relatively few restrictions imposed by federal law on the extent to which insurers can discriminate among insureds on the basis of risk characteristics.

a. The Fair Housing Act

According to the Fair Housing Act (FHA), it is unlawful "to refuse to sell or rent after the making of a bona fide offer, or to refuse to negotiate for the sale or rental of, or *otherwise make unavailable or deny, a dwelling* to any person because of race, color, religion, sex, familial status, or national origin." 42 U.S.C. §3604(a) (emphasis added).

It is also unlawful under the FHA "to discriminate in the sale or rental, or otherwise to make unavailable or deny, a dwelling to any buyer or renter because of a handicap of (A) that buyer or renter[;] (B) the person residing in or intending to reside in that dwelling after it is so sold, rented, or made available; or (C) any person associated with that buyer or renter." 42 U.S.C. §3604(f).

A number of federal courts have held that the FHA applies to homeowners' insurance in certain contexts, notwithstanding (a) the plain statement reverse preemption doctrine of the McCarran-Ferguson Act (MFA) and (b) the fact that the FHA nowhere mentions the business of insurance. For example, in *NAACP v. American Family Mut. Ins. Co.*, 978 F.2d 287 (7th Cir. 1992), the court held that the FHA applies to homeowners' insurance to forbid racial discrimination in the property/casualty insurance underwriting process, since the federal law is consistent with—and therefore does not "invalidate, impair, or supersede"—the Wisconsin law forbidding racial discrimination in the underwriting process by property/casualty insurers.[7] *See generally* Dana L. Kaersvang, *The Fair Housing Act and Disparate Impact in Homeowners Insurance,* 104 Mich. L. Rev. 1993 (2006) (arguing that FHA disparate impact analysis should be applied to homeowners' insurance). The more difficult cases involve the use by homeowners' insurers of credit scoring techniques, which have been expressly authorized in a number of states but that arguably create a racially disparate impact that runs

---

6. This section draws from Avraham, Logue, & Schwarcz, *Understanding Insurance Anti-Discrimination Laws,* 87 S. Cal. L. Rev. 195 (2014).

7. *But see Mackey v. Nationwide Insurance Cos.,* 724 F.2d 419 (4th Cir. 1984) (holding that the FHA does not apply to insurance). *Mackey* is the only appellate case contra to *American Family.* Arguably, HUD regulations issued after *Mackey* effectively overruled *Mackey.*

afoul of the FHA. Contrast *Dehoyos v. Allstate Corp.*, 345 F.3d 290 (5th Cir. 2003) (holding that the FHA applies) with *Ojo v. Farmers Group, Inc.*, 600 F.3d 1205 (2010) (holding that the reverse preemption provision of the MFA applies to disparate impact claims under the FHA if Texas state law permits credit scoring in situations in which there is a racially disparate impact); and *Ojo v. Farmers Group, Inc.*, 356 S.W.3d 421 (Tex. 2011) (on certification from the Ninth Circuit, holding that Texas law does in fact authorize the use of credit scoring even if it produces a racially disparate impact, so long as there is no disparate treatment). *See generally* Sarah L. Rosenblush, *Fair Housing Act Challenges to the Use of Consumer Credit Information in Homeowners Insurance Underwriting: Is the McCarran-Ferguson Act a Bar?* 46 Colum. J.L. & Soc. Problems 49 (2012) (arguing that courts should take a narrow approach to MFA reverse preemption to allow FHA disparate impact claims against homeowners' insurers to go forward).

The U.S. government has, since at least 2011, taken the position that the FHA does in fact apply to insurance. Specifically, among the rules promulgated by the U.S. Department of Housing and Urban Development (HUD) on April 1, 2011, was a prohibition on "[r]efusing to provide . . . property or hazard insurance for dwellings or providing such services or insurance differently because of race, color, religion, sex, handicap, familial status, or national origin." 24 C.F.R. §100.70(d)(4). Later in 2011, HUD formally adopted the disparate impact standard for claims under the FHA. *See* "Implementation of the Fair Housing Act's Discriminatory Effects Standard," 76 FR 70921-01 (November 15, 2011) ("Examples of a housing policy or practice that may have a disparate impact . . . include . . . the provision and pricing of homeowner's insurance.") (citing *Ojo*, 600 F.3d at 1207-8).

In 2014, however, a federal district court in the District of Columbia held that HUD's promulgation of a disparate-impact rule exceeded the agency's statutory authority, on the ground that the FHA prohibits only intentional discrimination. *See Am. Ins. Ass'n v. United States Dep't of Hous. & Urban Dev.*, 74 F. Supp. 3d 30, 39 (D.D.C. 2014). In a recent decision involving the distribution of federal low-income housing credits through designated state agencies in Texas, the U.S. Supreme Court disagreed. In *Texas Dep't of Hous. & Cmty. Affairs v. Inclusive Communities Project, Inc.*, 576 U.S. ___, 135 S. Ct. 2507 (June 25, 2015), the Court held that "disparate-impact claims are cognizable under the Fair Housing Act." *Id.* at 2525.

The Court also placed limitations on those claims, however. As the Court pointed out, "[i]n contrast to a disparate-treatment case, where a 'plaintiff must establish that the defendant had a discriminatory intent or motive,' a plaintiff bringing a disparate-impact claim challenges practices that have a "disproportionately adverse effect on minorities' and are otherwise unjustified by a legitimate rationale." *Ricci* v. *DeStefano*, 557 U.S. 557, 577 (2009). Therefore, the Court emphasized that disparate-impact claims under the FHA relying solely on statistical disparity in housing outcomes will fail and should be dismissed at the trial stage unless the plaintiffs can point to a policy or practice of the defendant that causes the statistical disparity and show a "causal connection" between that policy and unlawful disparity. *Id.* at 2523-24. Furthermore, even when courts do find disparate-impact liability, the Court noted that their remedial orders "should concentrate on the elimination of the offending practice that "arbitrar[ily] . . . operate[s] invidiously to discriminate on the basis of rac[e]." *Id.* (citing *Griggs* v. *Duke Power Co.*, 401 U. S. 424, 431 (1971)).

Note that the Court's decision in *Inclusive Communities Project* did not directly address the HUD regulation cited above. Thus, the decision does not directly address the question of under what circumstances, if any, the reverse-preemption rule in the McCarran-Ferguson Act might apply to block disparate-impact claims against insurers under the FHA. Is the HUD rule good law? Does HUD need to revise the rule in any way to satisfy the limitations articulated in the Court's holding? After the Supreme Court's opinion came down, the D.C. Circuit Court of Appeals in an unpublished opinion vacated and remanded the district court's decision in *Am. Ins. Ass'n*, ordering the district court to apply the *Inclusive Communities Project* disparate impact standard. *See Am. Ins. Ass'n v. United States Dep't of Hous. & Dev.*, 1:13-cv-00966-RJL, No. 14-5321 (September 23, 2015).

b. Section 1981 of the Civil Rights Act of 1866

Section 1981 states as follows:

All persons within the jurisdiction of the United States shall have the same right in every State and Territory to make and enforce contracts, to sue, be parties, give evidence, and to the full and equal benefit of all laws and proceedings for the security of persons and property as is enjoyed by white citizens, and shall be subject to like punishment, pains, penalties, taxes, licenses, and exactions of every kind, and to no other.

. . .

For purposes of this section, the term "make and enforce contracts" includes the making, performance, modification, and termination of contracts, and the enjoyment of all benefits, privileges, terms, and conditions of the contractual relationship.

. . .

The rights protected by this section are protected against impairment by nongovernmental discrimination and impairment under color of State law.

14 Stat. 27-30.

Section 1981 suits have rarely been used by plaintiffs against insurance companies, presumably because of the difficulty of proving discriminatory intent, which is a requirement of such suits. *Guidry v. Pellerin Life Insurance Co.*, 364 F. Supp. 2d 592 (W.D. La. 2005), was one of many class action Section 1981 lawsuits concerning racial discrimination that were brought in connection with the sale of industrial life insurance policies. Industrial life insurance policies, also referred to as "burial insurance," were insurance policies primarily targeted toward lower-income communities. Industrial insurance was traditionally sold door to door, with premiums based on outdated race-based actuarial tables. Industrial insurance was largely phased out during the 1970s and 1980s, but some well-known insurance companies still collected premiums on the policies decades later. Starting with a $206 million class action against American General Life Insurance in 2000 for violating Section 1981 and 1982 prohibitions against race-based underwriting, there have been many class action settlements against the insurers selling industrial life insurance. Few of these class actions were litigated past the certification of the class. *See, e.g., In re Monumental Life Ins. Co.*, 365 F.3d 408 (5th Cir. 2004) (holding that black policyholders' industrial life insurance discrimination claims may proceed as a class action); *Thompson v. Metropolitan Life Ins.*, 149 F. Supp. 2d 38 (S.D.N.Y. 2001) (denying insurer's motion for summary judgment); *Brown v. American Capital Ins. Co.*, No. Civ. A. 01-2079, 2004 WL 2375796 (E.D. La. Oct. 21, 2004). According to Robert Dilberato, one of the plaintiffs' lawyers involved in some of the litigation, most of the insurers seem to be more interested in settling the class actions and washing their hands of these old policies than fighting for them. In *Guidry*, however, the court concluded that the higher premiums for black policyholders did not violate the civil rights laws because census data showed that African Americans do die earlier than most other racial groups. This is the only reported case that we have found in which a court specifically authorized race-based underwriting practices so long as they were actuarially accurate. Apparently, *Guidry* was not appealed. *See* J. Gabriel McGlamery, *Race Based Underwriting and Death of Burial Insurance*, 15 Conn. Ins. L.J. 531 (2009). For a fictional but accurate first-person account of selling such insurance, see Allan Gurganus's story, *Blessed Assurance*, in his collection, White People (1991).

c.   Title VII of the Civil Rights Act of 1964

City of Los Angeles v. Manhart, 435 U.S. 702 (1978), is perhaps the most famous insurance discrimination case ever decided. The suit was brought as a class action on behalf of female employees of the Los Angeles Department of Water and Power, alleging that the department's requirement that female employees make larger contributions to its pension fund than male employees violated §703(a)(1) of Title VII of the Civil Rights Act of 1964, which, among other things, makes it unlawful for an employer to discriminate against any individual because of that individual's sex. The Department's pension plan had been based on mortality tables and its own experience showing that female employees had greater longevity than male employees and that the cost of a pension for the average female retiree was greater than for the average male retiree because more monthly payments had to be made to the former.

The Court held that the challenged differential in the department's pension plan violated Title VII as unlawful discrimination in employment on the basis of sex. The Court noted that the differential was discriminatory in its "treatment of a person in a manner which but for that person's sex would be different." The statute, which focuses on fairness to individuals rather than fairness to classes, precludes treating individuals as simply components of a group such as the sexual class here. Even though it is true that women as a class outlive men, that generalization cannot be used, the Court reasoned, to justify disqualifying an individual to whom it does not apply.

In reaching its conclusion that Title VII does not allow gender-based premiums and payouts in employer-provided retirement annuities, the majority opinion, written by Justice Stevens, reasoned as follows:

> [Title VII] makes it unlawful "to discriminate against any *individual* with respect to his compensation, terms, conditions, or privileges of employment, because of such *individual's* race, color, religion, sex, or national origin." 42 U.S.C. §2000e-2 (a)(1) (emphasis added). The statute's focus on the individual is unambiguous. It precludes treatment of individuals as simply components of a racial, religious,

sexual, or national class. If height is required for a job, a tall woman may not be refused employment merely because, on the average, women are too short. Even a true generalization about the class is an insufficient reason for disqualifying an individual to whom the generalization does not apply.

That proposition is of critical importance in this case because there is no assurance that any individual woman working for the Department will actually fit the generalization on which the Department's policy is based. Many of those individuals will not live as long as the average man. While they were working, those individuals received smaller paychecks because of their sex, but they will receive no compensating advantage when they retire.

It is true, of course, that while contributions are being collected from the employees, the Department cannot know which individuals will predecease the average woman. Therefore, unless women as a class are assessed an extra charge, they will be subsidized, to some extent, by the class of male employees. It follows, according to the Department, that fairness to its class of male employees justifies the extra assessment against all of its female employees.

But the question of fairness to various classes affected by the statute is essentially a matter of policy for the legislature to address. Congress has decided that classifications based on sex, like those based on national origin or race, are unlawful. Actuarial studies could unquestionably identify differences in life expectancy based on race or national origin, as well as sex. But a statute that was designed to make race irrelevant in the employment market, *see Griggs v. Duke Power Co.*, 401 U.S. 424, 436 (1971), could not reasonably be construed to permit a take-home-pay differential based on a racial classification.

Even if the statutory language were less clear, the basic policy of the statute requires that we focus on fairness to individuals rather than fairness to classes. Practices that classify employees in terms of religion, race, or sex tend to preserve traditional assumptions about groups rather than thoughtful scrutiny of individuals. The generalization involved in this case illustrates the point. Separate mortality tables are easily interpreted as reflecting innate differences between the sexes; but a significant part of the longevity differential may be explained by the social fact that men are heavier smokers than women.

Finally, there is no reason to believe that Congress intended a special definition of discrimination in the context of employee group insurance coverage. It is true that insurance is concerned with events that are individually unpredictable, but that is characteristic of many employment decisions. Individual risks, like individual performance, may not be predicted by resort to classifications proscribed by Title VII. Indeed, the fact that this case involves a group insurance program highlights a basic flaw in the Department's fairness argument. For when insurance risks are grouped, the better risks always subsidize the poorer risks. Healthy persons subsidize medical benefits for the less healthy; unmarried workers subsidize the pensions of married workers; persons who eat, drink, or smoke to excess may subsidize pension benefits for persons whose habits are more temperate. Treating different classes of risks as though they were the same for purposes of group insurance is a common practice that has never been considered inherently unfair. To insure the flabby and the fit as though they were equivalent risks may be more common than treating men and women alike; but nothing more than habit makes one "subsidy" seem less fair than the other.

In dissent, Justices Burger and Rehnquist stated:

Gender-based actuarial tables have been in use since at least 1843, and their statistical validity has been repeatedly verified. The vast life insurance, annuity, and pension plan industry is based on these tables. As the Court recognizes, it is a fact that "women, as a class; do live longer than men." It is equally true that employers cannot know in advance when individual members of the classes will die. Yet, if they are to operate economically workable group pension programs, it is only rational to permit them to rely on statistically sound and proved disparities in longevity between men and women. . . .

This is in no sense a failure to treat women as "individuals" in violation of the statute, as the Court holds. It is to treat them as individually as it is possible to do in the face of the unknowable length of each individual life. Individually, every woman has the same statistical possibility of outliving men. This is the essence of basing decisions on reliable statistics when individual determinations are infeasible or, as here, impossible.

Of course, women cannot be disqualified from, for example, heavy labor just because the generality of women are thought not as strong as men — a proposition which perhaps may sometime be statistically demonstrable, but will remain individually refutable. When, however, it is impossible to tailor a program such as a pension plan to the individual, nothing should prevent application of reliable statistical facts to the individual, for whom the facts cannot be disproved until long after planning, funding, and operating the program have been undertaken. . . .

It is perhaps unsurprising that the *Manhart* decision produced a lively scholarly debate. *See, e.g.,* Lea Brilmayer, Richard Hekeler, Douglas Laycock, & Teresa A. Sullivan, *Sex Discrimination in Employer-Sponsored Insurance Plans: A Legal and Demographic Analysis,* 47 U. Chi. L. Rev. 505 (1980); George J. Benston, *The Economics of Gender Discrimination in Employee Fringe Benefits:* Manhart *Revisited,* 49 U. Chi. L. Rev. 489 (1982); Lea Brilmayer, Douglas Laycock, & Teresa A. Sullivan, *The Efficient Use of Group Averages as Nondiscrimination: A Rejoinder to Professor Benston,* 50 U. Chi. L. Rev. 222 (1983); and George J. Benston, *Discrimination and Economic Efficiency in Employee Fringe Benefits: A Clarification of Issues and a Response to Professors Brilmayer, Laycock, and Sullivan,* 50 U. Chi. L. Rev. 250 (1983). *See generally* Jonathan Simon, *The Ideological Effects of Actuarial Practices,* 22 Law & Soc'y Rev. 771 (1988) (discussing arguments on both sides).

d. The Affordable Care Act

42 U.S. Code §300gg — Fair health insurance premiums
  (a) Prohibiting discriminatory premium rates
    (1) In general. With respect to the premium rate charged by a health insurance issuer for health insurance coverage offered in the individual or small group market—
      (A) such rate shall vary with respect to the particular plan or coverage involved only by—
        (i) whether such plan or coverage covers an individual or family;
        (ii) rating area, as established in accordance with paragraph (2);
        (iii) age, except that such rate shall not vary by more than 3 to 1 for adults (consistent with section 300gg-6(c) of this title); and
        (iv) tobacco use, except that such rate shall not vary by more than 1.5 to 1; and
      (B) such rate shall not vary with respect to the particular plan or coverage involved by any other factor not described in subparagraph (A).

(2) Rating area

   (A) In general. Each State shall establish 1 or more rating areas within that State for purposes of applying the requirements of this subchapter.

   (B) Secretarial review. The Secretary shall review the rating areas established by each State under subparagraph (A) to ensure the adequacy of such areas for purposes of carrying out the requirements of this subchapter. If the Secretary determines a State's rating areas are not adequate, or that a State does not establish such areas, the Secretary may establish rating areas for that State.

   (3) Permissible age bands. The Secretary, in consultation with the National Association of Insurance Commissioners, shall define the permissible age bands for rating purposes under paragraph (1)(A)(iii).

   (4) Application of variations based on age or tobacco use. With respect to family coverage under a group health plan or health insurance coverage, the rating variations permitted under clauses (iii) and (iv) of paragraph (1)(A) shall be applied based on the portion of the premium that is attributable to each family member covered under the plan or coverage.

---

   e.   State Insurance Antidiscrimination Laws

Only a few states have laws expressly forbidding insurers in all lines of insurance from engaging in any form of discrimination on the basis of race, religion, or national origin in the underwriting process. Even fewer states have outright cross-line bans on the use of other characteristics, such as location or gender or sexual orientation. Many states, however, impose some limitations on the use of some characteristics in one line of insurance or another, although there is enormous variation across states in terms which lines and which characteristics are regulated and how they are regulated. *See generally* Avraham, Logue & Schwarcz, *supra*.

   One source of consistency across states in insurance antidiscrimination laws is the NAIC Model Unfair Trade Practices Act, some version of which has been adopted by many states. This model law includes unfair discrimination as an unfair trade practice, and it defines "unfair discrimination" as follows:

   (1) Making or permitting any unfair discrimination between individuals of the same class and equal expectation of life in the rates charged for any life insurance policy or annuity or in the dividends or other benefits payable thereon, or in any other of the terms and conditions of such policy.

   (2) Making or permitting any unfair discrimination between individuals of the same class and of essentially the same hazard in the amount of premium, policy fees or rates charged for any accident or health insurance policy or in the benefits payable thereunder, or in any of the terms or conditions of such policy, or in any other manner.

   (3) Making or permitting any unfair discrimination between individuals or risks of the same class and of essentially the same hazard by refusing to insure, refusing to renew, canceling or limiting the amount of insurance coverage on a property or casualty risk solely because of the geographic location of the risk, unless such action is the result of the application of sound underwriting and actuarial principles related to actual or reasonably anticipated loss experience.

   (4) Making or permitting any unfair discrimination between individuals or risks of the same class and of essentially the same hazards by refusing to insure, refusing

to renew, canceling or limiting the amount of insurance coverage on the residential property risk, or the personal property contained therein, solely because of the age of the residential property.

(5) Refusing to insure, refusing to continue to insure, or limiting the amount of coverage available to an individual because of the sex, marital status, race, religion or national origin of the individual; however, nothing in this subsection shall prohibit an insurer from taking marital status into account for the purpose of defining persons eligible for dependent benefits. Nothing in this section shall prohibit or limit the operation of fraternal benefit societies.

(6) To terminate, or to modify coverage or to refuse to issue or refuse to renew any property or casualty policy solely because the applicant or insured or any employee of either is mentally or physically impaired; provided that this subsection shall not apply to accident and health insurance sold by a casualty insurer and, provided further, that this subsection shall not be interpreted to modify any other provision of law relating to the termination, modification, issuance or renewal of any insurance policy or contract.

(7) Refusing to insure solely because another insurer has refused to write a policy, or has cancelled or has refused to renew an existing policy in which that person was the named insured. Nothing herein contained shall prevent the termination of an excess insurance policy on account of the failure of the insured to maintain any required underlying insurance.

The following case represents one state court's effort to interpret and apply the state law prohibition on unfair discrimination.

TELLES v. COMMISSIONER OF INSURANCE

Supreme Judicial Court of Massachusetts
574 N.E.2d 359 (1991)

NOLAN, J.

Today we are asked to decide whether the Commissioner of Insurance (commissioner) may lawfully issue regulations which prohibit life insurers from considering gender-based mortality differences in the underwriting of life insurance. We hold that the commissioner is not authorized to promulgate the regulations in question, as they are in direct conflict with several statutes which expressly permit the very type of risk classification involved in this case.

Effective September 1, 1988, the commissioner issued regulations prohibiting a life insurer from considering gender-based mortality differences in the underwriting of life insurance. 211 Code Mass. Regs. §§35.00 et seq. (1987) ("unisex" regulations). Insurance underwriting is the process by which an insurer determines whether, and on what basis, to accept a risk. The regulations prohibited insurance companies from using any table or other statistical compilation as a basis for any action which classifies residents of the Commonwealth into separate classes based on race, color, religion, *sex,* marital status, or national origin. 211 Code Mass. Regs. §35.04(1) (emphasis supplied). The regulations also stated that "[n]o policy . . . shall, on the basis of . . . sex . . . treat any covered person . . . differently than it treats or would treat any other covered person . . . with respect to the availability, terms, conditions, rates, benefits or requirements. . . ." 211 Code Mass. Regs. §35.04(2).

Prior to the issuance of the regulations, Massachusetts insurance companies used gender-based mortality tables to classify individuals and to determine insurance rates. The mortality rates for males are generally higher than those for females. In the case of ordinary life insurance, which involves periodic premium payments until the policy matures, a woman would likely make payments for a longer period of time before death. Therefore, prior to these regulations, life insurance premiums were lower for females than they were for males. Pursuant to the unisex regulations, insurance companies must ignore gender in the determination of insurance rates, benefits, conditions, or requirements. The regulations, therefore, have resulted in higher life insurance premiums for women than for men. . . .

The parties agreed that there were no disputed issues of material fact. The judge below determined that the commissioner had the implicit authority, derived from art. 1 of the Massachusetts Declaration of Rights, as appearing in art. 106 of the Amendments,[8] to issue the regulations. The judge also determined that the regulations did not have a discriminatory purpose. Therefore, the judge allowed the commissioner's motion for summary judgment and denied the plaintiffs' cross motion. We granted the plaintiffs' application for direct appellate review. We now vacate the judgment.

The commissioner has conceded that the mortality rates for males are generally higher than those of females. He does not dispute that females as a class have fewer deaths than males as a class at every interval. In September of 1988, when the unisex regulations first barred the use of separate mortality tables based on gender, insureds of different risk classifications (men and women) were required to be grouped together. Given this, the unisex regulations are in direct conflict with several Massachusetts statutes which permit insurers to engage in the very type of risk classification involved in this case. *See* G.L. c. 175, §120; c. 176D, §3(7); c. 175, §144 (1988 ed.).

The statutory pattern which deals with insurance regulation authorizes insurers to "discriminate fairly." *Life Ins. Ass'n of Mass. v. Commissioner of Ins.,* 403 Mass. 410, 416, 530 N.E.2d 168 (1988). We stated in *Life Ins. Ass'n* that "[t]he basic principle underlying statutes governing underwriting practices is that insurers have the right to classify risks and to elect not to insure risks if the discrimination is fair." *Id.* at 415, 530 N.E.2d 168. We went on to acknowledge that "[t]he intended result of the [information gathering] process is that persons of substantially the same risk will be grouped together, paying the same premiums, and will not be subsidizing insureds who present a significantly greater hazard." *Id.* at 416, 530 N.E.2d 168.

Chapter 175, §120, and G.L. c. 176D, §3(7), illustrate the principle that insureds must be treated in accordance with their risk classification. Chapter 175, §120, states that "[*n*]*o life company* and no officer or agent thereof *shall make or permit any distinction or discrimination in favor of individuals between insurants of the same class and equal expectation of life* in the amount or payment of premiums or rates charged for policies of life or endowment insurance, or annuity or pure endowment contracts, or in the dividends or other benefits payable thereon, or

---

8. Article 1, as appearing in art. 106, states: "All people are born free and equal and have certain natural, essential and unalienable rights; among which may be reckoned the right of enjoying and defending their lives and liberties; that of acquiring, possessing and protecting property; in fine, that of seeking and obtaining their safety and happiness. Equality under the law shall not be denied or abridged because of sex, race, color, creed or national origin."

in any other of the terms and conditions of the contracts it makes" (emphasis supplied). Chapter 176D, §3(7), also has a provision that defines "[u]nfair discrimination" as that which treats individuals of the same class and equal expectation of life differently.

This statutory scheme requires the commissioner to treat equally insureds who are of the same risk classification. This may result in "fair discrimination." It is conceded that women are of a different risk classification than men, given their differences in life expectancy. Regulations which make it mandatory to place women in the same risk category as men, such as the unisex regulations, are in direct conflict with c. 175, §120 and c. 176D, §3(7).

Likewise, c. 175, §144(6A)(*h*), provides that "[a]ll adjusted premiums and present values referred to in this section shall for all policies of ordinary insurance be calculated on the basis of (*i*) the Commissioner[s'] 1980 Standard Ordinary Mortality Table. . . ." This table (CSO Table), published in 1980, and based on experience data from 1970 through 1975, treated males and females as distinct classes, with separate mortality tables. In 1982, the Legislature had amended G.L. c. 175, §144, to authorize directly the use of the CSO table. St. 1982, c. 334, §2. The unisex regulations expressly bar the use of separate mortality tables based on an insured's sex, in direct conflict with c. 175, §144.

It is settled that "an administrative board or officer has no authority to promulgate rules and regulations which are in conflict with the statutes or exceed the authority conferred by the statutes by which such board or office was created." *Bureau of Old Age Assistance of Natick v. Commissioner of Pub. Welfare*, 93 N.E.2d 267, 269 (Mass. 1950). The unisex regulations are in direct conflict with several statutes regulating insurance practices. These statutes have not been amended, and there is no judicial decision which states that the statutes are unconstitutional. The commissioner may not issue a regulation which is in conflict with statutes which control his authority. Accordingly, the commissioner was without power to issue the regulations in question.

The commissioner contends that, even in light of the statutory scheme, art. 1 bestows authority on him to promulgate the regulations. We disagree. The commissioner's authority to issue regulations is delegated by the Legislature and does not derive from the State Constitution. The Legislature has explicitly denied the commissioner the authority to issue the challenged regulation. It is the legislative, not the executive, branch which is given the power to make laws. Whatever the merits of the regulations may be, the doctrine of separation of powers embodied in art. 30 of the Massachusetts Declaration of Rights requires that an administrative agency receive a proper delegation of authority before promulgating rules of general application. An administrative body does not have any inherent authority to issue regulations. . . .

NOTES AND QUESTIONS

1. The Pennsylvania Supreme Court made the opposite decision in a case involving gender-based automobile insurance rates. *See Hartford Acc. & Indem. Co. v. Insurance Comm'r of Pennsylvania*, 482 A.2d 542 (Pa. 1984). The court affirmed the insurance commissioner's decision that Hartford Accident's

gender-based automobile insurance rates were "unfairly discriminatory," within the meaning of the Pennsylvania Casualty and Surety Rate Regulation Act, which prohibited "excessive, inadequate, or unfairly discriminatory" rates. The court upheld the commissioner's interpretation of the Rate Act's antidiscrimination clause and rejected Hartford Accident's argument that the clause be limited in meaning to "*actuarially* unfair." The court concluded the "fairness" of rates be recognized as "distinct from and transcending the need for sound actuarial justification" and approved the commissioner's reference to the Pennsylvania Equal Rights Amendment to the Pennsylvania state Constitution for his interpretation of the antidiscrimination clause. Shortly after the Pennsylvania Supreme Court's decision in *Hartford*, the state legislature attempted to reverse the Court's, and hence the commissioner's, decision by amending the state's insurance rating law as follows:

> This section shall not be construed to prohibit rates for automobile insurance which are based, in whole or in part, on factors, including, but not limited to, sex, if the use of such a factor is supported by sound actuarial principles or is related to actual or reasonably anticipated experience; however, such factors shall not include race, religion or national origin.

Section 3(e) of the Casualty and Surety Rate Regulatory Act, 40 P.S. §1183(e), as amended in 1986. But that wasn't the end of the story. The amended language was eventually struck down by the Pennsylvania courts as also being inconsistent with the Equal Rights Amendment to the state Constitution. *Bartholomew ex rel. Bartholomew v. Foster*, 541 A.3d 393 (Commonwealth Ct. 1988), *aff'd* 522 Pa. 489 (1989). How might the Pennsylvania courts respond to the statutory arguments relied on by the Massachusetts court in *Telles*?

2. The court in *Insurance Servs. Office v. Commissioner of Ins.*, 381 So. 2d 515 (La. Ct. App. 1979) affirmed a lower court decision overruling an order from the commissioner that held use of gender and age classifications to be unfairly discriminatory. The court noted statistics showing a higher rate of accidents in males and young people, and that Louisiana allowed insurers to use any classification as long as it was "reasonable." *Id.* at 517. The court also noted that although the classifications are discriminatory to some extent, they do not *unfairly* discriminate, and they are allowable because they are supported by a "sound statistical basis."

3. Following are sample cases addressing state-law-based "unfair discrimination" claims outside the gender context:

   - *State v. Insurance Services Office*, 434 So. 2d 908 (Fla. Dist. Ct. App. 1983), affirmed the striking down of an insurance department regulation prohibiting insurers from classifying on the basis of sex, marital status, or scholastic achievement. The court concluded that the department had exceeded its legislative grant of authority, and that the classifications in question did not *unfairly* discriminate. Legislative history and debate revealed the legislature had decided not to include sex, marital status, and scholastic achievement in the groups of classifications that unfairly discriminated. The court did not find persuasive the department's arguments that the classifications unfairly discriminated because they were completely unrelated to driving, and noted the legislature's statement that the classifications were unfair only if they were found to be actuarially unsound. *Id.* at 913.

- *Anzinger v. O'Connor,* 440 N.E.2d 1014 (Ill. App. Ct. 1982), held the insurers' classification scheme for insuring emergency room physicians to be excessive and unfairly discriminatory. The scheme classified physicians according to where they practiced in the emergency room and was the result of the insurers' lack of testable data, as this type of insurance was an emerging field at the time. The lack of sufficient loss data and lack of uniformity with other insurance companies created excessive rates. The rates were also unfairly discriminatory because they classified similarly situated physicians differently; some physicians were classified with surgeons, while others were not, for example. *See also Louisiana Med. Mut. Ins. Co. v. Green,* 657 So. 2d 1052 (La. Ct. App. 1995) (insurance company applied a $500 surcharge only to doctors using registered nurse anesthetists; *remanded*).

- *Lumbermen's Mutual Cas. Co. v. Insurance Commissioner of Maryland,* 487 A.2d 271 (Md. 1985), affirmed the insurance commissioner's conclusion that insurance companies in three consolidated cases unfairly discriminated against drivers who had two or three tickets in a defined time period. The insurance companies refused to renew the drivers' policies and argued that renewal would force them to face risks that they would not be compensated for. The commissioner and the court rejected this argument, asserting that the companies would be compensated, and that in any case, the asserted inadequacy of the rates did not fall within the insurance code's permitted justifications for nonrenewal.

- In February 1986, the Truck Insurance Exchange refused to offer a joint policy to a homosexual couple who otherwise qualified. The couple protested to the California Department of Insurance, which declined to take action. The couple then sued the Exchange, alleging violations of the Insurance Code as well as the Unruh Act, an antidiscrimination law. In *Beaty v. Truck Ins. Exch.,* 8 Cal. Rptr. 2d 593 (Ct. App. 1992), the court ruled that the couple was justifiably discriminated against as an unmarried couple and were treated as any unmarried couple would be; therefore, they were not discriminated against because they were homosexual. The court held that the couple refused to state a valid claim despite their allegation that homosexuals were effectively discriminated against by being grouped with unmarried couples. Since then, California has enacted the California Insurance Equality Act, which superseded the decision in *Beaty.* The Act states: "Every policy issued, amended, delivered, or renewed in this state shall provide coverage for the registered domestic partner of an insured or policyholder that is equal to, and subject to the same terms and conditions as, the coverage provided to a spouse of an insured or policyholder." Cal. Ins. Code §381.5 (West 2005).

RISK CLASSIFICATION PROBLEM

1. Consider classification on the basis of the following risk factors in the following kinds of insurance:

	Life Insurance	Health Insurance	Auto Insurance	Homeowners Insurance
Smoking				
Location of residence				
Number of unrelated adults in household				
Credit score				
Health status				
Gender				
Ethnicity				
Age				
Genetic test results				

2. Suppose that we decided to prohibit one or more of these classifications. How would that be done? How would that be enforced? Consider the role of targeted marketing.

3. Would an insurance company that charged different premiums based on distinctions such as those on the grid be committing an unfair trade practice under the NAIC Model Unfair Trade Practices Act? Would an insurance company that refused to make those distinctions be committing an unfair trade practice? Does the Act adequately address the use of underwriting, marketing, and insurance contract design to make classification decisions? Would an insurance company that made such a distinction violate the Fair Housing Act?

4. Do we need new federal legislation that would explicitly limit insurers' use of various characteristics in the sale and pricing of insurance? If so, what sorts of limitations should apply? Should they be outright prohibitions? On what lines of insurance, and for what characteristics?

5. Suppose that one or more of these classifications had a disparate impact on individuals protected by the FHA. Should that disparate impact require insurers to change their practices? The Supreme Court in Inclusive Communities Project recently held that plaintiffs may bring disparate-impact claims under the FHA. What type of causal connection might exist between these classifications and a disparate impact on a protected group in the FHA? If you were a lawyer representing an insurer in such a lawsuit, how would you make the case that the disparate-impact claim should be dismissed? If you were a lawyer representing the plaintiff, how would you counter that argument?

6. In 2007, the Federal Trade Commission (FTC) released a report on the use of credit scores in automobile insurance underwriting. The FTC press release on the report stated these findings:

    • Scores effectively predict the number of claims that consumers file and the total cost of those claims. Their use is likely to make the price of insurance better match the risk of loss that consumers pose. Thus, on average, as a result of the use of scores, higher-risk consumers pay higher premiums and lower-risk consumers pay lower premiums.

    • Use of scores may result in benefits for consumers. For example, scores permit insurers to evaluate risk with greater accuracy, which may make them more willing to offer insurance to higher-risk consumers for whom they otherwise would not be able to determine an appropriate premium. Scores also may allow insurers to grant and price coverage more efficiently, producing cost savings that could result in lower premiums. Little empirical data was submitted or available to the FTC that would allow the agency to quantify the magnitude of these benefits.

    • Scores are distributed differently among racial and ethnic groups, and these differences are likely to have an effect on the premiums that these groups pay, on average.

    • As a proxy for race and ethnicity in statistical models of insurance, scores have a 1.1 percent and 0.7 percent effect for African Americans and Hispanics, respectively. This means that most of their predictive power is not as a substitute for membership in racial or ethnic groups. In addition, scores effectively predict risk of claims within racial and ethnic groups.

    • The commission could not develop an alternative scoring model that would continue to predict risk effectively, yet decrease the differences in scores among racial and ethnic groups. The results of these efforts indicate that there is no readily available alternative scoring model that would achieve those results.

FTC Releases Report on Effects of Credit-Based Insurance Scores, *http://www.ftc.gov/opa/2007/07/facta.shtm* (last visited Oct. 1, 2007) (the report and accompanying statements can be downloaded from this page).

The report was controversial because it relied on a nonrandom selection of data provided voluntarily by the insurance industry. ("'The FTC's approach to collecting data for the analysis is like the federal government trying to do a study on the health impacts of tobacco use with data selected by tobacco companies for the study,' said Allen Fishbein of the Consumer Federation of America." Michelle Singletary, *FTC Dropped Ball on Study of Credit Scores, Insurance Premiums*, Denver Post, Aug. 5, 2007, *available at http://www.denverpost.com/headlines/ci_6541916*). For this reason, Commissioner Pamela Jones Harbour dissented from the release of the report. Commissioner Jon Leibowitz voted to release the report, but filed the following concurring statement:

> I voted to release this Report because staff's analysis of the data—albeit data primarily provided by a subset of insurers that elected to submit their data for the study—makes a substantial contribution to public discussion in this area. While the analysis demonstrates that credit-based insurance scores are correlated with risk, countering the hypothesis that scores are used principally

as a proxy for race or ethnicity, the results in today's Report are of course no cause for celebration. The differences in credit-based insurance scores across racial and ethnic groups are a disturbing reminder that our society is—still—not race blind, and that vestiges of our history of discrimination remain ever-present.

Table of Cases

Table of Authorities

————, Bonded Import Safety Warranties, in Import Safety: Regulatory Governance in the Global Economy 215 (Cary Coglianese et al. eds, 2009), 10

————, Constructing the Insurance Relationship: Sales Stories, Claims Stories and Insurance Contract Damages, 72 Tex. L. Rev. 1395 (1994), 63, 109, 117

————, Containing the Promise of Insurance: Adverse Selection and Risk Classification, in Moral Risks (Richard Ericson & Aaron Doyle eds., 2003), 688

————, Containing the Promise of Insurance: Adverse Selection and Risk Classification, in Risk and Morality (Richard Ericson & Aaron Doyle eds., 2003), 12

————, Containing the Promise of Insurance: Adverse Selection and Risk Classification, 9 Conn. Ins. L.J. 371 (2003), 690

————, Health Insurance, Risk and Responsibility After the Affordable Care Act, 159 U. Pa. L. Rev. 1577 (2011), 258

————, Insurance and the Law, in International Encyclopedia of Social and Behavioral Sciences 7587 (N.J. Smelser & Paul B. Baltes eds., 2001), 16

————, Insurance Liability Risks, 29 Geneva Papers on Risk & Ins. 128 (2004), 479

————, Liability Insurance as Tort Regulation: Six Ways That Liability Insurance Shapes Tort Law in Action, 12 Conn. Ins. L.J. 1 (2006), 604

————, Liability Insurance at the Tort-Crime Boundary, in Fault Lines: Tort Law as Cultural Practice (David M. Engel & Michael McCann eds., 2009), 417

————, Liability Insurance Contracts and Defense Lawyers: From Triangles to Tetrahedrons, 4 Conn. Ins. L.J. 101 (1997-1998), 569

————, Liability Insurance, Moral Luck, and Auto Accidents, 9 Theoretical Inquiries L. 165 (2008), 425

————, Medical Malpractice and the Insurance Underwriting Cycle, 54 DePaul L. Rev. 393 (2005), 604, 610

————, On the Genealogy of Moral Hazard, 75 Tex. L. Rev. 237 (1996), 6, 226, 244

————, Reconsidering Insurance for Punitive Damages, 1998 Wis. L. Rev. 557

————, Risk, Insurance and the Social Construction of Responsibility, in Embracing Risk: The Changing Culture of Insurance and Responsibility (Tom Baker & Jonathan Simon eds., 2002), 15, 17

————, Teaching Real Torts: Using Barry Werth's Damages in the Law School Classroom, 2 Nev. L.J. 386 (2002), 23

————, Transforming Punishment into Compensation: In the Shadow of Punitive Damages, 1998 Wis. L. Rev 211, 556

Baker, Tom, & Thomas O. Farrish, Liability Insurance and the Regulation of Firearms, in Suing the Firearms Industry (T. Lytton ed., 2005), 7

Baker, Tom, & Sean Griffith, Ensuring Corporate Misconduct: How Liability Insurance Undermines Shareholder Litigation (Univ. Chi. Press 2010), 475

————, The Missing Monitor in Corporate Governance: The Directors' and Officers' Liability Insurance, 95 Geo. L.J. 1765 (2007), 7

————, Predicting Corporate Governance Risk: Evidence from the Directors' and Officers' Liability Insurance Market, 74 Chi. L. Rev. 487 (2007), 467

Baker, Tom, & Karen McElrath, Whose Safety Net? Home Insurance and Inequality, 21 Law & Soc. Inquiry 229 (1996), 180

Baker, Tom, & Eva Orlebeke, The Application of Per Occurrence Limits from Successive Policies, 3 Envtl. Claims J. 411 (1991), 371

Barnes, Brian, Note, Against Insurance Rescission, 120 Yale L.J. 328 (2010), 93

Ben-Shahar, Omri, & Kyle D. Logue, Outsourcing Regulation: How Insurance Reduces Moral Hazard, 111 Mich. L. Rev. 197 (2012), 7, 102, 687

————, The Perverse Effects of Subsidized Weather Insurance, 184

Benston, George J., Discrimination and Economic Efficiency in Employee Fringe Benefits: A Clarification of Issues and a Response to Professors Brilmayer, Laycock, and Sullivan, 50 U. Chi. L. Rev. 250 (1983), 697

————, The Economics of Gender Discrimination in Employee Fringe Benefits: *Manhart* Revisited, 49 U. Chi. L. Rev. 489 (1982), 697

Bernstein, Peter L., Against the Gods: The Remarkable Story of Risk (1998), 5

Black, Bernard S., Brian R. Cheffins, & Michael Klausner, Outside Director Liability, 58 Stan. L. Rev. 1055 (2006), 606

Boardman, Michelle E., Contra Proferentem: The Allure of Ambiguous Boilerplate, 104 Mich. L. Rev. 1105 (2006), 37, 50, 63

Boyce, Lee, Blackbox Insurance May Be Cutting Young Drivers' Costs, but I Still Worry About the Spy in the Car, ThisIsMoney.co.uk (June 25, 2012), http://www.thisismoney.co.uk/ money/cars/article-2161658/Blackbox-insurance-helps-young-drivers-I-worry-spy-car. html, 8

Bragg, Michael, Concurrent Causation and the Art of Policy Drafting: New Perils for Property Insurers, 20 Forum 385 (1985), 176

Brilmayer, Lea, Richard Hekeler, Douglas Laycock, & Teresa A. Sullivan, Sex Discrimination in Employer-Sponsored Insurance Plans: A Legal and Demographic Analysis, 47 U. Chi. L. Rev. 505 (1980), 697

Brilmayer, Lea, Douglas Laycock, & Teresa A. Sullivan, The Efficient Use of Group Averages as Nondiscrimination: A Rejoinder to Professor Benston, 50 U. Chi. L. Rev. 222 (1983), 696

Brodeur, Paul, Outrageous Misconduct (1985), 341

Browne, Mark J., Ellen S. Pryor, & Bob Puelz, The Effect of Bad-Faith Laws on First-Party Insurance Claims Decisions, 33 J. Legal Stud. 355 (2004), 127

Burton, Steven J., & Eric G. Andersen, Contractual Good Faith: Formation, Performance, Breach, Enforcement (1995), 110

Butler, Richard J., et al., HMOs, Moral Hazard and Cost Shifting in Workers Compensation, 16 J. Health Econ. 191 (1997), 22

Cady, Thomas C., & Georgia Lee Gates, Post Claim Underwriting, 102 W. Va. L. Rev. 809 (2000), 102

Chandler, Seth, Reconsidering the Duty to Settle, 42 Drake L. Rev. 741 (1993), 547

Clark, Geoffrey, Betting on Lives: The Culture of Life Insurance in England, 1695-1775 (1999), 214, 223

Cohen, George M., Legal Malpractice Insurance and Loss Prevention: A Comparative Analysis of Economic Institutions, 4 Conn. Ins. L.J. 305 (1997–1998), 7

———, The Negligence-Opportunism Tradeoff in Contract Law, 20 Hofstra L. Rev. 941 (1992), 108-109

De Meza, David, & David C. Webb, Advantageous Selection in Insurance Markets, 32 Rand J. Econ. 249 (2001), 13

Diamond, Shari S., & Neil Vidmar, Jury Room Ruminations on Forbidden Topics, 87 Va. L. Rev. 1857 (2001), 607

Diller, Matthew, Entitlement and Exclusion: The Role of Disability in the Social Welfare System, 44 UCLA L. Rev. 361 (1996), 244

Duhigg, Charles, Late in Life, Finding a Bonanza in Life Insurance, N.Y. Times (Dec. 17, 2006), 226

Dunn, Richard M., David R. Hazouri, & Julie Rannik, Criminalization of Negligent Acts by Employees of U.S. and Foreign Corporations, 69 Def. Couns. J. 17 (Jan. 2002), 424

Dworkin, Ronald, What Is Equality? Part 1: Equality of Welfare, 10 Phil. & Pub. Aff. 185 (1981), 690

———, What Is Equality? Part 2: Equality of Resources, 10 Phil. & Pub. Aff. 283 (1981), 690

Eidsmore, Daniel C., & Pamela K. Edwards, Home Liability Coverage: Does the Criminal Acts Exclusion Work Where the "Expected or Intended" Exclusion Failed?, 5 Conn. Ins. L.J. 707, 414

Einav, Liran, Amy Finkelstein, Stephen P. Ryan, Paul Schrimpf, & Mark R. Cullen, Selection on Moral Hazard in Health Insurance (NBER Working Paper No. 16969, 2011), 240

Eisenberg, Melvin Aron, The Limits of Cognition and the Limits of Contract, 47 Stan. L. Rev. 211 (1995), 110

Ericson, Richard V., & Aaron Doyle, The Institutionalization of Deceptive Sales in Life Insurance, 46 Brit. J. Criminology 993 (2006), 139

———, Uncertain Business: Risk, Insurance and the Limits of Knowledge (2004), 226, 244, 250

Ericson, Richard V., Aaron Doyle, & Dean Barry, Insurance as Governance (2003), 226

Farrish, Thomas O., "Diminished Value" in Automobile Insurance: The Controversy and Its Lessons, 12 Conn. Ins. L.J. 39 (2005-2006), 195

Logue, Kyle D., & Ronen Avraham, Redistributing Optimally: Of Tax Rules, Legal Rules, and Insurance, 56 Tax L. Rev. 147 (2002), 15, 690

Lopucki, Lynn, The Death of Liability, 106 Yale L.J. 1 (1996), 605

Lynch, William H., *NAACP v. American Family,* in Insurance Redlining: Disinvestment, Reinvestment, and the Evolving Role of Financial Institutions 157 (Gregory D. Squires ed., 1997), 194

Macneil, Ian R., Bureaucracy and Contracts of Adhesion, 22 Osgoode Hall L.J. 5 (1984), 60

Mahoney, Martha R., Legal Images of Battered Women: Redefining the Issue of Separation, 90 Mich. L. Rev. 1 (1991), 210, 211, 691

Mathias, John H., Jr., et al., Directors and Officers Liability: Prevention, Insurance and Indemnification (4th ed. 2003), 478

Mayers, David, & Clifford W. Smith, Jr., On the Corporate Demand for Insurance, 55 J. Bus. 281 (1982), 475

McDowell, Banks, Choice of Law in Insurance: Using Conflicts Methodology to Minimize Discrimination Among Policyholders, 23 Conn. L. Rev. 117 (1990), 82

McGlamery, J. Gabriel, Race Based Underwriting and Death of Burial Insurance, 15 Conn. Ins. L.J. 531 (2009), 695

Merkin, Robert, Gambling by Insurance — A Study of the Life Insurance Act of 1774, 9 Anglo-Am. L. Rev. 331 (1980), 226

Moore, Christopher, Coyote Blue (1994), 226

Morris, Clarence, Waiver and Estoppel in Insurance Policy Litigation, 105 U. Pa. L. Rev. 925 (1957), 66-67

Moss, David A., When All Else Fails: Government as the Ultimate Risk Manager (2002), 5, 665, 670

Pearson, Robin, Thrift or Dissipation? The Business of Life Insurance in the Early Nineteenth Century, 43 Econ. Hist. Rev. 236 (1990), 214

Pepper, Steven, Applying the Fundamentals of Lawyers' Ethics to Insurance Defense Practice, 4 Conn. Ins. L.J. 27 (1997–1998), 569

Plevin, Liam, & Rachel Emma Silverman, Investors Seek Profits in Strangers' Deaths, Wall St. J. (May 2, 2006) at C1, 226

Posner, Richard A., Economic Analysis of Law (5th ed. 1998), 139

Powers, D.J., The Discriminatory Effects of Homeowners Insurance Underwriting Guidelines, in Insurance Redlining: Disinvestment, Reinvestment, and the Evolving Role of Financial Institutions (Gregory D. Squires ed., 1997), 194

Practicing Law Institute, Personal Injury Law and Technique Course Handbook, Automobile Insurance Problems (1968), 430

Pryor, Ellen, The Tort Liability Regime and the Duty to Defend, 58 Md. L. Rev. 1 (1999), 527

Pryor, Ellen Smith, & Charles Silver, Defense Lawyers' Professional Responsibilities: Part I — Excess Exposure Cases, 78 Tex. L. Rev. 599 (2000), 569

————, Defense Lawyers' Professional Responsibilities: Part II — Contested Coverage Cases, 15 Geo. J. Legal Ethics 29 (2001), 569

Rakoff, Todd, Contracts of Adhesion: An Essay in Reconstruction, 96 Harv. L. Rev. 1174 (1983), 112

Randall, Susan, Insurance Regulation in the United States: Regulatory Federalism and the National Association of Insurance Commissioners, 26 Fla. St. U. L. Rev. 625 (1999), 634, 639

————, Redefining the Insurer's Duty to Defend, 2 Conn. Ins. L.J. 221 (1997), 513

Rappaport, John, How Private Insurers Regulate Public Police, 130 Harv. L. Rev. (forthcoming 2017), 11

Resnick, Alan N., Bankruptcy as a Vehicle for Resolving Enterprise-Threatening Mass Tort Liabilities, 148 U. Pa. L. Rev. 2045 (2000), 605

Restatement (Second) of Conflict of Laws (2007), 437

Restatement (Second) of Contracts (1981), 42, 43, 50, 61, 75, 82

Restatement (Third) of the Law Governing Lawyers, 532, 566, 568, 569

Richmond, Douglas R., Bad Insurance Bad Faith Law, 39 Tort Trial & Ins. Prac. L.J. 1 (2003), 545, 548

Swisher, Peter N., Judicial Rationales in Insurance Law: Dusting Off the Formal for the Function, 52 Ohio St. L.J. 1037 (1991), 62

Sykes, Alan O., "Bad Faith" Breach of Contract by First-Party Insurers, 25 J. Legal Stud. 405 (1996), 129

——— , Judicial Limitations on the Discretion of Liability Insurers to Settle or Litigate: An Economic Critique, 72 Tex. L. Rev. 1345 (1994), 546

——— , Subrogation and Insolvency, 30 J. Legal Stud. 383 (2001), 312-313

Syverud, Kent, The Duty to Settle, 76 Va. L. Rev. 1113 (1990), 539

Talesh, Shauhin, Data Breach, Privacy, and Cyber Liability Insurance: How Insurance Companies Act as "Compliance Managers" for Businesses, Law & Social Inquiry (under review), 364

Tausend, Eric, "No-Prejudice" No More: New York and the Death of the No Prejudice Rule, 61 Hastings L.J. 497 (2009), 108

Teller, L.S., Measure of Recovery by Insured Under Automobile Collision Insurance Policy, 43 A.L.R.2d 327 (2007), 195

Thomas, Jeffrey E., New Appleman on Insurance Law Library Edition (Lexis 2012), 49-50

Treaster, Joseph B., Home Insurers Frown on Many Dogs, N.Y. Times (Mar. 30, 2002) at A11, 10

Van Noris, Bob, Fund Boss Spurns Huge Payout Gaps in Interview, Says He'll Seek Fairness, Nat'l L.J. (Dec. 10, 2001) at A1, 251

Wagner, Gerhard, ed., Liability in Tort and Liability Insurance (2005), 604

Wells, Bert, Rukesh Korde, & Teresa Lew, New Appleman on Insurance Law Library Edition (2015), 360

Werth, Barry, Damages (1998), 23, 562

Whitford, William C., & Spencer L. Kimball, Why Process Consumer Complaints? A Case Study of the Office of the Commissioner of Insurance of Wisconsin, 1974 Wis. L. Rev. (1974), 617

Wooten, James A., The Most Glorious Story of Failure in the Business: The Studebaker-Packard Corporation and the Origins of ERISA, 49 Buff. L. Rev. 683 (2001), 274

Works, Robert, Coverage Clauses and Incontestable Statutes: The Regulation of Post Claim Underwriting, 1979 U. Ill. L.F. 809 (1979), 217

——— , Excusing Nonoccurrence of Insurance Policy Conditions in Order to Avoid Disproportionate Forfeiture: Claims-Made Formats as a Test Case, 5 Conn. Ins. L.J. 505 (1998–1999), 103, 108, 351, 484, 490

Wortham, Leah, The Economics of Insurance Classification: The Sound of One Invisible Hand Clapping, 47 Ohio St. L.J. 835 (1986), 690

——— , Insurance Classification: Too Important to Be Left to Actuaries, 19 U. Mich. L.J. Reform 349 (1986), 690

Wriggins, Jennifer, Domestic Violence Torts, 75 S. Cal. L. Rev. 121 (2001), 413

——— , Flood Money: The Challenge of U.S. Flood Insurance Reform in a Warming World, 119 Penn. St. L. Rev. 361 (2014), 186

Zartman, Lester W., & William H. Price, Yale Readings in Insurance — Property Insurance (1921), 212

Zeiler, Kathryn, et al., Physicians' Insurance Limits and Malpractice Payments: Evidence from Texas Closed Claims 1990–2003, 36 J. Legal Stud. 59 (2007), 606

Zelizer, Viviana, Morals and Markets: The Development of Life Insurance in the United States (1979), 226

Index